International Encyclopedia of the Social Sciences, 2nd edition

International Encyclopedia of the Social Sciences, 2nd edition

VOLUME 8
SOCIOLOGY, PARSONIAN–VULNERABILITY

William A. Darity Jr.
EDITOR IN CHIEF

MACMILLAN REFERENCE USA
A part of Gale, Cengage Learning

Detroit • New York • San Francisco • New Haven, Conn • Waterville, Maine • London

International Encyclopedia of the Social Sciences, 2nd edition

William A. Darity Jr., Editor in Chief

LIBRARY OF CONGRESS CATALOGING-IN-PUBLICATION DATA

International encyclopedia of the social sciences / William A. Darity, Jr., editor in chief.—2nd ed. v. cm. Rev. ed. of: International encyclopedia of the social sciences / David L. Sills, editor. c1968–c1991.
   Includes bibliographical references and index.
   ISBN 978-0-02-865965-7 (set hardcover : alk. paper)—ISBN 978-0-02-865966-4 (v. 1 hardcover : alk. paper)—ISBN 978-0-02-865967-1 (v. 2 hardcover : alk. paper)—ISBN 978-0-02-865968-8 (v. 3 hardcover : alk. paper)—ISBN 978-0-02-865969-5 (v. 4 hardcover : alk. paper)—ISBN 978-0-02-865970-1 (v. 5 hardcover : alk. paper)—ISBN 978-0-02-865971-8 (v. 6 hardcover : alk. paper)—ISBN 978-0-02-865972-5 (v. 7 hardcover : alk. paper)—ISBN 978-0-02-865973-2 (v. 8 hardcover : alk. paper)—ISBN 978-0-02-866141-4 (v. 9 hardcover : alk. paper)—ISBN 978-0-02-866117-9 (ebook : alk. paper)
   1. Social sciences—Dictionaries. 2. Social sciences—Encyclopedias. I. Darity, William A., 1953– II. Title: Encyclopedia of the social sciences.
   H40.A2I5 2008
   300.3–dc22
                                                                   2007031829

0-02-865965-1 (set)   0-02-865970-8 (v. 5)
0-02-865966-X (v. 1)   0-02-865971-6 (v. 6)
0-02-865967-8 (v. 2)   0-02-865972-4 (v. 7)
0-02-865968-6 (v. 3)   0-02-865973-2 (v. 8)
0-02-865969-4 (v. 4)   0-02-866141-9 (v. 9)

This title is also available as an e-book.
ISBN 978-0-02-866117-9; 0-02-866117-6
Contact your Gale representative for ordering information.

Printed in the United States of America
3 4 5 6 7 8 14 13 12 11 10 09 08

Editorial Board

Contents

Contents

S

SOCIOLOGY, PARSONIAN

Talcott Parsons was an American sociologist whose work dominated English-speaking social theory from the end of World War II (1939–1945) until the mid- to late 1960s. Parsons elaborated a general theory of society believing that it would give sociology a distinctive subject matter of its own, while also securing a scientific status for the discipline alongside those other social sciences concerned with the activities of the individual as a member of a group. Parsons's work focused attention on the power of the social system to influence the social behavior of individuals.

THE PARSONIAN PERSPECTIVE

In Parsons's view, the primary task of sociology is to develop a set of abstract generalizing concepts capable of describing the social system. This provides all investigators with a common conceptual framework for empirical work in order to enable cumulative inquiry. These generalizing concepts are to be judged through their rational coherence as a basis for then making propositions about the world. Parsons's first major publication, *The Structure of Social Action* (1937), reviewed the work of some European theorists, namely Max Weber (1864–1920), Émile Durkheim, Vilfredo Pareto, and Alfred Marshall, whose works, Parsons claimed, converged around basically "the same system of generalized social theory … the voluntaristic theory of action" (p. 720). This theory views human beings as making choices between ends (or goals) and means (or ways) of achieving particular ends. These

choices, Parsons argued, are limited by shared values contained within the social environment. It is because individuals embrace values concerning the sacredness of human life and the family that tendencies towards pure self-interest are curbed and the need for external sanctions including legal punishments are reduced, though never totally eliminated. These values are expressed through concrete norms, or rules of behavior, which limit the lengths to which individuals will go when pursuing their chosen ends or goals.

Parsons's early critical investigation of the work of classical European sociologists provided a foundation for his later work, *The Social System* (1951), which asked, "how is order possible?" Parsons argued that values and normative expectations provide the context in which actors seek to maximize their personal desires. Behavior and relationships that facilitate the achievement of individual needs and desires become institutionalized into a system of status roles and sanctions that are articulated through the social system. The social system, in turn, includes a personality system (the individual actor) and a cultural system (broader values that make sense of the norms linked to status roles). These three systems form the general theory of action. Each system is linked to a functional prerequisite or set of needs that must be met in order for the system as a whole to continue working. Pattern variables are also closely bound up with this general theory of action. They refer to the choices that actors must make between alternative options as a necessary condition for meaningful action in any given situation. Pattern variables are important because they classify actors' modes of orientation in the personality, social, and cultural systems. This theory also provided the foundation for Parsons's concept of structural functionalism, which attempted to categorize any level of social life at any level of analysis.

INFLUENCE ON SOCIOLOGICAL THEORY

Parsons's major works have influenced the development of sociological theory in a number of ways. *The Structure of Social Action* introduced American sociologists to the work of Durkheim and Weber as general theorists, which not only established a common vocabulary for modern sociologists but also provided them with an important frame of reference. Parsons's analysis of convergence in the works of certain European theorists also set a precedent for other sociologists, for example Anthony Giddens, to make links between oppositions such as conflict/consensus, action/structure, and micro/macro in contemporary social theory. *The Social System* helped develop and further a systems analysis, or large-scale macro, approach in sociology in place of one that stressed the importance of individual or micro elements.

The dominance of Parsons's ideas in sociology declined around the mid- to late 1960s. A resurgence of interest in Parsons's work took place, however, in the 1980s. Jeffrey Alexander in the United States and Richard Münch in Germany, for example, attempted to build upon and resolve certain problems implicit in Parsons's original systems theory through their own distinctive works on neofunctionalism. The theory of neofunctionalism stresses the need to bring together action theory and systems theory while also emphasizing the key importance of collective or macro phenomena in establishing the conditions within which social action takes place.

Critics of Parsonian sociology have focused on its failure to engage with practical reality and empirical social problems. Parsons's work has been stigmatized as merely grand theory. Parsons's excessive concern with the power of the social system also led certain critics to argue that he saw human beings as oversocialized conformists whose individual behavior was largely determined by system constraints. Other commentators have suggested that Parsons's emphasis on social integration, conformity, and harmony disregarded inequalities and those material interests, power, and ideological elements that supported them.

SEE ALSO *Parsons, Talcott; Social System; Sociology, Macro-*

BIBLIOGRAPHY

Alexander, Jeffrey C., ed. 1985. *Neofunctionalism.* London: Sage.

Münch, Richard. 1987. *Theory of Action: Towards a New Synthesis Going Beyond Parsons.* London: Routledge.

Parsons, Talcott. [1937] 1949. *The Structure of Social Action: A Study in Social Theory with Special Reference to a Group of European Writers.* New York: Free Press.

Parsons, Talcott. 1951. *The Social System.* New York: Free Press.

Jonathan S. Fish

SOCIOLOGY, PIONEERS IN

SEE *Ibn Khaldūn; Weber, Max.*

SOCIOLOGY, POLITICAL

In a seminal article from 1969, Giovanni Sartori drew a sharp distinction between the sociology of politics and political sociology. The sociology of politics, Sartori argued, involved a reduction of politics to its social conditions and thus formed a subfield of sociology much like the sociology of religion or of the family. While a comprehensive analysis of political institutions and processes certainly would involve an analysis of social conditions, the sociology of politics was insufficient, Sartori argued, because it lacked political science's understanding of politics in its own terms and as a fundamental activity. Sartori's solution was thus that political sociology should be a genuine hybrid, though his main concern was to defend against "sociologists eager to expand to the detriment of political scientists" (1969). More interesting, however, was Sartori's argument that the reason this synthesis was so important was that the objective role of politics was increasing and hence the necessity of political analysis for larger social theory was as well: "The power of power is growing at a tremendous pace," he wrote. As a result, "the greater the range of politics, the smaller the role of 'objective [read sociological] factors'" (1969).

It is perhaps ironic, then, that virtually the only scholars who regularly use the term *sociology of politics* today are political scientists, when they want to highlight social variables, such as class or family structure. *Political sociology* is indeed usually used to refer to a subfield of sociology, but one that has long since adopted the kind of hybrid approach Sartori thought sociology lacked. Political sociologists thus study an array of political processes in their own terms, in terms of their social conditions, distributions, and effects, and in terms of their combination of these two sides. Moreover, in light of the robust theories of power that have developed since the late 1960s in virtually all varieties of social theory, political sociology has long since abandoned any clear separation of the social from the political.

The intellectual roots of political sociology reflect its cross-disciplinary reach from a time even before disciplines. The philosophers of classical antiquity, for instance, wrote extensively about the varieties of political possibility, including kingship, aristocracy, and, most important for modern discourse, democracy. But the ancients did not yet have a clear concept of society, such that politics and society could be seen to interpenetrate and covary in interesting ways. This conceptualization awaited the thinkers of the European Enlightenment, who theorized society as distinct from, but shaping and shaped by, political institutions. Thus Montesquieu (1689–1755) proposed a theory emphasizing the role of climate in shaping the basic forms of governance—republican, monarchic, and despotic; behind each of these forms was a particular "spirit," comprising the distinct manners and morals of people living in these particular conditions. A. R. J. Turgot (1721–1781), Condorcet (1743–1794), and others—perhaps most importantly the great Scottish economist Adam Smith (1723–1790)—advanced historical accounts emphasizing different aspects of social and economic development that corresponded to transformations in basic forms of governance. Jean-Jacques Rousseau (1712–1778) in particular introduced the contemporary notion of civil society, and outlined the ways in which the "General Will" of the collectivity might be propagated through "political religion."

Like their predecessors, social thinkers in the nineteenth and early twentieth centuries—the forerunners of contemporary political sociology—variously developed broad explanations by reconstructing the historical process, theorizing its motors, and delineating the features of key contemporary social structures and institutions. While a wide variety of thinkers—including philosophers, economists, politicians, natural scientists, and sociologists—contributed to the development of political and social thought in this period, Karl Marx (1818–1883) and Max Weber (1864–1920) have been the most important for the subsequent development of political sociology.

Beyond the political effects of his work, Marx's legacy for political sociology consists mainly in his approach to "political economy," which nevertheless in many respects most clearly embodies the reductionistic "sociology of politics" approach Sartori bemoaned. Because Marx saw the "material"—including the means and relations of production—as the key foundation for social forms, including the state, Marxist political sociology has always emphasized the basis of all politics in economic interests (though

the "economic" has sometimes been understood more narrowly, and sometimes more broadly). In the Marxist tradition, the modern state is thus conceived as an expression of the "interests" of the ruling class—the bourgeoisie. Nevertheless, the Marxist tradition—always more complex than either its denigrators or doctrinaires portrayed it—has evolved important accounts of the complex relations between state and civil society in the capitalist and postindustrial eras, of the state as a powerful player in class conflict, as well as an emphasis on the role of power, both economic and political, in the process of social reproduction.

Usually taken as a contrasting figure, Max Weber also developed a powerful account of social stratification in capitalism. But for Weber, disparities in wealth were not the only driving force behind this stratification; rather, differences in status and political power also came into play, potentially forming complicated groupings not reducible to class. In contrast to orthodox readings of Marx, Weber held that in modern times political institutions have become separated from economic and social structure, and thus developed a powerful analysis of the state as an agent and product of bureaucratic rationalization. Perhaps most famously, Weber developed a typology of political power, distinguishing traditional, bureaucratic, and charismatic legitimation as ideal types. In his pessimistic account of modernization, Weber traced a general trend toward bureaucratic rationality tending toward complete domination—the so-called iron cage—though the move from traditional to bureaucratic legitimation was punctuated, and would likely continue to be, by moments of charismatic consolidation. Over time, however, this charismatic authority also succumbed to the rationalization process, what Weber termed "the routinization of charisma."

While many-faceted, three legacies in particular define Weber's influence on political sociology: first, his broad comparative-historical method; second, his multidimensional theory of class, status, and party, which is usually taken as a refutation of Marxist reductionism; and third, his analysis of the bureaucratic operation of the state as part of his overall account of the "rationalization" process. One subsequent development adapting elements of Weber's theory was the theory of "the circulation of elites" by Gaetano Mosca (1858–1941), which emphasized the power exercised by competing small groups with superior knowledge and technical expertise, as well as the trenchant analysis of political parties as organizing forces of these elites by Robert Michels (1876–1936). But these are only two prominent immediate examples, and nearly all political sociology since Weber has manifested various residues of and engagements with his thought.

In the United States during the twentieth century, scholars in political sociology continued the traditions established by Marx and Weber, among other nineteenth-century thinkers, of conceptualizing their subject matter in broad, macrohistorical terms. For the two decades following World War II (1939–1945), political sociology thus reflected the broader division in sociology between *functionalism* and *conflict theory*.

Amalgamating insights developed by Émile Durkheim (1858–1917) into the forms of social solidarity with Weber's account of rationalization, as well as more traditional Anglo-Saxon liberal political thought, functionalism created a model of reality in which various social institutions exist in and sustain an orderly interrelated whole. A facet of this whole was a perceived clear analytical distinction between state and society, a perspective expressing the liberal outlook of this school. Political parties, according to this view, were the main institutions connecting state and society. A central aspect of this agenda, particularly as applied by political scientists, was the comparison between liberal-democratic regimes and communist regimes, in terms of multiple interrelated spheres of polity, economy, society, and culture. The functionalist approach to national socialism and communism, for instance, was associated with the theory of "totalitarianism," which was drawn in distinction to Marxist accounts that portrayed "fascism" as an extreme outgrowth of capitalism; totalitarianism theory saw the Nazis and the Soviets as one type, while fascism saw them as distinct. Where fascism theory gave overwhelming precedence to the economic sphere, functionalism saw "totalitarian" states as polycratic, and ascribed their power to homologies among analytically distinct societal subsystems. In less dramatic and politically charged efforts, functionalist research investigated "political culture"—first the norms and values that supported particular political institutions, then later a more interpretive analysis of political symbols and meanings—as well as topics relating to American institutions, such as the bureaucracy, media and information, the military, and political parties.

In contrast to functionalism, conflict theory borrowed basic tenets from Marx and many of its variants are characterized as "Marxist," particularly those that take a critical stand on the connection between social science and political action. Not all conflict theory is Marxist, however, since one can accept on purely analytical grounds that conflict is pervasive in social and political life. Nevertheless, holding conflict to be paramount, conflict theory questioned functionalism's emphasis on order and individual autonomy from politics. Social order, for conflict theorists, was not the result of functional interdependence but, where present, the outcome of competing social forces. Conflict theorists thus charge that the liberal separation between state and society was unfounded, and

pursued an analysis of many different bases of conflict, including race and gender along with class and other factors.

In contrast to the Manichean distinction between conflict and functionalist perspectives in the 1960s and 1970s, the theoretical landscape since then has been more inclusive of diverse theoretical perspectives. Beginning in the 1970s, then, and continuing in the 1980s and 1990s, political sociology developed a variety of thematic orientations, as opposed to building and defending a few grand theoretical positions. Thus new research agendas emerged. One such agenda argued that the state should be the central subject of comparative sociological and political inquiry. Studies in this vein examined the historical formation of the state with renewed comparative focus on states as autonomous actors with their own interests, while other studies put the state's organizational profile under comparative scrutiny.

A somewhat different research agenda was one that had primarily concerned historians earlier: the study of nationalism. While the methods and ideological orientations of studies of nationalism varied, they tended to have a broad historical scope that sought the genesis of what was usually taken to be a modern phenomenon.

A third research agenda regarded questions of economic-political development around the world, including differential patterns of development. Dominated by so-called dependency theory and world-systems theory, this approach produced a wide array of findings that, though typically having a historical outlook, found a place in more standard debates in sociology and comparative politics.

Yet a fourth research agenda gaining momentum during this period was one that focused on social movements and collective action—to many, the quintessential topic for political sociology. Though a key impetus for the spread of this research agenda was the interest in investigating the civil rights movement of the 1960s, research on social movements grew to cover diverse geographical, political, and historical contexts. Finally, a fifth research agenda pertained to the conceptualization and historical evolution of civil society and its related concept of social capital. Again, with considerable divergence in terms of theoretical and political vantage points, this line of inquiry has attracted attention from sociologists, political scientists, and historians, as well as philosophers and political practitioners, particularly since 1989, when political sociologists saw the development of a vibrant public sphere between the individual and the state as the linchpin of democratization after the collapse of communism in Eastern Europe.

Perhaps the most important topic toward which social scientists in general and political sociologists in particular have turned their attention since the 1980s is globalization. Referring in general to increasing economic, political, and social interconnectedness across the world, globalization puts many of the traditional concerns of political sociology in a new context. In the face of the expansion of global trade and investment capital, political sociologists have become interested in examining the repercussions of unequal global development, global inequality, and, more generally, the social adjustment to economic change. Political sociologists have extended this critical view to developments in the West as well, such as the spread of neoliberal ideology and the resistance to it through various antiglobalization social movements and other forms of protest. Further, political sociology has adjusted its traditional concerns in the face of emerging political global actors. Thus political sociologists are investigating the role of transnational corporations, nongovernmental organizations, and political and economic intergovernmental organizations. One theme that ties such various facets of investigation together is the question of the challenge these emerging actors pose to the maintenance of the state's modern form. In the face of globalization of culture, finally, political sociology revisits traditional concerns regarding identity, values, political loyalty, citizenship, and migration patterns. Under the influence of poststructural and postmodern theory, political sociology has inquired into the complex processes through which the basic units of its analysis are "constructed" as political actors and entities, including through the disciplinary practices of sciences like political sociology itself.

SEE ALSO *Civil Society; Class; Dependency Theory; Durkheim, Émile; Elite Theory; Fascism; Functionalism; Hierarchy; Inequality, Political; Marx, Karl; Merton, Robert K.; Michels, Robert; Parsons, Talcott; Political Science; Postmodernism; Poststructuralism; Poulantzas, Nicos; Sociology; State, The; Stratification; Structuralism; Weber, Max; World-System*

BIBLIOGRAPHY

Easton, David. 1965. *A Systems Analysis of Political Life*. New York: Wiley.

Michels, Robert. [1915] 1959. *Political Parties: A Sociological Study of the Oligarchical Tendencies of Modern Democracy*. Trans. Eden and Cedar Paul. New York: Dover.

Sartori, Giovanni. 1969. From Sociology of Politics to Political Sociology. *Government and Opposition* 4: 195–214.

Weber, Max. [1922] 1978. *Economy and Society: An Outline of Interpretive Sociology*. Eds. Guenther Roth and Claus Wittich, trans. Ephraim Fischoff et al. Berkeley: University of California Press.

Jeffrey Olick
Chares Demetriou

SOCIOLOGY, POST-PARSONIAN AMERICAN

Talcott Parson's functionalism became the dominant paradigm in American sociology after Word War II. Talcott Parsons (1902–1979) envisioned society as a coherent and auto-regulating social system separated from its environment by boundaries. A social system itself consisted of relatively autonomous but also interdependent subsystems responsible for the general functional imperatives of adaptation, goal attainment, integration, and latency. Functionalism held that social systems tended toward equilibrium, change being slow and evolutionary, oriented toward increasing complexity and differentiation. Robert Merton had already criticized his mentor's penchant for grand theorizing and assumption of systemic unity and integration in *Social Theory and Social Structure* (1949). This book distinguished between latent and manifest functions in social systems and stressed the unintended consequences of action. But Merton himself, in many respects, operated within the functionalist paradigm, which lost its hegemony only in the late 1960s and early 1970s. While functionalism had for at least two decades unified sociology with an overarching theoretical framework, competing paradigms emerged as both a cause and a result of its decline. American sociology became much more heterogeneous, pluralistic, and contentious. The main strands of post-Parsonian sociology are reviewed below. Research that is either theory driven or has theoretical implications for the discipline as a whole are privileged in this survey.

CONFLICT AND DOMINATION

A significant group of American sociologists attacked the integration and consensus premises of functionalism and made conflict and domination in society their focus. Inequality and its social reproduction have also become crucial issues. The politically charged environment of the 1960s undergirded this paradigm shift, and many sociologists took their cues from Karl Marx and Max Weber. Eric Olin Wright rejuvenated the classical Marxian theory of exploitation and class by taking into account not only control over the means of production but also control over how things are produced and control over labor power. Other Marxists, such as Michael Burawoy, studied accumulation processes and class conflict on the shop floor. Alvin Gouldner pointed to the ascent of a new social class formed by the cognitive elite. William Julius Wilson elucidated the logics of economic and racial inequality in the United States, and Douglas Massey dissected the segregation patterns in American cities.

In addition to class and race, gender also became a central research area. Nancy Chodorow's *The Reproduction of Mothering* (1978) combined psychoanalysis with sociology to examine gender dynamics in the nuclear family. Arlie Hochschild studied the feminine nature of emotional work in contemporary society, and Christine Williams undertook ethnographies of gender relations in the workplace. Domination and conflict also stimulated sophisticated theoretical work, such as Steven Lukes's influential treatise on power. The most ambitious theoretical form of conflict sociology has been provided by Randall Collins, who developed over the decades a potent model to study (among many other things) credentialism, geopolitical strife, and intellectual transformation. It is a testament to the empirical soundness of his general conflict model that Collins successfully predicted in the 1980s the breakdown of the Soviet empire.

HISTORICAL-COMPARATIVE SOCIOLOGY

Another strand in the post-Parsonian period focused on wide-scale historical transformations. In contrast with the evolutionary and integrative assumptions of functionalism, the burgeoning field of historical-comparative sociology mostly centered on dynamic political and economic structures and underlined the role of revolution, violence, and contention in social change. Barrington Moore's seminal book *The Social Origins of Dictatorship and Democracy* (1966) outlined the three routes to the modern world (the liberal, the fascist, and the communist) and the mechanisms through which preindustrial agrarian social structures and the course of industrialization mixed to determine regime outcomes. His student Theda Skocpol fashioned a robust theory of social revolution based on state structures, international forces, and class relations.

Immanuel Wallerstein's world-system theory pushed the capitalist division of labor to the global level and examined how the countries in the periphery are exploited by those at the core. Daniel Bell hailed the rise of postindustrial society. He also pointed to the contradictions between the economic and the cultural logics of late capitalism. Charles Tilly created models of contentious politics and state formation; his argument about the positive feedback between state making and war making has attained classic status. In the last decade of the twentieth century he also put forth relational theories of violence and inequality. Michael Mann has been fleshing out since the mid-1980s the interconnections between economic, political, ideological, and military power throughout history, and Jack Goldstone has significantly improved the understanding of revolutions by stressing demographic pressures on states and the role of intra-elite conflict. It is important to note, however, that not all cutting-edge historical-comparative sociology has been about politics. William J. Goode's *World Changes in Divorce Patterns*

(1993), for instance, constructed an ambitious theory to cross-culturally analyze and predict divorce.

SOCIAL STRUCTURES AND ORGANIZATIONS

Formal properties of social structures and organizations constituted the main research objects for the third sociological strand in the post-Parsonian era. The Simmelian geometry of social forms was an inspiration to many scholars. In the 1970s Donald Black developed a general social control approach, which he subsequently applied to behavior of law, formation of norms, coalition building, economic consolidation, and deviance. Harrison White's famous study of vacancy chains made a momentous contribution to the literature on organizational forms and mobility. Mark Granovetter's work on the strength of weak ties was decisive in making network analysis a major methodology in sociology. Network analysis has been successfully operationalized since the 1970s to depict and explain phenomena as disparate as collective action, organizational behavior, cultural and scientific diffusion, sexual behavior, and crime. Among the most brilliant practitioners in sociology are Peter Bearman, Ronald Burt, Roger Gould, Edward Laumann, and John Padgett.

Post-Parsonian sociology took an interest in both the formal and the symbolic structures of organizations. Prominent representatives of the neo-institutionalist perspective, Paul DiMaggio and Walter Powell analyzed organizational isomorphism, John Meyer and Brian Rowan considered the mythical and ceremonial dimensions of formal structures in organizations, and Frank Dobbin showed the effects of cultural meanings on industrial policy. There has also been considerable theoretical progress in research on social systems. Andrew Abbott, for instance, proposed an ecological model for studying professions in *The System of Professions* (1988). Abbott viewed ecology, in the Chicago tradition of urban sociology, as an interacting system, and he empirically showed how jurisdictional battles between professions have molded their individual trajectories. Abbott has also laid out an innovative research agenda with a stress on the radical temporality of all social phenomena, and he has created a fractal model to explain social change and even the development of sociology itself. Finally, functionalism itself underwent an overhaul after Parsons. The neo-functionalism of Jeffrey Alexander insisted on open-ended, pluralistic, and creative interactions between subsystems in society and added a conflict orientation to the Parsonian paradigm.

CULTURE

The fourth sociological strand after Parsons was spurred by the linguistic turn in the social sciences. Culture became a key concept, especially in the 1980s and the

1990s. Ann Swidler has claimed that, rather than being preferences or values, culture involves strategies of action incorporated in dispositions, styles, and skills. Bill Sewell worked out a semiotic model of action and a theory of social structure integrating both resources and transposable schemes. His theoretical work explores temporality and underscores the importance of events in the transformational social structures. Viviana Zelizer showed how social meanings govern economic interactions and how people use money to create and maintain intimate ties. Michelle Lamont emphasized the role of symbolic boundaries and moral vocabularies in social stratification. Alexander's cultural sociology highlighted the centrality of meaning systems and performative practices in civil society.

MICRO-SOCIOLOGY

Finally, concomitant with the studies of large-scale structures, institutions, and processes, the post-Parsonian era also witnessed a growing interest in micro-sociology. Two distinct micro paradigms challenged functionalism's vision of the "oversocialized concept of man," to use the words of Dennis H. Wrong (1961). The first of these is interactionism. The symbolic interactionism of Herbert Blumer argued that meaning is construed through social interaction and that individuals are interpretative beings with reflexivity. Howard Becker's labeling theory as well as his later groundbreaking work on art worlds followed, in many respects, the symbolic interactionist research program. In his work resisting all facile theoretical labels, Erving Goffman was probably the most important student of social interaction in the second half of the twentieth century. From the late fifties to his untimely death in 1982, he analyzed social interaction in all kinds of settings using a wide array of dramaturgical, game-theoretic, etological, and cognitive concepts. His studies of impression management, stigma, role distance, embarrassment, and total institutions have all become classics.

Again within the interactionist paradigm, Harold Garfinkel deployed ethnomethodology to uncover the practical and often unconscious rationality that guides quotidian routines, with a particular attention to how people give accounts. Conversation analysts have devised sophisticated tools to capture the logic of verbal interaction. Among signal work in the interactionist tradition are Jack Katz's subtle phenomenological analyses of violence and emotions and Randall Collins's theory of interaction rituals, which is exceptionally promising as it bridges the individual and institutional levels.

Utilitarianism has been the other major micro-paradigm in the post-Parsonian era. This paradigm itself consists of two interacting streams: exchange theory and rational choice theory. George Homans had already done behaviorist work in the 1950s on social exchange. Peter

Blau later extended Homans's model by exploring the structural implications of exchange, and Goode built on this paradigm to examine the production and distribution of prestige in society. The ways power relationships affect social exchange have been extensively investigated by Richard Emerson and Karen Cook. Parallel to these developments in exchange theory, an increasing number of researchers (usually referred to as rational-choice sociologists) were drawn to the promise of explaining social interaction and institutions from the assumptions of utility-maximizing actors and methodological individualism. These scholars were influenced by the work of economists such as Mancur Olson, who studied in the 1960s and the 1970s the collective action problems that groups face. In this vein Michael Hechter attempted to account for group solidarity from rational choice premises. James S. Coleman's magnum opus *Foundations of Social Theory* (1990) strived to erect a parsimonious rational choice foundation to explain all kinds of phenomena, including social capital, trust, collective action, and revolutions. Coleman applied his model also to the asymmetry between natural and corporate actors in contemporary societies.

As noted, the post-Parsonian period has been characterized by a multiplicity of theoretical orientations. While some have seen this as a cause for concern, there is reason to think that it is the absence of a hegemonic paradigm like the Parsonian functionalism that has allowed for the immense dynamism in the late twentieth century and early twenty-first century and that both the productive exchanges and the contentious struggles between the different strands sketched above have vastly enriched American sociology.

SEE ALSO *Blau, Peter M.; Critical Theory; Duncan, Otis Dudley; Functionalism; Merton, Robert K; Mills, C. Wright; Parsons, Talcott; Sociology; Sociology, Parsonian; Structuralism*

BIBLIOGRAPHY

Abbott, Andrew D. 1988. *The System of Professions: An Essay on the Division of Expert Labor.* Chicago: University of Chicago Press.

Chodorow, Nancy. 1978. *The Reproduction of Mothering.* Berkeley: University of California Press.

Coleman, James S. 1990. *Foundations of Social Theory.* Cambridge, MA: Harvard University Press.

Goode, William J. 1993. *World Changes in Divorce Patterns.* New Haven, CT: Yale University Press.

Merton, Robert King. 1949. *Social Theory and Social Structure.* Glencoe, IL: Free Press.

Moore, Barrington, Jr. 1966. *The Social Origins of Dictatorship and Democracy: Lord and Peasant in the Making of the Modern World.* Boston: Beacon.

Wrong, Dennis. 1961. The Oversocialization Conception of Man in Modern Sociology. *American Sociological Review* 26 (2): 183–196.

Ari Adut

SOCIOLOGY, RURAL

The discipline of rural sociology addresses how communities and areas with few people are socially and economically organized, what patterns of social interaction occur among residents within these areas and elsewhere, and why and how communities change over time. Its early practitioners were active members in the rural sociology section of the American Sociological Society (later renamed as the American Sociological Association) until 1937. In that year, they founded the independent Rural Sociological Society (RSS) to promote teaching, research, and extension outreach. Since then, membership in the Society increased from seventy-nine to slightly less than one thousand academic scholars, professionals, and students in the new millenium. The first newsletter of the rural section appeared in 1925. The RSS published the newsletter as *Newsline* from the 1970s through 1980 and subsequently as *The Rural Sociologist* with the purpose to spread news about the vitality of rural sociology among its practitioners and others interested in the discipline.

HISTORICAL CONTRIBUTIONS

Rural sociological scholarship has a long tradition involving people, communities, and natural resources due in part to its location in the university land-grant system. In 1997 Norwood Kerr discussed the founding of the American land-grant university system by the Morrill Land-Grant College Acts of 1862 and 1890, the latter for traditionally black institutions in southern states. These acts introduced the movement led by Connecticut and thirteen other states to establish agricultural experiment stations to specifically address the development of practical agricultural information for rural farmers and ranchers through scientific investigations. The movement culminated in 1887 with the passage of the Hatch Act that forged the federal-state partnership for funding "scientific agriculture." The public service counterpart to the Hatch Act followed in the Smith-Lever Act of 1914. It assigned to the new cooperative extension service the task providing to ordinary people access to their state universities for assistance regarding a broad array of issues affecting themselves, and their families, businesses, and local governments. Early rural sociology programs and their research were and continue to be mostly affiliated with institutional partnerships between universities and agricultural experiment stations along with cooperative extension both at the state level and with counterparts in the United States Department of Agriculture.

Following the pioneering the work of sociologists such as W. E. B. Du Bois and F. H. Gidding, rural sociology was significantly influenced by the Country Life Commission that was appointed by President Theodore Roosevelt. The Commission's 1909 report on twelve rural communities pointed to problems of poverty, crime, population change, and governance that many rural communities were experiencing at that time and revealed the need for the land-grant system to devote social science expertise to solve these problems. Funding for conducting this research languished for a while, but passage of the Purnell Act of 1925 expanded federal commitment to experiment station research by funding studies in agricultural economics, rural sociology, and home economics. As documented by Olaf Larson and Julie Zimmerman in 2003, this commitment was extended in the United States Department of Agriculture (USDA)'s Division of Farm Population and Rural Life, where rural sociologists such as Charles Galpin, Carl Taylor, and others pioneered national-level studies on social trends and conditions in rural areas. These studies were followed by more locally oriented studies conducted by academic rural sociologists such as Paul Landis, Carle Zimmerman, and Dwight Sanderson. Founded in 1936, the journal *Rural Sociology* became the flagship for reporting much of this research.

During the next quarter-century, the importance of rural sociology to the public policy process and programs diminished with the dismantling of New Deal programs in the 1940s and the Division of Farm Population's successor, the Bureau of Agricultural Economics (BAE), in 1953. The USDA no longer favored what it termed "cultural surveys" nor did it receive well Walter Goldschmidt's study of two rural California communities in 1944 wherein he reported that rural well-being was negatively affected by large farms and powerful farmers. Trends of an increasingly more urban and industrialized U.S. population in the post–World War II (1939–1945) era were among other factors that contributed to rural sociology's loss of stature.

CONTEMPORARY RESEARCH EMPHASES

Interest renewed in rural sociology in the last quarter of the twentieth century. Researchers continued their traditional interests in rural communities, population change, rural poverty, and social inequality. They rejuvenated work begun in the 1950s on the adoption and diffusion of agricultural innovations. In 1983 Everett Rogers, one of the foremost leaders of this area, reported that the number of empirical studies grew from a total of 405 in 1962 to slightly more than 3,000 twenty years later. The "sociology of agriculture" became the new label that drew on this research history. It also staked out new areas regarding the social significance of women in agriculture, new biotechnologies, the expansion of industrialized agriculture and agribusiness, and the globalization of agro-industrialized systems. In their 1988 book, *Rural Sociology and the Environment*, Don Field and William Burch Jr. recognized important connections among agricultural sociology, human ecology, and natural resource sociology. They termed the intersection of these research venues as "agroecology" (p. 114) and proposed that it serve in the broadest sense as a definitive guide for rural development and a critical component of applied environmental sociology. The most comprehensive inventory of rural sociological concepts, subject matter, and knowledge about American rural life appeared in 1997. Gary Goreham's *The Encyclopedia of Rural America: The Land and People* includes articles by prominent rural sociologists and other scholars on 232 topics that vary from agriculture and other rural industries to rural youth, the elderly, women and minority groups, crime, culture, technology, and natural resources and the environment.

INTERNATIONAL RURAL DEVELOPMENT

Community and economic development continue to be important research and policy issues that confront and connect rural communities and rural scholars in America and abroad. Economic globalization has stressed and challenged rural communities everywhere. While many businesses and manufacturing companies seek out lower-cost production areas and lucrative markets, rural communities strive to find ways to overcome infrastructural, capital, resource, and policy obstacles to promote development and competitiveness. In 1962 U.S. and European rural sociologists convened at the annual meeting of the RSS in Washington, D.C., to form the Committee for International Cooperation in Rural Sociology to address these issues.

After three world congresses, the Committee organized the International Rural Sociology Association (IRSA) in 1976 to spearhead concern and attention involving the impacts of globalization and rural development. The IRSA is a federation of regional rural sociological societies devoted to foster the development and application of rural sociological inquiry to improve globally the quality of rural life. In addition to the RSS, the Association includes the Australian and Oceania Network, the Asian Rural Sociological Association, the Latin America Rural Sociological Association, and the European Society for Rural Sociology. The IRSA met at the XI World Congress in 2004 in Trondheim, Norway, to explore the unevenness, risks, and resistance related to the globalization of production and to the identification of rural economies' and societies' agency to manage change in this process. IRSA congresses are held every four years.

SEE ALSO *Sociology*

BIBLIOGRAPHY

Buttel, Frederick H. 1997. Rural Sociology. In *Encyclopedia of Rural America: The Land and People*. Vol. 2, ed. Gary A. Goreham. Santa Barbara, CA: ABC-CLIO.

Buttel, Frederick H., Olaf F. Larson, and Gilbert Gillespie Jr. 1990. *The Sociology of Agriculture*. Westport, CT: Greenwood Press.

Field, Donald R., and William R. Burch Jr. 1988. *Rural Sociology and the Environment*. Westport, CT: Greenwood Press.

Fuguitt, Glenn V., and Alvin L. Bertrand. 1999. IRSA History. International Rural Sociology Association. http://www.irsa-world.org.

Goldschmidt, Walter R. [1947] 1978. *As You Sow: Three Studies in the Social Consequences of Agribusiness*. Mortclair, NJ: Allanheld, Osmun.

Goreham, Gary A., ed. 1997. *Encyclopedia of Rural America: The Land and People*. 2 vols. Santa Barbara, CA: ABC-CLIO.

Green, Gary. 1999. Development, Community, and Economic. In *Encyclopedia of Rural America: The Land and People*. Vol. 1, ed. Gary A. Goreham. Santa Barbara, CA: ABC-CLIO.

Kerr, Norwood Allen. 1987. *The Legacy: A Centennial History of the State Agricultural Experiment Stations, 1887–1997*. Columbia: University of Missouri.

Larson, Olaf F., and Julie N. Zimmerman. 2003. *Sociology in Government: The Galpin-Taylor Years in the U.S. Department of Agriculture, 1919–1953*. University Park: Pennsylvania State University Press.

McDowell, George R. 2001. *Land-Grant Universities and Extension: Into the 21st Century*. Ames: Iowa State University Press.

Rogers, Everett. 1983. *Diffusion of Innovations*. 3rd ed. New York: Free Press.

RSS Historian's Report. 2005. *The Rural Sociologist* 25 (1): 24–25.

John K. Thomas

SOCIOLOGY, SCHOOLS IN

In this entry, *school* will be understood as referring to a group of practitioners who are identified in terms of characteristic ways of acting upon the world. Such practices are derived from some general principles (analytical, theoretical, empirical premises of interpreting and putting into practice some basic ways of viewing reality), often formulated by a central figure or figures and amplified by their students or followers. If not in terms of some defining orientation to the world, a school may receive its identity in terms of either the name of the leader who formulated the basic approach, or else the setting where the group developed its coherence and overall unity.

Schools are fairly common categorizations of groups in the humanities, such as in philosophy (e.g., American pragmatism), the arts (e.g., cubism), and even history (e.g., the Annales school of Lucien Febvre [1878–1956], Marc Bloch [1886–1944], and Fernand Braudel [1902–1985]). In contrast, it is uncommon to find schools in the history and development of the natural sciences, however marked they are by controversies over priorities in scientific discoveries. In between, although it is more common in presenting the history of the discipline to deal with the work of individuals rather than that of schools, in the social and behavioral sciences (social anthropology, clinical and social psychology, and particularly sociology), schools have played a major role. To pursue this topic, however, it is necessary to provide further specification of what is taken to be a *school* by breaking the term into a *weak* sense and a *strong* sense.

By *weak* sense of school is meant a grouping of figures and their research and publications that share a general orientation to reality, a general way of dealing with and interpreting social reality, irrespective of whether these individuals have known or interacted with each other; the strength of their networks is thus weak, and there is no specific locale for their training. The collective identity of such a school is heuristic in providing some organization to the diversity of empirical and research orientations present in the discipline, but it does not have a clear focus. And *school* in this sense may fade into a looser grouping, such as *traditions* that may be analytical (e.g., Collins 1994) or geographical (e.g., Genov 1989).

Perhaps the best approach to schools in the weak sense noted above is the pioneering study of then-contemporary sociological theories conducted by Pitirim Sorokin (1889–1968). He proposed (1928, p. xvi) that social theories seeking scientific merit could be grouped in nine major *schools* (mechanistic, synthetic and geographical, geographical, biological, biosocial, biopsychological, sociologistic, psychological, and psycho-sociologistic), with some important varieties listed under several schools. The taxonomy of his study was intended to establish inductively and critically sociology as a multidimensional discipline seeking to deal factually with its subject matter and correlations between classes of social phenomena and between social and nonsocial phenomena. Fifty years later this perspective of the unity in diversity of sociology still held (as seen in Eisenstadt and Curelaru 1976).

Strong schools are those that have a recognizable central primary figure (or in some cases, figures) who elaborates the basic principles of approaching social reality in the search for valid knowledge (the ontology and epistemology of the research enterprise)—metaphorically, who prepares the basic structure of a cookbook of recipes that may be used by students. In turn, the practices of the students add to the corpus of the initial doctrines and principles, perhaps by taking this into new vistas of research. The networking among members of the school will be strong, and will often show a high degree of citation of works of one another, with the writings of the central figures given privileged attention. While cohesion and mutual support vis-à-vis the discipline is high, for example, in obtaining resources for members and new recruits, such as publication outlets, research grants, and even academic or related positions, it is by no means assured. Yet even strong schools may weaken after one or two generations, either due to internal bickering regarding leadership or intellectual direction, or because of apparent exhaustion of research potential in the basic formulations of the school. Ultimately, the appeal of a school may wane when its central problems and modes of operation become viewed as superannuated in relating to societal reality and its changing conditions.

Some strong schools at peak strength dominate subfields of sociology and take on the general name of their orientation, with subgroups as offings having their own identity. In social psychology-sociology, *symbolic interactionism* (coined by Herbert Blumer [1900–1987]) has stressed the significance of establishing and interpreting how actors make sense (find meaning) in interacting with one another, even if the objective meaning of their situation is ambiguous. This school, drawing on the initial theoretical writings of the pragmatist philosopher George Herbert Mead (1863–1931) and the pioneering social psychological studies of William I. Thomas (1863–1947), had new dimensions introduced in the 1960s and 1970s in the ethnographic studies of Erving Goffman (1922–1982) and Harold Garfinkel (the latter, aided by Aaron Cicourel, developing the frames of ethnomethodology), and further in the 1980s in the studies of Gary Fine on subcultures. Though it is still a viable orientation at the microlevel (of interacting individuals), it has not been an overarching orientation of broader segments of society.

Also in this rubric of strong schools might be included *world-system theory*, which in the 1970s and 1980s had a major formulator, Immanuel Wallerstein (assisted by Terence Hopkins and Chris Chase-Dunn), a center for training (at the State University of New York–Binghamton), and a journal (*Review*). The comparative-historical studies of this school derive from a Marxist perspective of the exploitation of labor, before as well as after the advent of modern capitalism, and the unequal distribution of world resources operating over time in zero-sum fashion with core capitalistic countries accumulating greater shares at the expense of "peripheries." The emergence of India and East Asia in recent decades has attenuated the appeal of this school, although it has made with its many scholars an important mark in the area of macrosociology.

There is perhaps a further set of *very strong* schools, which have practically dominated the entire field of sociology, or at least established some sort of intellectual hegemony for an entire generation or more. One might speak of the Marxist school drawing on the leadership of Karl Marx (1818–1883) and Friedrich Engels (1820–1895), with a basic presupposition that the social order rests on the expropriation of labor and the exploitation of workers, who are temporarily kept from realizing their true conditions by the smokescreens of the dominant class, but as conditions increasingly worsen, a point will be reached where a socialist revolution will shatter the capitalist system. There have been numerous variations of Marxism claiming legitimacy as successors, but the one that in addition to world-system theory has been most recognized in the United States and Germany is the Frankfurt school, which later evolved under the second-generation leadership of Jürgen Habermas (at the University of Frankfurt) as *critical theory*. The major figures of the school in the 1920s sought to amalgamate a Marxist orientation critical of capitalism (historical materialism) with a Freudian orientation on psychological and cultural maladaptations of the modern world that hinder personal freedom and generate alienation. At the Institute of Social Research, they—notably Theodore Adorno (1903–1969), Max Horkheimer (1895–1973), and Herbert Marcuse (1898–1979)—pursued philosophical and historical investigations, interrupted by the Nazi regime. After World War II (1939–1945), the renovated critical theory orientation found many adepts on both sides of the Atlantic, spearheaded by Habermas, who engaged in the mass media a wide variety of topics and whose writings on *communicative action* considerably widened the theoretical tools by an earnest engagement with non-Marxist orientations such as American pragmatism and Parsonian action theory.

The three other "hegemonic schools" (Tiryakian 1986) to be noted may each be said to have nearly dominated the field of sociology, either in their own country or in the entire discipline. Besides all the characteristics of strong schools noted above, they emerged in periods of national reconstruction following some major crisis, and their basic theoretical and methodological orientations offered new initiatives for sociological action.

The secular government of the French Third Republic (1870–1940), which gave a high premium to public education, science, and civic morality, favored the rise of the Durkheimian school (Besnard 1983), whose intellectual leader, Émile Durkheim (1868–1917), produced foundational works for modern sociology, established the teaching of sociology at the prestigious Sorbonne in Paris, attracted highly gifted students— Marcel Mauss (1872–1950), François Simiand (1873– 1935), Maurice Halbwachs (1877–1945), Marcel Granet (1884–1940), Robert Hertz (1881–1915), Henri Hubert (1872–1927)—who later found appointments in major areas of the public sector, and secured major publishing outlets (the publishing house Alcan and the world-class journal, the *Année Sociologique*, which greatly contributed to advancing comparative-historical sociology and tacitly is the model for the American *Annual Review of Sociology*). The school emphasized in diverse analyses the irreducibility of the social to individual causation such as *economic interests*, but sought to bring to light structures of social organization deeply imbedded in cognitive and ritual aspects of the collectivity itself.

In the United States, the University of Chicago became the locale of a new empirical orientation derived from (1) the pragmatism of Charles Sanders Peirce (1839– 1914), William James (1842–1910), and George Herbert Mead (1863–1931), and (2) the application of ecology in botany to the study of the dynamics of social organization of the human urban habitat, marked by competition and accommodation of various groups. With brilliant students under the analytical leadership of Robert Park (1864– 1944) and the quantitative leadership of his lieutenant, Ernest Burgess (1886–1966), the Chicago school emerged after World War I (1914–1918) as providing outstanding training in field research and participant-observation of interaction processes (Bulmer 1984; Abbott 1999; Chapoulie 2001). It obtained research grants for its students, enjoyed a major publication outlet for doctoral monographs with the University of Chicago Press, and has been the site of the continuous publication of a world-class journal, the *American Journal of Sociology*.

Finally, in the post–World War II era, from the mid-1940s until the mid-1960s, Talcott Parsons (1902–1979) at Harvard University provided the prolific intellectual leadership for a new and systematic analytical perspective intended to integrate sociology, social anthropology, and social and clinical psychology. As the United States took global leadership in a *pax Americana*, Harvard's Department of Social Relations provided new comparative and theoretical training that could be applied at micro- as well as macrolevels of analysis in what came to be termed *structural-functional analysis*. The historical development of this school and some of its major contributors—including Robert Merton (1910–2003), Kingsley Davis (1908–1997), Neil Smelser, and Robert Bellah—as related to but distinct from Parsons (whose later writings in what he saw as "action theory" went considerably beyond the initial mode of analysis he provided in the 1940s and 1950s) awaits to be written, beyond Parsons's intellectual biography (Gerhardt 2002). Such a history would entail the many resources the school made available (such as the publishing house the Free Press, and the research grants of the Ford Foundation) and the diffusion of many of its central theoretical ideas to related disciplines such as political science and social anthropology.

This necessarily skeletal account of schools needs two final points. First, some of the most important names in the history of sociology are not associated with schools, despite their intellectual worth and significance. Such is the case, for example, with Herbert Spencer (1820–1903), Max Weber (1864–1920), Georges Gurvitch (1894–1965), and Pitirim Sorokin. Second, schools do not flourish in sociology at all times; the contemporary period, for instance, seems to be a quiescent period bereft of a clearly recognized "hegemonic" school. Perhaps this presents an opportunity for a more objective examination of the rise and fall of schools, as well new research on their interconnecting networks.

SEE ALSO *Chicago School; Frankfurt School; Habermas, Jürgen; Marcuse, Herbert; Marx, Karl; Marxism; Mead, George Herbert; Merton, Robert K; Park, Robert E.; Parsons, Talcott; Race Relations Cycle; Sociology; Sociology, American; Wallerstein, Immanuel; Weber, Max; World-System*

BIBLIOGRAPHY

Abbott, Andrew. 1999. *Department & Discipline: Chicago Sociology at One Hundred.* Chicago: University of Chicago Press.

Besnard, Philippe. 1983. The "Année Sociologique" Team. In *The Sociological Domain: The Durkheimians and the Founding of French Sociology,* ed. Philippe Besnard, 11–38. Cambridge, U.K., and New York: Cambridge University Press; Paris: Editions de la Maison des Sciences de l'Homme.

Bulmer, Martin. 1984. *The Chicago School of Sociology: Institutionalization, Diversity and the Rise of Sociological Research.* Chicago: University of Chicago Press.

Chapoulie, Jean-Michel. 2001. *La Tradition sociologique de Chicago, 1892–1961.* Paris: Seuil.

Collins, Randall. 1994. *Four Sociological Traditions.* New York: Oxford University Press.

Eisenstadt, S. N., and M. Curelaru. 1976. *The Form of Sociology: Paradigms and Crises.* New York: Wiley.

Genov, Nikolai, ed. 1989. *National Traditions in Sociology.* London and Newbury Park, CA: Sage.

Gerhardt, Uta. 2002. *Talcott Parsons: An Intellectual Biography.* New York: Cambridge University Press.

Sorokin, Pitirim A. 1928. *Contemporary Sociological Theories.* New York and London: Harper.

Tiryakian, Edward A. 1986. Hegemonic Schools and the Development of Sociology. In *Structures of Knowing: Current Studies in the Sociology of Schools,* ed. Richard C. Monk, 417–441. Lanham, MD: University Press of America.

Edward A. Tiryakian

SOCIOLOGY, THIRD WORLD

Any discussion of the "third world" should begin with a definition of the term. *Third world* is commonly used to describe countries that are economically poor, lack adequate educational and health systems, suffer from the digital divide, and exhibit relatively little global political power. Although frequently used, the term is considered out-of-date and even derogatory in some circles. Many scholars, for instance, argue that "third world" implies that poor countries are less important than other ("first world") countries or are somehow not part of the global economic system. In their 2007 book *Global Inequalities,* York Bradshaw, Stephen Scanlan, and Michael Wallace said that instead of "third world" critics often use "developing world" or "developing nations" when referring to countries that are not fully developed from an economic and quality of life standpoint.

In his 1974 publication *The Modern World System,* Immanuel Wallerstein discussed one theoretical perspective concerned with development, which places countries into three different categories. The "core" is composed of rich, industrialized countries that also enjoy a relatively good quality of life in terms of education and health care. The "periphery" is composed of poor countries that lack industrial capacity and well-developed education and health care systems. The "semi-periphery" is composed of middle-income countries that are between the core and the periphery. The periphery and the semi-periphery make up the vast majority of the world's countries.

For this discussion, terminology is not a main concern. Terms come and go over time, but the reality is that *global inequality* remains an enormous problem. Much of the world lives amid extreme poverty. This article describes the developing world and then discusses how sociology studies it.

AN UNEQUAL WORLD

To begin, here is a quiz: What two developing countries account for 37 percent of the world's 6.5 billion people? If you answered China (1.3 billion) and India (1.1 billion), you win a prize. In fact of the ten most populated countries in the world, seven are considered developing and, together with China and India, they account for nearly 51 percent of the world's population. Of the 210 countries listed by the World Bank, three-quarters are considered low- or middle-income countries, and this represents the vast majority of the world's population. In fact if the issue is studied in reverse, there are only twenty-four true "core" countries in the world (11 percent of the world's countries), and they account for less than 20 percent of the global population. There are a number of other "high income" countries (e.g., Bahrain, Kuwait, Monaco, Slovenia), but they are mostly small and do not possess all of the characteristics of the core (World Bank 2007).

Another way to think about global inequality is to compare the resources of companies, countries, and individuals. Here is another quiz: What country has the twenty-second largest economy in the world, as measured by gross domestic product (output of total goods and services)? The answer: the core country Austria, which has a gross domestic product of $309.4 billion. Twenty-one countries have larger economies, and 188 have smaller ones (World Bank 2007). But wait a minute! Austria is not the twenty-second largest economic entity in the world; Wal-Mart is. That is right. According to Christopher Tkaczyk in his 2007 article "Fortune 500: The Top 50," Wal-Mart, the biggest multinational corporation in the world in terms of total revenue ($351.139 billion), is larger than all but twenty-one countries in the world. Wal-Mart is larger than several core countries, most semi-peripheral countries, and all peripheral countries. And incredibly the combined revenues of the top *two* multinational corporations (Wal-Mart [$351.139 billion] and Exxon Mobil [$347.254 billion]) are greater than the *combined* economic output of all fifty-three sub-Saharan African countries. Together Wal-Mart and Exxon Mobil are larger economic entities than the entire continent of Africa (Tkaczyk 2007; World Bank 2007).

Inequality is also evident when looking at personal wealth across countries and regions. A comprehensive study conducted in 2006 by the World Institute for Development Economics Research at the United Nations University in Helsinki, Finland, revealed that the richest 2 percent of the world's population owns more than half of the world's wealth. And the richest 10 percent of the population owns 85 percent of the world's wealth. By contrast, the bottom 50 percent of the world's population owns 1 percent of the total wealth on the planet. In fact 1.3 billion people around the world live on less than $1 per day, and 3 billion (nearly half the planet's population) live on less than $2 per day. By contrast, pointed out Luisa Kroll and Allison Fass in the 2007 article "The World's Billionaires," the extremely wealthy of the world—the 946 billionaires throughout the globe—are worth $3.5 trillion ($3,500,000,000). That is more than twice the

gross domestic product of all peripheral countries in the world combined (World Bank 2007).

And what are the consequences of poverty? One is disease and premature death. A primary development indicator is the child mortality rate in a country—the number of children who die before the age of five for every 1,000 children born. In economically developed countries, the average child mortality rate is only 8 (led by Sweden's 3), but in developing countries the rate is 89. In a pair of 2007 studies by UNICEF, it was found that in Africa the child mortality rate is 174, with a number of countries over 200 and some approaching 300 (UNICEF 2007a, 2007b). Each *day* around the world as many as 35,000 children die primarily from preventable diseases and malnutrition. Respiratory infections, diarrheal disease, tuberculosis, measles, malaria, and HIV/AIDS are some of the leading causes of death among children of the developing world. According to York Bradshaw, Stephen Scanlan, and Michael Wallace (2007), the vast majority of the world's HIV/AIDS cases are in developing countries, led by African countries.

SOCIOLOGY AND GLOBAL INEQUALITY

Sociology was slow to study international inequality and development. Until the 1970s the field was dominated by economists, anthropologists, and political scientists. All of this began to change in 1974, when the sociologist Immanuel Wallerstein published *The Modern World System*. Wallerstein argued that the current world economic and political structures have their origins in sixteenth-century Europe. His book and subsequent work established an entirely new theory (world-systems theory) that divides the world into the core, periphery, and semi-periphery, as mentioned previously. Although some people disagree with Wallerstein, just about everyone agrees that along with finding an innovative theory, he started a movement of young sociologists who wanted to study international inequality and development.

In response to Wallerstein's new theory, a number of sociologists began to conduct sophisticated statistical studies to examine the causes and effects of international inequality. The results of several studies are presented below. All are based on a large sample of developing countries.

- Foreign investment in poor countries does not reach the mass population and therefore creates more inequality in those places. This ultimately harms economic growth in the developing world (Bornschier and Chase-Dunn 1985).

- Expanding foreign debt and the accompanying structural adjustment policies implemented by the

International Monetary Fund (IMF) and others increase child mortality in poor countries (Bradshaw, Noonan, Gash, and Buchmann 1993).

- Likewise structural adjustment policies have increased riots and overall instability in a number of developing countries (Walton and Ragin 1990).

- Education is linked to greater economic growth and less inequality in the developing world (Buchmann and Hannum 2001; Hannum and Buchmann 2005).

- Child labor is detrimental to the quality of life in developing countries. Moreover education reduces child labor, again underscoring the necessity of schooling in developing nations (Bradshaw, Scanlan, and Wallace 2007).

Sociologists use two other types of studies to advance theoretical and substantive knowledge of development. First, some sociologists *compare* a few countries in great detail in order to address difficult questions and issues that often reflect inequalities of wealth and power. For example, in his book *Reluctant Rebels: Comparative Studies of Revolution and Underdevelopment* (1984), John Walton looked at revolts and revolutions in the Philippines, Colombia, and Kenya to answer this question: Why and when do people rebel? And in the book *Child Labor in Sub-Saharan Africa* (2004), Loretta Bass takes us across the continent of Africa to explain the causes and effects of child labor (including slavery). Inequality is again a key component in the explanation of this pressing challenge. Second, other sociologists engage in intensive *case studies* of particular developing countries to investigate especially important issues (Bradshaw and Wallace 1991). For example, in his highly regarded book *Underdeveloping the Amazon: Extraction, Unequal Exchange, and the Failure of the Modern State* (1985), Stephen Bunker relied on extensive fieldwork to show how local and international forces interacted to plunder the Amazon. And in *Growing Up Modern: The Western State Builds Third-World Schools* (1991), Bruce Fuller focused on the poor country of Malawi to demonstrate how the "fragile" national state tried (with mixed success) to implement a Western-style education system. National and global inequalities helped to explain the outcome.

In the early twenty-first century most internationally oriented sociologists are concerned with global inequality in one form or another. Although an occasional sociologist argues that global inequality is shrinking and globalization is a positive force (see, for example, Glenn Firebaugh's provocative book *The New Geography of Global Income Inequality* [2003]), most are concerned about the high level of inequality and its impact on the vast majority of the world's population. In terms of offer-ing solutions to global inequality, sociologists have joined others to advocate for more foreign aid to poor countries and forgiveness of the developing world's crippling debts. Perhaps the most well-known and passionate spokesperson for these positions is Bono, the lead singer for the Irish rock group U2. He has encouraged the United States and other countries to contribute 1 percent more of their federal budgets to the world's poor:

> One percent is the girl in Africa who gets to go to school—thanks to you. One percent is the AIDS patient who gets her medicine—thanks to you. One percent is the African entrepreneur who can start a small family business—thanks to you. One percent is not redecorating presidential palaces and money flowing down a rat hole. This one percent is digging waterholes to provide clean water. (Bono 2007, p. 41)

There is much more for sociologists to study. Over the next ten years sociologists will most likely devote substantial attention to three issues (among others). First, HIV/AIDS continues to ravage large parts of the developing world, and there is a huge need for research to study both the causes and effects of this pandemic in more detail. Second, information technology has the capacity to improve health, education, and overall quality of life in developing regions (Bradshaw, Fallon, and Viterna 2005). Commenting on a new e-school initiative in Africa, South African president Thabo Mbeki said, "Let us use this technology to do things better, develop African brain power that will pull our country and the African continent as a whole out of poverty" (Nepad 2007). Finally, many believe that the darkest side of globalization includes not the sale of products across national borders but the sale of human beings. Hundreds of thousands of people—especially women and girls—are sold each year in both the developing and the developed worlds. Sociologists are primed to lead the way in studying this enormous social challenge, another problem that emerges from an unequal world.

SEE ALSO *AIDS/HIV in Developing Countries, Impact of; Developing Countries; Development and Ethnic Diversity; Development in Sociology; Inequality, Gender; Inequality, Political; Inequality, Racial; Poverty; Sociology; Third World; United Nations; Wallerstein, Immanuel; World-System*

BIBLIOGRAPHY

Bass, Loretta E. 2004. *Child Labor in Sub-Saharan Africa.* Boulder, CO: Lynne Rienner.

Bono. 2007. *On the Move.* Nashville, TN: W Publishing Group.

Bornschier, Volker, and Christopher Chase-Dunn. 1985. *Transnational Corporations and Underdevelopment*. New York: Praeger.

Bradshaw, York, and Michael Wallace. 1991. Informing Generality and Explaining Uniqueness: The Place of Case Studies in Comparative Research. *International Journal of Comparative Sociology* 32: 154–171.

Bradshaw, York, Kathleen Fallon, and Jocelyn Viterna. 2005. Wiring the World: Access to Information Technology and Development in Poor Countries. *Research in Social Stratification and Mobility* 23: 369–392.

Bradshaw, York, Stephen Scanlan, and Michael Wallace. 2007. *Global Inequalities*. 2nd ed. Boston: Pine Forge.

Bradshaw, York, Rita Noonan, Laura Gash, and Claudia Buchmann. 1993. Borrowing against the Future: Children and Third World Indebtedness. *Social Forces* 71 (3): 629–656.

Bradshaw, York, Wanda Rushing, Stephen Scanlan, and Kristen Heck Sajadi. Submitted for publication. The End of Childhood: Children at Work and War in a Changing World.

Buchmann, Claudia, and Emily Hannum. 2001. Education and Stratification in Developing Countries: A Review of Theories and Research. *Annual Review of Sociology* 27: 77–102.

Bunker, Stephen G. 1985. *Underdeveloping the Amazon: Extraction, Unequal Exchange, and the Failure of the Modern State*. Urbana: University of Illinois Press.

Firebaugh, Glenn. 2003. *The New Geography of Global Income Inequality*. Cambridge, MA: Harvard University Press.

Fuller, Bruce. 1991. *Growing-Up Modern: The Western State Builds Third-World Schools*. New York: Routledge.

Hannum, Emily, and Claudia Buchmann. 2005. Global Educational Expansion and Socio-Economic Development: An Assessment of Findings from the Social Sciences. *World Development* 33 (3): 333–354.

Kroll, Luisa, and Allison Fass. 2007. The World's Billionaires. Forbes.com, March 8, 2007. http://www.forbes.com/2007/03/07/billionaires-worlds-richest_07billionaires_cz_lk_af_0308billie_land.html.

New Partnership for Africa's Development (Nepad). 2007. *Nepad Dialogue*. English ed. Issue 177, April 20, 2007.

Tkaczyk, Christopher. 2007. Fortune 500: The Top 50. CNNMoney.com. http://www.money.cnn.com/galleries/2007/fortune/0704/gallery.500top50.fortune/index.html.

UNICEF. 2007a. Monitoring the Situation of Children and Women. UNICEF. http://www.Childinfo.org.

UNICEF. 2007b. *The State of the World's Children 2007*. New York: UNICEF.

Wallerstein, Immanuel. 1974. *The Modern World System*. New York: Academic.

Walton, John. 1984. *Reluctant Rebels: Comparative Studies of Revolution and Underdevelopment*. New York: Columbia University Press.

Walton, John, and Charles Ragin. 1990. Global and National Sources of Political Protest: Third World Responses to the Debt Crisis. *American Sociological Review* 55 (6): 876–890.

World Bank. 2007. *World Development Report 2007*. Washington, DC: World Bank.

World Institute for Development Economics Research. 2006. *The World Distribution of Household Wealth*. Helsinki, Finland: United Nations University.

York W. Bradshaw

SOCIOLOGY, URBAN

As the cutting edge of change, cities are important for interpreting societies. Momentous changes in nineteenth-century cities led theorists to explore their components. The French word for place (*bourg*), and its residents (*bourgeois*), became central concepts for Karl Marx (1818–1883). Markets and commerce emerged in cities where "free air" ostensibly fostered innovation. Industrial capitalists thus raised capital and built factories near cities, hiring workers "free" from the feudal legal hierarchy. For Marx, workers were proletarians and a separate economic class, whose interests conflicted with the bourgeoisie. Class conflicts drove history. Max Weber's (1864–1920) *The City* (1921) built on this legacy but added legitimacy, bureaucracy, the Protestant ethic, and political parties in transforming cities. Émile Durkheim (1858–1917) similarly reasoned historically, contrasting traditional villages with modern cities in his *Division of Labor* (1893), where multiple professional groups integrated their members by enforcing norms on them.

British and American work was more empirical. British and American churches and charitable groups that were concerned with the urban poor sponsored many early studies. When sociology entered universities around 1900, urban studies still focused on inequality and the poor. Robert Park (1864–1944) and many students at the University of Chicago thus published monographs on such topics as *The Gold Coast and the Slum* (1929), a sociological study of Chicago's near north side by Harvey Warren Zorbaugh (1896–1965).

The 1940s and 1950s saw many efforts to join these European theories with the British and American empirical work. Floyd Hunter published *Community Power Structure* (1953), an Atlanta-based monograph that stressed the business dominance of cities, broadly following Marx. Robert Dahl's *Who Governs?* (1961) was more Weberian, stressing multiple issue areas of power and influence (like mayoral elections versus schools), the indirect role of citizens via elections, and multiple types of resources (money, votes, media, coalitions) that shifted how basic economic categories influenced politics. These became the main ideas in power analyses across the social sciences.

Parisian theorists like Michel Foucault (1926–1984), Pierre Bourdieu (1930–2002), and Henri Lefebvre (1901–1991) suggested that the language and symbols of upper-status persons dominated lower-status persons. Others, such as Jean Baudrillard, pushed even further to suggest that each person was so distinct that theories should be similarly individualized. He and others labeled their perspective *postmodernism* to contrast with mainstream science, which they suggested reasoned in a linear, external, overly rational manner. Urban geographers like David Harvey joined postmodernist themes with concepts of space to suggest a sea change in architecture, planning, and aesthetics, as well as in theorizing, although Harvey's main analytical driver is global capitalism.

Saskia Sassen starts from global capitalism but stresses local differences in such "world cities" as New York, London, and Tokyo. Why these? Because the headquarters of global firms are there, with "producer services" that advise major firms, and market centers where sophisticated legal and financial transactions are spawned. Individual preferences enter, via global professionals and executives who like big-city living, but hire nannies and chauffeurs, attracting global migrants, which increases (short-term, within city) inequality. Some affluent persons create gated housing, especially in areas with high crime and kidnapping, like Latin America.

These past theories stress work and production. A new conceptualization adds consumption. Walter Benjamin (1892–1940) theorized that the *flaneur* drove the modern capitalist economy, by shopping. Typified by the top-hatted gentleman in impressionist paintings, the *flaneur* pursued his aesthetic sensitivities, refusing standardized products. Mall rats continue his quest.

Theories have grown more bottom-up than top-down, as have many cities, although this is controversial, as some capital and corporations are increasingly global. The father of bottom-up theory is Alexis de Tocqueville (1805–1859), whose *Democracy in America* (1835–1840) stressed community associations like churches. Linked to small and autonomous local governments, these associations gave (ideally) citizens the ability to participate meaningfully in decisions affecting them. Such experiences built networks of social relations and taught values of participation, democracy, and trust.

In the late twentieth century, Tocqueville and civic groups became widely debated as nations declined and cities competed for investors, residents, and tourists. With the cold war over, globalization encourages more cross-national travel, communication, investment, and trade. Local autonomy rose. But nations declined in their delivery of egalitarian welfare benefits, since ideal standards are increasingly international. "Human rights" is a new stan-

dard. Yet the world is too large to implement the most costly specifics, even if they remain political goals.

Over the twentieth century, many organizations shifted from the hierarchical and centralized to the smaller and more participatory. The community power literature from Hunter (1953) to Dahl (1961) and beyond suggests a decline in the "monolithic" city governance pattern that Hunter described in Atlanta. Dahl documented a more participatory, "pluralistic" decision-making process, where multiple participants combine and "pyramid" their "resources" to shift decisions in separate "issue areas."

New social movements (NSMs) emerged in the 1970s, extending past individualism and egalitarianism and joining consumption and lifestyle to the classic production issues of unions and parties. These new civic groups pressed new agendas—ecology, feminism, peace, gay rights—that older political parties ignored. In Europe, the national state and parties were the hierarchical "establishment" opposed by NSMs. In the United States, local business and political elites were more often targeted. Other aesthetic and amenity concerns have also arisen—like suburban sprawl, sports stadiums, and parks; these divide people less into rich versus poor than did class and party politics.

Comparative studies emerged after the 1980s of thousands of cities around the world. They have documented the patterns discussed above, and generally show that citizens and leaders globally are more decentralized, egalitarian, and participatory. *The New Political Culture* (1998), edited by Terry Nichols Clark and Vincent Hoffmann-Martinot, charts these new forms of public decisions and active citizen-leader contacts via NSMs, consumption issues, focused groups, block clubs, cable-television coverage of local associations, and Internet groups. Global competition among cities and weaker nations makes it harder to preserve national welfare-state benefits. This encourages more income inequalities, individualism, and frustrated egalitarianism, which is registered in higher crime rates, divorce, and low trust. As strong national governments withdraw, regional and ethnic violence rises (e.g., in the former Soviet Union or diverse cities like Miami). Voter turnout for elections organized by the classical national parties (which still control local candidate selection in most of the world) thus declined, while new issue-specific community associations mushroomed in the late twentieth century. Urbanism has become global, carried by civic groups, diffused by the Internet, and operating in more subtle ways than past theories proposed.

SEE ALSO *Anthropology, Urban; Assimilation; Bourdieu, Pierre; Chicago School; Cities; Class Conflict; Community Power Studies; Dahl, Robert Alan; Economics, Urban; Elite Theory; Foucault, Michel;*

Geography; Hunter, Floyd; Marx, Karl; Metropolis; Pluralism; Social Movements; Street Culture; Tocqueville, Alexis de; Urban Renewal; Urban Riots; Urban Sprawl; Urbanization; Weber, Max

BIBLIOGRAPHY

Clark, Terry Nichols, and Vincent Hoffmann-Martinot, eds. 1998. *The New Political Culture.* Boulder, CO: Westview.

Dahl, Robert A. [1961] 2005. *Who Governs? Democracy and Power in an American City.* 2nd ed. New Haven, CT: Yale University Press.

Hunter, Floyd. 1953. *Community Power Structure: A Study of Decision Makers.* Durham: University of North Carolina Press.

Terry Nichols Clark

SOCIOLOGY, VOLUNTARISTIC VS. STRUCTURALIST

Voluntaristic sociology emphasizes the importance of free will, or agency, in social settings. Structuralist sociology emphasizes the importance of social settings in shaping and constraining free will. Tension between the two emphases has bedeviled and inspired sociology and related disciplines since the nineteenth century. Among the first to wrestle with this tension was Auguste Comte, who coined the term *sociology* in the 1830s. Human action is determined by the laws of society, in Comte's structuralist view, but understanding these laws will allow sociologists to help modify human action. Comte recognized the possible contradiction and discussed it in lecture 48 of his *Social Physics* ([1839] 1975, p. 132): if free will is able to make modifications, "what can [they] consist of, since nothing can alter either the laws of harmony or the laws of succession?" Comte's solution reflects his structuralist emphasis: free will can affect only the intensity of the operation of societal laws, not the laws themselves. Comte gives examples of powerful monarchs who had only a meager impact on the lives of their subjects.

Later scholars expanded the scope of voluntarism beyond monarchs and sociologists to encompass all of humanity. The most extreme statement of voluntarism within the sociological mainstream came from Herbert Blumer, who invented the term *symbolic interactionism* in 1937. Human behavior, Blumer insisted, is a creative act that cannot be reduced to structural causes: "even though it may well be a well-established and repetitive form of social action, each instance has to be formed anew" (1969, p. 17). This formulation implies that people may choose

not to behave as expected. Indeed, while symbolic interactionism generally focuses on conformity, Blumer also helped to establish the field of *collective behavior*, which focuses on deviance. In these writings Blumer argued that voluntaristic deviance, if it comes to be widely accepted, is the main mechanism through which societies evolve.

By the end of the twentieth century, voluntarism had, in one sense, conquered the field. It was considered improperly derogatory to imply that any person's choices are determined by social context. Even explicitly structuralist theories were increasingly concerned to accommodate free will to some degree, often through the use of the concept of *opportunities*. At the same time, the goal of most sociological explanation remained structuralist, focusing on contextual factors that predict individual outcomes. The radical voluntarism of symbolic interactionism and collective behavior analysis was not widely adopted and, indeed, came to be criticized for ignoring the persistent structures of inequality that characterize social life. In short, sociology was equally committed to voluntarism and structuralism. This paradox generated a variety of attempts to view structure and agency as mutually constitutive.

On one hand were efforts at combination. An influential version of this approach was Peter L. Berger and Thomas Luckmann's *The Social Construction of Reality* (1966), which argued that the two *moments* of institution–creation and institution–maintenance are analytically distinct even if they may in practice coincide. The creation of institutions involves the active working of human agency while maintenance involves the socialization of future generations to view the institutions created by their predecessors as legitimate and permanent. A contrasting approach is exemplified by Anthony Giddens's *The Constitution of Society* (1984), which argues that structure and agency should not be considered as distinct from one another but, rather, as two parts of the same process, which he labeled *structuration*. People produce and reproduce the rules of social life in ways that are patterned by the rules of social life.

On the other hand were efforts to privilege structuralism over voluntarism and vice versa while maintaining both. A sophisticated version of the former balance comes from the works of Pierre Bourdieu. Bourdieu argued that human agency is a variable product of social structure mediated by the bodily comportment and criteria of judgment that Bourdieu called *habitus*. Habitus structures individual preferences and actions and is itself structured by training within particular social contexts. Claims of agency—whether among academic observers or the people being observed—are in this view the result of structural processes. Alternatively, voluntarism may subsume structuralism, as in Patricia Hill Collins's *Black Feminist*

Thought (2000). Collins argued that the powerless are frequently canny observers of the workings of society and active agents of resistance. Ongoing subordination is the product of other people's continuous efforts to dominate, and even the powerless participate in this "matrix of domination" when they work to protect their privilege, meager as it may be (Collins 2000, pp. 227–229, 273–277). The implication is that structuralist claims—whether among observers or the observed—are voluntaristic acts of domination that obscure the radical potential of voluntaristic transformation.

These approaches are usually cited as a way of signaling intellectual affiliation and are only beginning to be juxtaposed and compared. It remains unclear what standards one might use to evaluate voluntarism and structuralism.

SEE ALSO *Blumer, Herbert; Bourdieu, Pierre; Comte, Auguste; Giddens, Anthony; Interactionism, Symbolic; Social Constructionism*

BIBLIOGRAPHY

Berger, Peter L., and Thomas Luckmann. 1966. *The Social Construction of Reality: A Treatise in the Sociology of Knowledge.* New York: Doubleday.

Blumer, Herbert. 1969. *Symbolic Interactionism: Perspective and Method.* Englewood Cliffs, NJ: Prentice-Hall.

Bourdieu, Pierre. 1990. *The Logic of Practice.* Trans. Richard Nice. Stanford, CA: Stanford University Press.

Collins, Patricia Hill. 2000. *Black Feminist Thought: Knowledge, Consciousness, and the Politics of Empowerment.* 2nd ed. New York: Routledge.

Comte, Auguste. [1839] 1975. *Physique sociale: Cours de philosophie positive, leçons 46 à 60* [Social physics: Course on positive philosophy, lessons 46–60]. Paris: Hermann.

Emirbayer, Mustafa, and Ann Mische. 1998. What Is Agency? *American Journal of Sociology* 103 (4): 962–1023.

Fuchs, Stephan. 2001. Beyond Agency. *Sociological Theory* 19 (1): 24–40.

Giddens, Anthony. 1984. *The Constitution of Society.* Berkeley: University of California Press.

Martin, John Levi. 2003. What Is Field Theory? *American Journal of Sociology* 109 (1): 1–49.

Charles Kurzman

SOCIOMETRY

Sociometry, by definition, measures the "socius"—the interpersonal connection between two people (Moreno 1951). The founder of sociometry, Jacob L. Moreno (1889–1974), conceived three levels of sociometry

(Moreno [1953] 1993), applying the term *sociometry* to each (tending to cause confusion). These levels are:

> theoretical system (alternately termed *sociatry*)—
> including role, social atom,
> spontaneity/encounter, psychodrama/enactment,
> and sociometry theories;
>
> subtheory of that system; and
>
> assessment method and intervention (Hale 1981;
> Remer 2006).

Historically sociometry was a central influence in sociology and related areas, even producing several dedicated journals. Over time, though, its influence has diminished to such a point that, at most, one of its central constructs—the sociogram—gets only passing mention in assessment texts (e.g., Cohen and Swerdlik 2005; Cronbach 1970; Gronlund 1971). However, a complete understanding of sociometry provides tremendously powerful structures and tools for use not only in small group interactions but also wherever and whenever interpersonal dynamics come into play.

Grasping the entire sociometric system is optimal, but popularly sociometry theory is focused on measuring relationships, the purview of both social atom theory (long-term relationships and their development and maintenance over time) and sociometry (fluctuation of interpersonal connections over short periods). The sociogram is the representation of sociometry (see Figure 1).

Beyond the conception of humans as essentially social beings, sociometry recognizes and uses the fact that all these connections are perpetually manifest in the social choices we make—for example, with whom we eat lunch; whom we marry; whom we sit next to in classes, receptions, and other meetings; whom we like and do not like (based on tele, warm-up, role reciprocity). Using both positive (choose/acceptance/attraction) and negative (not-choose/rejection/repulsion) choices, the connections between people and the patterns of connections throughout groups are made manifest, explored, and influenced (Remer 1995a, 1995b; Remer and Finger 1995; Remer, Lima, Richey, et al. 1995).

The key to using sociometry as an assessment and intervention (like Heisenberg's principle) most effectively is understanding Moreno's full conceptualization. The misconception is that sociometry stops with the production of the sociogram from choices expressed related to a specific criterion (e.g., "With whom would you most and least want to sit at a wedding reception?"). This level is what Moreno called "near ['weak'] sociometry" (my label). "Strong" sociometry requires two conditions beyond eliciting choices and depicting them: (1) The choices must be implemented (e.g., you must sit with whom you have chosen), and (2) the reasons for choosing must be made overt and explored. The last two conditions present many possibilities and difficulties.

Implementing the choices makes them real in the sense that the full impact of a choice is experienced (e.g., you can say I'll sit with Aunt Bertha to be nice, but actually sitting with her may inform you fully why others have not opted for that seat). So future choices will be influenced. Arriving at an optimal implementation is challenging because not everyone can have one of his or her positives, and some must endure a negative—regardless of how many selections are allowed (a phenomenon addressed by the theory).

Examining choice rationales presents other challenges. People tend to be uncomfortable with the process because, for example, they believe that feelings may be hurt or they are confused by their own ambivalences and lack of awareness of their reasons. Reservations have some validity but usually not nearly to the degree feared. The benefit derives from probing projections attendant—assumptions about the rationales and/or expectations for the choices. At worst, some perceptions are confirmed; at best and more often, the rationales do not conform to suppositions in informative ways (e.g., you are not chosen by a friend because you see each other frequently and he or she wants to visit with others, or you are chosen by someone because you are seen as the only less talkative person in the group). Negatives are not necessarily "bad," nor are positives necessarily "good." Learning reasons challenges assumptions and/or provides the basis for changing behaviors—a not inconsequential therapeutic value.

The sociograms (Figure 1) and the choices from which it is constructed (Figure 2) clarify these points and introduce terminology to illustrate the strengths of sociometry. The data are real, using the criterion "From whom would you like feedback?" based on two positive and two negative choices.

The pattern of choices shows that D is the "star" (that is, he or she receives the most choices) and F is a "rejectee" (he or she receives no positive choices and a number of negative choices); everyone else is a "member" (receiving some positive and perhaps some negative choices). No "isolate" (someone receiving no choices) appears. C, D,

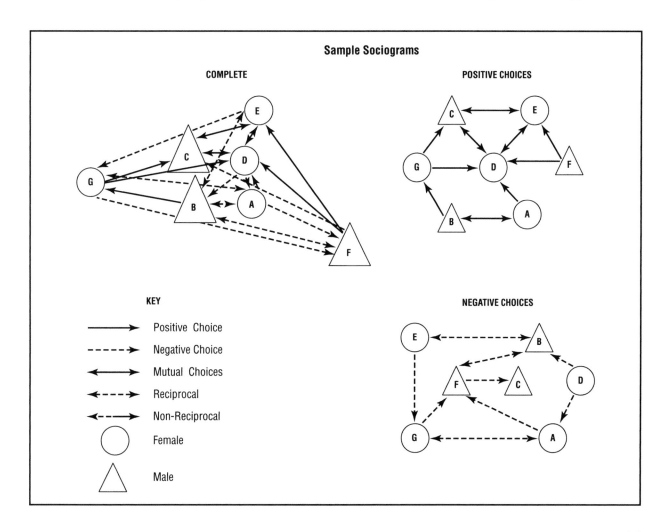

Sociometric Choice Matrix							
Chooser	Chosen						
	A	B	C	D	E	F	G
A		+		+		–	–
B	+				–	–	+
C				+	+		
D	–	–	+		+		
E		–	+	+			–
F		–	–	+	+		
G	–	+	+		–		
+ Choices Received	1	1	3	5	3	0	1
– Choices Received	2	3	1	0	1	3	2
Total Choices Received	3	4	4	5	4	3	3

and E form a "subgroup," having each reciprocally positively chosen each other. The centrality of D and F to the group dynamics is more obvious in seeing the positives and negatives separately, illustrating that energy of the group is demanded regardless of choice valence—both D and F have significant impacts.

The criterion implemented dyadically manifests practical difficulties. Who would be paired with D; who would be stuck with F? If C and E were paired, satisfying their desires, what then of D's desires? The optimal implementation satisfies the most choices of either valence. The process makes manifest exactly the dynamics experienced in all group situations (as anyone planning a wedding reception can attest). Knowing the reasons behind the choices and their strength (expanded schema) can help with optimal assignment. Some rationales indicate that "violating" a choice is not as detrimental as assumed (e.g., A and G reciprocally reject because they do not know each other).

With the particular criterion used (and its converse, "To whom would you like to give feedback?"), the implementation and rationale-sharing fit well together (i.e., sharing the rationales is giving feedback). With different criteria the sociometry will change, perhaps not greatly. For example, "To whom would you like to speak?" or "Whom would you like to know better?" could change the valence of the A–G choices and also demonstrates the difference between "actionable" criteria and "near" sociometry ones (e.g., "Whom in the group don't you know well?"). Choice of criteria influences the sociometry, revealing each individual's worth if done skillfully.

Lest sociometry be thought to be only small-group focused, Moreno's work with the U.S. Navy in forming more efficient and safer squads (Moreno 1951) and with the Hudson School for Girls, where cottages were formed and run sociometrically (Moreno [1953] 1993) were both large-scale sociometry interventions.

Sociometry as an assessment and intervention is a powerful tool. Sociometry the theory offers principles to predict and guide. More comprehensive and powerful, sociometry the system applies synergistically to the multiple foci and levels of human relatedness addressed by the interconnected subtheories.

SEE ALSO *Choice in Psychology; Groups; Networks; Prediction; Sociology*

BIBLIOGRAPHY

Cohen, Ronald J., and Mark E. Swerdlik. 2005. *Psychological Testing and Assessment.* 6th ed. Boston: McGraw-Hill.

Cronbach, Lee J. 1970. *Essentials of Psychological Testing.* 3rd ed. New York: Harper and Row.

Gronlund, Norman E. 1971. *Measurement and Evaluation in Teaching.* 2nd ed. New York: Macmillan.

Hale, Ann E. 1981. *Conducting Clinical Sociometric Explorations: A Manual for Psychodramatists and Sociometrists.* Roanoke, VA: Royal.

Moreno, Jacob L. 1951. *Sociometry, Experimental Method, and the Science of Society.* Ambler, PA: Beacon House.

Moreno, Jacob L. 1953. *Sociometry: A Journal of Interpersonal Relations and Experimental Design* 18 (4).

Moreno, Jacob L. [1953] 1993. *Who Shall Survive? Foundations of Sociometry, Group Psychotherapy, and Sociodrama.* Student ed. Roanoke, VA: Royal.

Remer, Rory. 1995a. Strong Sociometry: A Definition. *Journal of Group Psychotherapy, Psychodrama, and Sociometry* 48: 69–74.

Remer, Rory. 1995b. Using Strong Sociometry: Some Guidelines and Techniques. *Journal of Group Psychotherapy, Psychodrama, and Sociometry* 48: 79–84.

Remer, Rory. 2006. Chaos Theory Links to Morenean Theory: A Synergistic Relationship. *Journal of Group Psychotherapy, Psychodrama, and Sociometry* 59: 55–85.

Remer, Rory, and Vickey S. Finger. 1995. A Comparison of the Effects of Sociometry Components on Personal and Interpersonal Growth. *Journal of Group Psychotherapy, Psychodrama, and Sociometry* 48: 114–117.

Remer, Rory, Geraldo Lima, Stephen Richey, et al. 1995. Using Strong Sociometry as an Interpersonal Feedback Tool. *Journal of Group Psychotherapy, Psychodrama, and Sociometry* 48: 74–79.

Rory Remer

SOCIOMUSICAL THEORY

SEE *Music.*

SOFT SKILLS

Soft skills are core abilities and personal attributes that complement hard skills, that is, the technical knowledge required of an individual in the workplace. The term is often used synonymously with *generic skills* or *social competence*, though it refers in the strict sense only to key abilities that can be applied to job performance.

The term *soft skills* originated in the information technology sector and emphasizes the fact that soft skills are difficult to measure compared to technical skills, which have a straightforward or measurable impact on outcome. Due to the interdisciplinary character of the concept—it is used in the economic, social, and psychological sciences—a simple one-dimensional definition does not exist. There is broad consensus, however, concerning the division into *intrapersonal* skills and *interpersonal* skills. The former refer to self-regulating characteristics, such as time- and self-management, improvements in learning and performance, awareness of rights, and responsibility. The latter encompass those abilities and attitudes used in interactions with other people. Interpersonal skills can be further differentiated according to the individual's position in the interactive situation. Firm-internal collaboration requires leadership qualities and conflict-management skills with regard to subordinates as well as successful participation in a team of peers. Communication skills and negotiation competencies are important in interactions with customers and clients and are especially required in service-related activities. The concept also comprises personal attitudes, such as self-confidence, integrity, and respect; technical abilities, such as knowledge in information and communication technology; and language proficiency, even though the latter can be measured and could equally be considered a hard skill.

For the United States, the Secretary's Commission on Achieving Necessary Skills (SCANS) represents an extensive survey of abilities required to meet existing labor demands. Commissioned by the U.S. Department of Labor, SCANS identifies hard and soft skills that are essential in the workplace and ranks them according to the impact they have on job performance in different types of occupations. The survey also lists the most substantive literature on workplace skills for future research. A further important resource is the Occupational Information Network (O*NET), whose design reflects a systematic way to collect and analyze occupational information. Though both instruments show a similar categorization scheme at the broadest level, the term *soft skills* is not explicitly stated. Rather, SCANS uses the terms *personal qualities* and *interpersonal competencies*, while O*NET mainly uses *worker characteristics*. SCANS and O*NET constitute a relevant source for the development

and success of education and training programs, job analysis, and job design that goes far beyond the description of entirely technical and cognitive skill requirements.

EMPIRICAL EVIDENCE

The first attempts at measuring personal and interpersonal competence can be traced to the triarchic concept of intelligence introduced by the American psychologist Edward L. Thorndike (1874–1949). Thorndike distinguished between abstract, mechanical, and social intelligence and thus allowed for a multidimensional investigation of knowledge and traits that relied on psychometric procedures (1920). The wide-ranging term *soft skills*, entailing highly personal and subjective traits and qualities, requires a sensitive analysis of assessment tools. A common standard of measurement at the national level is not yet available, and the instruments already existing at the microeconomic level vary with respect to the set and definition of the indicators they use. The information collected from group discussions, simulations, and psychometric questionnaires does not contain all dimensions of soft skills and only considers a small cohort of individuals. Much work has been done in the sector of information systems (IS). The personal and interpersonal skills of workers employed in the IS field have been evaluated using simulated work situations. The findings indicate that work experience does not have a significant effect on self-management strategies or interaction with peers and superiors. However, IS professionals perform better in managing subordinates and interacting with customers (Damien et al. 1999).

At the macroeconomic level, research focuses on the analysis of the impact of soft skills on earnings. Greg J. Duncan and Rachel Dunifon (1998) suggest that soft skills are as good a predictor of labor market success as are levels of formal education.

Interpersonal skills can also be used to explain gender and racial pay gaps (Borghans et al. 2005; Fan et al. 2005). Such skills have a particularly positive impact on the job performance of women. Studies in intergenerational mobility take account of soft skills, but the results derived so far are vague. Samuel Bowles and Herbert Gintis (2001) suggest incorporating personal attitudes that are relevant to economic success into the analysis of intergenerational mobility. The American sociologist Melvin Kohn argued in *Class and Conformity* (1969) that, at least for some traits, experiences are passed via a process of vertical cultural transmission. For example, parents who operate relatively independently in the workplace automatically transfer some of their self-regulating strategies to their children.

SOFT SKILLS AND POLICY SIGNIFICANCE

With the shift in employment from manufacturing to services and with the diffusion of computer technology and information systems, the demand for soft skills in the labor market has increased. Soft skills not only affect the tools for recruitment, they also serve as a predictor for career progression if the type of occupation enforces a high level of social competence. Education programs have been adjusted as a reaction to changing workplace requirements. In addition, studies in the economics of aging emphasize the importance of soft skills as an instrument to compensate for the decline in cognitive and physic abilities with age, since social competencies remain relatively stable over one's lifetime. Numerous surveys indicate that training in interpersonal and communication skills raises individual productivity at all levels of qualification.

In order to assess the progressive potential of soft skills by a common standard, a clear definition that explicitly refers to employment still remains to be developed. However, the effects of soft skills in the workplace have to be analyzed with caution. Though the state of research definitely justifies and stimulates further work in this area, the socioeconomic value of soft skills tends to be overestimated. A pure focus on soft skills neglects their complementary character with respect to technical knowledge.

SEE ALSO *Cultural Capital; Educational Quality; Human Capital; Psychological Capital; Skill; Social Capital*

BIBLIOGRAPHY

Borghans, Lex, Bas ter Weel, and Bruce A. Weinberg. 2005. People People: Social Capital and the Labor-Market Outcomes of Underrepresented Groups. IZA Discussion Paper 1494.

Bowles, Samuel, and Herbert Gintis. 2001. The Intergenerational Transmission of Economic Status: Education, Class, and Genetics. In *Genetics, Behavior and Society*, ed. Marcus Feldman. Vol. 6 of *International Encyclopedia of the Social and Behavioral Sciences*, eds. Neil Smelser and Paul Baltes, 4132–4141. Oxford: Elsevier.

Damien, Joseph, Soon Ang, and Sandra Slaughter. 1999. Soft Skills and Creativity in IS Professionals. System Sciences, 1999. HICSS-32. *Proceedings of the 32nd Hawaii International Conference on System Sciences* 7: 1–5.

Duncan, Greg J., and Rachel Dunifon. 1998. Soft-Skills and Long-Run Labor Market Success. *Research in Labor Economics* 17: 123–149.

Fan, C. Simon, Xiangdong Wei, and Junsen Zhang. 2005. "Soft" Skills, "Hard" Skills, and the Black/White Earnings Gap. IZA Discussion Paper 1805.

Kohn, Melvin L. 1969. *Class and Conformity: A Study in Values.* Homewood, IL: Dorsey.

O*NET OnLine (Occupational Information Network). http://online.onetcenter.org.

Thorndike, Edward L. 1920. Intelligence and Its Use. *Harper's Magazine*, January, 227–235.

U.S. Department of Labor, Employment, and Training Administration. 2000. Workplace Essential Skills: Resources Related to the SCANS Competencies and Foundation Skills. 2000. Washington, DC: Author.

Rita M. Strohmaier
Wolfgang Eichert

SOLAR ENERGY

In a broad sense, most energy that individuals use is some form of solar energy. Other renewable energy sources (such as wind, hydropower, and wood) indirectly harness solar energy by using the atmosphere, oceans, and forests as solar collectors. Even exhaustible fossil fuels (oil, coal, and natural gas) are solar energy that was originally captured by plants and concentrated by geological processes into forms with high energy densities per unit of weight and volume.

In more common usage, *solar energy* refers to the two primary ways in which people harness and directly use solar energy using manufactured collectors: heating, and generating electricity.

Space and water heating systems for buildings can be either passive or active. Both approaches use glass to trap heat, as in a greenhouse. Passive design uses no moving parts or fluids; rather, it involves incorporating features into the siting and design of a building to take advantage of the natural solar radiation available. Such features include large windows facing south, heat-absorbent material such as brick or tile in floors and walls, and orienting a building on its site so as to maximize sun exposure.

Active heating systems use water or another liquid piped through collector units. The most common type of collector is a roof-mounted flat-plate design, consisting of an insulated glass-covered box painted black to maximize heat absorption. Water circulates in a loop between the collectors, where it is heated, and a tank, where it is stored until needed for either domestic uses or space heating.

There are two technologies for converting solar energy to electricity. Solar thermal-electric power plants (also called concentrating-solar-power, or CSP, power plants) use mirrors to gather solar radiation and focus it on a small area to produce high temperatures. The concentrating collectors may be parabolic troughs or dishes, or a system of mirrors that are spread over a wide area and that focus sunlight on a receiver at the top of a tower in what is called a power tower or central receiver system. A fluid circulates through a receiver unit at the parabola's focal point, where it is boiled. The resulting steam drives a generator as in a conventional power plant. Unlike solar-heating systems, which are installed at the point of energy consumption, CSP plants are typically large, central-station generating facilities.

The other solar-electric technology is photovoltaic cells. Photovoltaic cells are made of a semiconducting material, such as silicon, that releases electrons when struck by light. Cells are typically combined into modules, which in turn are assembled into larger arrays. Arrays can be sized for residential, industrial, or electric-utility use. The most commonly used material is crystalline silicon, but research since the 1970s has produced advances in such newer designs as thin-film cells using noncrystalline (amorphous) silicon, cadmium telluride, and other materials.

Interest in solar energy was stimulated in the 1970s by high oil prices and has been further stimulated by government policies, such as tax credits. Enthusiasm diminished in the 1980s and 1990s as the prices of oil and natural gas fell and many government subsidies lapsed. After the late 1990s interest was renewed by rising energy prices, but the use of solar energy remains limited. In *Renewable Energy* (2002), the International Energy Agency estimates that in the year 2000, solar heating made up 0.3 percent of world energy consumption and photovoltaic cells contributed less than 0.05 percent.

The major impediment to solar energy is cost. Though solar radiation is abundant and nonpolluting, the equipment required to gather and utilize it is expensive. Solar heating systems have found some commercial adoption in sunny locations for certain applications, especially for heating swimming pools. CSP technologies, though technologically proven, are not yet competitive with other sources of electricity. Perhaps the most promising technology is photovoltaics. By 2002, photovoltaic costs had fallen to about 20 to 30 percent of their 1980 levels. They have become cost-effective in some specialized applications, particularly in remote locations far from existing power lines. From 1992 to 2003, installed photovoltaic capacity worldwide grew by about 30 percent annually.

Economic theory predicts that as exhaustible energy resources are depleted, their prices will tend to rise, making renewable sources more attractive over time. The long-run prospects for solar energy will depend on how its cost compares with other energy sources.

For more information on solar technologies and research, see the Web sites for the International Energy Agency and the U.S. Department of Energy's National Renewable Energy Laboratory. On the economics of solar and other energy sources, see *Economics of the Energy Industries*, by William Spangar Peirce (1996).

SEE ALSO *Energy; Energy Sector*

BIBLIOGRAPHY

International Energy Agency. 2002. *Renewable Energy.* http://www.iea.org/.

International Energy Agency. 2004. *Trends in Photovoltaic Applications: Survey Report of Selected IEA Countries between 1992 and 2003.* Report IEA-PVPS T1-13:2004. http://www.iea.org/.

National Renewable Energy Laboratory. Solar Research. U.S. Department of Energy. http://www.nrel.gov/solar/.

Peirce, William Spangar. 1996. *Economics of the Energy Industries.* 2nd ed. Westport, CT: Praeger Publishers.

Renewable Energy Working Party. 2002. *Renewable Energy … into the Mainstream.* International Energy Agency. http://www.iea.org/.

Steven E. Henson

SOLDIERS

SEE *Militarism; Military.*

SOLIDARITY

Solidarity, often referred to as *social solidarity*, is a fundamental concept in the scientific study of human societies, cultures, and social relations. Researchers who were concerned to discover why societies cohere (and why they may disintegrate) hypothesized that social cohesion may be due to ideas or feelings people have about one another. Alternatively, structural conditions, such as a particular arrangement of social roles and relations, might foster conditions producing human unity.

Social theorist Émile Durkheim (1858–1917) first wrote about the problem of social solidarity in *The Division of Labor in Society* (1893). Durkheim considered society as a moral force characterized by a fundamental duality: Individual consciousnesses comprised the social entity even while society's norms imposed constraint on any single individual. As societies change, the type of solidarity that "glues" society together also changes. Social solidarity of undifferentiated societies, or *mechanical solidarity*, is based on likeness (e.g., the cultural similarity of each member of a tribe). Industrial societies cohere because of *organic solidarity*, based on the interdependency of dissimilar individuals (e.g., occupational diversity due to the division of labor).

Feelings of solidarity are encouraged when individuals strongly identify with a collectivity. Durkheim saw this as one of the bases for religious sentiments. In every religion, boundaries are drawn between the sacred and profane. Through this type of categorization, Durkheim explains, humans both create a moral ordering for social life and develop the conceptual apparatus necessary for rational thought. "The categories of the understanding" are "born in religion and of religion" (Durkheim [1915] 1965, pp. 21–22). Conceptualizations of time, space, class, causality, and so forth, although linked to brain function, are elaborated and interpreted differently in different cultures. The source of this variation is the social collectivity representing a *collective conscience*. In Durkheim's view, the collective conscience is expressed through "collective representations," or symbols. These cultural symbols "are the result of an immense cooperation, which stretches out not only into space but into time as well; to make them, a multitude of minds have combined their ideas and sentiments" ([1915] 1965, p. 29). Because collective representations express the heritage of an individual as well as provide the intellectual framework for his understandings, the person feels himself linked to a tradition and standards of behavior. Thus, the individual's ideas and feelings stem from a source beyond his personal experience; they come from society itself.

A stable social order rests on the solidarity of its people. What happens when social stability is threatened, through crime, for example? Durkheim argues, somewhat paradoxically, that crime and punishment (the reaction to crime) reinforce the social order. When an infraction is defined as criminal, it places the person who committed the crime outside the social order and deems him worthy of punishment. Those who have not transgressed are affirmed in their status as the law-abiding citizens. Durkheim argues that crime thus builds social solidarity and cohesiveness. Contemporary scholars counter that Durkheim's vision presents an oversocialized conception of humans. For example, Allen Liska and Barbara Warner's (1991) research shows that fear of crime may undermine social solidarity in U.S. neighborhoods where criminal behavior is not checked by authorities. Similarly, Teresa P. R. Caldeira's (2000) research on São Paolo indicates that multiple processes linking crime, poverty, and social status in a context of weak or corrupt policing can lead to increasing social isolation and the fragmentation of public spaces. This, in turn, undermines the potential for democratic development. Liska and Warner's research ultimately supports the Durkheimian position by arguing that the stabilization of crime in certain areas leads to social withdrawal, constraining "opportunities for crime, thereby decreasing both robbery and other crimes" (Liska and Warner 1991, p. 1441). Caldeira's research, by contrast, challenges the Durkheimian argument by suggesting that "social solidarity" under some repressive conditions is merely an expression of class, caste, or ethnic identification.

If excessive crime and lawlessness indicate the breakdown of society and solidarity, utopian or intentional communities present an idealized vision of a cohesive social order. In *Commitment and Community*, Rosabeth Moss Kanter identifies a social order of perfect solidarity where society is maintained through individual commitment, not coercion. This is an "imagined utopia," in which "humankind's deepest yearnings, noblest dreams, and highest aspirations come to fulfillment, where all physical, social, and spiritual forces work together, in harmony, to permit the attainment of everything people find necessary and desirable" (Kanter 1972, p. 1). History abounds with numerous attempts by religious or political idealists to create such societies in miniature. Despite repeated tries, none have found an ideology or set of social arrangements that invariably induces persons to want to do what they have to do: to follow society's rules without question or resistance. In short, there are limits to social solidarity's hold over the individual.

Whereas the ideational approach focuses on symbols, feelings, and identities, a structural approach to social solidarity identifies relational connections among individuals as key for maintaining social order and cohesion. James Moody and Douglas White articulate a social network conception of solidarity that defines structural cohesion formally as "the minimum number of actors who, if removed from a group, would disconnect the group." Society, in their view, is built up "through the hierarchical nesting of ... cohesive [network] structures" (Moody and White 2003, p. 103). The structural perspective is theoretically indebted to Durkheim's argument in *The Division of Labor* and Georg Simmel's (1858–1918) research on group formation, but methodologically, network analysis draws from graph theory in mathematics. This combination of theoretical and formal traditions allows for greater operational specification of the concept of social solidarity, as well as empirical analysis of how solidarity functions in reality. Using network analytic techniques, researchers are able to determine where, within a social network, relations are most stable and where they are likely to break down. This represents a scientific advance in the field, which is yielding promising results.

Since the nineteenth century, social theorists have viewed solidarity as a key factor underlying the problem of order in society. Durkheim's writings provided a strong impetus for two lines of theorizing: ideational and structural. Sociologists of religion and anthropologists were most interested in Durkheim's arguments about the religious basis of solidarity feelings, concepts, and symbols. Criminologists followed Durkheim in his interest in the social functions of crime. Social network theorists have drawn from Durkheim and others to develop a formal definition of social cohesion, or solidarity, in order to investigate varying social structures. Each line of investigation has increased human knowledge of the internal dynamics and power of social connection.

SEE ALSO *Caste; Class; Collective Action; Communalism; Communitarianism; Crime and Criminology; Durkheim, Émile; Ethnicity; Identity; Networks; Networks, Communication; Putnam, Robert; Race; Social Capital; Social Movements; Sociology*

BIBLIOGRAPHY

Caldeira, Teresa P. R. 2000. *City of Walls: Crime, Segregation, and Citizenship in São Paulo.* Berkeley: University of California Press.

Durkheim, Émile. [1893] 1933. *The Division of Labor in Society.* Trans. George Simpson. New York: Macmillan.

Durkheim, Émile. [1915] 1965. *The Elementary Forms of the Religious Life.* Trans. Joseph Ward Swain. New York: Free Press.

Kanter, Rosabeth Moss. 1972. *Commitment and Community: Communes and Utopias in Sociological Perspective.* Cambridge, MA: Harvard University Press.

Liska, Allen E., and Barbara D. Warner. 1991. Functions of Crime: A Paradoxical Process. *American Journal of Sociology* 96 (6): 1441–1463.

Merry, Sally Engle. 2002. Urban Danger: Life in a Neighborhood of Strangers. In *Urban Life: Readings in the Anthropology of the City*, eds. George Gmelch and Walter P. Zenner, 115–129. 4th ed. Prospect Heights, IL: Waveland.

Moody, James, and Douglas R. White. 2003. Structural Cohesion and Embeddedness: A Hierarchical Concept of Social Groups. *American Sociological Review* 68 (1): 103–127.

Maryjane Osa

SOLIDARNOŚĆ

The Independent Self-Governing Trade Union Solidarity (in Polish *Niezależny Samorządowy Związek Zawodowy "Solidarność"*) is a Polish trade union federation important historically for the role it played as a nonviolent, anticommunist mass social movement in Poland between 1980 and 1989. Solidarity was formed in Gdańsk, Poland, in August 1980 after a nationwide wave of strikes, sparked by price increases imposed by a government facing economic crisis, forced the ruling Communist Party to acknowledge the constitutional right of workers to form free trade unions. As a non-party-sponsored, legally recognized civil organization, Solidarity represented an unprecedented new development in state-society relations in the former Eastern bloc.

Prior to 1980 Poland had been convulsed by several economic and political crises accompanied by widespread social unrest. In each case, however, the party had been able to weather the crisis either by reorganizing its top leadership and introducing new, liberalizing economic and cul-tural policies (in 1956 and in 1970) and/or by targeting the most outspoken group with harsh reprisals, as occurred in 1968, 1970, and 1976. Signs of a broader, more concerted opposition to the regime came in 1976, with the formation of the *Komitet Obrony Robotników* (KOR; the Worker's Defense Committee), a group founded to provide legal and financial support to workers arrested in strikes in Warsaw and Radom of that year. Ranging in composition from former revisionist intellectuals and anticommunist left oppositionists to clergy, KOR became the focal point of a movement to establish links among workers, intelligentsia, and the Church and to form and defend an alternative public sphere outside the bounds of official, state-controlled institutions. If in 1970 striking workers had responded to state violence in kind by setting fire to Gdańsk party headquarters, the new opposition's strategy was that of peaceful self-organization, signaled by left KOR intellectual Jacek Kuroń's popular motto: "Don't burn down party committees, found your own!"

By 1980 striking workers were able to draw on a half-decade of experience in one of the most developed underground cultures of opposition in the Eastern bloc. Strikes broke out in Gdańsk's Lenin Shipyards on August 14, and by August 17 an Inter-Enterprise Strike Committee, formed under the leadership of electrician Lech Wałęsa and including KOR intellectuals in an advisory capacity, had drafted a list of twenty-one demands, many of which extended beyond immediate concerns and addressed fundamental injustices of Communist-Party rule in Poland. The demands called for, among other things, acknowledgment of the right to form free trade unions, for freedom of speech, access to government-controlled media, a halt to reprisals against outspoken critics of the regime, and economic and health care reform. Strikes spread quickly throughout Poland and by August 21, a hitherto recalcitrant government announced its readiness to negotiate. Between August 30 and September 1, state representatives signed a series of agreements recognizing the workers' right to self-government and obligating the regime to initiate a nationwide debate on the issues presented in the postulates.

The period of Solidarity's first legal existence (August 1980–December 1981) can be divided into three main stages, as detailed by Timothy Garton Ash in *The Polish Revolution: Solidarity* (2002, pp. 303–308), David Ost in *Solidarity and the Politics of Anti-Politics* (1990, pp. 78–79), and Jadwiga Staniszkis in *Poland's Self-Limiting Revolution* (1984, pp. 17–28). Initially, propelled by its success in Gdańsk, Solidarity emerged as a powerful social movement, while at the same time containing its opposition within the legal structure of the trade union and refraining from competition with the party for political power. In the second stage, confrontations with the state as well as internal disagreements between reformist and revolutionary factions revealed the inadequacy of this formula. Finally, in its third stage, Solidarity moved into the political arena, openly working for regime change.

Solidarity proved to be too much of a direct challenge to the Communist Party's monopoly, itself facing pressure from the Soviet Union, and on December 13, 1981, martial law was declared throughout Poland by recently appointed party secretary General Wojciech Jaruzelski. Prominent Solidarity leaders were arrested and interned, strikes and demonstrations were forcefully suppressed by armed riot police, and Solidarity was subsequently delegalized.

The early and mid-1980s saw Solidarity gradually reconstituting itself, now as an underground organization. In 1988 economic crisis forced the party back to the negotiating table with the opposition. This time, with the effects of *perestroika* being felt throughout the Eastern bloc, politics could be placed squarely on the agenda. Between February and April 1989, in an extraordinary series of negotiations known as the Roundtable Talks, state and Solidarity leaders hammered out an exit from communism for Poland. Free elections were to be held for a portion of seats in parliament, a new senate was to be formed, and a presidency was to replace the role played by the general secretary of the Communist Party. Though the party had insured that key elements of the new government would remain under its control for a transition period, Solidarity won the free portion of the elections by a landslide. With the opening of the Berlin Wall in November 1989, events in Eastern Europe soon outstripped the gradual exit from communism mapped out during the Polish Roundtable Talks, and new, free elections were held in Poland in 1990. Meanwhile, Solidarity, deprived of its opponent, collapsed dramatically as a unified formation, fragmenting into numerous smaller political parties.

The trade union returned to political prominence in 1997 as the animating force behind a coalition of conservative right parties, which won the parliamentary election of that year and governed until 2001.

SEE ALSO *Berlin Wall; Communism; Glasnost; Solidarity; Totalitarianism; Unions; Warsaw Pact; Working Class*

BIBLIOGRAPHY

Ash, Timothy Garton. 2002. *The Polish Revolution: Solidarity.* 3rd ed. New Haven, CT: Yale University Press.

Ost, David. 1990. *Solidarity and the Politics of Anti-Politics: Opposition and Reform in Poland since 1968.* Philadelphia: Temple University Press.

Staniszkis, Jadwiga. 1984. *Poland's Self-Limiting Revolution,* ed. Jan T. Gross. Princeton, NJ: Princeton University Press.

Christopher J. Caes

SOLOW, ROBERT M.
1924–

The American economist and 1987 Nobel laureate Robert Merton Solow was born on August 23, 1924, in Brooklyn, New York. Several years after his birth, economics, in the United States and globally, launched a great leap forward after the stock market crash of 1929 had created the Great Depression that attracted able minds to the study of economics rather than physics or biology. After Solow returned from army service in Europe during World War II (1939–1945), he joined in this movement under the mentorship of the economist Wassily Leontief (1906–1999) at Harvard. Such has been Solow's originality, wisdom, and energy that his imprint can be found in diverse corners of microeconomics, macroeconomics, and welfare policy.

The awarding to Solow of the Nobel Prize and the American Economic Association's prestigious John Bates Clark Medal (1961) presumably traces primarily to his seminal 1956 growth model that breathed new life into the earlier pioneering attempts of Paul H. Douglas (1892–1976) to explain statistically the growth of a society's real output in terms of its historical profiles of labor and of capital inputs. Because both of these time series were so positively correlated in trend, Douglas's linear-log regressions had been hopelessly ill-conditioned. At Massachusetts Institute of Technology (MIT), where Solow became an assistant professor in 1949 and remained until retiring as institute professor emeritus in 1995, he cut the Gordian knot by introducing into the statistical analysis independent information on market-factor shares. His principal finding was the hypothesis that much of historic gain in outputs was not plausibly connected with "deepening of the Capital/Labor ratio." Instead, an "exogenous residual" of Schumpeter-like technical innovation shifted upward "total factor productivity" to an important degree. A simplest Cobb-Douglas-Hicks example, à la Solow, would be $Q = (1.03)^t L^{.75} K^{.25}$. It is fitting that Solow as a Harvard student in Schumpeter's last lectures put the $(1.03)^t$ Schumpeterian parameter of innovation into growth theory, with emphasis upon rate of growth in total-factors productivity.

Fruitful tools of new mathematics—Dantzig linear programming, Kuhn-Tucker nonlinear programming, Bellman stochastic programming—came into wide use among economists after World War II, and Solow's diverse bibliography illustrates his role as a pioneer. Besides Solow's depth, his width is exemplified by his many analyses of post-Hotelling exhaustible resources. Besides putting his pen where his heart is, at Resources for the Future (a nonprofit organization focusing on the economic and social dimensions of environmental, energy, and natural resource issues) and similar organizations, Solow has put his shoulder to the wheels of conservation economics.

President John F. Kennedy's Council of Economic Advisers—Walter Heller (1915–1987), James Tobin (1918–2002), and Kermit Gordon (1916–1976)—and staff members Kenneth Arrow, Arthur Okun, and Solow set the high water mark for fruitful academic contributions to public policy in the early 1960s. In addition, Solow's facile pen over the years has reviewed contemporary debates in the public press, and he has expressed criticism of prominent economists, including John Kenneth Galbraith (1908–2006) and Milton Friedman. But his was never an in-your-face attack. Those to the right and the left of Solow generally respected his genial argumentation.

Solow's colleague at MIT and fellow Nobel laureate Paul Samuelson has dubbed Solow the Enrico Fermi (1901–1954) of economics. Fermi was both a great physicist-theorist and a great physicist-experimentalist; Solow has been both a creator of new theoretical economics and also one who subjected basic economic relations to statistical testing. Without his mathematical doodlings, Solow could not have been one of the wisest in the circle of Tobin, Arrow, and Franco Modigliani (1918–2003). Without his native DNA and mentors (Leontief, Talcott Parsons, Richard Goodwin, Abraham Wald), Solow would not have generated the wisdoms that were uniquely his.

BIBLIOGRAPHY

Arrow, Kenneth, Hollis B. Chenery, Bagicha S. Minhas, and Robert M. Solow. 1961. "Capital-Labor Substitution and Economic Efficiency." *Review of Economics and Statistics* 43 (3): 225–250.

Dorfman, Robert, Paul A. Samuelson, and Robert M. Solow. 1958. *Linear Programming and Economic Analysis.* New York: McGraw-Hill.

Hahn, Frank, and Robert M. Solow. 1995. *A Critical Essay on Modern Macroeconomic Theory.* Cambridge, MA: MIT Press.

Solow, Robert M. 1955–1956. "The Production Function and the Theory of Capital." *Review of Economic Studies* 23 (2): 101–108.

Solow, Robert M. 1956. "A Contribution to the Theory of Economic Growth." *Quarterly Journal of Economics* 70 (1): 65–94.

Solow, Robert M. 1957. "Technical Change and the Aggregate Production Function." *Review of Economics and Statistics* 39 (3): 312–320.

Paul A. Samuelson

SOLOW RESIDUAL, THE

A *growth accounting exercise* is used to break down the growth of output into the growth of the factors of production—capital and labor—and the growth of the efficiency in the utilization of these factors. The measure of this efficiency is usually referred to as *total factor productivity* (TFP). For policy purposes, it may matter whether output growth stems from factor accumulation or from increases in TFP.

The American economist Robert M. Solow set up the grounds for growth accounting in a 1957 article. Solow considered a neoclassical production function,

$$Y_t = A_t F(K_t, L_t) \tag{1}$$

where Y_t is aggregate output, K_t is the stock of physical capital, L_t is the labor force, and A_t represents TFP, which appears in a Hicks neutral way. After some simple transformations, this equation can be written in terms of the growth rates of these variables. For simplicity, consider a Cobb-Douglas production function $F(K_t, L_t) = K_t^{\alpha} L_t^{1-\alpha}$ with $0 < \alpha < 1$. Then, taking natural logarithms and differentiating both sides of (1) with respect to time t, the growth rate of aggregate output can be expressed as,

$$\dot{Y}/Y = \dot{A}/A + \alpha(\dot{K}/K) + (1-\alpha)(\dot{L}/L) \tag{2}$$

(For a variable $E = Y, A, K, L$, the term $\dot{E}$ stands for the derivative of E with respect to time t, and so $\dot{E}/E$ stands for the growth rate.) Note that the growth rates of physical capital and labor are weighted by α and $(1-\alpha)$. As is well known, these weights correspond to the respective shares of rental payments for capital and labor in total income. With available data on α and the growth rates for output, physical capital, and labor, TFP growth can be computed from (2) as the residual. Accordingly, TFP growth is the so-called Solow residual.

Solow carried out this exercise for the U.S. economy for the 1909–1949 period, during which output per man-hour approximately doubled. According to Solow's estimates, about one-eighth of the increment in labor productivity could be attributed to increased capital per man-hour, and the remaining seven-eighths to the residual. But the residual seemed too large.

To be sure, TFP is shaped by a broad range of influences—a variety of technological, economic, and cultural factors. These factors include innovations in technology, the shift of underemployed labor from agriculture to more productive sectors, economic policies aimed at liberalization and competition, and changes in shopping habits—from tiny shops to department stores. Usually, these changes will increase TFP, although TFP may fall for other reasons, such as trade union restrictions, environmental regulations, and safety measures that limit the use of production factors. (For example, suppose that to conduct weight-lifting exercises a gym requires a spotter; then, two people are needed for a single task, so this rule would decrease TFP.) Other factors that may influence TFP are frictions in financial markets, physical and human capital externalities, public expenditures, or any other element that affects the aggregate productivity of the economy.

Measurement is crucial for comprehending the Solow residual. First, observe that aggregate output is roughly the value of market goods and services produced in a society, but for most purposes this measure is too narrow because it leaves out many basic activities that enhance welfare. For instance, from the weight-lifting example we can see that a safety measure will usually decrease output for the benefit of protecting human lives, and it should be clear that the beneficial effects of this rule will not affect output directly. Moreover, output and other aggregate variables may be measured with error; indeed, many Internet activities are not satisfactorily treated in the national accounts. Second, there is the problem of quality adjustment. Various goods and services (e.g., cars, cellular phones) did not exist in the past or are now of much better quality, but these quality improvements are not well recorded in the statistics. Third, there are lags in the processes of innovation, learning, and implementation of technologies. Some current investments will see most of their payoffs far in the future and cannot be evaluated according to today's productivity. From 1973 to 1989, the United States and some other Western economies experienced a slowdown in TFP growth. Presumably, this productivity slowdown happened because these advanced economies were adjusting to the era of information and communication technologies; in the meantime, productivity—as shown in the statistics—was low.

In spite of these measurement problems, various studies have analyzed the determinants of the Solow residual (Denison 1962; Jorgenson and Griliches 1967) with emphasis on embodied and disembodied technological progress. Advances in technology may be embodied in the latest vintages of capital. Thus, new capital is better than old capital, not just because old capital has suffered wear and tear, but because of the quality improvement that comes with new capital. Therefore, a part of technological progress is embodied in K_t and failure to allow for this rise in quality may overstate the growth assigned to TFP. Similar considerations apply to labor: New generations entering the labor force are better educated and by all counts are more productive. In contrast, disembodied technological progress, included in TFP, will be associated with new modes of organization and operation of inputs, as well as other improvements not incorporated into the quality of factors of production. In practice, it has proved difficult to offer reliable estimates for the importance of embodied and disembodied technological progress. Sizable estimates have been reported for the contribution of embodied technological progress in physical capital to growth, but it is puzzling that many cross-country studies (Pritchett 2001) have found that the estimates for human capital to growth are insignificant or do not have the desired sign.

With the availability of broad sets of data in recent years, it has been possible to make cross-country comparisons of Solow residuals. These exercises offer new possibilities to test theories of economic growth. For a broad collection of countries, some studies contend that the growth process can be explained by factor accumulation. For instance, this suggests that the observed high growth rates for output in some fast-growing countries in Southeast Asia may not be long lasting, since there may be decreasing returns in the accumulation of these factors and further investments may become less productive. These studies have been criticized on the grounds of poor measurement of human capital, high physical capital shares, and biased estimates from endogeneity in the variables (Klenow and Rodríguez-Clare 1997; Easterly and Levine 2001). Therefore, the prevailing view is that to a great extent cross-country differences in output levels and growth rates should be attributed to the Solow residual.

In summary, the Solow residual is that part of output growth that cannot be attributed to the accumulation of capital and labor. There is a variety of factors that may contribute to output growth and hence the residual may be sizable. Quantifying the main determinants of the Solow residual may be instrumental in comparisons of growth experiences across countries and in testing theories of economic growth.

SEE ALSO *Accumulation of Capital; Change, Technological; Neoclassical Growth Model; Production Function; Solow, Robert M.*

BIBLIOGRAPHY

Denison, Edward F. 1962. The Sources of Economic Growth in the United States and the Alternatives Before Us. Supplementary Paper no. 13. New York: Committee for Economic Development.

Easterly, William, and Ross Levine. 2001. It's Not Factor Accumulation. *World Bank Economic Review* 15 (2): 177–219.

Jorgenson, Dale W., and Zvi Griliches. 1967. The Explanation of Productivity Change. *Review of Economic Studies* 34 (2): 249–280.

Klenow, Peter J., and Andrés Rodríguez-Clare. 1997. The Neoclassical Revival in Growth Economics: Has It Gone Too Far? *NBER Macroeconomics Annual* 12: 13–103.

Pritchett, Lant. 2001. Where Has All the Education Gone? *World Bank Economic Review* 15 (3): 367–391.

Solow, Robert M. 1957. Technical Change and the Aggregate Production Function. *Review of Economics and Statistics* 39: 312–320.

Fernando García-Belenguer
Manuel S. Santos

SOLOW-SWAN GROWTH MODEL

SEE *Neoclassical Growth Model.*

SOLZHENITSYN, ALEKSANDR
1918–

Born in southern Russia in 1918, Aleksandr Solzhenitsyn was brought up in highly straitened circumstances. By the time he graduated from Rostov University in 1941 with a degree in mathematics and physics, Solzhenitsyn was an enthusiastic champion of Marxist ideology who hoped to describe anew what he considered the glorious advent of the Russian Revolution. To this end Solzhenitsyn intended to pursue postgraduate literary studies, but the outbreak of hostilities in 1941 led to army service and eventual assignment to a sound-ranging battery on the front lines. In early 1945, Solzhenitsyn was arrested for critical comments on U.S.S.R. leader Joseph Stalin (1879–1953) in letters to a friend (the mail was censored) and sentenced to eight years imprisonment, to be followed by "eternal exile" in a remote area of the Union of Soviet Socialist Republics.

Solzhenitsyn served his sentence in various labor camps and prison research institutes, emerging in 1953 with his Marxist faith shattered and his head full of literary plans. *The First Circle*, composed mostly in the 1950s (after his exile was annulled), but published only in 1968, reflects his experience in a Moscow prison institute, *One Day in the Life of Ivan Denisovich* (1962) is based on his incarceration in Central Asia. *One Day*, Solzhenitsyn's first publication, appeared in Moscow by special permission of Communist Party leader Nikita Khrushchev (1894–1971), who deemed it useful for his campaign against Stalin. *One Day* caused a worldwide sensation by its depiction of a Stalinist concentration camp and generated hundreds of letters to Solzhenitsyn from former inmates of Soviet prisons and camps. Much of this material was later incorporated into *The Gulag Archipelago*, a three-volume indictment of the Soviet penal system that Solzhenitsyn published in Paris the following decade.

In the intervening years Solzhenitsyn gained prominence as a resourceful opponent of the Soviet regime, releasing bitterly critical statements that were distributed by the samizdat network and typically beamed back to the Soviet Union by Radio Liberty. *Samizdat* literally means "self-publishing house," an ironic term that refers to a method whereby privately typed materials were distributed chain-letter fashion among opposition-minded individuals who could not get access to the tightly controlled Soviet press. Apart from essays of this type, Solzhenitsyn produced *Cancer Ward* (1968) and an early version of *August 1914* (1971) during this period; both texts were published abroad to the great displeasure of the Soviet regime. In 1970 Solzhenitsyn was awarded the Nobel Prize in Literature, a decision the regime chose to interpret as one more hostile act. The Soviet leadership increasingly viewed Solzhenitsyn as a dangerous political opponent, and an unsuccessful assassination attempt by the KGB was launched in 1971.

The publication of *The Gulag Archipelago* (1973–1976) had a profound impact throughout the world and moved the regime to arrest Solzhenitsyn in 1974 and expel him from the Soviet Union. After two years in Switzerland, Solzhenitsyn moved to the United States, settling in Cavendish, Vermont, until his return to Russia in 1994. Apart from several high-profile appearances during this period (e.g., the commencement address at Harvard University in 1978), the writer's time was almost entirely dedicated to a cycle of narratives describing Russia's slide toward the revolutionary abyss. Entitled *The Red Wheel*, the cycle comprises ten volumes in the Russian edition (1983–1991) and encompasses the period between the outbreak of World War I in 1914 and April 1917. After his return to Russia, Solzhenitsyn published sketches of his two decades abroad, a number of short stories, essays on literary and political matters, and a two-volume study of the interactions of Russians and Jews in Russian history, *Dvesti let vmeste* (2001–2002). A thirty-volume *Complete Works* of Solzhenitsyn's work was published in 2006.

SEE ALSO *Concentration Camps; Gulags; Khrushchev, Nikita; Literature; Marxism; Prisons; Stalin, Joseph; Stalinism; Totalitarianism*

BIBLIOGRAPHY

Ericson, Edward E., Jr., and Daniel J. Mahoney, eds. 2006. *The Solzhenitsyn Reader: New and Essential Writings, 1947–2005.* Wilmington, DE: ISI Books.

Mahoney, Daniel J. 2001. *Aleksandr Solzhenitsyn: The Ascent from Ideology.* Lanham, MD: Rowman and Littlefield.

Scammell, Michael. 1984. *Solzhenitsyn: A Biography.* New York: Norton.

Solzhenitsyn, Aleksandr. 1978–1991. *Sobranie sochinenii* [Collected Works]. 20 vols. Paris: YMCA Press.

Alexis Klimoff

SOMBART, WERNER
1863–1941

German economist Werner Sombart was born in Ermsleben near the Harz mountains, the son of a prosperous landowner and liberal member of parliament. He studied law, economics, and history at the universities of Pisa, Rome, and Berlin. In 1888 he earned his doctorate in economics from the University of Berlin. After working for two years at the Bremen Chamber of Commerce, he became professor of political economy, first at the University of Breslau and later at the Berlin Business School. In 1918 he was appointed full professor at the University of Berlin.

Over his entire career Sombart tried to explain the origins and growth of the capitalist system of economic organization. In addition to his multivolume work on modern capitalism, he published four specialized books on the emergence of capitalism, relating it to such diverse factors as the bourgeois mentality, the Jewish people, warfare, and luxury consumption. To ground his theories Sombart employed a massive quantity of secondary historical material, varying from statistics and letters to novels and travel accounts. Because of his historical approach to economic issues, he is often seen as the last member of the German historical school to dominate economic thinking in Germany in the second half of the nineteenth century. It is difficult, however, to place Sombart in any school of thought, because his theories and political views changed repeatedly. He started his career as a Marxian economist, became a conservative, and ended as a sympathizer with Adolph Hitler's Nazi regime.

Undoubtedly, Sombart's masterpiece is *Der Moderne Kapitalismus* (Modern Capitalism), published in 1902, expanded in 1916–1917, and enlarged in 1927. This three-volume work, which has never been translated into English, explored the historical evolution of the European economy in the direction of modern capitalism. It was Sombart, not Karl Marx, who coined the word *capitalism* and described it as a unique economic system in human history characterized by the passion of entrepreneurs to build up pecuniary capital—in other words, to make money. He divided the capitalist era into three stages: (1) early capitalism (1500–1760), dominated by a handicraft mentality, (2) high capitalism (1760–1914), in which the Industrial Revolution spread from England to western Europe and the United States, and (3) late capitalism (starting with World War I), typified by growing state intervention. Next to the entrepreneurial pursuit of profit, Sombart identified major historical events such as the discovery of double-entry bookkeeping and the application of new technologies in industry as the main drivers of capitalist development. With its richness of facts and speculative notions, the book is "highly stimulating even in its errors," as renown economist Joseph Schumpeter (1883–1950) aptly put it.

One of the studies Sombart published in connection with *Der Moderne Kapitalismus* was *Die Juden und das Wirtschaftsleben* (1911), translated as *The Jews and Modern Capitalism* (1951). Unlike the well-known sociologist Max Weber (1864–1920), who linked the rise of capitalism to the Protestant work ethic, Sombart suggested a link between the Jews and capitalist development. As he saw it, the shift in entrepreneurial activity from southern to northern Europe between the fifteenth and seventeenth centuries resulted from the move of Jews from Spain, Portugal, and Italy to Germany, Holland, and England. For Sombart, it was no surprise that areas from which the Jews fled underwent economic decline, whereas those they entered gained strength; as he saw it, the Jewish character and religion had "the same leading ideas as capitalism" (1951, p. 205). Sombart's book did not express outright anti-Semitism; but his discussion of Jews as a group was rife with prejudices that clearly laid the ground for his later sympathy with the Nazis.

Although Sombart was the most productive German economist of his time, he did not achieve fame or earn widespread admiration. His work is overly descriptive, disproportionately concerned with history, sloppy with data, and lacking in theoretical rigor; moreover, his political positions were unsavory. Still, Sombart's historical approach to economic development influenced the first American institutional economists, the French historians of the Annales school, and, most importantly, the economist Schumpeter. For example, Sombart coined the popular term *creative destruction*, which, along with some of his insights on capitalism, is usually attributed to Schumpeter. Since the late 1990s there has been some renewed interest in Sombart's work, owing to the growing emphasis on the role of historical specificity in economics.

BIBLIOGRAPHY

Backhaus, Jürgen, ed. 1996. *Werner Sombart (1863–1941): Social Scientist.* 3 vols. Marburg, Germany: Metropolis-Verlag.

Hodgson, Geoffrey M. 2002. *How Economics Forgot History: The Problem of Historical Specificity in Social Science.* London and New York: Routledge.

Sombart, Werner. 1902–1927. *Der Moderne Kapitalismus: Historisch-Systematische Darstellung des gesamteuropäischen Wirtschaftslebens von seinen Anfängen bis zur Gegenwart.* 3 vols. Munich: Deutscher Taschenbuch Verlag, 1987.

Sombart, Werner. 1911. *Die Juden und das Wirtschaftsleben.* Leipzig: Duncker & Humblot. Trans. by Mortimer Epstein as *The Jews and Modern Capitalism.* Glencoe, IL: Free Press, 1951.

Gert-Jan Hospers

SOROS, GEORGE
1930–

George Soros, Hungarian-born American financier and philanthropist, is the second son of Tivadar and Erzebet Soros. He was thirteen years old when Nazi Germany invaded Hungary. To escape the German genocide of the Jews, the Soros family survived the occupation in secret hideouts under fake identities. In 1946 George Soros immigrated to England from the Russian-controlled country and attended the London School of Economics.

After graduation, Soros managed to break into the nepotistic merchant banking industry in London, where he was hired to be a trainee by a Hungarian managing director at Singer and Friedlander. In 1956 he was hired by another trainee's father to work in international arbitrage at his small brokerage firm in New York. In the European investment boom following the formation of the Coal and Steel Community, Soros made a name for himself as an analyst in European securities at Wertheim and Company and later at Arnold and S. Bleichroeder.

SOROS THE FINANCIER

In 1966 Soros started managing a $100,000 model portfolio of American securities for Arnold and S. Bleichroeder, which was later turned into an investment fund and, in 1969, a hedge fund. In 1973 Soros left the firm to start his own hedge fund, which evolved into the Quantum Fund. Assets under his management reportedly returned 3,365 percent from 1969 to 1980, compared to 47 percent for the Standard and Poor's stock index. The spectacular investment success caught public attention in 1981, when Soros was billed by *Institutional Investor* as "the world's greatest money manager." Unfortunately 1981 became the first year that he lost money. He subsequently left daily management of the fund to outside managers and later an internal staff, satisfied to be the owner and coach.

Soros is probably best known as "the man who broke the Bank of England." His fund bet heavily on the devaluation of the British pound in the fall of 1992 and made over $1 billion from the bet and other related derivatives transactions. The ensuing infamy left Soros undisturbed as he saw the devaluation as something bound to happen and insisted he operated within the rules. He is also widely believed to have been a force behind the currency speculations during the Asian financial crisis in 1997, an accusation he denied. The former Malaysian prime minister Mahatir Mohamad, one of Soros's fervent critics at the time, said in 2006 that he now believed Soros had not been involved.

SOROS THE PHILANTHROPIST AND PHILOSOPHER

Soros's philanthropic activities, which started long before his rise to fame, have centered around his pursuit of open societies. He has written extensively on the subject, which resonated deeply with his teenage experience. He believes that the markets are always wrong and that he himself is just as fallible. Society is inundated with similar fallibilities. He believes that, under an open society where free expression is cherished and differences in opinions are allowed, people are best equipped to keep their own biases to the minimum.

Soros believes the United States has justifiably pursued an open market policy thanks to its economic and political might. Developed legal systems, a business-friendly economic environment, and possession of the world's main trading currency have attracted capital to the United States. The negative effects on certain domestic industries have been limited by trade restrictions posed by the World Trade Organization.

Soon after he earned his first $25 million, Soros started giving his wealth away to promote the principles of open society. In 1979 he provided scholarships to black students at Cape Town University. South Africa's racial segregation policies at the time made it a prominent closed society. Soros thought the university championed open society by treating black students equally. He withdrew support eventually after he found out that scholarships were not all used to fund additional black students as he intended.

In 1984 Soros created the Soros Foundation in Hungary to provide financial support for scholars on a competitive basis. By 2006 the network had expanded to thirty-two foundations spanning eastern Europe, Africa, and Central America. The most profound impact has been in eastern Europe, where Soros funded scholarships for academics to study abroad and supported libraries and health education programs. Although each foundation developed its own program according to its specific needs, all operated under the expectation that they would be prototypes of open society. In 1991 Soros set up and financed the Central European University, with campuses in the early twenty-first century in Budapest, Prague, and Warsaw, to train graduate students in various subjects of the humanities in the hope that they would promote the practice of open society.

SEE ALSO *Apartheid; Currency; Development; Economic Crises; Exchange Rates; Financial Markets; Foundations, Charitable; Freedom; Holocaust, The; Mahathir Mohamad; Nazism; Philanthropy; Segregation*

BIBLIOGRAPHY

Open Society Institute and Soros Foundations Network. www.soros.org.

Slater, Robert. 1996. *Soros: The Life, Times, and Trading Secrets of the World's Greatest Investor.* Burr Ridge, IL: Irwin Professional Publishers.

Soros, George. 1995. *Soros on Soros: Staying Ahead of the Curve.* New York: Wiley.

Soros, George. 2002. *George Soros on Globalization.* New York: Public Affairs.

Shi Larry Cao

SOUTH, THE (GLOBAL)

SEE *North and South, The (Global).*

SOUTH, THE (USA)

Historically and culturally, the South is the most distinctive region of the United States. Once a center for African American slavery, the South is the only U.S. region to have fought for a separate national existence. Following defeat in the Civil War (1861–1865), poverty and legalized racial discrimination marked the southern states until the last decades of the twentieth century. While slavery and racial strife never dominated all parts of the South, they contributed to the economic, political, social, and cultural isolation of the entire region. As a result, W. J. Cash expressed a broad consensus when he called the South "not quite a nation within a nation, but the next thing to it" (1941, p. xlviii).

Like many other world regions, the South has no precise definition. It includes a variety of climates and geographical features, ranging from subtropical coastal swamps to the Appalachian Mountains, which include the highest peaks east of the Mississippi River. The border between Pennsylvania and Maryland (the Mason-Dixon Line) divides North from South traditionally, but does not define the entire region. Eleven states seceded to form the Confederate States of America in 1861: Virginia, North Carolina, South Carolina, Georgia, Florida, Tennessee, Alabama, Mississippi, Louisiana, Arkansas, and Texas. Four other slave states did not secede: Delaware, Maryland, Kentucky, and Missouri. The modern state of West Virginia broke away from Virginia during the Civil War, creating lasting disagreement over whether it should be considered southern. The U.S. Census defines the South as the former slave states (minus Missouri), plus Oklahoma and the District of Columbia. Accepting the reality that state lines have never circum-

scribed the cultural patterns of speech, food, politics, religion, and race relations that are widely associated with the South, the authoritative *Encyclopedia of Southern Culture* falls back on a circular definition: " 'The South' is found wherever southern culture is found" (Wilson and Ferris 1989, p. xv).

The South became a discrete region by an extended process linked to African American slavery. Slaves worked in all the American colonies, but especially on plantations growing tobacco in Virginia and rice in South Carolina. By the time of the first federal census in 1790, slaves comprised 31 percent of the U.S. population south of Pennsylvania, but less than 2 percent elsewhere. With the invention of the cotton gin in 1793, cultivation of the fiber expanded widely south of Virginia, spreading slavery and the plantation system across the southern interior and gradually tying the South together as the "Cotton Kingdom."

Representatives of the free and slave states clashed in the Constitutional Convention of 1787, but regional self-consciousness did not spread widely until after 1820, as southern whites reacted to a growing abolition movement in the North and to northern opposition to slavery's expansion. In 1860 a northern majority elected an avowedly antislavery president, Abraham Lincoln (1809–1865), prompting eleven slave states to leave the Union and form the Confederacy. Southern defeat in the ensuing Civil War brought the abolition of slavery, first by the Emancipation Proclamation (1863) and more fully by the Thirteenth Amendment to the U.S. Constitution (1865).

During Reconstruction (1865–1877), native southern whites used violence and intimidation to regain power over their state governments and the ex-slaves. The plantation system continued under tenancy arrangements that left blacks and many whites largely impoverished and uneducated. Beginning in the 1890s, white Democrats used poll taxes and literacy tests to strip most black men of the right to vote, followed by laws requiring the strict segregation of the races in all public facilities. In response, millions of black southerners fled to find better opportunities in the North and West. Until the civil rights movement of the 1950s and 1960s brought new federal legislation, widespread poverty, legal segregation, black disfranchisement, and exclusive control by an all-white Democratic Party characterized the so-called Solid South. Before these reforms, unique social and political institutions—and the prolonged struggle to maintain them—made the South unmistakably different from the rest of the United States, and fed a strong regional identity, especially among whites.

Despite these dominant regional patterns, diverse regional subcultures have long flourished in the South. The Appalachians and similar patches of hill country did not support plantations, but sustained a distinct white folk culture that became the seedbed of modern country-and-western music. Equally distinct African American cultures developed in the largely black plantation districts. African cultural survivals, including the unique Gullah language, marked the Sea Islands of South Carolina and Georgia, while other black communities developed special musical traditions, especially New Orleans jazz and the Mississippi Delta blues. Lying between the mountains and the coastal lowlands, the Piedmont South fostered industrial development with urban centers like Atlanta and Charlotte.

Isolation and distinctiveness have encouraged southern stereotypes. Racial prejudice and exploitation encouraged images of both black inferiority and universal white racism. Violence, ignorance, and laziness have been attributed to southern whites and blacks alike. Plantation owners have been credited with aristocratic gentility, and poor whites scorned for hopeless degradation. The roots of these stereotypes are slowly giving way, but popular images only die gradually.

The South has changed rapidly since the end of World War II (1939–1945). Vigorous industrial recruitment, often founded on low wages, weak regulations, and hostility to labor unions, attracted outside industry and led to massive urban and suburban growth. The civil rights movement ended legalized segregation and stimulated a two-party political system, as millions of new black voters entered the Democratic Party while many whites switched to the resurgent Republicans. Southerners of both parties acquired leading roles in national politics, as Democrats won presidential elections with Jimmy Carter (1976) and Bill Clinton (1992 and 1996) and came close with Al Gore (2000), while southern Republicans like Newt Gingrich, Trent Lott, and Jesse Helms exercised a powerful conservative influence on Congress from the 1990s onward. Black migration reversed direction, lifting the region's black population by 7.2 million between 1970 and 2000. Prosperity attracted millions of other newcomers as well, including northern-born whites and Hispanic immigrants, but the offshore flight of low-wage manufacturing has distressed many southern industrial communities.

Recent changes have led some observers to worry that the South may disappear as a distinct region, but change has come on top of deep-seated historical experiences that are likely to give distinct characteristics to southern development for a long time to come.

SEE ALSO *Benjamin, Judah P.; Bluegrass; Blues; Civil Rights Movement, U.S.; Confederate States of America; Davis, Jefferson; Democratic Party, U.S.; Desegregation; Jazz; Jim Crow; Johnson, Lyndon B.; Kefauver, Estes; Key, V. O., Jr.; Lincoln, Abraham; Migration; Politics; Politics, Southern; Poll Tax;* *Reconstruction Era (U.S.); Republican Party; Segregation; Slavery; Southern Bloc; Southern Strategy; Stereotypes; Supreme Court, U.S.; Thurmond, Strom; U.S. Civil War*

BIBLIOGRAPHY

Cash, W. J. 1941. *The Mind of the South.* New York: Knopf.

Cobb, James C. 2005. *Away Down South: A History of Southern Identity.* New York: Oxford University Press.

Cooper, William J., Jr., and Thomas E. Terrill. 2002. *The American South: A History.* 3rd ed. New York: McGraw-Hill.

Reed, John Shelton. 1974. *The Enduring South: Subcultural Persistence in Mass Society.* 2nd ed. Chapel Hill: University of North Carolina Press.

Wilson, Charles Reagan, and William Ferris, eds. 1989. *The Encyclopedia of Southern Culture.* Chapel Hill: University of North Carolina Press.

Harry L. Watson

SOUTH SEA BUBBLE

The South Sea Bubble was one of the first famous financial bubbles of modern times. The shares of the South Sea Company rose rapidly to ten times their par value within a few months in 1720, and even more swiftly fell back. These rapid fluctuations arose in the process of creating the first modern fiscal state. It was difficult to manage higher taxes and borrowing, and a bubble was the result.

The Glorious Revolution of 1688 brought King William (1650–1702) from the Low Countries to the English throne, together with his military ambitions and Dutch financial bureaucrats to help finance the resulting wars. The English government dramatically increased its taxes, creating a tax basis that assured investors that the government's bonds could and would be paid.

The English government then tried to figure out how to extend its borrowing. It issued a variety of securities that were not easily transferable; some were irredeemable. While the government's cost of servicing the national debt was substantial, most annuities traded at large discounts. Imitating the French model of John Law (1671–1729), the South Sea Company (which never traded in the South Seas) offered to exchange existing government debt for equity in the company that could be traded easily. The South Sea Company would buy and hold government debt, paying dividends on its stock from the interest it received on the bonds, and profiting by providing liquidity to holders of government debt. The company's first major venture was the debt conversion of 1719 in which it exchanged £1 million for newly issued stock. The government's debt payments fell, former debt holders saw the value of their securities rise, and the company earned a considerable profit.

The South Sea Company then proposed to exchange about £30 million of the national debt for its own shares, paying the English Treasury for the privilege. Parliament and the king approved the conversion by early April 1720, by which time the stock had more than doubled from January. The company obtained the right to issue new shares to finance the conversion, but the conversion ratio was not fixed, and the company could obtain government debt more cheaply as its share price rose. Public interest and company activities drove the price ever higher. Many investors bought South Sea shares knowing that they were overpriced; they hoped to sell the shares for even higher prices before the shares returned to a more reasonable level. The company issued fresh equity in four subscriptions, at higher and higher prices. It also lent generously against its own shares, reducing their supply and increasing demand for them.

The price of South Sea stock rose from around £140 in January 1720 to £300 at the start of April and £800 at the start of June. The price was near £1,000 in the summer, but it fell precipitously in September, back to £200 by October. The rapid fall of share prices in September 1720 probably was brought about by some small event that made it clear to many traders that buying opportunities based on expected price rises were coming to an end. The bubble collapsed, taking the prices of other stocks in London and Amsterdam down with the South Sea Company. The problem of providing liquid government debt was not solved until the introduction of consols (consolidated English government debt with no due date) a generation later.

SEE ALSO *Bubbles; Manias; Panics; Speculation*

BIBLIOGRAPHY

Dale, Richard. 2004. *The First Crash: Lessons from the South Sea Bubble.* Princeton, NJ: Princeton University Press.

Temin, Peter, and Hans-Joachim Voth. 2004. Riding the South Sea Bubble. *American Economic Review* 94 (5): 1654–1668.

Peter Temin

SOUTHERN BLOC

The term *southern bloc* refers to a coalition of southern Democratic representatives and senators who united with Republicans to advance shared legislative interests, principally to prevent federal involvement in race relations in the U.S. South. The seniority of many southern bloc members enhanced their legislative influence because they held so many congressional committee chairmanships. The "southern bloc" had political connections to the "southern strategy" in presidential politics that emerged in the 1960s.

The southern bloc was another instance of the sectionalism that had always unified southerners in both houses of Congress. From the beginning of the nation, southern interests had voted together regarding issues of slavery. Beginning in the 1930s in an effort to stop Franklin D. Roosevelt's plan to "pack" the Supreme Court, southern Democrats voted with Republicans against nonsouthern Democrats. The alliance of southern Democrats and Republicans formed a "conservative coalition." The southern bloc and the farm bloc also shared interests, for as V. O. Key Jr. noted about Congress in the 1940s: "Between the extreme of urban industrialism and of prosperous, rural Republicanism, the poor, southern Democracy occupies a position in the political center" (1949, p. 378). Recent instances of the southern sectionalism that shaped the southern bloc include the occasion during the Reagan years when several southern House Democrats ("boll weevils") joined with Republicans to enact the president's budget. In 1993 southern Democrats and Republicans coalesced to pass the North American Free Trade Agreement.

Southern U.S. senators, given the Senate rules allowing filibusters (unlimited debate), have played a critical role in the work of the southern bloc. Tom T. Connally of Texas (1877–1963) was among the first leaders of the bloc in the Senate, and Richard B. Russell Jr. of Georgia (1897–1971) led the Senate's southern bloc between 1945 and 1969. Before the 1960s, virtually all southern senators were members of the bloc. Some did not formally ally themselves with it: Lyndon B. Johnson of Texas, Estes Kefauver of Tennessee, and Ralph W. Yarborough of Texas. The Declaration of Constitutional Principles (March 12, 1956)—the so-called "southern manifesto"—which assailed the Supreme Court's *Brown v. Board of Education* decision (1954 and 1955) was signed by nineteen of the twenty-two southern senators (not signing were Kefauver, Johnson, and Albert A. Gore Sr. of Tennessee) and by 82 of the 106 southern House members.

Southern senators did not have majority support for voting against federal intervention in race relations. As a minority, the bloc resorted to delaying tactics allowed by the Senate rules in order to prevent passage of important civil rights legislation. Filibusters by the southern bloc that succeeded included those against anti-lynching bills in 1935 and 1938; anti–poll tax measures in 1942, 1944, and 1946; fair-employment practices legislation in 1946; and voting rights bills in 1960. In 1957, having significantly watered down a civil rights bill, the southern bloc did not filibuster it. But one of its members, then-Democrat Strom Thurmond of South Carolina, filibustered the bill for more than twenty-four hours.

Between 1938 and 1963 the southern bloc, allying with some western Democrats and Republicans beat back all eleven attempts to end filibusters on civil rights legislation. Such attempts seek to invoke cloture, a procedure to end debate and vote on the measure being discussed. From its enactment in 1917 to its amendment in 1975, Senate Rule XXII required a vote by two-thirds of the Senate to end debate; in 1975 that proportion was reduced to three-fifths, so that sixty senators could halt a filibuster. On June 10, 1964, after a filibuster lasting seventy-four days, the longest filibuster in history, the Senate successfully imposed cloture for the first time on a civil rights bill. The Senate also invoked cloture on filibusters against civil rights bills in 1965 (voting rights) and 1968 (open housing).

In presidential politics, a "southern strategy" sought to unite the white South and Republicans to mutual advantage. "Southern strategy" was a pejorative phrase charging Republicans with racist or at least political intentions to court southern white support by taking more pleasing positions on desegregation. In 1964 the Republican presidential nominee Barry Goldwater (1909–1998), who had voted against the 1964 Civil Rights Act, carried the five Deep South states with a hard-edged southern strategy, but lost in a landslide to Democratic nominee Lyndon Johnson. In 1968 the Republican nominee, Richard Nixon, employed a softer southern strategy to curb the threat posed by the American Independent Party candidate George C. Wallace (1919–1998). Senator Thurmond, who had run as the States' Rights Democratic Party (Dixiecrat) presidential candidate in 1948 and switched to the Republican Party in 1964, was a key ally in this strategy. Thurmond battled Wallace, claiming a vote for Wallace was essentially a vote for the Democratic candidate, Hubert Humphrey (1911–1978). The winner, Nixon, carried South Carolina and four other southern states not in the Deep South.

In the 2000 and 2004 presidential campaigns, with southern whites identifying more with the Republican Party, the Republican nominee, George W. Bush, abandoned the southern strategy of previous Republican presidential candidates to seek greater black and Hispanic support, and he did make some headway among Hispanic voters, but not among black voters.

Since the 1960s the political bases that supported the southern bloc have been changed by the growing black vote in the South, which is increasingly critical to the election of Democrats; by Republican gains in the former solidly Democratic South; and by the social and economic convergence of the South with the non-South. Conserva-

tive southern Democrats have largely vanished as conservative southern voters now ally more with Republicans. In the 1980s and later, civil rights measures received considerable support from southern Democrats, and the conservative coalition appeared less frequently in congressional voting. Indeed, *Congressional Quarterly* discontinued its annual report on conservative coalition voting after the 1998 session of Congress, in which the conservative coalition appeared on only 6 percent of the roll call votes.

SEE ALSO Brown v. Board of Education, *1954; Civil Rights Movement, U.S.; Democratic Party, U.S.; Dixiecrats; Johnson, Lyndon B.; Kefauver, Estes; Key, V. O., Jr.; Nixon, Richard M.; Politics; Politics, Southern; Republican Party; Roosevelt, Franklin D.; South, The (USA); Southern Strategy; Thurmond, Strom*

BIBLIOGRAPHY

Black, Earl, and Merle Black. 2002. *The Rise of Southern Republicans.* Cambridge, MA: Harvard University Press.

Fite, Gilbert C. 1991. *Richard B. Russell, Jr., Senator from Georgia.* Chapel Hill: University of North Carolina Press.

Key, V. O., Jr. 1949. *Southern Politics in State and Nation.* New York: Knopf.

Murphy, Reg, and Hal Gulliver. 1971. *The Southern Strategy.* New York: Charles Scribner's Sons.

Harold W. Stanley

SOUTHERN STRATEGY

In American politics, the "southern strategy" refers to efforts by the Republican Party and its candidates to win presidential elections since 1964 by appealing to conservative whites (especially white southerners) disaffected with the Democratic Party by its strong embrace of civil rights laws in the 1960s and its racially egalitarian policies since.

BEFORE 1960: THE UNSTABLE DEMOCRATIC PARTY COALITION

While racial discrimination existed nationwide before 1960, it was especially pervasive and severe in the South. Region-wide, but especially in the Deep South (Louisiana, Mississippi, Alabama, Georgia, and South Carolina), the politically and economically dominant white population enforced segregated schools, neighborhoods, and public establishments, severe discrimination in jobs and housing, and denial of voting rights for blacks. Virtually all southern Democratic politicians favored racial segregation and antiblack discrimination; candidates that did not were unelectable. Meanwhile, most white southerners vilified

Republicans as the party of the Union cause during the Civil War and of the hated Reconstruction era, when federal troops occupied southern states after the war. From 1932 into the 1940s, the Democratic Party's majority coalition nationwide was owed in part to intense Democratic loyalties among most white southerners.

Such support remained strong as long as Democrats did not push aggressively for civil rights for blacks. But in 1948 Democratic Party convention delegates supported this plank in the party platform: "The Democratic Party commits itself to continuing efforts to eradicate all racial, religious, and economic discrimination." In vehement opposition, delegate Strom Thurmond, then governor of South Carolina, stalked out of the convention, leading other Deep South delegates in tow (Edsall and Edsall 1991, p. 34). The dissidents formed the States' Rights Democratic ("Dixiecrat") Party, with Thurmond as their presidential candidate. The Dixiecrats carried several southern states in 1948, serving early notice to the national Democratic Party that aggressive action on civil rights would result in the party losing much white southern support. In 1954 Thurmond won a U.S. Senate seat from his native South Carolina; in 1964, he switched to the Republican Party.

1960 TO 1964: RACIAL ISSUES REEMERGE, AND REPUBLICANS MOVE TO THE RIGHT

During the 1950s events such as the Supreme Court's 1954 ruling ordering schools to desegregate (*Brown v. Board of Education*) and the 1957 crisis attending the integration of Central High School in Little Rock, Arkansas, kept civil rights issues on the national agenda. However, the Democratic and Republican parties equivocated on civil rights issues, until 1964. That year, President Lyndon B. Johnson and northern members of Congress from both parties overcame fierce southern Democratic opposition to pass the Civil Rights Act of 1964, which outlawed segregated public places, including most private businesses, and banned employment discrimination. Meanwhile, Republicans moved sharply rightward on racial issues (Carmines and Stimson 1989), nominating Arizona senator Barry Goldwater for the presidency in 1964. Far more conservative on racial issues than previous Republican candidates had been, Goldwater argued forcefully against the Civil Rights Act, emphasizing his view that proper jurisdiction over civil rights policy lay with the states, not the federal government. Goldwater's argument was not openly racist: He neither vilified blacks nor made openly segregationist appeals, as Thurmond and other southern Democratic politicians had for decades. Nonetheless, Goldwater's position was enormously attractive to white southerners enraged by the national Democratic Party's embrace of civil rights laws. President Johnson won a landslide reelection over Goldwater in 1964. But Goldwater carried five Deep South states that had not voted Republican in presidential elections since Reconstruction. The Democratic lock on the South was broken, and issues and developments after 1964 would continue to erode white southerners' loyalty toward the Democratic Party.

The southern strategy, then, first emerged in 1964 to attract white southerners by positioning the Republican Party as the new political home for racial conservatism (Carmines and Stimson 1989). Columnist Robert Novak (1965) described the southern strategy as encompassing staunch anti-Communism in foreign affairs and conservative appeals for a less activist federal government in domestic affairs, and deemphasizing civil rights without endorsing racial segregation or discrimination, to attract white southerners but avoid alienating moderate whites with raw racial appeals. After 1964 the southern strategy flowered, but with a changing issue focus, favoring more covertly racial issues such as social welfare programs, "law and order," school busing, and, in the 1980s, affirmative action and violent crime.

1965 TO 1972: YEARS OF TURMOIL AND NIXON'S SOUTHERN STRATEGY

By 1968 Republicans were refining their 1964 appeals and discourse and extending them to new issues. In 1965 President Johnson signed the Voting Rights Act of 1965, throwing the federal government's full weight into guaranteeing voting rights for southern blacks. The next three years were tumultuous, seeing the rise of black militant groups and major riots in Los Angeles (1965), Detroit (1967), and many other cities in 1966 and following the assassination of Martin Luther King Jr. in 1968. After another assassination—that of Democratic presidential candidate Robert Kennedy—the 1968 Democratic National Convention met in Chicago. Chaotic scenes of police beating demonstrators in Chicago's streets and parks echoed the tumult within the convention hall, as the party's delegates splintered over the issue of continuing the Vietnam War. Republicans sought to capitalize on the turbulence of the late 1960s by calling for "law and order." This appeal resonated strongly with conservative whites nationally, but especially white southerners. By 1965 almost all American homes had televisions, and televised footage of urban riots, assassinations, antiwar protests, black militant groups, recreational drug use and sexual activity among young people, and unrest at the Democratic Party convention fostered perceptions that under Democratic governance the nation and the social fabric were unraveling at the seams.

Guided by former Thurmond political advisor Harry Dent, the 1968 Republican nominee, Richard Nixon, sent unmistakable signals of sympathy to white southerners. Meeting with southern Republican delegates, Nixon supported limiting federal government intrusion into their region's affairs. He assured them his administration would not "ram anything down your throats," said he opposed school busing, promised to appoint "strict constructionists" to the Supreme Court, and opposed federal intervention in local school affairs (Carmines and Stimson 1989, p. 53). Nixon's candidacy was complicated by the American Independent Party candidacy of former Alabama governor George Wallace, who also appealed to white southerners with a populist, antigovernment, "law and order" campaign. Although Wallace carried several southern states, Nixon eked out a win in a divided nation exhausted by war in Vietnam and rocked by protests, assassinations and violence, and racial unrest at home.

1969 AND LATER: THE SOUTHERN STRATEGY EVOLVES, BUT CONTINUES

During the Nixon presidency directly racial issues, such as school busing, and covertly racial issues, such as social welfare spending, assumed center stage. Controversies over school busing arose owing to court rulings such as the 1971 *Swann v. Charlotte-Mecklenburg* decision requiring busing to achieve racial integration. Nixon won a landslide reelection in 1972, winning every southern state. Later Republican candidates continued to make covert racial appeals toward conservative whites nationwide, but especially conservative southern whites. Ronald Reagan launched his 1980 campaign with a speech emphasizing "states' rights" in Philadelphia, Mississippi, where the kidnapping and murder of three civil rights workers had shocked and galvanized the nation in 1964. Reagan also made racially charged remarks about "welfare queens" in stump speeches, tried to dismantle the U.S. Civil Rights Commission, opposed affirmative action programs, and advocated cutting federal aid to cities and social programs that especially benefited blacks.

In 1988 George H.W. Bush's campaign portrayed Democratic candidate Michael Dukakis as "soft" on violent crime in a racially charged campaign designed by Republican advisors including Lee Atwater, a native South Carolinian, protégé of Harry Dent, and former campaign director for Republican U.S. Senator (and 1948 Dixiecrat presidential candidate) Thurmond. The campaign featured the story of William "Willie" Horton, a black convict who, released from prison on a weekend furlough (a controversial program supported by Massachusetts governor Dukakis), escaped to Maryland, where he attacked a couple in their home. Republican strategists openly exploited the Horton case, with one TV ad showing a sinister and unruly-looking Horton in police custody. Political scientists Donald Kinder and Lynn Sanders (1996) and Tali Mendelberg (2001) demonstrate that the effect (if not the intent) of the Horton campaign was to stoke white fears of black violence and criminality for political gain. Atwater promised that "by the time this election is over, Willie Horton will be a household name." Later, he said "the Horton case is one of those gut issues that are value issues, particularly in the South, and if we hammer at these over and over, we are going to win."

In the four presidential elections between 1992 and 2004 racial issues have receded in importance, and moral and religious issues have become more prominent. These developments have fueled continued Republican realignment among white southerners, but generally for reasons remotely related to race. As the first southern conservative president since Andrew Jackson (Lind 2003), George W. Bush has enjoyed very high approval ratings from white southerners. Bush's social conservatism and eager use of force overseas since the September 11, 2001, attacks resonate strongly with the militarism (Nisbett and Cohen 1996) and social and religious conservatism (Smith 1997; Green et al. 2003) common among white southerners. For Democrats, the region is now forbidding territory. In the seven presidential elections since 1980, Republican candidates have swept every southern state four times (1984, 1988, 2000, and 2004), and won all but one southern state, Georgia, in 1980. In 1992 and 1996 Arkansas native Bill Clinton carried some southern states, but most southern electoral votes still went to the Republicans.

The southern strategy, launched in 1964 and refined with a panoply of racially charged issues from 1968 to 1988 and other, generally less race-related, issues since 1992, has borne fruit for Republicans. Most white southerners are now reliably Republican in voting for president, and increasingly in voting for Congress and state offices as well. Meanwhile, as reported by Mike Allen in the *Washington Post* (2005), Republican National Committee chairman Ken Mehlman tacitly admitted the racial basis of the southern strategy. In prepared remarks to the National Association for the Advancement of Colored People, Mehlman acknowledged that "some Republicans [were] trying to benefit politically from racial polarization," adding that "we were wrong" and calling it "not healthy for the country for the political parties to be so racially polarized."

Still, southern Republicans may be continuing efforts to polarize the party system by race. The Republican-led 2003 redistricting in Texas has nearly eliminated white Democrats in Texas's U.S. House of Representatives delegation. After the 2004 election, Texas's U.S. House delegation had eleven Democrats—one white and ten black or

Latino—and twenty-one Republicans—one Latino and twenty white. Similarly, in 2005 Georgia Republicans passed a controversial "Voter ID" law requiring would-be voters to show a driver's license or other state-issued photo identification. Georgia's black lawmakers walked out of the statehouse in angry protest over the law's passage. Civil rights groups charged the law would disproportionately suppress black voting, since blacks are less likely to own cars and thus have drivers' licenses. The law required those without drivers' licenses to purchase a state-issued identification card, but at offices that were scarce in heavily-black Atlanta. An injunction, passed later in the year, blocked the law from further being enforced.

SEE ALSO *Civil Rights Movement, U.S.; Dixiecrats; Nixon, Richard M.; Reagan, Ronald; Republican Party; Thurmond, Strom*

BIBLIOGRAPHY

Allen, Mike. 2005. RNC Chief to Say It Was "Wrong" to Exploit Racial Conflict for Votes. *Washington Post*, July 14: A4.

Carmines, Edward, and James Stimson. 1989. *Issue Evolution: Race and the Transformation of American Politics*. Princeton, NJ: Princeton University Press.

Edsall, Thomas Byrne, and Mary D. Edsall. 1991. *Chain Reaction: The Impact of Race, Rights, and Taxes on American Politics*. New York: Norton.

Green, John C., James Guth, Lyman Kellstedt, and Corwin Smidt. 2003. The Soul of the South: Religion and Southern Politics at the Millennium. In *The New Politics of the Old South*, 2nd ed., eds. Charles Bullock III and Mark Rozell, 283–298. Lanham, MD: Rowman and Littlefield.

Kinder, Donald R., and Lynn M. Sanders. 1996. *Divided by Color: Racial Politics and Democratic Ideals*. Chicago: University of Chicago Press.

Lind, Michael. 2003. *Made in Texas: George W. Bush and the Southern Takeover of American Politics*. New York: Basic Books.

Mendelberg, Tali. 2001. *The Race Card: Campaign Strategy, Implicit Messages, and the Norm of Equality*. Princeton, NJ: Princeton University Press.

Nisbett, Richard, and Dov Cohen. 1996. *Culture of Honor: The Psychology of Violence in the South*. Boulder, CO: Westview Press.

Novak, Robert. 1965. *The Agony of the GOP, 1964*. New York: Macmillan.

Smith, Oran P. 1997. *The Rise of Baptist Republicanism*. New York: New York University Press.

Fred Slocum

SOVEREIGNTY

Political scientists trace the conventional definition of sovereignty—supreme legal authority exercised over a particular territory and people—to the writings of European legal and political philosophers from the sixteenth to nineteenth centuries. Many view sovereignty as a defining feature of political modernity, and some critical and postmodern theorists regard sovereignty as a discursive practice and, as such, a central problem for contemporary politics, particularly world politics. It is argued that the discursive practice of sovereignty constructs and sustains the state as the supreme authority in a world in which human well being and social justice would be better served by finding ways of simultaneously holding states more accountable to people and by enlarging the role of global civil society. By some accounts, the sovereign state is the cause of war and international anarchy as well as the primary obstacle to the construction of a humane world order.

Writings on sovereignty over the past four centuries reflect two distinct views, one unlimited and absolute, the other restrictive and conditional. The works of Niccolò Machiavelli (1469–1527), Jean Bodin (1530–1596), Thomas Hobbes (1588–1679), and John Austin (1790–1859) fall into the first category. In Austin's view law is "the command of the sovereign." Machiavelli and Hobbes held that the recognition and exercise of sovereignty as supreme authority is necessary to the establishment of effective government. Bodin's conception was so absolute that, in his view, elected officials could not be said to hold sovereign power at all. Such absolute sovereignty was mitigated when it passed historically from the "divine right of kings" in the sixteenth through the eighteenth centuries to the state or government. Though Hobbes and Austin did not deny a role for the people, their emphasis on the state as the locus of sovereignty is evident today, as there are no requirements that states be democratic in order to be recognized as possessing sovereign authority accountable to no higher authority, hence the criticism of state sovereignty by today's human rights advocates. In contrast, John Locke (1632–1704) and Jean-Jacques Rousseau (1712–1778) argued for a shift in the locus of sovereignty from government to people.

Recent criticisms of sovereignty as a discursive practice stem largely from the work of the influential postmodernist Michel Foucault (1926–1984), who sought to unveil how sovereignty discourses both correspond to and constrain the way power is constituted in social relations in specific historical and cultural contexts. This exercise reveals the paradox of modernity, where sovereignty, said to reside within the individual, has a totalizing effect when exercised by the state. Philosopher Jacques Derrida (1930–2004) also notes the contradiction between, on the one hand, sovereignty understood as one group or individual exercising a superior power over others and, on the other, modernity's promise of democracy and equality.

Sovereignty can be viewed within particular contexts such as international law, international political relations, or through a network of legal relations within a federal state, such as the United States. In international law, an absolute concept of sovereignty is less relevant than the "sovereign equality" of states. States freely enter into legally binding agreements through treaties, but in doing so, they in effect agree to a diminishment of sovereignty. An example is the optional clause to the Statute of the International Court of Justice, which imposes compulsory jurisdiction on all states signing the clause. Some argue that the members of the European Union give up some state sovereignty in favor of "pooled" sovereignty. A distinction is also made between de jure sovereignty, that is, the legal status of sovereignty, and de facto sovereignty, which allows a state to act sovereign as a practical matter even if not supported by de jure, or legal, recognition.

Sovereign equality is a legal attribute of states in their legal and political relations with another. New states "come into existence" as a result of being recognized by existing states. Thus the success of a people or a secessionist movement in seeking recognition as a sovereign state will ultimately depend on the political will of existing states. States may also experience diminished sovereignty as a consequence of violating international norms or as a result of the enforcement of international law by other states. Following their defeat in World War II (1939–1945), for instance, Germany and Japan formed postwar governments under the supervision of the international community, and their ability to maintain military forces was curtailed as a condition of their defeat. More recently, following the United Nations Security Council enforcement action in 1991, Iraq's sovereignty was diminished by the International Atomic Energy Commission inspections and the U.N. designation of "no-fly zones."

In a federal system such as the United States, sovereignty can be reserved or shared between the federal and state or provincial governments. Additionally, indigenous peoples within a state can exercise or assert indigenous sovereignty. Although the term *indigenous* has gained widespread use internationally, U.S. law refers to "tribal sovereignty," while Canada and other settler states refer to "aboriginal" sovereignty. The history of tribal sovereignty in the United States has been troubled, uneven, and often inconsistent, in large part because U.S. law asserts congressional "plenary power" over indigenous peoples. U.S. law treats tribal sovereignty as a lesser or subordinate form of sovereignty. Though eroded through many of the court decisions during most of the twentieth century, in the later twentieth and early twenty-first centuries the right of self-determination has been strengthened as U.S. law recognizes that indigenous tribes and nations possess many attributes of sovereignty. A move toward international recognition of indigenous rights may further strengthen the legal and political basis of indigenous sovereignty, which indigenous peoples often regard as the ability to control one's own political destiny.

Sovereignty has no intrinsic moral authority. As a legal doctrine or norm, sovereignty is said to have settled the church-state authority crisis of the sixteenth century. Its legitimacy, however, rested at that time on the notion of divine right, whereby authoritative uses of power were grounded in the moral claims of religious loyalty. With the rise of nationalism in the eighteenth century, the moral basis shifted from the church to the people in the form of the nation, so that divine right gave way to popular sovereignty. It soon became evident that nationalism was exclusionary, and as an ideology it could be used to justify heinous atrocities against "others" who did not belong to the national group controlling the state.

Sovereignty today is the subject of much debate, with some calling for the "deterritorialization" of sovereignty and others heralding the erosion of the sovereign state in favor of a combination of simultaneously more local and more global societal relations.

SEE ALSO *Confederate States of America; Federalism; Monarchy; Totalitarianism*

BIBLIOGRAPHY

Austin, John. 1995. *The Province of Jurisprudence Determined*, ed. Wilfred E. Rumble. Cambridge, U.K.: Cambridge University Press. (Orig. pub. 1832).

Balke, Friedrich. 2005. Derrida and Foucault on Sovereignty. *German Law Journal* 6 (January 1). http://www.germanlawjournal.com/print.php?id=539.

Barker, Joanne. 2005. *Sovereignty Matters: Locations of Contestation and Possibility in Indigenous Struggles for Self-Determination*. Lincoln: University of Nebraska Press.

Bartelson, Jens, ed. 1995. *A Genealogy of Sovereignty*. Cambridge, U.K.: Cambridge University Press.

Bodin, Jean. 1992. *On Sovereignty: Four Chapters from the Six Books of the Commonwealth*. Trans. and ed. Julian H. Franklin. Cambridge, U.K.: Cambridge University Press. (Orig. pub. 1576).

Foucault, Michel. 2003. *The Essential Foucault*, eds. Paul Rabinow and Nikolas S. Rose. New York: New Press.

Hobbes, Thomas. 1982. *Leviathan*, ed. C. B. McPherson. New York: Penguin Books. (Orig. pub. 1651).

Ivison, Duncan, Paul Patton, and Will Sanders, eds. 2000. *Political Theory and the Rights of Indigenous Peoples*. Cambridge, U.K.: Cambridge University Press.

Kamuf, Peggy. 1991. *The Derrida Reader*. New York: Columbia University Press.

Krasner, Stephen. 1999. *Sovereignty: Organized Hypocrisy*. Princeton, NJ: Princeton University Press.

Krasner, Stephen. 2001. *Problematic Sovereignty*. New York: Columbia University Press.

Locke, John. 2003. *Two Treatises on Government and a Letter on Toleration*, ed. Ian Shapiro. New Haven, CT: Yale University Press. (Orig. pub. 1689).

Machiavelli, Nicolo. 1984. *The Prince*. New York: Bantam Classics. (Orig. pub. 1532).

Machiavelli, Nicolo. 2003. *The Art of War*. Trans. Christopher Lynch. Chicago: University of Chicago Press. (Orig. pub. 1520).

Nelsen, Brent F., and Alexander Stubb, eds. 2003. *The European Union: Readings on the Theory and Practice of European Integration*. Boulder, CO: Lynne Rienner.

Philpott, Daniel. 2001. *Revolutions in Sovereignty: How Ideas Shaped Modern International Relations*. Princeton, NJ: Princeton University Press.

Porter, Robert Odawi. 2004. *Sovereignty, Colonialism, and the Future of the Indigenous Nations: A Reader*. Durham, NC: Carolina Academic Press.

Rousseau, Jean-Jacques. 1968. *The Social Contract*. Trans and ed. Maurice Cranston. New York: Penguin Books. (Orig. pub. 1762).

Slaughter, Anne-Marie. 2004. *A New World Order*. Princeton, NJ: Princeton University Press.

Trask, Haunani Kay. 1999. *From a Native Daughter: Colonialism and Sovereignty in Hawaii*. Manoa: University of Hawaii Press.

Weber, Cynthia. 1994. *Simulating Sovereignty: Intervention, the State, and Symbolic Exchange*. Cambridge, U.K.: Cambridge University Press.

Wilmer, Franke. 1993. *The Indigenous Voice in World Politics*. Newbury Park, CA: Sage.

Franke Wilmer

SOWETO

SEE *Townships.*

SOWETO UPRISING OF 1976

SEE *Apartheid.*

SPACE EXPLORATION

The sociocultural status of space exploration has been contested for many years and remains uncertain. Although astronomy and related sciences have benefited greatly from the world's space programs, space exploration was motivated not by scientific curiosity but by the romanticism of a social movement and by competition between prestige-conscious nations. By the end of the nineteenth century, astronomy possessed a rough picture of the solar system, including the knowledge that objects like the Moon and Mars were worlds somewhat comparable to the earth, but realistic means for space travel had not yet been imagined. Then, autonomous intellectuals independently developed the correct theories for multi-stage liquid-fuel rockets.

SOCIAL ORIGINS

Konstantin Tsiolkovsky (1857–1935) was an impoverished schoolteacher in Russia who devoted many years of socially isolated work to developing fruitful ideas about spaceflight. American Robert H. Goddard (1882–1945) independently developed many of the same ideas, and possessing greater resources was actually able to build a working liquid-fuel rocket in 1926. Romanian-German Hermann Oberth (1894–1989) learned of the work of his colleagues just as he was about to publish his treatise, *The Rocket into Planetary Space*, in 1923. On the basis of the work of these pioneers, spaceflight societies were founded in Germany (1927), the United States (1930), Russia (1931), and Great Britain (1933). The German, U.S., and Russian groups independently duplicated Goddard's working liquid-fuel rocket, although Goddard refused to cooperate with the others in the vain hope that he could develop unaided the technology to send an unmanned rocket to the moon. United only by publications and occasional visits, these groups formed an international social movement dedicated to space travel for transcendent motives that were neither economic nor political.

As the financial troubles of the Great Depression deepened, the space-travel movement struggled to survive. Especially in Germany, and later in the United States and Russia, the movement entered into a marriage of convenience with the military. The Treaty of Versailles ending World War I (1914–1918) had limited German artillery and aircraft but did not mention rockets. Members of the movement, notably Oberth's young protégé Wernher von Braun (1912–1977), presented liquid-fuel rockets to the German army as effective weapons, although development of conventional solid-fuel rockets would have been a better choice for military purposes. Near the end of World War II (1939–1945), von Braun's team completed development of the 300-mile-range V-2 rocket, demonstrating the potential of liquid-fuel technology for spaceflight. Starting with the launch of Sputnik I in 1957, the Soviet Union and the United States competed for international prestige through aggressive space programs, until the landing of the Apollo 11 lunar module on the moon in 1969.

On the basis of a huge library of technical and scholarly publications, the facts of the history of space exploration to date are clear, but the social-scientific interpretation is hotly debated. The view around 1960 was that international propaganda competition was the main driver, as has been summarized by Vernon van Dyke (1964). Amitai Etzioni (1965) argued that the American space program was a useless extravagance through which the military-industrial complex looted the national treasury. Then, John Logsdon (1970) argued that President John F. Kennedy's (1917–1963) decision to go to the moon was a means for reviving the political spirit of his New Frontier program after defeats in 1961 with the aborted Bay of Pigs invasion of Cuba and in a meeting with the Soviet leader Nikita Khrushchev (1894–1971). William Bainbridge (1976) took the argument one step further, suggesting that in Germany and the Soviet Union, as well as in the United States, leaders of the transcendental spaceflight movement had cleverly manipulated beleaguered political leaders to invest in space as a symbolic solution to their inferiority in competition with other leaders. Michael Neufeld (1996) has argued against this thesis in the case of Germany, asserting that technically competent military engineers possessed a correct estimation of the military potential of the technology. Walter McDougall (1985) argued against this view in the case of the Soviet Union, stating that Marxist ideology naturally supported visionary technological projects. Most recently, Logsdon (2006) has argued that the American space program has been trapped in a vicious circle, as members of the movement convince political leaders to undertake technically demanding projects, but the public is not willing to invest enough to make them successful.

SOCIETAL IMPLICATIONS

Public opinion has long been generally favorable toward the space program but has never been a driving force in motivating development of the technology. In October 1947, a Gallup poll asked 1,500 Americans, "How long do you think it will be before man will be able to fly to the moon?" Only 21 percent guessed a particular year, 38 percent said "never," and the remainder had nothing to say on the topic. Throughout the Apollo program, a majority tended to feel the project was not worth the cost. Americans' enthusiasm for the actual moon landing faded fast after 1969, possibly accelerated by a general loss of confidence in science and technology that prevailed until the mid-1970s. Since then, majorities have tended to feel that the National Aeronautics and Space Administration (NASA) was doing a good job, but they give space exploration a low priority for funding. The responses of 1,400 Americans to the General Social Survey in 2004 were typical. Only 14.3 percent wanted funding increased, 43.4 percent wanted it kept at current levels, 36.8 percent wanted funding reduced, and the remaining 5.5 percent had no opinion.

Around 1970 there was considerable discussion of the potential terrestrial benefits of space, especially the second-order consequences from technology transfer, often called *spin-offs*. These were popularly conceptualized as distinct inventions made in the space program that found valuable uses in society. Many people count Tang powdered fruit drink, Teflon coatings on frying pans, and Velcro fasteners among these, but all existed before the space program. Real spin-offs actually are rare, but their stories fit popular misconceptions about how technological progress occurs, so they are legends that gain strength in the retelling. Far more important are the intended *applications* of space technology, the most prominent of which are communications satellites, navigation satellites (Global Positioning System), meteorology satellites, and military reconnaissance satellites. Difficult to measure, but probably of equal value, is the general stimulus to scientific and technological development achieved by the space program through increasing the technical expertise in the population, widely disseminating abstract technical ideas that may contribute to innovations far from their original sources, and inspiring young people to study science.

When Bainbridge (1991) asked two thousand students at Harvard University in 1986 to identify the possible goals for the space program, they came up with a list of 125 goals that could be clustered into groups that served different values. Some goals were technical and economic, including the benefits of satellites listed above, spin-offs, possible manufacturing in the vacuum and weightlessness of space, new knowledge for sciences like physics and astronomy, and preservation of the earth's environment. A different set of goals stressed emotional and idealistic values, such as spiritual fulfillment, personal inspiration, artistic and aesthetic transcendence, satisfaction of curiosity, and the building of world harmony. A small group of items concerned national pride, defense, and military capabilities in space. Finally, a number of far-out but reasonably popular goals envisioned colonization of the solar system and the discovery of extraterrestrial life.

The early decades of the twenty-first century appear to be a transition period, in which predictions would be especially hazardous. China has launched men into orbit, thereby demonstrating the quality of its technology, especially to the propaganda disadvantage of Japan, which has pursued a half-hearted and largely unsuccessful space program. Both Russia and the European Union have well-established space launch capabilities but lack ambitious goals. After failing twice to develop a successor to the space shuttle in the National Aerospace Plane and the X-33, and running more than fifteen years overdue in completing the space station, the U.S. space program clearly required fundamental redirection. The initial phase of reorganization, announced in 2004, severely cut back scientific research and technological development in favor of very long-term plans for adventurous but poorly motivated human voyages to the Moon and Mars.

As any science fiction fan would be happy to explain to any social scientist willing to listen, the long-term social implications of space exploration could possibly be profound. Despite daunting technical and economic hurdles, the colonization of Mars and of several large satellites in the solar system could lead to a time when more humans lived off the Earth than on it. Some think we will transform ourselves radically to become better adapted to those alien environments and better prepared for interstellar travel. If so, space travel could bring about a new adaptive radiation event comparable to that which produced the human species five million years ago in East Africa, what the science fiction writer Alfred Bester (1913–1987) called "arrival of the fittest" in his novel, *The Stars My Destination* (1956). If the social scientist scoffed at such ideas, the science fiction fan might comment there must have been chimpanzees five million years ago who scoffed as well.

SEE ALSO *Bay of Pigs; Industry; Mars; Science Fiction; World War II*

BIBLIOGRAPHY

Bainbridge, William Sims. 1976. *The Spaceflight Revolution: A Sociological Study.* New York: Wiley.

Bainbridge, William Sims. 1991. *Goals in Space: American Values and the Future of Technology.* Albany: State University of New York Press.

Bauer, Raymond. 1969. *Second-Order Consequences: A Methodological Essay on the Impact of Technology.* Cambridge, MA: MIT Press.

Etzioni, Amitai. 1964. *The Moon-Doggle: Domestic and International Implications of the Space Race.* Garden City, NY: Doubleday.

Ginzberg, Eli, James W. Kuhn, Jerome Schnee, and Boris Yavitz, eds. 1976. *Economic Impact of Large Public Programs: The NASA Experience.* Salt Lake City, UT: Olympus.

Launius, Roger D. 2003. Public Opinion Polls and Perceptions of U.S. Human Spaceflight. *Space Policy* 19: 163–175.

Logsdon, John M. 1970. *The Decision to Go to the Moon: Project Apollo and the National Interest.* Cambridge, MA: MIT Press.

Logsdon, John M. 2006. "A Failure of National Leadership": Why No Replacement for the Space Shuttle. In *Critical Issues in the History of Spaceflight*, ed. Steven J. Dick and Roger D. Launius, 269–300. Washington, DC: NASA.

McDougall, Walter A. 1985. *The Heavens and the Earth: A Political History of the Space Age.* New York: Basic Books.

Neufeld, Michael, 1996. *The Rocket and the Reich: Peenemunde and the Coming of the Ballistic Missile Era.* Cambridge, MA: Harvard University Press.

Ordway, Frederick I., III, Carsbie C. Adams, and Mitchell R. Sharpe. 1971. *Dividends from Space.* New York: Crowell.

Roy, Stephanie A., Elaine C. Gresham, and Carissa Bryce Christensen. 2000. The Complex Fabric of Public Opinion on Space. *Acta Astronautica* 47: 665–675.

Van Dyke, Vernon. 1964. *Pride and Power: The Rationale of the Space Program.* Urbana: University of Illinois Press.

William Sims Bainbridge

SPACESHIP EARTH

SEE *Fuller, Buckminster.*

SPANCE, MICHAEL

SEE *Signals; Screening and Signaling Games.*

SPANISH CIVIL WAR

The Spanish Civil War broke out on July 17, 1936, as a result of the revolutionary process begun under the democratic Second Republic of Spain, which had been inaugurated in 1931. Democracy had brought large-scale political and social mobilization, while the left launched a series of four revolutionary insurrections between 1932 and 1934. In 1935 an alliance of the moderate and the revolutionary left formed a Popular Front that won the election of February 1936. This produced a weak minority government of the moderate left that could not restrain the revolutionaries, whose violence, disorder, seizure of property, and corruption of electoral processes provoked a military revolt.

Though Spanish political society was strongly polarized between right and left, each polarity was badly fragmented. The military revolt brought scarcely more than half the army out in revolt, though it was assisted by rightist militia. The leftist Republican government in power abandoned constitutional rule and engaged in what was called "arming the people," which meant giving weapons and de facto power to the revolutionary organizations.

The result was the Spanish revolution of 1936–1937, the most intense and spontaneous outburst of worker revolution seen in modern Europe, not excepting the Russian Revolution of 1917. It collectivized much farmland and most of urban industry, and it was marked by an extensive Red Terror—the mass execution of political opponents, directed against all conservative organizations, and especially the Catholic Church—which destroyed countless churches. Nearly 7,000 clergy were killed, and at least 55,000 people perished in the Republican zone.

After two months, the military insurgents elected General Francisco Franco as their commander-in-chief. Franco also acted as dictator and permanent chief of state. By the second week of the Civil War, he had successfully sought military assistance from Nazi Germany and Fascist Italy, and he mounted a military drive on Madrid. The rebels quickly termed themselves Nationalists and mounted a savage repression of their own, which was more concerted and effective than that of the Republicans and eventually claimed even more victims.

General Franco organized a single-party state, partially modeled on that of Fascist Italy, in April 1937. He combined the Spanish fascist party with rightist groups to form the Falange Española Tradicionalista (Traditionalist Spanish Phalanx, or FET). Franco succeeded in establishing almost complete political unity among the rightist forces, enabling him to concentrate almost exclusively on the war effort, and in the process he developed a more effective and professionally led military force than did his opponents.

The revolutionary Republic proved ineffective militarily, relying on disorganized revolutionary militia. After the first two weeks it lost battle after battle, resulting in the organization of a new Republican government on September 4, 1936, led by the Socialist Francisco Largo Caballero. It eventually included all the leftist forces in a single government and began the creation of a new centralized Ejército Popular (People's Army).

Though France was led by a Popular Front government at this time, it was becoming dependent on Great Britain, which counseled against involvement in Spain. The French government therefore took the lead in organizing the Non-Intervention Committee, which gained the collaboration of nearly all European governments and took up deliberations in London in September 1936, though it was unsuccessful in ending the involvement in the war of the three major European dictatorships.

Germany and Italy were already intervening on behalf of Franco, and the Republicans urgently requested military assistance from the Soviet Union, the only other revolutionary state in Europe. Stalin finally decided to send assistance in September 1936, and Soviet military assistance began to arrive soon afterward. This assistance was paid for by shipping most of the Spanish gold reserve (the fifth largest in the world) to Moscow. Late-model Soviet planes and tanks, which arrived in large quantities, outclassed the weaponry provided by Hitler and Mussolini. These weapons, together with hundreds of Soviet military specialists, were accompanied by the first units of the International Brigades, a volunteer force organized by the Communist International, which eventually numbered approximately 41,000. By the end of

1936 the war was turning into a stalemate, and it promised to become a long struggle of attrition.

In this situation, the Spanish Communist Party, which had been weak prior to the war, expanded rapidly. Soviet assistance helped it become a major force on the Republican side, emphasizing the importance of restraining the revolution of the extreme left and concentrating all resources on the military effort. This provoked great tension, leading to the "May Days" of May 1937 in Barcelona, the center of the revolution. This was a mini–civil war within the civil war, with the extreme revolutionary left fighting the more disciplined forces of the Communists and the reorganized Republican state. The latter dominated, leading to the formation that same month of a new Republican government led by the Socialist Juan Negrín, which deemphasized the socioeconomic revolution and sought to concentrate all its activity on the military effort.

The Soviet escalation of military intervention in October 1936 was quickly countered by a counter-escalation from Mussolini and Hitler, who sent an Italian army corps of nearly 50,000 men and a 90-plane German aerial unit, the Condor Legion, to Spain. This guaranteed that Franco would continue to receive the support necessary to maintain the military initiative. In 1937 he conquered the Republican northern zone, and in April 1938 his army sliced through Aragon to the Mediterranean, dividing the remaining Republican zone in two. During the conquest of the northern zone, the most famous (and infamous) incident of the war occurred. This was the bombing of the Basque town of Guernica by German and Italian planes in April 1937.

Though Mussolini desired a quick and complete Nationalist victory to strengthen Italy's position in the Mediterranean, Hitler was in no hurry. He preferred that the Spanish war continue for some time. It had become the main focus of European diplomacy during 1936-1937, and it served to distract attention from the rearmament of Germany and the beginning of its expansion in central Europe. The French government covertly supported the Republican cause in a policy of "relaxed nonintervention," which served as a conduit for military supplies from the Soviet Union and other countries. By 1937, Stalin was in turn increasingly distracted by the Japanese invasion of China. In 1938 he sought disengagement from Spain, but he could find no terms that would not involve a loss of face.

Franco's forces slowly but steadily gained the upper hand. His government in the Nationalist zone maintained a productive economy and a relatively stable currency. The revolutionary Republican zone, by contrast, was wracked with inflation and suffered increasingly severe shortages, producing widespread hunger by 1938. The Communists, in turn, developed a political and military hegemony under the Negrín government, though never complete domination. The policy of both Negrín and the Communists was to continue resistance to the bitter end, hoping that a general European war would soon break out, during which France would come to the relief of the Republicans. This was increasingly resented by the other leftist parties, however, who finally rebelled in Madrid in March 1945, overthrowing Negrín and the Communists, and then soon surrendering to Franco, who declared the end of the war on April 1, 1939.

The Spanish Civil War was a classic revolutionary-counterrevolutionary civil war, somewhat similar to those that occurred in eastern and southeastern Europe after each of the world wars. It became a highly mythified event, often presented as a struggle between "fascism and democracy," "fascism and communism," or "Christian civilization and Asian barbarism." It has also been viewed as the "opening battle of World War II (1939–1945)." All such epithets are exaggerated, however. While there was fascism on the side of Franco's Nationalists, there was no democracy on the Republican side. In Spain, Hitler and Stalin were on opposite sides, but they joined forces in August-September 1939 to begin World War II in Europe. Germany and Italy did gain their goals in Spain, however, while Soviet policy failed.

Militarily, the war was notable for the introduction of late-model weaponry, especially new warplanes and tanks. The Soviet military studied the war with great thoroughness, but they sometimes drew the wrong conclusions from it, as did some other countries. Germany learned important lessons on the use of combined arms and air-to-ground support, but it failed to improve its armored forces. The victorious Franco regime skirted with involvement in World War II, but it never entered that conflict and endured until Franco's death in 1975.

SEE ALSO *Civil Wars; Fascism; Franco, Francisco; Hitler, Adolf; Mussolini, Benito; Stalin, Joseph; World War II*

BIBLIOGRAPHY

Bolloten, Burnett. 1991. *The Spanish Civil War: Revolution and Counterrevolution.* Durham: University of North Carolina Press.

Coverdale, John F. 1975. *Italian Intervention in the Spanish Civil War.* Princeton, NJ: Princeton University Press.

Payne, Stanley G. 1987. *The Franco Regime 1936-1975.* Madison: University of Wisconsin Press.

Payne, Stanley G. 2003. *The Spanish Civil War, the Soviet Union, and Communism.* New Haven, CT: Yale University Press.

Payne, Stanley G. 2006. *The Collapse of the Spanish Republic, 1933-1936. Origins of the Civil War.* New Haven, CT: Yale University Press.

Preston, Paul. 1993. *Franco. A Biography.* London: HarperCollins.

Thomas, Hugh. 1986. *The Spanish Civil War.* New York: Harper & Row.

Whealey, Robert H. 1989. *Hitler and Spain. The Nazi Role in the Spanish Civil War.* Lexington: University of Kentucky Press.

Stanley G. Payne

SPANISH-AMERICAN WAR
SEE *War of 1898.*

SPATIAL MAPPING
SEE *Geography.*

SPATIAL THEORY

Spatial theory is built on the concept of distance; this distance may be of an economic or ideological form. The foundations of spatial analysis span many disciplines, such as economics, urban studies, and political science. The seminal paper by Hotelling (1929) studied the equilibrium location of two sellers of a homogenous product in a *linear* town where all consumers are located on a single road. Hotelling's model is based on physical distance and demonstrates that if the sellers compete only in terms of location (spatial competition) and they are identical in all other dimensions such as quality, costs, and prices, then their optimum location will be the *median* of the town. Consumers try to minimize travel time when they choose between similar stores. The result is that the stores locate next to each other at the center of the town to capture the most customers. The implicit assumption of spatial models is that people are motivated mainly by self-interest—firms maximize profit and consumers maximize utility.

The notion of space can be extended beyond physical space to include "position" in product characteristics, as described by Lancaster (1979), and "position" in political platforms, as elaborated by Downs (1957). Similarly, in Chamberlain's (1933) model of monopolistic competition, space is seen as a tool to derive the demand curve faced by the monopolistic firm. Although Hotelling and Smithies (1941) are credited with originating the idea, Downs established spatial theory as a conceptual tool. The modern applications of spatial theory in economics, urban studies, and political science are based on the trade-offs between gains and losses as a result of changes in spatial position. Smithies modified Hotelling's model by introducing elastic demand so that people at the edges of town might stop shopping at the store if it moved too far to the center. Under perfect inelastic demand conditions, as suggested by Hotelling, consumers are assumed to travel to the center of the town regardless of the opportunity cost of transportation. To introduce a trade-off between the access and transportation cost, Smithies suggested that transportation costs lead to elastic demand at each point on the linear road. Thus, when consumers face an inverse demand function with respect to the distance from the center, they will stop traveling to the center if the cost of travel outweighs the benefit of access. Mills (1972) suggested that allocation of land to differing uses is determined primarily by transportation costs. He argued that variability in transportation costs is a key determinant in the distribution of people across a metropolitan area. The lower transportation costs are, the more decentralized the area is.

Political applications of the spatial model closely followed the spatial theories of economic competition. The electoral models developed by Downs essentially adopt the same principles that economists and social choice theorists use to analyze people's actions in the marketplace and collective decision making. The economic concept of locational equilibrium has been applied to the political world. Downs assumed that voters were distributed over policy dimensions and that political parties played the role of stores. The tendency of competing businesses toward imitation is applied to political parties during elections. When voters vote for the party closest to them on a single policy dimension, the parties converge to the median voter's preferences. Since the goal of a political party is to maximize votes, parties and candidates purposefully take positions in the center of the distribution of voter preferences. Restricting issues to a single policy dimension and assuming single-peaked preferences, the expected result is a spatial equilibrium at the position of the median voter (Downs 1957; Black 1958). Since the voters choose to support the candidate nearest to them on the ideological scale, the parties and candidates should adopt platforms that appeal to the median voter to win a majority of the votes. The Downs/Hotelling spatial theory of competition assumes that each voter votes for the candidate from whom he or she derives the highest utility. Downs's model is an example of the social choice theory; it introduces the electoral trade-off between the number of extremists each party loses by moving toward the center, as compared with the number of moderates it gains. As parties move toward the center of the political spectrum, the voters at the extremes are less likely to identify with mainstream parties and thus choose extremist alternatives or abstention.

Modern monocentric models were developed in the 1960s, largely by Alonso (1964), Muth (1969), and Mills (1972). These models assume the existence of a center in a geographic space to which access is scarce, and therefore valuable. To be close to the center for better access, businesses and consumers bid for land. Land prices are inversely related to distance to the center. Businesses and consumers face a trade-off between land prices and transportation costs. Those who value access to the center more will outbid the others and face higher land prices and lower transportation costs. In Beckmann's (1973) family choice model, distance to the center is inversely related to the number of dependents in a family unit. Similarly, the smaller size of the ratio of wage earners to family size determines an equilibrium location further from the center. Monocentric models are not concerned with why access is desirable but rather with its consequences, especially the manner in which the market allocates access. However, the need to interact turns out to be sufficient to generate a dense center that exhibits a single peaked-distribution of (homogenous) people across locations. There are many theories of why people want to develop and maintain lasting and positive relations. Beckmann (1976) was the first to focus on the trade-off between the average distance to those with whom one interacts and the amount of the land one consumes. In this model, the city or downtown emerges as a magnet for social relations.

Note that the spatial electoral model (Downs 1957) and the monocentric model (Alonso 1964; Muth 1969; Mills 1972) are also single-peaked as long as the voters are voting on one issue, the city has one center, and the spatial competition has only one dimension. In the real world, however, political discourse and campaign issues seldom fall into a single dimension and goods are different in other dimensions than distance. In this case single-peaked distributions are not possible and multiple equilibria result instead.

SEE ALSO *Borders; Cities; Geography; Metropolis; Mills, Edwin; Political Science, Behavioral; Political Theory; Public Choice Theory; Public Goods; Trade; Transportation Industry*

BIBLIOGRAPHY

Alonso, W. 1964. *Location and Land Use: Toward a General Theory of Land Rent.* Cambridge, MA: Harvard University Press.

Beckmann, M. J. 1973. Equilibrium Models of Residential Land Use. *Regional and Urban Economics* 3: 361–368.

Beckmann, M. J. 1976. Spatial Equilibrium in the Dispersed City. In *Mathematical Land Use Theory*, ed. Y. Y. Papageorgiou, 117–125. Lexington, MA: Lexington Books.

Black, D. 1958. *The Theory of Committees and Elections.* Cambridge, U.K.: Cambridge University Press.

Chamberlain, E. H. 1933. *The Theory of Monopolistic Competition.* Cambridge, MA: Harvard University Press.

Downs, Anthony. 1957. *An Economic Theory of Democracy.* New York: Harper & Row.

Hotelling, H. 1929. Stability in Competition. *Economic Journal* 39 (1929): 41–57.

Lancaster, K. 1979. *Variety, Equity, and Efficiency.* New York: Columbia University Press.

Mills, E. 1972. *Studies in the Structure of the Urban Economy.* Baltimore, MD: Johns Hopkins University Press.

Muth, R. 1969. *Cities and Housing: The Spatial Pattern of Urban Residential Land Use.* Chicago: University of Chicago Press.

Smithies, A. 1941. Monopolistic Price Policy in a Spatial Market. *Econometrica* 9 (1): 63–73.

Haydar Kurban
Makada Henry

SPEARMAN, CHARLES

SEE *Intelligence.*

SPEARMAN RANK CORRELATION COEFFICIENT

The Spearman rank correlation coefficient is a nonparametric (distribution-free) rank statistic proposed by Charles Spearman in 1904. It is a measure of correlation that captures the strength of association between two variables without making any assumptions about the frequency distributions of the underlying variables.

The computation of the Spearman rank correlation coefficient requires first that the values of the two variables be assigned ranks. When the data are not initially ranked, the first step is to separately rank the two variables (X and Y) under examination. Then the Spearman coefficient is calculated as the ordinary Pearson correlation coefficient r between the ranked values of X and Y. After ranking the two variables, for each case i we take the difference $d_i = X_i - Y_i$ for each pair, and then we calculate the Spearman coefficient. This coefficient of rank correlation measures the degree of association between the two sets of ranks. The formula of this statistic is

$$r_s = 1 - \frac{6\sum_{i=1}^{n} d_i^2}{n(n^2-1)}$$

where r_s = the Spearman rank correlation coefficient, d = the difference between each pair of ranks of corresponding values of the variables X and Y, and n = the number of pairs of values in the sample.

There are two properties of this coefficient. First, the values of the Spearman correlation coefficient will always vary between −1 and 1. When the value of the coefficient is 1, there is a perfect positive correlation or direct correlation. That is, large values of the one variable, for example, X, are associated with large values of the other, for example, Y, and small values of the X variable are associated with small values of the Y variable. When the coefficient is −1, there is a perfect negative correlation or indirect correlation. In this case, large values of the X variable are associated with small values of the Y variable and vice versa. When the value is equal to zero, it means that there is no relationship or correlation. This statistic shows only that two variables X and Y correlate positively or negatively; it does not offer any indication that one variable affects the other.

The second property of the Spearman rank correlation, and of its parametric counterpart, is that it is a pure number without units or dimensions. In using this coefficient we deal with two sets of ranks assigned to the variables X and Y. The original observations on the variables may be ranks, or they may be numerical values ranked by magnitude.

In addition to interpreting the magnitude and the direction of a correlation coefficient, the significance of a given value of correlation should also be tested. The null hypothesis states that no correlation exists and that whatever value of correlation is found between the two examined variables is due to sampling error.

A modern approach to testing the hypothesis that the value of the Spearman coefficient is significantly different from zero is to calculate the probability that it would be greater than or equal to the observed r by using a permutation test. This method is superior to the traditional ones in most cases, even when the dataset is large, because modern computing has the power to generate permutation.

The traditional approach for determining significance is still widely used. It involves the comparison of the calculated r with published tables for various levels of significance. It only requires that the tables have the pertinent values for the desired ranges.

An alternative approach for samples of large sizes is the approximation to the Student's t-distribution that is given by the following formula:

$$t = r_s / [(1 - r_s^2) / (n - 2)]^{1/2}$$

When the sample size (n) is less than 10, the above is not appropriate. For values of (n) less than 10, table 1 shows the critical values of r_s required for the significance

Critical values of Spearman rank correlation coefficient for N<10

N	Nondirectional test	Directional test
5	1.00	0.90
6	0.89	0.83
7	0.79	0.72
8	0.72	0.62
9	0.70	0.60

SOURCE: http://faculty.vassar.edu/lowry/corr_rank.html.

Table 1

at the 0.05 level for both a nondirectional and a directional test.

APPLICATIONS AND SHORTCOMINGS

The Spearman rank correlation coefficient can be used when the normality assumption of the two examined variables' distribution is violated. It also can be used when the data are nominal or ordinal. It may be a better indicator that a relationship exists between two variables when the relationship is nonlinear, even for variables with numerical values, when the Pearson correlation coefficient indicates a low or zero linear relationship. When there are three or more conditions, a number of subjects are all observed in each of them, and we predict that the observations will have a particular order. In this case, a generalization of the Spearman coefficient is useful.

As with all other nonparametric or distribution-free procedures or tests, the Spearman rank correlation coefficient is less powerful than its parametric counterpart, the Pearson product-moment correlation coefficient. In addition, there is no evidence of causality between the two variables that have been found to be related by this coefficient.

ALTERNATIVE CORRELATION COEFFICIENTS

There are other examples of correlation coefficients, including the Pearson product-moment correlation coefficient, which is used for making inferences about the population correlation coefficient, assuming that the two variables are jointly normally distributed. When this assumption cannot be justified, then a nonparametric measure such as the Spearman correlation coefficient is more appropriate. The Pearson correlation coefficient measures the linear association between two variables that have been measured on interval or ratio scales. The for-

mula that determines the Pearson product-moment correlation coefficient (r_{XY}) is

$$r_{xy} = \frac{\sum_{i=1}^{n}[X_i - E(X)][Y_i - E(Y)]}{\left\{\sum_{i=1}^{n}(X_i - X)^2(Y_i - Y)^2\right\}^{\frac{1}{2}}}$$

The significance of r, where the null hypothesis states that no correlation exists between the two variables X and Y ($r_{XY} = 0$), is found by the following t-statistic, with ($n - 2$) degrees of freedom:

$$t = \frac{r(n - 1)^{\frac{1}{2}}}{(1 - r^2)^{\frac{1}{2}}}$$

Another measure of degree of concordance that is closely related to the Spearman correlation coefficient is the Kendall tau rank correlation coefficient, given by the formula

$$\tau = \frac{1(4Q)}{n(n - 1)}$$

Similar to the Spearman coefficient, Kendall's tau lies between −1 and 1. When it is equal to +1, we assume that there exists complete concordance, whereas when it is equal to −1, there exists complete disagreement. This Kendall tau (τ) coefficient uses the same data as the Spearman correlation coefficient (r_s) but differs arithmetically, so they are not exactly similar.

In order to calculate the tau (τ) coefficient we go through the following steps.

We rank the values of variable X from 1 to n; similarly, we rank the values of variable Y, both in an ascending order.

We make pairs for every ranked value of X_i the equivalent Y_i.

We compute the variable S, which is equal to $S = \Sigma c_{ii}$ where $c_{ii} = 1$ if X_i and X_j have the same rank with the Y_i and Y_j and $c_{jj} = -1$ in the opposite case.

If there are no same-value cases among the X_i and Y_i (or there are few compared to the sample size (n)), then Kendall's tau coefficient is equal to $\tau = 2S / [n(n - 1)]$.

An advantage of the Kendall tau coefficient compared to the Spearman correlation coefficient is that the former can be generalized in order to determine the Kendall partial correlation coefficient, which is equivalent to the Pearson partial correlation coefficient in cases where nonparametric statistics are appropriate.

Another correlation coefficient, the correlation coefficient C of rank matrices (or "double-entrance matrix"), examines the degree of dependence between two variables X and Y, despite the facts that these variables could be ranked or not, that they could be continuous or discontinuous, and that they could have normal distributions or not. It can be calculated by the formula:

$$C = \left[\frac{x^2}{(n + x^2)} \right]^{\frac{1}{2}}$$

and it follows the chi-squared (χ^2) distribution with $v = (r - 1)(q - 1)$ degrees of freedom, where r and q are the numbers of rows and columns, respectively, of the rank matrix under examination. In order to test the null hypothesis that $C = 0$, or that the two variables X and Y do not have a significant relationship, we calculate the χ^2 and the χ_a^2, which is the critical value. The latter can be found in the tables of the χ^2 distribution for $v = (r - 1)(q - 1)$ degrees of freedom. If $\chi^2 \, \chi_a^2$, then the null hypothesis is rejected.

SEE ALSO *Pearson, Karl; Statistics*

BIBLIOGRAPHY

Hogg, Robert V., and Allen T. Craig. 1995. *Introduction to Mathematical Statistics*. 5th ed. New York: Macmillan.

Kendall, Maurice G. 1970. *Rank Correlation Methods*. 3rd ed. London: Charles Griffin.

Lehmann, Erich L., and H. J. M. D'Abrera. 1998. *Nonparametrics: Statistical Methods*, rev. ed. Englewood Cliffs, NJ: Prentice-Hall.

Pearson, Karl, and Alice Lee. 1903. On the Laws of Inheritance in Man. *Biometrika* 2 (4): 357–463.

Spearman, Charles. 1904. "General Intelligence" Objectively Determined and Measured. *American Journal of Psychology* 15:72–101.

Weisstein, Eric W. 2002. Spearman Rank Correlation Coefficient. Wolfram MathWorld Web site. http://mathworld.wolfram.com/SpearmanRankCorrelationCoefficient.html.

Katerina Lyroudi

SPECIAL PERIOD

SEE *Castro, Fidel.*

SPECIFICATION

The term *specification* is used in economics to denote the choice of a model in the context of empirical modeling. Unfortunately, the use of the term since the late 1950s (Theil 1957, Leamer 1990) is confusing because different types of models are conflated; the crucial confusion being between a *statistical* (a set of probabilistic assumptions) and a *structural* (substantive) model. The distinction between these two types of models is important because they raise very different issues with respect to the premises of inference in empirical modeling (see Spanos 2006a).

THEORY AND STRUCTURAL MODELS

It is widely recognized that most stochastic phenomena (the ones exhibiting chance regularity patterns—see Spanos 1999) are commonly influenced by a very large number of contributing factors, and that explains why theories are often dominated by *ceteris paribus* clauses. The idea behind a theory is that in explaining the behavior of a variable, say y_k, one demarcates the segment of reality to be modeled by selecting the primary influencing factors $\mathbf{x}_k$, cognizant of the fact that there might be numerous other potentially relevant factors $\boldsymbol{\xi}_k$ (observable and unobservable) that jointly determine the behavior of y_k via a *theory model*:

$$y_k = h^\star(x_k; \xi_k), \, k \in \mathsf{N} := \{1, 2; \ldots, n; \ldots\} \tag{1}$$

where $h^\star(.)$ represents the true behavioral relationship for y_k. The guiding principle in selecting the variables in x_k is to ensure that they collectively account for the *systematic behavior* of y_k and the *unaccounted factors* ξ_k represent nonessential disturbing influences which could only have a *nonsystematic* effect on y_k. This reasoning transforms (1) into a *structural model* of the form:

$$y_k = h(x_k; \varphi) + \epsilon(x_k, \xi_k), \, k \in \mathsf{N}. \tag{2}$$

By definition the error term process is:

$$\left(\varepsilon(\mathbf{x}_k, \xi_k) \Big|_{design}^{control} \right) = \varepsilon_k \sim IID(0, \sigma^2), \quad k = 1, 2, \ldots, n. \tag{3}$$

and represents all unmodeled influences, *intended* to be a nongeneric *white-noise* (nonsystematic) stochastic process; that is, $\{\varepsilon(\mathbf{x}_k, \boldsymbol{\xi}_k), k \in \mathbf{N}\}$ has (i) mean zero, (ii) variance $\sigma_\varepsilon^2 < \infty$; (iii) uncorrelated over k, and (iv) orthogonal to $h(\mathbf{x}_k; \varphi)$ for all possible values $(\mathbf{x}_k, \boldsymbol{\xi}_k) \in \mathbf{R}_x \times \mathbf{R}_\xi$. Note that (iv) aims to demarcate a "near isolation" condition for the phenomenon of interest.

In summary, a structural model provides an "idealized" substantive description of the phenomenon of interest, in the form of a "nearly isolated" mathematical system (Spanos 1995). The specification of a structural model comprises several choices: (a) the demarcation of the segment of the phenomenon of interest to be captured, (b) the important aspects of the phenomenon to be measured, and (c) the extent to which the inferences based on the structural model are germane to the phenomenon of interest.

The kind of *errors* one can probe for in the context of a structural model concern the choices (a)–(c), which include the form of $h(\mathbf{x}_k; \varphi)$ and the circumstances that render the error term $\varepsilon(\mathbf{x}_k, \boldsymbol{\xi}_k)$ potentially systematic, such as the omission of relevant factors, say w_k, in ξ_k that might have a systematic effect on the behavior of y_t (see Spanos 2006b for further discussion).

The problem with (3) is that assumptions (i)–(iv) of the structural error are nontestable because their assessment would involve verifying these assumptions for all possible values $(\mathbf{x}_k, \boldsymbol{\xi}_k) \in \mathbf{R}_x \times \mathbf{R}_\xi$. To render them testable one needs to embed this structural into a statistical model with a generic error term; a crucial move that often passes unnoticed. Not surprisingly, the nature of the embedding itself depends crucially on whether the data $\mathbf{Z} = (\mathbf{z}_1, \mathbf{z}_2, ..., \mathbf{z}_n)$ are the result of an experiment or they are nonexperimental (observational) in nature.

STATISTICAL MODELS WITH EXPERIMENTAL DATA

In the case where one can perform experiments, "experimental design" techniques might allow one to operationalize the "near isolation" condition, including the *ceteris paribus* clauses, and ensure that the error term is no longer a function of $(\mathbf{x}_k, \boldsymbol{\xi}_k)$, but takes the generic form

$$\mathcal{E}(\mathbf{x}_k, \xi_k) = \epsilon_k \sim \text{IID}(0, \sigma^2), \, k = 1, 2, ..., n, \quad (4)$$

where "IID" stands for Independent and Identically Distributed. For instance, *randomization* and *blocking* are often used to "neutralize" the phenomenon from the potential effects of $\boldsymbol{\xi}_k$ by ensuring that these uncontrolled factors cancel each other out (Fisher 1935). As a direct result of the experimental "control," via (4) the structural model (2) is essentially transformed into a *statistical model*

$$y_k = h(\mathbf{x}_k; \theta) + \epsilon_k, \, \epsilon_k \sim \text{IID}(0, \sigma^2), \, k = 1, 2, ..., n. \quad (5)$$

The statistical error terms in (5) are qualitatively very different from the structural errors in (2) because they no longer depend on $(\mathbf{x}_k, \boldsymbol{\xi}_k) \in \mathbf{R}_x \times \mathbf{R}_\xi$. The most important aspect of embedding the structural (2) into the statistical model (5) is that, in contrast to (i)–(iv) for $\{\varepsilon(\mathbf{x}_k, \boldsymbol{\xi}_k), k \in \mathbf{N}\}$, the probabilistic assumptions $\varepsilon_k \sim \text{IID}(0, \sigma^2)$ concerning the generic *statistical error term* are rendered *testable*. That is, (4) has operationalized the "near isolation" condition and the statistical model has been created as a result of the experimental design and control.

A crucial consequence of (4) is that the *informational universe of discourse* for the statistical model (5) has been demarcated to the probabilistic information relating to the observables $\mathbf{Z}_k := (y_k, X_k)$ as described by the joint distribution $D(\mathbf{Z}_1, \mathbf{Z}_2, ..., \mathbf{Z}_T; \varphi)$. A statistical model can be viewed as a parameterization of the presumed probabilistic structure of the process $\{\mathbf{Z}_t, t \in \mathbf{T}\}$ (Spanos 1986, 1999). This probabilistic structure is chosen so as to render the observed data $Z := (z_1, z_2, ..., z_n)$ a truly typical realization thereof. This introduces into the empirical modeling a *probabilistic perspective* which treats the data as realizations of generic stochastic processes devoid of any substantive information.

In contrast to a *structural model*, once $\mathbf{Z}_t$ is chosen by some theory or theories, a statistical model relies exclusively on the statistical information in $D(\mathbf{Z}_1, \mathbf{Z}_2, ..., \mathbf{Z}_T; \varphi)$ that "reflects" the chance regularity patterns exhibited by the data. Hence, a statistical model acquires a life of its own in the sense that it constitutes a self-contained generic generating mechanism defined exclusively in terms of the observables $\mathbf{Z}_k := (y_k, X_k)$. For example, in the case where $h(x_k; \varphi) = \beta_0 + \beta_1^T x_t$, the error assumptions $\varepsilon_k \sim \text{NIID}(0, \sigma^2)$ give rise to the *Gauss Linear* model which is given in table 1 (Spanos 1986).

In summary, a *statistical model* constitutes an "idealized" *probabilistic description* of a stochastic process $\{\mathbf{Z}_t, t \in \mathbf{T}\}$ giving rise to data $\mathbf{Z}$ in the form of an internally consistent set of probabilistic assumptions chosen to ensure that this data constitute a "truly typical realization" of $\{\mathbf{Z}_t, t \in \mathbf{T}\}$. Specification for the statistical model refers to choosing a parameterization and an associated complete set of testable probabilistic assumptions constituting the premises of inference. Specification error denotes departures from assumptions [1]–[5].

STATISTICAL MODELS WITH OBSERVATIONAL DATA

This is the case where the observed data on (y_k, x_k) are the result of an ongoing data generating process, undisturbed by any experimental control or intervention. In this case the route followed in (4), in order to render the statistical error term (a) free of $(\mathbf{x}_k, \boldsymbol{\xi}_k)$, and (b) nonsystematic in a statistical sense, is no longer feasible. However, as shown in Spanos (1986), sequential conditioning provides a general way to transform an arbitrary stochastic process $\{\mathbf{Z}_t, t \in \mathbf{T}\}$ into a *martingale difference process*, a modern form of a white-noise process. This provides the key to an alter-

---

Table 1 – The Gauss Linear (GL) Model

$$y_t = \beta_0 + \boldsymbol{\beta}_1' x_t + u_t, \, t \in \mathbf{N},$$

[1] Normality: $y_t \sim N(.,.)$.

[2] Linearity: $\varepsilon(y_t)\beta_0 + \boldsymbol{\beta}_1' x_t$ is linear in $(\beta_0, \boldsymbol{\beta}_1)$,

[3] Homoskedasticity: $Var(y_t) = \sigma^2$, free of x_t,

[4] Independence: $\{y_t, t \in \mathbf{N}\}$ is an independent process,

[5] t-invariance: $\theta = (\beta_0, \boldsymbol{\beta}_1, \sigma^2)$ do not vary with t.

---

native approach to specifying statistical models in the case of nonexperimental data by replacing the controls and interventions with the choice of the *relevant conditioning information set* D_t that would render the error term nonsystematic—a martingale difference. The technical aspects of specifying statistical models using sequential conditioning are beyond the scope of the present discussion (Spanos 2006b), but an example of how one can specify a statistical model as a reduction from $D(\mathbf{Z}_1, ..., \mathbf{Z}_T, \varphi)$ can shed some light on its practical aspects.

The *Normal/Linear Regression* (LR) model results from a reduction of $D(Z_1, ..., Z_T, \varphi)$ by assuming that $\{\mathbf{Z}_t, t \in \mathbf{T}\}$ is a NIID process. These reduction assumptions ensure that the appropriate conditioning information set is $D_t = \{X_t = x_t\}$, giving rise to a statistical error term:

$$(u_t | X_t = x_t) \sim \text{NIID}(0; \sigma^2); \ k = 1; 2; ..., n. \qquad (6)$$

This is analogous to (4) in the case of experimental data, but now the error term has been operationalized by a judicious choice of the conditioning information set $D_t = \{X_t = x_t\}$. The complete specification of the Linear Regression model is similar to the Gauss Linear model (table 1), but instead of $D(y_t; \theta)$, the underlying distribution is $D(y_t | X_t; \theta)$—assumptions [1]–[5] pertain to the probabilistic structure of $\{(y_t | X_t = x_t), t \in T\}$ (Spanos 1986). In this sense, $D(y_t | X_t; \theta)$ brings to the table the statistical information which supplements, and can be used to assess the appropriateness of, the substantive subject matter information carried by the structural model.

CONFRONTING SUBSTANTIVE WITH STATISTICAL INFORMATION

An important aspect of embedding a structural into a statistical model is to ensure (whenever possible) that the former can be viewed as a *reparameterization/restriction* of the latter. The structural model is then tested against the benchmark provided by a statistically adequate model. *Identification* refers to being able to define φ uniquely in terms of θ. Often θ has more parameters than φ and the embedding enables one to test the validity of the additional restrictions, known as overidentifying restrictions (Spanos 1990).

SEE ALSO *Specification Tests*

BIBLIOGRAPHY

Fisher, Ronald A. 1935. *The Design of Experiments*. Edinburgh, U.K.: Oliver and Boyd.

Leamer, Edward E. 1990. Specification Problems in Econometrics. In *The New Palgrave: A Dictionary of Economics*, eds. John Eatwell, Murray Migate, and Peter Newman, 238–245. New York: Norton.

Spanos, Aris. 1986. *Statistical Foundations of Econometric Modelling*. Cambridge, U.K.: Cambridge University Press.

Spanos, Aris. 1990. The Simultaneous Equations Model Revisited: Statistical Adequacy and Identification. *Journal of Econometrics* 44: 87–108.

Spanos, Aris. 1995. On Theory Testing in Econometrics: Modeling with Nonexperimental Data. *Journal of Econometrics* 67: 189–226.

Spanos, Aris. 1999. *Probability Theory and Statistical Inference: Econometric Modeling with Observational Data*. Cambridge, U.K.: Cambridge University Press.

Spanos, Aris. 2006a. Econometrics in Retrospect and Prospect. In *New Palgrave Handbook of Econometrics*, vol. 1, eds. Terence C. Mills and Kerry Patterson, 3–58. London: Macmillan.

Spanos, Aris. 2006b. Revisiting the Omitted Variables Argument: Substantive vs. Statistical Adequacy. *Journal of Economic Methodology* 13: 179–218.

Theil, Henri. 1957. Specification Errors and the Estimation of Economics Relationships. *Review of the International Statistical Institute* 25: 41–51.

Aris Spanos

SPECIFICATION ERROR

In the context of a statistical model, *specification error* means that at least one of the key features or assumptions of the model is incorrect. In consequence, estimation of the model may yield results that are incorrect or misleading. Specification error can occur with any sort of statistical model, although some models and estimation methods are much less affected by it than others. Estimation methods that are unaffected by certain types of specification error are often said to be *robust*. For example, the *sample median* is a much more robust measure of central tendency than the *sample mean* because it is unaffected by the presence of extreme observations in the sample.

For concreteness, consider the case of the linear regression model. The simplest such model is

$$Y = \beta_0 + \beta_1 X + U, \qquad (1)$$

where Y is the regressand, X is a single regressor, U is an error term, and β_0 and β_1 are parameters to be estimated. This model, which is usually estimated by *ordinary least squares*, could be misspecified in a great many ways. Some forms of misspecification will result in misleading estimates of the parameters, and other forms will result in misleading confidence intervals and test statistics.

One common form of misspecification is caused by nonlinearity. According to the linear regression model (1), increasing the value of the regressor X by one unit always increases the expected value of the regressand Y by β_1 units. But perhaps the effect of X on Y depends on the level of X. If so, the model (1) is misspecified. A more general model is

$$Y = \beta_0 + \beta_1 X + \beta_2 X^2 + U, \qquad (2)$$

which includes the square of X as an additional regressor. In many cases, a model like (2) is much less likely to be misspecified than a model like (1). A classic example in economics is the relationship between years of experience in the labor market (X) and wages (Y). Whenever economists estimate such a relationship, they find that β_1 is positive and β_2 is negative.

If the relationship between X and Y really is nonlinear, and the sample contains a reasonable amount of information, then it is likely that the estimate of β_2 in (2) will be significantly different from zero. Thus we can test for specification error in the linear model (1) by estimating the more general model (2) and testing the hypothesis that $\beta_2 = 0$.

Another type of specification error occurs when we mistakenly use the wrong regressor(s). For example, suppose that Y really depends on Z, not on X. If X and Z are positively correlated, we may well get what appear to be reasonable results when we estimate regression (1). But the correct regression

$$Y = \gamma_0 + \gamma_1 Z + U, \qquad (3)$$

should fit better than regression (1). A number of procedures exist for deciding whether equation (1), equation (3), or neither of them is correctly specified. These are often called *nonnested hypothesis tests*, and they are really a way of testing for specification error. In the case of (1) and (3), we simply need to estimate the model

$$Y = \beta_0 + \beta_1 X + \beta_2 Z + U, \qquad (4)$$

which includes both (1) and (3) as special cases. We can test whether (1) is correctly specified by using the t-statistic for $\beta_2 = 0$, and we can test whether (3) is correctly specified by using the t-statistic for $\beta_1 = 0$.

Of course, it is possible that Y actually depends on both X and Z, so that the true model is (4). In that case, if we mistakenly estimated equation (1), we would be guilty of omitting the explanatory variable Z. Unless X and Z happened to be uncorrelated, this would cause the estimate of β_1 to be biased. This type of bias is often called *omitted variable bias*, and it can be severe when the correlation between X and Z is high.

Another very damaging type of specification error occurs when the error term U is correlated with X. This can occur in a variety of circumstances, notably when X is measured with error or when equation (1) is just one

equation from a system of simultaneous equations that determine X and Y jointly. Using ordinary least squares in this situation results in estimates of β_0 and β_1 that are *biased* and *inconsistent*. Because they are biased, the estimates are not centered around the true values. Moreover, because they are inconsistent, they actually converge to incorrect values of the parameters as the sample size gets larger.

The classic way of dealing with this type of specification error is to use *instrumental variables* (IV). This requires the investigator to find one or more variables that are correlated with X but not correlated with U, something that may or may not be easy to do. The IV estimator that results, which is also called two-stage least squares, is still biased, although generally much less so than ordinary least squares, but at least it is consistent. Thus, if the sample size is reasonably large and various other conditions are satisfied, IV estimates can be quite reliable.

Even if a regression model is correctly specified in the sense that the relationship between the regressand and the regressors is correct and the regressors are uncorrelated with the error terms, it may still suffer from specification error. For ordinary least squares estimates with the usual standard errors to yield valid inferences, it is essential that the error terms be uncorrelated and have constant variance. If these assumptions are violated, the parameter estimates may still be unbiased, but confidence intervals and test statistics will generally be incorrect.

When the error terms do not have constant variance, the model is said to suffer from *heteroskedasticity*. There are various way to deal with this problem. One of the simplest is just to use *heteroskedasticity-robust* standard errors instead of conventional standard errors. When the sample size is reasonably large, this generally allows us to obtain valid confidence intervals and test statistics.

If the error terms are correlated, confidence intervals and test statistics will generally be incorrect. This is most likely to occur with time-series data and with data where the observations fall naturally into groups, or clusters. In the latter case, it is often a good idea to use *cluster-robust* standard errors instead of conventional ones.

When using time-series data, one should always test for *serial correlation*, that is, correlation between error terms that are close together in time. If evidence of serial correlation is found, it is common, but not always wise, to employ an estimation method that "corrects" for it, and there are many such methods. The problem is that many types of specification error can produce the appearance of serial correlation. For example, if the true model were (4) but we mistakenly estimated (1), and the variable Z were serially correlated, it is likely that we would find evidence of serial correlation. The right thing to do in this case would be to estimate (4), not to estimate (1) using a method that corrects for serial correlation.

The subject of specification error in regression models and other statistical models has produced a vast body of research in statistics, econometrics, and other fields. A graduate-level textbook that covers this topic extensively is *Econometric Theory and Methods* (2004) by Russell Davidson and James MacKinnon. A less-advanced book that treats many of the same topics at a lower level is Jeffrey Wooldridge's *Introductory Econometrics* (2006).

SEE ALSO *Least Squares, Ordinary; Measurement Error; Properties of Estimators (Asymptotic and Exact); Specification Tests*

BIBLIOGRAPHY

Davidson, Russell, and James G. MacKinnon. 2004. *Econometric Theory and Methods*. New York: Oxford University Press.

Wooldridge, Jeffrey M. 2006. *Introductory Econometrics: A Modern Approach*. 3rd ed. Mason, OH: Thomson/South-Western.

James G. MacKinnon

SPECIFICATION TESTS

The term *specification tests* is used in economics to denote tests for departures from the premises of inference in empirical modeling. This use of the term, however, is confusing because it conflates statistical with substantive specification errors (misspecifications), rendering the discussions of specification tests problematic (see Theil 1957).

In the context of a statistical model, the relevant misspecifications concern departures from the probabilistic assumptions constituting the statistical premises, such as [1]–[5] in Table 1.

In contrast, *specification errors* in relation to a structural model concern the model's inadequacies in relation

---

Normal/linear regression model

Statistical Generating Mechanism (GM): $y_t = \beta_0 + \beta'_1 x_t + u_t$, $t \in N$,
[1] Normality: $(y_t | X_t = x_t) \sim N(.,.)$
[2] Linearity: $E(y_t | X_t = x_t) = \beta_0 + \beta'_1 x_t$
[3] Homoskedasticity: $Var(y_t | X_t = x_t) = \sigma^2$,
[4] Independence: $\{(y_t | X_t = x_t), t \in N\}$ is an independent process,
[5] t-invariance: $\theta = (\beta_0, \beta_1, \sigma^2)$ are not changing with t.

Table 1

---

to: (a) the demarcation of the segment of reality to be modeled; (b) the crucial aspects of the phenomenon to be quantified; and (c) the extent to which the inferences based on the structural model are germane to the phenomenon of interest. In addition, reliable probing for such specification errors can only take place in the context of a statistically adequate model, that is, an estimated statistical model whose assumptions are (approximately) true for the data in question. Statistical inadequacy renders inference procedures (estimation, testing, prediction) unreliable because the procedures nominally differ from the actual error probabilities. A statistically adequate model provides reliable inference procedures to probe for substantive inadequacies.

Specification tests in the context of a structural model refer to assessing the adequacy of the three choices described above, including incongruous measurement and external invalidity (see Spanos 2006a). The quintessential form of a substantive specification error, however, is the omitted-variables problem. The issue is one of *substantive inadequacy* insofar as subject-matter information raises the possibility that certain influential factors W_t might have been omitted from the relevant factors X_t explaining the behavior of y_t (Leamer 1990). That is, omitting certain potentially important factors W_t may confound the influence of X_t on y_t, leading to misleading inferences. Stating the problem in a statistically coherent fashion, one is comparing the following two models:

$$[M_0]: y_t$$
$$= x'_t \beta + u_t, \; (u_t | X_t$$
$$= x_t) \sim NIID(0, \sigma^2), \; t \in N, \quad (1)$$

$$[M_1]: y_t$$
$$= x'_t \alpha + w'_t \gamma + \varepsilon_t, \; (\varepsilon_t | X_t$$
$$= x_t, W_t = w_t) \sim NIID(0, \sigma^2 \varepsilon), \; t \in N, \quad (2)$$

using the hypotheses:

$$H_0: \gamma = 0 \; \text{vs.} \; H_1: \gamma \neq 0. \quad (3)$$

Models (M_0, M_1) are based on the same statistical information $Z := (y, X, W)$, but M_0 is a special case of M_1 subject to the *substantive restrictions* $\gamma = 0$; M_0 can be viewed as a *structural* model embedded into the statistical model M_1. Assuming that the statistical model M_1 is statistically adequate, these statistical parameterizations can be used to assess the relationship between W_t, X_t, and y_t by evaluating the broader issues of *confounding* and *spuriousness* using hypothesis testing (see Spanos 2006b).

The statistical parameterizations associated with the two models, $\varphi = (\beta, \sigma_u^2)$ and $\theta = (\alpha, \gamma, \sigma_\varepsilon^2$, take the form:

$$\alpha = \beta - \Delta\gamma, \quad \gamma = \delta - D\alpha, \qquad (4)$$

$$\sigma_\varepsilon^2 = \sigma_u^2 - [(\sigma_{13} - \sigma_{12}\Delta)\textstyle\sum_{3.2}^{-1}(\sigma_{13} - \sigma_{12}\Delta)'],$$

$$\sigma_\varepsilon^2 = \sigma_{11} - \sigma_{12}\textstyle\sum_{22}^{-1}\sigma_{21}, \qquad (5)$$

$$\beta := \textstyle\sum_{22}^{-1}\sigma_{21}, \quad \delta := \textstyle\sum_{33}^{-1}\sigma_{31},$$

$$\Delta := \textstyle\sum_{22}^{-1}\sum_{23}, \quad D := \textstyle\sum_{33}^{-1}\sum_{32},$$

$$\textstyle\sum_{3.2} = \sum_{33} - \Delta'\sum_{23}, \quad \sum_{2.3} = \sum_{22} - D'\sum_{32}, \qquad (6)$$

where $\sigma_{11} = Var(y_t)$, $\sigma_{21} = Cov(X_t, y_t)$, $\sigma_{31} = Cov(W_t, y_t)$, $\Sigma_{23} = Cov(X_t, W_t)$, $\Sigma_{33} = Cov(W_t)$. The textbook omitted-variables argument attempts to assess the seriousness of this unreliability using the sensitivity of the estimator $\hat\beta = (X'X)^{-1}X'y$ to the inclusion/exclusion of W_t, by tracing that effect to the potential *bias/inconsistency* of $\hat\beta$. Spanos (2006b) argues that the sensitivity of point estimates provides a poor basis for addressing the confounding problem. Although the confounding and spuriousness issues are directly or indirectly related to the parameters α and β, their appraisal depends crucially on the values of all three covariances (σ_{21}, σ_{31}, Σ_{23}), and it can only be addressed adequately in a hypothesis-testing setup supplemented with a post-data evaluation of inference based on severe testing (see Spanos 2006b for details).

Specification (misspecification) tests in the context of a statistical model refer to assessing the validity of the probabilistic assumptions constituting the statistical model in question. Taking the normal/linear regression as an example (Table 1), *specification error* denotes any form of departures from assumptions [1]–[5] arising from viewing the observed data $Z := (y, X)$ as a truly typical realization of the stochastic process $\{(y_t \mid X_t = x_t), t \in \mathbb{N}\}$. This takes the form of Mis-Specification (M-S) tests, probing for departures from assumptions [1]–[5] (Spanos 1986, 1999).

To get some idea as to how these M-S tests can be viewed as probing for departures from the model assumptions, consider the linearity assumption [2]

Linearity: $E(y_t \mid X_t = x_t) = \beta_0 + \beta_1'x_t$

When this assumption is invalid, $E(y_t \mid X_t = x_t) = h(x_t) \neq \beta_0 + \beta_1'x_t$ for some non-linear function $h(.)$. For the comparison to be operational, we need to specify a particular form for $h(.)$, say:

Nonlinearity $\Rightarrow E(y_t \mid X_t = x_t) = \alpha_0 + \alpha_1'x_t + \alpha_2'\psi_t(x_t)$

where $\psi_t(x_t)$ includes, say, the second order terms $(x_{it}x_{jt})$, i, $j = 2, \ldots, k$; note that $x_{1t} = 1$. This comparison creates a situation of two competing models:

Model 1: $E(y_t \mid X_t = x_t) = \beta_0 + \beta_1'x_t$,

Model 2: $E(y_t \mid X_t = x_t) = \alpha_0 + \alpha_1'x_t + \alpha_2'\psi_t(x_t)$

which, superficially, resembles the initial setup of models (1) and (2) but is fundamentally different in the sense that $\psi_t(x_t)$ does not comprise different variables but functions of x_t. Subtracting Model 1 from Model 2 gives rise to the following auxiliary regression:

$$\hat u_t = (\alpha_0 - \hat\beta_0) + (\alpha_1' - \hat\beta_1')x_t + \alpha_2'\psi_t(x_t) + \varepsilon_t \quad (7)$$

where $\hat u_t$ denotes the residuals from Model 1, which can provide a basis for testing the linearity assumption using the hypotheses:

$$H_0 : \alpha_2 = 0, \ vs. \ H_1 : \alpha_2 \neq 0. \qquad (8)$$

The test of choice is the *F*-test (see Spanos 1986). Using the same type of reasoning, one can argue that the regression function will be affected by departures from other assumptions, such as [4] independence, leading to the auxiliary regression:

$$\hat u_t = (\gamma_0 - \hat\beta_0) + (\gamma_1' - \hat\beta_1')x_t + \gamma_2'z_{t-1} + \varepsilon_t, \quad (9)$$

where $z_{t-1} := (y_{t-1}, x_{t-1})$ (see Spanos 1986).

Pursuing the same reasoning further, one can derive an auxiliary regression to provide the basis for a joint test of how certain departures from assumptions [2] and [4] might affect the assumed regression function. This constitutes a combination of the previous two auxiliary regressions, leading to:

$$\hat u_t = (\delta_0 - \hat\beta_0)$$
$$+ (\delta_1' - \hat\beta_1')x_t + \delta_2'\psi_t(x_t)$$
$$+ \delta_3'z_{t-1} + \varepsilon_t, \qquad (10)$$

expressed in terms of the hypotheses:

$$H_0 : \delta_2 = 0 \ and \ \delta_3 = 0,$$
$$vs. \ H_1 : \delta_2 \neq 0 \ or \ \delta_3 \neq 0. \qquad (11)$$

All the M-S tests introduced above are *F*-type tests based on the joint significance of the coefficient of the omitted factors. The only reliable conclusion one can draw on the basis of each of these M-S tests is whether there is evidence that Model 1 is misspecified in the direction being probed (see Spanos 1999; Mayo and Spanos 2004).

SEE ALSO *Hausman Tests; Specification; Specification Error*

BIBLIOGRAPHY

Leamer, Edward E. 1990. Specification Problems in Econometrics. In *Econometrics: The New Palgrave*, ed. John Eatwell, Murray Milgate, and Peter Newman, 238–245. New York: Norton.

Mayo, Deborah G., and Aris Spanos. 2004. Methodology in Practice: Statistical Misspecification Testing. *Philosophy of Science* 71: 1007–1025.

Spanos, Aris. 1986. *Statistical Foundations of Econometric Modelling.* Cambridge, U.K.: Cambridge University Press.

Spanos, Aris. 1999. *Probability Theory and Statistical Inference: Econometric Modeling with Observational Data.* Cambridge, U.K.: Cambridge University Press.

Spanos, Aris. 2006a. Econometrics in Retrospect and Prospect. In *Palgrave Handbook of Econometrics*, ed. Terence C. Mills and Kerry Patterson. Vol. 1: *Econometric Theory*, 3–58. London: Macmillan.

Spanos, Aris. 2006b. Revisiting the Omitted Variables Argument: Substantive vs. Statistical Adequacy. *Journal of Economic Methodology* 13: 179–218.

Theil, H. 1957. Specification Errors and the Estimation of Economic Relationships. *Review of the International Statistical Institute* 25 (1/3): 41–51.

Aris Spanos

SPECULATION

Speculation is the acquisition of an asset exclusively for resale motivated solely by the anticipation of capital appreciation and gain. Most commonly, speculation occurs in anticipation of a price increase such that buying temporally precedes selling as speculators temporarily hold title to ("go long in") an asset. The possibility exists, however, of temporally reversing the trades in anticipation of a price decline through forward contracting. Here speculators would "short" an asset by agreeing to sell that to which they do not yet have title, planning the future acquisition of the anticipated cheaper asset in advance of the contracted delivery date. Speculation is similar to arbitrage insofar as arbitrage too involves the trade of commodities exclusively for capital gain. Arbitrageurs, however, trade across markets at a point in time so that opportunities for capital gains are much less risky than they are for speculators who conduct trades over time.

Any asset—as something that is capable of producing a stream of future material benefits—has the potential to be an object of speculation. Historically, real estate, precious metals, and financial instruments (stocks, bonds, currencies, and the like) have been the most common objects. At times, speculation in such assets has advanced at an especially feverish pace as Charles P. Kindleberger (2001) demonstrates in his discussion of the many histor-ical episodes of speculative manias and their recoil in panics and market crashes.

SPECULATION AND MARKET STABILITY

There is considerable debate centered on whether speculation will act as a stabilizing or destabilizing market force. A long-standing dispute about the desirability of flexible versus fixed exchange rates has been periodically most vigorous, turning on precisely this question. Since the 1980s, researchers have debated the presence of destabilizing speculation in the form of a speculative bubble—as a process denoting movements in asset prices that cannot be justified on any reasonable economic grounds—as an explanation for observed volatility in equity markets.

The question of whether speculation will stabilize or destabilize a market hinges critically on the manner in which speculators form their expectations of future price changes. It was thought originally that if speculators based their expectations of capital gains on anticipated future changes in the conditions affecting the demand for or supply of an asset, then the act of speculation would even out price fluctuations over time. If instead speculators extrapolated from recent price trends, their actions would serve to increase the amplitude of price fluctuations rather than dampen them down. While such a characterization remains broadly accurate, subsequent research in rational expectations modeling has shown that speculation will be destabilizing even with some forms of forward-looking expectations of price changes.

Extreme volatility in currencies, stocks, and other financial markets in the mid- to late 1920s stimulated an effective challenge to the traditional classical way of thinking about speculation. Logic had previously held that speculation of any significance must be a stabilizing force; otherwise, if speculators were indeed a destabilizing force in the market, it would mean that speculators had worse foresight than average, their losses would then be greater than average, and so their existence would be short-lived. As Milton Friedman (1953) would later argue, "speculation can be destabilizing in general only if speculators on the average sell when the currency is low in price and buy when it is high" (p. 175).

For such reasoning to be sufficient grounds on which to deduce the absence of destabilizing speculation, several conditions must hold. Price expectations must be formed independently of the opinion of others, there must be a consistency between short-term and long-term anticipated gains, and the act of speculation itself must not alter the underlying economic value of the asset. If the future is known or equivalent to such, as in the case when one can define the full range of outcomes and associated probabilities, speculation is essentially an exercise in inter-temporal arbitrage, and the foregoing conditions could reasonably hold. The opportunity to speculate would be then a constructive market force wherein producers with greater risk aversion shift price risk to less risk-averse speculators. Otherwise, when the future is uncertain (as distinct from risky), the problem is much more complicated and the dichotomy between stabilizing and destabilizing speculation unclear.

Addressing the implications of true uncertainty in the formation of long-term expectations, John Maynard Keynes (1936) discusses the manner in which interdependent opinions may confuse and complicate the expectations formation process. In his famous beauty contest metaphor, Keynes likens investment to a beauty competition in which the winner is the one who most closely predicts the outcome that will be the opinion of the majority. The challenge for contestants then "is not a case of choosing those which, to the best of one's judgment, are really the prettiest, nor even those which average opinion genuinely thinks is the prettiest. We have reached the third degree where we devote our intelligences to anticipating what average opinion expects the average opinion to be" (p. 156). Keynes reserves the term *speculation* for this activity of forecasting psychology to underscore the important influence of social convention in the determination of outcomes and differentiates it from the "activity of forecasting prospective yield of assets over their whole life," which Keynes terms *enterprise* (p. 158).

Nicholas Kaldor (1939) carefully examines the implication of speculation for market stability by distinguishing between price stability and income stability. Even if speculation can be shown to stabilize prices, depending on the reactions of producers and elasticities of supply, the action may yield a greater instability in economic activity and incomes. Kaldor further argues that where the proportion of speculative transactions in the total is large, it may well be more profitable for individual speculators to focus on forecasting the psychology of other speculators rather than on the trend of nonspeculative elements. "Even if speculation as a whole is attended by a net loss, rather than net gain, this will not prove even in the long-run, self-corrective" (p. 2). Rudiger Dornbusch (1976) captures mathematically this inconsistency between short-term and long-term anticipated gains in a model of exchange rate "overshooting" driven by speculators with myopic perfect foresight.

Alongside the debate about the effects of speculation on the stability of currency markets is a parallel debate about the effects of speculation on the stability of equity markets. In a mathematical approach similar to that of Dornbusch, Robert P. Flood and Peter M. Garber (1980) examine a model of the speculative bubble in which forward-looking "rational" expectations may or may not motivate destabilizing speculation. The source of instability is a fundamental indeterminacy in the formal mathematical model, which is resolved in the literature by variously reducing the liquidity of the traded asset, introducing slow to adjust expectations, or imposing what is in effect a transversality condition that precludes by assumption anything but stability and convergence to a steady state. The steady state outcome is "efficient" in the sense that market prices fully and accurately reflect all relevant information about the future net income earning prospects of the assets discounted to the present. Viewed differently, the various "solutions" serve, in one way or another, to alter either the elasticity of expectations or the elasticity of speculative stocks, which together, as Kaldor had earlier argued, determine "the degree of price-stabilizing influence of speculation" (p. 9).

NONORTHODOX VIEWS

Where the orthodoxy focus on debating the stability implications of speculation in a probabilistic framework, heterodox economists concentrate on the implications for economic stability of speculation under conditions of true uncertainty. For Hyman Minsky (1982), financial fragility occurs in a world in which speculation in fixed assets is debt-financed and investors have both severely constrained foresight and limited memories of past distress. In his financial instability hypothesis, the evolving margins of safety between the streams of asset income in relation to the contemporaneous changes in debt service costs (rather than discounted present values) both characterize and explain the path of business fluctuations.

In a similar framework, Brenda Spotton Visano (2006) explores how the norm of speculation—as a collective dynamic—emerges when a revolutionary innovation shatters common understandings of the economic environment. The rate at which speculation in liquid financial assets related to the innovation becomes fashionable and spreads—thus sending asset prices spiraling upward—parallels the nonlinear, path-dependent diffusion course of the precipitating innovation itself. Because here the speculative activity materially affects an innovation's potential, the material outcome is dependent on the collective assessment of that potential. In this case, what constitutes "excess" speculation is wholly unclear; in such environments, no criteria exist on which to base independent estimates of an asset's fundamental value.

It follows that those who believe that speculation causes greater market volatility and misallocations of investment will advocate for some form of market intervention. Minsky recommends the presence of a lender of last resort in critical credit markets. Paul Davidson (1998) argues for a buffer stock mechanism in the control of a market maker. It is James Tobin's proposal (1978) to levy a tax on foreign currency transactions, however, that has attracted the greatest attention. As a means of raising the cost of speculative transactions, levying a "Tobin tax" would "throw some sand in the wheels of our excessively efficient international money markets" (p. 154)—a proposal that is similar in practice and in purpose to the long-standing policy of levying stamp duty on the buying and selling of British property and shares.

By contrast, those who believe that speculation is predominantly a stabilizing market influence continue to advocate for less market intervention. The theoretical and policy debates persist with no clear agreement in sight.

SEE ALSO *Bubbles; Efficient Market Hypothesis; Finance; Financial Instability Hypothesis; Keynes, John Maynard; Manias; Panics; Stability in Economics; Tobin, James*

BIBLIOGRAPHY

Davidson, Paul. 1998. Volatile Financial Markets and the Speculator. *Economic Issues* 3 (2): 1–18.

Dornbusch, Rudiger. 1976. Expectations and Exchange Rate Dynamics. *Journal of Political Economy* 84(6): 1161–1176.

Flood, Robert P., and Peter M. Garber. 1980. Market Fundamentals versus Price-Level Bubbles: The First Tests. *Journal of Political Economy* 88 (4): 745–770.

Friedman, Milton. 1953. The Case for Flexible Exchange Rates. In *Essays in Positive Economics*, 157–203. Chicago: University of Chicago Press.

Kaldor, Nicholas. 1939. Speculation and Economic Stability. *Review of Economic Studies* 7 (1): 1–27.

Keynes, John Maynard. 1936. *The General Theory of Employment, Interest, and Money*. Reprinted in vol. VII of *The Collected Writings of John Maynard Keynes*, eds. Donald Moggridge and Elizabeth Johnson. London: Macmillan, 1974.

Kindleberger, Charles P. 2001. *Manias, Panics, and Crashes: A History of Financial Crises*. 4th ed. New York: Wiley.

Minsky, Hyman. 1982. The Financial Instability Hypothesis: Capitalistic Processes and the Behavior of the Economy. In *Financial Crises: Theory, History, and Policy*, eds. Charles P. Kindleberger and Jean-Pierre Laffargue, 13–39. Cambridge, U.K.: Cambridge University Press.

Spotton Visano, Brenda. 2006. *Financial Crises: Socio-economic Causes and Institutional Context*. London: Routledge.

Tobin, James. 1978. A Proposal for International Monetary Reform. *Eastern Economic Journal* 4 (3–4): 153–159.

Brenda Spotton Visano

SPECULATIVE FICTION

SEE *Science Fiction.*

SPECULATIVE MOTIVE

SEE *Money, Demand for.*

SPEECH ACT THEORY

Although the reflection on the performative dimension of language can arguably be traced back to the Sophists (Corax of Syracuse, Tisias, Gorgias, Protagoras, and Isocrates) of the fifth century BCE and their (lost) treatises on rhetoric and argumentation, it is John L. Austin (1911–1960) who usually is credited with being the first philosopher to systematically address this question. In his postmortem book titled *How to Do Things with Words* (1975), Austin showed that language can be used not only to *describe* states of affairs (as in *This kitchen is very clean*), but also to *do* things (in this case, *to note* that this kitchen is very clean). More specifically, Austin named the type of action a person performs *in* saying something an *illocutionary act*. For instance, in saying *Come here!* in specific contexts, I can be said to be giving my interlocutor an order, which is an illocutionary act. This act can also have consequences, such as my making my interlocutor come when I say *Come here!* Austin named this type of action a *perlocutionary act*, which is an act that comprises the intentional or nonintentional consequences that result from the illocutionary act.

Although Austin provided a detailed classification of speech acts, it is John R. Searle who developed the most thorough systematization of this theory of language (Searle 1969, 1979; Searle and Vanderveken 1985; Vanderveken 1990–1991). Searle identified five different types of illocutionary acts, which he called assertives (i.e., holding something to be true, as in *This kitchen is very clean*), commissives (i.e., committing oneself, as in *I'll be there*), directives (i.e., getting someone to do something, as in *Come here!*), expressives (i.e., expressing a psychological state vis-à-vis something that was done previously, as in *Sorry for stepping on your toes*), and declarations (i.e., transforming the world by making it conform to the propositional content, as in *I hereby declare that the session is open*). Searle also identified what he called *indirect* speech acts, which correspond to the speech acts by which one says more than what is literally said. For instance, when I say *Would you mind bringing me this chair?* I am *literally* asking my interlocutor if she is willing to bring me a chair. Searle calls this type of literal speech act a *secondary illocutionary act* by which a *primary* illocutionary act (or *indirect* speech act) is performed. In this case, the indirect speech act consists of (politely) asking my interlocutor to bring me a chair.

Several critiques have, of course, been addressed to this theory. For instance, Stephen C. Levinson (1981,

1983), Marina Sbisà (1984, 1987, 2002), and Emanuel A. Schegloff (1988) deplore that the orthodox speech act theory fails to capture the complexity and sequential character of human interaction, which, at first sight, renders its use relatively sterile to people interested in the detailed study of interaction (but see Cooren 2000, 2005; Geis 1995; Jacobs 1989; Sanders 1987; van Rees 1992). Another critique, coming from Jacques Derrida (1988), consists of highlighting the iterable character of speech acts, that is, their capacity of being repeated (or iterated) in a potentially infinite number of contexts. According to Derrida, this iterability undermines the identification made by Searle between what a speaker/writer means and the type of speech acts he or she produces (a monologism also denounced by Sbisà). According to this perspective, what the producer of a given speech act means is something that is conventionally reconstructed a posteriori by the participants and not something that defines a priori what a given speech act will count as. This reflection paves the way for a model of speech acts that would take into account the *speech agency* of things as diverse as documents, as in *This announcement invites a bid for the construction of their building*, where we attribute to a text the action of inviting; or spoken words, as in *His words blessed their union*, where the focus is on the agency of pronounced words (Cooren 2004).

SEE ALSO *Communication; Psycholinguistics*

BIBLIOGRAPHY

Austin, John L. 1975. *How to Do Things with Words.* 2nd ed. Eds. J. O. Urmson and Marina Sbisà. Oxford: Clarendon Press. (Orig. pub. 1962).

Cooren, François. 2000. *The Organizing Property of Communication.* Amsterdam: John Benjamins.

Cooren, François. 2004. Textual Agency: How Texts Do Things in Organizational Settings. *Organization* 11 (3): 373–393.

Cooren, François. 2005. The Contribution of Speech Act Theory to the Analysis of Conversation: How Pre-sequences Work. In *Handbook of Language and Social Interaction*, eds. Kristine L. Fitch and Robert E. Sanders, 21–40. Mahwah, NJ: Erlbaum.

Derrida, Jacques. 1988. *Limited Inc.* Evanston, IL: Northwestern University Press.

Geis, Michael L. 1995. *Speech Acts and Conversational Interaction.* Cambridge, U.K.: Cambridge University Press.

Jacobs, Scott. 1989. Speech Acts and Arguments. *Argumentation* 3 (4): 345–365.

Levinson, Stephen C. 1981. The Essential Inadequacies of Speech Act Models of Dialogue. In *Possibilities and Limitations of Pragmatics: Proceedings of the Conference on Pragmatics, Urbino, July 8–14, 1979*, eds. Herman Parret, Marina Sbisà, and Jef Verschueren, 473–492. Amsterdam: John Benjamins.

Levinson, Stephen C. 1983. *Pragmatics.* Cambridge, U.K.: Cambridge University Press.

Sanders, Robert E. 1987. *Cognitive Foundations of Calculated Speech: Controlling Understandings in Conversation and Persuasion.* Albany: State University of New York Press.

Sbisà, Marina. 1984. On Illocutionary Types. *Journal of Pragmatics* 8 (1): 93–112.

Sbisà, Marina. 1987. Speech Acts and Context Change. In *Process Linguistics*, eds. Thomas T. Ballmer and Wolfgang Wildgen, 252–279. Tübingen, West Germany: Max Niemeyer Verlag.

Sbisà, Marina. 2002. Speech Acts in Context. *Language and Communication* 22 (4): 421–436.

Schegloff, Emanuel A. 1988. Presequences and Indirection: Applying Speech Act Theory to Ordinary Conversation. *Journal of Pragmatics* 12 (1): 55–62.

Searle, John R. 1969. *Speech Acts: An Essay in the Philosophy of Language.* London: Cambridge University Press.

Searle, John R. 1979. *Expression and Meaning: Studies in the Theory of Speech Acts.* Cambridge, U.K.: Cambridge University Press.

Searle, John R., and Daniel Vanderveken. 1985. *Foundations of Illocutionary Logic.* Cambridge, U.K.: Cambridge University Press.

Vanderveken, Daniel. 1990–1991. *Meaning and Speech Acts.* 2 vols. Cambridge, U.K.: Cambridge University Press.

van Rees, M. Agnès. 1992. The Adequacy of Speech Act Theory for Explaining Conversational Phenomena: A Response to Some Conversation Analytical Critics. *Journal of Pragmatics* 17 (1): 31–47.

François Cooren

SPEED OF ADJUSTMENT
SEE *Flexibility.*

SPENCER, HERBERT
1820–1903

Herbert Spencer (1820–1903) was a nineteenth-century English social philosopher who sought to explain all domains of the universe in terms of some "cardinal" or "first principles" of evolution. He termed his approach "synthetic philosophy," and before he was done he wrote treatises on ethics (1851, 1892–1898), psychology (1855), biology (1864–1867), and, eventually, sociology (1874–1896). He also wrote a major work on methodology in the social sciences (1873) that was far superior to anything written at the time, and he commissioned the largest collection of data by a sociologist on human societies in the sixteen volumes of his *Descriptive Sociology* (under various authors from 1873 to 1934). This latter project served as the inspiration for the Human Relations Area Files initiated by George P. Murdock, which sought to categorize and quantify qualitative data from ethnographic studies of societies.

Spencer coined the phrase "survival of the fittest" almost a decade before the English naturalist Charles Darwin's analysis of natural selection appeared; in many ways, modern views of Spencer are colored by this phrase and the social advocacy it contains. In fact, Spencer's arguments about "ethics" taint present-day perceptions of his work because by today's political standards they appear conservative, although they were liberal in Spencer's time. Perhaps the most unfortunate impression of Spencer's sociology is its association of the rise of social Darwinism and the eugenics movement with Spencer's advocacy. Both of these movements gained traction long after Spencer's death; thus, Spencer cannot be seen as a key player in what they advocated.

Spencer's ideas were, however, used by some key advocates of social Darwinism or eugenics. For example, in his key work, *The Genetical Theory of Natural Selection* (1930), the English evolutionary biologist Ronald A. Fisher significantly advanced the field of genetics in the first half of the book, but used Spencer's ideas to promote a version of eugenics in the second half. The same is true for social Darwinists who often invoked Spencer's (and, more often, Darwin's) name to legitimate their advocacy that the natural competition among individuals should be allowed to play itself out within societies just as it does in the natural world. Spencer used the phrase "survival of the fittest" most often within sociology to address the topic of how war had historically allowed societies to evolve, with the more organized and fit society generally winning a war and advancing the level of organization of human societies. Still, he did advocate that competition among individuals and collective actors within societies should go unregulated, letting the more fit survive. In reading Spencer's more scholarly works, however, and particularly his sociology, there is very little of this latter form of advocacy. And yet, in the twenty-first century Spencer's reputation is often tied to discredited intellectual movements. Spencer was an ideologue when he wrote on ethics, to be sure, but he was also a scientist and scholar whose works have not received the attention that they deserve because of the prejudices against his ideological moments.

Thus, Spencer was more than an ideologue. His collected works comprise one of the most comprehensive collections of scholarship ever produced in the social sciences. His sociological works, which came late in his career, are perhaps his most important because they draw upon the vast body of data assembled by scholars under his financial sponsorship and patronage into the volumes of *Descriptive Sociology*. *The Principles of Sociology* (1874–1896) presents a functional approach, emphasizing that the evolution of human societies is the result of population pressures for structural and cultural differentiation around three main axes: operation (functional needs for production and reproduction), regulation (needs to consolidate power), and distribution (needs to create infrastructures and exchange systems for moving people, resources, and information about a society). What scholars often overlook in this analysis is the emphasis on power. Most of *The Principles of Sociology* examines the effects of concentrated power on increasing inequality which, in turn, shapes the structure of key institutional systems: economy, kinship, religion, and polity. He also developed a theory of microdynamics, revolving around ceremony under varying levels of concentrated power and inequality.

In *The Principles of Sociology*, Spencer presented a geopolitical theory of human evolution, emphasizing the effects of inter-societal conflict on social complexity and on concentrated power. War was the main referent for the phrase "survival of the fittest" in Spencer's sociology; with this idea, he documented that, in general, the more complex and better organized society will generally defeat the less complex and less organized society. With conquest, then, comes the successive ratcheting up of the level of societal complexity. However, war forces the centralization of power that, in turn, increases the level of inequality. Inequalities pose internal threats that, ironically, force more centralization of power to manage them—thereby escalating inequality in a cycle that ultimately leads to societal dissolution or deevolution. Still, despite this cyclical dynamic, societies have become larger and more differentiated over the long course of history. When differentiation of societies has produced free markets as the main mechanism for distribution, Spencer felt that war and its effects on centralization of power and inequalities in all institutional spheres work against further societal evolution. War and concentrated power create what in the 2000s is termed the "military-industrial complex" that deprives the economy of capital and limits innovation, thus serving as a drag on societal evolution.

Spencer was the most-read social philosopher of the nineteenth century, yet modern social scientists rarely consult his work because it is associated with discredited intellectual and social movements in which Spencer was not an active participant. In many ways, this state of affairs is a bit unfair to Spencer's legacy but it is also understandable given the extremes to which Spencer's ideas were taken by later ideologues. Still Spencer's collective works contain many useful insights that can still serve social science (for a detailed analysis of Spencer's sociology see Turner 1985; for a complete primary and robust secondary bibliography on Spencer's work see Perrin 1993).

BIBLIOGRAPHY

PRIMARY WORKS

Spencer, Herbert. 1851. *Social Statics; or, Conditions Essential to Human Happiness.* New York: Appleton-Century-Crofts.

Spencer, Herbert. 1855. *The Principles of Psychology.* New York: Appleton-Century-Crofts.

Spencer, Herbert. 1862. *First Principles.* New York: A. L. Burt.

Spencer, Herbert. 1864–1867. *The Principles of Biology.* New York: Appleton-Century-Crofts.

Spencer, Herbert. 1873. *The Study of Sociology.* London: Routledge, Kegan, Paul.

Spencer, Herbert. 1874–1896. *The Principles of Sociology.* New Brunswick, NJ: Transaction Books, 2002.

Spencer, Herbert. 1892–1898. *The Principles of Ethics.* New York: Appleton-Century-Crofts.

SECONDARY WORKS

Fisher, R. A. 1930. *The Genetical Theory of Natural Selection.* Oxford: Clarendon.

Perrin, Robert G. 1993. *Herbert Spencer: A Primary and Secondary Bibliography.* New York: Garland.

Turner, Jonathan H. 1985. *Herbert Spencer: A Renewed Appreciation.* Newbury Park, CA: Sage.

Jonathan Turner

SPENCER, MARGARET BEALE

SEE Brown v. Board of Education, *1954.*

SPHERE, PUBLIC

SEE *Public Sphere.*

SPIRITUALITY

The term *spirituality* is at the center of much debate on the shape and meaning of religion in the modern, or postmodern, world. Yet the term defies an easy or singular definition—it is an "attitude or principle that inspires, animates, or pervades thought, feeling, or action," to quote *Random House Webster's Unabridged Dictionary* (2nd ed., 1997). It is worthy of note that both the verbs and the spheres of activity to which the verbs point in this definition vary. Beyond spirituality's broad sweep in thought, feeling, and practice, all pointing to the inner, subjective world of religion, spirituality is also viewed as having emerged, as Ursula King points out, as "a general code word for the search of direction, purpose, and meaning related to the deepest dimension of human existence" and is thus "no longer exclusively based on an a priori theological standpoint, but is rooted in a search, in experimentation, questioning and exploring" (1998, p. 96).

Writing more than a century ago, the American psychologist William James (1842–1910) privileged this inner space in his classic definition of religion as "the feelings, acts, and experiences of individual men in their solitude, so far as they apprehend themselves to stand in relation to whatever they may consider the divine." James distinguished this personal, experiential element within religion from the "theologies, philosophies, and ecclesiastical organizations [that] may secondarily grow up" around the experience ([1902] 1985, p. 31).

Viewing religion broadly as a transcendent and often transforming experience, he left open the form of the experience itself and the devotional object at the center of that experience. Spirituality is thus the primary and motivating quality of religion—"whether the religion in question," writes Catherine L. Albanese commenting not specifically on, but in keeping with James's outlook, "is organized or of movement status or mostly individual; and whether it involves God, or other-than-human guides and spirits, or the center of the Self, or an almighty Nature, or an Ideal held to be worth living or dying for" (2001, p. 11).

Spirituality thrives in the context of a living religious tradition; indeed, the latter's constituent elements of symbol, doctrine, myth, ritual, text, and story all shape an experiential religious world. Belief and practice embedded within tradition "keep alive" a sense of transcendence, sacrality, and ultimacy. Put differently, religion is a symbolic and linguistic system that by its nature is powerfully evocative—it triggers experiences and emotions and at the cognitive level defines a meaningful universe including proper strategies of action. Encoded signs and symbols are the means by which experiences not only are generated but are described, even recognized and labeled, as religious. Historically, the major world religious traditions have relied upon symbolic forms for breaking outside of the profane world and into an alternative reality known only through its ecstatic qualities and interpretive frames. Even within contemporary, more secular social settings, research suggests that those persons most involved in their religious traditions are more likely to report having strong religious experiences (Yamane and Polzer 1994, pp. 1–25).

More appropriately, we should speak of spiritualities—emphasizing the plural—since they vary by tradition and social and personal circumstance. Monotheistic, and typically highly monarchical religious traditions such as Christianity, Judaism, and Islam image God as a distant powerful being, as a male, kinglike lawgiver and judge, and locate the central human problem as one of sin and guilt as measured against divine standards. Emphasis is upon what Marcus J. Borg describes as a "performance model" of spiritual practice, of trying to meet the requirements God expects (1997, pp. 62–71). Hence the dominant God is somewhat more distant as traditionally conceived. But in the many Hindu and Buddhist traditions with their numerous gods, male and female, or no god, stress is upon devotion and meditation in quest of inner peace, joy, and liberation. There are many spiritual paths toward a higher consciousness through the cultivation of experiences of connection, belonging, wholeness, and selflessness. Eastern spiritual diversity thus stands out in contrast to the more monotheistic Western styles.

Religious symbols, belief, and community generate spiritual energy, but social factors shape the form the spiritual dynamic will take. As Max Weber (1864–1920) observed, the spiritual styles and theodicies for ruling elites differ markedly from those who are either weak and powerless or socially mobile. The spiritual dynamics of elites typically focus more upon the blessedness and naturalness of the existing order; the powerless on otherworldly rewards that should come in the next life; and the socially mobile on the importance of getting ahead and doing well. Metaphysical spiritualities acknowledge these same features of the natural order but usually without fullblown justifications for dominance. Minorities are often, though not always, characterized by otherworldly spirituality. At times they are motivated spiritually by religiously inspired ethical ideals to engage in struggles against oppression and inequality, an obvious example being the civil rights movement led by the Reverend Martin Luther King Jr. (1929–1968). Rooted in the African American Christian experience, King exposed the gap between ethical ideals and social injustice; addressing a deep psychological dissonance between ideals and practice, he thereby mounted a "spiritual protest" without having to resort to the use of violence as a means of bringing about constructive social change.

In the contemporary world, spirituality takes increasingly diverse forms in response to changing social and cultural realities. One emerging pattern is described as *post-traditional*, characterized by the searching and experimenting Ursula King speaks of. Individuals acting with a great degree of autonomy explore spiritual truths from many sources, mixing and matching elements to their own choice. High levels of exposure to religious diversity contribute as well to a mixing of the codes. Cross-national research in Western countries suggests that this pattern holds broadly for the post–World War II (1939–1945) generation (Roof et al. 1995), and especially so in the United States. Seeker-oriented spirituality is compatible with life in modern, rapidly paced societies. Also, in these settings, ties to faith traditions are often weak. Social and religious conditions thus make for a thriving "spiritual marketplace" where innovative entrepreneurs compete with one another in defining spiritual needs and in supplying meaning and practice—all intended to assist the individual in his or her spiritual journey. Drawing upon the spiritual resources available to them, both within and outside of organized religion, people assume a considerable amount of self-direction in cultivating their spiritual lives.

A distinction between *spiritual* and *religious* is becoming more commonplace in advanced modern societies. Within the United States, for example, the number of people claiming to be "spiritual but not religious" is estimated variously (but with differing empirical measures) as 14 percent (Roof 1999) and 31 percent (Wuthnow 2005) of the adult population. To be religious implies faith in God or the divine, participation in institutionally based practices, and respect for the teachings of a tradition; to be spiritual puts emphasis upon the experience of connectedness, relationship, or oneness with God/Christ/a higher power/the sacred/nature and appreciation for personal growth and inner awareness in one's life journey. Various empirical measures of self-rated religiousness and spirituality are increasingly used by social scientists as a means of taping these differing responses. Self-rated religiousness is related to attendance at religious services and orthodox belief, whereas self-rated spirituality is associated with mystical experiences and New Age beliefs and practices, particularly among those with higher levels of education and income. An expanding body of research links these two to a broad range of social, psychological, and behavioral correlates, particularly in areas of psychotherapy, child-rearing philosophy, and lifestyle research (see Zinnbauer et al. 1997).

Research suggests that the vast majority of those claiming to be religious are also spiritual—indeed, the spiritual lies at the core of religious life. But if the post-traditional spiritual quests described above represent shifting styles of individual religious expression, a second pattern might be called *retraditionalizing*, or the deliberate cultivation of spiritual meaning through committed religious life and practice. Described as *engaged spirituality*, this effort is deeply grounded within congregational religious life and thus is less individualistic in style, and seeks to combine spiritual depth with social concern and responsibility (Wuthnow 1998; Stanczak 2006). A third, quite different pattern is the *neotraditional* response, or the attempt at reconstructing and enforcing older religious beliefs and values throughout a sociopolitical order. Protesting the erosions of modernity, efforts such as these typically arise in close alignment with political ideologies and mass movements, as with the mobilization of the

Religious Right in the United States or the rise of radical Islamic militants in various parts of the world. Spirituality of this kind arises out of a remythologizing of narratives of God, people, and nationality in search of religious certainty and a more secure moral universe.

SEE ALSO *Fundamentalism; Religion*

BIBLIOGRAPHY

Albanese, Catherine L., ed. 2001. Introduction. In *American Spiritualities: A Reader*, 1–15. Bloomington: Indiana University Press.

Borg, Marcus J. 1997. *The God We Never Knew: Beyond Dogmatic Religion to a More Authentic Contemporary Faith*. New York: Harper.

James, William. [1902] 1985. *The Varieties of Religious Experience: A Study in Human Nature*. New York: Penguin Classics.

King, Ursula. 1998. Spirituality in a Postmodern Age. In *Faith and Praxis in a Postmodern Age*, ed. Ursula King, 94–112. London: Cassell.

Roof, Wade Clark. 1999. *Spiritual Marketplace: Baby Boomers and the Remaking of American Religion*. Princeton, NJ: Princeton University Press.

Roof, Wade Clark, Jackson W. Carroll, and David A. Roozen, eds. 1995. *The Post-War Generation and Establishment Religion: Cross-Cultural Perspectives*. Boulder, CO: Westview.

Stanczak, Gregory C. 2006. *Engaged Spirituality: Social Change and American Religion*. New Brunswick, NJ: Rutgers University Press.

Wuthnow, Robert. 1998. *After Heaven: Spirituality in America since the 1950s*. Berkeley: University of California Press.

Wuthnow, Robert. 2005. *America and the Challenges of Religious Diversity*. Princeton, NJ: Princeton University Press.

Yamane, David, and Megan Polzer. 1994. Ways of Seeing Ecstasy in Modern Society: Experiential-Expressive and Cultural-Linguistic Views. *Sociology of Religion* 55 (1): 1–25.

Wade Clark Roof

SPIVAK, GAYATRI

SEE *Representation in Postcolonial Analysis.*

SPOCK, BENJAMIN
1903–1998

Benjamin Spock was, for a generation, the canonical authority in America on the raising of children. Even after Spock passed the apogee of his influence, he continued to be the point of reference for almost all writers on the subject for the next forty years and into the early twenty-first century. By almost any standard Spock was the most important American author of child-rearing advice of the twentieth century. His principal work, *Baby and Child Care*, went through seven editions, was translated into thirty-eight languages, and sold more than fifty million copies around the world. Aside from the Bible, it was the best-selling book of the twentieth century in America.

THE EARLY YEARS

Spock was born in New Haven, Connecticut, the son of a successful corporate lawyer. He graduated from Yale University, won a gold medal as an oarsman at the 1924 Olympics, and went to medical school at Columbia University. In the 1930s Spock studied at the New York Psychoanalytic Institute. He was the first psychoanalytically trained pediatrician in New York, where he maintained a private practice from 1933 to 1943.

Spock's Park Avenue practice brought him overtures from publishers, who pressed him to write a book setting forth his distinctive combination of pediatrics and child psychology. In 1946 he did. The first edition of *The Common Sense Book of Baby and Child Care* began, as did all subsequent editions: "Trust yourself. You know more than you think you do." It invited mothers to indulge their own impulses and their children's, assuring them on the basis of the latest scientific studies that it was safe to do so. In the process, the book overturned the expertise of the previous generation and authorized mothers to express their "natural" feelings toward their children.

Earlier advice, embodied in the convergence of the psychologist John Watson's *Psychological Care of Infant and Child* and the U.S. government's *Infant Care* pamphlets of the 1920s and 1930s, warned against parental deviation from rigid disciplinary schedules and undue display of fondness or physical affection. Spock urged spontaneity, warmth, and a fair measure of fun for parents and children alike. He insisted that there were no infallible rules and that each child had to be treated as a distinct individual.

A CHILD-CENTERED APPROACH

Baby and Child Care seemed predicated on an unprecedented child-centeredness that celebrated instinct in youngsters and their mothers as well. After decades during which parents had been told they would spoil the child disastrously if they yielded to the child's demands, Spock told parents they could trust the child's desires and their own. "What you instinctively feel like doing is best," he promised his readers, in deliberate defiance of Watson. If you "feel like comforting the child, do it." The very feeling would make it "natural and right."

Spock found parables of the reliability of desire in what was at the time the most current research on sleeping and eating. Those studies showed that infants stabilized a bedtime schedule on their own, without parental coercion, if given a little time. The studies demonstrated that somewhat older children worked out a feeding routine on their own, if they were indulged while they came to it. Older children even chose a balanced diet once past the first rush to sweets. Afforded free run of a smorgasbord, children pigged out for a few days on candy, cake, and ice cream but then of their own volition turned to proteins, greens, and grains. It turned out that, as Spock put it, the child "knows a lot." Parents could give in to their child "without worrying about the consequences," hard though it might be for them "to have this kind of confidence in [the child's] appetites." Modern mothers and fathers were "lucky" to be able to let go and be "natural."

Impulse—of both the child and the parents—could be safely followed. Spontaneous inclination was a virtue, deliberate control a vice. A mother angry at her child would do better to express her anger at once. Waiting until she calmed down and came to conscious mastery would be "grim" and "unnatural."

Conservative critics later complained that Spock promoted what they called permissive child rearing. In one of the earliest expressions of the "culture wars" that marked the last quarter of the twentieth century, critics held Spock responsible for the counterculture and the collapse of conventional morality. On their face, such charges were difficult to sustain. Spock never counseled permissiveness and soon enough advised against it. He simply had no stake in permissiveness per se. When critics of the 1946 edition assailed what they took to be Spock's undue indulgence of the child, Spock rewrote the permissive passages without a pang in the second edition. As Spock said in that revised version and in every revision that came after, the issue was not intrinsically important. Both strictness and permissiveness would work for "goodhearted" parents, neither for "insecure" ones. The only matter of any real moment was "the spirit that the parent [put] into managing the child."

Discipline and indulgence were not, for Spock, at odds. He trained as a psychoanalyst, but he never permitted Sigmund Freud's (1856–1939) tragic vision to inflect his advice. Civilization, in Spock's view, did not entail discontents. Conflict was not in the nature of things. Antagonism only appeared when parents mismanaged.

Spock's essential endeavor was to keep parents from activating the infantile ego. His deepest concern was to prevent pitched battles of will between mother and child. He resorted to permissiveness only as a tactic—one among several—in a larger strategy of conflict management. It was never a principle, only a ploy, driven by fear of the fallout of contention.

AN ACTIVIST LIFE

But if Spock did not espouse opposition in his pediatrics, he embraced it in his politics. Even before the war in Vietnam, he warned against the dangers of nuclear testing and served as cochairman of the National Committee for a Sane Nuclear Policy. He was a vocal opponent of the war, helped lead the march on the Pentagon in 1967, and was convicted and sentenced to jail for conspiracy to aid draft resisters in 1968. (His conviction was reversed on appeal.) He ran for president in 1972 as the candidate of the People's Party and continued as an activist long after. Past the age of seventy, Spock was arrested for protesting against a nuclear power plant in New Hampshire, budget cuts at the White House, and nuclear weapons at the Pentagon. Past eighty, Spock still gave as many as a hundred talks a year on the nuclear arms race.

Spock's child-rearing advice changed as his political views and American family life evolved. In successive editions of *Baby and Child Care*, he made a place for fathers as well as mothers in child care, allowed new gender roles for boys and girls, acknowledged divorce and single parenting, and explicitly urged vegetarianism on his readers.

But in essentials Spock's advice never changed. He always aimed to write a guide for living more than a medical reference book. He always challenged conventional notions of normality and sought to alleviate anxiety, in parents and children alike. He always offered reassurance in the down-to-earth manner in which he set forth his advice. He had a genius for popularization. No one ever explained Freud better in everyday language. No one ever wrote better gender-neutral prose.

Even as Spock set himself in militant antagonism to the status quo in politics, he endeavored to help parents accommodate their children to fit in the society and the economy the children would encounter. However inadvertently, he pushed mothers and fathers to prepare children for the corporate bureaucracies in which they would make their careers. He emphasized the cooperativeness and congeniality that organizational life demands. He held that parents "owe it to the child to make him likeable" and that they had to make the child be like others to be likable. He never did reconcile his dissident politics and his conformist child rearing.

SEE ALSO *Brazelton, T. Berry; Child Development; Parent-Child Relationships; Parenting Styles; Psychology; Socialization*

BIBLIOGRAPHY

PRIMARY WORKS

Spock, Benjamin. 1946. *The Common Sense Book of Baby and Child Care.* New York: Duell, Sloan, and Pearce.

Spock, Benjamin, and Mary Morgan. 1989. *Spock on Spock: A Memoir of Growing Up with the Century.* New York: Pantheon.

SECONDARY WORKS

Bloom, Lynn. 1972. *Doctor Spock: Biography of a Conservative Radical.* Indianapolis, IN: Bobbs-Merrill.

Mitford, Jessica. 1969. *The Trial of Dr. Spock, the Rev. William Sloane Coffin, Jr., Michael Ferber, Mitchell Goodman, and Marcus Raskin.* New York: Knopf.

Watson, John B. 1928. *Psychological Care of Infant and Child.* New York, Norton.

Zuckerman, Michael. 1993. Doctor Spock: The Confidence Man. In *Almost Chosen People: Oblique Biographies in the American Grain.* Berkeley: University of California Press.

Michael Zuckerman

SPOILS SYSTEM

SEE *Patronage.*

SPONTANEOUS ORDER

SEE *Hayek, Friedrich August von.*

SPORTS

Sport is a social phenomenon that deeply permeates societies throughout the world. Millions of people view, participate in, or discuss sporting events on a near daily basis. Further, sport has become a multibillion-dollar industry that employs thousands of people. As sport has become more pervasive and as the size and magnitude of the sport industry has grown, it has increasingly come under the scrutiny of sociological researchers. The purpose of this entry is to overview some of the major issues and insights developed from a sociological analysis of sport. This overview is categorized into two sections. First is a discussion of sociological studies of sports as an institution that has significant implications for the lives of participants, their families, and the communities in which they live. The second category of studies views sports as a microcosm of society, which provides a fertile field to test sociological theory and gain insights about society. This entry continues with an overview of both of these research agendas.

SPORT AS A SOCIAL INSTITUTION

Research on sports as a social institution has been guided by two very different theoretical perspectives. On the one hand, researchers using a systems model, largely derived from functional theory, tend to see sport as an institution that contributes to society by reinforcing major cultural values such as success, achievement, competition, work, and cooperation, and also increases community or school unity. Other sociologists examine sport from a conflict perspective where it is viewed as an "opiate of the masses" (Coakley 2001; Eitzen 2001).

Sport as an Inspiration: The Functional Perspective Numerous studies have been conducted that seek to determine the consequences of sports involvement for participants. Prominent among this research are studies seeking to understand the relationship between involvement in sports during childhood and adolescence and a variety of simultaneous and adult outcomes. While a variety of possible outcomes have been explored, two representative examples of this line of research are described herein. These examples include the relationship between sports participation and adult income and sports participation and the sexual behavior of teenage females.

A number of researchers have empirically explored the relationship between sports participation and adult income. These studies have consistently found that individuals who participate in youth or high school athletics generally have adult earnings that are higher than individuals who do not participate in sports. For the most part, these relationships remain significant when factors such as race, parents' socioeconomic status, and parents' educational attainment are statistically controlled.

Similarly, researchers such as Tamela McNulty Eitle and David J. Eitle (2002) have determined that sports participation is strongly associated with the sexual behavior of adolescent females. This research found that adolescent females who play sports are less likely to have ever had sexual intercourse (Miller et al. 1999), have an older age of onset of sexual activity (Brown et al. 1997; Miller et al. 1998), and have higher rates of contraceptive use (Miller et al. 1999). Even after adolescence, Eitle and Eitle found that those who participated in sports were less likely to become pregnant outside of marriage and to have had fewer lifetime sex partners.

Researchers have attempted to explain why participation in athletics tends to have these positive outcomes. Explanations include physical appearance; it is argued that being stronger and healthier provides advantages in both athletic participation and the work force. Christopher Shilling's 1992 findings maintain that the physical capital accrued through sports participation is convertible to other forms of advantage in other areas of life. Researchers James Curtis and colleagues argued in their 2003 work that athletes gain self-confidence, which leads to better choices; they learn important interpersonal skills, and athletic involvement provides visibility and social networks.

Sport as an Opiate: The Conflict Perspective Some scholars argue that sport is an institution that provides the illusion that success can be achieved by anyone with talent and who is willing to work hard. As a result, sport is one of the institutions that allows deep and persistent patterns of prejudice, discrimination, and inequality to continue. Thus, because a few minority athletes have become extremely famous and wealthy, society is lulled into thinking that prejudice, discrimination, and racism are largely problems of the past. In addition, some maintain that sport is a powerful reinforcer of a racist ideology. For example, African Americans are typically represented as being athletically superior. Unfortunately, concomitant is the belief that they are mentally inferior. Thus from an observation of sport one is given the impression that minority athletes succeed because of physical prowess, while white athletes succeed through perseverance, hard work, and intelligence. To show that this racist ideology persists into the twenty-first century, in 2004 J. R. Woodward examined the sports guides dedicated to critiquing collegiate players eligible for the annual National Football League draft. He found that African American players were more likely than white players of their same position to be described in physical rather than mental terms.

Also from the conflict perspective, sport can be viewed as a tool used by the advantaged to help them maintain their privileged positions. In his book *Beer and Circus* (2000), Murray Sperber discussed how modern college sports are used as an "opiate of the masses." He noted that since the mid-twentieth century the cost of college education at large state universities has increased dramatically. At the same time the quality of that education has diminished as class sizes have significantly increased and a much higher proportion of the classes are taught by graduate students or part-time faculty. Sperber argued that to distract students from the fact that they are paying more and getting less, colleges have placed greater emphasis on sports. Thus, rather than demanding academic change, students focus on the upcoming football or basketball game. Meanwhile, so-called "student-athletes" are recruited to fill the stadium and keep alumni donations flowing. The exploitation of these student-athletes is evident as the vast majority will not have the benefits of a career in professional sports and are placed in circumstances where academic success is unlikely. When their eligibility has expired, these former student-athletes leave college, often without a degree and lacking the skills necessary for success in life outside of athletics. Similarly, Douglas E. Foley's 1994 ethnographic study of a Texas high school describes how high school football is an agent of socialization that reinforces existing patterns of race and gender inequality.

SPORT AS A MICROCOSM OF SOCIETY

Some researchers in the sociology of sport argue that sport is a microcosm of society. A 2004 book by Franklin Foer (2004) describes how soccer can explain the world. Thus sport, like society, has become increasingly bureaucratized and commercialized and continues to exhibit patterns of racism and sexism. Further, because sport tends to be open and visible, it provides an excellent lens to study these issues and test relevant theories. To follow are several examples showing how studies of sports are used to gain insight about society.

Professional sport represents the epitome of capitalism, and much can be learned about labor relations in general by watching the conflict between professional sports team owners and athletes. The actions of professional athletes closely parallel the actions of other workers as they seek higher wages and better working conditions. Like other workers, professional athletes have sought redress in the courts and they have formed unions and organized strikes. At the same time, owners attempt to keep wages low so their profits will be greater.

In addition, much can be learned about race relations in the United States from sports as circumstances in sport generally reflect circumstances in the remainder of society. While sport appears on the surface to be a very meritocratic institution, where participants are rewarded strictly on the basis of their accomplishments, a careful examination reveals extensive patterns of inequality. For example, while minority athletes are visible and numerous in sports such as basketball and football, they are underrepresented in many other sports. Further, minorities are underrepresented in positions of power in virtually all sports. The owner of nearly every professional sports franchise is white, minorities are rare in the upper management of sports, and most coaches are white. For example, during the 2005 college football season, only 3 of the 117 teams playing Division I football had a minority head coach. Given these circumstances, it is not surprising that minority assistant college football coaches perceived less career-related opportunity, were less satisfied with their careers, and had greater occupational turnover expectations than their white counterparts.

Among players, sociologists have detected a phenomenon called "stacking." Racial stacking is the over- or underrepresentation of players of certain races in particular positions in team sports. For example, quarterbacks in football and pitchers and catchers in baseball have traditionally been white, while running backs and defensive backs in football and outfielders in baseball are much more likely to be minority. Again, this pattern reinforces a racist ideology as white athletes dominate positions of power where mental skills and leadership are essential, while minority athletes dominate positions where pure athletic skill is more critical.

There are also extensive differences by race in the sports that individuals play. In 2003 Pat Goldsmith conducted a study of the racial patterns of school sports participation and used these differences as a forum to test economic and cultural theories to explain these differences. Economic or structural theories predict that differences by race exist because of economic differences across races. Cultural or racial theories would predict that differences would exist even when socioeconomic status was equal. He found that economic theories best predict the sports that whites play, while cultural theories best predict the sports that blacks play.

It should also be noted that similar patterns of inequality in sports are found relative to gender. In college and high school, female sports generally receive only a minority of the athletic budget and the coaches of female teams have significantly lower salaries. In sum, the sociology of sport is a new and dynamic subdiscipline with the potential for significant insights about sociological theory and about societies in general.

SEE ALSO *Sports Industry*

BIBLIOGRAPHY

Adler, Patricia A., and Peter Adler. 1989. The Gloried Self: The Aggrandizement and The Constriction of Self. *Social Psychology Quarterly* 52 (4): 299–310.

Brown, J. T., L. Ellis, M. L. Guerrina, et al. 1997. The Relationship between the Frequency of Exercise and the Age of Onset of Sexual Intercourse in Adolescent Females. *Nurse Practitioner* 22: 16–18.

Coakley, Jay J. 2001. Sport in Society: An Inspiration or an Opiate. In *Sport in Contemporary Society*, ed. D. Stanley Eitzen. 6th ed. New York: Worth Publishers.

Cunningham, George B., and Michael Sagas. 2004. Racial Differences in Occupational Turnover Intent among NCAA Division IA Assistant Football Coaches. *Sociology of Sport Journal* 21: 84–92.

Curtis, James, William McTeer, and Phillip White. 2003. Do High School Athletes Earn More Pay? Youth Sport Participation and Earnings as an Adult. *Sociology of Sport Journal* 20: 60–76.

Eide, R., and N. Ronan. 2001. Is Participation in High School Athletics an Investment or a Consumption Good? *Economics of Education Review* 20: 431–442.

Eitle, Tamela McNulty, and David J. Eitle. 2002. Just Don't Do It: High School Sports Participation and Young Female Adult Sexual Behavior. *Sociology of Sport Journal* 19: 403–418.

Eitzen, D. Stanley. 1999. American Sport at Century's End. *Vital Speeches of the Day* 65: 189–191.

Eitzen, D. Stanley. 2001. *Sport in Contemporary Society*. 6th ed. New York: Worth Publishers.

Ewing, B. T. 1995. High School Athletics and the Wages of Black Males. *Review of Black Political Economy* 24: 65–78.

Foer, Franklin. 2004. *How Soccer Explains the World*. New York: HarperCollins.

Foley, Douglas E. 1994. *Learning Capitalist Culture: Deep in the Heart of Tejas*. Philadelphia: University of Pennsylvania Press.

Goldsmith, Pat Antonio. 2003. Race Relations and Racial Patterns in School Sports Participation. *Sociology of Sport Journal* 20: 147–171.

Hoberman, J. 1997. *Darwin's Athletes: How Sport Has Damaged Black America and Preserved the Myth of Race*. Boston: Houghton Mifflin.

Howell, F. M., A. W. Miracle, and C. R. Rees. 1984. Do High School Athletics Pay? The Effects of Varsity Participation on Socioeconomic Attainments. *Sociology of Sport Journal* 1: 15–25.

Loy, J. W., and Joseph F. McElvogue. 1970. Racial Segregation in American Sport. *International Review of Sport Sociology* 5: 1–23.

Miller, K. E., D. F. Sabo, M. P. Farrell, et al. 1998. Athletic Participation and Sexual Intercourse among Adolescents: Family, Peer, and Other Antecedents. *Youth and Society* 29: 54–83.

Miller, K. E., D. F. Sabo, M. P. Farrell, et al. 1999. Sports, Sexual Behavior, Contraceptive Use, and Pregnancy among Female and Male High School Students: Testing Cultural Resource Theory. *Sociology of Sport Journal* 16: 366–387.

Otto, L. B., and D. F. Alwin. 1977. Athletics, Aspirations, and Attainment. *Sociology of Education* 42: 102–113.

Picou, J. S., V. McCarter, and F. M. Howell. 1985. Do High School Athletics Pay? Some Further Evidence. *Sociology of Sport Journal* 2: 72–76.

Rees, R., and H. Brandl-Bredenbeck. 1995. Body Capital and the Importance of Sport: A Comparison of American and German Adolescents. *Journal of Comparative Physical Education and Sport* 17: 50–56.

Sage, George H. 1998. *Power and Ideology in American Sport*. 2nd ed. Champaign, IL: Human Kinetics.

Shilling, Christopher. 1992. Schooling and the Production of Physical Capital. *Discourse* 13: 1–19.

Sperber, Murray. 2000. *Beer and Circus*. New York: Henry Holt.

Woodward, J. R. 2004. Professional Football Scouts: An Investigation of Racial Stacking. *Sociology of Sport Journal* 21: 356–375.

Don E. Albrecht

SPORTS INDUSTRY

Athletic activities have long been part of all societies, but it was not until the early twentieth century that professional team sports began to develop. Since then, the top levels of basketball, football (soccer in North America), baseball, hockey, and North American football have become widely popular professional activities that have attracted the attention of economists.

While professional sports grew in the first half of the twentieth century, a major turning point came in the 1960s when lucrative television contracts began to greatly increase team revenues. Revenues were no longer limited by the number of seats in the stadium or arena. Players' salaries later increased rapidly. Economists' interest in the sports sector did not begin in earnest until the 1990s, largely as a result of the increased involvement of the public sector in financing professional sports facilities in the United States. The first economics journal in the field, the *Journal of Sports Economics*, began publication in 2000.

GROWTH OF PUBLIC FUNDING

The policy issue that has attracted the most attention from economists is the growth of public funding of stadiums and arenas in the United States, funding that is based on the proposition that professional teams have a significant economic impact on a city.

The sports industries argue that teams raise incomes and employment in host cities and that publicly funded facilities, and perhaps tax concessions, are a good investment for an urban area. If these benefits are the carrot, the stick is the threat to move a team to a more hospitable city. To make this a credible threat, leagues typically keep in reserve at least one city that is anxious to host a team. As a result, many cities have provided subsidized facilities, with price tags in the hundreds of millions of dollars.

Economists have undertaken many studies of whether these subsidies are warranted. There is little difference in their results, which conclude that teams have either a slightly negative or no discernable impact on a city's economy. Rodney D. Fort discussed some of these studies in his book *Sports Economics* (2006).

A number of factors explain these findings. Perhaps the most important is that team-related spending by local residents is still spent, but on other goods and services, in the absence of a local team. In addition, professional sports as a tourist attraction are overrated; while visitors attend games, they usually come to the city for other reasons and enjoy games while they are in town. Finally, much of a team's revenue is spent outside its city, both for away games and for the earnings of players who live elsewhere in the off-season.

PLAYER MARKETS

A second major area of interest to economists is the analysis of the markets for players. These markets provide examples of shifting market structures and changing claims to income. For many years, teams held monopsony power, the power that comes to a single buyer, in the market for players. This power came from player drafts and reserve clauses.

The player draft is a system in which teams in a league select ("draft") incoming players in an ordered fashion, usually in reverse order of finish in the last season: the team that finishes last gets the first draft choice for the next year. A player may sign only with the team that drafts him, and that rule applies even when a team trades or sells a draft choice to another team.

The reserve clause, which originated in professional baseball in 1877, bound a player to the team with which he signed his first contract, usually the team that drafted him. While the team had the power to trade the player or to sell his contract, the player was not able to sign with another team even when his contract expired. As the only buyer, a team held complete monopsony power and was thus able to keep salaries low.

Leagues argued that these restrictions on player movement improved competitive balance across teams. In fact, however, economic markets still functioned. Teams traded both draft choices and players. As Fort pointed out in *Sports Economics*, there is no statistically significant difference in competitive balance before and after draft systems were in place in the National Football League and in Major League Baseball. Rich, winning teams have tended to buy good players and maintain their winning ways.

Teams' monopsony powers were reduced by the growth of player unions in the 1960s and 1970s. There have been player strikes and owner lockouts in several sports. As a result, the markets for players have changed.

Reserve clauses began to break down in baseball in the late 1970s, and other sports followed. While player drafts still operate, reserve clauses bind a player to a team for a limited number of years. Players now become free agents after several years in the league and are able to change teams and to negotiate their own contracts.

As a result, salaries are much higher than they once were. Michael Leeds and Peter Von Allmen cited examples in *The Economics of Sports* (2005). Average annual salaries in the United States in 2002 ranged from a low of $1.3 million in the National Football League to a high of $4.5 million in the National Basketball Association. At the same time in Europe, ordinary soccer players earned from $600,000 to over $1 million dollars annually, plus bonuses. Star players in all sports earn far more, as they attract more fans and increase box office and television revenues. It is not clear whether these salary levels will continue in all sports, as the 2004 to 2005 season-long lockout in the National Hockey League has resulted in team salary caps.

SCANDALS

Two problems continue to plague major league sports, despite the efforts of many organizations. First, there are scandals arising from the use of performance-enhancing drugs; in 2006 alone, for example, there were widespread doping allegations in major league baseball and in the Tour de France cycling race. Doping scandals have led to questions regarding the legitimacy of records set by players or teams later found to have been using performance-enhancing drugs. Second, and more infrequently, there is game fixing, usually associated with gambling. In 2006, for example, a widespread game fixing scandal arose in football (soccer) in Italy, involving several of the country's top-level teams.

There are similar problems in amateur sports, where success may bring present or future financial rewards. In some sports it is lucrative advertising contracts for "amateur" athletes. In others, such as American football, universities are training grounds for professional athletes, and it is the promise of future benefits that tempts some players to use performance-enhancing drugs.

Politics plays a key role in international sports. At various times, countries have boycotted the Olympic Games, as in the Moscow Games of 1980. Votes to award the Olympic Games to a city are often a very political matter, sometimes associated with charges of bribery, as in the case of the 2002 Winter Games awarded to Salt Lake City, Utah.

These problems aside, markets in sports industries operate as understood by economic theory. Each team in a professional sport has some monopoly power as the only seller of the sport in its home city. A team also has some monopsony power as one of a small number of buyers of player talent. After a few years, ordinary players have market power in the sale of their services, augmented by union contracts. A very good player has considerable power as his marginal revenue product exceeds that of other players. But all this likely matters little to fans, the final purchasers of the industries' outputs. Fans, after all, do not cheer for markets, they cheer for their home team.

SEE ALSO *Entertainment Industry; Industry; Olympic Games*

BIBLIOGRAPHY

Fort, Rodney. 2006. *Sports Economics.* 2nd ed. Upper Saddle River, New Jersey: Pearson Prentice Hall.

Leeds, Michael, and Peter Von Allmen. 2005. *The Economics of Sports.* 2nd ed. New York: Pearson.

Lewis Soroka

SPOT MARKET

The point in time when a buyer and a seller agree to the terms of a transaction (the *contract date*) need not be the same as the point in time when the transaction occurs (the *execution date*). For example, on January 1 a buyer and a seller can agree on the terms of a transaction to be conducted on February 1. When the buyer and the seller agree to the terms of the transaction prior to the execution of the terms of the transaction, it is said that the transaction occurs on a *futures* or *forward* basis (wherein the distinction between the two involves specific terms as to how the transaction is to be handled). The agreed price is called a *futures* or *forward price*. Alternatively on January 1 a buyer and a seller can agree on the terms of a transaction to be conducted immediately. When the buyer and the seller agree to the terms of the transaction at the same time that the transaction is executed, it is said that the transaction occurred on a *spot basis*. The agreed price is called a *spot price*. Most consumer transactions, with the exceptions of major transactions such as home purchases, are conducted on spot bases.

The *spot market* is a formal market for buying and selling securities and commodities on a spot basis. In practice, while the physical transfer of the securities or commodities (called *settlement*) may take a day or more, for legal and accounting purposes the transaction is assumed to have occurred instantaneously. In a futures or forward market, it is not the securities and commodities that are sold but rather contracts for the purchase or sale of securities and commodities at some future date. The purpose of the futures or forward markets is to enable the buyers and the sellers to mitigate the risk of future price fluctuations by locking in the price prior to the transaction occurring. Forward and futures markets evolved as a means of transacting business when the physical delivery of the product was forced to take place in the future. Examples include selling a crop prior to the harvest and buying a product that must be shipped from overseas. If sellers seek to mitigate risk, then they will be willing to sell their products on a forward or futures basis for less than they would otherwise sell them for on the spot market. If buyers seek to mitigate risk, then they will be willing to pay more on a forward or futures basis than they would be willing to pay on a spot basis.

The purchase of a security on a spot market with the intent of reselling the security at a later date on a spot market resale at a higher price is called *speculation*; the purchase of a security on a spot market with the intent simultaneously to sell the security at a higher price on a different spot market is called *arbitrage*. For example, in arbitrage one might purchase €1,000 at a price of $1.25 per euro on the New York spot market and simultaneously sell the €1,000 at a price of $1.26 per euro on the

London spot market, making a profit of $10. In speculation one might purchase €1,000 at a price of $1.25 per euro on January 1 and sell the €1,000 at a price of $1.26 per euro on February 1, making a profit of $10.

Arbitrageurs (those who conduct arbitrage) serve an important role in financial markets. By constantly looking for and exploiting pricing discrepancies, arbitrageurs force prices in different markets to equate. For example, if euros sell for a higher price on London markets than on New York markets, arbitrageurs will step into the market, buying up euros on the New York spot market and simultaneously selling them on the London spot market. This increase in the demand for euros in New York causes an increase in the price of euros on the New York market. Simultaneously the increase in the supply of euros in London causes a decrease in the price of euros on the London market. The arbitrage will continue, and the prices will continue to move until the prices on the two spot markets become equal. (In practice the prices will not become exactly equal due to small costs for conducting the transactions.) At that point there is no further incentive to arbitrage, and so the arbitrage stops. There are enough people attempting arbitrage and financial markets are efficient enough that computers are usually required to conduct arbitrage because price discrepancies, when they occur, are quickly arbitraged away. The benefit that arbitrageurs play is to alleviate people seeking to buy currency on spot markets from having to compare prices across many markets. Virtually all the time (non-arbitrage) buyers and sellers are guaranteed that the price they see on one spot market is identical to the prices they would find on all other spot markets.

SEE ALSO *Arbitrage and Arbitrageurs; Equity Markets; Euro, The; Financial Markets; Interest Rates; Interest, Own Rate of; Returns; Speculation*

BIBLIOGRAPHY

Billingsley, Randall S. 2006. *Understanding Arbitrage: An Intuitive Approach to Financial Analysis.* Upper Saddle River, NJ: Wharton School Publications.

Cross, Samuel Y. 1998. *All About … the Foreign Exchange Market in the United States.* New York: Federal Reserve Bank of New York.

Cuthbertson, Keith, and Dirk Nitzsche. 2001. *Investments: Spot and Derivatives Markets.* New York: John Wiley.

Antony Davies

SPOT PRICES

SEE *Spot Market.*

SPRAWL

SEE *Suburban Sprawl; Urban Sprawl.*

SPREADS

In economics and finance the term *spread* is used in many different contexts. Generally, a spread involves calculating the difference between two related values. In the context of option contracts, for example, spreads involve the buying and/or selling of options of the same type with various exercise prices and expiry dates. John Hull, in his 2006 book, discusses a number of spreads—bull spreads, bear spreads, box spreads, butterfly spreads, calendar spreads, and diagonal spreads. For example, a bullish vertical spread can be constructed by buying one call option and writing one call option with the same expiry date but a larger exercise price. This is called a spread because it is made up of the same type of option, in this case call options. It is bullish because the investor profits from a rise in the price of the underlying asset and is called vertical because there are two different exercise prices involved. As an example, suppose that for $2 you buy a call with an exercise price of $20 and sell for $1 a call with an exercise price of $30. The cost of this bull strategy is $2 - $1 = $1 and the payoff is $10 if the stock price (at expiration) is greater than $30, zero if the stock price is below $20, and the difference between the stock price and $20 if the stock price is between $20 and $30.

In the context of bonds, the spread between the interest rate on risky corporate bonds and the interest rate on risk-free government bonds, both of the same maturity, is called the risk spread (or risk premium). Bonds with default risk always have a positive risk spread, and there is a positive relation between the risk spread and the risk of default. Moreover, the risk spread is a good measure of general economic activity because it is negatively correlated with the overall growth rate of the economy. For example, when the growth rate of the economy slows, the risk of default increases and the immediate impact is an increase in the risk spread. Because default risk is important to the size of the risk spread, credit rating agencies, such as Standard & Poor's, provide information on default risk by rating the quality of corporate bonds in term of their probability of default.

The spread also refers to the slope of the yield curve—the difference between long- and short-term interest rates. This spread is referred to as the term spread and describes the term structure of interest rates—the relationship among interest rates on bonds with the same risk of default but different terms to maturity. When the yield curve is upward-sloping (the most typical case), the term spread is positive (the long-term interest rate is above the short-term interest rate); when the yield curve is downward-sloping (referred to as an inverted yield curve), the term spread is negative (the long-term interest rate is below the short-term interest rate); and when the yield curve is flat, the term spread is zero (short- and long-term interest rates are the same). Frederic Mishkin and Apostolos Serletis, in chapter 6 of their 2007 study, discuss the yield curve and the term structure of interest rates.

Early investigations into the risk and term structure of interest rates looked at whether the slope of the yield curve—the spread between long- and short-term interest rates—helps predict future short-term interest rates. Studies, such as those by Robert Shiller and colleagues (1983) and Gregory Mankiw and Lawrence Summers (1984), found that the yield curve does not always help predict future short-term interest rates. Subsequent research, however, using better testing procedures, supports a different view. Studies by Eugene Fama (1984) and John Campbell and Shiller (1987, 1991), for example, show that the spread between long- and short-term interest rates contains useful information about future interest rates over the short run and the long run, but not over the intermediate term.

The slope of the yield curve also contains information about overall economic conditions. In fact, an extensive literature documents the usefulness of the yield curve in predicting future economic activity, such as Arturo Estrella and Gikas Hardouvelis's 1991 study and Estrella and Mishkin's 1996 and 1998 studies. However, twenty-first-century monetary policy procedures and globalization may be causing this relationship to loosen. In particular, the Federal Open Market Committee in the United States raised the target federal funds rate in seventeen consecutive meetings from June 2004 to July 2006, from 1 percent to 5.25 percent, but long-term interest rates in the United States declined for most of this period. In fact, long-term interest rates around the world have recently exhibited similar declines despite steady increases in short-term interest rates.

As Tao Wu argues in his 2006 study, the reason long-term interest rates have not been responding during the worldwide round of monetary tightening since the turn of the century is the adoption of an inflation-targeting approach to monetary policy as well as globalization. In particular, inflation targeting by many countries, including Australia, Canada, New Zealand, Sweden, and the United Kingdom, and increased international competition in labor and product markets have contributed to price stability and have put downward pressure on long-term interest rates. This has led to the decoupling of long-term interest rates from short-term interest rates with significant implications for monetary policy. In particular, most central banks use short-term interest rates as their operating instruments, but the effects of monetary policy on economic activity stem from how long-term interest rates respond to short-term interest rates. Hence, a deeper understanding of how inflation targeting and globalization affect the spread between long- and short-term interest rates is needed to evaluate the impact and timing effects of monetary policy.

SEE ALSO *Spreads, Bid-Ask; Yield*

BIBLIOGRAPHY

Campbell, John Y., and Robert J. Shiller. 1987. Cointegration and Tests of the Present Value Models. *Journal of Political Economy* 95 (5): 1062–1088.

Campbell, John Y., and Robert J. Shiller. 1991. Yield Spreads and Interest Rate Movements: A Bird's Eye View. *Review of Economic Studies* 58 (3): 495–514.

Estrella, Arturo, and Frederic S. Mishkin. 1996. The Yield Curve as a Predictor of U.S. Recessions. Federal Reserve Bank of New York, *Current Issues in Economics and Finance* 2: 1–6.

Estrella, Arturo, and Frederic S. Mishkin. 1998. Predicting U.S. Recessions: Financial Variables as Leading Indicators. *Review of Economics and Statistics* 80 (1): 45–61.

Estrella, Arturo, and Gikas A. Hardouvelis. 1991. The Term Structure as a Predictor of Real Economic Activity. *Journal of Finance* 46 (2): 555–576.

Fama, Eugene. 1984. The Information in the Term Structure. *Journal of Financial Economics* 13 (4): 509–528.

Hull, John C. 2006. *Options, Futures and Other Derivatives.* 6th ed. Upper Saddle River, NJ: Pearson/Prentice Hall.

Mankiw, N. Gregory, and Lawrence H. Summers. 1984. Do Long-Term Interest Rates Overreact to Short-Term Interest Rates? *Brookings Papers on Economic Activity* 1: 223–242.

Mishkin, Frederic S. and Apostolos Serletis. 2007. *The Economics of Money, Banking, and Financial Markets: Third Canadian Edition.* Toronto: Addison Wesley.

Shiller, Robert J., John Y. Campbell, and Kermit L. Schoenholtz. 1983. Forward Rates and Future Policy: Interpreting the Term Structure of Interest Rates. *Brookings Papers on Economic Activity* 1: 173–217.

Wu, Tao. Globalization's Effect on Interest Rates and the Yield Curve. 2006. Federal Reserve Bank of Dallas, *Economic Letter* 1: 1–8.

Apostolos Serletis

SPREADS, BID-ASK

The bid-ask spread is the difference between the ask (the lowest price at which someone is willing to sell an asset or security) and the bid (the highest price at which there is someone in the marketplace ready to buy it). The spread is often used as a measure of market uncertainty as well as market liquidity. The average of the bid-ask spread is also used as a measure of the consensus value of an asset. The term dates back to at least James Dolley, who used it in his March 1938 *American Economic Review* article to measure discontinuity in stock trading on the New York Stock Exchange, although the concept was probably in use before then.

The intuitive reason for the existence of a bid-ask spread is that there is disagreement among market participants as to the value of a security. However, there are other reasons for a bid-ask spread. For example, because buyers and sellers need not arrive simultaneously, market makers stand ready to buy securities from sellers and sell securities to buyers; the bid-ask compensates these market makers for the cost of holding inventory. Other causes could include the existence of an order-processing cost, or market makers might have to adjust their prices to protect themselves against the risk of trading with better informed agents; this is the *adverse selection cost.*

One problem with the use of the bid-ask spread is that the market might lack depth—that is, the ability of a trader to trade a large number of shares at the quoted price. Consequently, for average-sized trades, the bid-ask spread might not indicate expected transaction costs. Furthermore, if the potential price impact is asymmetric, the average of the bid-ask spread may not be useful as a measure of the current consensus value of the asset, either.

Alternate measures of liquidity have been suggested. Some of these are: (1) net trading range—that is, the difference between the high and low price less the change in price during a given trading period; (2) the effective bid-ask spread—that is, the distance between the average of the quoted bid-ask spread and the price at which the deal transacts; (3) turnover; and (4) the ratio of absolute returns to trading volume.

Empirically, bid-ask spreads have been linked to various factors such as the volume of trade, the cost of holding inventory, the degree of information asymmetry, and tick size. The first three factors follow immediately from the discussion above. The notion of tick size as a determining factor has acquired more prominence since the introduction of decimalization in secondary equity markets. Decimalization has led to smaller quoted and effective bid-ask spreads for most stocks. However, concomitantly, there have been more small trades and fewer large trades, and the depth of the market has suffered, exacerbating the problems listed above with the use of the bid-ask spread as a measure of liquidity.

SEE ALSO *Spreads*

BIBLIOGRAPHY

Angel, James. 1997. Tick Size, Share Prices, and Stock Splits. *Journal of Finance* 52 (2): 655–681.

Dolley, James C. 1938. The Effect of Government Regulation in the Stock-Trading Volume of the New York Stock Exchange. *American Economic Review* 28 (1): 8–26.

Korajczyk, Robert A., and Ronnie Sadka. 2006. Pricing the Commonality across Alternative Measures of Liquidity. August. Working Paper, Northwestern University. http://ssrn.com/abstract=900363.

Rhodes-Kropf, Matthew. 2005. Price Improvement in Dealership Markets. *Journal of Business* 78: 1137–1172.

P. V. Viswanath

SPYING

SEE *Hoover, J. Edgar.*

SRAFFA, PIERO
1898–1983

Piero Sraffa was born in Turin, Italy, on August 5, 1898. His father, Angelo Sraffa, was a well-known professor of commercial law and then rector of Bocconi University. Sraffa studied law in Turin and graduated with a dissertation titled "Monetary Inflation in Italy during and after the War," written under the supervision of future Italian president Luigi Einaudi.

INVOLVEMENT WITH KEYNES

During a stay as a research student at the London School of Economics from 1921 to 1922, Sraffa was introduced to the eminent University of Cambridge economist John Maynard Keynes, who was deeply impressed by the young Italian scholar. Keynes invited him to write an article on the Italian banking system for the *Manchester Guardian.* Upon receipt Keynes decided to publish the piece, titled "The Bank Crisis in Italy," in the *Economic Journal* and asked Sraffa to prepare a shorter version for the *Guardian.* Provoked by the article, Benito Mussolini asked Sraffa's father to make his son recant the opinion expressed in it, a request that was rejected. In 1923 Sraffa was appointed to a lectureship in political economy and public finance at the University of Perugia. In 1925 he published the influential paper "Sulle relazioni fra costo e quantità prodotta" (in *Annali di Economia*), which contains an analysis of the foundations of decreasing, constant, and increasing returns in the English economist Alfred Marshall's theory and a devastating criticism of the partial equilibrium method. Not least because of this essay, Sraffa obtained a full professorship in political economy at the University of Cagliari (Sardinia), a post he held in absentia to the end of his life. The English economist Francis Y. Edgeworth's high opinion of the essay led to an invitation to publish a related version in the *Economic Journal* in 1926 titled "The Laws of Returns under Competitive Conditions." The paper triggered a debate on monopolistic competition.

In 1927 Keynes arranged for a lectureship for Sraffa at Cambridge. Sraffa began teaching in 1928 on advanced theory of value. He also in the late 1920s began his interpretative and reconstructive work on the classical economists and his criticism of marginalist theory, which finally materialized in his 1960 book, *Production of Commodities by Means of Commodities*. His breakthrough, in the winter of 1927 to 1928, in regard to his novel interpretation of the classical theory of value and distribution, rendered the task of lecturing increasingly difficult for him. He resigned as lecturer and in 1931 was appointed to the position of librarian of the Marshall Library. In addition he was also placed in charge of the Cambridge program of graduate studies in economics. He gave up lecturing on value theory for good. The only lectures he was to give were devoted to continental banking in 1930 and to industry starting in 1942. In 1939 he joined Trinity College. He was on friendly terms with the Austrian-born British philosopher Ludwig Wittgenstein, who acknowledged to have been deeply influenced by Sraffa.

EDITORSHIP OF RICARDO PROJECT

In 1930 Sraffa was appointed to the editorship of *The Works and Correspondence of David Ricardo* on behalf of the Royal Economic Society. The project turned out to be much more difficult than Sraffa thought it would be when he assumed the task, not least because a well-known Ricardo scholar, Jacob H. Hollander, effectively boycotted the project for a while. Hollander did not disclose that several "Ricardiana" were in his possession, and when Sraffa proved that they must be, Hollander refused to show them to Sraffa (Gehrke and Kurz 2002). In preparing the edition, the first volumes of which were finally published in 1951, Sraffa was assisted by his friend Maurice H. Dobb. The last volume of the eleven-volume work, containing the general index, was not published until 1973. Sraffa's introduction to the first volume contains his novel, *surplus*-based interpretation of the classical approach to the theory of value and distribution. Sraffa held that the classical approach is fundamentally different from the marginalist, demand and supply one and cannot be interpreted as an early version of it. The Ricardo work is widely acknowledged to be a scholarly masterpiece. Interestingly, in 1961, long before the project's completion, the Swedish Royal Academy honored Sraffa for his work on the project by awarding him a Söderström gold medal in economics, an award that is considered to be a

precursor of the award commonly called the Nobel Prize in economics.

In the early 1930s Sraffa was also involved in the so-called Cambridge Circus discussing Keynes's 1930 work, *A Treatise on Money*, and his 1936 work, *The General Theory of Employment, Interest, and Money*. In his paper "Dr. Hayek on Money and Capital," published in the *Economic Journal* in 1932, Sraffa managed to effectively ward off an attack on Keynes's project by the Austrian-born economist Friedrich August von Hayek.

CRITICISM OF MARGINALIST THEORY

From an early time onward Sraffa was particularly critical of two closely related elements of contemporary economic theory. His critical attitude reflects the objectivist or materialist point of view he had developed in discussions with the Italian philosopher and politician Antonio Gramsci and during his intensive reading about recent breakthroughs in the sciences, especially quantum physics (Kurz and Salvadori 2005). The first element concerned the question of whether the parts should be seen as constitutive of the whole, or vice versa. Marginalist economics, starting from methodological individualism, advocated the former view. Sraffa implicitly rejected this position by developing his analysis not from given individual agents but a given "system of production." To take the whole as constitutive of the parts was also advocated by contemporary scientists, including the English mathematician and philosopher Alfred North Whitehead. Second, Sraffa was critical of the subjectivist element permeating contemporary economic theory and the corresponding concept of "real," that is, "psychic," cost (as advocated by Marshall). Sraffa deliberately sought to elaborate an *objectivist* alternative to marginalist theory revolving around the twin concepts of *physical real cost* and *social surplus* within the framework of an analysis that conceives of production as a *circular flow*.

Sraffa related his reconstructive work explicitly to the works of the English economist William Petty (1623–1687) and the French economist François Quesnay (1694–1774). In his *Political Arithmetick* (1690), Petty had insisted on expressing himself only "in Terms of Number, Weight or Measure; to use only Arguments of Sense, and to consider only such Causes, as have visible Foundations in Nature" (Petty 1986, p. 244). With the *Tableau économique* (1758), Quesnay had for the first time put forward a view of the processes of production and distribution of the economic system as a whole. Initially, Sraffa was highly critical of the labor theory of value, as advocated by Ricardo and Karl Marx, because in his view it involved a "corruption" of the earlier concept of *physical real cost* (Petty's "food"). It was only after Sraffa had turned to the case of an economic system with a surplus that is partly distributed to workers in proportion to the time worked that he realized he needed a concept of labor and that in very special conditions relative prices are proportional to labor values. This did not mean, however, that the labor theory of value played any constructive part in his analysis. On the basis of purely objective data (including the share of wages in net income), Sraffa showed that the general rate of profits, the rents of land, and the necessary prices corresponding to the given distribution of the product could be determined. This was an important finding in itself, which at the same time served as the basis for a critique of the alternative marginalist conceptualization. In particular, Sraffa showed that the rate of profits cannot generally be conceived of as determined by the "marginal productivity" of a given "quantity of capital."

In the second half of the 1950s Sraffa eventually found time to put together, revise, and complete his notes on the classical approach to the theory of value and distribution and publish them as *Production of Commodities by Means of Commodities* (1960). This book became one of the most often cited books in economics and was translated into several languages. Its findings played an important role in the so-called Cambridge controversies in the theory of capital. The importance of Sraffa's contribution lies in the fact that he pointed out the dark spots in the marginalist theory of value and distribution and elaborated an alternative to it rooted in the analyses of the classical authors.

Sraffa died on September 3, 1983, in Cambridge. An edition of Sraffa's hitherto unpublished papers is currently in preparation on behalf of Cambridge University Press.

BIBLIOGRAPHY

PRIMARY WORKS

Sraffa, Piero. 1925. Sulle relazioni fra costo e quantità prodotta. *Annali di Economia* 2 (1): 277–328. Trans. John Eatwell and Alessandro Roncaglia as On the Relations between Cost and Quantity Produced. In *Italian Economic Papers*, ed. Luigi L. Pasinetti, vol. 3, 323–363. Oxford: Oxford University Press, 1998.

Sraffa, Piero. 1926. The Laws of Returns under Competitive Conditions. *Economic Journal* 36 (144): 535–550.

Sraffa, Piero. 1932. Dr. Hayek on Money and Capital. *Economic Journal* 42 (165): 42–53.

Sraffa, Piero. 1960. *Production of Commodities by Means of Commodities: Prelude to a Critique of Economic Theory.* Cambridge, U.K.: Cambridge University Press.

SECONDARY WORKS

Eatwell, John, and Carlo Panico. 1987. Sraffa, Piero. In *The New Palgrave: A Dictionary of Economics*, eds. John Eatwell, Murray Milgate, and Peter Newman, vol. 4, 445–452. London: Macmillan.

Garegnani, Pierangelo. 1970. Heterogeneous Capital, the Production Function, and the Theory of Distribution. *Review of Economic Studies* 37 (3): 407–436.

Gehrke, Christian, and Heinz D. Kurz. 2002. Keynes and Sraffa's "Difficulties with J. H. Hollander": A Note on the History of the RES Edition of *The Works and Correspondence of David Ricardo. European Journal of the History of Economic Thought* 9 (4): 644–671.

Kurz, Heinz D., ed. 2000. *Critical Essays on Piero Sraffa's Legacy in Economics.* Cambridge, U.K.: Cambridge University Press.

Kurz, Heinz D., and Neri Salvadori. 1995. *Theory of Production.* Cambridge, U.K.: Cambridge University Press.

Kurz, Heinz D., and Neri Salvadori. 2005. Representing the Production and Circulation of Commodities in Material Terms: On Sraffa's Objectivism. *Review of Political Economy* 17 (3): 413–441.

Kurz, Heinz D., and Neri Salvadori, eds. 2003. *The Legacy of Piero Sraffa.* 2 vols. Cheltenham, U.K.: Edward Elgar.

Petty, William. 1986. *The Economic Writings of Sir William Petty.* 2 Vols. Ed. C. H. Hull. Cambridge, U.K.: Cambridge University Press, 1899. Reprinted in one volume, New York: Kelley.

Potier, Jean-Pierre. 1991. *Piero Sraffa, Unorthodox Economist (1898–1983): A Biographical Essay.* London: Routledge.

Ricardo, David. 1951–1973. *The Works and Correspondence of David Ricardo*, ed. Piero Sraffa with the collaboration of Maurice H. Dobb. 11 vols. Cambridge, U.K.: Cambridge University Press.

Heinz D. Kurz

SRAFFIAN ECONOMICS

SEE *Economics, Neo-Ricardian.*

ST. PETERSBURG PARADOX

SEE *Expectations; Utility, Von Neumann-Morgenstern.*

STABILITY, POLITICAL

Political stability can be defined as the reproduction of the status quo in political life. The term and its mirror image—*political instability*—have a decidedly behavioral connotation in most contemporary social science research. As seen by many scholars, political stability is the outcome of interactions by relevant political actors that reproduce the status quo in political life. Conversely, political instability results from interactions that challenge the status quo. To be empirically useful, however, the character of political behavior and whose values or expectations it fulfills (or violates) have to be specified.

The earliest theories of political stability concerned themselves with its societal prerequisites. The prominent sociologist Talcott Parsons (1902–1979) equated political stability with collective legitimacy and the systemic support it afforded. According to Parsons, legitimacy is "the higher normative defense against the breakdown of a system of social order" (Parsons 1963, p. 57). Parsons argued that if citizens did not view the political system as legitimate, they would be particularly prone to support political protest and other forms of antigovernment action. David Easton (b. 1917) further broadened the meaning of legitimacy to include citizen's perceptions of government institutions as fair, responsive, and valuable.

The difference between citizens who viewed the government as illegitimate but did not join in collective action and those who took part in political protest did not figure prominently in Parsons's work. For Parsons, the potential for disorder increased with the loss of public confidence in the government. Likewise, Easton argued, only diffuse support through the population gives the system political stability. In their concern with mass political attitudes, these social scientists went beyond a narrow focus on mass political behavior. Their theories, however, were judged as status quo–oriented and suffused with expectations of political behavior and functional roles characteristic of advanced industrialized democracies.

Beginning in the 1970s, social scientists turned their attention to political institutions and the patterns of political behavior they generate. Work on political stability has linked the durability and survival of political regimes with patterns of political behavior. The literature emphasizes institutional consistency and how it affects the behavior of political elites, but mass political attitudes can be used to explain the choices elites make given particular institutional configurations.

Scholars of political institutions have classified polities based on three attributes: (1) procedures for selecting the chief executive; (2) constraints on executive decision-making authority; and (3) extent of political participation. This classification results in three basic types of political systems: autocracies, anocracies, and democracies. Autocracies are polities where authority is concentrated and unchecked, whereas democracies are polities where power is diffused. According to scholars of political conflict, anocracies are institutional hybrids combining characteristics of both democracy and autocracy.

Fully autocratic and democratic regimes exhibit the greatest stability. This stability results from the compatibility of their institutions with the behavior of politically relevant actors. Institutionally inconsistent regimes (those exhibiting characteristics of both democracy and autocracy) lack these self-enforcing characteristics. Accordingly, the least stable political systems are autocracies with highly regularized procedures for selecting the chief executive and with high levels of political participation. The most unstable configuration for polities with an elected executive is one where the executive is highly constrained, but the electorate is very small.

The conclusions of institutional scholars can be summarized by a curve with an inverted-U shape: low and high levels of institutional development result in political stability; intermediate levels stimulate political instability. Institutions affect the cost-benefit analysis associated with challenges to authority. The interaction of political actors, in other words, is conducive or detrimental to the distribution of authority in a system of governance.

The work of institutional scholars highlights elite interests and behavior. Mass political behavior, as Parsons and Easton demonstrated, is also necessary to understand patterns of political stability. As the expectation that elites will respect the outcomes of democracy increases, the rewards for compliance with the rules of democracy also increase. This is another way of saying that what is important for a political system is whether institutional continuity is in the interest of the relevant political elites. By raising the cost of noncompliance with the democratic rules of the game, the public has a role to play in the cost-benefit analysis of elites.

One question that was not addressed in studies of political stability until the early twenty-first century is the compatibility of leadership survival with regime stability. Scholars have noted the apparent paradox that while democratic polities are durable forms of government, democratic leaders exhibit a high turnover rate. At the same time, autocratic leaders remain in office for remarkably long periods. The puzzle then is why autocrats tend to remain in power longer than democratic leaders even though autocracies as a group are not more stable than democracies.

According to the selectorate theory of political survival, elites and their supporters in stable democracies have more to lose in the long run by clinging on to power and suppressing their political opponents than by waiting for their turn to be (re)elected to office. Consequently, they choose democracy instrumentally and in the process help increase its legitimacy as a form of government. Autocrats, on the other hand, depend on a narrow coalition to win and remain in power and are widely perceived as illegitimate. As a result, democracies constitute a remarkably stable form of regime even though their leaders last half as long as autocrats.

The selectorate theory explains why protest is prevalent in democracies and rebellion predominates in authoritarian regimes. Because democracies are seen as more legitimate forms of government than autocracies, political protest does not level off as a country democratizes. Yet democracies do not have a demonstrable need to repress peaceful or routine protest. By reducing levels of socioeconomic and political inequality, democracies dampen the temptation to engage in rebellion, which is prevalent in authoritarian settings. Finally, democratization creates political opportunities to engage in more conventional forms of collective action, a point the selectorate theory is well equipped to explain.

SEE ALSO *Authoritarianism; Autocracy; Cold War; Democracy; Elections; Parsons, Talcott; Participation, Political; Political Instability, Indices of; Political Science; Political Science, Behavioral; Protest; Revolution*

BIBLIOGRAPHY

Boix, Carles. 2003. *Democracy and Redistribution.* Cambridge, U.K.: Cambridge University Press.

Bueno de Mesquita, Bruce, Alastair Smith, Randolph M. Siverson, and James D. Morrow. 2003. *The Logic of Political Survival.* Cambridge, MA: MIT Press.

Easton, David. 1965. *A System's Analysis of Political Life.* New York: Wiley.

Eckstein, Harry. 1973. Authority Patterns: A Structural Pattern for Inquiry. *American Political Science Review* 47 (December): 1142–1161.

Gates, Scott, Håvard Hegre, Mark P. Jones, and Håvard Strand. 2006. Institutional Inconsistency and Political Instability: Polity Duration, 1800–2000. *American Journal of Political Science* 50 (4): 893–908.

Gurr, Ted Robert. 1974. Persistence and Change in Political Systems, 1800-1971. *American Political Science Review* 68 (December): 1482–1504.

Parsons, Talcott. 1963. Some Reflections on the Place of Force in the Social Process. In *Internal War: Problems and Approaches,* ed. Harry Eckstein. New York: Free Press.

José A. Alemán

STABILITY, PSYCHOLOGICAL

Within any group at every age, human beings vary dramatically among themselves on any given psychological construct, structure, function, or process (let ψ stand for any such entity). It is commonly understood that variation in ψs, whether physical attributes or personality traits, appear in normal distributions in the population. It is important to assess whether differences between individuals in a ψ are fleeting or are stable through time. Thus, psychological science is centrally concerned with assessment of the stability of individual variation. Stability is consistency in the relative standing or rank of individuals in a group on some ψ through time (Figure 1). Stability is particularly pertinent to developmental science and the study of individual variation within a developmental trajectory. An individual with a stable personality trait (say, openness) will display a relatively high level of openness at one point in time vis-à-vis his or her peers and will continue to display a high level at a later point in time, where other individuals display lower levels at both times. Individuals show instability in a given ψ if they do not maintain their relative standing or order in the group through time.

Although developmental science emphasizes overall change and growth, the study of psychological stability is important for several reasons. First, the physiological systems of humans and other living organisms require certain stable conditions—physical, chemical, psychological, and environmental—to survive. These systems also allow for the maintenance of these conditions even in the face of ever-changing circumstances; stability in living organisms is generally in a state of *dynamic* and *adaptive equilibrium.* Second, stability provides basic information about the overall developmental course of a given ψ, insofar as individuals do or do not maintain their standing or order on ψ vis-à-vis others in the group through time. Third, it is generally assumed that to be meaningful, a ψ should show substantial consistency across time: a major predictor of ψ at a given age is ψ at an earlier age. Fourth, psychological stability affects the environment: Interactants often adjust to match a consistent ψ in another individual.

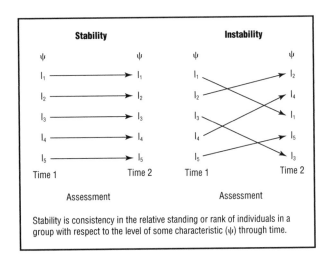

Stability is consistency in the relative standing or rank of individuals in a group with respect to the level of some characteristic (ψ) through time.

Figure 1

Development is governed by genetic and biological factors in combination with environmental influences and experiences. Stability of any ψ could be attributable to genetic or biological factors in the individual, or stability might emerge through the individual's transactions with a consistent environment. Personality traits tend to be stable across time and can serve as examples of a developmentally stable ψ. Current models describe personality as consisting of five factors, openness, neuroticism, extraversion, agreeableness, and conscientiousness. According to this five-factor trait theory, traits are endogenous dispositions that follow intrinsic paths of development essentially independent of environmental influences.

In the context of developmental science, consistency may have many applications and its evaluation may take many different forms. Longitudinal developmental design is requisite to addressing questions about consistency. Furthermore, it is desirable to distinguish between consistency among individuals, or *individual order consistency* (stability/instability), and consistency in a group, or *group mean level consistency* (continuity/discontinuity). Order consistency and mean consistency are independent or orthogonal constructs. Conceptually and empirically, the two can exist simultaneously, and both have been reported in the same longitudinal study of different ψs. Normally, stability is assessed using (Pearson or Spearman) statistical correlation.

It is further desirable to distinguish among types of stability. There are three prominent models of possible temporal association. One model describes *homotypic* (sometimes called *complete*) *stability*: the maintenance of order among individuals in the same ψ through time. This applies to some personality traits; individuals displaying high levels of openness in relation to others at Time 1 will display relatively high levels of openness relative to others at Time 2. A second model describes *heterotypic stability*, which is the maintenance of order among individuals on different manifest ψs through time where the different ψs are theoretically related and presumably share the same latent process (e.g., positive affectivity in personality, say, underlying the traits of openness and sociability). Thus, ψ_a (e.g., openness) at Time 1 relates to ψ_b (e.g., sociability) at Time 2. Models of heterotypic stability typically postulate that some shared ψ_c in the individual underlies stability between ψ_a and ψ_b. A third model of *mediated stability* describes the stability in ψ, or the stability between ψ_a and ψ_b, as explained by a mediating variable ψ_x that is not in the individual but remote from ψ. For example, ψ_a (e.g., openness) at Time 1 relates to ψ_a (e.g., openness) or ψ_b (e.g., sociability) at Time 2 because some ψ_x that is shared with each is itself stable (e.g., a positive environment). This model predicts that, once the contribution of ψ_x is removed, stability in individuals will attenuate.

Stability itself varies, and variation in stability depends on the ψ (some ψs may be more stable than others); on the age of the individual when the stability of ψ is assessed (a ψ may not be stable in infancy, but stabilize in adulthood—people are thought to become increasingly consistent in relation to one another as they age); on the assessment of ψ (the less information about ψ, the lower its stability estimate); on the temporal interval between assessments of ψ (the shorter the interassessment interval, the greater the stability estimate of ψ); and on whether assessments are made across consistent or inconsistent contexts (the former improves stability, and the latter attenuates stability).

Why might stability fail? If a ψ is not stable, there are two possible explanations: Either ψ is not stable, or ψ has not been assessed adequately. Barring measurement imprecision, we attribute instability to genetic and biological as well as environmental and experiential forces. The timing of biological phenomena is partially driven by genetic factors and tends to happen within a specific period of the life course for most people in any particular population. Change also arises because people engage in normative life tasks and roles, such as leaving home, establishing a family, and starting a career. The life span perspective in psychology specifies that human beings are open systems, and the plastic nature of psychological functioning ensures that people exhibit both stability and instability in many ψs throughout the life course.

SEE ALSO *Developmental Psychology; Equilibrium in Psychology; Personality; Psychology; Trait Theory*

BIBLIOGRAPHY

Bornstein, Marc H., Elizabeth Brown, and Alan Slater. 1996. Patterns of Stability and Continuity in Attention across Early Infancy. *Journal of Reproductive and Infant Psychology* 14: 195–206.

Kagan, Jerome. 1971. *Change and Continuity in Infancy*. New York: Wiley.

McCrae, Robert R., and Paul R. Costa Jr. 1999. A Five-Factor Theory of Personality. In *Handbook of Personality: Theory and Research*, ed. Lawrence A. Pervin and Oliver P. John, 139–153. 2nd ed. New York: Guilford.

Roberts, Brent W., and Wendy F. DelVecchio. 2000. The Rank-order Consistency of Personality Traits from Childhood to Old Age: A Quantitative Review of Longitudinal Studies. *Psychological Bulletin* 126: 3–25.

Wohlwill, Joachim F. 1973. *The Study of Behavioral Development*. New York: Academic Press.

Marc H. Bornstein
Lea Bornstein

STABILITY IN ECONOMICS

The concept of stability in economics is closely related to the concept of equilibrium and is one of the three properties of equilibrium that is routinely studied by economic theorists (the others being uniqueness and existence). Economists typically use the term *stability* to denote what mathematicians call *asymptotic stability*. Hence an economic system (such as a firm, a market, or even an entire economy) is stable if, following some displacement of the system from equilibrium, it adjusts so as to regain its original equilibrium position. The concept of stability can be demonstrated by the behavior of a conventional (Marshallian) commodity market, in which supply and demand interact to determine both price and quantity traded. If the price level in such a market is dislodged from its equilibrium (market-clearing) value, the resultant excess demand (or supply) gives rise to subsequent changes in the price level that will restore conditions of equilibrium.

A stable equilibrium may be either a point (such as a particular value of the unemployment rate) or a path (such as a limit cycle describing regular fluctuations in national income). Furthermore, an equilibrium may be either stable or unstable depending on initial disequilibrium conditions. Indeed, if stability is observed only when an economic system is not displaced "too far" from equilibrium, then the system is described as being only locally stable. In economic systems with multiple equilibria, for example, individual equilibrium positions can only be locally stable. If stability is observed regardless of the initial distance from equilibrium, however, the system is said to be globally stable.

Stability is not always regarded as an important or good thing in economic theory. For example, instability is sometimes essential to the motion of the economic system that is being theorized, as in the English economist John Hicks's famous theory of the business cycle. Elsewhere, saddle-point instability is important for solving the problem of the choice of disequilibrium adjustment path in certain models involving rational expectations. Some economists, meanwhile, argue that stability is an unnecessary feature of equilibrium analysis. They suggest that unstable equilibrium models generate the useful empirical claim that the current outcomes of an economic system will *not* persist in the future. Finally, as will become clear in the discussions of path dependence and resilience below, other economists regard stability as an analytical straitjacket that discourages routine exploration of the possibility that economic systems display richer dynamics.

SPEEDS OF ADJUSTMENT AND THE USEFULNESS OF EQUILIBRIUM

This having been said, the prevalence of equilibrium analysis in economic theory means that most economists seek to prove (or, very often, simply assume) the stability of equilibrium most of the time, and with good reason. First, it is essential that an economic system be able to "get into" equilibrium if the latter is to be useful as a description of the actual configuration of the system at any point in time. Second, the method of comparative statics/dynamics, on which so many of the results and policy conclusions of economic theory are based, is predicated on the stability of equilibrium.

The usefulness of equilibrium for describing the outcomes that one might expect to observe in an economic system depends, in fact, not just on stability but also on the speed of disequilibrium adjustment. Unless equilibrium is reached sufficiently rapidly, it may not be interesting as a description of system outcomes over a particular time horizon. Indeed, if adjustment is so slow that the data defining an equilibrium configuration autonomously change before the equilibrium itself is attained, then even an analytically stable equilibrium may never be reached in practice, rendering it meaningless as a description of system outcomes over *any* time horizon. The speed of disequilibrium adjustment is an issue to which economists who rely on equilibrium analysis seldom pay sufficient attention.

STRUCTURAL STABILITY AND PATH DEPENDENCE

The potential for the data defining an equilibrium position to change in the course of disequilibrium adjustment draws attention to two further issues connected with stability in economics. First, a stable economic system must also be structurally stable if it is to attain equilibrium. This means that, over the course of disequilibrium adjustment, the data defining the system must be subject to only small variations that do not fundamentally alter the character of the system's motion (by converting a stable system into an unstable one, for example). Structural stability is rarely addressed by economists, who instead usually assume that data remain literally constant in the course of disequilibrium adjustment.

Second, the adjustment dynamics of a system may be affected by path dependence. A conventional, stable equilibrium can be described as determinate in the sense that it is both defined and reached independently of the path taken toward it. But if disequilibrium adjustment changes the data defining an equilibrium and hence changes the equilibrium configuration itself, then the equilibrium is indeterminate or path-dependent. For example, if disequilibrium trading results in a particular consumption experience that would not have existed in the absence of disequilibrium conditions, and if this experience alters household preferences (a shortage may enhance the perceived desirability of a commodity, for instance), then the exact equilibrium configuration of a Marshallian commodity market will be affected by the history of its disequilibrium adjustment, and will thus be path-dependent. As this example illustrates, an indeterminate or path-dependent economic system may eventually reach an (historically contingent) equilibrium position, in which case it is said to be definite-indeterminate. Such a system may be said to display "weak" stability in the sense that, although its outcomes are path-dependent, a position of equilibrium is eventually attained. This contrasts with the "strong" stability characteristic of determinate systems, which converge onto fixed points or paths defined independently of the system's prior adjustments.

However, an indefinite-indeterminate system will never "settle down" into a state of equilibrium (thus lacking even "weak" stability), but will instead remain in continual, path-dependent motion. A path-dependent equilibrium position may exist at any point in time in an indefinite-indeterminate system, but such positions are continually being redefined and are never reached, so that they never serve as interesting descriptions of the system's outcomes. Note that indeterminacy or path dependence is not the same as instability. The latter involves movement away from a fixed point or path. Path dependence, on the other hand, involves redefinition of the equilibrium point/path in the course of disequilibrium adjustment. In path-dependent systems, an equilibrium may exist and attract the system toward itself. But the equilibrium will be redefined by the resulting motion of the system and, as a consequence of the system thus "chasing a moving target," may never be reached. Unfortunately, economists typically assume away path dependence when dealing with the stability properties of equilibrium models, with the result that any sense of the historical contingency of economic outcomes is lost. Work on hysteresis and lock-in in economics—concepts that show how events in the past can permanently affect current and future economic behavior and outcomes—can be understood as attempting to rectify this state of affairs.

STABILITY OR RESILIENCE

Finally, the behavior of indefinite-indeterminate systems prompts the question as to whether economists should pay more attention in future research to the *resilience* rather than the stability of economic systems. Stability analysis focuses on a precise outcome or configuration of a system, and the capacity of the system to return to this constant point or path over time. The concept of resilience, meanwhile, focuses on the durability of the system itself and hence its capacity for longevity. The key question addressed in the study of resilience is coarser and more qualitative than that addressed by stability analysis: Can the system as a whole reproduce itself in a sufficiently

orderly fashion, and thus persist over time? Hence an indefinite-indeterminate system—which displays neither "weak" nor "strong" stability properties—may nevertheless be very resilient. Whether stability or resilience is the more important property of an economic system is likely context-dependent. For example, if a concert hall is to be economically viable, it may be very important for that hall to ensure that the volume of its public address system remains essentially constant and that any variations in volume are rapidly eliminated by movement back toward equilibrium. However, it may be far more important for an exchange-rate regime to help reproduce orderly conditions of international trade and finance over time, than for it to ensure the movement of a particular exchange rate toward some predefined value identified by economists as an equilibrium.

SEE ALSO *Equilibrium in Economics; Steady State*

BIBLIOGRAPHY

Gandolfo, Giancarlo. 1996. *Economic Dynamics.* 3rd ed. Berlin and New York: Springer.

Hahn, Frank. 1973. *On the Notion of Equilibrium in Economics.* London: Cambridge University Press. Reprinted in Frank Hahn, *Equilibrium and Macroeconomics.* Cambridge, MA: MIT Press, 1984.

Holling, C. S. 1973. Resilience and Stability of Ecological Systems. *Annual Review of Ecology and Systematics* 4: 1–23.

Kaldor, Nicholas. 1934. A Classificatory Note on the Determinateness of Equilibrium. *Review of Economic Studies* 1 (2): 122–136.

Setterfield, M. 1997. Should Economists Dispense with the Notion of Equilibrium? *Journal of Post Keynesian Economics* 20 (1): 47–76.

Mark Setterfield

STABLE NODE

SEE *Node, Stable.*

STAGES OF DEVELOPMENT

Stage theories of development are sometimes called discontinuity theories. The premise is that development occurs in discontinuous stages: During a particular stage, a child will go through no significant changes in his or her abilities or capacities, and behavior will remain fairly stable within that stage. Later development will take the individual to a more mature stage, at which point there is again a kind of stability. This view is in direct contrast to continuity theories, which describe development as a continuous process without stages or phases.

FREUD

Freud presented one of the first stage theories of development, with different components of the personality developing in each. The theory focused on psychosexual development and described five stages: the oral stage, birth to eight months; the anal stage, eight to eighteen months; the phallic stage, eighteen months to six years; the latency stage, six to eleven years; and the genital stage, which is, in a sense, maturity. The id, a reflection of instinct and libido, is all important in the oral stage. The ego develops in the second stage. Both the Electra and Oedipal complexes occur in the third stage, as does the superego and thus the individual's conscience. The latency stage reflects a kind of loss of interest in sexual gratification; more important in this stage is the child's identification between him- or herself and the parent of the same sex. The genital stage allows the individual to develop adult sexual concerns. An individual may develop a fixation that prevents moving from one stage to another; for example, an individual with an oral fixation continues to seek pleasure through the lips and mouth, even as an adult. Various forms of regression may also occur when an individual returns to an earlier, less mature mode of psychic functioning.

ERIKSON

Although Freud's theory has been widely criticized and has remained the subject of much debate, its impact on subsequent developmental psychologists and clinicians is beyond doubt. Erik Erikson, the German developmental psychologist, studied with but then broke away from Freud to develop his own stage theory. Whereas Freud emphasized childhood and preadolescent development, Erikson's theory covers the life span, with eight stages; whereas Freud's psychosexual theory emphasized the libido and its expression in the different stages of development, Erikson's psychosocial theory emphasized the social environment. Each stage is characterized by a conflict or crisis, and each crisis has its origin in the interaction between the individual and the social environment. For example, in the first stage the crisis involves trust versus mistrust; Erikson felt that the individual must learn to trust others and him- or herself to develop a healthy personality. The eighth and final stage involves the crisis of integrity versus despair.

PIAGET

The most commonly cited cognitive stage theory was developed by the Swiss psychologist Jean Piaget. Piaget described four stages of development, each of which involves an idiosyncratic kind of thinking. Movement through these stages is typically completed sometime during adolescence. The first stage, the *sensorimotor*, lasts approximately two years, during which time the individual's cognition is processing only sensory and motoric information; he or she does not think beyond the here and now and cannot contemplate anything abstract or hypothetical. The individual adapts to the environment through the processes of *assimilation* (the individual manipulates information such that he or she can think about it and perhaps adapt to it) and *accommodation* (the individual's cognitive structures change in response to the experiences). Piaget used this adaptive process to explain all cognitive growth, deeming other kinds of what he termed *learning* superficial, almost a kind of memorization. Adaptation, on the other hand, requires a change in the individual's cognitive structures, and this depends on the adaptive process.

In the second stage, the *preoperational*, approximately ages two to seven, the individual moves beyond the here and now but still is not capable of cognitively operating on information. The third stage is the *concrete operational*, approximately ages seven to eleven, in which children begin to apply logical thinking to concrete events and objects. The fourth and final stage is the *formal operational*, from about age eleven on, at which point individuals are, for Piaget, "little scientists": they can take a number of variables into account when making logical decisions, and sometimes they are even scientific in the sense of reasoning about certain factors in isolation. The formal operator is, for Piaget, cognitively mature and able to apply logic to hypothetical (not just concrete) things, to reason sociocentrically (not egocentrically), and to think about various propositions. The formal operator also can be very effective with deductive logic. Piaget described how thinking in a deductive fashion (rather than relying on the less mature forms of transductive or inductive thought) depends on and supports hypothetical thinking. He referred to them as one process, the hypothetico-deductive process.

Several neo-Piagetians have proposed fifth and sixth stages of development in an effort to describe cognitive changes occurring in adulthood. Neo-Piagetians have also pointed to other skills, including *relativistic thinking*, a *problem-finding* capacity, and *dialectical thinking*. The first of these implies that the individual does not think in black and white or absolutes. The second implies that the individual not only can solve problems logically but can also identify them and define them in a manner that allows creative solution. The third, an ability to accept and reason dialectically, allows the individual to accept a thesis as well as its antithesis and integrate them, the result being a useful synthesis.

Piaget recognized that stages do not develop without particular experiences. They are dependent on genetic potentials, and indeed Piaget referred to his theory as a genetic epistemology. Epistemology is the study of knowledge; but by genetics Piaget was referring not to the chemical makeup of life—he was writing before technologies existed for the identification of genes themselves—but rather to the biological basis for development, and to potential. But adaptation is necessary for development. This is very important because it implies that individuals will not necessarily move through these stages; they move through them only when they are biologically ready and have had appropriate experiences. These experiences must challenge an individual and elicit adaptations.

In contrast to stage theories, continuity theories hold that development occurs unrestricted by stages. Learning theories reflect continuity theories, for they typically suggest that individuals have a stable potential to learn: the more experience one has, the more mature and capable the individual will become. In stage theories, biological or perhaps psychological factors interact with experience such that individuals can benefit from experience only if they are ready to do so.

SEE ALSO *Adolescent Psychology; Child Development; Erikson, Erik; Freud, Sigmund; Maturation; Oedipus Complex; Personality; Piaget, Jean; Psychology; Sexuality*

BIBLIOGRAPHY

Arlin, P. K. 1975. Cognitive Development in Adulthood: A Fifth Stage? *Developmental Psychology* 11: 602–606.

Erikson, Erik H. 1993. Childhood and Society. New York: Norton.

Freud, Sigmund, and James Strachey. [1923] 1962. *The Ego and the Id.* New York: Norton.

Piaget, Jean. 1962. Play, Dreams and Imitation in Childhood. New York: Norton.

Piaget, Jean. 1970. Piaget's Theory. In *Carmichael's Handbook of Child Psychology*, ed. Paul H. Mussen, 3rd ed., 703–732. New York: Wiley.

Piaget, Jean. 1976. *To Understand Is to Invent: The Future of Education.* Trans. George-Anne Roberts. New York: Penguin.

Mark A. Runco

STAGES OF ECONOMIC GROWTH

The attempt to search for a common set of general stages in the historical development of nations and their economies goes back to Adam Smith, who defined four stages of societal organization: the original stage of hunters, a second stage of "shepherds" or nomadic agriculture, a third stage of feudal "farming agriculture," and a fourth and final stage of commercial society.

The most commonly accepted set of stages are those postulated by Walt Whitman Rostow, who in *The Stages of Economic Growth* (1960) proposed the stages as a general model of economic change. Rostow's model assumes that it is possible that all societies during their development appear in one of five stages of economic development: the traditional society, the preconditions for takeoff, the takeoff, the drive to maturity, and the age of high mass-consumption. While this discussion will only consider the economic dimension of the stages, Rostow also outlined non-economic social, political, cultural, and psychological factors. However, in the classification of particular countries' development, he emphasized the economic factors.

DEFINITIONS OF ROSTOW'S STAGES

The first stage, the traditional economy, is characterized only by basic industries: agriculture and mining. The economy is unproductive, society is based on pre-Newtonian science and technology, and the labor force is unskilled. The attainable level of output per capita is limited. The second stage of growth, the preconditions for takeoff, finds economies in the process of transition, as the traditional society starts to exploit the results of modern science. While the society can still mainly be characterized by traditional low-productivity, there are already productivity improvements in agriculture and extractive industries that create savings that can be invested in infrastructure. The supportive role of government is very important at this stage. During the third stage, the "takeoff" stage, the rates of productive investment and saving rise further and new industries grow rapidly, using new techniques of production. The process of industrialization is driven by the leading sectors of industry, such as railroads and steel, and stimulates the growth of other industries. The fast growth of productivity in agriculture is an important condition for successful takeoff. The economy and its social and political structure are transformed so that the growth can be sustained. After the takeoff stage, as new and more advanced industries develop and modern technology is applied to all industries, the economy enters the fourth stage, the drive to maturity. The fifth and final stage of growth is that of high mass-consumption, when all the leading sectors move toward durable consumer goods and services and the service sector experiences rapid growth. The most developed countries, like the United States, are now considered to be in this stage.

Rostow tried to establish a general "theory" of development, based on a dynamic neoclassical theory of production. He did not, however, provide a formal "model" of the stages, but only a set of narrative descriptions, so that the result was "less a theory than a language" (Supple 1984, p. 114). Rostow "linked theoretical constructs (like production functions, capital-output ratios, propensities to invest and to consume) to the dynamics and narrative of historical change, and acknowledged the vital significance of sociopolitical attitudes, groupings, and discontinuities" (Supple 1984, p. 108).

Rostow presented and described empirical and historical evidence for the most advanced countries, especially Great Britain, to support the view that the modern development of these countries had gone through the same stages. This work gave impetus to more careful, longer-term empirical research that ultimately failed to support Rostow's conclusions—for example, it failed to "identify a takeoff in the economic history of countries such as France" (Crafts 2001, p. 308).

Aside from these theoretical criticisms, there were more general criticisms that may also be applied to current-day economic theories of growth and development. According to Edward S. Mason (1982), principal flaws include an overemphasis on discontinuity in historical processes, the teleological character of the conception of development, and problematic generalizations of political processes. R. de Oliveira Campos (1982) criticizes the presumption of the universality of economic motivations and of the inevitability of growth, without any space for economic decline and reversals. For W. Arthur Lewis (1982), what is missing is the crucial role of institutions; for Douglass C. North and Peter Temin (1982), it is the concept of transaction costs. Despite all these criticisms, Rostow's stages of growth undoubtedly contributed to or at least were consonant with the early thinking about economic development as a process, and concepts such as the *takeoff* or *leading sectors* have been accepted by the profession. As Supple remarks, "even Rostow's critics adopt his terminology" (1984, p. 108).

STAGES OF ENDOGENOUS GROWTH

Rostow's stages of growth have stimulated recent attempts in the field of growth theory to construct more general formal models able to capture the behavior of developed and less-developed economies. One of the first such models was developed by Costas Azariadis and Allan Drazen (1990), who used the endogenous growth model with human capital as an engine of growth, an approach first suggested by Robert Lucas (1988), but amended it by adding "threshold" externalities in the human capital sector. Such a model exhibited two steady states: the regime of the zero-growth, underdevelopment trap, and the regime of sustained growth. When the underdeveloped economy manages to accumulate a critical amount of human capital, it reaches an area of increasing returns stimulating even more investment in human capital, and the economy takes off into sustained growth. By explicitly modeling knowledge-diffusion, Fabrizio Zilibotti (2005) in the AK model and Michal Kejak (2003) in Lucas's model construct a model able to exhibit different stages of growth. (Mentioned here are only a handful of the numerous growth models with multiple steady states, as many of the others are not linked to Rostow's stages of growth.)

UNIFIED THEORY OF GROWTH AND DEVELOPMENT

Growth-theory literature on models with multiple steady states laid the grounds for the establishment of a "unified" theory of growth and development that aims to capture in a single unified framework the era of Malthusian stagnation, the modern stage of sustained growth, and the transition between these two regimes—industrial revolution. Lucas (2002) offers such a model of the industrial revolution, in which human capital serves as an engine of sustained growth. An important part of this model's mechanics is a Beckerian trade-off between the quantity and quality of the children responsible for demographic transition. A similar model with non-homothetic preferences is presented by Oded Galor and David N. Weil (2000). An alternative model of the industrial revolution in which new ideas are seen as an engine of growth can be found in the work of Charles I. Jones (2001). An even simpler model with exogenous growth in technology improvements is presented in works by Gary D. Hansen and Edward C. Prescott (2002) and Stephen L. Parente and Prescott (2004).

POLITICAL AND POLICY CONSEQUENCES

Rostow wrote *The Stages of Economic Growth* as an "Anticommunist Manifesto" (to quote the book's subtitle)—that is, as a liberal's reply to Marxist analysis (Solivetti 2005). He considered those societies in the transition from a traditional to a modern state especially vulnerable to communist development, which he calls "a disease of transition." Rostow's aim was to offer an attractive and achievable means of development for less-developed countries, as an alternative to dependency theory and development toward communism.

The ideological and political consequences of Rostow's stages of growth can best be guessed from his own political and policy-making activities. After publishing *The Stages*, he became an adviser to the American presidents John F. Kennedy and Lyndon B. Johnson and later the chairman of the policy Planning Council at the State Department. Rostow's theory "became a cornerstone in American international policy towards the Third World" (Solivetti 2005, p. 722).

The only policy recommendation derived from Rostow's stages of growth has been the principle that take-off into "self-sustained growth" requires a large increase in investment. Unfortunately, aside from the Marshall Plan for the reconstruction of Western Europe after World War II, this policy has not been successful in dealing with underdeveloped economies. As William Easterly (2001) points out—according to Solow's original insight—"capital fundamentalism" has failed to advance growth in poor countries. The foreign aid based on "financing the gap" has not delivered any results, and it has created wrong economic incentives.

Recent achievements in the unified theory of growth and development, besides contributing to a better explanation of past economic development, have also created strong claims for the effects of government policies on economic development. Despite the fact that empirical work on policies and growth, embodied mainly in cross-country growth regressions, has tended to confirm these claims, real-world experience has not satisfied expectations. In recent debates over this failure several shortcomings have been identified. In empirical studies on growth, it has been claimed, the conventional approach suffers from several statistical problems (Durlauf 2002), results are often driven by extreme observations (Easterly 2005), and there are nonlinear interactions between policy and growth once institutions are controlled for (Aghion and Howitt 2006). Furthermore, most existing theoretical development models ignore the informal sector (Easterly 2005) and/or do not properly model technological change (Aghion and Howitt 2006).

SEE ALSO *Capitalism; Communism; Development Economics; Economic Growth; Investment; Stagflation; Stagnation*

BIBLIOGRAPHY

Aghion, Philippe, and Peter Howitt. 2006. Appropriate Growth Policy: A Unifying Framework. Joseph Schumpeter Lecture. *Journal of European Economic Association* 4 (2–3): 269–314.

Azariadis, Costas, and Allan Drazen. 1990. Threshold Externalities in Economic Development. *Quarterly Journal of Economics* 105 (2): 501–526.

Campos, R. de Oliveira. 1982. Take-Off and Breakdown. In *Models and Methodology*, Vol. 1 of *Economics in the Long View: Essays in Honour of W. W. Rostow*, ed. Charles P. Kindleberger and Guido di Tella. London: Macmillan.

Crafts, Nicholas. 2001. Historical Perspectives on Development. In *Frontiers of Development Economics: The Future in Perspective*, eds. Gerald M. Meier and Joseph E. Stiglitz, 301–334. Oxford and New York: Oxford University Press.

Durlauf, Steven N. 2002. Policy Evaluation and Empirical Growth Research. In *Economic Growth: Sources, Trends, and Cycles*, eds. Norman Loayza and Raimundo Soto, 163–190. Santiago: Central Bank of Chile.

Easterly, William. 2001. *The Elusive Quest for Growth: Economists' Adventures and Misadventures in the Tropics.* Cambridge, MA: MIT Press.

Easterly, William. 2005. National Policies and Economic Growth: A Reappraisal. In *Handbook of Economic Growth*, vol. 1, eds. Philippe Aghion and Steven Durlauf, 1015–1059. Amsterdam: Elsevier.

Galor, Oded, and David N. Weil. 2000. Population, Technology, and Growth: From the Malthusian Regime to the Demographic Transition. *American Economic Review* 90 (4): 806–828.

Hansen, Gary D., and Edward C. Prescott. 2002. Malthus to Solow. *American Economic Review* 92 (4): 1205–1217.

Jones, Charles I. 2001. Was an Industrial Revolution Inevitable? Economic Growth over the Very Long Run. *Advances in Macroeconomics* 1 (2): 1–43.

Kejak, Michal. 2003. Stages of Growth in Economic Development. *Journal of Economic Dynamics and Control* 27 (5): 771–800.

Kindleberger, Charles P., and Guido di Tella, eds. 1982. *Models and Methodology.* Vol. 1 of *Economics in the Long View: Essays in Honour of W. W. Rostow*. London: Macmillan.

Lewis, W. Arthur. 1982. The Growth of Mature Economies. In *Models and Methodology*, Vol. 1 of *Economics in the Long View: Essays in Honour of W. W. Rostow*, eds. Charles P. Kindleberger and Guido di Tella. London: Macmillan.

Lucas, Robert E., Jr. 1988. On the Mechanics of Economic Development. *Journal of Monetary Economics* 22 (1): 3–42.

Lucas, Robert E., Jr. 2002. *Lectures on Economic Growth.* Cambridge, MA: Harvard University Press.

Mason, Edward S. 1982. The Stages of Growth Revisited. In *Models and Methodology*, Vol. 1 of *Economics in the Long View: Essays in Honour of W. W. Rostow*, eds. Charles P. Kindleberger and Guido di Tella. London: Macmillan.

North, Douglass C., and Peter Temin. 1982. The Theoretical Tools of the Economic Historian. In *Models and Methodology*, Vol. 1 of *Economics in the Long View: Essays in Honour of W. W. Rostow*, eds. Charles P. Kindleberger and Guido di Tella. London: Macmillan.

Parente, Stephen L., and Edward C. Prescott. 2004. A Unified Theory of the Evolution of International Income Levels. Research Department Staff Report 333. Minneapolis, MN: Federal Reserve Bank of Minneapolis.

Rostow, W. W. 1960. *The Stages of Economic Growth: A Non-Communist Manifesto.* Cambridge, U.K.: Cambridge University Press.

Solivetti, Luigi M. 2005. W. W. Rostow and His Contribution to Development Studies: A Note. *Journal of Development Studies* 41 (4): 719–724.

Supple, Barry. 1984. Revisiting Rostow. *Economic History Review*, new series, 37 (1): 107–114.

Zilibotti, Fabrizio. 2005. A Rostovian Model of Endogenous Growth and Underdevelopment Traps. *European Economic Review* 39 (8): 1569–1602.

Michal Kejak

STAGFLATION

Two main yardsticks of a modern economy's performance are the rate of growth in the production of goods and services and the inflation rate. When the production of goods and services is growing slowly or is falling (generally accompanied by a rising unemployment rate), stagnation occurs. When the prices of goods and services are rising, inflation occurs. *Stagflation*, a term attributed to the British politician Iain Macleod, refers to a situation in which an economy experiences stagnation and inflation simultaneously.

As recently as the 1960s, the conventional wisdom in macroeconomics was that inflation and stagnation could not appear at the same time. Economists generally believed that there was a stable, inverse relationship between the rate of inflation (the percentage change in the average level of prices) and the unemployment rate (the percentage of the labor force that is unemployed) as illustrated by the Phillips curve, made famous by the New Zealand economist A. W. H. Phillips (1914–1975). The Phillips curve presented policymakers with a trade-off: They could lower unemployment by stimulating demand but at the cost of higher inflation; or they could lower inflation but at the cost of higher unemployment. Policy discussions in the 1960s centered on which point on the Phillips curve was most desirable.

Consistent with the Phillips curve trade-off, the 1960s saw inflation in the United States increase and unemployment decline, with the unemployment rate falling to 3.5 percent by 1969 while inflation rose to 6.2 percent. In 1970, however, the unemployment rate increased substantially to 4.9 percent with little decrease in inflation. This was the start of a dismal decade for the large industrialized economies. As a whole, the Group of Seven (the seven largest capitalist economies) saw inflation double and real growth halve compared to the 1960s. This experience of relatively high inflation, slow growth, and high unemployment kindled interest in the causes of stagflation.

EXPLANATIONS FOR STAGFLATION

Economists developed two explanations for stagflation in industrialized economies. The first sees stagflation as a phase in an economic cycle that begins with excessive growth in spending, typically fueled by higher-than-normal growth in the money supply. Initially the growth in spending causes prices to rise and, in response, firms to expand production and employment so that the economy experiences higher inflation and lower unemployment. As argued by the American economists Milton Friedman (1912–2006) and Edmund S. Phelps (b. 1933), the decline in unemployment results from the higher inflation being unexpected so that real wages (i.e., wages adjusted for inflation) fall. Lower real wages lead workers to demand higher real wages, commensurate with higher expected inflation, in the second phase of the economic cycle, causing the unemployment rate to rise back toward what Friedman called the natural rate of unemployment, the level of unemployment that occurs when actual and expected inflation are equal.

The first explanation fits the U.S. stagflation of 1970. According to this view, the rising inflation of the 1960s caused expected inflation to increase, shifting the Phillips curve up in 1970, with the result that inflation remained high while the unemployment rate rose. The U.S. wage-price controls of the early 1970s were an attempt to lower expected inflation and shift the Phillips curve downward, in the hope of reducing inflation without having to increase unemployment.

The second explanation for stagflation focuses on autonomous events that make production more expensive and cause firms to raise their prices. This view is more relevant to the general stagflation of the later 1970s, the source of which is thought to have been the large increases in oil prices in 1973 and 1979. Given that energy is an important component of most goods, a large increase in energy prices increases the costs of production for most firms. Firms are willing to supply the same level of output only if their prices rise. The oil price increase is referred to as an *aggregate supply shock*. It triggers firms to raise prices and lower output. An adverse supply shock such as a large increase in energy prices shifts the Phillips curve upward and again results in both inflation and rising unemployment.

Not all economists believe that the stagflation of the later 1970s can be blamed on oil prices. Robert B. Barsky and Lutz Kilian (2002), for example, believe the first explanation holds for this episode too. They argue that the stagflation occurred largely because policymakers believed the natural rate of unemployment was lower than it actually was, leading them to overstimulate spending in a misguided attempt to push down the unemployment rate. The explanations are not mutually exclusive so that both may have contributed to the stagflation of the 1970s. An adverse supply shock should not cause sustained higher inflation unless accompanied by higher rates of growth in the money supply.

Developing countries, particularly in Latin America, have often suffered bouts of stagflation. An alternative explanation for stagflation in such economies focuses on the macroeconomic effects of exchange rate devaluations, as analyzed for example by Paul Krugman and Lance Taylor (1978). Most developing economies have fixed nominal exchange rates. If there is a balance of payments deficit, international agencies often prescribe a devaluation of the currency in order to reduce trade deficits. Such devaluations, however, may lead to short-run decreases in output along with higher inflation. Given rigidity in nominal wage rates and prices marked up from costs, the devaluation can result in reduced domestic aggregate demand because of the redistribution of income away from labor, which is assumed to have a higher marginal propensity to spend. Domestic demand can also fall from the decline in real money holdings as prices rise in response to higher import costs and from the increase in ad valorem taxes on imports. Thus devaluations can lead to periods of stagflation.

POLICY RESPONSES

The appropriate policy response to stagflation depends on its cause. If the stagflation is the result of policy-initiated excessive stimulation of spending so that the unemployment rate falls below the natural rate initially and then rises along with inflationary expectations, policymakers need to admit their error and to convince people that they should not build higher inflation rates into contracts. The problem, of course, is that people will be skeptical, so that the policymakers will need to establish credibility that they are truly adverse to inflation.

The suitable response to stagflation caused by aggregate supply shocks is less clear. One response is to do nothing and let the economy adjust as best it can to the shock. If energy prices will be permanently higher, the economy needs to make the changes to the new environment. The likely outcome is a short burst of inflation and a rise in unemployment followed by a gradual return to lower unemployment and stable prices. If energy price increases are temporary, policymakers may choose either to reduce the unemployment effects (by stimulating spending and increasing inflation) or to reduce the inflation effects (by restricting spending and increasing unemployment). The latter choice was the one taken by the administration of Gerald R. Ford after the 1973 oil price shock when it tightened monetary and fiscal policy in 1974 and exhorted households to cut spending as part of President Ford's famous "Whip Inflation Now" (WIN) campaign. The result was a large increase in unemployment with a peak unemployment rate of 8.5 percent in 1975.

Beginning in the early 1990s, inflation targeting by central banks has been advocated as a solution to the first cause of stagflation. If adopted, however, this policy will make the unemployment effects of supply shocks more severe because the response of policymakers will be to reduce spending growth in order to slow the inflation rate. A flexible inflation target that allows for short-run bursts of inflation from supply shocks is one possible remedy.

SEE ALSO *Inflation; Phillips Curve; Recession; Unemployment*

BIBLIOGRAPHY

Barsky, Robert B., and Lutz Kilian. 2002. Do We Really Know That Oil Caused the Great Stagflation? A Monetary Alternative. In *NBER Macroeconomics Annual 2001*, eds. Ben S. Bernanke and Kenneth Rogoff, 137–182. Cambridge, MA: MIT Press.

Blinder, Alan S. 1979. *Economic Policy and the Great Stagflation.* New York: Academic Press.

Bruno, Michael, and Jeffrey D. Sachs. 1985. *Economics of Worldwide Stagflation.* Cambridge, MA: Harvard University Press.

Krugman, Paul, and Lance Taylor. 1978. Contractionary Effects of Devaluation. *Journal of International Economics* 8 (3): 445–456.

Douglas K. Pearce

STAGNATION

Stagnation is a condition of an economy in which its rate of total output, or per capita output growth, is at—or close to—zero for a relatively long period of time. (Sometimes the term is applied to particular sectors, but in this entry it refers to the entire economy.) Stagnation is sometimes characterized by high rates of unemployment. It can be distinguished from other terms such as *recession* or *depression*, which usually refer to periods of low or even negative rates of growth but which are relatively short-lived phases of the business cycle. If stagnation is accompanied by high inflation, the phenomenon is called *stagflation* (although this may sometimes merely be a phase of the business cycle). The term *stagnation* is used both for economically advanced countries that have experienced growth in the past and have a high level of per capita income and for less-developed countries that have failed to grow.

The analysis of stagnation in this economic sense, as well as in broader terms, has a long history. The fourteenth-century Arab scholar Ibn Khaldun discussed the tendency of empires and societies to stagnate due to the erosion of solidarity and the spread of habits of luxury among rulers. In the twentieth century, this broad view about the rise and inevitable decline of civilizations was pursued by German philosopher Oswald Spengler (1880–1936), who analyzed stagnation in terms of factors like the domination of politics by the power of money and the concentration of populations in "barrack-cities" that turn people into mobs susceptible to demaguery. This view was also explored by historian Arnold Toynbee (1889–1975), who examined how mature civilizations, due to the "intractability of institutions," for instance, are unable to respond appropriately to challenges and therefore suffer stagnation. Heavy tax burdens and the corruption and excessive luxury of the ruling classes have often been highlighted in historical studies of stagnation. Stagnation in precapitalist countries was attributed by Adam Smith (1723–1790) to inadequate laws and institutions and to the neglect of foreign trade. Broad analyses of the problems of less-developed countries explain stagnation in terms of political and social factors. For instance, those enjoying political power and doing well outside of the economy are argued to be unwilling to makes changes to institutions and policies that are likely to worsen their own positions.

In more narrowly economic terms, stagnation in advanced economies has been explained both in terms of supply-side and demand-side factors. Factors on the supply side were stressed in the classical theory of the stationary state. In David Ricardo's (1772–1823) analysis of the growth process, as more capital is accumulated and more workers are hired, the demand for food to be consumed by workers increases, which drives agricultural production onto increasingly less fertile land, increasing the competition for land, driving up land rent, and reducing the profits out of which capital is accumulated, which eventually brings capital accumulation to a halt. While Ricardo may have underestimated the extent to which diminishing returns to agriculture can be offset by technological improvements, the main reason for his stationary state—that is, diminishing returns—continues to be stressed. In Robert M. Solow's 1956 model, for instance, as capital is accumulated, diminishing returns to capital set in to make saving and investment sufficient only to keep the capital-labor ratio constant, which implies a constant level of per capita income, unless exogenous technological change makes per capita output grow. The assumption of diminishing productivity of capital and other produced inputs has more recently fallen into disfavor, with empirical evidence suggesting that technological change and external economies can defeat the effects of diminishing returns, as usually assumed in new growth theory models. But structural changes increasing the weight of technologically lagging service sectors and environmental constraints remain possible causes of stagnation.

For the demand side, it was argued by John Maynard Keynes (1883–1946) that, in advanced economies, saving as a ratio of output tends to rise with increasing output and income as consumer wants are increasingly satiated, while investment incentives progressively decline with capital accumulation. With lower rates of investment and consumption, aggregate demand declines, and the rate of growth of output slows. These insights were used by Alvin Hansen (1887–1975) to develop a theory of U.S. stagnation in the 1930s due to inadequate aggregate demand. Subsequent events have shown that government aggregate demand policy can rescue economies from deficient aggregate demand and that there seems to be no inherent tendency for satiation in consumption. Nevertheless, governments may be unable or unwilling for political reasons to solve the problem of demand deficiency, and structural changes rather than any inherent tendency for consumption demand to become satiated may continue to make demand factors relevant. Josef Steindl (1912–1993) argued that the rise of monopoly power made possible by increasing industrial concentration tends to increase profit markups, which tends to increase saving in the economy, leading to a reduction in aggregate demand, a decline in capacity utilization, and a consequent decline in investment. Paolo Sylos-Labini (1920–2005) stressed problems created by the growth of oligopoly on the nature and consequences of technological change, which tended to increase profit margins of large firms and reduce aggregate demand.

Explanations of stagnation in less-developed countries sometimes focus on the demand side, for instance, stressing the absence of investment incentives due to the small size of markets and the high levels of uncertainty caused by external and internal shocks, and sometimes the supply side, emphasizing low saving and productivity. Many of the explanations invoke the concept of the vicious circle, according to which low per capita income, through a variety of channels, implies its persistence (see Nurkse 1953; Leibenstein 1957). The plethora of such mechanisms under discussion, in addition to low saving and investment incentives, include: poor nutrition and health and low productivity; low income, absence of collateral, and the inability to borrow and finance economic projects; and poverty, child labor, and low levels of education and human capital accumulation. More recently, vicious circles have been related to poor institutions, governance, corruption, and violence. Low levels of income may make corruption and violence more attractive, leading to poor economic performance. Some approaches examine how increases in per capita income may set off forces that lead to subsequent declines. Examples of such mechanisms include increases in population caused by better living conditions, which reduce per capita income; increases in consumption from very low levels when income increases; and the inability to adopt increasing-returns technologies that require a minimum size of the market (see Azariadis and Stachurski 2005). These mechanisms produce low-level poverty traps: if per capita income is initially below a critical minimum level, the economy will converge to a poverty trap, whereas if the economy happens to attain a level beyond that critical minimum, it sets off into self-sustained growth.

The newer approaches suggest that stagnation is not inevitable for advanced economies, and poor countries can escape from their low-level traps under certain circumstances. However, these approaches also suggest that broader political, social, and institutional factors emphasized in earlier approaches have continued relevance insofar as they interact with more narrowly defined economic factors in explaining stagnation.

SEE ALSO *Depression, Economic; Great Depression; Macroeconomics; Macroeconomics, Structuralist; Recession; Stagflation*

BIBLIOGRAPHY

Azariadis, Costas, and John Stachurski. 2005. Poverty Traps. In *Handbook of Economic Growth*, Vol. 1A, eds. Philippe Aghion and Steven Durlauf, 295–384. Amsterdam: Elsevier.

Hansen, Alvin. 1938. *Full Recovery or Stagnation?* New York: Norton.

Ibn Khaldun. [1375–1382] 1958. *The Muqaddimah: An Introduction to History*, 3 vols. Trans. Franz Rosenthal. New York: Pantheon.

Leibenstein, Harvey. 1957. *Economic Backwardness and Economic Growth: Studies in the Theory of Economic Development*. New York: Wiley.

Nurkse, Ragnar. 1953. *Problems of Capital Formation in Underdeveloped Countries*. Oxford: Oxford University Press.

Ricardo, David. [1817] 1962. *The Principles of Political Economy and Taxation*. Cambridge, U.K.: Cambridge University Press.

Smith, Adam. [1776] 1976. *An Inquiry into the Nature and Causes of the Wealth of Nations*. 2 vols. Oxford: Oxford University Press.

Solow, Robert M. 1956. A Contribution to the Theory of Economic Growth. *Quarterly Journal of Economics* 70 (1): 65–94.

Spengler, Oswald. 1926–1928. *The Decline of the West*. Trans. Charles Francis Atkinson. New York: Knopf.

Steindl, Josef. 1952. *Maturity and Stagnation in American Capitalism*. Oxford: Blackwell.

Sylos-Labini, Paolo. 1962. *Oligopoly and Technical Progress*. Trans. Elizabeth Henderson. Cambridge, U.K.: Cambridge University Press.

Toynbee, Arnold J. 1934–1961. *A Study of History*. Oxford: Oxford University Press.

Amitava Krishna Dutt

STAKEHOLDERS

Stakeholders are constituencies who are affected, voluntarily or involuntarily, by the actions taken by an organi-

zation, such as a corporation. Commonly cited examples of corporate stakeholders are employees, financial intermediaries, shareholders, customers, and suppliers, all of whom are affected by, respectively, a firm's compensation and hiring decisions, investment choices, dividend and share repurchase policies, product-related issues, and material purchases. The term, however, is often more broadly applied to include local, state, and federal governments because firms pay taxes and use public resources; it can also be extended to include the local community because firms interact with the natural environment and engage in philanthropic activities; and furthermore, because many firms operate on an international scale, it may even include the global community.

Stakeholders may raise issues of concern with corporations and suggest actions that corporations should take. For example, if shareholders are concerned that a corporation is holding too much money, they may argue for increased dividends. Constituents from a local community concerned with air quality may urge a corporation to invest in cleaner technologies. Even though they are not legally required to do so, corporations may consider and implement stakeholders' ideas because they provide a host of resources to corporations. Lenders and shareholders make financial resources available, employees and suppliers provide physical inputs, governments supply regulatory oversight, and citizens contribute to the social environment in which operations occur. In short, a corporation cannot exist without the support of a diverse set of stakeholders.

A corporation must consider the principles of stakeholder theory or stakeholder management when it decides which stakeholders to acknowledge and how to best respond to their often incompatible requests. The notion of stakeholders originated in the mid-1960s, but it was in the 1980s that, as evidenced by Edward Freeman's 1984 book *Strategic Management*, the idea of stakeholder management began to gain ground in the field of economics. Stakeholder theory represents a significant departure from the older principal-agent view of the firm, which effectively recognizes shareholders as the only legitimate constituency by nature of their ownership position. Stakeholder theory, in contrast, understands the corporation in law and in practice as more than an extension of shareholders with narrow, well-defined goals. Rather, the corporation is viewed as its own entity with its own rights and obligations. As the trustees of the firm, usually its board of directors, are responsible for the firm, they can and should serve other constituencies for the benefit of the corporation. Furthermore, in practice, the distinction between shareholders' and other stakeholders' concerns may not be so clearly defined: Shareholders themselves are often employees, consumers, and residents in the communities where corporations operate. Consequently, as James

Hawley and Andrew Williams argue in their 2000 study *The Rise of Fiduciary Capitalism*, shareholders may not be best served by the maximization of the share price alone and may be more concerned with a firm's employment opportunities, quality of goods, and impact on the environment.

It is not clear which stakeholders will most benefit and what changes in corporate activities are likely to result when corporations acknowledge them. The outcomes could range from managerial opportunism, as Michael Jensen notes in his 2000 article "Value Maximization, Stakeholder Theory, and the Corporation Objective Function," to economic democracy, as Paul Hirst suggests in his 1997 essay "From the Economic to the Political," and anything in between these extremes. In any case, the concept of stakeholders greatly broadens the theorization of the corporation in terms of its governance, objectives, and conditions of existence.

BIBLIOGRAPHY

Freeman, R. Edward. 1984. *Strategic Management: A Stakeholder Approach*. Boston: Pitman.

Hawley, James P., and Andrew T. Williams. 2000. *The Rise of Fiduciary Capitalism: How Institutional Investors Can Make Corporate America More Democratic*. Philadelphia: University of Pennsylvania Press.

Hirst, Paul. 1997. From the Economic to the Political. In *Stakeholder Capitalism*, eds. Gavin Kelly, Dominic Kelly, and Andrew Gamble, 63–71. Houndmills, Basingstoke, U.K.: Macmillan, and New York: St. Martins.

Jensen, Michael C. 2002. Value Maximization, Stakeholder Theory, and the Corporation Objective Function. *Business Ethics Quarterly* 12 (2): 235–256.

David M. Brennan

STALIN, JOSEPH
1878–1953

Joseph Stalin (Ioseb Jughashvili) was born in the Georgian town of Gori on December 6, 1878. The son of a shoemaker, he rose through the Russian revolutionary movement to become the unchallenged leader of the Soviet Union. He adopted the name "Stalin" from the Russian word *stal'* (steel) and advanced through the Bolshevik ranks after the movement's leader, Vladimir Lenin, commissioned him to write a pamphlet titled *Marxism and the National Question* (1913). When the Bolsheviks seized power in October 1917, Stalin was named People's Commissar of Nationalities. His rivalry with the head of the Red Army, Leon Trotsky, contributed to the growing fractures within the party. Just before a stroke incapacitated him in March 1923, Lenin fought with Stalin over the formation of the new Soviet Union, and he advised his comrades to remove Stalin from his post as General Secretary of the Communist Party. The other leaders did not heed Lenin's warning, however, and most of them paid with their lives a decade and a half later.

Stalin accumulated enormous power within the party through his skillful political manipulation and his willingness to resort to ruthlessness. By the early 1930s he had defeated all of his rivals for power. During the "Stalin Revolution" of 1928 to 1932, the state forced millions of peasants onto collective farms, exiled or killed the most productive peasants (the so-called *kulaks*), and rapidly industrialized the economy. The height of Stalinist terror was reached in the Great Purges of 1937 and 1938, when approximately 700,000 people were executed and millions more were exiled, imprisoned, or died in labor camps.

Despite Stalin's industrialization and militarization programs, the Soviet Union was not prepared for the German invasion of June 1941. Ultimately, the war was won by the tenacity and enormous sacrifice of the Soviet people, but Stalin provided inspiration for many, as well as the fear that one step backward would end in death. The Soviets lost some twenty-seven million people, but in the end the triumph over fascism provided the Communists with a new source of legitimation, and Stalin emerged with a new, uncontested authority.

Stalin's postwar policies were repressive at home and expansive abroad. While he sporadically used repression against individuals and groups and deported ethnic minorities from newly annexed territories, he did not engage in mass killing on the scale of 1937. In dealing with his former allies during the cold war, Stalin attempted to maintain the Grand Alliance with the Western Great Powers while maintaining a sphere of influence in Eastern Europe, where he could impose "friendly" governments. Western leaders refused to acquiesce in the expansion of Soviet influence, and the cooperation of the war years disintegrated into two hostile camps, each armed with atomic weapons.

In his last years, Stalin was enfeebled by strokes, and he deteriorated physically and mentally. His growing isolation, arbitrariness, and inactivity affected the entire country. The ruling elite engaged in plots and intrigues, while Stalin threatened his closest associates. He died of a massive stroke on March 5, 1953.

SEE ALSO *Bolshevism; Cold War; Communism; Iron Curtain; Lenin, Vladimir Ilitch; Russian Revolution; Trotsky, Leon*

BIBLIOGRAPHY

Fitzpatrick, Sheila, ed. *Stalinism, New Directions.* 2000. London: Routledge.

Gorlizki, Yoram, and Oleg Khlevniuk. 2004. *Cold Peace: Stalin and the Soviet Ruling Circle, 1945–1953.* Oxford: Oxford University Press.

Holloway, David. 1994. *Stalin and the Bomb: The Soviet Union and Atomic Energy, 1939–1956.* New Haven, CT: Yale University Press.

Lewin, Moshe. 1985. *The Making of the Soviet System: Essays in the Social History of Interwar Russia.* New York: Pantheon.

Service, Robert. 2005. *Stalin, A Biography.* Cambridge, MA: Harvard University Press.

Tucker, Robert C. 1973. *Stalin as Revolutionary, 1879–1929: A Study in History and Personality.* New York: W. W. Norton.

Ronald Grigor Suny

STALINISM

What is Stalinism? It is not the same as Communism. For if all Communist regimes were Stalinistic, how could one distinguish between Joseph Stalin's (1879–1953) mass terror, his annihilation policy, and the authoritarian Communist dictatorships in the Soviet Union and Eastern Europe after 1953? It is important to define the concept of Stalinism precisely, so that it can be clearly demarcated from other terms.

Several contemporaries observed that the Communist dictatorship in the Soviet Union of the 1930s and 1940s was different from other authoritarian dictatorships. Rather, it resembled the National Socialist regime in Germany, for it was characteristic of Bolshevik rule in the Stalin era to assert its claims to subdue the societies of the multiethnic empire, to dominate and control them. The Bolsheviks were trying to create new people and new orders from nothing, annihilating those they perceived as enemies of their new social order. The Bolsheviks allocated their enemies into social and ethnic groups, which were later to be isolated and annihilated. Already in the course of the civil war between 1918 and 1924, the Bolsheviks tried to stigmatize and annihilate ostensible class enemies. From 1929 to 1933 more than two million peasants were registered as *kulaks* (better-off farmers) and deported to Siberia, and more than ten thousand of them were killed. Former czarist elites and members of national minority groups suffered a similar fate. In 1937 and 1938 over a million people were arrested on Stalin's order; some of them were shot according to quotas. More than 680,000 people found their death simply because they belonged to a social or a national group that the leadership imagined to be on the side of its enemies.

The terror was not only directed against the subjects of the regime; it also destroyed the party and the political elites of the Soviet state. After the end of World War II (1939–1945), the violence and terror were directed primarily against ethnic minorities, collaborators, and former Soviet soldiers who had been in German captivity. Therefore, one can say that Stalinism was a regime of terror, violence, and annihilation. It started with the rise of Stalin as an autocrat and ended with his death in 1953.

The first people to speak about Stalinism were its contemporaries. Leon Trotsky (1879–1940), who lost the struggle for power to Stalin in the 1920s, interpreted Stalinism as the rule of a bureaucratic caste that had replaced the proletariat. In this view, Stalinism was a betrayal of the principles of "true" socialism, allegedly represented by Vladimir Lenin (1870–1924). This interpretation, however, could not explain why the party and the state apparatus would destroy themselves in the late 1930s; furthermore, it offered no explanation for the role of Stalin in Stalinism.

Hannah Arendt (1906–1975) and Carl J. Friedrich (1901–1984) were also influenced by the idea of the modern dictatorship of the twentieth century. They claimed that Stalinism was a form of totalitarian dictatorship, thus differentiating it from other traditional authoritarian dictatorships. According to this theory, Stalinism was a totalitarian dictatorship because it claimed total dominance, led to the disintegration and transformation of the society, subjected the society to total control, and atomized and effaced the individual as a subject. It has been argued that this interpretation mistook the claims of the regime for reality and assumed that the Stalinist state was capable of exercising total control over the society. Revisionists in American historiography claimed, in their turn, that the destructive potential of Stalinism resulted from the dynamics of a "society in motion." According to this concept, Stalinism was a result of the activity "from below" of competing groups within the power apparatus, which created social pressures to which the leadership had to respond.

After the opening of the Russian archives in the 1990s, the discussion about Stalinism took a new turn. There can be no further doubt that it was Stalin and his retinue who designed the strategies of mass terror and annihilation, although they could not consistently control the execution of those "policies." The origin of Stalinism was the desire of the leadership to transform the society and subject it to total control. In this respect, Stalinism was totalitarian in its claim. But the Bolsheviks only disposed of a weak state and thus were not capable of realizing their demands in a heterogeneous multinational empire. This was the reason they exercised violence to break resistance. Terror and annihilation occurred, however, under the conditions of premodern, personified power structures. Not only did these power structures make possible the rise of Stalin to the head of the party, they were also a prerequisite for a system in which a despot like Stalin could realize his violent fantasies. Stalinism bears the name of Stalin, who was the embodiment of the system; it is not possible to discuss Stalinism without considering Stalin himself.

SEE ALSO *Authoritarianism; Bolshevism; Bureaucracy; Communism; Lenin, Vladimir Ilitch; Leninism; Marx, Karl; Marxism; Oligarchy; Power; Russian Revolution; Socialism; Stalin, Joseph; Terrorism; Totalitarianism; Trotsky, Leon; Union of Soviet Socialist Republics; World War II*

BIBLIOGRAPHY

Baberowski, Jörg. 2004. *Der rote Terror: Die Geschichte des Stalinismus.* 2nd ed. Munich: DVA.

Davies, Sarah, and James Harris, eds. 2005. *Stalin: A New History.* Cambridge, U.K.: Cambridge University Press.

Fitzpatrick, Sheila, ed. 2000. *Stalinism: New Directions.* London: Routledge.

Service, Robert. 2004. *Stalin: A Biography.* London: Macmillan.

Jörg Baberowski

STALKING

SEE *Obsession.*

STANDARD CROSS-CULTURAL SAMPLE

The Standard Cross-Cultural Sample, or SCCS (Murdock and White 1969), is a cumulative and collaborative database of coded variables on maximally diverse and ethnographically best-described societies used by scholars in the social sciences. The champion of modern cross-cultural and statistical methods, George P. Murdock, in preparation for a standard sample, had classified the 1,267 societies in his coded *Ethnographic Atlas* into 200 distinctive world cultural provinces (Murdock 1962–1967, 1968). Douglas R. White (1968) had compiled a database of coded cross-cultural studies and done a concordance of previous samples (repeated by Ember 1992) that showed the fruitlessness of testing hypotheses that involved variables from different studies because there was little overlap between randomly drawn or ad hoc samples. White (1969), linked to the Columbia-Michigan historical-evo-

lutionary successor to the Boasian school, had just completed the first comparative historical study to use Murdock's *Ethnographic Atlas* codes in a regional study. The dual-authored approach to the SCCS signified a rapprochement between the Yale school of evolutionary functionalism and the historical anthropological schools at Columbia, Michigan, and Berkeley. Their founding of the Cumulative Cross-Cultural Coding Center (CCCCC) for the SCCS at the University of Pittsburgh (1968–1973), like their 1969 authorship, was coequal, although they were born nearly fifty years apart.

Both Murdock and White (1969) were advocates of multiple competing hypotheses (Chamberlain 1897). They designed the SCCS to be sufficiently large to test multivariate and competing hypotheses and sufficiently small to allow different investigators to code all the cases and so contribute to a cumulative database. Their evaluation of the literature on the 1,267 *Ethnographic Atlas* societies and other ethnographies led to their selection of the best and preferably earliest described representatives for 186 of Murdock's cultural provinces that were most independent of one another. Each society was pinpointed to specific dates and communities (White and Murdock 2006). Bibliographic recommendations for ethnographic sources (White 1986) were classified by focus and pertinence. The SCCS—the goal of which was to represent the cultural diversity of well-described human societies—ranges from contemporary hunter-gatherers such as the Kung to historical cities (e.g., Babylon, 1750 BCE; Rome, 110 CE; the Khmer capital of Angkor, 1292; Erevan, 1880; Abomey 1890) to communities of industrial nations (e.g., an Irish village, 1932; a Russian commune, 1955).

Construction of the SCCS reflected Murdock and White's concerns for sorting out alternative hypotheses. Correlations among variables in the SCCS cannot be taken as necessarily causal or functional relationships. As with similarities between the SCCS societies, they are affected by many factors, and the challenge is to separate out the different strands of influence, including measurement biases that may be studied by data quality controls (Naroll 1962; Whyte 1978b). Correlations or similarities may be influenced by functional associations, diffusion or borrowing from one society to another, or shared characteristics passed along through common ancestry. It is only the assumption of parallel independent inventions that supports the interpretation of a correlation between traits as functional adhesions in cultural systems. Murdock (1956), Harold E. Driver (1956), White (1968, 1975), and many other social scientists have long recognized the complementarities of different processes and the problems of inferences from correlational tests. History and science are integrally connected in this respect (Lyman and O'Brien 2004). The interpretation of intersocietal similarities and correlational analysis and of comparative distributional findings necessarily involves the different kinds of networks that mediate the effects of diffusion or borrowing on correlations or similarities: Intermarriage, migration, economic exchange, political, and other interactions may be involved. Likewise, shared "ancestry" may include common "stock" that is linguistic, political, or the result of outmigration or genetic origin, such as mitochondrial genes passed entirely through the maternal line, which have strong adaptive correlates to environment (Mishmar et al. 2003). A similar principle applies to strictly paternal genetic origin passing through the Y chromosome. Assortative genes also may be implicated in selection for correlates or similarities. Without large samples of cases, such as the SCCS, or even larger, such as Murdock's *Ethnographic Atlas*, the data are likely to be insufficient to separate or tease out different kinds of effects. From a statistician's point of view, many of the alternative kinds of effects fall under the general term of historical nonindependence of cases. Only one major attempt has been made so far, however, to implement a diachronic coding of variables such as those studied by Eric Wolf (1982), but there is no intrinsic constraint against doing so for researchers ambitious enough to try. Such an approach would remedy the defect of using the SCCS exclusively for a synchronic or snapshot approach to comparison rather than coding changes over time at spatially pinpointed and related sites.

Edward B. Tylor, although very familiar with diffusion and issues of common ancestry, was rightly critiqued for asserting that cross-cultural correlations represented functional evolutionary parallelisms in how traits are linked. Following Tylor's 1889 paper, statistician Francis Galton objected that because his cases were not historically independent, Tylor was not warranted to apply the usual tests of statistical significance to his correlational results. This is because when duplicates of the same originals are included in a sample (which does not necessarily change correlations, since that would depend on which kinds of cases are duplicated), the variance among the originals is much greater than it would appear from computing ordinary standard deviations. Variance is an *average*, divided by the number of cases, and so the variance increases in dividing the observed deviations by a smaller number of originals. The statistical significance of any correlation so affected is diminished accordingly. This critique, however, allows for a sample-size adjustment to recompute the effective variance for a smaller estimated number of independent cases. All this was well understood in the 1880s. In the 1889 oral discussion, H. W. Flower made an additional important comment: that any cross-cultural method "depended entirely upon the units of comparison being of equivalent value" (Tylor 1889, p. 272) as, for example, the contrast between individual

communities and larger religious, political, or regional units. The Galton and Flower problems may be linked in that if the traits of the smaller communities reflect those of the larger units, then the statistical significance of correlations of traits for the communities must be adjusted by reducing the effective *n* (estimated number of independent cases) to those of the larger units.

Galton's problem, as named by Raoul Naroll (1961)—that is, the problem of historically nonindependent cases—is not limited to cross-cultural research. It entails foundational statistical problems endemic to nonexperimental research in which the variance of statistics is underestimated when common historical factors or network interactions influence similarities of cases. Samples with historically nonindependent cases can still yield unbiased statistics (means and correlations, for example), but incorrect variance estimates of statistical estimates (and thus significance tests) require appropriate adjustment for Galton's problem, independently of the question of how to interpret statistics in the light of alternative hypothesis. Random sampling provides no escape.

There remains an unfortunate Tylorian tendency in cross-cultural research today, however, to try to interpret cross-cultural correlations as evidence of functional associations among traits *if* the sample is both small and random. Carol R. Ember and Melvin Ember (1998), for example, incorrectly argue that the independence of cases is strictly a matter of independent *selection* of cases in the sample, as if historical independence did not matter. This view (1998, p. 678)—that "independence of cases means only that the choice of one case is not influenced by the choice of any other case (which random sampling guarantees)"—is fundamentally mistaken. Simple random or cluster sampling of one or multiple cases from a sampling frame of well-described societies (e.g., Naroll 1967; Lagacé 1979) does not solve nonindependence problems. Nor does it solve the problem of representation of diversity where data for comparable descriptive coverage are lacking for the vast majority of cases in the underlying universe, as in cross-cultural research. The mistaken view that random sampling solves Galton's problem by guarding against sampling bias ignores the real problems, those of variance underestimates that skew significance and other tests in favor of the theory being tested. Malcolm Dow (1993) discusses the effects of ignoring Galton's problem on unwarranted saving of incorrect hypotheses, and shows that appropriate statistical controls can also help identify results that would otherwise be rejected. Without appropriate variance estimates, two independent tests of the same correct hypothesis can easily fail to replicate if confidence limits are underestimated.

Some researchers now refer to nonindependence of cases as "Galton's Opportunity" (Witkowski 1974) or

"Galton's Asset" (Korotayev and de Munck 2003) because historical nonindependence and network interactions invite further research into alternative hypotheses. More recently, cultural anthropologists have used the SCCS, along with methods from evolutionary biology, to address common historical ancestry, horizontal transmission, environmental adaptation, and functional interrelations in the distributions of cultural traits (Mace and Pagel 1994; Borgerhoff Mulder et al., 2001). Methods of independent contrasts (Nunn, Borgerhoff Mulder, and Langley 2006), for example, are sensitive to even small amounts of horizontal transmission in cultural datasets.

The SCCS was designed to provide some of the appropriate measurements for Galton's problem controls and for adjusting estimates of variance and significance tests accordingly. Murdock and White (1969) provided simple tests, following those proposed by Naroll (1961, 1965), to detect similarities among societies that depended on their relative geographic closeness and overall cultural affinities. They also provided a provisional phylogenetic language classification to help detect one of the types of common origin that might account for similarities among nonindependent cases. These allowed for estimates of the effective sample size of different variables. Benefits could increase for multivariate analysis if some of the new coding studies would expand ethnographic coverage to a new Extended SCCS, yet to be designed, with double the number of cases.

Hundreds of cross-cultural studies have by now contributed new codes for the pinpointed societies in the SCCS. Those resulting from Murdock and White's 1968–1973 CCCCC research projects are published along with others in Barry and Schlegel (1980). The thousands of authors who have used SCCS data for their research cover virtually every area in which cross-ethnographic comparisons are useful, including a great many subdisciplines of the social and related sciences. Assuming that a researcher avoids spurious findings that result from mistaken strategies such as cherry-picking high correlations and significance or ignoring Galton-type problems and opportunities, cumulativity can have exponential benefits when researchers, typically coding thirty or more new variables, can test relationships in a database with thousands of variables.

A sample of some findings of authors who treat their subject comprehensively at book length, using the SCCS, and who added coded data on their specialties, will illustrate how the SCCS is sufficiently large to test multivariate hypotheses. Sociologist Orlando Patterson (1982) carried out a magisterial study of the internal dynamics of slavery based on his own codings of slavery variables for the sixty-six slave societies in the SCCS. This was a first-of-its-kind study on the nature of slavery over time, world

and historical-comparative in scope: tribal, ancient, pre-modern, and modern. Slavery is shown to be "a parasitic relationship between master and slave, invariably entailing the violent domination of a natally alienated, or socially dead, person," and its internal dynamics to involve "a single process of recruitment, incorporation on the margin of society, and eventual manumission or death."

Economist Fred Pryor (2005a) carried out a similarly broad program of research in his comparative study of world economic systems. In his article (2005b) on the forty-one agricultural societies in the SCCS, he used clustering analysis of variables to cover a full range of variation in production, property, and distribution. He found evidence for only four basic agricultural systems among thirty-six clusterable cases and apart from the five that were unclusterable: herding plus, egalitarian farming, individualized, and semimarketized farming. Although "many anthropologists and historians consider agricultural systems to be the outcome of environmental, social, social-structural, and political variables, a statistical analysis indicates that very few such variables are correlated with the derived economic systems. The systems are thus revealed to stand as independent entities and worthy of more intensive study" (2005b, p. 2).

Anthropologist and Islamic specialist Andrey Korotayev (2004) was the first to code world religion for the SCCS. Two of the most powerful of his fertile set of findings are that world religion is the best predictor of large regional similarities in social structure, and that many of the major types of social structure (like Pryor, identified by a cluster analysis on the relevant variables) closely follow enduring regional boundaries such as the extent of the eighth-century caliphates resulting from the Arab/Islamic expansion.

Karen Paige and Jeffrey Paige (1981), teamed as sociologist and political scientist, succeeded in identifying systemic patterns in their study of gender roles by restricting their focus to the 108 prestate societies in the SCCS. They sharpened their hypotheses to focus on three determinative levels of resources: low-value, unstable, and stable. The hypotheses they tested showed how resource levels affect women and the womanly interests of men either in identification with females or in surveillance over female reproduction. With low material resources, females tend to be food producers and highly valued for the reproduction of children who add labor and enlarge the kin group and its prestige. With stable resources, property and inheritance become major issues for men as regards women: Children's paternity comes to be at stake, and men often form conflicting fraternal interest groups. The findings of these authors show high coherence with respect to their theory of the politics of reproductive issues and the effects of these issues on social organization generally.

Evolutionary biologist Laura Betzig (1986) focused on the starkest of Darwinian issues, power and the differential extremes of open or sub rosa control over female reproduction in harems and among concubines and mistresses, as documented by her coding of the 186 cases in the SCCS. Like Paige and Paige, she regarded men in societies with property as strongly concerned with the fidelity of their wives, but she went further to explore the vicious circle of links between differences in power and differences in reproductive success that are virtually without limit for the most powerful males in the historical era. Controversial and starkly sociobiological, her explanation as to why modern states become less despotic is that to attract mercenaries, specialists in defense, craftsmen, and those who run the state, people in power are forced to make concessions to others who still serve, directly or indirectly, to contribute to the reproductive efforts of men in power. Her philosophical predilection is to reject theories of further checks and balances in favor of an extreme: that the powerful dictate the laws in their own (reproductive) interests even in the absence of absolutist despotism.

Peggy Sanday (1981), exploring feminist issues, rejected arguments of universal female subordination, and after coding variables for different measures of relative male domination and female power, argued that dominance is not inherent in human relations but is socially constructed through deep symbolic mechanisms and not only as instituted in a people's secular power roles and behavior. Symbolic sources of male dominance, she argued, derive partly from ancient concepts of power, as exemplified by origin myths. Her hypotheses were designed to test the extent to which female power and male dominance are further determined by a people's adaptation to their environment, social conflict, and emotional stress. She illustrated her thesis through case studies of the effects of European colonialism, migration, and food stress, supported by statistical associations between aspects of sexual inequality and diverse forms of cultural stress.

The advantage of a database like SCCS is that, in spite of what theories authors are hoping to test, in so doing they contribute coded data and statistical hypothesis tests that can be revisited and challenged by others, using new data and that cumulated from the past. Some researchers are intent on coding variables that reflect the range of variability in the phenomena they study and on working more inductively from their findings, guided by theoretical questions. An example of a strongly inductive approach is that of Martin K. Whyte, who instructed his researchers to code half the SCCS societies for each of hundreds of gender-related variables relevant to the literature on gender roles. He summarized how his findings on male dominance contrast with those of Sanday, noting that his variables

have divergent cross-cultural distributions. Some, such as items for political leadership, are highly skewed in favor of men; others, such as property inheritance…, are more moderately skewed toward men; still others, such as the elaborateness of funerals or final authority over infants, show little or no male bias cross-culturally…. [Further], these different indicators are not associated with each other…. [and] some things that have been assumed in the … literature to have status implications for women may not. For example, there now seem to be no grounds for assuming that the relative subsistence contribution of women has any general status implications. (Whyte 1978a, p. 169)

Many of these authors address the Galton problem of controlling for nonindependence of cases. How prevalent is autocorrelation among the variables studied in cross-cultural research? Econometrician Anthon Eff (2004) tested 1,700 variables in the SCCS database to measure Moran's I for spatial autocorrelation (distance), linguistic autocorrelation (common descent), and autocorrelation in cultural complexity (mainline evolution). "The results suggest that … it would be prudent to test for spatial and phylogenetic autocorrelation when conducting regression analyses with the Standard Cross-Cultural Sample" (Eff 2004, p. 153). He illustrated the use of autocorrelation tests in exploratory data analysis, showing how all variables in a given study can be evaluated for nonindependence of cases in terms of distance, language, and cultural complexity. He explains the methods for estimating these autocorrelation effects, illustrates ordinary least squares regression using the Moran I significance measure of autocorrelation (options for Durbin-Watson tests are commonly available as an alternative), and shows how, when autocorrelation is present, it can often be removed so as to get proper estimates of regression coefficients and their variances. This is done by constructing a respecified dependent variable "lagged" by weightings on the dependent variable on other locations, where the weights are degree of relationship. Ordinary least squares regression will still bias the estimated coefficients when the dependent variable is respecified, but maximum likelihood methods (Anselin 1988) will give unbiased statistics and variances in which the effects of autocorrelation have been removed.

Use of the SCCS seems to encourage good research practices. Other methodological advances that would not have been made without the shared SCCS database include statistical entailment analysis, for example, of the sexual division of labor (White, Burton, and Brudner 1977; White 2000) and Murdock's (1980) use of this discrete-structure statistical method in his study of cultural theories of illness and their sociological entailments.

All of the cross-cultural articles and data published in the journal *Ethnology* for the SCCS and all the bibliographic, pinpointing, and coded data sets of the SCCS are in the public domain so as to facilitate scientific research. The journal *World Cultures*, edited by White from 1985 to 1990, has continued to publish SCCS cross-cultural codes and analytical articles. Google Scholar as of 2006 cites 413 online citations to articles referencing the SCCS, and the number unreferenced is perhaps four to six times that estimate. These works address a huge variety of topics. Their diversity, and their common references to a framework of variables and sample cases, along with the agreements and relatively clear bases for disagreements among authors, can be taken as indicators of success in the research design and cumulativity of the SCCS.

The SCCS is not about statistics or method but about science, and about broadly encompassing anthropological-cum-historical science that encompasses contending and often complementary theories of the social, biological, and physical sciences as they interact with questions about human societies and culture. The SCCS does not represent a narrowly conceived school of thought about what the assumptions or methods of this science ought to be, other than a good and far-ranging combination of science, history, and humanities. If one draws today from new findings about mitochondrial inheritance of energetic-environmentally adaptive genes in the maternal line, for example, and reconstructs the human matriline in its geographic migrations (and similarly for the Y chromosome patriline), is the SCCS a place to try to develop approaches to understanding the complexities and testing hypotheses about how human evolution has proceeded to the present? Or, taking Wolf's (1982) approach to world sociopolitical comparisons through a diachronic lens of world system histories and interactions: Is the SCCS not a suitable sample for entirely different kinds of codes that compare what is known about these societies through time, and through networks of interaction, not with one another but with larger entities of the global system and through the larger networks of sociopolitical and military interactions?

Recognizing that "each society is a process in time" (quoting Edmund Leach), Robert McC. Adams (2004 p. 353) reviews the vexing problems of using a mix of textual sources and archaeological data in coding or process modeling. To code or comprehend through space and time, however, also involves attention to the subjective positioning to the different texts that provide perspectives on history, and so opens into a whole set of other classical problems in anthropology that remain to be successfully integrated—at the level of the individual investigator, the research team, or a larger and more cumulative enterprise. Part of the success of the SCCS collectivity of researchers in relation to those who publish the data from investigators and from difference sources is not to try to edit out or reedit data but to respect the integrity of original data in correct form as originally presented from a particular standpoint. Thus different streams of data coming from different sources and investigators are not compromised. Rather these independent streams themselves can be compared for indicators of what might be missing, hinted at, biased, or interpreted as reliable through cross-validation and triangulation of methods of analysis.

Mindful of Flower's observation that any cross-cultural method depends entirely on the units of comparison and the problem under study, Murdock and White did not regard the SCCS as a unique touchstone for theory testing but only as a worthy example of what could be accomplished with collaborative construction of shared databases and efforts at comparable codings from ethnographic materials to facilitate new understandings in the human sciences.

BIBLIOGRAPHY

Adams, Robert McC. 2004. Review of Bruce G. Trigger, *Understanding Early Civilizations: A Comparative Study.* Cambridge, U.K., and New York: Cambridge University Press, 2003. *The International History Review* 26: 349–354.

Anselin, Luc. 1988. *Spatial Econometrics: Methods and Models.* Dordrecht: Kluwer Academic Publishers.

Barry, Herbert, III, and Alice Schlegel, eds. 1980. *Cross-Cultural Samples and Codes.* Pittsburgh, PA: University of Pittsburgh Press.

Betzig, Laura. 1986. *Despotism and Differential Reproduction: A Darwinian View of History.* New York: Aldine.

Borgerhoff Mulder, M., M. George-Cramer, J. Eshleman, and A. Ortolani. (2001). A Study of East African Kinship and Marriage Using Phylogenetically Controlled Comparison. *American Anthropologist* 103: 1059–1082.

Chamberlain, T. C. 1897. The Method of Multiple Working Hypotheses. *Journal of Geology* 39 (2): 155–165.

Dow, Malcolm. 1993. Saving the Theory: Chi-squared Tests with Cross-Cultural Survey Data. *Cross-Cultural Research* 27 (3–4): 247–276.

Driver, Harold E. 1956. An Integration of Functional, Evolutionary and Historical Theory by Means of Correlations. *Indiana University Publications in Anthropological Linguistics, Memoir* 12.

Eff, E. Anthon. 2004. Does Mr. Galton Still Have a Problem? Autocorrelation in the Standard Cross-Cultural Sample. *World Cultures* 15 (2): 153–170.

Ember, Carol R. 1992. With the assistance of Hugh Page, Jr., Timothy O'Leary, and M. Marlene Martin. *Computerized Concordance of Cross-Cultural Samples.* New Haven, CT: Human Relations Area Files.

Ember, Carol R., and Melvin Ember. 1998. Cross-Cultural Research. In *Handbook of Methodology in Cultural Anthropology,* ed. H. Russell Bernard, 647–687. Walnut Creek, CA: Altamira.

Frayser, Suzanne G. 1985. *Varieties of Sexual Experience: An Anthropological Perspective on Human Sexuality.* New Haven, CT: HRAF Press.

Gray, J. P. 1996. Is the Standard Cross-Cultural Sample Biased? A Simulation Study. *Cross-Cultural Research* 30 (4): 301–315.

Korotayev, Andrey. 2004. *World Religions and Social Evolution of the Old World Oikumene Civilizations: A Cross-cultural Perspective.* Lewiston, NY: Mellen.

Korotayev, Andrey, and Victor de Munck. 2003. Galton's Asset and Flower's Problem: Cultural Networks and Cultural Units in Cross-Cultural Research. *American Anthropologist* 105 (2): 353–358.

Lagacé, Robert O. 1979. The HRAF Probability Sample: Retrospect and Prospect. *Behavior Science Research* 14: 211–229.

Lyman, R. Lee, and Michael J. O'Brien. 2004. Nomothetic Science and Idiographic History in Twentieth-Century Americanist Anthropology. *Journal of the History of the Behavioral Sciences* 40 (1): 77–96.

Mace, Ruth, and Mark Pagel. 1994. The Comparative Method in Anthropology. *Current Anthropology* 35 (5): 549–564.

Mishmar, Dan, Eduardo Ruiz-Pesini, Pawel Golik, et al. 2003. Natural Selection Shaped Regional mtDNA Variation in Humans. *PNAS* 100 (1): 171–176.

Murdock, George Peter. 1956. How Culture Changes. In *Man, Culture, and Society*, ed. H. L. Shapiro, 247–260. New York: Oxford University Press.

Murdock, George Peter. 1962–1967. *Ethnographic Atlas.* Pittsburgh, PA: University of Pittsburgh Press. Published in installments of the journal *Ethnology.*

Murdock, George Peter. 1968. World Sampling Provinces. *Ethnology* 7: 305–326.

Murdock, George Peter. 1980. *Theories of Illness: A World Survey.* Pittsburgh, PA: University of Pittsburgh Press.

Murdock, George Peter, and Douglas R. White. 1969. Standard Cross-Cultural Sample. *Ethnology* 9: 329–369. http://repositories.cdlib.org/imbs/socdyn/wp/Standard_Cross-Cultural_Sample

Naroll, Raoul. 1961. Two Solutions to Galton's Problem. *Philosophy of Science* 28: 15–29.

Naroll, Raoul. 1962. *Data Quality Control: A New Research Technique.* Glencoe, IL: Free Press.

Naroll, Raoul. 1965. Galton's Problem: The Logic of Cross Cultural Analysis. *Social Research* 32: 428–451.

Naroll, Raoul. 1967. The Proposed HRAF Probability Sample. *Behavior Science Notes* 2: 70–80.

Nunn, Charles L., Monique Borgerhoff Mulder, and Sasha Langley. 2006. Comparative Methods for Studying Cultural Trait Evolution: A Simulation Study. *Cross-Cultural Research* 40 (2): 177–209.

Paige, Karen, and Jeffrey Paige. 1981. *The Politics of Reproductive Ritual.* Berkeley: University of California Press.

Patterson, Orlando. 1982. *Slavery and Social Death: A Comparative Study.* Cambridge, MA: Harvard University Press.

Pryor, Frederic L. 2005a. *Economic Systems of Foraging, Agriculture, and Industrial Societies.* New York: Cambridge University Press.

Pryor, Frederic L. 2005b. Rethinking Economic Systems: A Study of Agricultural Societies. *Cross-Cultural Research* 39 (3): 252–292. http://ccr.sagepub.com/cgi/content/abstract/39/3/252.

Sanday, Peggy. 1981. *Female Power and Male Dominance: On the Origins of Sexual Inequality.* New York: Cambridge University Press.

Stocking, George W., Jr. 1968. Edward Burnett Tylor. *International Encyclopedia of the Social Sciences*, ed. David L. Sills, 170–177. New York, Macmillan.

Tylor, Edward Burnett. 1889. On a Method of Investigating the Development of Institutions; Applies to Laws of Marriage and Descent. *Journal of the Anthropological Institute* 18: 245–272.

Wheeler [Nammour], Valerie. 1974. Drums and Guns: A Cross-Cultural Study of the Nature of War. PhD diss., University of Oregon, Eugene.

White, Douglas R. 1968. Societal Research Archives System: Retrieval, Quality Control and Analysis of Comparative Data. *Social Science Information* 7 (3): 78–94.

White, Douglas R. 1969. *Cooperation and Decision Making among North American Indians.* Ann Arbor, MI: Dissertation Reprints.

White, Douglas R. 1975. Process, Statistics and Anthropological Theory: An Appreciation of Harold E. Driver. *Reviews in Anthropology* 2: 295–314.

White, Douglas R. 1986. Focused Ethnographic Bibliography for the Standard Cross-Cultural Sample. *World Cultures* 2 (1):1–126.

White, Douglas R. 2000. Manual for Statistical Entailment Analysis 2.0: Sea.exe. *World Cultures* 11 (1): 77–90.

White, Douglas R., Michael L. Burton, and Lilyan A. Brudner. 1977. Entailment Theory and Method: A Cross-Cultural Analysis of the Sexual Division of Labor. *Behavior Science Research* 12: 1–24.

White, Douglas R., and George P. Murdock. 2006. Pinpointing Sheets for the Standard Cross-Cultural Sample. http://eclectic.ss.uci.edu/~drwhite/xc/SCCSPinpointing.html

Whyte, Martin K. 1978a. *The Status of Women in Preindustrial Societies.* Princeton, NJ: Princeton University Press.

Whyte, Martin K. 1978b. Cross-Cultural Codes Dealing with the Relative Status of Women. *Ethnology* 17: 211–237.

Witkowski, Stanley. 1974. Galton's Opportunity—Hologeistic Study of Historical Processes. *Behavior Science Research* 9 (1): 11–15.

Wolf, Eric. 1982. *Europe and the People without History.* Berkeley: University of California Press.

Douglas R. White

STANDARD DEVIATION

The standard deviation is found throughout the behavioral and social science literature. It is the average spread among a set of scores around their mean, and it is the most frequently used measure of variability in parametric datasets. Researchers analyze their data by looking at the variability and breaking that variability down into its component parts.

When we describe any set of data we use three characteristics: (1) the form of the distribution, (2) the mean or central tendency, and (3) the variability. All three are required, since they are generally independent of each other. In other words, knowing the mean tells us nothing of the variability.

Variability is a characteristic of all measures. In the social sciences, the people or groups that researchers study may be exposed to the same treatment or conditions, yet they show different responses to that treatment or condition. In other words, all the scores of the people or groups would be different. The goal of the scientist is to explain why the scores are different. If everyone were exactly the same, the standard deviation would be zero.

In addition to describing their data, researchers use the standard deviation in inferential statistics. When they manipulate conditions or treatments, researchers attempt to explain different scores between groups by looking at the variability between the groups. If the groups are different enough, then they are said to be statistically significantly different. This conclusion may be drawn based on the probability (odds) that the difference could have occurred by chance. Researchers use these samples as estimates of the true parameters in the population of interest, and the standard deviation is used (along with the sample size) to establish the precision of the estimates (Winer 1971). The smaller the standard deviation, the smaller the error (or the greater the precision of the estimate).

We also find variability that cannot be explained by the treatments or conditions applied to the people or groups. This variability must also be a part of all the explanations. This part of the variability is often called *error*, since experiments or studies do not indicate why it occurs.

The English mathematician and statistician Karl Pearson (1857–1936) introduced the procedure and the term *standard deviation* to statistics in 1892 (Magnello 2005). The standard deviation calculation is very straightforward. The standard deviation is defined as the square root of sum of the squared deviations from the mean, divided by the number of squared deviations. The equation for the standard deviation is $stdev = \sqrt{\dfrac{\Sigma(X - M)^2}{N}}$ where *stdev* is the standard deviation, X is a raw score, M is the mean of the scores, $X - M$ represents the deviation

of a score from the mean, and N is the number of scores. Many different symbols have been used to represent the elements of the equation, but in all cases the standard deviation is the square root of the average of the squared deviations from the mean.

At this point, new students of statistics often ask why researchers do not use the deviations from the mean directly. The deviations from the mean cannot be averaged since the sum of the deviations from the mean is always zero. It is possible to use the mean deviation score, which avoids the zero sum by employing absolute values, but this tends to be mathematically cumbersome (Weisstein 2003).

An example will illustrate the calculation of the standard deviation. Let us assume we have five scores for five individuals. The N is equal to 5. The scores are 10, 8, 6, 4, and 2. We must first calculate the mean, so we add all the scores and then divide by N. The sum of the scores (10 + 8 + 6 + 4 + 2) is 30, and the mean is 30 divided by 5, or 6. Next we must subtract the mean from each score to get the deviation score (10 − 6 = 4, 8 − 6 = 2, 6 − 6 = 0, 4 − 6 = −2, and 2 − 6 = −4). Note we cannot get the mean deviation score because the sum of the deviations is zero. This is always true. We solve this problem by squaring each deviation score (which eliminates the negative signs), then summing and dividing by N ($4^2 = 16$, $2^2 = 4$, $0^2 = 0$, $-2^2 = 4$, and $-4^2 = 16$; the sum of these deviation scores squared is 40; dividing 40 by 5 gives us 8). Since this result is the average of the squared deviations (also known as the *variance*), we must get back to the original score units by taking the square root of 8. The final result is a standard deviation of 2.8284 (rounded to four decimal places). We can say the average spread in the set of scores is about 2.8 (or as precise as we need to be).

A common way to help students and others visualize the standard deviation is to show a graph of a normal distribution, with the standard deviations as lines above and below the mean. We do this because many variables of interest to science are distributed normally (or approximately so) in the population of interest. In a large distribution (and a population), there are about three standard deviations above the mean, and three below the mean. Given these assumptions, we can say that approximately 68 percent of a population falls between −1 and +1 standard deviation of the normal curve; approximately 95 percent falls between −2 and +2 standard deviations; and better than 99 percent of the population falls between −3 and +3 standard deviations.

When the distribution of scores is not approximately normal, the use of the standard deviation, and the mean itself, may not be the preferred approach for describing the data. The reason for this is that extreme scores will have a large impact on the squared deviations from the mean, making the spread among scores appear quite large.

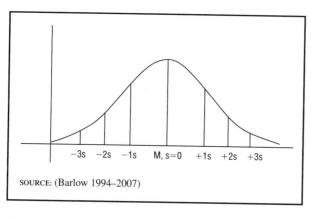

SOURCE: (Barlow 1994–2007)

Figure 1

Games, Paul, and George Klare. 1967. *Elementary Statistics: Data Analysis for the Behavioral Sciences.* New York: McGraw-Hill.

Magnello, M. Eileen. 2005. Karl Pearson and the Origins of Modern Statistics: An Elastician Becomes a Statistician. *The Rutherford Journal* 1 (December). http://rutherfordjournal.org/article010107.html.

Weisstein, Eric W. 2003. Mean Deviation. MathWorld—A Wolfram Web Resource. http://mathworld.wolfram.com/MeanDeviation.html.

Winer, B. J. 1971. Statistical Principles in Experimental Design. 2nd ed. New York: McGraw-Hill.

Samuel K. Rock Jr.

STANDARDIZATION

SEE *Modernism.*

STANDARDIZED TESTS

Standardized testing as a gateway to higher education was first established in the United States with the development of the College Entrance Examination Board in 1900. This board created a test designed to standardize admissions to elite universities in the northeastern United States and to encourage the development of a common curriculum among elite boarding schools (Chandler 1999; Lemann 1999). The original test consisted of essays and was not designed for mass testing. The College Board, however, created a broader test of IQ in 1926, the Scholastic Aptitude Test, commonly known today as the SAT I. This test was intended to help elite schools identify high-achieving students in nonelite high schools. In the early years, it also distinguished between white-collar students who were suitable for college and blue-collar students presumed to be ill prepared for such an education (Blau et al. 2003). By the mid-1950s, the demand for college education soared, spawning the development of the American College Testing Program (currently known as the ACT) in 1959. This test is the main alternative to the SAT. The origins of the SAT and ACT clarify their differing approaches. The SAT test was originally based on Army IQ tests as a measure of intelligence, whereas the ACT was historically designed to measure achievement rather than intelligence or aptitude.

Despite these differences in intent, the tests are similar in structure. The SAT I (also known as the SAT Reasoning Test) is designed to measure students' critical thinking and problem-solving skills. The test consists of three sections. The critical-reading section includes ques-

Skewed population data, such as income, may best be described using the median for central tendency and the mean absolute deviations from the median as the measure of spread. Another approach is to use the semi-interquartile range (also called the interquartile range) to describe the spread in skewed distributions. Extreme scores do not particularly affect this index, but it is more susceptible to sampling fluctuation and should not be used if the distribution is approximately normal. Box plots are often used to show both central tendency and dispersion using the semi-interquartile range. Unfortunately quartiles and box plots do not have the mathematical properties of the standard deviation and limit further analyses.

The standard deviation is used widely throughout the social sciences. In economics, the description of variations in stock prices employs the standard deviation. In political science, the assessment of voter preference is described as a percentage plus or minus, where the plus or minus amount is derived from the standard deviation. In psychology and sociology, variability among individuals and groups is routinely expressed in standard deviation units. In these days of powerful computer-based statistical tools that are available for laptop computers (arguably the two most widely used are SAS and SPSS), obtaining standard deviations (and most other statistical results) is quick and precise. Other programs, designed more for business use, also provide built-in formulas for calculating the standard deviation (often these are not considered accurate for scientific reporting).

SEE ALSO *Frequency Distributions; Measurement; Pearson, Karl; Social Science; Statistics; Test Statistics; Variance; Variation*

BIBLIOGRAPHY

Barlow, Kathleen. 1994–2007. Standard Deviation. In *The Encyclopedia of Educational Technology,* ed. Bob Hoffman. http://coe.sdsu.edu/eet/Articles/standarddev/start.htm.

tions on analytical reading, reading comprehension, and sentence completion. The writing section evaluates students' ability to write clearly, concisely, and competently. It also assesses students' ability to critically assess sentence and paragraph structure, as well as grammar. Finally, the mathematics section includes questions covering algebra, geometry, statistics, and advanced data analysis.

The ACT is similar to the SAT, but it has four broad sections. The English section evaluates writing and rhetorical skills. The mathematics section includes questions on algebra, geometry, and trigonometry. The reading section measures reading comprehension. The science section tests scientific skills including reasoning, analysis, and problem solving. Finally, the writing section tests writing skills.

The SAT and ACT are widely utilized among students and colleges. In 2006 about 1.5 million high school seniors took the SAT and approximately 1.2 million students took the ACT. Most colleges accept either the SAT or ACT for admissions since standards for comparing these scores are easily accessible.

The importance to higher education of standardized testing persists into graduate school, but testing tools are more diverse for graduate admissions than for undergraduate admissions. Professional schools require standardized tests that emphasize skills required by their specific disciplines. These include the Law School Admission Test (LSAT), the Medical College Admission Test (MCAT), and the Graduate Management Admission Test (GMAT). A more general and widely used standardized testing tool is the Graduate Record Examination (GRE). In 2005 nearly 500,000 persons took the GRE, accounting for 35 percent of persons with bachelor's degrees (National Center for Education Statistics 2006). The GRE has three sections. The verbal-reasoning section tests the respondent's ability to recognize concepts and to analyze information and relationships among parts of sentences. The quantitative-reasoning section tests algebra, geometry, data analysis, and quantitative reasoning. Finally, the analytical-writing section assesses the respondent's ability to write clearly, effectively, logically, coherently, and competently.

Key criticisms of standardized testing that have generated widespread sociological interest are: (1) the neglect of environmental differences among students, particularly those associated with cultural and racial differences; and (2) testing bias and validity. Criticisms of cultural and racial bias abound within the literature. One notable example is Tukufu Zuberi's *Thicker than Blood* (2001). Zuberi contends that the IQ test, the predecessor of modern standardized testing, developed out of the eugenics movement. This movement was committed to identifying biological differences between the races and classes. Proponents posited that racial inequalities in society were biologically determined because whites were perceived to be genetically superior. According to Zuberi, IQ tests provided statistical support for eugenics because white students scored higher on these tests than black and immigrant students.

During this period, many scholars argued that IQ tests, which measured math and verbal skills, accurately reflected biological differences in intelligence. Scholars influenced by this tradition purport that differences in test scores between blacks and whites reflect inherent biological differences between the races (Herrnstein and Murray 1994). However, sufficient data have not been provided to support this hypothesis. Today, most scholars acknowledge that standardized testing is biased and reflects more than biological differences between students.

Christopher Jencks, an influential scholar in this debate, has identified multiple biases in standardized testing. First, he argues that standardized tests neglect environmental differences between students, which creates bias. Comparisons of scores among racial groups are problematic because the IQ test was originally designed to compare the mental ability of students who were raised in comparable environments with similar levels of educational opportunity. Yet mass testing neglects environmental differences between students. This proposition has received widespread empirical support. William Rodgers and William Spriggs (1996) offer one of the most methodologically sophisticated assessments of environmental background factors by showing that a consideration of family and educational background reduces racial differences in test scores. However, they also find that the impact of the environment on test scores varies by race. Furthermore, racial biases exist in the measurement of standardized tests because components of these tests have different long-term effects on individuals' wages, depending on race and gender. Thus, Rodgers and Spriggs argue that standardized tests are racially biased because they measure different factors for different races.

Standardized tests are also biased in content (Jencks 1998). This is obvious when considering the language of the test. For students whose primary language is not English, standardized testing measures both English proficiency and scholastic achievement. As a result, these tests do not accurately reflect the achievement or readiness for college of language-minority students (LaCelle-Peterson 2000). Less-obvious content biases are prevalent in vocabulary words and essay topics.

Standardized tests are also biased methodologically if they claim (or are assumed) to measure ability because groups historically subjugated in society, including blacks, women, and the poor, are disadvantaged in this situation (Jencks 1998). Indeed, researchers have found that these tests create anxiety among African Americans and students of low socioeconomic status, who underperform on tests perceived to measure intellectual ability (Croizet and Dutrevis 2004; Steele and Aronson 1998). Additionally, women underperform when gender stereotypes are made salient (Benbow 1988).

Judith Blau and colleagues argue that blacks and whites place different significance on achievement tests. Whites believe that these tests measure ability, while blacks perceive unfair discrimination in testing practices. Thus, they conclude that black students and their parents place less weight on standardized test scores when considering postsecondary educational goals. Blau finds that test scores are a better predictor of educational attainment for white students than for black students. Furthermore, low-scoring black students are more likely than low-scoring white students to pursue postsecondary education. Thus, low scores are more likely to discourage white students, suggesting cultural differences in the value placed on tests (Blau et al. 2003). Further research is needed to determine how Blau's theory applies to gender and class issues. Preliminary research suggests that females place less value on mathematical portions of standardized test scores due to stereotype threats (Lesko and Corpus 2006).

Differences in the ability of standardized tests to predict future outcomes highlight an additional criticism of standardized testing: The tests are not valid because they are not accurate predictors of students' success in college or graduate school (Jencks 1998). Indeed, many scholars have found that standardized test scores do not predict grade point average in college (Gandara and Lopez 1998; Fleming 2000, 2002) or in graduate school (Oldfield 1994, 1996), and they do not predict success in the labor market (Blackburn 2004; Rodgers and Spriggs 1996).

The effect of the debates on standardized testing is evident. The title of the SAT has changed multiple times from the Scholastic Aptitude Test (a test of ability) to the Scholastic Assessment Test (this more general term suggests that the test measures more than ability) and finally to simply the SAT. In addition, the College Board has altered testing questions on the SAT to reduce cultural bias introduced from disparate knowledge and interests between groups in society. Furthermore, it has cut sections of the test to reduce reliance on vocabulary and increase reliance on verbal problem-solving skills. Even with these changes, however, racial and gender disparities persist. In 2004 the average SAT verbal score was 508 for college-bound high school seniors, ranging from 430 for black seniors to 451 and 528 for Mexican American and white seniors, respectively. Similarly, mathematics scores ranged from an average of 427 for black students to 531 for white students. ACT scores also vary by race. Average English ACT scores were 20.4 in 2004, ranging from 17.2 for black students to 18.3 for Mexican-American students and 22.5 for white students (Freeman and Fox 2005).

The persistence of the race gap is attributable to differences in family background and educational opportunity. Black students are generally raised in families with fewer resources than white students. Indeed, according to Melvin Oliver and Thomas Shapiro (1995), 63 percent of black households have zero or negative financial assets, meaning that their debt outweighs their assets. Only 28 percent of white families have negative financial assets. Furthermore, white median net worth (defined as the sum of all assets minus debt) is nearly twelve times black median net worth. This has important implications for test scores because students raised in families with greater wealth have the financial resources to prepare for standardized testing and attend college. Indeed, parental wealth and education are the two most important predictors of college attendance (Conley 1999).

The racial gap in test scores also persists because black students have fewer opportunities to prepare for the test. Schooling in the United States is highly segregated by race and socioeconomic status. Roslyn Mickelson (2006) found that predominantly black schools offer fewer SAT prep courses than integrated or predominantly white schools. Furthermore, even when black and white students study in the same schools (i.e., in integrated schools), they are offered different educational opportunities because they are grouped into classes by ability. Black students are more likely to be assigned to "lower-ability" classes than white students with the same grades and test scores. These classes are often taught by less-experienced teachers, and the courses offer a more general education rather than a college-preparatory education. Thus socioeconomic resources and educational opportunities explain the existing gap in standardized test scores by race.

As for gender, the standardized test score disparity is not uniform. Historically, boys and girls had equivalent verbal scores, but boys scored higher in math (Benbow 1988). The math score gap has diminished over time, in part because girls' educational opportunities have expanded, and they are taking more advanced math courses in high school. In 2004 boys and girls scored 538 and 504, respectively, on the math section of the SAT. Much of this remaining gender gap in test scores develops during high school because women continue to study in less rigorous math courses, and they are less likely than boys to participate in mathematically oriented extracurricular activities (Leahey and Guo 2001; Pallas and Alexander 1983; Vogt Yuan 2005).

It is important to understand what standardized tests measure because standardized testing has gained national recognition with the passage of the No Child Left Behind Act in 2002. This policy initiative requires standardized testing for students in the third through eighth grades and at least once during high school. The primary goal of the legislation is to reduce achievement gaps between students, particularly by race, poverty status, disability, ethnicity, and English proficiency. This act magnifies the significance of standardized testing. By neglecting the impacts of the environmental differences, testing biases, and validity issues discussed here, standardized testing will be of limited use to educators and policymakers as they seek to close achievement gaps.

SEE ALSO *Education, USA; Race and Education*

BIBLIOGRAPHY

ACT. http://www.act.org.

Benbow, Camilla Persson. 1988. Sex Differences in Mathematical Reasoning Ability in Intellectually Talented Preadolescents: Their Nature, Effects, and Possible Causes. *Behavioral and Brain Sciences* 11: 169–183.

Blackburn, M. L. 2004. The Role of Test Scores in Explaining Race and Gender Differences in Wages. *Economics of Education Review* 23: 555–576.

Blau, Judith, Stephanie Moller, and Lyle V. Jones. 2003. Going to College. In *Race in the Schools: Perpetuating White Dominance?* ed. Judith R. Blau, 177–202. Boulder, CO: Lynne Reinner.

Chandler, Michael, dir. 1999. *Frontline: Secrets of the SAT.* Boston. WGBH Educational Foundation. http://www.pbs.org/wgbh/pages/frontline/shows/sats/.

College Board. http://www.collegeboard.com.

Conley, Dalton. 1999. *Being Black, Living in the Red: Race, Wealth, and Social Policy in America.* Berkeley: University of California Press.

Croizet, Jean-Claude, and Marion Dutrevis. 2004. Socioeconomic Status and Intelligence: Why Test Scores Do Not Equal Merit. *Journal of Poverty* 8: 91–107.

Educational Testing Service: GRE—Graduate Record Examinations. http://www.ets.org/gre.

Fleming, Jacqueline. 2000. Affirmative Action and Standardized Test Scores. *Journal of Negro Education* 69: 27–37.

Fleming, Jacqueline. 2002. Who Will Succeed in College? When the SAT Predicts Black Students' Performance. *Review of Higher Education* 25: 281–296.

Freeman, Catherine, and Mary Ann Fox. 2005. *Status and Trends in the Education of American Indians and Alaska Natives.* NCES 2005–108. Washington, DC: National Center for Education Statistics, Department of Education.

Gandara, Patricia, and Elias Lopez. 1998. Latino Students and College Entrance Exams: How Much Do They Really Matter? *Hispanic Journal of Behavioral Sciences* 21:17–38.

Herrnstein, Richard J., and Charles Murray. 1994. *The Bell Curve: Intelligence and Class Structure in American Life.* New York: Free Press.

Jencks, Christopher. 1998. Racial Bias in Testing. In *The Black-White Test Score Gap*, eds. Christopher Jencks and Meredith Phillips, 55–85. Washington, DC: Brookings Institution Press.

LaCelle-Peterson, Mark. 2000. Choosing Not to Know: How Assessment Policies and Practices Obscure the Education of Language Minority Students. In *Assessment: Social Practice and Social Product*, ed. Ann Filer, 27–42. London: Routledge.

Leahey, Erin, and Guang Guo. 2001. Gender Differences in Mathematical Trajectories. *Social Forces* 80: 713–732.

Lemann, Nicholas. 1999. *The Big Test: The Secret History of the American Meritocracy.* New York: Farrar, Straus and Giroux.

Lesko, Alexandra, and Jennifer H. Corpus. 2006. Discounting the Difficult: How High Math-Identified Women Respond to Stereotype Threat. *Sex Roles: A Journal of Research* 54: 113–125.

Mickelson, Roslyn. 2006. Segregation and the SAT. *Ohio State Law Journal* 67: 157–199.

National Center for Education Statistics. 2006. *Digest of Education Statistics: 2005.* NCES 2006–030. Washington, DC: Department of Education. http://nces.ed.gov/programs/digest/d05.

National Center for Education Statistics. 2005. *Trends in Educational Equity of Girls and Women: 2004.* NCES 2005–016. Washington, DC: Department of Education. http://nces.ed.gov/pubsearch/pubsinfo.asp?pubid=2005016.

Oldfield, Kenneth. 1994. On the Importance of Informing Students about the Potential Risk Associated with Taking the Graduate Record Exam. *Journal of Thought* 29: 61–70.

Oldfield, Kenneth. 1996. The Political and Economic Reasons the Graduate Record Examination Persists Despite Its Generally Low Predictive Validity. *Journal of Thought* 31: 55–68.

Oliver, Melvin L., and Thomas M. Shapiro. 1995. *Black Wealth/White Wealth: A New Perspective on Racial Inequality.* New York: Routledge.

Pallas, Aaron M., and Karl L. Alexander. 1983. Sex Difference in Quantitative SAT Performance New Evidence on the Differential Coursework Hypothesis. *American Educational Research Journal* 20: 165–182.

Rodgers, William M., and William E. Spriggs. 1996. What Does the AFQT Really Measure: Race, Wages, Schooling, and the AFQT Score. *Review of Black Political Economy* 24: 13–47.

Steele, Claude, and Joshua Aronson. 1998. Stereotype Threat and the Test Performance of Academically Successful African Americans. In *The Black-White Test Score Gap*, eds. Christopher Jencks and Meredith Phillips, 401–430. Washington, DC: Brookings Institution Press.

Vogt Yuan, Anastasia. 2005. Sex Differences in School Performance During High School: Puzzling Patterns and Possible Explanations. *Sociological Quarterly* 46: 299–321.

Zuberi, Tukufu. 2001. *Thicker than Blood: How Racial Statistics Lie.* Minneapolis: University of Minnesota Press.

Stephanie Moller
Stephanie Potochnick

STANFORD PRISON EXPERIMENT

SEE *Prison Psychology; Zimbardo, Philip.*

STANTON, ELIZABETH CADY

SEE *Suffrage, Women's.*

STAR TREK

Although not popular during its original run in the late 1960s—it was cancelled after three low-rated seasons—the television program *Star Trek* developed a cult following that is still vibrant forty years later. Over the years, fans have appreciated the *Star Trek* saga's compelling stories and characters, idealistic and progressive view of the future, and confrontation with relevant political and cultural issues.

Gene Roddenberry created *Star Trek*, and the NBC network launched it in September 1966. The show centered on the twenty-third-century pangalactic travels of the USS *Enterprise*, the flagship of Starfleet—the military sector of the United Federation of Planets. The composition of the *Enterprise* crew itself was a social commentary on the advancements in civil rights and the nascent, albeit modest, recognition of gender equality. The ship was commanded by a white male, Captain James T. Kirk (William Shatner), but his supporting crew was considerably more diverse than the casts of other contemporary television shows. Using the fictional *Star Trek* universe, the show's episodes addressed the controversial issues of the late 1960s, including the Vietnam War, the cold war, and race relations. The show also broke new ground, most notably in featuring the first televised interracial kiss. Despite *Star Trek's* critical success, NBC cancelled it in 1969 because of low ratings.

Cancellation after only three seasons would be the death knell for most television programs, but *Star Trek's* cancellation marked only the beginning of one of the most successful science fiction ventures ever. Almost immediately, *Star Trek* reruns aired in syndication, earning high ratings and drawing new fans, known as "Trekkies" or "Trekkers." This fan base grew larger and more organized, and in 1972 Trekkies began holding *Star Trek* conventions. The show's actors, writers, and producers, along with thousands of fans, attend these conventions to discuss *Star Trek*, to trade memorabilia, and to socialize. With this demonstrable level of support, in 1979 Paramount Studios released a movie, *Star Trek: The Motion Picture*, which was produced by Roddenberry. The movie reunited the original cast, and it allowed the *Star Trek* legacy to continue. Throughout the 1980s subsequent *Star Trek* movies tackled social issues; for example, *Star Trek IV: The Voyage Home* (1986) was a parable on environmentalism and species protection.

Star Trek's increasing popularity gave Roddenberry the opportunity to create a new television program, *Star Trek: The Next Generation*, which debuted in September 1987. *The Next Generation* featured the twenty-fourth-century crew of the *Enterprise*, commanded by Captain Jean-Luc Picard (Patrick Stewart). As with the original *Star Trek* series, *The Next Generation* addressed important political, cultural, and social issues of its time. Anticipating the end of the cold war, the United Federation of Planets made a lasting, albeit tenuous, peace with its former archrivals the Klingons. In addition, *The Next Generation* reflected advancements in gender equality that had been achieved since the 1960s; whereas the original series relegated women to supporting roles, women in *The Next Generation* served as ships' doctors, security chiefs, and even admirals. *The Next Generation* episodes also addressed sexual orientation, the struggles of subjugated peoples, and ethical issues concerning animal experimentation. Unlike the original series, *The Next Generation* was well funded and highly rated, and it aired for seven seasons. Gene Roddenberry died in 1991 and did not see the full run of *The Next Generation*, but others ensured that the *Star Trek* legacy would continue.

The Next Generation's success led to more movies during the 1990s featuring the cast of *The Next Generation*. By 2006 there had been ten *Star Trek* movies. Additionally, *The Next Generation's* success spawned two more television series: *Star Trek: Deep Space Nine* (1993–1999) and *Star Trek: Voyager* (1995–2001). Neither show took place on the *Enterprise*, but each continued with the basic *Star Trek* themes; for example, at a time when few television programs featured women in charge, a woman commanded the *Voyager* ship. In 2001 yet another *Star Trek* series, *Star Trek: Enterprise* (2001–2005), was launched. This show took place in the twenty-second century, during the early years of the *Enterprise* and Earth's entry into the United Federation of Planets. Low ratings and less popularity among fans brought the cancellation of *Enterprise* in 2005. Although to date there are no more television programs planned, *Star Trek* remains part of the American cultural lexicon, with academics using the show as a vehicle for their social criticism (e.g., Johnston 2002; Roberts 1999). Reruns of the television programs and movies remain popular, and *Star Trek* conventions are still held worldwide.

SEE ALSO *Science Fiction; Television*

BIBLIOGRAPHY

Johnston, Steven. 2002. The Architecture of Democratic Monuments. *Strategies* 15: 197–218.

Roberts, Robin. 1999. *Sexual Generations: Star Trek The Next Generation and Gender.* Urbana: University of Illinois Press.

Star Trek Web site. http://www.startrek.com.

Steven Tauber

STAR WARS

George Lucas's film *Star Wars* (1977) had a lasting impact on the genre of science fiction films, the film industry in general, popular culture, and the political culture during and after Ronald Reagan's presidency. Lucas had established Lucasfilm Ltd. in 1971 and later founded Industrial Light and Magic, a special effects company. The revolutionary special effects in Lucas's films set a standard for future science fiction and action films. The new technologies used to make *Star Wars* included a new type of motion camera, innovations in sound technology, and developments in digital and computerized sequencing. Before *Star Wars*, possibly the last science fiction film to revolutionize the genre was director Stanley Kubrick's *2001: A Space Odyssey* (1968). The financial success of *Star Wars* changed Hollywood's negative perception of science fiction films, making possible the production of other such films, including *Star Trek: The Motion Picture* (dir. Robert Wise, 1979).

Lucas eventually made six *Star Wars* films, the original trilogy and a prequel trilogy. The titles and years of release are: *Star Wars* (later retitled *Star Wars: Episode IV–A New Hope*, 1977); *Star Wars: Episode V–The Empire Strikes Back* (1980); *Star Wars: Episode VI–Return of the Jedi* (1983); *Star Wars: Episode I–The Phantom Menace* (1999); *Star Wars: Episode II–Attack of the Clones* (2002); and *Star Wars: Episode III–Revenge of the Sith* (2005). By 2005 the two *Star Wars* trilogies and all merchandising and franchising had earned close to $20 billion, making it among the most popular and profitable film series in U.S. film history. Many of the episodes were nominated for and won Oscars and other film awards.

The plot of the films centers around Luke Skywalker, his family, the Jedi Knights, and the turbulent history of an intergalactic empire struggling from opposing totalitarian and democratic forces. Luke's character, his independent spirit, and tensions between him and his father (and surrogate fathers) hearken back to stories from the American West, Dickensian tales, and chivalry and medieval romances. The films also embody Joseph Campbell's structuralist approach to mythology. A subtext underlying the films pits a romantic notion of mysticism and the divine in nature against an overreliance on technology. Though futuristic and featuring such "technology" as light sabers, warp drives, androids, and sky cities, the story takes place "a long time ago in a galaxy far, far away," a setting that shrouds *Star Wars* in an ambiance of legend and mythology. In technical terms, the films are more science fantasy than science fiction and created a genre labeled "space opera."

A variety of influences have been identified. These include Japanese director Akira Kurosawa's *The Hidden Fortress* (1958); author Isaac Asimov's *Foundation* trilogy (1951–1953); Frank Herbert's *Dune* books; and Jack Kirby's *Fourth World* series published by DC Comics in the early 1970s. The relationship between Luke and his Jedi mentor Yoda is reminiscent of author Carlos Casteneda's *Don Juan* books about shamanistic initiation. The films' opening credits, with a scrolling tilted text that moves outward, is an homage to the *Flash Gordon* cinematographic serials from the late 1930s. Lucas indicated that he wanted to create a modern mythology, and the popularity of the films suggests that he succeeded. As evidence of this popularity are the many *Star Wars*–themed books and novelizations, comic books, syndicated comic strips, video and computer games, Web pages, and blogs, in addition to action figures and other *Star Wars*–related franchising and merchandizing.

Perhaps the most striking influence of Lucas's films was on American political culture during and after the Reagan administration (1981–1989). Reagan was at times dubbed "Ronald Ray-Gun" in underground comic strips from the 1960s because, as an actor, he had played Steve Coe in Lewis Seiler's *Murder in the Air* (1940). In this film, Reagan's Coe tests an experimental "ray" weapon called the Inertia Projector. Reagan was reportedly a fan of *Star Wars*, and he incorporated various allusions to the film into his foreign policy. In particular, he referred to the Soviet Union as the "Evil Empire," advocated a missile defense system that was later labeled "Star Wars," and drew parallels between communism and the Rebel Alliance of *Star Wars*.

Reagan's two Evil Empire speeches were delivered on June 8, 1982, at the British House of Commons and on March 8, 1983, to the National Association of Evangelicals. On March 23, 1983, Reagan delivered what became known as the "Star Wars speech," in which he enjoined "the scientific community … those who gave us nuclear weapons … to give us the means of rendering these nuclear weapons impotent and obsolete." Reagan's Strategic Defense Initiative, which proposed the development of ground- and satellite-based laser weapons that could target and destroy ballistic missiles, was termed "Star Wars" by a skeptical press and scientific community. The program was seen as heightening cold war tensions and militarizing space.

Star Wars allusions continued during the George H. W. Bush and George W. Bush administrations. During the Persian Gulf War (1991), for example, military officials called themselves Jedi Knights. Research, development, and funding for "Star Wars" missile defense technology continued through 2006, generating several books, including Francis FitzGerald's *Way Out There in the Blue: Reagan, Star Wars, and the End of the Cold War* (2000); *The Phantom Defense: America's Pursuit of the Star Wars Illusion* (2001) by Craig Eisendrath, Melvin A.

Goodman, and Gerald E. Marsh; and Loring Wirbel's *Star Wars: US Tools of Space Supremacy* (2003).

SEE ALSO *Popular Culture; Science Fiction*

BIBLIOGRAPHY

Jenkins, Garry. 1997. *Empire Building: The Remarkable Real Life Story of Star Wars.* Secaucus, NJ: Carol.

Meyer, David S. 1992. Star Wars, *Star Wars*, and American Political Culture. *Journal of Popular Culture* 26 (2): 99–115.

Reagan, Ronald. 1983. Address to the Nation on Defense and National Security. March 23. http://www.reagan.utexas.edu/archives/speeches/1983/32383d.htm.

Seed, David. 1999. *American Science Fiction and the Cold War: Literature and Film.* Chicago: Fitzroy Dearborn.

Jeff Williams

STARE, THE

The ancient Greeks explored the dialectics of the gaze in the form of the myth of Medusa, who can turn people to stone with a single glance. The Medusan story symbolically condenses a range of experiences of looking and being looked at in the graphic image of the "petrifying gaze" (*petrification* meaning literally the turning of the other into an inert object), and the Medusa, being a female deity, introduces the idea that "looking" implicates sexual and gendered phenomena of some social and cultural importance.

The human sciences have demonstrated that "looking" is a profoundly social and political phenomenon that obliges the analyst to distinguish between different modalities and practices of seeing ("looking," "gazing," "staring," "glancing," and so forth). It is thus important to distinguish the physical and physiological properties of "seeing" from the culturally defined forms of "looking." For example, very young infants tend to stare at objects and others (particularly other persons with a distinctive physical attribute); as children are socialized they learn to sublimate this natural inclination into the more civil act of glancing and looking away. Children are taught that certain forms of eye contact are regarded as impolite, that looking is subject to appropriateness norms.

We are not far from Jean-Paul Sartre's analysis of voyeurism and the attendant social relations of masochism and sadism in his work *Being and Nothingness* (1956). Here the Medusan imagery is elevated into a description of the human condition as consciousness seeks to objectify the other person and thereby escape from the petrifying glance of another consciousness. Simone de Beauvoir

(1908–1986) built upon Sartre's phenomenology of the gaze by formulating the topic in explicitly gendered terms, distinguishing between the aggressive masculine gaze and the defensive feminine look. Frantz Fanon explored similar phenomena by identifying the racialized perspective that projects the other as the object of racial oppression and prejudice (Fanon 1967).

Today the cultural construction of the gaze has led to a number of significant lines of research. Feminism's critique of patriarchal modes of experience, including the phallocentric ways in which women's bodies and female experience are cast into "objective" terms, is frequently formulated in "objective" terms, resulting in representations of women as an "object" of male desire. In a similar vein, John Berger has explored the male gaze and its role in creating representations of the female body in the history of Western art and, more particularly, in the history of the two- and three-dimensional nude figure (Berger 1972). Noteworthy in the field of media and film studies is Laura Mulvey's psychoanalytically inspired work on the voyeuristic conventions of Hollywood cinema, and more especially her theory of the phallocentric links between male visual pleasure and narrative cinema (1989). Erving Goffman's investigations of the "interactional work" of seeing and being seen—for example, the blank "stare-into-the-distance" assumed by urban passengers (the kind of neutral stare adopted in situations such as sharing an elevator, traveling on the subway, standing in line, etc.)—led him to his concept of "civil indifference." Goffman's research (1963, 1970) was prefigured by the German sociologist Georg Simmel (1858–1918), who is well known for pioneering work in the social phenomenology of the blasé attitude of cosmopolitan life. For Simmel, the urban metropolis creates forms of life where the self lives in a world of strangers, is continuously observed by the disinterested eyes of crowds, and loses the potential of creativity envisionment.

The look and its social analysis continues to play an important role within the field of visual culture theory and research. Popular culture is increasingly defined as a culture of global visuality, where all signifiers are either explicitly or implicitly reconfigured in voyeuristic terms—a multimedia world-industry of images designed to be looked at. Today computer-based communications, TV, film, and digitized multimedia provide the ultimate technological means that extend the social relationships embodied in gazing to a planetary stage. The related concepts of "the society of the spectacle," "simulacral culture," and the surveillance society have been developed to explore new geographies of power as these are redefined by the electronic media of watching, staring, and controlling the social field.

BIBLIOGRAPHY

Berger, John. 1972. *Ways of Seeing*. Harmondsworth, U.K.: Penguin.

De Beauvoir, Simone. 1970. *The Second Sex*. New York: Bantam.

Fanon, Franz. 1967. *Black Skin, White Masks: The Experience of a Black Man in a White World*. New York: Grove.

Goffman, Erving. 1961. *Encounters: Two Studies in the Sociology of Interaction*. Indianapolis, IN: Bobbs-Merrill.

Goffman, Erving. 1963. *Behavior in Public Places: Notes on the Social Organization of Gatherings*. New York: Free Press.

Goffman, Erving. 1970. *Strategic Interaction*. Oxford, U.K.: Blackwell.

Mulvey, Laura. 1989. Film, Feminism, and the Avant-Garde. In *Visual and Other Pleasures*, 111–126. London: Macmillan.

Sartre, Jean-Paul. 1956. *Being and Nothingness*. Trans. Hazel E. Barnes. New York: Philosophical Library.

Barry Sandywell

STATE, THE

All human communities have some type of political organization that governs the behavior of its individual members. However, state forms of government are distinct from other forms of political organization such as tribes, clans, and gens. As Brian Nelson states in his 2006 study, the state is best defined in terms of its basic structural characteristics, which are territoriality, sovereignty, law, centralization, legitimation, and class stratification. And as both Elman Service (1975) and Ted Llewellen (1983) note, in contrast to earlier forms of political organization, which were based on lineage and heredity, the state is a form of political organization based on territorial jurisdiction. The state is also a sovereign entity, which means it claims a monopoly of the legitimate use of physical force within a given territory, as argued by Max Weber (1978). The state's sovereignty depends on its ability to successfully enforce a monopoly of coercive force in relation to all inhabitants of its territory, against the claims of neighboring states, and against the claims of competing forms of political organization (e.g., tribes) within the same territory. Thus, for a state to exist, it must centralize the coercive powers of law, administration, and military force because sovereignty does not exist when governmental authority is retained by competing social units, such as clans or tribes, or where inhabitants' political loyalties are retained by local units of government that function independently of the state's central authority. Consequently, Charles Tilly observes (1975), "state-building" has been a lengthy and violent historical process involving the subordination of competing forms of political organization to the state's sovereign authority and the defense of its territorial boundaries against rival states.

The state's structural characteristics of territoriality, sovereignty, and centralized government are exercised through the application of general laws that are considered authoritatively binding on the territory's inhabitants. These laws are always reinforced by a corresponding form of state consciousness or ideology of legitimation. The state always derives its legitimacy from an operative myth of the state's origin or foundation, such as a belief that the law is received by a state's priests or wise men directly from the gods, or that the state is founded by heroes with exceptional virtues, or that the state was established by contract among its citizens. Yet, as a matter of fact, all states arise from a system of class stratification, which is reproduced by the state as one of its main political and economic functions. Class, as Friedrich Engels (1972) argued, is not the only kind of social stratification that exists in state societies—it generally coexists with gender, racial, or ethnic forms of stratification—but class stratification is a unique attribute of state forms of governance.

ORIGINS AND FORMS OF THE STATE

Scholars have proposed many different typologies of state forms, but historically, as Nelson (2006) states, there are four fundamental forms of state: (1) ancient city-states, (2) ancient empire-states, (3) modern city-states, and (4) the modern nation-state. The origins of the state are generally traced to the late Neolithic period (3000–4000 BCE), or about 34,000 years after the first *homo sapiens*. The first archaic states emerged on the banks of the Tigris and Euphrates Rivers (Mesopotamia), the Nile River Valley (Egypt), the Yellow River Valley (China), and the Indus River Valley (India).

Geography was a key factor in the origins of the state, because the fertility of these river valleys supported large settled agricultural populations, while the agricultural surpluses generated by these peoples made it possible to store and redistribute crops and to support the specialized craftsmen, warriors, priests, and administrators critical to state formation. Karl Wittfogel's (1957) hydraulic thesis of state formation notes that complex irrigation and flood control systems were necessary to realize these agricultural surpluses, while the construction and maintenance of these systems required increasingly centralized forms of political control. As Morton Fried (1967) and Jonathan Haas (1982) observe, this centralization of political authority and the emergence of social differentiation based on function mark the origins of the archaic state.

ANCIENT CITY-STATES

The first archaic states were created by the Sumerians of Mesopotamia about 3500 BCE, but within a few hundred years (3100–2320 BCE) many of these archaic states had evolved into fully developed city-states. The first real states were city-states, and the largest among them sometimes had tens of thousands of inhabitants. The ancient Sumerian city-states were typically warlike and in some cases expansionary. The fact that many ancient cities were defended by walls and fortifications suggests that the city-state, which quickly spread to other parts of Mesopotamia, did so partly as a result of the conquest of other peoples and partly as a way to defend against the threat of the Sumerian city-states. Significantly, these states not only centralized political authority within a defined territory, but eventually developed concepts of law that were first enunciated in the Hammurabic Code, a code of written law promulgated by Hammurabi, a king of Babylonia (1792–1750 BCE). Hammurabi's Code influenced the emergence of legal systems in other Near Eastern states and was transmitted as a model to other empires in the Near East, Mediterranean, and later Europe.

The Egyptian state emerged almost simultaneously with the Sumerian city-states in 3100 BCE. In both regions, the sovereign authority of the state and its legitimizing religious myth were embodied in the person of a king, who claimed power either as a deity (Egypt) or as the voice of the gods (Sumeria). The centralized bureaucratic, military, economic, and ideological power of these kings far surpassed that of any previous tribal chieftain or clan elder. These kings commanded a formal state-military hierarchy, sat atop a rigid class system, and exercised preeminent religious influence within the state.

The Indus Valley Civilization emerged at about the same time (3300 BCE) on the Indian subcontinent, but this civilization did not achieve a state-level society until about 2600 BCE. Romila Thapar (2002) explains that, as in Sumeria and Egypt, the irrigation of the Indus River Valley generated large agricultural surpluses that supported burgeoning urban centers by 2500 BCE, and, over the next six hundred years, Indus Valley Civilization spread to the Ganges River basin and northern Afghanistan. However, it was not until 1000 BCE that the first recognizable city-states appeared on the Indian subcontinent, although by 500 BCE there were sixteen monarchies known as the Mahajanapadas covering the Indian subcontinent. These city-states, Vincent Smith (1981) notes, followed the earlier pattern of legitimizing the right of a king to his throne with genealogies devised by priests that ascribed divine origins to the rulers.

In their history of China, John Fairbank and Denis Twitchett (vol. 1, 1978) note that the Huang He Valley emerged as the first cultural center in China in the late Neolithic period (2100–1800 BCE); by the end of the second millennium BCE, the Zhou Dynasty (1027–771 BCE) was established in the Yellow River Valley and later in the Yantgtze River Valley (770–221 BCE). The first Zhou king invoked "the Mandate of Heaven" to legitimize his rule, a concept that would influence almost every subsequent Chinese dynasty. During the Zhou Dynasty, the city-state spread throughout China until several hundred warring states were finally consolidated into seven states toward the end of the fifth century BCE.

ANCIENT EMPIRE-STATES

The ancient city-states were aggressive and expansionary regardless of where they originated, and their wars resulted directly in the formation of the first ancient empire-states. In most cases, Nelson (2006) observes, the basis of early state formation was the city, with empires arising as a secondary state formation from a city-state's imperial expansion. The Assyrians built the first empire-state, starting with Sargon of Akkad, who became the first king to successfully assert political control over inhabitants living beyond his city-state (2371 BCE). Assyrian kings gradually asserted hegemony over all of Mesopotamia and the Fertile Crescent (2371–612 BCE), including Egypt for a short period (745–612 BCE). In building an empire of city-states, the Assyrians established the model for all subsequent ancient and classical empires, including the Persian, Macedonian, and Roman Empires, as well as many smaller empires, such as the Athenian, Phoenician, and Carthaginian Empires.

In India and the Far East, comparable configurations emerged from the warring city-states. During the time that large parts of India were subjected to the Persian and Macedonian Empires, the first Indian empire-state was the kingdom of Magadha, which emerged as a major power in northeastern India after subjugating two neighboring states (684–26 BCE). Numerous empires rose and fell in different parts of the Indian subcontinent, including the Satavahana Empire (230 BCE–199 CE) in southern and central India, and the Gupta Empire (240–550 CE), which united northern India. In 1526 Babur established the Mughal Empire, which was the first empire-state to unite most of the Indian subcontinent by 1600 CE. Its successor, the Maratha Empire, stretched across the entire subcontinent by 1760 but was eventually displaced by the British Empire (1757–1947 CE).

In China, the Qin Dynasty (221–207 BCE) was the first to subdue large parts of the core Han Chinese homeland and unite them under a centralized Legalist government. It also imposed a common system of writing and developed a state ideology based on Confucianism. China was an empire-state for most of its history, although historians generally divide its political development into early imperial (221 BC–588 CE), classical imperial (580–1234 CE), and later imperial (1279–1911 CE) phases. However, as Peter Farb (1968) explains, there is considerable debate as to whether the Meso-American empires, including those established by the Olmecs (1200–400 BCE), Mayans (250–900 CE), Incas (1197–1533 CE), and Aztecs (1248–1521 CE) should be considered ancient empire-states, archaic states, or a distinct tribal (i.e., non-state) form of tributary empire.

MODERN CITY-STATES

The ancient empire-states were often disorganized and short-lived in comparison to modern states. As S. N. Eisenstadt (1963) observes, it was not uncommon for empires to be conquered by rival empires, nor was it uncommon for empires to disintegrate back into warring city-states or into forms of feudalism because of weak political leadership, natural catastrophe, invasion, or rebellion. However, city-states and empire-states are the only known forms of state until the emergence of the modern state.

The basic structural characteristics of the modern state are identical to those of earlier state forms. However, most modern states tend to manifest these characteristics on a different territorial scale (the nation) and to vest sovereignty in an impersonal legal system. In the modern state, sovereignty is asserted to reside in the impersonal state form, and not in the ruler as conceived in the archaic and ancient states. Thus, in the modern state, there is a firm distinction between the state and its government (rulers), which is a distinctive ideological characteristic of the modern state compared to earlier forms of state. As Nelson (2006) notes, the modern state has also evolved in tandem with the capitalist form of economy and is therefore generally linked to the reproduction of specifically capitalist forms of class stratification.

The origins of the modern state are found in the medieval towns of Europe, which, as a general rule, stood outside the stateless feudal system of political relationships based on personal rule. The medieval towns developed their own governing system based on the idea that the town (i.e., the state) was an abstract entity (corporation or *universitas*) that was by right free from outside control. Joseph Strayer (1970) notes that these commercial centers evolved into independent states, most notably in Italy and Germany in the fourteenth and fifteenth centuries. The German city-states of the Hanseatic League, which emerged from the mid-fourteenth century onward, constituted a trading and military alliance of modern city-states but never became a true state in itself. Venice is the only modern city-state to build a commercial empire-state (800–1797 CE) by asserting control over other cities and islands in the Mediterranean and Aegean Seas. Despite being largely displaced by the nation-state, Singapore, Monaco, and Luxembourg survive today as successful and prosperous modern city-states.

THE MODERN NATION-STATE

The modern state became largely synonymous with the nation-state beginning in Europe in the early 1300s. In parts of the world, such as Europe in the medieval era, China, and Japan, there was sometimes a concept of "the nation" or "the people," which was united by geography, language, literature, custom, and religion; but there were not actual states with territorial boundaries coinciding with this legitimating idea. Indeed, following the collapse of empires in Europe, China, Japan, and India, and their disintegration into feudalism, the state often ceased to exist as a form of political organization. Feudal forms of political organization were premised on structural characteristics that are the opposite of a state: (a) extreme decentralization *and* (b) the privatization of social, economic, and political power.

The modern nation-state originated in Europe as powerful monarchs in France, England, Russia, Spain, Sweden, and Denmark waged continuous wars to unify their "nations." The political and religious wars that engulfed Europe for four centuries finally culminated in 1648 in the Peace of Westphalia, which codified the modern system of nation-states as international law by recognizing fixed national boundaries and the sovereignty of states within their territories. However, the system of European nation-states was not actually completed until the unification of Germany and of Italy in 1871.

It has been argued that, because most of the major and minor European nation-states were all colonial and imperial powers from the 1500s onward, the major nation-states have always been nation-state-empires. In fact the nation-state as codified in the Westphalian system was largely transferred to other regions of the world through European colonial and imperial expansion. Some of these postcolonial states, such as those in North America (1700s), Latin America (1800s), China (1911), India (1947), and Africa (1950s–1970s), were established by revolutions of national independence. Other states established in Africa and the Middle East were artificial "nations" created by the retreating colonial powers after World War I and World War II. For this reason, however, many of the postcolonial states lack the fundamental characteristics of either a nation or a state, such as a founding or heroic myth to legitimize the state. These "nations" often have a stronger history of internal tribal and religious conflict, while they sometimes lack a common language or religion except as a legacy of the colonizing state. The shared characteristics of nationhood are often most common among political and economic elites but are not shared evenly by inhabitants, who continue to speak local dialects, follow traditional religious practices, or retain political loyalties to local tribes and clans.

THE FUTURE OF THE NATION-STATE

New nation-states have proliferated in the late twentieth and early twenty-first centuries as resurgent nationality and ethnic groups withdraw from artificially constructed nation-states or reassert their independence from nation-state empires. Membership in the United Nations increased from 51 members in 1945 to 191 members in 2002. However, as Martin Van Creveld argues in his 1999 study, the future of the nation-state appears uncertain: Many existing states are combining into new forms of transnational political association, while many of the state's economic and military functions are being taken over by organizations that are not states.

The reassertion of ethnic and religious identities within and against established nation-states has also led to the proliferation of failed states among many of the artificial postcolonial states. This has resulted in a number of tenuous governing entities best described as quasi-states or proto-states; in other cases it has resulted in long periods of stateless anarchy, where small areas are governed by competing warlords in a system sometimes described, as by Gianfranco Poggi in his 1990 study, as modern feudalism.

On the other hand, many nation-states are responding to the contemporary challenges of a new era of globalization by delegating or ceding partial sovereignty to transnational, international, or supranational organizations that perform the statelike functions of internal governance (European Union), economic regulation (World Trade Organization), health and welfare provision (United Nations), and military defense (North Atlantic Treaty Organization); but these organizations, as both Kenichi Ohmae (1990) and Martin Shaw (2000) point out, are neither nations nor states. It is not yet clear whether this emerging network of political, economic, and military organizations foreshadows the end of the nation-state or the establishment of a new global state.

SEE ALSO *Authority; City-State; Ethnicity; Gender; Globalization, Anthropological Aspects of; Globalization, Social and Economic Aspects of; Government; Law; Military; Nationalism and Nationality; Political Science; Political System; Politics; Race; Sovereignty*

BIBLIOGRAPHY

Eisenstadt, S. N. 1963. *The Political Systems of Empires.* London and New York: Free Press.

Engels, Friedrich. 1972. *The Origins of the Family, Private Property and the State.* New York: International Publishers.

Fairbank, John K. and Denis Twitchett, eds. 1978-2003. *The Cambridge History of China.* 12 vols. Cambridge, U.K., and New York: Cambridge University Press.

Farb, Peter. 1968. *Man's Rise to Civilization as Shown by the Indians of North America from Primeval Times to the Coming of the Industrial State.* New York: Dutton.

Fried, Morton H. 1967. *The Evolution of Political Society: An Essay in Political Anthropology.* New York: Random House.

Haas, Jonathan. 1982. *The Evolution of the Prehistoric State.* New York: Columbia University Press.

Llewellen, Ted C. 1983. *Political Anthropology: An Introduction.* South Hadley, MA: Bergin and Garvey.

Nelson, Brian R. 2006. *The Making of the Modern State: A Theoretical Evolution.* New York: Palgrave Macmillan.

Ohmae, Kenichi. 1990. *The End of the National State.* New York: Free Press.

Poggi, Gianfranco. 1990. *The State: Its Nature, Development, and Prospects.* Cambridge, U.K.: Polity Press, and Stanford, CA: Stanford University Press.

Service, Elman R. 1975. *Origins of the State and Civilization: The Process of Cultural Evolution.* New York: Norton.

Shaw, Martin. 2000. *Theory of the Global State: Globality as Unfinished Revolution.* Cambridge, U.K., and New York: Cambridge University Press.

Smith, Vincent A. 1981. *The Oxford History of India.* 4th ed. Delhi and New York: Oxford University Press.

Strayer, Joseph R. 1970. *On the Medieval Origins of the Modern State.* Princeton, NJ: Princeton University Press.

Thapar, Romila. 2002. *Early India: From the Origins to AD 1300.* Berkeley: University of California Press.

Tilly, Charles, ed. 1975. *The Formation of National States in Western Europe.* Princeton, NJ: Princeton University Press.

Van Creveld, Martin. 1999. *The Rise and Decline of the State.* Cambridge, U.K.: Cambridge University Press.

Weber, Max. 1978. *Economy and Society*, eds. Guenther Roth and Claus Wittich, trans. Ephraim Fischoff et al. 2 vols. Berkeley: University of California Press.

Wittfogel, Karl. 1957. *Oriental Despotism: A Comparative Study of Total Power.* New Haven, CT: Yale University Press.

Clyde Barrow

STATE, STATIONARY

SEE *Stationary State.*

STATE ENTERPRISE

A state enterprise is a large, complex economic organization owned and operated by a government rather than by a private individual or organization. Though an economic entity, it is totally encapsulated by the polity, with no separation of state and market. And very importantly, it also may transfer goods and services among suborganizations without explicit pricing of those transactions.

The problem posed by state enterprise is determining a single decision rule governing the economic behavior of multiple suborganizations controlled by a single decision maker, a rule that will lead to the realization of maximum profit for the entire group. It has been proven in the socialist calculation debate that maximizing the excess of revenue over cost from operations is the most fundamental economic problem, whether the economy is centralized or decentralized, privately or publicly owned, and whether this excess is labeled surplus, surplus value, or profit.

Although this form of economic organization dates to ancient times, this article will (1) trace briefly the development of such enterprises, and (2) trace equally briefly the development of the economic theory underlying the management of such enterprises from the Industrial Revolution in Europe to the present. Although state enterprises have developed in former European colonies in Africa, America, and Asia since decolonization, these are derived largely from metropolitan examples.

THE ECONOMIC HISTORY OF STATE-OWNED ENTERPRISES IN EUROPE, 1600–2000

In the early seventeenth century, the Dutch, Portuguese, Spanish, English, and French developed large, state-chartered multinational trading companies that lasted until the late eighteenth century.

The best example of the potential of state enterprise in this period was in ancient régime France. Richelieu established the model for an autarchic mercantilist state with new industries, a network of canals, and international trading companies on the model of the Dutch East India Company. He formed four chartered companies for the purpose of colonization but was unable to effectuate the entire system. His successor, Mazarin, appointed as finance minister Colbert, who expanded the principle of government control of enterprises to a wider range of industries and activities, enacting a much greater part of the system. Colbert established ten more trading companies. He systematically established royal monopolies for the production of luxury goods and government regulation of all commerce and production. The heyday of this policy, called mercantilism by its critics and later by economic historians, was between 1613 and 1767. Colbert was so successful at it that it is sometimes known as Colbertism. To conceptualize this French mercantilist economy mathematically, Quesnay, a critic of the system, developed his *Tableau Économique*. In 1954 Joseph Schumpeter called this a *planned economy*.

The practice of state control of enterprises survived the French Revolution and continued through the nineteenth, twentieth, and early twenty-first centuries, the state assuming ownership of such enterprises as canals, toll roads, toll bridges, toll tunnels, railroads, energy and electric utility companies, and airlines. In the post–World War II era, the state controlled over 50 percent of new investment based upon its ownership of enterprises. To optimize the output of these enterprises, it instituted an indicative central economic plan. That is, although private investors and consumers were not obligated to follow the government's economic plan because of the overwhelming government importance in the economy, there were strong incentives to do so.

Prussia under Bismarck in the nineteenth century showed the greatest reliance on state enterprise to finance the operation of the state. In one year in the 1870s, Prussia received 398 million francs from state enterprise, most from state railways but also from state-owned mines, factories, salt works, state forests, and state farms. The Bank of Prussia, state mint, toll roads, and toll canals also yielded substantial revenue to the state. This Bismarckian system of enterprise ownership was continued and extended by all subsequent German governments and included such important state enterprises as Lufthansa, VEBA, VIAG, Volkswagen, and Salzgitter. After World War II, the United States enforced a quasi-competitive economy on the West Germans under their control that did not require the dismantling of the state enterprises just named. In contrast, the Soviet Union forced a system of state enterprise upon East Germany, largely the former Prussia. In its centrally planned economy, state-owned enterprises produced about 97 percent of total net national income in 1985, this proportion continuing until about 1994.

The Marx-Kautsky concept that the economy was a single enterprise that should be controlled by the state was adopted by the Bolshevik Party in Russia and applied to the Soviet economy after 1917. Between 1917 and 1921, the Bolshevik government transferred 37,000 enterprises from private to state control in Russia, including all firms employing over ten workers. Among these enterprises were Aeroflot and those of the Oil Syndicate, Petroleum Syndicate, or Naphtha Syndicate, organized in 1918. In 1965, there were about 200,000 enterprises in operation in the USSR. In 1988, Aeroflot was split into smaller groups of enterprises. Azneft, Grozneft, and Embaneft, the state production trusts in the Oil Syndicate, were privatized after 1991.

The economic planning agency in the USSR, established in February 1921, was known as Gosplan, an advisory agency to the Council of Labor and Defense (STO). From 1925 until 1927, Gosplan was structured with two levels of central ministries above production enterprises. Cycles of decentralizing restructuring occurred, with peaks in 1957 under Khrushchev, in 1961–1965 under

Kosygin, in 1985–1990 under Gorbachev, and in 1991–2000 under Yeltsin. Putin succeeded Yeltsin in 2000 and remained in office as of 2007. He attempted to arrest the free-market trend and reestablish some state enterprises.

ECONOMIC THEORY OF STATE ENTERPRISES

Economic theories associated with the historical development of state enterprises include those of Augustin Cournot, Jules Dupuit, Léon Walras, Maurice Allais, and Gérard Debreu in France; Vilfredo Pareto and Enrico Barone in Italy; Karl Marx and Karl Kautsky in Germany; Vladimir Groman, Vladimir Popov, Wassily Leontief, and Leonid Kantorovich in the USSR; Jan Tinbergen in the Netherlands; Ragnar Frisch in Norway; Oskar Lange and Leonid Hurwicz in Poland; and Donaldson Brown, Alfred Bradley, Paul Samuelson, and Kenneth Arrow in the United States. Of these theorists, eight have been awarded the Nobel Memorial Prize in Economic Science since its establishment in 1969.

Interestingly, given the lead taken by France in the practice of mercantilist policy, there were few French academic writings on the doctrine in the sixteenth, seventeenth, and eighteenth centuries. Cournot in his 1838 *Recherches* introduced marginal cost pricing in government enterprises (toll roads, toll canals, and railroads, which were completely state owned by the 1870s), defining the marginal revenue and marginal cost functions to be the derivatives of the total revenue and cost functions, and prescribing a most efficient price as that attained at the equality of these two derivatives.

Dupuit in 1844 extended Cournot's marginal analysis from production to consumer utility. Using taxation as an example, he argued that total revenue from a new public utility (state enterprise) would be greatest where marginal revenue from a change in a price (toll) was zero. He distinguished between the utility to the nation as a whole (social or state utility), and the utility of a consumer of a service (private utility). Private utility varied with the consumer, and state utility could be maximized by price discrimination, charging different prices to consumers based on their individual utility functions.

Following Marx's 1859 lead in theory and the policy of the First International, which he cites, Walras from 1874 to 1877 developed a static model of a pure exchange economy of many sectors arrayed as an *m*-by-*n* plane matrix of linear demand and supply equations. When solved as a simultaneous equation system, this model yielded the quantity of output of all sectors used as inputs to each other sector and the prices at which these transactions took place. To begin operating the model, one was required to guess at the initial quantity of commodities held by each participant in the economy, and the prices of those commodities. The model then proceeded to final equilibrium by successive approximation.

The first explicit theoretical extension of the Marxian and Walrasian models was undertaken by quasi-socialist engineers Pareto and Barone in the 1890s. Pareto approved of the theory of class struggle and historical materialism but questioned the labor theory of value. In his 1896–1897 *Cours d'economie politique*, Pareto argued, using Walras's general equilibrium model, that as an equilibrium was simply the solution to a set of equations, this solution could be calculated by a socialist planner as well as worked out in practice through a market. In 1897, Pareto said he had been able "vigorously to prove that the coefficients of production are determined by the entrepreneurs in a regime of pure competition precisely in the same way as a socialist government would have to fix them if it wanted to realize a maximum of ophelimity" (Pareto 1897, pp. 485–502). In his 1906 *Manuel d'economie politique*, Pareto, analyzing only production in a collectivist economy, stated that "prices and net interest on capital disappear as actual entities … but they will remain as accounting entities; without them the ministry of production would proceed blindly and would not know how to plan production." Therefore, "[t]he phenomena we have just studied suggest, in an abstract way and without taking into account the practical difficulties, is an important argument in favor of collectivist production." In the 1909 French revised edition of this book by Bonnet, all four sets of Walrasian mathematical equations, including the consumption set, were presented explicitly, but only in a 113-page appendix. For consumer utility, however, he substituted an Edgeworth indifference curve for a Walrasian (cardinal) utility function. Mathematically, this substitution made no difference in the equilibrium equations. However, the ordinality of the utility or individual preference equations meant that no empirical (numerical) solution could be calculated representing his maximum of ophelimity. His focus thus shifted from the Walrasian problem of proving the existence of a solution to a set of equations to maximizing satisfaction, a preliminary statement of economic optimization, the linear programming problem. This optimum was defined as the state at which no one can be made better off without making someone else worse off. The solution assumed that all equations in the system were differentiable.

French economic planning after World War II was based on the theory Allais provided in 1943. He proved that a general equilibrium was Pareto optimal and that it could be attained by a centrally planned economy. If monopoly exists, however, these results are vitiated, for Walrasian general equilibrium assumes perfect competition in all markets. From 1937 to 1943, he was administrator of Nantes state enterprises, in control of railroads for five of the eighty-nine French departments.

Debreu in 1951 published an article in which he stated: "In an economy provided with a central planning board incarnating a social welfare function there is only one consumption unit. The whole economic system can be divided into nations among which consumption units are distributed." In 1959, objectively following Hegel and Arrow, Debreu published an axiomatic analysis of the development of a perfectly competitive economy. He utilized topology to extend the input-output analysis from the Euclidean plane to the solid, from two dimensions to a potentially infinite number of dimensions. Arrow and Debreu went on to show that a Pareto optimum could be calculated based on an analysis of ordinal preferences.

In 1908, Barone set up a general equilibrium model with four groups of linear equations similar to that of the Walras-Pareto model, and set up successive approximations as the solution process. The number of variables was found to be equal to the number of equations so that the system was formally (mathematically) solvable, that is, determinate. The market prices of the purely competitive system were found to be equivalent to the Paretian accounting exchange ratios among commodities in a collectivist system established solely by the Ministry of Production.

Unlike Walras and Pareto, Barone in his mathematical model focused solely on the production sector. His equations represented empirically observable magnitudes—quantities, costs, and exchange ratios (accounting prices)—among the *n* kinds of capital (enterprises) in this sector. Cournot marginal cost equality in all two-by-two-enterprise transactions was required for equilibrium. This represented Walrasian classical economics and Austrian capital theory

Marx and Engels in 1848 called for the centralization in the hands of the state of the means of production, credit, transportation, and communication. In 1859, Marx referred to Petty's 1699 statement that the entire country is "one large scale industrial establishment." Marx here stated, "The exchange-value of this particular commodity can therefore be exhaustively expressed only by the infinite number of equations in which the use-values of all other commodities form its equivalent." In 1863 and 1885 the first and second volumes of *Das Kapital* appeared, in the second of which Marx stated, "from the standpoint of society as a whole, the aggregate capital appears as the capital of a single joint-stock company." This was all a neomercantilist analysis, a systematic updating of Colbertism in mathematical terms.

Kautsky, the leading socialist theoretician after Engels's 1895 death, argued in the 1891 Erfurt Program, "The whole machinery of production will be turned into a gigantic concern subject to a single master [the state]." In a 1902 speech, he added that this required "systematic direction of production from a single point."

The earliest attempt to construct an empirical table of the Quesnay sort, as suggested by Marx, was by the Menshevik V. G. Groman in 1923. STO ordered the Central Statistical Administration to construct a "balance of the national economy" for 1923–1924. Preliminary results were released in 1925. In 1926–1928, Pavel I. Popov, assisted by Lev N. Litoshenko and M. Barenholz, developed a rudimentary input-output model based upon Quesnay's Tableau and Marx's two-sector model of expanded reproduction. It attempted to build an "inter-branch balance of productive links." In 1935 Leontief began research that led to the development of the input-output table and an economic theory underlying it. He recast the Walras model into an "input-output" form that facilitated actual calculation. Defining industries and sectors in terms of available statistical data series, he then constructed such a table to estimate coefficients of the U.S. economy in 1941 and 1953. In 1949, he constructed a 500-sector model of the U.S. economy, each sector modeled as a linear equation.

Kantorovich in 1939 showed that problems of economic allocation of resources can be reduced to maximizing a function subject to constraints, a linear programming approach to determining the optimum price in enterprises, a procedure foreshadowed by Pareto. He also introduced the distinction between the primal and dual in linear programming. He developed the "method of decisive multipliers," which were interpreted as "shadow prices." With regard to the necessary use of prices to achieve an optimum under socialism, he was objectively a follower of Lange, and through him of Pareto and Barone.

Tinbergen in 1936 constructed a twenty-four- or twenty-seven-equation input-output (econometric) model of the Dutch economy and in 1939 developed a thirty-eight-equation model of the U.S. economy for the League of Nations. These models used prices imposed by the central planner to imitate the operation of the purely competitive market, thus creating what came to be called *market socialism*. After World War II, he served for a decade as head of the central planning bureau of the Netherlands.

Frisch constructed theories of a price-driven socialist plan, a form of market socialism, but never actually held an official position in the planning office. To solve the input-output matrix, he developed in the early 1930s aspects of the technique later called *linear programming*.

In 1936 and 1937, Lange set out a socialist economy in which there were markets for consumer goods and labor services but not for capital goods. Prices for capital and nonlabor goods were not market prices but "mere indices of alternatives available, fixed for accounting purposes." He thus adopted the Pareto-Barone focus on accounting prices. For equilibrium, both market prices and accounting prices were determined by the condition that the quantity of each commodity demanded is equal to the quantity supplied. Each plant must produce the quantity of output that minimizes average cost, and each industry must produce the quantity that can be sold to consumers at that minimum average cost of production. These two rules make prices given by the Central Planning Board appear to consumers precisely as prices given by a perfectly competitive market. The solution to the allocation problem begins with random (guessed) prices chosen by the Central Planning Board and proceeds by iteration to a final solution. In a centrally planned economy without any markets, prices would be determined in precisely the same way. The socialist planning method, in either the decentralized or centralized form, would reach an equilibrium faster than a perfectly competitive market because the Planning Board would have more information about the network of prices and quantities than any individual enterprise could possibly have.

In the 1920s, Donaldson Brown and Alfred Bradley, economists at General Motors Corporation (GMC), took on the task of developing a price policy for the recently divisionalized firm, and following the lines of Pareto and Barone, they visualized GMC as a socialist economy of the Marx, Kautsky, and Soviet kind. Each division was viewed as an independent enterprise. All transfers between divisions within the firm were therefore priced, as previously all transactions between GMC and outside firms had been priced. This allowed GMC to allocate resources within the firm more precisely and hence to function more efficiently. The Brown-Bradley program corroborated from the capitalist side the theory being developed nearly simultaneously in the Soviet Union. Clearly implicit in all these findings was that the method of optimizing returns was the same for a privately owned enterprise as it was for a collectively owned (state-owned) one. Optimization required a "visible hand," that is, management of the enterprise, or economic planning.

Samuelson in 1941 and 1947 defined economic equilibrium to be a mathematical optimization problem, following Pareto. He introduced from physics the use of Langrangian multipliers in solving constrained optimization problems, defining these as either prices or costs. He explicitly equated this price to conceptions of Pareto, Barone, Hotelling, and Lange in the socialist planning debate. He attributed the compensation principle to Barone and not as have others to Kaldor and Hicks. He adopted Pareto's differentiability assumption and showed that the operation of the model was equivalent to solving a system of differential equations.

Arrow in 1951 amalgamated many individual preferences into one social preference, setting the problem as one of choosing alternative "social states," that is, income and wealth distributions, and concluding that the rational decision criterion is Pareto optimality. In 1959 Arrow introduced the concept that for exchanges between the divisions of a capitalist firm, "the same price should be charged as if it were a transaction with another firm." Adopting von Neumann's proof that the Lagrange multiplier was equivalent to the shadow price, he argued that only a process of successive approximations could determine the shadow price. He also redefined the concept of profit maximization as maximization of "the sum of the discounted profits" of the firm over time. This made profit maximization a dynamic rather than a static process. In 1969, he returned to the application to enterprises, stating, "An incentive for vertical integration is the replacement of buying and selling on the market by the cost of intrafirm transfers; the existence of vertical integration may suggest that the costs of operating competitive markets are not zero, as is usually assumed in our theoretical literature."

The chief mathematical tool used by all those writing from 1838 to 1956 was calculus and matrix algebra. Samuelson in the 1940s, and Arrow, Debreu, Hurwicz, and Hirshleifer in the 1950s, experimented with more powerful methods of analysis, including dynamical systems and topology. The last four showed that it is possible to reach a solution to the general equilibrium model without the assumption of universal differentiability.

SEE ALSO *Arrow, Kenneth J.; Communism; Debreu, Gerard; Enterprise; Entrepreneurship; Frisch, Ragnar; General Equilibrium; Hicks, John R.; Hurwicz, Leonid; Lagrange Multiplier; Markets; Marx, Karl; Mercantilism; Pareto, Vilfredo; Petroleum Industry; Planning; Prices; Programming, Linear and Nonlinear; Russian Economics; Samuelson, Paul A.; Socialism; State, The; Tinbergen, Jan; Union of Soviet Socialist Republics; Walras, Léon*

BIBLIOGRAPHY

Arrow, Kenneth. 1951. *Social Choice and Individual Values.* New York: Wiley; London: Chapman and Hall.

Arrow, Kenneth. 1959. *A Time Series Analysis of Inter-Industry Demands.* Amsterdam: North-Holland.

Arrow, Kenneth. 1969. *Total Factor Productivity Growth in Individual Industries and in the Economy.* Cambridge, MA: Harvard University, Center for International Affairs, Project for Quantitative Research in Economic Development.

Braudel, Fernand. 1982. *The Wheels of Commerce.* Vol. 2 of *Civilization and Capitalism, 15th–18th Century.* 3 vols. Trans. Siân Reynolds. New York: Harper and Row.

Coornaert, E. L. J. 1967. European Economic Institutions and the New World: The Chartered Companies. In *The Expanding Europe in the Sixteenth and Seventeenth Centuries.* Vol. 4 of *The Cambridge Economic History of Europe*, 2nd ed., ed. E. E. Rich and C. H. Wilson, 223–275. Cambridge, U.K.: Cambridge University Press.

Dobb, Maurice. 1966. *Soviet Economic Development Since 1917.* 6th ed. New York: Routledge and Kegan Paul.

Dolan, Edwin G. 1967. Structural Interdependence of the Soviet Economy before the Industrialization Drive. *Soviet Studies* 19 (1): 66–73.

Frisch, Ragnar. 1933. Propagation Problems and Impulse Problems in Dynamic Economics. In *Economic Essays in Honor of Gustav Cassel*, 171–205. London: Allen and Unwin.

Jasny, Naum. 1954. A Soviet Planner—V. G. Groman. *Russian Review* 13 (1): 52–58.

Jasny, Naum. 1962. The Russian Economic "Balance" and Input-Output Analysis: A Historical Comment. *Soviet Studies* 14 (1): 75–80.

Kantorovich, Leonid. 1939. *Matematicheskie metody; organizatsii I planirovaniia proizvodstva.* Leningrad: Izd. Leningradskogo Gos. Univ.

Lange, Oskar. 1938. *On the Economic Theory of Socialism.* Minneapolis: University of Minnesota Press.

Pareto, Vilfredo. 1897. The New Theories of Political Economy. *Journal of Political Economy* 5 (4): 485–502.

Rima, Ingrid H. 1972. *Development of Economic Analysis.* Homewood, IL. Richard D. Irwin.

Schumpeter, Joseph. 1954. *History of Economic Analysis*, rev. ed. New York: Oxford University Press.

Spulber, Nicholas. 1964. *Foundations of Soviet Strategy for Economic Growth: Selected Soviet Essays, 1924–1930.* Trans. Robert M. Hankin. Bloomington: University of Indiana Press.

Spulber, Nicholas, and Kamran Moayed Dadkhah. 1975. The Pioneering Stage in Input-Output Economics: The Soviet National Economic Balance, 1923–1924, After Fifty Years. *Review of Economics and Statistics* 57 (1): 27–34.

Julian Ellison

STATE OF NATURE

State of nature refers to a condition in which there is no established political authority. It is essentially a state of complete freedom. Political theorists have used it to better understand human nature and, typically, to justify the rationality of a particular type of government. Proponents claim that the state of nature provides insight into the inherent dispositions and inclinations of human beings. Because individual conduct is not coerced by political authority, it will reflect how humans behave naturally.

Social contract theorists commonly speculate about what life would be like in the state of nature. Based on their understandings of human nature, they argue that individuals in the state of nature face certain threats to their well-being. Consequently, rational people should consent to recognize the authority of a state in exchange for protection from these threats. The extent of the state's authority and the safeguards it is responsible for providing are functions of the theorist's view of human nature. Generally, an optimistic view of human nature leads to the advocacy of a state with limited powers, while a more pessimistic view is associated with a more powerful state.

Thomas Hobbes (1588–1679), in *Leviathan* (1651), first used the state of nature to justify the authority of the state. He claims that the state of nature would be a war of "every man against every man" (p. 76). Hobbes's characterization of the state of nature results from his view of human nature (see chapter 13). He believed that all people are basically equal physically and mentally, so no individual is safe from the machinations of others. Moreover, humans are innately competitive, diffident, and glory seeking. Therefore, they are prone to attack others for gain, preemptive self-defense, and recognition. Given this view of human nature, he envisioned the state of nature as a place in which violence would always be a threat, that is, a state of "war." There would be no industry, culture, knowledge, or society and "worst of all, continual fear, and danger of violent death" (p. 76). Hobbes famously concludes that, in the state of nature, "the life of man" is "solitary, poor, nasty, brutish, and short" (p. 76).

The solution to this state of war, according to Hobbes, is the creation of an overawing government, that is, a leviathan. Because human nature disposes people to conflict and violence, only an all-powerful state can maintain order. Consequently, people should give up almost all personal autonomy, retaining only their right to self-defense. Hobbes contends that an authoritarian government is not only necessary but preferable to a state of nature.

John Locke (1632–1704), in *Two Treatises of Government* (1690), also uses the state of nature in his justification of limited government. He claims that the state of nature would be characterized by "inconveniences" (p. 276). Human beings, according to Locke, are rational creatures able to understand the law of nature using reflective reason (see chapter 2, *Second Treatise*). This law requires that people not harm another individual's natural right to "Life, Health, Liberty, or Possessions" (p. 271). It also obligates them to help preserve the lives of others when possible. Finally, it gives people the right to enforce the law and punish transgressions only so far as to deter future crime. Locke believes that humans in the state of nature are typically inclined to respecting the natural right of others. The problem is that people are unable to be objective when their own interests are at stake. Humans are naturally disposed to overpunishing transgressions against themselves, family members, or friends. Retaliation inevitably creates an escalating cycle of violence.

Government, according to Locke, can provide a remedy, restraining "the partiality and violence of Men" (pp. 275–276). By objectively adjudicating violations of natural law, it can prevent the cycle of violence resulting from subjective enforcement. Rational people should be willing to give up their natural right to enforce the law of nature to the state. In exchange, the state becomes responsible for enforcing their natural rights to life, liberty, and property. Because the state of nature is merely a state of inconvenience, it does not warrant the establishment of a more intrusive and powerful government.

Jean-Jacques Rousseau (1712–1778), in the *Second Discourse on the Origin of Inequality* (1754), provides a much more brutish understanding of the human condition in the state of nature. He claims that previous theorists mischaracterized the state of nature because they had mistaken socialized inclinations for natural attributes. "They spoke about savage man, and it was civil man they depicted" (p. 38). Rousseau claimed that humans in the state of nature have only three basic physical desires: food, sex, and sleep. Their only fears are hunger and pain. No significant human conflict arises in the state of nature because people have very limited desires and an inborn sentiment of pity, which inspires a form of natural goodness. All other human passions and desires, along with such qualities as rationality and virtue, are acquired in society. Human beings in the state of nature, therefore, are simply animals, albeit with unrealized civilizing potential. They are in essence noble "savages."

The state of nature is a thoroughly modern approach to studying human nature and justifying the responsibilities of the state. It embodies three basic principles of liberal political theory: the priority of the individual, equality, and personal freedom. First, the state of nature's asocial condition suggests that humans should ultimately be understood as abstract individuals. Second, humans in the state of nature are considered morally equal, with no person having the authority to dominate anyone else. Third, people are portrayed as autonomous, self-determining creatures, thus emphasizing freedom as a natural human quality. This depiction of the human condition is quite contrary to the classical view, which assumes that human beings cannot be understood outside of the society in which they live.

The state of nature was a particularly popular thought experiment during the seventeenth and eighteenth centuries before falling out of vogue. Nonetheless, it continues to influence contemporary academic and public discourse. For example, the "original position" in John Rawls's *Theory of Justice* (1971) is a conceptual variation of the state of nature. In international relations, some scholars use the idea of a state of nature to theorize about the relationships and interactions between political states. The imagery produced by state-of-nature theories also maintains a grip on the popular imagination, from Hobbes's nightmarish war of all against all to Rousseau's romanticized noble savage. Locke's natural rights in the state of nature have also been passed down through the American Declaration of Independence as unalienable rights to "life, liberty, and the pursuit of happiness."

SEE ALSO *Civilization; Discourse; Enlightenment; Government; Hobbes, Thomas; Law; Locke, John; Philosophy, Political; Property, Private; Representation; Rousseau, Jean-Jacques; Social Contract; Society*

BIBLIOGRAPHY

Hobbes, Thomas. [1651] 1994. *Leviathan: With Selected Variants from the Latin Edition 1668*, ed. Edwin Curley. Indianapolis, IN: Hackett.

Locke, John. [1690] 1988. *Two Treatises of Government*, ed. Peter Laslett. Cambridge, U.K.: Cambridge University Press.

Rousseau, Jean-Jacques. [1754] 1987. *Second Discourse on the Origin of Inequality*. In *The Basic Political Writings*, trans. and ed. Donald A. Cress, 25–82. Indianapolis, IN: Hackett.

Johnny Goldfinger

STATE-DEPENDENT RETRIEVAL

State-dependent retrieval describes the experimental finding that subjects who learn something in one state (e.g., a drug, nondrug, or mood state) remember more if they recall in the same state, rather than in a changed state. *Context-dependent retrieval* describes the same phenomenon. Numerous states or contexts can act as retrieval cues to facilitate remembering if reinstated at recall. Graham Davies and Donald Thomson (1988) provide an excellent reference source describing the different contexts found to influence memory. These include external states, where the learning environment is reinstated (e.g., the room, or a crime scene), and internal states, where the inner experiential state is reinstated (e.g., with alcohol, drugs, or mood states). In one experiment with subaqua divers, the divers who learned and recalled word lists in the same context (on land or under water) remembered 50 percent more words. In another experiment, subjects performed memory tasks while sober or under the influence of alcohol. Twenty-four hours later they were tested under the same or different conditions; those who learned and recalled in the same state remembered more than those who changed states. Endel Tulving and Donald Thomson proposed that specific retrieval cues facilitate recall if the information about them is encoded and stored at the same time as the material to be remembered (Tulving and Thomson 1973). Their "Encoding Specificity" principle states that a cue must reinstate information present in the original memory trace to be effective at retrieval.

State-dependent retrieval has been studied extensively in animals using drugs to induce state changes. Donald Overton (1974) commented that many experiments using pharmacologically induced states suffer from methodological problems. Eric Eich (1980) reviewed fifty-seven experiments of human drug state-dependent retrieval and noted that the phenomenon is not always reproducible; it is also unclear whether drugs exert an influence directly on memory or indirectly through changes in mood.

Researchers became interested in the effects of mood on memory, particularly the perpetuation of depressive mood states. Mood was thought to have a state-dependent effect on memory. This suggestion arose from the findings of studies in the 1980s by John Teasdale (1983) and others that happy past memories were significantly more likely to be retrieved in happy moods and sad memories more often in depressed moods. These *mood congruity* effects were thought to result from mood state acting as a context; support for the mood-state-dependent retrieval explanation came from experiments demonstrating that similarity of mood state at time of encoding and retrieval produced less forgetting of emotionally neutral material than changed mood states. Gordon Bower (1981) advanced his "Associative Network Theory of Memory and Emotion" to explain these findings, but controversy surrounded mood-state-dependent retrieval; the effect was elusive and unpredictable (Blaney 1986; Kuiken 1991). Analysis of experiments investigating mood-state-dependent retrieval identified methodological problems that contributed to the controversy surrounding the reliability of the effect (Kenealy 1997). In particular, designs confounded encoding and retrieval by not measuring (or reporting) initial learning scores; some lacked objective measures of mood manipulation; and others used the same method of mood induction at encoding and retrieval, confounding the effects of mood and induction procedure. The phenomenon is intriguing, but the evidence does not allow definitive statements to be made concerning the generality and reliability of state-dependent retrieval.

BIBLIOGRAPHY

Blaney, Paul H. 1986. Affect and Memory: A Review. *Psychological Bulletin* 99: 229–246.

Bower, Gordon H. 1981. Mood and Memory. *American Psychologist* 36: 129–148.

Davies, Graham M., and Donald M. Thomson, eds. 1988. *Memory in Context: Context in Memory.* Chichester, U.K.: John Wiley and Sons.

Eich, Eric. 1980. The Cue-Dependent Nature of State-Dependent Retrieval. *Memory amd Cognition* 8: 157–173.

Gerrards-Hesse, Astrid, Kordelia Spies, and Friedrich W. Hesse. 1994. Experimental Inductions of Emotional States and Their Effectiveness: A Review. *British Journal of Psychology* 85: 55–78.

Haaga, David A. F. 1989. Mood-State-Dependent Retention Using Identical or Non-Identical Mood Inductions at Learning and Recall. *British Journal of Clinical Psychology* 28: 75–83.

Kenealy, Pamela M. 1997. Mood-State-Dependent Retrieval: The Effects of Induced Mood on Memory Reconsidered. *Quarterly Journal of Experimental Psychology* 50A: 290–317.

Kuiken, Don, ed. 1991. *Mood and Memory: Theory, Research, and Applications.* Newbury Park, CA: Sage.

Peeters, Rudi, and Géry d'Ydewalle. 1987. Influences of Emotional States Upon Memory: The State of the Art. *Communication & Cognition* 20: 171–190.

Teasdale, John D. 1983. Negative Thinking in Depression: Cause, Effect or Reciprocal Relationship? *Advances in Behavious Research & Therapy* 5: 3–25.

Tulving, Endel, and Donald M. Thomson. 1973. Encoding Specificity and Retrieval Processes in Episodic Memory. *Psychological Review* 80: 353–373.

Pamela M. Kenealy

STATELESSNESS

A state, or more broadly in the Anglo-Saxon tradition, a nation-state, comprises a population living on a delineated territory with internationally respected boundaries and under a state apparatus whose prime and most distinguishing characteristic is the monopoly of violence. This definition follows that of Max Weber, whose original 1922 formulation of the monopoly of *Gewaltsamkeit* (physical violence) implies a potential use of that violence. At best a state carries international and internal legitimacy and thus is widely respected.

Stateless people are without legally enforceable claims to any internationally recognized state. The "host states" usually withhold the supply of public goods like security, law and defense from stateless people, at least to some extent. People can be or become stateless, i.e., are not recognized as belonging to a specific territory that meets the initially stated requirements. Stateless persons may be registered as nonnational residents, foreigners or categorized as nationals of another state even when that state does not accept them as nationals and thus will not protect them.

On the other hand, they might have advantages in avoiding taxes and the military draft.

The United Nations, early in 2006, reported 2,381,900 stateless people around the world, which was more than a 50 percent increase over 2005. The United Nations High Commissioner for Refugees (UNHCR) notes that precise numbers are difficult to ascertain, and that the actual number may be much higher, of even more than 11 million stateless people.

Four broad categories emerge: first, people that never were taken care of in their own state or that never have raised such claims. These are mostly members of small ethnic tribes living at a subsistence level, such as natives of the Amazonas region or the Pygmies of Africa. Frequently, these people were driven into their current settlement areas by more powerful contenders (e.g., Brazilian settlers or colonists in South Africa). In cases like the Aborigines of Australia and the Maoris of New Zealand, the new conquering state eventually granted them passports.

Second, people lose their attachment to their state for temporary reasons such as external conquest or internal strife, epidemic diseases or natural catastrophes. They may still have their personal documents but their state territory may not be accessible for them due to the given reasons. Losing personal documents in these situations makes claims for return even more difficult.

Third, a state may have ceased to exist due to external subjugation or exhaustion of the soil. This either forces the indigenous population to become (second-class or slave) citizens of the new state as, e.g., under Mongolian rule, leads to their annihilation in that territory, as with most of the Jews after Titus' victory in the first Jewish-Roman War (66–73 CE), or forces them abroad. If the new state will be widely recognized internationally, the third category of stateless people merges to refugees who carry no longer internationally recognized documents.

In cases of state collapse (Rotberg 2004) citizens may still carry a passport but have no state authority to protect them. A partial recovery of a state as in Lebanon or sort of a foreign protectorate is one of the possible outcomes here, as in Somalia on the part of the Ethiopian government in 2007, as is the permanent intermingling of internal and external ethnic divisions (Carment and James 2004).

There is a fourth category of people who cannot guarantee their economic survival in their home state, throw away all their documents (*Sans-Papières*) to avoid sanctioning on the part of the recipient states, and try to enter another state illegally as a refugee. From these four basic categories many more combinations can be derived, in particular with respect to forms of diaspora (Shain and Sherman 1998).

The lower the level of development in the lost or given up territory, the fewer and less recognized the documents and skills of these refugees, the harder the economic consequences for them in having to accept *Lumpenproletariat* jobs in their new states. Their status of illegal (and often unwanted) immigrants is permanently insecure. The numbers of these immigrants swell (now a sizable nine-digit figure), the larger the persistence of the North-South divide (Mediterranean connex, influx from Mexico, and *mutatis mutandis* of the Chinese in Eastern Russia). In general, the somatic and psychic illnesses are severe among these exile-driven people, even though a sizeable portion of this group is composed of rather robust and resilient young men. Their success for integration into a new culture depends on family networks and middle-men-minorities helping out with jobs and shelters, and, last but not least, on the pull-effects a generous and highly-developed welfare-state exerts on citizens of underdeveloped economies.

There can be vast overlap between these four categories of stateless people. The first dividing line is whether these individuals possess a valid passport. Otherwise the likelihood diminishes rapidly that any state will claim these people. There is also a small numbers effect here making for more benevolent reactions on the part of recipient states. Sometimes, e.g., with the Vietnamese boat-people or the Algerian Harkis, this is an offspring of joint fighting in an external war. Thus, there is a two-dimensional space formed by the dimension of passport-ownership (yes, restricted in various degrees, no) and the dimension of a claiming/recipient state (yes, with restrictions, no). The matter becomes more complicated when some family or clan members of an ethnic group that does not have its own state, like the Roma or the Kurds, live with their passport-owning brethren. A continuum of severity, or in a different terminology: a property space of legality and legitimacy, stretches from (1) no passsport and no-state-claim people (like the Bushmen) via (2) (restricted) passport-ownership and no state claim (German Jews driven into exile under Nazi rule), (3) the lack of a passport, but a claiming state (e.g., tourists abroad in a catastrophe like the tsunami of 2004) to the (4) full protection of a passport and a claiming state.

In any case, a claiming state is more important for ultimate safety than possession of a formal passport. In that respect, emphasis has been duly laid on a functioning state apparatus as a variable in its own (Linz and Stepan 1996).

As to Kurdish and Palestinian refugees, it is not only their stronger "host" states that do not concede a joint state for the across-border population. The major powers of the world in this power rivalry, above all the United

States, turn down claims for an independent state on the historically claimed territory.

Under conditions of globalization with workers and tourists seeing the world, the need for shelter in a home state with its guaranteed jurisdiction becomes even more important, paradoxically the more often the boundary of one's own state is crossed. The risks intensify for children born and raised in a third country that has not issued a passport to either parent.

SEE ALSO *Civil Rights; Diaspora; Human Rights; Jews; Lumpenproletariat; Migration; Nationalism and Nationality; Nation-State; Palestinians; Refugee Camps; Refugees; Roma, The*

BIBLIOGRAPHY

Carment, David, and Patrick James. 2004. Third-Party States in Ethnic Conflict: Identifying the Domestic Determinants of Intervention. In *Ethnic Conflict and International Politics: Explaining Diffusion and Escalation*, eds. Steven E. Lobell and Philip Mauceri, 11–34. New York: Palgrave Macmillan.

Diamond, Jared M. 2005. *Collapse: How Societies Choose to Fail or Succeed*. New York: Viking.

Linz, Juan J. and Alfred Stepan. 1996. *Problems of Democratic Transition and Consolidation: Southern Europe, South America, and Post-Communist Europe*. Baltimore, MD: Johns Hopkins University Press.

Rotberg, Robert I., ed. 2004. *When States Fail: Causes and Consequences*. Princeton, NJ: Princeton University Press.

Shain, Yossi, and Martin Sherman. 1998. Dynamics of Disintegration: Diaspora, Secession and the Paradox of Nation-States. *Nations and Nationalism* 4 (3): 321–346.

Weber, Max. [1922] 1964. *Wirtschaft und Gesellschaft*. Studienausgabe. Köln: Kiepenheuer & Witsch.

Ekkart Zimmermann

STATIONARY PROCESS

A *times series* is a set of data ordered in time, usually recorded at regular time intervals. In probability theory, a time series $\{x_t\}$ is a collection of random variables indexed by time. In the social sciences, examples of time series include the quarterly level of the gross domestic product, the monthly inflation rate, the annual level of crime, and the annual population growth. One of the main features of time series is the interdependency of observations over time. This interdependency needs to be accounted for in the modeling of time series data, in order to improve understanding of their temporal behavior and forecasting of their future movements.

The class of all models for time dependent data is far too large to enable methods of analysis to be designed that would be suitable for all these models. The modeling of the interdependence becomes an impossible task, and a certain degree of stability or invariance in the statistical properties of the time series becomes essential for its modeling.

Stationarity broadly refers to some form of statistical stability or equilibrium. Stationarity is a key concept in the analysis of time series data, as it allows powerful techniques for modeling and forecasting to be developed. There are different forms of stationarity, depending on which of the statistical properties of the time series are restricted. The two most widely used forms of stationarity are: *weak stationarity* and *strict stationarity*.

WEAK AND STRICT STATIONARITY

A time series $\{x_t\}$ is said to be *strictly stationary* when the *probability density function* of the collection of the random variables $x_{t_1}, \ldots, x_{t_k}$ is the same as that of the random variables $x_{t_1 + h}, \ldots, x_{t_k + h}$ for all integers $t_1, \ldots, t_k$ and positive integers k and h. The strict stationarity property restricts the probabilistic properties of any collection of random variables to be invariant to time shifts, which implies that the probabilistic behavior of each random variable is the same across time.

A time series $\{x_t\}$ is said to be *weakly stationary*, sometimes referred to as *second-order* or *covariance stationary*, when

$$E(x_t) = \mu < \infty, \text{ for all integers } t,$$
$$Var(x_t) = \sigma^2 < \infty, \text{ for all integers } t,$$
$$Cov(x_t, x_{t+h}) = \gamma(h), \text{ for all integers } t \text{ and } h.$$

The weak stationarity property restricts the *mean* and *variance* of the time series to be finite and invariant in time and takes the linear dependence between two distinct observations (as measured by the *covariance*) to be a function of the time distance between them. The function $\gamma(h)$, for integers h, is called the *autocovariance function*. The function $\rho(h) = \gamma(h)/\sigma^2$, for integers h, is the *autocorrelation function*.

Strict stationarity implies weak stationarity when the mean and variance of the time series exist. The two forms of stationarity are equivalent if the time series follows the *normal* distribution. Overall, weak stationarity is less restrictive than strict stationarity. Moreover, it turns out that the weak stationarity condition is sufficient for most of the statistical results derived for *cross-sectional* data to hold. For these reasons, weak stationarity is employed more often than strict stationarity. Various authors use the term *stationarity* to refer to weak stationarity. Figure 1 shows one hundred simulated data from a weakly stationary time series.

A simple example of a weakly stationary time series is the *white noise* sequence, a sequence of zero mean, con-

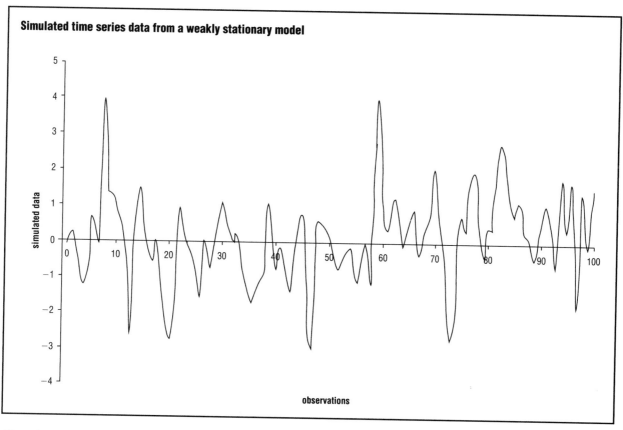

Simulated time series data from a weakly stationary model

Figure 1

stant variance, and *uncorrelated* random variables. Probably the most well-known model for weakly stationary time series is the *autoregressive moving average of orders p and q*, or ARMA(*p,q*), model with appropriate restrictions on its coefficients, where the variable under consideration is written as a linear combination of its own *p* past values, an error term (usually taken to be a white noise sequence), and *q* past values of the error term. The ARMA(*p,q*) model was popularized by George Box and Gwilym Jenkins (1970).

Stationarity plays an important role in the forecasting of time series data. Suppose that at time *t* we are given a set of data $x_{t-n}, ..., x_t$ and we wish to forecast the future value x_{t+h}. In predicting the value x_{t+h}, we would make use of the given data, and we would predict the value x_{t+h} by some function *f* of the given data. To determine which function *f* gives the best forecast, a measure of accuracy or *loss function* is needed to evaluate how accurate a forecast is. The most commonly used measure in prediction theory is based on the *mean squared error* (MSE) of the forecast, and the function *f* is chosen so that the MSE is minimized. It turns out that the function *f* that produces the smallest MSE is the *conditional mean* of x_{t+h} given the available information $x_{t-n}, ..., x_t$,

$E(x_{t+h}|x_{t-n}, ..., x_t)$. If the time series were normally distributed, then the conditional mean $E(x_{t+h}|x_{t-n}, ..., x_t)$ is a linear combination of the data $x_{t-n}, ..., x_t$. In general, the conditional mean is unknown, and it is common in prediction theory to consider only predictors $\hat{x}_{t+h}$ for x_{t+h} that are a linear combination of the available data $x_{t-n}, ..., x_t$,

$$\hat{x}_{t+h} = a_0 x_t + a_1 x_{t-1} + ... + a_n x_{t-n},$$

where $a_0, a_1, ..., a_n$ are parameters that need to be estimated. The assumption of weak stationarity of the time series $\{x_t\}$ guarantees that the parameters $a_0, a_1, ..., a_n$ are invariant in time and therefore can be easily estimated from the data.

A detailed discussion of the properties, modeling, and forecasting of stationary time series can be found in Peter Brockwell and Richard Davis (2002).

NONSTATIONARITY

The conditions for stationarity, weak or strong, can be violated in many different ways. Time series that do not have the stationarity property are called *nonstationary*. Examples of nonstationary time series data include the levels of the gross domestic product and population, which do not fluctuate around a constant level, but show overall an upward time trend. For these series, the average behavior for the beginning and the end of the sample differs, which rules out the possibility that the time series is stationary. A trend component in the data is one of the most common cases of nonstationarity in economic time series. Popular models for capturing trend behavior are the *linear trend* and *random walk* models.

The linear trend model assumes that the random variable x_t of the time series can be written as the sum of a deterministic linear trend $\alpha + \beta t$ and a white noise random variable ε_t,

$$x_t = \alpha + \beta t + \varepsilon_t, \qquad (1)$$

where α and β are constant parameters. Under the linear trend model (1), x_t is regarded as being scattered randomly around the trend line $\alpha + \beta t$, with the fluctuations around the trend line having no obvious tendency to increase or decrease. It follows that the mean of x_t depends on time t, $E(x_t) = \alpha + \beta t$, so that the time series $\{x_t\}$ is nonstationary. Deterministic nonlinear functions of time t could also be considered to describe the trend of $\{x_t\}$.

The random walk model assumes that the random variable x_t of the time series can be written as the sum of its previous value x_{t-1} and a white noise random variable ε_t,

$$x_t = x_{t-1} + \varepsilon_t. \qquad (2)$$

Under the random walk model (2), from one period to the next, the current observation of the time series takes a random step away from its last recorded value. The random walk model (2) can be extended to include an additive constant δ, and becomes the *random walk with drift δ* model,

$$x_t = \delta + x_{t-1} + \varepsilon_t. \qquad (3)$$

If it is assumed that the time series $\{x_t\}$ starts from some initial value x_0, then it can be shown for the random walk with drift model (3) that the mean and variance of x_t depend on time t, $E(x_t) = x_0 + \delta t$ and $Var(x_t) = tVar(\varepsilon_t)$. Therefore, a time series $\{x_t\}$ following the random walk without or with drift models (2) and (3) is nonstationary.

The trend component in the linear trend model (1) falls in the category of *deterministic trends*, as it is assumed that the trend of the time series is a deterministic function

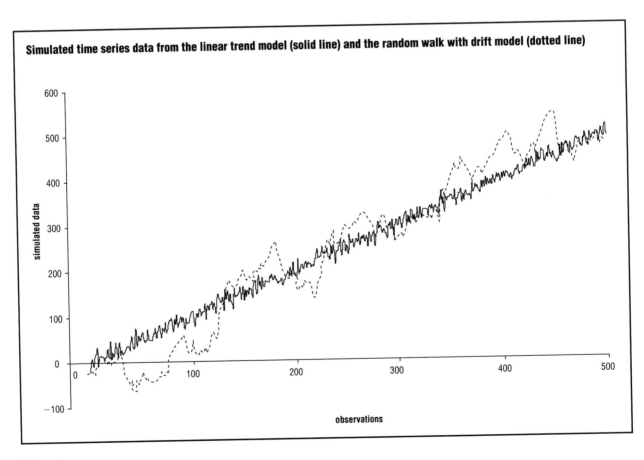

Simulated time series data from the linear trend model (solid line) and the random walk with drift model (dotted line)

Figure 2

of time. On the other hand, the trend component in the random walk without or with drift models (2) and (3) belongs in the category of *stochastic trends*, since for these models the trend of the time series is taken to be driven by the lagged time series, which is stochastic.

The difference between deterministic and stochastic trends can be seen from the models (1) and (3). The mean of x_t is a linear function of time t for both the linear trend and random walk with drift models (1) and (3), but the variance of x_t is increasing in time t for the random walk with drift model (3), and is constant in time t for the linear trend model (1). Another difference between the two models is the nature of the effect of shocks to future values of the time series. For the random walk with drift model (3) the effect of a shock is permanent, while for the linear trend model (1) it wears off. Figure 2 shows five hundred simulated data from the linear trend and random walk with drift models (1) and (3) with parameters $\alpha = x_0 = 0$ and $\beta = \delta = 1$.

A detailed discussion on nonstationary time series and the various models for the trend can be found in James D. Hamilton (1994).

TRANSFORMING NONSTATIONARITY TO STATIONARITY

The analysis of nonstationary time series is more complicated than that of weakly stationary ones. Moreover, statistical inference that involves nonstationary data is usually nonstandard, in contrast to weakly stationary ones. For these reasons, if nonstationarity is evident in the data, it is common practice to apply some transformation to the data that makes them weakly stationary and then apply statistical analysis on the transformed data.

For example, if a time series $\{x_t\}$ follows the linear trend model (1), then if one subtracts the trend $\alpha + \beta t$ from x_t, the transformed series is a white noise sequence, which is weakly stationary. Nonstationary time series that become weakly stationary after extraction of a deterministic trend are described as *trend-stationary*.

Another important transformation that can make nonstationary data into weakly stationary is the *difference* operator. The difference operator, denoted usually by Δ, is such that when applied to x_t the result is $x_t - x_{t-1}$,

$$\Delta x_t = x_t - x_{t-1}.$$

If it is assumed that the time series $\{x_t\}$ follows the random walk without or with drift models (2) and (3), then the difference operator transforms the data into a white noise sequence without or with an additive constant (the drift), which is weakly stationary. In some cases, it could be required that the difference operator is applied more than

once to the data to achieve weak stationarity. Nonstationary time series that become weakly stationary after applying the difference operator are referred to as *difference-stationary*.

Difference-stationary time series are often described as being *integrated of order d*, denoted as I(d). The parameter d is the *order of integration* and is the number of times that the difference operator has to be applied to the data in order to achieve weak stationarity. In the case that we take d differences and the resulting time series follows a weakly stationary ARMA(p,q) model, then the original time series follows the *autoregressive integrated moving average of orders p, d, and q*, or ARIMA(p,d,q), model of Box and Jenkins (1970).

For nonstationary economic time series, it is common that the order of integration is $d = 1$, and in a few cases is $d = 2$. Time series that are integrated of order 1 are referred to as having a *unit root*. Examples include the random walk with or without drift and the ARIMA(p,d,q) with $d = 1$ models. Time series having a unit root have attracted particular attention in the literature of theoretical and applied econometrics.

More information on the topic of unit root time series can be found in William Greene (2003), including testing procedures to discriminate between weakly stationary and unit root time series.

SEE ALSO *General Equilibrium; Nash Equilibrium; Partial Equilibrium; Stability in Economics; Steady State; Unit Root and Cointegration Regression*

BIBLIOGRAPHY

Box, George E. P., and Gwilym M. Jenkins. 1970. *Time Series Analysis: Forecasting and Control*. San Francisco: Holden-Day.

Brockwell, Peter J., and Richard A. Davis. 2002. *Introduction to Time Series and Forecasting*. 2nd ed. New York: Springer.

Greene, William H. 2003. *Econometric Analysis*. 5th ed. Upper Saddle River, NJ: Prentice Hall.

Hamilton, James D. 1994. *Time Series Analysis*. Princeton, NJ: Princeton University Press.

Violetta Dalla

STATIONARY STATE

Classical political economy, from William Petty, the Physiocrats, Adam Smith, and David Ricardo, to John Stuart Mill and Karl Marx, analyzed the dynamics of capitalist economies and investigated the sources of economic growth and development. In this analysis, a *progressive* or *advancing* state is one in which capital accumulation is proceeding, whether smoothly or erratically—in other words, it is a condition of positive economic growth, usually associated with high and rising profits and wages. An economic system experiencing negative growth is said to be in a *declining* state. Thomas Malthus and Ricardo focused much attention on various scenarios associated with decline—leading Thomas Carlyle to dub political economy "the dismal science"—while Marx made prognostications about its inevitability. A *stationary* state is one in which growth is neither positive nor negative. Until John Stuart Mill, the stationary state was, like the declining state, considered unwelcome, and growth was thought to benefit all three great classes of society: capitalists, landlords, and workers.

In his *Principles of Political Economy* (1848), Mill for the first time raised the possibility that the stationary state could be desirable (and economic growth undesirable). In addition, whereas in all the earlier classical authors the system's movements were seen as governed by internal "laws of motion" that, while they could be identified and interpreted, *could not be altered*, in Mill, for the first time, the possibility that human intervention into the system could affect its outcomes was contemplated. Marx, of course, also put forward the idea that people make their own history (though "not exactly as they please"), but for Marx capitalism must grow ("Accumulate or die!"), and his analysis also viewed capitalism as incapable of being reformed, so change meant a transition to socialism. Strictly speaking, outcomes could be influenced by human interference even in Ricardo, where, for example, repeal of the corn laws could allow cheaper corn to be imported, supporting profits that otherwise were being squeezed by the artificially high price of corn—but this is a case not of affecting the laws themselves, but of clearing the way for the "laws of motion" to operate to their fullest.

In *Principles*, Mill begins by affirming that the laws of production are, like the laws of physics, unalterable (although some might be guided within strict limits), but then suggests that the laws of distribution are capable of being guided by human institutions. For Mill, distribution is governed by the laws and customs of society. The nature of distribution varies from society to society and is subject to historical change. Like his predecessors in Classical political economy, Mill saw a tendency toward a falling rate of profit that would lead to a stationary state. However, whereas the earlier writers associated the stationary state with gloom and poverty, Mill saw it as the blissful final result of economic progress. Mill also considered the idea that a society could *choose* to adopt a stationary state, rather than wait for a stationary state to be imposed on it.

In the ideal stationary state, society would have achieved a sufficiently high level of wealth accumulation. Workers would be educated to realize the negative effects of population growth, and they would control their numbers voluntarily. As population growth reached a stationary stage, there would be no tendency for wages to fall and no reason for further growth in production. Mill was sure to note that a "stationary condition of capital and population implies no stationary state of human improvement" (Mill [1848] 1987, p. 751), thus making the distinction between quantitative growth and qualitative development. He also pointed out that his analysis applied only to the presently industrialized nations, and that what would later be called "developing" countries have not yet reached the level of economic well-being necessary to turn to zero growth.

Recently, ecologically oriented economists have cited Mill and put forward their vision of a *steady-state economy*, which is more or less the same idea conceived by Mill (see, for example, Daly's notion of "an economy with constant stocks of people and artifacts" [1978, p. 17]). This is somewhat confusing, because in traditional growth theory the term *steady-state* refers not to zero growth, but to proportional growth. Frank Knight (1921) noted, for example, that John Bates Clark's "static state," which is an abstraction for methodological purposes, is not the same as the classical authors' stationary state. Ludwig von Mises also expressed the sentiment that "[t]he idea of a stationary state is an aid to theoretical speculation. In the world of reality there is no stationary state, for the conditions under which economic activity takes place are subject to perpetual alterations which it is beyond human capacity to limit" ([1922] 1951, p. 196]). In neoclassical economics, the term *steady-state* is used to indicate not a state of zero growth, but rather a kind of equilibrium growth, as in the "golden rule," in which the propensity to save is such that per capita consumption is equalized across generations. This is obviously not what the classical economists meant by the stationary state.

SEE ALSO *Development Economics; Economic Growth; Economics, Classical; Equilibrium in Economics; Malthus, Thomas Robert; Mill, John Stuart; Mises, Ludwig Edler von; Ricardo, David; Stability in Economics; Steady State*

BIBLIOGRAPHY

Daly, Herman E. 1977. *Steady-State Economics: The Economics of Biophysical Equilibrium and Moral Growth.* San Francisco: Freeman.

Knight, Frank H. 1921. *Risk, Uncertainty, and Profit.* Boston: Hart, Schaffner, and Marx; Houghton Mifflin.

Mill, John Stuart. [1848] 1987. *Principles of Political Economy.* New York: Kelley.

Mises, Ludwig von. [1922] 1951. *Socialism: An Economic and Sociological Analysis.* Trans. J. Kahane. New Haven, CT: Yale University Press.

Mathew Forstater

STATISM

Statism is a more complex, quirky phenomenon than is often supposed. It is a more cerebral, less emotive concept—and a more recent one—than nationalism, patriotism, and xenophobia. Quentin Skinner, a prominent contemporary political theorist, regards the very use of the word *state* in early modern theory as a "decisive confirmation" of his thesis that "the state," as opposed to "the ruler," as the monopolizer of "legitimate" disposition over the means of violence, is foundational to what he terms "modernity" (Skinner 1978). Henceforward, rulers alternate in manning the state apparatus, but the state itself persists *en permanence*. Skinner explicitly follows Max Weber: "Modernity" involves the separation of the ruler from ownership of the means of rulership.

This leads to a problem. Whereas, in the words of Jens Bartelson (2001), "Skinner and other(s) … have accounted for the emergence of the modern state concept … it could be argued that their accounts … are themselves inherently statist, since they have posited a modern notion of the state as the end towards which early modern political reflection evolved.… It is as though all roads in the past led to Weber but none further beyond" (p. 9). Moreover, if one characterizes statism as predicated not just on the presence but also on the centrality of the modern state, one runs into an unexpected paradox. This paradox assumes a variety of guises, all of them marked by denial and avoidance. The USA Patriot Act of 2001, to give one egregious example, was designed to bolster the national security state, but did so by transposing "state" into "homeland." The verbal legerdemain involved here is by no means without precedent: Euphemisms for "state" (Motherland, Fatherland, *la patrie*—the list goes on) have long abounded. This in turn is part of the reason why the unwieldy (and often inaccurate) composite, the "*nation*-state," has become so familiar, as have such formulations as the United *Nations*, the Inter*national* Monetary Fund, and the Communist Inter*national*. None of these could have been engendered by nations; all are examples both of inter-state organization and, once again, of an intriguing, fastidious avoidance of the word "state." Political scientists have proved adept at introducing semantically equivalent locutions for the state (e.g., the "governmental process," the "political system"). These subterfuges are invariably unconvincing. By reintroducing the state through the back door, they inadvertently attest to the hold or centrality of a concept they had started out by trying to avoid. Not for nothing was there a recent debate within the recondite reaches of political science about "bringing the state back in": Where, one has to ask, did participants in this debate think it had ever gone away to?

But if the state was there all along, we must at this point ask questions about its oddly elusive centrality.

Nothing sensible can be said about statism without doing so. As Bartelson (2001) states, "within large parts of our legacy of political theorizing, the state is both posited as an object of political analysis and presupposed as the foundation of such analysis.… [This] makes it inherently difficult to take political theorizing out of its statist predispositions" (p. 5). Anarchist theorizing, to take one extreme, fails at the level of significance in that "the state" is both the object and the condition of its critique (Thomas 1985). At another extreme, to regard "the state" as the *telos* (ultimate end) toward which political reflection as well as political innovation was moving would make early instances of state institution-building, such as cameralism, presentiments of statism too—which would make about as much sense as regarding the Magna Carta of 1215 as the fountainhead of present Western liberties. The state, one should remember, is an institution. Statism is a concept, one that would make of the state what it is not: the be-all and end-all of political life, or "the sole source of its intelligibility."

States differ. All of them may appear as unitary entities when viewed from the outside, looking in: They are conditioned by the absence of their features—authority and sovereignty—in what is (incorrectly) called the "international" sphere. The state is also distinct from civil society, when viewed from the inside, looking out. The state and the international sphere, on the one hand, and the state and civil society, on the other, are binaries in which each term is always already defined in terms of the other term of the couplet. But it follows from none of this that states are best understood as constructs or resultants of parallelograms of forces that predated them, constructs that, once established, change the rules of the game once and for all. States are also entities that have tasks to perform—things to do, that is, other than satisfy definitional requirements. States do not often do these well. They make universalist claims on their own behalf while restricting popular participation in "their" affairs. Their record in addressing, let alone confronting, citizens' claims are at best mixed. These claims are themselves not of a piece. Personal rights (such as freedom of speech and assembly) are distinct from political rights (which center around claims to participate in the workings of the state), and both are distinct in their turn from what T. H. Marshall (1964) calls the rights of "social citizenship" (guaranteed education, full employment, decent housing, free medical care—the foundation of the twentieth-century "welfare state").

It is noteworthy that the early-twenty-first-century U.S. national security state (the "homeland") trumps the rights of social citizenship (which have never counted for much in the United States) with a mixture of personal and political rights that are trumpeted and reified as the consummation of what is called "freedom," this being one of many stratagems to which modern states can, with frightening ease, resort. Statism is of great help to such sleight of hand. It is content to award the state a set of purely formal credentials. Citizenship as outlined above is, nevertheless, not a formal category but the site of substantive demands and rights. Because it is the state's job to deliver on these, and not to fulfill formal definitional requirements, states on all but statist characterizations may be found wanting—and this gives everyone a great deal of work to do.

SEE ALSO *Anarchism; Citizenship; Corporatism; Cosmopolitanism; Internationalism; Magna Carta; Modernity; Monarchy; National Security; Nationalism and Nationality; Nation-State; Patriotism; State; Weber, Max; Xenophobia*

BIBLIOGRAPHY

Bartelson, Jens. 2001. *The Critique of the State.* Cambridge, U.K.: Cambridge University Press.

Marshall, T. H. 1964. *Class, Citizenship, and Social Development.* Garden City, NY: Doubleday.

Skinner, Quentin. 1978. *The Foundations of Modern Political Thought.* 2 vols. Cambridge, U.K.: Cambridge University Press.

Thomas, Paul. 1985. Introduction. *Karl Marx and the Anarchists.* London: Routledge and Kegan Paul.

Paul Thomas

STATISTICAL BIAS

SEE *Properties of Estimators (Asymptotic and Exact).*

STATISTICAL EFFICIENCY

SEE *Properties of Estimators (Asymptotic and Exact).*

STATISTICAL NOISE

Statistical noise refers to variability within a sample, stochastic disturbance in a regression equation, or estimation error. This noise is often represented as a random variable.

In the case of a regression equation

$$Y = m(X \mid \theta) + \varepsilon,$$

with $E(\varepsilon) = 0$, the random variable ε is called a disturbance or error term and reflects statistical noise. Noise in this context is usually viewed as arising from omitted explanatory variables; as such, the error term is a proxy for variables not included in the regression. Variables may be omitted from the regression for several reasons. The theory determining the behavior of the dependent variable Y may be incomplete, or perhaps some variables known to influence Y are unavailable to the researcher. Variables that have only slight influence on Y might be eliminated from the regression in order to maintain a parsimonious model. If the conditional mean function $m(x \mid \theta)$ is specified parametrically (e.g., as in ordinary least squares), the error term might reflect error in this specification, which is perhaps only an approximation to the true form of $m(x \mid \theta)$.

Even if the regression equation includes all relevant variables, and if the conditional mean function is correctly specified, the error term may reflect either measurement error in Y or intrinsic randomness in Y. Intrinsic randomness might be the result of nonsystematic variation in human behavior if Y describes the action of individuals. Tastes, preferences, and the like may be explained partly by other variables, but notions of bounded rationality in microeconomic theory suggest that some behavior is inexplicable.

In the typical estimation paradigm, a finite sample of size n is drawn and used to compute an estimate $\hat{\theta}$ of some quantity θ that is of interest. Even if the estimator is statistically consistent, the estimate that is obtained will typically differ from the true quantity θ because the researcher does not have an infinite amount of data, but only a finite sample. The difference between $\hat{\theta}$ and θ can be expressed by writing

$$\hat{\theta} = \theta + \varepsilon,$$

where again ε represents statistical noise, which can be positive or negative. In principle, one could draw many samples of size n and compute estimates of θ from each sample; each estimate would differ from the true θ. These random differences constitute a form of statistical noise. In this case, the noise arises from the fact that each sample of size n will not have exactly the same characteristics (e.g., the means, variances, etc. of observations on individual variables will differ across samples, and will also differ from the mean, variance, etc. of the underlying population from which the data are drawn).

Statistical noise plays a large role in determining what can be learned from a sample of data in any estimation setting. The variance of regression residuals determines, in part, the goodness of fit of an estimated regression line as well as the variance of estimators of regression parameters and other quantities. The variance of an estimator determines the precision of estimates that are obtained from data, which in turn affects the width of confidence intervals and the ability to reject null hypotheses of the form $H_0: \theta = 0$. Statistical noise is often assumed to be normally distributed, but this assumption is inappropriate in many settings.

SEE ALSO *Least Squares, Ordinary; Measurement Error; Properties of Estimators (Asymptotic and Exact); Sampling; Semiparametric Estimation; Specification Error; Variables, Random; White Noise*

BIBLIOGRAPHY

Cook, R. Dennis. 1982. *Residuals and Regression.* New York: Chapman and Hall.

Paul W. Wilson

STATISTICS

Statistics is a discipline that deals with data: summarizing them, organizing them, finding patterns, and making inferences. Prior to 1850 the word *statistics* simply referred to sets of facts, usually numerical, that described aspects of the state; that meaning is still seen in the various sets of government statistics, for example the monthly report on the nation's unemployment rate and the voluminous tables produced in the wake of each decennial census. During the twentieth century, as a result of the work of Karl Pearson, Ronald Fisher, Jerzy Neyman, Egon Pearson, John Tukey, and others, the term came to be used much more broadly to include theories and techniques for the presentation and analyses of such data and for drawing inferences from them. Two works by Stephen Stigler, *The History of Statistics: The Measurement of Uncertainty before 1900* (1986) and *Statistics on the Table: The History of Statistical Concepts and Methods* (1999) offer broad and readable accounts of the history of statistics.

Although often taught in departments of mathematics, statistics is much more than a branch of applied mathematics. It uses the mathematics of probability theory in many of its applications and finite mathematics and the calculus to derive many of its basic theoretical concepts, but it is a separate discipline that requires its practitioners to understand data as well as mathematics.

VARIABILITY

In a sense, statistics is mainly concerned with variability. If every object of the same class were the same, we would have no need for statistics. If all peas were indeed alike, we could measure just one and know all about peas. If all families reacted similarly to an income supplement, we would have no need to mount a large scale negative income tax experiment. If all individuals held the same opinion on an issue of the day, we would only need to ask one person's opinion and we would need to take no particular care in how we chose that person. Variability, however, is a fact of life and so statistics is needed to help reveal patterns in the face of variability.

Statistics is used in the collection of data in several ways. If the data are to be collected via an experiment, statistical theory directs how to design that experiment in such a way that it will yield maximum information. The principles of replication (to allow the measurement of variability), control (to eliminate known sources of extraneous variability), and randomization (to "even out" unknown sources of variation) as enunciated by Fisher in his 1935 book *The Design of Experiments* help ensure that if differences are found between those receiving experimental treatment(s) and those in control group(s), those differences can be attributed to the treatment(s) rather than to preexisting differences between the groups or to experimental error. If the data are to be collected via a sample survey, the principles of probability sampling ensure that the findings can be generalized to the population from which the sample was drawn. Variations on simple random sampling (which is analogous to drawing numbers out of a hat) take advantage of known properties of a population in order to make the sampling more efficient. The technique of stratified sampling is analogous to blocking in experimental design and takes advantage of similarities in units of the population to control variability.

Once data are collected, via experiments, sample surveys, censuses, or other means, they rarely speak for themselves. There is variability, owing to the intrinsic variability of the units themselves or to their reactions to the experimental treatments, or to errors made in the measuring process itself. Statistical techniques for measuring the central tendency of a variable (e.g., means, medians) clear away variability and make it possible to view patterns and make comparisons across groups. Measures of the variability of a variable (e.g., ranges and standard deviations) give information on the spread of the data—within a group and in comparisons between groups. There are also summarization techniques of correlation and regression to display the patterns of relations between variables—for example, how does a nation's GDP per capita relate to its literacy rate? These numerical techniques work hand in hand with graphical techniques (e.g., histograms, scattergrams) to reveal patterns in the data. Indeed, using numerical summaries without examining graphical representations of the data can often be misleading. Of course, there are many more complicated and sophisticated summary measures (e.g., multiple regression) and graphical techniques (e.g., residual plots) that aid in the summarization of data. Much of modern data analysis, especially as developed by John Tukey, relies on less conventional measures, on transformations of data, and on novel graphical techniques. Such procedures as correspondence analysis and data mining harness the power of modern computing to search for patterns in very large datasets.

FREQUENTIST AND BAYESIAN INFERENCE

Perhaps the most important use of statistics, however, is in making inferences. One is rarely interested merely in reactions of subjects in an experiment or the answers from members of a sample; instead one wishes to make generalizations to people who are like the experimental subjects or inferences about the population from which the sample was drawn. There are two major modes of making such inference.

Classical or frequentist inference (the mode that has been most often taught and used in the social sciences) conceptualizes the current experiment or sample as one from an infinite number of such procedures carried out in the same way. It then uses the principles codified by Fisher and refined by Neyman and Pearson to ask whether the differences found in an experiment or from a sample survey are sufficiently large to be unlikely to have happened by mere chance. Specifically it takes the stance of positing a null hypothesis that is the opposite of what the investigator believes to be true and has set out to prove. If the outcome of the experiment (or the sample quantity) or one more extreme is unlikely to have occurred if the null hypothesis is true, then the null hypothesis is rejected. Conventionally if the probability of the outcome (or one more extreme) occurring when the null hypothesis is true is less than .05 (or sometimes .01), then the result is declared "statistically significant."

Frequentists also carry out estimation by putting a confidence interval around a quantity measured from the sample to infer what the corresponding quantity in the population is. For example, if a sample survey reports the percentage in the sample who favor a particular candidate to be 55 percent and gives a 95 percent confidence interval as 52 to 58 percent, the meaning is that a procedure has been followed that gives an interval that covers the true population percent 95 percent of the time. The frequentist does not know (and is not able to put a probability on) whether in any particular case the interval covers the true population percent—the confidence is in the procedure, not in the interval itself. Further, the interval takes into account only what is known as *sampling error*, the variation among the conceptually infinite number of replications of the current procedure. It does not take into account non-sampling error arising from such problems in data collection as poorly worded questions, nonresponse, and attrition from a sample.

In order for these mechanisms of classical statistics to be used appropriately, a probability mechanism (probability sampling or randomization) must have been used to collect the data. In the social sciences this caution is often ignored; statistical inference is performed on data collected via non-probabilistic means and even on complete enumerations. There is little statistical theory to justify such applications, although superpopulation models are sometimes invoked to justify them and social scientists often argue that the means by which the data were accumulated resemble a random process.

Since the 1970s there has been a major renewal of interest in what was historically called inverse probability and is currently called Bayesian inference (after the English nonconformist minister and—during his lifetime—unpublished mathematician Thomas Bayes [1701?–1761]). Admitting the experimenter's or analyst's subjective prior distribution formally into the analysis, Bayesian inference uses Bayes' theorem (which is an accepted theorem of probability for both frequentists and Bayesians) to combine the prior distribution with the data from the current investigation to update the probability that the hypotheses being investigated is true. Note that Bayesians do speak of the probability of a hypothesis being true while frequentists must phrase their conclusions in terms of the probability of outcomes when the null hypothesis is true. Further, Bayesians construct credibility intervals, for which, unlike the frequentists' confidence intervals, it is proper to speak of the probability that the population quantity falls in the interval, because in the Bayesian stance population parameters are viewed as having probability distributions. For a frequentist, a population parameter is a fixed, albeit usually unknown, constant. Much of the revival of interest in Bayesian analysis has happened in the wake of advances in computing that make it possible to use approximations of previously intractable models.

While the distinction between Bayesians and frequentists has been fairly sharp, as Stephen E. Fienberg and Joseph B. Kadane (2001) note the two schools are coming together, with Bayesians paying increasing attention to frequentist properties of Bayesian procedures and frequentists increasingly using hierarchical models.

Two much more detailed descriptions of the field of statistics and its ramifications than is possible here are given by William H. Kruskal (1968) and Fienberg and Kadane (2001).

SEE ALSO *Bayes' Theorem; Bayesian Econometrics; Classical Statistical Analysis; Econometric Decomposition; Mathematics in the Social Sciences; Methods, Quantitative; Path Analysis; Pearson, Karl; Probability; Random Samples; Recursive Models; Sampling; Surveys, Sample; Variance; Variance-Covariance Matrix*

BIBLIOGRAPHY

Fienberg, Stephen E., and Joseph B. Kadane. 2001. Statistics: The Field. In *International Encyclopedia of the Social and Behavioral Sciences*, ed. Neil J. Smelser and Paul B. Baltes, 15085–15090. Oxford, U.K.: Elsevier.

Fisher, Ronald A. 1935. *The Design of Experiments*. Edinburgh: Oliver and Boyd.

Kruskal, William H. 1968. Statistics: The Field. In *International Encyclopedia of the Social Sciences*, ed. David L. Sills, vol. 15, 206–224. New York: Macmillan.

Stigler, Stephen M. 1986. *The History of Statistics: The Measurement of Uncertainty before 1900*. Cambridge, MA: Harvard University Press.

Stigler, Stephen M. 1999. *Statistics on the Table: The History of Statistical Concepts and Methods*. Cambridge, MA: Harvard University Press.

Judith M. Tanur

STATISTICS, BAYESIAN

SEE *Bayesian Statistics.*

STATISTICS, INFERENTIAL

SEE *Hypothesis and Hypothesis Testing.*

STATISTICS, TEST

SEE *Test Statistics.*

STATISTICS IN THE SOCIAL SCIENCES

Social science research generally relies on statistical analyses for the understanding of behavioral phenomena. Data analysis generally begins with an examination of descriptive statistics, then proceeds to inferential statistics.

DESCRIPTIVE STATISTICS: CENTRAL TENDENCY AND VARIABILITY

The arithmetic *mean* is the most common measure of central tendency. It is calculated by adding all the scores in a distribution and dividing by the number of scores. A less frequently used average is the *median*; it is calculated by ordering the numbers by size and identifying the middle-most score. The least used measure of central tendency is the *mode*, the most frequently occurring score.

When scores fall in a normal distribution, the mean is the most useful average because it gives a good sense of typical scores and because researchers can use it in subsequent sophisticated statistical tests. However, if a group of numbers is non-normal or has extreme values, the mean may not give a good sense of typicality; extreme scores have an inordinate impact on the mean, elevating or reducing it to give a false sense of typical values. In such a situation, researchers may use the median. Finally, the mode can be useful when an investigator is interested simply in getting a count of the number of observations in a given category.

To get a sense of the degree to which scores disperse, researchers calculate a measure of variability. The most common measures of variability are the *variance* and the *standard deviation* (SD); the SD is the square root of the variance. The SD tells, on average, how far any given score is likely to fall from the mean. Researchers prefer these measures with the mean because they can be used with sophisticated data analyses.

When investigators compute the median, they are likely to make use of a different measure of variability, the *semi-interquartile range* (SIQR). To compute the SIQR, the researcher identifies the scores at the twenty-fifth and the seventy-fifth percentile ranks and averages the two.

The least sophisticated, and least employed, measure of variability is the *range*. It is simply the difference between the highest and lowest score. It is greatly affected by extreme scores, so the range does not provide a useful measure of the degree to which scores cluster.

A final type of descriptive statistic is the *standardized score*, commonly the *z*-score. A standardized score indicates how far a given number in a distribution falls from the mean in standard deviation units. Thus, if a score fell one standard deviation above the mean, its standardized *z*-score would be +1.00. Or if a score fell half a standard deviation below the mean, its *z*-score would be –0.50. This descriptive *z*-score is used differently from the inferential statistic by the same name.

INFERENTIAL STATISTICS FOR TESTING DIFFERENCES BETWEEN MEANS

After an assessment using descriptive statistics, researchers conduct inferential tests designed to determine whether the obtained results are likely to generalize beyond the sample of subjects tested. Most of the statistics are based on certain assumptions regarding the data. In order for the tests to be maximally informative, data should be normally distributed and the variances of different groups should be equal. For some tests, there is an additional assumption of equal sample sizes across groups. Although the tests are robust enough to permit some violation of assumptions, the greater the departure from the assumptions, the less optimal the information provided by the tests.

The most commonly used statistical tests in the social and behavioral sciences are the analysis of variance (ANOVA) and related tests, including the Student's *t*-test; Pearson product-moment correlation; regression analysis; and the chi-square test. All of these except the chi-square test fall conceptually within the domain of the general linear model (GLM). ANOVA is a specific case of linear regression that is, in turn, a special case of the GLM. The basic premise of the GLM is that one can express the value of a dependent variable as a linear combination of the effects of a set of independent (or predictor) variables plus an error effect.

For historical reasons, researchers have treated ANOVA and related models and linear regression as different statistical approaches. Theoretically, these various tests are closely related, but in application, they are algebraically different. Hence, many researchers have not known of the close relation between them. As computer-based analyses have become nearly ubiquitous, however, a merging of the different approaches has begun (Howell 2007).

Researchers use the ANOVA and the Student's *t*-test to assess whether reliable differences exist across groups. Historically, the *t*-test is the older of the two approaches, but the ANOVA is used more frequently. The two tests lead to identical conclusions. In fact, for a two-group *t*-test, there is an identity relation between an obtained *t*-value and the *F*-value, namely, $t^2 = F$.

The *z*-test is conceptually similar to the *t*-test, addressing the same questions, but is much less frequently used because the *z*-test requires that the investigator know the population mean and variance (and standard deviation). The *t*-test requires only estimates of the population mean and standard deviation, which the researcher can discern from the data. It is rare for researchers to know the population parameters.

The ANOVA is useful for comparing means of multiple groups in studies with a single independent variable and for comparing means of two or more groups in studies with multiple independent variables. The advantage of ANOVA for single-variable research is that it permits a global assessment of potential differences with a single test. The advantage of ANOVA with multiple independent variables is that the investigator can spot interactions among variables.

The ANOVA lets the researcher know if means of any two groups differ reliably, but it does not specify exactly which of the means differ. In order to determine which of multiple means differ from one another, researchers employ post hoc analyses. When a study has multiple

dependent variables, or outcome measures, researchers use an extension of the ANOVA, the multivariate analysis of variance (MANOVA).

INFERENTIAL STATISTICS FOR IDENTIFYING RELATIONS AMONG VARIABLES

Sometimes investigators are interested in whether two factors covary. That is, is there an association between them such that by knowing a value of a measurement on one variable, one can make a reasonable prediction about the value on the second variable? Researchers use the Pearson product-moment correlation to identify the strength of an association between variables and regression analysis for making predictions.

Correlations can be positive, wherein as the score by a subject on one variable increases in magnitude, so does the magnitude on the second variable. Correlations can also be negative, as when increasing scores on one variable are paired with decreasing scores on the other variable. Or there can be no relation between the two variables. The sign, positive or negative, of the correlation does not indicate the strength of a relation, only the relative direction of change of scores on the two variables. The strength of a relation between variables is signaled by the absolute value of the correlation coefficient. These coefficients range from −1.00 to +1.00.

In some research, the investigator tries to predict a dichotomous outcome (e.g., success versus failure). In this instance, the appropriate test is known as logistic regression.

NONPARAMETRIC STATISTICS

The commonly used statistical tests make assumptions about characteristics of data. When the assumptions are not tenable, researchers can use nonparametric statistics, sometimes called distribution-free tests because they do not make any assumptions about the nature of the data in a distribution. Their advantage is that they do not require that data be normally distributed or that different groups have equal variability. Their disadvantage is that they discard some information in the data; thus they are, statistically speaking, less efficient. There are nonparametric statistics that correspond to the commonly used parametric tests.

When a two-sample *t*-test is inappropriate because of the nature of the distribution of scores, researchers can use either the Wilcoxon rank-sum test or the Mann-Whitney U. Instead of a one-sample paired *t*-test, one could use Wilcoxon's matched-pairs signed-ranks test or the sign test.

A replacement for the ANOVA is the Kruskal-Wallis one-way ANOVA for independent samples. When there are repeated measurements of subjects, Friedman's rank test for k correlated samples can be appropriate to replace the ANOVA.

When a study involves observations of the frequency with which observations fall into various categories, a common nonparametric test is the chi-square test. There are two varieties in common use, depending on whether the research design involves a single variable or two variables. The one-variable chi-square is a goodness of fit test, indicating whether the predicted number of observations in specified categories matches the observed number. The two-variable chi-square test assesses whether the frequencies of observations in different categories are contingent upon values of the second variable.

HYPOTHESIS TESTING

The logic of inferential tests of statistical significance is to establish a null hypothesis, H_0, that specifies no relation between variables or no differences among means, then to see if there is enough evidence to reject H_0 in favor of the experimental (or alternate) hypothesis. Rejection of H_0 is associated with an a priori probability value that the researcher establishes. Most researchers select a probability value of .05, meaning that they will reject H_0 if the probability of having gotten the obtained results is less than 5 percent if H_0 is actually true.

When rejecting H_0, researchers note that their results are *statistically significant*. Nonscientists often erroneously interpret the word *significant* to mean *important*. This technical wording is not intended to convey a sense that the results are important or practical. This wording simply means that the results are reliable, or replicable.

One objection to null hypothesis testing is that the cutoff for statistical significance is traditional and arbitrary. A probability value of .051 conveys much the same effect as a statistically significant value of .05, yet researchers have traditionally claimed that the slightly higher probability value puts their results into a different category of results, one reflecting no interesting findings and insufficient information to reject H_0.

The approach of most researchers is to question the likelihood of obtaining the results if H_0 is true. Thus, any conclusion specifies how rare the results were if the H_0 is true, but, logically, this approach says nothing about whether H_0 actually is true. The logic of traditional tests of the null hypothesis is often confused with the question of whether H_0 is true, given the results that were obtained. These two questions are conceptually very different. As a result, the traditional tests also say nothing about whether an experimental hypothesis, presumably the one of interest, is true.

Controversy currently exists regarding the adequacy of such tests of the null hypothesis. Theorists have argued

that H_0 is, strictly speaking, never true. That is, there will always be differences across groups or relations among variables, even if the differences are small or the relations weak. As a result, researchers have proposed alternate strategies for answering research questions.

One suggestion is to report effect sizes rather than simple probability values. Generally speaking, there are two families of effect sizes, *d-families* for questions of difference and *r-families* for questions of association (Rosenthal 1994). In an experiment, an effect size is a statistic that assesses the degree of variability due to treatments compared to variability caused by unknown factors like measurement error. A common measure of effect size when two groups are compared is Cohen's d. For more complex designs, investigators assess effect size through measures like eta-squared, η^2, and omega-squared, Ω^2.

Effect sizes in correlational analyses include r^2, which indicates the percentage of common variability among correlated variables. (In linear regression analysis, r^2 has a different meaning, relating to error in predicting the value of a criterion variable from predictor variables. It is conceptually related to the similarly named statistic in correlations.)

A different supplement to traditional hypothesis testing involves the use of confidence intervals (CI). A CI specifies the range of scores that can be considered plausible estimates of some population parameter. The parameter most often estimated is the mean. Thus a CI for a mean gives the investigator a sense of values of the population mean that seem reasonable, given sample values.

Some investigators have suggested that CIs be used to increase the information provided by null hypothesis testing because CIs give information about potential effect sizes, about the statistical power of a study, and about comparability of results across different studies. As with any emerging statistical technique, there are controversies associated with the use of CIs (Cohen 1994; Cumming and Finch 2005), including the fact that researchers in the social and behavioral sciences are still relatively untutored in the use of CIs (Belia et al. 2005).

One recent approach to hypothesis testing has been to replace the traditional probability value (i.e., what is the probability that the result occurred given that H_0 is true?) with the probability that an effect can be reproduced if a study were replicated (Killeen 2005). Theorists have argued that social and behavioral researchers are typically interested in whether their effects are real and will replicate, not whether the researcher can reject a statement of no effect. Thus it makes more sense to use a statistic that allows a prediction about how likely a result is to recur if a study is repeated.

A final, alternate approach to hypothesis testing involves Bayesian statistics. This approach relies on an investigator's prior knowledge and beliefs about the outcome of research. Given certain a priori assumptions, it is possible to compute the probability that H_0 is true, given the data, instead of merely the likelihood of obtaining the data, assuming that H_0 is true. Unfortunately, accurate probability values that would make the Bayesian approach feasible in the social and behavioral sciences are very difficult to ascertain, so few researchers have adopted this approach.

SCALES OF MEASUREMENT

The noted psychologist S. S. Stevens (1906–1973) identified four scales of measurement, each in increasing order of mathematical sophistication. Nominal scales are simply categorical (e.g., female-male). Ordinal scales are ordered in magnitude, but the absolute magnitude of the difference between any two observations is unspecified (e.g., the number of votes of the first-, second-, and third-place candidates in an election). With interval scales, a given difference between any two scores means the same at all points along the scale (e.g., the difference on a seven-point rating scale from one to two is equivalent to the difference between six and seven). A ratio scale involves the equality of differences between scores but also equality of ratios among scores (e.g., a task taking four seconds requires twice as much time as a task taking two seconds, and ten seconds is twice as long as five).

Behavioral researchers have sometimes claimed that parametric statistics require interval or ratio data. In reality, determining the scale of measurement of data is not always straightforward. Furthermore, statisticians do not agree that such distinctions are important (Howell 2007; Velleman and Wilkinson 1993). In practice, social researchers do not pay a great deal of attention to scales in determining statistical tests. Furthermore, some tests that purport to be useful for one type of scale (e.g., the phi coefficient for categorical data) are actually algebraic variations on formulas for parametric tests (e.g., Pearson's r).

SEE ALSO *Bayesian Statistics; Central Tendencies, Measures of; Chi-Square; Classical Statistical Analysis; Cliometrics; Data, Longitudinal; Data, Pseudopanel; Econometrics; General Linear Model; Hypothesis and Hypothesis Testing; Least Squares, Ordinary; Logistic Regression; Mean, The; Measurement; Methods, Quantitative; Mode, The; Probability; Psychometrics; Regression; Regression Analysis; Social Science; Standard Deviation; Statistics; Student's T-Statistic; Test Statistics; Variability; Variance; Z-Test*

BIBLIOGRAPHY

Belia, Sarah, Fiona Fidler, Jennifer Williams, and Geoff Cumming. 2005. Researchers Misunderstand Confidence Intervals and Standard Error Bars. *Psychological Methods* 10 (4): 389–396.

Cohen, Jacob. 1994. The Earth Is Round ($p < .05$). *American Psychologist* 49 (12): 997–1003.

Cumming, Geoff, and Sue Finch. 2005. Inference by Eye: Confidence Intervals and How to Read Pictures of Data. *American Psychologist* 60 (2): 170–180.

Howell, David. C. 2007. *Statistical Methods for Psychology*. 6th ed. Belmont, CA: Wadsworth.

Killeen, Peter. R. 2005. An Alternative to Null-Hypothesis Significance Tests. *Psychological Science* 16 (5): 345–353.

Rosenthal, Robert. 1994. Parametric Measures of Effect Size. In *The Handbook of Research Synthesis*, ed. Harris Cooper and Larry V. Hedges, 231–244. New York: Russell Sage Foundation.

Velleman, Paul. E., and Leland Wilkinson. 1993. Nominal, Ordinal, Interval, and Ratio Typologies Are Misleading. *The American Statistician* 47: 65–73.

Wilkinson, Leland, and the Task Force on Statistical Inference. 1999. Statistical Methods in Psychology: Guidelines and Explanations. *American Psychologist* 54: 594–604.

Bernard C. Beins

STATUS SYMBOLS

SEE *Prestige.*

STATUS-BEHAVIOR LINK

SEE *Role Theory.*

STEADY STATE

The concept of the "steady state" refers to a long-term, dynamic equilibrium, where diminishing returns have exhausted all the gains from capital deepening (i.e., increasing capital per worker). In the absence of technological progress, growth in per-worker output stops. A related concept of "dynamic equilibrium" was central to classical theory, particularly to David Ricardo's growth theory. This dynamic equilibrium was called the "stationary state." In the stationary state, all growth ends; both income and the size of the population are static. The stationary state occurs because diminishing returns in agriculture eventually lead to the end of growth. In this state the rate of profits is driven to zero, and rent captures all the economic output in excess of the output required to support the population at a subsistence wage rate. Policy proposals were often justified in part by whether they would postpone the emergence of the stationary state.

After a century of neglect, interest in growth theory reemerged with the Harrod-Domar model, which was developed independently by Roy Harrod in 1939 and Evsey Domar in 1946. This model did not have a dynamic equilibrium, however, because it did not allow for the possibility of diminishing returns. It was not until the Solow model emerged in 1956 that a dynamic equilibrium was introduced into neoclassical economics. The steady state in the Solow model occurs because the production function has diminishing returns. In this model, growth potentially has three sources: growth in capital per worker, growth in the labor force, and technological change. The latter two sources of growth are exogenous and are constant, as is the saving rate. For a linearly homogeneous production function, growth rates will converge to a steady-state growth rate, where all the positive effects of saving and investment on growth have been exhausted and where only the rate of population growth and the rate of technological progress impact the growth rate. This steady-state growth rate is expressed as $g = \dot{Y}/Y = \lambda + n$, where g is the rate of growth of income (GDP), λ is the rate of technological change, and n is the rate of growth of the labor force.

This steady-state growth rate can best be understood by considering a linearly homogeneous production function, $Y = F(K, L)$, where K is capital and L is labor. Output per unit of labor is $Y/L = y = f(k)$. The labor input can increase either because the number of workers, N, rises, or because Harrod-neutral technological change makes each worker more productive. Assume that N grows at a constant rate, n, and that there is a constant rate of technological change, λ. Then L will grow at the rate $n + \lambda$. With a constant marginal and average propensity to save and invest, s, capital per worker, k, will change by $k = sy - (n + \lambda + \delta)k$, where δ is the rate of depreciation. Increases in k will increase $y = f(k)$, and k will increase if $sy > (n + \lambda + \delta)k$. In other words, there will be capital deepening, which increases capital per augmented worker, L, if investment is sufficient to offset depreciation and provide each augmented worker with the same capital as before.

Policies that affect saving and investment will only have a temporary impact on growth, but since s does not affect steady-state growth, policy will have no impact on growth in the long run. Policy will, however, affect the steady state level of income per augmented worker, y. Consider an economy that is at a steady state. An increase in the saving rate will temporarily increase the growth rate because it will increase sy. Eventually a new steady-state level of y is reached and the growth rate will fall to its original level of $\lambda + n$. The economy is said to conditionally converge to an equilibrium y. The level of y is conditional on the saving rate, the labor force growth rate, and the technology.

Endogenous growth models have challenged this notion of the steady state by introducing models where policy matters in the long run because certain types of saving and investment affect λ through positive externalities. If these externalities exhibit constant returns, then policies that affect the saving rate will influence steady-state growth, and growth rates will not converge. Convergence is one of the most tested implications of the neoclassical steady state. If all countries share the same technology because knowledge is freely available, then per capita income should depend only on the rate of saving. Furthermore countries or regions that were late to develop should conditionally converge to countries that began to develop earlier. In other words, everything else being equal, poor countries should experience faster growth than rich countries. Robert Barro and others have tested for this convergence in cross-sectional estimates of growth. One of the explanatory variables is real per capita income for some earlier year. A negative coefficient for past income is evidence that convergence is occurring. Many empirical studies have found a negative coefficient, indicating conditional convergence, but they have also found that the rate of convergence is slow.

Conditional convergence does not necessarily imply a narrowing of gaps in per capita income between rich and poor nations. Many countries, both rich and poor, may be at or close to their conditional steady state, where per capita income is determined by structural variables, such as population growth rates, saving rates, and structural and institutional factors that determine λ, the rate of technological change (see Jones 1997; Darity and Davis 2005). Structural, institutional, and historical differences are receiving attention in the literature on economic development (see Grabowski, Self, and Shields 2007).

SEE ALSO *Stability in Economics*

BIBLIOGRAPHY

Barro, Robert J. 1991. Economic Growth in a Cross-Section of Countries. *Quarterly Journal of Economics* 106 (2): 407–433.

Darity, William, Jr., and Lewis S. Davis. 2005. Growth, Trade, and Uneven Development. *Cambridge Journal of Economics* 29 (1): 141–170.

Domar, Evsey. 1946. Capital Expansion, Rate of Growth, and Employment. *Econometrica* 14 (2): 137–147.

Grabowski, Richard, Sharmisha Self, and Michael P. Shields. 2007. *Economic Development: A Regional, Institutional, and Historical Approach.* Armonk, NY: Sharpe.

Harrod, Roy F. 1939. An Essay in Dynamic Theory. *Economic Journal* 49 (193): 14–33.

Jones, Charles I. 1997. On the Evolution of the World Income Distribution. *Journal of Economic Perspectives* 11 (3): 19–36.

Jones, Charles I. 2002. *Introduction to Economic Growth.* 2nd ed. New York: Norton.

Lucas, Robert E., Jr. 1988. On the Mechanics of Economic Development. *Journal of Monetary Economics* 22 (July): 3–42.

Ricardo, David. [1817] 1965. *The Principles of Political Economy and Taxation.* London: Aldine.

Romer, David. 2006. *Advanced Macroeconomics.* 3rd ed. Boston: McGraw-Hill.

Romer, Paul M. 1986. Increasing Returns and Long-Run Growth. *Journal of Political Economy* 94 (5): 1002–1037.

Solow, Robert M. 1956. A Contribution to the Theory of Economic Growth. *Quarterly Journal of Economics* 70 (1): 65–94.

Solow, Robert M. 2000. *Growth Theory: An Exposition.* 2nd ed. New York: Oxford University Press.

Michael P. Shields

STEEL INDUSTRY

The steel industry has a rich history. It exhibited remarkable technological dynamism and entrepreneurship and enjoyed significant economic, political, and strategic importance. With globalization and emergence of high technology sectors the industry has lost its clout. Western nations no longer dominate the industry due to changing costs and diffusion of technology and favorable government policy by selected high growth developing countries.

RISE OF AN INDUSTRY

The modern steel industry is inseparable from the second Industrial Revolution of the nineteenth century. From simple, small-batch production, new technologies such as the Bessemer process (developed in England in 1854) contributed to the mass production of steel. The industry diffused throughout Europe and the United States. The depression of the 1890s and subsequent mergers consolidated the American industry. In 1901 U.S. Steel, then the world's largest company, was formed. Scale of production increased dramatically in the twentieth century with large-scale blast furnaces to melt iron ore, its reduction in open hearth furnaces, followed by larger and more efficient basic oxygen furnaces (developed in Austria in 1954), continuous casting of molten steel, and port-based mills (in Japan and South Korea), which relied on massive ships capable of transporting imported raw materials and exports of finished steel products inexpensively. In the United States in the 1980s Kenneth Iverson adopted German innovations in electric arc furnace (EAF) technology. These mini-mills relied on recycled scrap or natural gas–based directly reduced iron (DRI) and thin slab casting. Mini-mills' smaller scale added to its flexibility

and competitiveness compared to blast furnace–based integrated producers.

The geographical location of steel mills was dictated by the availability of coal and iron ore. For the United States in the mid-1800s coal fields in eastern states such as Pennsylvania, Ohio, New York, and New Jersey attracted major iron works. Similarly, the availability of iron ore and coal around Birmingham, Alabama, and later in the late nineteenth century in Minnesota and Michigan influenced the location of steel mills in the Great Lakes region with Chicago as a major market. Such patterns have been found in other countries such as Brazil and India where mills were located near mines. However, in East Asian countries such as South Korea, Taiwan, and Japan, devoid of raw materials, a new pattern of plant location emerged, targeting coastal locations to source raw materials from and export finished steel to the world economy.

The post–World War II (1939–1945) American industry was characterized by oligopolistic competition at home, slow technological change, and little international competition. A handful of firms led by U.S. Steel dominated the industry. Supportive Keynesian policies propped up the U.S. economy, maintained industry profits, and accommodated high wages for steel workers. A major steel strike in 1959 paralyzed the economy, which was soon followed by brief controls of steel prices during the Vietnam War under the Kennedy administration (1961–1963) to stem inflationary pressures. John F. Kennedy asked steel workers to restrain their wage demands on the condition that steel corporations such as U.S. Steel would not raise prices. While workers kept their part of the bargain the companies did not as prices increased by $6 a ton. An infuriated Kennedy found such action as "wholly unjustifiable and irresponsible defiance of the public interest" (Kennedy 1962). Such price controls have been maintained worldwide through subsidies and public ownership because of the industry's dense intersectoral linkages. Not only are investments and employment encouraged in other industries but also economy-wide inflation is restrained. Steel is also a strategic industry with direct links to the defense sector.

GOVERNMENT POLICY AND SHIFTS IN THE INDUSTRY

Strikes in the steel industry were commonplace as conflict over wages and working conditions became paramount under rapid growth. The violent Homestead strike of 1892 in Pennsylvania turned into a complex battlefield with Andrew Carnegie using scab African American labor to crush the largest craft union, the Amalgamated Association of Iron and Steel Workers. In 1919 steel workers fought U.S. Steel and the movement was labeled a "Red Scare," unleashing an anti-Bolshevik and anti-radical hysteria. In Europe and in India, pro-labor social democratic governments and public ownership of many steel mills protected workers, while in South Korea unions were either banned or co-opted by the government-controlled Federation of Korean Trade Unions (FKTU), which was also infiltrated by the Korean Central Intelligence Agency. In the early twenty-first century, steel unions persist but most have lost their clout due to global competition from developing countries, declining membership, and the relative insignificance of the industry in economies driven by services and high technology. Unionization of American workers as a whole declined from 50 percent in the 1950s to about 13 percent by 2004.

Reconstruction of Western Europe and Japan and the rapid adoption of new steel technologies around the world eroded the American industry's competitiveness. The industry has been protected and promoted by governments worldwide as it has dense backward (ore, coal, heavy equipment) and forward linkages (construction, machinery, automobiles, shipbuilding). Some of the leading steel firms in Western Europe, such as British Steel and French Usinor-Sacilor, have been state owned. In late industrializing countries state ownership was routine as part of their import substitution industrialization strategy. Steel Authority of India (SAIL) in India, Siderurgia Brasileira (SIDERBRAS) in Brazil, the highly successful Pohang Iron and Steel Corporation (POSCO) in South Korea, and China Steel Corporation (CSC) in Taiwan were all state-owned. The former Soviet Union, Eastern bloc countries, and China, though outside the capitalist world economy until the late twentieth century, also relied on the industry for national development. The American industry was caught off guard by new mills, often with newer technologies. Since the late 1950s, the United States has been a net importer of steel. By 1987 Japan and South Korea supplied 28 percent of U.S. imports, mostly in high value flat products, while Western Europe, saddled with excess capacity, had a similar U.S. share. In the mid-2000s imports constitute 21 percent of the U.S. market.

In periods of high economic growth steel unions in the United States secured high wages, exceeding the average industry wage. Employment in the industry ensured working-class members middle-class living standards. However, by the 1970s technological obsolescence in the United States, excess global capacity, and lower operating costs in East Asia and Brazil made American steel jobs insecure. As foreign companies targeted the large U.S. market in cyclical downturns, the United States adopted a variety of protectionist policies. It started with voluntary restraint agreements (VRAs) in 1968, then the Trigger Price Mechanism (TPM) during the Carter administration (1977), and additional VRAs during the Reagan, Clinton, and the Bush Sr. administrations (1982–1992). The TPM was designed to penalize countries selling below cost, while VRAs forced foreign firms to restrain exports to a preset market share. Plagued by cumulative losses, including large debts and pension fund obligations, these policies merely deferred restructuring but did not prevent plant shutdowns and investments in non-steel sectors. The ensuing production imbalances compelled U.S. producers to obtain new technologies from capital surplus Japanese producers to supply better quality steel to auto producers in the United States, including Japanese auto transplants, while debt-ridden countries such as Brazil sought foreign investments for steel exports. Unable to maintain the high-wage workforce, the American steel industry shed nearly 300,000 steel jobs over the past quarter century and consequently improved labor productivity considerably. U.S. productivity also increased due to the diffusion of mini-mills. With lower capital and labor costs than the integrated segment and the hiring of nonunion workers in the southern United States, about 54 percent of American steel is produced with mini-mill technology.

STATE OF THE INDUSTRY AND FUTURE TRENDS

In the mid-2000s the major steel-producing countries are China, Japan, the United States, Russia, and South Korea with 272, 113, 99, 66, and 48 million metric tons respectively. Major exporters are Japan, Russia, Ukraine, Western Europe, South Korea, and Brazil. The most noteworthy development is the unprecedented growth of the Chinese economy since economic liberalization in 1979. Not only does China produce two-and-one half times more steel than Japan, but between 1998 and 2004 Chinese consumption of steel increased from 111 to 265 million metric tons. High demand in China moderates competition arising from excess global capacity and could prompt occasional shortages. While there is considerable intra-European steel trade, Russia, Japan, and South Korea have found the Chinese market attractive.

Globalization and neo-liberal policies have increased steel trade, cross-national investments and mergers, and privatization of state firms. Mittal Steel, founded by an Indian entrepreneur, has become the world's largest steel company through its acquisition of mills in the United States, Europe, Central Asia, and Mexico. In 2006 after many rebuffs, Mittal Steel acquired Arcelor, the world's largest steel firm revenue-wise, located in Luxembourg. Arcelor itself is a product of a merger between Spanish Aceralia, French Usinor, and Luxembourg's Arbed. Arcelor-Mittal is the largest steel venture with considerable expansion plans in India and elsewhere. In 2005 POSCO of South Korea, with several steel ventures in Asia and Latin America, announced a $12 billion iron and steel project in India. With declining steel intensity (share of steel to gross domestic product) in mature economies such as the United States, the growth of services, high technology industries (the new economy), and material substitutions, the steel industry is unlikely to witness a major resurgence in OECD economies. Both investment requirements and environmental concerns have dampened construction of large steel mills. The Clean Air Act implemented by the U.S. Environmental Protection Agency has made substantial improvements in steel plant emissions. Smaller plants using alternative technologies are feasible, but the supply of scrap, natural gas, and electricity may limit their diffusion in developing countries.

As long as mature economies are saddled by excess capacity, trade conflicts will persist. The use of Section 201 to assist American steel workers allegedly injured by subsidized steel imports is perceived by foreigners to be hypocritical since trade barriers and bailouts of firms of their pension obligations slow industrial adjustment. Higher steel prices resulting from protection could lead to job losses in steel-using industries, benefiting shareholders rather than workers. In the end, shared global prosperity is likely to ease the adjustment process, while any slowdown in China will exacerbate the excess capacity problem. High growth developing or exporting countries such as China, India, and Brazil are good candidates for the future expansion of the industry, while Japan and South Korea will remain important global suppliers of steel and steel technologies.

SEE ALSO *Industry; Railway Industry; Transportation Industry*

BIBLIOGRAPHY

Adams, W., and H. Mueller. 1980. The Steel Industry. In *The Structure of American Industry*, ed. W. Adams. 8th ed. New York: Macmillan.

Amsden, A. H. 1989. *Asia's Next Giant: South Korea and Late Industrialization*. New York: Oxford University Press.

Barnett, D. F., and R. W. Crandall. 1986. *Up from the Ashes: The Rise of the Minimill in the United States*. Washington, DC: Brookings Institution.

D'Costa, Anthony P. 1993. State-Sponsored Internationalization: Restructuring and Development of the Steel Industry. In *Trading Industries, Trading Regions: International Trade, American Industry, and Regional Economic Development*, eds. H. Noponen, J. Graham, and A. R. Markusen, 92–139. New York: Guilford Press.

D'Costa, Anthony P. 1999. *The Global Restructuring of the Steel Industry: Innovations, Institutions, and Industrial Change*. London: Routledge.

Hogan, William T. 1994. *Steel in the 21st Century: Competition Forges a New World Order*. New York: Lexington Books.

International Iron and Steel Institute, World Steel in Figures. http://www.worldsteel.org.

Kennedy, John F. 1962. Statement on the Steel Crisis. John F. Kennedy Library and Museum. http://www.cs.umb.edu/~rwhealan/jfk/j041162.htm.

Markusen, A. 1985. *Profit Cycles, Oligopoly, and Regional Development*. Cambridge, MA: MIT Press.

Anthony P. D'Costa

STEELE, CLAUDE M.
1946–

One of the most influential social scientists of the past five decades, the American social psychologist Claude Mason Steele is best known for two conceptually related lines of research and theorizing: the effects of negative stereotypes on the achievement and identities of minorities and women and people's psychological adaptation to self-image threats. He has also conducted research on the psychological effects of alcohol consumption.

SELF-AFFIRMATION THEORY

In 1988 Steele published what would become the most widely embraced modification of Leon Festinger's theory of cognitive dissonance, arguably social psychology's most influential theory of human motivation. Festinger (1957) had proposed that when people become aware of holding two inconsistent cognitions (e.g., I smoke cigarettes and smoking is unhealthy), they are motivated to reduce the resulting psychological discomfort by restoring consistency (e.g., by persuading themselves that smoking is not really very harmful). Steele challenged the central tenet of dissonance theory—that people find inconsistency per se uncomfortable and have a fundamental need for consistency between cognitions. Steele proposed that people are bothered not by mere psychological inconsistency but by the negative portrayal of the self that the inconsistency implies. Like earlier dissonance revisionists (e.g., E. Aronson 1969), Steele stressed the critical role of the self-concept in mediating the induction and reduction of dissonance, but unlike them, he rejected any inherent human preference for consistency, relegating inconsistency to a mere signal that the integrity of the self-image is under threat. For Steele, the psychic origin of dissonance phenomena is the actor's desire to maintain a sense of global "self-integrity," and this desire supersedes any need for consistency.

Steele further posited a self-system comprising self-conceptions, values, talents, and so on, which make up a pool of resources upon which the actor may draw to restore a sense of self-integrity when self-image threats arise. This fact, Steele proposed, gives the actor a great deal of flexibility in responding to self-threats. Employing Festinger's oft-used example of the cigarette smoker who reduces dissonance by downplaying the risks of smoking,

Steele argued that the smoker can maintain a sense of global integrity by reminding himself or herself of virtues in other domains of his or her life (I'm a great father, I'm a valuable member of the church, etc.). Such self-affirmations restore global self-esteem, thus allowing the individual to tolerate the self-threat implied by smoking despite the evidence that smoking is unhealthy.

Steele and his students tested the self-affirmation formulation by replicating standard dissonance paradigms in which a person is induced to engage in dissonance-arousing behavior (choosing between equally attractive gifts, writing a counter-attitudinal essay in support of an unpopular social policy, etc.) and then has his or her attitudes (e.g., toward the gifts or social policy) measured. If participants were given a self-affirmation of some sort (e.g., writing a few sentences about an important value), they showed no evidence of dissonance; in a wide variety of studies (Steele 1988), self-affirmations eliminated the attitude change that typically results from inducing dissonance.

Self-affirmation became influential as much for its highly transportable methodological paradigm—using value affirmations, for example—as for its theoretical alternative to dissonance. Examining the role of self-esteem threat has since become a thriving enterprise, as researchers can easily induce self-affirmation into the study of a variety of social-psychological phenomena, such as persuasion (e.g., Cohen, Aronson, and Steele 2000), prejudice (e.g., Fein and Spencer 1997), health (e.g., Creswell et al. 2005), and underachievement (e.g., Cohen et al. 2006). Although debate still continues on the role of inconsistency in cognitive dissonance, self-affirmation theory has established itself as a staple in current social psychology.

STEREOTYPE THREAT

Dissatisfied with the standard explanations for African Americans' lagging test scores and achievement and viewing many phenomena through the hospitable lens of self-affirmation theory, Steele proposed a social-psychological alternative to the standard explanations that focused either on poverty or genetic differences in average intelligence. Steele proposed that black students face a self-threatening situational predicament that occurs as a result of their awareness of unflattering racial stereotypes. In a widely read article published in the *Atlantic* (Steele 1992), he proposed the possibility that African Americans are hampered by the stigma of intellectual inferiority—a phenomenon that later came to be called "stereotype threat" (Steele and Aronson 1995). In situations where the stereotype is applicable, such as during an intelligence test, African Americans face an extra psychological burden not felt by a comparable white student taking the same test, a sense of risk that the test may confirm a racial inferiority

coupled with a heightened motivation to disprove the stereotype. Such a situation, Steele argued, generates anxiety, distraction, and other psychological impediments to test performance. Steele further proposed that, over time, students would defend against stereotype threat by disidentifying with academics, that is, reducing the extent to which they based their self-esteem on doing well academically.

A series of experiments performed with Joshua Aronson (Steele and Aronson 1995) offered strong support for the predictions about test performance. In each of the experiments African American college students performed significantly better on a standardized verbal test when the test was presented in a way that minimized the concern with confirming the stereotype. For example, in one experiment the test takers were told that the test was either a measure of their intelligence or that it was a nonevaluative laboratory problem-solving exercise. While this difference had no effect on white test takers, African American test takers performed nearly twice as well when the test was portrayed as nonevaluative.

These experiments drew national attention among educators and were referred to in two U.S. Supreme Court cases debating the use of affirmative action policies in hiring and college admissions. A publicized disagreement about the wisdom of affirmative action between Steele and his twin brother, Shelby Steele, the noted conservative scholar, drew additional attention to the research. Subsequent research confirmed the utility of the theory for understanding gender gaps in mathematics achievement, demonstrating that stereotype threat had similar effects on the mathematics performance of females (Spencer, Steele, and Quinn 1999).

In the decade after 1995 well over a hundred replications of stereotype threat effects on test performance were published, marking it as one of the most influential theories in the history of social psychology. Critics of the theory debate the degree to which stereotype threat underlies test-score gaps in the real world, but the theory has generated a handful of successful intervention studies that demonstrate that by reducing stereotype threat, race and gender test-score gaps are significantly reduced (Aronson, Fried, and Good 2002; Cohen et al. 2006; Good, Aronson, and Inzlicht 2003).

ALCOHOL MYOPIA

Steele and his students also conducted research on the psychological effects of alcohol consumption, documenting what they referred to as "alcohol myopia," (Steele and Josephs 1990), the effect of narrowing the drinker's focus upon immediate events and stimuli and reducing focus upon distant events, stimuli, or thoughts. Steele and his students documented that this narrowed focus plays a role in alcohol's well-known reduction of social inhibitions and reduction of emotional stress. After holding positions at the University of Utah, the University of Washington, the University of Michigan, and Stanford University, Steele became the director of the Center for the Advanced Study in the Behavioral Sciences.

SEE ALSO *Achievement Gap, Racial; Alcoholism; Cognitive Dissonance; Festinger, Leon; Intelligence; Motivation; Priming; Self-Affirmation Theory; Self-Concept; Self-System; Social Psychology; Stereotype Threat; Stereotypes; Underachievers*

BIBLIOGRAPHY

Aronson, E. 1969. The Theory of Cognitive Dissonance: A Current Perspective. In *Advances in Experimental Social Psychology*, vol. 4, ed. L. Berkowitz, 1–34. New York: Academic.

Aronson, J., G. Cohen, and P. R. Nail. 1998. Self-Affirmation Theory: An Update and Appraisal. In *Cognitive Dissonance: Progress on a Pivotal Theory in Social Psychology*, ed. E. Harmon Jones and J. Mills, 127–147. Washington, DC: APA Books.

Aronson, J., C. Fried, and C. Good. 2002. Reducing the Effects of Stereotype Threat on African American College Students by Shaping Theories of Intelligence. *Journal of Experimental Social Psychology* 38: 113–125.

Cohen, G., J. Aronson, and C. M. Steele. 2000. When Beliefs Yield to Evidence: Reducing Biased Evaluation by Affirming the Self. *Personality and Social Psychology Bulletin* 26 (9): 1151–1164.

Cohen, G. L., J. Garcia, N. Apfel, and A. Master. 2006. Reducing the Racial Achievement Gap: A Social-Psychological Intervention. *Science* 313: 1307–1310.

Creswell, J. D., W. Welch, S. E. Taylor, et al. 2005. Affirmation of Personal Values Buffers Neuroendocrine and Psychological Stress Responses. *Psychological Science* 16 (11): 846–851.

Fein, S., and S. J. Spencer. 1997. Prejudice as Self-Image Maintenance: Affirming the Self through Derogating Others. *Journal of Personality and Social Psychology* 73: 31–44.

Festinger, L. 1957. *A Theory of Cognitive Dissonance*. Stanford, CA: Stanford University Press.

Good, C., J. Aronson, and M. Inzlicht. 2003. Improving Adolescents' Standardized Test Performance: An Intervention to Reduce the Effects of Stereotype Threat. *Journal of Applied Developmental Psychology* 24: 645–662.

Spencer, S. J., C. M. Steele, and D. M. Quinn. 1999. Stereotype Threat and Women's Math Performance. *Journal of Experimental Social Psychology* 35: 4–28.

Steele, C. M. 1988. The Psychology of Self-Affirmation: Sustaining the Integrity of the Self. In *Advances in Experimental Social Psychology*, vol. 21, ed. L. Berkowitz, 261–302. New York: Academic.

Steele, C. M. 1992. Race and the Schooling of Black Americans. *Atlantic Monthly*. April: 68–78.

Steele, C. M. 1997. A Threat in the Air: How Stereotypes Shape Intellectual Ability and Performance. *American Psychologist* 52: 613–629.

Steele, C. M., and J. Aronson. 1995. Stereotype Threat and the Intellectual Test Performance of African-Americans. *Journal of Personality and Social Psychology* 69 (5): 797–811.

Steele, C. M., and R. A. Josephs. 1990. Alcohol Myopia: Its Prized and Dangerous Effects. *American Psychologist* 45: 921–933.

Joshua Aronson

STEELE, SHELBY
SEE *Race-Blind Policies.*

STEINEM, GLORIA
1934–

Gloria Steinem, a leader in the twentieth-century struggle for women's rights, was born on March 25, 1934, in Toledo, Ohio. Because of her father's penchant for traveling to warmer climates each winter, Steinem and her sister, Suzanne, had little time for formal schooling. Her mother, who had been educated as a teacher, provided some homeschooling for the girls, long before homeschooling was widely accepted. When Steinem was eleven years old, her parents divorced, and with her older sister away at college, Steinem was left alone to care for her mother, who suffered bouts of deep depression, accompanied by dementia. At seventeen, Steinem went to live with Suzanne in Washington, D.C., where she finished high school and completed her education at Smith College, where she graduated Phi Beta Kappa in 1956.

After spending a year in India, Steinem returned to the United States and worked as a public relations officer for a group later associated with the Central Intelligence Agency (CIA), although she claims to have had no knowledge of the association at that time. She later wrote for *Esquire, Glamour,* and *Show* magazines, where her exposé of life as a Playboy bunny earned her not only accolades but also fame. At *New York* magazine she worked with many of the budding writers of the New Journalism movement, including Tom Wolfe, Norman Mailer, and Gay Talese.

When the National Organization for Women was founded in 1966, Steinem, like many other women, saw the movement as a vehicle for white, middle-class housewives wanting to achieve independent goals outside traditionally male-controlled marriage. She saw no merit in the movement for herself, a single sophisticate, working in New York. But in 1969, Steinem attended a rally on abortion held by the feminist organization the Red Stockings, and after hearing other women detail the pain and humiliation they had endured, she had an epiphany. She had had an abortion herself and was harshly judged by the medical personnel who attended her procedure. Stories told by the women at the rally were even more horrific and included tales of emotional and physical pain and even death. Through the rally, Steinem came to see that not only married middle-class white women, but all women, including women of color, deserved to be treated as individuals, with rights equal to those enjoyed by men.

From that time forward, Steinem would devote much of her time and energy to furthering the cause of "reproductive freedom" and spoke at rallies around the country, recruiting women for the cause. She was a major catalyst in the movement's long-term success and provided a strong voice in the ongoing struggle through *Ms.* magazine, which she and her partners founded in 1971.

By that time, Steinem had also become respected as a political writer and activist, and in 1972 she helped found the Women's Action Alliance. She backed presidential candidates Shirley Chisholm and George McGovern, for whom she wrote several speeches. She also wrote five books, *Outrageous Acts and Everyday Rebellions* (1983), *Marilyn: Norma Jeane* (1986), *Revolution from Within: A Book of Self-Esteem* (1992), *Moving Beyond Words* (1994), and *Doing Sixty and Seventy* (2006).

Though she was credited with saying that "a woman needs a man like a fish needs a bicycle," Steinem was not the originator of this phrase. She told *Time* magazine in 2000, "In fact, Irina Dunn, a distinguished Australian educator, journalist and politician, coined the phrase back in 1970 when she was a student at the University of Sydney." Yet, the quip did define Steinem's outlook on marriage until 2000, when she married David Bale, a British entrepreneur and avid animal rights activist. The marriage, however, was to be short-lived. Bale died of brain cancer at the end of 2003, leaving Steinem to her lifelong quest of helping women find personal power and inner peace.

SEE ALSO *Feminism; Journalism*

BIBLIOGRAPHY

Cohen, Marcia. 1988. *The Sisterhood: The True Story of the Women Who Changed the World.* New York: Simon and Schuster.

Heilbrun, Carolyn G. 1995. *The Education of a Woman: The Life of Gloria Steinem.* New York: Dial Press.

Steinem, Gloria. 1983. *Outrageous Acts and Everyday Rebellions.* New York: Holt, Rinehart, and Winston. 2nd ed., New York: Henry Holt, 1995.

Patricia Cronin Marcello

STEM CELLS

A stem cell has two special qualities: the ability to produce offspring of itself indefinitely, and the ability to differentiate into different types of specialized cells. "Adult" stem cells are found in various organs of fully formed organisms. For example, umbilical cord blood and bone marrow contain stem cells capable of producing the various cells found in the blood, such as red blood cells, white cells, and platelets.

Public debate about ethical, social, religious, and legal issues involving stem cells has centered on a different kind of stem cell, so-called embryonic stem cells, usually obtained from excess embryos created by in vitro fertilization (IVF), but sometimes created specifically for research or therapeutic purposes. These human embryonic stem cells (hESCs) have the capacity to form any tissue in the body; that is, they are totipotential.

HESCs are of scientific and medical interest for three reasons: (1) they provide an opportunity to do laboratory research on normal and abnormal differentiation; (2) they provide an opportunity to test experimental therapies, including drugs and genes, at a cellular level, without exposing living animals or humans to risk; (3) they present an opportunity to develop and transplant cell lines that can replace vital molecules such as insulin (for patients with diabetes mellitus) or dopamine (for patients with Parkinson's disease), or to replace damaged tissue in the heart, nervous system, or elsewhere.

HESCs from residual IVF embryos are unlikely to be sufficient for all research and therapeutic interests. If, for example, stem cells are to be useful in treating diabetes, it will be important to create a cell line that is genetically identical to the recipient, so that it will not be rejected after transplantation. This can be accomplished by removing the nucleus of an egg, replacing it with the nucleus from a cell obtained from the potential recipient, and allowing the egg to grow to a stage when stem cells can be removed. This is called "somatic cell nuclear transfer" (SCNT).

SCNT is also of interest for laboratory research on genetic disorders such as cystic fibrosis or Tay Sachs disease. An embryo is created using the nucleus from a somatic cell of a patient with the disorder being studied, and then stem cells with the abnormal gene are obtained from the early embryo. This is sometimes called "research cloning." SCNT for the purpose of creating a cell line that would be used for treatment is sometimes called "therapeutic cloning."

Objections to research involving hESCs involve several concerns. First, some believe that an embryo has the same moral status as a fully formed human and is entitled to the same protections. Destruction of an embryo, in this view, is morally equivalent to murder. Proponents of hESC research point out that residual embryos are used only when the parents intend to destroy them anyway, and are not destroyed because of the interest in stem cell research. They also point out that tens of thousands of residual IVF embryos are destroyed annually without similar objection.

Second, opponents also argue that there are alternative approaches to obtaining totipotential stem cells, such as using adult stem cells. Most experts believe adult stem cells are not totipotential and therefore should not divert research funds from the more promising embryonic stem cells.

Third, opponents object to SCNT combined with hESC research because of concerns that it is a critical technical step for reproductive cloning, the creation of genetically identical replicas of existing persons. Advocates of hESC research argue that reproductive cloning is nearly universally opposed at the present time, largely because of concerns about biologic safety, and that "slippery slope" arguments are insufficient to prohibit research that can help alleviate suffering, disability, and death from diseases affecting large numbers of existing persons.

Fourth, concerns have been raised that the transfer of human cells into the developing brain of laboratory animals could result in an animal capable of human experience and therefore with moral status comparable to a human. Although most neuroscientists consider this to be unlikely, some groups have proposed prohibiting full gestation of nonhuman primates if human stem cells have been implanted in their central nervous systems early in embryonic development.

Governmental policies reflect a range of approaches in different countries and states, and policies within any jurisdiction are often in flux, subject to the success of politicians with various views. Some prohibit human embryonic stem cell research; some permit it but have restrictions on use of public funds; some permit research using existing embryos but prohibit creation of embryos for research; and some restrict somatic nuclear cell transfer because of concerns that it may accelerate human reproductive cloning.

SEE ALSO *Ethics in Experimentation; Medicine; Neuroscience; Public Policy; Reproductive Politics*

BIBLIOGRAPHY

McHugh, Paul R. 2004. Zygote and Clonote—The Ethical Use of Embryonic Stem Cells. *New England Journal of Medicine* 351 (3): 209–211.

National Academy of Sciences. 2006. Understanding Stem Cells: An Overview of the Science and Issues from the National Academies. http://dels.nas.edu/bls/stemcells/booklet.shtml.

Sandel, Michael J. 2004. Embryo Ethics: The Moral Logic of Stem-Cell Research. *New England Journal of Medicine* 351 (3): 207–209.

Walters, LeRoy. 2002. Human Embryonic Stem Cell Research: An Intercultural Perspective. *Kennedy Institute of Ethics Journal* 14 (1): 3–38.

Norman Fost

STEPFORD WIVES

The 1975 film *The Stepford Wives* begins with photographer Joanna Eberhart (Katharine Ross) leaving the urban malaise of New York City with her two children and her husband Walter (Peter Masterson) and moving to the picture-perfect village of Stepford, Connecticut, ready to start life anew and raise their brood in peace and tranquility. Strong, intelligent, with an independent streak, Joanna, we learn, has been a proponent of equal rights for women if not a strident feminist, and she is surprised to find that the housewives she meets are throwbacks to the 1950s, obsessed with homemaking and wanting nothing more from life than to please their husbands. Only her like-minded friend Bobbie Markowitz (Paula Prentiss) appreciates that something is clearly wrong here. Bobbie, too, thinks that the wives of Stepford are behaving more like life-size Barbie dolls than women of their own generation, and Bobbie is suspicious as well of why all their husbands spend so much time at the local men's association.

Gradually, Joanna learns. Threatened by the women's liberation movement, the men of Stepford have taken matters into their own hands. They are doing away with their wives one by one and replacing them with "gynoids," android duplicates. Unfortunately, by the time Joanna discovers this, Bobbie has become the latest of these "trophy wives," and the movie's epilogue, delivered at the supermarket no less, suggests a similar fate for Joanna.

Directed by Bryan Forbes and scripted by William Goldman, this first movie version of Ira Levin's best-selling 1972 novel did very well at the box office, earning a substantial $4 million from its domestic release alone, and it introduced into the American lexicon the term *Stepford wife*, a phrase meaning not simply "mindlessly deferential" but also "robotically conformist."

The 2004 remake, also titled *The Stepford Wives*, fared less well, both with critics and the public. Frank Oz, who was chosen to direct, and Paul Rudnick, who wrote the script, both were best known for their ways with a comedy, and together they created a broad, campy farce. In their version, Joanna Eberhart (Nicole Kidman) is a cold, driven television executive who has been fired when one of the reality shows she produces ends in disaster. Joanna and her ineffectual husband Walter, here a network vice president played by Matthew Broderick, move to a gated Connecticut community where they are immediately greeted by a Martha Stewart–perfect realtor, Claire Wellington (Glenn Close), and her husband Mike (Christopher Walken), who welcome them into their plastic paradise.

Once again, Stepford proves to be a community where all the women Joanna's age seem to awaken each morning wearing makeup, wanting nothing more than to bake their brownies and scrub their toilets and be there at the door when hubby gets home. The husbands are different, however. Goldman's script depicted the husbands as sinister, manipulative, eerily efficient corporate types, whereas Rudnick's makes them out to be men whose masculinity has been diminished by the highly successful women they married.

Joanna cannot understand why these women have forfeited their careers and embraced a model of pliant domesticity last seen in the Eisenhower era. Only two others in Joanna's circle think this is odd as well: a feminist author, Bobbie Markowitz, and half of a newly arrived gay couple, Roger Banister. Rudnick's specialty is sarcastic dialogue, the piercing one-liner, and the movie is well cast in this regard, for Bette Midler (Bobbie) and Roger Bart (Roger) deliver their lines with perfect aim as if they were poisonous darts. It is a truly funny movie, and, to their credit, the filmmakers achieve this without mocking the original. There is little or no suspense in this version, however. How could there be? The term *Stepford wives* is so deeply imbedded in the American psyche that everyone in the audience already knew the story. That may well be why Oz and Rudnick chose to end the film as they did, to catch the audience off-guard.

Their ending, which reportedly had to be rethought and then reshot before the film was released, is more upbeat than the original's, for theirs spares Joanna, and it has a brilliant woman behind the scheme in question. But such departures from the original are problematic. What does it say about us that a cautionary tale about the gender war has been turned into a battle of the sexes fought for laughs? Is it somehow a tribute to female capability that it is Claire who is the villain, rather than her husband Mike, as the script leads us to suspect for much of the movie? What are we to make of men so desperate to wear the pants in the family that they would "cybertize" their wives? What made those pants worth wearing to begin with? The first third of the movie is the movie at its best, for Kidman reprises much of what she achieved in *To Die For* (1995), once again giving a dangerously ambitious woman a high, lethal sheen. Joanna is not a particularly

sympathetic character though. Nor is Bobbie in this version. Nor is anyone else.

Viewed decades later, the original, with its hip clothes and burn-your-bra politics, seems seriously dated. The remake, on the other hand, gives us pause to think about how much has changed between men and women in the past quarter century, and whether those changes were all for the better. One can only hope that was what the filmmakers intended.

SEE ALSO *Conformity; Feminism; Feminism, Second Wave; Gender; Inequality, Gender; Marriage; Women and Politics; Women's Liberation; Women's Movement*

BIBLIOGRAPHY

Fowler, Douglas. 1988. *Ira Levin.* Eugene, OR: Starmont House.

Goldman, William. 1983. *Adventures in the Screen Trade.* New York: Warner Books.

Thomson, David. 2006. *Nicole Kidman.* New York: Knopf.

Jay Boyer

STEREOTYPE THREAT

Stereotype threat is a term coined by social psychologists Claude Steele and Joshua Aronson that refers to the fear people experience when they are at risk of confirming a negative stereotype that is held about their group. This psychological threat can undermine successful performance of tasks and activities.

Typically stereotype threat is examined by asking people to perform a challenging task that evaluates their ability in an area. Before the task, some people are given a prompt designed to activate a stereotype. For example, when women are reminded of the stereotype that men are better than women at math, they score lower on a difficult math test. Similarly African American students who are told that a test reflects their verbal ability perform worse on the test than do equally capable white students. Mere mention that the test diagnoses verbal ability is enough to conjure up a debilitating belief among some African American students that their score will be lower. But a person need not be socially stigmatized, feel intellectually inferior, or belong to a minority group to be vulnerable to stereotype threat. In one study, white men from a prestigious university were asked to take a difficult math test on which, some were told, Asians typically perform better. The men in this *threat* condition performed worse on the exam than did those who received no information about how others perform. Indeed stereotype threat can impair the cognitive functioning of anyone who is in a negatively stereotyped group (e.g., drug users, the elderly, athletes, the economically disadvantaged).

Stereotype threat is situation-dependent and is not a general attitude or expectancy that affects individuals across contexts. A threatening situation can occur any time a negative stereotype is brought to mind, even when a person is alone. Experimenters have also shown that priming positive stereotypes about one's group can actually enhance performance. In one experiment, for example, Asian American women performed well on a mathematics test when their ethnicity was made prominent, but poorly when their gender was made prominent.

What makes people vulnerable to the threat of fulfilling a stereotype? First, people are likely to experience a threat in those areas in which they care about performing well. When a woman who values success in math is being evaluated, she will feel more threatened by a stereotype than will someone who dismisses math as unimportant. Also at risk are people who feel a strong sense of identification with and attachment to their group. Merely having to indicate one's race on the first page of an evaluation can be enough to activate a threat and impair performance. When one is in the numerical minority (e.g., the only African American student in a group of white students), group identity is made even more salient. People who expect discrimination or suspect that a stereotype may be valid are also more easily triggered by threatening situations.

The fear of confirming a negative stigma has been shown to lower students' performance on items from the Graduate Record Examination (GRE), the Texas Assessment of Academic Skills (TAAS), Raven's Progressive Matrices, and high school Advanced Placement (AP) exams. Stereotype threat has also been shown to limit important cognitive resources such as working memory and self-monitoring capabilities. Students who feel threatened may enlist strategies to safeguard their self-esteem, such as opting for less challenging school work, making excuses for their school failures, resisting feedback others give them about their work, or disassociating with school-related activities altogether. As a consequence, the effects of stereotype threat may be far-reaching, influencing placement in advanced classes, college admissions, people's career choices, and, ultimately, their earnings. Some argue that stereotype threat is in part to blame for the black-white achievement gap prevalent in U.S. schools.

Researchers have suggested a number of ways in which people can offset the detrimental effects of stereotype threat. Leaders and decision makers, whether in schools or elsewhere, can emphasize cooperative working environments that reduce prejudice, foster trusting interpersonal relationships, and value others as individuals. Placing an emphasis on the malleable nature of academic ability will also help individuals see the potential for intellectual growth and academic success. Researchers have also shown that individuals who are good self-monitors—that is, those who are sensitive to their social surroundings and able to regulate their behavior to negotiate them—show resilience in the face of stereotype-threatening situations. Helping individuals to become self-affirming may provide them with an interior source of strength and assurance needed to withstand environmental stressors.

SEE ALSO *Achievement Gap, Racial; Cognition; Diathesis-Stress Model; Prejudice; Priming; Racism; Self-Esteem; Self-Monitoring; Standardized Tests; Steele, Claude M.; Stereotypes; Stigma; Stress; Stress-Buffering Model*

BIBLIOGRAPHY

Aronson, Joshua, and Claude M. Steele. 2005. Stereotypes and the Fragility of Academic Competence, Motivation, and Self-Concept. In *Handbook of Competence and Motivation*, eds. Andrew J. Elliot and Carol S. Dweck, 436–456. New York: Guilford Press.

Spencer, Steven J., Claude M. Steele, and Diane M. Quinn. 1999. Stereotype Threat and Women's Math Performance. *Journal of Experimental Social Psychology* 35 (1): 4–28.

Steele, Claude M. 1997. A Threat in the Air: How Stereotypes Shape Intellectual Identity and Performance. *American Psychologist* 52 (6): 613–629.

Steele, Claude M., and Joshua Aronson. 1995. Stereotype Threat and the Intellectual Test Performance of African-Americans. *Journal of Personality and Social Psychology* 69 (5): 797–811.

Ellen L. Usher

STEREOTYPES

Stereotypes constitute a person's set of expectations about a social group's characteristics, including traits, behaviors, and roles. They are the categorical associations perceivers make to group members based on their membership. Although cognitive in form, stereotypes are interlocked with affect and behavior: Along with prejudice and discrimination, stereotypes make up the tripartite foundation for the breakdown of intergroup relations.

Stereotyping stems from categorization processes that involve the self. Social identity theory contends that people conceptualize the self at different levels of inclusiveness that range from the subordinate to the superordinate. At each level of abstraction, the corresponding identity (personal, social, or collective self) is salient, with reference to each varying by context. In perceiving the self through a social identity, the person views the self as part of an in-group that is distinctive and, under many circumstances, more subjectively positive than out-groups. Self-categorization theory continues this narrative:

Depersonalization of the self via in-group and out-group differentiation triggers group phenomena that include stereotyping.

Two principles of self-categorization theory structure stereotypes: comparative fit and normative fit. In the former, also known as meta-contrast ratio fit, the smaller the perceived intragroup difference in comparison to intergroup differences, the more the group embodies a coherent unit. Thus, people are categorized into groups that minimize within-group differences and maximize between-group differences. Furthermore, normative fit requires that these differences, both within and between, align with the perceiver's normative beliefs about the group—that the group fits expectations. An interaction between comparative fit and normative fit processes guides stereotype construction. Under the first principle, within-group variability decreases, increasing perceived homogeneity between group members; under the second, perceived group categories reflect a perceiver's expectations about that group or the content of normative beliefs.

A two-dimensional framework inherited from person perception literature illustrates the content of stereotypes. Person and group perception use two recurring dimensions that are variations of warmth/morality and ability/competence. One example, the stereotype content model, argues that stereotypes immediately answer two key questions for the perceiver: Do out-group members intend good or ill toward me and my group? and Are they able to act on these intentions? The answers to these questions produce stereotypes in four quadrants: ambivalent (or cross-dimensional) stereotypes (e.g., elderly people are stereotypically nice but incompetent, rich people are stereotypically competent but not nice); stereotypically neither warm nor competent (e.g., poor people); and stereotypically both warm and competent (e.g., middle class).

UTILITY: FORM FITS FUNCTION

Because stereotypes stem from the differentiation of "us" from "them," stereotype targets usually fall outside the cultural default (in the United States): not young, not white, not male, not heterosexual, not middle class, and not Christian. Groups whose members are the least (visibly) representative of the default receive the most stereotypes. The high prevalence of age, racial or ethnic, and gender stereotypes results in part from the speed of categorizing people on these dimensions.

Stereotyped targets are not exclusive to the visibly different. Stereotypes also form when a person perceives an *illusory correlation* between a group and a particular characteristic; in actuality, group membership and the characteristic might covary by chance or because of historical development, or not even covary at all, but perceiving a

fundamental connection strengthens the stereotypic quality of the characteristic for that group. Stereotypes may reflect the perceiver's knowledge of power relations in society. Some national stereotypes exemplify such contextual influences on stereotype formation, with perceivers relying on features of a nation—political, economic, religious, geographic, and status vis-à-vis one's own nation, among others—to characterize its residents. Because they are shaped by the social context, stereotypes reflect cultural beliefs. As such, they shift over time—when social conditions change, societies update their stereotypes of groups because the social relations of those groups transform. As an example, many ethnic groups in the early twenty-first-century United States receive more favorable stereotypes than they did in the 1930s, including originally mistrusted immigrants (e.g., Irish, Italian, Jewish) who now join the mainstream.

Whatever their origins, stereotyping serves cognitive, motivational, and social purposes. For example, in the *cognitive miser* view, stereotyping saves mental effort. Facing cognitively overwhelming tasks and limited attention and effort, people rely on stereotypes to increase available on-line resources. People's social interaction priorities also influence stereotyping. Many models of stereotyping posit two modes of impression formation, with some models arguing for an either-or competition between the two, and others placing them on the ends of a continuum. In either case, one mode emphasizes the need to make quick decisions through categorical information, whereas the other underscores the need to be accurate through effortful use of individuating information. The perceiver who must prioritize between these interaction goals is dubbed the *motivated tactician*. Using stereotypes can smooth interactions if both people agree on the stereotype or if the interaction is brief and inconsequential for the holder of the stereotype.

Because they are convenient, stereotypes often actively motivate perceivers to maintain them. Creating exceptional subtypes is one way to maintain an overall stereotype despite a few salient people who do not conform neatly to the group. Subtyping allows the perceiver to cognitively isolate people who are stereotype-inconsistent by explaining that while they belong to the stereotyped group, they do not entirely represent the group.

At the societal level, system justification theory argues that people stereotype to maintain the status quo, even at the expense of one's own group. Some researchers argue that minority groups' own negative stereotypes demonstrate the system-justifying effects of stereotypes. Some researchers also suggest that complementary stereotypes (e.g., poor but happy, rich but miserable) increase support for the status quo because they satisfy people's desire to perceive their world as fair and legitimate.

MEASUREMENT: THE EXPLICIT
AND THE IMPLICIT

Although stereotypes may reflect a cultural belief, the individual with that knowledge does not necessarily endorse such a belief, as argued by the dissociation model of stereotypes. Nevertheless, regardless of one's explicit prejudice level, a person may be primed to think of groups stereotypically. For example, the presentation of a group label facilitates the activation of subsequent stereotype-consistent associations for both low- and high-prejudiced people. Implicit stereotypes can persist, even when explicit stereotypes do not.

Incongruent results from explicit and implicit stereotype measures illustrate the dissociation between personal endorsement and cultural knowledge. They also demonstrate that perceivers are often unaware of their own cognitive associations, particularly if they are automatic. In addition, when egalitarian cultural norms discourage unfavorable prejudgments of others, and perceivers have a self-interest to refrain from these expressions, implicit measures can extract more information than can explicit measures. In short, implicit measures may detect what remains elusive from explicit measures. Regardless of whether a measure is explicit or implicit, stereotype measures reveal biases toward stereotype-consistent information.

Explicit measures are straightforward. As with other attitude measures, researchers can assess stereotypes through self-reports of impressions about target groups. For example, perceivers can express their impressions of immigrants in their own words, which the researchers then code into manageable categories. Stereotypes might include immigrant groups' traits, behaviors, socioeconomic status, and life satisfaction, for example. Alternatively, perceivers can rate on a scale of how characteristically immigrants are hard-working, engage in criminal behaviors, experience poverty, feel welcome in the host nation, and so on.

Implicit measures reveal attention, attribution, and memory biases toward stereotype-consistent information. People prefer to confirm their stereotypes, at an immediate perceptual level, detecting stereotype-consistent information more easily. Although they then attend to stereotype-inconsistent information, if present, they tend to explain it away: The out-group's success was a fluke, the successful out-group individual is not typical, and so on. In general, an out-group's stereotype-consistent behavior elicits internal attributions to the group's enduring dispositions; stereotype-inconsistent behavior elicits external attributions to chance or temporary circumstances. If a particular negative trait stereotype afflicts a target group, that group's failures could be attributed to the supposed negative trait. If an out-group member does behave negatively and stereotypically (e.g., the criminal activity of a black person), situational factors will likely be disregarded in explaining that person's behavior. People also better recall and recognize stereotype-consistent information than stereotype-inconsistent information if they are busy and operating in the complex environments typical of everyday interactions.

Researchers also devise priming methods to study automatic stereotypic associations. Some involve subliminal presentation of priming stimuli. Study participants then perform various tasks—including word searches, lexical decision tasks, fluency-manipulated tasks, and interpretations of ambiguous behaviors—in which they might produce responses that indicate stereotypic associations to the primes. Reaction speed, performance quality, and stereotypicality of responses indicate level of stereotype activation. Compared to this preconscious (subliminal) presentation of stimuli, other priming manipulations explicitly present stimuli; thus the perceiver postconsciously produces the activated associations. The implicit association test consciously primes two categories and then measures differential reaction times to concepts that are stereotype-consistent to one of the primes but not the other. People often react more quickly to negative words following out-group primes and to positive words following in-group primes. Also using postconscious priming, neuroimaging studies show increased amygdala (vigilance) activation to images of out-groups. Automatic associations escape a person's conscious awareness, but implicit measures subtly detect what lurks beneath the surface.

CONSEQUENCES: THE GOOD, THE
BAD, AND MORE BAD

Stereotypes might result from historical accidents, unduly generalize across people, and mostly derogate, yet they persist. Nevertheless, the costs of stereotyping have more extensive effects, especially for the target. First, the perceiver glosses over individuating information about a target (preference for stereotype-consistent information foregoes potential knowledge gain). On their side, targets are evaluated at the category level and not according to individual characteristics. They might even be classified with others in a group with which they do not identify.

Inaccuracies of three types plague stereotypes. Stereotypic inaccuracy refers to the overestimation of the target group's stereotypicality or the underweighing of its stereotype-inconsistent qualities. Valence inaccuracy entails exaggeration of the negativity or positivity of the group's stereotypes. Dispersion inaccuracy results from over- or undergeneralizing the variability between group members. Nonetheless, some other researchers argue for studying the accuracies contained within stereotypes because in this view they reflect reality.

The effects of stereotyping increase concomitantly with prejudice. Stereotypes along with prejudice strongly predict discrimination, so prejudiced perceivers are much more likely to act on their prejudice to negatively stereotyped groups.

Stereotypes reach beyond themselves. *Stereotype threat* describes targets' awareness of their group's negative stereotypes in a particular and consequential performance domain; they can ironically perform worse than those who do not care about that domain. Furthermore, stereotype threat leads to the targets fulfilling the stereotype that haunted them in the first place. Some examples are black students in an academic setting and women in mathematical tasks, for whom performance was labeled as diagnostic of their ability. Stereotype-threat effects differ from self-fulfilling prophecies because they affect people without encountering a prejudiced person.

Self-fulfilling prophecies, also called *behavioral confirmation*, perpetuate stereotypes through the perceiver's expectancies of confirmation and the target's behavioral confirmations of the expectancy. For the perceiver, one utility of stereotypes is in making the cognitive and social load more manageable. Stereotypes may also be useful for targets who want to fulfill their interaction partner's expectancies so that they can avoid conflict or focus on an aspect of the interaction they deem more important. The process, however, perpetuates stereotypes in society.

SEE ALSO *Attitudes; Attribution; Discrimination, Racial; Merton, Robert K.; Perception, Person; Prejudice; Self-Fulfilling Prophecies; Steele, Claude; Stereotype Threat*

BIBLIOGRAPHY

Devine, Patricia G. 1989. Stereotypes and Prejudice: Their Automatic and Controlled Components. *Journal of Personality and Social Psychology* 56 (1): 5–18.

Fiske, Susan T., Amy J. C. Cuddy, Peter Glick, and Jun Xu. 2002. A Model of (Often Mixed) Stereotype Content: Competence and Warmth Respectively Follow from Perceived Status and Competition. *Journal of Personality and Social Psychology* 82 (6): 878–902.

Greenwald, Anthony G., and Mahzarin R. Banaji. 1995. Implicit Social Cognition: Attitudes, Self-Esteem, and Stereotypes. *Psychological Review* 102 (1): 4–27.

Jost, John T., and Mahzarin R. Banaji. 1994. The Role of Stereotyping in System Justification and the Production of False Consciousness. *British Journal of Social Psychology* 33 (1): 1–27.

Macrae, C. Neil, Charles Stangor, and Miles Hewstone, eds. 1996. *Stereotypes and Stereotyping*. New York: Guilford Press.

Tajfel, Henri, and John C. Turner. 2004. The Social Identity Theory of Intergroup Behavior. In *Political Psychology: Key Readings*, eds. John T. Jost and Jim Sidanius, 276–293. New York: Psychology Press.

Turner, John C., and Penelope J. Oakes. 1989. Self-Categorization Theory and Social Influence. In *The Psychology of Group Influence*, ed. Paul B. Paulus, 233–275. 2nd ed. Hillsdale, NJ: Erlbaum.

Tiane L. Lee
Susan T. Fiske

STERILE CLASS

SEE *Physiocracy.*

STERILIZATION, ECONOMIC

The term *sterilization* is used in international economics and macroeconomics to describe the actions a central bank undertakes in order to neutralize the effects of central bank interventions in the foreign exchange market on the supply of domestic currency in the economy. Sterilization usually takes the form of an open market operation, in which a central bank sells or purchases government bonds on an open market in the amount it purchases or sells foreign currency on the foreign exchange market, so that the amount of domestic currency in circulation remains unchanged.

Suppose for example that it takes \$1.35 to purchase €1; that is, it takes 1.35 American dollars to purchase 1 euro (the currency of the European Union). Suppose further that the Federal Reserve System (the United States' central bank) wishes to keep the exchange rate from rising from its current level to say \$1.50 for €1. To accomplish this task the American central bank must sell euros (foreign exchange) out of its reserves. Since the euros will be purchased with dollars, the supply of dollars in circulation will decrease and the supply of euros in circulation will increase. Thus the value of the euro will not rise relative to the dollar. But this action reduces the amount of domestic currency in circulation in the United States, which might not be desirable. For example interest rates might rise. In order to counteract this effect, the central bank may simultaneously purchase domestic (American) bonds in order to put domestic currency back in circulation. Similarly if a central bank is buying foreign currency to keep the value of domestic currency low, it can sterilize such intervention by selling bonds and removing from circulation domestic currency that was introduced by such foreign exchange market intervention.

If an intervention in a foreign exchange market is accompanied by a sterilization operation, it is called a sterilized intervention. International economics theory states that a sterilized intervention has occurred when: (1) international assets are perfect substitutes; (2) there is full capital mobility; and (3) the uncovered interest parity holds (that is, if one tries to make money by borrowing at a low interest rate in one currency and investing at a high interest rate in another currency, any gains will be offset by the change in the exchange rate). However if international assets are not perfect substitutes, or there are barriers to the flows of capital across borders, sterilized intervention can be effective in maintaining a certain level of exchange rate while minimizing the effect of interventions on the supply of domestic currency. In his 2003 article "Is Official Foreign Exchange Intervention Effective?" Michael Hutchison argued that in practice sterilized interventions have been effective.

One recent example of a central bank actively engaged in sterilized interventions is the People's Bank of China, China's central bank. In order to prevent the value of RMB, Chinese currency, from rising too fast against the U.S. dollar in the early 2000s, the People's Bank of China was actively purchasing dollars while at the same time issuing its own central bank bills. As a result the effect of foreign exchange interventions on the supply of domestic currency was neutralized, and the People's Bank of China accumulated foreign reserves, while Chinese commercial banks accumulated their holdings of central bank bills, claims on the People's Bank of China. The reason sterilized interventions were effective in China is limited capital mobility in and out of China, as a result of which Chinese and foreign assets are not perfectly substitutable.

Less frequently the term *sterilization* is used to describe the actions a central bank might take in order to reduce the effects of international capital inflows on the supply of domestic currency in the country. This type of sterilization was important during the lending boom of the 1990s when many emerging markets experienced a surge in international capital inflows, which was accompanied by the rise in domestic money supply and therefore inflation. In his 1997 article "Sterilizing Capital Flows" Jang-Yung Lee provided a detailed discussion of the sterilization of international capital inflows.

SEE ALSO *Capital Controls; Capital Flight; Economics, International; Euro, The; Federal Reserve System, U.S.; Macroeconomics; Policy, Monetary*

BIBLIOGRAPHY

Hutchison, Michael. 2003. Is Official Foreign Exchange Intervention Effective? *Federal Reserve Bank of San Francisco Economic Letter*, July 18. http://www.frbsf.org/publications/economics/letter/2003/el2003-20.html.

Lee, Jang-Yung, 1997. Sterilizing Capital Flows. *International Monetary Fund Economic Issues* (7). http://www.imf.org/external/pubs/ft/ISSUES7/issue7.pdf.

Galina Hale

STERILIZATION, HUMAN

Sexual sterilization can be effected through various surgical operations designed to prevent a person from reproducing. In its most radical form, sterilization involves castration, which is the removal of the testes (male) or ovaries (female) and the consequent destruction of the capacity to produce human germ cells (sperm or ova). Late in the nineteenth century advances in surgical technique provided alternatives to castration as the sole means of sterilizing humans. These new operations were simpler for surgeons to perform, were less dangerous for patients to endure, and had a much more limited impact on health.

In the 1880s the Scottish surgeon Lawson Tait initiated the operation of salpingectomy for women. Tait's technique was introduced as a therapy for ectopic pregnancy, a potentially fatal condition that sometimes occurs when a fertilized ovum lodges unexpectedly in a fallopian tube. Removal of a section of each fallopian tube prevents any ovum from traveling to the uterus (womb), hence ruling out any future pregnancy.

Soon after Tait introduced salpingectomy, the Chicago surgeon Albert Ochsner developed the operation of vasectomy as a treatment for problems of the male prostate gland. Ochsner described how he removed a portion of the cord known as the *vasdeferens*, removing the route a sperm travels. He endorsed vasectomy as a surgical option that would avoid objections raised against castration. Ochsner's surgery was also innovative because he specifically prescribed it as a means of preventing convicted criminals from having children. Soon the operation was being recommended as a way to prevent parenthood among chronic alcoholics, sex criminals, the mentally impaired, and the poor.

Ochsner's technique became popularized just as the eugenics movement began to take root in the United States. The term *eugenics* was coined by the English scientist Francis Galton in 1883. Galton believed that most human characteristics, from physical and mental traits to moral predispositions, were inherited. *Eugenics* was his name for the science that aimed to increase the number of "well-born"—healthy and productive people—in future generations. Many of Galton's followers believed, as he did, that societies should eliminate the future births of hereditarily tainted unhealthy and dependent people. The emergence of new technologies for surgical sterilization during Galton's lifetime made that goal appear more feasible.

In the last decade of the nineteenth century, the state of Michigan debated the adoption of a law to mandate "asexualization" (castration) of some repeat criminals as well as inmates of asylums and homes for the mentally impaired to prevent the birth of children with similar disorders. That law and similar efforts in Kansas and Pennsylvania were rejected between 1897 and 1905.

Two years later the Indiana prison doctor Harry C. Sharp, working in collaboration with J. N. Hurty, secretary of the Indiana Board of Health, convinced their state legislature to adopt what became the first involuntary sterilization law in the world. Sharp had introduced vasectomy into his practice at the Indiana Reformatory as a therapy to cure male inmates of *onanism* or habitual masturbation. After several hundred experimental surgeries, Sharp convinced legislators that the procedure was also valuable as an efficient means to prevent the reproduction by hereditarily diseased parents of criminals and similarly "defective" children. Following Indiana's lead, by 1926 twenty-one other states had passed laws that allowed governmental boards, commissions, or officials of state prisons, asylums, or other institutions to choose people who would be sterilized.

In 1927 the practice of salpingectomy for "eugenic" purposes was endorsed by the U.S. Supreme Court in the case of *Buck v. Bell*. The lawsuit pitted the Virginia teenager Carrie Buck against the state doctor who directed the Virginia Colony for Epileptics and Feebleminded. Buck was sent to the colony because she was an unmarried mother—a "moral degenerate"—whose condition was supposedly inherited from her mother, Emma Buck, already a colony inmate. Testimony in the case suggested that Carrie Buck's seven-month-old baby was abnormal as well, prompting an opinion for the Supreme Court by Justice Oliver Wendell Holmes Jr. that upheld the Virginia sterilization law, concluding: "Three generations of imbeciles are enough." Later research disclosed that Carrie Buck had no hereditary "defects," and her daughter Vivian eventually earned a spot on her grade-school honor roll.

With the *Buck* decision as precedent, ten more American states passed eugenic sterilization laws by 1937. More than 60,000 surgeries were performed in the United States under the authority of eugenics laws between 1907 and the late 1970s. Ten other laws sanctioning involuntary sterilization were enacted in countries in the Americas, Europe, and Asia. The most notable was the 1933 German law that was applied to almost 400,000 people in less than ten years.

In 1942 the U.S. Supreme Court revisited the issue of coercive sterilization, striking down an Oklahoma law that authorized surgery on habitual criminals. Jack Skinner, the prisoner who challenged the law, had convictions for armed robbery and chicken theft. He argued that no scientific evidence proved the trait of "criminality" to be an inherited characteristic. The Court overturned the sterilization law, calling it a violation of the Constitution's equal protection clause because it applied to common crimes like Skinner's chicken theft but provided an exception for tax evasion, embezzlement, or political graft. At the same time the Court did not disturb the *Buck* ruling, which stood as continued justification of operations on the disabled.

Other operations, often targeting ethnic or racial minority populations, occurred without legal sanction. Jews and the Sinti and Roma ("Gypsies") were sterilized using X-rays or caustic chemicals as part of the Nazi death camp program of "research" during World War II (1939–1945). From the mid-1950s until the 1970s, reports surfaced of widespread sterilization of Latinas, African Americans, and American Indians in several states. In the wake of these revelations, most American laws with "eugenic" language were repealed in the 1970s. Several European countries instituted programs of restitution for victims of sterilization policies; the Canadian provinces of Alberta and British Columbia later paid reparations following lawsuits. In the United States, the Virginia General Assembly, which in 1924 had enacted the law used to sterilize Carrie Buck, became in 2001 the first state legislature to condemn the sterilization law it had passed in the name of eugenics. Apologies followed in Oregon, North and South Carolina, and California, the state where more than one-third of all U.S. sterilizations took place. In 2007, to mark the centennial of U.S. sterilization laws, both the first state to pass such a law (Indiana, 1907) and the last state (Georgia, 1937) repudiated their earlier sterilization laws. Reports of sterilization abuse focused on minority populations in Peru, the Czech Republic, and Brazil have continued to appear in the first decade of the twenty-first century.

SEE ALSO *Crime and Criminology; Determinism, Biological; Determinism, Genetic; Ethics; Eugenics; Fertility, Human; Galton, Francis; Genocide; Heredity; Mental Retardation; Morality; Reparations; Reproduction; Reproductive Politics; Reproductive Rights*

BIBLIOGRAPHY

Kevles, Daniel J. 1985. *In the Name of Eugenics: Genetics and the Uses of Human Heredity.* Cambridge, MA: Harvard University Press.

Lombardo, Paul A. 2003. Facing Carrie Buck. *Hastings Center Report* 33 (2): 14–17.

Reilly, Phillip R. 1991. *The Surgical Solution: A History of Involuntary Sterilization in the United States.* Baltimore, MD: Johns Hopkins University Press.

Paul A. Lombardo

STERNBERG, ROBERT

SEE *Multiple Intelligences Theory; Intelligence.*

STEROIDS

The generic term *steroids* refers to a group of substances sharing a common basic chemical structure, many of which function as hormones in the human body. The two best-known classes of human steroid hormones are *corticosteroids* and *anabolic-androgenic steroids.* Corticosteroids are hormones secreted by the adrenal gland, such as cortisol, which modulate a range of physiologic functions, such as inflammatory responses and blood pressure. Many synthetic corticosteroids have been developed, such as hydrocortisone, beclomethasone, and dexamethasone; these synthetic substances have effects similar to those of naturally occurring corticosteroids and are widely prescribed in medicine for a range of conditions. For example, hydrocortisone is often a component of skin creams used to treat poison ivy reactions or other inflammatory skin conditions; beclomethasone is a common component of inhalers used in the treatment of asthma; and high doses of corticosteroids are administered to recipients of organ transplants to prevent rejection of the foreign tissue. In low dosages, corticosteroids have few psychiatric effects, but higher doses may sometimes cause manic symptoms (e.g., euphoria, hyperactivity, increased self-confidence, and impaired judgment) or even psychotic symptoms (e.g., delusions or hallucinations) in some predisposed individuals. Corticosteroids have very little potential for abuse and are rarely ingested by illicit substance abusers.

Anabolic-androgenic steroids represent an entirely different class of hormones. The prototype hormone of this class is the male hormone testosterone, which is secreted primarily by the testes in males. Anabolic-androgenic steroids produce masculinizing (androgenic) effects—such as beard growth, male pattern baldness, and male sexual characteristics—together with muscle-building (anabolic) effects. These latter effects account for the greater muscle mass and lower body fat of men as compared to women. Many synthetic anabolic-androgenic

steroids have been developed over the last fifty years. Like testosterone, these synthetic substances produce both anabolic and androgenic effects; there are no purely anabolic or purely androgenic compounds. In medical practice, the principal use of testosterone is in the treatment of hypogonadal men—men who do not secrete sufficient testosterone in their own bodies, and who therefore require testosterone supplementation to maintain normal masculine characteristics. Aside from this application, anabolic-androgenic steroids have only very limited medical uses, such as in the treatment of certain forms of anemia.

Unlike corticosteroids, anabolic-androgenic steroids are widely abused by individuals wishing to gain muscle and lose body fat. The great majority of these illicit users are male; women generally do not abuse anabolic-androgenic steroids because of the drugs' undesirable masculinizing characteristics, such as beard growth, deepening of the voice, and shrinkage of the breasts. Men generally do not have to worry about these masculinizing effects and therefore may take doses far in excess of the amounts naturally present in the body. Specifically, an average man secretes between 50 and 75 milligrams of testosterone per week in his testes, whereas illicit anabolic-androgenic steroid abusers often ingest the equivalent of 500 to 1,000 milligrams of testosterone per week. When taken in these very high doses, anabolic-androgenic steroids can produce dramatic increases in muscle mass and strength, making it possible for users to far exceed the upper limits of muscularity attainable under natural conditions, without these drugs. Because of these properties, anabolic-androgenic steroids are widely used by athletes in sports requiring strength or muscle mass for feats such as hitting home runs in baseball or playing line positions in American football. In the United States there have been many recent well-publicized cases of prominent professional athletes who were found to be taking anabolic-androgenic steroids, and this issue became a subject of several congressional hearings in 2005. In addition, anabolic-androgenic steroids are increasingly abused by boys and young men who have no particular athletic aspirations, but who simply want to look more muscular. This pattern of abuse is particularly prevalent in North America, Australia, and some European countries—cultures where muscularity is sometimes portrayed as a measure of masculinity. By contrast, anabolic-androgenic steroids are rarely abused for purposes of body image in Asia, probably because Asian cultural traditions do not emphasize muscularity as an index of masculinity. However, anabolic-androgenic steroids are certainly used by some Asian athletes, especially at the elite level because these individuals are seeking a performance advantage, rather than a body-image effect.

In Europe and North America illicit anabolic-androgenic steroid use represents a significant and probably growing public health problem. Taken in massive doses, these hormones may pose long-term medical risks, especially because of their adverse effects on cholesterol levels, which may greatly increase the risk of heart attacks or strokes at an early age (sometimes in the forties or fifties). In addition, high doses of anabolic-androgenic steroids may have psychiatric effects such as irritability, aggressiveness, and even violent behavior (sometimes popularly called "roid rage") in some individuals. Thus, these drugs may pose a danger not only to users themselves, but even to some nonusers—particularly women—who may become victims of such violence. Men who use anabolic-androgenic steroids for long periods may also suffer depressive symptoms, sometimes accompanied by suicidal thoughts or even successful suicide, if they abruptly stop these drugs. Despite these risks, however, it appears unlikely that illicit anabolic-androgenic steroid use will decline in the near future because these drugs are readily available on the black market and offer a great temptation to men seeking muscle and strength gains.

SEE ALSO *Masculinity Studies; Sports; Sports Industry*

BIBLIOGRAPHY

Kanayama, Gen, Harrison G. Pope Jr., Geoffrey Cohane, and James I. Hudson. 2003. Risk Factors for Anabolic-Androgenic Steroid Use among Weightlifters: A Case-Control Study. *Drug Alcohol Dependence* 71 (1): 77–86.

Pope, Harrison G., Jr., and Kirk J. Brower. 2005. Anabolic-Androgenic Steroid Abuse. In *Comprehensive Textbook of Psychiatry*, vol. 3, eds. Benjamin J. Sadock and Virginia A. Sadock, 1318–1328. Philadelphia: Lippincott Williams and Wilkins.

Yesalis, Charles E., ed. 2000. *Anabolic Steroids in Sport and Exercise*. 2nd ed. Champaign, IL: Human Kinetics.

Harrison G. Pope Jr.
Gen Kanayama

STICKY PRICES

Price stickiness, the failure of prices to adjust fully in the face of evolving equilibrium conditions, reflects a lack of responsiveness to changes in supply and demand. This phenomenon has received considerable empirical and theoretical attention. To begin with, Barro and Grossman (1980), an early New Keynesian exposition on general disequilibrium, establishes the potential macroeconomic implications of such stickiness as divergence from equilibrium in the form of price rigidity in one market spilling over to others. For instance, they demonstrate how excess demand or supply in labor or commodity markets can stimulate more general macroeconomic shifts.

Approaching the question from a slightly different perspective, John Taylor (1980) adopts a rational expectations framework with staggered wage contracts (the sole source of wage rigidities in his model) to explain the persistent unemployment observed during postwar business cycles.

While Barro and Grossman (1980), Taylor (1980), and related work generally takes for granted price stickiness (typically by assuming some mechanism for it), to explore its larger macroeconomic implications, most theoretical work has been concerned with finding plausible microeconomic foundations for the emergence of price rigidities. These efforts have generated two principal veins of inquiry: one focused on price stickiness as a possible consequence of government intervention and the other on rigidities introduced by contractual commitments set by optimizing agents.

Several avenues of state intervention have received theoretical attention. First, governments frequently regulate the prices of various goods and services. To be meaningful (i.e., consequential), these restrictions must be binding in the sense that the resulting price in the market differs from what might otherwise have emerged under ordinary equilibrium circumstances. For instance, a legally mandated minimum wage (a kind of price floor) would influence prevailing wages only in sectors of the labor market where the equilibrium wage is below that mandated minimum. Such regulations undermine the full impact of many potential shifts in supply and demand, as changes in equilibrium price that would be evident in the absence of them are no longer so in their presence. Another important form of government interference with market prices comes in the form of attempts to fix (or peg) exchange rates. This has given rise to a literature (e.g., Krugman 1979, who builds on the work of Salant and Henderson 1978) focusing on the idea that such policies drive a wedge between the prevailing exchange rate (which is determined by the government's peg) and the "fundamental" exchange rate (that which would prevail in an unfettered foreign exchange market). If the two diverge sufficiently, the government's ability to defend the fixed rate may be overwhelmed by speculative pressure.

On balance, however, more theoretical attention has been directed toward the possibility that stickiness might arise as a result of contract setting (the consequences of which in terms of price rigidities are straightforward) and other purposeful behavior by optimizing agents. For instance, "menu costs" have received a great deal of attention (see, for instance, Mankiw [1985] for a thorough review of menu costs). Essentially, this approach is rooted in the idea that prices might not respond to shifts in supply and demand if the transaction costs (in a variety of senses) associated with adjusting prices are sufficiently high. At the most trivial level there is a cost associated with adjusting menus and price labels. For instance, in markets characterized by monopoly or oligopoly, shifts in demand might yield changes in the prevailing market price only if the transaction costs associated with adjusting price are less than the erosion of profits that would occur if firms simply maintained their prices. On a more subtle level, frequent adjustment in prices might undermine consumer confidence or trust (e.g., if they believe that the frequent price changes represent some effort at manipulation).

Another popular line of inquiry revolves around "efficiency wages" (see Akerlof and Yellen 1986), which are set above the labor market equilibrium with the intention of promoting higher worker productivity. Frequently cited justifications for paying efficiency wages include discouraging shirking (because the financial penalty associated with being fired is greater), avoiding adverse selection (since workers with higher capabilities may be more inclined to apply for jobs with a higher wage), and reducing turnover costs (as individuals may be reluctant to quit a job with a higher-than-market wage).

A large body of empirical work is concerned with price stickiness. The principal objectives of this literature are to determine whether price stickiness actually arises in practice and whether the various theoretical explanations of price stickiness are consistent with observed empirical patterns. Rotemberg (1982) is one among many reporting evidence of price stickiness. Using U.S. data, he finds that it arises because of the transaction costs that firms incur when they change prices.

Despite the extensive empirical and theoretical literature concerned with it, the concept of price stickiness has met with skepticism. Lucas and Sargent (1978) and other New Classical economists challenge the idea that prices (or wages) are slow to adjust, suggesting instead that rational agents formulate price expectations using all available information in such a fashion that prices and wages should quickly readjust to equilibrate the market.

SEE ALSO *Adverse Selection; Akerlof, George A.; Distortions; Economics, New Classical; Economics, New Keynesian; Expectations; Expectations, Rational; Lucas, Robert E., Jr.; Macroeconomics; Microeconomics; Sargent, Thomas; Transaction Cost; Wages*

BIBLIOGRAPHY

Akerlof, George A., and Janet Yellen, eds. 1986. *Efficiency Wage Models of the Labor Market.* Cambridge, U.K.: Cambridge University Press.

Barro, Robert J., and Herschel I. Grossman. 1971. A General Disequilibrium Model of Income and Employment. *American Economic Review* 61 (1): 82–93.

Froyen, Richard T. 1993. New Classical and New Keynesian Directions. In *Macroeconomics: Theories and Policies*, 341–362. New York: Macmillan.

Krugman, Paul. 1979. A Model of Balance of Payments Crises. *Journal of Money, Credit, and Banking* 11(3): 311–325.

Lucas, Robert E., Jr., and Thomas Sargent. 1978. After Keynesian Macroeconomics. In *After the Phillips Curve: Persistence of High Inflation and High Unemployment.* Boston. Federal Reserve Bank of Boston.

Mankiw, N. Gregory. 1985. Small Menu Costs and Large Business Cycles: A Macroeconomic Model. *Quarterly Journal of Economics* 100 (2): 529–538.

Rotemberg, Julio. 1982. Sticky Prices in the United States. *Journal of Political Economy* 90 (6): 1187–1211.

Salant, Stephen, and Dale Henderson. 1978. Market Anticipation of Government Policy and the Price of Gold. *Journal of Political Economy* 86: 627–648.

Taylor, John B. 1980. Aggregate Dynamics and Staggered Contracts. *The Journal of Political Economy* 88 (1): 1–23.

Mai Noguchi Hubbard

STIGLER, GEORGE JOSEPH
1911–1991

The years following World War II (1939–1945) saw a generation of remarkable economists who managed among themselves to remake the economics discipline and profession. Of this group, perhaps none possessed a better economic intuition or a keener economic mind than George Stigler. Though not as much of a public figure as his close colleague and longtime friend, Milton Friedman (1912–2006), Stigler did as much, if not more, to form what became known as the Chicago school of economics. It was at Chicago that Stigler would conduct research that not only gained him a Nobel Prize in 1982 but also ultimately changed the course of economic analysis. He had a rare talent for asking the right questions and putting forth provisional answers that inevitably provoked the profession and caused it to reconsider commonly held truths. At the same time, no economist was more a reflection of the ideological struggles of postwar America than Stigler.

George Joseph Stigler was born in Renton, Washington, on January 17, 1911, to immigrant parents. His choice to attend the graduate program at the University of Chicago in 1933 was perhaps his most fateful decision. It was there that he formed a lasting friendship with Friedman as well as becoming acquainted with Aaron Director (1901–2004), a young lecturer in the Department of Economics. These two would be among the very few who ever managed to significantly influence Stigler's thinking.

Despite his early and continuing contributions in the field of the history of economic thought, his lasting contributions were in industrial organization and government regulation, two fields he essentially helped form. It is perhaps easiest to understand Stigler's lifework by grasping its essential consistency. In some sense he was a self-appointed white knight dedicated to defending the innocent damsel of traditional price theory against all and any attacks. He developed a knack for demonstrating the efficiency of markets despite and against all appearances to the contrary.

His pioneering work in industrial organization reinforced the core idea that markets work. Two noted works make this amply clear. "The Economics of Information" (1961) analyzes how markets use available information in the most efficient way. His "Theory of Oligopoly" (1964) essentially concludes that the traditional theories of perfect competition and monopoly could amply handle any issue dealing with market structure. (He would later push this further and eliminate the need for monopoly theory as well, indicating that competitive markets were sufficient to encompass the needs of economic analysis.)

If the first part of his postwar research helped to define the field of industrial organization by emphasizing the efficiency of markets, the second half demonstrated the inability of governments to improve outcomes through regulation. "What Can Regulators Regulate? The Case of Electricity" (1962), jointly written with his long-time associate Claire Friedland, empirically indicated that government regulation of public utilities made no real difference in cost. What were then unexpected results helped to precipitate research that ultimately led to the deregulatory movement in public policy. In the same way, Stigler's analysis of the political market for government regulation, "The Theory of Economic Regulation" (1971), led to new research exploring how politicians operated and how and why government regulation became law. By ascribing narrow self-interest as the motivation for politicians, Stigler made a major contribution to the expanding field of public choice.

His final work on the role of government, exemplified by the posthumously published "Law or Economics," is perhaps his most controversial. Logically, political markets should resemble economic ones in that they are both under the sway of the test of time. If an existing arrangement is not the most efficient one, then this should create a situation in which economic agents could benefit through improving the status quo. Therefore whatever is, must by definition be efficient. Otherwise it would change. Such an approach follows perfectly from Stigler's lifetime drive to become increasingly more consistent in his analysis. At the end of his career, he surveyed an economic world where competitive markets ruled and provided the only useful analytical key.

Unlike Friedman, his close friend, Stigler deliberately eschewed a public presence. Yet without Stigler providing micro-based research, Friedman and his counterrevolution against the forces of Keynesianism and other non-mainstream approaches would have failed to achieve its singular success. Stigler remained active and at his beloved University of Chicago from 1958 until his untimely death on December 1, 1991. He was a scholar of great but cutting wit who had a talent for forming either fierce friendships or lasting animosities. Anything lacking intensity was never his style.

BIBLIOGRAPHY

PRIMARY WORKS

Stigler, George J. 1961. The Economics of Information. *Journal of Political Economy* 69 (3): 213–225.

Stigler, George J. 1964. A Theory of Oligopoly. *Journal of Political Economy* 72 (1): 44–61.

Stigler, George J. 1971. The Theory of Economic Regulation. *Bell Journal of Economics and Management Science* 2 (1): 3–21.

Stigler, George J. 1988. *Memoirs of an Unregulated Economist.* New York: Basic.

Stigler, George J., and Claire Friedland. 1962. What Can Regulators Regulate? The Case of Electricity. *Journal of Law and Economics* 5: 1–16.

Stigler, George J. 1992. Law or Economics. *Journal of Law and Economics* 35 (October): 455-468.

Craig Freedman

STIGLITZ, JOSEPH E.
1943–

Joseph E. Stiglitz, born in Gary, Indiana, received his PhD from the Massachusetts Institute of Technology in 1967. A winner of the John Bates Clark Award for young economists, he has taught at Yale, Princeton, Stanford, MIT, Oxford, and Columbia University. In 1986 he founded the *Journal of Economic Perspectives.* In 2001 he was awarded the Nobel Prize in economics.

Stiglitz's initial academic output, including his first two published articles in 1967, focused on how economic growth is affected by investment, risk, and income and wealth levels. In the early 1970s he and Michael Rothschild developed important insights into the nature of risk in financial and insurance markets. By the mid-1970s he was exploring problems of exhaustible natural resources, sharecropping, efficiency wages, and discrimination, even while looking more deeply into the nature of information and risk in insurance and financial markets.

Working simultaneously on theoretical problems and on applied issues led Stiglitz to his breakthrough insight regarding the importance for economics of *imperfect information*, a term Stiglitz first used in two 1976 papers. As discussed by Stiglitz and Andrew Weiss in their 1981 article, this notion, sometimes denoted *asymmetric information*, refers to situations in which some participants in a market know more than others and can use their informational advantage to affect the efficiency of market outcomes. This informational advantage is often held by "agents" who hope to contract with "principals" controlling scarce resources—for example, applicants seeking jobs from potential employers and prospective borrowers seeking credit from lenders. Principals can then often best achieve their goals by supplying fewer loans (or fewer jobs) than are demanded. As Stiglitz argued in his 1987 article, prices are not in these cases permitted to rise to levels at which demand equals supply; indeed, in these models the quality of the commodity traded (the productivity of workers or default level of borrowers) depends on price. Their profits are often largest at a "rationing equilibrium"—a price wherein the quantity that agents seek to buy (or sell) exceeds the quantity that the principal supplies (or buys). At rationing equilibria, market forces will generally not equalize supply and demand.

These insights generated what Stiglitz calls the *economics of information*, which explores the consequences of information asymmetries in credit, financial, product, and labor market. New information-based paradigms have been developed in development economics, trade theory, and other fields; and information-based models have been central to the emergence of the microfoundational "New Keynesian" (named for the preeminent economist John Maynard Keynes) approach to macroeconomics.

The economics of information suggests that selective government interventions and/or nonmarket institutions can enhance growth and reduce poverty. Stiglitz became increasingly involved in the policy implications of these ideas, triggered by an extended period in public service. He served on the Clinton administration's Council of Economic Advisers from 1993 to 1997, the last two years as chair. He then became chief economist and senior vice-president of the World Bank from 1997 to 2000. While at the World Bank, he publicly challenged the so-called Washington Consensus, that is, the then-prevailing practice at the World Bank and International Monetary Fund of using full-information, competitive-economy models to understand global and developing-country economic outcomes. In Stiglitz's view, more realistic models would show that global economic forces have often jeopardized

viable local governmental and institutional economic arrangements. Amid considerable controversy, as Ha-Joon Chang notes in his 2001 book, the World Bank made some changes in its modeling and policy approaches. Stiglitz tells his side of the story in his bestselling 2002 book, *Globalization and Its Discontents.*

Two articles summarizing Stiglitz's work in light of his Nobel prize are Chang's (2002) and J. Barkley Rosser's (2003); Stiglitz's own summary of his ideas and their implications for the change in the economics paradigm appears in his 2003 and 2004 articles.

SEE ALSO *Discrimination; Economics, New Keynesian; Economics, Nobel Prize in; Information, Asymmetric; Information, Economics of; Insurance; International Monetary Fund; Natural Resources, Nonrenewable; Risk; Sharecropping; Structural Adjustment; Uncertainty; Wages; Washington Consensus; World Bank, The*

BIBLIOGRAPHY

Chang, Ha-Joon, ed. 2001. *Joseph Stiglitz and the World Bank: The Rebel Within.* London: Anthem Press.

Chang, Ha-Joon. 2002. The Stiglitz Contribution. *Challenge* 45 (2): 77–96.

Rosser, J. Barkley, Jr. 2003. A Nobel Prize for Asymmetric Information: The Economic Contributions of George Akerlof, Michael Spence and Joseph Stiglitz. *Review of Political Economy* 15 (1): 3–21.

Stiglitz, Joseph E. 1987. The Causes and Consequences of the Dependence of Quality on Price. *Journal of Economic Literature* 25 (1): 1–48.

Stiglitz, Joseph E. 2002. *Globalization and Its Discontents.* New York: Norton.

Stiglitz, Joseph E. 2003. Information and the Change in the Paradigm in Economics: Part 1. *American Economist* 47 (2): 6–21.

Stiglitz, Joseph E. 2004. Information and the Change in the Paradigm in Economics: Part 2. *American Economist* 48 (1): 17–49.

Stiglitz, Joseph E., and Andrew Weiss. 1981. Credit Rationing in Markets with Imperfect Information. *American Economic Review* 71 (3): 393–410.

Gary A. Dymski

STIGMA

Although the term originally described a mark made through branding to designate a person of undesirable moral character, *stigma* was introduced into the psychological literature by Erving Goffman in 1963 to refer more broadly to any attribute or characteristic that makes its bearer tainted or devalued by others. Jennifer Crocker, Brenda Major, and Claude M. Steele (1998) refined the definition, noting that stigmatized characteristics convey "a social identity that is devalued in a particular social context" (p. 505). This definition highlights two important properties of stigma. The first is that the stigmatized characteristic is attributed meaning beyond the characteristic itself—it is often assumed to be broadly reflective of the person or his or her identity. The second property is that personal characteristics lead to stigma through their context-specific symbolic value, rather than through inherent properties of their own. Wrinkles and white hair, for example, may be revered as a sign of wisdom and experience when it comes to relationship advice, but may lead to undeserved assumptions of incompetence when it comes to navigating computers.

Goffman distinguished among three types of stigmas: tribal stigmas (e.g., racial, ethnic stigmas), blemishes of individual character (e.g., drug addict, criminal offender), and abominations of the body (e.g., weight, body scars). Despite enjoying wide recognition, Goffman's typological approach has given way to a more dimensional approach to stigma, one relying more on general principles that help understand the underlying differences and commonalities among stigmas. In 1984 Edward E. Jones and colleagues proposed six such dimensions: degree of concealability, degree of change over time, degree of disruptiveness, how aesthetic others find the attribute, how the stigma originates, and degree of peril the stigma poses.

IMPACT OF STIGMA ON ITS TARGETS

The psychological impact of these dimensions, particularly concealability and responsibility, has been a topic of intense study. Research on the dimension of responsibility in particular has shed light on the *internalization hypothesis*—the notion that people internalize society's negative ascriptions about their group, with negative consequences for their self-concept. Early studies included Kenneth B. and Mamie P. Clark's 1947 doll study, which found that young African American children preferred to play with white dolls rather than black dolls. Although the children's responses may have stemmed from their efforts to please the researchers or an unfamiliarity with black dolls, the findings were widely interpreted as evidence for the deleterious effects of stigma on the self-concept.

This interpretation remains popular despite empirical evidence to the contrary. Research consistently shows that the self-esteem of African Americans is, on average, higher than the self-esteem of U.S. whites. In 1989 Crocker and Major proposed that stigmatization may actually protect self-esteem, such that when people know they are the targets of stigma, negative outcomes can be attributed to the prejudice of others rather than to one's talents or efforts (thereby protecting self-esteem). Nevertheless, attributions to prejudice are protective only to the extent that people believe that they are not to blame or that the prejudice is undeserved. For example, overweight women, when rejected on the basis of their weight, nevertheless show a drop in self-esteem, presumably because they endorse the notion that weight is controllable and a matter of willpower. Thus perceptions of responsibility/controllability may influence the impact of stigma on the self. A thus-far unresolved puzzle is whether and how stigma affects the self-esteem of Asian Americans, Latinos, and Native Americans in the United States, who show lower self-esteem than U.S. whites.

Importantly, one does not need to believe or internalize relevant stereotypes in order for them to have adverse consequences. This is evident from research on *stereotype threat*, which shows that performance (e.g., on tests) is affected following the mere awareness that one might be viewed or judged according to a stereotype. For example, whereas women underperform relative to men in a math task when reminded about gender differences, performance differences disappear when the same task is framed as gender-neutral—that is, when the threat is removed. These data, also replicated among stigmatized minorities in the academic domain, are powerful demonstrations against nativist views of performance differences. Subsequent research shows that the cognitive and emotional disruption of having to contend with stereotypes plays a critical role in explaining group-based performance differences where stereotypes are involved.

Individuals may use a variety of strategies to cope with the threat of stigmatization. Behaviorally, people may avoid situations or contexts in which a particular identity is devalued. Psychologically, individuals may disengage, and ultimately disidentify, from the domain in which their group is stigmatized. Proactive strategies may include efforts to disprove the stereotype, as well as social activism. Thus, people are not merely passive recipients of social judgments and evaluations, but rather they psychologically construe and physically shape their social worlds to actively cope with the problem of stigma.

WHAT LEADS PEOPLE TO STIGMATIZE OTHERS?

Approaches to stigmatization from the perceiver's perspective have a longer history and fall into two broad approaches: motivational and cognitive. They both encompass stereotypes, prejudice, and discrimination, terms that roughly correspond respectively to beliefs, attitudes, and behavior. The cognitive approach conceptualizes stigmatization as a by-product of human information-processing biases. The basis for this approach is that people naturally use schemas, or mental categories, to reduce the potentially limitless number of stimuli in the world into more manageable groupings. Schemas provide not only an organizing principle to help individuals navigate the world, but also a way for people to "fill in the blanks" as needed: A person assumes a new chair will have the properties to support his or her weight, even though the person has never sat on it. According to the cognitive approach, similar processes apply when a person stigmatizes others: A person may assume, for example, that a new female acquaintance cannot read a map though the former has no experience or information on this woman's map skills. Despite being unfair or even harmful to the perceived (by eliciting stereotype threat, for example), these cognitive processes perpetuate stigma because they confer to the perceiver the benefit of having to use relatively few mental resources. Further, some mental associations may be relatively automatic, that is, outside of awareness, so that even people who are motivated to be egalitarian and sincerely believe they are not prejudiced can stigmatize others unwittingly.

By contrast, the central idea behind the motivational approach is that people stigmatize others to feel better about themselves. Research shows that individuals receiving negative feedback about themselves are more likely to discriminate against stigmatizable others, and that this restores self-esteem. Existentially oriented work proposes that people use symbolic means, including a deep investment in cultural or societal ideals, to transcend death. Thus, when reminded of their mortality, people are more likely to be less tolerant of others who subscribe to different worldviews (e.g., religion, political orientations). Newer views suggest that specific intergroup attitudes and behavior depend on the amount of intergroup competition as well as the group's perceived status. A high-status group that one competes for resources with, for example, tends to be viewed as competent and cold, eliciting envy. By contrast, a low-status group that does not represent a competitive threat tends to be seen as incompetent and warm, eliciting pity. Thus the field is moving toward identifying specific emotions and attitudes associated with different manifestations of stigma. Together with an increasing volume of research identifying processes related to being the target of stigma, the field is moving toward a more precise, balanced science.

SEE ALSO *Clark, Kenneth B.; Discrimination; Goffman, Erving; Prejudice; Racism; Stereotype Threat; Stereotypes*

BIBLIOGRAPHY

Clark, Kenneth B., and Mamie P. Clark. 1947. Racial Identification and Preference in Negro Children. In *Readings in Social Psychology*, eds. Theodore M. Newcomb and Eugene L. Hartley, 169–178. New York: Holt.

Crocker, Jennifer, and Brenda Major. 1989. Social Stigma and Self-Esteem: The Self-Protective Properties of Stigma. *Psychological Review* 96 (4): 608–630.

Crocker, Jennifer, Brenda Major, and Claude M. Steele. 1998. Social Stigma. In *The Handbook of Social Psychology*, 4th ed., eds. Daniel T. Gilbert and Susan T. Fiske, 504–553. Boston: McGraw-Hill.

Goffman, Erving. 1963. *Stigma: Notes on the Management of Spoiled Identity*. Englewood Cliffs, NJ: Prentice-Hall.

Jones, Edward E., Amerigo Farina, Albert H. Hastorf, et al. 1984. *Social Stigma: The Psychology of Marked Relationships*. New York: Freeman.

Kunda, Ziva. 1999. *Social Cognition: Making Sense of People*. Cambridge, MA: MIT Press.

Steele, Claude M. 1997. A Threat in the Air: How Stereotypes Shape Intellectual Identity and Performance. *American Psychologist* 52 (6): 613–629.

Twenge, Jean M., and Jennifer Crocker. 2002. Race and Self-Esteem: Meta-analyses Comparing Whites, Blacks, Hispanics, Asians, and American Indians and Comment on Gray-Little and Hafdahl (2000). *Psychological Bulletin* 128 (3): 371–408.

Rodolfo Mendoza-Denton

STIMULUS, UNCONDITIONED

SEE *Classical Conditioning.*

STOCHASTIC FRONTIER ANALYSIS

Stochastic frontier analysis (SFA) refers to a body of statistical analysis techniques used to estimate production or cost functions in economics, while explicitly accounting for the existence of firm inefficiency. The operative word in this definition is *inefficiency*, which implies producers may behave suboptimally in their decisions to maximize or minimize some objective function (e.g., profits, production, revenue, or costs). The intellectual underpinnings of inefficiency in economics can be traced to the writings of John Hicks (1938), who argued that monopolists possess motivations other than those of pure profit maximization; these motivations may lead to suboptimal production. (See Kumbhakar and Lovell [2000] for other rationalizations for inefficiency in equilibrium and a discussion of its intellectual underpinnings.)

The empirical departure point for SFA is the production frontier model, originally formulated by Aigner,

Lovell, and Schmidt (1977) and Meeusen and van den Broeck (1977). Let

$$y_i = x_i' \beta + v_i - u_i,$$

$$i = 1, ..., N$$

where firm i seeks to maximize production of observable output y_i, employing linear production function $x_i' \beta$. Observable production inputs (e.g., labor and capital) are in column vector x_i and marginal products are the corresponding column vector of unknown parameters, β. The v_i is a zero-mean, symmetric error. The salient feature of the model is non-negative error, u_i, representing unobserved inefficiency, so the specification is a leading case of an error-component model. The deterministic portion of the specification, $x_i' \beta$, represents the frontier of maximal output for a given set of inputs x_i. The symmetric error, v_i, causes the frontier to be stochastic. The one-sided inefficiency term, u_i, can only reduce output and represents departure from this frontier.

If the inputs and outputs are in natural logarithms, then equation 1 is a Cobb-Douglas production function. Other common functional forms, such as the translog, can be modeled with appropriate selection of the components of x_i. For example, a cost frontier can also be estimated if y_i is total cost and x_i are total output and input prices. Depending on the specification, u_i can be technical (production), revenue, profit, or cost inefficiency.

Estimation of the parameters in equation 1 is complicated by the fact that the mean of inefficiency is nonzero, but either a modified ordinary least squares or a maximum likelihood algorithm are typically employed. For this particular specification, identification is achieved from an independence assumption on x_i, v_i, and u_i and by specific distributional assumptions on the error components, such as v_i normal and u_i truncated normal, exponential, or gamma (Greene 1990). These assumptions may be difficult to justify. In particular, it has been argued that inefficiency is correlated with input mix and that specific distributions for the errors are too restrictive. Schmidt and Sickles (1984) relax these assumptions by considering panel data (firms observed over multiple time periods) and fixed-effect estimation, where inefficiency is nonstochastic and time-invariant.

Methods for quantifying inefficiency itself are due to Jondrow et al. (1982), whereas Horrace and Schmidt (1996, 2000) develop methods from inference on inefficiency. Generalizations of the basic model are plentiful. Semi- and nonparametric estimation techniques have been considered (Fan, Li, and Weersink 1996). Time-varying inefficiency was first considered by Cornwell, Schmidt, and Sickles (1990) and Kumbhakar (1990). Applications are unlimited but include estimation of frontiers for industries in the manufacturing and services sectors, for government entities, and for samples of countries. There is also a complementary Bayesian estimation literature (van den Broeck et al. 1994). Finally, there is a competing, purely deterministic methodology called *data envelopment analysis*, or DEA, developed by Charnes, Cooper, and Rhodes (1978).

BIBLIOGRAPHY

Aigner, Dennis, C. A. Knox Lovell, and Peter Schmidt. 1997. Formulation and Estimation of Stochastic Frontier Production Function Models. *Journal of Econometrics* 6: 21–37.

Charnes, Abraham, William W. Cooper, and Edwardo Rhodes. 1978. Measuring Efficiency of Decision-Making Units. *European Journal of Operational Research* 2: 429–444.

Cornwell, Christopher, Peter Schmidt, and Robin Sickles. 1990. Production Frontiers with Cross-Sectional and Time-Series Variation in Efficiency Levels. *Journal of Econometrics* 46: 185–200.

Fan, Yanqin, Qi Li, and Alfons Weersink. 1996. Semi-parametric Estimation of Stochastic Production Frontier Models. *Journal of Business and Economic Statistics* 14: 460–468.

Greene, William. 1990. A Gamma Distributed Stochastic Frontier Model. *Journal of Econometrics* 46: 141–164.

Hicks, John R. 1935. The Theory of Monopoly: A Survey. *Econometrica* 3: 1–20.

Horrace, William C., and Peter Schmidt. 1996. Confidence Statements for Efficiency Estimates from Stochastic Frontier Models. *Journal of Productivity Analysis* 7: 257–282.

Horrace, William C., and Peter Schmidt. 2000. Multiple Comparisons with the Best, with Economic Applications. *Journal of Applied Econometrics* 15: 1–26.

Jondrow, James, C. A. Knox Lovell, Ivan S. Materov, and Peter Schmidt. 1982. On the Estimation of Technical Efficiency in the Stochastic Production Function Model. *Journal of Econometrics* 19: 233–238.

Kumbhakar, Subal C. 1990. Production Frontiers, Panel Data, and Time-Varying Technical Inefficiency. *Journal of Econometrics* 46: 201–211.

Kumbhakar, Subal C., and C. A. Knox Lovell. 2002. *Stochastic Frontier Analysis*. Cambridge, U.K.: Cambridge University Press.

Meeusen, Wim, and Julien van den Broeck. 1977. Efficiency Estimation from Cobb-Douglas Production Functions with Composed Error. *International Economic Review* 18: 435–444.

Schmidt, Peter, and Robin Sickles. 1984. Production Frontiers and Panel Data. *Journal of Business and Economic Statistics* 2: 367–374.

Van den Broeck, Julien, Gary Koop, Jacek Osiewalski, and Mark F. J. Steel. 1994. Stochastic Frontier Models: A Bayesian Perspective. *Journal of Econometrics* 61: 273–303.

William C. Horrace

STOCHASTIC TREND

SEE *Unit Root and Cointegration Regression.*

STOCHASTIC VARIABLE

SEE *Variables, Random.*

STOCK EXCHANGES

Stock exchanges are organized markets where investors buy and sell shares of corporate stock and bonds. Some of the better-known stock exchanges are the New York Stock Exchange (established in 1792), the Tokyo Stock Exchange (1878), and the London Stock Exchange (1698). Stock exchanges are important insofar as they promote economic efficiency. They offer private investment opportunities to individuals and direct a large part of production in capitalist societies. If stock exchanges work well, this efficiency will promote efficiency in the general economy.

Corporations promote economic efficiency by producing goods that consumers want most urgently and keeping production costs to a minimum. Investors speculate over which corporations will be most efficient and profitable before they buy corporate stocks. After buying shares of stock, investors must monitor the activities of corporate officers to see that their company is operating efficiently to earn the highest potential profit. Corporate officers can mismanage their businesses in several ways. First, they can form faulty business plans. Management can invest in producing products that consumers do not want or invest in a production plan that is excessively costly. Second, corporate officials can mismanage the execution of essentially sound business plans. Third, corporate officials can commit deliberate fraud or deception for personal gain. In any case, stockholders in a mismanaged corporation will lose money.

Competition in stock exchanges determines who plans much of production. When corporate executives plan and carry out efficient production, profits rise and the price of the corporation's stock increases. When corporate executives form defective business strategies or mismanage the execution of sound strategies, stockholders have an interest in replacing them. If stockholders do not replace incompetent corporate executives, then the price of the stock will likely fall. That is, if stockholders do not deal with inefficient corporate executives, the stock exchange can penalize stockholders by cutting the value of their stock. This is how stock exchanges pressure corporate shareholders to terminate incompetent corporate managers. Of course, stockholders may not respond to such pressure from the stock market. However, if stockholders fail to remove incompetent corporate managers, the low price of that corporation's stock will make it an easy target for a takeover bid or leveraged buyout. In other words, a new group of investors could move to buy out some or all of the old stockholders and replace the existing management. Takeovers and leveraged buyouts often transfer ownership of a corporation from a large number of inattentive stockholders to a small number of large investors, who demand better performance from their executives. One of the more famous examples of such a move is when Henry Kravis bought out RJR Nabisco for $25 billion in 1989 and ejected CEO Ross Johnson.

Investors compete in stock exchanges to earn money for themselves. Yet competition between investors promotes the careers of efficient corporate executives and ruins the careers of incompetent ones. This is how stock exchanges determine who plans production. Of course, it always takes some time for pressure from the stock exchange to remove inept management from any particular corporation. However, stock exchanges do not tolerate incompetence indefinitely.

There are reasons to question the efficiency of stock exchanges. The key issue in stock exchange efficiency is information. A stock exchange is efficient if the price of each stock reflects all relevant and available information on that stock. Any stock that is undervalued, given available information, will be coveted—and its price will rise. Any stock that is overvalued will be sold off and its price will fall. In theory, such buying and selling of stocks will push stock prices to their true values.

Ideally, stock prices will reflect the actual performance of the corporate management. In actual stock exchanges, the price of corporate shares can overestimate or underestimate the performance of corporate management. Since investors have incomplete, and sometimes inaccurate, information regarding corporations, there will always be some inaccuracy in stock prices. Investors do, however, profit from being accurately informed, and this prompts them to eliminate serious deficiencies in their information. Stock prices move toward levels that reflect the true performance of corporate officers, but it always takes some time for pertinent information to be uncovered.

Efficient stock exchanges adjust to a continuous flow of new information, but the fact that this information is always incomplete means that stock prices are never perfectly accurate measures of executive performance. Trading with incomplete information is speculative, but unavoidable. The lack of perfect information means that stock exchanges can never achieve 100 percent efficiency, yet stock exchanges are *relatively* efficient if they adjust to new information as it becomes available. Some studies indicate that stock markets are efficient. Yet other studies of stock exchanges indicate inefficiency. Stocks of small firms tend to earn excess returns in January, and returns tend to be low on Mondays. Also, upswings and crashes in aggregated stock prices (bull and bear markets) indicate that stock prices deviate from their true values, based on market fundamentals. For example, on October 19, 1987, the Dow Jones Index declined 22 percent. Some argue that this and other crashes are evidence of irrationality in stock exchanges, while others claim that the October 19 crash was triggered by the proposal by the House Ways and Means Committee to limit the deductibility of interest on corporate debt.

While it is obvious that stock exchanges are not perfect, the case for regulating stock exchanges is less clear. Some insist that anomalies in stock exchanges indicate a need for government regulation. Given the importance of stock exchanges in modern economies, governmental regulation that improves stock exchange performance can improve overall economic conditions. On the other hand, government regulation is sometimes flawed and will sometimes impair market performance. Expert opinion is divided over the issue of stock exchange regulation, but there is a considerable amount of evidence indicating that current regulations are excessive.

We can illustrate the importance of stock exchanges by examining the economic performance of countries where they do not exist. Stock exchanges are particular to capitalism. Socialist economies prohibit private ownership of stocks, private dividends, and stock exchanges. In a socialist society, all citizens have an equal stake in all parts of industry and all are paid a *social dividend* as equal owners of industry. Since socialist societies lack stock and other financial markets, socialist production gets directed by central authorities. This is a critical difference between socialism and capitalism. Twentieth-century experience with Soviet-style central planning indicates that Wall Street does a better job of directing industry than do central authorities. While there is room for doubt concerning the need for regulation of stock exchanges, there is far less doubt about the need for some kind of market for trading equities. Stock exchanges are an indispensable part of modern economies because they provide an efficient means of planning production in an efficient manner. Without stock exchanges, capital investment would be far less efficient.

Some recent proposals for socialism would allow people to own shares of stock in particular businesses. However, every citizen would be limited to an equal amount of stocks that could be traded only for other stocks. Advocates of this proposal believe that this sort of limited stock exchange would improve managerial performance, while approximating equal ownership of the means of production. However, a "socialist stock exchange" would not be as effective at removing inept

managers, simply because it would eliminate hostile takeovers and leveraged buyouts at the hands of large professional investors.

Stock exchanges promote overall economic efficiency, despite the occasional appearance of significant flaws. Improvement in information technology has improved the efficiency of stock markets, and this trend will most likely continue. The general public often misunderstands the role that stock exchanges play in modern economies. People often see stock trading as a purely financial matter, but stock exchange activity is important for planning real production. Stock exchanges have and will continue to play a central role in modern economies because of their indispensable role in promoting economic efficiency.

SEE ALSO *Bubbles; Capitalism; Corporations; Efficient Market Hypothesis; Finance; Financial Instability Hypothesis; Financial Markets; Information, Asymmetric; Lender of Last Resort; Modigliani-Miller Theorem; Panics; Socialism; South Sea Bubble; Speculation; Stock Exchanges in Developing Countries; Stocks; Tobin's Q; Veblen, Thorstein*

BIBLIOGRAPHY

Borough, Bryan, and Helyar, John. 1991. *Barbarians at the Gate: The Fall of RJR Nabisco.* New York: Harper.

Fama, Eugene, and Kenneth French. 1988. Dividend Yields and Expected Stock Returns. *Journal of Finance* 22 (1): 3–25.

Grossman, Sanford. 1989. *The Informational Role of Prices.* Cambridge, MA: MIT Press.

Malkiel, Burton G.. 2003. *A Random Walk Down Wall Street: The Time-tested Strategy for Successful Investing.* New York: Norton

Mises, Ludwig von. [1922] 1981. *Socialism: An Economic and Sociological Analysis.* Trans. J. Kahane. Indianapolis, IN: Liberty Fund.

Mitchell, Mark, and Jeffrey Netter. 1989. Triggering the 1987 Stock Market Crash: Anti-takeover Provisions in the Proposed House Ways and Means Tax Bill. *Journal of Financial Economics* 24: 37–68.

Roemer, John. 1994. *A Future for Socialism.* Cambridge, MA: Harvard University Press.

D. W. MacKenzie

STOCK EXCHANGES IN DEVELOPING COUNTRIES

Stock exchanges play an important role in developing countries. One of the major challenges that developing countries face is capital formation. In economic terms, capital consists of equipment and machinery used to make consumer goods. The capital structure of developed nations consists of many different types of capital goods organized in factories and industries. Developed countries have capital goods arranged in stages of production. For example, iron ore is first mined, then it is refined, then it is made into steel. Steel is then shaped and assembled into final products, like cars and buildings. Workers use capital equipment at each stage to produce final goods for consumers.

Capital goods derive from financial investment. In order to develop a modern capital structure, someone must invest in buying capital goods. Stock exchanges provide a source of funding for capital investment. When a corporation forms or expands, it needs money to invest in capital (as well as labor and other supplies). The executives of the corporation can raise money for capital by selling new shares of stock in a stock exchange. Each share of stock entitles its owner to part of a corporation's future profits. Sales of new shares in stock exchanges serve two purposes. Stock exchanges enable individuals to invest their own money for private gain. Stock exchanges also enable businesses to raise money to buy capital equipment. This is important for many developing countries that lack advanced capital equipment. The alternative to development through private investment is government funding for investment projects. Government-funded investment projects can be financed either by a nation's own government or through direct foreign aid.

Stock trading also determines who runs corporations. If a corporation is run well, its stockholders will earn a high dividend or capital gains on the price of their stock. If corporate management runs a corporation badly, the price of the corporation's stock will fall. When a corporation's stock price falls dramatically, it is easy for new investors to buy up shares of the stock and replace the management. This is how stock exchanges get rid of incompetent corporate executives. Stock exchanges thus help developing countries to avoid waste from incompetent corporate management.

Stock exchanges played an important role in the development of industrial western Europe and North America. The London Stock Exchange emerged in the eighteenth century. Initially, brokers traded stocks in coffeehouses and private clubs. The stock market in Amsterdam emerged in the seventeenth century. The financial system of Belgium dates to at least the fourteenth century, but the Brussels Stock Exchange opened in 1801. Initially, these stock exchanges were informal and simple. With the passage of time, these early stock exchanges developed into sophisticated institutions with formal rules. Eventually, stock exchanges in major cities began to direct capital investment throughout the West and in

parts of Asia. For example, Belgium developed rapidly during the nineteenth century. Statistical studies indicate that the economic development of Belgium was driven by the development of Belgian financial markets, including the Brussels Stock Exchange. Financial development in Belgium began with the country's independence in 1830, and was accelerated by the liberalization of the Belgian stock market in 1867. This pattern was paralleled in many nations. Statistical studies show that well-developed stock exchanges have enhanced long-run economic growth, increased capital investment, and raised productivity throughout the industrialized world.

Since the 1970s many developing nations have begun to form more advanced financial markets. One study (Agarwal 2001) of nine African nations indicates that stock exchange development has led to increased economic growth. Another study (Mohtadi and Agarwal 2007) of twenty-one developing nations shows that the development of stock exchanges increases private investment and economic growth. This study indicates that stock exchanges contribute to economic development by stabilizing productivity and liquidity shocks.

As stock exchanges develop, the issue of financial regulation arises. Some evidence supports the case for liberalization of stock exchanges. Peter Henry (2003) finds that deregulating stock exchanges reduces capital costs and increases investment and per worker productivity. Liberalized stock exchanges can also facilitate the adoption of new technologies in developing nations. Some distortions in the international financial system led investors to hold too much debt and too little equity (Henry 2006). The liberalization of stock exchanges has caused a shift from debt to equity holding during the 1990s. This shift from debt to equity caused a short run increase in economic growth. Henry (2000) also finds that liberalizing stock exchanges can reduce the cost of equity capital by allowing risk-sharing between foreign and domestic investors.

Some scholars point to examples of stock market crashes as evidence of need for regulation. The 1929 crash on Wall Street is well known, but there are more recent examples of stock exchange panics to examine. The Kuwaiti stock market crash of 1982 is often cited as an example of how stock markets need regulation. The Kuwaiti crash left investors with over $90 billion of debt and put serious strain on the Kuwaiti banking system. The Kuwaiti example indicates that stock exchanges can malfunction badly. It should be noted that the Kuwaiti crash represents only a single incident of stock exchange failure. While the Kuwaiti crash supports the case for stock exchange regulation, this incident does not prove the case for regulation.

Investment in stock exchanges typically leads to financial inequality as some investors earn fortunes, but stock exchange activity also promotes economic development and rising living standards for all. The inequality that arises from stock exchange activity may be an unavoidable part of economic progress. Stock exchanges appear to contribute to economic development in developing nations significantly. Regulation of emerging stock exchanges might yield some benefits, but there is a strong case for opening stock exchanges up to free competition and foreign investment.

SEE ALSO *Bubbles; Developing Countries; Development Economics; Equity Markets; Finance; Investment; Speculation; Stock Exchanges*

BIBLIOGRAPHY

Agarwal, Sumit. 2001. Stock Market Development and Economic Growth: Preliminary Evidence from African Countries. *Journal of Sustainable Development in Africa* 3 (1): 48–56.

Atje, Raymond, and Boyan Jovanovic. 1993. Stock Markets and Development. *European Economic Review* 37: 632–640.

Ayittee, George B. N. 1992. *Africa Betrayed.* New York: St. Martin's Press.

Barro, Robert J. 1991. Economic Growth in a Cross Section of Countries. *Quarterly Journal of Economics* 106 (2): 407–443.

Bauer, P. T. 1981. *Equality, the Third World, and Economic Delusion.* Cambridge, MA: Harvard University Press.

Bauer, P. T. 1984. *Reality and Rhetoric: Studies in the Economics of Development.* Cambridge, MA: Harvard University Press.

Caporale, Guglielmo Maria, Peter G. A. Howells, and Alaa M. Soliman. 2005. Stock Market Development and Economic Growth, the Causal Linkage. *Journal of Economic Development* 29 (1): 33–50.

Demirguch-Kunt, Asli, and Ross Levine. 1996. Stock Market Development and Financial Intermediaries: Stylized Facts. *World Bank Economic Review* 10: 291–321.

El-Erian, Mohamed A., and Manmohan Kumar. 1995. Emerging Equity Markets in Middle Eastern Countries. Working Paper 94/103. *IMF Staff Papers* 42: 313–343.

Greenwood, Jeremy, and Bruce Smith. 1997. Financial Markets in Development, and the Development of Financial Markets. *Journal of Economic Dynamics and Control* 21 (1): 145–181.

Henry, Peter. 2000. Stock Market Liberalization, Economic Reform, and Emerging Market Equity Prices. *Journal of Finance* 55 (2): 529–564.

Henry, Peter. 2003. Capital Account Liberalization, the Cost of Capital, and Economic Growth. *American Economic Review* 93 (2): 91–96.

Henry, Peter. 2006. Capital Account Liberalization: Theory, Evidence and Speculation. Center on Democracy, Development, and the Rule of Law Working Paper. http://iis-db.stanford.edu/pubs/21498/No_72_Henry-Liberalization.pdf.

Levine, Ross. 1991. Stock Markets, Growth, and Tax Policy. *Journal of Finance* 46 (4): 1445–1465.

Levine, Ross, and Sara Zervos. 1998. Stock Markets, Banks, and Economic Growth. *American Economic Review* 88: 537–558.

Mohtadi, Hamid, and Sumit Agarwal. 2007. Stock Market Development and Economic Growth: Evidence from Developing Countries. Working paper. http://www.uwm.edu/~mohtadi/PA1-4-01.pdf.

Nieweburgh, Stijn van, Frans Buelens, and Ludo Cuyvers. 2006. Stock Market Development and Economic Growth in Belgium. *Explorations in Economic History* 43 (1): 13–38.

Strigham, Edward. 2002. The Emergence of the London Stock Exchange as a Self-Policing Club. *Journal of Private Enterprise* 17 (2): 1–19.

Strigham, Edward. 2003. The Extralegal Development of Securities Trading in Seventeenth-century Amsterdam. *Quarterly Review of Economics and Finance* 43 (2): 321–344.

D. W. MacKenzie

STOCK OPTIONS

A stock option, also known as a derivative, is a contractual right, but not an obligation, to purchase (call) or sell (put) shares of a company's stock at a future date and at a predetermined, or strike, price. A stock option fulfills two purposes simultaneously: It serves as a hedging instrument designed to reduce the financial risk of an investor holding a particular financial asset, and it serves as a speculative financial instrument by requiring a second investor to assume more risk in return for a potentially higher financial reward.

Employee stock options are call options and are not publicly traded. Employee stock options must be held by the employee for a specified period of time, termed the vesting period, before the option can be exercised. Employee stock options in the United States consist of two types: incentive stock options and nonqualified stock options. The difference between the two is that the profits from incentive stock options are taxed as a capital gain while those from nonqualified stock options are taxed as ordinary income.

Stock options have long been a component of corporate executive compensation packages. They have become increasingly popular over the past few decades as U.S. companies shifted away from accounted earnings to stock price as the primary measure of corporate performance. Granting stock options to corporate executives, it is argued, helps align their interests with those of shareholders by linking executive compensation to company stock price performance. In the 1990s employee stock options became more widely used in typical employee compensation packages for two reasons. First, unlike salaries, employee stock options did not cost companies anything. Second, they were used to attract and retain motivated and entrepreneurial employees, especially in booming high-tech and cash-strapped start-up companies.

But employee stock options have been criticized for their potential to become worthless, or "underwater," should the company stock price deteriorate. This was often the case after the dot-com crash in the late 1990s, which left many employees holding worthless stock options. Another criticism claims that the rules for reporting and accounting employee stock options are insufficient. This criticism arose after evidence surfaced that major corporations routinely backdated executive stock options in order to ensure higher financial rewards for those executives. Furthermore, there are criticisms of the Black-Scholes pricing model that is used in valuing stock options, and questions pertaining to whether employee stock options should be valued at the time they are granted or when they are exercised. These criticisms arose after the 2002 Sarbanes-Oxley Act strengthened compensation reporting and accounting measures and required companies to expense employee stock options. The act was a response to the wave of corporate scandals that surfaced in the United States between 1999 and 2001, in which corporate executives at such notable companies as Enron and WorldCom cashed in their stock options after artificially inflating their company's stock price. Finally, employee stock options have been criticized as contributing to the increasing polarization of wealth, since the median total realized compensation (including gains from stock options) of the top *Fortune* 500 chief executive officers since the 1970s has nearly quadrupled while the real wages of workers has declined.

SEE ALSO *Bull and Bear Markets; Equity Markets; Expectations; Financial Markets; Hedging; Risk; Stock Exchanges; Stocks; Stocks, Restricted and Unrestricted; Uncertainty*

BIBLIOGRAPHY

Hall, Brian J., and Kevin J. Murphy. 2003. The Trouble with Stock Options. *Journal of Economic Perspectives* 17 (3): 49–70.

Jayson J. Funke

STOCKHOLM SCHOOL

The Stockholm School was a macroeconomic school that was parallel to but independent of the employment theory developed by John Maynard Keynes during the 1930s. It consisted of a number of Swedish economists who were all influenced by Knut Wicksell's theory of the cumulative process of 1898. In Wicksell's theory, increases in the price level are followed period by period, and inflation is assumed to be driven by the gap between the natural rate (profitability of investments) and the loan rate of interest. If the natural rate exceeds the loan rate of interest, investments and consequently demand for goods and labor will increase and so will the price level. This is in contrast to the quantity theory of money, which says that increases in the price level are caused by increases in the supply of money. Gunnar Myrdal's analysis of expectations in his dissertation of 1927 forms a second influence on the Swedish economists.

The Stockholm School developed in three stages. In the first stage Myrdal and Erik Lindahl in the early 1930s discussed Wicksell's criteria of monetary equilibrium (macroeconomic equilibrium), namely, that the natural rate of interest should equal the loan rate of interest, that saving should equal investments, and that the price level should be constant. One outcome of the discussion was that the second condition for monetary equilibrium should be formulated as equality between planned saving and planned investments—that is, ex ante, not between realized saving and investments, that is, ex post.

The second stage is connected with the unemployment commission of the Swedish government and the fact that Sweden during the 1930s was hit by the worldwide Great Depression. Myrdal (1934) wrote a report in which he discussed how fiscal policy (variations of government expenditure and of taxes) could be used to even out the business cycle. Bertil Ohlin (1934) discussed how monetary policy and custom duties could be used for the same purpose. The analyses of Myrdal and Ohlin are rather similar to that of Keynes in *The General Theory of Employment, Interest and Money* of 1936. For example, Ohlin's contribution discusses multiplier effects of public expenditure (i.e., increased public expenditure may increase gross national product more than the original increase of expenditure).

The Swedish government took the advice of members of the Stockholm School, which some believe is the main reason Sweden was comparatively mildly affected by the Great Depression. However, the devaluation by 30 percent of the Swedish krona in 1931 probably had a much greater impact.

The third stage took place in the end of the 1930s when the analysis of the Stockholm School was refined. One example is Erik Lundberg's dissertation from 1937; in anticipation of Paul Samuelson's mathematical analysis of 1939, Lundberg demonstrated numerically that a combination of the acceleration principle (a theory that says that investments depend on the change of consumption) and the multiplier theory can be used to explain the business cycle.

The creative phase of the Stockholm School lasted to the end of the 1930s. After that only a few contributions were published. Like the Austrian business cycle theory of Mises and Hayek, the Stockholm School was surpassed by Keynesian economics. Whereas the Keynesian equilibrium theory was easy to use and to generalize, this was not the case for the Swedish analysis.

SEE ALSO *American Dilemma; Austrian Economics; Cumulative Causation; Economics, Keynesian; Equilibrium in Economics; Expectations; Great Depression; Hayek, Friedrich August von; Keynes, John Maynard; Lundberg, Erik; Macroeconomics; Mises, Ludwig Edler von; Multiplier, The; Myrdal, Gunnar; Quantity Theory of Money; Samuelson, Paul A.; Wicksell Effects*

BIBLIOGRAPHY

Jonung, Lars, ed. 1991. *The Stockholm School of Economics Revisited.* Cambridge, U.K: Cambridge University Press.

Lundberg, Erik. 1937. *Studies in the Theory of Economic Expansion.* London: P. S. King.

Myrdal, Gunnar. 1927. *Prisbildningsproblemet och föränderligheten* [The Pricing Problem and Change]. Uppsala and Stockholm: Almqvist & Wicksells Förlag.

Myrdal, Gunnar. 1934. *Finanspolitikens ekonomiska verkningar* [Economic Effects of Fiscal Policy]. SOU 1934:1. Stockholm: P. A. Norstedt & Söner.

Ohlin, Bertil. 1934. *Penningpolitik, offentliga arbeten, subventioner och tullar som medel mot arbetslöshet* [Monetary Policy, Public Works, Subsidies and Custom Duties as Means Against Unemployment]. SOU 1934:12. Stockholm: P. A. Norstedt & Söner.

Siven, Claes-Henric. 2006. Monetary Equilibrium. *History of Political Economy* 38 (4): 665–709.

Claes-Henric Siven

STOCKHOLM SYNDROME

SEE *Traumatic Bonding.*

STOCKS

Stocks are a type of financial instrument that represent ownership in a business organization. Ideally, the price of any stock is equal to the present value of expected future cash payments to the stockholder. Stocks perform specific and important functions in financial markets and in the economy generally. From the perspective of private investors stocks are a form of financial investment. Ownership of stock in a business entitles a person to part of the profits generated by the operation of that business. When a corporation realizes profits, it pays a dividend to its stockholders, though it will often retain some profits to finance additional business operations.

Stocks differ from other financial instruments mainly in terms of risk. For example, bond owners are paid interest according to their bond's annual yield. Companies that issue bonds enter into a contract with bondholders to pay a specific amount of money over a specific time period. Once a bond matures, the company that issued the bond returns the money that it borrowed to the bondholders. Stockholders, in contrast, are the owners of that company. Since corporations are legally obligated to pay bondholders interest, bondholders risk default if the issuing company goes bankrupt. Since the dividend paid by the company varies with the performance of that company, stockholders can realize a poor rate of return without the company actually going bankrupt.

Economists view stocks as a particular type of institution that performs specific social functions. Stocks, and other financial instruments, play an important role in the functioning of capitalist societies. Stocks, bonds, and other types of loans are alternative means of financing the operations of a business. Stocks represent a means of raising financial capital for business investment. Anytime a business sells new shares of stock, the investors who buy them provide funding for new entrepreneurial business projects. Investors who buy new shares of stock in a company are speculating about the future profits of that company. If the projects that a company undertakes realize or exceed expected profits, its stockholders (unlike bondholders) will earn high dividends and capital gains. So the capitalists who buy shares of stock are speculators who attempt to predict future trends in the economy. Efficient businesses produce products that consumers want most urgently at a low cost. Efficient businesses will earn the most profits for their stockholders.

Capitalists who speculate accurately concerning different businesses can earn new fortunes for themselves by providing finance to efficient businesses. Capitalists who err in predicting future economic trends can lose previously accumulated fortunes. In this way stock ownership can work as a regulating mechanism to direct money into efficient businesses that need additional funding to expand and away from inefficient businesses whose operations should be curtailed.

Most stock trading involves previously owned shares of stock rather than newly issued shares. Trading of existing shares of stock is also important to the functioning of businesses. The price of existing shares of stock tells a company how much money it can raise by issuing new shares. Of course, businesses need not use this method of finance, and many businesses buy up existing shares of stock to increase the value of the remaining shares. Yet stock ownership still affects the business's performance.

It is important to note that stock ownership implies a separation of ownership and control. Stockholders own a corporation, but the chief executive officer (CEO) or president actually manages the daily operations and plans the future operations of any corporation. Separation of ownership and control in a corporation, though, poses a potential problem. The CEO and other top executives may abuse their authority at the expense of stockholders. Both bondholders and stockholders have an interest in the efficient operation of the corporation in which they have invested. Under specific circumstances, bonds and stocks are virtually identical. If investors have perfect information on the activities of corporate officers, if taxes affect bonds and stocks equally, and if the costs of transacting for stocks and bonds are equal, then stocks and bonds will be perfect substitutes as far as investors are concerned. The logic behind this proposition is simple. If people have perfect information about the activities of corporate officers, then they will know exactly what the future stream of dividends will be. If a stock will pay more than a bond with certainty, then investors will buy more of that stock. When investors own more shares of a stock, its price will rise, and its dividend will fall. The rate of return of a stock will therefore be equal to the interest rate on bonds—if investors have perfect information on the operation of that corporation by its top executive officers. Investors might prefer stocks or bonds for tax reasons or because of differences in transactions costs. But given our three assumptions, bonds and stocks will appear identical to investors.

The idea that investors have perfect information is completely unrealistic, but it does tell us much about the real world. Stocks are different from bonds because of the differences in information needed to profit from these two types of investments. All bondholders need to know is that corporate officers are doing their jobs well enough so that the corporation can avoid bankruptcy and pay interest on its bonds. With stockholders things are different. Every penny that the corporate officers waste or take for themselves is money lost to the stockholders. Consequently, stockholders need to be much better informed about the activities of corporate officers than do bondholders. Bonds are a good investment for people who want a decent rate of return without much bother. Stocks can deliver a higher rate of return but require more attention from investors. Consequently, owners of stocks act as corporate watchdogs to make sure that corporations run efficiently. Of course, some stockholders fail to pay proper attention to their corporate officers. But many stockholders do pressure corporate executives to run their businesses more efficiently, and this pressure contributes to the overall efficiency of the economy.

SEE ALSO *Bubbles; Capitalism; Corporate Social Responsibility; Corporations; Efficient Market Hypothesis; Financial Instability Hypothesis; Financial Markets; Information, Asymmetric; Lender of Last Resort; Modigliani-Miller Theorem; Panics; Risk; Socialism; Speculation; Stock Exchanges; Stock Exchanges in Developing Countries; Tobin's Q; Veblen, Thorstein*

BIBLIOGRAPHY

Jensen, Michael, and William Meckling. 1976. Theory of the Firm: Managerial Behavior, Agency Costs and Ownership Structure. *Journal of Financial Economics* 11: 5–50.

Miller, Merton. 1977. Debt and Taxes. *Journal of Finance* 32: 261–275.

Modigliani, Franco, and Merton Miller. 1958. The Cost of Capital, Corporation Finance and the Theory of Investment *American Economic Review* 48 (3): 261–297.

D. W. MacKenzie

STOCKS, RESTRICTED AND UNRESTRICTED

Restricted and unrestricted stocks are important components of corporate executive compensation packages. Restricted stocks have particular conditions that must be fulfilled before they can be transferred or sold, whereas unrestricted stocks have no such conditions.

There are two types of restricted stocks. The first type is often referred to as unregistered stocks, which are not legally registered with the Securities and Exchange Commission (SEC) for the purpose of public transactions. The Federal Securities Act of 1933 requires that all stocks be registered with the SEC prior to any public transaction unless the transaction or the stocks are exempt. In 1972 the SEC implemented Rule 144, which identified restricted stocks as any privately issued company stocks, or company stocks publicly purchased by company "insiders" (powerful employees like company executives). According to the SEC, restricted stocks must be held for a certain period of time before they can be publicly sold. However, restricted stocks may be sold privately at any time, though such transactions are strictly regulated.

Restricted stocks are commonly used in executive compensation packages to ensure a balance of long- and short-term incentive rewards. Whereas unrestricted stocks are often considered to be short-term incentive rewards because they can be immediately sold, restricted stocks are usually considered to be long-term incentives given the length of their vesting periods (the length of time the stocks must be legally held before they can be publicly sold). However, there is disagreement about the actual effectiveness of restricted stocks as long-term incentives. Restricted stocks are also often granted to insiders after corporate mergers and acquisitions to prevent adverse effects on company performance. Venture capitalists are also often given restricted stocks in pre-initial public offerings to help ensure long-term commitment.

The second type of restricted stock is also commonly used in company compensation plans as incentives or rewards for employee performance or service. These stocks are similar to unrestricted stocks in the sense that they are not legally restricted. However, they are restricted in the sense that they cannot be transferred or sold by employees until they have fulfilled certain conditions set by the company. These conditions are often related to specific employee performance goals or are satisfied after an employee remains with a company for a set period of time. For example, a company may grant one thousand shares of restricted stock to an employee who can sell those shares when a certain performance goal is fulfilled. Alternatively, it may grant one thousand shares of restricted stock to an employee who can sell those shares two years after the date the shares were issued.

Although both restricted and unrestricted stocks have long played a role in executive compensation packages, the popularity of restricted stocks increased dramatically in the United States after the passing of the 2002 Sarbanes-Oxley Act, which required companies to expense stock options granted to all employees through compensation plans. The act followed a wave of corporate scandals between 1999 and 2001 in which prominent company executives at companies like Enron, WorldCom, Tyco, and Adelphia artificially inflated their company's stock prices to cash in their stock options for their own financial gain.

SEE ALSO *Stocks*

BIBLIOGRAPHY

Besner, Gregory. 2004. Restricted Stock: Regulations, Trends and Technologies. *Compensation and Benefits Review* 36 (1): 52–59.

Ellig, Bruce R. 2006. The Evolution of Executive Pay in the United States. *Compensation and Benefits Review* 38 (2): 55–61.

Longnecker, Brent M., and Christopher S. Crawford. 2006. *The Power of Restricted Stock*. Updated ed. Scottsdale, AZ: WorldatWork.

Jayson J. Funke

STOCKS AND FLOWS

In economics and business, the concept of stocks and flows is crucial to understanding the development of economic variables. It is most commonly used in macroeconomics, labor economics, and accounting. More generally, the concept of stocks and flows is central in system dynamics theory, which describes the development of complex systems.

Most economic variables are either stocks or flows. Stock variables describe the state of the economy at a given point in time, whereas flow variables describe the changes in the economy over a period of time. If one looks at an extremely small period of time, flows will be close to zero, whereas stocks could have any value. Stocks are accumulated or depleted over time by flows, whereas flows represent the rate of movement of items in and out of stocks. Frequently, stocks are characterized by nouns and flows, which represent processes, by verbs.

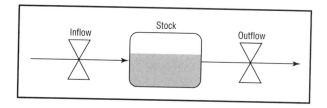

Flows can be divided into inflows—flows that add to stocks—and outflows—flows that deplete the stocks. The difference between inflows and outflows is called net inflows. The figure illustrates the relationship between stocks and flows. If the inflow is greater than the outflow or net inflow is positive, the stock will be rising; if the inflow is less than the outflow, net inflow is negative, and the stock will be falling.

The simplest illustration of stocks and flows is a bathtub. The level of water in the bathtub is a stock, the water coming from the faucet is an inflow, and the draining of the water through the drain is an outflow. If we plug the drain and turn on the faucet, the net inflow will be positive, and the stock of water in the bathtub will be rising. If, instead, we close the faucet and open the drain, the net inflow of water will be negative, and the stock of water in the bathtub will fall.

STOCKS AND FLOWS IN MACROECONOMICS

Economic development cannot be well described or understood without knowledge of which variables represent stock and which variables represent flows. Most macroeconomic variables reported by statistical agencies are flow variables. Gross Domestic Product (GDP) represents the value of final goods produced by the economy during a given year. GDP is a flow that is measured in dollars, euros, or other currency units per year. GDP is an inflow to the stock of inventory in the economy. The stock of inventory is not large as most of GDP is either consumed by individuals or by the government, invested in production by firms, or exported. Consumption, government spending, and exports are outflows. The remaining GDP is accumulated as additional inventory.

An important stock that plays a big role in macroeconomics is a stock of government debt. It is accumulated by the flows of government budget deficits (the difference between budget spending and budget revenues); it is depleted by the repayment of the debt, through budget surplus (negative budget deficit). If the government runs a budget deficit for many years in a row, it will accumulate a large stock of government debt. Because the interest needs to be paid on the stock of debt and the interest payments are part of budget spending, it becomes harder to stop accumulating the debt when the stock is already large. This provides an example of how the stocks themselves can affect the flows: the larger the stock of debt, the larger the interest spending that is a flow contributing to the stock of debt.

Another important example of stocks and flows in macroeconomics is unemployment. At any given point in time a number of people in the economy are unemployed. The total number of unemployed is a stock. In each period a number of people lose their jobs and join the ranks of unemployed, representing an inflow to unemployment, and a number of unemployed people find jobs and leave unemployment, representing an outflow from the unemployment. If the rate at which workers lose their jobs (job separation rate) is higher than the rate at which unemployed find jobs (job finding rate), unemployment will increase because the net inflow to unemployment will be positive. Thus policies designed to lower the unemployment rate must take into account the effects of certain measures on both job finding rate and job separation rate. For example, if a policy makes it harder for firms to fire workers, it would lower the job separation rate. However, such a policy would also make firms more reluctant to hire new workers, lowering the job finding rate. The overall effect of such a policy on unemployment is uncertain.

STOCKS AND FLOWS IN MICROECONOMICS

Each individual's wealth is a stock. It is accumulated by the inflow of income and depleted by the outflow of spending. The best way to picture this is by thinking about a bank account. The balances in the bank account represent the stock of cash available to the individual; the direct deposit of the salary is an inflow to the account, and check and cash withdrawals are the outflow. If the net

inflow is positive, the balances in the bank account will rise. Of course, individuals can hold other assets in addition to bank accounts. Frequently, the largest portion of an individual's wealth is the value of his or her house. Economists believe that the stock of wealth affects the flow of consumer spending—the higher the wealth, the larger portion of income the consumers are willing to spend, which lowers the net inflow of income. This is a mechanism through which economists at the beginning of the 2000s linked the U.S. housing boom to the nation's low savings rate.

Firms also have a stock of wealth, usually referred to as the firm's net worth, or capital stock, which is the difference between a firm's assets and liabilities. If a firm is publicly traded, individuals and financial institutions can buy shares of that firm's stock, which would give the buyer an ownership share of the stock of the firm's wealth. Firms accumulate their capital through the inflow of investment. The stock of capital depletes through the outflow of depreciation and capital that is used up in production.

Galina Hale

STOLEN GENERATIONS (AUSTRALIA)

Stolen Generations, a term coined by Australian historian Peter Read in 1981, refers to those Australian Aboriginal and Torres Strait Islander people who were taken from their indigenous families and communities as children. In its widest interpretation, Stolen Generations might encompass all those indigenous children taken away from their communities since the earliest days of British settlement to the present day, but it is more generally understood to refer to the estimated 100,000 people taken forcibly under extraordinary government legislation targeting children of Aboriginal descent.

Such legislation was first enacted in the 1880s by the Victorian colonial parliament, as the key to its aim of concentrating "full-blood" Aboriginal people, presumed to be on the verge of extinction, on reserves, while forcing off those of mixed descent. Similar legislation was enacted around Australia by the six state governments after federation in 1901, enabling removal and indenturing of Aboriginal and mixed-descent children at the discretion of the authorities, without requiring parental consent or a court ruling. The national Commonwealth government, taking over administration of the Northern Territory in 1911, demonstrated its own commitment to indigenous child removal by introducing such legislation itself. These early policies were couched as "protection." Introduced in response to Aboriginal land reservation in the southeastern states, child removal under this legislation peaked in the 1920s in accompaniment with a second dispossession as these reserved lands were revoked. Focusing disproportionately on girls, who were placed in private domestic service, the practice revealed an intent to "absorb" the Aboriginal population by removing their children to be brought up as "white."

Authorities used the threat of child removal to ensure submission on the now government-controlled reserves, though the child of *any* person of Aboriginal descent could be taken. Where white settlement was sparser, child removal accompanied the expansion and consolidation of white control, alongside violent destruction of Aboriginal communities, and tended to target children of non-Aboriginal fathers to prevent the growth of a mixed-descent Aboriginal population. Institutions were established around Australia to hold removed children. Aboriginal organizations in the southeast protested, and attempted to raise wider awareness and support in the interwar period, with feminist and humanitarian organizations playing a role in campaigns against child removal.

An important conference of state and federal Aboriginal authorities held in 1937 partly in response to such criticisms prefigured a postwar shift to "assimilation." The influx of non-British migrants from former enemy lands and a shift to cultural theories of race created a new emphasis on the social assimilation of Aboriginal people to an "Australian way of life," even as Australia ratified an international treaty that defined forcible removal of children as a crime in international law in 1949. Boys were now taken in equal proportions to girls, and adoption to white families replaced the older systems of institutionalization and apprenticed labor. Though indigenous people might claim exemption from the provisions of government legislation, subject to proof one had assimilated by having cut ties with the broader indigenous community, a parent's exemption certificate did not cover the children. Indigenous children continued to be arbitrarily removed on no other grounds than their race for decades, with repeal of such discriminatory legislation only starting in 1964, and continuing, slowly, until the last was removed in 1984. By that time, generations of indigenous children had been removed from their families and communities. While many would eventually return to the broader Aboriginal and Torres Strait Islander community, the effects of repeated dislocations, disruption, and trauma were immense, for individuals and for the diverse indigenous communities around Australia. The impact of child expropriation on indigenous Australia has been as devastating as that of land dispossession, if not more so.

Australia entered the millennium with the Stolen Generations at the forefront of political debate. The 1997 Report of a National Inquiry into the Separation of Aboriginal and Torres Strait Islander Children had found that the "actions were genocidal," a number of civil cases had been fought and lost, and there were calls to make restitution a part of the process of national reconciliation. Approximately 250,000 people walked across the Sydney Harbor Bridge in 2000 on Sorry Day, one of the largest public demonstrations in Australian history. State governments and other groups formally apologized to Aboriginal and Torres Strait Islander people. Prime Minister John Howard controversially refused to apologize, arguing that an official apology might constitute liability for compensation claims. Though the term itself was fiercely contested, the history of the Stolen Generations nevertheless became part of the curricula in many schools.

SEE ALSO *Colonialism; Discrimination; Indigenous Rights; Race; Racism; Truth and Reconciliation Commissions; Whiteness*

BIBLIOGRAPHY

Haebich, Anna. 2000. *Broken Circles: Fragmenting Indigenous Families, 1800–2000*. Perth, Australia: Fremantle Arts Centre Press.

National Inquiry into the Separation of Aboriginal and Torres Strait Islander Children from Their Families (Australia). 1997. *Bringing Them Home: Report of the National Inquiry into the Separation of Aboriginal and Torres Strait Islander Children from Their Families*. Sydney: Human Rights and Equal Opportunity Commission.

Mellor, Doreen, and Anna Haebich, eds. 2002. *Many Voices: Reflections on Experiences of Indigenous Child Separation*. Canberra: National Library of Australia.

Read, Peter. 1999. *A Rape of the Soul So Profound: The Return of the Stolen Generations*. Sydney: Allen and Unwin.

Victoria K. Haskins

STOLPER-SAMUELSON THEOREM

In 1941 Wolfgang Stolper (1912–2002) and Paul Samuelson (b. 1915) put forward a proposition relating changes in the real incomes of workers and of capitalists to changes in the level of protection from import competition. They showed that lowering protection lowered the real income of the scarce factor used intensively in the import-competing sector and raised the real income of the other factor. Previously, international economists believed that opening an economy to international trade would, by increasing the aggregate supply of goods available, enable all income earners to be better off.

Stolper and Samuelson constructed a model of an economy in which only two factors, capital and labor, are used to produce two goods. Households either own capital or supply labor. The home economy cannot change world prices, but it can change the relative price of the two goods by changing the taxes levied on the imported good. In a neoclassical economy in which prices adjust smoothly and all factors are fully employed, a change in goods prices induces a change in the real income of the households owning the factors that produce the goods so that one group of factor owners is better off and the other is worse off.

The crux of the theorem is the link between the changes in the relative price of the goods and the changes in the prices of factors thereby induced. Since 1941 other international economists have stressed that this link has nothing to do with factor scarcity or the cause of the change in goods prices, but rather that it applies generally whenever relative prices change. The importance of the theorem derives from its fundamental message that changes in goods prices necessarily create conflict between households owning different factors. A vast literature developed in response to Stolper and Samuelson seeking to generalize the theorem to a world in which there are many goods and many factors. However, unless very strong restrictions were imposed on the technology of the producers, generating general propositions linking factor income changes to goods price changes proved difficult.

A later model that uses a criterion of real income change corresponding to the change in the utility of the income earner has obtained general propositions. Subject to a weak restriction that there is some diversity among households in their preferences and/or their ownership of factors, a change in any goods price will make some households better off and some worse off. Conversely, for any household there is some goods price change that will make it better off and some that will make it worse off. This generalizes the essential message of the original theorem. It shows that there are universal incentives for households to lobby government to change policies to yield benefits for them, and for other households to oppose them.

As an example, take the original Stolper-Samuelson model in which two factors produce two goods. Suppose the shares of capital and labor in the costs of producing a unit of good 1 (clothing) are 6/10 and 4/10 respectively and that the corresponding shares in producing a unit of good 2 (machinery) are 3/10 and 7/10. Thus, clothing is the good that uses a relatively labor-intensive technique of production. Then, if the price of clothing is raised by 1 percent, the wage rate of workers goes up by 2.3 percent, and the rate of return on capital goes down by 1 percent. Conversely, if the price of a unit of machinery goes up by 1 percent, the wage rate of workers goes down by 1.3 per-

cent, and the rate of return on capital goes up by 2 percent. As predicted by the theory, both workers or capital-owners will benefit if the price of the good which uses their factor intensively rises because of some government intervention in markets.

The theorem has applications to changes in goods prices that originate because of changes in any government taxes or policies or supply shocks. In particular, the theorem is the foundation of models of political economy that seek to explain patterns of government taxes and expenditures. It has been applied empirically to models that explain the structure of national tariffs, other taxes, subsidies, and transfers to households.

SEE ALSO *Economics, International; Heckscher-Ohlin-Samuelson Model; International Economic Order; Rybczynski Theorem; Tariffs*

BIBLIOGRAPHY

Deardorff, Alan V., and Robert M. Stern, eds. 1994. *The Stolper-Samuelson Theorem: A Golden Jubilee.* Ann Arbor: University of Michigan Press.

Lloyd, Peter J. 2000. Generalizing the Stolper-Samuelson Theorem: A Tale of Two Matrices. *Review of International Economics* 8 (4): 597–613.

Stolper, Wolfgang F., and Paul A Samuelson. 1941. Protection and Real Wages. *Review of Economic Studies* 9 (1): 58–73.

Peter Lloyd

STORYTELLING

Storytelling may be broadly defined as an ancient method of conveying ideas, intimations, and emotions in a narrative form with or without the accompaniment of music or visual art. Originally an oral tradition, storytelling has evolved from its earliest form to include a variety of multimedia applications. Folklorists generally do not approve of such inclusive definitions. In her scholarly analysis of the history of storytelling, *The World of Storytelling* (1990), Anne Pellowski defines storytelling as:

> the art or craft of narration of stories in verse/and or prose, as performed or led by one person before a live audience; the stories narrated may be spoken, chanted, or sung, with or without musical, pictorial, and/or other accompaniment and may be learned from oral, printed, or mechanically recorded sources; one of its purposes may be that of entertainment. (Pellowski 1990, p.15)

Storytellers may have also collected stories from various people they encountered while telling the stories they had learned or created from observations and life experiences. Stories may have been used to entertain, but they were also used to educate audiences. Folklorists discuss oral tales of two main types: *Märchen* and *Sagen*, which are German terms with no exact English equivalents. *Märchen* is both singular and plural, and means something akin to *fairy tale*. These tales, which are not presented as true, are set in the timeless/placeless world of *once-upon-a-time*. The *Sagen*, or legends, however, are presented as factual, with powerfully specific times and places. The common folk may have told their stories at home, at work, and at festival times. Folk stories were told repeatedly and handed down through generations from one teller to the next, making use of storytelling for teaching purposes. Collectors of folktales, such as the Brothers Grimm, Charles Perrault, Joseph Jacobs, Peter Christian Asbjornsen, Jorgen Moe, Andrew Lang, Joel Chandler Harris, and Richard Chase seem to have gathered tales, in part, for the purpose of cultural enrichment.

What is the purpose of storytelling? Pellowski, in line with other theorists, says that storytelling may have started as informal entertainment or play, and only gradually became intertwined with religious rituals, historical recitations, and educational functions. Most theorists suggest that storytelling fulfills the desire for playacting and meets entertainment needs while helping to explain the surrounding physical world or helping honor or placate the supernatural force(s) believed to be present in the world. Storytelling can help explain and express strong emotions and experiences in memorable, long-lasting ways through the intricate use of rhythm, rhyme, and repetition. Storytelling can help preserve traditions, customs, and societal standards, while bestowing immortality on leaders or ancestors. Pellowski notes the earliest evidence of storytelling may be found in the Westcar Papyrus of the Egyptians, which includes tales of encounters between a pyramid builder named Khufu or Cheops and his sons. One of the most famous tales recorded on papyrus is known as *The Shipwrecked Sailor.*

Pellowski traces the development of the bardic tradition, defining the bard as, "a storyteller whose function is to create and/or perform poetic oral narrations that chronicle events or praise the illustrious forebears and present leaders of a tribal, cultural, or national group" (Pellowski 1990, p. 21). The bard was a storyteller, a poet, and a musician. The term *bard* had its introduction through Greek and Roman tales of the Celts. Bards have also been known as *rhapsodes, minstrels,* or *jongleurs.*

Tales from a variety of cultures have been preserved because of storytelling traditions. Some examples are: *Beowulf,* an Anglo-Saxon tale of courage in the face of brute strength; *Gilgamesh,* a Sumerian epic tale of the Sumerian king, Gilgamesh, and his friendship with Enkidu, the half-beast, half-man being created to destroy him; *The Iliad,* a Greek epic tale of the Trojan War; *The Odyssey,* a Greek epic tale of Odysseus on his homeward journey from Troy; *Story of Sigurd (Siegfried),* a Norse legend; *The Volsunga Saga,* the adventures of Sigurd, including the killing of a dragon named Fafnir; *The Merry Adventures of Robin Hood* and *King Arthur and His Knights,* legendary English tales of daring and bravery; *Song of Roland,* legendary French tales; *Sundiata, The Epic of the Lion King,* a legendary African tale of how Sundiata became King of Mali; *The Tain,* an Irish tale of the legendary hero Cuchulain, his birth, battles and ultimate death; and *The Ramayana* of India, a religious tale.

SEE ALSO *Communication; Ethnography; Ethnology and Folklore; Media; Narratives; Tradition*

BIBLIOGRAPHY

Pellowski, Anne. 1990. *The World of Storytelling,* expanded and rev. ed. Bronx, NY: H. W. Wilson.

Geraldine Cannon Becker

STOUFFER, SAMUEL

SEE *Tolerance, Political.*

STOWE, HARRIET BEECHER
1811–1896

As an active figure of the nineteenth century and the so-called "feminine fifties," Harriet Beecher Stowe lived and wrote, negotiating between extremes of unfolding cultural elements. During that time, young girls commonly learned that the meek could and should inherit the world by practicing self-discipline and humility. As they matured, women might learn that they could through their own wit and activity earn a place in an emerging capitalist economy. Stowe's life and writings approach such cultural contradictions as played out in the realms of race, sex, class, religion, and changing ideas of what constitutes noble identity and behavior.

Stowe's best-selling *Uncle Tom's Cabin; or, Life Among the Lowly,* first appeared as serialized in 1851–1852 in the abolitionist newspaper *The National Era.* In 1852 these "sketches" were published in book form and widely translated into theater and over forty languages. As Stowe states in her preface, "The object of these sketches is to awaken sympathy and feeling for the African race, as they exist among us; to show their wrongs and sorrows, under a system necessarily cruel and unjust." Appealing to her readers' various faculties, Stowe shows that the institution of slavery is fundamentally incompatible with Christianity. By 1862 when she met with President Abraham Lincoln, the cultural impact of *Uncle Tom's Cabin* had become so great that Lincoln is said to have acknowledged, "So you're the little woman who wrote the book that started this great war!"

Public reaction to Stowe's million-seller in large part reflects debates in American racial history. After receiving scathing contemporary pro-slavery reviews, she documented her sources by publishing the five-hundred-page *A Key to Uncle Tom's Cabin* (1854). Later, Harlem Renaissance writers and others have sharply criticized Stowe's Christ-like portrayal of the martyr Uncle Tom as obsequious and a role model obstacle in the struggle for racial equality.

Born on June 14, 1811, Stowe's early life prepared her well for facing slavery and women's issues head-on and resolutely. She gained rhetorical skills early from her austere and demanding Protestant evangelist father, Lyman Beecher, and later from her brother, abolitionist and theologian Henry Ward Beecher. Available to her were books, sermons, and philosophical discussions. In a home peopled by siblings, relatives, and boarders, she developed a lively mind as well as a reverence for an idealized image of womanhood. Stowe attended the Hartford Female Seminary—founded and run by her sister Catherine Beecher—and later taught there. Unlike other women's schools that prepared women for marriage, Beecher's seminary taught women to use their own judgment and to become socially useful. Such teachings evolve as a concluding lesson in *Uncle Tom's Cabin* as readers are urged to see to it that in their actions they "feel right." In 1836 Harriet Beecher married the Bible scholar Calvin Ellis Stowe and subsequently bore seven children before moving to Bowdoin, Maine, in 1850.

Later in life Stowe spoke and wrote to protect the women's rights movement from those who advocated free love and free divorce. Her later works question the cultural bases of capitalism and consumerism by revisiting the early 1850s virtues of humility, charity, self-discipline, and social usefulness, but these works generally lack the fire that had established her earlier place in literary history. She died on July 1, 1896.

SEE ALSO *Feminism; Slave Resistance; Slavery; Suffrage, Women's; U.S. Civil War; Uncle Tom; Women's Movement*

BIBLIOGRAPHY

Hedrick, Joan. 1994. *Harriet Beecher Stowe, a Life*. New York: Oxford University Press.

Henning, Martha L. 1996. Harriet Beecher Stowe's *Uncle Tom's Cabin*: Modeling Communal Willfulness. In *Beyond Understanding, Appeals to the Imagination, Passions, and Will in Mid-Nineteenth-Century American Women's Fiction*. New York: Peter Lang Publishing.

Knox, Thomas W. 1887. *Life and Work of Henry Ward Beecher*. Hartford, CT: The Hartford Publishing Company.

Parker, Rev. E. P. 1869. Harriet Beecher Stowe. In *Eminent Women of the Age*, eds. James Parton et al., 296–331. Hartford, CT: S. M. Betts & Company.

Sklar, Kathryn Kish. 1973. *Catharine Beecher; A Study in American Domesticity*. New Haven, CT: Yale University Press.

Sundquist, Eric J., ed. 1986. *New Essays on Uncle Tom's Cabin*. Cambridge, U.K.: Cambridge University Press.

Martha L. Henning

STRATEGIC BEHAVIOR

In economics, the term *strategic behavior* usually refers to decision-making that takes into account the actions and reactions of other economic agents. Its essential feature is the recognition of the direct interdependence between one's behavior and that of others.

The difference between strategic and nonstrategic behavior can be highlighted by the following example: Suppose a consumer enters a store and encounters a product with a particular marked price. This consumer's decision to buy or not buy the product depends solely on their preference for the product. On the other hand, suppose the store allows bargaining. In this case, the price for the product is not fixed, but depends rather on the process of negotiation between the buyer and the seller. In this process of negotiation and purchase, the consumer presumably not only takes into account their own likes and dislikes for the product, but also tries to anticipate such factors as the lowest price the seller would be willing to accept. Whereas in the first situation personal preference is the only factor influencing the consumer's decision, in the latter case the consumer also has to take into account the seller's behavior in deciding what offer to make or accept and consequently whether to buy or not. This latter process is an example of strategic behavior.

In economics, the first formal discussion of the concept of strategic behavior is believed to be in Augustin Cournot's 1838 book *Recherches sur les principes mathématiques de la théorie des richesses* (published in English as *Researches into the Mathematical Principles of the Theory of Wealth*). In a chapter on the competition between producers, Cournot considers how each producer, when making output decisions, takes into account the impact their own output and that of other producers has on the market price and thereby on profits.

The concept of strategic behavior is now recognized in many diverse academic fields, ranging from economics and business to politics and international relations. In the present day, a counterpart of Cournot's above-mentioned example with an impact on our day-to-day life is competition between producers of oil. There are only a handful of big oil-producing countries in the world, and in deciding whether to increase or reduce production, each takes into account the impact of their decision on the price of oil in the global market and consequently on their own revenues. R&D races, bidding in auctions, trust in societies, contracts, and social insurance are a few of the many prominent applications of the concept in economics and business. Strategic voting and the formulation of election platforms are two examples of strategic behavior in politics, while in international relations, strategic behavior is found in arms races, trade, and in negotiations between nations. The outcome of interaction between the strategic behaviors of a set of agents is a subject examined by game theory.

SEE ALSO *Competition, Imperfect; Game Theory; Strategic Games; Strategy and Voting Games*

BIBLIOGRAPHY

Cournot, Augustin A. 1838. *Recherches sur les principes mathématiques de la théorie des richesses.* Paris: Hachette. Published in an English translation by Nathaniel T. Bacon as *Researches into the Mathematical Principles of the Theory of Wealth* (New York: Macmillan, 1927).

Sumon Majumdar

STRATEGIC GAMES

The concept of a strategic game forms part of the central idea behind the theory of games. A strategy is a plan of action that a player can use to guide the player in selecting moves throughout the game. It may be trivially simple, such as "whenever you are called on to move, select randomly among the moves," or it may contain detailed complex instructions to cover all contingencies.

With few exceptions, virtually all games of any interest have a strategic component. Even tic-tac-toe, which is often utilized to illustrate an inessential game, or one that is not worth playing, has a strategic component. It is regarded as inessential because with only a little thought both players can enforce a draw; nevertheless, it has a set of strategies from which each player can select his actions. Even in a game as simple as this it is possible to select a losing strategy.

In the formulation and mathematical analysis of games of strategy, John von Neumann and Oskar

Morgenstern (1944) made the great contribution of providing a complete language for the study of individual and multiperson conscious strategic choice. Concepts that had been extremely vague were defined precisely and operationally in a manner so that they could be analyzed mathematically. This includes the precise meanings of the terms *choice, move, information, strategy, outcome,* and *payoff.* But in many of the social sciences, particularly political science, sociology, and anthropology, some research questions are rather abstract, taking into account context and much of the richness and intangibles of areas of investigation. For many of the critical problems in the disciplines these subtleties cannot be ignored, and unfortunately the formal language of strategic games does not pick them up. With its mass markets and anonymous rational conscious behavior, economics has many more questions that are congenial to the strategic game analogy than do the other social sciences.

When the analogy is made between formal games of strategy and strategic behavior in politics or society, the gap between them is manifested in the assumptions that are made concerning knowledge of the rules of the game and common knowledge. When we consider the game chess, two implicit assumptions are made: It is assumed that all players know the rules of the game, and that each player knows that the other player knows the rules of the game. In society, even the best politicians know that much is unknown.

In the formal definition, strategy is defined as a complete book of instructions that a player could give to a delegate to play for him that describes what he wants the delegate to do under every contingency that might arise. A game as simple as chess has a hyper-astronomical number of strategies, so large that there is no way that they can all be enumerated in practice. It is clear that chess could be considered an inessential game in the sense that if a player could calculate all strategies it would be simple to select an optimal strategy, and if each player did that he would not bother playing—he would merely submit his optimal strategies and the game would be declared a draw or a win for the first mover. Yet years of experience and calculations on the size of the calculations tell us that the way chess is actually played by the best of human chess players is not by the enumeration of all strategies.

The difference between the abstraction of certain concepts and their manifestation in everyday life is nicely illustrated in the formal concept of strategy and how it is manifested in both military and corporate arenas. A strategy in the military or at the top of a corporation is an overall plan that, in its scope, bears some resemblance to the ideal strategy utilized in strategic games, but it has at least two critical modifications: It recognizes the critical role of delegation and aggregation. The general knows that neither he nor his opponent knows all the rules of the game, and he knows that he has to delegate decision-making to those who have greater special information than he does.

In spite of these caveats, there are many questions in economics, political science, social psychology, and even law, biology, and anthropology that can use the formal game structure profitably. Two basic applications to political science serve as examples. The first is the Condorcet Paradox and the second the Shapley-Shubik Power Index.

The Condorcet Paradox was established in 1785 by Marquis de Condorcet (b. 1743). His *Essay on the Application of Analysis to the Probability of Majority Decisions* describes describes the intransitivity of majority preference. According to the Condorcet Paradox majority wishes can be in conflict with each other. Consider three individuals named A, B, and C and the issues called I, II, and III to be put to the vote. The preferences of A are given by I pr II pr III (where *pr* means "preferred to"), the preferences of B are III pr I pr II, and the preferences of C are II pr III pr I. Consider a simple majority vote between any two social choices. By a 2:1 majority, a vote between I and II selects I, a vote between I and III selects III, and a vote between II and III selects II.

The Shapley-Shubik Power Index (Shapley and Shubik 1954) gives an intrinsic measure for how power varies with the accumulation of votes. Consider a committee with five votes. If there are three individuals with one person having three votes and the other two people having one each, and the rule was simple majority vote, the individual with three votes would have all the power. If there were five individuals, each with one vote, the power would be spread evenly. The index gives the nonlinear formula to measure power as a function of distribution of the votes. For example, in the five-vote simple-majority voting game, if there were four individuals with one having two of the five votes and the others having one each, the first person's power would be one-half, and the others' would be one-sixteenth each. This measure provides a benchmark, assuming that all individuals have equal chances of forming any coalition. In application, a correction for coalition possibilities must be made. A natural application of this is in predicting outcomes in Supreme Court cases.

SEE ALSO *Strategic Behavior; Strategy and Voting Games; Subgame Perfection*

BIBLIOGRAPHY

Condorcet, Jean-Antoine-Nicolas de Caritat, Marquis de. 1785. *Essai sur l'application de l'analyse à la probabilité des décisions rendues à la pluralité des voix* (*Essay on the Application of Analysis to the Probability of Majority Decisions*). Paris: Impr. Royale. New York: Chelsea, 1972.

O'Neill, Barry. 1999. *Honor, Symbols, and War*. Ann Arbor: University of Michigan Press.

Schelling, Thomas C. 1960. *The Strategy of Conflict*. Cambridge, MA: Harvard University Press.

Shapley, Lloyd S., and Martin Shubik. 1954. A Method for Evaluating the Distribution of Power in a Committee System. *American Political Science Review* 48, no. 3 (September): 787–792.

von Neumann, John, and Oskar Morgenstern. 1944. *Theory of Games and Economic Behavior*. Princeton, NJ: Princeton University Press.

Martin Shubik

STRATEGIES, SELF-HANDICAPPING

People might be expected to reach for any and every advantage to facilitate performance, including eliminating any obstacle or disability that might interfere with success. Nevertheless, individuals are sometimes willing to strategically create impediments to performance, and this has been termed *self-handicapping*. Self-handicapping is a strategy undertaken to escape the implications of an impending failure, should it occur, on an individual's sense of self-worth. It is an anticipatory self-protective strategy, the goal of which is to guide performance-relevant attributions. Those who make use of this tactic place excessive significance on ability. They feel that competence can be demonstrated but not improved, and while they perceive their own self-worth as hinging on personal aptitude, they are uncertain of their capacity to succeed. Thus, self-handicappers possess a fragile, doubt-ridden sense of self, which they work to bolster. By erecting barriers to achievement, self-handicappers aim to discount personal competence as the causal agent in any subsequent failure. The presence of such obstacles also serves to enhance any personal responsibility for successful outcomes occurring in spite of the handicap.

Two distinct forms of self-handicapping have been investigated: behavioral and claimed. Behavioral handicaps involve actively sabotaging one's own performance. The athlete who fails to practice in the weeks leading up to an important match may be using lack of preparation as an explanation for an impending loss. However, an athlete who complains of illness, fatigue, or injury prior to a match may satisfy the same goal of providing a justification for failure, but these are merely claims, where the individual does not actively undermine his or her performance, but instead provides an a priori excuse. In general, males are more likely to engage in behavioral self-handicapping than females, but both genders make use of claimed handicaps.

As originally conceptualized, self-handicapping was thought to stem entirely from an individual's desire to sustain positive self-views. However, research shows that impression management or maintenance of esteem in the eyes of others is also an influential motive. As such, self-handicapping can involve self-deception as well as self-presentation.

Some individuals are more likely to employ this strategy than others. Situational factors can also increase the likelihood that self-handicapping will occur. Most notably, situations involving noncontingent success (e.g., undeserved praise, inexplicable victory) or private failure are also more likely to induce self-handicapping. Earned or expected successes are liable to be seen as repeatable (and thus are unlikely to produce the feelings of uncertainty necessary for self-handicapping). Further, whereas private failure leaves open the possibility of being viewed positively by others, public failure leaves no positive image to preserve, and makes the introduction of additional handicaps useless.

Though employed as a means to protect the self from undesirable consequences, in the long run self-handicapping may actually cause more harm than it prevents. Some handicaps are injurious in and of themselves (e.g., drug and alcohol abuse). Further, although self-handicapping does bolster immediate self-regard, habitual use of this strategy actually undermines self-esteem by underscoring a person's self-doubt. In addition, high self-handicappers tend to demonstrate poorer academic performance. Ironically, the desire to appear capable seems to actually drive self-handicappers to undermine their competence over time.

SEE ALSO *Depression, Psychological; Self-Concept; Self-Defeating Behavior; Self-Esteem; Self-Presentation*

BIBLIOGRAPHY

Arkin, Robert M., and Kathryn C. Oleson. 1998. Self-Handicapping. In *Attribution and Social Interaction: The Legacy of Edward E. Jones*, ed. John M. Darley and Joel Cooper, 313–347. Washington, DC: American Psychological Association.

Pettit, Jeremy W., and Thomas E. Joiner. 2006. Self-Handicapping. In *Chronic Depression: Interpersonal Sources, Therapeutic Solutions*, ed. Jeremy W. Pettit and Thomas E. Joiner, 85–94. Washington, DC: American Psychological Association.

Strube, Michael J. 1986. An Analysis of the Self-Handicapping Scale. *Basic and Applied Social Psychology* 7: 211–224.

Robert M. Arkin
Karen E. MacGregor

STRATEGY AND VOTING GAMES

In game theory, a player's strategy refers to a complete contingent plan for all possible scenarios that might arise. When voting is modeled in a game theoretical framework, voters are treated as strategic players, and the framework describes the strategic interactions among the voters. A voting game is characterized by three key elements: the set of voters, the set of strategies available to each voter, and each voter's preferences on the set of voting outcomes. The set of feasible strategies in a particular voting game depends on the voting system in use. For example, under the plurality voting system, each voter can vote for only one candidate. With preferential voting, each voter ranks a list of candidates in order of preference. Therefore, a voter's strategy in a plurality voting game specifies which candidate to vote for each combination of other players' votes, whereas in a preferential voting game, a strategy specifies a preference list for each combination of other players' rankings. A voting outcome is determined by all voters' strategies (called a strategy profile) under a particular voting system. For example, in a single-winner plurality voting game, the candidate with the most votes wins the election. In proportional representation systems, the percentage of votes received by a party determines the percentage of seats allocated to the party. A voter's preference on the set of voting outcomes is usually represented by a payoff function that assigns a numeric value to each strategy profile.

The concept of strategy, together with strategic game (or normal form game), was first formally introduced in 1944 in *The Theory of Games and Economic Behavior*, by John von Neumann and Oskar Morgenstern. Later, in 1950, John F. Nash Jr. developed the solution concept of the Nash equilibrium, which describes any stable state in which each player's strategy is optimal (in the sense that it maximizes a player's payoffs among his or her other strategies) given other players' equilibrium strategies. Since then, game theory has become an important tool for analyzing problems in various fields, including economics, biology, and political science. An early application of game theory to voting situations was offered by Robin Farquharson in his influential 1969 book, *Theory of Voting*. Farquharson's approach departed from earlier studies, which usually assumed sincere voting by disregarding the strategic aspects of voting. A voter's strategy is sincere if the person votes according to his or her true preferences regardless of other voters' strategies. In general, a sincere voting profile does not constitute an equilibrium for a voting game. Allan Gibbard (1973) and Mark Allen Satterthwaite (1975) proved a theorem showing that strategic voting is universal in common democratic systems. Consequently, modeling voting as a strategic game has been widely accepted in economics and political science.

Although strategic voting modeling has its theoretical attractiveness, the degree of empirical support varies for different voting systems. In addition, two lines of criticism of game theoretical voting models have arisen. From a descriptive view, it is not clear whether real-life voters have full knowledge of game structures and are able to perform complex strategic calculus. Normatively, strategic voting rationalizes manipulations of systems by voters who misrepresent their preferences, and accordingly by candidates who use media influence to shape voters' perceptions. Such manipulations are generally considered undesirable for a democratic system.

SEE ALSO *Strategic Behavior; Strategic Games; Strategy*

BIBLIOGRAPHY

Farquharson, Robin. 1969. *Theory of Voting.* New Haven, CT: Yale University Press.

Gibbard, Allan. 1973. Manipulation of Voting Schemes: A General Result. *Econometrica* 41 (4): 587–601.

Nash, John F., Jr. 1950. Equilibrium Points in *n*-Person Games. *Proceedings of the National Academy of Sciences of the United States of America* 36 (1): 48–49.

Neumann, John von, and Oskar Morgenstern. 1944. *Theory of Games and Economic Behavior.* Princeton, NJ: Princeton University Press.

Satterthwaite, Mark Allen. 1975. Strategy-Proofness and Arrow's Conditions: Existence and Correspondence Theorems for Voting Procedures and Social Welfare Functions. *Journal of Economic Theory* 10 (2): 187–217.

Yuelan Chen

STRATIFICATION

The term *stratification* refers to the system of inequalities within and between societies, the processes of assignment to positions within a social hierarchy, and the means by which resources are allocated. Various theories have tried to explain how and why stratification systems emerged. The most prominent of these were developed in the nineteenth and early twentieth centuries following industrialization, which altered the social structures of traditional feudal and agrarian societies and gave rise to more complex urban societies. Before industrialization, societies were more stable and had much less economic inequality, and clear, fixed boundaries separated groups like the nobility from their subjects (see Lenski 1966).

In his pioneering account, Karl Marx explained stratification as a product of the mode of production—the principal system of market organization (e.g., capitalism). He outlined a progressive transition from feudalism to capitalism and finally to socialism. Marx claimed that the organization and development of modern, industrial capitalist societies were driven by class relations. He argued that capitalist societies would grow increasingly divided between a capitalist class that owns the capital and therefore controls the means of production and a growing labor class (proletariat) that sells its labor to capitalists in order to survive. Marx predicted a struggle between capitalists and workers leading to the destruction of the capitalist system and the formation of a socialist society free of classes. Moving beyond his historical prediction, modern Marxists have reconceptualized his class schema to focus on authority, the inherently antagonistic relations between workers and owners/managers, and the exploitative nature of capitalism (see, for example, Wright 1997).

In the early twentieth century, Max Weber added a focus on social status and political power to Marx's more purely economic perspective. He proposed class, status, and party as the three dimensions of stratification in modern societies, though he also discussed the role of castes and professions. Though Weber's writings conceptualizing class were not very developed or novel, he has been deployed widely in class schemas focused on prestige, occupations, status, and skill. Weber's present-day influence can most be seen in the use of his concept of *closure*—that is, the process by which organizations define boundaries that establish which members receive certain benefits and which do not.

Structural functionalism, which traces its roots to the work of Émile Durkheim, perceived stratification systems as universal to every society, from simple hunter-gatherer tribes to complex, modern industrial societies. Kingsley Davis and Wilbert E. Moore (1945) offered a particularly influential account of the "functional necessity of stratification." Structural functionalist theories were criticized for neglecting conflict and for failing to address the possible lack of stratification in small egalitarian tribes or the reduction of stratification in modern social democracies. Today, structural functionalism has few followers in the social sciences.

A common characteristic of these early attempts was the effort to develop general laws. During the post–World War II (1939–1945) period, however, social scientists have moved away from grand, all-encompassing theories of stratification toward more flexible perspectives, which perceive stratification as a result of the interplay between multiple actors and multiple dimensions of inequality. One of the main new issues gaining attention was that of gender. Scholars argued that gender played a central role in the formation and functioning of stratification systems. They showed that women's exclusion from social life placed them in an inferior position, resulting in lessened life chances and status. While women's standing in social and economic life has improved over the past half-century, women are still restricted by gender roles and patriarchy. Rich literatures examine the impact of family structure, occupational segregation, devaluation of women's work, and sex-based pay gaps.

Other issues that came under greater scrutiny were race and ethnicity. Scholars demonstrated that one's racial and ethnic background greatly influences one's life chances. U.S. sociologists have devoted a great deal of attention to black-white differences in residence, educational achievement, and employment status. Many focused on residentially segregated ghetto communities where unemployment, poverty, and single parenthood were highly concentrated. Though many sociologists have demonstrated that some racial and ethnic differences can be explained by class-based factors like income level, there is an emerging literature on how race, gender, and class intersect to shape disadvantage.

There also has been great interest in the actors and processes that reproduce and maintain social inequalities. Many sociologists focused on the role of elites in the reproduction and maintenance of social inequalities. American sociologist C. Wright Mills (1956) argued that a "power elite" controls the economy, state, and military. Some scholars have described elites as a conscious, homogenous social class, which actively reproduces itself and guards the privileges it possesses. Perhaps the most productive line of inquiry has concentrated on the linkages between social origins and levels of attainment. Peter M. Blau and Otis Dudley Duncan (1967) famously analyzed the relationship between paternal occupation, education, and attained occupation. Debates about modeling techniques and historical and cross-national patterns of mobility and attainment dominated analyses of stratification from the 1970s to the early 1990s. Some scholars took the study of reproduction, mobility, and attainment in new directions and emphasized the role of social ties and culture. French sociologist Pierre Bourdieu argued that access to high culture and learned practices, which he referred to as *cultural capital*, enable the children of the privileged to get ahead and facilitate the reproduction of social inequalities. Bourdieu also offered the concept of *habitus* to account for the embodied disposition that dominant classes exercise instinctively to reproduce their higher status. The concept *social capital* emerged to refer to the resources that flow through social networks.

In recent years, with the rise of globalization and the expansion of neoliberalism across the globe, debates about the global stratification system gained a great deal of attention. World systems theorists, led by Immanuel Wallerstein, contend that industrial core countries have an exploitative relationship with the less-developed periphery. The perseverance of poverty in the Third World, the weakening position of traditional labor classes in industrialized countries, and rising income inequalities within nearly every country lead many to believe that we are now facing a global system benefiting a small minority while hurting the rest. While many note the massive levels of inequality between countries, there has been a lively debate about whether global inequality is increasing or decreasing. Glenn Firebaugh (2003), for example, claims that inequality between countries has decreased, while Branko Milanovic (2005) contends it has increased. Regardless, global inequality in income, health, and well-being remains enormous and in the future stratification scholars are likely to focus more on the plight of the disadvantaged in less-developed countries, where the majority of the world's population resides.

SEE ALSO *Education, Unequal; Inequality, Income; Inequality, Political; Race Relations; Sociology, Political*

BIBLIOGRAPHY

Blau, Peter M., and Otis Dudley Duncan. 1967. *The American Occupational Structure.* New York: Wiley.

Bourdieu, Pierre, and Jean-Claude Passeron. [1970] 1990. *Reproduction in Education, Society, and Culture.* 2nd ed. Trans. Richard Nice. London: Sage.

Davis, Kingsley, and Wilbert E. Moore. 1945. "Some Principles of Stratification." *American Sociological Review* 10 (2): 242–249.

Firebaugh, Glenn. 2003. *The New Geography of Global Income Inequality.* Cambridge, MA: Harvard University Press.

Lenski, Gerhard E. [1966] 1984. *Power and Privilege: A Theory of Social Stratification.* Chapel Hill: University of North Carolina Press.

Milanovic, Branko. 2005. *Worlds Apart: Measuring International and Global Inequality.* Princeton, NJ: Princeton University Press.

Mills, C. Wright. [1956] 2000. *The Power Elite.* New York: Oxford University Press.

Wallerstein, Immanuel. 1974. *Capitalist Agriculture and the Origin of the European World-Economy in the Sixteenth Century.* Vol. 1 of *The Modern World-System.* New York: Academic Press.

Wright, Erik Olin. 1997. *Class Counts: Comparative Studies in Class Analysis.* New York: Cambridge University Press.

Yunus Kaya
David Brady

STRATIFICATION, POLITICAL

If social stratification usually refers to the kind and degree of distribution of resources (e.g., wealth, status, prestige, and privilege) within a social system, then political stratification is best understood as the extent to which such inequalities are encapsulated in, or influenced by, political structures and processes (i.e., involving influence, authority, or power). In this sense power is understood not only in relation to achieving desired results, even against opposing interest, but also in terms of the ability to frame and set agendas. Conceived of and measured as an absolute, or relative, entity, political stratification is often used in studies on societal change, egalitarian opportunity structures, democratization, the distribution of power and equality, and the efficiency of social and political justice. Linking political, economic, and social inequality structures, the concept is central to the social sciences and social policy.

Narrower conceptualizations of political stratification, favored particularly by political scientists in the 1960s and 1970s, usually focus on stratified political activities, positions, and influence of individuals, groups, parties, or nation-states. Studies in this vein tend to explore a variety of topics including political elites, the electorate, conceptions of democracy and citizenship, political activism, and new social movements. However, this narrow conception is rarely accompanied by a clear overarching theoretical model about political stratification. Indeed, attempts to distinguish political from social stratification are only partially successful and not widely accepted in the social sciences, due in part to the complex yet profound interdependence between the political, social, economic, and cultural spheres. Political stratification in a wider sense, however, has permeated the social and political sciences. Indeed, most modern studies on social stratification are steeped in a political discourse.

POLITICAL STRATIFICATION FROM AN INSTITUTIONAL PERSPECTIVE

From an institutional perspective political stratification can be related to norms, values, class structures, status groups, associations, and laws, which structure the relations between individual and collective actors. For example, this perspective would suggest that associations are based on social and economic interests, which in turn give rise not only to a stratification order due to differential capacities and influence, but also to cooperation and conflict according to these pursuits. Based on differing relations to the means of production, the German political philosopher Karl Marx (1818–1883) predicted that the bourgeoisie would protect its economic interests by repressive laws. This would create a class consciousness;

cause the resolution of regional, ethnic, and other conflicts among the proletariat; lead to a unified and politically organized labor movement; and ultimately result in the overthrow of the capitalist system by revolution, to be replaced by a classless, communist society. Critics argue that class theory fails to account for the growing presence of a strong middle class, the absence of antagonistic relations between classes, the continued success of elites to set agendas, and the triumph of capitalism over socialism as an economic-political system. This criticism is not as convincing as it appears at first. On the one hand neo-Marxists are able to overcome at least part of these criticisms by emphasizing the exploitative nature of economic interactions also within the growing middle class, which, based on differential access to wealth, authority, skills, or credentials, become at once exploiters and exploited within a capitalistic system. Beyond this, systematic economic exploitations and political paternalism continue to take place based on differential access to resources between nations of differing economic development levels, social groups differentiated by ethnicity or gender, and the transfer of advantage and privilege from one generation to another. On the other hand there exist other class theories that do not share the assumptions of Marxist class structures. For example, class structure can relate to the social positions of actors as identified by their integration into the labor market. This is distinct from a social hierarchy, and usually borrows from German sociologist Max Weber's (1864–1920) notions of class. In this sense, class does not imply a single hierarchical dimension. A nonhierarchical class schema as developed by, for instance, British sociologist John Goldthorpe and his colleagues, differs from class schemata based on some vertical (i.e., ascending/descending) dimension. For example, skilled industrial workers, small proprietors, and minor officials may occupy a similar position in a hierarchy, but may be separated by class in that they are subjected to very different technical and economic realities due to innovations or governmental policies. A second Weberian approach to institutional structures consists of his distinction between different authority-types: traditional, legitimated by heredity and traditions; charismatic, based on inspirational leaders; and legal-rational, based on law and rationality.

Another important tradition from an institutional perspective relates to the subjective assessment of status or prestige. The ranking or rating of occupations according to their subjectively perceived prestige and its resulting access to social, economic, and political resources started most likely with American educator George S. Counts (1889–1974) in the 1920s but was popularized by the National Opinion Research Center (NORC) in the 1940s. While some argue that it is the subjectively attributed qualities to these titles themselves that structure society, and while others suggest that subjective aspects are merely proxies for an underlying social and economic structure, Weber emphasized the interdependence between class, status, and prestige. According to Weber power has different bases that interact with each other: class based on economics, status based on prestige and honor, and party based on political power and domination via associations. An important variant to this theme was presented by the French sociologist Pierre Bourdieu (1930–2002), who explored the convertibility between economic, cultural, social, and symbolic capital.

POLITICAL STRATIFICATION FROM A RELATIONAL PERSPECTIVE

From a relational perspective political inequality structures emerge from differentiated interactions between agents. At the base are actors such as individuals, political bodies, associations, and nation-states, which interact with each other. These interactions are patterned not only according to institutionalized rules but such interactions, never a perfect reproduction of institutional blueprints, also create, maintain, and transmute these rules. Societal structures from this perspective are based on and created from the recurring patterns of relations. Based in part on the study of religious and political characteristics of groups, German philosopher and sociologist Georg Simmel (1858–1918) proposed that society exists only as social representations, or collective ideas, which provide the basis for social relations as societies' external form (i.e., rejecting the idea of society as something that can have a substantive existence). Indeed, the objectification of the church or the state is created from complex relations and interactions among the members of large, heterogeneous groups. In this vein democratization and social equality can be understood as the reduction of systematic power differences between group members within a social system, while the distribution of power also gives rise to the structuring of social relations in terms of cooperation, conflict, and competition. Differential relations between agents within a social system were initially studied with simple sociograms in order to understand power structures and relations. These have been replaced by more sophisticated forms of network analysis, in which power structures are explored in terms of differing relations between nodes and their quality, reciprocity, density, intensity, and durability within a network structure. This approach can be found in studies focusing on cliques, associations, interest groups, and elites.

POLITICAL STRATIFICATION FROM AN EMBODIED PERSPECTIVE

From an embodied perspective political stratification can be understood in a number of different ways. Here individuals are at the forefront as they, through continuous acts of self-definition, interpret and make sense of norms and values, and as they interact with each other. Based on the symbolic interactionist perspective of American philosopher and social psychologist George Herbert Mead (1863–1931), the "socio-physiology" of individuals underpins self-awareness, interactions, and behavior. Interactions and the thus-derived structures are based on the interpretation and internalization of rules by individuals. Or structures and stratification are based on interaction according to a system of rules, yet these interactions concurrently reproduce and transform the rules and thus the underlying structures. For French philosopher Michel Foucault (1926–1984), organizations and institutions (e.g., schools, asylums, medicine) are invested within individual bodies through discipline and punishment of their bodily activities. As such, individuals in modern societies no longer require the policing of their thoughts and activities by others but become their own guards. Connected to this notion is governmentality, which also plays a role in conceptualizing political stratification from a poststructural perspective. Governmentality refers to power as tactical and continuous negotiations between actors and institutions (e.g., markets). Meaning and knowledge are shaped via the interconnection between discursive strategies and practices. From this perspective, power is omnipresent and embedded in all forms of discourse and actions. Knowledge thus produced and internalized has the power to regulate and discipline the self. Also, Bourdieu's notion of different forms of capital could be understood as part of embodied structures because such capitals are connected to personal fields of power and the habitus of the individual.

In sum, political structures can be conceived of in terms of institutions, relations, and bodies, although these perspectives are best understood as ways to organize different theoretical approaches rather than implying differences in kind. Throughout, controversies about political stratification center on questions such as: What is stratified? How is it stratified? What causes such stratification? and What are its consequences? Postmodern, particularly poststructural, theorists would argue that due to technological innovations and the increased speed and efficiency of mobility of information, goods, and people, all social, economic, political, and cultural structures are dissolving. In the absence of dominant political structures and social order, individuals no longer have positions and trajectories but are either encouraged or forced to construct themselves and to interpret their environment according to context-dependent, ephemeral, media-dominated, lifestyle and consumption choices.

Such suggestions may point at important dynamics associated with modernization and globalization, but empirical evidence continues to illustrate the persistence of structures. Part of the criticisms against structural approaches is based on three misunderstandings: inability for (privileged) individuals to perceive the constraints of structures, structures as something static, and determinacy of structures. However, individuals' subjective experience of structures is not necessary for structures to exist. Structures do not necessary imply stability as even highly dynamic and changing systems can be based on structures. And the presence and influence of structures rarely determines completely the thoughts and actions of individuals. Despite the demonstrable social, economic, and political changes that modern (and all other societies) are experiencing, structures themselves continue to exist as they persist, adapt, or transmute. Modern questions about political structures should not be based on whether they exist but rather in what form and in which context they exist.

SEE ALSO *Class; Foucault, Michel; Globalization, Social and Economic Aspects of; Hierarchy; Inequality, Political; Mead, George Herbert; Modernization; Political Science; Postmodernism; Stratification; Structuralism; Weber, Max*

BIBLIOGRAPHY

Blau, Peter M., and Otis D. Duncan. 1967. *The American Occupational Structure*. New York: Wiley.

Bourdieu, Pierre. 1979. *La distinction: critique sociale du jugement*. Paris: Éditions de Minuit.

Erikson, Robert, and John H. Goldthorpe. 1992. *The Constant Flux: A Study of Class Mobility in Industrial Societies*. Oxford: Clarendon.

López, José, and John Scott. 2000. *Social Structure*. Philadelphia: Open University Press.

Verba, Sidney, Norman H. Nie, and Jae-on Kim. 1978. *Participation and Political Equality: A Seven-Nation Comparison*. Cambridge, U.K.: Cambridge University Press.

Wright, Erik Olin. 1997. *Class Counts: Comparative Studies in Class Analysis*. Cambridge, U.K. and New York: Cambridge University Press.

Manfred Max Bergman

STRATIFICATION, SOCIAL

SEE *Stratification*.

STREAM OF CONSCIOUSNESS

The science of psychology in large part investigates the activities of individuals and groups as they function in a social system. Many social scientists share the conviction that a psychological understanding requires not only systematic observation of behavior that occurs in a social context but also study of the mental life of the individuals involved. Human beings have access of a direct kind to part of their mental life. They are normally in a position to communicate to others a great deal of firsthand information concerning that part. Specifically they apprehend their own stream of consciousness as it is proceeding within them. William James (1842–1910) is one of the original creators of the science of psychology and is famous for the perspicacious account presented on the stream of consciousness in his masterwork *The Principles of Psychology* (1950 [1890]). The following is from James's *Talks to Teachers on Psychology: And to Students on Some of Life's Ideals* (1916 [1899]) and encapsulates his concept of the stream of consciousness:

> Now the *immediate* fact which psychology, the science of mind, has to study is also the most general fact. It is the fact that in each of us, when awake (and often when asleep), *some kind of consciousness is always going on*. There is a stream, a succession of states, or waves, or fields, (or of whatever you wish to call them), of knowledge, of feeling, of desire, of deliberation, etc., that constantly pass and repass, and that constitute our inner life. The existence of this stream is the primal fact, the nature and origin of it form the essential problem, of our science. (p. 15)

I spell out here James's concept of the stream of consciousness (cf. Natsoulas 1999, 2001) using interchangeably the terms *state of consciousness* and *consciousness state* for the basic durational components that James proposes to constitute the stream of consciousness one at a time in tight succession.

A consciousness state is generally an awareness of a number of items. It is no less an integral state given the number of its "objects." These include states of consciousness as well as, for example, environmental properties and bodily aspects of the individual. A highly recurrent feature of the mental life of humans is the direct apprehension of states of consciousness as they occur. James holds that this "inner awareness" is a matter of one consciousness state's having another consciousness state belonging to the same stream among its objects. It is impossible for a state of consciousness to be itself among the items it directly apprehends. James insists on the latter point notwithstanding his equally central thesis that a consciousness state commonly has many distinct objects. Not every consciousness state is an object of inner awareness. But such a state transpiring unbeknownst is no less a basic durational component of its stream. A sincere report of one's being unaware of x does not on its own entail that one did not experience a state of consciousness with x among its objects.

A stream of consciousness consists of momentary states of consciousness one after another in a series that subjectively seems tightly adjacent. Inner awareness does not detect any interruption in the flow of consciousness however long or brief it may be. Such a stoppage must subsequently be inferred to have taken place if it is to be known of at all. Some of James's remarks suggest that the stream of consciousness is continuous in the sense of expanding in the dimension of time through internal growth rather than by a series of external accretions. But I argue at length elsewhere that his more consistent view is that pulses of change in the brain yield pulses of mentality (Natsoulas 1992–1993). The latter series is proposed to be continuous. Each state directly follows upon the consciousness state right before it "with absolutely nothing in between" just as long as no "time-gap" intervenes. Such time-gaps do happen, according to James, owing to what is taking place in the brain. But they are not noticeable because consciousness totally ceases during any time-gap. In *The Principles of Psychology* James advances a dualist interactionist theory as to the relation of the mental to the physical (cf. Natsoulas, 2005). The brain generates the consciousness states, but they can in turn influence the ongoing physical process that produces them and thus indirectly affect the course that the stream of consciousness is taking. Yet no state constituting the stream is a state of the brain. Nor is any state of consciousness any kind of feature belonging intrinsically to the brain itself.

One's consciousness is at any moment comprised completely of a single consciousness state. This is James's (1950 [1890]) view with one exception. In the same individual a second consciousness may simultaneously flow, consisting of its own distinct states of consciousness (cf. James 1982 [1902]). Yet every state of consciousness is integral in the sense that each one of them is a unitary awareness, albeit usually possessing many objects but never compounded of distinct mental experiences or mental acts. James describes the individual complexity of the large majority of human states of consciousness (calling them "fields" and "states" interchangeably):

> The concrete fields are always complex. They contain sensations of our bodies and of the objects around us, memories of past experiences and thoughts of distant things, feelings of satisfaction and dissatisfaction, desires and aversions, and other emotional conditions, together with determinations of the will, in every variety and permutation and combination. In most of our concrete states of consciousness all these different classes of ingredients are found simultaneously present to some degree, though the relative proportion they bear to one another is very shifting. (1916 [1899], p. 17)

One should not understand these many ingredients of James's consciousness states to be separate mental acts as traditionally conceived of. They are not mutually distinct cases of someone's being aware of something. Any object of a state of consciousness is apprehended therein in relation to all other objects of that consciousness state. James's ingredients of the states of consciousness are (1) abstractions from individual concrete states that have them among their features, (2) features of how a consciousness state's multiple objects are apprehended altogether, and (3) nonexistent except in the form of features of states of consciousness. Thus an auditory or a visual experience does not exist except as an ingredient of one or more consciousness states (cf. Natsoulas 2001).

From James's standpoint references to someone's being aware of this or that is very likely to be misleading. It is not meant to imply that the experiential features of consciousness states have a subject or an ego who is aware. This is not to say that a stream of consciousness and all of the consciousness states involved are not someone's. Rather it is to maintain that the consciousness states themselves are the only location that there is of consciousness. Neither the brain nor any kind of spiritual entity is what experiences, thinks, feels, apprehends, or issues one's states of consciousness and is in that sense the source or agent of one's mental life. One's brain does indeed bring one's states of consciousness into existence, but it is aware of nothing at all including its doing so and the states it produces. James distinguishes the material self, the social self, and the spiritual self but identifies the spiritual self concretely with the stream of consciousness and not with any entity or operation external to the stream that causes it to be as it is or that oversees it or puts it to use. "The passing Thought [i.e., state of consciousness] itself is the only *verifiable* thinker" (James 1950 [1890], p. 346). It is states of consciousness in themselves that provide mental life with subjective temporal unity. They do so by appropriating immediately past consciousness states that are now objects of inner awareness and more distant consciousness states that are currently objects of remembrance.

Is James's understanding of the consciousness states consistent with its seeming firsthand that consciousness is a "fighter for ends"? That a state of consciousness has a certain goal or type of goal among its objects is owed directly to the brain state responsible for the consciousness state's occurrence. The influence of past states of consciousness is limited to their having reinforced or inhibited (furthered or checked) the ongoing brain process and thereby affected the course it was taking. A state of consciousness and its successors may come to intend some new goal but not as a consequence of their effects on how the ongoing brain process is proceeding. James asserts that a consciousness state can produce nothing absolutely new. But a consciousness state can help to maintain a certain goal as an object of the stream at the expense of alternative goals and to increase thereby the chance of related actions since the brain process determines such actions and is suitably affected.

Is the stream of consciousness illusory? James (1950 [1890]) raises this question himself as he discusses the spiritual self and concretely identifies the spiritual self to be no other than the stream of consciousness itself. From certain of his own introspective efforts James surmises that all one can know of oneself in an immediate rather than an inferential way is objective (e.g., bodily states) and requires perceptual observation. Consciousness states and the streams of which they are parts are not directly apprehended and therefore are inferred constructs. James sets this skeptical position aside for practical reasons and continues to use the deliverances of inner awareness as though he has no doubts. The following questions indicate what I believe is a better reason for his going on just as he does. How can James be aware of observing *x* if he has no inner awareness of any state of consciousness with *x* among its objects? Can James tell he is observing *x* by making behavioral observations? Would a certain piece of James's behavior give away to him or to others that he is observing *x*? But then how can anyone be aware of observing a piece of James's behavior if there cannot occur in anyone inner awareness of any consciousness state having that piece of behavior among its objects?

SEE ALSO *James, William; Psychotherapy*

BIBLIOGRAPHY

James, William. 1916. *Talks to Teachers on Psychology: And to Students on Some of Life's Ideals.* New York: Holt. (Orig. pub. 1899.)

James, William. 1950. *The Principles of Psychology.* New York: Dover. (Orig. pub. 1890.)

James, William. 1982. *The Varieties of Religious Experience.* Ed. Martin E. Marty. Harmondsworth, U.K.: Penguin. (Orig. pub. 1902.)

Natsoulas, Thomas. 1992–1993. The Stream of Consciousness: I. William James's Pulses. *Imagination, Cognition, and Personality* 12 (1): 3–21. (Series published 1992–2006 in same journal.)

Natsoulas, Thomas. 1998. On the Intrinsic Nature of States of Consciousness: James's Ubiquitous Feeling Aspect. *Review of General Psychology* 2 (2): 123–152.

Natsoulas, Thomas. 2001. On the Intrinsic Nature of States of Consciousness: Attempted Inroads from the First-Person Perspective. *Journal of Mind and Behavior* 22 (3): 219–248.

Natsoulas, Thomas. 2005. On the Intrinsic Nature of States of Consciousness: A Thesis of Neutral Monism Considered. *Journal of Mind and Behavior* 26 (4): 281–306.

Thomas Natsoulas

STREET CULTURE

A primary issue for urban sociologists is the disproportionate poverty in ghettoes, defined as parts of American cities that are composed of mostly poor African Americans. These economically and socially alienated communities often suffer from high rates of unemployment, crime, and drug use, creating images of these areas and their occupants that mask differences among residents and the structural conditions that affect them. Several studies have attempted to disentangle these issues by identifying systematic inequalities and the ways inner-city residents respond to them. Many note the integral role of street cultures in such neighborhoods, which help disadvantaged residents to cope with inner-city life by offering alternative methods for attaining social order.

In his 1999 ethnography, *Code of the Street*, Elijah Anderson argued that the problems of poor, inner-city black communities are exacerbated by deindustrialization, the outsourcing of jobs, the flight of the middle class, an ineffective law enforcement system, and a prominent underground economy. Anderson argued that these structural changes and the alienation they breed promote an oppositional culture whereby inner-city residents rely on the code of the street, or "a set of informal rules governing interpersonal public behavior, particularly violence" (p. 33) to distribute respect and ensure order. While this code provides residents with a mechanism to organize the community, its success relies on the use of violence to gain social status, creating a culture where the paths to money and respect reflect deviant lifestyles.

Anderson argued that within these neighborhoods, knowledge of the code becomes necessary for all individuals to maintain respect and ensure survival. Familiarity with the code holds whether individuals self-identify as *decent* individuals, or those who tend to hold mainstream values, or *street* individuals, or those who embrace and enforce the code and its use of violence. This requires decent people who do not fully embrace the code to be streetwise, or to engage the code to gain respect and to prevent challenges to their person or status. This may require individuals to challenge someone else's power by taking that person's belongings or through physical attack or to display material possessions, which suggests that they not only have money but also that they are willing to defend it. Such issues are particularly salient for adolescents who must negotiate their identities within public spaces, making them vulnerable to stereotyping by people who live outside these neighborhoods and who are unable to distinguish between residents who engage the code only when necessary and those who always live by it.

As an oppositional culture, the code of the street also has implications for cultural forms created in urban spaces such as hip-hop and rap music. As Mark Anthony Neal suggested in his 2004 article, "Up from Hustling: Power, Plantations, and the Hip-Hop Mogul," in its onset, hip-hop and rap music offered a critical voice capable of accurately portraying the black urban experience and affecting social change within these impoverished neighborhoods. Over time, however, these musical forms have been transformed into a mainstream and stylized version of black culture that no longer resembles the ghetto public it sought to represent. Neal suggested that, "what is bought and sold in the open market of commodified blackness is anything but authentic, but rather stylized perceptions of black life, packaged for mass consumption" (p. 166). This hip-hop image, which glorifies excessive consumerism, the underground drug economy, and misogynistic practices, fails to affect social change in the ways originally envisioned by hip-hop artists. Instead, these images influence public policies aimed at monitoring black urban youth, providing justifications for further discrimination against impoverished inner-city residents and legitimizing the oppositional culture posed by the code.

While previous works, such as Elliot Liebow's 1967 ethnography, *Tally's Corner*, have reached similar conclusions to Anderson's thesis regarding the role of the street corner in redefining limited life chances, they have also been critiqued for their emphasis on oppositional culture, which suggests that in certain ways, poor, inner-city blacks contribute to their own blocked mobility. Many urban researchers have reached alternative conclusions in studies of inner-city black communities, suggesting instead that street cultures are integral resources used by disadvantaged residents to enhance their abilities to achieve middle-class status. For instance, in his 1980 book, *Alley Life in Washington*, James Borchert wrote that, following the Civil War (1861–1865), alley residents developed invaluable community networks that allowed them to survive through periods of intense urbanization and institutionalized racism. These ideas have also been noted in international works such as Steve Hall, Simon Winlow, and Craig Ancrum's 2005 article, "Radgies, Gangstas, and Mugs: Imaginary Criminal Identities in the Twilight of the Pseudo-Pacification Process." In their study of British, lower-class males, they found that these individuals do not engage in violence and criminality to resist normalization, but instead, to enhance their life chances. Studies such as these suggest that while street cultures have formed in various times and spaces, they do not always exhibit subcultural or oppositional characteristics, providing opportunities for further research that delineates the structural, spatial, and individual relations between street cultures and mainstream values.

SEE ALSO *Anthropology, Urban; Culture; Culture of Poverty; Culture, Low and High; Ethnography;*

Ethnomethodology; Sociology; Sociology, Urban; Tally's Corner

BIBLIOGRAPHY

Anderson, Elijah. 1999. *Code of the Street: Decency, Violence, and the Moral Life of the Inner City*. New York: W. W. Norton.

Borchert, James. 1980. *Alley Life in Washington: Family, Community, Religion, and Folklife in the City, 1850–1970*. Chicago: University of Illinois Press.

Hall, Steve, Simon Winlow, and Craig Ancrum. 2005. Radgies, Gangstas, and Mugs: Imaginary Criminal Identities in the Twilight of the Pseudo-Pacification Process. *Social Justice* 32 (1): 100–112.

Liebow, Elliot. 1967. *Tally's Corner*. Boston: Little, Brown.

Neal, Mark Anthony. 2004. Up From Hustling: Power, Plantations, and the Hip-Hop Mogul. *Socialism and Democracy* 18 (2): 157–182.

M. Bess Vincent

STRESS

Stress is often used to describe overwhelming or threatening situations or the pressure that human beings encounter when experiencing such circumstances. The American physiologist Walter Cannon introduced the term stress in 1929 as an acute emergency reaction that could help the organism mobilize energy for fight-or-flight responses in dangerous situations. In 1936, the Austrian-born Canadian endocrinologist Hans Selye first used the term stress when describing threatening conditions capable of producing chronic changes in the homeostatic balance of an organism if lasting long enough. It is now known that stress and stressor exposure can elicit a complex array of physiological changes. Stress can be physical or psychological, controllable or uncontrollable, acute or chronic, and the word stress is often used imprecisely referring either to a stressor or a stress response.

Originally, the main stressors for human beings related to physical injury, predators, and starvation. Acute physical stressors required emergency reactions helping the organism mobilize energy for fight-or-flight responses, that is, physiological reactions that prepare an individual for the strenuous efforts required by fighting or running away. Threatening situations usually call for vigorous activity, and the autonomic and endocrine responses that accompany them help mobilize the body's energy responses. During emergencies, the sympathetic branch of the autonomic nervous system is activated to help mediate arousal, activation, and mobilization. The activated sympathetic nervous system speeds up the heart rate and diverts blood flow to the muscles, and the adrenal glands release epinephrine.

This type of acute mobilization of biological resources is clearly advantageous during short-term physical emergencies. In the contemporary world, however, people often react in this acute manner to stressor exposure that does not involve life-endangering situations. When encountering psychological or social stressors, the same physiological responses may be activated, which is likely not adaptive or appropriate. For example, the acute stress response can occur in relation to academic exams, traffic jams, relationship breakups, family feuds, or simply worrisome situations. Such activations are likely harmless in the short term but can potentially be harmful when chronically provoked. Physiological reactions to stressor exposure are also often accompanied by psychological reactions such as anxiety, worry, anger, inability to relax, and poor concentration, which again may be harmless in the short term but potentially detrimental in the long run.

SOURCES OF STRESS

The sources of stress can be infinite. Research has often focused on major life events, job-related stress, daily hassles, environmental stress, and sociocultural factors as sources of stress, among others. Major life events such as changing careers, getting married, or losing a loved one can entail a serious challenge. Such events luckily rarely occur, but everyday hassles such as having car trouble, getting to work late, missing a deadline, or having to run in order to catch the bus can obviously happen more frequently. Environmental stress such as pollution, noise, or natural disasters can also take its toll on people, as can job-related stress such as an unhappy boss, a manipulating co-worker, or simply a stressful and demanding working environment.

Because of evidence that stress responses are specific and may vary based on how a particular stressor is perceived, researchers have proposed models highlighting the interaction of biological and psychological factors in health and illness. One such model, the diathesis-stress model, proposes that two continuously interacting factors jointly determine an individual's susceptibility to stress and illness. One factor involves predisposing (diathesis) factors establishing a person's vulnerability to illness, for example, genetic vulnerability, and the other involves precipitating factors from the environment, such as traumatic experiences. The diathesis-stress model highlights the fact that different people have different vulnerabilities, resulting in possible health consequences because of stress combined with diathesis. Other models have proposed that how people perceive themselves and the stressor at hand may impact how they react mentally as well as physiologically when exposed to stressors. For example, if a stressor is perceived as a serious threat, this will elicit more complex reactions than if the stressor is perceived as a daily event. Another model, the stress-buffering model, posits that certain factors, such as individual differences or social support, may protect, or "buffer," people from the impact of stressful events. In this model, individuals under stress with little or no social support, for example, experience negative health effects, whereas the negative effects of stress for individuals with high levels of social support are reduced or eliminated. Clearly, a number of factors can affect how people perceive and react to stressor exposure.

IMPACT ON HEALTH

Stressors are part of daily life. However, when energy is constantly mobilized at the cost of energy storage, one can never store any surplus energy. If stressor exposure is long term or overtaxes coping resources, stress can have adverse impact on health. For example, the long-term effects of prolonged secretion of glucocorticoids have been shown to involve increased blood pressure, damage to muscle tissue, growth inhibition, and suppression of the immune system. Research has also found links between stressor exposure and physiological health issues such as heart disease and cancer. This is not to say that stress causes heart disease or cancer; it is possible, however, that prolonged stressor exposure may be a contributing factor in the development of a number of physiological problems. Research has also found an effect on wound healing: Studies have found, for example, that stressor exposure can slow the healing of wounds significantly (Glaser et al. 1999), which supports the hypothesis that prolonged stressor exposure may suppress the immune system.

Stressor exposure may also contribute to psychological disorders such as post-traumatic stress disorder (PTSD). PTSD is caused by exposure to a situation of extreme danger and stress, such as acts of war, assault, injury, death of a loved one, and so on. Symptoms of PTSD include recurrent dreams or recollections, and the disorder can interfere with social activities and produce a feeling of hopelessness. Research has also indicated a link between stress and depression, as stress and glucocorticoids appear to be intertwined with the biology of depression. Sympathetic arousal is a relative marker of anxiety and vigilance, while heavy secretion of glucocorticoids is more a marker of depression, and statistically, people who are undergoing significant life stressors are more likely to become depressed, and people who are depressed are more likely to have undergone a recent significant stressor. Symptoms of PTSD as well as depression are often treated with medication to adjust the serotonin and/or epinephrine systems, either alone or in combination with some form of psychotherapy. PTSD and depression can also be treated with some form of psychotherapy alone.

Despite the impact that stressors can have on health, research has not established a clear connection between stressor exposure and health-related issues. In fact, when exposed to the same type of stressor, one person might get sick while another will not. Apparently, stress and the consequences of stress may arise from how people appraise the events rather than from the events themselves. How people appraise and cope with stressor exposure may again depend on factors such as individual differences, coping styles, perception of control, and social support. Individual differences such as dispositional optimism and explanatory style have been linked to better psychological and physiological adjustment to stressors. Dispositional optimists generally expect positive outcomes in life, while explanatory style refers to a person's general propensity to always attribute outcomes either to positive or negative causes. A person's resilience may also impact how stressors are perceived and met. Resiliency often refers to a person's ability to develop coping strategies despite being in a difficult situation or the ability to bounce back when bad things happen. In general, it appears that people who see stressors as challenges to be overcome rather than insurmountable problems tend to cope with stressors in the most adaptive way.

COPING STYLES AND STRATEGIES

Coping usually refers to the cognitive, behavioral, or emotional way that people deal with stressful situations and is seen as a dynamic process involving a series of responses entailing the interaction of a person and the environment. In general, coping styles that approach the problem in order to deal with it have been found to be more adaptive than coping styles avoiding the problem. People with a strong sense of personal control are also more likely to engage in adaptive problem-focused coping. Personal control is the belief that people make their own decisions and also that an individual determines what others do to that person or what the person does him- or herself. The opportunity to control aversive events or the belief that aversive events can be controlled may play a crucial role in determining how a person might react during stressor exposure.

The degrees of social support people receive or perceive may also play an important role in how people cope with stressors. Social support is the companionship of others and the emotional or practical support of others. Research has shown social support to be important for faster recovery and fewer medical complications from surgery or illness, for lower mortality rates, for less distress in the face of terminal illness, and for reduced vulnerability to illness and mortality. It appears that people's outcome expectancies, their coping strategies, their sense of control, and their perceived or actual social support act as factors

in how they appraise stressors or as buffers against the impact of the stressor exposure.

Stress appears to be an unavoidable part of life in the contemporary world. Stressor exposure is not necessarily harmful; nevertheless, depending on the characteristics of the stressor, the length of exposure, individual differences, and coping strategies, stressors may have adverse physiological and psychological impacts on a person's life.

SEE ALSO *Coping; Diathesis-Stress Model; Hypertension; Life Events, Stress; Optimism/Pessimism; Psychoneuroimmunology; Psychosomatics, Social; Resiliency; Stress-Buffering Model; Trauma*

BIBLIOGRAPHY

Cannon, Walter B. 1929. *Bodily Changes in Pain, Hunger, Fear, and Rage. An Account of Recent Researches into the Function of Emotional Excitement.* 2nd edition. New York: D. Appleton.

Carver, Charles S., and Michael F. Scheier. 1998. *On the Self-Regulation of Behavior.* Cambridge, U.K.: Cambridge University Press.

Glaser, Ronald, Janice K. Kiecolt-Glaser, Philip T. Marucha, et al. 1999. Stress-Related Changes in Proinflammatory Cytokine Production in Wounds. *Archives of General Psychiatry* 56 (May): 450-456.

Lazarus, Richard S. 1990. Stress, Coping, and Illness. In *Personality and Disease*, ed. Howard S. Friedman, 97–120. New York: Wiley.

Rabin, Bruce S. 1999. *Stress, Immune Function, and Health: The Connection.* New York: Wiley-Liss.

Sapolsky, Robert M. 2004. *Why Zebras Don't Get Ulcers.* 3rd edition. New York: Times Books.

Segerstrom, Suzanne C. 2000. Personality and the Immune System: Models, Methods, and Mechanisms. *Annals of Behavioral Medicine* 22 (3): 180–190.

Segerstrom, Suzanne C., and Gregory E. Miller. 2004. Psychological Stress and the Human Immune System: A Meta-analytic Study of Thirty Years of Inquiry. *Psychological Bulletin* 130 (4): 601–630.

Selye, Hans, A. 1936. A Syndrome Produced by Diverse Nocuous Agents. *Nature* 138: 32.

Lise Solberg Nes

STRESS-BUFFERING MODEL

The concept of the *stress-buffering model* is that certain resources help to reduce the impact of negative life events on an individual's health status. An accumulation of adverse occurrences can be related to health problems, but life stress may have less effect among people who have more psychosocial resources. In this sense, the resource serves as an insulating factor, or *buffer*, between the stressors and the disease outcome, so that people who have more resources are less affected by stress.

Stress is typically measured by the number of major negative events that a person has experienced in the past year. These include events such as loss of a loved one or experiencing severe financial difficulty. Job strains, in an occupation in which demands are high but control is low, can serve as a stressor, and criminal victimization (assault or theft) can be quite distressing. High levels of stress have been linked to anxiety, depression, and physical health problems in studies of general populations, but buffering resources can reduce the relation between stress and disease.

One type of stress-buffering agent is *social support*. Social support can be defined as resources provided by others that help a person to cope better with problems. Research has shown that persons with more social support are less affected (or unaffected) by negative life events. Supportive relationships contribute to well-being because they provide a source of intimacy, acceptance, and confiding about emotions (emotional support), which provides buffering effects across a broad range of life stressors. Supportive persons may also offer useful advice and guidance (informational support). By providing such resources, personal relationships help to reduce the impact of stress on depression and anxiety. Some studies have also suggested that social support can provide buffering effects that reduce the risk of mortality from cardiovascular disease or cancer.

Personality characteristics also may serve as a stress-buffering resource. For example, a personality complex termed *hardiness* has been found to provide buffering effects. Hardiness is defined as scoring high on attributes of commitment (being involved with other people rather than detached or alienated), control (taking control over one's decisions and actions, rather than passivity and powerlessness), and challenge (the ability to tolerate uncertainty and see life events as a challenge rather than a threat). Persons who score higher on hardiness show less illness at high levels of stress, compared with persons low on hardiness. Thus individuals who score higher on this personality complex are more resistant to stress.

An implication of the stress-buffering model is that interventions to enhance available social support or to teach persons positive attitudes about commitment, control, and challenge can help make persons less vulnerable to negative events. Such interventions can be conducted in school, clinic, or community settings so as to improve people's coping ability and thereby improve the mental and physical health of the population.

SEE ALSO Anxiety; Coping; Psychosomatics, Social; Stress

BIBLIOGRAPHY

Ouellette, Suzanne C., and Joanne DiPlacido. 2001. Personality's Role in the Protection and Enhancement of Health. In *Handbook of Health Psychology*, eds. Andrew Baum, Tracey E. Revenson, and Jerome E. Singer, 175–193. Mahwah, NJ: Erlbaum.

Wills, Thomas Ashby, and Marnie Filer. 2001. Social Networks and Social Support. In *Handbook of Health Psychology*, eds. Andrew Baum, Tracey E. Revenson, and Jerome E. Singer, 209–234. Mahwah, NJ: Erlbaum.

Thomas Ashby Wills
Don Mendoza

STRIKES
SEE *Unions.*

STRONG AXIOM OF REVEALED PREFERENCE
SEE *Revealed Preference.*

STRONG SEPARABILITY
SEE *Separability.*

STRUCTURAL ADJUSTMENT

Developing or emerging market economies may face periods of severe economic instability. This may involve a stagnant or declining economy, perhaps accompanied by high rates of inflation, a falling currency, and unsustainable foreign debt obligations. In these circumstances and often as a last resort, member countries may look for financial support from the world's two main multilateral aid and financial institutions, the World Bank and the International Monetary Fund (IMF).

Financial support from these institutions often requires the successful negotiation of a structural adjustment loan (SAL) with the member country. These loan programs link disbursements of funds to the meeting of specified conditions (performance criteria) through the implementation of a combination of economic policy reform measures. The International Monetary Fund allows member countries to borrow, subject to agreed-upon conditions, on their economic policies. The IMF has always had conditions on their loans, but since 1982 the number of these loans has expanded. Similarly, the World Bank pays a great deal of attention to helping countries improve their economic policies. In 1980 the World Bank began to make structural adjustment loans that carried conditions on economic policies—so-called adjustment lending. A significant part of its lending was for structural adjustment, namely loans to support reforms rather than specific investments.

The IMF and World Bank made 958 adjustment loans to developing countries between 1980 and 1998. Argentina alone was the recipient of thirty adjustment loans during this period. While these loans are often negotiated in the context of economic crisis and attempt to restore balance of payments viability and macroeconomic stability, they are geared to increasing international competitiveness and improving economic efficiency in the use of domestic resources—the term *Washington Consensus* is often associated with this reform package.

Often the country in crisis faces considerable economic turmoil and may have no option but to accept painful economic remedies in order to receive external funding. This may involve a menu of higher interest rates, government spending cuts and higher taxes, and the abolition of various subsidies on consumption items. These policies are unlikely to be popular, and so the programs are extremely controversial. The SALs often include trade liberalization measures that place fewer restrictions on foreign trade. These measures include reducing or abolishing tariffs and quotas on imports, a less restrictive stance toward foreign investment, a more realistic exchange rate, and capital account liberalization that reduces controls on capital flows across national boundaries. The internal market-oriented structural reforms promote deregulation of domestic markets and the privatization of government enterprises.

THE EFFECTIVENESS OF STRUCTURAL ADJUSTMENT PROGRAMS

Restoring macroeconomic stability in times of crisis is critical. Indeed the ability to restore and maintain macroeconomic stability in the face of often-turbulent external conditions is one of the most important factors accounting for the diversity of economic performance in the developing world. The effectiveness of SALs in achieving this objective is a hotly debated issue. In his 2001 book, *The Elusive Quest for Growth*, William Easterly notes that

> "In the 1980s, the World Bank and the IMF gave an average of six adjustment loans to each country in Africa, an average of five adjustment loans to each country in Latin America, an average of four adjustment loans to each country in Asia, and an

average of three adjustment loans to each country in Eastern Europe, North Africa and the Middle East. The operation was a success for everyone except the patient. There was much lending, little adjustment, and little growth in the 1980s and 1990s. The per capita growth rate of the typical developing country between 1980 and 1998 was zero." (pp. 102–103)

Some studies even suggest that a higher IMF loan-participation rate reduces economic growth and conclude that the typical country would be better off economically if it committed itself *not* to be involved with IMF loan programs.

A number of concerns arise about the effectiveness of SALs. One issue relates to the speed of the structural adjustment required. Should all of these policies be implemented immediately or only gradually? Governments may stall in implementing the required policies, use creative financial accounting to avoid real adjustment, or reverse the policies once the program is over. A second issue relates to the sequencing of structural reforms. Many commentators point to the crucial role of foreign capital inflow during the structural reform period to reduce the frictions that will emerge during the transition. It may be preferable, however, that controls on foreign capital be relaxed only after trade and other industrial-sector distortions have been dismantled. The reason for this is that capital inflow will result in a real exchange rate appreciation that disadvantages exporters. Meanwhile, the tariff reductions will disadvantage domestic producers facing lower-priced imports.

Privatization policies as part of a SAL have also been questioned, particularly in the transitional economies of eastern Europe. Public assets may be sold off below their real value in order to find a buyer and to generate quick cash flow, with a loss of public accountability. Privatization might also mean that income-generating assets are sold, leaving behind all the residual "unproductive" activities, plus a new layer of watchdog agencies to regulate the newly privatized activities.

In the context of the 1997 Asian financial crisis, further debate escalated on the effectiveness of SALs, particularly the financial deregulation requirements. In this context the views of Joseph Stiglitz have been well publicized, particularly his stinging condemnation of the response of the IMF and the U.S. Treasury to the Asian crisis in his 2002 book, *Globalization and Its Discontents*. Stiglitz rails against the IMF's "market fundamentalism," its "one-size-fits-all" approach to crisis management, and "its mistakes in sequencing and pacing, and the failure to be sensitive to the broader social context" (p. 73). Rescue packages were overly contractionary and pushed the economies deeper into recession. Inadequate attention was given to the social dimensions of the crisis. In particular, greater efforts were needed to ensure food security and preserve the purchasing power of vulnerable households. Finally, there was a lack of appreciation of the potential for irreversible social breakdown in the midst of economic crisis, with rising ethnic and factional violence. The impacts of SALs on social sectors and the poor have been particularly troublesome, and the IMF and World Bank have incorporated social safety nets into their programs (Cornia, Jolly, and Stewart 1987–1988).

The IMF has staunchly defended the economic policies that it recommended to the crisis-affected countries of Asia. It argues that the causes of the crisis were internal or homegrown, reflecting underlying structural distortions and macroeconomic imbalances. The use of high interest rates on a temporary basis was essential to correct the excessive competitive devaluations in the crisis countries. Insolvent financial institutions had to be closed down and belt-tightening was essential. The IMF notes that the recoveries of some of these countries point to the effectiveness of its policy advice.

One of the interesting empirical findings relating to the effectiveness of SALs is that the results often depend on the characteristics of the specific country concerned. Countries have generated a variety of responses to basically similar SALs. This seems to reflect the importance of differences in institutional, social, and historical conditions between countries (Taylor 1988).

A REASSESSMENT

The disappointing response to repeated structural adjustment lending has led to much soul searching. At the IMF, poverty reduction and growth facilities have replaced structural adjustment loans. Reducing the microeconomic interventions and concentrating on core macroeconomic concerns have streamlined conditionality. There is also now a focus on pro-poor growth and social safety nets. There was a perceived need to move beyond Washington Consensus policies to so-called second-generation reforms, following the growing recognition that market-oriented policies may be inadequate without more serious institutional transformation. The expectations placed on lending to developing countries conditional on their making policy reforms proved unrealistic. There is a growing recognition that structural adjustment should promote growth and capacity expansion and not just efficiency. The recommendation now is for a more strategic focus, concentrating on the key barriers to growth, rather than employing a scattergun approach to abolishing all market distortions.

SEE ALSO *Liberalization, Trade; Privatization; Washington Consensus*

BIBLIOGRAPHY

Corbo, Vittorio, Morris Goldstein, and Mohsin Khan, eds. 1987. *Growth-Oriented Adjustment Programs.* Washington, DC: International Monetary Fund and World Bank.

Cornia, Giovanni Andrea, Richard Jolly, and Frances Stewart, eds. 1987–1988. *Adjustment with a Human Face.* 2 vols. Oxford: Clarendon Press.

Easterly, William. 2001. *The Elusive Quest for Growth: Economists' Adventures and Misadventures in the Tropics.* Cambridge, MA: MIT Press.

Stiglitz, Joseph. 2002. *Globalization and Its Discontents.* London: Allen Lane.

Taylor, Lance. 1988. *Varieties of Stabilization Experience: Towards Sensible Macroeconomics in the Third World.* Oxford: Clarendon Press.

John Lodewijks

STRUCTURAL EQUATION MODELS

Structural equation modeling (SEM) is a general method for modeling systems of effects among three or more variables. Structural equation models can vary greatly in complexity. At its base, SEM is an extension of linear regression (or, linear regression is a special case of SEM) in which a number of regression equations are solved simultaneously. This process allows for the explicit modeling of many quantities not typically a part of linear regression, including the covariances (or absence thereof) among predictors, the residual variances of the endogenous (predicted) variables, and measurement error in both the exogenous and endogenous variables.

COMPONENTS OF A STRUCTURAL EQUATION MODEL

A full structural equation model consists of a measurement part and a structural part. It is the measurement part that allows for the modeling of measurement error. As in factor analysis, the modeler typically assumes that some latent construct is measured by its influence on one or more (usually at least three, for model identification purposes) observed variables. A latent construct is some unmeasured, and perhaps unmeasurable, variable of substantive interest. In a traditional measurement model, the latent construct is established by its effects on the observed indicator variables; for example, self-esteem as a construct might be measured by several items on a questionnaire covering a range of related content. Each item is modeled as being fully determined by two quantities: the self-esteem latent construct and an item-specific residual, or disturbance, usually considered uncorrelated with the residuals of the other items and other variables in the model. Thus, the observed covariances among the items are fully determined by their common cause, the latent construct; alternatively, the latent construct is defined by that portion of the variance of the indicators that is in common.

MEASUREMENT MODELS

Such a model, with one or more latent constructs, each with its own indicators, can stand by itself as a *confirmatory factor analysis* (CFA). CFA is a special case of SEM. In CFA, the measurement models for the constructs of interest are estimated, and the covariances among the constructs are freely estimated; that is, there are no hypothesized constraints on relations among the latent constructs. Importantly, these covariances are estimated incorporating correction for measurement error. As the latent variable is that variance which is common among the observed indicators, the indicator-specific residual variances (error) have been removed from consideration. Many social science researchers conduct a CFA on their data before moving to a full structural equation model.

A CFA is distinct from an *exploratory factor analysis* (EFA) in that, for CFA, the latent constructs are conceptualized a priori, as are the patterns of relations between constructs and indicators. EFA is statistically very similar to CFA but has a different purpose. If the researcher does not have an a priori model, or, perhaps, the CFA results in a poor fit to the data, EFA might be used. In EFA, all observed indicators are modeled as having been caused by all latent constructs (of a number specified by the researcher, often based on empirical aspects of the data), with only certain identifying restrictions. In contrast, most CFAs in the social sciences model each indicator as being caused by exactly one latent construct (though there is no statistical necessity to do this), resulting in a more clear definition of the latent construct. Latent constructs in EFA can be more difficult to describe, as the description is determined by the researcher's interpretation of the pattern of loadings (regression coefficients) relating each indicator to the construct.

STRUCTURAL MODELS

The second part of a full structural equation model is the structural part: the model of the relations among the latent constructs. Each construct can be modeled as having multiple effects on and/or multiple causes from other constructs. Thus, each endogenous, or downstream, construct is the outcome variable in a multiple regression equation and may well be a predictor variable in one or more multiple regression equations for other outcomes. These relations are typically represented pictorially in a diagram with directional arrows representing modeled effects, and curved, bidirectional arrows representing covariances among the exogenous variables (as in path analysis; indeed, path analysis is a special case of SEM in which there is no measurement model, for the constructs of interest are the measured variables). In most cases, all the exogenous variables are modeled with all possible correlations among them represented. A failure to include such a correlation would in effect be a hypothesis that that correlation equals zero, which is rarely applicable to exogenous variables. Observed variables (indicators) are usually diagrammed as labeled rectangles, latent variables as ovals.

As in the measurement part, residual variance is explicitly modeled. In all but rare cases, each endogenous variable has an exogenous disturbance associated with it— a latent variable that is the "cause" (actually the pooled causes) of all variance not determined by the regression relations.

MODEL ESTIMATION

When the full model has been established, the next step is to estimate the coefficients for each covariance, effect, and loading (the measurement coefficients). Each effect and loading estimate is a partial regression coefficient: the regression of the specified endogenous variable on the specified "upstream" variable, controlling for the other variables that have effects leading to the endogenous variable. And thus the coefficients are interpretable as partial regression coefficients: the change in the downstream variable per unit change in the upstream variable, holding all other variables constant. Certain hypotheses involving the path coefficients can be tested as in regression, such as the null hypothesis that the path coefficient equals zero, which is tested by the ratio of the coefficient to its standard error.

Structural equation modeling software routinely calculates a number of indices of fit of the model. A fitted model allows for the calculation, from the various path coefficients and estimated variances, covariances, and residual covariances, of a model-implied variance/covariance matrix of the original variables—that is, a covariance matrix that is consistent with the fitted model. Broadly speaking, the fit of the model is an assessment of how well the model, with its estimated coefficients, implies a covariance matrix that matches the original matrix from the data. If there is no significant discrepancy, as measured by a chi-squared statistic, then it may be concluded that the path model is consistent with the data. Note that this does not necessarily indicate that the model is an accurate depiction of causation in reality, but only that it is not inconsistent with reality as indicated by the covariance matrix.

There has been, however, much debate over the utility of the chi-squared statistic. It is widely agreed that, assuming an adequate sample size, a nonsignificant chi-square results in a failure to reject the model. However, there may be cases where the chi-squared statistic is sensitive to small deviations between the actual and implied covariance matrices that are not of practical importance to the researcher; this is especially true when the sample size is large. As a result, numerous statistics have been developed to assess approximate or close fit. Among the more prominent of these are the comparative fit index, the Tucker-Lewis index, and the root mean squared error of approximation.

HYPOTHESIS TESTING

The test of model fit is one of the primary results of estimating a model. Other hypotheses of interest in SEM frequently involve constraints on the structural coefficients: for example, that two coefficients are equal to each other, or that a set of three coefficients are all equal to zero. These can readily be tested in structural equation modeling software by the estimation of *nested models*. In this situation, the fit of a full model (without the constraints) is compared with a restricted model (with the constraints applied in the estimation process). Two such models are nested if the restricted model can be created strictly by imposing constraints on the full model. If the full model fits the data well, then the difference between the chi-squared statistics for the two models is itself distributed as a chi-squared statistic, with degrees of freedom equal to the number of constraints applied. A significant chi-squared statistic indicates that the restricted model fits significantly less well than the full model.

SEE ALSO *Factor Analysis; Hypothesis and Hypothesis Testing; Hypothesis, Nested; Least Squares, Ordinary; Linear Regression; Linear Systems; Methods, Quantitative; Nonlinear Regression; Nonlinear Systems; Regression; Regression Analysis; Statistics in the Social Sciences*

BIBLIOGRAPHY

Bollen, Kenneth A. 1989. *Structural Equations with Latent Variables.* New York: Wiley.

Loehlin, John C. 1998. *Latent Variable Models: An Introduction to Factor, Path, and Structural Analysis.* 2nd ed. Hillsdale, NJ: Erlbaum.

Marsh, Herbert W., and John Balla. 1994. Goodness of Fit in Confirmatory Factor Analysis: The Effects of Sample Size and Model Parsimony. *Quality and Quantity* 28: 185–217.

Patrick S. Malone

STRUCTURAL TRANSFORMATION

There is considerable debate across and even within theoretical perspectives and social science disciplines as to the nature of "social structures." Nonetheless, there is also general consensus that structures are more or less fixed aspects of social life that cannot be significantly altered by isolated actions. The division of labor, modes of production, state institutions, and even aspects of symbolic culture, such as language, can all be seen as structures that individuals face as fixed, stable, and resistant to change. Nonetheless, as William Sewell (1992), among others, has pointed out, too often social-scientific notions of structure reify such social forms, implying their domination of agency and their imperviousness to change. Permanent and unmoving as they may seem from any given time or vantage point, structures are far from immutable. Instances of macrosocial change in the foundations or basic architecture of any given social form, and in the patterns of agency associated with that form, are often referred to as structural transformations. The term is too widely and loosely used in the social sciences to give it a precise, comprehensive meaning, but it is possible to speak of some prevalent usages.

Perhaps most famously, Jürgen Habermas wrote of the "structural transformation of the public sphere." Habermas identifies a moment in the histories of Britain, France, and Germany in which there developed public arenas for rational political debate (at least among middle-class men) within emerging democratic cultures. These arenas effectively mediated between private life and the state, cultivating both critical rational discourse among participants and a forum for ideas and debate as to how democratic governance could be achieved. Habermas identifies several key social processes that undermined and transformed the public sphere into something quite different, including the tremendous growth in the size and scale of the public sphere that accompanied democratization, the blurring of the lines between private and public that accompanied the growth of the welfare state, and the development of political parties, professionalized politicians, and a mass media oriented toward marketing rather than public debate.

Habermas's work on the public sphere has sparked a lively literature on the nature of democratic processes, rational discourse, and communication in modern societies. Among others influenced by Habermas, for example, Craig Calhoun (2006) has argued that higher education is currently undergoing a structural transformation characterized by skyrocketing costs, the marginalization of teaching, and the shift in focus from public goods production to private goods distribution, with dramatic consequences for the role of higher educational institutions in the economy and public life. Calhoun identifies three key processes fostering this transformation: (1) the massive increase in the size and scope of universities, which has, among other things, intensified status-driven enrollment competition; (2) declining public funding; and (3) related trends toward privatization, most obviously in the rapidly intensifying pursuit of intellectual property revenues.

In addition to Habermas's and Calhoun's identification of rapid increases in social scale (we might also include Max Weber's account of the rise of bureaucratic organization as a transformative response to this problem of size), other key processes seen as primary contributors to structural transformations involve the intermixing of different kinds of people and the development of new modes of economic, political, and cultural activity. Contemporary observers may connect such social changes to globalization, but of course this is not a uniquely modern phenomenon. Anthropologists speak of the structural transformation of linguistic communities (Silverstein 1998) and hunter-gatherer institutions (Riches 1995) as sometimes wrought by confrontations of new peoples in contexts of exploration, migration, and war.

Economists, of course, are most closely associated with the transformations of economic structures. Used in this context, the term is most often understood to involve the change from one sort of economic production system to another, perhaps most prominently the change from an agriculturally based economy to an industrial one or from a nonmarket to a market-based economy (Johnston 1970; Gollin et al. 2002). The processes involved in such shifts are too numerous, complex, and contested to be discussed here, potentially arising from a host of economic (e.g., the rise of national and international markets, the influence of the International Monetary Fund), political (e.g., elections, revolutions, and wars), and cultural factors (e.g., the rise of the "Protestant ethic"). Nonetheless, such changes, as with other sorts of structural transformations, are commonly seen as having massive consequences for the societies and individuals experiencing them, not the least of which are a fundamentally altered division of labor and the social mobility system. Out of such transformations, new patterns of social relations and social forms arise that condition social action in various but profound ways.

SEE ALSO *Anthropology; Bureaucracy; Development Economics; Development, Rural; Economics; Habermas, Jürgen; Industrialization; Market Economy; Urbanization; Weber, Max*

BIBLIOGRAPHY

Calhoun, Craig. 2006. Is the University in Crisis? *Society* (May/June): 8–18.

Gollin, Douglas, Stephen Parente, and Richard Rogerson. 2002. The Role of Agriculture in Development. *American Economic Review* 92 (2): 160–164.

Habermas, Jürgen. 1989. *The Structural Transformation of the Public Sphere: An Inquiry into a Category of Bourgeois Society*. Trans. Frank Burger with Frederick Lawrence. Cambridge, MA: MIT Press.

Johnston, Bruce F. 1970. Agriculture and Structural Transformation in Developing Countries: A Survey of Research. *Journal of Economic Research* 8 (2): 369–404.

Riches, David. 1995. Hunter-Gatherer Structural Transformations. *Journal of the Royal Anthropological Institute* 1 (4): 679–701.

Sewell, William, Jr. 1992. A Theory of Structure: Duality, Agency, and Transformation. *American Journal of Sociology* 98 (1): 1–29.

Silverstein, Michael. 1998. Contemporary Transformations of Linguistic Communities. *Annual Review of Anthropology* 27: 401–426.

Kent Redding

STRUCTURALISM

Structuralism is the theoretical position that finds meaning in the relation between things, rather than in things in isolation. In other words, it gives primacy to pattern over substance. To take a crude example, the colors red, green, and amber take on the meanings "stop," "go," and "caution" in relation to each other, in the context of a traffic light. In some other context, and in opposition to other colors, red may mean something completely different, such as socialism or communism, or humanity or sacrifice. Such meanings may be either part of a universal pattern or culturally determined.

SAUSSURE AND EARLY APPROACHES IN LINGUISTICS

Structuralism began in linguistics and spread to anthropology, philosophy, literary criticism, and other fields. Its founder was Ferdinand de Saussure (1857–1913), a Swiss linguist who wanted to move beyond the historical interests that dominated his field in the early twentieth century. Although the work he published during his lifetime was entirely in the historical tradition, he left behind lectures given between 1906 and 1911 that set the scene for a new synchronic, structural analysis of language. These were published posthumously as the *Course in General Linguistics* (1916).

In the *Course*, Saussure made four distinctions which are now commonplace both in language studies and in many social sciences. The most important is the distinction between synchronic (at the same time) and diachronic (through time). His own interest in the (synchronic) structure of language was thus contrasted to others' interests in the (diachronic) history of languages. The second was between *langue* and *parole*—the French words always being used for this distinction. *Langue* refers to "language" in the sense of linguistic structure or grammar and, by extension (e.g., later, in anthropology or sociology), to the "grammar" of a culture or society. *Parole* means "speech" or actual utterances of individuals and, by extension, the actual actions of individuals in a social structure. The third distinction was between syntagmatic and associative (later called paradigmatic) relations. The former are relations between words or smaller units within a sentence and, by extension, the relations between elements with a cultural "sentence" such as the traffic light sequence mentioned above. The latter marks the relation between those elements and what they mean. Finally, Saussure considered the relation between signifier (a word or symbol that stands for something) and signified (what it means), these two elements together making up what he called the sign. He stressed that the sign is arbitrary: It depends on knowing the language. In his example, if I speak French, I call the dog *le chien*, but if I speak German, I call him *der Hund*.

Later structuralists in linguistics developed Saussure's ideas further, including, for example, the French Indo-Europeanist Émile Benveniste (1902–1976), who studied under one of Saussure's students. Benveniste added the distinction between *énoncé* (a statement independent of context) and *énunciation* (a statement in context), the latter exemplified by the subject/object opposition of first- and second-person pronouns. This, in turn, suggested the further understanding of language as discourse.

Another major development is credited to Roman Jakobson (1896–1982), Nikolai Trubetzkoy (1890–1938), and others of the "Prague school," active first in Prague in the 1930s and later in the United States and elsewhere. They applied Saussurian distinctions at the level of phones (sounds), which are grouped slightly differently into phonemes (meaningful units of sound) by different languages according to the presence or absence of certain distinctive features. English, for example, distinguishes the *unvoiced* labiodental fricative /f/ from its *voiced* equivalent /v/: "Fat" is a different word from "vat." Jakobson was also important for his emphasis on the distinction between metaphor (relations of similarity, such as a crown as in the trademark of a beer company) and metonymy (relations of contiguity, such as a crown standing for sovereignty). In studies of the acquisition of language, he found that aphasics have difficulty with this aspect of language function.

APPROACHES IN ANTHROPOLOGY

In anthropology, there have been three main approaches in structuralist thought. First, the classic French structuralism of Claude Lévi-Strauss and his followers maintains a search for universal principles. In his kinship studies, for example, Lévi-Strauss sought the system of all possible systems and the structural principles that differentiate one kinship system from another: positive or negative marriage rules, marriage to one kind of cousin or another, and the effects of such marriage principles, when repeated, on relations among social units within a society. A rule of marriage of men to the category of the mother's brother's daughter, for example, would create a system of "generalized exchange" in which group A gives its daughters in marriage to group B, and group B to group C (not to group A). The same pattern is repeated through the generations. Marriage to the father's sister's daughter, however, creates a demographically unstable pattern of "delayed direct exchange" in which women marry in one direction in one generation and in the opposite direction in the next generation. The latter systems are virtually nonexistent or break down easily when created. A system that allows marriage to either of these kinds of cousin, by contrast, fosters "direct exchange" between just two groups, sometimes with men exchanging their sisters with other men.

Second, J. P. B. de Josselin de Jong (1886–1964) and his students from the 1930s onward, working mainly in the East Indies, were interested in patterns occurring within that culture area. Later scholars in Holland, Belgium, and Britain sought similar patterns elsewhere, and the idea was that each cluster of cultures had its own system, and an anthropologist could better understand a society in terms of its contrast to related cultures within that area rather than on its own. There are elements of this regional approach too in Lévi-Strauss's work on South American Amerindian mythology.

Third, British structuralists, such as Sir Edmund Leach (1910–1989) and Rodney Needham (1923–2006), in the 1960s and 1970s emphasized relations between elements within a given culture. Both the Dutch and the British structuralists had an interest in kinship structures, which for the Dutch especially involved a search for regional patterns and large cultural associations, and for the British usually more specific ones, as, for example, in Needham's reanalysis of symbolic associations among Purum in eastern India between wife-givers/wife-takers: superior/inferior, private/public, east/west, life/death, sacred/profane, village/forest, prosperity/famine, and moon/sun.

Much of this work, including Lévi-Strauss's, was based on the application of Jakobson and Trubetzkoy's notion of "distinctive features" to culture. The idea was that the same structural principles that govern language also govern culture and that simple "binary oppositions" defined by the presence or absence of some feature were significant especially for the understanding of kinship, symbolism, and mythology. Famously, Lévi-Strauss's work on North and South American myths, such as his four-volume *Mythologiques* (literally, "mytho-logics"), sought explanations for the meaning of myth through such simple distinctions and their transformations. Elements in mythology, such as different kinds of animals and their actions, say, one flies up, the other down, can be dissected by the structuralist, who thereby can understand the cultural code of the mythological system from the people who possess it.

OTHER STRUCTURALISTS

Among other structuralists were the psychoanalyst Jacques Lacan (1901–1981) and the Marxist writer Louis Althusser (1918–1990). Lacan stressed the importance of language in defining identity. He reinterpreted Sigmund Freud through Saussure, arguing that the unconscious has a structure not unlike language. Lacan emphasized opposition (e.g., love is the opposite of hate), thereby suggesting that language is never complete but implies what is left out. In a similar vein, Althusser reinterpreted Karl Marx, arguing for a deep "symptomatic" reading to move beyond the "surface" reading of his contemporaries. He suggested that one needs to understand the structure of the whole in order to explain modes of production. For Marx, he says, there is no distinct individual because the individual is embedded in the social context. Likewise, one should not see in Marx economic determinism (the Marxian base as determining the superstructure) because both the base and the superstructure are part of the same system.

At least implicitly, structuralism remains at the root of much of early twenty-first-century thinking in the social sciences, although its specific tenets are often now overshadowed by new interests and its simplistic vision attacked as misleading. It remains a touchstone even for its critics because so much in poststructuralism depends on understanding structuralist thought at its root and so much in postmodernism requires an understanding of what it is that is being rejected.

Linguists moved on from structuralism through Noam Chomsky's work, which from the 1960s has emphasized universals over the structural features of particular languages. Yet in linguistics, phonemes and other structural elements of language, though sometimes defined differently than they were by Jakobson and Trubetzkoy, remain essential. Anthropology has decidedly moved on in several directions, and there have been interesting criticisms of structuralist thought in that field. One

of the most important was that of the French anthropologist-sociologist Pierre Bourdieu (1930–2002), who attempted to break down the static notion of structure he saw in Saussure and Lévi-Strauss—dependent on oppositions such as *langue/parole*, as well as system/event and rule/improvisation. Bourdieu wished to emphasize individual action, not within the structure, but in what he called the *habitus* or environment of "dispositions." The French historian of science Michel Foucault (1926–1984) had a similar impact. Early in his career, he stressed the absence of order in history and suggested that *parole* rather than *langue* is its essence. Later he came to emphasize "discourse" over structure. Again, this linguistic concept is used in a metaphorical sense, implying a way of talking about something or the body of knowledge implied. Inherent in this, as in much poststructuralist and postmodernist thinking, is a notion of power that is absent in classic structuralist concerns.

SEE ALSO *Lévi-Strauss, Claude; Social Science; Social Structure*

BIBLIOGRAPHY

Althusser, Louis. 1969. *For Marx.* Trans. Ben Brewster. London: Allen Lane.

Deliège, Robert. 2004. *Lévi-Strauss Today: An Introduction to Structural Anthropology.* Trans. Nora Scott. Oxford: Berg.

Lacan, Jacques. 1977. *Écrits: A Selection.* Trans. Alan Sheridan. London: Tavistock Publications.

Lévi-Strauss, Claude. 1969. *The Elementary Structures of Kinship.* Rev. ed. Trans. James Harle Bell, John Richard von Sturmer, and Rodney Needham. Boston: Beacon Press. (Orig. pub. 1949.)

Lévi-Strauss, Claude. 1978. *Myth and Meaning.* London: Routledge and Kegan Paul.

Saussure, Ferdinand de. 1974. *Course in General Linguistics.* Rev. ed. Ed. Charles Bally and Albert Sechehaye. Trans. Wade Baskin. London: Fontana. (Orig. pub. 1916.)

Alan Barnard

STUDENT NONVIOLENT COORDINATING COMMITTEE

On February 1, 1960, four black freshmen from North Carolina A & T College (now University) went to the Woolworth's 5 and 10 cent store in downtown Greensboro, North Carolina. After shopping for a few items they proceeded directly to the store's lunch counter, their real objective. They all took seats and were promptly ignored. The students were not surprised by the waitress's refusal to serve them. In fact they knew they were flirting with danger by flagrantly violating the local segregation ordinance barring African Americans from service in white restaurants, because they had recently spent several weeks talking about the options available to them to combat segregation.

The Greensboro students were not the only ones discussing protest strategies during the 1959–1960 school year. On the contrary, black students all over the South were holding discussion groups and workshops on the topic. In the days and weeks following the Greensboro sit-ins, African American students from other schools began to sit in at segregated downtown lunch counters. Adult leaders soon recognized that a full-fledged student movement had begun. One of those who appreciated the effectiveness of the fledgling student movement was longtime activist Ella Baker (1903–1986). Previously, Baker had worked with the National Association for the Advancement of Colored People (NAACP). Some time later she advocated the creation of a permanent organization in the wake of the Montgomery bus boycott in Montgomery, Alabama, resulting in the establishment of the Southern Christian Leadership Conference in 1957.

In April 1960 Baker urged student leaders to attend a conference that she planned to hold at her alma mater, Shaw College (now university) in Raleigh, North Carolina. Before the students left Raleigh they had established the Student Nonviolent Coordinating Committee (SNCC). By the spring of 1961, the young organization became involved in civil rights campaigns of national scope such as the Freedom Rides (when members of the SNCC rode interstate buses through the Deep South to test a 1960 law forbidding racial segregation in interstate transportation). By the end of the summer, two competing strategies emerged in SNCC: nonviolent direct action and voter registration. At a particularly stormy meeting in August 1961, the group decided that it would do both.

As the organization matured over the next few years, SNCC activists were involved in virtually every major campaign of the Civil Rights movement from the March on Washington in 1963 to Mississippi Freedom Summer, a voter registration campaign in African American communities in Mississippi. During these tumultuous years, the young people of SNCC did the grueling and dangerous work of confronting every aspect of segregation from black disfranchisement to black economic inequality. SNCC organizers were threatened, jailed, brutalized, and a few were even killed. Along the way some of them denounced the Vietnam War, as well. The FBI placed them under surveillance, and the organization was harassed by the IRS. After several years of working for reform in some of the most isolated areas of the rural

South, some members of the organization began to rethink their position on a number of issues, including their support for integration. This critical philosophical shift soon resulted in a very public expression of support by some members of SNCC for the concept of Black Power, a political movement that sought to bolster racial consciousness among African Americans. Consequently, many members of the group began to shift their focus to issues of black economic equality and black political education. As the 1960s drew to a close, SNCC members drifted to pursue individual goals. For a brief time in the late 1960s, some attempted to form an alliance with the Black Panther Party, a political organization founded to promote civil rights and self-defense, but it was short-lived, and the Student Nonviolent Coordinating Committee soon passed out of existence. But in many of the communities where SNCC worked, black people still remember and appreciate the efforts of the SNCC kids to help them organize for social change.

SEE ALSO *Black Panthers; Black Power; Civil Rights; Civil Rights Movement, U.S.; Davis, Angela; Desegregation; Forman, James; Jim Crow; National Association for the Advancement of Colored People (NAACP); Passive Resistance; Protest*

BIBLIOGRAPHY

Carson, Clayborne. 1981. *In Struggle: SNCC and the Black Awakening of the 1960s.* Cambridge, MA: Harvard University Press.

Fleming, Cynthia Griggs. 2004. *In the Shadow of Selma: The Continuing Struggle for Civil Rights in the Rural South.* Lanham, MD: Rowman & Littlefield.

Cynthia G. Fleming

STUDENT'S *T*-STATISTIC

In measuring social and economic progression, statistical methods that take into account various magnitudes of uncertainties are used for inference and decision-making. One of the tasks in statistical inference is to estimate population mean from a sample of observations. For example, one may want to estimate the mean value of the retail price (μ) of a gallon of unleaded gasoline based on prices (X's) from a few gas stations in a large city. A natural estimate of μ is the arithmetic sample mean $\bar{X} = \sum_{i=1}^{n} X_i / n$. The estimator $\bar{X}$ has many desirable statistical properties, especially when X_i's are independent and identically distributed as a normal (Gaussian) random variable with mean μ and variance σ^2. From properties of normal distribution, the following Z-statistic

$$Z = \frac{\bar{X} - \mu}{\sigma / \sqrt{n}} \qquad (1)$$

is a standard normal random variable with mean $\mu = 0$ and variance $\sigma^2 = 1$. This Z-statistic has been used to make statistical inferences and decisions when variance σ^2 is known or the number of observations n is large. However, in most applications, the variance σ^2 is usually unknown and the number of observations n may be small. William Sealy Gosset (1876–1937), a chemist at the brewery of Arthur Guinness Sons and Co. (Boland 1984), studied the small sample property of

$$T = \frac{\bar{X} - \mu}{S / \sqrt{n}}, \qquad (2)$$

where $S^2 = \Sigma_{i=1}^{n}(X_i - \bar{X})^2/(n-1)$ is the sample variance. Gosset's work resulted in the birth of Student's T-statistic. Gosset published his work in *Biometrika* in 1908 under the pseudonym "Student" from his 1904 report to the company titled "The Application of the Law of Error to Work of the Brewery." Gosset's employer was against the work done for the company being made public but allowed him to publish it under a pseudonym. Gosset's original statistic was

$$\frac{\bar{X} - \mu}{\sqrt{\Sigma_{i=1}^{n}(X_i - \bar{X})^2/n}}. \qquad (3)$$

The Student's T-statistic used in the current formulation in expression (2) is due to English statistician Ronald Aylmer Fisher (1925).

Student's T-statistic was one of the important breakthroughs in statistical sciences in the twentieth century (Kotz and Johnson 1992). The density function of the Student's T-statistic with ν (integer) degrees of freedom is

$$\frac{\Gamma(\frac{\nu+1}{2})}{\sqrt{\nu\pi}\Gamma(\frac{\nu}{2})}\left(1 + \frac{t^2}{\nu}\right)^{-\frac{\nu+1}{2}}, \qquad (4)$$

where $\Gamma(a)$ is the Gamma function defined as

$$\Gamma(a) = \int_0^{\infty} x^{a-1} e^{-x} dx.$$

Density functions of the Z-statistic and Student's T-statistic are bell-shaped curves with Student's T having a heavier tail. The density function of Student's T-statistic relative to the density function of the standard normal is shown in Figure 1.

The distribution of the Student's T-statistic is the Student's T-distribution and statistical tests based on the

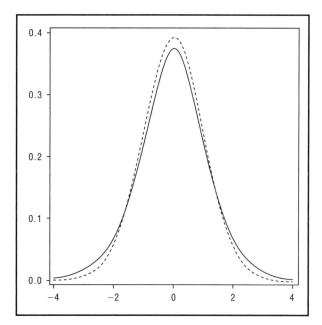

Figure 1: The Density Function of the Student's T Statistic (Solid Line) with 6 Degrees of Freedom Relative to the Density Function of Standard Normal (Dashed Line)

Student's T-statistic form various Student's T-tests. The expectation (mean) of the Student's T-statistic is 0, and the variance is $\nu/(\nu - 2)$ for $\nu \geq 2$. When $\nu = 1$, the Student's T-statistic becomes the Cauchy random variable, which does not have a variance. The Student's T-statistic has infinite variance when $\nu = 2$. The degrees of freedom of the Student's T-statistic defined in expression (2) are $n - 1$.

Student's T-statistic has been used for estimation and decision-making in many fields of science ranging from agriculture, biology, economics, public health, and zoology. As a simple illustration, to estimate the average unleaded retail gasoline price per gallon in a large city, the author of this entry conducted an informal random sample survey on his way (seventeen miles) home at the end of April in 2006. He observed prices of $2.999, $2.879, $2.959, $2.839, $2.899, $3.019, and $2.919 without including the duplicates. The sample mean ($\bar{X}$) of these seven observations was $2.930. Under normality assumption of the gasoline price, the sample mean is usually a good point estimator of the underlying mean value μ. Because of the randomness of the sample, a better approach for statistical inference is to construct an interval estimator. A classic method is to find the $100(1 - \alpha)\%$ confidence interval for the underlying mean gasoline price based on the Student's T-statistic:

$$(\bar{X} - t_{1-\alpha/2, \, n-1} S/\sqrt{n}, \ \bar{X} + t_{1-\alpha/2, \, n-1} S/\sqrt{n}), \quad (5)$$

where $t_{1 - \alpha/2, \, n - 1}$ is the critical value that satisfies

$$P(|T| \geq t_{1 - \alpha/2, \, n - 1}) = \alpha$$

and α is the probability that the confidence interval does not cover the true underlying mean value μ. The critical values of Student's T-statistic for various values of α and degrees of freedom are available in all statistical software packages and in most basic statistical books. A commonly used confidence is 95% ($\alpha = 0.05$) for interval estimation. From our sample observations, the 95% confidence interval for μ is

$$(2.930 - 2.447 * 0.065/ \sqrt{7}, \ 2.930 + 2.447 * 0.065/ \sqrt{7}),$$

which is (2.870, 2.990).

In addition to estimation, Student's T-statistic is also useful for hypothesis testing. The hypothesis to be tested is the null hypothesis. For example, the null hypothesis may be H_0: $\mu = \mu_0$ and the alternative hypothesis can be set as H_α: $\mu \neq \mu_0$ (two-sided test). One may commit two types of errors in testing statistical hypotheses. Rejecting the null hypothesis when it is true is the Type I error and accepting the null hypothesis when it is false is the Type II error. The probability of making Type I error is denoted by α, which is the same value used above for constructing a confidence interval. The probability of making Type II error is denoted by β. Type I error and Type II error are inversely related. The power of the test is $1 - \beta$, which is the probability of rejecting the null hypothesis when it is false. The upper bound of α is the size of the test, and the critical (rejection) region for a given Student's T-test of size α with ν degrees of freedom is $\{| T| \geq t_{1 - \alpha/2, \, \nu}\}$. The p-value is the probability of the test statistic as contradictory to the null hypothesis as the observed Student's T-statistic. Using the above seven observations, we can conduct a two-sided Student's T-test on the null hypothesis H_0: $\mu = 3.000$ vs $\mu \neq 3.000$ by constructing the test statistic:

$$T = \frac{\bar{X} - \mu}{S/\sqrt{n}} = \frac{2.930 - 3.000}{0.065/\sqrt{7}} = -2.8493.$$

The absolute value of the observed Student's T-statistic $| T| > 2.447 = t_{1 - 0.05/2, \, 6}$. That is, the observed Student's T-statistic (-2.8493) is in the critical region, which leads to rejecting the null hypothesis. A very popular way of performing statistical hypothesis testing is by computing the p-value. The two-sided p-value from the above example is $2P(T \leq -2.8493) = 0.0292$, which is less than the commonly used size of 0.05. Therefore, one would reject the null hypothesis of $\mu = 3.000$ and conclude that the underlying mean retail price for unleaded gasoline in that city was different from $3.000 per gallon.

The above simple example on estimation and hypothesis testing is formulated based on a two-sided Student's T-statistic. Similar estimation and hypothesis testing can be done for a one-sided test. In planning a scientific investigation, scientists need to decide how many samples are needed in order to control both Type I and Type II errors. Student's T-statistic plays a fundamental role in designing scientific investigations. Alan Agresti and Barbara Finlay (1997) provide an introduction to statistical estimation and hypothesis testing.

Student's T-statistic can be extended in many directions. For example, if X_i denotes the difference of the gasoline prices of a gas station at two different occasions, one can conduct a paired Student's T-test for quantifying the changes. If one wants to make a statistical comparison of the gasoline prices in two cities, one may construct a two-sample Student's T-statistic

$$\frac{\bar{X}_1 - \bar{X}_2}{\sqrt{S_1^2 / n_1 + S_2^2 / n_2}}, \tag{6}$$

where n_1, n_2 are the number of observations from sample (city) one and two, respectively, $\bar{X}_1 = \sum_{i = 1}^{n_1} X_{1i}/n_1$, $\bar{X}_2 = \sum_{i = 1}^{n_2} X_{2i}/n_2$, $S_1^2 = \sum_{i = 1}^{n_1}(X_{1i} - \bar{X}_1)^2/(n_1 - 1)$, $S_2^2 = \sum_{i = 1}^{n_2}(X_{2i} - \bar{X}_2)^2/(n_2 - 1)$. If the two samples have equal variances, one can form the pooled Student's t-statistic as

$$\frac{\bar{X}_1 - \bar{X}_2}{S_p\sqrt{1/n_1 + 1/n_2}}, \tag{7}$$

where

$$S_p^2 = \frac{(n_1 - 1) S_1^2 + (n_2 - 1) S_2^2}{n_1 + n_2 - 2}$$

is the pooled sample variance. Under the null hypothesis of equal means of X_{1i}'s and X_{2i}'s (H_0: $\mu_1 = \mu_2$), the two-sample Student's T-statistic in expression (7) follows the Student's T-distribution with $n_1 + n_2 - 2$ degrees of freedom if X_{1i}'s and X_{2i}'s are independent and identically normally distributed.

For more advanced statistical inferences, such as in correlation analysis, linear regression, and generalized linear models, the estimators of the parameters are approximately of Student's T-distribution. Hence, one can perform a statistical analysis on the estimated parameters based on Student's T-statistic.

As the sample size increases, the degrees of freedom increase and the Student's T-statistic converges to the standard normal random variable (Z). Asymptotically, one may use the Z-test to replace the Student's T-test when degrees of freedom are large ($n \geq 30$). Student's T-statistic is widely used for small sample analysis. One of the fundamental assumptions in deriving the distribution of Student's *T*-statistic is the normality of X_i's. This assumption is not easy to check for a small sample size. Many nonparametric (distribution-free) procedures have been proposed for conducting statistical inference without assuming normality of X_i's (Hollander and Wolfe 1999). For multiple sample inferences, Fisher (1925) extended the two-sample Student's *T*-test to analysis of variance (ANOVA) when X_i's are normally distributed. Without assuming normality, many rank-based techniques were developed for nonparametric versions of the two-sample Student's *T*-test and Fisher's ANOVA (Hollander and Wolfe 1999). A great many statistical methods have been invented in the twentieth century. Student's *T*-statistic is one of the most widely used statistical tools not only by professional statisticians but also by all scientists involved in data analysis and decision making.

SEE ALSO *Descriptive Statistics; Distribution, Normal; Hypothesis and Hypothesis Testing; Probability Distributions; Test Statistics*

BIBLIOGRAPHY

Agresti, Alan, and Barbara Finlay. 1997. *Statistical Methods for the Social Sciences.* 3rd ed. Upper Saddle River, NJ: Prentice Hall.

Boland, Philip J. 1984. A Biographical Glimpse of William Sealy Gosset. *American Statistician* 38: 179–183.

Fisher, Ronald A. 1925. *Statistical Methods for Research Workers.* Edinburgh, U.K.: Oliver and Boyd.

Hollander, Myles, and Douglas A. Wolfe. 1999. *Nonparametric Statistical Methods.* 2nd ed. New York: Wiley.

Kotz, Samuel, and Norman L. Johnson, ed. 1992. *Breakthroughs in Statistics: Methodology and Distribution.* Vol. 2. New York: Springer.

Student (William Sealy Gosset). 1908. The Probable Error of a Mean. *Biometrika* 6 (1): 1–25.

Dejian Lai

STUNTED GROWTH

Linear growth or height is influenced by genetic factors, environmental factors, and medical conditions. The National Center for Health Statistics (NCHS) has developed age- and gender-specific growth charts for health professionals to track children's height over time. Height is converted to *height-for-age*, often expressed as a percentile. Children growing between the fifth and ninety-fifth percentiles are considered to be growing within normal limits.

Children whose height is below the fifth percentile may be classified as stunted or of short stature. *Stunting*, defined as height-for-age that is more than two standard deviations below the NCHS or World Health Organization (WHO) International Growth Reference, serves as a general indicator of a child's nutritional status over long periods of time. Growth stunting is a gradual process that occurs in response to chronic biological insults, including malnutrition and infectious diseases, during periods of linear bone growth. It often begins in utero and extends through the first two years. Childhood stunting is closely associated with poverty and is often used as a population-based indicator to compare nutritional adequacy across countries. Without environmental changes, such as adoption, stunting can lead to a permanent reduction in growth. Thus, children who experience stunting early in life are often shorter during childhood and adulthood than peers who had adequate early growth.

The term *short stature* (SS) usually refers to children whose height is compromised by medical problems, such as Turner's syndrome, growth hormone deficiency, renal insufficiency, or Prader-Willi syndrome. The term *idiopathic short stature* (ISS) is used when there is no apparent explanation for a child's short stature. ISS can include children with short familial stature or a constitutional/maturational delay in development.

STUNTING

In the absence of adequate nutrients, a child's body conserves energy by limiting weight gain and then by limiting linear growth. Cross-sectional and longitudinal studies from multiple countries have found associations between stunting and children's health and development, caused by underlying factors such as malnutrition and infections. The consequences associated with early stunting include metabolic changes, depressed immune function, morbidity, mortality, delayed motor skills, delayed and irregular school attendance, low cognitive scores, and poor academic achievement. Adults with a history of stunting are at risk for obesity, reduced glucose tolerance, coronary heart disease, hypertension, and osteoporosis, as well as decreased work performance and productivity, thereby limiting economic capacity. In settings in which stunting is prevalent, the economic capacity of the entire society may be diminished.

The United Nations Standing Committee on Nutrition estimated that in 2004 approximately 148 million preschool children (27 percent under five years of age) in developing countries were stunted. Malnutrition is a serious global concern, and in some countries rates of stunting among children exceed 50 percent. In 2000, 70 percent of stunted children were from Asia, primarily

South Central Asia, and 24 percent were from sub-Saharan Africa.

The primary causes of stunting are nutrient deficiencies and infection. Recent evidence has shown that cow's milk intake is linked to linear growth, primarily by stimulating insulin-like growth factor (IGF-1). Although several nutrients have been linked to stunting, including protein, iron, zinc, copper, calcium, and vitamins D, A, and C, supplementation trials have not yielded clear findings, with the exception of 2002 meta-analysis by Brown et al. showing small but significant effects of zinc supplementation on linear growth. Intestinal infections can lead to stunting by reducing the absorption of nutrients. In environments with poor hygienic conditions, frequent infections can directly impact metabolism, particularly during infancy when nutritional demands are high and complimentary foods are introduced.

Caregiving practices can influence stunting through feeding patterns, food choices, and household stress. In food-insecure households, families may rely on foods low in macro- and micronutrients. When food is readily available, stunting rates are low. Stunting related to nutrient deficiencies can be minimized by exclusive breastfeeding for the first six months of life, as recommended by the WHO. However, in much of the world, complimentary foods are introduced before six months, often with liquids and cereals that are low in nutrients. If animal-source foods are not available, it can be difficult to provide sufficient nutrients for adequate growth. Finally, there is some evidence that severe family stress can result in diminished linear growth.

Stunting can continue into later childhood, adolescence, and adulthood, generally as an extension of prior stunting. Latin America has high rates of stunting in middle and late childhood, particularly in economically depressed areas. Although malnourished girls may have extended growth periods due to delayed menarche, they generally remain shorter than peers due to past stunting. Growth during adolescence does not typically compensate for earlier stunting.

Catch-up growth is defined as growth that is greater in velocity than expected. Although catch-up growth typically occurs during periods of rapid growth in infancy and toddlerhood, it can occur in middle childhood, particularly if there are nutritional or environmental improvements. There is recent controversy about the promotion of catch-up growth, as rapid weight gain has been linked with metabolic syndrome later in life.

Historically, stunting has been addressed through nutrition supplement programs, with inconsistent success in reducing stunting and increasing linear growth. Supplementation, combined with psychosocial stimulation, can also lead to improvements in cognitive performance into early adulthood.

In Peru, where food availability is adequate and stunting is primarily caused by dietary patterns, a randomized controlled trial of a nutrition education intervention from birth found that feeding practices and dietary intake improved, and the stunting rate was reduced by two-thirds among children eighteen months of age.

Economic progress has also been linked with decreased stunting rates. For example, Southeast Asia has seen a significant decrease since 1990 corresponding with economic improvements. National factors such as energy availability, female literacy, safe water rate, amount of economy derived from agriculture, and gross national product largely explain stunting prevalence within nations.

SHORT STATURE

The health and developmental consequences of SS/ISS are generally less severe than stunting, depending on the underlying causes. Although early studies raised concerns about the emotional well-being of SS/ISS children, recent studies with adequate comparison groups have not found difficulties in emotional well-being or self-image related to SS/ISS.

INTERVENTION AND TREATMENT

Children with growth hormone deficiency have been treated effectively with recombinant growth hormone. Growth hormone therapy (GHT) has been approved for treatment of children with ISS, but it is expensive and requires injections six or seven times a week until adult height is achieved. A 2003 Cochrane review by Jackie Bryant, C. Cave, and R. Milne found nine randomized controlled trials of GHT among children with ISS, most with only short-term effects. Although GHT can contribute to short-term increases in height (ranging from 0 to 0.7 standard deviations per year), children with ISS will be shorter than peers in adulthood. There is debate on the merits of GHT among children with ISS, particularly because treatment with GHT does not appear to alter children's quality of life. More research is needed to examine the long-term consequences of GHT, including adult stature, quality of life, and costs.

There have been concerns regarding the relation between long-acting stimulations given to children with attention-deficit/hyperactivity disorder and children's growth. Although most studies have found no long-term negative effects on children's height, the findings are not consistent and there are some data suggesting diminished gains in height after four years of treatment.

OTHER CONDITIONS

Severe dieting and anorexia nervosa result in inadequate weight gain (including weight loss) and may alter the sex hormones and menarche. However, there is not a clear relation between anorexia nervosa and stunting/SS. Growth history, timing of onset (before or after puberty), and duration of anorexia nervosa can impact nutritional status and growth outcomes, but have not been studied systematically.

In summary, stunting occurs early in life and can have lifelong consequences on cognition, academic performance, work capacity, and economic potential. Ensuring adequate nutrition and care through the promotion of breastfeeding; access to nutrient-rich food, including cow's milk; and developmentally and culturally appropriate feeding practices may be effective strategies to prevent stunting.

SEE ALSO *Body Mass Index; Child Development; Development; Disease; Hypertension; Malnutrition; Nutrition; Obesity; Undereating; World Health Organization*

BIBLIOGRAPHY

Branca, Francesco, and Marika Ferrari. 2002. Impact of Micronutrient Deficiencies on Growth: The Stunting Syndrome. *Annals of Nutrition and Metabolism* 46 (suppl. 1): 8–17.

Brown, Kenneth H., Janet M. Peerson, Juan Rivera, and Lindsey H. Allen. 2002. Effect of Supplemental Zinc on the Growth and Serum Zinc Concentrations of Prepubertal Children: A Meta-analysis of Randomized Controlled Trials. *American Journal of Clinical Nutrition* 75: 1062–1071.

Bryant, Jackie, C. Cave, and R. Milne. 2003. Recombinant Growth Hormone for Idiopathic Short Stature in Children and Adolescents. *Cochrane Database of Systematic Reviews* (4): CD004440.

Frongillo, Edward A., Mercedes de Onis, and Kathleen M. Hanson. 1997. Socioeconomic and Demographic Factors are Associated with Worldwide Patterns of Stunting and Wasting of Children. *Journal of Nutrition* 127: 2302–2309.

Lee, Mary M. 2006. Idiopathic Short Stature. *New England Journal of Medicine* 354: 2576–2582.

Milman, Anna, Edward A. Frongillo, Mercedes de Onis, and Ji-Yun Hwang. 2005. Differential Improvement among Countries in Child Stunting is Associated with Long-term Development and Specific Interventions. *Journal of Nutrition* 135: 1415–1422.

Penny, Mary E., Hilary M. Creed-Kanashiro, Rebecca C. Robert, et al. 2005. Effectiveness of an Educational Intervention Delivered through the Health Services to Improve Nutrition in Young Children: A Cluster-Randomised Controlled Trial. *Lancet* 365: 1863–1872.

United Nations System: Standing Committee on Nutrition. 2004. *Fifth Report on the World Nutrition Situation: Nutrition for Improved Development Outcomes.* Geneva, Switzerland: Author. http://www.unsystem.org/scn/Publications/html/RWNS.html.

Margo A. Candelaria
Maureen M. Black

STYLIZED FACT

The original idea of a stylized fact was introduced by Nicholas Kaldor (1908–1986) and applied to macroeconomic growth theory. Beyond the original application, the idea of a stylized fact is used throughout economics and the social sciences (and also in other scientific disciplines) as a simplifying abstraction of some social or economic process or fact. Being only a stylized fact, it is not a fact proper, but an assertion of what a researcher believes to be more or less true for a whole class of objects in question and with no reference to any concrete empirical finding. As Kaldor stated the problem of empirical observations, these "are always subject to numerous snags and qualifications" (Kaldor 1961, p. 178). Thus empirical observations and statistics distilled from them have always to be interpreted in the light of some theory. "[T]he theorist should be free to start off with a stylized view of the facts" (Kaldor 1961, p. 178)—this stylized view being a mental or verbal and in most cases still informal model of the domain of research. Empirical details, even contradictory ones, can be neglected in this early stage of research. Thus a first hypothesis explaining the stylized (and not the detailed empirical) facts can be generated.

Two stylized facts as quoted from Kaldor's paper illustrate what Kaldor may have meant with this term:

> As regards the process of economic change and development in capitalist societies, I suggest the following "stylized facts" as starting point for the construction of theoretical models: (1) The continued growth in the aggregate volume of production and in the productivity of labour at a steady trend rate; no recorded tendency for a falling rate of growth of productivity. (2) A continued increase in the amount of capital per worker, whatever statistical measure of "capital" is chosen in this connection. (Kaldor 1961/1968, p. 178)

Both of these stylized facts neglect details in the time series for measurements of productivity and capital per worker and are not even interested in the details of measurements ("whatever statistical measure … is chosen"). Moreover, a "steady trend rate" is observed—obviously a continuous deterministic function of time, as the "steady trend rate" can hardly be otherwise formalized.

Obviously, Kaldor's stylized facts are statements about the outcome of some abstract social or economic process, not about the outcome of any concrete or real process. Thus stylized facts are not statements that aggregate the knowledge gained from the statistical analysis of many concrete social processes, but the interpretation of what a researcher distills from his or her experience of some social or economic processes. The problem with this view is that it is in a way immune to falsification, as any real economic process that is not in line with the stylized fact can be declared as something like noise (cf. Boland 1994, p. 536). Robert Solow even commented on Kaldor's paper, saying, "there is no doubt that they are stylized, though it is possible to question whether they are facts" (Solow 1970, p. 2).

Thus, stylized facts can only be seen as starting points for further empirical and theoretical research. Recently, stylized facts have also been discussed as starting points for formal modelling and computer simulation of abstract social processes (compare, e.g., Gilbert 2000; Schwerin and Werker 2003). As Bernd-O. Heine et al. observe, the "value added by simulation models can be assessed by comparing the explanatory power of these models with respect to the relevant stylised facts to those using established methods" (2005, p. 2.11). In this sense the term is also used by Joshua Epstein (2006, p. 16), who lists several "stylized facts" such as the right-skewed wealth distributions (Epstein and Axtell 1996, pp. 7, 33–34) that were generated by the Sugarscape simulation model using a number of specified rules describing the behavior of individual agents. This is in any case an extension of Kaldor's idea of stylized facts, as the simulation models mentioned provide microfoundation for stylized facts on the macro level.

BIBLIOGRAPHY

Boland, Lawrence A. 1994. Stylized Facts. In *The New Palgrave Dictionary of Economics*, Vol. 4, repr. with corrections, ed. John Eatwell, Murray Milgate, and Peter Newman, 535–536. London: Macmillan.

Epstein, Joshua M. 2006. *Generative Social Science*. Princeton, NJ: Princeton University Press.

Epstein, Joshua M., and Robert Axtell. 1996. *Growing Artificial Societies: Social Science from the Bottom Up*. Cambridge, MA: Massachusetts Institute of Technology Press.

Gilbert, Nigel. 2000. Modeling Sociality: The View from Europe. In *Dynamics in Human and Primate Societies: Agent-Based Modeling of Social and Spatial Processes*, ed. Timothy A. Kohler and George J. Gumerman, 355–372. New York: Oxford University Press.

Heine, Bernd-O., Matthias Meyer, and Oliver Strangfeld. 2005. Stylised Facts and the Contribution of Simulation to the Economic Analysis of Budgeting. *Journal of Artificial Societies and Social Simulation* 8 (4). http://jasss.soc.surrey.ac.uk/8/4/4.html.

Kaldor, Nicholas. 1961. Capital Accumulation and Economic Growth. In *The Theory of Capital*, ed. Friedrich A. Lutz and Douglas C. Hague, 177–222. Reprint ed. 1968. London: Macmillan.

Schwerin, Joachim, and Claudia Werker. 2003. Learning Innovation Policy Based on Historical Experience. *Structural Change and Economic Dynamics* 14 (4): 385–404.

Solow, Robert M. 1970. *Growth Theory: An Exposition*. New York: Oxford University Press.

Werker, Claudia, and Thomas Brenner. 2004. Empirical Calibration of Simulation Models. Papers on Economics and Evolution 2004-10. Jena, Germany: Max Planck Institute for Research into Economic Systems.

Klaus G. Troitzsch

SUBALTERN

The term *subaltern* derives from Latin *sub-* (below, under) plus *alter* (other) or *alternus* (alternate), which produced *subalternus* (subordinate). It designated a lower-ranking, even an inferior, individual. In the eighteenth and nineteenth centuries, *subaltern* was employed as a military term. In the twentieth and twenty-first centuries, under the influence of Marxism, nationalism, postcolonialist theory, and feminism, *subaltern* has come to be used broadly to represent subordination in social, political, religious, and economic hierarchies. Diverse aspects of societies, histories, and other human situations have been examined at the national, communal, and individual levels to recover the roles of marginalized or subaltern participants displaced by stratification. In particular the term has come to symbolize disruption and distortion of indigenous history, values, and polity in the wake of external conquest, colonization, and prominence given to Westernization at the expense of indigenous mores.

MILITARY USAGE

In martial contexts, the term was applied to commissioned military officers below the rank of captain. Essentially it denoted a junior officer, particularly at the various grades of lieutenant. Temporary command would be handed over to a subaltern officer during "trooping the colors" in honor of a monarch's birthday.

The term was employed regularly by the British army until the Cardwell reforms in 1871. The senior subaltern rank was captain lieutenant. The junior subaltern rank in the cavalry was cornet, while its counterpart in the infantry was ensign. During the American Revolutionary War (1775–1783), the colonial army had ranks such as cornet, subaltern, and ensign—marked by green cockades in their hats. The rank of second lieutenant eventually replaced that of subaltern.

SOCIOPOLITICAL USAGE

Antonio Gramsci (1891–1937), an Italian political theorist, prominent socialist, founding member of the Communist Party in Italy (the Partito Comunista d'Italia), parliamentarian, and prisoner under the fascist regime of Benito Mussolini (1883–1945), provided the intellectual impetus for transforming the notion of subaltern into a political and social concept through his writings. He wrote of workers in Europe as belonging to classes that had been subordinated through sociopolitical hegemony, were exploited through economic methods, and were excluded from meaningful participation in the offices and benefits of the nation-state. A binary, almost dualist, relationship was said to arise between dominant and suppressed groups. Gramsci noted that such subaltern or proletarian classes could be exploited because they lacked unity and common cause and would remain oppressed unless they developed a unifying ideology that would lead them to alter the balance of power and form a new state or governing institutions that embodied and represented their wills and wishes. Gramsci, elaborating on Karl Marx (1818–1883), postulated that the working classes could and would under conditions of political coercion, economic exploitation, and social marginalization eventually develop a collective consciousness or common philosophy. That collective ideology would serve to transform them by generating self-awareness of their subordinate situations and galvanize them into resistance—thereby relocating the agency of change from the elite classes to the proletariat.

Another important intellectual influence was the notion that all forms of discourse are shaped—both overtly and inadvertently—by ideology. The literary theorist Edward Said (1935–2003) argued that the dominant views of politics, literature, religion, and history plus writings on those topics reflect Occidental, imperialist permutations. The loci of those ideological foundations were supposed to have been England and France during the colonial period of the fifteenth through twentieth centuries and the United States from the mid-twentieth century onward. The consequences of ideologies have permeated individual and collective assumptions and actions, it was suggested.

Drawing upon Gramsci's theories and influenced by Said's writings, an academic subdiscipline called *subaltern studies* developed in the late 1970s and early 1980s. Other influences on the development of the concept of subaltern into a theoretical framework that has displaced previous radical frameworks, such as the notion of history as an accurate record of the past, include postcolonial historiography (on which it became a major influence as well) and deconstructionism. Subaltern studies attempt to offer a theory of change grounded in notions of dominance; colonialism; subservience; alienation, including loss of self-identity; resistance; confrontation; and transformation. It postulates that even when marginalized, those who are oppressed can display agency. The common people are regarded as closely if not completely synonymous with the subaltern classes within each society. The elite of each society, whether of indigenous or expatriate origins, are designated as the dominant groups. Exploitation of the subaltern by the elite is considered an existing precondition that must be acknowledged and investigated in order to comprehend the masses in each society. The field of subaltern studies can therefore be viewed as a form of postcolonial studies.

Ranajit Guha, a historian studying South Asia, has been highly influential in popularizing the term *subaltern*, in defining its mandate and intellectual parameters, and in applying resultant concepts to historical and contemporary sociopolitical issues. He also edited several volumes of *Subaltern Studies* and anthologies drawn from those volumes. Guha and other scholars working on subalterns, such as Gayatri Chakravorty Spivak, Dipesh Chakrabarty, and Homi Bhabha, have suggested that attempts to reconstruct past events—that is, the process of historiography that produces historical accounts—is inextricably bound with and constantly reflects the impact of interactions between dominant or elite and subordinate or subaltern groups. Guha critiqued elitism by colonialists and nationalists while urging that historiography be constructed from below, not above. Spivak raised the issue of agency among the subordinate. Chakrabarty has examined reasons for historical accounts remaining centered on the state. Partha Chatterjee and Gyanendra Pandey have focused on the fragmentary aspects of history, memory, and historiographical accounts. Shahid Amin analyzed relationships between peasants and capitalists in economic production. Amin also demonstrated how and why accounts of the past are reshaped by individual and collective memory to fit new predilections. Focusing largely on the historiographies of colonialism in India and of subsequent Indian nationalism, they have proposed that those accounts were shaped by elitist British feudatory imperialism and by neo-elitist Indian bourgeois patriotism, respectively. As such, they conclude that established historiography and histories should be rejected as unrepresentative and inaccurate. The spotlight of inquiries into societies should be on the contributions of the people rather than on the accomplishments of the elites, according to scholars utilizing methodologies that incorporate the concept of the subaltern.

INTELLECTUAL IMPACTS OF SUBALTERN STUDIES AND SUBALTERN AS A CONCEPT

The term *subaltern* has come to be used to denote the underclasses of societies and often replaces other designations for those lower classes. Those groups are thereby distinguished from members of the ancien régime and from members of the new elites. The term has been employed in the contexts of investigations into political, religious, and social interactions between dominant and subordinate groups. Such studies have examined not only agencies of change but also how and why particular ethnoreligious communities, societal classes, and economic clusters are displaced by the might, convictions, organization, and vitality of other, emergent new elites. Moving beyond a rejection of established methodologies for analyzing societies, the study of subalterns has expanded to include investigations of social transformation and inquiries into how and why some groups developed into elite classes who control resources and perpetuate stereotypes, while other groups become subaltern communities experiencing crisis and displacement. Studies of the subaltern have suggested that the actions of elites and subalterns are affected by regional religiopolitical and socioeconomic factors and that therefore neither group can develop homogeneously. Indeed conflation and separation of modes of domination and subordination seem to have differentially determined the relationships that arose between elites and subalterns living in diverse areas.

It has been recognized that the presence of elitist and subaltern classes affects not only the patterns of interaction between groups but also influences the historiography of each community. The official historical record, often crafted by elites and instilled with a sense of social dominion and political hegemony, must be read not simply as a record of the past but also as an elite ideological product of rule that may have slowly but surely appropriated aspects of the subordinated people's past. This increasing marginalization of subordinate communities and individuals could even eventually reduce references to members of the indigenous confessional group to fleeting stereotypical images.

Examples from historical contexts to which the term has been applied by modern scholars include the *dhimmi* or protected minority communities of Jews, Christians, and Zoroastrians in the medieval Middle Eastern Islamic caliphates of the Umayyads (661–750) and the Abbasids (750–1258), the peasants and workers of early modern France (1492–1789) and tsarist Russia (1721–1917), and the indigenous working classes of British India (1858–1947).

Reassessment of the concept of the subaltern and of the field of subaltern studies has commenced with deliberations regarding their significant contributions and limitations. Indeed the representativeness of subaltern studies can be questioned in terms of selectivity of topics, choice of source materials, and parameters of inquiry. Sumit Sarkar in particular has noted a reductionist tendency that excludes the complexities inherent in historical events while simultaneously being "simplistic and retrogressive" in paying short-shrift to the impacts of precolonial hierarchies (1997, p. 51). An original founder of subaltern studies turned critic, Sarkar perceives subaltern studies as mired among forms of Marxism recast in the guises of cultural, class-based, and minutia or fragment-focused investigations. Achin Vanaik, who approaches disenchantment for subaltern studies from the viewpoint of a political scientist, conflates it with postmodernism and post-structuralism. He notes a tendency to ground many studies on the subaltern in an assumed notion of secularism. Vinay Lal has raised the issue of why studies of the subaltern constantly utilize Western theories to comprehend Eastern data rather than turning to Oriental models to comprehend those who were and are subordinated. Lal also pushed for a more nuanced appreciation of the nexus between history and myth and of influences by the latter on the former's creation, propagation, and preservation. Dane Kennedy and Richard Eaton have critiqued the rigid framework of the subaltern specifically and the amorphousness of cultural studies generally. Moreover the disillusionment and radical dissent with historiography that spawned and shaped inquiry into the situations of subalterns have become relatively mainstream in academia and broader intellectual settings.

Overall it could be suggested that historiography and other analyses of past and present societies benefited from being reshaped through inclusion of the subaltern or subordinate within the basic repertory of historical themes, events, and agents.

SEE ALSO *Fascism; Feminism; Gramsci, Antonio; Hegemony; Hierarchy; Marx, Karl; Marxism; Memory; Mussolini, Benito; Nationalism and Nationality; Postcolonialism; Resistance; Stratification; Working Class*

BIBLIOGRAPHY

Amin, Shahid. 1995. *Event, Metaphor, Memory: Chauri Chaura, 1922–1992.* Berkeley: University of California Press.

Bhabha, Homi K. 1994. *The Location of Culture.* London: Routledge.

Chakrabarty, Dipesh. 1992. Postcoloniality and the Artifice of History: Who Speaks for "Indian" Pasts? *Representations* 37: 1–26.

Chakrabarty, Dipesh. 1992. The Death of History. *Public Culture* 4 (2): 47–65.

Chatterjee, Partha. 1994. *The Nation and Its Fragments: Colonial and Post-Colonial Histories.* Delhi: Oxford University Press.

Chaturvedi, Vinayak, ed. 2000. *Mapping Subaltern Studies and the Postcolonial.* London: Verso.

Choksy, Jamsheed K. 1997. *Conflict and Cooperation: Zoroastrian Subalterns and Muslim Elites in Medieval Iranian Society.* New York: Columbia University Press.

Das, Veena. 1989. Subaltern as Perspective. In *Subaltern Studies,* ed. Ranajit Guha, vol. 7, 310–324. Delhi: Oxford University Press.

Eaton, Richard M. 2000. (Re)Imag(in)ing Other[2]ness: A Postmortem for the Postmodern in India. *Journal of World History* 11 (1): 57–78.

Gramsci, Antonio. 1967. *The Modern Prince and Other Writings.* Trans. Louis Marks. London: Lawrence and Wishart; New York: International.

Gramsci, Antonio. 1992–1996. *Prison Notebooks.* Trans. Joseph A. Buttigieg and Antonio Callari. New York: Columbia University Press.

Guha, Ranajit. 1988. On Some Aspects of the Historiography of Colonial India. In *Selected Subaltern Studies,* ed. Ranajit Guha and Gayatri C. Spivak, 37–44. New York: Oxford University Press.

Guha, Ranajit. 2002. *History at the Limit of World-History.* New York: Columbia University Press.

Kennedy, Dane K. 1996. Imperial History and Post-Colonial Theory. *Journal of Imperial and Commonwealth History* 24: 345–363.

Lal, Vinay. 2001. Subaltern Studies and Its Critics: Debates over Indian History. *History and Theory* 40: 135–148.

Ludden, David E., ed. 2002. *Reading Subaltern Studies: Critical History, Contested Meaning, and the Globalization of South Asia.* London: Anthem.

Pandey, Gyanendra. 1992. In Defense of the Fragment: Writing about Hindu-Muslim Riots in India Today. *Representations* 37: 27–55.

Said, Edward. 1978. *Orientalism.* New York: Pantheon Books.

Sarkar, Sumit. 1994. Orientalism Revisited: Saidian Frameworks in the Writing of Modern Indian History. *Oxford Literary Review* 16: 205–224.

Sarkar, Sumit. 1997. *Writing Social History.* Delhi: Oxford University Press.

Spivak, Gayatri C. 1988. Can the Subaltern Speak? In *Marxism and the Interpretation of Culture,* eds. Cary Nelson and Lawrence Grossberg, 217–313. Urbana: University of Illinois Press.

Spivak, Gayatri C. 1988. Subaltern Studies: Deconstructing Historiography. In *Selected Subaltern Studies,* eds. Ranajit Guha and Gayatri C. Spivak, 3–32. New York: Oxford University Press.

Vanaik, Achin. 1997. *The Furies of Indian Communalism: Religion, Modernity, and Secularization.* London: Verso.

Jamsheed K. Choksy

SUBGAME PERFECTION

In a Nash equilibrium strategy profile, every player plays the best response against the other players' strategies specified in the profile. For extensive form games where players move sequentially, one may use this notion, treating players' strategies as complete plans of action before the play begins. However, this concept ignores the sequential structure, and hence, sometimes may not be justifiable.

Consider the entry-deterrence game in Figure 1, in which there are two firms (players): a possible entrant (player 1) to an industry in which there is an incumbent (player 2). The potential entrant moves first and has two choices—to enter (*E*) or to stay out (*O*). If player 1 does not enter, the game ends. If player 1 enters, the incumbent then has two options—to accommodate (*A*) or to fight (*F*).

The game in Figure 1 has two Nash equilibria: (*O, F*) and (*E, A*). Indeed, in the equilibrium profile (*O, F*), the entrant is playing the best response *O*, because the entrant believes that the incumbent will choose *F*. However, this belief is based on an *incredible threat*. *F* is not optimal in the unreached *subgame* (intuitively, the "game" below a nonterminal node) in which the incumbent has to make a choice (the incumbent does not make a choice when the entrant chooses *O* because the game ends).

A subgame perfect equilibrium (SPE), as defined by Reinhard Selten (1965), is a strategy profile that induces a Nash equilibrium in every subgame of the original game, even if it is off the equilibrium path. Clearly, SPE refines the set of Nash equilibria. In the above example, (*E, A*) is a SPE, while (*O, F*) is not.

Any finite extensive form game with perfect information is solved using *backward induction*. Backward induction finds the optimal actions of the players in the "last" subgame first, and then, given these actions, works backward to the beginning to find the SPE of the game.

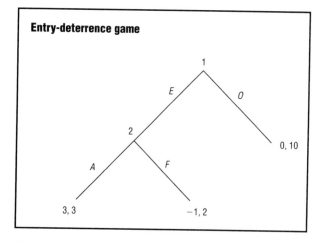

Entry-deterrence game

Figure 1

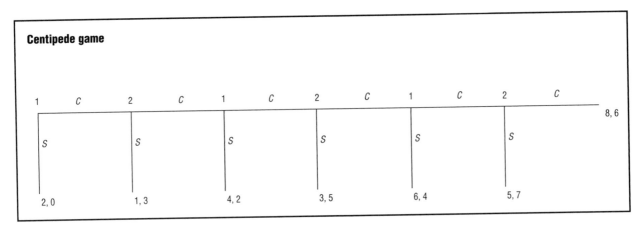

Figure 2

Consider the two-player "centipede" game in Figure 2, in which each player sequentially chooses either to continue (*C*) or to stop (*S*). Backward induction implies that the unique SPE is *S* for both players in every stage.

The backward induction solution is not observed in experiments where the players continue the game for a few stages (McKelvey and Palfrey 1992). This finding questions whether rational players follow backward induction. Robert Aumann (1995), however, proved that "common knowledge of rationality" implies backward induction.

Another criticism of SPE comes from the experiments on the ultimatum game, as in Figure 3, in which player 1 offers a fraction (*x*) of a pot of money to player 2, who has a choice to accept (*A*) or to reject (*R*).

The SPE outcome is for player 1 to offer the smallest money unit (say, 1*c*) and for player 2 to accept it. However, in experiments, offers are about 40 percent, and low offers are rejected (Guth et al. 1982). This is a violation of SPE only if we assume that the players care only about money. One may, however, test the outcomes using revealed preferences in games (Ray and Zhou 2001).

For games with imperfect information, subgame perfection is not enough to justify a solution. One should consider sequential equilibrium (Kreps and Wilson 1982).

SEE ALSO *Game Theory; Nash Equilibrium; Strategic Behavior; Strategic Games; Strategy and Voting Games*

BIBLIOGRAPHY

Aumann, Robert J. 1995. Backward Induction and Common Knowledge of Rationality. *Games and Economic Behavior* 8: 6–19.

Guth, Werner, Rolf Schmittberger, and Bernd Schwarze. 1982. An Experimental Analysis of Ultimatum Bargaining. *Journal of Economic Behavior and Organization* 3: 367–388.

Kreps, David M., and Robert B. Wilson. 1982. Sequential Equilibria. *Econometrica* 50: 863–894.

McKelvey, Richard D., and Thomas R. Palfrey. 1992. An Experimental Study of the Centipede Game. *Econometrica* 60: 803–836.

Ray, Indrajit, and Lin Zhou. 2001. Game Theory via Revealed Preferences. *Games and Economic Behavior* 37: 415–424.

Selten, Reinhard. 1965. Spieltheoretische Behandlung eines Oligopolmodells mit Nachfragetragheit. *Zeitschrift fur die Gesamte Staatswissenschaft* 121: 301–324, 667–689.

Indrajit Ray

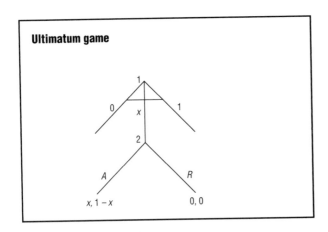

Figure 3

SUBJECT/SELF

Many social scientists argue that the modern Western conception of the self is a social construction. In "The Subject: The Person" (1979) anthropologist Marcel Mauss wrote that the history of the modern Western self began with the ancient Roman concept of the persona. Originally *persona* simply meant a "mask," as in the mask that a dramatic actor would wear during ritual performances. But as time went on the notion of persona became inscribed into Roman law as an individual with rights, duties, and obligations. Every male Roman citizen was considered a "person" with ancestors, a name, a clan or family, and a right to the protections of Roman law. At the same time, a slave had no personality, no ancestors, no right to property, no "self." Emerging during the final days of the Roman Empire, the early Christian Church democratized this notion of selfhood by investing every human being with a "soul." While in the human world fundamental differences in social status remained, in the eyes of God all were equal. But this early Christian self was still distant from the modern Western notion of the person as a psychological being.

According to sociologist Max Weber, the next stage in this conceptual evolution came with the Protestant Reformation of the sixteenth century. Within the Catholic Church, persons invested with souls depended upon the mediating power of the priest for salvation. The priest took confession, provided communion, and offered contrite sinners salvation through his power to dispense God's forgiveness. When Martin Luther and John Calvin turned against the Catholic Church, they eliminated the priest's mediating power. The sinner's salvation depended upon individual conscience, not the priest's magic. With this emphasis on conscience and personal responsibility, a new notion of self emerged, a psychological being with a complex interior life visible to God but concealed from the world at large.

The Protestant notion of a rational self invested with personal responsibility became one foundation for the ideas of individuality promulgated by Enlightenment philosophers and the early classical political economists. Beginning with John Locke, the quasi-divine quality of the self became indissolubly linked with private property and a new conception of political rights. For Locke, and later for Adam Smith, a natural object became personal property when the individual mixed his or her labor with the thing. This early "labor theory of value" made it clear that the self was sacred and its holiness could be transferred to things, transforming them into individual possessions. Further, this new sacred self had the capacity to challenge the so-called divine right of the absolutist sovereigns that had ruled Europe for almost a thousand years. Now every individual had the same God-given right to self-government and individual rationality. During the eighteenth and nineteenth centuries, a wave of republican revolutions washed over Europe and the Americas. Under these new republican regimes, the state was considered a servant of the people; the people were thought to be a collection of self-governing, self-possessed individuals.

But beginning in the late nineteenth century, notions of the centered, rational subject were increasingly called into question by philosophers and social scientists. For instance, Friedrich Nietzsche conceived of the individual as an instinctual cauldron propelled by the "will to power." This will to power drove the first human beings to excesses of bloodlust and cruelty as they expressed their individual sovereignty through the domination of others. But this changed as the original sovereigns entered human society. Social discipline no longer allowed the free expression of the will to power, and the instinct for domination turned inward. That repression of instinct led to the rational, centered, subject conscious of her or his guilt— the bad conscience of antisocial desire. Building on Nietzsche's notion of the disciplinary self, twentieth-century scholar Michel Foucault produced a series of historical studies documenting techniques that created the modern subject. In *Madness and Civilization* (1965), Foucault argued that while madness had often been punished in early modern Europe, it was not until the late eighteenth and early nineteenth centuries that the modern asylum took shape. This institution operated differently than earlier forms of incarceration. A disciplinary arrangement, in which the "insane" subject was made to feel guilt for "transgression" against reason, created a new kind of person, a self whose interior life was governed by a persistent internalized self-surveillance. As a site for the inscription of social power, the subject internalized the asylum.

More recently, many feminists and postmodernists argued that the "will to power" itself was the product of this rational, alienated individuality. In her essay "The Feminist Standpoint" (2004), Nancy Hartsock wrote that as "a consequence of this experience of discontinuity and aloneness, penetration of ego-boundaries, or fusion with another is experienced as violent" (p. 46). The self seeks to escape its internalized prison through contact with others, but the only escape seems to be through violence, violation, and domination. Sexuality itself becomes tangled in this process, and the masculine self often sees the object of its desire as a thing to be conquered. But another path is possible. Mutuality, rather than domination, could satisfy the desire for fusion. Such mutuality, however, depends on a new kind of subjectivity, a self decentered, continuous, and open to transformation.

SEE ALSO *Alienation; Feminism; Foucault, Michel; Locke, John; Madness; Nietzsche, Friedrich; Postmodernism; Religion; Sexuality; Slavery; Smith, Adam; Social Science; Subjectivity: Overview; Weber, Max*

BIBLIOGRAPHY

Foucault, Michel. 1965. *Madness and Civilization: A History of Insanity in the Age of Reason.* Trans. Richard Howard. New York: Vintage.

Hartsock, Nancy. 2004. The Feminist Standpoint: Developing the Ground for a Specifically Feminist Historical Materialism. In *The Feminist Standpoint Theory Reader: Intellectual and Political Controversies*, ed. Sandra Harding, 35–53. New York: Routledge.

Mauss, Marcel. 1979. The Subject: The Person. In *Sociology and Psychology*. Trans. Ben Brewster. London: Routledge.

Nietzsche, Friedrich. 1887. *On the Genealogy of Morals*. Trans. Walter Kaufmann and R. J. Hollingdale. New York: Vintage, 1967.

Weber, Max. 1958. *The Protestant Ethic and the Spirit of Capitalism*. Trans. Talcott Parsons. New York: Schribner's.

Graham Cassano

SUBJECTIVE PROBABILITY

SEE *Probability, Subjective.*

SUBJECTIVE VALUE

SEE *Value, Subjective.*

SUBJECTIVITY: OVERVIEW

In emulating the success of the physical sciences, the social sciences have traditionally been committed to the paradigm of objective knowledge. The norm of objectivity was understood as an ideal of disinterested, factual, replicable, lawlike knowledge of social reality, a type of knowledge that would demonstrably transcend both ideological controversies and commonsense knowledge, indeed a knowledge wholly independent of human interests, passions, and all subjective entanglements. Not surprisingly, this image of science polarized epistemological disputes into two extreme camps, the objectivist persuasion defending the ideal and a range of dissenting voices questioning the possibility or desirability of a purely objective knowledge of social life. Perspectives from the latter camp shared the belief that an authentic social science must accept the radically subjective nature of its research fields and devise methods and approaches to capture the phenomena of subjective life. What follows is a brief survey of some of these approaches to subjectivity.

Given the importance of human emotions, intentions, and reasoning in modern thought, it is useful to begin with philosophy. The founding moment of modern philosophy lies in René Descartes's (1596–1650) defense of the *cogito*, the irreducible moment of subjective consciousness that persists as a foundation of objective, mathematical knowledge. Following Descartes's lead, we see the "philosophy of subjectivity" branching into its various forms: the explorations of Immanuel Kant (1724–1804) and Johann Fichte (1762–1814) of the transcendental subject; G. W. F. Hegel's (1770–1831) historicized vision of subjectivity as a genetic formation of "spirit" (in the 1807 *Phenomenology of Spirit*); Karl Marx's (1818–1883) materialist account of the subject of history exemplified by revolutionary agency and praxis; and the emergence in the first part of the twentieth century of phenomenology as a descriptive philosophy of lived experience (in the work of Edmund Husserl [1859–1938] and his students).

There were also parallel movements within the human sciences. The debate between objectivism and subjectivism first came to public attention in the dispute at the end of the nineteenth century within German sociology between the *Naturwissenschaft* and *Geisteswissenschaft* images of science. Where the "natural science" model aspired to uncover objective laws, the "human sciences" foregrounded the "spirited" realms of human action, conscious agency, and the intentional life of singular individuals embedded in particular historical contexts. The well-known defense of subjective cognition in the work of Wilhelm Windelband (1848–1915), Heinrich Rickert (1863–1936), and Wilhelm Dilthey (1833–1911) entered modern sociology in Max Weber's (1864–1920) version of a "sociology of action" based upon understanding actors' motives (the so-called *Verstehen* or "understanding" approach to historical and social explanation). The subjective experience of historical agents is not to be reduced or discounted; rather, it is to be recovered through situationally sensitive contextual methodologies. Alongside the legitimate claims of quantitative methodologies, the social sciences must construct new and imaginative "qualitative" approaches to intersubjective experience.

Weber's methodological writings were given a phenomenological grounding in the work of Husserl's student, Alfred Schutz (1899–1959). Essentially Schutz followed Husserl's argument that all scientific knowledge has its foundations in the pretheoretical world of practical action, the *Lebenswelt* or lifeworld of everyday experience (Husserl [1954] 1970). Rather than treating subjectivity as an irrelevance or hindrance to objectivity, the social sciences could only achieve rigorous knowledge by making this "subjective world" of practical life its central topic. The human sciences, in other words, presuppose a phenomenology of the social world (Schutz 1967).

Other traditions had come to the same conclusion from different routes. One of the most notable of these is the tradition of American pragmatism and its sociological correlate, symbolic interactionism. Theorists such as William James (1842–1910), John Dewey (1859–1952), and George Herbert Mead (1863–1931) viewed the social world as the outcome of the reflexive interaction of conscious agents. Human beings act and relate to one another through communicative, symbolic means. Because individuals symbolically construct their lifeworlds, the interactional processes involved must form the first topic of a genuine social science. When combined, European phenomenological sociology and American interactionist sociology have given rise to a wide range of approaches to subjective experience. Among the most influential of these are phenomenological sociology interpreted as a radical sociology of knowledge (exemplified by the work of Peter Berger and Thomas Luckmann [1966]); the ethnomethodological sociology of Harold Garfinkel (1967) and Aaron Cicourel; the language-based perspectives of conversation analysis; the interactionist sociology of Erving Goffman (1922–1982) (1974) and the microsociology of subcultures and personal worlds influenced by Goffman's work (e.g., Becker 1964; Glaser and Strauss 1967; Sudnow 1972); phenomenological psychology and humanistic psychology (Psathas 1973); social studies of science as a "subjective construction"; and so on. In addition, we might mention the interdisciplinary-wide movements of qualitative methodology, feminist epistemology, structuration theory, and recent forms of critical theory (influenced by the work of Jürgen Habermas).

In the tradition of "continental philosophy," the subject and subjectivity occupy a fundamental role in a number of theoretical perspectives—most notably in the development of semiotic and structuralist ways of thinking that rejected the Cartesian *cogito* and "humanist" subject, and more recently in various strands of poststructuralist thought in which we find something like "the return of subjectivity."

In the tradition of metaphysical humanism, the transcendental subject is thought to constitute the "object" through its active processes of representation (Kant, Arthur Schopenhauer [1788–1860]) or intentional syntheses (Husserl, Max Scheler [1874–1928], Jean-Paul Sartre [1905–1980], Maurice Merleau-Ponty [1908–1961], Paul Ricoeur [1913–2005], and others). The "world" is the totality of phenomenal appearances given to the constituting subject. Objects are "correlated" to subjective activities, functions, representations, and practices. This has been called the "philosophy of consciousness." Questioning the primacy of consciousness produces a range of antisubjective positions. In this context, we might view psychoanalysis as the key to the rejection of the primacy of pure consciousness, with Sigmund Freud's (1856–1939) attempt to dethrone the privileged position of subjectivity by exploring the anonymous functions of desire and unconscious experience. Psychoanalytically ori-

ented thought contests the primacy of the ego, particularly in the guise of the subject understood as a stable, proprietorial center of conscious acts. The structuralism of Roland Barthes (1915–1980) and Louis Althusser (1918–1990), for example, has extended this criticism by seeing the self as a "subject-position" created by ideological practices and social discourses.

This critique of the subject opened the way for a much more complex and diverse problematic of subjectivity—emphasizing the changing historical, institutional, and cultural forms adopted by the subject within different fields of power (here the work of Martin Heidegger [1889–1976] and Michel Foucault [1926–1984] can be mentioned). More recent theorizing has criticized the Cartesian subject as an ideological pillar of masculine, Eurocentric culture. As black feminist and postcolonial theory has argued, the "white mythology" of the occidental subject helps to sustain patriarchy, women's oppression, colonialism, and phallocentric institutions more generally. Rather than positing a disembodied, essentialist, and metaphysical "subject," the task poststructuralist and postmodern thought has set for itself is to deconstruct all essentialist conceptions of the subject in order to investigate the concrete relations and discourses that create different historical forms of embodied subjectivity.

SEE ALSO *Goffman, Erving; Intersubjectivity; Objectivism; Objectivity; Structuralism*

BIBLIOGRAPHY

Becker, Howard S. 1964. *Outsiders: Studies in the Sociology of Deviance.* New York: Free Press.

Berger, Peter L., and Thomas Luckmann. 1966. *The Social Construction of Reality: A Treatise in the Sociology of Knowledge.* Garden City, NY: Doubleday.

Foucault, Michel. 1972. *The Archaeology of Knowledge.* Trans. A. M. Sheridan Smith. London: Tavistock.

Foucault, Michel. 1973. *The Birth of the Clinic: An Archaeology of Medical Perception.* Trans. A. M. Sheridan Smith. London: Tavistock.

Garfinkel, Harold. 1967. *Studies in Ethnomethodology.* Englewood Cliffs, NJ: Prentice-Hall.

Glaser, Barney, and Anselm Strauss. 1967. *The Discovery of Grounded Theory: Strategies for Qualitative Research.* Chicago: Aldine.

Goffman, Erving. 1974. *Frame Analysis: An Essay on the Organization of Experience.* New York: Harper.

Husserl, Edmund. [1954] 1970. *The Crisis of European Sciences and Transcendental Phenomenology: An Introduction to Phenomenological Philosophy.* Trans. David Carr. Evanston, IL: Northwestern University Press.

Husserl, Edmund. 1991. *Cartesian Meditations: An Introduction to Phenomenology.* Trans. Dorion Cairns. Dordrecht, Netherlands: Kluwer.

Psathas, George, ed. 1973. *Phenomenological Sociology: Issues and Applications.* New York: Wiley.

Sandywell, Barry. 1996. *Logological Investigations.* 3 vols. London: Routledge.

Schutz, Alfred. 1967. *The Phenomenology of the Social World.* Trans. George Walsh and Frederick Lehnert. Evanston, IL: Northwestern University Press.

Schutz, Alfred, and Thomas Luckmann. 1974. *The Structures of the Life World.* Trans. Richard M. Zaner and H. Tristram Engelhardt Jr. London: Heinemann.

Sudnow, David, comp. 1972. *Studies in Social Interaction.* New York: Free Press.

Barry Sandywell

SUBJECTIVITY: ANALYSIS

The terms *subject* and *subjectivity* are employed in the humanities and social sciences in contradistinction to the notion of the self or selfhood. The latter terms traditionally suggest the idea of identity as a personal possession and of individuality as both unique and autonomous. The notion of the subject is more ambivalent in that the term at once denotes a person under the control or influence of other people or external forces—that is, a being literally or figuratively subjected to such forces and influences—and an individual agency that thinks, feels, perceives, intends, and acts in its interaction with other people and the outside world. In contrast to the self, regarded as a stable human essence and the controlling center of its own actions, the subject in contemporary critical theory is conceived as at once active and passive, and as the product of its inscription in language, politics, and culture. This so-called de-centered subject is the result of a thorough rethinking of the notion of subjectivity during the second half of the twentieth century. As such, it forms a radical break with some of the earlier theories of the subject in which it nonetheless finds its foundations.

The term *subject* in relation to human consciousness finds its origins in German idealism. Idealists, such as Georg Wilhelm Friedrich Hegel (1770–1831) and Immanuel Kant (1724–1804), assume, albeit with considerable differences in their accentuations, that only mental entities are real. Physical things, therefore, exist only in the sense that they are perceived by the controlling center of the mind. Similarly, René Descartes (1596–1650), firmly rooted in the historical intellectual movement the Enlightenment or the Age of Reason, posits that the only immediately and directly perceptible forms and objects of knowledge are those that are part of one's state of mind. External realities merely exist as ideas or pictures in the mind. The only incontestable truth-claim pertains to one's consciousness, hence Descartes's famous dictum: *Cogito, ergo sum*—"I think, therefore I am." Descartes's model forms the basis of all subsequent theories of the subject as an autonomous being that, in being aware of its capacity for thought, is conscious of its existence. Although there are considerable differences between Descartes's position and idealist notions of the subject, they share in common an emphasis on the human powers of perception, rationality, and free agency—on the central position of human consciousness from which all forms of knowledge and meaning are suggested to spring.

MODERNIST INFLUENCES

While philosophers such as Søren Aabye Kierkegaard (1813–1855) and Arthur Schopenhauer (1788–1860) were among the earliest contestants of idealist and rationalist notions of subjectivity, the most immediate precursors of the postmodern de-centering of the subject are three disruptive thinkers who can be jointly associated with the rise of modernism in mid–nineteenth-century western Europe: Nietzsche, Marx, and Freud.

Friedrich Nietzsche (1844–1900) took Schopenhauer's notion of the subject as a figment of the philosophical imagination a step further by claiming that "subjectivity is the product of repressive value systems" (Cavallaro 2001, p. 88). Arguing that there is "no doer behind the deed," Nietzsche attacks the subject in its foundations, exposing the Cartesian notion of its essential autonomy and rationality to be based on a questionable premise since the existence of thinking can never be fully proved. As a grammatical fiction, the subject has no existence as a stable substance or essence but is only the product of dominant ideologies.

The psychoanalyst Sigmund Freud (1856–1939) further undercut the presumed self-presence and unitary nature of subjectivity by introducing the notion of the unconscious and exploring its operations as among the most powerful forces in psychic life. The Freudian subject is split and divided against itself both because of the separation between conscious and unconscious psychic contents and because of the fundamentally contradictory and divisive drives that go into the subject's making. Largely unknowable to itself and profoundly determined by its early experiences within the family situation, the psychoanalytic subject defies any form of self-determination and self-knowledge, explains Mikkel Borch-Jacobsen in *The Freudian Subject* (1988).

The political economist and socialist revolutionary Karl Marx (1818–1883) saw the Cartesian notion of the subject as an ideological ruse that merely served to sustain the liberal theory of the social contract. Instead of conceiving the subject's consciousness of itself as the only verifiable reality, he argued that the material world is real and that people's ideas about and perceptions of the world are the results, not the causes, of their experience of its realities.

Postmodern thinkers, however diverse in their emphases in approaching the problem of the subject, all take their cues from these three fundamental challengers of Enlightenment thought. Michel Foucault (1926–1984), for example, follows in Nietzsche's footsteps by investigating the processes through which the subject is produced within specific historical and ideological contexts. Ladelle McWhorter explains in *Bodies and Pleasures: Foucault and the Politics of Sexual Normalization* (1999) that Foucault takes structures of knowledge and power to be equally enabling as constraining forces to produce subjectivity. Foucault therefore focuses on the ways in which even the human body cannot be said to have any meaningful and socially intelligible existence outside the discourses—sets of statements that define a cultural object, thereby calling it into being—that produce it.

Jacques Lacan (1901–1981) builds on the Freudian notion of the subject by making language central to psychic development. The Lacanian subject is alienated from its physical reality and the plenitude of its initial indivisibility from the mother in two stages. The first comes when the subject (mis)recognizes itself in the mirror and begins to identify with this image, thus building up an essentially imaginary sense of itself. The second and even more decisive moment at which the Lacanian subject is split from the Real is when it enters the realm of language and can henceforth exclusively identify and know itself in symbolic terms (Grosz 1990).

Taking Marx's analysis of class relations as his point of departure, Louis Althusser (1918–1990) locates the emergence of the subject in ideological structures—or belief systems—which, he maintains, "seduce" individuals to take up their socioculturally determined positions within the system of social relations (Hall 2004, p. 85). Constituted through the process of interpellation—the process by which ideology addresses the individual subject and therewith effectively produces him or her as an effect—the Althusserian subject likewise flies in the face of the classical definition of the subject as cause and substance.

THE POSTMODERN SUBJECT AS SOCIAL CONSTRUCT

Whether defined as the product of power/knowledge (Foucault), language (Lacan), or ideology (Althusser), the postmodern subject is essentially a social construction, the result or effect of systems of meaning and knowledge that always precede him or her, both individually and collectively. Since such systems are both multiple and sociohis-torically specific, changing over time, and cross-culturally diverse, subjectivity can neither be seen as unitary nor as a universal phenomenon transcending historical and social boundaries. What is more, the location of the emergence of the subject in systems that precede it, and whose operations necessarily exceed any individual's control, definitively puts paid to the Cartesian notion of human consciousness as the center of control over its own being. While postmodernists thus emphasize the subject's subjugation to the structures that produce him or her, thereby privileging the passive aspects of the term, this is not to say that individual subjectivity is denied any possibility for activity. Since ideological systems and structures of meaning and knowledge can only operate through their bearers, even the de-centered, split subject of postmodernity can be considered potentially endowed with a certain form of agency. The ambivalence of the term *subject* is ultimately maintained by the fact that subjects, though variously produced by external forces and thus by no means masters of their selves, also actively function within their constitutive outsides, whether in conformity with prevailing norms and meanings or in deviation from or actual defiance of their regulatory operations. As a produced effect of discourse, language, or ideologies, the postmodern subject is constituted in a double bind.

SEE ALSO *Althusser, Louis; Enlightenment; Foucault, Michel; Freud, Sigmund; Hegel, Georg Wilhelm Friedrich; Humanism; Idealism; Intersubjectivity; Kant, Immanuel; Marx, Karl; Objectivism; Rationalism; Social Constructs; Subject/Self*

BIBLIOGRAPHY

Borch-Jacobsen, Mikkel. 1988. *The Freudian Subject.* Trans. Catherine Porter. Stanford, CA: Stanford University Press.

Cavallaro, Dani. 2001. *Critical and Cultural Theory: Thematic Variations.* New Brunswick, NJ: Athlone.

Grosz, Elizabeth. 1990. *Jacques Lacan: A Feminist Introduction.* New York: Routledge.

Hall, Donald E. 2004. *Subjectivity.* New York: Routledge.

McWhorter, Ladelle. 1999. *Bodies and Pleasures: Foucault and the Politics of Sexual Normalization.* Bloomington, IN: Indiana University Press.

renée c. hoogland

SUBLIMATE

The Latin word *sublimis* means lifted up, elevated, lofty, eminent, distinguished, a verbal chain containing the movement of going from lower to higher. The *Oxford English Dictionary* defines the verb *sublimate* as "to raise to high place, dignity or honor"; "to act upon (a substance) so as to produce a refined product"; "elevation to a higher state or plane of existence; transmutation into something higher, purer, or more sublime." In *Civilization and Its Discontents*, Freud uses this metaphorical structure to address how humans sublimate their instincts toward the higher plane of culture, or civilization: "Sublimation of instinct is an especially conspicuous feature of cultural development; it is what makes it possible for higher psychical activities, scientific, artistic or ideological, to play such an important part in civilized life" (Freud 1930, p. 97). In an earlier work, Freud had specified that he was addressing sexual drives: "Sublimation … consists in the instinct's directing itself towards an aim other than, and remote from, that of sexual satisfaction" (Freud 1914, p. 94). The sublimation of instincts—deflecting them away from sexuality—is aided by developmental processes of identification, inhibition, and displacement, which change libidinal instincts into "impulses of affection" (Freud 1924, p. 177). Although many individuals never reach this developmental level, sublimation still plays a role in their lives; hence the wide range of psychoanalytic formulations that attempt to take into account the multiple functions of sublimatory activity.

In Freud's formulations he presumes the individual has already achieved a separate existence from family members and has established his or her status as an individual with stable boundaries. Many other psychoanalytic texts address an earlier set of developmental issues in which stable boundaries between self and other have not yet been established. For example, John Gedo (1996) discusses the role of sublimation in individuals coping with psychotic disintegration. Edward Glover suggests that sublimation is a "process which affords the maximum protection from illness with the minimum expenditure of energy" (Glover 1931, p. 280). Heinz Kohut (1976) notes the function of sublimation in maintaining self-object relations in which an art object serves to restore a sense of self-cohesion by fulfilling a function the self cannot provide. Melanie Klein views sublimation as an attempt to repair the damage done to an internalized object as a result of hate and aggression: "The attempts to save the loved object, to repair and restore it, attempts which in the state of depression are coupled with despair, since the ego doubts its capacity to achieve this restoration, are determining factors for all sublimations" (Klein [1935] 1948, p. 290).

Once stable boundaries have been established, the individual is capable of relating to others as separate, capable of "object relationships" with all their complexity of desire, frustration, approach, avoidance, and expectation. Some formulations address the function of sublimation in sustaining the capacity for object relationships or even providing substitute objects. Michael Balint writes that

"all sublimations, and especially the form of sublimation called art, are a kind of deception, are underhand ways of getting back to real personal objects" (Balint 1959, p. 115). For Volney Gay sublimation is a form of "object relatedness" protecting us "from the terrors of schizoid loneliness" (Gay 1992, pp. 292–293). The work of Gedo and Arnold Goldberg (1973) suggests four levels of sublimation: (1) Sublimation serves to prevent psychotic disintegration by providing desperate measures of marking a differentiated status. (2) Sublimation assists in sustaining psychological cohesion by providing self-objects that serve the self's narcissistic needs. (3) Sublimation affords object relationships. (4) In Freud's terms, sublimation enables one to bypass repression and experience gratification without guilt.

In his works D. W. Winnicott describes sublimation as beginning with the union of baby and mother and continuing throughout life "in the intense experiencing that belongs to the arts and to religion and to imaginative living, and to creative scientific work" (Winnicott [1951] 1975, p. 242). This view is "post-Freudian" in the sense that sublimation is not about bypassing repression so as to avoid guilt but rather taking stock of separateness and achieving an experience of re-joining. Hans Loewald views sublimation in these terms, observing that sublimation aims to restore, at least partially, the "original unity" of baby and mother; sublimation "is a kind of reconciliation of the subject-object dichotomy" (Loewald 1988, p. 20). For Jacques Lacan sublimation provides access to an archaic experience preceding the subject-object distinction, the point marking the loss of immediacy with the mother's body.

SEE ALSO *Culture; Freud, Sigmund; Loneliness; Narcissism; Obsession; Oedipus Complex; Psychology; Sexuality*

BIBLIOGRAPHY

Freud, Sigmund. [1914] 1957. On Narcissism: An Introduction. In *The Standard Edition of the Complete Psychological Works of Sigmund Freud*, ed. and trans. James Strachey, Vol. 14, 73–102. London: Hogarth.

Freud, Sigmund. [1924] 1959. The Dissolution of the Oedipus Complex. In The Standard Edition of the Complete Psychological Works of Sigmund Freud, ed. and trans. James Strachey, Vol. 19, 171–179. London: Hogarth.

Freud, Sigmund. [1930] 1961. Civilization and Its Discontents. In *The Standard Edition of the Complete Psychological Works of Sigmund Freud*, ed. and trans. James Strachey, Vol. 21, 64–125. London: Hogarth.

Freud, Sigmund. [1933] 1964. New Introductory Lectures on Psycho-analysis. In *The Standard Edition of the Complete Psychological Works of Sigmund Freud*, ed. and trans. James Strachey, Vol. 22, 5–182. London: Hogarth.

Gay, Volney P. 1992. *Freud on Sublimation: Reconsiderations.* Albany: State University of New York Press.

Gedo, John E. 1996. *The Artist and the Emotional World: Creativity and Personality.* New York: Columbia University Press.

Gedo, John, and Arnold Goldberg. 1973. *Models of the Mind: A Psychoanalytic Theory.* Chicago: University of Chicago Press.

Glover, Edward. 1931. Sublimation, Substitution and Social Anxiety. *International Journal of Psycho-Analysis* 12: 263–297.

Klein, Melanie. [1935] 1948. A Contribution to the Psychogenesis of Manic-depressive States. In *Contributions to Psycho-Analysis, 1921–1945*, 282–310. London: Hogarth.

Kohut, Heinz. 1976. Creativeness, Charisma, Group Psychology: Reflections on the Self-analysis of Freud. In *Freud: The Fusion of Science and Humanism*, ed. John E. Gedo and George H. Pollock, 379–425. New York: International Universities Press.

Lacan, Jacques. 1992. *The Ethics of Psychoanalysis, 1959–1960.* Vol. 7 of *The Seminar of Jacques Lacan*, ed. Jacques-Alain Miller, trans. Dennis Porter. New York: Norton.

Loewald, Hans W. 1988. *Sublimation: Inquiries into Theoretical Psychoanalysis.* New Haven, CT: Yale University Press.

Muller, John. 1999. Modes and Functions of Sublimation. In *The Annual of Psychoanalysis,* Vol. 26–27, ed. Jerome A. Winer, 103–125. Hillsdale, NJ: Analytic Press.

Winnicott, D. W. [1951] 1975. Transitional Objects and Transitional Phenomena. In *Through Paediatrics to Psycho-Analysis,* 229–242. New York: Basic Books.

Winnicott, D. W. 1967. The Location of Cultural Experience. *International Journal of Psycho-Analysis* 48: 368–372.

John P. Muller

SUBLIMINAL SUGGESTION

Subliminal suggestion occurs when messages or ideas that are perceived below (sub) the threshold or limen of conscious awareness influence thoughts, feelings, or actions. A message, object, concept, idea, or other stimulus is perceived *subliminally* when it is processed at a sensory level (visual or auditory) without an accompanying conscious sensory experience. When environmental stimuli (words, symbols, sounds) are subliminally perceived and encoded, mental representations of these stimuli and associated mental constructs are activated. The internal activation of mental representations makes schematically related constructs, goals, and behavioral tendencies more accessible in memory. Consequently, subliminally perceived messages may be "suggestive" of those behaviors that are mentally activated, as their heightened accessibility increases the likelihood that they will be enacted.

Auditory or visual stimuli may be processed nonconsciously under a variety of conditions. Images embedded within complex patterns and vocal messages that are masked by surrounding noise may not be consciously recognized, but implicit tests of familiarity demonstrate that these messages or signals were subliminally perceived and processed. Laboratory studies investigating the limits of subliminal influence most commonly prime behavioral tendencies by flashing words or images on a computer screen for 100 to 300 milliseconds—too quickly to be consciously perceived.

In the late 1950s, subliminal suggestion was claimed to be a commonly used method of influencing consumer purchase behavior at a nonconscious level. This notion was largely popularized by Vance Packard's 1957 book, *The Hidden Persuaders.* This book detailed a study conducted by James Vicary in which theatergoers were subliminally exposed to the messages "buy popcorn" and "drink Coca-Cola" as they were flashed, for a third of a millisecond, onto the picture screen during the movie. Vicary claimed that subliminal exposure to these advertisements caused a rise in Coca-Cola and popcorn sales of 18 percent and 58 percent respectively.

Vicary later admitted that his study was fabricated and hence there was no substance to the claim that subliminal messages were an effective means of persuasion. In 1973, however, Wilson Bryan Key's book *Subliminal Seduction* generated great public concern that subliminal suggestion was practiced widely among advertisers in the United States. Consequently, the Federal Communications Commission declared that the insertion of subliminal messages in advertising was a form of intentional deception that was contrary to the public interest. Hence, marketing professionals concur that the use of subliminal messages in advertising is unethical and could have potentially disastrous consequences for public relations if uncovered.

Beyond these ethical considerations, the effectiveness of advertising with subliminal suggestions is scientifically questionable. Extensive research into implicit (nonconscious) cognition and behavior in the psychological sciences demonstrates that the "suggestive" influence of subliminally perceived messages is limited to words, images, or sounds that are highly familiar, abstract, and simple.

The meaning of a perceived cue cannot be processed at a subliminal level unless there is a preexisting mental representation of this cue. Consequently, it is unlikely that novel images, words, or concepts will influence thoughts and behaviors when they are subliminally processed. Thus unfamiliar product brands will not reliably influence consumption or purchase behavior if they are not consciously perceived.

The meaning or behavioral message associated with subliminally perceived cues is general, not specific. Mental representations of the meaning of such perceptual cues are categorical; that is, the meaning of subliminally perceived cues is construed abstractly. Consequently, subliminally perceived messages may only succeed in influencing one to engage in a *related* activity, if at all. For instance, the subliminal perception of a Coca-Cola brand name may bring the idea of "drink" or "thirst" to consciousness and activate a desire to purchase a drink, but the drink purchased will not necessarily be Coca-Cola. Therefore, subliminal messages are at best suggestive, but never persuasive.

Implicit cognition research has consistently demonstrated that the meaning of complex messages cannot be processed at a subliminal level (Greenwald 1992). The meaning of the words *eat* and *drink* may be processed subliminally, thereby increasing the likelihood that the perceiver will engage in these behaviors. However, more complex messages that include brand names, punctuation, or sentences are not likely to have such a suggestive effect.

SEE ALSO *Advertising; Attitudes; Attitudes, Behavioral; Cognition; Consciousness; Hidden Persuaders; Persuasion; Persuasion, Message-based; Want Creation; Wants*

BIBLIOGRAPHY

Greenwald, Anthony G. 1992. New Look 3. Unconscious Cognition Reclaimed. *American Psychologist* 47 (6): 766–779.

Key, Wilson Bryan. 1973. *Subliminal Seduction: Ad Media's Manipulation of a Not So Innocent America.* Englewood Cliffs, NJ: Prentice-Hall.

Moore, Timothy E. 1982. Subliminal Advertising: What You See Is What You Get. *Journal of Marketing* 46 (2): 38–47.

Underwood, G. 1994. Subliminal Perception on TV. *Nature* 370: 103.

Claire E. Ashton-James
Tanya L. Chartrand

SUBSIDIES

A subsidy is a benefit, in some form, which one would not otherwise receive, but the concept is more complex than such a simple definition implies. The twin cruxes of the problem are the determination of the basis of comparison by which a subsidy is reckoned and whether the comparison is treated positively or normatively and if the latter negatively or affirmatively. Consider the following examples:

A rich uncle will pay your college tuition and living expenses if you go to college.

Parents arrange for one child to inherit more than the other, where the norm is equal shares.

A polluting firm may be offered a payment if it will stop its polluting activities.

A firm producing multiple outputs allocates costs on paper so that they differ from what they actually are; for example, residential customers pay telephone rates below their cost of service and business subscribers pay more than their cost of service, or, more specifically, poor residential customers benefit from below-cost rates that are financed by the higher rates paid by wealthier customers.

An industry is given payments by government so that it will expand, or not contract, thus providing more employment than it otherwise would.

A shift from one costing procedure to another increases some measured costs and decreases others.

A change from one institution to another changes the distribution of gains and losses.

Whether or not a subsidy exists in each of the examples depends on the choice of basis; in the last two examples, the subsidy depends on the cost procedure or the institution used as the basis of comparison.

Accordingly, a decrease in business telephone rates implies a subsidy to business if one believes the lower residential rates are proper; if one thinks that low residential rates involve an improper subsidy to householders, an increase in those rates (and a decrease in business rates) will end the subsidy. A change in rates based on a shift in costing procedure means gainers are being subsidized if you posit that the initial costing procedure is correct; but if you consider the initial costing procedure to be erroneous, those people are now not being subsidized and others are. A change from one costing procedure to another creates a subsidy to gainers if you assume that the initial costing procedure is proper; they are getting more than they should. If you think the second costing procedure is correct, then the gainers are not being subsidized; they are getting what they should. Non-normatively, changes in costing procedures bring about different net income changes.

The foregoing examples are stated in largely non-normative terms. The concept of subsidy often has a negative normative connotation when it could have an affirmative one—it depends on the choice of base as to what people are entitled. The "choice of base" is illustrated in the following examples.

The rich uncle may be spoiling you or he may be contributing to the family's practice of taking care of its own, depending on what view, or base, one takes.

The parents may be punishing one child or they may be providing for a child so ill that he or she cannot support himself or herself. If one feels that children should be treated equally, the ill child is being subsidized. If one feels that distribution of an estate should be a matter of relative need, then no subsidy in a pejorative, i.e., negative, sense is created.

One may feel that polluters should not be rewarded for polluting by paying them not to pollute; indeed, they should be taxed if they pollute. Yet, the tax and payment policies are analytically equivalent. Imposing a tax on pollution lowers the polluters' profits, thereby inducing them to spend money to install pollution-preventing equipment to avoid paying the tax; similarly, providing a subsidy to install such equipment can induce the firm to enhance its income position by receiving the subsidy. In each case, the firm is led to change its behavior, and the result is less pollution.

An alternate definition of a subsidy is a benefit, in some form, that is not received through the market. This definition posits market distribution as the base. Several problems arise with this definition. Firstly, the market is not the only decisional arrangement in society; government and nonprofit organizations are other modes of distributing gains and losses, and positing market distribution negates these other modes. Secondly, there is no such thing as "the market"; there can be different markets, all of which are the result of the actions, plans, and strategies of firms and of governments to influence the structure and performance of markets. Distribution through one market is a subsidy if an individual considers another market to be proper. Different structures of power lead to different structures of rights and of markets; whether a subsidy exists will depend on the structure posited as proper.

For the rich uncle, one may substitute one's church or the government or other nonprofit educational and charitable institutions. These may receive voluntary donations and transfer the money to people who qualify on the basis of perceived capabilities, needs, or redistributive goals, to create and give effect to a sense of community—payments giving effect to people's social preferences. Programs to encourage the integration of immigrants into the community may involve short-run subsidies, but they avoid the costs of unemployment dislocation and enhance productivity in the long run by improving working and other skills. The benefit so transferred may qualify as a subsidy under the definition of subsidy as a benefit which one would not receive through the market. That privileges market determination, or, more properly, the power structure that produces certain actual markets and not others, and debases other, nonmarket decisional processes.

The negative connotation of a subsidy may be warranted in the case of "pork" politics and the "Christmas tree" collection of payments and other benefits to interest groups having influence in the legislature. This view is only partly in conflict with those that see the role of government as helping to solve problems in the social interest and enabling people to receive their just due. It may be that a distinction has to be made between transfers/subsidies that represent returns to political fund contributors and those that represent putative solutions to social problems; however, the language of political symbolism is elastic enough to blur the distinction.

SEE ALSO *Unemployment*

BIBLIOGRAPHY

Boulding, Kenneth E. 1972. *Redistribution to the Rich and the Poor.* Belmont, CA: Wadsworth.

Buchanan, James M. 1987. *Public Finance in Democratic Process.* Chapel Hill: University of North Carolina Press.

Lasswell, Harold D. 1936. *Politics: Who Gets What, When, How.* New York: McGraw-Hill.

Musgrave, Richard A. 1986. *Public Finance in a Democratic Society.* New York: New York University Press.

Page, Benjamin I. 1983. *Who Gets What from Government.* Berkeley: University of California Press.

Sen, Amartya K. 1999. *Commodities and Capabilities.* New York: Oxford University Press.

Warren J. Samuels

SUBSIDIES, FARM

Farm subsidies are monetary transfers from taxpayers and consumers to producers of agricultural commodities, and they are mostly a characteristic of high- and middle-income countries. They were first introduced in the United States on a large scale shortly after the 1929 crisis, mainly in response to fears of inadequate food supplies (Gardner 2002). Since then, subsidies have been renewed by the U.S. Congress every five to six years under legislation, the so-called Farm Bills. Farm subsidies were introduced in Europe after World War II, again as means to prevent food shortages, and were institutionalized after the introduction of the Common Agricultural Policy following the Treaty of Rome. Other countries with considerable levels of farm subsidies are Korea, Japan, Mexico, and Turkey. Farm subsidies achieved their objective of increasing food availability. However, despite huge food surpluses during the last three decades of the twentieth century, not only have they remained in place but they have been increased and applied to more commodities.

Based on their source of funding, farm subsidies are categorized as either taxpayer financed or consumer financed. Taxpayer-financed subsidies are direct transfers from the treasury to commodity producers; most payments are based on quantity produced or area planted, while some are based on input use or other requirements, such as conservation measures. However, because these types of subsidies cause considerable distortions to world commodity markets, countries have attempted to decouple payments from current production and instead give subsidies in the form of direct income support as a way to make them less trade distortionary (Baffes and de Gorter 2005). Consumer-financed subsidies are typically associated with tariffs imposed on imports or subsidies on exports.

Farm subsidies are monitored by the Organization of Economic Cooperation and Development (OECD), which publishes detailed figures each year. During 2002–2005 total transfers to agricultural producers or consumers of agricultural products in OECD countries averaged $357 billion, of which 56 percent were financed by consumers, while the remaining 46 percent were financed by taxpayers. The European Union accounts for 39 percent of subsidies, while the United States and Japan account for 27 percent and 16 percent, respectively. The remaining 17 percent are accounted for by Korea, Turkey, Mexico, and Canada. On a commodity basis, the largest beneficiary is the milk industry, followed by producers of beef, rice, and wheat.

Because farm subsidies induce overproduction, which in turn depresses world prices, there have been attempts to limit them (Aksoy and Beghin 2004). Limiting the level of farm subsidies was first considered during the Uruguay Round (1986–1994) of multilateral trade negotiations under the aegis of the General Agreement of Tariffs and Trade (GATT). It was agreed that taxpayer-financed subsidies with the most distortionary impact on trade would be gradually reduced from their 1986–1988 level. It was also agreed that export subsidies should be eliminated, while tariffs on imports should be reduced by approximately one-third of their initial level. However, because the formulas for calculating such reductions were complicated, most countries were able to fulfill their obligations by changing the nature of subsidies rather than undertaking real reductions. The issue of subsidies was reconsidered during the Doha Development Agenda, which was launched in 2001. However, farm subsidies turned out to be one of the most contentious issues of the agenda, and the negotiations were suspended.

SEE ALSO *Agricultural Economics; Agricultural Industry; Distortions; European Union; General Agreement on Tariffs and Trade; Subsidies; Tariffs; Taxes*

BIBLIOGRAPHY

Aksoy, M. Ataman, and John C. Beghin. 2004. *Global Agricultural Trade and Developing Countries.* Washington, DC: World Bank.

Baffes, John, and Harry de Gorter. 2005. Disciplining Agricultural Support through Decoupling. Policy Research Working Paper 3533. Washington, DC: World Bank.

Gardner, Bruce L. 2002. *American Agriculture in the Twentieth Century: How It Flourished and What It Cost.* Cambridge, MA: Harvard University Press.

John Baffes

SUBSISTENCE AGRICULTURE

The peasant concept of the good life is the minimum expenditure of physical labor. When applied to food production, peasants expend only enough labor to grow enough food to last until the next harvest. Labor expenditures are matched to the food needed for a subsistence diet. This defines the subsistence compromise and explains why peasant societies experience endemic seasonal hunger and are vulnerable to famine conditions in consecutive poor crop years. Seasonal hunger and peacetime famine conditions affect all peasant societies regardless of race, religion, climate, population density, cultivation practices, and subsistence crops grown. Even peasant societies with low population densities that cultivate fertile soils experience endemic hunger and famine conditions.

Three social values govern subsistence agriculture: (1) equalized opportunities for qualifying households to share cultivation rights on village land, (2) minimal labor expenditures in food production (subsistence labor norms) on the assumption that every crop year will be normal, and (3) equalized sharing of harvests in poor crop years to ensure the survival of all village households. Only by analyzing the operation of the subsistence compromise at the village level can scholars and political leaders understand why seasonal hunger is endemic in peasant societies and why famine conditions recur.

LAND

The primary source of subsistence food safety for peasant households is communal land tenure, the equalized allocation of cultivation rights on land controlled by village councils. The purpose of communal tenure is to distribute enough land to qualifying households to grow subsistence amounts of food with subsistence labor norms.

Partible inheritance is the usual way for equalizing subsistence opportunities. Customary law mandates equally dividing land among surviving sons at the death of the household head. Inheriting households acquire cultivation rights to equal portions of each category of land. Each household gets a parcel in the most fertile field (irrigated or best drained) and in as many other fields as there are variations in fertility. A common result of partible inheritance is households cultivating several parcels that are scattered on village land. As population densities increase, village land is divided into many small parcels (morselation).

Equalized access to land use is also often enforced by periodic redistribution of land by lot. Redistribution may be done annually or every second, third, fourth, or tenth year. Customary law mandates that land in communal tenure is a perpetual reservoir for periodic redistribution. It cannot be sold by occupying households because they do not own it; nor can fences be built because they would impede periodic redistribution.

When a village's land can no longer be physically divided without drastically impairing productivity, the number of parcels is stabilized. Harvest sharing, however, continues. Clifford Geertz in his 1963 book calls land and harvest sharing "agricultural involution" because it seeks to maximize the number of households that can be fed from a fixed area of arable land.

LABOR

As long as communal tenure operates, customary law protects the performance of subsistence labor norms. Control of land use allows landholding households to control labor expenditures through several strategies, the most common of which is parents' transferring as much labor as possible to dependents. All peasant societies have high birthrates because households desire many children so that large amounts of agricultural labor can be transferred to them at a young age. Transferring agricultural labor to dependents also occurs through the use of slaves; the use of sharecroppers; the assignment of gender tasks; having multiple wives; and in India, through the Hindu caste system. These practices rely on the least motivated or physically weakest members of peasant societies to perform agricultural labor. Seasonal hunger is often an annual event in normal crop years because their inefficient labor is combined with minimal agricultural labor performed by adult male heads of households.

Peasants believe that a fixed amount of annual labor will produce adequate subsistence harvests in normal crop years although they know that not all crop years are normal. Nonetheless, they willingly risk seasonal hunger to preserve subsistence labor norms. Households always calculate how much labor is required to feed their households until the next harvest, and after this labor is performed, peasants view indolence as the proper use of time.

HARVEST SHARING

In poor crop years, customary law mandates harvest sharing, which most clearly visible in densely populated villages that must practice intensive cultivation. Landless households acquire claims to shares of harvests, usually through sharecropping, by performing disproportionately large amounts of agricultural labor for landholding households.

The ethic of harvest sharing dampens the motivation of a small minority of households to respond to commercial incentives to grow enlarged food surpluses for sale on anonymous markets. Harvest sharing is a leveling institution that enforces a near equality in food-producing capabilities. Preventing households from growing enlarged harvests for market sale ensures that food loans (however small) are available for hungry households. The result is that households that are receptive to commercial incentives do not perform the necessary labor to grow enlarged harvests because any surpluses they produce will not be theirs to sell. Although certainly not economic, harvest sharing is the moral economy of the peasantry. It sustains subsistence agriculture because it tries to ensure that all village households will have enough food to survive poor crop years.

CULTIVATION PRACTICES

The fixed amount of agricultural labor required to produce subsistence-sized harvests is proportional to population density. Labor expenditures are minimal in shifting cultivation but increase as land is more intensively cultivated. Shifting cultivation, practiced where land is abundant and people are few, requires less per capita labor than any other cultivation practice because there is no ground preparation. Trees are cut and burned and women and children dibble the seeds of food grains (rice, barley, rye, maize, sorghum) into the ground among charred stumps and a tangle of partially burned branches. Thereafter weeding is haphazard and is done by women and children. Land is cultivated for two, three, or four years and then allowed to revert to secondary forest. In eight to twenty years the canopy of the secondary forest shades grasses to death. The forest is recut and burned and the ground replanted. Yields are low, but so too are labor inputs.

As population increases, shifting cultivation is replaced by continuous cultivation; and as population further increases, continuous cultivation evolves into intensive cultivation. The most visible signs of continuous cultivation are fields and terraces without stumps and ground preparation by plows pulled by oxen or water buffalo. Rice cultivators build terraces to retain a water cover to drown competing weeds, and seeds are broadcast sown. When rice cultivation intensifies, women plant germinated blades one at a time. Further intensification requires irrigation, double cropping, intense weeding, and fertilization. Ester Boserup (1965, 1970) has documented that a high percentage of the additional labor required for intensive cultivation is done by women.

TRADE

All contemporary peasant societies are monetized. As long as peasants control enough land to achieve subsistence diets in normal crop years, their money needs are minimal. Cultural anthropologists have documented that peasant households produce only enough exchange commodities to acquire target sums of money. Typically exchange commodities are one or two bags of grain, but they can be seed cotton, wool, unprocessed coffee beans, tobacco, cinnamon bark, latex sheets, or fowls.

The money acquired through trade is used to purchase a limited variety of manufactured products. Typically these products are textiles, edged tools, cooking pots, plastic pails, and plastic sandals. Manufactured products substitute for fragile handicraft products that need continuous replacement. Peasants compute the durability and utility of manufactured products over handicraft products by comparing the amount of labor required to make handicraft products with the amount of labor required to produce exchange commodities. If the terms of trade are favorable, measured in the amounts of labor saved, peasant households produce commodities specifically for sale. Often these products—coffee, tea, latex sheets—have minimal or no household use, and frequently much of the labor is done by children. Target sums of money are not incomes because in poor crop years little money is acquired and peasant households make few purchases. The welfare of peasant households does not depend on money incomes but rather on control of land use.

ECONOMIC DEVELOPMENT

Economists like Theodore W. Schultz observed subsistence agriculture without understanding the revolutionary differences between subsistence and commercial social values, between subsistence and commercial labor norms, or between communal and freehold tenure. Nor do most economists understand how assured food surpluses came to be produced in some European nations after 1600 with fewer laborers working longer hours.

Schultz's analysis of peasant agriculture is based on the false assumption that commercial social values and commercial labor norms are universal and that they operate in peasant villages. On the basis of this assumption, Schultz claimed that peasants were eager to adopt green revolution technologies, improved seed, mechanical plowing, fertilizers, all of which must be purchased if investments made them available. For Schultz and economists who followed his lead, the green revolution was technology that could magically end peasant privation. But peasant privation was not in fact ended because Schultz and most economists did not understand that peasant societies have huge amounts of unused male labor. Assured food surpluses can be produced by supervising agricultural labor—similar to labor performed on plantations. Some of this labor entails better ground preparation, timely seeding, more weeding, and better feeding of draft animals. Peasants reject green revolution technologies because increased per capita yields require adopting these technologies as a package, and applying the package requires much more labor. Only when more people must be fed from the same area of land are some green revolution technologies adopted, because they are necessary to sustain a subsistence level of food production and consumption.

W. Arthur Lewis was an experienced observer of peasant labor norms. He understood that the first step in ending subsistence privation was more agricultural labor performed by males. Unfortunately, policies prescribed by international aid agencies continue to be guided by Schultz's misconception that peasants are eager to adopt green revolution technologies. In most peasant societies per capita food production remains stationary.

SEE ALSO *Agricultural Economics; Agricultural Industry; Food; Habits; Lewis, W. Arthur; Migration, Rural to Urban; Peasantry; Tradition*

BIBLIOGRAPHY

Boserup, Ester. 1965. *The Conditions of Agricultural Growth: The Economics of Agrarian Change under Population Pressure.* Chicago: Aldine.

Boserup, Ester. 1970. *Woman's Role in Economic Development.* New York: St. Martin's Press.

Geertz, Clifford. 1963. *Agricultural Involution: The Process of Ecological Change in Indonesia.* Berkeley: University of California Press.

Lewis, W. Arthur. 1955. *The Theory of Economic Growth.* New York: Harper Torchbooks.

Schultz, Theodore W. 1964. *Transforming Traditional Agriculture.* New Haven, CT: Yale University Press.

Seavoy, Ronald E. 1973a. The Shading Cycle in Shifting Cultivation. *Annals of the Association of American Geographers* 63: 522–528.

Seavoy, Ronald E. 1973b. The Transition to Continuous Rice Cultivation in Kalimantan. *Annals of the Association of American Geographers* 63: 218–225.

Seavoy, Ronald E. 1977. Social Restraints on Food Production in Indonesian Subsistence Culture. *Journal of Southeast Asian Studies* 8: 15–30.

Seavoy, Ronald E. 1980. Population Pressure and Land Use Change: From Tree Crops to Sawah in Northwestern Kalimantan, Indonesia. *Singapore Journal of Tropical Geography* 1: 61–67.

Seavoy, Ronald E. 1986. *Famine in Peasant Societies.* Westport, CT: Greenwood Press.

Seavoy, Ronald E. 2000. *Subsistence and Economic Development.* Westport, CT: Praeger.

Ronald E. Seavoy

SUBSTITUTABILITY

Substitutability is a fundamental concept in economics and is encountered in both consumer theory and producer theory. To illustrate, assume a finite number of commodities (say *n*) and consider the following (direct) utility function,

$$u = f(x_1, x_2, ..., x_n),$$

where $(x_1, x_2, ..., x_n)$ is the commodity vector. Commodities *i* and *j* are said to be *substitutes* if

$$\frac{\partial^2 f(x_1, x_2, ..., x_n)}{\partial x_i \partial x_j} < 0,$$

that is, if increased consumption of x_j reduces the marginal utility of x_i, and vice versa. If the second-order partial derivative is positive, then x_i and x_j are *complements*, and if it is zero, then x_i and x_j are *independent*.

Although the sign of the above second-order partial derivative is invariant under linear transformations of the utility function, it is not invariant under monotonic increasing transformations of the utility function. The demand system, however, has the advantage of being invariant under monotonic increasing transformations of the utility function. The demand system is obtained by maximizing $u = f(x_1, x_2, ..., x_n)$ subject to the budget constraint,

$$p_1 x_1 + p_2 x_2 + ... + p_n x_n = y,$$

where $(p_1, p_2, ..., p_n$, is the vector of prices and *y* is income. The demand systems is given by

$$x_i = x_i(p_1, p_2, ..., p_n, y), \quad i = 1, 2, ..., n$$

and gives the quantity demanded (of each commodity) as a function of the prices of all commodities and income.

In terms of the demand system, we can find out how the demand for good x_i changes if the price of good x_j changes. In particular, if $\Delta x_i / \Delta p_j > 0$, then x_i is a *gross substitute* for x_j, meaning that when x_j becomes more expensive the consumer switches to consuming x_i; in other words, the consumer substitutes away from the relatively more expensive good towards the relatively less expensive good. If $\Delta x_i / \Delta p_j < 0$, then x_i is a *gross complement* for x_j, meaning that when x_j becomes more expensive the consumer reduces the consumption of x_j and also of x_i; complements are goods that are consumed together (as, for example, coffee and sugar).

The definitions given above are in gross terms because they ignore the *income effect*—that is, the change in demand of good x_i due to the change in purchasing power as a result of the change in the price of good x_j. The

Slutsky equation—see Mas-Colell, Whinston, and Green (1995) for more details—decomposes the total effect of a price change on demand into a substitution effect and an income effect, as follows:

$$\frac{\partial x_i}{\partial p_j} = k_{ij} - \frac{\partial x_i}{\partial y} x_j,$$

where $\partial x_i / \partial p_j$ is the total effect of a price change on demand, k_{ij} is the substitution effect of a compensated price change on demand, and $-\partial x_i / \partial y)x_j$ is the income effect, resulting from a change in price (not in income). Hicks (1956) suggested using the sign of the cross-substitution effect (that is, the change in compensated demand) to classify goods as substitutes whenever k_{ij} is positive. In fact, according to Hicks (1956), $k_{ij} > 0$ indicates substitutability, $k_{ij} < 0$ indicates complementarity, and $k_{ij} = 0$ indicates independence.

One important property of the Slutsky equation is that the cross-substitution effects are symmetric, that is

$$k_{ij} = k_{ji}$$

This symmetry restriction may also be written in elasticity terms, as follows

$$\frac{\eta_{ij}}{s_j} + E_i = \frac{\eta_{ji}}{s_i} + E_j$$

where η_{ij} is the elasticity of demand of good *i* with respect to the price of good *j*, E_i is the income elasticity of demand of good *i*, and $s_j = p_j x_j / y$ is the proportion of total expenditure devoted to good *j*.

The symmetrical terms in the above equation are the Allen elasticities of substitution, so that the equation can be written as

$$\sigma_{ij}^a = \frac{\eta_{ij}}{s_j} + E_i = \frac{\eta_{ji}}{s_i} + E_j = \sigma_{ji}^a$$

where σ_{ij}^a denotes the Allen elasticity of substitution between goods *i* and *j*—see Allen (1938) for more details. If $\sigma_{ij}^a > 0$, goods *i* and *j* are said to be Allen substitutes, in the sense that an increase in the price of good *j* causes an increased consumption of good *i*. If, however, $\sigma_{ij}^a < 0$, then the goods are said to be Allen complements, in the sense that an increase in the price of good *j* causes a decreased consumption of good *i*.

The Allen elasticity of substitution is the traditional measure and has been employed to measure substitution behavior and structural instability in a variety of contexts. When there are more than two goods, however, the Allen elasticity may be uninformative and the Morishima elasticity of substitution,

$$\sigma_{ij}^{m} = s_i(\sigma_{ji}^{a} - \sigma_{ii}^{a}),$$

is the correct measure of substitution elasticity—see Morishima (1967) and Blackorby and Russell (1989). Notice that σ_{ij}^{m} measures the net change in the compensated demand for good j when the price of good i changes. Goods will be Morishima complements (substitutes) if an increase in the price of i causes x_i/x_j to decrease (increase).

In the producer context, the producer's problem can be formulated as

$$C(w_1, w_2,\ldots, w_n, y) = \min_x w_1 x_1 + w_2 x_2 + \ldots + w_n x_n$$

subject to

$$y = f(x_1, x_2, \ldots, x_n),$$

where w_i denotes the price for input i, y denotes output, and x_i denotes input i. Inputs i and j are said to be *substitutes* if

$$\frac{\partial^2 C(w_1, w_2, \ldots, w_n, y)}{\partial w_i \partial w_j} > 0.$$

If the second-order partial derivative is negative, then x_i and x_j are *complements*.

As in the consumer context, the degree of substitutability between any pair of factors in the producer context is also measured using the elasticity of substitution. The Allen elasticity of substitution in the cost minimization framework can be obtained by

$$\sigma_{ij}^{a} = \frac{C \times C_{ij}}{C_i \times C_j} = \frac{\varepsilon_{ij}}{s_j},$$

where C_i is the partial derivative of the cost function with respect to the price of the i th factor, and C_{ij} is the partial derivative of C_i with respect to the price of the j th factor. $\varepsilon_{ij} = \partial \ln x_i / \partial \ln w_j$ is the elasticity of the demand for the i th factor (x_i) with respect to the price of the j th factor (w_j). $s_j = w_j x_j / \sum_k w_k x_k$ is the cost share of input j.

Again, as in the consumer context, when there are more than two goods, the Allen elasticity may be uninformative and the Morishima elasticity of substitution, calculated as

$$\sigma_{ij}^{m} = \frac{w_j \times C_{ij}}{C_i} - \frac{w_j \times C_{jj}}{C_j} = \varepsilon_{ij} - \varepsilon_{jj},$$

is the correct measure of substitution elasticity—see Morishima (1967) and Blackorby and Russell (1989).

The conceptual foundations of the Allen and Morishima elasticities of substitution are different. The Allen elasticity of substitution classifies a pair of inputs as direct substitutes (complements) if an increase in the price of one causes an increase (decrease) in the quantity demanded of the other, whereas the Morishima elasticity of substitution classifies a pair of inputs as direct substitutes (complements) if an increase in the price of one causes the quantity of the other to increase (decrease) relative to the quantity of the input whose price has changed. For this reason, the Morishima elasticity of substitution leans more toward substitutability. To put it differently, if two inputs are direct substitutes according to the Allen elasticity of substitution, theoretically they must be direct substitutes according to the Morishima elasticity of substitution, but if two inputs are direct complements according to the Allen elasticity of substitution, they can be either direct complements or direct substitutes according to the Morishima elasticity of substitution.

BIBLIOGRAPHY

Allen, R. G. D. 1938. *Mathematical Analysis for Economists.* London: Macmillan.

Blackorby, Charles, and R. Robert Russell. 1989. Will the Real Elasticity of Substitution Please Stand Up? (A Comparison of the Allen/Uzawa and Morishima Elasticities). *American Economic Review* 79 (4): 882–888.

Hicks, John R. 1956. *A Revision of Demand Theory.* Oxford: Clarendon Press.

Mas-Colell, Andreu, Michael D. Whinston, and Jerry R. Green. 1995. *Microeconomic Theory.* Oxford and New York: Oxford University Press.

Morishima. M. 1967. A Few Suggestions on the Theory of Elasticity (in Japanese). *Keizai Hyoron* (*Economic Review*) 16: 144–150.

Apostolos Serletis

SUBURBAN SPRAWL

Suburbanization, the movement of resources and people out of cities, has increased sprawl: the overdevelopment, congestion, and environmental degradation of regions. Suburbanization and suburban sprawl are the result of several factors, including economic change—such as deindustrialization—that acts as a centrifugal force that propels private investment and people outward into the suburbs, large public and private investments in highways, government subsidies for low interest mortgage loans, and suburban housing development. Simultaneously, resources and people are pushed outward to the suburbs by the concentration of problems and poverty in urban

America—unemployment, crime, poorly performing schools, poor services, and decaying infrastructure—which are partly due to a dwindling tax base and comparatively low per-capita government spending. Thus, the growth of the suburbs, which tend to be more affluent and mostly white compared to urban areas, not only has exacerbated residential segregation by race, ethnicity, and class, it has also contributed to the creation of suburban sprawl.

The concentration of poverty in central-city neighborhoods—where 20 to 40 percent of a typical region's population lives—destabilizes families, schools, and neighborhoods. It produces dramatic increases in a host of social ills and the loss of economic and social opportunity. As population and businesses flee, poverty and racial segregation grows. Property values and revenue income erode and deplete needed local social services and government capacity.

Older working class inner-ring and middle-income adjacent suburbs—where 20 to 30 percent of a typical region's population lives—soon become riddled with similar problems. While poverty rates are twice as high in central cities than in the suburbs, 30.5 percent of the nation's poor live in the suburbs. Ironically, however, many of these areas—particularly in the older inner-ring suburbs—are less able to address such growing problems because their local governments have fewer resources than the more affluent suburbs. Per capita they have the lowest sales, property, and income tax bases but higher tax rates and lower spending on services. Suburban sprawl spreads out even further to growing middle-class communities—where another 20 to 40 percent of a typical region's population resides—that often do not have a sufficient property tax base to support the growing needs for schools and other public services. Although some of these suburbs are growing in population, they are not always able to maintain levels of tax revenues needed to meet growing demand for services, including schools, police, fire, utilities, and sanitation, particularly in the context of declining fiscal support from the federal and state governments. These fiscally and environmentally stressed communities become declining suburbs.

The stable, secure, and affluent suburbs—where only 15 to 30 percent of a region's population live—captures the lion's share of infrastructural investment and spending, economic growth and jobs, usually paid in part by other parts of the region. They enjoy many benefits: funding for roads, wastewater treatment, airports, shared labor, and product markets. Their tax base expands and per-capita spending soars, while their housing markets exclude others. But their prosperity is not due only to their hard work and good fortune. It has been subsidized by federal and state policies.

The rapid expansion of the number of political jurisdictions to over 90,000 in the early 2000s is mostly due to the creation of new suburbs. Suburban political incorporation allows suburbs to insulate themselves from cities, protect their tax base and property values, build better schools, and siphon off transportation dollars and business investment. Affluent suburbs avoid most regional responsibilities and burdens. They do not pay for central city services and infrastructure that commuters use, including sanitation, police, bridges, airports, sports complexes, and so on. At the same time these affluent suburbs deplete remaining green space and endanger fragile and precious environmental resources.

As a result, the racial composition and quality of life of metropolitan areas has concomitantly shifted dramatically: suburban dwellers, who remain largely white, score higher than inner-city residents, who are predominantly people of color, in nearly every opportunity category—including income, employment, assets, quality of education, and housing—and with lower crime rates.

Conventional explanations of suburban sprawl include: (1) individual choices and cultural differences; (2) poorly designed urban renewal and social programs; and (3) deindustrialization, changing market forces, and globalization.

But others have shown that suburban sprawl is also a consequence of a host of historically created and contemporarily sustained sets of public policies and private practices. Following World War II (1939–1945), billions of dollars wielded by national, state, and local governments provided pathways out of cities for millions of white working and middle-class residents. For example, the GI Bill, the Interstate Highway Act, and home mortgage loan programs contributed to suburban sprawl. Without aid for home buying and highway construction, white middle-class exodus would not have occurred on such a large scale. In short, suburban sprawl has been subsidized. Moreover, inner-city poverty and suburban prosperity are not coincidental; they are two sides of the same coin.

Ironically, the fate of suburbs, central cities, and older suburbs are inextricably linked. Both suburbanites and inner-city residents have a stake in regional developments, partly because regional economies prosper or falter as a whole. Their destinies are intertwined. Thus, regional level solutions may be necessary to address inner-city poverty and suburban sprawl.

BIBLIOGRAPHY

Benfield, F. Kaid, Matthew D. Raimi, and Donald D. T. Chen. 1999. *Once There Were Greenfields: How Urban Sprawl Is Undermining America's Environment, Economy, and Social Fabric.* Washington, DC: National Resources Defense Council.

Dreier, Peter, John Mollenkopf, and Todd Swanstrom. 2001. *Place Matters: Metropolitics for the Twenty First Century.* Lawrence: University of Kansas Press.

Jackson, Kenneth. 1985. *Crabgrass Frontier: The Suburbanization of the United States.* New York: New York University Press.

Katz, Bruce, ed. 2000. Introd. to *Reflections on Regionalism.* Washington, DC: Brookings Institution Press.

Lindstrom, Matthew J., and Hugh Bartling. 2003. *Suburban Sprawl: Culture, Theory, and Politics.* Lanham, MD: Rowman & Littlefield.

Orfield, Myron. 1997. *Metropolitics: A Regional Agenda for Community and Stability.* Washington, DC: Brookings Institution Press.

Pastor, Manuel. 2001. Geography and Opportunity. In *America Becoming: Racial Trends and Their Consequences*, vol. 1, eds. Neil Smelser, William Julius Wilson, and Faith Mitchell. Washington, DC: National Academy Press.

Rusk, David. 1993. *Cities without Suburbs.* Washington, DC: The Woodrow Wilson Center Press.

Ron Hayduk

SUBURBS

"Every true suburb is the outcome of two opposing forces, an attraction toward the opportunities of the great city and a simultaneous repulsion against urban life" (Fishman 1987, p. 26). Though suburbs are defined by the U.S. Census Bureau as any territory within a metropolitan area yet outside of the central city, the formation of suburbs is not simply based on geographic location. Suburbs are largely the product of people's desire for separation based on social factors. These factors vary between instances of suburb formation, but frequently include separation of class, religious, cultural, ethnic, or racial groups. The traditional pattern of white populations and wealth found in U.S. suburbs is not mirrored internationally, although the common feature of suburbs around the world is separation of populations. For instance, the suburbs of Mumbai, India, house many of the city's poor, while in Paris the suburbs are ethnically stratified, with suburban ethnic minority populations suffering from high rates of unemployment and other forms of discrimination.

The early suburbs of London, as well as several in the United States, were built around the separation of different economic classes. During the eighteenth century, wealthy business owners in London began to use landholdings around Westminster as a way to avoid the lower classes within urban areas. A century later, the same happened in the United States around the cities of New York, Philadelphia, and Boston. Suburbs such as these, based on class separation, can best be described as bourgeois enclaves. Here the wealthy could establish communities that reflected their own values and beliefs (Fishman 1987).

The formation of middle-class suburbs in the United States beginning in the early twentieth century and expanding rapidly after World War II (1939–1945) is the result of a number of factors. A strong economy at the beginning of the century made the suburban lifestyle more accessible to many Americans. The development of lower-cost homogenized housing, such as the Sears Catalog home, made purchasing a house a realistic prospect for the middle class. In the 1920s, U.S. suburban growth surpassed urban growth for the first time (Weeks 1981). Economic factors during the Great Depression caused the growth of suburbs to decline drastically. In the late 1940s and 1950s, however, suburban growth rates resurged and reached their highest levels (Rothblatt and Garr 1986). This resurgence is frequently attributed to strong economic growth and social programs like the GI Bill that provided opportunities to service members after the war.

In 1947 construction began on Levittown on Long Island, New York, a project considered the start of the middle-class suburban revolution in America. The rapid expansion of the freeway system during the early 1950s made possible the development of many similar communities, as is evident in the expansion of freeways and homes in the Los Angeles area (Fishman 1987; Weeks 1981). *Levittown* has since become a term used to describe various social problems accompanying the formation of suburbs, including white flight, cultural wasteland, and separate spheres of family and economic life (Keller 1998).

Home ownership, achieved through the development of suburbs, is the most important factor of wealth accumulation in American society. While economic factors played a significant role in the formation of suburbs, they do not explain why middle-class Americans felt the need to escape urban areas that had previously been acceptable to them. In fact, economic factors have helped constrain suburban growth that has been driven by other factors, such as race. Prior to the twentieth century, there had been a relatively small African American population in U.S. cities. However, the migration of African Americans from rural areas in the early twentieth century brought significant white resistance and a push for racially segregated housing areas (Massey and Denton 1998). *White flight*, the mass migration of whites out of the cities, was hindered by economic factors during the Great Depression. Following World War II, however, the movement of whites to the peripheral areas around cities, coupled with social and institutional policies of racially restrictive housing, resulted in high degrees of racial segregation. White flight became a major factor in school desegregation policy; in the mid-1970s a debate arose over whether busing for the purpose of school desegregation would lead to increases in white flight.

School desegregation has had numerous effects on the formation and structure of America's suburbs. In the midst of the period of white flight, the U.S. Supreme Court decision in *Brown v. Board of Education* (1954) led to the integration of many schools in neighborhoods that had previously been white enclaves. A number of measures were taken by white communities and conservative local and state governments to resist school integration. School busing during the 1960s and 1970s became a strongly debated issue, and residents of suburbs found they could maintain racial segregation of schools more effectively than had been possible in inner-city areas. Due to the effectiveness of suburbs as residential enclaves, white residents could gerrymander school districts in order to halt integration (James 1989). By the late 1970s, school busing had become a less pressing issue (Woodard 1998). While affirmative action policies remained in effect, opposition to such policies rose during the 1980s with the idea that the United States had transcended racial issues. As a result, there has been an increase in school segregation in suburban areas since 1989 (Reardon et al. 2000). In addition, policies still in place to aid school integration are being challenged throughout the country, despite the fact that public schools remain heavily segregated. In 2006 the Supreme Court heard arguments in two cases regarding school integration policies that some parents considered discriminatory. Cases from Seattle, Washington, and Louisville, Kentucky, reviewed whether public schools can take race into consideration in campus assignments in order to achieve racial integration. In a 5–4 decision the Court declared that schools attempting to achieve or maintain racial integration cannot do so by measures that take explicit account of the students' race (Greenhouse 2007).

Despite the passage in 1968 of the Fair Housing Act, little progress has been made toward racial integration of suburbs (Orser 1998). The Fair Housing Act prohibited owners, real-estate agents, and renters from denying access to housing on the basis of race. The act also outlawed lying about the availability of a dwelling, and prevented *blockbusting* (telling white residents that minorities are moving into a neighborhood in an effort to convince them to sell) (Sidney 2003). As of 1990, only 20 percent of Americans lived in desegregated neighborhoods (Darden 1998). Housing segregation between whites and Hispanics, as well as between whites and Asians, has risen since 1980. However, studies have shown that suburbanization is tied to socioeconomic status among Hispanics and Asians, but suburbs have remained mostly closed to blacks whatever their socioeconomic status (Darden 1998). Housing discrimination has also contributed to higher levels of poverty, a lower average income, and lower life chances for those trapped in declining inner-city neighborhoods.

One result of the formation of suburbs was that people who were left behind in urban neighborhoods were forced to deal with urban decay brought about by the flight of millions out of the cities. Buildings were left empty, and businesses were forced to close and move to more profitable areas. Resources previously available within cities were shifted to peripheral areas as suburbs grew. The 1949 Housing Act was designed to facilitate redevelopment in areas that had been affected by urban decay; this process came to be known as *urban renewal*. The act sparked a debate over how to handle such renewal. Federal subsides were given to private developers in order to generate new business within urban areas. But development was centered heavily around the interests of those in suburban areas, and little attention was paid to the needs of those living within urban areas. In addition, most urban development took place in residential areas, forcing many out of their homes. Eventually, a compromise was reached, and developers were required to find alternative housing for those displaced by urban renewal (Hays 1995). Urban-renewal plans have consistently favored the interests of the suburbs. As far back as 1766 an urban-renewal plan for London was designed around the needs of business owners with little regard for workers and lower-class citizens (Fishman 1987). Today, urban renewal still often functions in the interests of suburban residents over the poor and minorities who remain in inner cities.

From 1970 to 1990, the number of high-poverty metropolitan areas doubled; these areas are more likely to be home to traditionally disadvantaged minorities (Sidney 2003). American suburbs formed out of a desire for racial segregation. In the twenty-first century, continuing housing discrimination in America's suburbs leads to a continuation of racial segregation with increases in economic stratification.

SEE ALSO *Segregation, Residential; Sociology, Urban; Towns*

BIBLIOGRAPHY

Barnes, Robert. 2006. Supreme Court to Review Two School Integration Plans. *Washington Post,* December 3: A3.

Darden, Joe T. 1998. Desegregation of Housing. In *Encyclopedia of Urban America: The Cities and Suburbs,* ed. Neil Larry Shumsky, 247–249. Santa Barbara, CA: ABC-CLIO.

Fishman, Robert. 1987. *Bourgeois Utopias the Rise and Fall of Suburbia.* New York: Basic Books.

Greenhouse, Linda. 2007. Justices Limit the Use of Race in School Plans for Integration. *New York Times,* June 29.

Hays, R. Allen. 1995. *The Federal Government and Urban Housing: Ideology and Change in Public Policy.* 2nd ed. Albany: State University of New York Press.

James, David R. 1989. City Limits on Racial Equality: The Effects of City-Suburb Boundaries on Public-School

Desegregation, 1968–1976. *American Sociological Review* 54 (6): 963–985.

Keller, Mollie. 1998. Levittown. In *Encyclopedia of Urban America: The Cities and Suburbs*, ed. Neil Larry Shumsky, 431–432. Santa Barbara, CA: ABC-CLIO.

Massey, Douglas, and Nancy Denton. 1998. *American Apartheid: Segregation and the Making of the Underclass.* Cambridge, MA: Harvard University Press.

Orser, W. Edward. 1998. White Flight. In *Encyclopedia of Urban America: The Cities and Suburbs*, ed. Neil Larry Shumsky, 877–878. Santa Barbara, CA: ABC-CLIO.

Reardon, Sean F., John T. Yun, and Tamela Mcnulty Eitle. 2000. The Changing Structure of School Segregation: Measurement and Evidence of Multiracial Metropolitan-Area School Segregation, 1989–1995. *Demography* 37 (3): 351–364.

Rothblatt, Donald N., and Daniel J. Garr. 1986. *Suburbia an International Assessment.* New York: St. Martin's Press.

Sidney, Mara S. 2003. *Unfair Housing: How National Policy Shapes Community Action.* Lawrence: University Press of Kansas.

Weeks, John R. 1981. *Population: An Introduction to Concepts and Issues.* 2nd ed. Belmont, CA: Thomason Wadsworth. 9th ed., 2005.

Woodard, J. David. 1998. Busing. In *Encyclopedia of Urban America: The Cities and Suburbs*, ed. Neil Larry Shumsky, 113–114. Santa Barbara, CA: ABC-CLIO.

Ben Snyder
Paul Ketchum

SUDRAS

Sudras (also Sudhra or Shudra) are people occupying a position next to the bottom of the Hindu caste system in India. Most Sudras are menial workers. At times it is difficult to distinguish Sudras from untouchables (Dalits), who stand below them and are considered to be so polluted that they are regarded as outside the caste system entirely. The Vaisya (Vaishya) or merchant caste stands directly above the Sudras in India's cast hierarchy.

Identifying a member of the Sudra class is a matter of recognizing subtle distinctions with which one becomes familiar after living around Sudras. They are usually identified by their vocabulary, which may include vulgarities; by the towns where they live or were born; by their occupations or by their personal names, which may include a reference to their occupations; and by other subtle characteristics. By tradition when a Sudra dies, the body is taken to the burial place through a south gate because all other gates are reserved for the upper castes. There have been times when the jobs performed by Sudras were considered to be so polluting that Sudras were considered equivalent to untouchables. Strictly speaking, this would not be their

status by birth but by economic actions. In addition Sudras could be exiled or slain at will.

Caste, or *varna* (literally, "color"), is affirmed by the Vedas as an expression of cosmic law (*rita*). Sudras are associated with the color black, which may have originated in the colors assigned to the various *varna*. One Hindu justification for the caste system rests in the belief that people were created from parts of the body of the god Purusha. Social standing is defined by the part of Purusha from which a person and his or her line is descended. Sudras are said to come from the feet.

In the Hindu Rig-Veda, the *dvijas* (twice-born) are identified as members of the Brahman, Kshatriya, and Vaisya castes. At about twelve years of age, members of these castes underwent a ceremony that made them "twice-born," and they were thereafter permitted to study the Vedic scriptures. The Sudras were not *dvijas* and therefore were not allowed to study the Vedas. Such study usually consisted of listening to recitations or readings of the Vedas because the very sounds were believed to have religious power. Some ancient legal books report that Sudras caught listening to Vedic recitations had molten lead poured into their ears. A Sudra could also have been forced to drink boiling oil if he or she claimed to have taught someone something learned from the Vedas.

The ancient Hindu *Laws of Manu* discusses castes in great detail. This text gives names to the offspring of unions of men with wives of the different castes and to those born to unmarried parents. The *Chandalas* were produced by the union of a Sudra father and a Brahman mother. A *Nishada* (or *Parasava*) was produced by a Brahman father and a Sudra mother. A Sudra father and a Vaisya mother produced an *Ayogava*. A Sudra father and a Kshatriya mother produced a *Kshattri*. In addition the son of a Sudra man by a Nishada woman was identified as a *Kukkutaka*, among the many such designations outlined by the *Laws of Manu*.

The powerless Sudras were assigned to the rank of servants in India, and most service and menial jobs became their duties. According to the *Laws of Manu*, a Sudra faced with starvation could engage in handicrafts. However, the best way of life for a Sudra was to serve a Brahman, because this was the best occupation and prepared one for the next life. A Sudra is unable to lose caste, being already at the bottom; however, Sudras can prepare for the next world by imitating the virtuous.

Although Indians traditionally organized people into four major, rigidly defined social classes or castes, contemporary Indian society includes several thousand subcastes called *jati*, meaning "birth," "lineage," or "race." Most *jati* probably developed from hereditary occupational practices. Many *jati* are regionally based. Some *jati* groups comprise only a few hundred families, while others may include thousands of families. Usually these are endogamous status groups.

Another function of *varna* is that it creates a complex system of purity and impurity. The ritual purity one acquires at birth may be enhanced by the practice of rituals during life. The higher the caste, the purer are its members. However, the higher castes are also considered to face the grave danger of ritual contamination from members of the lower castes. Purity regulations codify many areas of Indian life, especially those involving intimacy, such as drinking, eating, touching, and marriage. According to the *Laws of Manu*, drinking from a vessel after a Sudra used it would cause spiritual pollution of members of the higher castes. Purification requires a three-day regimen of drinking water in which *kusa* grass has been boiled. In addition twice-born Indians are forbidden to eat food prepared by a Sudra because it is considered to be impure. If a Brahman died with Sudra food undigested in his or her stomach, that person would be reborn as a Sudra. Sudras were urged to fast and eat only the leftovers of the *dvijas*. To become Vaisyas in the next life, Sudras had to abstain from meat.

Practices regarding touch have remained a sensitive area. If a Sudra should accidentally touch someone of a higher caste, such as a Brahman, then the Brahman would consider himself or herself contaminated, and extensive rites of purification would be necessary to remove the stain. Marriage is permitted only between members of the *jati* of a particular *varna*. According to the *Laws of Manu*, mixed-caste marriages violate the cosmic law of dharma that orders the world. Such marriages would therefore cause chaos.

In Tamil-speaking areas of South India, the population is made up mostly of Sudras, with only a few Brahmans and almost no Kshatriyas or Vaisyas living in many areas. Tamil-speaking Sudras have developed practices unknown to the original caste system of northern India. Among the numerous rankings of agricultural Tamil, the success of many Sudras has in practice put them above other castes in wealth and power.

Discrimination on the basis of caste has been against the law in India since the country achieved independence from Britain in 1947. However, the Hindu system requires castes, so the lives of many Sudras in tradition-bound rural India have barely changed. Many still belong to agricultural *jati* in which they are landlords or members of particular skill groups, giving them an incentive to maintain the caste system.

In urban areas the pace of life makes it more difficult to practice caste discrimination. While discrimination still exists in many rural areas, it is breaking down in India's cities. Urban Sudras have been able to organize and use political power to advance the status of their caste. Their success has been limited, however, by their numerous *jati* and the continuance in many areas of Hinduism's *varna* belief. Long practice enforces personal and informal discrimination despite the laws, but in many areas prosperous Sudras are marrying into higher castes. When this occurs, Sudras often change their names to disguise their Sudra origin.

SEE ALSO *Brahmins; Caste; Caste, Anthropology of; Dalits; Distinctions, Social and Cultural; Hierarchy; Hinduism; Kshatriyas; Purification; Stratification; Vaisyas*

BIBLIOGRAPHY

Anand, Dinesh S. 2000. *Who Is a Sudra?* New Delhi: Blumon.

Bandyopadhyay, Sekhar. 1997. *Caste, Protest, and Identity in Colonial India: The Namasudras of Bengal, 1872–1947*. London: Taylor and Francis.

O'Brien, Desmond. 1979. *RASAS and Lament of the Sudra*. College Park, MD: SCOP.

Pfaffenberger, Bryan. 1982. *Caste in Tamil Culture: The Religious Foundations of Sudra Domination in Tamil Sri Lanka*. Syracuse, NY: Syracuse University Press.

Sharma, Ram Sharan. [1958] 2002. *Sudras in Ancient India: A Social History of the Lower Order down to circa A.D. 600*. Delhi: Motilal Bananrsidass.

Andrew J. Waskey

SUEZ CRISIS

The Suez Crisis of October 1956, which involved a coordinated attack by British, French, and Israeli forces on Egyptian positions in the Sinai Peninsula and along the Suez Canal, was a pivotal moment not only for interstate relations within the region, but also for interactions between the superpowers within the larger context of the cold war. Triggered by numerous factors and settled by an uneasy cease-fire, the Suez Crisis left a great deal of "unfinished business" on the table between Israel and the Arab States. It also saw the first full engagement of the United States into the region.

The political environment in the region had been deteriorating for an extended period prior to the actual invasion. Among the elements that contributed to this situation were: (1) the 1955 establishment of the Baghdad Pact between Turkey and Iraq; (2) the completion of an extensive arms deal between Czechoslovakia and Egypt; (3) the prospect of the sale of modern weaponry to Iraq and possibly to other future Baghdad Pact members; (4) the nationalization of the Suez Canal by Egypt in June 1956, which included provisions that excluded Israeli shipping from passing through the canal and a blockade of the Gulf of Aqaba and Straits of Tiran (which cut off all shipping into Israel's southern port city of Eilat); (5) increased incursions into Israel by Palestinian guerillas known as the *fedayeen* (whom Israel labeled as terrorists); and (6) the October 1956 expansion of the Syrian-Egyptian joint military command to include Jordan. As a result of these events, the Israelis believed that they were "under siege" and that action was needed.

For the Israelis, there were three main goals behind any action undertaken in late 1956: (1) the restoration of freedom of navigation through the Gulf of Aqaba and Straits of Tiran, (2) cessation of *fedayeen* raids, and (3) the elimination or reduction of the threat posed by the Egyptian army deployed in Sinai. The British and French were not happy with the situation either, but they were focused on the implications of Egypt's nationalization of the Suez Canal and Nasser's support for Algerian nationalists fighting against the French.

Although their motives were different, the three sides agreed that the situation was intolerable and action needed to be taken. In fact, the Israelis had considered taking unilateral preemptive action, but they were instead "invited" to participate in the action already being planned by the British and French. The timing of the operation was also influenced by perceptions that both the United States and the Soviet Union were distracted or involved with other things at the time, and that they would therefore not "interfere" with the operation. For the United States, 1956 was a presidential election year, and the British, French, and Israelis believed that the Americans would be wrapped up in their own electoral cycle, and that President Eisenhower would not risk his chances of winning re-election by getting involved in an international conflict. It was also believed that the Soviets had their hands full dealing with rising national sentiments in both Poland and Hungary.

The actual invasion of Egyptian territory by Israeli forces began on October 29, 1956. By November 7, a cease-fire was brokered. Part of the cease-fire agreement included the establishment of a peacekeeping force under the auspices of the United Nations. Known as the United Nations Emergency Force (UNEF), these troops were intended to serve as a buffer between Egypt and Israel. They were charged with ensuring that freedom of navigation throughout the Straits of Tiran was maintained, and that there would be no cross-border raids by guerrilla forces. These were two of the primary Israeli concerns that led to the outbreak of armed hostilities. UNEF also supervised the withdrawal of Israeli forces from Egyptian territory, a process that was completed by March 1957. UNEF remained deployed in the area until May 1967, when President Gamal Abdel Nasser expelled the force from Egyptian territory.

The Suez Crisis also had larger implications for the region and for the international system as a whole. For the first time, the United States was brought into the Arab-Israeli conflict, although the Americans tended to view the situation in terms of the larger cold war context. In early 1957, concerns about Nasser and Soviet influence in the region led the Eisenhower administration to formulate what would become known as the Eisenhower Doctrine. According to this policy, the United States would provide assistance, when requested, to any country in the Middle East threatened by international Communism. In this respect, the Eisenhower Doctrine set the stage for active U.S. involvement in the region.

SEE ALSO *Arabs; Eisenhower, Dwight D.; Nasser, Gamal Abdel; War*

BIBLIOGRAPHY

Kyle, Keith. 1991. *Suez.* New York: St. Martin's Press.

Troen, Selwyn Ilan, and Moshe Shemesh, eds. 1990. *The Suez-Sinai Crisis, 1956: Retrospective and Reappraisal.* London: Frank Cass.

Rachel Bzostek

SUFFRAGE MOVEMENT, WOMEN'S

SEE *Suffrage, Women's; Women's Movement.*

SUFFRAGE, WOMEN'S

With few exceptions, women were not allowed to vote before the twentieth century. In 1900, however, only twenty-five nations held regular elections for at least some of their political leaders, and only six recognized the right of suffrage for most of their adult male citizens. Several American states and territorial governments granted women voting rights between 1855 and the 1890s; Sweden and Great Britain offered a limited right in local elections to some women in the 1860s; but New Zealand in 1893 was the first to guarantee a national right of woman's suffrage. About two dozen European nations as well as Australia and Canada extended the right to vote to women by 1919. In 1920 the Nineteenth Amendment to the U.S. Constitution barred gender-based prohibitions of the right to vote in the United States. Other democracies recognized voting rights for women only after World

War II, France in 1944, Italy and Japan in 1945, and other nations still later, India (1950), Switzerland (1971), Portugal (1976), Taiwan (1996), and Kuwait (2005). In 1945 the newly established United Nations recognized "the equal rights of men and women" in its charter, and its 1948 *Universal Declaration of Human Rights* specified that "the will of the people shall be the basis of the authority of government; … [as] expressed in periodic and genuine elections" and "by universal and equal suffrage." Moreover, the declaration continues, these rights and freedoms are to be honored "without distinction of any kind, such as race, colour, sex, language, religion, political or other opinion, national or social origin, property, birth or other status." At the beginning of the twenty-first century, more than half of all nations and approximately 60 percent of the world's population live under some form of electoral democracy; among these nations, the full recognition of women's voting rights has become a common baseline for assessing the presence of democracy.

The woman suffrage movement in the United States is commonly traced back to a women's rights meeting convened in Seneca Falls, New York, in 1848. This point of origin, although significant, overlooks the ways the idea of women's suffrage extends and gains much of its force from the principles of equality, consent, and liberty that emanate from democratic forms of government, however imperfect these forms or political practices may be at a particular time. For the democratic ideal that requires the equal treatment, consent, and empowerment of more than a select few within a society offers a suggestive logic supportive of efforts to include others, if not ultimately all persons, in the democratic process of self-governance. However self-evident this inclusionary logic may be to some, democratization is almost never self-executing or easy because most social relations in the world have been and remain ordered principally in nondemocratic ways.

EARLY HISTORY

From this perspective, the efforts of Margaret Brent, a Catholic immigrant to the colony of Maryland in 1638, offer the first instructive case of a woman who demanded full recognition of her right to vote along with her male peers. Brent was a prominent, unmarried property owner, businesswoman, and attorney in colonial Maryland. She also served as the legal executor of the estate of Maryland governor Leonard Calvert. Under the leadership of the Calvert family, Maryland was founded in the 1630s as the first American colony to recognize the freedom of religion. In 1645 the colony suffered extensive political and sectarian religious strife after Puritan militants invaded the colony, imprisoned several Catholic leaders, and plundered their estates.

Governor Calvert succeeded in defeating the militants in 1647, but he died the same year, leaving Brent to assume a leading role in restoring order within the colony. To aid her efforts, Brent in 1648 requested two votes in the Maryland colonial assembly. The first vote she claimed for herself, the second she claimed as the legal executor of Calvert's extensive property interests in Maryland. Brent's claims to a right to vote were rejected, but the assembly commended her critical contributions to the survival of the colony. Brent protested her exclusion from the assembly's proceedings and later elected to resettle in neighboring Virginia. Although Brent's attempt to secure her right to vote failed, historical records indicate that at least a small number of American colonial women—most likely all widowed or unmarried property owners—successfully asserted their right to vote in several colonial elections.

The subsequent democratic advances initiated by the American and French Revolutions in 1776 and 1789 supported similarly instructive associations between the principles carried by the democratic form and the advocacy of new women's rights, including the right to vote. On the eve of American independence, for example, Abigail Adams appealed to her husband, John Adams, then a Massachusetts delegate to the Continental Congress and later the second U.S. president. "Remember the Ladies," Abigail famously wrote, "and be more generous and favourable to them than your ancestors.… [For] if perticuliar care and attention is not paid to the Ladies we are determined to foment a Rebelion, and will not hold ourselves bound by any Laws in which we have no voice, or Representation." (Abigail Adams to John Adams, March 31, 1776, Adams Family Papers, The Massachusetts Historical Society).

Although Abigail Adams failed in 1776 to convince her husband that democratic government required the consent of all, including women, the logic of her argument was repeated and became commonplace among subsequent advocates of women's suffrage reform, including the French revolutionary thinker Marquis de Condorcet in the 1790 essay "On the Admission of Women to the Rights of Citizenship." Ironically, the more radical French Revolution never yielded robust efforts to extend voting rights for French women—despite their critical role in national events. American women, by contrast, possessed the right to vote in New Jersey state elections from 1776 until 1807, when a state constitutional amendment limited the suffrage to white, adult males. In addition propertied widows with school-age children were permitted to vote in local school board elections in Kentucky in 1838. These limited and highly exceptional American examples vividly demonstrate how little progress was made on effecting the idea of women's suffrage during the first half of the nineteenth century.

THE SENECA FALLS CONVENTION

Several propitious conditions in the 1830s and 1840s sustained the idea and hope for women's suffrage. The most important of these conditions was the emergence of more activist and organized antislavery and temperance movements in the United States. Women were core elements in both movements, and many in turn gained deeper commitments to the democratic principles of equality and liberty as well as invaluable experiences regarding the organizational mechanics and difficulties of social reform. Coincident with these movements, voting rights and mass forms of political participation expanded to include a greater portion of the adult male populations in the United States, Great Britain, and parts of Europe. Social reformers of all sorts were encouraged by these democratic developments, which paralleled new educational, economic, and social opportunities afforded to a small but growing number of women. The advances of this period, however, also made manifest to some the inequity and democratic contradictions of the continued exclusion of women from voting and other forms of public participation. U.S. women's rights advocates, such as Angelina Grimké and Sarah Grimké, initiated public discussions of these issues, which inspired wide public fascination, numerous critics, and a generation of future woman suffrage activists.

Against this historical backdrop, more than 300 women and men, including Frederick Douglass and other abolitionists, met in Seneca Falls in 1848. Inspired by the abolitionist movement, Quaker egalitarian ideals, and the Declaration of Independence, the organizers of this meeting (Elizabeth Cady Stanton, Lucretia Mott, Mary Anne McClintock, and others) proposed that the convention discuss the "social, civil and religious rights of women." Attendees heard numerous speeches, but the most important was Stanton and Mott's "Declaration of Sentiments," which proclaimed "that all men and women are created equal" and that "it is the duty of the women of this country to secure to themselves their sacred right to the elective franchise." Convention members vigorously debated the latter claim before they ultimately endorsed it and the declaration as a whole. With few exceptions, public reactions were hostile to the convention's advocacy of woman suffrage, and many who endorsed its declaration publicly retracted their support. Over the next decade additional women's rights conventions met, which along with new pro–women's rights publications attracted greater public attention for the movement and strengthened a small but activist network of leaders that included Stanton, Susan B. Anthony, Paulina Wright Davis, and Lucy Stone. Despite these developments, suffragists garnered no additional political advancements before the U.S. Civil War, although Kansas extended school board election voting rights to women in 1861.

THE POST–CIVIL WAR PERIOD

The conclusion of the Civil War opened new opportunities for political, economic, and social change in the United States. Foremost among these widely anticipated changes were the amendments required in the U.S. Constitution and most state constitutions. Woman suffrage leaders appealed directly to those who possessed the most influence over these expected constitutional changes: members of Congress, state legislators, party leaders, and abolitionist groups. Suffrage leaders also founded the American Equal Rights Association (AERA), which jointly promoted women and African American rights within a single "human rights" agenda framed, according to Anthony, by "the farthest bound of the principle of the 'consent of the governed.'" At both the state and federal levels, however, not a single women's suffrage amendment or popular referendum won political support. Stanton moreover ran (although she was not permitted to vote) for a U.S. House seat in New York in 1866. She lost, receiving only 24 votes of 22,450 cast. The political weakness of the woman suffrage movement also was evidenced by the fact that the Fourteenth Amendment to the U.S. Constitution (ratified in 1868) formally recognizes each state's power to limit the right to vote to "male inhabitants," an engendered description of the right to vote not present in the original U.S. Constitution.

Some women suffragists found partial consolation in the language of the Fifteenth Amendment of the U.S Constitution (ratified in 1870) because it used gender-neutral language to prohibit states from denying or abridging voting rights of U.S. citizens based upon race, color, or previous condition of servitude. Other activists, such as Stanton and Anthony, were embittered and radicalized by their political failures, and they withheld support for the ratification of the Fourteenth and Fifteenth Amendments, thereby severing themselves from other suffrage supporters and many of their former abolitionist and Republican Party allies.

After 1868 fissures among woman suffrage advocates grew more prominent. Stanton, Parker Pillsbury, and Anthony founded a new women's newspaper, abandoned the AERA, and led efforts to create the National Woman Suffrage Association (NWSA). Under the leadership of Stanton and Anthony, the NWSA focused on securing a national constitutional amendment, but the two advocates and others aligned with them increasingly became involved in the promotion of other social reforms too. Their efforts won praise from some, greater opposition from entrenched and popular social interests, and no immediate political results related to the suffrage issue. For example, between 1869 and 1889 no women's suffrage constitutional amendment won approval in either branch of Congress. In addition to its constant lobbying of members of Congress, the

NWSA experimented with other constitutional reform tactics, which included civil disobedience and the federal judiciary. The latter hope was encouraged by a novel and expansive interpretation of the Fourteenth Amendment's protections of the "privileges or immunities" of American citizens. In 1872 Anthony and other women were arrested for attempting to vote in state elections. Their trials attracted considerable media attention for the idea of women's suffrage and ultimately the desired opportunity to press their claim before the U.S. Supreme Court. In *Minor v. Hapersett* (1875), however, the Court determined that the term *citizens* in the Fourteenth Amendment did not grant women the right to vote.

Woman suffrage advocates not aligned with the NWSA formed other organizations, including the American Woman Suffrage Association (AWSA). Established in 1869 and led by Henry Ward Beecher, Henry Blackwell, Stone, and others, the AWSA published a weekly national newspaper, the *Woman's Journal.* Unlike the NWSA, its principal focus was state and local suffrage reform movements; yet the record of political achievements also was limited over the next twenty years. Despite sustained organizational efforts, most states did not vote on suffrage amendments or referenda; where they did, the male electorate rejected women's suffrage in Kansas in 1867, Nebraska in 1871, Michigan in 1874, Colorado in 1876, Oregon in 1884, Rhode Island in 1887, and Washington in 1889. Several successes were sufficient to encourage reform efforts in other states, yet only four western American territorial states granted women full voting rights: Wyoming (1869), Utah (1870), Washington (1883–1887), and Montana (1887). In 1867 Michigan women taxpayers received a limited right to vote in school trustee elections; women in Kansas received full voting rights in municipal elections in 1887. By 1889 American women could vote in school-related elections in about a dozen states and territories.

THE TWENTIETH CENTURY AND THE NINETEENTH AMENDMENT

In 1890 the NWSA and AWSA merged into the National American Woman Suffrage Association (NAWSA). Like its predecessors, the new organization continued its lobbying and grassroots efforts, but it too achieved mixed political results. Over the next two decades additional states granted women's suffrage in school, municipal, and tax-related elections, but only five states—Wyoming (1890), Colorado (1893), Utah (1896), Idaho (1896), and Washington (1910)—recognized a woman's right to vote in all elections. Despite persistent opposition to the idea of women's suffrage, progressive social, economic, and political conditions in the United States and Europe accelerated the woman suffrage movement in the 1910s. President

William H. Taft spoke to the 1910 NAWSA annual convention. Although he did not endorse women's suffrage, his presence at the meeting was perceived as an endorsement by NAWSA members and the media. In 1912 former president Theodore Roosevelt publicly supported woman suffrage, and the social reformer and NAWSA activist Jane Addams seconded Roosevelt's nomination for president at the 1912 Progressive Party convention. The Democrat Woodrow Wilson won the presidency in 1912 without supporting woman suffrage, but Progressive Party legislators in Illinois proved critical for the passage of legislation in 1913 that recognized women's voting rights in presidential and municipal elections. By mid-decade about one-third of American states fully recognized a woman's right to vote, but only five national democracies did: New Zealand (1893), Australia (1902), Finland (1906), Norway (1913), and Denmark (1915).

World War I (1914–1918) and its aftermath corresponded with renewed efforts by national woman suffrage organizations and a further consolidation, especially in Europe, of the relationship between democracy and recognition of women's voting rights. The United Kingdom recognized the right for women thirty years or older in 1918; Austria, Germany, Hungary, Ireland, and Poland recognized national rights of women's suffrage in 1918, as did Belgium, the Netherlands, and Sweden in 1919. In the United States the NAWSA and the Congressional Union worked to win congressional approval of an amendment to the U.S. Constitution. In addition to lobbying members of Congress and President Wilson, these organizations effectively orchestrated mass marches, petition campaigns, and political candidate endorsements designed to exert electoral pressure on the national political parties and those running for office. In 1917 the National Woman's Party, led by Alice Paul and Lucy Burns, supported widely publicized protests and acts of civil disobedience in which some were arrested and imprisoned for chaining themselves to the White House fence. Publicly President Wilson remained uncommitted, refusing to endorse constitutional amendment efforts in Congress. But by January 1918 Wilson's conceptions of a more peaceful and democratic postwar world were clear, and he argued before the U.S. Senate on September 30, 1918 that a women's suffrage amendment was "clearly necessary to the prosecution of the war and the successful realization of the objects for which the war is being fought" (*Cong. Rec*). The U.S. House of Representatives endorsed the amendment by the required two-thirds majority, but the U.S. Senate stalled the amendment until June 1919, when it too passed the Nineteenth Amendment. By August 1920 three-quarters of the states required by the U.S. Constitution had ratified the Nineteenth Amendment.

BIBLIOGRAPHY

Abigail Adams to John Adams, March 31, 1776, Adams Family Papers. The Massachusetts Historical Society, Boston.

Carr, Lois Green. 2004. *Margaret Brent, A Brief History.* Annapolis, MD: Maryland State Archives.

Congressional Record, 65th Cong., 2nd sess., 1918, vol. LVI, pt. 10928.

Dinkin, Robert. 1977. *Voting in Provincial America: A Study of Elections in the Thirteen Colonies, 1689–1776.* Westport, CT: Greenwood.

DuBois, Ellen. 1978. *Feminism and Suffrage: The Emergence of an Independent Women's Movement in America, 1848–1869.* Ithaca, NY: Cornell University Press.

Frost-Knappman, Elizabeth, and Kathryn Cullen-Dupont. 2005. *Women's Suffrage in America.* Rev. ed. New York: Facts on File.

Kromkowski, Charles. 2002. *Recreating the American Republic: Rules of Apportionment, Constitutional Change, and American Political Development 1700–1870.* New York: Cambridge University Press.

Charles A. Kromkowski

SUFISM

SEE *Islam, Shia and Sunni.*

SUGAR INDUSTRY

Sugar has been an important commodity historically due to a variety of factors, including the human appetite for sweet foods and drinks, the complementarity that sugar brings to the other flavors in food, its preservation and fermentation properties, and the calories it provides. Sugar (or more precisely sucrose) was first prepared in India. It was brought back to the Western world by the Greek conqueror Alexander the Great in 325 BCE. Trade in sugar was further expanded in the Mediterranean region by the Arab conquest of the sixth century CE. Improvements in the crystallization process expanded the sugar trade (especially in the form of molasses) in the twelfth century. However, the limited supply of sugar in the international market caused refined sugar to be relatively costly until the production of sugar by European colonies in the Americas grew after 1700. This expansion, coupled with improvements in refining technologies that reduced unwanted tastes in the sweetener, caused sugar to replace other sweeteners such as honey, becoming the dominant sweetener over time. While demand for sugar remained relatively unaffected by the introduction of non-nutritive sweeteners, in the early twenty-first century the dominance has been challenged, particularly in the United States, by high fructose corn syrup (HFCS). The competition between sugar and HFCS raises several policy questions.

HISTORICAL TRADE PATTERNS

The fact that the expansion of production and trade of sucrose was largely linked to the European colonization of the Americas had significant implications for the institutional arrangements in the international sugar market in place at the beginning of the twentieth century. Specifically colonization of the Americas as well as other parts of the globe in the eighteenth and nineteenth centuries was at least partially driven by economic considerations of the countries involved. Restrictions were placed on the countries with which colonies could trade. Raw goods produced in the colonies were required to be sold in the mother country and significant import restrictions existed to encourage the purchase of manufactured goods to each respective European power. This enabled the European powers economic benefits from the colonization of the New World.

Another byproduct of the rise of sugar in European colonies in general and in the Americas in particular was the linkages between sugar and slavery. As described by B. W. Higman in his 2000 article for *Economic History Review*, the rise of the sugar economies in the seventeenth through the nineteenth centuries in the Caribbean has been labeled as "The Sugar Revolution." This revolution has been associated with several empirical facts, including the increased importance of monoculture, the replacement of small farms with plantations, and the increased use of black slaves. The movement toward monoculture and increased farm size has proven not to be unique to sugar; however, certain characteristics of sugar production may make the crop more susceptible to the establishment of plantations. The relationship between sugar and slavery may be more systematic. The exact reason for this linkage is unclear. One explanation for this linkage could be the presence of scale economies. In 1977 Mark Schmitz found evidence of significant economies of scale in Antebellum sugar production in Louisiana, which used slavery. Further evidence of the economies of slavery-based agriculture can be found in Robert Fogel and Stanley Engerman's 1977 work.

The elimination of slavery in the colonial powers and the United States in the nineteenth century changed the institutions in the labor relationship. Slaves were replaced with contract labor, but the use of contract labor in the sugar plantations implied a radical change in the source of that labor. Before 1770 one-half to two-thirds of the contract labor destined for the British Caribbean and other North American colonies came from Europe. However, the contract labor for the sugar plantations was predominantly non-white. This shift also implied significant changes in the terms of the labor contract. In addition, the reduction of the availability of contract labor from countries such as India undoubtedly accelerated the introduction of labor-saving technology to the industry.

The entanglement of European powers in the trade of sugar also contributed to the first significant alternative sweetener. The British blockade of European ports during the Napoleonic wars led to the development of a viable sugar beet industry in France. In the twenty-first century sucrose from sugarcane and sugar beets share the global market for refined sugar. The expansion of sugar beet production in the second half of the nineteenth century followed a host of factors—including the abolition of slavery in Britain and France and the expansion of grain imports from Russia—that reduced the profitability of grain crops in Europe.

The decline in the price of sugar had two divergent impacts on the economy. First, lower sugar prices reduced the cost of a primary input for a variety of industries (i.e., bakeries, breweries, and the makers of jams). Second, lower sugar prices impoverished producers in the colonies. The same policy scenario applies to the present-day United States. Sugar tariffs pit the interest of sugar producers against the interests of confectionary manufacturers. The ultimate dispensation of this debate depends on the relative political power of each sector through rent-seeking behavior. One response to the declining sugar prices both in the nineteenth and in the twenty-first centuries is the establishment of import tariffs or quotas to increase the domestic price and, thereby, protect domestic sugar producers.

MODERN SUGAR MARKET

Despite the end of European colonial rule, many of the tariff agreements continue to follow the trade patterns established in colonial times. With the emergence of the European Union (EU) as an economic union in the closing years of the twentieth century, agricultural policy coalesced into the Common Agricultural Policy (CAP) of Europe. The CAP established a system of tariffs to protect domestic producers from foreign competition. Historically, African, Caribbean, and Pacific (ACP) sugar producers were given access to the European market under the CAP through the Sugar Protocol of the Lomé Convention and its successor the Cotonou Agreement.

At the beginning of the twenty-first century, most countries that support their internal sugar price use a form of the tariff rate quota (TRQ) which is allowed under the Uruguay Round Agreement on Agriculture. The TRQ is a system of two tariffs. The first tariff allows the sale of a fixed quantity (or minimum access) of a commodity at a lower or first tier tariff. Any quantity of that commodity imported above this fixed quantity is charged a higher

(typically prohibitive) tariff. Given that the second tariff level is prohibitive, the country can increase the price received by domestic producers by reducing the fixed quantity imported under the first tier tariff. This is the policy instrument used by both the United States and the EU to increase the price of sugar for their respective producers. However, apart from supporting domestic producers, the TRQ gives countries in the EU a mechanism to honor its commitments to the ACP. Specifically, former colonies can be allocated portions of the minimum access quantity, in essence giving ACP countries access to a higher internal price of sugar at a low tariff rate. The United States allocates its first-stage quota in a similar way to a group of forty countries.

Apart from its grounding in historical trade patterns, the international sugar market is also affected by a myriad of regional and global trade agreements. Regional trade agreements involve a small number of countries in the same geographic region. In this context, the agreements forming the EU are a regional trade agreement. Other regional trade agreements include the North American Free Trade Agreement (NAFTA) and proposed trade agreements such as the Free Trade Area of the Americas (FTAA). The effect of each of these trade agreements on sugar markets is dependent on the role sugar plays in each group of economies.

An example of the ambiguous role regional trade agreements play in the sugar market can be found in NAFTA. As discussed, the sugar price in the United States is protected by a system of tariffs. From this perspective both freer trade with both Canada and Mexico raise critical issues. First, while Canada does not pose a direct threat to the U.S. sugar industry from production, the TRQ on sugar prohibits pass-through imports of sugar into the United States through Canada. However, NAFTA still allows for the importation of sugar containing products from Canada, increasing the competition for confections in the United States and reducing the demand for sugar. For example, lower sugar prices contributed to Kraft Foods' decision to move the production of Life Savers candy entirely to Canada in 2003.

A different set of problems was raised by the potential effects of Mexican sugar production on the U.S. sugar market. Mexico's government has historically been involved directly in its sugar industry through its ownership of its sugar mills and other policies but had divested these holdings as a part of its economic liberalization program in the late 1980s. In recognition of the potential competition from Mexico, NAFTA includes specific provisions governing Mexico's access to the U.S. sugar market. Many of these provisions are concerned with Mexico's status as a net sugar producer. Specifically, since Mexico imports sugar and other sweeteners, the domestic producers wanted to be protected from pass-through sugar (i.e., sugar purchased at lower world market prices for sale at protected U.S. prices). Hence, Mexico was granted duty-free access to the U.S. market for 7,258 metric tons of sugar. If Mexico obtained the status of a net sugar-surplus producer, the quota would be expanded to 25,000 metric tons in years 1 to 6 and 250,000 metric tons in years 7 to 15. Some controversies have arisen in the implementation of these provisions. Specifically, the original provisions were restricted to becoming a net sugar-surplus producer, ignoring the potential impact of alternative sweeteners such as HFCS. This raised the possibility of substituting HFCS for sugar especially in the manufacture of soft drinks to enhance Mexico's net surplus of sugar.

In the mid-2000s the URAA of the WTO remains the most relevant multilateral trade agreement facing the international sugar market. Within this context, it is important that the TRQ format of the EU and the United States is the sanctioned agricultural policy and thus completely legal under the WTO. The primary question is then whether significant changes to these accepted instruments will occur in the Doha round of WTO negotiations started in 2001. At its inception, increases in market-access were primary to the Doha round discussion on agricultural trade. One idea is to increase market access by expanding the minimum access portions of the TRQs.

SUGAR PRODUCTION

Various domestic factors affect the production of sugar and institutions within the U.S. sugar market. As discussed, sugar prices in the United States are supported by a TRQ. Adding a layer of complication, the government supports the domestic price of sugar by providing a non-recourse loan for raw sugar at 18 cents per pound and refined sugar produced from sugar beets at 22.9 cents per pound, according to 2002 statistics (Haley and Suarez 2002). If the market price falls below 18 cents per pound, producers (or more accurately sugar mills) store their raw sugar and receive a loan from the government of 18 cents for every pound of raw sugar placed in storage. If the market price for sugar rises over 18 cents per pound plus any interest accrued, they take the sugar out of storage, sell it at the prevailing market price, and repay the loan. However, if the market price for sugar does not exceed 18 cents per pound plus accrued interest during the marketing year, producers simply forfeit sugar in storage to the government in fulfillment of the loan. While the non-recourse loan program for sugar is typical for agricultural commodities in the United States, it is encumbered by the Dole Amendment, which requires the sugar program to be operated at no cost to the government.

Certain characteristics of sugar production have implications for vertical integration in the market channel

for sugar. Sugar is produced from two different primary crops: sugarcane and sugar beets. While the end product (i.e., sucrose) is identical for each process, each crop implies a different market channel. The production of sugarcane typically occurs in tropical or subtropical climate zones. The stalks containing the sucrose are removed from the field for milling that produces a raw form of sugar that is relatively stable. The raw sugar is then later refined into table sugar, removing impurities that may affect the flavor. Technical considerations require that these mills be located close to production. When the stalks are harvested in the field the sucrose content of the sugarcane starts to deteriorate. Further, the sucrose content of standing sugarcane deteriorates after a freeze.

Following Coases's paradigm (1937) that the boundaries of the firm are determined by the comparison of transaction costs with the diseconomies of scope, the technical characteristics of sugarcane are conducive to the vertical integration of production of processing of sugarcane. Specifically, in Coases's paradigm the boundaries of a firm are dictated by a comparison of transaction costs and diseconomies of scope. In this case transaction costs include the possibility of using a thin market to extract monopolistic rents while the diseconomies of scope involve the economic costs of carrying out an activity that is outside of the firm's specialization. In the case of sugarcane, the potential deterioration of quality gives rise to the possibility of monopolistic rents. The possible economic losses of economic rents more than offset the economic costs of diversification into processing facilities. Viewing the transaction from the other side, the diversification into sugarcane production insures a steady supply of sugarcane into the future, reducing the risk of investment.

Production of sucrose from sugar beets does not face the same climatic constraints as sugarcane. Further, the sucrose content of sugar beets is more stable than sugarcane, extending the period for the extraction of sucrose from sugar beets. Thus sugar beet producers have less impetus for vertical integration than producers and processors of sugarcane.

Finally, any discussion of the sweetener markets, particularly in the United States, is not complete without reference to HFCS. HFCS is a liquid sweetener derived from corn that can be used in production of soft drinks and other industrial uses. It is typically conceded that sugar tariffs in the United States provided the incentives for the commercial development of HFCS production. However, while HFCS is a perfect substitute for sugar in many applications, it lacks the baking quality to replace sugar completely. The interaction between sugar and HFCS prices is then dependent on the saturation of specific sweetener markets. For example, HFCS is easily used in the production of soft drinks and, because it is typically priced lower than sugar, dominates the sweetener market for this market. Thus the relationship between HFCS and sugar prices depends on the substitutability of the use at the margin.

SEE ALSO *Agricultural Industry; Caribbean, The; Industry; Plantation; Slave Trade; Slavery; Slavery Industry*

BIBLIOGRAPHY

Coase, Ronald H. 1937. The Nature of the Firm. *Economica* 4 (16): 386–405.

Engerman, Stanley L. 1983. Contract Labor, Sugar, and Technology in the Nineteenth Century. *Journal of Economic History* 43 (3): 635–659.

Fogel, Robert W., and Stanley L. Engerman. 1977. Explaining the Relative Efficiency of Slave Agriculture in the Antebellum South. *American Economic Review* 67 (3): 275–296.

Greene, Gretchen. 1998. Transitions in the Mexican Sugar Industry. PhD diss., University of Florida.

Haley, Steven L., and Nydia R. Suarez. 2002 U.S. Sugar Policy and Prospects for the U.S. Sugar Industry. In *Sugar and Related Sweetener Markets in the Twenty-First Century: International Perspectives*, eds. Andrew Schmitz, Thomas H. Spreen, William A. Messina Jr., and Charles B. Moss, 241–258. London: CAB International.

Higman, B. W. 2000. The Sugar Revolution. *Economic History Review* 53 (2): 213–236.

Josling, Timothy. 2002 The Place of Sugar in Regional and Multilateral Trade Negotiations. In *Sugar and Related Sweetener Markets in the Twenty-First Century: International Perspectives*, eds. Andrew Schmitz, Thomas H. Spreen, William A. Messina Jr., and Charles B. Moss, 13–30. London: CAB International.

Moss, Charles B., and Andrew Schmitz. 2002 Trade in HFCS: Cointegration with Substitute Goods. In *Sugar and Related Sweetener Markets in the Twenty-First Century: International Perspectives*, eds. Andrew Schmitz, Thomas H. Spreen, William A. Messina Jr., and Charles B. Moss, 299–314. London: CAB International.

Polopolus, Leo C. 2002 World Sugar Markets and Entangled Government Programs. In *Sugar and Related Sweetener Markets in the Twenty-First Century: International Perspectives*, eds. Andrew Schmitz, Thomas H. Spreen, William A. Messina, Jr., and Charles B. Moss, 1–12. London: CAB International.

Pryor, Frederic L. 1982. The Plantation Economy as an Economic System. *Journal of Comparative Economics* 6: 288–317.

Schmitz, Andrew, and Charles B. Moss. 2001. Vertical Integration in Production and Marketing: The Case of Sugar in the United States. *International Sugar Journal* 103 (1234): 443–446, 461.

Schmitz, Mark D. 1977. Economies of Scale and Farm Size in the Antebellum Sugar Sector. *Journal of Economic History* 37 (4): 959–980.

Charles B. Moss

SUICIDE

Suicide can be the outcome of an individual's difficult and stressful experiences or a response to an unbearable situation. Sometimes suicide is complicated by drug and/or alcohol use. The scope of suicide includes all ages, classes, races, and sexes, although some groups are at more risk than others. Children or family members of those who have attempted or completed suicide are more likely themselves to attempt or complete suicide, as suicide has a ripple effect and can convey the idea that self-destruction is an acceptable solution to distress. Casualties of suicide, or those left behind, experience traumatic grief, guilt, shame, stress, and self-doubt—sometimes keeping them from speaking of the event at all. Statistics of suicide are underrepresented and not always reliable because the action can be classified in some other way; legally, suicidal components must be established beyond a doubt. Additionally, it is sometimes difficult to categorize the intentionality of death.

Suicide rates are higher for those who suffer from depression or other psychiatric problems; use drugs or alcohol when depressed; suffer from physical, especially irreversible, illness; are divorced; have lost an important relationship through death or breakup; and live in certain areas. War combatants also face a high rate of suicide because of post-traumatic stress disorders. People with HIV/AIDS are at risk, with the decision of suicide based on the fear of loss of function or increase in suffering and the feeling of being isolated. In "suicide by cop" incidents, an armed suicidal individual forces a law officer to use deadly force resulting in death. Individuals name various other reasons for suicide, including as a means to reunite with the dead, a means to ensure rest and refuge, a way to take revenge, and a penalty for failure.

DURKHEIM'S STUDIES

In 1897 the French sociologist Émile Durkheim (1858–1917) conducted a study of suicide in France. He found lower suicide rates among women, Catholics, Jews, and married people and higher rates among men, Protestants, wealthy people, and unmarried individuals. Based on the data, he argued that categories of people with strong social ties had low suicide rates, and that categories of people with the lowest social integration had the highest suicide rates. Durkheim believed that too much or too little integration or regulation (cohesion) was unhealthy for society and accordingly established four conditions that can lead to suicide: (1) altruism, or too much integration, a willingness to sacrifice the self for the group's ostensible interest (e.g., suicide bombers); (2) egoism, or too little integration (e.g., those not bound to social groups left with little guidance); (3) fatalism, or too much regulation with no perceived way out of a situation (e.g., slaves); and (4) anomie, or too little regulation and no fulfillment of needs (e.g., those coping with the death of a spouse, economic depression, institutional failure, or wealth insufficient to provide happiness). Durkheim focused on anomie as an unhealthy and destructive pathological state for society, resulting in a "milky-way-galaxy" of choices for normative behavior (read "normlessness") and a lack of social regulation.

AMERICAN DEMOGRAPHIC DATA

In the United States, suicide ranks eleventh on the list of causes of death. Suicides occur most often among white males, and the rate increases with age; older white males have the highest suicide rates in the nation. Females and nonwhite males reach their peak for suicide vulnerability earlier in adult life. Suicide is the third leading cause of death in the age group fifteen to twenty-four. Bad economic times are usually associated with an increase of suicide rates. Rates for Native Americans are the highest of any ethnic population in the nation.

Suicide rates tend to be higher in areas where people live far apart from each other; more densely populated states have lower suicide rates. Accordingly, the highest suicide rates are in the western states, with Wyoming and Alaska at the top of the list, although California is ranked as having one of the lowest rates. The middle and eastern states are ranked lower in suicide rates than the western states (with the District of Columbia and Massachusetts as the lowest), although Vermont, West Virginia, and Oklahoma are ranked as high. Most of the New England states are ranked as having the lowest rates of suicide.

SUICIDE AMONG THE ELDERLY

Since 1990, in the United States there has been an increase in suicide rates in individuals eighty-five years or older, although suicide in the elderly does not elicit the same response as it does in younger individuals. Elderly individuals are more likely to be socially isolated for a longer time before death and are more likely to experience physical illness, other sources of distress and depression, and loss of relationships, making them at higher risk for suicide. Elders are less likely to give warning signs of suicide.

TEEN SUICIDE AND THE FAMILY

Since the 1980s the general incidence of suicide has increased in the United States; the rate for those between the ages of fifteen and twenty-four has tripled. Although suicide among adolescents is seriously underreported, researchers generally consider it to be the second- or third-most common cause of death in that group. More than eight out of ten kids who threaten suicide attempt it;

females make more suicide attempts, although more males complete suicide, with firearms or explosives the most common method of self-destruction. Half of all children who have made one suicide attempt will make another, sometimes as many as two a year until they succeed. The majority of suicide attempts are expressions of extreme distress and not merely bids for attention; this distress is often related to others prior to suicide. Additionally, some children who take their own lives are indeed the opposite of the rebellious teen. They are anxious, insecure kids who have a desperate desire to be liked, to fit in, and do well. Their expectations are so high that they demand too much of themselves, thereby condemning themselves to constant disappointment. A traumatic event (such as the loss of a valued relationship or a change of residence), which can seem minor viewed from an adult perspective, is enough to push children and adolescents over the edge into a severe depression. Alcohol and drug use are associated with heightened suicide risk in youth.

The role of the family is also a variable in teen suicide. Two-thirds of suicidal teens report poor relationships with their parents. Increased levels of suicidal behavior in adolescents is associated with certain family characteristics: rigid rules, poor communication, overbearing parents, and long-term patterns of family dysfunction such as alcoholism and mental illness.

PHYSICIAN-ASSISTED SUICIDE

In some cases an individual may be too incapacitated by illness to end his or her life without assistance. The ethics of physician-assisted suicide, or euthanasia, has been the subject of vigorous debate. *Active euthanasia* refers to direct action being used to end a life; *passive euthanasia* refers to not taking steps to prolong life or "letting die." Some argue that active euthanasia respects the principle of individual autonomy and the right to self-determination, that its foremost concert is the patient's well-being, and that it adheres to the physician's Hippocratic Oath to do no harm, where doing no harm means alleviating pain and respecting the wishes of a rational person. Many argue that a decision to kill oneself with the assistance of a physician is a private choice that society has no right to regulate; others argue that assisted suicide threatens the moral foundations of society.

INTERNATIONAL DEMOGRAPHIC DATA

Suicide rates vary from nation to nation, with Belarus, Estonia, Hungary, Kazakhstan, and the Russian Federation having the highest suicide rates in the world. Suicide rates for men are substantially higher in all countries and are also high for indigenous populations who have been exploited, discriminated against, and deprived of their previous cultural existence. China is undergoing a national suicide crisis, with 21 percent of the world's population, 44 percent of the world's suicides, and 56 percent of the world's female suicides. Those in China at a higher risk of suicide live in rural areas or areas where the government has policies that have increased stress through the disruption of traditional family patterns. Some argue that this level of suicidal behavior has changed attitudes in China about suicide, with self-destruction coming to be seen as an acceptable action.

OTHER MANIFESTATIONS OF SUICIDE

Suicide can also occur as a group response to extreme situations, notable examples being the mass suicide at the Masada fortress in 73 CE by besieged Jews choosing death over defeat by the Romans; the Jonestown cult's mass murder-suicides in Guyana in 1978; and the Heaven's Gate cult suicides in southern California in 1997.

Suicide bombings by terrorist groups became a phenomenon in the late twentieth century. Terrorism constitutes random acts of violence or the threat of such violence as a political or religious strategy, and suicide bombing is one of these strategies. The attacks of September 11, 2001, show how self-destruction can be used as a weapon.

The act of suicide has been interpreted in many ways and given various meanings. In Christianity and Judaism, suicide is sinful and forbidden. Historically, many societies have viewed suicide as a crime and have enacted laws to regulate the act and punish those who attempt it. Those who attempt or commit suicide have often been seen as psychotic or mentally ill; by contrast, in some cultures suicide is viewed as an honorable and glorious death. Some approve of suicide when it is seen as the only option left to alleviate pain and suffering from severe illness. Freud understood suicide as a drive or death instinct; from an existentialist standpoint, suicide removes the necessary choice for authentic existence.

SEE ALSO *Alienation; Alienation-Anomie; Assisted Death; Death and Dying; Depression, Psychological; Durkheim, Émile; Euthanasia and Assisted Suicide; Morbidity and Mortality; Native Americans; Suicide Bombers*

BIBLIOGRAPHY

Beckerman, N. L. 1995. Suicide in Relation to AIDS. *Death Studies* 19 (3): 223–234.

Brock, Dan W. 1994. Voluntary Active Euthanasia. In *Contemporary Issues in Bioethics*, 4th ed., eds. Tom L. Beauchamp and LeRoy Walters. Belmont, CA: Wadsworth.

Colt, George Holt. 1991. *The Enigma of Suicide*. New York: Summit.

Conwell, Y. 2001. Suicide in Later Life: A Review and Recommendation for Prevention. *Suicide and Life-Threatening Behavior* 31 (Suppl.): 32–47.

Crosby, A. E., M. P. Cheltenham, and J. J. Sacks. 1999. Incidence of Suicide Ideation and Behavior in the United States, 1994. *Suicide and Life-Threatening Behavior* 29 (2): 131–140.

Durkheim, Émile. 1951. *Suicide*. Trans. John A. Spaulding and George Simpson, ed. George Simpson. Glencoe, IL: Free Press.

Freud, Sigmund. [1917] 1959. Mourning and Melancholia. In *Collected Papers*. Trans. Joan Riviere, Vol. 4, 152–172. New York: Basic Books.

Hendin, Herbert. 1995. *Suicide in America*, expanded ed. New York: Norton.

Kastenbaum, Robert. 2000. *The Psychology of Death*. 3rd ed. New York: Springer.

Kochanek, Kenneth D., et al. 2004. Deaths: Final Data for 2002. *National Vital Statistics Report* 53 (5). Hyattsville, MD: National Center for Health Statistics.

Leenaars, Anton A., and Susanne Wenckstern. 1991. *Suicide Prevention in Schools*. New York: Hemisphere.

Mancinelli, I., A. Comparelli, P. Girardi, and R. Tatarelli. 2002. Mass Suicide: Historical and Psychodynamic Considerations. *Suicide and Life-Threatening Behavior* 32 (1): 91–100.

Minois, Georges. 1999. *History of Suicide: Voluntary Death in Western Culture*. Trans. Lydia G. Cochrane. Baltimore, MD: Johns Hopkins University Press.

Murray, Alexander. 1998–2000. *Suicide in the Middle Ages*. 2 vols. Oxford and New York: Oxford University Press.

National Household Survey on Drug Abuse. 2002. *Substance Use and the Risk of Suicide Among Youths*. http://www.oas.samhsa.gov/2k2/suicide/suicide.htm.

National Vital Statistics Reports: Deaths (2002). http://www.cdc.gov/nchs/data/nvsr/nvsr54/nvsr54_10.pdf.

Osgood, Nancy J. 1992. *Suicide in Later Life*. New York: Lexington.

Pedahzur, Ami. 2004. *Suicide Terrorism*. Cambridge, U.K.: Polity Press.

Pellegrino, Edmund D. 1994. The Virtuous Physician and the Ethics of Medicine. In *Contemporary Issues in Bioethics*, 4th ed., eds. Tom L. Beauchamp and LeRoy Walters. Belmont, CA: Wadsworth, 1994.

Phillips, M. R., H. Liu, and Y. Zhang. 1999. Suicide and Social Change in China. *Medicine and Psychiatry* 23 (1): 25–50.

Rachels, James. 1994. The Distinction between Active Killing and Allowing to Die. In *Contemporary Issues in Bioethics*, 4th ed., eds. Tom L. Beauchamp and LeRoy Walters. Belmont, CA: Wadsworth.

Reisman, David. [1961] 2000. *The Lonely Crowd*. New Haven, CT: Yale University Press.

Reuter, Christoph. 2002. *My Life Is a Weapon: A Modern History of Suicide Bombing*. Trans. Helena Ragg-Kirkby. Princeton, NJ: Princeton University Press.

Ryan Ashley Caldwell

SUICIDE BOMBERS

A suicide bomber (or suicide attacker) is a person who participates in a suicide attack. Boaz Ganor, the cofounder of the International Policy Institute for Counter-Terrorism, has defined a suicide attack as one whose success depends on the death of the person or persons who carry it out. Suicide attacks are one of the tactics employed by terrorists, and since the early 1980s such attacks have become familiar worldwide, having been adopted by some thirty-two terrorist organizations and groups in twenty-eight countries.

The increasing use of suicide attacks by terrorist organizations is explained by the strategic and tactical advantages of such attacks:

1. The bombers themselves plan and carry out the attacks according to circumstances, and, because they operate as "smart bombs," they can delay or cancel an operation if necessary.

2. The attack plan is relatively simple, since there is no need for an escape route.

3. The suicide bomber is a threat to morale and has a significant psychological effect on the target population.

4. The victimized population feels it is facing an enemy who does not budge from death, which in turn leads this population to pressure its government into negotiating with the terrorist organizations.

5. Attacks are also used to make the communities that support the terror organizations appear stronger and more powerful. This implants the idea that such attacks are the best way to fight a more powerful enemy.

6. Suicide attacks cause more casualties than any other types of terror attacks. For example, between 1982 and 2005, the average number of fatalities in shooting attacks worldwide was 3.2, bombing attacks killed an average of 6.92 persons, and suicide attacks killed an average of 81.48.

Historically, suicide attacks predate the modern period. The Moslem Hashashin of the late Middle Ages used this tactic, as did the Sulu who attacked the Spanish colonialists in the Philippines in the eighteenth century. In modern times, the Japanese kamikaze pilots used suicide attacks against the Allied fleet during World War II. From the first attack on October 25, 1944, until the last one on August 15, 1945, kamikaze pilots carried out more than 2,500 suicide attacks.

The first modern terrorist organization to employ suicide bombers was Hezbollah, an Islamic Shiite group based in Lebanon, which attacked the American Embassy in Beirut on April 18, 1983. On October 23, 1983, they attacked again, this time targeting the barracks of American and French soldiers. These attacks caught the attention of the entire world, not only due to the high number of victims (300 killed and 96 wounded), but also because of the consequent withdrawal of the multinational peacekeeping force from Lebanon. According to Robert Pape, a political scientist at the University of Chicago who has made an extensive study of suicide terrorism, this encouraged other organizations to adopt the use of suicide bombers, and throughout the 1980s other guerrilla groups used them against Israeli forces and their allies in Lebanon (2003, 2005).

The Liberation Tigers of Tamil Eelam (LTTE) in Sri Lanka have used suicide bombers more often than any other group. Between 1987 until 2006, they perpetrated over 200 suicide attacks. The frequent use of suicide bombers forced LTTE to adapt and develop the tactics of its attacks, which have ranged from simple attacks on military and civilian targets to more sophisticated attacks on the Sri Lankan Navy and Air Force.

In the late 1990s, and even more so in the early 2000s, other terrorist groups started to employ suicide bombers. During this period, most of these terrorist groups were concentrated in the Middle East region. Groups such as the PKK (Kurdistan Workers Party) in Turkey, the GIA (Armed Islamic Group) in Algeria, and the Egyptian Islamic Jihad used suicide bombers briefly during their struggle against state governments. The Palestinian organizations, however, are the only ones in the region to use this tactic for a long period of time. The first suicide attack in Israel was carried out by Hamas in April 1993, and over the years other Palestinian factions, such as Palestinian Islamic Jihad and PFLP (Popular Front for the Liberation of Palestine), have perpetrated many more attacks, with the peak coming in 2002. During al-Aqsa Intifada (2000–2005) the Palestinian factions carried out 145 suicide bombings. Following the beginning of the second Russia-Chechnya war, Chechen terrorist groups also began to use suicide bombers against the Russian Army, both in Chechnya and in Russia itself.

The group most closely identified with suicide bombings involving a large number of victims, however, is al-Qaeda, whose attacks on the World Trade Center in New York and the Pentagon in Washington, D.C., on September 11, 2001, killed nearly three thousand people. This attack is considered the most deadly suicide attack to date. Moreover, since the American-led coalition troops invaded Iraq in March 2003, al-Qaeda suicide bombers have attacked them repeatedly.

One of the most interesting features of suicide attack in modern times is the large percentage of women used as suicide bombers. Groups such as PKK, and various Chechen factions, have used mostly women for suicide missions, whereas LTTE and Palestinian organizations have used both men and women. The use of women in such missions stems from the operational advantage of using women, who are considered less likely to be terrorists. In addition, in traditional cultures, women are not obliged to undergo security inspections, so they can often get closer to the target of attack more easily. The use of women in these missions has been justified by various claims, raging from sex liberation and equal rights in nationalistic groups to religious justifications in the case of religious terrorist groups. However, many believe that these women have been forced to participate in suicide bombing against their will.

Car, truck, motorcycle, and boat bombs are all operational variations of the suicide attack. In each case, a vehicle filled with explosives and detonators is driven up to or rammed into the target. The "bag bomb" is carried to the scene of an attack, as is the more frequently used explosive belt. Packed with explosives and scrap metal to increase the damage when the wearer detonates it, an explosive belt has been used in 46.2 percent of terror attacks, while car and truck bombs have been used in 37.7 percent (Database on Suicide Terrorism 1982–2003). The choice of tactics depends on the surroundings, so that Hezbollah has generally used car and truck bombs to attack Israeli army convoys and installations, while LTTE has crashed boat bombs into Sri Lankan military vessels.

Suicide attacks have led to interdisciplinary studies investigating the motives behind them. The first attempts by researchers to explain the suicide bomber phenomenon, in the early 1990s, concentrated on the personal and socio-environmental motives of the individuals involved. More recently, however, the focus has shifted to the motives of the organizations. The increase in terrorist attacks carried out by organizations with a network structure, like al-Qaeda, has led researchers to focus on the immediate environment of the suicide bomber and the social network in which he operates. As a result, the spotlight is now on the dynamics within the social network, and on the effect of this network on the bomber's decision to carry out an attack.

In addition to scientific research, which concentrates on analyzing the phenomenon of suicide attacks, there are a growing number of attempts to analyze the cultural motives behind the bombers themselves. The most widely known such attempt is the movie *Paradise Now* (2005), directed by Hany Abu-Assad, in which two brothers decide to sacrifice themselves as suicide bombers but are unable to follow through with their plan. These attempts have therefore been criticized as glorifying suicide bombers and not giving adequate attention to the perspective of the victims of suicide attacks.

SEE ALSO *Fundamentalism, Islamic; Terrorism; Terrorists; War; World War II*

BIBLIOGRAPHY

Bloom, Mia M. 2005. *Dying to Kill: The Allure of Suicide Terror.* New York: Columbia University Press.

Database on Suicide Terrorism. 1982–2003. National Security Studies Center at the University of Haifa.

Gambetta, Diego, ed. 2005. *Making Sense of Suicide Missions.* New York: Oxford University Press.

Pape, Robert. 2003. The Strategic Logic of Suicide Terrorism. *American Political Science Review* 97 (3): 343–361.

Pape, Robert. 2005. *Dying to Win: The Strategic Logic of Suicide Terrorism.* New York: Random House.

Pedahzur, Ami. 2005. *Suicide Terrorism.* London: Polity Press.

Ami Pedahzur
Alexandr Bialsky

SUN YAT-SEN
1866–1925

Born into a peasant family in Canton (Guangzhou), raised in Hawaii, and educated at colleges in Hawaii and Hong Kong, Sun Yat-sen (Sun Wen or Sun Yixian or Sun Zhongshan) played a key role in the overthrow of China's Qing or Manchu dynasty (1644–1911), in the politics of the early Chinese Republic, and in the shaping of post-1949 regimes in Beijing and in Taipei. Sun came to be venerated in Taiwan as the "father of the nation" (*guofu*) and in the People's Republic of China as a "pioneer of the revolution" (*xianxingzhe*). The cult of Sun seems to be one common denominator across the hostile Taiwan Strait. Retreating to Taiwan after his defeat in the civil war, Chiang Kai-shek (Jiang Jieshi, 1887–1975) legitimized his Guomindang (Nationalist Party) by mythologizing Sun. Beijing stresses Sun's anti-imperialist campaign and his cooperation with Soviet Russia and the Communist Party. Such accolade is not shared by Western scholars, who have tried to demythologize Sun. Marie-Claire Bergère, for instance, dubs Sun "a traveling salesman of the revolution" (1998, p. 139), hardly present at the countless late Qing uprisings as he shuttled among nations to raise funds from overseas Chinese communities and foreign sources. It is telling, nevertheless, that Sun was from coastal China, which was long exposed to foreign influence, and that overseas Chinese were considered the "mothers of the revolution." Modernization in China has invariably followed the pattern of spreading from coastal areas inland, with Sun as an early symbol for what has continued into the twenty-first century.

In the chaotic times of the late Qing and early Republic, Sun, above all else, emerges as a paragon of revolution not necessarily because of his leadership in uprisings and politics but because of his writings. *The Three Principles of the People* is a compilation of his speeches, the 1924 version rendered definitive by his death more than anything else. It is an irony of history that this hodgepodge of ideas, by no means systematic and insightful, and derivative of American government apparatus, should become the sacred text for school children and university programs in Taiwan. Even the first line of Taiwan's national anthem is a dull drone of "The Three Principles of the People." On the other hand, *The International Development of China* (1922) was prescient in merging capitalism with socialism in the wake of World War I (1914–1918). Sun also emphasized international "cooperation," urging Western powers to abolish unfair treaties that subjugated China as a subcolony (*cizhimindi*) and to treat China as a market for investment and a "dumping ground" and factory. The unfortunate choice of "dumping ground" revealed the psychological complex of a Westernized Chinese patriot bent upon saving China, while either pretending to identify or subconsciously identifying with Western interests. Most brilliant is Sun's utopian vision for China's economic and industrial modernization: a network of railways; coastal development based on three major ports in the northern, central, and southern regions; mining and heavy industry; and dams and river transportation. It was yet another unfortunate choice that Sun used *colonization* for his plans regarding Tibet and Xinjiang, but it was a sign of the times. Sun's grandiose dreams have earned him the mocking appellation Big-Gun-Sun (*Sun dabao*) in China, yet Deng Xiaoping's (1904–1997) Four Modernizations program (in agriculture, industry, science and technology, and the military) echoed Sun's plan closely, and the contemporary westward movement to exploit energy reserves and other resources, as well as the economic zones revolving around major Chinese seaports, coincide with Sun's blueprint. In charting out a path for modernization, Sun Yat-sen was indeed visionary.

BIBLIOGRAPHY

Bergère, Marie-Claire. 1998. *Sun Yat-sen*. Trans. Janet Lloyd. Stanford, CA: Stanford University Press.

Sun Yat-sen. [1922] 1953. *The International Development of China*. Taipei, Taiwan: China Cultural Service.

Sun Yat-sen. 1965. *Guofu quanji* [Complete works of Sun Yat-sen]. Taipei, Taiwan: Archives of Guomindang.

Sheng-mei Ma

SUPER MARIO BROTHERS

SEE *Video games.*

SUPEREGO

SEE *Equilibrium in Psychology; Freud, Sigmund; Psychoanalytic Theory.*

SUPERORDINATE GOALS

Social organizations are formed to accomplish specific goals, such as the acquisition of valued resources necessary for the survival of the group in question. Crucial to this process is the recognition that some goals are more important than others, and that some people are better equipped than others to aid in their acquisition. As a consequence, hierarchies of both people and goals are frequently established to facilitate group functioning, whether that group is a small social unit such as a family, or a larger cultural, religious, or political group.

This pursuit of specific goals sometimes results in conflict when a goal involves a valued resource that cannot be shared by competing subgroups. Hostilities are further exacerbated by self-categorization, which uses status or physical attributes to characterize "in-group" people (those like me) and "out-group" people (those not like me) for the purpose of treatment or differential allocation of resources. Such self-categorization occurs in (1) nation-states that compete for human and natural resources, (2) corporations that compete for customers and sales, and (3) other groups that are physically distinguishable and that compete for services and opportunities within the same society. This conflict between groups has no simple cause, and no totally effective solution. Nevertheless, Muzafer Sherif (1958) did demonstrate that it is possible to achieve harmony between opposing social groups, by introducing what he called "superordinate goals." These are goals for both groups that can be achieved only through the cooperation of both.

In Sherif's "Robbers Cave" experiment (so named for its site, Robbers Cave State Park in Oklahoma), boys attending a summer camp were, in the first phase of the study, divided into two groups that functioned independently of each other. In the second phase, the groups opposed each other, participating in competitive and frustrating activities in which only the winning group could have valued resources. The experiment demonstrated that (1) members developed unfavorable attitudes and derogatory stereotypes of the out-group, (2) social distance developed to the point of mutual avoidance, and (3) hostile attacks sometimes occurred. In the final phase of the experiment, the technique—superordinate goals—proved effective in reducing tension between groups by introducing goals that were shared by members of both groups and required collaborative efforts.

Several recent studies have identified aspects of Sherif's technique that contribute to the effectiveness of superordinate goals in reducing conflict. One of the most critical aspects is the ability of superordinate goals to create a sense of shared identity. John Dovidio and colleagues (2001) intervened in the functioning of two groups to change people's conceptions of their membership from that of diverse membership (in different groups) to common membership in a single, more inclusive group. The study revealed that if members of different groups are induced to conceive of themselves more as a single, superordinate group rather than as two separate groups, attitudes toward former out-group members will become more positive. Thus, cooperative relationships between groups, such as those established in Sherif's Robbers Cave study, can reduce bias not only by ameliorating realistic group threat, but also by establishing a more inclusive, superordinate group identity (Gaertner et al. 2000).

There is little doubt among scholars regarding the ultimate benefits of the pursuit of superordinate goals rather than goals peculiar to nationalistic or individualistic interests. Superordinate goals enable people from opposing sides to come together and work toward a common end. In the everyday work environment, for example, the alignment of employer and employee goals with regard to job security can minimize conflict (Worchel and Simpson 1993). Within corporations there are superordinate goals that emphasize, in the words of AT&T's slogan, "being the best." The adoption of such a common goal has served to boost morale as well as minimize labor-management conflict. Superordinate goals also can be introduced to minimize group conflict at the level of large social groupings; at the global level these include activities such as space exploration, medical research, pollution control, and nuclear disarmament (Frank 1983).

SEE ALSO *Conflict; Cooperation; Corporations; Diversity; Interest Groups and Interests; Mobilization; Nation-State; Organizations; Politics; Self-Classification; Sherif, Muzafer; Stereotypes*

BIBLIOGRAPHY

Dovidio, John F., Samuel L. Gaertner, Yolanda F. Niemann, and Kevin Snider. 2001. Racial, Ethnic, and Cultural Differences in Responding to Distinctiveness and Discrimination on Campus: Stigma and Common Group Identity. *Journal of Social Issues* 57 (1): 167–188.

Frank, Jerome D. 1983. Nuclear Arms and Violence toward Children: Sociopsychological Aspects of the Nuclear Arms Race. *Political Psychology* 4 (2): 393–408.

Gaertner, Samuel L., John F. Dovidio, Brenda S. Banker, et al. 2000. Reducing Intergroup Conflict: From Superordinate Goals to Decategorization, Recategorization, and Mutual Differentiation. *Group Dynamics: Theory, Research, and Practice* 4 (1): 98-114.

Sherif, Muzafer. 1958. Superordinate Goals in the Reduction of Intergroup Conflict. *American Journal of Sociology* 63 (4): 349–356.

Sherif, Muzafer, O. J. Harvey, B. Jack White, et al. 1961. *Intergroup Conflict and Cooperation: The Robbers Cave Experiment.* Norman: University of Oklahoma Press.

Worchel, Stephen, and Jeffry A. Simpson. 1993. *Conflict between People and Groups: Causes, Processes, and Resolutions.* Chicago: Nelson-Hall.

Carolyn B. Murray

SUPPLY

In economic theory, supply is the relationship between the price of a product and the number of units of product that producers are willing to offer for sale per unit time (called *quantity supplied*) when all other relevant factors, excluding the price of the product, remain fixed. The concept of supply ignores the effect of consumers on the market by assuming that consumers purchase as many units as producers offer for sale. The assumption that other factors remain fixed is known as the *ceteris paribus* assumption. For example, suppose that when the price of a product is $10 per unit, producers are willing to offer one million units of product for sale each month (the quantity supplied). Holding all other things constant, if the price of the product were to rise to $12, producers would make more profit on each unit and so producers would be enticed to offer more units for sale—the quantity of units supplied would rise. Similarly, holding all other things constant, if the price of the product were to fall to $8, producers would make less profit on each unit and so producers would be enticed to offer fewer units for sale—the quantity supplied would fall. Supply is this positive relationship between price and quantity supplied. Plotting various prices against the corresponding quantities supplied yields a graph called the *supply curve*. The supply curve is a pictorial representation of supply.

A shift in supply (also called a change in supply, or a supply shock) occurs when the number of units producers are willing to offer for sale changes for a reason unrelated to the price of the product. A shift in supply represents a new relationship between price and quantity. For example, suppose producers are willing to offer one million units of product for sale each month when the price per unit is $10. An increase in the costs of labor and materials reduces the producers' profit margins and so reduces the producers' incentives to produce. As a result, even if the price of the product were to remain fixed at $10, producers would no longer be willing to offer one million units of product for sale each month. Alternatively, suppose that a change in technology enables producers to produce at a fraction of the cost at which they used to produce. The new technology increases the producers' profit margins and so increases the producers' incentives to produce. As a result, even if the price of the product were to remain fixed at $10, producers would be willing to offer more than one million units for sale each month.

Most supply shocks (or violations of the *ceteris paribus* assumptions for supply) can be categorized as:

- changes in the prices of factors;
- changes in the technology the firm employs; and
- changes in the number of firms in the industry.

Factors are things the firm uses in producing its product. Examples of factors are labor, materials, energy, buildings, machinery, and land, the last three of which are a special type of factor called capital. Capital factors are factors that are used in the production of the product but that are not used up in the production (except in the sense of depreciating). Noncapital factors (labor, materials, energy) are used up in the production. For example, a firm uses steel and robots to produce cars. The steel that is used to produce one car cannot be used to produce a second car because the steel was used up in the production of the first car. The robot, however, can be used to produce one car and then used to produce a second car. The robot is not used up when the first car is produced. Therefore, the robot is a capital factor and the steel is a noncapital factor.

When the price of a factor declines, it becomes more profitable for producers to produce, so quantity supplied increases even if the price of the product remains constant. This is an increase in supply. Similarly, when the price of a factor increases, it becomes less profitable for producers to produce, so quantity supplied decreases even if the price of the product remains constant. This is a decrease in supply.

Technology is an intangible that represents the sophistication of the production process. For example, one hundred workers can produce one car every six months when each worker works on his own car. But, when the workers are arranged in an assembly line with each worker performing a specialized task, the one hundred workers can produce one car every day. The rearrangement of the workers into an assembly line is an improvement in technology. Prior to the invention of the

Bessemer process, it was so difficult to refine aluminum that aluminum was more expensive than gold. In the 1800s Henry Bessemer discovered that injecting oxygen into the aluminum while it was melted allowed far more aluminum to be refined for the same cost. This discovery was an improvement in technology.

When technology improves, it becomes more profitable for producers to produce and so quantity supplied increases even if the price of the product remains constant. This is an increase in supply. If technology were to devolve, it would become less profitable for producers to produce, so quantity supplied would decrease even if the price of the product remained constant. This would be a decrease in supply.

The number of firms in the industry typically changes as the industry's profitability changes. If the industry becomes more profitable than other industries of comparable risk, new firms will enter the industry, thereby increasing supply. If the industry becomes less profitable than other industries of comparable risk, existing firms will leave the industry, thereby decreasing supply.

When the number of firms in an industry declines, the quantity supplied decreases even if the price of the product remains constant. This is a decrease in supply. When the number of firms in an industry increases, the quantity supplied increases even if the price of the product remains constant. This is an increase in supply.

Supply (sometimes called industry supply) typically refers to the aggregate production of all firms in an industry. One can refer to the supply of a single firm (the individual supply, or firm's supply). In a perfectly competitive environment, a single firm's supply curve is the portion of the firm's marginal cost curve that is above the firm's average variable cost curve. That is, assuming that the price of the firm's product is high enough so that it is more profitable for the firm to produce than to shut down (i.e., the price is greater than the firm's average variable cost), the minimum price required to entice the firm to offer one more unit of product for sale is the cost to the firm of producing that additional unit (i.e., the marginal cost). Individual supply curves can be combined to form industry supply via the method of horizontal addition. At each price, the quantities supplied by the various firms are added to attain a single quantity supplied for the industry as a whole. When supply is represented graphically, the price is typically shown on the vertical axis and the quantity supplied is shown on the horizontal axis. Thus combining the quantities supplied of the various firms entails adding the quantities shown on the horizontal axis while holding the numbers on the vertical axis fixed. In the example below, when the price of the product is $10 per unit, Firm #1 offers 200 units and Firm #2 offers 100 units. If these are

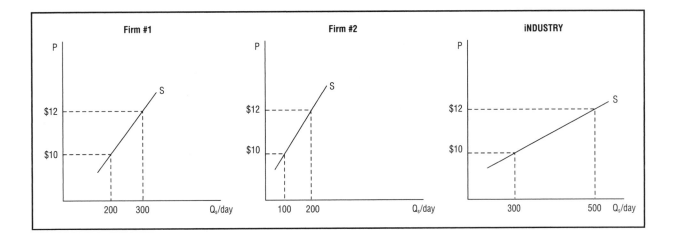

the only two firms in the industry, then the industry as a whole offers 300 units when the price is $10.

The steeper the slope of the industry supply curve, the less responsive the quantity supplied to changes in the price of the product. In the extreme case of a vertical supply curve, the quantity supplied remains fixed regardless of how high or low the price of the product might go. For example, the supply of seats at a stadium is vertical. Regardless of how high the price of tickets might go, the number of seats cannot change (at least not in the short run).

The concept of supply, and its linkage via demand to equilibria, was first formalized by the British economist Alfred Marshall (1842–1924) in his 1890 book *Principles of Economics.* Marshall was one of the first to conceptualize the behavior of producers and consumers independently. The approach, though common today, was not intuitively obvious. The data economists observed was equilibrium data—prices and quantities that arise only after the forces of demand and supply interact. To conceive of supply as an independent force required intuiting the existence of forces that could not be observed directly, but only inferred theoretically. Today, modern econometric techniques allow economists to obtain statistical estimates of supply and demand, but such techniques, even had they existed in 1890, would have been virtually impossible to implement without computers.

In the same way supply ignores the effect of consumers, demand ignores the effect of producers. The result is two behavioral paradigms: Supply summarizes the behavior of producers who exist (relative to consumers) in a vacuum; demand summarizes the behavior of consumers who exist (relative to producers) in a vacuum. Economists then combine demand and supply together to predict what price and quantity will result when consumers and producers are allowed to interact. The resultant price and quantity is called the equilibrium.

SEE ALSO *Average and Marginal Cost; Demand; Equilibrium in Economics; Excess Demand; Excess Supply; Input-Output Matrix; Marginalism; Partial Equilibrium; Productivity; Profitability*

BIBLIOGRAPHY

Eissa, Nada, and Jeffrey B. Liebman. 1996. Labor Supply Response to the Earned Income Tax Credit. *Quarterly Journal of Economics* 111 (2): 605–637.

Lucas, Robert E., Jr. 1990. Supply-Side Economics: An Analytical Review. *Oxford Economic Papers* 42 (2): 293–316.

Parkin, Michael. 2005. *Microeconomics.* 7th ed. Boston: Pearson Addison Wesley.

Antony Davies

SUPPLY, AGGREGATE
SEE *Aggregate Supply.*

SUPPLY, EXCESS
SEE *Excess Supply.*

SUPPLY, LABOR
SEE *Labor Supply.*

SUPPLY OF MONEY
SEE *Money, Supply of.*

SUPREMACY, WHITE

SEE *White Supremacy.*

SUPREME BEING

Supreme being is a seventeenth-century descriptor for God. Given that the social sciences are a modern phenomenon, this designation is appropriate. In an attempt to accommodate the growing awareness of the pluralism of beliefs in the world, *supreme being* became a generic term for the entity that underpins the various world faiths.

CONCEPT OF THE SUPREME BEING

The concept of a supreme being starts with a sense that "something" must be responsible for this world around us. The idea of a creator is key, for this creator requires worship (i.e., an acknowledgement of human dependence on and love for the creator). It is this combination of creator and worship that drives most religious traditions to monotheism. Even in Hinduism, there is an emphasis on the underlying unity of the many in the *one.*

For the sake of simplicity, theistic traditions talk about an omnipotent, omniscient, and perfectly good God. Unlike a limited God (where the issue of the limits of God's power or knowledge could be endlessly debated), theism invites us to affirm an unlimited God, where each attribute is stretched out to infinity.

A crucial area of discussion involves the relationship of the supreme being to time. In Judaism, Moses Maimonides (1135–1204), for example, addressed the issue; in Islam, Ibn Sina (980–1037); and in Christianity, Thomas Aquinas (c. 1225–1274). There is agreement that God is outside time—so there is no duration in the life of God (see Burrell 1986). In addition, God has timeless knowledge of the future—God knows the beginning to the end. However, in the modern period, we find in all three traditions a growing sympathy with the view that God is everlasting (i.e., time is part of God, but there was never a time when God was not and will never be a time when God ceases to be).

Under the influence of Alfred North Whitehead (1861–1947), a movement known as *process theology* emerged that suggests that God's omniscience does not include the decisions of free-will creatures because, by definition, genuinely free decisions are not known until they are made (see Whitehead [1929] 1960). The concept of the supreme being that emerges from this account is often *pantheist* (God and the world are identified together) or *panentheist* (God and the world are identified together, but God is more than the world). This view has more in common with Hindu traditions than with classical Christianity.

ARGUMENTS FOR A SUPREME BEING

For those traditions heavily influenced by Hellenistic thought (i.e., Greek learning), certain arguments emerged to defend the rationality of belief in God. In the Islamic, Jewish, and Christian traditions, two arguments came to the fore. The first is the *design* argument. With its roots in the *Timaeus* of Plato (427–347 BCE), it flourished in the writings of Aquinas and William Paley (1743–1805). The argument seeks to draw a parallel between a human artifact (for Paley it was a "watch") and the world. A watch is clearly intended for and serves certain purposes (even if you do not know what a watch is for, its purpose could be deduced). The cosmos, with all its complexity, is the same. From a watch, we can infer a watchmaker; so from the cosmos, we can infer a designer.

Contemporary defenders of the design argument abound. The Muslim thinker Bediuzzaman Said Nursi (c. 1877–1960) constructs the argument in *The Words* (1928). For many Western philosophers, it is widely believed that David Hume (1711–1776), in *Dialogues Concerning Natural Religion* (1779), effectively undermined the design argument. Hume's first problem is the analogy: Is the world really like a human artifact? The whole argument depends on this analogy: If one likens the world to a giant vegetable, then the human mind does not automatically leap to design and order. Instead, we shall find ourselves thinking of gradual growth—an image that does not require a creator. Hume's second problem is that the argument does not get back to God. At best, explains Hume, the argument takes us back to a designer, but we have no reason to assume that this designer is omnipotent, omniscient, or perfectly good. Indeed, given evil and suffering in creation, we have good reason to assume that the designer is not omnipotent or perfectly good. Hume's third problem is that there are naturalistic explanations for the world's order. Hume was living before Charles Darwin (1809–1882) formulated the natural selection hypothesis. However, other writers have explored the ways in which Darwin undermines the design argument. Richard Dawkins (2006), a biologist at Oxford University, argues that the order in the world is due to the fact that those things that do not fit in do not survive. The world's order is not due to a creator organizing everything in advance.

The *cosmological* argument takes a variety of forms. Among the best known is the Islamic *Kalām* argument for a first cause to the universe. The presumption is that one cannot have an infinite regress of causes. So the universe must have an immaterial first cause that is responsible for everything that follows. Scholars have contested the presumption that there cannot be an infinite regress of causes; after all, no one complains that 22/7 (pi) must finish somewhere before it can be considered intelligible. In addition, Stephen Hawking (1988) has suggested that the combination of cosmology and quantum mechanics might create the conditions for a universe to just start.

Given all this, there is more interest in the argument of Thomas Aquinas. In the *Summa Theologica*, Aquinas explains that he believes that the universe has a start only because of the Genesis story; his instinct is to follow his Greek masters and affirm that matter is eternal. However, he still accepts that rationally it is necessary to posit the existence of God to explain "why anything is" and "how it continues to be." The third of his "five ways" (arguments) to God's existence insists that the intelligibility of the universe depends on a necessary being. If everything is contingent (could be otherwise), then ultimately it would remain unexplained (because we would still have questions about the "why" and the "how"). So, for the universe to make sense, it depends on a necessary being (a being who contains within itself the reason for its own existence). Debate around this form of the argument hinges on the coherence of the idea of a necessary being. Recent defenders of this argument have linked it with the nature of truth (see Markham 1998).

Brief mention should be made of the *ontological* argument. Formulated by Saint Anselm (1033–1109) and then popularized by René Descartes (1596–1650), the ontological argument is an exploration of the meaning of the word *god*. Anselm points out that even the atheist understands the concept of God (otherwise atheists would not know what they were denying). Given that the concept of God includes perfection—the greatest conceivable being—(or in Anselm's terminology, "that than which nothing greater can be thought"), it follows that an imaginary God would not be the greatest conceivable being because the greatest conceivable being would be one that exists both in the mind and reality. Therefore, if the idea of the greatest conceivable being makes sense, then such a being must exist. This argument continues to provoke considerable debate. Recent defenders include Alvin Plantinga (1965).

There are several other arguments for belief in a supreme being. Immanuel Kant (1724–1804) in his *Critique of Practical Reason* (1788) insists that the existence of a supreme being is a necessary postulate of moral discourse. C. S. Lewis (1898–1963) argued that moral discourse does not make sense unless it is grounded in a transcendent being, which is the locus of such values. More recently, some have suggested that there is a pointer to the transcendent in music, beauty, or art (see Steiner 1989).

One major objection to belief in a supreme being is the problem of evil. The traditional form of the problem is a logical one: If God is all powerful, then God must be able to abolish evil; if God is all loving, then God must wish to abolish evil. Yet evil exists, so God cannot be all powerful and all loving. This problem has generated a vast literature on *theodicy* (an attempt to justify God in the light of evil) (see Hick 1977). For some, the social sciences have undermined religion by providing a naturalistic explanation for the religious phenomenon.

BELIEF IN A SUPREME BEING

It is not clear how influential these arguments are on belief in a supreme being. Belief in God is a result of a web of practices that take an elaborate social form. Despite secular expectations to the contrary, belief in a supreme being is widespread. As children learn a language, so, running parallel, a religious worldview is formed. For many people, the concept of the supreme being is nebulous, and there is little clarity about the arguments for a supreme being's existence. Yet there are rich resources in the different world faiths; these can provide both a coherent account and some strong arguments for the supreme being.

SEE ALSO *Christianity; Church, The; Darwin, Charles; Hinduism; Hume, David; Islam, Shia and Sunni; Judaism; Kant, Immanuel; Lay Theories; Monotheism; Nation of Islam; Natural Selection; Religion; Theism; Totemism*

BIBLIOGRAPHY

Burrell, David B. 1986. *Knowing the Unknowable God: Ibn-Sina, Maimonides, Aquinas.* Notre Dame, IN: University of Notre Dame Press.

Dawkins, Richard. 2006. *The God Delusion.* London: Bantam.

Hawking, Stephen W. 1988. *A Brief History of Time: From the Big Bang to Black Holes.* New York: Bantam.

Hick, John. 1977. *Evil and the God of Love.* London: Macmillan.

Hume, David. [1779] 1990. *Dialogues Concerning Natural Religion.* London: Penguin.

Kant, Immanuel. [1788] 1976. *Critique of Practical Reason, and Other Writings in Moral Philosophy.* Trans. and ed. Lewis White Beck. New York and London: Garland.

Lewis, C. S. [1952] 1977. *Mere Christianity.* London: Collins.

Markham, Ian. 1998. *Truth and the Reality of God: An Essay in Natural Theology.* Edinburgh, U.K.: Clark.

Nursi, Bediuzzaman Said. [1928] 1992. *The Words.* Trans. Şükran Vahide. Istanbul, Turkey: Sözler Neşriyat.

Plantinga, Alvin, ed. 1965. *The Ontological Argument.* Garden City, NY: Anchor.

Steiner, George. 1989. *Real Presences.* Chicago: University of Chicago Press.

Whitehead, Alfred North. [1929] 1960. *Process and Reality: An Essay in Cosmology.* New York: Harper.

Ian Markham

SUPREME COURT, U.S.

Article III of the U.S. Constitution states that "[t]he judicial Power of the United States, shall be vested in one supreme Court, and in such inferior Courts as the Congress may from time to time ordain and establish." While the Constitution establishes a Supreme Court, it does little to describe what the Court will look like or what it will do. Nevertheless, the Supreme Court has developed over time to become a key player in the U.S. policy process.

COMPOSITION AND FUNCTION OF THE COURT

With respect to composition, the Constitution provides that the justices of the U.S. Supreme Court will be appointed by the president, with the advice and consent of the Senate, and absent some malfeasance in office (which might result in their impeachment), they enjoy life tenure. As a result, appointing Supreme Court justices provides presidents with an opportunity to leave an enduring policy legacy; William Rehnquist was appointed by Republican president Richard Nixon in 1972, yet he remained a strong conservative force on the Court until his death in 2005.

The number of members of the Supreme Court is determined by statute rather than spelled out in the Constitution. During the first century of the Court's history, the number of justices varied from five to ten. In 1869, the number was set at nine, and it has held constant ever since.

Of the nine members, eight are associate justices and one serves as the chief justice. The position of chief justice must be filled specifically by the president. Thus, when Chief Justice Warren Burger retired in 1986, President Ronald Reagan nominated William Rehnquist—who was already serving as an associate justice—to the position of chief justice; although the Senate had confirmed Rehnquist as an associate justice in 1972, they had to confirm him as chief justice again in 1986.

People sometimes refer to the chief justice as "first among equals." The chief justice's vote does not count more than that of any other justice. However, regardless of his actual time served on the Court, he automatically has more seniority than any associate justice. As a result, he speaks first at conferences—meetings to discuss the merits of cases—and, if the chief justice is in the majority, he determines who will write the Court's opinion. The position of chief justice also entails some additional administrative and ceremonial responsibilities.

With respect to function, the Constitution provides that the Supreme Court has original jurisdiction—the ability to hear the case first, before any other court—over disputes between states, disputes between states and the federal government, and cases involving foreign diplomats. In all other cases, the Supreme Court exercises appellate jurisdiction; that is, it can only review the decision of another court. Because fact-finding is generally relegated to trial courts—courts with original jurisdiction—the Supreme Court is generally limited to resolving disputes over the meaning and application of the law.

Among the cases over which the Supreme Court exercises appellate jurisdiction, the overwhelming majority are brought to the Court through a petition for a writ of certiorari. The Court has complete discretion over whether to grant the petition and hear the case or not. Indeed, the Supreme Court grants relatively few of the petitions filed with it. During the Court's 2002 term, 8,225 cases (including appeals, original jurisdiction cases, and extraordinary writs) were brought before the Supreme Court, yet the Court granted full review to fewer than 100.

A significant body of scholarship is devoted to determining how and why the Court chooses which cases it will hear. Empirical evidence suggests that the Court chooses to hear cases that give it the greatest opportunity to make policy: cases that present significant legal issues that will have broad impact on the legal landscape and, in particular, cases the court below decided "wrongly." In other words, as long as the state and lower federal courts are deciding legal issues in a way that is consistent with the policy and legal preferences of the Supreme Court justices, the justices will generally let those lower court decisions stand. The Court is far more likely to accept a case to correct a perceived error on the part of the lower courts.

JUDICIAL REVIEW AND U.S. POLICY

While determining who wins and who loses legal disputes is arguably an inherently political activity, the U.S. Supreme Court plays its most active role in the American political process when it exercises judicial review. Judicial review is the power to evaluate whether state and federal government actions, both legislative and executive, comport with the Constitution and, if they do not, declare those actions void.

The U.S. Supreme Court first exercised judicial review in the 1803 case of *Marbury v. Madison*. In February 1801, outgoing president John Adams signed a number of judicial commissions, but his secretary of state, John Marshall, did not deliver them before the end of Adams's term. When the new president, Thomas Jefferson, took office, his secretary of state, James Madison, refused to deliver the commissions. William Marbury, one of the individuals who did not receive his commission, brought a claim directly to the U.S. Supreme Court. Interestingly, by this point, John Marshall had taken office as the chief justice of the Supreme Court.

Marbury brought his claim directly to the Supreme Court because a provision of the Judiciary Act of 1789 gave the Supreme Court the power of original jurisdiction over such matters. When the Supreme Court finally issued its decision in 1803, Chief Justice John Marshall concluded that the Court could not compel the president to deliver the commission to Marbury because Congress could not expand the Supreme Court's original jurisdiction beyond that described in the Constitution. The Court was unable to help Marbury, but it achieved its result by declaring an act of Congress unconstitutional and void.

The *Marbury* decision was relatively uncontroversial when it was issued. Chief Justice Marshall made it clear that the Court's role in exercising judicial review was limited to making legal, rather than political, determinations. In its earliest incarnation, judicial review was considered an almost ministerial function that gave the Court relatively little policymaking prerogative. As time passed, however, the potential for policymaking through the exercise of judicial review became clear.

In the late 1920s and early 1930s, the full power of judicial review was revealed. Specifically, as Congress began to pass social legislation in response to the Progressive movement and as President Franklin Roosevelt began to implement his New Deal economic policies, the Supreme Court stood squarely in the way of elected-branch policymaking. The Court issued a number of decisions striking down social and economic legislation on the grounds that it violated constitutional notions of federalism and individual liberty.

In 1937, following a string of Supreme Court decisions striking down New Deal programs, Roosevelt proposed a plan to "pack" the Court: On the pretext of assisting an overworked and elderly Supreme Court, Roosevelt proposed creating a new seat on the Supreme Court for every justice who was seventy years old or older and who remained on the Court. The result would have been to add six new seats, and those seats would, of course, be filled by judges friendly to Roosevelt's New Deal programs.

Within weeks of Roosevelt's proposal, Justice Owens Roberts abandoned the Court's anti–New Deal faction to create a narrow majority that supported the constitutionality of Roosevelt's programs. Roberts's apparent about-face is often referred to as the "switch in time that saved nine" because his change in position helped preserve the nine-member Supreme Court. Historical examination of the Court's deliberations from this time period indicate that Roberts had cast his pro–New Deal votes on the cases in question weeks before Roosevelt announced his plan; in other words, the coincidence between the threat to pack the Court and Roberts's change of position was just that—a coincidence.

Still, the Court's ability to stall implementation of significant social and economic programs highlights the potential of judicial review as a political force. Moreover, the shift in Supreme Court policy during the 1930s emphasizes the amount of discretion that the Court has in interpreting the Constitution. Although Chief Justice Marshall described judicial review as a mechanical application of clear legal principles, the events surrounding the New Deal demonstrate the extent to which the Constitution is subject to a wide range of interpretation. Indeed, since the 1930s, there has been an increasing awareness of the political implications of Supreme Court membership, and the nomination and confirmation process has become quite politically charged.

Any lingering doubt about the political dimension of the Court's exercise of judicial review was dispelled during the tenure of Chief Justice Earl Warren. Warren was appointed by a conservative president—Dwight Eisenhower—but his time on the Court was marked by a clear liberal agenda. Warren was particularly interested in expanding the rights of criminal defendants, and his time on the Court is marked by numerous decisions that broadly construe the individual rights the Constitution guarantees to criminal defendants.

Among the cases that make up Chief Justice Warren's legacy are *Miranda v. Arizona* (1966) and *Gideon v. Wainwright* (1963). In *Miranda*, the Supreme Court held that the Fifth Amendment protection against self-incrimination requires police to inform any criminal suspect in their custody of their constitutional rights; specifically, *Miranda* requires the police to inform suspects in custody that they have the right to remain silent and decline to answer any questions. The *Miranda* decision is particularly striking because it delves into the nuts and bolts of police procedure, setting fairly "bright line" requirements for the policy to follow.

In *Gideon v. Wainwright* (1963), the Supreme Court ruled that the Sixth Amendment guarantee of effective assistance of counsel requires states to provide attorneys to indigent criminal defendants. In other words, the state must pay attorneys to represent criminal defendants who are too poor to hire attorneys on their own. Implementation of the *Gideon* decision has imposed considerable financial burdens on the states.

Both the *Gideon* and *Miranda* decisions reflect Chief Justice Warren's personal ideological agenda. First, both decisions give higher priority to the rights of the individual than to the rights of the state; procedural and financial burdens placed on government take second chair to the rights guaranteed individuals by the Constitution. Second, both decisions reflect Warren's belief that the U.S. Supreme Court plays a countermajoritarian role in U.S. politics. While the legislative and executive branches respond to the will of the majority, Warren (and many others) viewed the courts as providing a voice and a forum to those who are socially marginalized, such as the poor.

THE SUPREME COURT AND CONSTITUTIONAL DIALOGUE

Two politically charged issues—race and abortion—highlight both the political aspect of judicial review and the role of the Supreme Court in a broader political dialogue. In both issue areas, the Supreme Court has played a key role in setting U.S. policy. Yet in both issues, the constraints placed on the Court and the dialogue between the Court and other political actors is apparent.

In 1857, the Supreme Court issued a decision in the case of *Scott v. Sandford* (better known as the "*Dred Scott* decision"). Legally, *Dred Scott* was a significant statement about the importance of states' rights. Politically, however, *Dred Scott* was important because the Court held, essentially, that even emancipated slaves could not be full citizens of the United States. In an already tumultuous political climate, the *Dred Scott* decision became a rallying point for abolitionists and contributed to the outbreak of the U.S. Civil War and, ultimately, to the enactment of the Fourteenth Amendment's guarantee of equal protection of the laws.

In *Plessy v. Ferguson* (1896), the Court considered a Louisiana statute that required separation of the races on all railroads. In finding that the Louisiana statute did not violate the Fourteenth Amendment, the Court explicitly rejected Plessy's argument that segregation marginalized African Americans and perpetuated the belief that African Americans were inferior. Yet in *Brown v. Board of Education of Topeka* (1954), the Court outlawed segregated schools precisely because of the social stigma associated with segregation. What changed? The political climate had changed dramatically; between 1896 and 1954, African Americans had gained considerable electoral strength. Moreover, the composition of the Court had changed. Specifically, the *Brown* decision was vetted by a newly appointed Chief Justice Earl Warren.

The change in jurisprudence between *Plessy* and *Brown* illustrates both the importance of the ideology of individual members of the Court and the importance of a favorable political climate for the Court's exercise of power. The Court's decision in *Brown* could be implemented only with the support of the president, who mobilized the National Guard to force southern states to integrate their public schools.

The issue of race provides further illustration of the interplay between the Court and the elected branches. The Supreme Court has struggled to articulate a clear, concise position on the issue of affirmative action, leaving states to formulate their policies through a process of trial and error. In 1978, the Court first addressed the issue of affirmative action in higher education with the case of *Regents of the University of California v. Bakke*. In *Bakke*, the Court indicated that some affirmative action programs might be constitutionally acceptable, but the University of California program was not. Over the next twenty-five years, public universities across the country attempted to develop constitutionally acceptable yet effective affirmative action policies, but the Court failed to provide clear guidance. In 2003, the Court issued two decisions on the issue of affirmative action, and universities hoped that the issue would finally be resolved. In *Gratz v. Bollinger*, the Court struck down the University of Michigan's affirmative action program for undergraduate admissions; in *Grutter v. Bollinger*, the Court upheld the affirmative action program for the University of Michigan's law school. Taken together, the two decisions indicate that diversity in education is a compelling government interest, that public schools can consider racial diversity in admissions decisions, but that race cannot be given any precise, explicit weight in the decision process. The decisions provide guidance, but they are far from defining exactly when and how public universities may consider race in admissions.

While the issue of race illustrates the interplay and interdependence of the courts and elected government over the course of more than a century, the issue of abortion provides a more succinct yet equally compelling illustration. In 1973, following the relaxation of numerous state anti-abortion laws, the Supreme Court issued its landmark decision in *Roe v. Wade*. In *Roe*, the Court held that the right to privacy—which is not enumerated in the Constitution but which the Court had previously inferred from a number of constitutional provisions—protected the right of a woman to obtain an abortion. In a remarkably "legislative" opinion, the Court expounded that a woman's right to privacy completely dominated the state's interests during the first trimester of pregnancy but the two obtained more equal footing as the pregnancy progressed.

The *Roe* decision ignited a firestorm of controversy. It mobilized anti-abortion activists and helped solidify a full-fledged anti-abortion movement in American politics. It prompted conservative state governments to enact increasingly restrictive anti-abortion legislation in an effort to test the boundaries of *Roe* and lead to the Court overturning its decision. It made the issue of abortion and the right to privacy a sort of litmus test in judicial nominations and confirmations. In the wake of *Roe*, the effect of the Court on politics and that of politics on the Court are stark.

SEE ALSO Brown v. Board of Education, *1954;* Brown v. Board of Education, *1955;* Constitution, U.S.;

Dred Scott v. Sanford; *Eisenhower, Dwight D.; Great Depression;* Grutter *Decision;* Hernandez v. Texas; *Jefferson, Thomas; Judicial Review; Judiciary; Law; Madison, James; Marshall, Thurgood; New Deal, The; Public Policy;* Roe v. Wade; *Roosevelt, Franklin D.; Separation of Powers; Warren, Earl*

BIBLIOGRAPHY

Baum, Lawrence. 2004. *The Supreme Court.* 8th ed. Washington, DC: CQ Press.

Devins, Neal. 1992. Judicial Matters. *California Law Review* 80: 1027–1069.

Lazarus, Edward. 2005. *Closed Chambers: The Rise, Fall, and Future of the Modern Supreme Court.* Rev. ed. New York: Penguin.

Nelson, William Edward. 2000. *Marbury v. Madison: The Origins and Legacy of Judicial Review.* Lawrence: University of Kansas Press.

O'Brien, David. 2005. *Storm Center: The Supreme Court in American Politics.* 7th ed. New York: Norton.

Rosenberg, Gerald. 1993. *The Hollow Hope: Can Courts Bring About Social Change?* Chicago: University of Chicago Press.

Wendy L. Watson

SURPLUS

In the history of economic thought there are, broadly, two approaches to the study of prices and income distribution. The neoclassical, or marginalist, approach is the dominant modern theory. But there is an older approach rooted in the writings of William Petty and François Quesnay (in his *Tableau Economique*) and in those of authors in the classical school of political economy such as David Ricardo and Karl Marx. Classical economists considered the surplus to be that portion of the annual social product left over after deducting one part to replace the means of production used up and another part to pay workers for their consumption. The classical economists generally took the view that wealth creation is the productive combination of direct human labor and means of production, where the latter was considered to be indirect labor because it was the result of previous periods' labors.

While the centrality of labor in the production process was a theme that was common to the writings of most classical economists (Hunt 2002, chapter 2) it was in the writings of Marx that the labor theory of value (LTV) reached its fullest level of development. The LTV states that the value of a commodity is equal to the total amount of direct and indirect labor time (or *labor value*) that is necessary for its production, given demand and technology. Further, in the Marxian perspective money prices are

assumed to be regulated by labor values. It is quite simple to understand this, for if in the production of a good the direct labor productivity rises and/or the labor productivities in the industries that supply its inputs rise, then its unit labor value will fall. Consequently, given wage rates, its unit costs will also fall, thereby allowing firms to lower their unit selling prices.

Let c = labor time needed to produce the means of production used up daily and l = the direct labor time per day needed to produce a given amount of output. If money prices are proportional to the total labor time, as assumed by Marx (*Capital* Volume I), then unit money price will be proportional to $c + l$. Let v = labor time needed to produce wage-goods so that money wages are proportional to v. Then unit money cost of production will be proportional to $c + v$. Thus unit money profits or *surplus value* will arise if and only if $c + l > c + v$, that is to say, $l > v$. Hence collectively workers need to work for a length of time that exceeds the time needed to produce wage goods (Shaikh 1987).

MODERN DEBATES

Nonetheless, not all contemporary authors who subscribe to the surplus approach consider the LTV to be valid. These authors base their position on Piero Sraffa's (1960) reevaluation of the Ricardian LTV. Ricardo's struggles with the LTV can be understood by remembering that the general rate of profit equals the aggregate surplus divided by the aggregate capital advanced. However, in a world of heterogeneous commodities the numerator cannot be divided by the denominator in this equation unless they are rendered commensurate in value terms. That is, one needs to know their prices beforehand. However, prices themselves are affected by changes in income distribution between wage and profit rates, thereby introducing an element of circular reasoning into the theory. This was the basis of Ricardo's attempts to search for an invariant measure of value that would be immune to the changes in the distribution of income.

Contemporary Sraffian authors reject the relevance of labor values and take the position that physical production data and cost structures are sufficient to simultaneously determine relative prices and profit rates (Kurz 2006, p. 9). Authors in this school consider the LTV to be redundant because of the apparent autonomous movements of prices and profits (Steedman 1977). On the other hand, Shaikh (1982, 1984) argues that this autonomy is an illusion, as random fluctuations of market prices around values will bring about transfers of surplus value between different sectors that will result in only limited deviations of actual profits from surplus value.

To understand Shaikh's argument it is necessary to draw on Marx's distinction between the circuit of industrial capital and the capitalist circuit of revenue. In the former *variable capital* is advanced to hire workers who are combined with raw materials and machinery (or *constant capital*) to produce an output. In the latter circuit capitalist households use all or part of the surplus value produced in the first circuit to purchase a portion of the output. One may further subdivide the circuit of capital into three departments that respectively produce raw materials and machinery (Department I), workers' consumption goods (Department IIA), and capitalist households' consumption goods (Department IIB).

Let prices be initially equal to values in all three departments. Then a decrease only in the aggregate price of the output of Department I will lower input costs in all departments, as constant capital is a common input. A price decrease in only Department IIA output will have the same effect because, given real wages, lower prices of Department IIA output will also lower advances for variable capital, another common input, in all three sectors.

The drop of price below value in Department I will squeeze profits only in that department and will create excess profits in the other two departments. The same will hold true for a price decrease only in Department IIB. Then in both situations the price-value deviation will be accompanied by a transfer of value within the circuit of capital from one department to another.

In contrast, a fall in the price of only department IIB output will leave all sectors' production costs unaffected but will entail a revenue gain on capitalists' personal accounts, as the money-value that they pay to purchase goods will be lower than the value of these goods. In other words, there will be a transfer of surplus value from the circuit of capital to the capitalist circuit of revenue, producing a fall of aggregate profits in the latter. However, if such transfers between the two circuits are ignored then an illusion is created that profits vary independently of surplus value (Marx 1971, p. 347).

IMPLICATIONS

It should now be clear that the extent of profits–surplus value deviations will depend on price-value deviations in Department IIB and on surplus value transfers between the two circuits. If all surplus value is consumed as revenue by capitalists the profit–surplus value deviation will be a maximum; conversely if all surplus value is reinvested there is no circuit of revenue and the profit–surplus value deviation will be zero.

More generally, an important implication of this framework is that the balance between production and non-production activities determines an economy's growth rate. Production activities are those that create surplus value while non-production activities are ones that subsequently utilize it or use it up in some way (Shaikh

and Tonak 1994, chapter 2). This distinction between these two types of activities has some implications for the role of the State if the aim is to raise the growth rate. First, non-productive expenditures by the State should grow at a rate which is slower than the growth of production activity. Second, there could be a policy of increasing the proportion of production activity (e.g., generation of electricity) by the State. Finally, along the lines discussed by Nicholas Kaldor (Palma and Marcel 1989), taxation policies could be implemented to squeeze (luxury) consumption spending by capitalist households and encourage the retention of a greater proportion of surplus value within the circuit of capital.

SEE ALSO *Class, Leisure; Class, Rentier; Economics, Neo-Ricardian; Labor Theory of Value; Profitability; Profits; Rate of Exploitation; Rate of Profit; Relative Surplus Value; Ricardo, David; Sraffa, Piero; Surplus Value*

BIBLIOGRAPHY

Hunt, E. K. 2002. *History of Economic Thought: A Critical Perspective*. Armonk, NY: Sharpe.

Kurz, Heinz. 2006. The Agents of Production Are the Commodities Themselves: On the Classical Theory of Production, Distribution and Value. *Structural Change and Economic Dynamics*, 17: 1–26.

Marx, Karl. 1971. *Theories of Surplus Value, Part III*. Moscow: Progress Publishers.

Palma, Gabriel, and Mario Marcel. 1989. Kaldor on the "Discreet Charm" of the Chilean Bourgeoisie. *Cambridge Journal of Economics*, 13(1): 245–272.

Ricardo, David. 1951–1973. *The Works and Correspondence of David Ricardo*, 11 volumes, ed. Piero Sraffa with the collaboration of M. H. Dobb. Cambridge, U.K.: Cambridge University Press.

Shaikh, Anwar M. 1982. Neo-Ricardian Economics: A Wealth of Algebra, a Poverty of Theory. *Review of Radical Political Economics*, 14(2): 67–83.

Shaikh, Anwar M. 1984. The Transformation from Marx to Sraffa. In *Ricardo, Marx, Sraffa: the Langston Memorial Volume*, ed. Ernest Mandel and Alan Freeman, 43–84. London: Verso.

Shaikh, Anwar M. 1987. Surplus Value. In *Marxian Economics: The New Palgrave*, ed. John Eatwell, Murray Milgate, and Peter Newman, 344–349. New York: Norton, 1990.

Shaikh, Anwar M., and E. Ahmet Tonak. 1994. *Measuring the Wealth of Nations*. Cambridge, U.K.: Cambridge University Press

Sraffa, Piero. 1960. *Production of Commodities by Means of Commodities*. Cambridge, U.K.: Cambridge University Press.

Steedman, Ian. 1977. *Marx after Sraffa*. London: New Left Books.

Jamee K. Moudud

SURPLUS, SOCIAL

SEE *Social Surplus.*

SURPLUS LABOR

SEE *Labor, Surplus: Marxist and Radical Economics.*

SURPLUS POPULATION

For classical political economists, the poverty and unemployment generated in the early stages of capitalist development denoted the existence of a surplus population caused by the inability of the poor to postpone marriage and behave in a rational and virtuous manner.

MALTHUS

The most influential exponent of this view was T. R. Malthus (1766–1834), author of the "population principle," or "the constant tendency in all animated life to increase beyond the nourishment prepared for it" (Malthus [1798] 1933, p. 5)—widely invoked to legitimate poverty and inequality on the grounds of "natural laws." According to Malthus, the principle's "natural and necessary effects [are] … a very considerable portion of that vice and misery, and of that unequal distribution of the bounties of nature which it has been the unceasing object of the enlightened philanthropists in all ages to correct" (p. 5). Malthus based his principle of population on a "natural law," the tendency of all forms of life, including human life, to increase beyond the available means of subsistence: When unchecked, he argued, population increases geometrically, doubling every twenty-five years, whereas food can increase only arithmetically (p. 8). That technological change and growth in the productivity of labor in agriculture and other areas of economic activity have proven Malthus wrong have not undermined, however, the continuing ideological value of his principle as a tool for legitimating poverty, inequality, underdevelopment, war, and human misery in all its forms. For example, Robert Kaplan (1994), writing about the conditions in West Africa in the mid-1990s—which, in his view, portended a twenty-first century engulfed in anarchy, disease, and overpopulation—states: "It is Thomas Malthus, the philosopher of demographic doomsday, who is now the prophet of West Africa's future. And West Africa's future, eventually, will be that of most of the world" (p. 48).

MARX

Marx's alternative to Malthus's principle of population is the principle of the reserve army or relative surplus population, which captures the effects of changing patterns of capital accumulation upon the working population (Marx [1867] 1967, chapter 25). Theoretically, the process of capital accumulation entails increases in the demand for labor, which, in turn, lead to increases in the value of labor power; that is, as the supply of labor declines, capitalists are compelled to offer higher wages to entice workers to their enterprises. The effect of higher wages is a reduction in profits. In practice, wages tend to rise together with capital accumulation, but they never rise enough to endanger the system itself. For the classical political economists and for Malthus, in particular, the mechanism that kept wages equal to their "natural" price (that is, equal to the minimum level of subsistence) is embodied in the principle of population. When wages rise, workers overreproduce themselves, and this increase in the size of the population produces a supply of labor greater than the demand, so wages fall to their "natural" price, that is, to a minimum level of subsistence. Under these conditions, workers could improve their situation only by controlling their numbers, thereby raising the price of labor. Poverty and unemployment are, therefore, the result only of workers' "natural propensity" to reproduce beyond the available means of subsistence.

Against Malthus, Marx observes that capital accumulation does not automatically entail increases in the demand for labor because as the forces of production develop, the organic composition of capital changes. From the perspective of its value composition, capital is composed of constant capital (the value of the means of production) and variable capital (the value of labor power). From the perspective of its technical composition, capital is composed of the means of production and living labor. Changes in the technical composition produce changes in the value composition, and this correlation between the two is the organic composition of capital (Marx [1867] 1967, p. 612). In the process of capital accumulation, the organic composition of the total social capital changes; the constant increases at the expense of the variable component, and "since the demand for labor is determined not by the amount of capital as a whole but by its variable constituent alone, that demand falls progressively with the increase of total capital.… It falls relatively to the magnitude of the total social capital and at an accelerated rate" (p. 629). The logic of capital accumulation inexorably produces unemployment, the constant presence of a "relative surplus population" or "reserve army of labor" whose size and composition will vary with the specific needs of capital accumulation in a given social formation. It follows that the relationship between the level of employment and the size of the population is not determined by the latter but by the organic composition of capital invested at a given time: "the more or less favorable circumstances in which the wage-working class supports and multiplies itself, in no way alter the fundamental character of capitalist production" (p. 615). Capital accumulation, therefore, is indifferent to and independent from rates of population growth (pp. 640–641).

SURPLUS POPULATION IN THE TWENTIETH AND TWENTY-FIRST CENTURIES

In the two centuries after the publication of Malthus's work, the capitalist mode of production has penetrated even more deeply in all social formations. World capitalist accumulation has internationalized the reserve army of labor. Within advanced capitalist social formations, such as that of the United States, changes in the organic composition of capital resulted in automation, downsizing, outsourcing, deindustrialization, decline in the demand for skilled blue-collar labor, growth in the service and information-technology sectors of the economy, and increases in the demand for technical, professional, and managerial labor. As it could not be otherwise, such qualitative shifts in capital investment necessarily contributed to the existence and reproduction, through time, of a surplus population of fluctuating size and composition.

Changes in the organic composition of capital, however, are not the only cause of surplus populations. Welfare-state policies, the product of successful class struggles (especially in western Europe) and of the capitalist classes' effort (especially in the United States) to avert social unrest and even revolution in the aftermath of the Great Depression, had unintended demographic consequences. By providing social services and minimal income payments to the unemployed, disabled, and poor, such policies contributed to the growth, through natural increase, of a large and relatively stable population of poor and near-poor people, unemployed and largely unemployable. Therefore, the surplus population in advanced capitalist societies is heterogeneous, including the recent and the long-term unemployed and a varying proportion of people who have never been employed and are likely to be unemployable. Illiteracy, lack of skills, age, responsibility for the care of small children or elderly relatives, criminal records, drug addictions, disability, mental illness, and so forth are some of the reasons millions of people have never or seldom entered the labor force. Also part of the surplus population are the homeless, prostitutes, and those who make a living through illegal activities, the "lumpenproletariat." Finally, as the effects of globalization are felt more strongly among the more vulnerable sectors of the working classes, Latino immigrants—particularly the undocumented—have become the more visible and stigmatized sector of the surplus population. Even if most of them work in poorly paid manual jobs that most U.S. citizens refrain from doing, they are contradictorily perceived both as dangerous, unhealthy, idle, a burden for the taxpayers, and, at the same time, the cause of declining wages for low-skilled workers.

In racially heterogeneous societies such as the United States, blacks and other "nonwhite" populations have been deemed superfluous by the white elites or managerial classes (Darity 1983), a view reflecting the resilience and pervasiveness of racism across all social classes and the disproportionate presence of racial and ethnic minorities in the poverty population. And, given the economic and political interests of U.S. and European capitalist classes in the so-called developing world, their populations also were deemed superfluous, a drain on the world's resources, the main cause of "underdevelopment," political unrest, and revolutionary, anticapitalist and anticolonial struggles. Consequently, national and international strategies were devised to control the size of these surplus populations (Demerath 1976; Mass 1976; Gimenez 1977; Michaelson 1981; Bandarage 1997).

Within the United States, in the early twentieth century scientists lent support to eugenic theories of racial differences in intelligence and promoted immigration and sterilization policies designed to keep "inferior" (that is, non-"Nordic") races from entering the country and to discourage the "unfit" (that is, the poor, Native Americans, blacks, Puerto Ricans, criminals, the mentally ill, alcoholics) from reproducing (DeFine 1997). While such government-sponsored policies are no longer in place, the practice of government-funded sterilization, made easily available to poor and nonwhite women, continues unabated; it has become the most widespread form of birth control among women older than twenty-five in the United States (Petchesky 1976) and, for all practical purposes, can be viewed as an effect of a "doctrine of preemptive extermination" aimed at the surplus population (Darity 1983). Presumably, sterilization is done with the women's consent, but consent cannot be taken for granted when women are not fully informed of alternatives or when the alternatives—efficient use of contraceptives or abortion—are placed beyond their reach. Furthermore, the women who "choose" sterilization tend to be poor, Puerto Ricans, Latinas, African Americans, and Native Americans (Petchesky 1976; DeFine, 1997). The high incidence of sterilization constitutes a form of abuse and a strategy to control the growth of populations deemed superfluous because it is a form of birth control that, conservative rhetoric about the value of life notwithstanding, is made easily available and paid by federal and state funds. Abortion, on the other hand, though legal, is unavailable for most poor women, for the Hyde Amendment, passed in 1976, "excludes abortion from the comprehensive health care services provided to low-income people by the federal government through

Medicaid ... Currently, only seventeen states fund abortions for low income women" (ACLU 2004).

Besides sterilization, poor women, especially women on welfare, are encouraged to use long-term forms of contraception, such as Depo-Provera, Norplant, or quinacrine (Chamberlain and Hardisty 2006) with problematic side-effects. These practices, supported by the political right, have affected the consciousness of people of color, women and men, who become suspicious of family planning programs and even perceive legalized abortion as part of a genocidal strategy against people of color. The political right exploits this perception, claiming to be "allies of these communities ... pointing to 'shared values' on abortion and other social issues" (Chamberlain and Hardisty 2006).

Wishful thinking about the role of abortion in cutting down the size of the surplus population is epitomized in the notion that the legalization of abortion caused a decline in the crime rate: "In the early 1990s, just as the first cohort of children born after *Roe v. Wade* was hitting its late teen years—the years during which young men enter their criminal prime—the rate of crime began to fall. What this cohort was missing ... were the children who stood the greatest chance of becoming criminals.... Legalized abortion led to less unwontedness; unwontedness leads to high crime; legalized abortion, therefore, led to less crime" (Levitt and Dubner 2005, p. 139). They assumed that, as safe abortions had been available to middle-class women before legalization, the women most likely to have had abortions after *Roe v. Wade* would be poor, in their teens, unmarried, or all three (p. 138) because now "any woman could easily obtain an abortion, often for less than $100" (p. 138). Their findings have been criticized and shown to be misleading because of statistical flaws; they ignored changes in the crime rate that would have undermined their arguments, and by focusing on the crime rates of 1985 and 1997 only, they ignored "the 800-pound gorilla of crime trends: the rise and fall of the crack epidemic during the intervening years ... which first drove violent crime up in the late '80s and early '90s, then drove it down in the mid and late '90s" (Sailer 1999). They should have been criticized also because they ignored the effects of the Hyde Amendment, which, after 1976, kept poor women—presumably those likely to give birth to potential criminals—in most states from having access to abortions. Regardless of the flaws in their research, their argument is ideologically powerful, strengthening racial stereotypes among whites and suspicion about abortion among nonwhites. What gets lost in the midst of these arguments is the need of all women, regardless of class, race, or ethnicity, to attain some control over their bodies. Women's reproductive rights, their right to make free and informed decisions about childbearing, are endangered by the contradictions and ideological effects inherent in political discourses and practices that celebrate motherhood and urge white, middle-class women to reproduce and reject abortion while making abortion unavailable and pushing sterilization as the birth control of "choice" for poor, especially nonwhite, women.

Besides population control, prisons (many of them turned into workplaces) and the army are the other two strategies the dominant classes use to deal with the surplus population. The Malthusian spirit, captured in Scrooge's reply to someone requesting a donation for the poor at Christmastime, is still alive: When told that many of the poor and destitute would rather die than go to the work house or prison, Scrooge said: "If they would rather die, ... they had better do it, and decrease the surplus population" (Dickens [1843] 1876, p. 12).

SEE ALSO *Labor, Surplus: Conventional Economics; Labor, Surplus: Marxist and Radical Economics; Lumpenproletariat; Malthus, Thomas Robert; Marx, Karl; Overpopulation; Proletariat; Unemployment*

BIBLIOGRAPHY

ACLU. 2004. Public Funding for Abortion. http://www.aclu.org/reproductiverights/lowincome/16393res20040721.html.

Bandarage, Asoka. 1997. *Women, Population, and Global Crisis: A Political-Economic Analysis.* London: Zed Books.

Chamberlain, Pam, and Jean Hardisty. 2006. Reproducing Patriarchy: Reproductive Rights Under Siege. *The Public Eye Magazine* 14 (1). http://www.publiceye.org/magazine/v14n1/ReproPatriarch-12.html#P134_63036.

Darity, William, Jr. 1983. The Managerial Class and Surplus Population. *Society* 21 (1): 54–62.

DeFine, Michael Sullivan. 1997. A History of Governmentally Coerced Sterilization: The Plight of the Native American Woman. http://www.geocities.com/CapitolHill/9118/mike2.html.

Demerath, Nicholas J. 1976. *Birth Control and Foreign Policy: The Alternatives to Family Planning.* New York: Harper & Row.

Dickens, Charles. [1843] 1876. *Christmas Stories.* New York: Harper & Brothers, Publishers.

Gimenez, Martha E. 1977. Population and Capitalism. *Latin American Perspectives* 4 (4) (Fall): 5–40.

Kaplan, Robert D. 1994. The Coming Anarchy. *Atlantic Monthly* 273 (2): 44–76.

Levitt, Steven D., and Stephen J. Dubner. 2005. *Freakonomics: A Rogue Economist Explores the Hidden Side of Everything.* New York: William Morrow.

Malthus, T. R. 1798. *On the Principle of Population,* vol. 1. New York: E. P. Dutton, 1933.

Marx, Karl. 1867. *Capital: A Critique of Political Economy,* vol. 1, *The Process of Capitalist Production.* New York: International Publishers, 1967.

Mass, Bonne. 1976. *Population Target: The Political Economy of Population Control in Latin America.* Brampton, Ontario, Canada: Charters Publishing.

Michaelson, Karen, ed. 1981. *And The Poor Get Children: Radical Perspectives on Population Dynamics.* New York: Monthly Review Press.

Petchesky, Rosalind Pollack. 1976. "Reproductive Choice" in the Contemporary United States: A Social Analysis of Female Sterilization. In *And The Poor Get Children: Radical Perspectives on Population Dynamics,* ed. Karen Michaelson, 50–88. New York: Monthly Review Press.

Sailer, Steve. Does Abortion Prevent Crime? *Slate,* 1999. http://www.slate.com/id/33569/entry/33575.

Martha E. Gimenez

SURPLUS VALUE

For Karl Marx, surplus value is critical to the expansion of capital. In the money circuit $M - C - M'$, capitalists purchase commodities (C) with money (M) in order to sell these commodities for more than their initial outlay (M'). Surplus value is the difference $M' - M$, the profit that the capitalist makes at the end of the money circuit. Instead of hoarding this profit, as would a miser, the capitalist reinvests it in a new, enhanced circuit of money. The conclusion of each circuit, with more value produced, provides the starting point for the expansion of capital in each subsequent circuit.

The problem that Marx (1867) sets himself in *Capital,* volume 1, is how capitalists can sell for more than they buy. Are some commodities sold for more than they cost? The answer is yes and no. Marx assumes that capitalists pay for the full cost of inputs such as raw materials, which are used in the production process. The yarn that is used by the weaver is paid for at full cost. However, there is one commodity that does beget more value than its cost: labor power.

On the one hand labor power, which is sold by workers to capitalists, has a capacity to produce output. The capitalist makes use of a worker's labor power, say for eight hours per day, adding eight hours of value to the commodity produced. On the other hand it has a cost, which for the capitalist is the outlay of wages that enable workers, and their families, to subsist. Crucially, the value of this labor power is less than the value of the worker's output. The worker may have to work only four hours per day to produce value that is equivalent to the goods required for subsistence. But, exercising control over the labor process, the capitalist requires an eight-hour day: the worker is robbed of four hours of labor power that is extracted by the capitalist as surplus value. For Marx, sur-

plus value entails the exploitation of workers by the capitalist class.

From a political point of view, the theory of surplus value has been an ideological weapon for exposing the injustice of the capitalist production process. The capitalist seeks to extend the working day to extract what Marx refers to as absolute surplus value (a reduction in the value of labor power would increase relative surplus value). To this day, in capitalist economies workers suffer adverse health effects from excessive hours of work. The Japanese have their own word for it: *karoshi*—death from overwork. In response to this problem, the European Union has imposed a forty-eight-hour-maximum workweek. Marx's theory of surplus value provides the basis for arguing for a reduction in working hours. As Philp (2005) has shown, however, the surplus-value approach does not always have to be associated with a sharpening of the class struggle. The reduction in hours can benefit capitalists if less unemployment reduces the burden of taxation.

In making the argument that workers are exploited, the problem is that on the surface, workers seem to be paid a wage for the full working day. Before capitalism, the extraction of a surplus was much more obvious. The feudal peasant gave one day's worth of corn to the landlord, and another to the priest. Under capitalism, however, surplus value is located in the circulation of money, where workers freely exchange their labor power for wages and where capitalists seem to make profits as a natural reward for risking their money in the spirit of enterprise.

Key to the analytical power of surplus value is Marx's assumption, maintained in the first two volumes of *Capital,* that commodities are sold at their values. The money value of consumption goods purchased by workers, using money wages, is the same as the labor embodied in those commodities; the money value of the output produced by workers is the same as the labor embodied in that output. Hence there is an assumed equivalence between surplus value, measured in units of labor time, and money profits, located in the circulation of money.

Critics of Marx, however, have argued that in *Capital,* volume 3, where he allows prices to diverge from values, the equivalence between surplus value and profits is not successfully maintained. Marx develops a procedure for transforming values into prices that is generally considered to be incomplete. Whereas the outputs of each branch of production are transformed from values to prices, the transformation is not carried out for inputs. Inspired by Piero Sraffa, and the earlier input-output approach of Wassily Leontief, Marx's critics have shown that when the values of inputs are transformed into prices the consequences are severe. Total money profits are different from total surplus value, there being no reason why the category of embodied labor value should be at all useful. Since capitalists only care about money profits, why should Marxists use the irrelevant category of surplus value?

In recent years, the main reaction to this Sraffian critique of Marx has been to downplay the role of value as embodied labor time. Goods can only have value if they are sold in the marketplace, so what matters is the form that value takes in exchange—the value-form of commodities. Proponents of the value-form approach argue that in *Capital*, volume 1, Marx uses both labor embodied and value-form definitions of the value of labor power. In the "new solution" to the transformation problem, the value-form definition is preferred, with the share of wages in money income interpreted to be the value of labor power. In this approach, the equivalence between money profits and surplus value is established, even when both inputs and outputs are transformed from value to prices. A number of different variants to the value-form approach have emerged, with some dispute over the extent to which labor-embodied categories are replaced across all commodities, not just labor power, and whether the analysis should be recast in a dynamic or non-equilibrium setting (Foley 2000).

A problematic issue with the value-form approach is that by abandoning labor-embodied values, Marx's approach is drained of all content. Is a real exploration beneath the surface offered by interpreting money categories as a form of value? There are two ways in which the value-form approach can provide a useful basis for future research.

First, by emphasizing the importance of money in Marx's economics, it provides an alternative to neoclassical general equilibrium theory, which has limited relevance to a barter-exchange economy. The value-form approach can be used to model a genuinely capitalist system with credit money providing the vehicle for capital expansion (see Trigg 2006). The role of credit in the recent economic boom in the United States, for example, has been related to the extraction of surplus value in China. With no trade-union rights and high productivity, there is a structural relationship between the production of vast quantities of surplus value by the emerging Chinese proletariat and the credit boom associated with China's purchase of U.S. financial assets.

Second, the value-form approach provides a possible starting point for Marxian empirical research. By working with money categories, Marxists are able to interpret national accounts data from a value-theoretic perspective. The secular fall of the rate of profit since the 1960s, which has been observed throughout the developed economies, can be empirically examined in the light of Marx's theory of the falling rate of profit. In contrast to neoclassical economics, in which profits are assumed to be zero under perfect competition, the surplus-value approach offers a systematic analysis of how the rate of profit is determined.

SEE ALSO *Exchange Value; Labor Theory of Value; Value*

BIBLIOGRAPHY

Foley, Duncan K. 2000. Recent Developments in the Labour Theory of Value. *Review of Radical Political Economics* 32 (1): 1–39.

Leontief, Wassily W., et al. 1953. *Studies in the Structure of the American Economy.* New York: Oxford University Press.

Marx, Karl. [1876] 1976. *Capital.* Vol. 1. London: Penguin.

Philp, Bruce. 2005. *Reduction, Rationality, and Game Theory in Marxian Economics.* London: Routledge.

Sraffa, Piero. 1960. *Production of Commodities by Means of Commodities.* Cambridge: Cambridge University Press.

Trigg, Andrew B. 2006. *Marxian Reproduction Schema: Money and Aggregate Demand in a Capitalist Economy.* London: Routledge.

Andrew B. Trigg

SURPRISES
SEE *Shocks.*

SURVEY

Social scientists investigate people who lived in the past or are living in the present. Surveys are one tool they use to gather information about a population of interest. Social scientists use surveys to assess people's behavior, knowledge, opinions, attitudes, or abilities. Surveys can be conducted orally or in written form, and they can be administered to individuals or groups. Group surveys offer an advantage over other methods of investigation, such as interviews or observation, in that they can collect sensitive data while keeping participants' identities confidential. In addition a large amount of data can be collected at once, rather than collecting data from each participant individually. Edward Laumann and colleagues (1994) designed and administered a survey to assess the sexual behavior of American adults. The survey was administered nationwide to over 3,000 men and women, addressing such sensitive topics as typical sex practices, number of sex partners, and contraction of sexually transmitted diseases. Two of the most important properties that must be assessed in the development and use of a survey are its reliability and validity.

RELIABILITY AND VALIDITY

Reliability is the extent to which a survey is accurate, meaning that it is free of measurement error. While this psychometric property can be calculated using a variety of methods, reliability is theoretically the ratio of true score variance to observed score variance. It is determined by calculating a correlation coefficient on relevant data. Common methods of determining reliability include the *test-retest* method, in which scores from two different administrations of the same test are correlated to detect error from time sampling, and the *split-half* method, in which a correlation coefficient is calculated between two halves of the survey in order to determine internal consistency (Kaplan and Saccuzzo 2005).

Validity is the extent to which the survey measures what it is intended to measure or gathers the information it is designed to gather. A psychometrically sound survey is one that has been shown, through empirical research, to have several kinds of evidence for validity, such as construct-related evidence (the extent to which the instrument measures what it is claimed to measure) and content-related evidence (the extent to which the instrument includes content representative of the construct being investigated) (Mitchell and Jolley 2004). In addition to these types of evidence for validity, a survey is said to have *face validity* if it is obvious from the questions what the survey is designed to measure. Face validity may or may not be a desired quality for a given survey, depending on the nature of the research. That is, some surveys, particularly those addressing controversial or sensitive issues, are more effective when questions address the central topic in a covert manner. This reduces the probability of *response bias*, a potential disadvantage of the survey method discussed below.

SAMPLE

Once a valid and reliable survey has been designed, social scientists must administer it to people. In some situations it is possible to survey all members of the population in question. However, more often researchers are interested in a large population for which it is impossible to survey everyone. In that case, the researcher must acquire a sample of people from the population who are willing to complete the survey. To ensure the accuracy of the data, the sample should be *representative*, meaning it adequately reflects the actual population with regard to variables that are related to the construct(s) in question. For example, the proportion of women and men in the sample should be similar to the proportion in the population, particularly if there is reason to believe that men and women would respond differently to the survey.

There are many sampling strategies aimed at ensuring a representative sample. With the *random sampling method*, the sample is acquired in such a way that each member of the population has an equal chance of being selected, and the selection of each respondent is independent of the selection of all other respondents. A representative sample is important to protect research from *sampling bias*, the tendency for a sample to systematically exclude certain members of the population while overrepresenting others.

ADVANTAGES AND DISADVANTAGES

The survey method has advantages and disadvantages when compared to other methods of investigation. The greatest advantage of this method is the ability to collect a large amount of information from many people simultaneously. Surveys can be administered to a room full of people, a mass e-mail list, or a large telephone pool with relatively little work on the part of the researcher. A second advantage of this method is its ability to gather the exact information that is sought, since researchers write the questions they want answered. However, this advantage assumes that respondents do all of the following when completing a survey: (1) read or hear the question and interpret it as it was meant to be interpreted; (2) reflect on their personal experiences related to the question; and (3) answer the question honestly. The latter is most likely to be a problem, particularly with surveys that ask about sensitive or controversial topics. In such cases, respondents may practice *impression management*, wherein they answer questions so as to present themselves in a particular way. Giving socially desirable responses is a common type of impression management in which respondents present themselves in an unrealistically favorable or virtuous light. In addition to impression management, the validity of survey data may be reduced by response bias, in which respondents tend to respond to questions in a certain way (e.g., in the affirmative or negative) regardless of the actual content of the questions. Finally, because surveys are voluntary, they are subject to the willingness of respondents to complete them. Thus the *response rate*, or the percentage of individuals contacted who complete the survey, is important, particularly since survey response rates have declined since the early 1990s (Tourangeau 2004).

SEE ALSO *Methods, Quantitative; Observation, Participant; Panel Studies; Random Samples; Reliability, Statistical; Social Science; Statistics; Surveys, Sample; Validity, Statistical*

BIBLIOGRAPHY

Kaplan, Robert M., and Dennis P. Saccuzzo. 2005. *Psychological Testing: Principles, Applications, and Issues.* 6th ed. Belmont, CA: Thomson Wadsworth.

Laumann, Edward, John H. Gagnon, Robert T. Michael, and Stuart Michaels. 1994. *The Social Organization of Sexuality:*

Sexual Practices in the United States. Chicago: University of Chicago Press.

Mitchell, Mark, and Janina Jolley. 2007. *Research Design Explained.* 6th ed. Belmont, CA: Thomson Wadsworth.

Tourangeau, Roger. 2004. Survey Research and Societal Change. *Annual Review of Psychology* 55: 775–801.

Angela K. Fournier

SURVEY OF INCOME AND PROGRAM PARTICIPATION

The Survey of Income and Program Participation (SIPP) is a continuous panel survey of samples of people aged fifteen and older who reside in households or noninstitutional group quarters (e.g., college dormitories, rooming houses). Each sample person is asked to provide information every four months for a period of three to four years. Information is also gathered for people who join a SIPP sample member's household and for children in the household. The U.S. Census Bureau collects, processes, and disseminates SIPP data. SIPP began in fall 1983 and is scheduled to undergo a major re-engineering beginning with a panel introduced in 2011 or 2012.

EVOLUTION

SIPP's origins date to the late 1960s when government program analysts became increasingly dissatisfied with the available information on household income, assets, tax liabilities, and participation in public assistance programs. A proposal in 1970 for a new income survey led to the inauguration in 1975 of the Income Survey Development Program (ISDP) in the Office of the Assistant Secretary for Planning and Evaluation, U.S. Department of Health, Education, and Welfare (now the Department of Health and Human Services). The ISDP carried out four major field tests, of which the largest and most complex was the 1979 Research Panel.

Plans to implement the full SIPP, under the sponsorship of the Social Security Administration, were derailed when funding for the program was deleted from the federal budget in 1981. The new Census Bureau director, Bruce Chapman, convinced the Reagan administration to revive SIPP at the Census Bureau. The 1984 SIPP panel began in fall 1983; it followed adult members of about 21,000 original sample households every four months for eight or nine waves of interviewing (thirty-two to thirty-six months). Another SIPP panel began each February

from 1985 through 1993. A hiatus occurred until April 1996 when a new four-year panel began, followed in 2001 by a three-year panel and in 2004 by a planned four-year panel. The 1990 and 1996–2004 panels oversampled households expected to have low incomes.

The first decade of SIPP was difficult. Budget cuts necessitated reductions in sample size or in the number of interviews, or both, for the 1984–1991 panels. Conversion from paper-and-pencil to computer-assisted personal interviewing (CAPI) drove a decision to forego new panels after 1993 until 1996, when the survey design changed. Instead of an overlapping design with two or three panels in the field at the same time, SIPP adopted an abutting panel design in which one panel ends before another begins.

CONTENT AND DESIGN FEATURES

SIPP's primary purpose is to provide detailed information on the economic situation of people in the United States. The core questionnaire in each wave asks about demographic characteristics, amounts for over seventy sources of cash income and in-kind benefits, health insurance coverage, and labor force activity (most items are asked on a monthly basis). Topical modules included once or twice in each panel cover assets and liabilities, income taxes paid, annual income, program eligibility, and personal histories. A module with variable content included once in each panel to meet the needs of federal agencies has ranged over many topics, including child-care expenses, health-care use, housing costs, child support, and extended measures of well-being.

SIPP has a true panel design in that original sample members are followed for the life of their panel, even if they change addresses, thus permitting longitudinal analysis with the core data. The current abutting design permits longer panels with larger sample sizes than the original overlapping design.

The primary products from SIPP are data files that are available via the Internet. For every panel, the Census Bureau produces files for the core data for each wave and topical module, and a longitudinal file for the entire panel. The Census Bureau also publishes occasional reports from SIPP on such topics as child-care arrangements, changes in poverty status and well-being, and the financial return to schooling. Generally, the release of data files lags considerably behind the completion of data collection for a wave or an entire panel.

ADVANTAGES AND DISADVANTAGES

SIPP is an immensely rich source of data on the social and economic characteristics of the U.S. household population and how people's living situations change over a three- to four-year window. Researchers have used the core SIPP data to study spells of poverty and participation in public assistance programs within and across years, the extent to which people rely on multiple assistance programs at the same time or in sequence over time, and family composition changes (for example, the likelihood of young adults leaving and moving back to their parents' households). Researchers have used the topical module data for analyses of many issues of public policy concern.

SIPP data must be used with caution for three main reasons. First is the increasing loss of original sample members over the life of a panel, which not only is greater for low-income households and some other groups, but also has been worsening across successive panels. Thus, 32 to 33 percent of the 1996 and 2001 panels were lost by wave nine, compared with 22 percent of the 1984 panel. Second, a "seam bias" affects the monthly core data; it results because people most often report a transition, such as moving onto or off the food stamp program, at the time of the preceding interview and not within the four-month recall period of the current interview. Finally, the SIPP data are complex and difficult to use. Researchers are urged to consult carefully the file documentation, the *SIPP User's Guide*, and the *SIPP Quality Profile* and to contact other knowledgeable users.

Compared with the Panel Study of Income Dynamics, a heavily used longitudinal survey that began in 1968, the 2004 SIPP sample is almost six times larger, and it provides intrayear data. However, SIPP has a much shorter window of observation. Compared with the Current Population Survey (CPS) Annual Social and Economic Supplement (ASEC), the source of official income and poverty statistics, SIPP has much more information and supports short-term longitudinal analyses that the CPS cannot. However, the CPS ASEC has over twice as large a sample as the 2004 SIPP panel, is released promptly, and is relatively easy to use.

SEE ALSO *Current Population Survey; Panel Study of Income Dynamics*

BIBLIOGRAPHY

Citro, Constance F., and Graham Kalton, eds. 1993. *The Future of the Survey of Income and Program Participation*. Panel to Evaluate the Survey of Income and Program Participation, Committee on National Statistics, National Research Council. Washington, DC: National Academy Press.

David, Martin H., ed. 1983. *Technical, Conceptual, and Administrative Lessons of the Income Survey Development Program (ISDP): Papers Presented at a Conference*. New York: Social Science Research Council.

U.S. Bureau of the Census. Survey of Income and Program Participation (SIPP). http://www.bls.census.gov/sipp/.

U.S. Bureau of the Census. 1998. *Survey of Income and Program Participation Quality Profile*. 3rd. ed. SIPP Working Paper 230. Washington, DC: U.S. Department of Commerce, Bureau of the Census. http://www.bls.census.gov/sipp/workpapr/wp230.pdf.

U.S. Bureau of the Census. 2001. *Survey of Income and Program Participation Users' Guide*. 3rd. ed. Washington, DC: U.S. Department of Commerce, Bureau of the Census. http://www.bls.census.gov/sipp/usrguide/sipp2001.pdf.

C. F. Citro

SURVEYS, SAMPLE

Surveys are instruments that researchers use to measure attitudes, tastes, viewpoints, and/or facts from a specific population. Most populations (or groups) are too large and widespread geographically to allow researchers to obtain information on each group member. To compensate, researchers have devised several methods by which they make inferences about a population by using information gathered from a selected sample of the population.

Various government agencies (including the U.S. Census Bureau) and academic disciplines (including economics, political science, and sociology) make frequent use of survey sampling to better understand the prevailing characteristics of specific populations. This entry examines survey sampling through the two most common formats in which it is conducted: questionnaires and interviews. Before moving to this discussion, however, it is worthwhile to describe the central methodology that makes survey sampling of populations so effective—drawing the actual sample.

The most commonly used procedure in drawing a survey sample is the simple random sampling (SRS) method. In order to make effective inferences about a population, survey researchers must be confident that the sample they are using is representative of the population in which they are interested. If the sample is not representative then bias (the misrepresentation of a population's characteristics) can result. SRS provides assurance that the sample represents the population because each sampling unit (a person) has an equal probability of being selected to participate in the survey.

Though an equal probability of random selection helps mitigate response bias in survey samples, most populations of interest to researchers have such significant variation that SRS alone does not provide enough confidence that the sample is truly representative of a population. In order to address population variation, national polling techniques, such as those practiced by Gallup, require an initial stratification of the population before the random sample is drawn. Stratification is the division of a population into homogenous groups according to a specific set of dimensions or stratums (e.g., geographic location, age, sex). Once the population is divided in this manner, SRS is applied to each stratum. In most cases, survey researchers draw a proportionate stratified sample, which helps to keep the sampling units from each stratum closely resembling their proportion in the overall population. Most surveys, whether delivered in questionnaire or interview format, make use of a stratified SRS methodology.

QUESTIONNAIRES

Questionnaires are impersonal surveys used to collect data from respondents that have been targeted as part of a sample. Questionnaire surveys have traditionally been delivered through the mail to sample respondents. The growing popularity of e-mail in the late 1990s allowed researchers to employ this method of delivery more frequently. Despite its growing popularity, however, most survey questionnaires do not use the e-mail method because of the relatively large number of people with limited or no e-mail access as of the early twenty-first century.

The primary advantage of questionnaires, regardless of delivery method, is that they are relatively low cost. In stark contrast to interviews, questionnaires do not require the assistance of trained staff. In addition, because it costs the same to mail a survey three miles or three thousand miles, there are financial advantages to conducting national surveys. Access to bulk mail rates can provide even greater savings for researchers. Another advantage to questionnaires is that they reduce bias errors that personal interviewers may introduce. Whenever one person is talking to another to obtain information, an interpersonal dynamic is introduced that can alter the way a respondent answers questions. Since questionnaires are delivered through paper or computer, this missing human element is a welcome absence. Finally, questionnaires provide greater anonymity, in large part because there is no interviewer aware of respondent identity.

There are also disadvantages to questionnaires. Primary among these is that survey questions must be fairly simple so as to be understood by the vast majority of intended respondents. If questions are too complex or vague, respondents may miss the point of a question entirely, thereby introducing response bias. Also problematic is the inability of researchers to probe respondents for more specific information on topics. Question answers are final. In addition, researchers have no control over who actually completes the questionnaire since they have no direct contact with the respondent. Finally, researchers face low response rates (20 percent to 40 percent) when using questionnaire-based surveys. Most published research using

data collected from mail surveys reports a response rate between 20 to 30 percent, although the rate is sometimes higher for targeted populations. The Internet's popularity has helped to increase response rates by allowing researchers to follow-up with respondents through a hybrid approach in which both mail and e-mail requests for questionnaire completion are transmitted to respondents.

INTERVIEWS

Personal interviews form the backbone of modern opinion polling. Usually conducted by a team of well-trained interviewers, these interviews enable polling companies to receive respondent data in a much shorter time frame than is required for questionnaires. Most interviews in opinion polling are of the schedule-structured variety, in which all respondents are asked the same questions, in the same order, in the same way so as to reduce response bias. Other interview forms include the focused (which allows the interviewer to ask probing questions depending upon how a respondent answers) and nondirective (in which the interviewer provides little structure or form). The focused and nondirective approaches are usually employed by academics focusing on a small sample of respondents in order to build empirical theories.

The primary advantage of the structured interview is that it gives researchers better control over the interview situation. The most direct improvement of interviews over questionnaires is that it is unlikely someone other than the respondent will provide question responses. Concomitantly, interviews have a much higher response rate than questionnaires (usually 95%), adding to their usefulness when time is of the essence. Of course, there are disadvantages, not the least of which is the interview bias referenced above. Cost is also a disincentive.

SEE ALSO *Attitudes; Internet; Methods, Research (in Sociology); Polls, Opinion; Random Samples; Research; Research, Survey; Social Science; Survey; Tastes*

BIBLIOGRAPHY

Frankfort-Nachmias, Chava, and David Nachmias. 2000. *Research Methods in the Social Sciences.* 6th ed. New York: Worth.

Richardson, Stephen, Barbara S. Dohrenwend, and David Klein. 1965. *Interviewing: Its Forms and Functions.* New York: Basic Books.

Schaffer, David R., and Don A. Dillman. 1998. Development of a Standard E-Mail Methodology. *Public Opinion Quarterly* 62: 378–397.

Weisberg, Herbert F., Jon A. Krosnick, and Bruce D. Bowen. 1996. *An Introduction to Survey Research, Polling, and Data Analysis.* 3rd ed. Thousand Oaks, CA: Sage.

Brian Calfano

SURVIVAL ANALYSIS REGRESSION

Survival analysis is a statistical methodology to study the occurrence of an event over time. It is referred to as survival analysis because it was originally derived in contexts where the event was death, but the event under study need not be death. Examples from the social sciences where survival analysis can be used are studies that investigate time from marriage until separation or divorce and intervals between births.

A graphical representation of typical survival data is depicted in Figure 1, which shows study recruitment over time. For each of four participants, study entry is indicated as t_0. Occurrence of an event is indicated by a square. If no event is observed during the study period, the last known event-free time point is marked with a circle. For these participants the "time until the event occurred" cannot be specified. Such observations are said to be censored. A censored observation can arise from the fact that a participant is lost to follow-up during the observation period or from a limited observation period, that is, the event might occur some time after the observation period has ended. Censoring of this type is called right censoring. A right censored observation indicates that occurrence of the event, if it happens, will take place after the time that contact is lost with the participant or after the end of the observation period. Analysis of the data is not based on chronologic time but on a different time scale—the "time from t_0" (Figure 2).

Survival analysis regression aims at investigating and quantifying the impact subject and study factors have on the time until the event occurs. These factors are often measured at study entry (t_0) for each individual participant, and their effect on time to event is quantified via the hazard function of the survival time distribution. The hazard function models the rates at which events occur as a function of subject and study factors. Parametric and semiparametric methods are available for survival analysis regression. For details see Hosmer and Lemeshow (1999) or Kleinbaum and Klein (2005). The most frequently used model for analyzing survival data is the Cox proportional hazards model (a semiparametric model). It assumes that hazard rates are proportional over time but does not make distributional assumptions regarding survival times. Examples of parametric methods are the Weibull and accelerated failure time models, which assume specific statistical distributions for survival times in addition to assuming proportional hazards. Standard models assume independence between observations, but extensions of the models are available to accommodate dependencies (frailty models) between observations. Such dependencies might arise if participants, for example, are family members. Extensions also exist to accommodate multiple events, competing events, and factors that might change over time. On one hand the extension to multiple events and competing events is conceptually straightforward. Analysis involving factors that might change over time, on the other hand, are both technically and conceptually more involved. Survival analysis regression has been

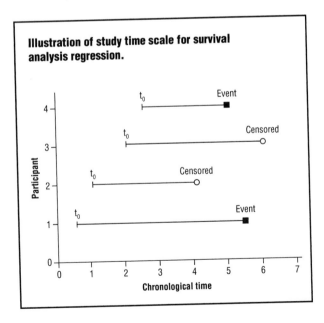

Illustration of study time scale for survival analysis regression.

Figure 1

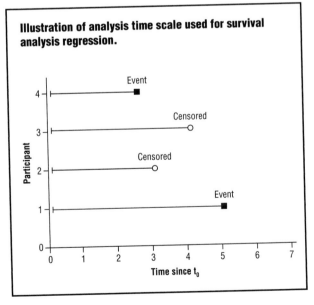

Illustration of analysis time scale used for survival analysis regression.

Figure 2

used extensively and successfully in various fields to quantify the impact of different factors on time to event.

SEE ALSO *Censoring, Left and Right; Censoring, Sample; Regression*

BIBLIOGRAPHY

Hosmer, David W., Jr., and Stanley Lemeshow. 1999. *Applied Survival Analysis: Regression Modeling of Time to Event Data.* New York: Wiley.

Kleinbaum, David G., and Mitchel Klein. 2005. *Survival Analysis: A Self-Learning Text.* New York: Springer.

Susanne May
David W. Hosmer Jr.

SURVIVOR FUNCTION

SEE *Duration Models.*

SWASTIKA

SEE *Rituals; Nazism.*

SWEATSHOPS

Sweatshops, commonly defined today as workplaces violating multiple labor laws, have always been a part of the economic landscape, as have attempts to eliminate sweatshop conditions. Public outrage following the 1911 Triangle Shirtwaist fire in New York, for example, led to creation of a Factory Investigating Commission and the passage of thirty-six laws reforming the state labor code.

U.S. federal labor law is embodied in the Fair Labor Standards Act, originally passed in 1938. This act, too, responded to the prevalence of poor working conditions, calling for elimination of "conditions detrimental to the maintenance of the minimum standard of living necessary for health, efficiency, and general well-being of workers" (U.S. Department of Labor 2004, p. 1). Recent laws such as the U.S. Victims of Trafficking and Violence Protection Act of 2000 extend protection from exploitative practices.

Internationally, the 1998 United Nations Declaration on Fundamental Principles and Rights at Work provides the foundation for global labor standards. The Declaration defines four core types of labor standards: freedom from forced (trafficked) labor, nondiscrimination, abolition of child labor, and freedom of association/collective bargaining. Additional standards appear in the United Nations Anti-Trafficking Protocol, which recognizes that trafficked workers are victims of a crime and not illegal immigrants (United Nations 2000).

Despite these laws and agreements, violations of labor standards like those exposed by the Triangle fire persist and may well be increasing with globalization. In the United States sweatshop production is closely related to international flows of labor. Sectors such as agriculture, services, and clothing, in which immigrant labor constitutes larger shares of the workforce, are most likely to violate labor laws (Free the Slaves 2004).

While the extent of trade globalization as a new phenomenon is a subject of much debate (Sutcliffe and Glynn 1999), developing countries indisputably have only recently become major producers and exporters in such labor-intensive sectors as clothing and electronics. Companies in sectors that are very sensitive to wages and other costs of protecting workers may find relocation to low-wage countries a profitable response to global competitive pressure.

In developing countries, labor laws and enforcement are typically weak and labor is highly skewed toward the informal sector (Singh and Zammit 2003), defined by the International Labour Office (2002) as paid work not "recognized, regulated or protected by existing legal or regulatory frameworks" (p. 12). As a result, both wages and nonwage labor costs are lower than in rich countries. While labor costs are not always the only or even primary reason companies move out of developed countries (Chang 1998), for labor-intensive firms, moving offshore and subcontracting to informal producers clearly have become key elements of competitive strategy.

That sweatshop conditions still exist even in the United States is evidence that economic incentives for violating labor standards can be compelling to employers facing competitive threat. Opponents to sweatshops, recognizing the economic incentive to firms of low labor standards, have focused on raising the cost of using sweated labor. The International Confederation of Free Trade Unions and national trade unions emphasize ratification of and compliance with existing national and United Nations labor standards (International Confederation of Free Trade Unions 2006). Additional pressure comes from popular antisweatshop movements, often supported by trade unions, that target consumers. By exposing sweatshop producers and encouraging consumer boycotts, these movements hope to raise the cost of exploitative labor practices.

While the scope of consumer-based economic punishment of sweatshop producers is limited (Gibson 2005; Elliott and Freeman 2003), empirical evidence suggests that consumers in at least some sectors are willing to pay higher prices to support better labor conditions (Pollin,

Burns, and Heintz 2004). In clothing, popular movements have had considerable success in gaining acceptance of codes of conduct designed to raise standards. Many agreements and partnerships specifying in detail acceptable working conditions have emerged between producers and antisweatshop organizations representing consumers, both in the United States and in Europe.

Negotiated agreements and codes of conduct mark a dramatic step forward in recognizing basic human rights at work. A similar change is occurring in economic analysis of labor standards, with leading international institutions now linking protection of core labor standards to democracy and therefore to economic development (International Labour Office 2004; World Bank 2007).

Despite considerable progress, significant challenges remain. Government policy can have a strong impact on compliance, but mainly in large formal-sector firms (Weil 2004). Given the high level of informal labor and the difficulty of monitoring even formal-sector small producers scattered throughout the world, enforcement of laws and agreements continues to be weak.

Countries themselves raise objections to externally imposed standards, fearing loss of sovereignty and competitiveness. As one telling example, the U.S. government has ratified only two of the eight ILO core labor rights: It has not ratified the convention on the right to organize, the convention on equal remuneration, or the convention on discrimination. For poor countries, the economic consequences are not insubstantial. Some standards, such as eliminating child labor and improving health and safety, can be prohibitively expensive in competitive export sectors. Even developing countries strongly in favor of raising labor standards may argue (with much evidence to support their case) that economic growth rather than outside intervention is the best path to sustainable improvement in wages and working conditions (Singh and Zammit 2003). Where intervention reduces competitiveness, growth is retarded and the intervention becomes self-defeating.

In any case, even complete compliance with existing laws and codes of conduct would not settle disagreements over sweatshops. Current laws define core standards but not cash standards (Elliott and Freeman 2003), which would mandate wage minimums designed to establish a living wage, considered by many a critical component of working conditions. Thus, although frameworks for higher labor standards are evolving rapidly, serious limitations persist. A narrow definition of sweatshops excluding cash standards and the difficulty of monitoring working conditions in an increasingly globalized economy both pose daunting obstacles to further progress. Poor countries urgently require international support to finance the improved standards that all too often they desire but cannot afford.

SEE ALSO *Child Labor; Economic Growth; Globalization, Social and Economic Aspects of; Labor Law; Labor Union; Occupational Safety; Unions; Wages*

BIBLIOGRAPHY

Chang, Ha-Joon. 1998. Globalization, Transnational Corporations and Economic Development: Can the Developing Countries Pursue Strategic Industrial Policy in a Globalizing World Economy? In *Globalization and Progressive Economic Policy*, ed. Dean Baker, Gerald Epstein, and Robert Pollin. Cambridge, U.K.: Cambridge University Press.

Elliott, Kimberly Ann, and Richard B. Freeman. 2003. *Can Labor Standards Improve under Globalization?* Washington, DC: Institute for International Economics.

Free the Slaves. 2004. *Hidden Slaves: Forced Labor in the United States.* Washington, DC: Free the Slaves, and Berkeley: University of California, Human Rights Center.

Gibson, William. 2005. Monitoring Labor Standards in a Macroeconomic Context. In *Interactions in Analytical Political Economy: Theory, Policy, and Applications,* ed. Mark Setterfield, 67–104. Armonk, NY: M.E. Sharpe.

International Confederation of Free Trade Unions. 2006. *Internationally Recognised Core Labour Standards in the United States: Report for the WTO General Council Review of Trade Policies of the United States.* Geneva, Switzerland: Author.

International Labour Office. 2002. *Women and Men in the Informal Economy: A Statistical Picture.* Geneva, Switzerland: Author.

International Labour Office. 2004. *Organizing for Social Justice: Global Report under the Follow-up to the ILO Declaration on Fundamental Principles and Rights at Work.* Geneva, Switzerland: Author.

Pollin, Robert, Justine Burns, and James Heintz. 2004. Global Apparel Production and Sweatshop Labor: Can Raising Retail Prices Finance Living Wages? *Cambridge Journal of Economics* 28 (2): 153–171.

Singh, Ajit, and Ann Zammit. 2003. Globalisation, Labour Standards and Economics Development. In *The Handbook of Globalisation,* ed. Jonathan Michie, 191–215. Cheltenham, U.K.: Edward Elgar.

Sutcliffe, Bob, and Andrew Glynn. 1999. Still Underwhelmed: Indicators of Globalization and Their Misinterpretation. *Review of Radical Political Economics* 31: 111–131.

United Nations. 2000. *The Protocol to Prevent, Suppress and Punish Trafficking in Persons, Especially Women and Children, Supplementing the United Nations Convention against Transnational Organized Crime.* Geneva, Switzerland: Author.

U.S. Department of Labor. 2004. *The Fair Labor Standards Act of 1938, as Amended* (WH publication 1318). Washington, DC: Author.

Weil, David. 2004. Improving Labor Standards in the Apparel Industry: Can Government Make a Difference? Working

Paper, Boston University/Harvard Center for Textile and Apparel Research.

World Bank. 2007. *Global Economic Prospects: Managing the Next Wave of Globalization.* Washington, DC: Author.

Diane Flaherty

SWEDISH SCHOOL OF ECONOMICS
SEE *Stockholm School.*

SYMBOLIC ANALYSTS
SEE *New Class, The.*

SYMBOLIC INTERACTIONISM
SEE *Interactionism, Symbolic.*

SYMBOLIC INVERSION
SEE *Rites of Passage.*

SYMBOLS

Culture is based on symbols. Flags, traffic lights, diplomas, and mathematical notation are all, in their various ways, symbols. So foundational is symbolism to humans that without it communication would be impossible. The most symbolic aspect of culture is language, but symbolism also plays a role in religion, politics, art, and literature as well as in kinship, commerce, and science. Symbolism is basic to the construction and conveyance of gender, ethnic, and national identities. It is the primary way by which humans create meaning, classify knowledge, express emotion, and regulate society. The ineluctably human ability to generate and interpret symbols is, for example, what allows us to differentiate winks from blinks (Sapir 1932, p. 493). Although both are roughly identical movements involving the rapid closing and opening of the eye, the former is a meaningful gesture transmitting the conspiratorial message that the winker is in on a secret, whereas the latter is a meaningless twitch. The difference is significant but wholly symbolic. Because symbolism is funda-

mental to human thought and interaction, it is of concern to the social and cognitive sciences, particularly anthropology and linguistics, though it is also studied by psychology, philosophy, and sociology, and to a lesser extent political science and even economics.

At its most basic level, a symbol is anything that represents another thing by virtue of customary association due to a conceptual connection or perceived resemblance. The English word *symbol* derives etymologically from the Greek *súmbolon*, meaning "tally," "contract," or "ticket," which referred originally to a token that was broken in two so that each half could be used to confirm the identity of the other. The word stems from the Greek roots *syn-* ("together") and *ballein* ("to throw"), and thus has the approximate connotation of "to throw together."

UNIVERSAL VERSUS CULTURE-BOUND DIMENSIONS OF SYMBOLISM

Because virtually anything can serve as a symbol and because a symbol conveys information only insofar as it has meaning to a specific community, the connection between a symbol and its referent is not intrinsic to the symbol itself but rather is a function of agreed upon use, custom, or convention. It is in this sense that language is symbolic. The word *water* designates the liquid object only insofar as members of the English speech community agree that it does. The liquid has no inherent property that compels us to call it by that name. It could just as well be designated by other sounds, for instance *agua* in Spanish, *mayim* in Hebrew, or *vo'* in Tzotzil Maya. Exceptions to this arbitrariness may exist in ethnobiological classification (see Berlin 1992) and onomatopoeia.

The meaning of political and religious symbols, often charged with emotion, are likewise dependent on cultural contexts, even when the same or similar signs are employed across cultures. For Christians the Eucharist is a holy sacrament symbolizing the Body and Blood of Christ, yet pagans may see the consumption of bread and wine as a representation of ritual cannibalism. Or again, the swastika has come to be taboo in much of Europe and the United States due to its historic association with Nazi Germany and contemporary white supremacists, but elsewhere, as in the cases of Hinduism, Buddhism, and Native American religions, it remains a sacred symbol with positive connotations. In religions of Indic origin it is a symbol of auspiciousness, as reflected by its original Sanskrit name *svasti,* meaning luck, well-being, and fortune; in Hindu traditions it is a solar symbol, and in Buddhist regions it adorns the entrance to some temples. The swastika design is also seen in Native American traditions. To the Navajo the symbol is known as the "whirling winds," and was used in curing ceremonies, and as a motif woven into textiles; among the neighboring Hopi it was a conventional sign associated with clan migrations. In short, symbols are without specific meanings aside from the connotations assigned to them.

Depth Psychology Still, certain studies suggest that some symbolism is universal, due to its rootedness in unconscious processes, developmental stages, or panhuman experiences of the body, eating, and sexuality. Sigmund Freud (1989) maintained that the symbolism found in dreams, myths, fairytales, and linguistic utterances expresses in disguised form unresolved childhood conflicts or taboo urges surrounding sexuality and violence that are repressed in the subconscious of individuals. Jung (1964) viewed certain symbols as archetypes of the "collective unconscious." Thus, one encounters universal archetypes—the Trickster, Rebirth, the Hero's quest, the Great Mother, and so on—not only in the myths and rituals of tribal peoples, the art of the high Renaissance, and modern science fiction, but also in the dream-work, projective fantasy, and free-associations of the patient involved in psychotherapeutic individuation.

The Human Body Many researchers have posited that the human body provides a template for another set of experiences held in common by all people. Throughout the world, pre-eminence is accorded to the right-hand side in systems of lateral symbolism and dual classification (Needham 1973), while hair is freighted with multiple symbolic meanings and therefore is a focus of ritual in almost all societies. The fact that the same three colors predominate in ritual symbolism cross-culturally may reflect a psychobiological substrate: the common experience of body fluids, through which black is linked to feces, white to semen or breast milk, and red to blood (Turner 1967). However, a caveat is warranted here, for these colors are also worked through local categories of meaning. While black may be associated with feces and therefore ideas of pollution, night, and death in many cultures, in Hinduism it is white, not black, that is associated with death, funerals, and mourning.

Others have suggested that the human body is a "natural symbol" for any bounded system, not the least of them the well-known organic model of society, in which the categories of the physical body provide the model for the experience of the social body and vice versa (see Douglas 1970).

Alimentary Classification Food constitutes another universal plane of symbolic classification. Claude Lévi-Strauss, who founded the structuralist approach to the analysis of symbols, theorized that the opposition between raw food and cooked food, elaborated symbolically in myths and rituals around the world, is an expression of the universal dichotomy between Nature and Culture (1970). Because in all societies people must not only eat but also marry, he overlays the rules of kinship and marriage on the classification of food. Building on the idea that the boundaries of the natural body and social body reinforce each other reciprocally, Lévi-Strauss demonstrates that eating and intercourse are symbolically equated (although not always consciously) in many societies, making culinary and sexual codes mirror images of each other (1966). In a related vein, Mary Douglas famously argued that the dietary laws in the Old Testament reflect a typology in which the animals prohibited as food to the ancient Israelites were taxonomic anomalies that cross-cut the socially construed ideal categories of creation just as "mixed marriages" were prohibited because they similarly would produce "hybrid" children that transected the ideal social divisions ordained by God (1966).

TERMINOLOGY AND THE LOGIC OF SYMBOLISM

The study of symbolism deals with two different but related issues. One concerns *what* symbols mean, the other *how* they work, or the logic by which they come to mean anything in the first place. Analysis depends on a differentiation between *signifier* (the perceptible vehicle or external form), *signified* (the meaning, referent, connotation, etc.) and *signification* (the relation between the two). Some scholars, such as Clifford Geertz, use the word *symbol* as a blanket term "for any object, act, event, quality, or relation which serves as a vehicle for a conception" (1973, p. 91). Yet because the word *symbol* has been used in an enormous variety of ways, other researchers find it necessary to distinguish between *symbol, sign,* and *signal,* sometimes making further distinctions by adding *index* and *icon* to the list. Despite a large literature on the topic, there is, however, a lack of uniformity as to how this terminology is employed. Still, if one considers the distinctions between *symbol, sign,* and *signal* to represent differences in degree rather than kind, there is some consensus as to the way the definitions are drawn.

Signal, Sign, and Symbol A *signal* generally expresses a relationship between signifier and signified that is dynamic or causal. Animals as well as humans make use of signals, and in both cases the signifiers trigger or incite certain actions—as, for instance, when a male bird arouses the female by signaling with a mating call or car brake lights signal motorists behind to stop. A *sign* tends to have a singular meaning, in that signifier and signified are closely connected and typically come from the same context, and the signification itself is mostly *metonymic*—that is, a part or attribute stands for the whole. When, for example, a hunter sees a hoofprint of the deer he is pursuing, the hoofprint is a sign of his quarry. In military, technical, and commercial fields signs are often employed as codes, such as Morse code or the North American Industrial Classification System used to designate business type. When signs are used as codes it is because the relation between signifier and signified is conventional rather than intrinsic and because the signification is precise.

Symbols expand the notions of signs and signals. Symbols are characterized by rich meanings that are multiple, fluid, diverse, layered, complex, and frequently predicated on metaphorical associations that assert an analogy between things from different contexts that normally may not be connected. Given that the referents of symbols tend to be general, abstract, and ambiguous, their personally or socially constructed significations may not be apparent except to those who make them.

Whether a signifier is a symbol, signal, or sign is determined not by the object itself but rather by how it is used. In fact, the same signifier can function as all three depending on the situation; for example, the color red functions as a signal in stoplights, as a sign of blood in a painting of the crucified Christ, and as a symbol in a national flag. Moreover, the meanings of symbols, insofar as they are conventional, are context-dependent and variable, both across and within cultures. In ancient Rome red was associated with the god of war, Mars, whereas in China red is an auspicious color associated with luck, money, success, happiness, and traditional wedding attire. In the United States, a red rose is a statement of love, but being "in the red" means one has suffered economic losses, and "seeing red" means one is angry.

Icons and the Problem of "Likeness" Symbols are usually *iconic*—that is, "a sensory likeness-relation is intended or interpreted" (Firth 1973, p. 75). Of course, from an anthropological perspective, what is seen as the associated or analogous "sensory likeness-relation" between signifier and signified is culturally determined; as Victor Turner appositely remarks, "one culture's analogy is another culture's puzzle" (1975, p. 151). Therefore, because iconicity is culturally constructed, many scholars prefer to use the term *icon* only when there is a geometrical similarity between signifier and signified, as with formal pictures, portraits, or models. Typical icons of this sort, which often involve a change in scale between signified and signifier, include maps, the Roman numeral *II*, and religious images of the Buddha, Christ, and saints.

While such icons clearly manifest *likenesses*, or analogous qualities, much symbolism rests on the predication of resemblance between things that are neither ostensibly similar nor physically in contact. Even science relies on symbolism when, associating things that are profoundly

unlike, it uses analogies to explain causation, whereas magic uses analogies to connect unlike things through associations of co-occurrence.

Metaphor and Metonym A distinction between *metaphor* and *metonym* is basic to symbolism. Metaphor is "principally a way of conceiving one thing in terms of another, and its primary function is understanding." Metonymy, on the other hand, has "primarily a referential function, that is, it allows us to use one thing to *stand for* another" (Lakoff and Johnson 1980). Metonymy is a form of signification in which an attribute or name of something is used to denote the wider semantic field to which the thing belongs, signifier and signified being drawn from the same general context. Thus, the word *brass* is a metonym for "military officers," just as *crown* is used metonymically for "kingship." Metaphors, on the other hand, are comparisons, similes, or analogies, and rely on a sensory resemblance or asserted conceptual similarity between things belonging to different cultural contexts, and imply the transference of qualities from one context to another. For instance, when a brand of beer uses a crown on its label to assert that it is the "king of beers," it is making a metaphoric association, as royalty and alcoholic beverages belong to different domains (Leach 1976, p. 14). Metonyms and metaphors, like signs and symbols, frequently co-occur in the same communication event, with one level of meaning characteristically being played off the other.

FEATURES OF SYMBOLIC COMMUNICATION

Symbols are especially useful in *showing* what one cannot *say*; that is, they express ineffable concepts, abstract ideas, and particularly complex emotional significations that are difficult or impossible to fully articulate. Because they powerfully sum up many things at once, symbols are frequently deployed in political and, especially, religious domains. While the existence of different political parties shows that not everyone agrees about what their country stands for, everyone does agree that their country's flag stands for their country. One way in which symbols can be used to condense a constellation of meanings is through the invocation of physical attributes that are associated with moral character: The "straight" or "upright" man can be contrasted with a man who is "crooked" or "low."

Multivocality Symbols predominate in political and religious contexts because their wide spectrum of connotations, which permits multiple understandings among subdivisions within a population, allows them to appeal to a broad audience. The more public a symbol is, the wider is its range of referents—and the broader its range of signification, the richer and more complex its meaning becomes, allowing for diverse and sometimes even contradictory interpretations. "Key symbols" (Ortner 1973), those that characterize whole peoples, nations, religions, and political movements, tend to be among the most abstract and polysemous, yet still provide basic orientations for thought and action—such as with the Virgin of Guadalupe, who is used to symbolize Mexico.

The radical polysemy of symbolic signification led anthropologist Victor Turner to conclude that an outstanding feature of all symbols was what he termed their *multivocality*; that is, "they stand for many objects, activities and relationships; there is not a one-to-one relationship between symbol and referent but a one-to-many relationship" (1967, p. 284). According to Turner, one must consider three fields of meaning: the *exegetical* meaning, or what members of the culture say the symbol means; the *operational* meaning, revealed by how the symbol is used; and the *positional* meaning, which derives from the relation between a symbol and other objects and symbols in the same or related cultural complexes (pp. 20, 284–285). Symbols are further characterized by a *polarization of meaning* (p. 28), one pole having to do with the symbol's sensory aspects or the emotional impulses it arouses, the other indexing related normative values or principles of ideology or social organization.

The Logic of Binary Oppositions

For Lévi-Strauss in his studies of symbols in myth, totemism, and other systems of symbolic classification (1966), symbols cannot be interpreted as having meaning in themselves but only in terms of structural opposition, a binary logic that exists in culture because it is in fact a reflection of the binary structure of the human mind. Drawing intellectual capital from the structural linguistics of Saussure (1966) and Jakobson (1956), as well as mathematics and the natural sciences, Lévi-Strauss reasoned that meaning was created symbolically in culture in a way that was analogous to the way it was created in information theory and in language. In the digital world of computers, everything from words to pictures to music is based on a binary logic that involves only two numerical symbols, *1* and *0*. In linguistic phonemic analysis, meaning comes about through discerning phonetic differences within minimal pairs. For instance *b* and *p* in English are both labial stops, the only difference being that the former is voiced and the latter is not, yet it is that minimal difference that allows us to differentiate between a *bat* and a *pat*. So too, in culture, symbols have meaning because they also are based on binary oppositions—raw/cooked, hot/cold, high/low, rough/smooth, light/dark, right/left, and so on—that reflect sensory contrasts and ultimately relate back to the primary symbolic opposition between nature and culture. Moreover, not just oppositions but also the logical relations between sets of oppositions are important to the

analysis of symbolic systems. These logical relations may be expressed in terms of reciprocity, analogy, homology, reflection, inversion, isomorphism, and so on.

Models of and Models For

Another anthropologist, Clifford Geertz, took his cues not from the sciences but instead from literature, philosophy, and the humanities generally. He takes an "interpretive" approach to culture, which in his view is essentially a system of symbols, the analysis of which is akin to formulating a critical reading of a manuscript or interpreting a poem, as culture itself is likened to an assemblage of texts. Geertz proposes that "cultural patterns, that is, systems or complexes of symbols" are artifacts in the public domain; they are not private cognitions or meanings accessible only through the specialized techniques of psychologists and philosophers (1973, pp. 91–92). Geertz also holds that cultural patterns are models composed of sets of symbols whose relations to one another "model" relations among other psychological, social, and physical entities, activities, processes, and so forth by paralleling or simulating them. Geertz's most novel insight, however, comes from his observation that the term *model* has two senses, an "of" sense and a "for" sense, and it is this dual aspect that gives symbols their special quality, for when they are configured together into cultural patterns they are both a model *of* reality and a model *for* reality; that is, they both reflect the world and shape it. If one sees religion as a "cultural system," as Geertz does, and as a complex of symbols, then the models on which these constructs are based have this dual aspect in that they both *describe* the world as it *is* and *prescribe* the way it *ought* to be.

Multiplex and Transflective Displays

Symbols display two other noteworthy characteristics: They are *multiplex* as well as *transflective*. Both ideas derive from the electrical sciences. As used in electronics, telecommunications, and computer networking, the term *multiplex* refers to the simultaneous transmission of two or more signals along one communications channel or the sharing of information in a single medium. Symbols can be thought of as wires or channels. When, for example, a man sends a red rose to the object of his affection, two messages symbolizing love are being communicated simultaneously through the same communications channel, yet they are being modulated via different sensory receptors (namely, vision and smell): The red color connotes the heart and passion and the scent connotes the sweetness of romance. This multiplex modulation or *sensory fusion* causes many symbols, especially metaphors, to evoke experiences comparable to *synesthesia*—the coupling of different bodily sensations or the crossing of sensory wires—compelling persons to hear colors, taste sounds, or in the case of the rose, simultaneously *see* as well as *smell* something *felt*.

The term *transflective* is used in electrical engineering to refer to a type of liquid crystal display (LCD) screen in which the pixels are illuminated from both the front of the monitor's screen by ambient light and from behind the screen by an internal light. Analogously, symbols, especially in ritual, are regarded as both transmitting and reflecting the spiritual effluence that animates them and makes them foci of intense cultural meaning. A symbol is "illuminated from behind" in that it transmits general meanings, moods, energy, and radiance from a source that is internal to it—that is, from a power that is "within" or "behind" the symbol. It is also reflective, or "illuminated from the front," in that it absorbs the particular conditions, meanings, emotions, and intentions projected onto it in a particular moment and reflects these back out again. In the study of ritual, one can think in terms of the dual illumination coming from and reflected on the Christian cross, or coming from and reflected on quartz crystals used in Navajo rituals. In varying degrees all symbols, but especially sacred symbols, both transmit public meanings and reflect private ones, and it is this dual aspect that makes them boundless sources of meaning, energy, and significance.

SEE ALSO *Anthropology; Anthropology, Linguistic; Communication; Critical Theory; Culture; Disease; Food; Freud, Sigmund; Geertz, Clifford; Hinduism; Identity; Lévi-Strauss, Claude; Myth and Mythology; Nazism; Philosophy; Psychology; Rhetoric; Rites of Passage; Rituals; Romance; Science Fiction; Semiotics; Signals; Sociology; Totemism; Turner, Victor; Universalism*

BIBLIOGRAPHY

Berlin, Brent. 1992. *Ethnobiological Classification: Principles of Categorization of Plants and Animals in Traditional Societies.* Princeton, NJ: Princeton University Press.

Douglas, Mary. 1966. *Purity and Danger: An Analysis of Concepts of Pollution and Taboo.* New York: Praeger.

Douglas, Mary. 1970. *Natural Symbols: Explorations in Cosmology.* London: Barrie & Jenkins; New York: Basic Books.

Firth, Raymond. 1973. *Symbols: Public and Private.* Ithaca, NY: Cornell University Press.

Freud, Sigmund. [1917] 1989. *Introductory Lectures on Psycho-Analysis.* Trans. and ed. James Strachey. New York: Norton.

Geertz, Clifford. 1973. *The Interpretation of Cultures: Selected Essays.* New York: Basic Books.

Jakobson, Roman, and Morris Halle. 1956. *Fundamentals of Language.* Janua Linguarum: Series Minor 1. The Hague: Mouton.

Jung, C. G., ed. 1964. *Man and His Symbols.* Garden City, NY: Anchor Books/Doubleday.

Lakoff, George, and Mark Johnson. 1980. *Metaphors We Live By.* Chicago: University of Chicago Press.

Leach, Edmund. 1976. *Culture and Communication: The Logic by Which Symbols Are Connected: An Introduction to the Use of Structuralist Analysis in Social Anthropology.* Cambridge, U.K.: Cambridge University Press.

Lévi-Strauss, Claude. 1966. *The Savage Mind.* Chicago: University of Chicago Press.

Lévi-Strauss, Claude. 1970. *The Raw and the Cooked: Introduction to a Science of Mythology.* Vol. 1. Trans. John and Doreen Weightman. New York: Harper and Row.

Sapir, Edward. 1932. "Symbolism." In *Encyclopedia of the Social Sciences,* ed. Edwin R. A. Seligman and Alvin Johnson, Vol. 14, 492–495. New York: Macmillan.

Saussure, Ferdinand de. 1966. *Course in General Linguistics.* Ed. Charles Bally and Albert Sechehaye, with Albert Reidlinger; trans. Wade Baskin. New York: McGraw-Hill Paperbacks.

Turner, Victor. 1967. *The Forest of Symbols: Aspects of Ndembu Ritual.* Ithaca, NY: Cornell University Press.

Turner, Victor. 1975. "Symbolic Studies." *Annual Review of Anthropology* 4: 145–161.

Jerome M. Levi

SYMPATHY

Sympathy is an emotional response that involves both understanding and being moved by the suffering or joy of another. Perhaps the most famous illustration of this response occurs in the biblical parable of the Good Samaritan, where a certain Samaritan stops to help a man left half dead by thieves on the way from Jerusalem to Jericho. Sympathy, then, as this parable suggests, is a kind of positive response to another's suffering and is distinct from other negative responses, such as schadenfreude, a kind of joy or pleasure at another's misfortune. Further, sympathy, as we commonly understand it, is also distinct from empathy—although this distinction is not always observed. Empathy involves the sharing of another's feelings or the processes by which we come to feel as another feels. Sympathy, in contrast, involves, first, an awareness of another's suffering as theirs and not ours and, second, being moved to relieve that person's suffering.

To talk of "positive" and "negative" responses to the suffering of others indicates yet another widely attributed (though contestable) feature of sympathy: that it is a kind of moral emotion or response. Sympathy, or equivalently now compassion, understood as a kind of moral response to the suffering of another, has had a significant influence on moral thought and practice, specifically in the moral theories of several modern philosophers, including in the eighteenth-century David Hume and Adam Smith, in the nineteenth-century Arthur Schopenhauer, and in the twentieth-century Max Scheler. Such figures, however, do not necessarily understand sympathy quite as we would.

Hume, for instance, sees sympathy as a kind of mechanism through which the feelings of others are transferred to us (the two analogies he uses are the reverberation of sound and the reflection of light in a mirror), which seems closer to empathy as described earlier.

The idea that sympathy is an attribute important to morality extends, however, beyond the modern world. One obvious earlier reference to sympathy as a morally significant attribute comes to us from Buddhism, though this is hardly the only one. One explanation of why sympathy should feature in the moral thought and practice of different cultures is perhaps that human suffering is such a basic evil that its relief (except in certain highly specific circumstances, such as those related to criminal punishment) is thought across cultures to be an unqualified moral good. Even in societies where sympathy does not figure prominently in moral thought and practice (as was plausibly the case in various ancient societies, including ancient Greece and Rome), it would generally still be recognized as an important human quality in some sense. A person completely devoid of sympathy would in almost any human society be viewed as lacking a critical human attribute—indeed in terms of modern psychological categories, we would describe such a person as a sociopath, a person devoid of any moral sense or conscience.

Sympathy, then, seems to be a fundamental human psychological attribute or state. Indeed its presence seems central to normal human psychological development. Even infants, for example, become distressed at witnessing the distress of others. While this response may simply be an early form of empathy, it seems plausible to suggest, as some psychologists have done, that sympathy as a more cognitively complex emotional state develops from this simpler emotional response. Thinking of the development of sympathy as a part of normal human psychological development may then be thought to provide support for a kind of naturalistic explanation of morality. It is our natural capacity for sympathy (a capacity that we develop from infancy to adulthood) that makes certain moral cultural practices—including, for example, our recognition of claims on us derived from other's needs—possible. But while a number of moral philosophers (including Hume and Smith) have advanced moral theories in which sympathy plays something like this naturalistic explanatory role, other moral theorists, most notably those influenced by Immanuel Kant, would deny that sympathy has this sort of moral foundational role. According to the Kantian view, morality is founded not on our emotional capacities but on our capacity for reason alone.

SEE ALSO *Buddhism; Developmental Psychology; Emotion; Hume, David; Kant, Immanuel; Moral Sentiments; Smith, Adam; Stages of Development*

BIBLIOGRAPHY

Hume, David. [1739–1740] 1978. *A Treatise of Human Nature*, ed. L.A. Selby-Bigge, 2nd ed., rev. and variant readings by P. H. Nidditch. Oxford: Oxford University Press.

Kant, Immanuel. [1785] 1964. *Groundwork of the Metaphysic of Morals*. Trans. H. J. Paton. New York: Harper and Row.

Scheler, Max. [1913] 1954. *The Nature of Sympathy*. Trans. Peter Heath. New Haven, CT: Yale University Press.

Schopenhauer, Arthur. [1839] 1995. *On the Basis of Morality*. Trans. E. F. J. Payne. Providence, RI: Berghahn Books.

Smith, Adam. [1759] 1976. *The Theory of Moral Sentiments*, eds. D. D. Raphael and A. L. Macfie. Oxford: Clarendon Press; New York: Oxford University Press.

Craig Taylor

SYNDICALISM

Syndicalism—and its cognates, known as anarcho-syndicalism or revolutionary syndicalism—was a radical movement linked to the rise of trade unionism and socialism in the late nineteenth and early twentieth centuries. Syndicalists traced their origins and beliefs to Marxian political thought. They believed that in society and the economy there was a split between capitalists (employers) and labor (workers) and that these two contending classes were engaged in a perpetual struggle over the proper division of an economy's total product. Syndicalists and socialists maintained that the class struggle between capital and labor would persist until workers seized the full fruits of their productivity by eliminating production for profit. Syndicalists differed from socialists in their insistence that workers could liberate themselves from capitalism only through self-activity and direct action at the point of production, without resort to politics and legislation. Syndicalists shared with trade unionists an ideology that stressed worker self-activity and direct action above politics and parliamentarianism; indeed, the term is derived from *syndicat*, the French word for trade union. What most sharply distinguished syndicalists from other trade unionists was the former's commitment to the abolition of capitalism through revolutionary direct action.

Syndicalism achieved its largest membership and peak influence between 1905 and 1919. The first workers' organization to adopt a syndicalist program was the French Confederation Generale du Travail (CGT), which in its 1905 Charter of Amiens declared its autonomy from the Socialist Party and other political bodies that sought parliamentary representation. Instead of seeking to advance workers' interests through electoral activity and legislative reforms, the CGT called upon its members to combat their class enemies through direct action on the job. That same year a select group of radicals in the United States created the Industrial Workers of the World (IWW). At its 1905 founding convention, the IWW included members of the Socialist Party of America (SPA) and the Socialist Labor Party among its most prominent delegates and platform speakers, but by 1908 the organization had severed all formal relations with socialist and other political parties. During the same years, syndicalist organizations emerged in Germany, the Netherlands, Scandinavia, Great Britain, Italy, Spain, Argentina, Chile, and Mexico, among other places. Yet except for France, Italy, and the Spanish-speaking nations, syndicalism represented only a minority tendency within a much broader worker and radical movement. This was especially true in those nations with more developed economies and powerful trade union movements, such as Germany, Great Britain, and the United States. In Germany, syndicalism was overshadowed by the Deutsche Gewerkshaften Bund (DGB) and the Socialist Party (SPD). In Britain, syndicalism existed largely as the personal cause of a single prominent labor leader, Tom Mann, whose Industrial Syndicalist Education League published pamphlets but lacked members. And in the United States, the IWW rarely built a substantial membership. Only in France, Italy, Spain, and the Latin American nations, which all had far smaller and weaker labor movements, did syndicalism emerge as a dominant tendency, and even in these nations it existed more clearly among leaders than followers.

Between 1905 and 1913, no transnational or international body united the movement's separate national manifestations. Yet syndicalists shared a common ideology and common strategy and tactics. Moreover, syndicalist leaders regularly crossed national borders to promote their cause. Tom Mann traveled often to Australasia, South Africa, and North America; the American syndicalists William D. Haywood and William Z. Foster visited Britain and France; and French, Italian, and Spanish syndicalists crossed their respective borders and traversed the Atlantic. A common set of ideas and assumptions united all syndicalists. Whether they claimed to find their original inspiration in the French anarchist Pierre Proudhon's tirades against property and the state or Mikhail Bakunin's battles with Marx and Engels about the role of political parties and the state, they insisted that workers must liberate themselves from capitalism through direct action, with the strike as the workers' most effective weapon.

For a syndicalist, no strike brought failure or defeat. If workers won their struggle, they learned the lesson of solidarity and worker power. If a strike failed, they discovered that employers were their enemies and that class struggle remained the essence of existence. Thus, even defeated strikers could return to their jobs without relinquishing the class struggle. Back on the job, workers could harass their employers and diminish their profits by strictly applying work rules to slow production, declining to use inferior materials, refusing to maintain machines in optimum condition, regulating the pace of work, and, in some instances, damaging the machinery, tools, and goods with which they worked. Syndicalists defined these tactics as "sabotage," and they taught workers concrete lessons in the application of their power, without casting ballots or seeking legislative reforms. Indeed, syndicalists believed that as workers assimilated the lessons of direct action and applied them in practice, they could eliminate capitalism. The culmination of direct action would be the social "general strike," in which all workers left their jobs or laid down their tools simultaneously, paralyzing the economy and demonstrating that labor, not capital, wielded power. In the aftermath of the general strike, workers' organizations would administer the economy, eliminate production for profit, and reorganize the economy. As a result, political parties and the state would vanish.

In 1913 the separate national syndicalist movements united to create their own international body, a counterpart to the socialist Second International. And like the Second International, the Syndicalist International failed to survive the outbreak of World War I (1914–1918). Another result of the war—the Bolshevik Revolution in Russia—brought more grief to syndicalists. Most syndicalists initially found vindication in the triumph of the Bolsheviks, which they perceived as a victory for workers. Indeed, syndicalists considered the Soviets to be the Russian version of the self-governing workers' institutions that would govern society and economy in the aftermath of revolution, and they enlisted enthusiastically in the Comintern and its trade union affiliate, the Profintern. But as Lenin and his comrades established their dictatorship of the proletariat and used the party and the state apparatus to dominate the new Soviet Republic, many syndicalists felt that the Bolsheviks had subjected workers to new forms of subjugation. Other syndicalists, such as Mann and Haywood, remained loyal to the Bolshevik cause. A majority of syndicalists, however, including the anarchist Emma Goldman, served as the most vitriolic critics of the Bolshevik dictatorship.

In 1923 the anti-Bolshevik syndicalists formed a second Syndicalist International. By then, however, the separate syndicalist national movements formed, at best, marginal and often minuscule worker movements compared to the dominant trade union movements. In Britain, syndicalism disappeared as a living presence, while in Germany, the Netherlands, Scandinavia, France, and the United States it survived as a marginal, minority movement. Only in Spain did syndicalism—in its anarcho-syndicalist form—maintain a vital presence. Here, it dominated the national labor movement until its crushing defeat by Franco and the Falangists in the Spanish Civil War of the 1930s. Since then, wherever syndicalism has survived, it has done so solely as a concept of worker self-activity esteemed by small circles of intellectuals or as a minuscule movement among workers.

SEE ALSO *Bolshevism; Capitalism; Class Conflict; Labor; Labor Union; Marxism; Socialism; Unions*

BIBLIOGRAPHY

Joll, James. 1980. *The Anarchists.* 2nd ed. Cambridge, MA: Harvard University Press.

Stearns, Peter. 1971. *Revolutionary Syndicalism and French Labor: A Cause without Rebels.* New Brunswick, NJ: Rutgers University Press.

Thorpe, Wayne. 1989. *"The Workers Themselves": Revolutionary Syndicalism and International Labor, 1913–1923.* Amsterdam, Netherlands: International Institute of Social History.

Van der Linden, Marcel, and Wayne Thorpe, eds. 1990. *Revolutionary Syndicalism: An International Perspective.* Aldershot, England: Scolar Press.

Melvyn Dubofsky

SYSTEM ANALYSIS

System analysis, system inquiry, or systems theory is the study of the interdependence of relationships. A system is composed of regularly interacting or interrelating parts that, when taken together, form a new whole with properties distinct from its constituent parts. Systems are seen to be structurally divisible but functionally indivisible wholes with emergent properties. Central to system analysis is the recognition that the structure of any system—the many interlocking, sometimes time-delayed, sometimes circular interrelationships among its components—is often just as important, if not more important, than the individual components themselves in determining the system's behavior.

Systems are characterized by complexity, a set of boundaries, and the ability to regenerate. Complexity refers to a large number of densely connected parts and multiple levels of embeddedness and entanglement. A system is defined by a set of parametric conditions or boundaries that delimit it or set it apart from its environment. No system can be completely closed or else we could not perceive it; there are only varying degrees of closure set by boundaries. A system regenerates itself through the self-reproduction of its own elements and of the network of interactions that characterize them in a process known as autopoiesis. Thus an autopoietic system renews, repairs, and replicates or reproduces itself in a flow of matter and energy.

Systems can change through an evolutionary process with a tendency toward greater structural complexity and organizational simplicity, more efficient modes of operation, and greater dynamic harmony. Change is enacted through a process of feedback where information concerning the adequacy of the system, its operation, and its outputs are introduced into the system. Negative feedback signals that there is a discrepancy between what the system produces and what it should produce. It tells us that we should change something in the system so that we can reduce the deviation from the norms stated in the system's output model. Positive feedback signals that the whole system should change, that we should increase the deviation from the present state and change the output model. Functionalism is based on this adaptation. To survive or maintain equilibrium with respect to its environment, any system must to some degree adapt to that environment, attain its goals, integrate its components, and maintain its latent pattern, a cultural template of some sort.

A system can be ordered as a hierarchy or a heterarchy. A hierarchy is a vertical arrangement of entities within systems and their subsystems. A heterarchy is an ordering of entities without a single peak or leading element, and which element is dominant at a given time depends on the total situation. Systems may be understood through holism, where attention is focused on the emergent properties of the whole rather than on the behavior of the isolated parts, or reductionism, where phenomena are understood by breaking them down into their smallest possible parts.

Several fields utilize system analysis. Cybernetics, chaos theory, and social dynamics, for example, are among the disciplines that apply system analysis. Some areas of education and environmental sustainability also utilize system analysis. The systems framework is also fundamental to organizational theory, as organizations are complex, dynamic, goal-oriented processes; in anthropological studies, notably those incorporating positive and negative feedback; and in cybernetics, catastrophe theory, chaos theory, and complexity theory, all of which have the common goal of explaining complex systems that consist of a large number of mutually interacting and interrelated parts. In biology the living systems theory of James Grier Miller is a general theory about how all living systems work, maintain themselves, develop, and change. Living systems can be as simple as a single cell or as complex as a supranational organization such as the European Union. In sociology the structural functionalism of Talcott Parsons argues that the largest system is "the action system" consisting of interrelated behaviors of individuals, embedded in a physical-organic environment with others, with each part in a social system arranged in a pattern of interpenetrating relationships influenced by a socializing culture that constitutes standards and channels for guiding actions. Societies (which are highly complex), like systems and organisms, have functional needs that must be met if the society is to survive. Parsons says that all societies have four basic needs: adaptation, goal attainment, integration, and pattern maintenance (i.e., inertia, latency, or self-maintenance).

The deterministic or restrictive nature of systems is addressed by aspects of structuralism. Structuralism rejects the concept of human freedom and choice and focuses instead on the way human behavior is determined by various structures. Thomas Kuhn, for example, notes how scientists operate under a standard praxis of "normal science," deviating from a standard "paradigm" only in instances of irreconcilable anomalies. In political science the structural realism of Kenneth Waltz describes international politics as a systemic interaction of states within an anarchical environment. States first seek survival and are socialized by an anarchical environment to act and react based on threats to survival and to form self-help alliances with like units. The system effects described by Robert Jervis notes how political relations among states in a system, similar to biological interactions among cells and other scientific phenomena, can produce effects different from the sum of individual actions.

SEE ALSO *Catastrophe Theory; Chaos Theory; Cyberspace; Functionalism; Heterarchy; Hierarchy; Models and Modeling; Parsons, Talcott; Sociology, Post-Parsonian American; Stability, Political; Structuralism; Waltz, Kenneth*

BIBLIOGRAPHY

Banathy, Bela. 1996. *Designing Social Systems in a Changing World.* New York: Plenum.

Bateson, Gregory. 1979. *Mind and Nature: A Necessary Unity.* New York: Dutton.

Bausch, Kenneth C. 2001. *The Emerging Consensus in Social Systems Theory.* New York: Kluwer Academic/Plenum.

Bertalanffy, Ludwig von. 1968. *General System Theory: Foundations, Development, Applications.* New York: George Braziller.

Churchman, C. West. 1968. *The Systems Approach.* New York: Delacorte.

International Society for System Sciences (ISSS). http://www.isss.org/

Jantsch, Erich. 1980. *The Self-Organizing Universe: Scientific and Human Implications of the Emerging Paradigm of Evolution.* New York: Pergamon.

Jervis, Robert. 1997. *System Effects: Complexity in Political and Social Life.* Princeton, NJ: Princeton University Press.

Kahn, Herman. 1956. *Techniques of System Analysis.* Santa Monica, CA: Rand Corporation.

Kuhn, Thomas. 1996. *The Structure of Scientific Revolutions.* 3rd ed. Chicago: University of Chicago Press.

Miller, James Grier. 1978. *Living Systems.* New York: McGraw-Hill.

Parsons, Talcott. [1937] 1967. *The Structure of Action.* New York: Free Press.

Parsons, Talcott. 1977. *Social Systems and the Evolution of Action Theory.* New York: Free Press.

Parsons, Talcott, and Neal J. Smelser. 1956. *Economy and Society.* Glencoe, IL: Free Press.

System Dynamics Society. http://www.systemdynamics.org/

Waltz, Kenneth. 1979. *Theory of International Politics.* Reading, MA: Addison-Wesley.

Weinberg, Gerald M. 1975. *An Introduction to General Systems Thinking.* New York: Wiley-Interscience.

Anastasia Xenias

SYSTEMATIC PROCESSING
SEE *Attitudes.*

SYSTEMIC DESENSITIZATION
SEE *Psychotherapy.*

SYSTEMS THEORY

Systems theory is a philosophy and worldview arising from the belief that aspects of the world are not independent of each other but interdependent on one another. This results in a research view and approach that it is difficult if not impossible to separate components of a question from logically related material in the world at large. "Logically related" depends on the question under examination and changes as the research question changes. Systems theory is sometimes called structural functionalism or holism.

Systems theory approaches understanding a problem as understanding a set of relationships among disparate factors. This contrasts to classic scientific analysis, where a set of independent variables is compared to dependent variables. Examining interactions among the independent variables approaches but is not systems theory. Systems theory requires two things. First, there must be a web of interactions among all the elements under study. Second, there are complex patterns as a result of these interactions. Sometimes systems theory includes such concepts as feedback systems and chaos theory. However, not all systems theorists include these research approaches within systems theory. Organizational and social network research is included in systems theory.

Because of the interactions among components, systems analysis tends to involve more complex analytical techniques. For example, instead of least squares analysis, systems theory might employ computer modeling and simultaneous equations techniques. System theory's strength and weakness arises from this. The methodology is harder to learn and understand, but the explanatory power can be greater. Also systems theory tends to be interdisciplinary, especially in the social sciences. A planetary system can be isolated for study and still be a system. The reasons behind results in a particular election can involve individual and group psychology, economics and market analysis, history, religion, and communications theory because all of these are known electoral factors.

This can lead to the complaint that systems theory overcomplicates problems and research. This complaint is not without some validity. In certain analysis situations systems theory can be overkill. In other situations systems theory can be necessary for understanding the problem.

The basic concept of systems theory can be traced back to philosophers in ancient Greece and China. As a research approach, systems theory is much more recent. Modern systems theory dates to just after World War II and such researchers as Margaret Mead and Gregory Bateson. Their work is based on concepts developed by Rudolf Virchow, Adolf Bastian, and Franz Boas. In turn this work is based on the philosophic concepts of G. W. von Leibniz in the 1600s. Modern systems researchers include Niklas Lehmann and Robert Axelrod.

Simple systems in modern use include such things as the feedback concept of a household thermostat that turns on or off a heating or cooling unit depending on the temperature inside, the temperature outside, and the desired temperature. Complex systems include chaos theory and its applied forms in different disciplines.

SEE ALSO *Boas, Franz; Mead, Margaret; Social Science; Social System; System Analysis*

BIBLIOGRAPHY

Eve, Raymond A., Sara Horsfall, and Mary E. Lee, eds. 1997. *Chaos, Complexity, and Sociology: Myths, Models, and Theories.* Thousand Oaks, CA: Sage.

Harrison, Neil E., ed. 2006. *Complexity in World Politics: Concepts and Methods of a New Paradigm.* Albany: State University of New York Press.

Sebeok, Thomas A., and Marcel Danesi. 2000. *The Forms of Meaning: Modeling Systems Theory and Semiotic Analysis.* New York: Mouton de Gruyter.

Smith, John, and Chris Jenks. 2006. *Qualitative Complexity: Ecology, Cognitive Processes, and the Re-Emergence of Structures in Post-Humanist Social Theory.* New York: Routledge.

David Conklin

T

TABLEAU ECONOMIQUE
SEE *Quesnay, Francois.*

TABOOS

The term *taboo* is derived from a Micronesian word that means "reserved" and originally alluded to objects or things that contained so much supernatural power that only trained religious specialists could handle them safely. The word *taboo* was first mentioned as a native term in Captain James Cook's (1728–1779) accounts of his voyages to the Pacific islands. It quickly entered English popular usage and has been used in comparative anthropology since then. This conception of taboo is illustrated in Old Testament accounts of laypersons who were afflicted with disease or even killed on the spot after touching the sacred Ark of the Covenant. More generally, however, the term is used to describe a wide range of vernacular beliefs that forbid certain actions for fear that they will lead to a catastrophe afflicting the surrounding community. The seeming disparity between the apparent triviality of the forbidden actions and the extent of the feared consequences distinguishes taboos from the more pragmatic magical beliefs describing contraindicated actions with certain consequences. Psychoanalyst Sigmund Freud (1856–1939), in his influential collection of essays *Totem and Taboo* (1912–1913), also adapted *taboo* to refer to a form of compulsive behavior among modern-day persons.

The most common and best-studied taboos deal with sexual and dietary precautions and may well derive from pragmatic experience. One of the most widespread cate-gories of taboos concerns limiting marriage to partners outside of one's family or clan. The myths explaining these taboos tend to portray the associated disaster in terms of a divine punishment, as in a Zuni myth that associates a catastrophic flood with inbreeding within clans, or the well-known Greek myth of Oedipus, whose unwitting marriage with his mother was the cause of a decimating plague. However, given the ubiquity of such taboos, it is clear that they were based on prescientific observations linking genuinely risky actions to cultural misfortunes that occurred later. It took no knowledge of genetics to recognize that inbreeding among family or clan members was associated with a higher rate of lethal birth defects and genetic illnesses.

Similarly, many dietary restrictions may be based on a recognition that close contact with certain food animals, especially pigs, was associated with a wide variety of diseases, some (like trichinosis) parasitic in nature, others (like influenza) communicated directly from live animals to susceptible humans. However, as Mary Douglas (1966) noted, such food taboos are often associated with images of the culture's own identity. Thus a meal such as the "kid seethed in its mother's milk" (the basis of the kosher division between dairy and meat products), may have been in origin a ritual meal of a rival culture. Hence both marriage and dietary taboos became, in practice, ways of maintaining the boundaries of a culture's membership.

Taboos are often enforced by institutional religions, frequently through dominating secular institutions. In Islamic cultures, religious taboos against the consumption of alcohol and indiscreet behavior by females are strongly enforced by secular authorities, even among non-Islamic visitors. Similarly, restrictions on certain forms of incestuous marriage are normally written into legal codes. But many cultures add to these codes prescriptions against other forms of marriage, such as interracial or same-sex unions, which involve no risk to the partners or their cultures but which are seen as irreligious and so dangerous to the safety of the commonwealth.

However, many taboos are privately enforced, especially among those practicing professions with high degrees of danger or risk, particularly sailors and miners. Violating such a taboo may lead to a spontaneous work stoppage by coworkers, who fear risking a serious accident. A number of these taboos reflect vernacular understanding of religious practices. The Jewish restriction on work during the Sabbath clearly underlies the common superstition tabooing the start of any major project (such as a ship's voyage) on a Friday because the work involved would usually stretch past sundown and so into the forbidden time. The proscription on speaking the sacred names of God, particularly in private rituals of magic, is commonly extended to purely mundane uses of divine words in trivial oaths and exclamations. However, many other words, such as *pig* (often forbidden in mariners' conversations) may show an extension of the dietary taboos into the realm of language. Other taboos, such as miners refusing to work on a day when their hands or feet were unusually cold on rising (the origin of the proverbial phrase "got cold feet") may reflect popular psychology. The common taboo on allowing women to participate in such risky professions, or even to be present onboard ship or in a mine shaft, is probably linked to the common practice of soldiers and male athletes avoiding sex before action, originally a religious act of renunciation in return for divine favor and increased strength.

An especially widespread class of taboos reflects cultural attitudes toward death. Many such practices forbid the explicit mention of dying or overly free use of objects associated with funerals. Hence, in Japan the number four (pronounced "shi," which also means "death") is a common taboo, being omitted in hospital rooms and flight numbers. Similarly, in Italy, the number seventeen is often skipped because it could be expressed in Roman numerals as XVII, which is an anagram of the Latin past perfective verb "VIXI," which literally means "I have ceased to be alive," or, more bluntly, "I died." Flowers associated with funerals, such as lilies (in North America) or chrysanthemums (in Asian countries), should not be given to the living for fear of putting them at risk. Common legends assert that wearing an article of clothing worn by a corpse may lead to one's own death, and buildings or even automobiles in which death occurred may become too contaminated for the living to use. Behind all of these taboos is the belief, especially strong in Western cultures, that the living need to be insulated from the concept of mortality.

Overall, taboos are best understood as parallel to magic: magical actions are ways of managing one's perception of risk or danger by *doing* something, whereas observing taboos minimizes risk by *not* doing something. Of course, refraining from a tabooed action often involves choosing actions with religious and magical overtones (such as the preparation of kosher meals).

SEE ALSO *Cultural Relativism; Disease; Freud, Sigmund; Islam, Shia and Sunni; Kinship; Magic; Norms; Religion; Rituals; Sanitation; Sin; Totemism*

BIBLIOGRAPHY

Diamond, Jared M. 1997. *Guns, Germs, and Steel: The Fates of Human Societies.* New York: Norton.

Douglas, Mary. 1966. *Purity and Danger: An Analysis of Concepts of Pollution and Taboo.* New York: Praeger.

Freud, Sigmund. [1912–1913] 1950. *Totem and Taboo: Some Points of Agreement between the Mental Lives of Savages and Neurotics.* Trans. James Strachey. New York: Norton.

Iwasaka, Michiko, and Barre Toelken. 1994. *Ghosts and the Japanese: Cultural Experience in Japanese Death Legends.* Logan: Utah State University Press.

Mullen, Patrick. 1978. *I Heard the Old Fishermen Say: Folklore of the Texas Gulf Coast.* Austin: University of Texas Press.

Poggie, John J., Jr., Richard B. Pollnac, and Carl Gersuny. 1976. Risk as a Basis for Taboos among Fishermen in Southern New England. *Journal for the Scientific Study of Religion* 15 (3): 257–262.

Bill Ellis

TAINO

The Taino Indians are a subgroup of the Arawakan Indians of northeastern South America. They were living in the Greater Antilles (Hispaniola, Jamaica, Cuba, and Puerto Rico) when Christopher Columbus (1451–1506) arrived in the New World in 1492. The Arawak had a complex and highly ceremonial culture. While they had neither a written language nor an advanced system of counting, the Arawak people had a highly developed culture, including a universal language, a system of ceremonial dances, sculpture, jewelry, weaving, music, and poetry. They grew fruit such as guava, papaya, and pineapple, as well as beans, squash, chilies, and tobacco. They played a ceremonial ball game called *batu*, which, like stickball in many southeastern American Indian nations, was also used as a form of conflict resolution. They were governed by a village-based theocracy and were organized around a three-tiered class structure: Each village had a single *cacique*, or chief; *nitainos*, or noblemen; and *nabo-*

rias, or the working class. Villages also had *bohiques*, who functioned as priests and healers.

Taino culture was integral to the development of the postcontact region. Taino place names are still used in many areas (such as the Puerto Rican towns of Utuado and Mayaguez). The Taino also introduced to Europeans the *hamaca*, or hammock; and the *barbacoa*, or barbecue; the musical instrument maracas, and a way of making cassava bread. Tainos named the *yuca* among other plants and the iguana as well as other animals.

Mostly agricultural, seafaring, and peaceful, the Taino had been engaged in a series of conflicts with the more aggressive Caribs for about one hundred years prior to European contact. The Europeans probably confused the Taino with the Caribs and considered them a threat, subject to the Spanish Crown and liable to forced conversion to Catholicism. There is always considerable debate over the size of precontact indigenous populations and the degree to which those populations were reduced by Europeans. When the Spanish arrived on Puerto Rico (or Boriken) in 1508, it is estimated that there were between 20,000 and 50,000 Tainos. The vicious combination of disease, flight, and the wages of an unsuccessful rebellion in 1511 reduced that number to about 4,000 by 1515.

As with many other indigenous people of the Americas, these numbers allowed Europeans to assume that all Tainos had been decimated and no longer existed, although there was and is debate over whether "absorption" or "extermination" is the cause. However, there is no evidence that the Taino were eradicated. Many contemporary Puerto Ricans claim Taino heritage. The Taino are now asking for official recognition as indigenous and sovereign peoples from the government of Puerto Rico and have formed at least two organizations: the United Confederation of Taíno People and the Jatibonicu Taino Tribal Nation of Boriken. There is also a growing movement of Taino revivalism, connected to a broader movement for indigenous resurgence across the Caribbean. Members of the movement advocate cultural preservation and promotion, correction of historical misconceptions, the preservation and maintenance of sacred sites, and environmental protection.

SEE ALSO *Boricua; Indigenismo; Indigenous Rights; Native Americans; Nuyoricans*

BIBLIOGRAPHY

Forte, Maximilian C., ed. 2006. *Indigenous Resurgence in the Contemporary Caribbean: Amerindian Survival and Revival.* New York: Peter Lang.

Jatibonicu Taino Tribal Nation of Boriken. http://www.taino-tribe.org.

Rouse, Irving. 1992. *The Tainos: Rise and Decline of the People Who Greeted Columbus.* New Haven, CT: Yale University Press.

United Confederation of Taíno People. http://uctp.org/.

Mary E. Stuckey

TAIT, LAWSON

SEE *Sterilization, Human.*

TALENT

The social sciences can have an enormous impact on society by identifying talented individuals and finding methods to fulfill the potentials implied by that talent. *Talent* generally refers to particular potentials. It can be contrasted with the general ability estimated with tests of intelligence (IQ). Talent is both domain and culture specific.

Exceptional talents have been studied for many years. In his seminal study titled *Hereditary Genius* (1869), Sir Francis Galton presented data suggesting that talent is inborn. He concluded that talent ran in families, the implication being that there was not much that could be done if an individual was not born into the right family. Galton's data were derived from archival sources, which did indeed show that the more closely family members were related (e.g., sons and fathers versus cousins), the more likely they would share the same level of ability. The data were biased, however, in that only certain fields were represented. Also, gender bias, common in Galton's time, meant that only certain careers were open to women and only certain skills were developed in girls. Indeed, educational advantages were at that point given almost entirely to boys and men. The conclusion about heredity seems to have been unwarranted as well. This is because both nature and nurture run in families. Just because talent runs in families does not mean that it is genetically based. Certain experiences are also more common in some families than others. Socioeconomic status, for instance, shows continuity across generations, and this means that certain families will have educational advantages in every generation, while other families will not. In short, talent might appear to be inherited because it runs in families, but that can just as easily be explained in terms of experiences (e.g., educational) that are common to certain families.

It is most realistic to recognize both nature and nurture as influences on talents. Certain biological givens, for example, characterize the entire human race. There is also some indication that the human nervous system has specializations for different talents and that these might vary from person to person. Recent evidence suggests that certain talents are tied to particular genes and alleles, such as the dopamine receptor DRD2. Biological influences on talent determine what potentials any one individual will have. Everyone has potentials, but clearly the range of potentials varies dramatically from person to person. If these potentials are recognized, perhaps as a kind of precociousness or giftedness, they may be reinforced and fulfilled through formal and informal educational experiences.

Some talents may require more reinforcement (and more experience) than others. Musical talent, for example, is apparent very early in life, in part because the individual need not master a huge corpus of information. Mathematical talent is not apparent quite as early, but still is manifest by approximately age ten. Other fields may require the individual to master a large knowledge base, and for that reason more experience is necessary. Talent in an area such as physics, then, would not be fulfilled until adulthood.

Although talent often develops to the degree that it is valued and reinforced, sometimes the causality is the other way around and the talent has an impact on the experiences obtained. This occurs when parents or teachers recognize a child's potential and react to it by providing optimal experiences. Talent is not, then, entirely dependent on nurturance; it can also determine what experiences are most likely to occur. In short, talent and experience have a *bidirectional* causal relationship.

One of the most influential theories of talent was presented by Howard Gardner (1983). Often called the theory of *multiple intelligences*, his view distinguishes eight domains of talent: verbal-symbolic, mathematical-logical, musical, spatial, bodily-kinesthetic, interpersonal, intrapersonal, and naturalistic. Gardner's theory is widely recognized in part because it is based on data from experimental, psychometric, cognitive, biographical, and developmental investigations, and in part because it avoids common cultural biases. In Western culture, for example, the emphasis is on verbal-symbolic and mathematical-logical talents. These are emphasized in the schools much more than the other domains. But other cultures (and eras) emphasize other talents.

Even within one culture, views of talent vary with the passage of time. Athletic skills such as hitting or catching a ball, for example, were probably not greatly valued in the early part of American history, though now these skills can lead to scholarships and lucrative careers. What may be most important is the implication that some talents are presently not recognized. This further implies that there are human potentials that are not being fulfilled. Some of these may be extremely important for world peace and the preservation of the environment.

Talent is probably best identified and nurtured by looking beyond cognitive ability. Certainly cognitive ability plays a role, but there is much more to it. A potential talent will not even be fulfilled unless the individual invests time in the domain in question. Joseph Renzulli recognized cognitive and extracognitive aspects of exceptionality. Here, general ability plays a role, as does creative potential and task commitment. The last of these reflects interest, motivation, and persistence. Clearly educators should look for each of these contributions to talent (general ability, creative ability, and motivation).

The domain-specific view of talent is also useful in the educational setting. If educators recognize a variety of different talents, the potentials of each child can be fulfilled. Instead of identifying as gifted only children who are exceptional in verbal or mathematical skills, each individual's talents can be reinforced.

SEE ALSO *Cognition; Creativity; Culture; Gifted and Talented; Heredity; Intelligence; Intelligence, Social; Multiple Intelligences Theory; Nature vs. Nurture*

BIBLIOGRAPHY

Gardner, Howard. 1983. *Frames of Mind: The Theory of Multiple Intelligences.* New York: Basic Books. Tenth anniversary ed., 1993.

Sternberg, Robert, and Janet Davidson, eds. 1986. *Conceptions of Giftedness.* Cambridge, U.K.: Cambridge University Press.

Mark A. Runco

TALIBAN

The Taliban is a radically militant Islamic movement that controlled some 90 percent of Afghanistan between 1996 and 2001. The Taliban emerged from their base in Kandahar in southwestern Afghanistan in reaction to the lawlessness caused by infighting between rival mujahideen forces in the wake of the Soviet withdrawal in 1989. The Taliban's declared aims included the restoration of peace, rigid enforcement of Islamic law, disarming the population, and defending the Islamic character of Afghanistan.

In 1994 the Taliban, under the leadership of Mullah Mohammed Omar, began its territorial conquest with the seizure of the Afghan border post of Spin Boldak and subsequent takeover of the city of Kandahar. The fall of Kandahar provided the Taliban with a nucleus of fighters as thousands of Afghan refugees, mostly students at madrassas (Islamic religion schools) near the Afghan-Pakistani border, joined the movement. The Taliban's swift military successes launched a surprising advance that culminated in the capture of the Afghan capital, Kabul, in 1996.

The Taliban set out to create the world's most pure Islamic regime by introducing a disturbing and deeply revolutionary form of Muslim culture that came at a tremendous cost to human freedom. Men were ordered to keep their beards to a specific length, and subjected to punishment for defiance. Members of minority groups wore labels to distinguish them as non-Muslims, a measure the Taliban argued was to protect them from religious police enforcing Islamic law. Frivolities such as television, the Internet, music, and photography were outlawed. Punishments including amputation of the hands of thieves and the stoning to death of women convicted of adultery, considered severe by European standards, were common under the Taliban.

It was the Taliban's anti-woman agenda, however, that caused mounting concern around the world. Under the Taliban women were forbidden to work outside the home, were compelled to wear a head-to-toe covering known as a burka, and could not leave the home without a male guardian. Such issues, along with restrictions on women's access to health and education, caused resentments among ordinary Afghans and drew the ire of the international community. To the Taliban, however, the restrictions served to preserve the honor and dignity of women who had previously been preyed upon.

Despite their strict beliefs and anti-drug profile, the Taliban could not resist using opium to fund its activities, underlining the movement's poor understanding and interpretation of Islamic law. Though the Taliban leaders led an austere life in contrast to the ostentatious lifestyle of the mujahideen warlords, their economic policy was left in the hands of chance and fate, culminating in Afghanistan's slide into economic backwardness.

Only three countries, the United Arab Emirates, Pakistan, and Saudi Arabia, established diplomatic ties with the Taliban government. Both Pakistan and Saudi Arabia distinguished themselves among foreign powers by the scale of their efforts and support for the regime. Although it is officially denied, there is widespread agreement that the Taliban gained crucial early support from the Pakistani army and intelligence services, especially in helping make the Taliban a highly effective military force. Pakistan, influenced by its geopolitical and economic interests, remained a strong diplomatic and economic lifeline for the regime.

In Saudi Arabia the Taliban's push for a pristine Islamic society was in accord with the Saudi's strict form of Wahhabi theology and law. Saudi Arabia bankrolled the madrassas in Pakistan that provided an ideological guide for the Taliban. A great deal of uncertainty remains about the extent of Saudi Arabia's assistance to the Taliban but the consensus appears to be that their aid was largely financial.

The Taliban enjoyed a cozy relationship with Al-Qaeda and found in the group a useful ally, especially in the significant boost Al-Qaeda provided to the Taliban's military campaigns against the Northern Alliance. Al-Qaeda enjoyed a comfortable refuge in Afghanistan under the Taliban regime.

The Taliban made giant strides in uniting the country but ultimately was unable to end the civil war. The strongest opposition to the Taliban came from the Northern Alliance, who controlled the northeast region of Afghanistan. This group backed the U.S.-led coalition that ousted the Taliban from power in 2001.

SEE ALSO *Al-Qaeda; Arabs; Fundamentalism, Islamic; Government; Islam, Shia and Sunni; Muslims; Radicalism; Sexism; Union of Soviet Socialist Republics*

BIBLIOGRAPHY

Marsden, Peter. 1998. *The Taliban: War, Religion, and the New Order in Afghanistan.* London: Zed Books.

Rashid, Ahmed. 2002. *Taliban: Islam, Oil, and the New Great Game in Central Asia.* New ed. London: Tauris.

Rubin, Michael. 2002. Who Is Responsible for the Taliban? *Middle East Review of International Affairs* 6 (1). http://meria.idc.ac.il/journal/2002/issue1/jv6n1a1.html.

Charles Ebere

TALLY'S CORNER

Tally's Corner: A Study of Negro Streetcorner Men (1967), by the American anthropologist Elliot Liebow (1925–1994), represented a breakthrough for its time in studies dealing with poverty and race. *Tally's Corner* was originally written as Liebow's PhD dissertation in anthropology for the Catholic University of America.

For twelve months in 1962 and 1963, Liebow and a group of researchers studied the behavior of a group of young black men who lived near and frequently hung around a street corner in a poor black neighborhood in downtown Washington, D.C. Liebow's participant observation revealed the numerous obstacles facing black men on a day-to-day basis, including the structural and individual levels of racial discrimination propagated by whites in society.

Liebow's observations about young black men in the ghetto, a complex system comprised of an overabundance of liquor stores, pool halls, and pawnshops, directly parallel similar research by notable scholars, such as William Foote Whyte (1914–2000) in *Street Corner Society* (1943). In this respect, *Tally's Corner* represents one of the first ethnographic attempts at understanding how groups navigate extreme poverty in the inner cities. The book shares some similarities with W. E. B. Du Bois's (1868–1963) *The Philadelphia Negro* (1899) in that throughout *Tally's Corner*, Liebow elaborates on the cultural deficiencies of blacks in the ghetto and is quick to attribute these deficiencies as the root cause of their perpetual poverty. Unlike Du Bois, however, Liebow fails to factor in the effects of racial discrimination against blacks in the employment sector and in access to quality education and how these structural elements affect the lives of black people living in the ghetto.

Nevertheless, *Tally's Corner* is unique in how it looks at not only poverty and its effects on inner-city people but specifically on the systemic and long-term effects of poverty on black men and black families. In the five main chapters that make up *Tally's Corner*, Liebow discusses how black men deal, on a daily basis, with issues of work, their relationships, their children, and their friends and networks. His portrait of how inner-city blacks navigate the racial waters of their neighborhoods is both gloomy and sad, revealing a number of examples of how whites are apathetic and often discriminatory toward black workers. Black men's constant struggle to succeed and their frequent failures translate for Liebow into a self-perpetuating cycle of doubt, where blacks become tired of trying to beat white society at its own game and thus accept failure as a way of life.

The sociologist and ethnographer Elijah Anderson, following Liebow's tradition of urban ethnographic research into black lives in the inner city, has spent a lifetime studying race and class issues in urban communities. An explicit example of the continuity of Liebow's work is in Anderson's *Code of the Street* (1999), an ethnographic study examining morality, teen pregnancy, the search for respect, and other issues central to people living in the inner city.

Although Liebow's study offers valuable insight into the lives of young and poor black men in the early 1960s, his analysis caters to what the psychologist William Ryan (1923–2002) labeled a "blaming-the-victim" mentality or what the anthropologist Oscar Lewis (1914–1970) referred to as a "culture of poverty," whereby the structural inequalities in society are not questioned. Rather, blame for persistent social ills is placed directly onto the victims themselves. A clear example of the use of a blaming-the-victim argument is in the 1965 Moynihan Report, which argued that unemployment and a lack of educational success among black Americans could be traced to dysfunctional black families. Hence the burden of misfortune is shifted directly onto black Americans.

In a similar vein, Liebow argued that the relentless patterns of racial discrimination by whites had left black men with low self-esteem and thus a desire to remain uneducated and unattached to their children or families. The problem with this argument is that it fails to account for the real and pervasive racial dilemmas faced by blacks in the United States. For example, Liebow argued that as long as black Americans failed to become educated, they would remain ignorant of the opportunities provided many whites. Thus education is a key, for Liebow, in lifting black men out of poverty. However, what is left out of Liebow's equation is that the racial discrimination that occurs in the school system is real and that for blacks education may not necessarily equal opportunities for success. As Joe Feagin, Amanda Lewis, Judith Blau, and many other researchers have noted, the American education system is a racialized institution that fundamentally caters to middle-class whites while routinely denying blacks and other nonwhites equal opportunities for learning and advancement. Likewise, Liebow ignores the impact of racial discrimination in employment as a major factor affecting blacks' opportunities for upward social and economic mobility. Thus for blacks living in the ghetto, the racial structure of society is such that even should they succeed in navigating the educational obstacle course, they will continue to suffer penalties in rewards vis-à-vis comparably educated whites. This fact not only affects the social and economic mobility of black Americans, it also has an adverse impact on the motivation of blacks living in the ghetto to follow through on their education.

Numerous studies have criticized *Tally's Corner* for its failure to consider the impact of institutional and systemic racism on the lives of blacks in the United States. For example, Steven Gregory's *Black Corona* (1998) argues against the idea that the black ghetto is dysfunctional and socially disorganized. Rather, like Kenneth B. Clark (1914–2005) in *Dark Ghetto* (1965), Gregory maintains that the black community has been rendered powerless by urban political processes, even as black Americans continue to organize and fight for social justice. A more direct critique of *Tally's Corner* is in James Borchert's *Alley Life in Washington* (1980). Borchert finds order and stability in his examination of alley housing in Washington, D.C., and he directly rejects the view of lower-class black life as pathological.

SEE ALSO *African Americans; Culture of Poverty; Ethnography; Ghetto; Moynihan Report; Poverty*

BIBLIOGRAPHY

Anderson, Elijah. 1999. *Code of the Street: Decency, Violence, and the Moral Life of the Inner City.* New York: Norton.

Blau, Judith R. 2003. *Race in the Schools: Perpetuating White Dominance?* Boulder, CO: Lynne Rienner.

Borchert, James. 1980. *Alley Life in Washington: Family, Community, Religion, and Folklife in the City, 1850–1970.* Urbana: University of Illinois Press.

Clark, Kenneth B. 1965. *Dark Ghetto: Dilemmas of Social Power.* New York: Harper and Row.

Du Bois, W. E. B. 1899. *The Philadelphia Negro: A Social Study.* New York: Lippincott.

Gregory, Steven. 1998. *Black Corona: Race and the Politics of Place in an Urban Community.* Princeton, NJ: Princeton University Press.

Lewis, Amanda E. 2003. *Race in the Schoolyard: Negotiating the Color Line in Classrooms and Communities.* New Brunswick, NJ: Rutgers University Press.

Lewis, Oscar. 1959. *Five Families: Mexican Case Studies in the Culture of Poverty.* New York: Basic Books.

Liebow, Elliot. 1967. *Tally's Corner: A Study of Negro Streetcorner Men.* Boston: Little, Brown.

Ryan, William. 1971. *Blaming the Victim.* New York: Pantheon.

Van Ausdale, Debra, and Joe R. Feagin. 2001. *The First R: How Children Learn Race and Racism.* Lanham, MD: Rowman and Littlefield.

Whyte, William Foote. [1943] 1993. *Street Corner Society: The Social Structure of an Italian Slum.* 4th ed. Chicago: University of Chicago Press.

David G. Embrick

TANGO

SEE *Dance.*

TARIFFS

Tariffs are discriminatory taxes collected at the border on imported goods but not levied on similar goods originating domestically. Tariffs are sometimes very large (everywhere in the 1930s and in some developing countries in the early twenty-first century) and sometimes very low (Hong Kong in the early twenty-first century). Tariffs are substantially discriminatory between international trading partners. Regional trade agreements such as the European Union (EU) and the North American Free Trade Agreement (NAFTA) remove tariffs between the members while imposing tariffs on nonmembers. Tariffs also significantly discriminate between goods. Tariff schedules of most countries contain over 10,000 lines with tariffs ranging in some cases from 0 percent to over 100 percent.

Tariffs come in specific and ad valorem forms. Specific tariffs are charges per unit, for example, $1,000 per automobile. Ad valorem tariffs are levied as a percentage of invoice value. A 5 percent tariff levied on a $20,000 automobile yields a $1,000 specific tariff equivalent. The automobile example also illustrates how to calculate the ad valorem equivalent of a specific tariff: divide the specific tariff by the invoice price. Ad valorem tariffs are much easier to use for comparison purposes across goods and countries. Comparison including specific tariffs requires prices to deflate the specific duties, which is often extremely burdensome.

Both specific and ad valorem tariffs are common. Ad valorem tariffs are the only sensible type when there is no natural quantity unit (boxes of parts). But ad valorem tariffs are disadvantageous where corrupt border officials are suspected; underinvoicing will lower the tax paid, with importer and border official splitting the difference. History also matters: The United States has many specific tariffs despite the likely honesty of its customs officials.

Some tariffs vary with the level of trade. The tariff quota is a tariff that steps upward when trade passes a preset amount. Another example is an antidumping duty, which is equal to the difference between last year's price differential between the exporting firm's cost (or foreign price) and its U.S. sale price.

TARIFF COSTS AND BENEFITS

Tariffs provide revenue to the government that levies them. This benefit is offset by the cost to users of paying the tax. Less obviously tariffs provide a benefit to domestic producers who experience less stringent competition from imports. The balance of these three effects is typically calculated to yield a net loss to the economy. A tariff reduction is typically calculated to reduce net loss by the height of the tariff times the increase in imports induced by the tariff reduction. The marginal net cost of tariffs is thus proportional to the height of the tariff.

A potentially important complication is that import competition may cause periods of unemployment for domestic workers; hence, tariffs provide a benefit by employing more workers. Typical calculations for the U.S. economy show that the costs of employment-increasing tariff hikes per job saved are greater than the wage paid in the job—usually several times the wage.

What explains the use of tariffs in view of their cost to the economy? Politics. The pressure of domestic producers and trade unions that gain from tariffs is largely unopposed. Consumers are unorganized whereas producers who import intermediate goods often refrain from resisting tariffs as they push for tariffs on the import of goods that compete with their output. Two contrary forces push tariffs down. Most importantly, politicians tempted to grant higher tariffs also know that the resulting reduction in general prosperity harms their prospects of retaining power (at the next election or, less certainly, against a coup). More subtly, the interest groups themselves bear a share of the overall cost of tariffs, tending to restrain their demands. Political economy models that view tariffs as objects for sale in political markets with these forces at work have been fitted to data on the pattern of protection, and the model appears to statistically explain the pattern well.

The discriminatory aspect of tariffs (differing across trading partners and across goods) typically adds to the cost of tariffs. Discrimination across trading partners results in costly trade diversion. The purchase of goods shifts from the lowest cost source (increasing net loss in proportion to the tariff if the source is not a partner) to the favored partner (with marginal net benefit equal to the zero tariff). Discrimination across goods imposes a more subtle cost on the economy with a similar structure. Think about increasing the dispersion of tariffs while preserving the average tariff. The increase in tariffs on already high-tariff goods reduces trade where it is most costly whereas the reduction in tariffs on low-tariff goods increases trade where it is least costly.

Discrimination across trading partners and across goods is substantial and has increased with the overall liberalization of trade since the mid-1900s. Regional trade agreements have proliferated even as multilateral negotiations have reduced overall tariffs. Wide tariff reductions have exempted certain product categories, such as agriculture and apparel, in rich countries.

INTERNATIONAL TRADE RELATIONS

Tariffs tend to reduce prices of exports from foreign economies. This spillover implies that part of the cost of tariffs is borne by foreigners. Since national governments will thus be tempted to overuse tariffs, nations agree to restrict their tariffs in international negotiations and enforce their agreements through international institutions such as the World Trade Organization (WTO). The dispute settlement process of the WTO generates frequent headlines and gives a false impression that international relations are becoming more acrimonious. As with family therapy, if the parties are arguing, it is better than if they are not talking. Imperfections in particular negotiation rounds or institutions should not obscure their very positive role in preventing much worse outcomes, such as the tariff wars of the 1930s.

Two basic principles of the WTO and its predecessor institutions are nondiscrimination between partners and reciprocity. Reciprocity means that the parties alter their tariffs to balance the exchange of market access provided. For example, a round of tariff negotiations might increase U.S. imports by one trillion dollars while reciprocally increasing access to foreign markets by one trillion dollars. Importantly, the WTO permits the United States to withdraw market access of, say, one billion dollars, by raising its tariffs in a particular product while reciprocally authorizing the foreign countries to withdraw one billion dollars of market access by raising foreign tariffs.

Regional trade agreements are the great exception to nondiscrimination. The principles of the WTO permit it on the reasoning that a move toward free trade between the members is better than the move away from liberal trade due to trade diversion. Opinions among trade economists diverge over whether regional agreements are a building block or a stumbling block to multilateral liberalization.

SEE ALSO *Barriers to Trade; Liberalization, Trade; Quotas, Trade*

BIBLIOGRAPHY

Anderson, James E., and Eric van Wincoop. 2004. Trade Costs. *Journal of Economic Literature* 42: 691–751.

Anderson, James E., and J. Peter Neary. 1992. Trade Reform with Quotas, Partial Rent Retention and Tariffs. *Econometrica* 60 (1): 57–76.

Bagwell, Kyle, and Robert W. Staiger. 2002. *The Economics of the World Trading System.* Cambridge, MA: MIT Press.

Krugman, Paul, and Maurice Obstfeld. 2006. *International Economics: Theory and Policy*, 7th ed. Boston: Addison-Wesley.

James E. Anderson

TARSKI, ALFRED

SEE *Logic, Symbolic.*

TASTES

It is telling that economists use a term reserved for one of the five senses, *taste*, to denote human desires and motives. This indicates first that economists consider human desires as private and therefore not subject to moral valuation. One cannot be scolded for having taste buds that prefer sour cream, for example, to yogurt. Similarly one cannot be scolded for liking pushpin (a triviality, a children's game) better than poetry—the examples used by the founders of utilitarianism, Jeremy Bentham (1748–1832) and John Stuart Mill (1806–1873). Second, this signifies that economists consider human desires as personal and therefore not subject to interpersonal utility comparison. As much as it is supposedly impossible to compare A's taste buds for sour cream with B's, one cannot compare A's utility from consuming an extra automobile with B's. Third, this suggests that economists consider desires as fixed and therefore not to be tampered with to explain behavioral puzzles.

Whether neuroscientists regard the taste buds as private, personal, or fixed is another matter. At issue is the accuracy of the economists' assumption of tastes as private, personal, and fixed. It is easy to see the limits of each of these assumptions, as many social scientists have shown. Nonetheless, they persist in mainstream welfare analysis and in economics textbooks. They have proved impervious to criticism because they lend themselves easily to the thrust of economic analysis. Namely, it is about rationality: how agents respond to incentives so they can maximize a given end by a given set of means (Robbins 1935).

Economists have identified several axioms as the necessary conditions of rationality. The most important are two axioms concerning how agents compare alternative bundles of goods according to their own tastes; that is, how tastes become "preferences." According to the transitivity axiom, the preferences must be consistent. If an agent prefers A to B and B to C, then he or she must prefer A to C. According to the completeness axiom, the agent must be complete with his or her tastes. He or she must know how to rank all the bundles within his or her feasible set. This allows the agent to be decisive.

Empirical and experimental findings by behavioral-decision researchers in psychology and behavioral economists have questioned the axiom of transitivity. For instance, how one values a product may change depending on whether or not one owns the product, called the "endowment effect" (Thaler 1980) or "loss aversion" (Tversky and Kahneman 1991). It seems that agents value something more if they happen to own the item; the price at which they are willing to sell the item is higher than the price they are willing to pay for it. Some researchers have questioned this endowment effect on different grounds (Shogren, Shin, Hayes, and Kliebenstein 1994; Hanemann 1991; List 2001). Concerning the axiom of completeness, the parable of Buridan's ass illustrates the problem of indecision. Agents may simply fail to rank two equally appealing bundles (Khalil 1997).

Economists are still in disagreement about how to interpret the empirical and experimental findings that question these axioms. This short entry tackles the assumptions about tastes from another angle: by directly examining the assumptions that tastes are private, personal, and fixed.

TASTES AS PRIVATE

The assumption that tastes are private allows economists to treat all tastes—such as pushpin, cockfight, Aristotle's *Politics*, altruism, and poetry—as fungible. This allows economists to place them as elements in a single utility function. In this manner, an agent would buy more poetry if the price of cockfight tickets increased. If an agent holds irreconcilable utility functions, as the multiple-self approach maintains (Elster 1986), the agent's ability to economize across all tastes will be compromised.

The treatment of tastes as private comes at a price. It means that there is no room for educators and public figures to try to upgrade the tastes of the citizens. The upgrade would be deemed as arrogant and constitute interference in the citizens' private lives.

However, this may not be necessarily the case. It is possible to maintain the fungibility of tastes, and hence allow for the calculus of optimization to proceed, without the tastes-as-private assumption. That is, it is possible to recognize a qualitative difference between pushpin and poetry without undermining utilitarianism or the idea of a single utility function. For instance, John Harsanyi (1997) and Yew-Kwang Ng (1999, 2003) distinguish between actual preferences, on the one hand, and informed preferences, on the other. Ng identifies ignorance as one reason, out of several others, that agents would fail to choose the more welfare-enhancing, informed preferences. For Ng, agents would want informed preferences in place of actual ones because the informed preferences would afford happiness. Also one can argue that agents, with sufficient practice and education, would find no discontinuity between coarse entertainment and high-culture entertainment.

TASTES AS PERSONAL

The assumption of tastes as personal permits economists to avoid thorny political issues concerning the distribution of income. Economists usually restrict themselves to policies that avoid interpersonal utility comparison, based on what is known as the Pareto welfare criterion. This criterion stipulates that a policy maker can reallocate resources as long as it makes at least one agent better off without reducing the welfare of anyone else.

However, as Adam Smith (1723–1790) amply shows in *The Theory of Moral Sentiments* (1759), humans have the capacity to place themselves in the shoes of others, a quality he called sympathy. Sympathy, which can be extended to nonhuman animals, is a method of interpersonal utility comparison. It allows the agent to judge whether the pleas of others are justifiable, given the costs involved (see Khalil 2006).

TASTES AS FIXED

The assumption of tastes as fixed involves two separate flavors: first, fixity of tastes across agents or cultures; second, fixity of tastes across time for the same agent.

Fixity across Agents or Cultures The fixity of tastes across agents or cultures allows economists to explain differences in behavior solely on the basis of differences in income and relative prices. This prevents scientists from inventing tastes in an arbitrary fashion. For George Stigler and Gary Becker (1977), to explain differences in behavior in terms of differences in taste amounts to an intellectual retreat. For instance, cohabitation in place of marriage in the United States and western Europe is currently free from stigma. In many other cultures, and in the historical past of Euro-American culture, cohabitation amounts to living in sin. It has been punished by ostracism or even death, known as honor killing. To explain the disappearance of the stigma surrounding cohabitation, it would be an intellectual retreat to state: "Oh, Europeans and North Americans are now humane; they shed the backward values." Also if we see Agent Z suddenly buying more oranges than usual, it would be an intellectual retreat to hypothesize: "Oh, Agent Z suddenly started to like oranges more." Such answers are intellectually unsatisfying because they beg certain questions: Why did the rest of the people in the world not become as enlightened as the North Americans and the Europeans? Why did Agent Z change his or her taste?

It is a better strategy to assume that tastes are stable, that is, the same tastes prevail across cultures and agents and to examine instead changes in incentives. Concerning cohabitation, there are several candidates: the introduction of the contraceptive pill in 1964, the spread of the welfare state, and an increased division of labor that facilitates female participation in the workforce. Each of these factors lowers the risk or cost of pregnancy and therefore lowers the cost of cohabitation relative to marriage. Also, concerning oranges, there are several candidates: lower prices of oranges, higher prices of all other fruits, or new information about the health benefits of oranges, for example. All of these candidates deal with the change of constraints and therefore avoid the intellectual retreat.

It would also be an intellectual retreat to evaluate the economic performance among countries by appealing to differences in cultural tastes (Khalil 2007a). If we witness one economy performing better than another, it would be an arbitrary assumption to suppose that the people of the better-performing economy had different tastes from the other. A more challenging task is to look for differences in climate, endowment, or relative prices. In fact it is crucial for analysis to maintain the fixity of tastes across cultures. Of course cultures have different tastes for how to prepare coffee or what to eat for breakfast. But such differences are trivial in comparison to fundamental issues, such as investment, innovation, and entrepreneurship. These issues are of universal concern for human survival. Given this, it is important to resist the rising tide of culturalist economics that tries to explain the debacles of, for example, Latin America or Islam in terms of fundamental cultural values (North 2005).

In the same vein, if one sees a person indulging in gambling or alcohol to the point of dysfunction, one should not invent new tastes, such as the theory that some people have a weak will toward present consumption while others have a strong will. This would be an intellectual retreat (Khalil 2007b). To see how or why some agents become addicted to or indulge in reckless activity, it is more intellectually appropriate to assume first that agents have the same tastes. Of course agents have different tastes, but such differences should be accounted for endogenously rather than as the entry point of analysis. This is especially the case if one intends to analyze actions that lead to the dysfunction of the agent, broadly called weakness of will, such as addiction and recklessness. It is important, then, to resist the rising tide of behavioral economics that tries to explain weakness of will as simply the result of present-bias tastes, which amounts to quasi-hyperbolic discounting (Laibson 1997; O'Donoghue and Rabin 1999).

Also the behaviorist onslaught has created new tastes, aside from the ones to explain weakness of will. It has created tastes for envy, jealousy, fairness, social preferences, and so on (Gintis, Bowles, Boyd, and Fehr 2005). In this manner, behavioral puzzles are not interrogated in relation to welfare or well-being (Khalil 2000, 2004). Rather, the puzzles are "solved" by the question-begging invention of new tastes. In fact economists are not short of evolutionary stories about the stability of populations with such new tastes (Francois and Zabojnik 2005; Gintis 2003a; Gintis 2003b; Bowles 2004, chap. 2). Such stories fundamentally depend on the variability of lineages of tastes across agents—true to the neo-Darwinian assumption of diverse lineages in the population as the prerequisite of natural selection. Such evolutionary stories then proceed to show why a lineage, such as a social preference toward trustworthiness, can become dominant. Namely, the lineage becomes dominant if it already exists in the population above a critical frequency. But such evolutionary stories amount to establishing the stability of the new taste at hand. They do not provide an endogenous account of the origin of the lineage. Worse, it is unlikely that members of a population would simultaneously experience a mutation of the same kind at a scale that is required to reach a critical mass.

Fixity across Time The fixity of tastes across time for the same agent, which can be called the "economics Archimedean rock," affords the celebrated assumption of consumer sovereignty. This assumption allows economists to undertake a static welfare comparison. If an agent's tastes are manipulated by powerful entities, such as firms and their advertising arms (Galbraith 1958) or the culture of competitive markets (Bowles 1998), the result is that the tastes of the consumer are not stable enough over time to afford welfare comparisons. If a monopolist M "brainwashes" or "educates" consumers to love C more if it is in its container M than if it is any other container, M'—$U(CM) > U(CM')$, then consumers suffer when CM' replaces CM as a result of the breakup of the monopoly. Thus researchers cannot capture the welfare benefit, such as lower prices of C, as a result of the breakup of the monopoly.

The problem of change of tastes across time is about innate change. The problem, as discussed here, is not about fashion or fad. The issue of fashion deals with a covariation of tastes across consumers that is not prompted by a change of income, relative prices, or the innate change of taste. The change of tastes due to fashion, as Edi Karni and David Schmeidler (1990) suggest, does not threaten the idea of fixed tastes. They trace the phenomenon of fashion to the social aspect of the consumption of the goods under question, which explains the cyclical behavior.

The problem of change of tastes across time discussed here is, rather, due to the development of the agent, which is usually path dependent, where habits play a supreme role. Gary Becker (1996, chap. 1) proposes the notion of personal capital that is augmented through consumption. Past consumption enhances the marginal utility of current consumption, which becomes the basis of habit formation. Becker argues that the endogenous change of tastes across time does not result in unstable tastes. While the subutility function changes as a result of habit formation, the extended utility function is stable. Given the stability of the extended utility function, consumer sovereignty is preserved, so static welfare comparison is possible. Along a different vein, Ng (2003) uses the analysis of happiness, based on informed and nondeceiving preferences, to help researchers to judge welfare when there is a change of tastes.

Robert Sugden (2004) also deals with consumer sovereignty in the face of changing tastes. For Sugden, however, tastes change because they are reference dependent, where the reference can be the endowment (endowment effect) or the present (weakness of will). Given that tastes change with arbitrary factors, such as endowment or temptations afforded by the present, tastes amount to incoherent preferences. The normative economics Archimedean rock cannot be the satisfaction of preferences. Sugden suggests that consumer welfare should be evaluated according to the opportunity or freedom that the consumer has to assert his or her right to take care of himself or herself. Welfare therefore is not primarily about preference satisfaction. It is primarily about the freedom to pursue one's preferences, which can be incoherent. Such freedom, possessed by the individual, should be the true meaning of "consumer sovereignty."

CONCLUSION

Economics would greatly benefit from dropping the assumptions that tastes are private, personal, and fixed across time for the same individual. The only assumption about tastes that, at first approximation, is worth preserving is the fixity of tastes across agents or cultures. This should not mean that, at second and tertiary approximations, cultures and agents have identical tastes. However, for fundamental issues—such as weakness of will, trustworthiness, entrepreneurship, and cohabitation—it is imperative not to explain differences in practice in terms of differences in taste. Such an explanation would be an intellectual retreat.

SEE ALSO *Altruism; Becker, Gary; Behaviorism; Bentham, Jeremy; Cultural Relativism; Distinctions, Social and Cultural; Economics, Behavioral; Economics, Neoclassical; Galbraith, John Kenneth; Happiness; Individualism; Marginalism; Mill, John Stuart; Needs; Pareto Optimum; Rationality; Sen, Amartya Kumar; Smith, Adam; Socioeconomic Status; Stigler, George Joseph; Stigma; Sympathy; Utilitarianism; Utility Function; Want Creation; Wants; Welfare Analysis; Welfare Economics*

BIBLIOGRAPHY

Becker, Gary S. 1993. Nobel Lecture: The Economic Way of Looking at Behavior. *Journal of Political Economy* 101 (3): 385–409.

Becker, Gary S. 1996. *Accounting for Tastes.* Cambridge, MA: Harvard University Press.

Bowles, Samuel. 1998. Endogenous Preferences: The Cultural Consequences of Markets and Other Economic Institutions. *Journal of Economic Literature* 36 (1): 75–111.

Bowles, Samuel. 2004. *Microeconomics: Behavior, Institutions, and Evolution.* New York: Russell Sage.

Elster, Jon, ed. 1986. *The Multiple Self.* Cambridge, U.K.: Cambridge University Press.

Francois, Patrick, and Jan Zabojnik. 2005. Trust, Social Capital, and Economic Development. *Journal of the European Economics Association* 3 (1): 51–94.

Galbraith, John Kenneth. 1958. *The Affluent Society.* Boston: Houghton Mifflin.

Gintis, Herbert. 2003a. The Hitchhiker's Guide to Altruism: Gene-Culture Coevolution and the Internalization of Norm. *Journal of Theoretical Biology* 220: 407–418.

Gintis, Herbert. 2003b. Solving the Puzzle of Prosociality. *Rationality and Society* 15 (2): 155–187.

Gintis, Herbert, Samuel Bowles, Robert Boyd, and Ernst Fehr, eds. 2005. *Moral Sentiments and Material Interests: The Foundations of Cooperation in Economic Life.* Cambridge, MA: MIT Press.

Hanemann, W. Michael. 1991. Willingness to Pay and Willingness to Accept: How Much Can They Differ? *American Economic Review* 81 (3): 635–647.

Harsanyi, John C. 1997. Utilities, Preferences, and Substantive Goods. *Social Choice and Welfare* 14 (1): 129–145.

Karni, Edi, and David Schmeidler. 1990. Fixed Preferences and Changing Tastes. *American Economic Review* 80 (2): 262–267.

Khalil, Elias L. 1997. Buridan's Ass, Risk, Uncertainty, and Self-Competition: A Theory of Entrepreneurship. *Kyklos* 50 (2): 147–163.

Khalil, Elias L. 2000. Symbolic Products: Prestige, Pride, and Identity Goods. *Theory and Decision* 49 (1): 53–77.

Khalil, Elias L. 2004. The Gift Paradox: Complex Selves and Symbolic Goods. *Review of Social Economy* 62 (3): 379–392.

Khalil, Elias L. 2006. Introduction: Smith the Hedgehog. *Adam Smith Review* 2: 3–20.

Khalil, Elias L. 2007a. The Roadblock of Culturalist Economics: Douglass North and the Retreat of Economics. Working paper.

Khalil, Elias L. 2007b. New Behavioural Economics: Is Economics in Retreat? In *New Behavioural Economics*, ed. Elias L. Khalil. Cheltenham, U.K.: Edward Elgar.

Laibson, David. 1997. Golden Eggs and Hyperbolic Discounting. *Quarterly Journal of Economics* 112 (2): 443–477.

List, John A. 2001. Do Explicit Warnings Eliminate the Hypothetical Bias in Elicitation Procedures? Evidence from Field Auctions for Sportscards. *American Economic Review* 91 (5): 1498–1507.

Ng, Yew-Kwang. 1999. Utility, Informed Preference, or Happiness: Following Harsanyi's Argument to Its Logical Conclusion. *Social Choice and Welfare* 16 (2): 197–216.

Ng, Yew-Kwang. 2003. From Preference to Happiness: Towards a More Complete Welfare Economics. *Social Choice and Welfare* 20 (2): 307–350.

North, Douglass C. 2005. *Understanding the Process of Economic Change*. Princeton, NJ: Princeton University Press.

O'Donoghue, Ted, and Matthew Rabin. 1999. Doing It Now or Later. *American Economic Review* 89 (1): 103–124.

Robbins, Lionel Charles. 1935. *An Essay on the Nature and Significance of Economic Science*. 2nd ed. London: Macmillan.

Sen, Amartya. 1992. *Inequality Reexamined*. Cambridge, MA: Harvard University Press.

Shogren, Jason F., Seung Y. Shin, Dermot J. Hayes, and James B. Kliebenstein. 1994. Resolving Differences in Willingness to Pay and Willingness to Accept. *American Economic Review* 84 (1): 255–270.

Smith, Adam. 1759. *The Theory of Moral Sentiments*. London: A. Millar.

Stigler, George J., and Gary S. Becker. 1977. De Gustibus Non Est Disputandum. *American Economic Review* 67 (2): 76–90.

Sugden, Robert. 2004. The Opportunity Criterion: Consumer Sovereignty without the Assumption of Coherent Preferences. *American Economic Review* 94 (4): 1014–1033.

Thaler, Richard H. 1980. Toward a Positive Theory of Consumer Choice. *Journal of Economic Behavior and Organization* 1 (1): 39–60.

Tversky, Amos, and Daniel Kahneman. 1991. Loss Aversion in Riskless Choice: A Reference-Dependent Model. *Quarterly Journal of Economics* 106 (4): 1039–1061.

Elias L. Khalil

TÂTONNEMENT

Tâtonnement, a concept introduced by French economist Léon Walras (1834–1910), is a trial-and-error process by which equilibrium prices and stability are reached in competitive markets. Walras found that "the markets which are best organized from the competitive standpoint are those in which purchases and sales are made by auction" (Walras 1954, pp. 83–84).

In an auction market, the *tâtonnement* process starts when the price is fixed (called out), and then demand and supply states are revealed. One possibility is that demand and supply conditions are balanced, establishing normal prices. The most likely state is disequilibrium, where the market will show excess supply or demand, causing deviation of the actual from the natural price. If equilibrium prices are not obtained, then *tâtonnement* requires the auctioneer to increase or lower prices, depending on the demand or supply conditions. In this groping process, the market mechanism would make the actual price gravitate to its natural level, establishing equilibrium. As long as equilibrium is not achieved, no contracts for selling or buying will be executed. The modern literature has conferred the name *nontâtonnement* on the situation where trading does take place at false prices. An unsolved problem with the *tâtonnement* process is whether to make it compatible with the solutions of equation systems by counting equations and unknowns as Walras did, or through more complex general equilibrium solutions such as fixed-point methods.

Walras's analysis of the *tâtonnement* process was challenging because both equilibrium levels and stability conditions were required. Walras compared the stability analysis to a pendulum-like mechanism in which "the center of gravity lies directly beneath the point of suspension, so that if this center of gravity were displaced from the vertical line beneath the point of suspension, it would automatically return" (1954, pp. 109–112). That concept of stability remains in vogue. John Hicks's (1904–1989) research (1946) was an early attempt to make Walras's arguments transparent to economists. With two commodities, X and Y, Hicks explained that equilibrium required that the supply of X be equal to the demand for

X. Stability requires that a fall in the relative price of *X* to *Y*, which will make *X* cheaper, will increase the demand for *X* above its supply. For multiple commodities, Hicks realized that when the relative price of *X* to a standard commodity changed, we need to know what will happen to the prices of the other commodities, which can be assumed fixed, or assumed to move to their equilibrium levels. The classical economist Alfred Marshall (1842–1924) simplified this with his introduction of ceteris paribus assumption, which held changes in all other prices constant.

Paul Samuelson improved the process by making Hicks's contribution more dynamic. For a one-commodity case, Samuelson (1941, p. 102) wrote a price differential equation of the form $\frac{dp}{dt} = H(q_d - q_s)$, where the rate of change in prices, dp, with respect to changes in time, dt, is a proportion, H, to the difference between demand and supply, $q_d - q_s$. This model addresses multiple markets by allowing the demand and supply variables to depend on the prices of say *n* commodities, $p_1, \ldots, p_n$. In the commodities case, the model implies that if we plot excess demand for good 1 against the relative prices, p_1/p_2, we obtain solutions for the prices when the excess demand function crosses the relative price axis. Stable conditions are obtained only when the excess demand cuts the relative price axis from above, implying that the excess demand function is downward. Stability is obtained because if the actual price ratio is higher than the equilibrium price ratio, then excess supply of good 1, and excess demand for good 2, are obtained, and prices will adjust accordingly so that the actual price ratio goes back to equilibrium.

For more than two goods, the Samuelsonian development of the *tâtonnement* process cannot be generalized. While Samuelson improved upon Hicks's model in the dynamic realm, his correspondence principle shows that static and dynamic relations are both useful concepts. Samuelson (1960, p. 368) also developed the Le Chatelier principle to explain adjustment to equilibrium after an initial displacement. Increases in demand will cause the relative price, say, of goods H_n to increase. If the prices of the other goods, H_{n-1}, increase, then it will lower the increase in the price of H_n. The increased price of H_n will be smaller if the price of H_{n-2} is also unchanged. The metaphor for this process is that squeezing a balloon will decrease its volume more with constant temperature than if we let its temperature warm up during the squeezing.

As Franklin Fisher (2006, pp. 143–144) pointed out, this treatment represents the *tâtonnement* process when only prices adjust and trade does not take place at disequilibrium prices. The solution is, therefore, unsatisfactory, because many prices are fixed and auctioneers are not present in all markets.

SEE ALSO *Equilibrium in Economics; General Equilibrium; Market Clearing; Prices; Stability in Economics; Walras' Law; Walras, Léon*

BIBLIOGRAPHY

Cournot, A. A. 1897. *Researches into the Mathematical Principles of the Theory of Wealth*. Trans. Nathaniel T. Bacon. New York: Macmillan.

Fisher, Franklin, M. 2006. Paul Samuelson and the Stability of General Equilibrium. In *Samuelsonian Economics and the Twenty-First Century*, ed. Michael Szenberg, Lall Ramrattan, and Aron A. Gottesman, 142–145. New York: Oxford University Press.

Hicks, John R. 1946. *Value and Capital: An Inquiry into Some Fundamental Principles of Economic Theory*. 2nd ed. Oxford: Clarendon.

Newman, Peter. 1965. *The Theory of Exchange*. Englewood Cliffs, NJ: Prentice Hall.

Samuelson, Paul A. 1941. The Stability of Equilibrium: Comparative Statics and Dynamics. *Econometrica* 9 (2): 97–120.

Samuelson, Paul A. 1960. An Extension of the Le Chatelier Principle. *Econometrica* 28 (2): 368–379.

Samuelson, Paul A. 1966. *The Collected Scientific Papers of Paul A. Samuelson*, ed. Joseph E. Stiglitz. Cambridge, MA: MIT Press.

Walras, Léon. 1954. *Elements of Pure Economics or the Theory of Social Wealth*. Trans. William Jaffé. Homewood, IL: Irwin.

Lall Ramrattan
Michael Szenberg

TAWNEY, R. H.
1880–1962

Richard Henry Tawney, teacher, social scientist, journalist, and political moralist, was born in Calcutta in 1880. Of upper-middle-class origin, Tawney was sent to Rugby School in England, where he developed something of the moral thoughtfulness for which Thomas Arnold (1795–1842) had made that institution famous. After Oxford University, where he attached himself to reform-minded circles, and social work at Toynbee Hall, a settlement house in London, Tawney found his vocation in education. He spent most of his career at the London School of Economics and Political Science and was also pedagogically and administratively active in the adult education movement. An English patriot, Tawney served in both world wars. His childless marriage to Annette Jeanie Beveridge, sister of a prominent Liberal politician, lasted from 1909 until her death in 1958. Tawney himself died in London in 1962.

Tawney's discipline was history, specifically economic history, a field that he helped to establish. He produced several scholarly monographs, including *Religion and the Rise of Capitalism* (1926), a study of religious social thought of the sixteenth and seventeenth centuries and its relationship with emergent economic forces. In a celebrated footnote, Tawney questioned Max Weber's (1864–1920) thesis of a simple causal relationship between a homogeneous Protestantism and the growth of entrepreneurialism, suggesting instead that the capitalist spirit, as well as being of older vintage, had additional, nonreligious influences. While its arguments and strongly didactic style were themselves controversial, *Religion and the Rise of Capitalism* became a minor classic that has been translated into at least seven languages.

However, it was in a nonprofessional capacity that Tawney made his greatest mark. He became an important theoretician of the democratic Left, guiding the philosophy and tactics of the Labour Party through books, articles, policy documents, and editorials (principally for the *Manchester Guardian*) as well as by an irreproachable personal example. Two works were outstanding in this regard. *The Acquisitive Society* (1920) challenged the individualism and greed that Tawney associated with the system of industrial capitalism, proposing in their place a society based on principles of cooperation, professionalism, and service. His most important political volume was *Equality*, first published in 1931 and updated in 1938 and 1952. Here Tawney indicted the maldistribution of resources in Britain and set out a strategy for equality comprising progressive taxation, extensive public ownership, and a generous welfare state.

Another key text is Tawney's private diary of 1912 to 1914. Unencumbered by the elaborate, irony-laden erudition of his published writings, Tawney's *Commonplace Book* (published posthumously in 1972) contains in brilliant aphoristic outline the germs of his mature social philosophy. In particular, it reveals that Tawney's political idealism was securely anchored in profound Christian convictions. The final entry, for example, identifies an urgent imperative "to make society, when it is at peace, a field in which mere power, ruthlessness, [and] ambition, can*not* override the merciful and gentle" (p. 83).

Elements of Tawney's approach have been overtaken by such postindustrial trends as the decline of manufacturing (at least in the developed world) and the coming of a global information society. Nevertheless, the essence of his position—an ethically grounded, scrupulously honest argument for a free, fair, and fraternal society—has remained persuasive to many sections of the moderate Left in Britain, the United States, and elsewhere. The passing of time thus confirms Tawney's central place in the canon of democratic socialism.

SEE ALSO *Socialism*

BIBLIOGRAPHY

Dennis, Norman, and A. H. Halsey. 1988. *English Ethical Socialism: Thomas More to R. H. Tawney*. Oxford: Clarendon.

Duff, Alistair S. 2004. The Sickness of an Information Society: R. H. Tawney and the Post-Industrial Condition. *Information, Communication and Society* 7 (3): 403–422.

Ormrod, David, ed. 1990. *Fellowship, Freedom and Equality: Lectures in Memory of R. H. Tawney*. London: Christian Socialist Movement.

Tawney, R. H. 1972. *R. H. Tawney's Commonplace Book*, eds. J. M. Winter and D. M. Joslin. Cambridge, U.K.: Cambridge University Press.

Terrill, Ross. 1973. *R. H. Tawney and His Times: Socialism as Fellowship*. Cambridge, MA: Harvard University Press.

Wright, Anthony. 1987. *R. H. Tawney*. Manchester, U.K.: Manchester University Press.

Alistair S. Duff

TAX BURDEN

SEE *Tax Incidence.*

TAX CREDITS

A tax credit is an amount that reduces payable taxes during a specific time period. Tax credits occur because a particular expense is tax deductible or because of a public policy that provides a credit up to a fixed amount. In order to calculate a tax credit, we use the following equation: Tax Credit = (Tax deductible expense) * (Tax rate).

In some countries interest expenses, depreciation, labor costs, and raw materials costs are tax deductible from a company's taxable profits. Hence equivalent tax credits are estimated based on these expenses. Tax credits have a meaning only when a company (or an individual person) has enough profits to be taxed. Specifically in Australia, Canada, the United Kingdom, and the United States, a tax credit is considered a disbursement (payment) toward taxes owed by a company or individual. There is a similar item in the French tax system, though under another name.

A tax credit differs from a tax deduction, tax allowance, or tax relief because the latter three reduce taxable income, whereas the tax credit decreases tax liability unit for unit—in other words, it reduces the tax itself. Tax credits can be divided into two categories. The first consists of refundable (or non-wastable) tax credits, which can decrease owed taxes below zero and which thus lead to a net payment to the taxpayer, greater than their payments into the tax system. Hence they function like a moderate form of negative income tax. Examples of this type of tax credit in the U.S. tax system are the Earned Income Tax Credit and the Child Tax Credit. In the United Kingdom tax system examples include the Working Tax Credit and the Child Tax Credit. The second category consists of nonrefundable (or wastable) tax credits, which cannot reduce owed taxes below zero and thus do not allow the taxpayer to get a refund in excess of his or her payments into the tax system. Examples of this type of tax credit in the U.S. system include two educational tax credits, the Hope Tax Credit and the Lifetime Learning Tax Credit. Examples in the United Kingdom tax system include the former Children's Tax Credit and the Declared Gifts Tax Credit, given to registered charities under the Giftaid scheme.

TAX CREDITS IN THE UNITED STATES

Principal tax credits in the U.S. tax system include the Child Tax Credit, the Federal Tax Credit for Energy Efficiency, the Earned Income Tax Credit, and the Low Income Housing Tax Credit. The Child Tax Credit (CTC) is based on the number of children in a family. In 2005 an individual could claim $1,000 of CTC per child. According to Internal Revenue Service (IRS) regulations, a child must be claimed as a dependent. To be eligible to be declared as a dependent, a child must have a Social Security number, be related to the taxpayer, be less than seventeen years old, and be a citizen or resident of the United States. The CTC is not available to wealthy people or to those who do not pay any taxes. For a couple (filing a joint return) the maximum adjusted gross income (i.e., combined income) is $110,000. For a single parent it is $75,000, and for a married couple filing separately it is $55,000 each. Finally, it should be noted that if a couple or single parent gets the CTC, this does not prohibit them from getting any other tax credit they qualify for.

The Earned Income Tax Credit (EITC) is a refundable tax credit that decreases or eliminates the taxes paid by low-income people. In some respects it can be considered a wage subsidy for low-income workers. The EITC was established in 1975 and expanded in 1986, 1990, 1993, and 2001. In 2006 this tax credit was one of the major antipoverty tools the U.S. government had and was widely supported.

The EITC has a three-stage structure: the phase-in stage, in which the tax credit increases as earnings increase; the plateau stage, in which the maximum range

has been reached and the amount of credit is not affected by an increase in earnings; and the phase-out stage, in which the tax credit decreases as earnings increase. For instance, in 2006 the EITC for a four-member family was equal to 40 percent of the first $10,750 earned, the maximum credit was $4,400, the EITC decreased as earnings passed $15,000, and it became zero when earnings went beyond $35,000.

In 2004 the EITC cost the federal government approximately $36 billion. According to the General Accounting Office and the IRS, 15 to 20 percent of Americans who qualify for the EITC do not claim it. For this reason several nonprofit organizations, with the help of the government, have initiated special programs all over the United States to make the EITC known to taxpayers and to help taxpayers claim it. In addition to the federal EITC, eleven states and some other areas offer local EITC.

Overall the EITC has increased the percentage of people who join the labor force. There is some evidence that this rise in worker supply has caused a decrease in wages (on a per hour basis) for those that qualify for this particular tax credit.

The Federal Tax Credit for Energy Efficiency, which was established by the Energy Policy Act of 2005, applies to people and companies in four categories:

> Consumers who make home improvements to save energy, such as insulation, window replacement, or the instillation of heating or cooling systems; or who buy energy-efficient cars, such as hybrid gasoline-electric, diesel, battery-electric, alternative fuel, and fuel cell vehicles, or who install solar water heating, photovoltaic, fuel cell, and microturbine systems.

> Homebuilders who, in order to construct energy-efficient homes, pay for building-envelope improvements and energy-efficient heating and cooling systems.

> Appliance manufacturers who manufacture energy-efficient washing machines, dishwashers, and refrigerators. This in turn can lead to a price reduction for these types of appliances.

> Owners or designers of commercial buildings in which lighting, heating, and cooling systems meet efficiency standards. Credits in this category go up to $1.80 per square foot.

Another category of tax credit is the Low Income Housing Tax Credit (LIHTC), which was established by the Tax Reform Act of 1986 (TRA86). This tax credit aims to give low-income Americans incentives to own a house rather than rent. TRA86 offered incentives to investors to buy homes by changing the treatment of imputed rent, local property taxes, and mortgage interest payments. These changes, however, negatively affected low-income people, who usually lived in rented homes. Hence the LIHTC was established along with the TRA86 to mitigate these negative consequences. The LIHTC directly subsidizes the development costs of low-income residential units, excluding land acquisition costs. Tax credits are claimed as an annuity for a period of ten years (the credit period) and not as a lump sum as with other tax credits. Since 2002, 40 to 50 percent of new construction of family residences has been developed under the LIHTC program at a cost to the federal government of approximately $3 billion per year.

TAX CREDITS IN CANADA

In the Canadian tax system, one important tax credit is the Canada Child Tax Benefit (CCTB). The CCTB is a monthly tax-free payment available to qualifying Canadian families made in order to help defray some of the costs of raising children. The CCTB can incorporate the National Child Benefit and the Child Disability Benefit. The former is a monthly payment to low-income families with children. The latter is a monthly payment to families with children that have severe and prolonged mental or physical disabilities.

Another tax credit that has existed since 1980 is the Scientific Research and Experimental Development Tax Incentive Program (SR&ED or SRED). This tax credit applies to businesses in Canada and is intended to support and encourage applied research and experimental development leading to new or improved goods and services. The program costs the Canadian government approximately $1.8 billion per year. The Ministry of Finance is responsible for legislation of the SR&ED tax credit, and the Canada Revenue Agency is responsible for its administration.

Even if SR&ED expenses have already been deducted from revenue, businesses may qualify for Investment Tax Credit (ITC) if those expenses are associated with experimental development, applied research, basic research, or research support work. Relevant expenditures include wages, materials, equipment overhead, and SR&ED contracts arising from the aforementioned activities. The amount of the ITC depends on how much of a business's SR&ED expenses were incurred in Canada and on the business's legal status. Furthermore each region in Canada has the right to provide provincial or territorial tax credits to qualifying businesses that pursue SR&ED activities in those regions.

TAX CREDITS IN THE UNITED KINGDOM

In the United Kingdom tax system significant tax credits include the Working Tax Credit and the Child Tax Credit.

To qualify for these credits, a person must be older than sixteen and live in the United Kingdom—either as a British citizen or as a European Economic Area citizen working in the country—or receive a United Kingdom state pension while living abroad. The Child Tax Credit (CTC) is given to people who are responsible for at least one child or qualifying young person. It is paid directly to the person who is responsible for child care. A single parent can claim individually, but a couple must make a joint claim. The Working Tax Credit (WTC) is given to people who are employed or self-employed (either alone or in a partnership) if they meet the following criteria:

> they usually work sixteen or more hours per week;
>
> they are paid for that work;
>
> they expect to work for at least four weeks;
>
> they are older than sixteen and responsible for at least one child, or are sixteen years old and disabled, or are above twenty-five and work at least thirty hours per week on average.

If both people in a couple are working sixteen hours or more per week, only one can receive the WTC. There is, however, also a child care component of the WTC, which is always paid to the person responsible for raising a child, in addition to CTC payments. Before 2003, when the WTC and the CTC were established, the Working Families Tax Credit, created in 1999, combined the functions of the WTC and CTC. Before that, from 1986 to 1999, United Kingdom taxpayers received the Family Credit.

The amount of tax credits received depends on annual income. For instance, a family with income below £58,000 can claim the CTC in addition to child benefits. If a child or children are disabled, higher rates are paid. If the income is below £50,000, the CTC is £545 per year for the family (£1,090 if there is a baby under twelve months old). For low-income families, there is an additional £1,765 per child per year. The CTC can be claimed even by families that are rich. Both the WTC and the CTC are made up of components (elements) according to individual cases that form the basic amount of tax credit receivable. For instance, the basic element is £1,665 for the year 2006–2007, then other elements follow, such as the couple and lone parent element £1,640, the thirty hour element £680, the disabled worker element £2,225, and so on. For the CTC, the family element is £545, and then follow the family element, baby addition £545, the child element £1,765, the disabled child element £2,350, and so forth that are applied according to individual cases. Both these tax credits are paid based on the gross household income earned during the previous tax year.

WTC and CTC tax credits were not well administered when they were first established, and many cases of overpayment were observed. Nevertheless, tax credits are considered an important means of encouraging low-income employees, as they help avoid the disincentive to work that occurs when wages amount to little more than unemployment benefits.

SEE ALSO *Earned Income Tax Credit; Research and Development; Taxes*

BIBLIOGRAPHY

Canada Revenue Agency. Child and Family Benefits. http://www.cra-arc.gc.ca/benefits/menu-e.html.

Canada Revenue Agency. SR&ED Program: About Our Program. http://www.cra-arc.gc.ca/taxcredit/sred/aboutus-e.html.

Congressional Budget Office, U.S. Congress. 2007. Letter to Charles E. Grassley, Chairman of the U.S. Senate's Committee on Finance. http://www.cbo.gov/ftpdocs/77xx/doc7721/01-09-MinimumWageEITC.pdf.

Congressional Research Service Reports. The Earned Income Tax Credit (EITC): Percentage of Total Tax Returns and Credit Amount by State. http://www.digital.library.unt.edu/govdocs/crs/data/2005/meta-crs-7962.tkl.

Department of the Treasury, Internal Revenue Service. Earned Income Credit (EIC). http://www.irs.gov/pub/irs-pdf/p596.pdf.

Energy Star. Federal Tax Credits for Energy Efficiency. http://www.energystar.gov/index.cfm?c=products.pr_tax_credits.

Government of Canada. 2005. Taxation Info-Guide. http://www.cbsc.org/servlet/ContentServer?cid=1089652659441&pagename=CBSC_FE%2Fdisplay&lang=en&c=GuideInfoGuide.

Government of Newfoundland and Labrador, Canada. Scientific Research and Experimental Development Tax Credit. http://www.fin.gov.nl.ca/fin/scientific.html.

Greenstein, Robert, and Isaac Shapiro. 1998. New Research Findings on the Effects of the Earned Income Tax Credit. Center on Budget and Policy Priorities Report. http://www.cbpp.org/311eitc.htm.

HM Revenue and Customs. Rates and Allowances: Tax Credits/Child Benefit. http://www.hmrc.gov.uk/rates/taxcredits.htm.

HM Revenue and Customs. What Are Tax Credits? http://www.taxcredits.inlandrevenue.gov.uk/qualify/WhatAreTaxCredits.aspx.

HM Treasury. 2005. 2005 Pre-Budget Report. http://www.hm-treasury.gov.uk/pre_budget_report/prebud_pbr05/press_notices/prebud_pbr05_press02.cfm.

Motley Fool. The Child Tax Credit. http://www.fool.com/personal-finance/taxes/2003/02/21/the-child-tax-credit.aspx.

Katerina Lyroudi

TAX EVASION AND TAX AVOIDANCE

Tax evasion is the use of unlawful means by individuals and firms to reduce their taxes. It refers to taxpayers' intentional actions that misrepresent or conceal the true state of their financial affairs to tax administrators. An example of tax evasion is taxpayers' deliberate understatement of their income. Tax fraud is a kind of evasion that involves the falsification of records. In most countries tax evasion is a crime punishable by fines or imprisonment.

Tax avoidance is the use of lawful means by individuals and firms to decrease their taxes. In some countries a distinction is made between tax planning and avoidance. Acceptable tax planning satisfies both the wording and the intent of the tax law. Tax avoidance (abusive tax planning) is consistent with the letter but not the spirit of the law. It usually involves the exploitation of loopholes in tax legislation to the advantage of taxpayers. An example of tax avoidance is transforming highly taxed income into preferentially taxed capital gains. The boundary between tax planning and avoidance is sometimes fuzzy, and so is that between tax avoidance and evasion.

Under the self-interest and rationality assumptions, taxpayers would engage in evasion or avoidance so long as their incremental benefits from such activities exceed their incremental costs. However, many individuals and firms appear to be inherently honest and comply more fully than is anticipated by this approach. This suggests that taxpayers' observed compliance levels depend not only on economic incentives but also on their sense of moral and social obligations. The determinants of tax evasion and avoidance broadly include:

> taxpayers' sense of community association and perception of the tax system's fairness;
>
> the tax rate (higher rates may induce evasion and avoidance, while the difference between personal and corporate rates encourages avoidance);
>
> opportunities to evade or avoid taxes (tax withholding and third-party reporting reduce evasion, while access to skilled tax practitioners increases avoidance);
>
> tax practitioners' approach to reporting decisions;
>
> taxpayers' compliance costs;
>
> tax administrators' effectiveness (including detection, penalty, and enforcement).

In developing countries, entry into the formal economy may be blocked by legal, regulatory, and bureaucratic barriers. This blockage gives rise to tax evasion and avoidance.

The extent of tax evasion and avoidance can be approximated by the tax gap, which is the difference between the tax that is meant to be paid and that which is paid. The quantification of the tax gap, especially tax avoidance by businesses, is beset with both conceptual and empirical difficulties. Numerical estimates nevertheless suggest that tax evasion and avoidance are serious in industrialized countries. In the United States the federal tax gap (which includes tax evasion, unintentional errors, nonfiling, and tax underpayment) in 2005 was estimated by the U.S. Treasury to be 14 percent of the total federal tax revenue or $345 billion, most of which is attributable to underreporting of individual incomes (U.S. Treasury 2006). Studies of the black market economy suggest that, generally speaking, countries in the Organisation for Economic Co-operation and Development (OECD) face even higher relative tax gaps than the United States. Although there are no reliable estimates of tax gaps in industrializing countries, it seems plausible to argue that, compared with developed economies, developing nations suffer higher relative tax gaps because of their poorer tax administration and larger informal sectors.

SEE ALSO *Crime and Criminology; Offshore Banking; Taxes*

BIBLIOGRAPHY

Schneider, F. 2006. Shadow Economies of 145 Countries All over the World: What Do We Really Know? http://www.econ.jku.at/Schneider/ShadEconomyWorld145_2006.pdf.

U.S. Department of the Treasury. 2006. A Comprehensive Strategy for Reducing the Tax Gap. http://www.ustreas.gov/press/releases/reports/otptaxgapstrategy%20final.pdf.

Woellner, Robin H., Stephen Barkoczy, Shirley Murphy, and Chris Evans. 2006. *Australian Taxation Law*. Sydney: CCH.

Binh Tran-Nam

TAX HAVENS
SEE *Offshore Banking.*

TAX INCIDENCE

The objective of tax incidence analysis is to determine who ultimately bears the burden of a tax. It is therefore an important concept for evaluating the equity of the tax system.

Statutory incidence assigns the burden of paying a tax to either an individual or a business, depending on the tax. However, the burden of the tax may be shifted because individuals and firms adjust their behavior when taxes are introduced or changed. As a result, economic incidence (our subject here) may differ from statutory ("legal") incidence. A simple example is an excise tax on gasoline. As shown in Figure 1, before a tax is imposed, the equilibrium supply (S) and demand (D) is achieved at price P_0 and quantity consumed of Q_0. If a $1 per gallon tax is imposed, the statutory incidence is borne by the consumer when he or she pays "at the pump." However, the consumer will not pay the full amount of the tax, because the supplier will now receive a lower after-tax price per gallon. In effect, suppliers are faced with a new demand curve, D', representing the price they will receive net of tax. This is denoted as the new demand curve, D', in Figure 1. This demand curve is shifted down from the original demand curve, D, by $1 per unit. Per gallon of gas, the consumers now pay P_g (the gross price), producers receive P_n (the net price), and government receives $P_g - P_n$, or the amount of the tax (T). In the case demonstrated in Figure 1, the producer receives a lower price per unit than before the tax is imposed, and the consumer pays a higher price than in the no-tax case. Therefore, part of the tax is paid by consumers in the form of a high pump price, and part is paid by the producer in the form of a lower after-tax price received.

The economic incidence of a tax is largely determined by the elasticities of supply and demand, that is, by

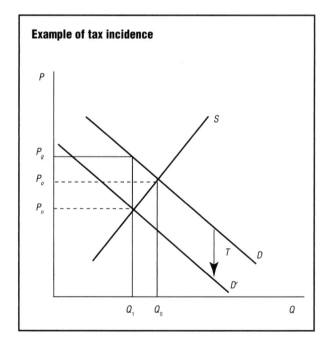

Example of tax incidence

Figure 1

the change in the quantity consumed or produced when the price of that good changes because of the imposition of the tax. When the price elasticity of supply is very small, the supply curve becomes more vertical and the supplier tends to bear a larger portion of the burden of the tax. When demand is very price inelastic, the consumer tends to bear a larger share of the burden of the tax (because there are few substitutes for the taxed good). This type of analysis can also be done for taxes on factors—that is, for taxes levied directly on labor and capital, such as a corporate profits tax or a payroll tax.

The analysis of tax incidence becomes more complicated when we consider the impact of a tax in one market on the supply and demand for goods in other markets. Arnold Harberger (1962), a pioneer of the study of general equilibrium tax incidence, demonstrated the theory that taxes levied in one market can be borne by productive factors in another market. Harberger's model evaluated the impact of a corporate income tax as a tax on capital in one sector of the economy (a "partial factor tax"). By using a model in which the demand and supply for output adjusted to a new equilibrium after a tax was imposed, the impact of a corporate income tax on the price of capital, labor, and output could be analyzed. The results show that, depending on the elasticities of demand and supply and the ability of producers to substitute labor for capital in the production process, the burden of a corporate income tax could be fully or partially borne by labor or capital, or shifted forward in terms of higher output prices. Harberger's model has been used since the 1960s to estimate the burden of taxes, and it is also a model for analyzing the excess burden or "welfare loss" of taxes.

Even more complicated, intertemporal models that consider the incidence of taxes over a lifetime have been developed using sophisticated models of the economy. John Shoven and John Whalley (1984) were among the first economists to use computer models to analyze the incidence of a system of taxes. These types of models are now regularly used as a means to incorporate many markets into the tax incidence analysis.

Joseph Pechman and Benjamin Okner (1974) produced one of the first comprehensive incidence analyses of the U.S. tax system, using incidence assumptions based on general equilibrium results. They compared the distribution of income before and after taxes (imposing various assumptions about the economic incidence of the tax) and showed that at that time, the tax system had little impact on the after-tax distribution of income. The Congressional Budget Office produces regular analyses of the distribution of the burden of U.S. federal taxes. Their 2006 analysis shows that when all federal taxes are considered, the tax system is somewhat progressive—that is, as incomes increase, so too does the percentage of income paid in tax.

BIBLIOGRAPHY

Congressional Budget Office. 2006. Historical Effective Federal Tax Rates: 1979–2004. Washington, DC: Author. http://www.cbo.gov/ftpdoc.cfm?index=7000&type=1.

Harberger, Arnold C. 1962. The Incidence of the Corporate Income Tax. *Journal of Political Economy* 70 (June): 215–240.

Pechman, Joseph A., and Benjamin A. Okner. 1974. *Who Bears the Tax Burden?* Washington, DC: The Brookings Institution.

Shoven, John B., and John Whalley. 1984. Applied General Equilibrium Models of Taxation and International Trade: An Introduction and Survey. *Journal of Economic Literature* 22 (September): 1007–1051.

Sally Wallace

TAX RELIEF

The term *tax relief* is widely used to refer to tax cuts, tax rebates, tax subsidies, tax breaks, and tax write-offs that reduce the amount of tax due or otherwise provide concessions to taxpayers. Usually, tax relief is targeted toward income and ownership taxes, consumption taxes, commodity taxes, and taxes on business establishments in apparent need of such financial makeups.

Tax relief is as old as modern-day government and is primarily born out of a government's genuine concern to bridge the wide gap between low-income and high-income earners by exempting those earning below the national minimum income from paying tax. Tax relief is also often meant to protect local infant industries by giving them tax holidays so they can better compete with foreign companies. In addition, tax relief can be informed by the need to redirect the economy toward a path of balanced growth and development. In this light, tax relief can be a useful tool in the hands of economic planners who wish to effect necessary adjustments in development parameters so as to achieve projected development objectives.

Tax relief is premised on the belief that it will be used for policing the economy and for bridging the gap between local industry and foreign industry. In addition, tax relief is seen as having the effect of stabilizing an economy, since a rise in the tax rate is likely to encourage workers to work less, knowing full well that they will be taxed. Tax relief may also stimulate the economy by raising the aggregate level of savings and consequently investment.

Empirical evidence shows that tax relief is often granted to individuals and corporate organizations who are victims of natural disasters. Tax relief may also be granted to citizens of states involved in bilateral or multilateral trade agreements as concessions in response to their development needs. For example, third world countries such as Gambia and Nigeria have been granted tariff concessions from GATT (General Agreement on Tariffs and Trade).

Tax-break programs may also help reduce the tax obligations of homeowners. In fact, some countries may offer tax relief to individuals who rent the property in which they reside and also to individuals earning a certain level of income. The Republic of Ireland, for example, offers such concessions to renters.

In some cases, tax relief may increase national income because it may encourage more work, saving, investment, risk taking, and entrepreneurship. If taxes are excessively or inappropriately levied, then a tax reduction may motivate people to be more productive and create wealth. Moreover, when people earn more income, they are able to spend more and save more.

Tax relief has been widely criticized for being politically popular despite a lack of clear economic benefits from such policies. After all, what is the rationale for granting tax relief that in the long run will be withdrawn? Tax relief is also criticized for having adverse effects on the economy in the long run. In technical terms, the government faces an intertemporal budget constraint, which means that when taxes are cut, other offsetting adjustments are required to make up for the cut. If the government decides to raise taxes later, effectively making the tax cuts temporary, the initial tax relief could lead to lower economic output over time. Tax cuts put money in people's pockets, but they do not pay for themselves. The government eventually has to pay its bills, and taxes are the primary source of government revenue.

SEE ALSO *Earned Income Tax Credit; Tax Credits; Tax Evasion and Tax Avoidance; Tax Incidence; Tax Revolts; Taxes*

BIBLIOGRAPHY

Anderton, Alain. 2000. *Economics*. 3rd ed. Ormskirk, U.K.: Causeway.

Anyaele, Johnson Ugorji. 2003. *Comprehensive Economics*. New ed. Lagos, Nigeria: Johnson.

Boyes, William, and Michael Melvin. 2005. *Fundamentals of Economics*. 3rd ed. Boston: Houghton Mifflin.

Culyer, A. J. 1985. *Economics*. New York: Blackwell.

Forster, Bruce, and Geoffrey Whitehead. 2003. *Economics*. London: ICM.

Sloman, John. 2006. *Economics*. 6th ed. London: Pearson.

Whitehead, Geoffrey. 1994. *Business Studies*. 2nd ed. London: Butterworth Heinemann.

Cajetan Nnaocha

TAX REVOLTS

Tax revolts are interesting because taxation—a claim made upon the property of individuals—is one of the two distinguishing features of government, the other being its monopoly on the legitimate use of force. Thus, when citizens rebel against taxes, their actions may represent something far more fundamental than when they reject other kinds of public policies. Tax revolts are also interesting because they seem to be ubiquitous. Peasant revolts against land taxes have been documented from medieval Japan (White 1995) to contemporary Africa (Kelsall 2000) and China (Bernstein and Lu 2003). In Europe, voters have rebelled against both British prime minister Margaret Thatcher's poll tax proposal that was regressive in incidence by bearing relatively more heavily on the poor than the wealthy (Burns 1992) and the progressive tax program of the Danish welfare state (Kirschelt 1997). And in the United States, the tax rebellion label has been applied to both the revolution of 1776, as illustrated by the Boston Tea Party, and the wave of tax reduction and tax caps adopted following California's passage of Proposition 13 in 1978 (Sears and Citrin 1985).

Given the importance and ubiquity of tax revolts, it is not surprising that scholars have spent considerable time trying to explain why they occur. The very ubiquity of "tax revolts" suggests that not all of the events so labeled are the same kind of phenomenon. Therefore, no single explanation is likely to explain all tax revolts. Indeed, there seem to be several different kinds that vary in terms of the breadth of issues they address. At the narrowest level are voter rejections of specific referendum proposals to raise taxes or to adopt bond issues. In such cases, the issue is narrowly defined and the forces determining voters' decisions are typically the same kinds of socioeconomic, attitudinal, and partisan variables found to be important in day-to-day politics (Cataldo and Holm 1983; Listhaug and Miller 1985). Thus, we do not need a special kind of explanation for some kinds of tax revolts. Indeed, it is not clear that such events constitute "revolts," since voters are making their preferences heard on specific policies through routine mechanisms of political choice.

The tax revolt label, in contrast, usually refers to something more unusual or unexpected. In some cases, as in voter agitation over property-tax-assessing practices in California in the early 1970s, the focus of the tax revolt might still be narrowly defined as a tax issue, even if it was a somewhat unusual sort (Paul 1975). But in other cases, tax revolts may represent a more general challenge to the government in power, as seems to have been the case in Britain's rejection of Thatcher's regressive poll tax and the Danish People's Party rejection of high levels of progressive taxation to support the welfare state. Even further, tax revolts may represent a rejection of the political regime itself, as some argue is the case with rural protests in China. In these broader episodes of tax revolution, taxes are merely the specific focus of a larger rebellion. Given this complexity, determining what citizens are saying when they revolt against taxes is easy neither for the politicians who must respond to rebellions or for scholars trying to explain them.

Perhaps the broadest and most unusual type of tax revolt occurred in the United States during the late 1970s and early 1980s, starting with the passage of California's Proposition 13. This event was certainly unusual. Californians had rejected by large margins two similar proposals in the previous decade. And nationally, while no tax revolt referendum had passed prior to Proposition 13, none failed in the ensuing five years, and none were successful thereafter. Within a short period, more than one hundred scholarly papers appeared purporting to interpret what voters were saying to politicians. These explanations covered all of those noted earlier for other tax revolts, from a rejection of big government (Rabushka and Ryan 1982) to symbolic racism (Sears and Citrin 1985). But none proved capable of explaining the boom and bust cycle of the great American tax revolt (Lowery and Sigelman 1981). Or rather, all of these explanations were true to some degree. That is, the U.S. tax revolt was an unusual kind of comprehensive single-issue politics in which grievances of all kinds were linked to a single policy solution—limiting taxes (Lowery 1982). In effect, tax revolution was a magic bullet that would solve a problem, no matter what the problem was. Once the tenuous connection between the many different kinds of grievances motivating voters and the specific tax proposals before them became obvious, support for the movement collapsed.

Irrespective of their origin, the consequences of tax revolts can be significant. Thatcher left office shortly after the failure of her poll tax proposal. In Denmark, the tax revolt movement evolved into the Danish People's Party, which has since taken a lead in promoting anti-immigration policies. In the United States, few tax revolt referendums actually cut taxes. Indeed, only one state followed California's Proposition 13 by sharply cutting property taxes. The other nineteen state referendums passed during the tax revolt period imposed fiscal caps that set limits on the future growth of government. But nearly all state legislatures cut taxes during this period so that for the first time in decades aggregate state tax burdens actually declined for several years. And the results of tax-revolt-induced policies can sometimes be surprising. As yet, the fiscal caps adopted by the states have not seriously impinged on government spending, although they may do so in the future (Cox and Lowery 1990). As for the hundreds of tax cuts adopted by legislatures, their consequences were often surprising. State government budgets were, as expected, highly constrained for several years. But

state taxes were also marginally less complex and more progressive and elastic after the tax revolt than before, something that neither supporters nor opponents of tax cut proposals had anticipated (Lowery 1986).

SEE ALSO *American Revolution; Poll Tax; Protest; Social Movements; Taxation; Taxes; Taxes, Progressive; Taxes, Regressive*

BIBLIOGRAPHY

Bernstein, Thomas P., and Xiaobo Lu. 2003. *Taxation without Representation in Contemporary Rural China.* New York: University of Cambridge Press.

Burns, Danny. 1992. *Poll Tax Rebellion.* Stirling, Scotland: AK Press.

Cox, James, and David Lowery. 1990. The Impact of Tax Revolt Era State Fiscal Caps. *Social Science Quarterly* 71: 492–509.

Kelsall, Tim. 2000. Governance, Local Politics and Districtization in Tanzania: The 1998 Arumeru Tax Revolt. *African Affairs* 99: 533–551.

Kitschelt, Herbert. 1997. *The Radical Right in Western Europe: A Comparative Analysis.* Ann Arbor: University of Michigan Press.

Listhaug, Ola, and Arthur H. Miller. 1985. Public Support for Tax Evasion: Self-Interest or Symbolic Politics? *European Journal of Political Research* 13: 265–282.

Lowery, David. 1982. Interpreting the Tax Revolt: A Review of the Literature and an Alternative Explanation. *State and Local Government Review* 14: 110–116.

Lowery, David. 1986. After the Tax Revolt: Some Positive, If Unintended, Consequences. *Social Science Quarterly* 67 (4): 736–750.

Lowery, David, and Lee Sigelman. 1981. Understanding the Tax Revolt: Eight Explanations. *American Political Science Review* 75 (4): 963–974.

Paul, Diane. 1975. *The Politics of the Property Tax.* Lexington, MA: Lexington Books.

Rabushka, Alvin, and Pauline Ryan. 1982. *The Tax Revolt.* Stanford, CA: Hoover Institute.

Sears, David, and Jack Citrin. 1985. *Tax Revolt: Something for Nothing in California.* Cambridge, MA: Harvard University Press.

White, James. 1995. *Ikki: Social Conflict and Political Protest in Early Modern Japan.* Ithaca, NY: Cornell University Press.

David Lowery

TAXATION

Taxation is as old as recorded history. The earliest forms of writing, pictographs from the ancient Near East, are records of taxpayer accounts, paid and owed, to the king. *Taxation* is the taking of economic resources by a political entity from an individual or collective who is subject to its authority. It is a *taking* in that taxation is not a freely voluntary exchange, because resources are given under threat of coercion. *Economic resources* can take the form of money, goods, or service. *Political entity* refers to an individual (chief, prince), group (tribe, caste), or institution (state, government) that makes claims on and decisions for those from whom economic resources are sought. Their *authority* to claim economic resources is derived by consent, law, or force. The subjects of taxation are usually territorial based, including social collectives (tribes, villages, colonies, castes), economic collectives (guilds, mercantile companies, incorporated businesses), and individuals and households.

There are two general forms of taxation, direct and indirect. Direct taxation refers to tax claims made on fixed entities, such as a person, a business, land, and property. Indirect taxation refers to tax claims made on economic transactions, such as the sale of goods and services, trade, and commerce. For much of preindustrial history, taxes were direct, such as the poll tax. They were imposed on collectives and paid in kind with service (labor) or goods (a percentage of agricultural harvests). With the rise of capitalist cash economies in the modern period, taxation increasingly was directed toward money and financial assets. The modern state has shown a preference and capacity for indirect taxes as well as direct taxes claimed from individual households and business collectives.

Taxation is a type of exchange relationship between a political entity and its claimed subjects. Exchange is what distinguishes taxation from plunder. The political entity is supposed to provide something in exchange for economic resources. In the earliest forms of taxation, political entities claimed tribute in exchange for protection from physical harm, both from the political entity itself and from others in warfare or robbery. As the relationship evolved historically, taxation became more varied in form and routinized in collection; in exchange, political entities provided more public goods, such as dispensation of justice, enforcement of law and property rights, establishment of economic infrastructure and cultural institutions, and provision of social and economic welfare goods. Some taxes are imposed not just to raise revenue but also to promote or discourage social behavior. For example, a reduced tax burden is meant to encourage charitable donations, while higher tax rates are meant to discourage smoking and drinking.

Taxation serves as the arena where power and wealth collide and connive in society. Each society develops its own system of distribution of tax burdens, progressive or regressive, which inevitably penalizes some and benefits others. Quasi-voluntary compliance occurs when political authorities succeed in providing sufficient goods in exchange and maintain a perception of fairness in the tax burden and a threat of coercion against those who do not pay. If these three factors are not in place, the tendency for evasion and noncompliance increases. Also income tax compliance was enhanced when employers were made to share responsibility for payment with employees. Tax burdens are sometimes effectively hidden in the final costs of goods. Resistance to the revenue claims of political authorities in the form of tax revolts provides some of history's most notable political conflicts, including the English civil war, the French Revolution, and the American War of Independence.

SEE ALSO *Poll Tax; Tax Credits; Tax Relief; Tax Revolts; Taxes; Taxes, Progressive; Taxes, Regressive*

BIBLIOGRAPHY

Adams, Charles. 1993. *For Good and Evil: The Impact of Taxes on the Course of Civilization*. London and New York: Madison Books.

Burg, David. 2004. *A World History of Tax Rebellions: An Encyclopedia of Tax Rebels, Revolts, and Riots from Antiquity to the Present*. New York: Routledge.

Webber, Carolyn, and Aaron Wildavsky. 1986. *A History of Taxation and Expenditure in the Western World*. New York: Simon and Schuster.

Gerald Easter

TAX-BASED INCOMES POLICY

SEE *Wage and Price Controls.*

TAXES

Taxation is the principal means by which governments get the resources to pay for activities such as armed forces, a court system, a health care program, and programs aimed at transferring resources to the destitute or the elderly. Taxation is not, however, the only means by which a government gains control of resources; for example, many countries draft people into the military. Among developed countries, taxation accounts for between 25 and 50 percent of national income. Taxation in developing countries generally raises substantially less than this, primarily due to the difficulty the tax authorities encounter in collecting taxes. Although tax receipts in many countries fall well short of covering current expenditures, the resulting deficits do not imply that the expenditures are costless; payment is simply delayed, and future generations bear the costs of the expenditure.

Taxation is as old as government itself. Indeed, the first known written records, made by the Sumerians about 5,000 years ago, are apparently tax records. Before money was widely used, taxes were paid in kind with grain, cattle, labor, and other valuable objects. Compulsory labor is the earliest form of taxation for which records exist; indeed, in the ancient Egyptian language the word *labor* was a synonym for *taxes*.

In Europe before the seventeenth century, most taxes were levied directly on people, depending on their status in society or on the land they owned. About that time, new taxes arose that were associated with the rising tax bases related to commerce, transactions, and urban markets. Some advocated such taxes as a way of introducing equality in taxation, because the privileged classes had managed to obtain virtual immunity from the existing status-based tax system.

Beginning in the nineteenth century, the growing scale and cost of war greatly expanded the revenue needs of many Western countries, and the tax systems expanded to keep up with these needs. The modern income tax began in Great Britain around 1800 to help pay for wars with France. Financing wars was then the major expense of government—from the twelfth to the nineteenth century, between 75 and 90 percent of the English government's expenditure went to financing wars. The income tax was also a response to a concern that a tax system that relied on land as a tax base was failing to reach the growing commercial wealth and income that arose during the Industrial Revolution.

Resistance to taxes was a theme of the American Revolutionary War (1775–1783). In keeping with that spirit, taxes in the United States were relatively low until the twentieth century and are still among the lowest of all developed countries. In 1900 U.S. federal taxes amounted to just 3.1 percent of gross domestic product (GDP), while state and local taxes comprised another 4 to 5 percent. The U.S. income tax was introduced in 1913, after the passage of the Sixteenth Amendment to the Constitution, which set aside the constitutional provision that all direct taxes must be levied across states in proportion to their population.

The role of the U.S. federal government expanded greatly during the first half of the twentieth century, and by 1943 federal taxes increased to 19.7 percent of GDP. World War II (1939–1945) was clearly the critical juncture, although the New Deal years of the 1930s were also important. Many programs, particularly Social Security, were introduced during the 1930s and would require much higher taxes in later years. By 2003 federal tax receipts (including social insurance payroll taxes) amounted to 17 percent of GDP, with state and local taxes adding another 8.8 percent. The total share had been roughly constant since the 1970s, but since 2001 federal taxes as a share of GDP have fallen notably due to a series of tax cuts enacted during the George W. Bush administration.

In modern tax systems, a wide range of activities and circumstances can trigger tax liability—the purchase of a good from a retailer triggers a sales tax, the payment of wages for a business to a worker triggers an income tax, or the passing of wealth from one generation to the next triggers estate and inheritance taxes. Although there are a large variety of taxes, certain kinds predominate. Among developed countries, which raise on average about 37 percent of GDP in taxes, slightly more than one-third of tax revenue comes from income taxes; slightly less than one-third comes from various taxes on consumption, including value-added taxes remitted by all businesses; and about one quarter comes from social insurance taxes. The United States stands out among developed nations for its relatively low taxes and for making much less use of consumption taxes. The United States is also the only member country of the Organisation for Economic Cooperation and Development, a group of thirty developed countries, without a value-added tax.

On average, poorer developing countries collect taxes that amount to a substantially lower percentage of their national income. Of the tax revenue they do collect, a smaller share comes from income taxes and a larger share from both consumption taxes and, especially, taxes on international trade. The reliance of developing countries on trade taxes reflects the relative ease with which goods can be observed and valued as they cross international borders, which is important in countries where administrative resources are scarce. It also reflects the use of import taxes as a deliberate economic strategy to promote domestic industrial development, as well as the prevalence of easily taxed exports of primary products such as oil, food, and industrial crops. This lower reliance on income taxes is largely due to the difficulty of collecting income taxes in countries with large informal sectors; unlike developed countries, only a small proportion of the workforce is employed by well-established, financially sophisticated companies whose existence facilitates collection of taxes on the income of both businesses and employees.

There are two key aspects to all taxes: Who bears the burden, and what is the effect on the economy? Ascertaining who bears the tax burden is not simply a matter of keeping track of who writes the checks to the government. For example, in the United States most of the income tax liability of employees is remitted by employers in the form of withholding, although it is widely believed that it is the employee, not the employer, who bears the burden through lower take-home pay. The filing of an employee's tax return reconciles his or her actual tax liability to what has already been remitted, on the worker's behalf, by the employer.

Taxes can also impose burdens by changing the prices of what people buy, as occurs with cigarette taxes. Taxes can even have an impact on individuals buying untaxed goods. For example, a tax on butter may cause some consumers to switch to margarine, driving up the price of margarine and shifting some of the tax to people who prefer margarine for health reasons.

Some types of taxes, such as the corporation income tax, are legally owed by a business entity, but the tax burden will be shared among the company's shareholders, workers, and customers to the extent that the company is able to "pass on" the tax burden by, for example, paying lower or charging higher prices for their products. Assessing the burden of the corporation income tax is one of the most controversial questions in the study of taxation, made more difficult by the advent of multinational corporations that have operations, customers, and shareholders in many countries.

The question of who *should* bear the burden of taxes is separate from who *does* bear the burden. It is a perennially contentious issue for which there is no right or wrong answer. One aspect is how the burden should be shared across income classes, an issue often referred to as *tax progressivity*. Intuitively appealing but vague principles—for example, taxes should match the benefits one receives from government activities, or taxes should equalize sacrifice—do not offer much practical guidance, and modern economics has for the most part given up on refining such principles to instead focus on the consequences of different levels of progressivity. Moreover, it is not clear why, in assessing the distributional consequences of government, it makes sense to focus on tax progressivity rather than the progressivity of what the government provides its citizens and how it assesses taxes to pay for those programs.

Aside from progressivity, tax systems should avoid arbitrary distinctions in tax burden based on people's tastes or characteristics, whether intended or capricious. In the past, such arbitrary taxes have been imposed on minorities; examples include the poll tax collected from Jewish communities in the Holy Roman Empire and the poll tax levied on non-Muslims in the eighth-century Abbasid caliphate of Persia. Modern tax systems often make tax-burden distinctions among families of the same income level, based, for example, on such factors as family size, charitable inclinations, or tastes for cigarettes.

The second question to ask about any tax system is what costs it imposes. The first and most obvious cost is that every dollar of taxes remitted to the government leaves one less dollar for taxpayers to spend on goods and services. For this reason, a responsible government will only raise taxes to provide programs whose value exceeds the private consumption that is given up.

But there are costs over and above the money taxed away. For one thing, collecting taxes requires a substantial bureaucracy. The Internal Revenue Service (IRS) budget is over $10 billion per year, although that amounts to only about 0.5 percent of the revenue it collects. Dwarfing that are the costs borne directly by the taxpayers—called *compliance costs*—which include the value of their time spent on tax matters and money spent on tax software and professional tax preparers and planners. This cost has been estimated to exceed $100 billion a year for the U.S. income tax system, ten times the administrative cost for all taxes combined and about 10 percent of revenues collected.

Administration of a legitimate, nonarbitrary tax system is facilitated when there are observable, measurable things that can serve as tax bases. For example, it is notoriously difficult to enforce taxes on food products grown and consumed by farmers and on the income of self-employed individuals. Most modern tax systems rely on businesses that withhold taxes on employees' earnings and provide information reports to the tax authority that can be matched with employees' tax returns. Withholding and information reports are supplemented by random audits, with penalties for noncompliance. In many countries, the employee-withholding system is exact and final so that no tax return need be filed by most employees; the British pay-as-you-earn system is an example.

In spite of these measures, substantial tax evasion occurs. According to the IRS, about 16 percent of the federal taxes that should be paid are not. The noncompliance rate varies widely by the type of income; it is less than 2 percent for wages and salaries and as much as 50 percent for self-employment income, the stark difference reflecting the availability of withholding and information reports for the former but not the latter type of income.

Taxes impose another kind of cost on an economy because they alter the costs and rewards of various behaviors. For example, both income and consumption taxes reduce the incentive to work by reducing the consumption reward per hour of labor supplied to the market. Income taxes, but not consumption taxes, also reduce the reward and therefore the incentive of individuals to save and businesses to invest. These behavioral responses represent costs because they channel resources in socially unproductive directions. For example, from society's point of view it is costly if income taxes dissuade someone from joining the labor force. Much economic analysis has tried to quantify these behavioral responses; the consensus view is that the overall labor supply response is not large and the saving response is not well understood, but certain other behaviors, such as the timing of capital assets sales to anticipated tax changes, are highly responsive to the tax system. The bigger the behavioral response, the higher the economic cost per dollar raised. Some have estimated that, all in all, the behavioral responses to the U.S. income tax system generate an extra forty cents of social cost for every additional tax dollar raised.

TRADEOFFS

Tax policy is controversial because the objectives often conflict. Although the economic costs could arguably be reduced by making the tax burden less progressive (i.e., reducing how much the tax burden rises with income), many would find such a system to be an unfair shifting of the burden toward low-income people. Simplifying the tax system could save substantial administrative and compliance costs, but a simplified system might render the tax burden less finely tuned to individual circumstances. Many of the debates about tax policy involve such choices. For example, would lowering taxes on entrepreneurial income stimulate enough economic activity to offset the fact that (successful) entrepreneurs are often among society's wealthiest citizens?

The twentieth-century expansion of the role of government, and the associated need for more tax revenues, seems to have peaked in the 1980s, and on average the worldwide ratio of tax collections to GDP has not changed much since that time. Looking ahead, as national economies become more interconnected, it may become more difficult to collect taxes without substantial cross-country cooperation. Furthermore, governments may compete to attract businesses by offering lower taxes. Some view this development as a dangerous "race to the bottom" that will undermine the ability of governments to provide public goods and social insurance, while others applaud it as a way to discipline otherwise profligate governments in the same way that competition among companies promotes cost-minimizing business operations.

Especially in the last two decades, the U.S. income tax system has become much more than a way to raise revenue; it also delivers a wide range of social programs. Thus, it is misleading to associate government expenditure programs with what the government *does* and the tax system with how it pays for what it does because much of what government does is achieved via the tax system. For example, the U.S. income tax subsidizes charitable giving by making it deductible from taxable income. It also promotes homeownership through its favorable tax treatment, and it delivers the country's biggest antipoverty program via the earned income tax credit. These programs add to the complexity of the tax system, and thus to its administrative and compliance costs, and the constituencies that benefit often oppose efforts to simplify the tax system that would eliminate these programs.

SEE ALSO *Earned Income Tax Credit; Inheritance Tax; Negative Income Tax; Tax Credits; Tax Evasion and Tax Avoidance; Tax Relief; Taxes, Progressive; Taxes, Regressive; Transaction Taxes*

BIBLIOGRAPHY

Auerbach, Alan J., and Kevin A. Hassett, eds. 2005. *Toward Fundamental Tax Reform*. Washington, DC: American Enterprise Institute Press.

Brownlee, W. Elliot. 2004. *Federal Taxation in America: A Short History*. 2nd ed. Washington, DC: Woodrow Wilson Center; Cambridge, U.K., and New York: Cambridge University Press.

Messere, Ken, Flip de Kam, and Christopher Heady. 2003. *Tax Policy: Theory and Practice in OECD Countries*. New York: Oxford University Press.

President's Advisory Panel on Federal Tax Reform. 2005. Final Report. *Simple, Fair, and Pro-growth: Proposals to Fix America's Tax System*. http://www.taxreformpanel.gov/final-report/.

Rosen, Harvey. 2004. *Public Finance*. 7th ed. New York: McGraw-Hill.

Slemrod, Joel, and Jon Bakija. 2004. *Taxing Ourselves: A Citizen's Guide to the Debate over Taxes*. 3rd ed. Cambridge, MA: MIT Press.

Webber, Carolyn, and Aaron B. Wildavsky. 1986. *History of Taxation and Expenditure in the Western World*. New York: Simon & Schuster.

Joel Slemrod

TAXES, PROGRESSIVE

A progressive tax is one for which the rates vary according to one's ability to pay. Thus, those who possess more highly valued economic assets, such as property or income, are taxed at a higher percentage than those whose economic assets are valued less.

Historically, progressive taxes were exceptional in that they were aimed at an elite class that was often exempt from paying certain taxes. In ancient times, progressive taxes were often associated with extraordinary circumstances, especially military campaigns. Republican Rome's *tributum* is an example of a war-related progressive tax.

Progressive taxation became a norm in the modern period with the emergence of a direct relationship between the state and individuals in society. The increased demands of modern states to raise revenue from individuals led to the introduction of citizenship, which brought enhanced political and legal rights to the individual and greater obligations of the individual to the state. These obligations included new revenue claims, such as personal income, capital gains, and inheritance taxes. These individual-based taxes form the basis of a progressive tax scheme, which is applied at ascending rates relative to the economic value of the targeted assets. The United States's personal income tax was meant to be progressive, with top marginal rates reaching above 90% in the 1960s.

The progressive tax was created as a fiscal means by which political authorities gained greater access to the economic resources of the wealthiest members of society. The arguments in favor of progressive taxation stress a sense of social fairness in that the wealthier members of society have a disproportionately higher ability to pay for those public goods and services from which they benefit, directly and indirectly. These arguments are associated with the ideological programs of political populism and socialism. By contrast, the arguments against progressive taxation stress a sense of individual fairness in that those with wealth are being penalized for their personal ingenuity, risk taking, labor, and luck. These arguments are associated with the ideological programs of free-market capitalism and neoliberalism.

In the advanced industrial economies, progressive tax systems went into place incrementally in the late nineteenth century. By the mid-twentieth century, they reached their limits with extremely high marginal rates and the spread of the progressive tax burden to the middle classes. This tax policy practice caused unintended negative consequences, including a rise in tax avoidance and capital flight and a decline in economic productivity and growth. Progressive taxation was viewed critically less as a fair means of allocating the tax burden and more as an unfair means of reallocating wealth. In the late twentieth century, a political reaction was led by Margaret Thatcher, the Conservative prime minister of the United Kingdom, and Ronald Reagan, the Republican president of the United States, who began a reverse trend to ease the tax burden on the wealthy with tax reforms of a more modified progressive and even regressive character in the advanced industrial economies.

SEE ALSO *Taxes; Taxes, Regressive*

BIBLIOGRAPHY

Griffith, Thomas D. 2004. Progressive Taxation and Happiness. *Boston College Law Review* 45 (5): 1363–1398.

Slemrod, Joel, ed. 1994. *Tax Progressivity and Income Inequality.* Cambridge, U.K.: Cambridge University Press.

Gerald Easter

TAXES, REGRESSIVE

A regressive tax is one that has a disproportionately more negative economic effect on the poorer members of soci-ety than the wealthier members. Regressive taxes usually have fixed rates, and are thus not sensitive to one's ability to pay. Likewise, a tax is considered regressive if the wealthy are able to avoid compliance more readily than the poor.

Because of the limited capabilities of premodern political authorities to assess value and monitor transactions, the earliest forms of taxation tended to be regressive. The preference was for taxes that were relatively simple to compute and collect. The head tax, such as the British poll tax and the Russian soul tax, was a direct tax with regressive distributional consequences. It was a levy applied at a fixed rate on each individual, regardless of income and property status. Likewise, the French *gabelle*, or salt tax, was an indirect tax with regressive distributional consequences. This tax was set at a fixed rate and administered by royal agents in the sale of this consumption necessity, even though the cost was a significantly greater burden for poor households.

In the modern period, regressive tax schemes remained common in economies with narrow elites, wide income disparity, underdeveloped industrial bases, and authoritarian political regimes. In the advanced industrial democracies, however, regressive taxation eventually fell out of favor. This was a consequence of political reforms that expanded voting rights, leading to the enactment of more progressive forms of taxation. An additional factor was an increase in technological and bureaucratic capabilities that enabled modern governments to keep track of economic activities and income sources.

More recently, arguments have gained ground in favor of tax reforms with regressive tendencies in the industrial democracies. Fiscal arguments stress the complex and opaque nature of contemporary tax systems and contend that the simplification of tax policy would facilitate taxpayer compliance and state collection. Economic arguments stress that a more regressive tax code would create greater incentives for the investment and activity that would stimulate economic growth to the benefit of all. In the United States, however, the reduction of high progressive tax rates in the 1980s and the first decade of the twenty-first century did not result in a decline in tax-avoidance practices among wealthier taxpayers.

National sales taxes and flat rate income taxes are the most common types of tax reforms that have regressive distributional consequences. The European economies rely heavily on the value-added tax (VAT), which is a kind of national sales tax, where a fraction of the total tax is added at each stage of production and distribution, instead of all at once at the last stage. If the price of necessary goods and services is relatively constant, then a sales tax is regressive. To illustrate, Denmark has a 25% VAT without exception. Thus, if two persons buy an identical bag of groceries each week for 20 Danish krones (DK), they both pay DK5 in VAT. But if the first person's weekly income was DK100 and the second's was DK1000, then the first person paid a higher percentage of their weekly worth (5%) than the second person (0.5%). Most European governments, however, provide exemptions on the VAT for basic necessities. Support for a flat income tax has grown in Europe and United States with the enactment of flat tax rates in the transition economies of central and eastern Europe, including Estonia, Slovakia, and Russia. The flat tax was instituted in the transition economies largely because of the weakness of the state tax administration to monitor and extract revenue from the emerging private sector and households.

SEE ALSO *Taxes; Taxes, Progressive*

BIBLIOGRAPHY

Hall, Robert E., and Alvin Rabushka. 1995. *The Flat Tax.* 2nd ed. Stanford, CA: Hoover Institution Press.

Kato, Junko. 2003. *Regressive Taxation and the Welfare State.* Cambridge, U.K.: Cambridge University Press.

Gerald Easter

TAYLOR, LANCE
1940–

Lance Taylor is an economist who has contributed widely to development economics and nonorthodox economic theory. After receiving his PhD in economics at Harvard in 1968, he taught at the leading economics departments of Harvard and Massachusetts Institute of Technology and then moved to a self-proclaimed heterodox department at the New School, a university in New York.

Taylor's early work deals with mainstream development topics, such as the econometric and simulation modeling of changes in the sectoral distribution of production in the course of development. He also explored development planning models, including research on numerical methods in nonlinear programming. While working in Chile in the 1970s, Taylor was exposed to the heterodox structuralist ideas of the United Nations Economic Commission for Latin America, and he observed firsthand how distributional conflict affects the economy. His subsequent models are more heterodox, departing from the orthodox neoclassical "closure" with full employment of labor; instead, they stress the role of aggregate demand and distributional conflict.

These ideas crystallized into what Taylor (1983, 1991) calls the *structuralist* approach to development

macroeconomics. The starting point is a model of demand-determined output along Keynes-Kalecki lines that examines the relationship between output growth and income distribution. The model is then extended to deal with interactions between industrial and agricultural sectors, asset markets and financial fragility, wage-price inflation due to distributional conflict, fiscal constraints on growth, international issues including debt and foreign exchange problems, and the interaction between rich and poor countries. Drawing on these theoretical contributions, Taylor, with his colleagues, developed structuralist computable macroeconomic models for a number of developing countries. From a sole focus on developing countries, Taylor's (1991, 2004) emphasis shifted to macroeconomic theory more generally, as applied to both developed and developing countries. Thus, while in mainstream economics there has been a trend toward applying theories constructed for developed countries to development issues, for Taylor there is a reverse tendency.

Taylor also worked extensively on economic policy in developing countries, leading numerous projects with collaborators from many countries. He provided some of the most rigorous and comprehensive criticisms of International Monetary Fund stabilization policies (see Taylor 1988). He also addressed the macroeconomic, distributional, and environmental consequences of economic liberalization policies adopted by developing and postsocialist economies, as well as the impact of such policies on the international financial system. This work not only draws on his theoretical models, but also his broader political economy perspective and his deep knowledge of the institutions of developing countries.

Taylor's opposition to neoliberal one-size-fits-all policies has been very influential, both because of his firm analytical grounding and his insistence that appropriate policies should take into account the specific structures and institutions of individual countries. His theoretical contributions, however, have not received the attention from mainstream economists that they deserve because of his departure from their protocol of using optimization as a basis of economic theorizing. But his structuralist alternative—of starting with macroeconomic accounting identities, then adding appropriate equations representing the behavior of relevant groups and the institutional attributes of particular economies based on careful historical and empirical work—may yet prove to be a more productive way of analyzing the operations of actual economies.

SEE ALSO *Economic Commission for Latin America and the Caribbean (ECLAC); International Monetary Fund; Macroeconomics, Structuralist; North-South Models; Structural Adjustment*

BIBLIOGRAPHY

Taylor, Lance. 1983. *Structuralist Macroeconomics: Applicable Models for the Third World.* New York: Basic Books.

Taylor, Lance. 1988. *Varieties of Stabilization Experience: Towards Sensible Macroeconomics in the Third World.* Oxford: Clarendon.

Taylor, Lance. 1991. *Income Distribution, Inflation, and Growth: Lectures on Structuralist Macroeconomic Theory.* Cambridge, MA: MIT Press.

Taylor, Lance. 2004. *Reconstructing Macroeconomics: Structuralist Proposals and Critiques of the Mainstream.* Cambridge, MA: Harvard University Press.

Amitava Krishna Dutt

TAYLOR RULE

In the late 1950s the Phillips curve became the dominant policy model, prescribing a trade-off between the wage and inflation rate against the unemployment rate. In the 1960s the parameters of the Phillips curve began to drift. Adaptive expectation with and without the natural rate and NAIRU (nonaccelerating inflation rate of unemployment) hypotheses was added to the curve. Later, the rational expectations hypothesis, which brought into question the assumptions of full information and variation between the actual and theoretical parameters of models, became popular. In 1979 and 1993, to improve predictions in line with the Phillips curve, the American economist John B. Taylor (b. 1946) introduced the Taylor curve, which specifies variance, rather than rate, in output and inflation to explain the great moderation in macroeconomic data since the 1970s.

Taylor advanced policy arguments—including that the variance of inflation and real gross domestic product (GDP) could be reduced to minimum levels—and empirical justifications for the Taylor rule. The rule is, where r is the federal fund rate, p is the inflation rate, and y is the percentage deviation of real GDP from a potential level. The Federal Open Market Committee (FOMC), the committee within the Federal Reserve that sets the target federal fund rate, can use this rule as a guide. The evidence shows a high correlation between the actual federal fund rate and estimates from the rule for the period from 1987 to 2005, with peaks and troughs matching up closely in most years.

The Taylor rule has many novel features. It transcends the "either/or" nature of the rules versus discretion debate by making room for discretionary policies as well. It is neither a fixed rule nor one that expands the money supply to approximately the growth rate of output as Milton Friedman (1983) proposed. A fixed policy rule would not be useful to the FOMC because, besides lacking a feedback mechanism, it would shun the Fed's responsibility to stabilize cyclical swings, rendering the Fed passive. Even when the public acts with rational expectations and policymakers have full information, the Fed may want to choose a time-inconsistent or suboptimal policy such as when a change in administration occurs. A new administration may want changes, encouraging the FOMC to choose sequentially, such as setting interest rate targets meeting-by-meeting.

Another novelty is that the Taylor rule is not necessarily optimal in the sense of a single point on the trade-off in the production-possibility-like frontier. While Robert M. Solow argued for precise estimates, Taylor inferred robust estimates for a broader group of models. Generally, rules are considered prescriptive or normative in nature, as Taylor originally intended them to be, but the Taylor rule turned out to be very descriptive as well.

One area for further research is to find the reliable equilibrium federal fund rate and potential GDP estimates in a more forward-looking environment. This may mean that changes in the money supply advocated by other rules should be considered. Just as patents require laws to encourage inventiveness, the Taylor rule requires commitment to make it credible. In the early twenty-first century, the Taylor rule is an active research program that is attracting much attention in the literature

SEE ALSO *Economics, New Classical; Economics, New Keynesian; Expectations, Rational; Federal Reserve System, U.S.; Macroeconomics; Monetarism; Monetary Theory; Phillips Curve; Policy, Monetary; Rules Versus Discretion; Variance*

BIBLIOGRAPHY

Blanchard, Olivier. 2006. *Macroeconomics.* 4th ed. Upper Saddle River, NJ: Pearson Prentice Hall.

Friedman, Milton. 1983. The Case for a Monetary Rule. In *Bright Promises, Dismal Performance: An Economist's Protest,* ed. William R. Allen, 225–227. San Diego: Harcourt Brace Jovanovich.

Kydland, Finn E., and Edward C. Prescott. 1977. Rules Rather than Discretion: The Inconsistency of Optimal Plans. *Journal of Political Economy* 85 (3): 473–492.

Poole, William. 1998. Comments. In *Inflation, Unemployment, and Monetary Policy,* by Robert M. Solow and John B. Taylor, 78–88. Cambridge, MA: MIT Press.

Solow, Robert M., and John B. Taylor. 1998. *Inflation, Unemployment, and Monetary Policy,* ed. Benjamin M. Friedman. Cambridge, MA: MIT Press.

Taylor, John B. 1979. Estimation and Control of a Macroeconomic Model with Rational Expectations. *Econometrica* 47 (5): 1267–1286.

Taylor, John B. 1993. Discretion versus Policy Rules in Practice. *Carnegie-Rochester Conference Series on Public Policy* 39: 195–214.

Taylor, John B. 1999. A Historical Analysis of Monetary Policy Rules. In *Monetary Policy Rules*, ed. John B. Taylor, 319–341. Chicago: University of Chicago Press.

Lall Ramrattan
Michael Szenberg

TAYLORISM

A traditional social science, sociology, informs this entry. Sociology is subdivided into areas of specialization that may overlap. Areas relevant to this topic include historical sociology, economic sociology, organizations and work, and theory.

The term *Taylorism* is synonymous with *scientific management*, both named after the American industrial engineer Frederick Winslow Taylor (1856–1915) and his 1911 monograph, *The Principles of Scientific Management*. Taylor provided the framework for a management philosophy and method and for the organization of work. He based his framework on scientific law, breaking work into parts and separating mental from physical labor. His principles involved the following: (1) Developing a science of production; (2) carefully selecting and training workers; (3) connecting the science and the workers; and (4) splitting responsibility between management and workers. Taylor's ideas contributed to a movement across industrialized countries. The Germans called it the *rationalization movement*.

Taylor's framework rested on the assumption that workers are motivated by money. Through his time-and-motion studies, he established specific standards for how long each particular job should take and which kinds of physical routines it should involve. These efficiency guidelines were used as bases against which each worker's output was measured, and pay was calculated once workers were selected in terms of their work ethic and trained consistent with established standards. The greater the worker's output, the more pay the worker received. Taylor's equation incorporated breaks during the workday at specific intervals and for a specified length of time because he realized breaks increased productivity and workers' stamina. He saw breaks as efficient and effective for both workers and management.

Management was charged with the mental work in this hierarchical division of labor. In planning rooms above the shop floor and sometimes housed behind plate glass windows, management delegated responsibility, designed products, set the production schedule, and checked performance.

As a consequence of Taylorism, the organization of production became compartmentalized and control became centralized. Product design and production were separated. Work became task specific and mechanical as workers were turned into quasi machines. According to some critics, deskilling resulted, and the engineering of workers replaced the engineering of materials. In addition, productivity declined.

This model of economic organization lends itself well to mass production, historically the dominant form of industrial production in the United States. It catered to waves of immigrants and a growing middle class. With its focus on efficiency, the model emphasizes quantity over quality and innovation. This focus affected even the design and production of American machine tools, necessary for the production of most other products. Machine tools were designed for convenience of operation and to minimize motion and the operators' need for skill. These machine tools were adequate for mass production, but not for flexible production or custom production.

The negative outcomes of Taylorism are consistent with Adam Smith's (1723–1790) concerns. While Smith embraced the division of labor because he believed when works specialize, they become more productive, he emphasized that oversimplification of a worker's tasks may have inhuman, demoralizing effects. Although famous for advocating a free market economy, Smith argued for government intervention if it is necessary for enhancing the quality of life, particularly for those with the least resources, to ensure the common good.

Karl Marx (1818–1883) preceded Taylor in history and did not address Taylorism specifically. Marxist theory, however, regards the mode of production as rooted in the economic system. Individuals must consume in order to survive, and they cannot consume unless they produce. They must therefore enter into relations they cannot control, such as economic relations. According to Marx, this differentiates them from nature, from their own kind, and leads to alienation. Marxist theory rejects Taylorism as a strident form of worker exploitation under capitalism that strips workers of control over their work. Workers become mere means to capitalists' ends.

Fordism is a form of mass production linked to Henry Ford (1863–1947) of the Ford Motor Company during the early twentieth century. Fordism adopted the same principles as Taylorism, including the separation of mental and physical labor and the segmentation of work. Both pivot on quantity and speed. Using Taylor's principles, Ford introduced the assembly line, which automated the control of work. The speed of the assembly line controlled workers' movements and output and dictated the timing of breaks during the workday. The method of Fordism preceded the social scientific concept of *Fordism*, a term coined by the French regulation school. This school arose in the context of the first significant post-war recession during the 1970s as a critique of the capitalist mode of regulation, regarded as co-opting social and political life.

Globalization means interdependence of nations, groups, and individuals around the world. One dimension of such interdependence is economic globalization, which is fueled by capital's search for cheap labor internationally. Cheap labor equals cheap technology; poor countries provide cheap labor and rich countries provide technological innovations. This division of labor between poor and rich countries represents a separation of physical from mental labor that is rooted in Taylorism. Technological innovations, like the Internet, facilitate speed by compressing time and space. A more holistic, flexible, and less hierarchical approach to the economic enterprise is required, however, for continuous innovation. Such an approach may provide the potential for the reintegration of physical and mental labor across the globe.

SEE ALSO *General Motors; Time and Motion Study*

BIBLIOGRAPHY

Neary, Brigitte U. 1993. Management in the U.S. and (West) German Machine Tool Industry: Historically Rooted and Socioculturally Contingent. PhD diss., Duke University, Durham, NC.

Sachs, Jeffrey. 2000. A New Map of the World. *The Economist* (June 24): 81–83.

Taylor, Frederick Winslow. 1911. *The Principles of Scientific Management.* New York: Harper.

Taylor, Frederick Winslow. 1947. *Scientific Management: Comprising* Shop Management, The Principles of Scientific Management, *and Testimony Before the Special House Committee.* New York: Harper.

Brigitte U. Neary

TEA INDUSTRY

Modern tea comes from *Camellia sinensis*, a tree native to China and India. In today's commercial tea trade there are three main varieties of *Camellia sinensis*: China, Assam (northeastern India), and Cambodia, each named for the area in which it was first grown commercially. The China variety is a hardy, 3-meter-high bush with a useful lifespan of one hundred years. The Assam and Cambodia varieties are tall single-stem trees with a commercial life of forty years. Typically, tea trees are kept short through frequent trimming for easy plucking (i.e., the picking of tea leaves).

Although tea can be grown in a variety of agroclimatic conditions, the best teas are grown at altitudes between 1,000 and 2,000 meters.

Green leaf, the farm product, is sent for processing at tea factories and becomes *made tea*—sometimes called *black tea* or *dry tea*—the internationally traded commodity. Tea companies then blend tea from various origins to make what is often called *packed tea*, the beverage that consumers drink. The ratio of green leaf to made tea is about five to one, that is 5 kilograms of green leaf are required to make 1 kilogram of made tea. Three processing methods are used to convert green leaf to three types of made tea: black, green, and oolong (Forrest 1985).

To make black tea, tea leaves are spread on racks to dry and then put through a machine that breaks up the leaf cells, frees the oils, and ejects a twisted lump of leaves. These are sent to a fermenting room, where they are spread thinly and left to absorb oxygen. The leaves are then exposed to a continuous blast of hot dry air for fifteen to thirty minutes, which turns them black. Black tea accounts for three-quarters of global tea output and is supplied mostly by East African and South Asian countries.

Green tea has a less processed flavor than black tea. The leaves are steamed and heated immediately after plucking. Because the leaves are dried without going through fermentation, they remain green. After being separated by grade, the leaves are packed in chests lined with aluminum foil. Green tea, which accounts for a quarter of global tea output, is supplied primarily by China and to a lesser degree by Japan, Vietnam, and Indonesia.

Oolong tea is traditionally prepared in South China and Taiwan from a special form of the China tea plant—the *chesima*. It has large leaves and a distinct flavor. Preparation is similar to black tea but with a much shorter fermentation process. Oolong teas, which account for only a small fraction of the global market, are often scented with flowers.

While people often refer to almost anything steeped in hot water as "tea," only *Camellia sinensis* is properly given this designation. Teas made with herbs and berries are more properly called *tisanes* or *infusions*. Leaves from several other plants are consumed like tea. For example, Paraguay tea, often called *yerba maté*, is made from the leaves of a species of holly found primarily in Argentina, Brazil, and Paraguay. The Indians of North Carolina used to prepare a tea called *yaupon* from the leaves of another holly-like tree. *Trinidad tea* is made from the leaves of the pimento or allspice tree.

PRODUCTION AND TRADE

Tea is produced in both tropical and temperate zones. Because it grows at high altitudes, it typically does not compete with food or other cash crops. Asia accounts for about three-quarters of global production, Africa for half the remainder, and several Middle Eastern and Latin American countries for the rest. During 2002–2005 China and India produced more than half of the world's tea (26 and 27 percent, respectively), followed by Sri Lanka (10 percent) and Kenya (9 percent). Global tea production during this period was 3.25 million tons.

Tea is produced by both smallholders and estates. Tea estates are owned by large companies producing large quantities of tea, normally exceeding 1,000 tons of made tea (sometimes as much as 10,000 tons). Tea estates employ both permanent and seasonal laborers. Often, the permanent laborers reside in living quarters within the estate and receive other benefits, such as basic health care and schooling for their children. The conditions for employment on tea estates are considered very good, and permanent workers are often considered to be "privileged" compared to their seasonal counterparts. Although wages are low compared to Western standards (about $2 per day), they are considered high enough for, say, Africa, where two working adults at this wage rate are able to lift a family of four to five above the poverty level. Conditions of employment are also considered good because estates, often owned by multinational companies, must adhere to international standards and scrutiny concerning wages, hours, and conditions of employment. In addition to the International Labor Organization which sets labor standards, numerous international and local non-governmental organizations and advocacy groups (such as the International Labor Rights Fund) monitor employment conditions.

Global tea production from 2000 to 2004 exceeded three million tons, valued between $4 and $5 billion annually. Growth in tea production, as high as 4 percent in the 1970s and 3 percent in the 1980s, slowed to 1.6 percent in the 1990s. Almost half of global tea production is traded internationally. Sri Lanka (22 percent), China (18 percent), Kenya (16 percent), and India (16 percent) account for almost three-quarters of world exports. The United Kingdom used to be the largest tea importer (during the 1960s it accounted for almost 40 percent of world imports, but by the early 2000s it accounted for only about 10 percent). The dominant tea importer is Russia, which accounted for 12 percent of world imports in 2005.

TEA PRICES

Unlike most primary commodities whose prices are determined in futures exchanges, tea prices are established at auctions (located in tea-producing countries), which trade about one-third of global tea output. India has six auctions, but the two largest are in Colombo, Sri Lanka; and Mombasa, Kenya. Other producer-country auctions are held in Chittagong, Bangladesh; Jakarta, Indonesia; and Limbe, Malawi. The Colombo and Mombasa auctions trade tea mostly for export, and their prices (especially Mombasa's) are considered the world price indicators.

Auctions in consumer countries, which operated during the 1970s and 1980s, have been less successful, with the exception of the London auction, once the world's most influential. Until the early 1970s, London held the world's dominant tea auction. London's last auction took place on June 29, 1998, bringing to a close a 319-year-old tradition. Tea auctions had been held in London since the East India Company's first auction in 1679. Aside from brief interruptions during the war years, auctions had been held at least once a week since 1864.

Kenya's tea auction system began in November 1956 in Nairobi under the auspices of the East African Tea Trade Association. It initially traded small quantities of secondary-grade teas, but following increased interest from producers and buyers the auction moved to Mombasa in 1969 and started trading main grades of tea. A turning point for the Mombasa auction came on October 26, 1992, when, following relaxation of foreign-exchange controls, transactions began taking place in U.S. dollars. With other major tea auctions trading in local currency (including the one in London), this change probably accounts for Mombasa's position as the world's dominant tea auction.

The global tea market is not subject to the types of trade impediments faced by other commodity markets (e.g., cotton). Furthermore, unlike the markets for commodities such as cocoa, coffee, and rubber, there has been no United Nations–backed international price stabilization scheme in the tea market in the post–World War II (1939–1945) period. There have been two voluntary supply-restriction schemes (Wickizer 1951). The first, running from 1920 to 1921, grew out of the sharp price decline of 1920 and was led by India and Sri Lanka (then Ceylon). A second restriction went into effect in 1930, led by the same countries and for the same reason. A five-year International Tea Agreement was launched in April 1933 to support tea prices through export quotas, backed by India, Indonesia, and Sri Lanka. The agreement occurred in response to the collapse of tea prices during the Great Depression—they declined by 70 percent between 1927 and 1932 (Sarkar 1972).

THE OUTLOOK

Because most tea is consumed in low- and middle-income countries, the long-term outlook for tea depends mostly on income growth in these countries. The UN Food and Agriculture Organization (FAO 2001), for example, estimated that the growth in global tea demand for the 2000–2010 decade is unlikely to exceed 1 percent, which is close to the rate of demand growth during the 1990s. Most demand growth is expected to come from increased imports by countries of the former Soviet Union. On the supply side, the FAO expects China, Kenya, and Vietnam to increase their exports. Because tea competes with coffee, as well as soft drinks such as Coca-Cola, tea consumption depends on the growth of these industries. Some growth is also expected to take place in niche markets, such as organic tea and iced tea, both of which are mostly consumed in high-income countries. Another dimension of tea is its perceived health benefits, implying that as consumers become more health conscious, they are more likely to drink more tea. This may be especially the case for green tea, which undergoes less processing at tea factories, and is hence considered a more "natural" drink.

SEE ALSO *Agricultural Industry; Colonialism; Imperialism; Industry*

BIBLIOGRAPHY

Food and Agriculture Organization: Committee on Commodity Problems. 2001. Medium-Term Outlook for Tea. Fourteenth Session of the Intergovernmental Group on Tea, New Delhi, India, October 10–11.

Forrest, Denys. 1985. *The World Tea Trade: A Survey of the Production, Distribution, and Consumption of Tea.* Cambridge, U.K.: Woodhead-Faulkner.

Sarkar, Goutam K. 1972. *The World Tea Economy.* Delhi: Oxford University Press.

Wickizer, Vernon D. 1951. *Tea under International Regulation* 2nd ed. Stanford, CA: Food Research Institute.

John Baffes

TEACHER EXPECTATIONS

Can the academic expectations that teachers develop for their students become self-fulfilling prophecies? Can predictions made about another individual actually *cause* outcomes that confirm the original prophecy, and if so, how and under what conditions? This question has generated considerable research as well as controversy in the social sciences. The volatile nature of the inquiry stems from the special obligation inherent in teaching. As with the healing professions, teachers are given the responsibility and held accountable to promote positive changes in their charges. If teacher prophecies about *differential* capability among students could explain the observed achievement gap between groups of students (a gap that disadvantages poor and ethnic minority children), this social-influence process carries large societal implications.

The expectancy concept and its potential for confirmation have a long history in literature and social science,

beyond education. Categorization of people, settings, and events reduces the complexity of social stimulation. It enables people to quickly sort experiences, identify essential features, predict outcomes, and plan actions. Although categorization can provide clarity, it can also blind a person when faulty or stereotyped beliefs, either positive or negative, are applied. An example of positive expectancy effects is found in the ancient Greco-Roman myth about the sculptor Pygmalion whose love for the statue Galatea brought her to life. Reference to negative expectancy effects is found in a 1948 paper by the sociologist Robert K. Merton, who coined the term *self-fulfilling prophecy.* Using the bank failures of the economic depression as one example, Merton defined the component parts as "a *false* definition of the situation evoking a new behavior which makes the original false conception come *true*" (p. 195).

In *Pygmalion in the Classroom* (1968), the psychologist Robert Rosenthal and the elementary school principal Lenore Jacobson conducted the first experimental test of a positive self-fulfilling prophecy. Teachers were given false test information about a randomly selected group of children who were labeled intellectual bloomers and expected to show greater growth in their learning. At the end of the year, the children identified as bloomers outperformed other children on intelligence tests—an effect documented in the early grades. This study fueled controversy over methodological problems, numerous experimental replications, and interest in the investigation of naturally occurring expectations in classrooms.

Evidence supports a causal connection between teacher expectations and student achievement, although the debate continues regarding the magnitude of the effect. The expectancy effect is more powerful under certain conditions, with the factors that moderate the effect under study (Brophy 1998; Rosenthal 2003; Weinstein 2002). The causal model proves complex, highlighting differences in susceptibility of both teachers and students to such effects and the magnifying role of the developmental stage of the children as well as of contextual features. There exists potential for teacher *perceptual* confirmation regardless of student behavioral confirmation and for student *disconfirmation* of negative or even positive teacher expectations.

Other vital questions include the mechanisms by which expectations can exert effects on student achievement, the factors that shape the formation of academic expectations and for whom, and the methods by which negative self-fulfilling prophecies might be reduced. Many social science fields have explored teacher expectations and expectancy effects, using varied methods at multiple levels of analysis.

Studies have documented that teachers treat high- and low-expectancy students differently, favoring highs with greater opportunity to learn and more positive interactions (Brophy 1998). Even young children are aware of differential treatment by teachers, which communicates information about the relative smartness of students in the classroom (Weinstein 2002). Thus, the mechanisms that bring about expectancy effects include the opportunity structure provided students, which directly impacts achievement, and ability messages, which through their shaping of student self-view and motivation to learn, ultimately impact achievement. Studies have also shown that differential expectations and differential treatment are expressed not only toward individual students but also toward groups of students—members of ability-based instructional groups within classrooms, academic tracks within schools, or high-poverty schools. Further, expectancy communication is evident not only in interpersonal interactions but also in the culture of classrooms and schools, where ability differences may be made publicly salient and instructional differentiation, such as a less rigorous curriculum for some students, may be a pervasive reality.

There also exists evidence of teacher bias in the formation of expectations—less clear with regard to gender, but more apparent in the stereotype-based underestimation of the ability of low-income, ethnic and linguistic minority, and special needs children. There is debate about the accuracy of teacher expectations, when judged against achievement scores, and the appropriateness of differentiated treatment. While it can be argued that expectations may play a larger self-maintaining role than self-fulfilling role, this debate also raises the question about the purpose for education—that is, whether a society is obligated to reach higher for all students.

Far less research has focused on how to reduce the occurrence of negative self-fulfilling prophecies in schooling. Intervention approaches have included increasing teacher awareness of biased expectations and promoting equitable interactions with students, schoolwide reform efforts to alter multilayered components of a negative expectancy climate, and policy mandates to raise academic standards (expectations) and reduce the achievement gap. Multidisciplinary research on this social-influence process has demonstrated the limits of behavioral and social-cognitive explanatory models and the importance of systemic and ecological approaches. When schools are structured to sort students for differential opportunities rather than for the development of talent in all students, expectancy processes no longer lie simply in the minds of teachers but rather are fueled by educational policy.

SEE ALSO *Education, USA; Gifted and Talented; Merton, Robert K.; Pygmalion Effects; Schooling; Schooling in the USA; Self-Fulfilling Prophecies*

BIBLIOGRAPHY

Brophy, Jere, ed. 1998. *Expectations in the Classroom.* Vol. 7 of *Advances in Research on Teaching.* Greenwich, CT: JAI Press.

Merton, Robert K. 1948. The Self-Fulfilling Prophecy. *Antioch Review* 8 (2): 193–210.

Rosenthal, Robert. 2003. Covert Communication in Laboratories, Classrooms, and the Truly Real World. *Current Directions in Psychological Science* 12 (5): 151–154.

Rosenthal, Robert, and Lenore Jacobson. 1968. *Pygmalion in the Classroom: Teacher Expectation and Pupils' Intellectual Development.* New York: Holt, Rinehart, and Winston.

Weinstein, Rhona S. 2002. *Reaching Higher: The Power of Expectations in Schooling.* Cambridge, MA: Harvard University Press.

Rhona S. Weinstein

TEACHER-CHILD RELATIONSHIPS

Attachment theorist John Bowlby (1969) argued that self-concept and understanding of relationships are determined, in part, by experiences in early relationships with caregivers, particularly parents. The nature and quality of these relationships are important, specifically the degree to which caregivers are available and responsive to children's needs. Although children's first significant relationships are typically formed with parents, alternative relationships formed with teachers and other primary caregivers are also critical to child and adolescent development. In fact, a national survey of adolescents (Resnick et al. 1997) revealed that the single most common factor associated with positive youth outcomes was a supportive relationship with an adult, and teachers were among the adults most frequently mentioned as the source of this support. The following sections provide a brief overview of what teacher-child relationships look like, the factors associated with the quality of these relationships, and the importance of teacher-child relationships in promoting children's academic and socio-emotional competencies.

WHAT IS A TEACHER-CHILD RELATIONSHIP?

As children enter school, teachers play an important role in shaping children's experiences outside of the home environment and early on can assist in supporting young children's adaptation to new challenges and demands during the transition into a classroom environment. Aside from their formal role of teaching academic skills, teachers are often responsible for regulating activity level, communication, and contact with peers (Howes and Hamilton 1993; Howes, Matheson, and Hamilton 1994; Pianta 1997). Teachers also provide behavioral support and teach coping skills (Doll 1996). In contrast to parent-child relationships, relationships between teachers and children are more likely to be time-limited in nature. Yet, teacher-child relationships are deemed important by children of all ages (Pianta, Hamre, and Stuhlman 2001) and are associated with later academic and social functioning (Hamre and Pianta 2001).

Teachers' perceptions of their relationships with children typically are shaped by the level of conflict or closeness—that is, the degree of discord or warmth within a relationship (Ladd and Burgess 1999; Pianta 1994; Pianta and Steinberg 1992). Similarly, children's perceptions revolve around the degree of emotional closeness and support, or negativity, within relationships with teachers (Bracken and Crain 1994; Ryan, Stiller, and Lynch 1994; Wentzel 1996). These perceptions of teacher-child relationships also appear to be consistent with observations of teachers and children interacting in the classroom (Howes et al. 1994; Pianta et al. 1997).

FACTORS THAT INFLUENCE TEACHER-CHILD RELATIONSHIPS

Research clearly indicates that the quality of teacher-child relationships is influenced by unique characteristics and previous relational experiences that both teachers and children bring to the classroom. Teacher-child relationships are frequently affected by children's behavioral problems, though there are some important gender differences. Teachers often characterize their relationships with female students as closer and less conflictual than their relationships with male students (Bracken and Crain 1994; Hamre and Pianta 2001; Ladd, Birch, and Buhs 1999; Ryan et al. 1994), which may be related to the fact that boys more frequently display antisocial behaviors, such as verbal and physical aggression. Several studies suggest that children's academic and socio-emotional competencies, or lack thereof, are linked to the quality of their relationships with teachers (Ladd, Birch, and Buhs 1999; Murray and Greenberg 2000). One report showed that teachers are most likely to report conflictual relationships with children whom they also view as having significant problem behaviors.

Several studies support the idea that teacher beliefs, experiences, and expectations also contribute to the quality of teacher-child relationships (Pianta, Hamre, and Stuhlman 2001). For instance, one report shows that teachers who report feeling depressed and unable to influence the development of children in their classrooms, and

who are observed to offer less emotional support, are more likely to report significant teacher-child conflict, even in the absence of reports of problem behaviors.

The race or ethnicity of both teachers and children also seems to play some role in determining teachers' perceptions of the quality of teacher-child relationships, though the evidence supporting this view is far from conclusive. In particular, an ethnic or racial match between child and teacher may be influential in the formation of positive, less conflictual relationships (Hall and Bracken 1996; Ladd, Birch, and Buhs 1999; Saft and Pianta 2000). Although teacher-child relationships are to some degree a function of characteristics of and interactions between individuals, it is important to recognize that they also have their own identity apart from specific, individual characteristics and interactions (Sroufe 1989).

IMPORTANCE OF TEACHER-CHILD RELATIONSHIPS

Positive, trusting, and low-conflict relationships with teachers from preschool through high school are key contributors to children's adjustment to their social and academic environment. Bridget Hamre and Robert Pianta (2001) report that teacher-child relationships in kindergarten are highly predictive of long-term educational outcomes (into middle school). Specifically, teacher-child conflict appears to be associated with negative feelings about school and school avoidance, lower levels of self-directedness and cooperation in the classroom, and poor academic outcomes (Birch and Ladd 1997). Additionally, teacher reports of relational conflict are related to increases in children's problem behaviors and decreases in competence behaviors over time (Pianta, Steinberg, and Rollins 1995). In contrast, young children whose teacher-child relationships are characterized by closeness show greater levels of overall school adjustment (Birch and Ladd 1997; Pianta et al. 1995). Similarly, Kathryn Wentzel (1998) reports a correlation for middle school students between teacher support and interest in school and suggests that teacher-child relationships may be particularly predictive of classroom functioning during transition points, such as the move from elementary into middle school. Importantly, children at risk for academic and behavioral difficulties are particularly well served by positive teacher-child relationships (Pianta et al. 1995). In summary, supportive, reciprocal relationships with teachers influence child development in multiple fashions and serve to promote positive emotional and academic outcomes, while protecting children from a variety of potential educational and socio-emotional risks.

SEE ALSO *Achievement; Adolescent Psychology; Bowlby, John; Education, Unequal; Education, USA;*

Mentoring; Parent-Child Relationships; Peer Effects; Peer Influence; Schooling

BIBLIOGRAPHY

Birch, Sondra H., and Gary W. Ladd. 1997. The Teacher-Child Relationship and Children's Early School Adjustment. *Journal of School Psychology* 35 (1): 61–79.

Birch, Sondra H., and Gary W. Ladd. 1998. Children's Interpersonal Behaviors and the Teacher-Child Relationship. *Developmental Psychology* 34 (5): 934–946.

Bowlby, John. 1969. *Attachment*. Vol. 1 of *Attachment and Loss*. New York: Basic Books.

Bracken, Bruce A., and R. Michelle Crain. 1994. Children's and Adolescents' Interpersonal Relations: Do Age, Race, and Gender Define Normalcy? *Journal of Psychoeducational Assessment* 12 (1): 14–32.

Doll, Beth. 1996. Children without Friends: Implications for Practice and Policy. *School Psychology Review* 25 (2): 165–183.

Drevets, Roma K., Stephen L. Benton, and Fred O. Bradley. 1996. Students' Perceptions of Parents' and Teachers' Qualities of Interpersonal Relations. *Journal of Youth and Adolescents* 25 (6): 787–802.

Hall, Wanda N., and Bruce A. Bracken. 1996. Relationship between Maternal Parenting Styles and African American and White Adolescents' Interpersonal Relationships. *School Psychology International* 17 (3): 253–267.

Hamre, Bridget K., and Robert C. Pianta. 2001. Early Teacher-Child Relationships and the Trajectory of Children's School Outcomes through Eighth Grade. *Child Development* 72 (2): 625–638.

Howes, Carollee, and Claire E. Hamilton. 1993. The Changing Experience of Child Care: Changes in Teachers and in Teacher-Child Relationships and Children's Social Competence with Peers. *Early Childhood Research Quarterly* 8 (1): 15–32.

Howes, Carollee, Claire E. Hamilton, and Catherine C. Matheson. 1994. Children's Relationships with Peers: Differential Associations with Aspects of the Teacher-Child Relationship. *Child Development* 65 (1): 253–263.

Howes, Carollee, Catherine C. Matheson, and Claire E. Hamilton. 1994. Maternal, Teacher, and Child-Care History Correlates of Children's Relationships with Peers. *Child Development* 65 (1): 264–273.

Ladd, Gary W., Sondra H. Birch, and Eric S. Buhs. 1999. Children's Social and Scholastic Lives in Kindergarten: Related Spheres of Influence? *Child Development* 70 (6): 1373–1400.

Ladd, Gary W., and Kim B. Burgess. 1999. Charting the Relationship Trajectories of Aggressive, Withdrawn, and Aggressive/Withdrawn Children during Early Grade School. *Child Development* 70 (4): 910–929.

Murray, Christopher, and Mark T. Greenberg. 2000. Children's Relationship with Teachers and Bonds with School: An Investigation of Patterns and Correlates in Middle Childhood. *Journal of School Psychology* 38 (5): 423–445.

Pianta, Robert C. 1994. Patterns of Relationships between Children and Kindergarten Teachers. *Journal of School Psychology* 32 (1): 15–31.

Pianta, Robert C. 1997. Adult-Child Relationship Processes and Early Schooling. *Early Education and Development* 8 (1): 11–26.

Pianta, Robert C., Bridget K. Hamre, and Megan W. Stuhlman. 2003. Relationships between Teachers and Children. In *Educational Psychology*, Vol. 7 of *Comprehensive Handbook of Psychology*, ed. William M. Reynolds and Gloria E. Miller, 199–234. New York: Wiley.

Pianta, Robert C., and Sheri L. Nimetz. 1991. Relationships between Teachers and Children: Associations with Behavior at Home and in the Classroom. *Journal of Applied Developmental Psychology* 12 (3): 379–393.

Pianta, Robert C., and Michael S. Steinberg. 1992. Relationships between Children and Kindergarten Teachers from the Teachers' Perspective. In *Beyond the Parent: The Role of Other Adults in Children's Lives*, ed. Robert C. Pianta, 61–80. San Francisco: Jossey-Bass.

Pianta, Robert C., Michael S. Steinberg, and Kristin B. Rollins. 1995. The First Two Years of School: Teacher-Child Relationships and Deflections in Children's Classroom Adjustment. *Development and Psychopathology* 7 (2): 297–312.

Resnick, Michael D., et al. 1997. Protecting Adolescents from Harm: Findings from the National Longitudinal Study of Adolescent Health. *Journal of the American Medical Association* 278 (10): 823–832.

Ryan, Richard M., Jerome D. Stiller, and John H. Lynch. 1994. Representations of Relationship to Teachers, Parents, and Friends as Predictors of Academic Motivation and Self-Esteem. *Journal of Early Adolescence* 14 (2): 226–249.

Saft, Elizabeth W., and Robert C. Pianta. 2001. Teachers' Perceptions of Their Relationships with Students: Effects of Child Age, Gender, and Ethnicity of Teachers and Children. *School Psychology Quarterly* 16 (2): 125–141.

Sroufe, L. Alan. 1989. Relationships and Relationship Disturbances. In *Relationship Disturbances in Early Childhood: A Development Approach*, ed. Arnold J. Sameroff and Robert N. Emde, 97–124. New York: Basic Books.

Wentzel, Kathryn R. 1998. Social Relationships and Motivation in Middle School: The Role of Parents, Teachers, and Peers. *Journal of Educational Psychology* 90 (2): 202–209.

Jason Downer
Kate Driscoll
Robert Pianta

TEACHERS

Psychologists and other social scientists since the early twentieth century have been concerned with learning and effective teaching. A century ago, education in the United States was a troubled institution. School curricula were seen as outdated and irrelevant, teachers were often ill-prepared, and students often displayed low levels of motivation. In light of these circumstances, social scientists began to investigate ways to improve the educational system. The move toward more progressive educational policies based on psychological research has continued to the present.

Early questions revolved around the nature of the classroom. That is, what were the relative merits of lectures, classroom discussions, and demonstrations and activities? When the move from prepared lectures to discussion took place, there was initial enthusiasm for discussions as fostering greater learning. Similarly, the introduction of demonstrations and activities engendered considerable enthusiasm. Unfortunately, the research on the different approaches has been inconclusive; students show an aptitude for learning across a wide variety of classroom formats.

Just as educators have tried to restructure classroom dynamics, they have engaged in a constant quest to adopt the latest technologies for their pedagogy. Teachers have made use of radio, television, and even the telephone for delivery of educational information. The adoption of the Internet in education continues the technological innovation. So far, however, different classroom formats and technologies have not led to systematic improvements in pedagogy. Each technology appears to have strengths, but widespread and generalized improvements in learning resist easy development.

One of the earliest, successful pedagogical innovations was the Personalized System of Instruction (PSI) developed by the psychologist Fred Keller (1899–1996). This approach was based on behavioral theory and featured self-pacing geared toward mastery of a task. Keller proposed including lectures and demonstrations only as vehicles of motivation, not as information delivery systems. Even though the approach was thoroughly grounded in behaviorism, Keller stressed the importance of the personal and social aspects of the learning situation.

Empirical research has documented PSI as an effective pedagogical approach. However, teachers never adopted it universally, even at the height of its popularity. Nonetheless, this system still has adherents who use it successfully.

Theories in cognitive psychology prevalent in the early twenty-first century highlight the idea that the creation of cognitive schemas enhances learning. Further, the use of so-called deep processing (e.g., self-reflective thought, integration of ideas, writing to learn) appears to benefit learners. One little-known, but promising, phenomenon that was rediscovered and applied to educational research in the late 1980s, the testing effect, is explicable in cognitive theory results. The act of taking a test can itself foster better retention than actually studying the material. The advantage of testing accrues when learners must generate answers and process multiple concepts in essay-type items. In contrast, recognition tests, such as those featuring multiple-choice items, and repetitive studying do not reliably lead to as complete learning.

The apparent advantage of repetitive studying is evident for tests taken immediately after studying, but this spurious advantage disappears with delayed testing. Theorists speculate that the immediate reinforcement associated with repeated exposure to material to be learned leads to misplaced feelings of confidence and mastery on the part of students. Further, the difficulty associated with generating answers on tests creates in the learner the impression that learning is incomplete and insufficient, even as it actually benefits the person. Researchers have suggested that learning is enhanced when students have to overcome difficulties. The paradox is that when students encounter such difficulties, it facilitates memory for the material but results in the subjective feeling of lack of progress toward the learning goal.

The fundament that unifies the various types of active learning is the creation of a network of interrelated ideas. In the early twenty-first century, cognitive and learning theory takes it as an article of faith that a cognitive schema provides interconnections among related information, a structure that facilitates assimilation of new information and effective retrieval of already-learned material.

ACTIVE LEARNING

Psychologists and educators have adopted the principles of active learning as critical components of classes. Historically, demonstrations by a teacher that illustrated a particular phenomenon constituted the approach to active learning, even though it may have been only the teacher who was active. Engagement on the part of the students is the concept of active learning that prevails in the early twenty-first century, and it can take a variety of forms. Some common types of active learning include writing to learn, cooperative learning, interteaching, and just-in-time teaching.

In writing to learn, the main purpose is not communication; rather, it is learning. Writing about a topic enables a student to ruminate on the ideas and to synthesize information, thereby solidifying learning. When students engage in low-stakes writing, a teacher does not assess the content or the style. The focus is on the development of ideas. Subsequently, high-stakes writing can be a means of assessing the quality of the writing and the knowledge of ideas. In theory, writing to learn involves students' evaluating ideas and information, which presumably helps them develop schemas and networks of interrelated ideas.

Cooperative learning involves the creation of a social setting to foster knowledge acquisition and retention. Educators have developed several different variations. The actual classroom process may differ significantly across the different types of cooperative learning. Empirical research has revealed a consistent, sometimes large, effect for cooperative learning compared to either competitive learning or individualistic learning. Investigators have documented the advantages of cooperative learning at all academic levels.

In cooperative learning, several students work together, taking responsibility not only for their own learning but also for that of the other group members. The critical components of cooperative learning include shared responsibility so that all members of the group learn, individual accountability for progress toward learning, face-to-face interaction, development of interpersonal skills, and self-monitoring by the group. Thus, cooperative learning relies on elements of cognitive theory and social psychological theory of group processes.

A development originating in the early 2000s that has its origins in Keller's PSI approach and involves structure, active learning, and cooperation is called interteaching. Interteaching places the responsibility for learning largely on the student, rather than on the teacher disseminating information via a lecture. In this approach, the instructor provides questions to guide students in a focused activity, and students then review the material to be learned and discuss it with fellow students in small groups. Finally, the students can request that the teacher address questions they have regarding the material.

Interteaching, like its predecessors, may not introduce elements that do not already exist in the classroom. What it involves is a rearrangement of behaviors and a redistribution of time devoted to individual and group work, discussion, lecturing, and out-of-class preparation. Like the other types of active learning, interteaching draws on cognitive theory but relies on a significant element of behavioral theory in its application.

Just-in-time teaching (JiTT), whose conceptual basis developed in the 1960s but was made practical through computer technology in the 1990s, involves student learning combined with the use of the Internet. Students take responsibility for learning specified material and for recognizing what aspects of that material they do not understand. JiTT relies on students to begin learning the material before class. Then the student communicates uncertainties to the teacher shortly before class time so the teacher can use class time most effectively to address the weaknesses in student learning. Class can be oriented toward what students do not know. Ideally, JiTT also engenders a spirit of cooperation between the students and the teacher.

TECHNOLOGY

Psychologists are often on the forefront of adopting new teaching technologies. The Internet and presentation software have become staples of the contemporary classroom. Preliminary evidence suggests that computer-based teaching can lead to greater learning than standard lectures when multimedia presentations are constructed so that the different components of a presentation are pedagogically integrated. The presence of excessive sound and graphics can lead to cognitive overload and reduced learning.

Theorists have speculated that multimedia presentations can enhance learning because the presentations foster multiple dual coding, that is, a combination of visual and verbal learning. This approach can increase student motivation while helping students encode concepts.

Presentation software can produce increased learning, but it has received criticism as being essentially a static medium that reduces teacher creativity and flexibility in the classroom. Some educators have responded to this criticism by noting that the software itself is not the problem; rather, the use of the software can be problematic if it does not lead students to process the material deeply.

Historically, new technologies have emerged and have become widely used in the classroom. Initial research often supports the efficacy of the new approaches, but sometimes it is not clear whether the increased student achievement stems from the new technology or from the additional enthusiasm of the teacher for the innovation.

BIBLIOGRAPHY

Bjork, Robert A. 1994. Memory and Metamemory Considerations in the Training of Human Beings. In *Metacognition: Knowing about Knowing*, eds. Janet Metcalfe and Arthur P. Shimamura, 185–205. Cambridge, MA: MIT Press.

Boyce, Thomas E., and Philip N. Hineline. 2002. Interteaching: A Strategy for Enhancing the User-Friendliness of Behavioral Arrangements in the College Classroom. *Behavior Analyst* 25 (2): 215–226.

Novak, Gregor M., Evelyn T. Patterson, Andrew D. Gavrin, and Wolfgang Christian. 1999. *Just-In-Time Teaching: Blending Active Learning with Web Technology*. Upper Saddle River, NJ: Prentice Hall.

Bernard C. Beins

TEACHING THEORIES

SEE *Teachers.*

TEATRO BUFO
SEE *Blackface*.

TECHNICAL CHANGE
SEE *Change, Technological*.

TECHNOCRACY

Initially and most generally, a technocracy was a form of organizational structure or system of governance in which decision makers were selected on the basis of technological knowledge. In the past, such individuals were called *technocrats*, a term used frequently in the twenty-first century by, for example, journalists, but differently, to refer to individuals exercising governmental authority because of their knowledge rather than political profile (e.g., "a government of technocrats, not politicians"). When used in the twenty-first century, the term *technocracy* is more likely to mean governance exercised by technological systems themselves than by experts.

Sharing connotations with theocracy (government by a divinity or its representatives), autocracy (ruleless governance by a lone individual), and bureaucracy (governance via routinized exercise of authority by humans), technocracy contrasts with democracy, rule by the citizenry. In addition to having a high estimation of applications of science-based learning, advocates of technocracy (such as the engineer/social activist Howard Scott) view governmentality as problematic, the complexity of technological systems being itself an important contributor of difficulty. They believe that, where possible, decisions should be designed into systems, because direct application is most effective and efficient. If humans have to be involved in governance, they should be highly familiar with the systems, rather than those with the authority of office, divinely inspired, with charisma, or by the people at large.

Late twentieth-century social studies of technoscience (such as those of the scholar Bruno Latour) tried to broaden the notion of technology, applying the term to any routinized complex of artifacts, agents, and practices. Users of technocracy generally think of technology in a more restricted sense, as the highly complex systems distinctive feature of "high tech" social formations.

In 1919 the American engineer W. H. Smith claimed to have coined the term technocracy, but Scott, founder of the arguably fascistic social movement Technocracy, Inc., asserted that he had heard the term as early as the 1880s. Used explicitly in this period by diverse Progressive political movements in the United States, technocracy was pre-sumed to be a natural and inevitable consequence of social evolution. Society was dependent on increasingly ubiquitous complex systems—like the railroad, those providing clean water, or those promoting public health—that themselves needed public support to function. Because systems were best understood by experts, technological expertise came to be seen as essential. The social chaos of the Great Depression of the 1930s exacerbated the perceived democracy crisis following from immigrant access to a broadened franchise. Giving governance to those who best understood technology (initially, engineers, such as Thorstein Veblen and Scott), but, later, managers (including James Burnham) would naturally promote scientific governance. Consonant with the positive social sciences, especially political science, technocracy also drew heavily on Western Utopian traditions (as in the work of novelist Harold Loeb) and a long American tradition of technological determinism.

A second period of the concept's popularity came with the 1960s rise of postindustrial theorizing, which fostered talk of an "information society" based in knowledge rather than manufacturing. For Daniel Bell, author of *The Coming of Post Industrial Society* (1973) technocracy was marked by the increasing power of professionals, as a consequence of which society was taking a more self-conscious, planned trajectory. The chief legacy of this second wave period, however, is that technocracy has come to mostly be used critically, to acknowledge an unfortunate necessity, not to be advocated. In his book *Autonomous Technology* (1977), for example, Langdon Winner developed an "alternative conception of technocracy," by adding "reverse adaptation" to the earlier technological imperative. Via technocracy, technologies have become ends, not means, displacing even the experts: "…[I]t matters little who in specific obeys the imperative or enacts the adaptation" (p. 258).

With today's widely shared sense that any human agency is marginalized by technology, technocracy is arguably common sense, even though its negative connotations mean only the critical freely use the term itself. Still, advocates of new systems feel compelled to justify them as democratic. Even though computing's implications for democracy, as in many other social arenas, are contradictory, the democratic implications of automated information and communications technologies (AICTs) were the ones that were stressed. Indeed, if networked, digitized representations at least theoretically democratize access to knowledge, and on-line plebiscites can extend opportunities for direct democracy, their disintermediation lessening the need for representation.

However, increasingly ubiquitous, self-governing smart machines, having artificial intelligence, can govern affairs autonomously, thus decreasing any need for democracy. Similarly, a perceived technology-enabled, rapidly proceeding globalization seems to lessen the need for any state.

Is computing the triumph of technocracy? This may depend on the ultimate cultural correlates of the new governance model emerging in cyberspace. This model takes institutional form in entities like the Internet Society and the World Wide Web Consortium, as well as in Free/Libre and Open Source Software development networks. Here governance focuses on devising technical standards, decisions about which are made whenever possible by consensus. Ostensibly democratic, such activities are open to the participation, either physical or electronically mediated, of anyone, as long as the participant can demonstrate the requisite technical expertise.

Perception of the technocratic affordances of new technologies has also spawned forms of resistance. As described by Richard Sclove in *Democracy and Technology* (1995) and especially in Scandinavia, AICTs are themselves used to support democratic technology consensus conferences, which aim to achieve broad social agreement before mega-projects begin. In these, cross-sections of the populace are encouraged to draw on their own experience, supplemented by expert responses to the citizens' own questions, to develop independent positions with regard to proposed technological ventures.

As argued by cyberspace ethnographers like David Hakken, technocratic presumptions filter what "impacts" are seen as likely to follow from AICTs. The same presumptions interfere with seeing how social factors shape the technologies themselves. The increased centrality of technological systems to the reproduction of capital is one of several important factors promoting the building of technocracy into computerized life. Still, as the success of consensus conferences show, this tendency can be contested. It must be for democracy to be more than mere posturing. Once implementation begins, the broader social correlates of using complex technological systems can be very hard to reverse. To avoid technocracy, it is essential to insert democratic participation early in the design of complex technological systems.

SEE ALSO *Internet; Technology; Technotopia*

BIBLIOGRAPHY

Bell, Daniel. 1973. *The Coming of Post-Industrial Society: A Venture in Social Forecasting.* New York: Basic Books.

Hakken, David. 2003. *The Knowledge Landscapes of Cyberspace.* New York: Routledge.

Sclove, Richard. 1995. *Democracy and Technology.* New York: Guilford Press.

Scott, Howard, et al. 1933. *Introduction to Technocracy.* New York: John Day Company.

Winner, Langdon. 1977. *Autonomous Technology: Technics-out-of-Control as a Theme in Political Thought.* Cambridge, MA: MIT Press.

David Hakken

TECHNOCRAT

A technocrat, according to the most basic meaning of the word, is someone who advocates or governs a technocracy—the rule of technical experts. The roots of the word *technocrat* lie in the classical Greek words for "skill" or "craft" (*techne*) and "rule" (*kratos*). The word *technocrat* is typically used to convey derogatory or ironic attitudes about technology and about the authority or power of those who understand and use technologies. Thus a technocrat is one who advocates technological or technical, rather than political, solutions to collective problems and who fails to consider the humanistic, historical, symbolic, moral, or personal elements of collective decisions. In France, for example, the word *technocrate* ("technocrat") is used by both the political left and right as an epithet for one who is said to administer or manage an organization on the basis of narrow technical expertise, and who lacks class consciousness, democratic commitments, moral conscience, and basic humanity (for example, Hecht 1998).

Daryush Sheyagan in *Cultural Schizophrenia* (1992) characterizes technocrats as "the managers of the technical, political, economic and scientific spheres of a modern society. They … take on the depersonalized, neutral quality of the world for whose efficiency they are responsible. They symbolize pure function stripped of all personal connotations … they are indifferent to the ethical purposes of what is produced" and can serve one type of political regime as well as another (pp. 148–149). However, if, as Jacques Ellul (1964) and Langdon Winner (1977) have suggested, technology is autonomous and technological imperatives determine decision outcomes, then in principle technocracy would not involve the authority of technocrats, for the real sources of authority and power would be impersonal and systemic.

Unlike the term *bureaucrat*, which since introduced by Max Weber has had a well-established place in the conceptual vocabulary and research of the social sciences, *technocrat* has had little use in social science research. Moreover, while a technocrat may also be a bureaucrat, *technocrat* can refer more generally to anyone who exercises scientific, technological, economic, administrative, or environmental authority.

The term is also used to refer to a member of a movement or organization that advocates governance by engineers or other technically trained experts instead of by politicians. Since 1933 in the United States, Technocracy, Inc. has been the principal research and educational organization representing the technocracy movement. Its predecessor, the Technical Alliance, was founded in 1919 by Howard Scott (1890–1970), who had been inspired by the writings of Thorstein Veblen (1857–1929). The official publication of Technocracy, Inc. is *North American Technocrat*. Henry Elsner Jr. (1967) has traced much of the history of the technocratic movement in the United States.

SEE ALSO *Bureaucrat; Democracy; Technocracy; Technology*

BIBLIOGRAPHY

Ellul, Jacques. 1964. *The Technological Society.* Trans. J. Wilkinson. New York: Vintage Press.

Elsner, Henry, Jr. 1967. *The Technocrats: Prophets of Automation.* Syracuse, NY: Syracuse University Press.

Hecht, Gabrielle. 1998. *The Radiance of France: Nuclear Power and National Identity after World War II.* Cambridge, MA: MIT Press.

Shayegan, Daryush. 1992. *Cultural Schizophrenia: Islamic Societies Confronting the West.* Trans. J. Howe. Syracuse, NY: Syracuse University Press.

Technocracy, Inc. Web site. www.technocracy.org.

Veblen, Thorstein. 1921. *The Engineers and the Price System.* New York: B.W. Heubsch.

Winner, Langdon. 1977. *Autonomous Technology: Technics-out-of-Control as a Theme in Political Thought.* Cambridge, MA: MIT Press.

Harlan Wilson

TECHNOLOGICAL CHANGE
SEE *Change, Technological.*

TECHNOLOGICAL DETERMINISM
SEE *Determinism, Technological.*

TECHNOLOGICAL DIFFUSION CURVE
SEE *Technology, Adoption of.*

TECHNOLOGICAL PROGRESS, ECONOMIC GROWTH

Technological progress is the fundamental force underlying the long run rise in real income per person. Technological progress reflects the growth of human knowledge, from advances in basic science such as the discovery of the laws of thermodynamics to highly practical and applicable ideas regarding production, like the design of an airplane wing or the mechanization of repeated actions or management and workplace organization, like double-entry accounting, just-in-time production, and the techniques of modern inventory management. It is nearly impossible to overstate the role of technology in economic life. Imagine, for example, how one's life would be different without such everyday inventions as computers and telephones, anesthesia and antibiotics, automobiles and airplanes, and electricity and petrochemicals.

Economic growth occurs because individuals have either more resources at their disposal or better ideas for turning resources into goods and services. Increases in resources alone cannot drive persistent economic growth. Natural resources are limited in a finite world, and while education can dramatically increase the productivity of human resources, such gains are constrained by human lifespans. Countries have doubled the education of their workforce, going from five years of schooling to ten, but it is hard to imagine repeating this accomplishment. The gains available from mechanization are also limited. If industry increases the number of machines per worker, growth will slow as each machine adds less to output than the one before. Indeed, estimates pioneered by Nobel laureate Robert Solow attribute less than half of U.S. economic growth to increases in resources. The lion's share of growth stems from technical progress.

In addition to playing a central role in persistently rising income levels, the advance of scientific and technical knowledge have driven a number of important economic trends. In production, technological progress has been the primary force underlying the shifts from manual to mechanized production methods, from natural to synthetic materials, from human and animal to mineral sources of power, and from raw labor to highly educated and specialized workers. The adoption of new technologies often drives the expansion of markets. Larger markets are required to allow workers and firms to concentrate on highly specialized activities and increase the return to innovations that involve investments in specialized knowledge or machinery. Innovations in transportation and communication have induced correspondingly dramatic changes in the organization of economic activity, shifting production out of the home, raising the average size of business enterprises, concentrating production in cities, and increasing the geographic extent of trade and the role of international transactions in local and national economies.

SOURCES OF TECHNOLOGICAL PROGRESS

The Industrial Revolution, which marks the beginning of a unique economic era of persistent increases in per capita incomes, is inextricably linked to the scientific revolution, and the world's current economic prosperity is difficult to imagine in the absence of fundamental advances in knowledge of biology, physics, and chemistry. Not all new technologies come from the scientific community, however. Private firms devote tremendous resources to applied research and development. In addition, many economically valuable ideas are the result of practical experimentation and the gradual accumulation of production experience. Even such high profile "inventions" as the Fulton steam engine—the mobile power source of the Industrial Revolution—drew on more than one hundred years of incremental improvements on earlier designs.

Unlike a hammer or a tractor, an idea can be used by many people at the same time. Indeed, because commercial success tends to attract attention, good ideas usually are hard to conceal. Once Henry Ford demonstrated that inexpensive cars could be mass produced on assembly lines, his production methods were widely copied. While early gains from an idea go to the inventor, as an idea spreads throughout an industry competitive pressure drives down prices, creating gains for society at large. Indeed, attempts to make use of the constant stream of new ideas generated by their competitors plays an important role in the tendency of firms in a given industry to locate close to each other, forming industrial clusters like Silicone Valley, Wall Street, and Hollywood.

Scientific research often generates insights that are valuable in many lines of business. Because of this, basic research is supported with public funds and new discoveries are widely disseminated. In more narrow and applied areas of knowledge, research is supported through the protection of intellectual property rights. These grant inventors a temporary monopoly on the use of their ideas, allowing them to recoup their research expenditures. Intellectual property rights attempt to balance the desire to reward successful research with the social benefits that derive from competitive markets and the widespread adoption of good ideas. In the pharmaceutical industry, drug prices typically fall by around 80 percent when a patent expires.

In addition to intellectual property rights, an educated workforce is essential to successful public and private research. Perhaps less obvious is the role of international trade. Access to large markets allows firms to spread the fixed cost of inventing a new idea thinly over a large number of units of output, raising the return to resources devoted to research. It is probably no accident that at the time of its Industrial Revolution, England had both the only European system of intellectual property rights and, due to an extensive network of roadways and canals, the most integrated national market in Europe.

INTERNATIONAL TECHNOLOGICAL TRANSFERS AND ECONOMIC DEVELOPMENT

For countries that are not on the technological frontier, technological progress owes more to imitation than innovation. Late industrializers—from the United States in the nineteenth century to China and India in the twenty-first—have always borrowed from the technological leaders of their day. The persistence of dramatic international disparities in income levels, however, testifies to the fact that successfully adopting existing technologies is neither easy nor automatic. Many technologies need to be adapted to fit local conditions including labor force skills, regulatory environment, availability of vital resources, and cultural differences.

Openness to international markets and an efficient legal system that protects the rights of foreign investors play important roles in attracting multinational companies that employ advanced technologies. Many developing countries, including China and India, have seen a marked increase in their growth rates directly following opening to international trade and foreign investment. On the other hand, international trade may lead developing countries to specialize in less technologically dynamic economic activities, such as agriculture and mining, and foreign investment in these areas may do little to promote ongoing technological transfers.

Because the introduction of a new technology generally creates both winners and losers, international technology transfers may also face deliberate and well-organized opposition. New technologies are often opposed by preindustrial elites that fear the loss of leadership to a new industrial class, by existing industries that are invested in older technologies, and by labor unions who fear the loss of jobs.

MANAGING THE CHALLENGES OF TECHNOLOGICAL PROGRESS

While technological progress raises average incomes over the long run, the costs and benefits of new technology are generally unevenly spread, creating a number of challenges for countries experiencing rapid technological progress. The introduction of new goods and processes often competes directly with established economic firms, causing them to adapt or be driven out of business, a process termed *creative destruction* by economist Joseph Schumpeter. The rise of the personal computer in the

1980s provoked a serious crisis at IBM, the leading maker of mainframe computers.

Technologies that raise output per worker are labor-saving by definition. Since the end of the Civil War (1861–1865), ongoing technical progress has reduced the share of agriculture in U.S. employment from 50 percent to less than 2 percent, and a similar process is currently underway in manufacturing. This release of labor from agriculture to other sectors has been an important force in rising U.S. living standards, but these large sectoral shifts have been a painful process for those directly involved.

Because the costs and gains from technical progress are unevenly shared, periods of rapid technical progress often see dramatic increases in income inequality such as characterized the European countries during their Industrial Revolutions. Because they were better able to adapt to the challenges of the computer revolution, educated workers have seen their wages rise quickly while other workers' wages have stagnated.

In addition to managing the labor market turbulence and larger sectoral shifts brought about by technological progress, technologically dynamic economies may face a host of unanticipated challenges that call for innovative economic, legal, and regulatory responses. The spread of the automobile gave rise to the suburbs and fundamentally altered American cities. The development of household appliances reduced the time required for routine housework, contributing to the rise in female labor force participation and changes in family structure. Advances in information technology may require new regulatory and legal responses to protect intellectual property rights in media, deter identity theft, and cope with the challenges of increased global competition.

These are nontrivial challenges, but technological progress has also provided the world with a greater capacity to meet them. Industrialization has provided both industrial pollution and the means to manage it, and the economic surplus created by increasing output per person has provided management with the ability to support and retrain workers who lose their jobs to technical progress. As in the realm of technology itself, the ability to meet the challenges raised by ongoing technological progress is limited ultimately by human creativity itself.

SEE ALSO *Business Cycles, Real; Change, Technological; Research and Development; Technological Progress, Skill Bias; Technology; Technology, Adoption of; Technology, Transfer of*

BIBLIOGRAPHY

Abramovitz, Moses. 1986. Catching Up, Forging Ahead, and Falling Behind. *Journal of Economic History* 46 (2): 385–406.

Jones, Charles I. 1995. R&D-Based Models of Economic Growth. *Journal of Political Economy* 103 (4): 759–784.

Mokyr, Joel. 1990. *The Lever of Riches: Technological Creativity and Economic Progress.* New York: Oxford University Press.

Romer, Paul M. 1990. Endogenous Technical Change. *Journal of Political Economy* 98 (5): S71–S102.

Solow, Robert M. 1956. A Contribution to the Theory of Economic Growth. *Quarterly Journal of Economics* 70 (1): 65–94.

Solow, Robert M. 1957. Technical Change and the Aggregate Production Function. *Review of Economics and Statistics* 39 (3): 312–320.

Lewis S. Davis

TECHNOLOGICAL PROGRESS, SKILL BIAS

This entry will discuss the different approaches to total factor productivity measurement and define skill-biased technical change. Let t denote a technology index and x and y denote inputs and output, respectively. Then the production function can be written as

$$y = f(x, t).$$

Technological change is then defined as a change in the technology index t that affects the relationship between inputs x and output y. Given a change in t (say from t_1 to t_2), technological change is said to take place if

$$\frac{\partial f(x,t)}{\partial t} \neq 0.$$

Assuming that $t_2 > t_1$, technological change is called *technological progress* if

$$\frac{\partial f(x,t)}{\partial t} > 0,$$

that is, if technological change allows the production of more output y with the same quantity of inputs x. Alternatively, technological change is called *technological regress* if

$$\frac{\partial f(x,t)}{\partial t} < 0.$$

Technological progress is usually measured in terms of the *rate of technological progress*

$$\frac{\partial \ln f(x,t)}{\partial t}. \tag{1}$$

Under the assumption of constant returns to scale (which is the maintained assumption in this article), the rate of technological progress is also referred to as the *growth rate of total factor productivity* (TFP) or *total factor productivity growth.*

There are four alternative approaches to the measurement of the rate of technological progress: growth accounting, the index number approach, the econometric approach, and the distance function approach.

The growth accounting approach to the measurement of the rate of technological progress was pioneered by Moses Abramovitz (1956) and Robert M. Solow (1957). It requires the specification of a neoclassical production function, $y = f(x, t)$. Totally differentiating the production function with respect to t and rearranging yields the rate of technological progress

$$\frac{\partial \ln f(x,t)}{\partial t} = \frac{d \ln y}{dt} - \sum_j \left(\frac{\partial \ln f(x,t)}{\partial x_j} \frac{dx_j}{dt} \right). \quad (2)$$

As an example, consider the Cobb-Douglas production function $Y = AK^\alpha L^{1-\alpha}$, where K is capital, L is labor, α is the share of capital in output, and A is a measure of the current level of technology, referred to as total factor productivity. With this production function, equation (2) implies

$$\frac{\dot{A}}{A} = \frac{\dot{Y}}{Y} - \alpha \frac{\dot{K}}{K} - (1-\alpha)\frac{\dot{L}}{L},$$

according to which the rate of growth of A is just the rate of technological progress (under constant returns to scale). Intuitively, $\dot{A}/A$ is the growth in output that cannot be accounted for by growth in capital and labor and is often called the *Solow residual,* after Robert Solow, who suggested this method of estimating the rate of total factor productivity growth.

Pioneered by W. Erwin Diewert (1976), the index number approach is an extension of growth accounting (from a continuous-time framework to a discrete-time framework). Under the assumption of cost minimization and constant returns to scale, equation (2) can be rewritten as

$$\frac{\partial \ln f(x,t)}{\partial t} = \text{Total factor productivity growth}$$

$$= \ln (I_y) - \ln (I_x)$$

where I_y is a (real) output quantity index and I_x an input quantity index. Equivalently,

$$\text{Total factor productivity growth} = \frac{I_y}{I_x},$$

according to which the rate of technological progress is a function of the ratio of an output quantity index to an input quantity index. Clearly, the index number approach does not require the specification of a production function, although we did use it above to establish the equiva-

lency between the growth accounting approach and the index number approach.

The index number approach is widely used by the majority of statistical agencies that produce productivity statistics (see Diewert and Nakamura 2003 for details). One critical issue regarding this approach is the selection of the appropriate indexes. Statistical indexes are mainly characterized by their statistical properties. These properties were examined in great detail by Irving Fisher (1922) and serve as tests in assessing the quality of a particular statistical index. They have been named, after Fisher, as *Fisher's system of tests* (see Eichhorn 1976 for a detailed analysis as well as a comprehensive bibliography of Fisher's "test" or "axiomatic" approach to index numbers).

The econometric approach involves estimating the parameters of a production, cost, or profit function. With a production function, the rate of technological progress can be measured directly using equation (1). With a cost function, $C(r, y, t)$, where r is the vector of input prices and the assumption of constant returns to scale, the rate of technological change can be shown to be

$$\frac{\partial \ln f(x,t)}{\partial t} = -\frac{\partial \ln C(r,y,t)}{\partial t},$$

where $\partial \ln C(r, y, t)/\partial t$ is the "dual rate of cost diminution." With a profit function, $\pi(r, y, t)$, and the assumption of constant returns to scale, the rate of technological progress can be shown to be the product of the dual rate of profit growth and the ratio of profit to revenue, as follows,

$$\frac{\partial \ln f(x,t)}{\partial t} = \frac{\partial \ln \pi(r,y,t)}{\partial t} \times \frac{\pi(r,y,t)}{py},$$

where p is the price of output. While the econometric approach provides deep insights into the production structure (i.e., the price elasticities as well as the elasticities of substitution), it assumes that the firms or industries in question are fully efficient (i.e., operating on the production frontier), which has been proved not to be the case by studies on technical and allocative efficiency.

Finally, the distance function approach to measuring total factor productivity, introduced separately by Ronald Shephard (1953) and Sten Malmquist (1953), seeks to separate total factor productivity into two components: changes resulting from a movement toward the production frontier and shifts in the frontier. Mathematically, the Malmquist total factor productivity index is given by

$$m_o^t (y_t, y_{t+1}, x_t, x_{t+1}) =$$

$$\frac{d_o^{t+1}(y_{t+1}, x_{t+1})}{d_o^t(y_t, x_t)} \times \left[\frac{d_o^t(y_{t+1}, x_{t+1})}{d_o^{t+1}(y_{t+1}, x_{t+1})} \times \frac{d_o^t (y_t, x_t)}{d_o^{t+1}(y_t, x_t)} \right]^{\frac{1}{2}},$$

where the term outside the brackets on the right-hand side measures the change in relative efficiency between years t and $t + 1$ and the geometric mean of the two ratios inside the brackets measures the shift in technology (technological progress) between the two periods evaluated at x_t and $x_{t + 1}$. This approach has several advantages. It does not require a specific functional form, and it does not assume that firms are operating at their efficient level. However, implicit in the approach is the assumption that all units (firms, industries, or countries) being compared have the same production function, when in fact evidence suggests that even firms in the same industry do not have identical production functions.

In our discussion so far of the four approaches to the measurement of technological progress, we implicitly assumed that technological progress is factor-neutral in the sense that the marginal rate of substitution between any two inputs (measured along a ray through the origin) is not affected by technological progress. Studies, however, find that technological progress is not factor-neutral; rather, it is skill-biased. *Skill bias* occurs when a shift in the production function (technological change) favors skilled over unskilled labor by increasing its relative productivity and therefore its relative demand and skill premium.

SEE ALSO *Growth Accounting; Machinery; Production Function; Returns to Scale; Technological Progress, Economic Growth; Technology; Technology, Adoption of*

BIBLIOGRAPHY

Abramovitz, Moses. 1956. Resource and Output Trends in the United States since 1870. *American Economic Review* 46: 5–23.

Diewert, W. Erwin. 1976. Exact and Superlative Index Numbers. *Journal of Econometrics* 4: 115–145.

Diewert, W. Erwin, and Alice Nakamura. 2003. Index Number Concepts, Measures of Decompositions of Productivity. *Journal of Productivity Analysis* 19: 127–159.

Eichhorn, W. 1976. Fisher's Tests Revisited. *Econometrica* 44 (2): 247–256.

Fisher, Irving. 1922. *The Making of Index Numbers: A Study of Their Varieties, Tests, and Reliability.* Boston: Houghton Mifflin.

Malmquist, Sten. 1953. Index Numbers and Indifference Surfaces. *Trabajos de Estadística* 4: 209–242.

Shephard, Ronald W. 1953. *Cost and Production Functions.* Princeton, NJ: Princeton University Press.

Solow, Robert M. 1957. Technical Change and the Aggregate Production Function. *Review of Economics and Statistics* 39: 312–320.

Apostolos Serletis

TECHNOLOGY

Technology refers to the underlying production methodology through which inputs or resources are converted into output (goods and services). At a point in time there is one best way to produce a good or service. In other words, there is a well-defined production technology at a point in time. Over time, the technology can change as better, more efficient, and cheaper means of production are invented. Such changes might be due to deliberate attempts by businesses and governments (called "endogenous technical change") or they may be accidental (due to serendipity). In the long term, new technologies build upon previous technologies to yield better, more refined products and process. In that context, it is widely argued that perhaps man's greatest innovation was the wheel.

Sometimes technology is treated as another input in the production process, like labor or capital, and in other instances it is viewed as a catalyst that makes existing inputs more productive. Two unique features that set technology apart from other factors are that it has the potential to yield disproportionate returns for inventors, and there is uncertainty associated with the invention and use of new technology. Inventors are able to earn disproportionate returns when they have a unique product that confers a monopoly upon them. The uncertainty associated with technology might be related to the race to invent first, or it might be with respect to research resources necessary for innovation success, or with the potential audience (who will use the new technology and how fast?).

Some technologies improve the product processes (by making them more efficient and, consequently, cheaper), whereas others introduce entirely new products. The Internet has enabled process improvements in a number of instances (e.g., via online brokerages or online travel agencies), whereas a new pharmaceutical drug for an illness previously without a cure may be viewed as a product innovation. More fundamentally, process technologies affect production costs, whereas product innovations have the ability to create new markets.

The ingredients to new technology are the research and development (R&D) resources. These include scientists and engineers and related physical resources (research laboratories and so on). The output of R&D is generally measured in the number of patents granted. The number of patents, however, is an imperfect measure because it does not account for inventions that are not patented, and it treats patents of varying importance qualitatively the same.

The development of new technology can be seen as a process involving three distinct stages—invention, development, and diffusion. Invention involves the conception of a new idea about a new product or a new process.

Development refers to the building of a prototype and testing its usability, possible side effects, and longevity. Diffusion is the marketing stage, when the new technology is dispersed to the potential audience or users. Cooperation among private firms or between the public and private sectors can occur at one or all of these stages.

Some technologies are more flexible than others. Flexible technologies enable substitution among inputs; for example, grocery stores can employ a large number of checkout clerks and have relatively few (or no) automated checkout machines, or they can have few clerks and more automated machines. Inflexible technologies, on the other hand, do not permit substitution among inputs; for example, a cab company should have at least one driver for each cab to deliver viable service—two (or more) drivers and no cars are as useless as two (or more) cars and no drivers. Over time, however, improvements in technologies can alter the substitutability among inputs—think about what will happen to the car-driver substitutability as "smart" highways become a reality. Furthermore, there might be differences in the nature of technologies as production expands. In some cases there might be an equal bang for the buck as inputs are increased—that is, doubling of all inputs doubles output (technically called "constant returns to scale"); in other cases there might be less than (or more than) proportionate returns—that is, doubling of all inputs less than doubles output—decreasing returns to scale.

As the importance of technologies has come to the forefront, so has the attention of researchers on the process of technological change. One interesting aspect in this regard is the premature technological obsolescence. Joseph Schumpeter foresaw this many decades ago when he referred to this as the "gale of creative destruction" (Schumpeter 1950). In industries susceptible to rapid technological progress (e.g., the electronics industry), successful technologies might become prematurely obsolete as they are overtaken (or "leapfrogged") by newer technologies before full benefits have been realized. While this is somewhat of a concern, governments generally have tried to let the markets work by not blocking or delaying premature obsolescence.

Market competition can play a crucial role in the production and use of technologies. The Schumpeterian hypothesis posits that monopolies, due to their reserves from past profits, are perhaps better equipped than their competitive counterparts to deal with the uncertainties of research and innovation. However, competitive pressures might induce firms to seek out better production methods and new products, either through their own research or via licensing the technology of others. Some software companies choose to develop their own software, whereas others license some software from others. The empirical evidence regarding the role of competition and firm size is rather mixed. Many large competitive firms have been quite innovative (e.g., Canon, 3M), whereas small inventors have also contributed useful technologies. The classic example in this instance is the development of the Apple computer in a garage. Firms might cooperate in the development of technologies among themselves, or there might be cooperation between the public and private sectors. Some governments such as the U.S. government have relaxed laws to check anticompetitive practices to allow cooperation in research. These moves have led to the emergence of consortia to jointly engage in research in pursuit of new technologies.

A number of new technologies can have implications for workers as they tend to be capital-using and labor-saving. Examples of such technologies include online banking, which might affect the jobs of bank tellers, and online travel agencies, which threaten the jobs of travel agents.

Full benefits of technologies are realized when they are optimally diffused. The diffusion of technologies occurs over time, because in some instances users have to incur monetary and learning costs (consider a new type of software that requires the user to spend time to learn what the software can do). Governments sometimes subsidize these learning costs directly (e.g., with cash grants for adopting energy-saving building technologies) or indirectly (e.g., with free user-education clinics by agriculture extension services). The transfer of technologies might occur via legal or illegal means. Legal means include research joint ventures among firms pursuing new technologies or licensing agreements where firms authorize others to use their technologies for a fee. Sometimes, however, these licensing arrangements can have harmful effects when firms refuse to license complementary technologies. In such instances, the pace of technological change is somewhat slowed. Internationally, developing nations generally seek to adopt technologies from developed countries by inviting foreign investments. But developed nations often are reluctant to offer the latest technologies because the existence and enforcement of intellectual-property protection laws is typically lax in developing nations. In recent years international treaties have tried to bring various nations onto a somewhat equal footing in regards to the protection of intellectual property. Illegal transfer of technologies occurs when rival firms are able to copy or use technologies without approval. Such spillovers of technologies are partly driven by the nature of technology (some technologies are easier to copy than others). Common means of technology spillovers include industrial espionage, reverse engineering (unraveling a product or process to learn about its construction), and hiring scientists and engineers from the inventor firm. Governmental ability to check technology spillovers is limited by the nature of technologies and by jurisdictional constraints. Government-sponsored technologies sometimes overcome these issues by making certain new technologies freely available in the public domain.

Often, choosing between alternate technologies can have long-term implications that can render some choices inefficient and very costly to alter over time. In other words, technological choice can have inertia when production processes are locked into specific technological streams. Two glaring examples of this are the keyboard settings of typewriters (and now computers) and the width of railroad tracks. The QWERTY settings of the manual typewriters were historically chosen so that the keys would be least likely to lock up, hence the choice, given the state of the technology at the time, was efficient. However, over time, the manual typewriters evolved into electric, then electronic, typewriters, and finally into computers. These iterations did not face the problem of keys locking, but the QWERTY format for keys has almost universally persisted, in spite of some alternate formulations that have been shown to be more efficient. In the other example, the choice of the width of rail tracks has implications for how far the rail network can ply and is very costly to change over time. Even today, a number of countries continue to have tracks of more than one width, creating networking problems within the country (these issues are even more pronounced in an intercountry setting). It seems, however, that governments have learned from past mistakes, and in some cases international standardization bodies (such as the one to manage the spread of the Internet) are being formed in early stages of technologies to avoid bottlenecks in the future.

Government involvement in the production, marketing (or diffusion), monitoring, and protection of technologies varies a great deal. Governments might need to monitor certain technologies for their effects. For example, in the United States new drugs have to undergo extensive testing for possible side effects and have to be approved by the Federal Drug Administration (FDA) before being made available publicly. Other technologies have to be tested for their effects on the environment. A key aspect of government technology policy deals with ensuring adequate returns to inventors (to preserve incentives for undertaking the risks of technology development) and creating conditions for long-term technological growth. Governments generally have policies to deal with intellectual-property protection and with subsidies to research. Patents that grant monopolies to inventors for a specific time period (currently twenty years for most patents in the United States) have proven quite popular despite their shortcomings. Patent applicants have to prove their own and the invention's credentials (i.e., uniqueness of their invention and their priority of discovery). The underlying rationale behind patents is that they balance the costs of monopoly grants against the long-term benefits that are realized when the secret patent formulae become public knowledge at the time of patent expiry, spurring future innovations. In practice, there is an interesting difference between U.S. patent policy and how patents are granted in (most of) the rest of the world. The United States grants a patent to the first person (or institution) to invent a new product or process; this person might not be the first to file the patent application. Most other countries, however, award a patent to the first to file, who might not be the original inventor. Both systems have merits and shortcomings. The U.S. system follows the essence of how patents should be granted, but leads to costly and socially wasteful litigation, especially in instances where the social value of patents is rather small. The rest of the world system avoids costly litigation, but can result in grave injustices when original inventors are slow to file the paperwork.

In recent years, the Internet, or more generally, "soft" technologies, have generated an interesting set of issues both for market participants and for governments trying to regulate technologies. Unlike "hard" or physical technologies (e.g., a tractor or an airplane), soft technologies are difficult to monitor (protect) and easy to transfer. Which aspects of a new software are like a language (and thus cannot be protected), and which aspects are like commercial products (and thus can be protected)? Transmission of soft technologies also makes convenient the separation of production and marketing over large geographical areas and eliminates the use of middlemen or substantial transactions costs. For example, soft technologies such as computer software, music, and e-books can be produced in one corner of the world and marketed in another via the Internet without the need of a middleman. Governments in such instances are somewhat powerless to monitor (and tax) these transactions. In effect, innovations in instruments of regulation have failed to keep pace with the speed of technological change.

The United States has been the world leader in technology since the end of World War II (1939–1945). Many important inventions and discoveries originated in the United States, and a number of these were byproducts of the U.S. defense and space programs. In the early 1980s, however, there were some concerns about the United States' declining technological leadership. It became evident that although many inventions were still originating in the United States, other countries were taking the lead in perfecting these technologies by making them more user-friendly. (For example, although the microwave oven was invented in the United States, there are hardly any domestic manufacturers of these ovens left.) These concerns prompted the U.S. government to strengthen intellectual-property protection in some cases and to stress better commercialization strategies for new technologies.

Two noteworthy developments in this regard were the provision of patents to semiconductor chips and the introduction of legislation that makes it easier for federally sponsored innovations to be commercialized. Universities in the United States are also now able to hold patents and benefit from commercialization of the technologies invented by their staff. It remains to be seen, however, how the world's technological leadership will evolve, especially with the advent of soft technologies that are difficult to control and not geographically constrained. Another key issue concerns the extent and speed of technological "trickle down" from developed nations to developing nations.

SEE ALSO *Technology, Adoption of; Technology, Transfer of*

BIBLIOGRAPHY

Goel, Rajeev K. 1999. *Economic Models of Technological Change.* Westport, CT: Quorum Books.

Kamien, Morton I., and Nancy L. Schwartz. 1982. *Market Structure and Innovation.* Cambridge, U.K.: Cambridge University Press.

Reinganum, Jennifer F. 1989. The Timing of Innovation: Research, Development, and Diffusion. In *Handbook of Industrial Organization*, eds. Richard Schmalensee and Robert Willig, 849–908. New York: Elsevier Science.

Schumpeter, Joseph. 1950. *Capitalism, Socialism, and Democracy.* 3rd ed. New York: Harper and Row.

Von Hippel, Eric. 1987. *The Sources of Innovation.* Oxford: Oxford University Press.

Rajeev K. Goel

TECHNOLOGY, ADOPTION OF

The adoption of technology is represented in the popular imagination as a straightforward process whereby the best technology wins in the marketplace, satisfying consumer needs. However, this superficial understanding neglects a number of important issues that shape technological adoption and the mechanisms of the process itself.

TECHNOLOGY AND THE DIFFUSION MODEL

The classic representation of technology adoption is Everett M. Rogers's technological diffusion curve, which he outlines in his 2003 book *The Diffusion of Innovations.* This s-shaped curve is broken up into three phases: innovation and early adoption, accelerating adoption, and saturation. In the first phase the technology is rare, unknown, and untested. First phase users are often very different from the general public or mass consumers, whether in their general interest in novelties and new gadgets, or their specific organizational or occupational needs. For example, "Segway" personal transporters are not moving into mass circulation as fast as their inventor might hope, but airports and others with the need for moving security personnel have adopted them more readily. Similarly, being the first to adopt a fax machine or a cell phone was a risky proposition at first: There was no one to communicate with and it was not clear that the technology would be successful. In accelerating adoption more broad markets for innovations emerge, and new groups of potential adopters engage the technology, which rapidly spreads. At saturation the rate of new adoption slows and the market for a new technology is relatively stable, although economic activities such as replacement, repair, and accessorization may be quite dynamic. The diffusion model of technology adoption is a very effective model for describing successful consumer products, and it originated in Rogers's studies of the communication of new ideas.

The origin of the diffusion model in studies of the dissemination of ideas leads to weaknesses in the model. The first is a pro-diffusion bias that is part of the core language of the model. For example those who are hesitant to adopt new technologies are described as "laggards," which positions them as irrationally risk-averse and resisting new technologies adopted by risk-taking "early adopters," rather than as hesitant to expend scarce resources on an untested new product.

The second problem with diffusion as a model of new technologies is that it leaves the design process for technologies unexamined, as well as the organizational contexts of technology adoption. Bruno Latour found in his 1996 study that when discussing contemporary corporate settings in particular, the designers and inventors interact with many different social groups (which may or may not be end users), and the earliest "adopters" of a new technology are the financiers, designers, managers, and suppliers and manufacturers who must be "enrolled" into supplying the resources for bringing the technology to a point of relative stability and maturity before it can move into the market. Within this process, asserts Robert J. Thomas in his 1994 book *What Machines Can't Do: Politics and Technology in Industrial Enterprise*, the organizational contexts of technology's design and implementation are most important, and internal politics, relationships with suppliers, employment markets and expertise, and other factors shape design and implementation or non-adoption of new technologies.

This points to the final issue with the mainstream diffusionist models of technology adoption: the assumption that the technologies that are moving into the marketplace are somehow the "best" in some unambiguous technical sense. But "best" can only be defined in relation to a particular group's interests and activities. Any Apple™ user will argue that the near monopoly that Microsoft™ enjoys in the marketplace does not reflect that the "best" operating system has been adopted. Therefore, proposes Wiebe E. Bijker in his 1995 study, social and economic power dynamics shape the processes that produce new technologies to be adopted and defined as "working," and the potential adoption patterns of those technologies across different user groups. Technology adoption discourses also assume that the technology is stable as a material and symbolic configuration: that there is closure of the technology. This assumption is not necessarily warranted: Sometimes in the process of the adoption a technology is adapted both materially changed, in terms of modifications or rebuilding, and certainly symbolically reconfigured, as the imagined and intended meanings and uses of the technology are reworked in different settings. In other cases, such as computers and cellular telephones, rapid changes in versions and models disrupt a smooth diffusion curve, as new features render technologies apparently obsolete, and closure and compatibility are not achieved.

TECHNOLOGY AND COMPATIBILITY

The issue of compatibility points to the complexity of the adoption of technology in varying social contexts. In all contexts of technology adoption, a new technology must fit within existing manufacturing and use infrastructures, meet perceived needs, be nominally affordable, and be convergent with important cultural ideals. Each of these five elements presents different barriers to adoption in diverse cultural, particularly international, contexts. A technically functional technology that disrupts important social processes or relies on scarce resources will not be adopted. This is part of the reason that patent offices are full of descriptions of technologies that "work" in a technical sense, but are not adopted and are not seen as "working" by their intended users.

SEE ALSO *Luddites; Productivity; Solow Residual, The; Technology; Technology, Transfer of; Technophobia*

BIBLIOGRAPHY

Bijker, Wiebe E. 1995. *Of Bicycles, Bakelites, and Bulbs: Toward a Theory of Sociotechnical Change.* Cambridge, MA: MIT Press.

Latour, Bruno. 1996. *Aramis, Or, The Love of Technology.* Trans. Catherine Porter. Cambridge, MA: Harvard University Press.

Rogers, Everett M. 2003. *Diffusion of Innovations.* 5th ed. New York: Free Press.

Thomas, Robert J. 1994. *What Machines Can't Do: Politics and Technology in the Industrial Enterprise.* Berkeley: University of California Press.

Jennifer L. Croissant

TECHNOLOGY, CELLULAR

Japan developed the world's first analog mobile phones in 1979. They spread rapidly, outstripping the world's landline systems within fifteen years. By 2006 the majority of the citizens of Europe, North America, and the wealthier nations of Asia, Africa, the Caribbean, and Latin America owned mobile phones. The United Kingdom had more mobiles than people, and there were 207 million users in the United States. More than twenty manufacturers produced them, and most nations had converged on GSM transmission, which was designed for European compatibility, although it coexisted with CMDA and iDen standards in the United States, Australia, Japan, and South Korea.

Most innovations have come from Japan, where a dense population that commutes to work, a high-tech industry long focused on miniaturization, and conducive social and consumer relationships led to early adoptions of camera and video phones, GPS (global positioning systems), text messaging, Internet, and music player capabilities. In Japan third-generation (3G) systems were the norm by 2005. Europe, South Korea, Taiwan, and coastal China are said to lag behind Japan by eighteen months, and North America lags three years behind. Elsewhere, developing nations rejected landlines in favor of cheaper mobile systems. The rollout of 4G systems is anticipated in Japan around 2010.

Mobile phones are not without problems. Many studies confirm the higher risk of auto accidents while using mobiles, even hands-free systems. Some scientific evidence shows increases in cancerous tumors among heavy, long-time users. Transmission towers are unwelcome sights in residential areas. Mobiles are also used in identity theft and credit card crime, in the coordination of terrorist attacks, and as detonators for bombs. Due to possible radio-wave interference, their use is banned in airplanes, hospitals, and some high-tech facilities. Theft of mobiles is common, with black markets on the Internet and in major cities.

Despite their problems, mobile phones have changed human communication profoundly, freeing it from the ancient constraints of physical proximity and spatial immobility. They have been rapidly adopted across cultures, age groups, and literacy and income levels, though in polyvalent modes. Mobile use initially was similar to the use of pagers by doctors and business people. Later mobiles became status items, especially among teenagers, who engaged in a "personalization culture" that included the use of faceplates, hand cords, stickers, and ringtones. For adults, status shifted to broadband Internet access.

Mobiles have become a basic technology of emergency response. Drivers use them to report accidents, police and fire departments use them as a back channel in disasters, and the elderly carry them "just in case." Australian studies show that high percentages of mobile users are "cellular Samaritans" who use their phones to summon help for those in difficulty. Camera and video phones allowed instant reporting on the 2005 Indian Ocean tsunami and Hurricane Katrina. Japanese users can even be informed of impending earthquakes.

Sociologists have noted across cultures, genders, and age groups an increase in "grooming calls," by which members of a family or group show concern and "nearness." These short, frequent calls reinforce bonds of affection. Immigrant families and diasporic clans in particular do this. However, the "universal availability" of mobile users also allows the reinforcement of hierarchy. Bosses call employees outside work hours, parents monitor children, and couples monitor each other: "If you are without a mobile phone it means that no one depends on you for urgent direction" (Bautsch et al. 2001, p. 3).

The location of mobile use is problematic. Mobiles have been banned from theaters, religious institutions, funerals, airplanes, and many restaurants, and their use is frowned upon in museums, bookstores, trains, and buses. A dynamic of "civil inattention" has arisen in which bystanders pretend to ignore mobile conversations and speakers use vague or euphemistic language. Mobiles are also used as symbolic bodyguards in public areas to ward off unwanted attention or to refuse to participate in public space: "Public space is no longer lived in all of its aspects, stimuli and prospects, but is kept in the background of an itinerant cellular intimacy" (Fortunati 2000, p. 11).

Receiving mobile calls is an area without norms. Phones may be on, off, or in message-only mode, as users determine their degree of availability. Users decide whom to give their numbers to, whom to block, whom to answer immediately, and who hears a busy signal. Finnish studies show that men are more likely than women to turn mobiles off to avoid social control. Because calls arrive unpredictably but habit dictates that they be answered, face-to-face conversations and other calls must be "suspended." Such interruptions cause anxiety for both parties, leading to anomie and difficult restarts. Users must also manage facial expressions and body language for multiple audiences, indicating primary and secondary importance to those present and absent. Such "managed availability," however, has increased the capacity of parents in particular to coordinate various roles. But managing role conflicts and the discrepant awareness of conversation partners may be difficult for older users, and may promote broad but shallow relationships among younger users.

One alternative is SMS (short message systems), or "text messaging." SMS patterns tend to follow earlier pager use, though today's users can communicate through emoti-cons or delay responses via timers. Finnish studies, however, show that feedback is expected within 15-30 minutes. In Asia SMS users tend to be young and to belong to linguistic subcultures, and they are often killing time in public places or transport. SMS offers friendship tryouts, invitations without risk, and the cost is shared by sender and receiver. Some Japanese teens maintain multiple personae for hundreds of *meru tomo* (email friends), and SMS is the common channel for arranging *enjo kosai*, or paid "dates," between businessmen and high school girls.

The mobile's impact on individuality is also an area of concern. Traditional feelings of longing, homesickness, sadness, or insecurity are assuaged by calls and thus leveled out. Mobiles diminish the number of true hellos and goodbyes. Lost are reflective periods when people review past actions and plan future ones. This culture of "nomadic intimacy" may portend more peripheral relationships, but fewer deep ones (Fortunati 2000). The deregulation of social life is another implication. "Nights out [are] characterized by endless deferrals and reshuffling of meetings and events which might never occur," writes Sadie Plant (2003, p. 64), and "freedom from punctuality is permitted by constant ability to update other parties as to your status" (Townsend 2000, p. 94). In Italy the popularity of the mobile "seems to be associated with its support for a spontaneous, disorganized lifestyle that has always reigned among most of the country's population" (Geser 2004).

The mobile has also made covert information exchange more possible. Some critics call this gossip, but others see it as decentralizing or democratizing. Parents communicate with other parents about children's attitudes and whereabouts; employees engage in a similar dynamic about bosses; and law officers speak to each other rather than through dispatchers or superiors. In China mobile networks have spread news censored by the government and allowed seemingly spontaneous demonstrations. But studies show that mothers and wives act as the mobile information hubs of most families, so although mobiles may reduce the number of shared family experiences, they seem to be assimilated to traditional roles.

In the future, as the distribution of antennas grows denser, the location of every mobile will be determinable by GPS. In Japan, location within 30 feet was the norm by 2006, whereas in the United States the few GPS-enabled systems were accurate to 300 feet. GPS will be standard in 4G systems and, combined with built-in compasses, will allow users to point phones at buildings to find addresses, businesses, and friends, as well as to navigate roads. One side effect may be a barrage of business advertising. Barcode scanners may also become standard on mobiles, so that consumers concerned about food safety and product origin can "source" their purchases on databases before buying. Pocket-sized mobiles with SIMs (subscriber identity modules) will serve as credit cards that can be passed over sensors, like RFID (radio frequency interface devices) tags (Kohiyama 2005). Because SIMs are removable, users may have different mobiles for different occasions; they may even use friends' phones, because their SIM carries their rate plans and caller lists. Batteries may become universally available, recharged, or swapped cheaply at kiosks or vending machines. Increased demand for Internet uses will lead to multilayered rate plans, and SMS will prevail underground on trains and in subsurface rooms. South Korea has announced plans to send out traffic tickets, fines, and even indictments by SMS. All mobiles will connect to nearby workplace, school, or community LANs to make use of the Internet when possible. Future architectural designs will change, allowing for ubiquitous mobile phone niches. World cities such as Tokyo, New York, London, and Paris may consist of people whose work requires face-to-face proximity for deals and transactions, whereas mobiles will allow others to work nomadically.

SEE ALSO *Technology, Video*

BIBLIOGRAPHY

Bautsch, Holly, Julien Ganger, Timothy Karnjate, et al. 2001. An Investigation of Mobile Phone Use: A Socio-technical Approach. Unpublished research report, Department of Industrial Engineering, University of Wisconsin–Madison. http://www.mobilesociety.net/uploadi/editor/IE449_0108.pdf.

Brown, Barry, Nicola Green, and Richard Harper, eds. 2002. *Wireless World: Social and Interactional Aspects of the Mobile Age*. London: Springer-Verlag.

Dziesinski, Michael J. 2003. What Is "Keitai Culture"?: Investigations into the Social Impact of Mobile Telephony with Society in Contemporary Japan. http://towakudai.blogs.com/Keitai.Research.Survey.pdf.

Fortunati, Leopoldina. 2000. *The Mobile Phone: New Social Categories and Relations*. Trieste, Italy: University of Trieste.

Geser, Hans. 2004. Towards a Sociological Theory of the Mobile Phone. http://socio.ch/mobile/t_geser1.htm.

Goffman, Erving. 1963. *Behavior in Public Places: Notes on the Social Organization of Gatherings*. New York: Free Press.

Ito, Mizoko, Daisuke Okabe, and Misa Matsuda, eds. 2006. *Personal, Portable, Pedestrian: Mobile Phones in Japanese Life*. Boston: MIT Press.

Katz, James E., and Mark A. Aakhus 2002. *Perpetual Contact: Mobile Communication, Private Talk, Public Performance*. Cambridge, U.K.: Cambridge University Press.

Kohiyama, Kenji. 2005. The Future of the Ketai. *Japan Media Review*, August 11. http://www.japanmediareview.com/japan/stories/050811kohiyama/.

Lasen, Amparo. 2005. *The Social Shaping of Fixed and Mobile Networks: A Historical Comparison*. Surrey, U.K.: University of Surrey.

Markoff, John, and Martin Fackler. 2006. With a Cellphone as My Guide. *New York Times*, June 28.

Plant, Sadie. 2003. On the Mobile: The Effects of Mobile Telephones on Social and Individual Life. http://www.motorola.com/mot/doc/0/234_MotDoc.pdf.

Sloane, Andy, and Felix van Rijn, eds. 2000. *Home Informatics and Telematics: Information, Technology, and Society*. Boston: Kluwer.

Townsend, Anthony M. 2000. Life in the Real-Time City: Mobile Telephones and Urban Metabolism. *Journal of Urban Technology* 7 (2): 85–104.

Tsai, Michelle. 2006. What's a Phone For? *Wall Street Journal* (Eastern edition), June 19: R 12.

Wellman, Barry. 2001. Physical Place and Cyber Place: The Rise of Personalized Networking. *International Journal of Urban and Regional Research* 25 (2): 227–252.

Wellman, Barry, Janet Salaff, Dimitrina Dimitrova, et al. 1996. Computer Networks as Social Networks: Collaborative Work, Telework, and Virtual Community. *Annual Review of Sociology* 22: 213–238.

William Marling

TECHNOLOGY, TRANSFER OF

The first humans developed new and better ways of production, and those around them watched and imitated. When the new and better ways became more complex, then the innovator would often teach the innovations to others. Since the beginning the transfer of technology has followed innovation. Technology is transferred from parents to children, from masters to apprentices, from teachers to students, from managers to workers, and from workers to workers. Technology spreads both horizontally (to competitors) and vertically (to suppliers and buyers) from a given innovating firm. It even spreads to seemingly unrelated industries (consider the case of the transistor that was developed for hearing aids but ended up in radios, TVs, computers, and space crafts).

However, the origin of the term *technology transfer* and its study as a separate phenomenon can be traced to the massive gifts of technology from the United States to Europe and Japan immediately following World War II (1939–1945). Many U.S. firms freely opened their doors so that European companies could come and study their production processes. Blueprints and patents were freely shared.

During the cold war between the United States and the Union of Soviet Socialist Republics (USSR), both sides encouraged the transfer of their technology to lesser-developed countries in order to help the recipients develop and to win allies. It was assumed that economic development required acquisition of modern technology. During the 1950s and 1960s, international organizations (such as the United Nations' Expanded Program of

Technical Assistance) and private foundations (such as the Ford and Rockefeller Foundations) were the primary conduits of international technological flows.

Many hoped that the farther a country lagged behind cutting-edge technology the more they would gain from acquiring that technology. Unfortunately this hope was misplaced. Experts discovered that countries closer to the technology frontier were better able to absorb cutting-edge technology than countries that lagged far behind. For example, countries needed reliable electricity before they could efficiently use any technology, such as computers, that was electrically driven. Furthermore, countries needed educated indigenous people who could understand both the new technology and the country's special needs in order to modify the technology so that it could work efficiently in the new environment. In the late 1970s and 1980s, literature emerged on *appropriate* technology where appropriate usually meant small-scale, simpler, and often manually powered technology such as hand pumps instead of electrically driven pumps. However, this appropriate technology was not always well received because it was viewed as inferior to what the developed world used.

During the 1980s and 1990s, some hoped that multinational companies would somehow find a way of successfully taking the most advanced technologies to the poorest countries in order to get the greatest profits from closing the largest technological gaps (and from paying lower wages). Contrary to this hope, most multinationals did not set up operations in the poorest countries; instead, they set up subsidiaries in countries that were already clearly on the path to economic development. Furthermore, multinationals have a strong incentive to keep their technology from any competitors. Some of a multinational's technology is expected to leak to competitors through migration of workers from multinational to domestically owned firms, through reverse engineering, or through industrial espionage. To minimize the risk of competitors acquiring their technology, many multinationals pay their workers significantly more than domestic firms pay (to keep workers from leaving) and do not give their best technologies to their foreign subsidiaries.

In the 1990s and early 2000s, a large literature emerged trying to estimate the relationship between foreign direct investment and growth rates of developing nations via technology spillovers. This literature assumes that technology naturally spills over the borders of a firm to neighboring firms and is plagued by problems with:

1. how to measure technology,

2. determining to what extent the foreign investment caused the growth or the growth attracted the foreign investment,

3. modeling and estimating the interaction between domestic development of technology and the foreign technology, and

4. explaining how and why the spillover effect occurs, especially because the firm has a strong profit motive to stop it.

The policy implication of many of these studies is that governments of lesser developed nations should actively encourage foreign direct investment. However, the problems listed above may invalidate that conclusion. Furthermore, this literature tends to consider only the positive effects of foreign direct investment and ignore potentially negative effects such as dependency, loss of sovereignty, increased corruption, disruption of native culture, and risk of capital flight, which can cause financial crises such as the one that swept Asia in 1997–1998.

SEE ALSO *Technology; Technology, Adoption of*

BIBLIOGRAPHY

Fan, Emma Xiaoqin. 2002. *Technology Spillovers from Foreign Direct Investment—A Survey.* Manila: Asian Development Bank.

Keller, Wolfgang. 2004. International Technology Diffusion. *Journal of Economic Literature* 42 (3): 752–782.

Saggi, Kamal. 2002. Trade, Foreign Direct Investment, and International Technology Transfer: A Survey. *World Bank Research Observer* 17 (2): 191–235.

Seely, Bruce E. 2003. Historical Patterns in the Scholarship of Technology Transfer. *Comparative Technology Transfer and Society* 1 (1): 7–48.

Jonathan E. Leightner

TECHNOLOGY, VIDEO

Video technology was developed as an adjunct to centralized television systems. Its widespread adoption since the 1970s has had the profound impact of integrating film and television culture into global everyday life. Initially many hoped that video technology would lead to greater diversity of programming and an expansion of television's function beyond ephemeral entertainment and would empower the ordinary viewer. The empowerment that has occurred has increased cultural fragmentation and an isolation of viewers from each other. Thus video technology contributes to the general post-1970s trend of privatizing life spheres.

Video is not a precise term. It most commonly refers to those technologies that record or download electronic images, but the general reference to all electronic images remains. In analog systems the recording is achieved by breaking down reflected light into a series of electrical impulses typically recorded on a magnetic tape. In digital systems the electrical impulses are further refined by a computer into a series of numbers that are recorded and that can be retrieved by other computers and displayed as images.

The American corporation Ampex first demonstrated a working video recorder in 1956. In the early 1960s video technology was used for instant replays in sports and the breaking events of President John F. Kennedy's 1963 assassination. Video cameras and systems were developed for surveillance and other uses. The Japanese manufacturers took the lead in developing consumer video recorders. Sony introduced the ½-inch Portapack in 1965 and the ¾-inch U-matic cassette system in 1969. These were adopted in the educational market and also in the adult film market. But it was in 1975 that the ½-inch cassette systems captured the global consumer market. At first there were two formats, Sony's Betamax and JVC's VHS, but within five years VHS dominated. The digital versatile disc (DVD) became the dominant video format after its introduction in 1997.

The video revolution was sparked by a pent-up desire of people throughout the world to change their use of television. Television critics were scornful of television's "vast wasteland" of poor choices in the United States and no choice in other countries. However, enhanced choice was a secondary reason for most VHS purchasers. The most important motivation was to watch shows at the time and place that was convenient for the viewers (*time shifting*). Thus video technology became part of the sociological phenomenon of a time crunch. This function of video was not imposed by corporations but was the result of a "consumption junction" (a term coined by Ruth Cowan in "The Consumption Junction" [1987]) among users, manufacturers, and content providers.

There was some experimentation with original programming for video. But video's overwhelming use was to extend the global market for Hollywood films and television shows and the mainstream values they convey, fitting a general pattern of "suppressing [video's] radical potential" (Winston 1998, p. 11). Raymond Williams's concept of mobile privatization is an influential way to understand video use. He deduced that broadcasting was a culmination of a century-long pattern of privatizing popular culture. People use television to make their homes the center of their lives. Video dramatically accelerated this trend. The additions of downloading movie and television clips on the computer, the cell phone, and the I-pod have gone even further in the private viewing of filmed entertainment.

Diaspora communities use video technologies for ready access to their home cultures. However, this direct access has weakened specialized movie theaters and has lessened the opportunities for theater bookers to introduce the audience to unknown titles.

The art of filmmaking has changed. The mainstream American film industry dramatically merged into transnational media conglomerates attracted by the new video revenue (Wasser 2001). Video became the most important market, surpassing the theatrical box office. Story lines and characters are sold across a variety of media, from games to merchandise.

Video games have influenced narrative film aesthetics toward visceral effects that seduce the audience into experiencing the repetitive thrills and spills of movement and sound at the expense of character development and plot logic. To make people feel the experience of the movie, filmmakers have increasingly turned toward another aspect of video technology, computer generated images (CGI). Video shifted experimental filmmaking from the art house to the art gallery. Adult filmmaking is entirely in video.

Video technology has enabled the large trends of mass culture. On the industrial end, industries have consolidated. The promise of grassroots video making has rarely caught the mass public's attention. One interesting example is the explosion of cheap fictional videos in Nigeria. On the consumer end, audiences have fragmented as viewers use video to facilitate a flexible work and leisure balance focused on consuming culture in isolated domestic spaces.

SEE ALSO *Modernization; Technology, Cellular*

BIBLIOGRAPHY

Cowan, Ruth Schwartz. 1987. The Consumption Junction: A Proposal for Research Strategies in the Sociology of Technology. In *The Social Construction of Technological Systems*, eds. Wiebe E. Bijker, Thomas P. Hughes, and Trevor J. Pinch, 261–280. Cambridge, MA: MIT Press.

Levy, Mark R., ed. 1989. *The VCR Age: Home Video and Mass Communication*. Newbury Park, CA: Sage Publications.

Wasser, Frederick. 2001. *Veni, Vidi, Video: The Hollywood Empire and the VCR*. Austin: University of Texas Press.

Williams, Raymond. 1992. *Television: Technology and Cultural Form*. Hanover, NH: University Press of New England. (Orig. pub. 1974).

Winston, Brian. 1998. *Media, Technology, and Society: A History*. New York: Routledge.

Frederick Wasser

TECHNOPHOBIA

The word *technophobia* derives from the Greek words *techne*, an art or craft, and *phobia*, fear. As Hal Hellman notes, this word is most often used to refer to fear: "fear of technology, fear of science, fear of change in general" (Hellman 1976, p. xi). The customary use of the word has been pejorative. Thus Daniel Dinello remarks that technophobia has been "deployed mainly by rabid technophiles who believe that questioning technology's direction is crazy if not satanic" (Dinello 2005, p. 8). However, the word has come to refer not only to fear of technology or dislike of particular technologies but to general critiques of technology.

Champions of technology like Hellman allege that critics of technology are motivated by fear and anxiety, a charge implying that technology critics suffer from a psychological condition. In his 1998 publication the psychologist Mark J. Brosnan elevated this ad hominem approach to academic respectability by developing a model of the cognitive and psychosocial factors that might account for feelings of fear and anxiety about technology.

Like the word *technocrat*, technophobia can be used ironically. Dinello, for example, appropriates the label *technophobe* for the critic of technology. Rather than pursue questions of definition further, however, a brief and selective discussion of critiques of technology follows.

Technology critics represent various ethical and social perspectives. Some, such as Jacques Ellul and Martin Heidegger, see technology as dehumanizing or as an expression of inauthenticity or idolatry. Others, such as Langdon Winner, critique technology because of its political or social effects, for example, its threat to political values such as freedom and democracy. Still others, such as Carolyn Merchant and Nancy Lublin, examine technology largely on account of its gendered qualities or its damaging environmental effects.

All these lines of critique share the view that there exists a unified ensemble called "technology" as such, a phenomenon that is in some sense "autonomous" (Winner 1977), operating through a logic of its own in which human decisions do not count. This view challenges technological optimism on the part of liberals and Marxist socialists (e.g., Karl Marx's optimism that what matters is not technology as such but which class controls technology). "Technophobes" do not merely allege that technologies are evil because oppressors control them and would be beneficial under a different form of social organization. Rather, they claim that an irresistible logic of technological autonomy trumps all forms of social organization and political agency, both individual and collective. The technology critic Winner, for example, refers to "reverse adaptation" (Winner 1977, pp. 226–251), a perverse logic in which political and other social ends have become determined by the means necessary to achieve them. For Winner, this and other characteristics of autonomous technology render democratic self-governance virtually impossible. As Henry Jenkins (1999)

notes, technology as such may be said to constitute, not merely reinforce, systems of power and social control, leading to violations of human freedom and civil liberties. Ironically, the claim that technology erodes freedom may be encouraged by technophile arguments that technological development is historically irresistible and hence uncontrollable by political or other means.

The term *Luddite* is commonly used to characterize technophobes. Yet the early-nineteenth-century Luddites did not fear all technology. Rather, they attacked the specific technologies of textile production that they saw as oppressive. Over two centuries, however, technology critiques shifted from a focus on production technology to an emphasis on the technologies of consumption, entertainment, education, and so forth. In the early twenty-first century the technologies especially arousing "technophobic" hostility include biotechnology (genetic manipulation, cloning, and eugenics), nanotechnology and robots, nuclear energy, and of course computers and cyber technology, all of which provoke distrust because of their places in the sphere of consumption.

Whereas in the nineteenth century the Romantic movement was responsible for much technology critique, in the twentieth century technophobia became associated with the political left (Heidegger and Ellul are prominent exceptions), especially those portions of the cultural left not identifying with orthodox Marxism. Social critics, such as Max Horkheimer and Theodor Adorno, and radical environmentalists, such as ecologists and ecofeminists, for example, Merchant, have frequently expressed deep suspicion about technology and its "conquest of nature." Conservatives, such as Thomas R. DeGrigori, especially in the United States with its market-libertarian traditions, tend to embrace technology or at least oppose government regulation of technology. Digital technology in particular flourishes in unregulated markets. On the other hand, certain technologies, such as biomedical technologies, are regarded by many conservatives as incompatible with religious faith. Of course the Old Order Amish are known for their avoidance of technologies associated with electricity and internal combustion on grounds of religion and community life.

The technological revolution shows no signs of abating. Hence technophobia in both senses—the psychological fear of technology and social critiques of technology—can be expected to flourish as well.

SEE ALSO *Bureaucrat; Conservatism; Digital Divide; Globalization, Social and Economic Aspects of; Libertarianism; Luddites; Marxism; Neoliberalism; Post-Traumatic Stress; Technocracy; Technocrat; Technology; Technology, Adoption of; Technology, Cellular; Technotopia*

BIBLIOGRAPHY

Binfield, Kevin, ed. 2004. *Writings of the Luddites*. Baltimore, MD: Johns Hopkins University Press.

Brosnan, Mark J. 1998. *Technophobia: The Psychological Impact of Information Technology*. New York: Routledge.

DeGrigori, Thomas R. 2002. *Bountiful Harvest: Technology, Food Safety, and the Environment*. Washington, D.C.: Cato Institute.

Dinello, Daniel. 2005. *Technophobia! Science Fiction Visions of Posthuman Technology*. Austin: University of Texas Press.

Ellul, Jacques. 1964. *The Technological Society*. Trans. John Wilkinson. New York: Knopf.

Heidegger, Martin. 1977. *The Question concerning Technology, and Other Essays*. Trans. William Lovitt. New York: Garland.

Hellman, Hal. 1976. *Technophobia: Getting out of the Technology Trap*. New York: M. Evans.

Horkheimer, Max, and Theodor W. Adorno. 2002. *Dialectic of Enlightenment*. Trans. Edmund Jephcott. Stanford, CA: Stanford University Press.

Jenkins, Henry. 1999. The Work of Theory in the Age of Digital Transformation. Massachusetts Institute of Technology. http://web.mit.edu/cms/People/henry3/pub/digitaltheory.htm.

Lublin, Nancy. 1998. *Pandora's Box: Feminism Confronts Reproductive Technology*. Lanham, MD: Rowman and Littlefield.

Merchant, Carolyn. 1980. *The Death of Nature*. San Francisco: Harper and Row.

Santana, Beatriz. 1997. Introducing the Technophobia/Technophilia Debate: Some Comments on the Information Age. University of California, Los Angeles, Department of Education. http://www.gseis.ucla.edu/courses/ed253a/beatriz.htm.

Winner, Langdon. 1977. *Autonomous Technology: Technics-out-of-Control as a Theme in Political Thought*. Cambridge, MA: MIT Press.

Harlan Wilson

TECHNOTOPIA

A technotopia is a governance model in which policy decisions would be made by a technocracy, a depoliticized branch of government that is staffed by highly educated scientific and technical specialists, to the exclusion of politicians or interest groups. Admission is based purely on scientific and technical expertise, as demonstrated in open, competitive examinations. Free from political interference, the technocracy makes decisions based solely on scientific evidence and instrumental rationality. At the core of technotopian thought is the conviction that technocrats will make better decisions than politicians. In their view, scientific and technological advances are inevitable and potentially beneficial, but only if they are managed by experts who can make scientifically driven decisions, free from political interference. In technotopian thought, scientific and technological advances broaden the relevance of scientifically driven decision making until the technocracy wholly supplants conventional political systems. The wealth and abundance created by a correctly managed technological infrastructure, it is argued, would eliminate the inequities that made conventional politics necessary.

The various components of technotopian thought are by no means new. For 1,300 years (605–1905), admission to the civil bureaucracy in dynastic China was based on a rigorous examination system. In *New Atlantis* (1627), the English philosopher and author Francis Bacon (1561–1626) envisioned a utopian society dedicated to fostering science and celebrating the achievements of explorers and inventors. In the eighteenth century, the French sociologist Henri de Saint-Simon (1760–1825) developed a recognizably technocratic governance model, in which an elite class of scientists and engineers would replace existing political institutions and make decisions on rational principles; Saint-Simon's student, Auguste Compte (1798–1857), added a sense of historical inevitability to Saint-Simon's formulation: Because the utility of the scientific method is matchless, it will ultimately be extended to all aspects of governance. In 1888, with the publication of Edward Bellamy's Utopian novel *Looking Backward*, technocratic thought reached mass audiences in the United States and Europe; in the United States *Looking Backward* sold more than 1 million copies by the end of the nineteenth century. The novel describes a future utopian society in which a technocratically controlled industrial sector has been redesigned to serve human needs, resulting in abundance, leisure, learning, and social peace. In the early twentieth century (1919–1933), the Technical Alliance of North America, a group of New York–based scientists, architects, and engineers, called for the restructuring of the entire U.S. economy on scientific principles and the replacement of conventional politics by technocratic rule.

Although there has never been a society in which technocrats have wholly supplanted politicians, technocratic principles inform the civil administration of science and technology in most of the world's advanced industrial economies, if to varying degrees. Closest to the technotopian ideal, arguably, is the modern civil administration of France, founded in 1945 in the wake of the Nazi occupation. Entry into the highest levels of the administration requires a diploma from the École Nationale d'Administration (ENA); its graduates are called *énarques*, and they take positions in one of the two "grand corps of the state," the administrative corps. Graduates of the leading French engineering school, the École Polytechnique, qualify for the better positions in the second of the two grand corps, the engineering corps. Both are designed to insulate the civil administration from political interference. Entry into either of the two diploma-granting institutions is based solely on competitive examinations. A host of administrative regulations and civil statutes prevent a too-cozy relationship between civil servants and business interests, especially the practice of *pantouflage*, in which bureaucrats who rule in industry's favor are rewarded with lucrative private-sector positions. However, there are no such rules against civil servants going into politics; indeed, Jacques Chirac and Valéry Giscard d'Estaing, who have both served as presidents of France, are graduates of ENA.

The intent of France's regulatory structure is clear: it is far better to have science and engineering affect politics than to have politics affect science and engineering. Although French citizens occasionally chafe at the perceived arrogance of their technocratic elite, it is also true that, in general, they trust the elite to make the right decisions concerning technology, and they take pride in France's impressive record of postwar technological advances. For this reason, French government decisions to commit to nuclear power and to build high-speed rail lines throughout the country have met with little public opposition; in consequence, France is now a net exporter of electricity and is regarded as the world leader in railway technology.

Criticisms of technotopia focus on the risks of taking the public (and their elected representatives) out of the state's decision-making apparatus. As part of their effort to stake out an autonomous zone of technocratic decision making, technocrats are tempted to elaborate and mystify their expertise in ways that make it appear to be far beyond the reach of the less educated; in so doing, they may be trying to cover up their inadequacies. At the same time, some technocrats express contempt for ordinary citizens who try to involve themselves in policy decision processes, believing that people with less-than-stellar educations could not possibly grasp the underlying science. Yet the public may question whether technocrats possess sufficient breadth of vision to make wise policy choices. Ultimately, technocrats must make policy decisions by trying to strike a balance between incommensurable factors, such as safety versus cost; critics of technocracy argue that these decisions need to be made transparently so that the public can evaluate them. Because technocrats are mainly drawn from the middle and upper classes, they may be suspected, as well, of class, gender, and racial biases. In the United States, for example, it has been argued that new hazardous waste disposal sites are disproportionately located within African American and Hispanic communities.

More fundamental criticisms question whether science and engineering are capable of providing an appro-

priate foundation for public policy decisions. Scholarship in science and technology studies (STS), for example, has repeatedly shown a picture of science at sharp variance with the naïve view of science underlying technotopian thought. STS research has repeatedly shown that, within scientific communities, scientific evidence is susceptible to multiple interpretations, in which political and social values can easily be shown to play significant roles. Even if technocrats are protected from outright manipulation by politicians and political parties, their decisions are nevertheless driven by more subtle political, social, and professional values; these need to be brought to light so that they can be evaluated by affected communities. Still, it seems clear that the public's interests are best served by keeping outright political manipulation out of technocratic decision-making processes. In the United States, for example, staff-recommended scientists were rejected from a Bush administration panel considering acceptable levels of lead in drinking water; they were replaced by appointees with financial ties to the lead industry.

SEE ALSO *Internet; Technocracy*

BIBLIOGRAPHY

Akin, William E. 1977. *Technocracy and the American Dream: The Technocrat Movement, 1900–1941.* Berkeley: University of California Press.

Burris, Beverly H. 1993. *Technocracy at Work.* Albany: State University of New York Press.

Cozzens, Susan E., and Edward J. Woodhouse. 1995. Science, Government, and the Politics of Knowledge. In *Handbook of Science and Technology Studies*, eds. Sheila Jasanoff, Gerald E. Markle, James C. Pattern, and Trevor Pinch, 533–553. Thousand Oaks, CA: Sage.

Radaelli, Claudio M. 1999. *Technocracy in the European Union.* London: Longman.

Bryan Pfaffenberger

TELECOMMUNICATIONS INDUSTRY

The term *telecommunications* is defined as communicating over distance. Technological advancements in this area have enabled a large share of the world's population to instantaneously communicate with others located all over the globe. Indeed, it is quite common to observe individuals in developed countries using electronic communication devices such as modular telephones, cellular phones, and personal computers to share ideas and information. But the widespread use of such equipment is a relatively new occurrence in the history of communications.

The modern telecommunications system uses a centralized network that relies on transmission facilities to send information between different locations. The origin of this network system developed from postal courier services established as early as the sixth century BCE in China (Xiong-jian and You-nong 1994). Postal service at that time was used primarily by the state to transmit commands and deliver orders to citizens and members of the armed forces. Providing an efficient long-distance communications system was key to governing a large geographic region and promoting economic growth. In succeeding years governments commonly sanctioned a single provider of courier service. Limiting communications services to one provider advanced efficient long-distance delivery of information by reducing costly duplication of services. Origins of a government-sanctioned monopoly can be traced back to Hapsburg's Emperor Maximilian I in 1505. Establishment of the state-owned monopoly soon followed in 1614, as Prussia established a state-run courier service that handled letters and parcels for the entire empire (Stephan 1859). Prussia's postal model served as the prototypical organizational structure for modern communications systems.

Over time, new technology such as the telegraph and telephone were generally integrated into the communications monopolies to form state-run post, telegraph, and telephone (PTT) companies in many countries. The development of the organizational structure of communications services in the United States is a notable exception to this form of integration. By the early nineteenth century privately owned telegraphic services in the United States were provided by Western Union, and postal service remained state-owned. Compared to postal delivery, telegraphy was a much faster way to transmit information because telegraphy used cables to transfer signals between locations. The invention of the telephone in 1876 by Alexander Graham Bell enhanced long-distance communications even further because it provided users the ability to transmit voice information over cable.

TELECOMMUNICATIONS GROWTH IN THE TWENTIETH CENTURY

Following the 1876 patent award for the telephone, Alexander Graham Bell, with support from a group of Boston financiers, established the Bell Telephone company. During its first years of operation Bell Telephone provided local communications services, and Western Union became the sole provider for telegraph communications. Over the next fifteen years Bell strengthened its monopoly status by extending its patent protection and developing a long-distance network to interconnect its operating companies. These operating companies formed the American Telegraph and Telephone Company

(AT&T). The Bell system also integrated vertically into equipment production by acquiring Western Electric from Western Union. At the turn of the century Bell was continuing a pattern of acquiring independent companies and also had merged horizontally into telegraphy through partial acquisition of Western Union. These acquisitions contributed to the upsurge in the number of telephones in the Bell system, from 2,231,367 in 1905 to more than 15,000,000 by 1920.

Parallel industry growth occurred in other industrialized countries in western Europe and in Japan. By the late 1950s these countries had developed extensive wireline network systems that provided most of their citizens and businesses access to affordable telecommunications services. Protected from significant international and domestic competition, telecommunications monopolies became major employers offering high-wage jobs to telephone linemen, cable splicers, station installers, switchboard operators, and construction workers. The provision of well-paying jobs contributed to the expansion of these nations' dynamic economies. Providing businesses the ability to communicate instantaneously over long distances created a competitive advantage domestically and internationally that further supported economic growth in industrialized countries.

Although maintaining an affordable and universal telecommunications system benefited society, government regulation of rates and subsidization of services introduced inefficiencies that grew as services expanded. The intent of rate regulation was to suppress price increases. In the United States this was achieved by setting maximum limits on telecommunications carriers' returns on investment. This type of a regulation, however, lowers the incentive to contain costs by encouraging overinvestment in capital and equipment in an attempt to generate greater profits (Averch and Johnson 1962). Government-approved subsidization of less lucrative sectors of the telecommunications monopoly was intended to allow carriers to finance expensive services with revenue from more profitable ones. In the United States relatively high prices in the long-distance sector helped support low prices for local services. Revenue from telecommunications services often supported more costly postal operations in countries with PTT-integrated systems (Noam 1992).

TECHNOLOGICAL ADVANCEMENTS AND TELECOMMUNICATIONS POLICY REFORM

New low-cost microwave technology changed the telecommunications industry because it became an economically attractive alternative to traditional long-distance services. The introduction of this technology in the late 1950s enhanced the competitiveness of long-distance carriers by nearly removing the additional cost of transmitting information over additional distances (Waverman 1975). In the United States the 1982 AT&T consent decree required Bell operating companies to provide all long-distance carriers the same access to local customers that AT&T enjoyed. The decree also required the 1984 divestiture of the Bell operating companies from AT&T, and provided these companies the option of purchasing telecommunications equipment from suppliers other than AT&T's manufacturing business.

Divestiture had the desired effect of promoting competition in the long-distance market. At the time of the breakup in 1984, AT&T had 96 percent of the business; by 1994 that share had fallen to 61 percent (Hendricks 1998). Long-distance users benefited tremendously from competitive prices offered by AT&T's rivals. Ten years after divestiture, interstate long-distance prices had fallen 22 percent. This competitive pricing environment also promoted significant growth in this sector, as the overall value of long-distance service rose from $34 billion in 1984 to $64 billion in 1994.

Twelve years after divestiture, the 1996 Telecommunications Act continued the shift toward less government intervention in telecommunications by providing additional support for competitive pricing of local services. Encouraged by the increasing array of potential competitors for local telephone service—made possible by technical advances in switching technology, cable, and cellular services—this act allowed long-distance and cable providers access to local markets (Crandall and Waverman 1995). This act also made it easier for local carriers to enter the long-distance market.

REGIONAL TELECOMMUNICATIONS MARKETS

Technological advancements that contributed to the changing telecommunications market in the United States also helped bring about changes in telecommunications services in the rest of the world. Many regions have privatized their PTT monopoly in an attempt to promote greater production efficiency. The pace of change toward privatization varies considerably across regions, though, and is influenced in large part by the quality of their network infrastructures.

Europe By the latter part of the twentieth century, greater demand for specialized telecommunications services made the maintenance of a large integrated system increasingly impractical, especially for European carriers operating extensive wireline systems. Encumbered by the use of older equipment, telecommunications companies faced high costs associated with extending the network system to provide universal service to businesses and residential customers. In addition, heavy reliance on in-house equipment manufacturing limited access to alternative cost reducing technology (Noam 1992, pp. 81–82). Pressure from the United States and the European Union to open markets, and the opportunity to provide low-cost competitive services encouraged privatization of services.

A shift toward market-oriented policy in Europe originated in the United Kingdom with the 1981 British Telecommunications Act. This act separated telecommunications services from the postal service, privatized the public telecommunications network system, and liberalized the equipment sector. Funding accrued from selling shares of British Telecommunications, the newly privatized company, helped to finance acquisition of new equipment. Liberalization of the equipment sector gave British Telecommunications the opportunity to take advantage of competitive bidding from equipment suppliers. In this more competitive telecommunications industry British businesses benefited from lower rates and lower waiting time for phone installation (Noam 1992, pp. 129–131).

Asia Although changes in telecommunications policy and the industry's growing significance as an engine for economic growth is nearly global, since the 1980s the transformations have been most marked in Asia. Societal support for change in this region is tied to overall support for growth in electronics and technology, especially in the Pacific Rim (Noam et al. 1994, pp. v–vi). The geography of this region—where countries along the Pacific Rim are physically separated by vast amounts of water, and immense countries such as China and India have inhabitants that live great distances from each other—underscores the importance of constructing a reliable system for transmitting information over long distances (Noam et al. 1994, p 13).

Policies aimed at developing reliable, low-cost telecommunications operations varied greatly during the last quarter of the twentieth century. For instance, Japan was the Asian front-runner in privatizing its domestic and international services in 1984. Greater competition led to declining rates, to more efficient self-selection of carriers, and to easier interconnection of networks (Ito and Iwata 1994, pp. 449–451). In contrast, the Chinese government limited foreign participation in the operations of telecommunications networks by investing heavily in this industry through the extension of loans and preferential tax policies in the mid 1980s. Carriers in the telecommunications industry were exempt from repaying 90 percent of government loans, and could retain 90 percent of their profits, which translates to a tax rate of 10 percent compared to a rate of 55 percent for nonpreferred industries (Wauchkuhn 2001). Under this policy, telecommunications in China grew at an annual rate of 24.6 percent by 1999.

Latin America The lack of an extensive network system presented a major challenge to the growth of Latin American economies, and the need for funding to finance the upgrading of systems created openness toward privatization. This openness was also influenced by trade liberalization policies such as the North American Free Trade Agreement (NAFTA).

Early privatization during the 1980s saw heavy investment in wireline systems by foreign owners, but the more significant growth in telecommunications services occurred with a second wave of international operators investing in wireless technologies (Hughes 2002). Research on postprivatization telecommunications in Latin America shows appreciable modernization of network systems and marked reductions of phone rates for differing market structures. For instance, following privatization, the Mexican government supported a single dominant provider of telecommunications services, whereas Brazil divested its former state-owned monopoly into separate competing companies (Hughes 2002). Both of these countries enjoyed declining prices for telecommunications services. These findings reveal that a large number of competitors is not always necessary to achieve low phone rates; rather, the low-cost operations associated with modernization contribute to higher profits from increasing customer demand at low prices. This prospect of greater profits creates an incentive for price reductions, even in industries dominated by a single firm. However, for the longer term, price pressures from competitors may be needed to help ensure the continuance of low prices (Hughes 2002).

Africa Countries in Africa, especially those in sub-Saharan Africa, face a daunting task in developing their telecommunications industry. By the late 1990s African nations accounted for only 2 percent of the world's telecommunications, even though these nations comprised 12 percent of the world's population (Noam 1999, p. 3). The absence of an extensive telecommunications network can be traced to the lack of infrastructure investment by colonialists during the early and mid-twentieth century. Following decolonization in the 1960s, African governments were left with outdated telecommunications equipment and a severely undertrained workforce. In response to the need for improved intra-African telecommunications services, African nations agreed to the development of the Pan-African Telecommunications Network (Panaftel) in 1962. This project resulted in significant expansion of the continent's network. Gains from this project slowed dramatically by the late 1980s as problems arose with standardizing switching systems, and incompatibility among carrier techniques hampered further development (Nuruddin 1999, pp. 258–259). These difficulties ulti-

mately led to the discontinuation of international funding for the Panaftel project.

International support for modernizing the telecommunications system in Africa did not stop with the decline of the Panaftel project, though: international development organizations such as the World Bank have pushed cooperation and privatization schemes for public telecommunications operations (Kone 1999, p. 161). Advanced wireless technology that avoids the need for heavy investment in wireline equipment offers the promise of speedy progress toward modernization for developing nations in Africa and elsewhere.

SOCIETAL BENEFITS

Modernization of telecommunication services provides important societal benefits other than simple economic growth; for example, modern systems make it easier to quickly obtain vital information needed to provide quality healthcare, and they provide quick access to critical information needed to lower safety and security risks. In addition, new technologies provide workers with well-paying jobs (Peoples 1998). These employment gains do come at a cost, though, as labor-saving technology such as digital-switching systems have significantly reduced demand for switchboard operators. Jobs as union telecommunications workers are also less prevalent in this industry as liberalization policies facilitated an influx of nonunion carriers in the United States. Nonetheless, policies promoting competition have contributed to increased industry employment.

Despite the impressive societal gains associated with modernization and competition in telecommunications, challenges still remain. The disparity in the quality and availability of telecommunications services between developed and developing countries remains high, even though mobile service has made access to the telecommunications network easier for citizens in developing countries. There is room for greater societal gains even in developed countries. For instance, phone rates for local service increased following liberalization policies in the United States in large part because the high cost of connecting to access lines presents a significant entry barrier into local telecommunications markets. Still, if the recent history of this industry is a reasonable guide, it is highly probable that technological advances will contribute to overcoming these lingering challenges.

SEE ALSO *Communication; Industry*

BIBLIOGRAPHY

Averch, Harvey, and Leland Johnson. 1962. Behavior of the Firm under Regulatory Constraint. *American Economics Review* 52 (4): 1053–1069.

Crandall, Robert, and Leonard Waverman. 1995. *Talk Is Cheap.* Washington, DC: Brookings Institution.

Hendricks, Wallace. 1998. Labor Negotiations with Regional Monopolies: The Telecommunications Industry. In *Regulatory Reform and Labor Markets*, ed. James Peoples, 249–276. Boston: Kluwer Academic.

Hughes, Robert. 2002. Privatization and Modernization of Telecommunications in Latin America. Working Paper. Center of International Studies, University of St. Thomas.

Ito, Youichi, and Iwata Atsushi. 1994. Japan: Creating the Domestic and International Network. In *Telecommunications in the Pacific Basin, An Evolutionary Approach*, eds. Eli Noam, Seisure Komatsuzaki, and Douglas A. Conn, 440–457. Oxford: Oxford University Press.

Kone, Hugues. 1999. The Ivory Coast (Côte d'Ivoire). In *Telecommunications in Africa*, ed. Eli Noam, 141–162. Oxford: Oxford University Press.

Noam, Eli. 1992. *Telecommunications in Europe.* Oxford: Oxford University Press.

Noam, Eli, ed. 1999. *Telecommunications in Africa.* Oxford: Oxford University Press.

Noam, Eli, Seisure Komatsuzaki, and Douglas A. Conn, eds. 1994. *Telecommunications in the Pacific Basin, An Evolutionary Approach.* Oxford: Oxford University Press.

Nuruddin, Mansur. 1999. Models for the Development of Regional Telecommunications Networks in Africa. In *Telecommunications in Africa*, ed. Eli Noam, 257–278. Oxford: Oxford University Press.

Peoples, James. 1998. Deregulation and the Labor Market. *Journal of Economic Perspectives* 12 (3): 111–130.

Stephan, Heinrich. 1859. *Geschichte der Preussischen Post von ihrem Ursprunge bis auf die Gegenwart* [History of the Prussian Post: From Its Origin to the Present]. Berlin: Verlag der Koniglichen Geheimen Ober-Hofbuchdruckerei.

Wauschkuhn, Markus. 2001. Telecommunications and Economic Development in China. Working Paper no. 16, Universität Bremen.

Waverman, Leonard. 1975. The Regulation of Intercity Telecommunications. In *Promoting Competition in Regulated Markets*, ed. Almarin Phillips, 201–239. Washington, DC: Brookings Institution.

Xiong-jian, Lian, and Zhu You-nong. 1994. China. In *Telecommunications in the Pacific Basin, An Evolutionary Approach*, eds. Eli Noam, Seisure Komatsuzaki, and Douglas A. Conn, 73–85. Oxford: Oxford University Press.

James Peoples

TELEOLOGY

The term *teleology* (from the Greek *telos*, meaning *end*) refers broadly to end-directedness, the idea that some things exist, have certain traits, or do certain things for the sake of some end. Many familiar cases of teleology are directly psychological, as when someone goes to the store

in order to get milk. Here the behavior is intentional and the end is the object of the agent's intention. In other cases, involving artifacts, psychology plays an indirect but equally crucial role through design and use. For example, a spark plug exists, is present in the engine, and sparks at a certain point in the combustion cycle for the sake of igniting the fuel. Though such objects have no intentions of their own, they have proper functions—things they may be said to do for the sake of some end, as opposed to other things they just happen to do (such as the spark plug's making a noise when it sparks).

The most interesting questions about teleology concern living things. We commonly apply teleological concepts to the parts and features of organisms. The heart, for example, is said to have the proper function of pumping the blood, which in turn occurs for the sake of blood circulation and the biological ends of nutrient distribution and waste removal; pumping the blood is what the heart is *for* in the organism, as opposed to other things it does merely as side-effects (such as making a *lub-dub* noise). This is a teleological claim analogous to claims about artifacts, and it licenses similar function-based evaluations: Just as a spark plug that does not fire under the right conditions is a defective spark plug, so too a heart that fails to pump in certain ways under the right conditions is a defective heart. Similar points may be made even about the parts and features of plants—for example, a color pattern on a flower may have the biological function of attracting pollinating insects, this being what that adaptation is for in the life of such plants. The question is whether it is legitimate to apply teleological concepts to the natural world in this way and, if so, how this application is to be understood.

It might at first seem that all uses of teleological concepts in biology are ruled out by neo-Darwinian evolutionary theory. Certainly the theory does reject the idea that the process of evolution is teleological. It is another question, however, whether the products of evolution— the parts and features of evolved organisms—might stand in teleological relations. In fact, many philosophers of biology agree that natural selection itself provides a basis for teleological judgments about adaptations and their relevant effects. This is because natural selection mimics design in an important respect. A designer makes a spark plug the way it is and puts it in the engine so that it will spark and ignite the fuel, and this means that these effects partly explain (via the designer's intentions) the presence of the spark plug in the engine, setting them apart as proper functions and ends served by the spark plug. Natural selection does not, of course, deliberately do anything or act with any foresight, but it still yields a similar relation between an adaptation and certain effects it has. In the case of the evolved color pattern, for example, the effect of attracting pollinating insects partly explains (via natural selection) the trait's coming to be a standard feature of the evolved species, setting this effect apart as specially relevant to the formation and life of this species of plant. Many have argued that this provides a basis for sensible talk of proper functions and ends in connection with biological adaptations.

The above approach sharply contrasts with any approach that seeks to explain teleological facts about organisms by attributing teleology to the processes by which species are formed. A common form of creationism, for example, posits direct creation of each species by a divinity, giving organisms a design-based teleology analogous to that of artifacts. Intelligent design theory, by contrast, may accept evolution and common ancestry, but still posits supernatural direction of evolutionary processes on the grounds that neo-Darwinism alone "cannot possibly" explain the evolution of certain complex structures. Proponents of intelligent design argue, for example, that providence guides the genetic mutations upon which natural selection acts.

While the doctrine of special creation has been discredited by a wealth of empirical evidence for evolution, intelligent design theory is trickier. Because there is no way to demonstrate the absence of divine intervention in historical processes, the theory can never be disproved. For this very reason, however, it also falls plainly outside the scope of science. The biological work cited by proponents of intelligent design would remain within science if it were used simply to point out puzzles and shape scientific research projects to try to solve them. But by treating the puzzles as grounds for embracing supernatural hypotheses, intelligent design becomes a religious alternative to the scientific enterprise rather than a scientific alternative to neo-Darwinism, as its proponents often claim it to be when advocating its inclusion in public school curricula.

Historically, the track record for the *God-of-the-gaps* approach—that is, appeals to the supernatural to explain whatever is currently difficult to explain scientifically—has not been impressive, as claims about what science cannot possibly explain are steadily overturned. Still, despite its not being science, intelligent design theory could of course turn out to be true. If it did, it would provide for a partially design-based biological teleology and a purposive direction for evolution itself. Strictly speaking, theists could have this general result even without embracing intelligent design at the level of natural processes. They could, for example, posit divine influence in the shaping of the background laws, allowing for a more general divine purpose behind creation without the micromanagement of evolution. It is worth noting that at least for part of his career Darwin himself was not averse to that idea, and similar claims have been advanced outside of

biology as well. Some have argued, for example, that a divine intelligence is necessary to explain the highly unlikely confluence of "finely tuned" physical laws, physical constants, and cosmological conditions that was crucial for the eventual emergence and evolution of life in the universe. According to such a view, which is not logically inconsistent with neo-Darwinian evolutionary theory, there could be a very general design-based teleology in addition to the teleology rooted in natural selection.

SEE ALSO *Creationism; Darwin, Charles; Hegel, Georg Wilhelm Friedrich; Idealism*

BIBLIOGRAPHY

Allen, Colin, Mark Bekoff, and George Lauder, eds. 1988. *Nature's Purposes: Analyses of Function and Design in Biology.* Cambridge, MA: MIT Press.

FitzPatrick, William. 2000. *Teleology and the Norms of Nature.* New York: Garland Publishers.

Neander, Karen. 1991. Functions as Selected Effects: The Conceptual Analyst's Defense. *Philosophy of Science* 58: 168–184.

Orr, H. Allen. 2005. Devolution: Why Intelligent Design Isn't. *New Yorker*, May 30: 40–52.

Polkinghorne, John. 1998. *Belief in God in an Age of Science.* New Haven, CT: Yale University Press.

Wright, Larry. 1976. *Teleological Explanations: An Etiological Analysis of Goals and Functions.* Berkeley: University of California Press.

William J. FitzPatrick

TELEVISION

Television is one of the most significant communications inventions. Television has fundamentally changed the political process, our use of leisure, as well as social relations among family and friends.

Television was not developed by any single individual or even a group of people working together. Scientists and visionaries imagined a device that would capture images with sound and transmit them into homes since the 1880s. The word *television* was first used at the 1900 Exhibition in Paris. Scottish inventor John Logie Baird (1888–1946) was the first person to provide a television transmission in October 1925, and he subsequently demonstrated it to the British public on January 26, 1926. On December 25, 1926, Kenjiro Takayanagi (1899–1990) displayed the first image in Japan. The technology improved slowly with athletes participating in the 1936 Olympic games in Berlin able to see some poor quality images of the games. In 1936 France and

Germany began television programming. In Great Britain King George VI's coronation from Hyde Park Corner on May 12, 1937, was the first broadcast of its kind, and the first U.S. election reported on television was on November 8, 1941, where news of Franklin Delano Roosevelt's victory was transmitted to an estimated 7,500 sets.

The development of television was halted during the Second World War in Europe and North America where manufacturers directed their attentions to munitions. Regular television service reached ninety-six countries by 1973.

Many of the things we associate with modern television technology were patented or devised in television's infancy. In 1928 Vladimir Zworyking (1889–1982) owned the first U.S. patent for an all-electronic color television; however, the development did not come to fruition for another twenty-five years. During the 1939 World's Fair in New York, television could not only receive audio and video images, but it was also designed to record those images, foreshadowing video recording devices (VCRs). And Baird later patented a 600-line electronic high definition color system in Britain in 1945.

TELEVISION'S GOLDEN AGE

The golden age of television is associated with the years 1949 to 1960 when American television viewing consisted of a variety of entertainment programming. The burgeoning prosperity and optimism of post–World War II influenced the spread of television. As more people were able to purchase televisions the demand for content grew. Early television programs offered revamped radio programs. There was some news and information programming, but those tended to be of short duration. A similar golden age is associated with British television. Early programs were reworked vaudeville acts and radio shows. Later situational comedies such as *I Love Lucy* and *The Honeymooners* would create new talent and genres.

The shared experience of watching key television programming provided an avenue for discussion and next-day water cooler conversation. As television matured so did the content, with programs such as *All in the Family* offering political and social commentary on issues ranging from race relations to the Vietnam War. Television's depiction of the family changed through time as well. While initial programming presented unified traditional families with bread-winning fathers and stay-at-home mothers, later programs depicted the breakdown of the traditional family dealing in both fiction and nonfiction with divorce, remarriage, blended families, and later, with same-sex unions.

Not only did television provide scripted programming, but it also broadcasted major sporting events. The first televised hockey game between the Montreal Canadiens losing six-to-two to the New York Rangers in Madison Square Gardens was seen on February 25, 1940. Television is also closely associated with the increasing popularity of the Olympic games, soccer, American football, and baseball.

With technological improvements, viewing time increased as well as television's influence on the public and politics. In 1947 there were only 60,000 American homes with television sets; by 1950 this figure grew to 12.5 million. Televisions are now found in nearly every home in the United States and Europe. In the developing world, the allure of television is so great that some want television before other communications devices such as telephones.

The hold of major networks on audiences soon dissipated with the advent of cable and specialty television programming. Rather than having a system where the networks catered to a common denominator of programming, the proliferation of specialty programs allowed people to view content that interested them specifically. Moving from analog to digital signals allowed for a so-called 500-channel universe where any specific interest could be satisfied, from golf to cooking; from sport to fashion; and from all news to pornography. As a result of these technological changes, the era of the mass audience was over. While there remain a few programs that can attain mass audiences, the market has been so fragmented that networks must compete for an ever-shrinking television audience.

EFFECTS ON CHILDREN

The rapid adoption of television fundamentally changed modern society. Television has been blamed for the decline in civil society, the breakdown of the family, suicide, mass murder, childhood obesity, and the trivializing of politics.

Children have been the target of broadcasters since the 1950s. Initially American broadcasters provided twenty-seven hours a week of children's television programming. By the 1990s there was twenty-four hour a day programming available to children. Children in Canada spend fourteen hours per week (Statistics Canada) watching television, while American children spend twenty-one hours per week (Roberts et al. 2005, p. 34). Some surveys suggest that British children have the highest rate of television viewing in the world. There are several concerns associated with television and children's viewing patterns. Many researchers have noted the link between the advent of television and increasing obesity and other weight-related illnesses. The time spent watching television is time not spent playing outdoors or in other physically challenging activities.

High television viewership of violence is linked to an increase in violent children. Prolonged exposure to violent television programming has shown that children can become more aggressive, become desensitized to violence, become accepting of violence as a means to solve problems, imitate violence viewed on television, and identify with either victims or victimizers.

Despite the negatives associated with television, it remains a powerful tool in shaping and educating children. While many point to the destructive nature of television, there are others who acknowledge television's positive impact. Researchers and programmers have developed content that has positively influenced children. Early studies on the PBS program *Sesame Street* found that children who viewed the program were better readers in grade one than students who had not watched the program. Programs were developed not only to help with literacy, but with other subjects as well as socialization, problem solving, and civic culture.

Notwithstanding the positive effects of children and television viewing, high television viewing has been associated with a decline in civic culture. As people have retreated to their homes to watch television, they have been less inclined to participate in politics either by voting or by joining political parties. In addition television viewing means that people are not interacting as much with friends or neighbors. What is more, television viewing also has been associated with an overall decline in group participation as well as volunteerism.

ADVERTISING AND OWNERSHIP

The issue of ownership of content and transmission was debated from television's onset. In 1927 the U.S. Radio Act declared public ownership of the airways. They argued that the airwaves should "serve the PICN—public interest, convenience, and necessity." Because of this understanding of the public owning the airwaves, it set the stage for regulatory bodies around the world licensing stations according to content regulations. Taking the issue of public interest one step further, the British government founded the British Broadcasting Corporation (BBC) in 1927. Other countries followed establishing their own public broadcasting systems. The United States lagged behind other nations by adopting a Public Broadcasting Service (PBS) in 1968. With the increasing adoption of television, many countries found the need to create new regulatory agencies. In the United States, the U.S. Federal Communications Commission (FCC) was created as an act of Congress on June 19, 1934.

The most successful television enterprises are closely associated with advertising. From the outset the way in which television content was funded was through the pursuit of advertising dollars. As a result it has often been said that television does not bring content to audiences, but instead it brings audiences to advertisers. The *propaganda*

model of the media, coined by Edward Herman and Noam Chomsky in their 1988 publication *Manufacturing Consent: The Political Economy of the Mass Media*, argues that the media uphold the dominant ideology in America. The five pillars of the model focus on ownership, advertising, sourcing, flak, and anticommunism. This model has been linked to other western media systems, but is most fitting in the United States where the power of the media rests with the owners.

Television's hold on the public imagination stems in part because of its ease of transmission. No one needs any special skill to receive the messages. All that is required is a television that can pick up a signal. More important, television influences our view of the world precisely because images are transmitted into people's homes. Since its inception, television transmissions have had the power to change our perceptions of world events. Starting with the Vietnam War and continuing to a myriad of events from the arms race to Tiananmen Square, and from the Civil Rights movement to the war in Iraq, television has become synonymous with the phrase "the whole world is watching."

SEE ALSO *Children; Chomsky, Noam; Communication; Cultural Studies; Entertainment Industry; Hidden Persuaders; Internet; Media; Medium Is the Message; Politics; Race Relations; Sports; Sports Industry; Subliminal Suggestion; Vietnam War; Violence*

BIBLIOGRAPHY

Giltan, Todd. 1980. *The Whole World Is Watching: Mass Media in the Making and Unmaking of the New Left.* Berkeley: University of California Press.

Gunter, Barrie, and Jill L. McAleer. 1990. *Children and Television: The One Eyed Monster?* New York: Routledge.

Herman, Edward S., and Noam Chomsky. 1988. *Manufacturing Consent: The Political Economy of the Mass Media.* New York: Pantheon Books.

Liebert, Robert M., and Joyce Sprafkin. 1988. *The Early Window: Effects of Television on Children and Youth.* 3rd ed. New York: Pergamon Press.

Postman, Neil. 1986. *Amusing Ourselves to Death: Public Discourse in the Age of Show Business.* New York: Penguin Books.

Putnam, Robert D. 2000. *Bowling Alone: The Collapse and Revival of American Community.* New York: Simon & Schuster.

Roberts, Donald F., Ulla G. Goehr, and Victoria Rideout. *Generation M: Media in the Lives of 8-18 Year-olds.* Kaiser Family Foundation Study, March 2005. http://www.kff.org/entmedia/7251.cfm.

Signorielli, Nancy. 1991. *A Sourcebook on Children and Television.* New York: Greenwood Press.

Statistics Canada. 2004. Average Hours per Week of Television Viewing by Children 2 to 11 Years. Table no. 5020002. http://www40.statcan.ca/l01/cst01/arts23.htm.

Van Evra, Judith. 1990. *Television and Child Development.* Hillsdale, NJ: Erlbaum.

Lydia Miljan

TEMPERAMENT

In contrast to theories that attribute variation in behavior primarily to socialization influences, temperament refers to early-appearing emotional, physiological, and attentional tendencies that, in interaction with the environment, organize the development of stable traits. Because a common focus on consistency of traits over time unites concepts of personality and temperament, temperament has been construed as an intrinsic core around which personality emerges.

A useful distinction between temperament and personality is that the latter includes a broader array of constructs involving more socially constructed cognitive attributes, such as morality, self-concepts, and beliefs. Temperament refers to more basic and overt behavioral tendencies. The more specific nature of temperament allows for coordination of adult research with investigations of infants and nonhuman animals, including the exploration of neural systems associated with temperament traits.

Although ideas regarding temperament appear in the writings of Greco-Roman physicians, the preeminence of the socialization models inherent in learning and psychoanalytic theories in the first half of the twentieth century prevented temperament concepts from receiving substantial attention from developmental psychologists until the 1960s. Two developments contributed to increased consideration of temperament during the latter half of the twentieth century. The first involved observations made by Alexander Thomas and Stella Chess (1977) of children experiencing psychological dysfunction despite being raised in well-functioning homes. A second and more recent advance concerns increasing sophistication of neuroscience measures and corresponding theories that have allowed for greater precision in linking activity in the brain to individual differences in behavior.

TEMPERAMENT DEFINED

Subtle differences exist in the boundaries researchers have used to define temperament. Early descriptions of temperament primarily considered susceptibility to, and severity and pervasiveness of, affective displays and included evidence of genetic origins and appearance during the first year as hallmarks (Goldsmith et al. 1987). More contemporary perspectives soften these boundaries, additionally focusing on attentional and behavioral processes that alter the course of emotional responses, and allowing for environmental influences.

In the early twenty-first century, the most frequently cited definition of temperament is that proposed in 1981 by Mary K. Rothbart and Douglas Derryberry: constitutionally based, relatively stable individual differences in emotional, motor, and attentional reactivity and self-regulation. The term *constitutionally* refers to the role of biological underpinnings, shaped by heredity, maturation, and interactions with the environment. *Stable* refers to consistency both over situations and over time. *Reactivity* involves latencies, intensity, and duration of behavioral, affective, and physiological reactions to changes in the environment. *Self-regulation* refers to attentional processes, such as orienting and focusing, and behaviors, such as approach and withdrawal, that modulate reactivity.

METHODOLOGY AND DIMENSIONS OF TEMPERAMENT

Temperament is assessed through structured and naturalistic observations made in the laboratory and the home, and through parent- and self-report questionnaires (the latter from older children and adults). Naturalistic observations maximize external validity but are time-consuming and often demonstrate low consistency across measurement periods. Laboratory assessments allow for tighter control of eliciting contexts, but ethical and practical limitations constrain the type of traits that can be assessed and may result in carryover effects from one procedure to another. The use of questionnaires allows for measurement of child behavior across a wide range of situations but can be contaminated by reporting bias. Despite the differences among assessment strategies, Rothbart and John E. Bates, in their 2006 examination of several studies, demonstrated convergence across measures.

Because of their ability to efficiently assess multiple aspects of behavior, questionnaires have been instrumental in identifying important temperament dimensions. Studies conducted in the late 1990s and early 2000s have used factor analysis of finely differentiated attributes to elucidate high-order traits. In a 2001 paper, Samuel P. Putnam, Lesa K. Ellis, and Rothbart describe three similar factors that have emerged from different questionnaires and across the lifespan. These factors also bridge gaps between personality and temperament traditions, as they bear resemblance to three of the "Big Five" traits commonly reported in adult personality studies. The first, labeled *surgency* and resembling the personality construct of extraversion, includes activity level, sociability, impulsivity, and enjoyment of high-intensity activities. The second, *negative affectivity*, is conceptually similar to neuroticism and includes sadness, anger, fear, and discomfort. The third, referred to as *orienting/regulating* in infancy and as *effortful control* thereafter, includes enjoyment of low-intensity activities, attentional focusing and shifting, and inhibitory control, and bears similarity to the personality construct of conscientiousness.

TEMPERAMENT STABILITY AND DEVELOPMENT

Rothbart and Bates (2006) review studies of twins and adopted children that indicate significant genetic effects on temperament, as well as describe more recent molecular genetic investigations that suggest specific genes underlying temperamental traits. Evidence of biological underpinnings suggests that temperament traits should be stable across time, and this is true to an extent. Several studies have supported predicted associations between infancy and middle childhood, but these relations are often fairly modest. More robust stability is found after the age of three years, and longitudinal studies conducted by Avshalom Caspi and colleagues (2003) have confirmed relations between temperament at age three and personality at age twenty-six. In their 2000 review, Brent W. Roberts and Wendy F. DelVecchio found that stability estimates increase throughout much of adulthood.

Multiple factors account for increasing estimates of stability with age. The first concerns the difficulty of measuring the same construct at differing developmental points, as both the expressions and elicitors of temperament change with maturation. The second explanation is that real change in the traits may occur because of environmental influences, and plasticity in systems underlying temperament may decrease over time. Finally, it is now recognized that temperament itself develops. Of primary importance is the emergence of regulatory capabilities that modulate earlier-appearing reactive tendencies. One such shift occurs in the second half of the first year, as fear-related behavioral inhibition alters the expression of approach motivation. Throughout the toddler and preschool periods, dramatic increases in effortful attentional and behavioral control allow for greater flexibility in the expression of other predispositions. Individual differences in maturation rates compound the appearance of instability.

The dominance of learning theories in explaining individual differences has given way to greater appreciation for inborn, biologically mediated predispositions that shape personal characteristics. Several temperament characteristics exhibit normative developmental change but also demonstrate interindividual stability over long periods. With advances in both measurement of genetic and neural processes and in theories explaining how biology and environment interact to form developmental pathways, our understanding of temperament is sure to show dramatic gains in the near future.

SEE ALSO *Personality; Trait Theory*

BIBLIOGRAPHY

Caspi, Avshalom, HonaLee Harrington, Barry Milne, et al. 2003. Children's Behavioral Styles at Age 3 Are Linked to Their Adult Personality Traits at Age 26. *Journal of Personality* 71 (4): 495–513.

Goldsmith, H. Hill, Arnold H. Buss, Robert Plomin, et al. 1987. Roundtable: What Is Temperament? Four Approaches. *Child Development* 58 (2): 505–529.

Putnam, Samuel P., Lesa K. Ellis, and Mary K. Rothbart. 2001. The Structure of Temperament from Infancy through Adolescence. In *Advances in Research on Temperament*, eds. Andrzej Eliasz and Alois Angleitner, 165–182. Lengerich, Germany: Pabst Scientist Publisher.

Roberts, Brent W., and Wendy F. DelVecchio. 2000. The Rank-Order Consistency of Personality Traits from Childhood to Old Age: A Quantitative Review of Longitudinal Studies. *Psychological Bulletin* 126 (1): 3–25.

Rothbart, Mary K., and John E. Bates. 2006. Temperament. In *Social, Emotional, and Personality Development*, ed. Nancy Eisenberg, 99–166. Vol. 3 of *Handbook of Child Psychology*, eds. William Damon and Richard M. Lerner. 6th ed. Hoboken, NJ: Wiley.

Rothbart, Mary K., and Douglas Derryberry. 1981. Development of Individual Differences in Temperament. In *Advances in Developmental Psychology*, vol. 1, eds. Michael E. Lamb and Ann L. Brown, 37–86. Hillsdale, NJ: Erlbaum.

Thomas, Alexander, and Stella Chess. 1977. *Temperament and Development*. New York: Bruner/Mazel.

Samuel P. Putnam

TEMPORALITY BIAS
SEE *Research, Cross-Sectional.*

TEMPORARY ASSISTANCE FOR NEEDY FAMILIES (TANF) 1997
SEE *Culture of Poverty.*

TEMPTATION
SEE *Sin.*

TENDENCIES
SEE *Trait Theory.*

TERM LIMITS

A "term limit" is a rule that prevents government officials from serving for more than a specified number of terms. More than a technical electoral regulation, a term limit reflects the manner in which citizens envision their leaders: Should politicians be temporary servants of the public who rotate relatively quickly into and out of office, or a corps of experts who remain in power as long as they earn majority support? The main rationale behind mandating turnover through a term limit is that it will bring fresh perspectives to government and ensure responsiveness to voter demands, at the potential cost of losing knowledgeable veterans. Term limits have been debated, and intermittently enacted, throughout the history of democracy.

One ancient Athenian legislature, the *Boule*, placed a one-term limit on service, an idea argued for by Greek philosopher Aristotle in the fourth century BCE. There were term limits in the first U.S. Congress established under the Articles of Confederation, although the idea was later rejected at the Constitutional Convention because many of the Founding Fathers thought it made Congress weak. The constitutions of Mexico and Costa Rica impose short term limits on both their legislators and presidents. The president of the United States is limited to two terms in office, as are most state governors. The term limit laws that have provoked the fiercest debate and had the most profound effects in America have been the limits enacted since 1990 on state legislators.

In 1990, voters in California, Colorado, and Oklahoma passed citizen initiatives, which for the first time imposed term limits on their state representatives. Two years later, ten more states enacted limits, all of them through initiatives and many of them spurred by the efforts of the "U.S. Term Limits" organization. Predictably, this reform was much less popular among state legislators themselves. Louisiana's state legislators were the only ones to impose limits on their own term lengths even though they did not face the threat of an initiative. By the end of the decade, twenty-one states had passed term limits. In four of them (Massachusetts, Oregon, Washington, and Wyoming), judges overturned these initiatives on technical grounds, and legislators repealed limits in Utah and Idaho. The term limits that remained in effect in fifteen states varied considerably in lengths and strictness. Michigan's initiative prevented state legislators from serving more than six years in the state's House and eight years in the Senate, banning them for life afterward. Louisiana's law, crafted by legislators themselves, imposed a twelve-year limit in each house, and only mandated that legislators sit out a single term before they are eligible to run again. But regardless of these important provisions, all term limit laws proposed were based on a similar line of reasoning and have faced a common set of criticisms.

Proponents of term limits contended they would bring a return to the ideal of the "citizen legislator" who carries the concerns of average voters into office, then quickly leaves to rejoin their ranks. Mandating turnover would replace entrenched incumbents with representatives who were closer to the people. These new lawmakers would not be tainted by allegiances to interest groups or captured by the bureaucracy, the argument went. Because new lawmakers could not plan a long future representing one district, they would be freed from catering to the whims of a narrow constituency and would make decisions with the common welfare in mind. To the supporters, term limits would make it more likely that exiting legislators "would anticipate careers in the private sector and therefore would, as they legislate, think about what it is like to live under the laws they make" (Will 1992, p. 201).

Those who argued against the imposition of term limits in the states and upon members of Congress warned that these laws would throw out of office many legislators with decades of institutional knowledge. Losing this expertise would leave the legislative branch impotent against a massive and well-informed executive branch. Some opponents predicted that after jettisoning their most senior parliamentarians legislatures would see their lawmaking process grind to a halt. Lobbyists and unelected staff would fill the vacuum of information and power, leaving voters poorly represented. One opponent compared the career paths of termed-out legislators to that of Cincinnatus, a Roman farmer much admired by the founders of the United States, who has become the archetype of the citizen legislator, charging that limits "would put at risk the independence of legislators contemplating exit who, rather than returning Cincinnatus-like to their waiting plow, prefer some sort of future elsewhere. Even Cincinnatus might be tempted to send a farm subsidy or two homeward in advance of his return" (Polsby 1993, p. 7).

Given that term limits have removed hundreds of legislators from office in many states, it is possible to judge the predictions made by both term limits' boosters and adversaries against the empirical record, gleaned from election statistics, surveys of legislators and statehouse observers, and state legislative archives. Not surprisingly, term limits have had their intended effect of greatly increasing turnover. This has brought new faces and perspectives into office, and accelerated gains in representation for racial and ethnic minorities in the states with changing demographics. Yet getting rid of incumbents has not made state legislative elections more competitive; term limits did not cut into the average margin of victory in these contests or lead to more seats changing party hands.

When new legislators come to office after term limits, surveys show, they do tend to think more about statewide concerns than about the demands of their districts. But they also spend less time keeping in touch with voters and working to solve constituent problems, compared to legislators who do not face limits. Although the legislative process has not devolved into chaos anywhere, committees tend to give bills less scrutiny after term limits and the laws that are ultimately produced are usually shorter and narrower. One of the clearest findings about term limits, confirmed in examinations of archival records as well as in interviews with a range of political observers, is that they dramatically reduce the power of the legislative branch. Governors exert more influence over crafting state budgets once limits are imposed, and legislators spend less time on oversight of the executive branch.

In many states as in the federal government, the chief executive also faces term limits. Since the ratification of the Twenty-second Amendment in 1951, U.S. presidents have been allowed to serve for only two elected terms in office. Thirty-four states imposed term limits on governors, with all but one state preventing governors from serving for more than two terms—Virginia's one-term limit is the exception. Such limits have been motivated less by the desire to bring new perspectives into office and more by concerns about halting the accumulation of power over time into the hands of a single leader. The Twenty-second Amendment was proposed by a Republican Congress not long after Democrat Franklin Delano Roosevelt (1882–1945) had won his fourth term. The amendment was proposed in order to prevent similarly popular future presidents from holding the office for life. Enacted for similar reasons, term limits on governors have had less profound effects than limits on legislators because they rarely bring political newcomers into office and serve to solidify rather than disrupt the normal rate of turnover.

In American statehouses, by contrast, term limits do much to shape the legislative landscape. It appears term limits will be a permanent feature of state political life since the courts have affirmed term limits in principle (in the *Bates v. Jones* decision) and most attempts to repeal or relax limits have met with staunch public opposition. The spread of term limits across the nation has also apparently come to a stop because they have been passed in nearly every state with an initiative process and the courts have made it clear that states cannot impose term limits on their members of Congress (in *U.S. Term Limits, Inc. v. Thornton*). This leaves the nation in the midst of a large-scale experiment with a central rule of democracy. Approximately a third of state legislatures operate under the same sorts of limits that were imposed under the Articles of Confederation, while two-thirds follow the guidance of the Constitutional Convention to leave legislators unhindered. The coming decades will test the wisdom of each system.

SEE ALSO *Aristotle; Democratic Party, U.S.; Elections; Initiative; Interest Groups and Interests; Judicial Review; Republican Party; Supreme Court, U.S.; Voting*

BIBLIOGRAPHY

Cain, Bruce, Richard Niemi, and Karl Kurtz, eds. 2007. *Institutional Change in American Politics: The Case of 130 Term Limits.* Ann Arbor: University of Michigan Press.

Carey, John M. 1996. *Term Limits and Legislative Representation.* Cambridge, UK: Cambridge University Press.

Carey, John M., Richard G. Niemi, and Lynda W. Powell. 2000. *Term Limits in the State Legislatures.* Ann Arbor: University of Michigan Press.

Carey, John M., Gary F. Moncrief, Richard G. Niemi, and Lynda W. Powell. Term Limits in the State Legislatures: Results from a New Survey of the 50 States. *Legislative Studies Quarterly* XXXI (1): 105–136.

Kousser, Thad. 2005. *Term Limits and the Dismantling of State Legislative Professionalism.* Cambridge, UK: Cambridge University Press.

National Conference of State Legislatures. Legislative Term Limits Overview. http://www.ncsl.org/programs/legismgt/ABOUT/Termlimit.htm.

Petracca, Mark. 1992. Rotation in Office: The History of an Idea. In *Limiting Legislative Terms,* eds. Gerald Benjamin and Michael Malbin. Washington, DC: CQ Press.

Polsby, Nelson W. 1993. Restoration Comedy. *The Yale Law Journal* 102: 1515–1526.

Will, George F. 1992 *Restoration: Congress, Term Limits, and the Recovery of Deliberative Democracy.* New York: Free Press.

Thad Kousser

TERM STRUCTURE OF INTEREST RATES

SEE *Interest Rates.*

TERMS OF TRADE

By terms of trade, economists generally mean commodity terms of trade (CTT), or net barter terms of trade (NBTT), given as a price or unit value ratio. For this ratio, it is appropriate to use the term *unit value* rather than *price* because different heterogeneous commodities are aggregated into a single commodity category such as exports or imports.

Commodity terms of trade of a country are defined as the unit value (price) of exports of the country divided by its unit value (price) of imports. Commodity terms of trade between two regions, say, the North (industrially developed) and the South (less developed), is defined as the unit value (price) of exports of the North to the South divided by the unit value (price) of exports of the South to the North. The commodity terms of trade index measures unit gains from the trade amount—imports (i.e., the volume of imports) that are available for one unit of exports.

INCOME TERMS OF TRADE

The income terms of trade (ITT) is an index of the value of exports divided by the unit value (price) of imports—the value of exports measured in terms of import goods. It corresponds to the commodity terms of trade multiplied by the volume of exports. ITT measures the purchasing power of exports—the amount of imports that can be financed by the total exports.

The use of ITT is often recommended in order to correct shifts in the commodity terms of trade for changes in the volume of exports. A fall in the terms of trade may be desirable if it leads to a significant expansion in export volumes so that the value of exports rises. As a result the capacity to import rises. The income terms of trade index is designed to measure the net effect of a change in the commodity terms of trade on the capacity to import or on the purchasing power of exports.

In the dynamic context of world economic growth, the volume of exports of a country or region often shows a trend growth exceeding the rate of decline (if any) of the commodity terms of trade, leading to a rise in its ITT. The ITT of a country or region can rise along with its trading partner as both can experience absolute gains from trade. To measure the relative gains from trade, Prabirjit Sarkar (1986b) recommended the use of the ITT of one country or region as a ratio of that of the other.

FACTORIAL TERMS OF TRADE

In the process of growth, technical progress takes place and factor productivity improves. As a result, the cost of production may decline and prices may fall. A decline in the commodity terms of trade may be precisely attributable to this technical progress and cost reduction. To net out this effect of technical progress on commodity terms of trade, the concept of factorial terms of trade is used. If the effect of technical progress on export prices or export unit values is taken into consideration, this leads to single factorial terms of trade. If the effects of technical progress on both export and import prices or unit values are taken into account, this leads to double factorial terms of trade.

To construct single factorial terms of trade (SFTT) of a country or region, its CTT is multiplied by some index of factor productivity in its export sector. To construct

double factorial terms of trade (DFTT) of a country or region, the SFTT is deflated by the index of factor productivity in the export sector of its trading partner. So DFTT is CTT multiplied by the ratio of the indexes of factor productivity in the export sectors of the trading partners.

Because the factorial terms of trade is used as an indicator of changes in welfare, which means changes in real income per head, labor productivity is often used in the calculation of factorial terms of trade. The SFTT index bears on a country's absolute welfare, while the DFTT index bears on relative welfare between trading countries as pointed out by the British economist John Spraos (1983).

THE PREBISCH-SINGER HYPOTHESIS

There is much controversy regarding the long-term movements of the terms of trade of the South vis-à-vis the North. This dispute centers on the Prebisch-Singer (PS) hypothesis, which is associated with the works of two United Nations economists, Raúl Prebisch and Hans W. Singer. The essence of the PS hypothesis is the long-term decline in the DFTT of the South vis-à-vis the North. In the absence of appropriate historical data since the last quarter of the nineteenth century both Prebisch and Singer used CTT of primary products vis-à-vis manufactures as the proxy of the DFTT of the South vis-à-vis the North for two reasons. First, the South constituted mainly primary-product exporting countries in contrast to the manufacture exporting countries constituting the North. Second, presuming that the technical progress and labor productivity improvements took place at a higher rate in the North than in the South, a decline in the CTT of the South would imply a further decline in the DFTT of the South.

The Prebisch-Singer hypothesis was virtually discarded in mainstream economics in the face of strong statistical objections against it. Since the 1980s, a series of studies undertaken by Spraos (1980), David Sapsford (1985), Sarkar (1986a, 1986b), Sarkar and Singer (1991), Grilli and Yang (1988), and many others questioned the validity of the criticism and provided strong statistical support for the Prebisch-Singer hypothesis, thereby bringing it back into the limelight.

The core of the PS hypothesis has a divergence implication: In the process of long-term decline in the terms of trade of the South, the standard of living of the poor South cannot be expected to catch up with that of the rich North. Both Prebisch and Singer argued that the fruits of technical progress taking place in the northern export sector were distributed among the northern people through higher wages and profits, leading to rising standards of living because of strong labor unions and high monopoly power of the capitalists. But the fruits of technical progress in the southern export sector were transmitted to the North through lower export prices because of surplus labor, leading to weak labor unions and the lack of monopoly power of the southern capitalists vis-à-vis their northern counterparts. Thus the process of evolution and growth of the world economy through technical progress led to uneven development (as observed by Sarkar in 2000) and a long-term decline in the DFTT of the South.

SEE ALSO *Development Economics; Prebisch, Raúl; Prebisch-Singer Hypothesis; Singer, Hans; Trade; Unequal Exchange*

BIBLIOGRAPHY

Grilli, Enzo R., and Maw Cheng Yang. 1988. Primary Commodity Prices, Manufactured Goods Prices, and the Terms of Trade of Developing Countries: What the Long Run Shows. *World Bank Economic Review* 2: 1–47.

Prebisch, Raúl. 1950. *The Economic Development of Latin America and Its Principal Problems.* Lake Success, NY: United Nations, Department of Economic Affairs.

Sapsford, David. 1985. The Statistical Debate on the Net Barter Terms of Trade between Primary Commodities and Manufactures: A Comment and Some Additional Evidence. *Economic Journal* 95 (379): 781–788.

Sarkar, Prabirjit. 1986a. The Singer-Prebisch Hypothesis: A Statistical Evaluation. *Cambridge Journal of Economics* 10 (4): 355–371.

Sarkar, Prabirjit. 1986b. Patterns of Trade and Movements of Interregional Terms of Trade between the Developing and the Developed Market Economies, 1950–1980. *Economic Bulletin for Asia and the Pacific* 37 (2): 1–13.

Sarkar, Prabirjit. 2000. North-South Uneven Development: What the Data Show. *Review* 23 (4): 439–457.

Sarkar, Prabirjit, and Hans W. Singer. 1991. Manufactured Exports of Developing Countries and Their Terms of Trade since 1965. *World Development* 19 (4): 333–340.

Singer, Hans W. 1950. The Distribution of Gains between Investing and Borrowing Countries. *American Economic Review* 40 (2): 473–485.

Spraos, John. 1980. The Statistical Debate on the Net Barter Terms of Trade between Primary Commodities and Manufactures. *Economic Journal* 90 (357): 107–128.

Spraos, John. 1983. *Inequalising Trade? A Study of Traditional North/South Specialisation in the Context of Terms of Trade Concepts.* London: Clarendon Press.

Prabirjit Sarkar

TERROR

Although all living things must die, humans are the only species who are aware of this unfortunate fact. How does this knowledge affect us? Inspired by Ernest Becker's influential book, *The Denial of Death* (1973), social psychologists Sheldon Solomon, Jeff Greenberg, and Tom Pyszczynski developed *terror management theory* to explore the role that awareness of the inevitability of death plays in diverse aspects of human behavior. As of 2006, more than three hundred studies conducted in at least fourteen countries have supported the central ideas of this theory and have shown that awareness of death influences a broad range of behaviors that, on the surface, bear no obvious relation to the problem of human mortality.

Terror management theory suggests that the awareness of death in an animal that wants to live creates the potential for paralyzing terror. Humankind "solved" the problem of death by using its sophisticated intellectual abilities to give life meaning, value, and permanence, and by so doing, provided a means of managing the potential for terror that awareness of death creates. People manage terror by immersing themselves in a *cultural worldview* that provides a theory of reality, standards for valued behavior that confer *self-esteem*, and the promise of literal or symbolic immortality to those who live up to these standards. Literal immortality is provided by the religious aspects of the worldview that promise some form of afterlife; symbolic immortality is attained by contributing to and being part of something that continues long after one's individual death, such as families, nations, or other valued groups. To effectively protect against existential terror, cultural worldviews and self-esteem requires ongoing validation by others. Those who share one's worldview and believe in one's value increase faith in the worldview and self-esteem, whereas those who disagree with one's worldview or one's value undermine this faith. To maintain the anxiety-buffering effectiveness of these structures, people exert great effort to keep their self-esteem and faith in their worldview strong and to ward off any threats to these beliefs that might arise.

Consistent with the theory, research has shown that: (1) bolstering self-esteem or faith in one's worldview makes people less prone to anxiety; (2) reminders of death increase one's striving for self-esteem and meaning, one's structuring of information about oneself and the world, and one's favorable reactions to people and ideas that support one's worldview and unfavorable reactions to people and ideas that threaten it; (3) threats to one's self-esteem or worldview bring thoughts of death closer to consciousness; and (4) increasing self-esteem, faith in one's worldview, or belief in an afterlife reduce the effects of reminders of death on defensive behavior. The effect of death awareness on human behavior is largely unconscious. People use self-esteem and their worldviews to defend against death-related anxiety when thoughts of death are on the fringes of consciousness; conscious thoughts of death are defended in ways more directly related to the problem of death, by denying one's vulnerability to disease or accident and promising to pursue a healthy lifestyle. When death-related thoughts come close to conscious awareness, this signals a potential increase in anxiety, which leads people to cling especially strongly to their worldviews and self-esteem and defend these structures against threat. These defensive reactions occur so rapidly that conscious fear of death is typically averted.

This work suggests that the problem of death lies at the root of the human quest for meaning and self-esteem, and that much human behavior is driven by the protection from existential anxiety that meaning and self-esteem provide. It also suggests that prejudice, hatred, and violence are often rooted in the threat to one's protective shield posed by those with worldviews different from one's own. Support for this view comes from studies showing that reminders of death increase stereotyping, hostility, and aggression toward those with different worldviews, favoritism toward one's group, and prejudice toward those from different cultures, nations, and religions. These processes have been shown to play an important role in international conflict and terrorism. Studies have shown, for example, that reminders of death have led young Iranians, who normally oppose terrorist violence, to increase their support for such tactics, and reminders of death have led young Americans, who normally oppose extreme military action, to support preemptive war and the use of weapons that would kill thousands of innocent civilians as part of the struggle against terrorism. This research shows that fear plays an important role in promoting support for violent solutions to the ongoing conflict in the Middle East.

This research also suggests that individual psychological problems are often rooted in breakdowns in the protection from core human anxiety that results when one's self-esteem or worldview is undermined. Reminders of death increase the severity of psychological symptoms, such as spider phobias and obsessive hand-washing, among those prone to these problems. People tend to be most happy and well-adjusted when they are able to view themselves as valuable contributors to a meaningful world. Although people have little conscious awareness of its impact, the problem of death exerts an important influence on most of what they do.

SEE ALSO *Anxiety; Death and Dying; Self-Esteem*

BIBLIOGRAPHY

Becker, Ernest. 1973. *The Denial of Death*. New York: Free Press.

Greenberg, Jeff, Sheldon Solomon, and Tom Pyszczynski. 1997. Terror Management Theory of Self-Esteem and Social Behavior: Empirical Assessments and Conceptual Refinements. In *Advances in Experimental Social Psychology*, vol. 29, ed. Mark P. Zanna, 61–139. New York: Academic Press.

Pyszczynski, Tom, Sheldon Solomon, and Jeff Greenberg. 2003. *In the Wake of 9/11: The Psychology of Terror*. Washington, D.C.: American Psychological Association.

Solomon, Sheldon, Jeff Greenberg, and Tom Pyszczynski. 1991. A Terror Management Theory of Social Behavior: The Psychological Functions of Self-Esteem and Cultural Worldviews. In *Advances in Experimental Social Psychology*, vol. 24, ed. Mark P. Zanna, 93–159. New York: Academic Press.

Tom Pyszczynski

TERROR MANAGEMENT THEORY

Terror management theory (TMT; Solomon, Greenberg, and Pyszczynski 1991) was derived from the work of the cultural anthropologist Ernest Becker (1924–1974), who in such books as *The Birth and Death of Meaning* (1962), *The Denial of Death* (1973), and *Escape from Evil* (1975) argued that the uniquely human awareness of death underlies a substantial proportion of human behavior. TMT posits that although human beings share with all life-forms a biological propensity toward survival, humans are unique in their awareness of the inevitability of death, that death can occur at any time, and that we are corporeal creatures no more important or enduring than barnacles, beets, and beavers. To assuage the potentially paralyzing terror engendered by this knowledge, humans embed themselves in cultural worldviews: humanly constructed beliefs shared by individuals in groups that provide a sense of meaning and significance and promises of symbolic and literal immortality to those who adhere to the standards of value prescribed by their culture.

While cultures vary considerably, they share the same defensive psychological function: to provide meaning and value and in so doing bestow psychological equanimity in the face of death. All cultural worldviews can ultimately be viewed as shared fictions, in the sense that none of them are likely to be literally true, and their existence is generally sustained by social consensus. Individuals surrounded by people believing the same things as themselves can be quite confident of the veracity of their beliefs. However, when one encounters people with different beliefs, this is posited to pose a challenge to one's death-denying belief systems; TMT proposes that this challenge is a primary reason that people are generally quite uncomfortable around, and hostile toward, those who are different. Additionally, because no symbolic cultural construction can actually overcome the physical reality of death, residual anxiety might well be unconsciously projected onto other groups of individuals as scapegoats, who are designated all-encompassing repositories of evil. Thus, responses to people with different beliefs might be to scapegoat them or berate them, or try to convert them to one's own system of beliefs. In some instances, these dynamics might well lead to terrorism, war, and killing.

Empirical support for TMT (see Solomon, Greenberg, and Pyszczynski [2004] for a recent review) has been obtained in over two hundred experiments, primarily by demonstrating that reminders of death (mortality salience) instigate cultural worldview defense. For example, after a mortality salience induction, Christian participants reminded of death liked fellow Christians more and Jewish people less, Germans sat further away from a Turkish person and closer to a fellow German, and people were more physically aggressive toward someone with different political beliefs. Research conducted after September 11, 2001, demonstrated that reminders of death or the events of 9/11 increased Americans' support for President George W. Bush and his policies in Iraq and conservative Americans' support for the use of nuclear and chemical weapons in preemptive military strikes. Additionally, Iranians reminded of death were more supportive of suicide bombers and more willing to engage in martyrdom actions.

Most recently, TMT theorists have been devising ways to minimize or eliminate the adverse effects of death denial while exploring how confrontations with mortality can elicit what is most noble in the human animal.

SEE ALSO *Anxiety; Salience, Mortality; Self-System; Terror*

BIBLIOGRAPHY

Solomon, Sheldon, Jeff Greenberg, and Tom Pyszczynski. 1991. A Terror Management Theory of Social Behavior: The Psychological Functions of Self-Esteem and Cultural Worldviews. In *Advances in Experimental Social Psychology*, vol. 24, ed. Mark Zanna, 93–159. Orlando, FL: Academic Press.

Solomon, Sheldon, Jeff Greenberg, and Tom Pyszczynski. 2004. The Cultural Animal: Twenty Years of Terror Management Theory and Research. In *Handbook of Experimental Existential Psychology*, eds. Jeff Greenberg, Sander L. Koole, and Tom Pyszczynski, 13–34. New York: Guilford Press.

Sheldon Solomon

TERRORISM

The study of terrorism is complicated by the fact that terrorism is a political rather than an analytical concept. The concept is closely related to major power conflicts, such as the cold war, nationalist conflicts, and—most recently—religious-political polarization; and its political use and

academic definitions have changed accordingly. As a result, scholars of terrorism have not only looked at terrorism as a particular kind of political violence, such as assassinations, hijackings, or—most recently—suicide bombings, but have also been sensitive to the discursive use and impact of the term *terrorism*. What both lines of study have in common, however, is the notion that terrorism—both as a practice and a discourse—is meant to terrify. Both the perpetrators of terrorist violence and those who have the power to name a particular kind of violence as terrorism do so to create fear. The study of terrorism has therefore not only focused on those branded as *terrorists* but also on those who do the naming, such as the media, policymakers, and academics, as well as on how the term *terrorism* is itself a highly contested label.

Precisely because terrorism is a political term, there is little consensus on how to define the phenomenon. According to an often-used definition, terrorism resembles guerrilla warfare to some extent while being distinctively different from it in others. Both are unconventional forms of warfare in which the state is attacked by groups of combatants lacking a fully armed military apparatus in order to bring about political change. However, whereas guerrilla fighters primarily target military objects, terrorists also attack "soft" civilian targets in order to paralyze society. According to this definition, the Oklahoma City bombing by Timothy McVeigh in 1995 is terrorist, whereas the suicide attack by Shi'a combatants on American and French U.N. troops in Beirut, Lebanon, in 1983, killing 241 marines, is an act of guerrilla warfare. Similarly, the Viet Cong fighting the U.S. army in Vietnam or the Algerian Front de Libération Nationale fighting the French colonial army in the 1950s were guerrilla fighters, whereas the Irish IRA, the Basque ETA, or the West German Red Army Faction also attacked civilians and are therefore defined as terrorist.

Scholars who have focused on the perpetrators of "terrorist" violence have used various perspectives. Richard Rubenstein (1987), among others, analyzes terrorism as a political strategy with a particular genealogy rooted in the French Revolution's *regime de la terreur* and nineteenth-century anarchism. Maximilien Robespierre and Louis Antoine Saint-Just as well as Sergej Nechaev and Michael Bakunin thus appear as the ideologues of terrorism. The thinking of the latter as to how to fight the all-powerful modern state, including the notion of the revolutionary vanguard, the provocation of the state, and the revolutionary moment, has subsequently influenced nationalist militants and left-wing revolutionaries of the twentieth century.

Another line of study has considered terrorism in relation to utopian belief systems and political eschatology. Rather than a strategy, terrorism is seen as a testimony, an act of faith, and the outcome of radical collective fantasies about ideological, ethnic, or religious purity. These studies focus on processes of radical "othering" and satanization, the political use of traditions of martyrdom and sacrifice, and the "mytho-logics" of political violence. Specific attention is given to the symbolism of the time and space of terrorism, such as the symbolism of particular days, buildings, or public spaces.

Partly in response to this, others have argued that while terrorism is usually informed by strong convictions, it should also be understood in terms of ulterior motives such as status, glamour, friendship, and money. Martha Crenshaw (1988) argues that terrorist groups can be analyzed as communities accommodating a variety of individual needs, such as the needs for recognition, excitement, and material benefits. The militant group is as much driven by the need to maintain itself as by its ideological objectives. These observations are used to argue that those militant groups whose existence is threatened by internal friction or outside aggression are usually the most violent. Others examine individual motives for joining a militant organization. Joseba Zulaika (1988) in a study on the ETA describes militant groups as the continuation of friendship in already existing peer groups. In a similar vein, recent terrorism has been explained as an attempt by religiously inspired militants to overcome existential anxieties caused by alienation, humiliation, and marginalization.

A growing body of work concerned with aspects of terrorism is the study of state terror. Michael Taussig (1984) has used the term *cultures of terror* to denote societies that are under constant threat of state violence and intimidation. This line of work focuses on the systematic use of torture and death squads, rumors, secret intelligence, and other forms of intimidation by state institutions, as well as on individual and collective coping strategies used by the victims of state terror. State terrorism can also include the deployment of terrorist actions by one state against another state, as shown, for example, by Libya's involvement in the explosion of Pan Am flight 103 over Lockerbie, Scotland, in 1988. In terms of numbers of victims, state terror is a much more serious problem than the terrorism of revolutionary or religiously inspired militants.

The study of terrorism-related discourse focuses on the use of the terrorism concept in the media, by policy makers, and by "terrorists" themselves. Studies on the "symbiotic relationship" between terrorists, the media, and state propaganda portray terrorist violence as "spectacle," as "theater" and "performative," or as "ritual." Without denying the reality of death and destruction, these studies focus on how the media frames terrorism in terms of Good and Evil, leaving little room for anything other than one-dimensional conceptions of terrorism and counterterrorism. The way terrorism was reported on dur-

ing the cold war, for example, created a fear of totalitarianism and of incomprehensible technology. More recently, and especially since the attacks of September 11, 2001, terrorism discourse resonates with the fear of religious fanaticism. Most of these studies also trace the complex relations between the media and state policy. Governments often brand their enemies as "terrorist" in order to legitimize an excessive use of force and the violation of human rights. At the same time, the perpetrators of "terrorist" violence themselves evoke collective fears and fantasies associated with terrorism in an effort to become "larger than life."

Following the September 11, 2001 attacks on the World Trade Center and the Pentagon, the study of terrorism has changed significantly, not only in quantitative terms, but also substantively. Book titles like *Terror in the Mind of God* (Juergensmeyer 2000) and *Terror in the Name of God* (Stern 2003) indicate an increased interest in the relationship between terrorism and religion. Studies of religious militancy largely fall into one of three categories. A culturalist approach tries to explain recent Islamist militancy in terms of long-standing traditions of violence and intolerance in Islam. A more empirical approach examines religious extremism per se, comparing Islamist militants with, for instance, American antiabortionists and Zionist extremists. Rather than being rooted in age-old and supposedly unchanging traditions, recent religious militancy is said to draw inspiration from renewed and redefined notions of purity and holy war, fostered by anxieties and inequalities caused by globalization and political or social marginalization. A historical approach examines religious radicalism as political ideology and religious militant groups as political organizations. Such studies analyze the rise of Islamic radicalism, the history of Al-Qaeda, or the life of bin Laden against the backdrop of geopolitical developments in the Middle East and Asia since the 1980s. Gilles Kepel (2002), for instance, explains the "9-11" attacks by Al-Qaeda as a sign of disillusion and an attempt to reverse a process of decline after various failed attempts to retain political power for the Islamist ideology.

Post-"9-11" studies of terrorism not only center on religion, but also focus on the sites, the organization, and the methods of modern terrorism. Today's terrorism is often transnational in scope, objective, and organization, and transcends the boundaries of the nation-state. Stephen Graham (2004) studies modern terrorism explicitly as an *urban* phenomenon, exploring the ways in which terrorism and counterterrorism are shaped by, and transform, the public life of global cities. As for the study of terrorist organizations, the emphasis has shifted from cell-structured and network organizations to the "rhizomatic" character of transnational terrorism. Some of the best-known terrorist phenomena like Al-Qaeda are franchises, allowing loosely connected "freelancers" to operate in their name, as much as they are organizations or networks. Finally, Walter Laqueur (1999), among others, in a book predating "9-11," explores the ways in which terrorist methods may evolve from the traditional methods of assassinations and hijacking to new forms of chemical, biological, nuclear, and cyber terrorism.

SEE ALSO *Fundamentalism, Islamic; Guerrilla Warfare; Revolution; Terrorists; Violence; Violence, Frantz Fanon on; War*

BIBLIOGRAPHY

Crenshaw, Martha. 1988. Theories of Terrorism: Instrumental and Organizational Approaches. In *Inside Terrorist Organizations*, ed. David C. Rapoport, 13–31. London: Frank Cass.

Feldman, Allen. 2002. Ground Zero Point One: On the Cinematics of History. *Social Analysis* 46 (1): 110–117.

Graham, Stephen. 2004. *Cities, War, and Terrorism: Towards an Urban Geopolitics*. Malden, MA: Blackwell.

Juergensmeyer, Mark. 2000. *Terror in the Mind of God: The Global Rise of Religious Violence*. Berkeley: University of California Press.

Kepel, Gilles. 2002. *Jihad: The Trail of Political Islam*. London: Tauris.

Laqueur, Walter. 1999. *The New Terrorism: Fanaticism and the Arms of Mass Destruction*. New York: Oxford University Press.

Rubenstein, Richard E. 1987. *Alchemists of Revolution: Terrorism in the Modern World*. London: Tauris.

Stern, Jessica. 2003. *Terror in the Name of God: Why Religious Militants Kill*. New York: HarperCollins.

Taussig, Michael. 1984. Culture of Terror, Space of Death: Roger Casement's Putumayo Report and the Explanation of Torture. *Comparative Studies in Society and History* 26 (3): 467–497.

Zulaika, Joseba. 1988. *Basque Violence: Metaphor and Sacrament*. Reno: University of Nevada Press.

Oskar Verkaaik

TERRORISTS

Terrorists are nonstate actors who pursue random unconventional violence targeted at noncombatants to achieve political objectives. The labeling of who is a terrorist depends heavily on who is making the distinction. President Ronald Reagan's observation that one man's terrorist is another man's freedom fighter implies the difficulty in objectively labeling certain people as terrorists. It is only nonstate actors who are defined as terrorists because according to current standards of international law, governments cannot engage in terrorism. Though some states support and even sponsor terrorism, acts of

violence committed by states against noncombatants are considered by international law to be crimes against humanity or war crimes, not terrorism.

The term *terrorist* is pejorative, and implies that persons so-labeled are immoral, evil, and criminal. Whereas criminals are considered innocent until proven guilty in the judicial systems of many democratic countries, there is no defined legal threshold to prove someone is a terrorist. Rather, individuals or groups are identified as terrorists precisely because they are labeled as such, regardless of whether these individuals or groups have actually engaged in random violent actions against noncombatants. Therefore, the burden of proving guilt is not on the government as with nonpolitical criminals. Rather, the burden of proving innocence is on the individuals who are accused of pursuing terrorism. Because it is nearly impossible to prove innocence, governments tend to eagerly label anyone who could be linked to acts of violence as terrorists.

In fact, individuals who engage in violent actions deemed as terrorism often perceive and label themselves as freedom fighters, resistance fighters, soldiers of God, or liberators. They also perceive their actions as the best means available to achieve the political objectives of the group to which they belong. Terrorists do not perceive their actions to be illegitimate or immoral. Rather, terrorists often argue that they must pursue violent actions in order to provoke a response, primarily from the government of a state, because the status quo has prevented them from achieving their political objectives.

Besides the actual individuals who engage in or attempt violent acts, terrorists can also be members of a group that provides tactical support—planning, funding, training, and ordering violent acts. In order to be considered a terrorist, an individual must be a member of a group with some type of political agenda. Individuals acting without any political agenda are not considered terrorists, but rather murderers, kidnappers, or other types of criminals. Though terrorists can simultaneously be guerrillas, the two designations are distinct in that guerrillas are defined as those who deliberately target military targets rather than noncombatants.

Terrorists engage in violence that is criminal in nature and illegal in most countries. Typical violent acts pursued by terrorists include the use of explosives, suicide bombing, the hijacking of an airplane, kidnapping, and murder. Terrorist groups are inherently clandestine due to their need to stay below the radar of government officials seeking to eradicate such organizations. Because it is difficult to remain clandestine, terrorists often seek support and assistance from governments that support their political agenda or objectives. Therefore, many terrorist groups maintain training camps in countries such as Syria, Libya,

Sudan, and Iran, all of which have been known to provide support to terrorists. To prevent discovery, terrorists often use e-mail and temporary cell phones when communicating and false identification papers when traveling. Though all strategic and tactical planning is pursued clandestinely, the actual terrorist activities are by necessity pursued publicly in order to draw mass attention and terrorize society.

The immediate objective of terrorists is to terrorize society by pursuing random violence, while the long-term objective is to persuade a government to change policies or take certain actions. Typical political objectives of terrorist groups include the release of political prisoners, improved political and civil rights, greater political autonomy, and territorial sovereignty.

Many terrorist groups are based in countries with governments that tend to be oppressive, repressive, intolerant of cultural diversity, and sometimes racist, denying political and civil rights to certain groups. As a result, terrorists and their supporters often argue that they have a legitimate right to resist such governments and to throw off the yoke of governmental persecution, just as many revolutions succeeded in doing in Western countries like the United States and France. Many non-Western governments are unwilling to label individuals seeking political freedom, sovereignty, rights, and so on as terrorists, and perceive their embrace of violence as exercising a right of resistance. This has led to a division between Western and non-Western governments and has prevented the United Nations from arriving at an agreed-upon definition of terrorism.

Governments seeking to eradicate or prevent future terrorism and to prosecute terrorists have created extensive counterterrorism policies. Such policies include the sanctioning of states suspected of supporting and hosting terrorist groups; arresting and trying individuals suspected of direct or indirect involvement in activities deemed terrorist; the collection of intelligence internationally and domestically, through monitoring communication, spying, using informants, and so on; increasing security at transportation hubs and government buildings; and sometimes even assassinating suspected terrorists. Though governments spend significant sums of money on counterterrorism efforts, terrorism continues to increase as the political objectives of terrorists expand. As a result, some governments are willing to address such political objectives in order to prevent future terrorist attacks.

SEE ALSO *Coup d'Etat; Defense; Defense, National; Destabilization; Dissidents; Guerrilla Warfare; Stability, Political; Terrorism*

BIBLIOGRAPHY

Anderson, Sean, and Stephen Sloan. 1995. *Historical Dictionary of Terrorism.* Metuchen, NJ: Scarecrow Press.

Combs, Cindy C. 2005. *Terrorism in the Twenty-First Century.* 4th ed. Upper Saddle River, NJ: Prentice Hall.

Crenshaw, Martha, and John Pimlott. 1997. *Encyclopedia of World Terrorism.* Armonk, NY: Sharpe Reference.

Henderson, Harry. 2001. *Global Terrorism: The Complete Reference Guide.* New York: Checkmark Books.

Kegley, Charles W., Jr., ed. 2003. *The New Global Terrorism: Characteristics, Causes, Controls.* Upper Saddle River, NJ: Prentice Hall.

Schmid, Alex P., and Albert J. Jongman. 2005. *Political Terrorism: A New Guide to Actors, Authors, Concepts, Data Bases, Theories, and Literature.* New York: Transaction Press.

Krista E. Wiegand

TEST STATISTICS

Hypothesis testing or significance testing is undoubtedly one of the most widely used quantitative methodologies in empirical research in the social sciences. It is one viable way to use statistics to examine a hypothesis in light of observations or sample information. The starting point of hypothesis testing is specifying the hypothesis to be tested, called the *null hypothesis*. Then a test statistic is chosen to summarize the sample information, and its value is taken as an indication of the strength of sample evidence against the null hypothesis.

Modern hypothesis testing dates to the 1920s and the work of Ronald Aylmer Fisher (1890–1962) on the one hand, and Jerzy Neyman (1894–1981) and Egon Pearson (1895–1980) on the other. Fisher (1925) refers to hypothesis testing as *significance testing* (this entry does not distinguish between the two terms). In the Fisherian approach, the observed test statistic is converted to the *P*-value, which is the probability of obtaining the observed or more extreme value of the test statistic under the null model; the smaller the *P*-value, the stronger the sample evidence against the null hypothesis. An early example of Fisher's significance testing was conducted in 1735 by the father and son Swiss mathematicians Daniel Bernoulli (1700–1782) and John Bernoulli (1667–1748). They tested for the random/uniform distribution of the inclinations of the planetary orbits. A detailed discussion of their original results and subsequent modifications of their results can be found in Anders Hald (1998).

In the Neyman and Pearsonian (1928, 1933) approach, an alternative hypothesis is specified and the null hypothesis is tested against this alternative hypothesis. The specification of an alternative hypothesis allows the computation of the probabilities of two types of error: Type I error (the error of falsely rejecting a null hypothesis) and Type II error (the error of incorrectly accepting a null hypothesis).

Type I error is also referred to as the *significance level* of the test, and one minus Type II error the *power* of the test. Given that the two types of error cannot be minimized simultaneously, the common practice is to specify the level of significance or Type I error and then use a test that maximizes its power subject to the given significance level. In the Fisherian approach, the *P*-value is reported without necessarily announcing the rejection or nonrejection of the null hypothesis, whereas in the Neyman and Pearsonian approach, the null hypothesis is either rejected in favor of the alternative hypothesis or not rejected at the given significance level. E. L. Lehmann (1993) provides a more detailed comparison of the two approaches.

In empirical research, a mixture of the two approaches is typically adopted. Consider the linear regression model:

$$Y_i = \beta_1 + \beta_2 X_{i2} + \beta_3 X_{i3} + \cdots$$
$$+ \beta_K X_{iK} + \varepsilon_i, \, i = 1, \cdots, n, \qquad (1)$$

where $\{Y_i, X_{i2}, ..., X_{iK}\}_{i=1}^n$ is the set of observations on the dependent variable Y and the explanatory variables X_2, ..., X_K, and ε_i is the unobserved error term. The parameters β_2, ..., β_K measure the *ceteris paribus* effects of the explanatory variables on the dependent variable. The significance of these effects is routinely tested by the *t*-tests and *F*-test. The *t*-test was discovered by William Sealy Gosset (1876–1937) for the mean of a normal population and extended by Fisher in 1925 to other contexts, including regression coefficients. Gosset's result was published in *Biometrika* under the pseudonym "Student" in 1908. The *F*-test was originally developed by Fisher in the context of testing the ratio of two variances. Fisher pointed out many other applications of the *F*-test, including the significance of the complete regression model.

For a given $j = 2, ..., K$, the null hypothesis for the corresponding *t*-test is $H_{0j}:\beta_j = 0$ and the *t*-statistic is

$$t_j = \frac{b_j}{se(b_j)},$$

where b_j denotes the ordinary least squares estimator of β_j and $se(b_j)$ denotes the standard error of b_j. Note that if the null H_{0j} is true, the explanatory variable X_{ij} would be absent from the regression model (1) and thus considered to be insignificant in explaining the dependent variable given the presence of the other explanatory variables. This is why *t*-tests are referred to as tests for the significance of individual variables as opposed to the *F*-test, which tests for the significance of the complete regression. The null hypothesis for the *F*-test is

$$H_0 : \beta_2 = \beta_3 = \cdots = \beta_K = 0.$$

There are several equivalent formulas for computing the *F*-statistic, one of which is

$$F = \frac{R^2/(K-1)}{(1-R^2)/(n-K)},$$

where R^2 is the coefficient of determination. Since under H_0, all the explanatory variables can be dropped from (1), the *F*-test is a test for the significance of the complete regression.

Much packaged computer software routinely calculates the *t*-statistics and the *F*-statistic. For a given sample, the observed value of t_j (F) summarizes the sample evidence on the significance of the explanatory variable X_j (the significance of the regression (1)). To either convert the observed value of t_j (F) to the *P*-value or make a binary decision on the rejection or nonrejection of the null hypothesis H_{0j} (H_0) at a given significance level, the distribution of t_j (F) under the corresponding null hypothesis is required. On the basis of the null hypothesis being true and further assumptions on the nature of the sample and on the normality of the error in (1), the distribution of t_j is known to be Student's *t* with $(K-1)$ degrees of freedom, denoted as $t_{[K-1]}$, and the distribution of F is the so-called *F*-distribution with $\{(K-1),(n-K)\}$ degrees of freedom denoted as $F_{[K-1, n-K]}$ (see Goldberger [1991] for details). The known distribution of t_j (F) under the null hypothesis allows the computation of the *P*-value or the computation of the appropriate critical value at a prespecified significance level with which the observed test statistic can be compared.

Like *t*-tests and the *F*-test, standard tests rely on further assumptions in addition to the truth of the null hypothesis, such as the assumption of a random sample and the normality of the error term. These further assumptions may not be met in typical applications in social sciences, and modifications are required of tests designed on the basis of these assumptions. For example, when normality of the error term is not met, the distributions of the *t*-statistic and *F*-statistic are no longer $t_{[K-1]}$ or $F_{[K-1, n-K]}$. Fortunately, their asymptotic distributions are known under general conditions and may be used to perform these tests. Alternatively, resampling techniques, such as the bootstrap and subsampling, may be used to approximate the distributions of the test statistics under the null hypothesis (see Efron and Tibshirani [1993] and Politis et al. [1999] for an excellent introduction to these methods).

The issue that has generated the most debate in hypothesis testing from the beginning is the choice of significance level (Henkel 1976). Given any value of the test statistic, one can always force nonrejection by specifying a low enough significance level or force rejection by choosing a high enough significance level. Although reporting the *P*-value partly alleviates this arbitrariness in setting the significance level, it is desirable to report estimates of the parameters of interest and their standard errors or confidence intervals so that the likely values of the unknown parameters and the precision of their estimates can be assessed.

SEE ALSO *Hypothesis and Hypothesis Testing; Student's T-Statistic*

BIBLIOGRAPHY

Efron, Bradley, and Robert J. Tibshirani. 1993. *An Introduction to the Bootstrap.* New York: Chapman and Hall.

Fisher, Ronald Aylmer. 1925. *Statistical Methods for Research Workers.* Edinburgh, U.K.: Oliver and Boyd.

Goldberger, Arthur S. 1991. *A Course in Econometrics.* Cambridge, MA: Harvard University Press.

Hald, Anders. 1998. *A History of Mathematical Statistics from 1750 to 1930.* New York: Wiley.

Henkel, Ramon E. 1976. *Tests of Significance.* Beverly Hills, CA: Sage.

Lehmann, E. L. 1993. The Fisher, Neyman-Pearson Theories of Testing Hypotheses: One Theory or Two? *Journal of the American Statistical Association* 88: 1242–1249.

Neyman, Jerzy, and Egon S. Pearson. 1928. On the Use and Interpretation of Certain Test Criteria for Purposes of Statistical Inference. *Biometrika* 20A: 175–240, 263–294.

Neyman, Jerzy, and Egon S. Pearson. 1933. On the Problem of the Most Efficient Tests of Statistical Hypotheses. *Philosophical Transactions of the Royal Society of London.* Ser. A: 231, 289–337.

Politis, Dimitris N., Joseph P. Romano, and Michael Wolf. 1999. *Subsampling.* New York: Springer.

Student (William Sealy Gosset). 1908. The Probable Error of a Mean. *Biometrika* 6 (1): 1–25.

Yanqin Fan

TEXTILE INDUSTRY

The textile industry is the world's oldest branch of consumer goods manufacturing and covers the entire production chain of transforming natural and chemical fibers (such as cotton, wool, and oil) into end-user goods, including garments, household goods, and industrial textiles. In the twelfth century China already produced cotton and fabrics. In the early seventeenth century India and Japan had domestic cotton industries. Modern textile manufacturing originated in Great Britain during the Industrial Revolution around 1780. The mechanization of spinning and weaving alongside a rising demand for clothing from the colonies contributed to the growth of "king cotton." In the early nineteenth century textile production spread from Britain over western Europe and the United States. Ever since that time, the textile industry has been one of the most competitive and geographically dispersed industries across the world.

Accounting for 5.6 percent of world trade flows and employing at least twenty million workers worldwide, the modern textile industry is a significant economic sector. Despite its geographical dispersion, large concentrations of textile production can be found in China, followed by India, the United States, the Russian Federation, Japan, and western Europe. Since the 1970s a gradual shift of production has taken place to newly industrializing countries in East and Southeast Asia, Latin America, eastern Europe, and North Africa.

The textile industry is typically the leading sector of industrialization. Usually, textiles manufacturing is labor intensive and employs relatively low skills and simple technologies. Moreover the capital investment needed is only modest in comparison with other types of industry. Some developing countries also benefit from local supplies of raw materials (e.g., cotton) that foster the development of textiles production. Thanks to low labor costs, the newly industrializing countries have become fierce competitors for producers in Europe and North America. This rivalry, combined with saturated home markets, has induced corporate restructuring in the European Union and the United States, making the textile industry progressively an industry of large, transnational corporations.

Growing competitive pressure has led to a variety of corporate strategies in American and European textiles. Some companies attempt to cut costs by producing standardized goods that benefit from economies of scale. Other firms pursue offshore strategies and relocate part of their operations to low-labor-cost countries. Most producers, however, choose for focused differentiation: They search for market niches where specialized goods can be sold for a premium price. For that purpose many textile firms invest in quality improvement, innovation, design, marketing, and retailing. Some of the firms also focus on the production of technical textiles (e.g., artificial grass). All these differentiation strategies ask for sophisticated skills, knowledge of local markets, and flexible production facilities. Textile firms increasingly have to cope with a trade-off between labor costs and the need for market proximity.

Since the 1960s governments in western Europe and America have protected domestic textile producers by means of trade arrangements. After the Long-Term Arrangement in 1962, the Multi-Fibre Agreement was negotiated in 1973. The aim of both agreements was to create an "orderly" development of global textiles trade— not only for developed but also for developing countries—by restricting imports that "disrupted" domestic markets. In practice merely the European and North American nations profited from the rules, because in most cases the cheap exports from developing countries were considered to be disruptive for the matured textile industry in the developed world. However, thanks to World Trade Organization (WTO) rules, which aim for nondiscrimination between all trading partners, and following a ten-year transition period (1995–2004), the global textile industry is liberalizing more and more. The protectionist strategies of older, established textile nations and the lack of attention of transnational firms for good labor and environmental circumstances at offshore locations are often criticized. Further liberalization should contribute to an improvement of these conditions in the textile industry across the globe.

SEE ALSO *Industrialization; World Trade Organization*

BIBLIOGRAPHY

Abernathy, William, John Dunlop, John Hammond, and David Weil. 1999. *A Stitch in Time: Lean Retailing and the Transformation of Manufacturing: Lessons from the Apparel and Textile Industries.* New York: Oxford University Press.

Dicken, Peter. 2003. *Global Shift: Reshaping the Global Economic Map in the Twenty-first Century.* 4th ed. London: Sage.

World Trade Organization. 2005. *International Trade Statistics 2004.* Geneva, Switzerland: World Trade Organization.

Gert-Jan Hospers

THANT, U.
1909–1974

U. Thant, the United Nations' third secretary-general and its first non-European, was born in Burma (Myanmar) in the small town of Pantanaw on January 22, 1909. Thant began his career as a schoolteacher in Pantanaw, eventually rising to the positions of headmaster and school superintendent. Following World War II (1939–1945) and the end of British colonial rule, his close friend, U. Nu (1907–1995), prime minister of the newly independent state of Burma, drew him into government service. There followed a number of important government appointments, culminating in Thant's designation as Burma's ambassador to the United Nations (1957–1961). Thant was selected as secretary-general on November 3, 1961, following the death of Dag Hammarskjold (1905–1961) in a plane crash in Africa.

Thant's ten years as UN secretary-general unfolded within the context of a continuing cold war rivalry between the United States and Soviet Union and the emergence onto the world scene of scores of newly independent states, drawn primarily from Africa and Asia. He managed during his two terms to secure the legitimacy of the position of secretary-general, which had come under assault from the Soviet Union during the last year of Hammarskjold's life, but he did little to expand the powers of the office. He proved himself a vigorous advocate for the economic concerns of third world nations and a vocal opponent of colonialism in southern Africa, but when he left office, in December 1971, the inequitable distribution of global wealth and continuing colonial situations in South Africa, Rhodesia, Namibia, and Angola remained as intractable as ever.

Thant's early years in office found him working in cooperation with the United States to quell a secession in the Congo and to fashion major peacekeeping initiatives in West New Guinea, Yemen, Malaysia, Cyprus, and Kashmir. His role as diplomatic facilitator during the Cuban missile crisis of 1962, although modest, earned him the respect of both superpowers and an extended first term as secretary-general. However, by the time of his reappointment to a second term, in 1966, Thant was expressing increasing frustration with his role. The UN's effectiveness was threatened by the refusal of the Soviet Union and France to contribute to peacekeeping operations. The fiscal crisis that emerged escalated into a political crisis when the United States, invoking Article 19 of the UN Charter, sought unsuccessfully to deny the Soviets a vote in the General Assembly. Further frustrating Thant was his inability to broker an end to the Vietnam War (1957–1975), despite his publicly voiced opposition to the American war effort.

Thant's last years in office were characterized by renewed frustrations. In 1967 he quickly surrendered to Egyptian demands that he remove UNEF (United Nations Emergency Force) from Egypt's border with Israel, thus earning widespread blame for the ensuing Arab-Israeli war. In 1971 the United Nations and Thant stood by helplessly as insurrection in the eastern part of Pakistan led to war between Pakistan and India and the dismemberment of Pakistan. Although pressed to assume a third term, Thant retired from office in December 1971.

Thant died on November 25, 1974. Denied a state funeral by the military junta that had ousted U. Nu in 1962, Thant's body was seized by antigovernment students who buried him, with full honors, at Rangoon University and used the occasion to stage antigovernment demonstrations. Government forces reclaimed Thant's body in a bloody confrontation with the student protesters and buried him near a major Buddhist pagoda in Rangoon.

SEE ALSO *Arab-Israeli War of 1967; Cold War; Colonialism; Secession; United Nations; Vietnam War*

BIBLIOGRAPHY

Condier, Andrew, and Max Harrelson, eds. 1976. *Public Papers of the Secretaries-General of the United Nations*, Vols. 6–7. New York: Columbia University Press.

Firestone, Bernard J. 2001. *The United Nations under U Thant, 1961–1971*. London: Scarecrow Press.

Thant, U. 1978. *View from the UN*. Garden City, NY: Doubleday.

Bernard J. Firestone

THATCHER, MARGARET
1925–

Margaret Thatcher's political career was marked by a series of "firsts." In June 1979 she became the first female prime minister of the United Kingdom. She was the first U.K. prime minister in the twentieth century to win three consecutive general elections (1979, 1983, and 1987), and upon her resignation in November 1990, she had become Britain's longest continuously serving prime minister since 1827.

Thatcher was also unique in having her name associated with a set of ideas, policies, and style of governance known as *Thatcherism*. Yet the extent to which Thatcherism as an ideology guided the policies of Thatcher's governments in office has been disputed. What is not in dispute is that these policies fundamentally altered the trajectory of the United Kingdom's economy, society, and polity and continued to impact upon policy outputs, political discourse, and electoral competition long after the demise of the Thatcher government.

Thatcherite economic policies were broadly labeled *monetarist* even though, technically, a monetarist strategy was only pursued for a limited initial period. In an attempt to reverse Britain's long-term economic decline, Thatcher challenged the basis of the postwar Keynesian social democratic consensus by attempting to restructure patterns of property ownership, taxation, and social attitudes toward welfare. An ambitious program of privatization transferred major state-owned industries and public services into the private sector, and 1.5 million public-sector houses were sold to their tenants. A parallel program of marketization promoted the use of market criteria by public-sector service providers—especially local authorities and the National Health Service. Taxation policies sought to reward "initiative" and "enterprise" through reduced rates of income tax. In parallel, welfare and social benefits were restructured, reduced, and increasingly means tested; and social attitudes toward collective welfare provision were challenged, most famously in Thatcher's

phrase "there is no such thing as society" (from an interview with Douglas Keay, 1987).

A hallmark of Thatcher's period in office was her style of governance. She confronted most of the powerful social and political institutions in the United Kingdom. Major state institutions—most particularly the civil service and local government—were reformed, and a wide range of regulatory bodies was introduced. A "community charge" (known as the poll tax) was imposed to reform the system of local government financing. This tax was extremely unpopular and prompted widespread nonpayment and, ultimately, riots in London in November 1990. The legal position and standing of trade unions was altered radically by five major legislative acts. Thatcher's foreign policies also revealed her combative nature. Her condemnation of Soviet-style communism earned her the epithet "the Iron Lady" in the Soviet press. Her support for Ronald Reagan (1911–2004), and for a close relationship with the United States, was reflected in mutual transatlantic perspectives on the cold war. Her general hostility to further European integration and her specific resistance to the creation of a federal European Union earned the United Kingdom the title "the awkward partner." However, the Falklands War, waged in 1982 against Argentina, secured Thatcher's status as a "warrior queen" in the popular press in the United Kingdom. The war lasted for seventy-four days, between April and June, and ended when British troops successfully reclaimed the British dependency of the Falkland Islands in the South Atlantic after an invasion by Argentina. Thatcher's image as a decisive war leader strengthened her poll ratings and was emphasized successfully in the Conservative Party's 1983 election slogan "the resolute approach."

After her resignation in 1990, Thatcher remained a member of Parliament until the 1992 general election. Thereafter she joined the House of Lords as Baroness Thatcher, and after a series of strokes she retired from public speaking in 2002. However, the legacy of Thatcher was profound, not least because of her impact upon her political opponents. Indeed the policies pursued by the Labour Party under Tony Blair were variously described as sub-Thatcherite, neo-Thatcherite, or simply Thatcherite.

SEE ALSO *Blair, Tony; Conservative Party (Britain); Economics, Keynesian; European Union; Falkland Islands War; Inequality, Political; Labour Party (Britain); Monetarism; Nationalism and Nationality; Neoconservatism; Privatization; Reagan, Ronald*

BIBLIOGRAPHY

Campbell, John. 2000. *The Grocer's Daughter*. Vol. 1 of *Margaret Thatcher*. London: Cape.

Campbell, John. 2003. *The Iron Lady*. Vol. 2 of *Margaret Thatcher*. London: Cape.

Keay, Douglas. 1987. AIDS, Education, and the Year 2000. *Woman's Own.* (October 31): pp. 8–10. http://www.margaretthatcher.org/speeches/displaydocument. asp?docid=106689.

David Judge

THATCHERISM

SEE *Thatcher, Margaret.*

THEATER

Contemporary British director Peter Brook wrote of theater and its essence in his book, *The Empty Space* (1968), "A man walks across this empty space (a bare stage) whilst someone else is watching him, and this is all that is needed for an act of theater to be engaged" (p. 9). By Brook's reckoning, the actor, the stage space, and the audience are the minimal necessary components for the art of the theater. At its most basic level, *theater* is a story presented in public by a performer or performers, for an audience.

There exists a distinction between the related art forms of *drama* (the written text) and *theater* (the process of performing the written text within a designated space). A difference must also be drawn between theater as a form of artistic or cultural entertainment and the existence of theatrical components within a culture. Performance occurs regularly in daily life (e.g., sporting events, political campaigns, weddings, and other social rituals), but these are not considered theater in the strictest sense. These routine presentations form the basis of performance studies, a discipline that uses terminology from the theater and that of anthropology in an effort to analyze how it is that people and cultures stage rituals and events.

Theater as society has come to think of it is a live artistic form, featuring many artists (dramatist, actor, director, designers, and audience) who collaborate to create performance events. Theater is also considered from a conventional viewpoint to be the most complete of all the art forms, in that it integrates many disciplines (dance, music, acting, visual spectacle, language, sculpture) in the presentation of a story. Theater occurs in a staging space, in front of an audience, regardless of the dramatic location of the event being enacted. Moreover, theater is performed in real time and usually requires a compression of the dramatic timeline, rather than a moment-to-moment literal reenactment of the event. Theater is an imitation of the human experience, drawing its characters and plotlines from dramatic events recognizable to the audience. The Greek philosopher Aristotle, in his critical text *Poetics*, described theater (or drama) as an imitation of men in action. Theater is an artistic form that lends itself easily to critiques of social problems, heralding the possible transformation of society in the wake of a public performance expressing new ideas for change.

One explanation for theater's origins lay in the ceremonial rituals of primitive cultures, usually linked to religious worship. Storytelling is an alternative explanation for theatrical origins, a performance in which a narrator such as a tribal leader or shaman recalled episodes important to the history of the tribe, acting out the events while interpreting the different characters for the shared enjoyment of the audience. The theatrical ritual achieved greater aesthetic sophistication as the cultures advanced, utilizing multiple actors, spectacle, dance, music, and costuming in an effort to make the performances more enjoyable. Society eventually began to prize these performances as much for their inherent entertainment and artistic values, as for their ritual significance.

FORM AND STYLE

Theater has developed different approaches to the creation of dramatic structure, utilizing a multitude of various styles and performance traditions. The play's *form* is the clearly identifiable organization of the plot elements, while the play's *style* is the means by which the form is interpreted for a contemporary audience. A theatrical form (e.g., comedy or tragedy) is a specific identifying plot structure as it demonstrates typical themes of human experience. A theatrical style (e.g., Shakespearian or expressionistic) is the representative interpretation of a form, based on audience expectations determined by place and time. Style may be associated with a specific historical period, playwright, culture, or artistic movement, whereas form is more universal and changes little from one culture to another.

The four distinct dramatic forms are: tragedy, comedy, drama, and mixed-forms. Tragedy concerns the fate of a main character who is caught up in events beyond his or her control, and is subsequently ruined as a consequence of a moral weakness or an inability to cope with difficult circumstances. Comedy—be it satire or farce—requires the happy or ironic resolution of a conflict involving an individual or a community. Aristotle wrote in his *Poetics* that the main difference between the tragedy form and the comedy form is that "one imitates people better, the other one people worse, than the average" (1967, p. 18). Tragedy and comedy were the dominant forms of theater until the eighteenth century. The form of drama emphasizes the moral seriousness of social issues, often through depictions of characters and situations drawn from daily life. Eighteenth-century French dramatic theorist Denis Diderot (1713–1784) advocated in his

Encyclopedia (c. 1755–1780) that this new drama "will encourage the light of reason, which everywhere grows brighter … and the spirit of the century will advance the revolution it began" (1967, p. 91). A mixed-form dramatic text combines elements of the comedy and tragedy forms and is a very uncommon form of theater. Theatrical styles, on the other hand, are many in number. Each style is associated with a specific time period (e.g., Restoration comedy such as William Congreve's *The Way of the World*), author (e.g., Shakespearian tragedy like *Hamlet*), or artistic movement (e.g., realistic drama, as an example Anton Chekhov's *The Cherry Orchard*).

HISTORY

Although the essential nature of theater is constant, the theatrical art form developed differently during various historical periods and throughout the regions of the world. Eastern (Asian) theater traditions predate Western (European) theater and utilize vastly different conventions (i.e., agreed-upon performance techniques). Asian theater forms rely heavily on the elements of musical performance and bodily expression to relate the story line to the audience. Chinese theatrical forms were first recorded in 1767 BCE during the Shang Dynasty. Popular entertainments of the time included shadow-play and puppet theaters, and live entertainers often performed at teahouses. Chinese theater was performed on a bare stage, accompanied by music, and characterized by a strict adherence to traditions. The most prolific contemporary expression of Chinese theater is the *Beijing Opera*, which employs a strictly ordered system of dance, singing, and acting to enhance the performance. Indian theater dates from the first century CE, and included Sanskrit dramas in which Indian actors performed specific codified gestures and chanted intonations with musical accompaniment designed to cultivate a balanced aesthetic, emotional state called a *rasa* within the spectators. Formal Japanese theater dates from the sixth century CE and includes variations such as Noh theater (1374), a stylized musical dance-drama with choreographed movements and masks; Bunraki theater (early seventeenth century), a puppet theater; and Kabuki theater (1603)—the most popular form—in which dance and spoken dialogue are used in conjunction with sets, stylized make-up, and costuming, to achieve the desired theatrical effect.

The formal Western theater tradition began in Greece with the ritual worship of Dionysus, the God of wine and revelry. The word *tragedy* evolved from the Greek word *tragoidia* (goat-song), the performance that accompanied ceremonies of ritual animal sacrifice. In 534 BCE, the city of Athens organized a contest to determine the best tragedy during the religious festival of the City Dionysia. At the festival, tragedies were performed in sets of three

linked stories drawn from either history or myth, followed by a satyr play (a short farcical comedy utilizing burlesque). Comedies were introduced at the City Dionysia after 487 BCE. The earliest Greek theaters were temporary wooden structures built into hillsides. Permanent theaters made of stone began to appear in the fourth century and were capable of seating more than ten thousand spectators. Greek actors performed on a small circular area called the *orkestra* (dancing place), which featured a *thymele* (small altar) for the ritual sacrifice, surrounded by the risers of the audience area, called the *theatron* (seeing place). The first *skene* (small scenic house) appeared in 458 BCE. The fifth century is recognized as the Golden Age of Greek Theater, with more than one thousand different plays believed to have been performed. Only thirty-one tragedies survive from the period—all written by three playwrights: Aeschylus (525–456 BCE), Sophocles (c. 496–406 BCE), and Euripides (c. 484–406 BCE). The Athenian playwright Aristophanes (c. 450–c. 388 BCE) is the only comic playwright of the time whose works have survived. Greek tragedies were written originally for just two actors, but in 468 BCE the use of a third actor was established. Each actor would play multiple roles, indicated by distinctive masks and representative props. Greek dramas also were the first to feature the chorus, a group of performers who chanted rhythmically, danced, and commented on the course of the action in the play.

Greek theater was appropriated by the Romans after 240 BCE but eventually gave way to more popular forms of entertainment. Roman citizens preferred spectacular and bloody events such as chariot races, armed contests between gladiators, wild animal fights, and mock naval battles (often staged in flooded amphitheaters). The rise of the Christian Church in the fourth century CE signaled a fierce opposition to theatrical practices, due to their origins in pagan rituals and their licentious subject matter. Organized theater all but disappeared by the sixth century, following the fall of Rome to the Visigoths, though some entertainment forms such as mimes, minstrels, and festivals continued in local communities until the Middle Ages and the re-emergence of theater as an art form. Liturgical dramas were performed during church services as a means of imparting religious doctrine to illiterate parishioners. The earliest recorded liturgical drama occurred during an Easter service around 925 CE, and included monks performing the discovery at the tomb. Plays moved out-of-doors and became part of religious festivals after 1300 CE, with performances staged on small, movable structures known as mansions. Local trade guilds took over the staging and financing of cycle plays (a group of plays featuring biblical story interpretations). Local vernacular language eventually replaced Latin as the spoken language of the performances, which also began to feature more secular subjects.

Religious strife and internal church conflicts changed the face of Europe in the fourteenth through sixteenth centuries. Religious theater was eventually outlawed, and entertainments began to be provided by a new professional theater during the Renaissance. Permanent theaters blossomed in London during the late sixteenth century and were staffed by acting troupes maintained by wealthy noblemen. The performances had a broad and popular appeal and were attended by the titled and commoners alike. The most famous English playwright of the period was William Shakespeare (1564–1616), who is believed to have penned an estimated thirty-eight plays. The English Civil War closed the London theaters in 1642. Meanwhile, opera emerged in Italy as a popular Renaissance form and prompted innovations such as scenic stage sets incorporating perspective drawing, machinery for changing background scenery in view of the audience, and rigging created for the purpose of flying people and scenic pieces around the stage. A new style called neo-classicism emerged in France during the sixteenth and seventeenth centuries, in which drama was made to conform to critical principles based on contemporaneous interpretations of classical theater. Most important were the unities of time, place, and action (each play should have a single plot action that could occur within a twenty-four-hour period and in locations that could realistically be reached during a single day of travel). Neoclassicism also demanded that the characters practice decorum (behaving according to strictly established social etiquette) and was centered on the notion of verisimilitude (the appearance of truth).

This preoccupation with realistic action/behavior onstage foreshadowed the early nineteenth-century development of romanticism. Romanticism was a revolt against the rules of the neoclassical theater and featured plotlines inclined toward emotional truth rather than rational knowledge and characters drawn from the lower social classes rather than the nobility. Romanticism flourished through the 1850s, followed at the end of the century by realism. Realism was the result of two modes of intellectual thought: The first involved the application of scientific thought to theatrical life, resulting in lifelike portrayals; while the second mode centered on democratic political ideals precipitating the need for social transformation. Theater was viewed as a laboratory of humanity, a place to test new ideas of social behavior and reform. The theater of the period exposed contemporary social ills (such as the plight of women in *The Doll's House*, the best known of Norwegian playwright Henrik Ibsen's realistic works), and made suggestions for reform (freedom from outmoded social structures). The director emerged as an artistic force during this period, bringing creative and visual unity to the stage performance. Also important during the late nineteenth century was the origination of musical theater (which uses song, dance, music, and spoken dialogue to relate a story). Musical theater remains one of the most popular entertainments into the twentieth and twenty-first centuries.

TWENTIETH-CENTURY THEATER

The avant-garde theater (also known as anti-realistic theater) was a strong presence in the early twentieth century, as writers and performers rejected realism and tried to reinvent the ideas of what constituted art. Avant-garde art pushed the boundaries of what is accepted as real, while at the same time attempting to document an individual's perceptions of reality. Twentieth-century avant-garde theater styles include expressionism, futurism, dadaism, and surrealism. Absurdism (life cannot be logically explained) is a style of the avant-garde that became very influential in theater following World War II. This eventually led to a backlash of radical experimental theater in the 1960s, meant to mingle political significance with aesthetic creation. This experimentation laid the groundwork for the contemporary post-modernism movement, which signals a break with the modernist movement and traditional portrayals of experience. Post-modernism theater utilizes a mixture of styles and advocates the primacy of the audience response to the formation of the work. Despite this growth and evolution of alternative styles, however, realism and musical theater remain the dominant mainstream theater fare of the twentieth and early twenty-first centuries.

BIBLIOGRAPHY

Aristotle. 1967. *Poetics.* Trans. Gerald Else. Ann Arbor: University of Michigan Press.

Brockett, Oscar G., and Franklin J. Hildy. 2003. *History of the Theatre.* 9th ed. Boston: Allyn and Bacon.

Brook, Peter. 1968. *The Empty Space.* New York: Simon and Schuster.

Carlson, Marvin. 1984. *Theories of the Theatre: A Historical and Critical Survey from the Greeks to the Present.* Ithaca, NY: Cornell University Press.

Carlson, Marvin. 1996. *Performance: A Critical Introduction.* London: Routledge.

Cole, Toby, and Helen Krich Chinoy, eds. 1949. *Actors on Acting.* New York: Three Rivers Press.

Diderot, Denis. 1967. *Encyclopedia: Selections*, ed. Stephen Gendzier. New York: J and J Harper Editions.

Dukore, Bernard. 1974. *Dramatic Theory and Criticism: Greeks to Grotowski.* New York: Holt, Rinehart, and Winston.

Esslin, Martin. 1961. *The Theatre of the Absurd.* New York: Doubleday and Company.

Jones, Robert Edmond. 1941. *The Dramatic Imagination.* New York: Theatre Arts Books.

Roach, Joseph. 1993. *The Player's Passion: Studies in the Science of Acting.* Ann Arbor: University of Michigan Press.

Stanislavski, Constantin. 1989. *An Actor Prepares*. New York: Routledge.

Vince, Ronald. 1984a. *Ancient and Medieval Theatre: A Historiographical Handbook*. Westport, CT: Greenwood Press.

Vince, Ronald. 1984b. *Renaissance Theatre: A Historiographical Handbook*. Westport, CT: Greenwood Press.

Vince, Ronald W. 1988. *Neoclassical Theatre: A Historiographical Handbook*. New York: Greenwood Press.

Margaret Coyle

THEIL, HENRI

SEE *Theil Index.*

THEIL INDEX

The Theil index, named for Dutch econometrician Henri Theil (1924–2000), is a special case of the family of inequality measures called the Generalized Entropy Measures. In its aggregate form, the Theil index is a measure of overall inequality. In addition, it lends itself to additive decomposability, a property that is extremely useful for simultaneously examining three aspects of inequality in a society divided into mutually exclusive and completely exhaustive social groups (e.g., based on gender, caste, race, religion, and so forth). Economists have used the decomposed version of the Theil index effectively to identify and highlight important sources of inequality in a given population. (e.g., Mookherjee and Shorrocks 1982; Conceição and Galbraith 2000). While this exercise is indeed efficacious, it is important to bear in mind that this is essentially an *ex-post* accounting of inequality as constituted by intergroup and intragroup inequalities, rather than a statement of causation.

With the assumption that individuals are grouped into m mutually exclusive and completely exhaustive groups $g_1, ..., g_m$, each with n_j individuals, overall inequality can be represented as follows:

$$T = \sum_{j=1}^{m} p_j R_j \log R_j + \sum_{j=1}^{m} p_j R_j T_j \qquad (1)$$

$$T_j \equiv \frac{1}{n_j} \sum_{i \varepsilon g_j}^{m} r_i \log r_i \qquad (2)$$

The decomposed version as stated above has two components that are interpreted below. However, it should be noted that inequality measures, such as those in equations (1) and (2), can be defined with respect to any number of classifications. For instance, Pan Yotopoulos

and Jeffrey Nugent (1976) report Fisher's index with respect to income classes i, sector j, educational attainment k, age m, and region n. The number of terms in the equation will be equal to the number of levels of stratification considered. For instance, in the expression above, the number of levels is two: society divided into groups, and groups comprising individuals. Fisher's index will accordingly have five levels of stratification.

These equations can be interpreted in multiple ways. For instance, William Darity and Ashwini Deshpande (2000) have interpreted these equations differently from Pedro Conceição and James Galbraith (2000). In both interpretations, T is treated in (1) as a measure of the general degree of inequality in a society or country, but the former characterization of the right side of the equation differs from the latter. The first term on the right hand side of (1) represents the extent of *between-group* inequality (B) across all ethnic groups in the population of focus. R_j is the ratio of the mean income for the jth group to the mean income for the entire population, while p_j is the jth group's population share. The second term represents the extent of *within-group* inequality (W) across all ethnic groups in the population. R_j and p_j have the same definition, but T_j is the *group-specific* Theil index measure, defined in (2). Here n_j is the absolute number of persons in group j. $i \in g_j$ indicates that T_j is generated by summing over all persons comprising group j, and r_j is the ratio of individual income or wealth to mean income or wealth for group j.

Conceição and Galbraith compute the between-group component of Theil's T from wage or earnings data aggregated by industrial sectors in a very large number of countries, and by lopping off the within-industry component of wage variation in Theil's T, they arrive at a lower bound estimate of dispersion (Conceição and Galbraith 2000). Darity and Deshpande, instead of focusing on industrial variations in compensation, consider the Theil's T from the perspective of variations in income or earnings across the major racial and ethnic groups that comprise a given society. They also presume that the identity of the groups is understood within the norms and conventions of the society in question. Note that under this interpretation, the weights in the Theil index virtually compel us to think of subaltern groups as minorities, or at most, modest majorities. Certainly, the interpretative validity becomes cloudy when the subaltern group is a substantial majority, as in South Africa.

The relationship between these three components is of more than just academic interest. The conventional interpretation of this equation would read it from left to right, where overall inequality would be the factor in exacerbating intergroup and intragroup inequality. However, Darity and Deshpande (2000) argue that the right-to-left reading can be equally important. Thus, *B* and *W* can actually drive overall inequality, or, more broadly, group affiliation and allegiance are independently salient in explaining overall inequality. Seen this way, any analysis of overall inequality will be necessarily incomplete without reference to *B* and *W*. However, given the caveat mentioned above, namely, that this is an ex-post accounting of overall inequality, the decomposed version of the Theil index cannot be used as a basis for inferring any kind of causation. Estimation over time is important to give clues about the relative contribution of *B* and *W* to a change in overall inequality. Darity and Deshpande raise the following questions suggested by this construction of the Theil index: Is it group difference or the general level of stratification across a population that is more decisive in shaping economic disparity? Does a higher degree of intergroup inequality necessarily produce greater levels of general inequality, or is the higher level of intergroup inequality mitigated by lower levels of within-group inequality? Does a higher level of general economic inequality produce greater levels of intergroup inequality?

The calculated values of individual components of *B* and *W* in equation (1) above need to be interpreted with care. Given that the mean incomes of the subaltern groups will necessarily be less than the overall mean incomes, the *R*s will be less than unity. Thus, the logs will be negative, and that, by construction, will make the overall *B* less than the overall *W*. Numerically, this will imply that the relative contribution of *B* to overall inequality will be substantially less than that of *W* (Paul [1999] finds the same for Australian household expenditure survey data). Before drawing the prima facie inference that *W* matters more than *B*, it would be good to remember that this outcome is a consequence of the construction of the index, and does not *necessarily* reflect the relative importance of *B* and *W*.

SEE ALSO *Gini Coefficient; Income Distribution; Inequality, Gender; Inequality, Income; Inequality, Political; Inequality, Racial; Inequality, Wealth; Kuznets Hypothesis*

BIBLIOGRAPHY

Conceição, Pedro, and James K. Galbraith. 2000. Constructing Long and Dense Time-Series of Inequality Using the Theil Index. *Eastern Economic Journal* 26 (1): 61–74.

Darity, William, Jr., and Ashwini Deshpande. 2000. Tracing the Divide: Intergroup Disparity across Countries. *Eastern Economic Journal* 26 (1): 75–85.

Mookherjee, Dilip, and Anthony F. Shorrocks. 1982. A Decomposition Analysis of the Trend in UK Income Inequality. *Economic Journal* 92 (368): 886–902.

Paul, Satya. 1999. The Population Sub-group Income Effects on Inequality: Analytical Framework and an Empirical Illustration. *Economic Record* 75 (229): 149–155.

Yotopoulos, Pan A., and Jeffrey B. Nugent. 1976. *Economics of Development: Empirical Investigations.* New York: Harper and Row.

Ashwini Deshpande

THEISM

The Greek word *theos* means "god" or "divine power." Hence, *theism* is the belief in a god, or the view that there is a god. Generally, theists think of *god* as a very powerful, personlike being who has control over some or all of the natural universe. To say that a god is personlike is to say that god is capable of thinking, acting, and communicating with other persons, especially human beings. Hence, theists typically refer to god by using pronouns such as "he" or "she" rather than "it." Theists believe that god has a personality, that is, a set of character attributes or traits in accord with which god acts. To varying degrees, theists think of god as interested in some or all of the affairs of human beings.

Theism may be contrasted with *atheism, deism,* and *agnosticism.* Atheism is the belief that there is no god. Deism is the belief in a very powerful being who created or designed the world but who is not concerned with the affairs of human beings. Deists tend to conceive of this being as an impersonal force. Agnosticism is the view that one cannot know whether there is a god. Some agnostics hold that it is in principle impossible ever to know whether or not there is a god; others hold more provisionally that it is currently impossible to tell whether there is a god.

There are various forms of theism. *Polytheism* is the belief in more than one or many gods. *Monotheism* is the belief in one god, usually capitalized as "God" and used as proper noun to refer to this one being. This convention is used in the discussion that follows.

Many people in the ancient world were polytheists. Polytheists developed elaborate belief systems according to which there are many gods who rule over different parts of nature. Often, one god is thought to be the supreme ruler, such as Zeus for the ancient Greeks or Jupiter for the Romans. In some cases, a human king or emperor could be identified as a god himself. Polytheists tend to understand the gods as imperfect in both their power and moral qualities. The gods are not in complete control of nature or themselves, and they do not always act with moral consistency. They are not interested in all the affairs of mankind, but they do intervene on occasion, especially if propitiated by worship and devotion. A hallmark of polytheism is the practice of representing the gods in the form of idols or graven images, which are then used in the context of ritual worship.

The most populous form of polytheism in the world is a certain form of Hinduism. However, at least one form of Hinduism (articulated by Ramanuja in the eleventh century) is monotheistic. If the traditional Hindu gods are viewed as ultimate and independent entities, Hinduism is polytheistic; if the gods are viewed as outward manifestations of one underlying, personlike reality, Hinduism is monotheistic. Buddhism is generally polytheistic, but some forms of Buddhism, such as Zen Buddhism, are usually understood to be atheistic. If the gods are viewed as ultimate powers, Buddhism is polytheistic; if the gods are considered illusory or unreal, Buddhism is atheistic. Aside from Hinduism and Buddhism, many other forms of polytheism are still found elsewhere, such as in sub-Saharan Africa and among Native Americans.

While polytheists tend to understand the gods as limited and imperfect, monotheists tend to understand the one God as unlimited and perfect. Many monotheists think of God as all-powerful, all-knowing, and all good. God is thought to be the creator, king, and judge of the universe. Generally, monotheists believe that God has made certain demands on all humans, and that God directs human history with providence toward some great cosmic end.

Judaism, Christianity, and Islam are the most well known forms of monotheism. In Judaism and Islam, God is conceived as not having bodily form. Linked with this view is a strict ban on any representation of God in the form of an idol and a ban on any form of idol worship. Although the sacred scriptures in these two traditions use bodily language to describe God, these are generally interpreted as metaphors. In Christianity, the oneness and nonmateriality of God is complicated by the belief in the divinity of Jesus, who is understood by traditional Christians to be both divine and human. Traditional Christians maintain that in some sense God is a nonmaterial being who became incarnate in the person of Jesus. Others tend to view the incarnation less literally.

For theists, the highest purpose in life is for humans to develop an interpersonal relationship with God. Precisely what form that relationship takes and how one goes about attaining that relationship differ from one tradition to another. In Judaism, the most intimate relationship with God is found through the observance of the commandments of the Torah, which Jews believe to be God's revealed teaching to the people of Israel. In Christianity, the most intimate relationship is found through good works and through faith in Jesus as the

manifestation of God. In Islam, the best relationship is found through submission to God and obedience to divine law as expressed in the Qur'an, which Muslims believe to be the revelation of God's word to the prophet Muhammad. All three forms of theism teach that respect or love for one's fellows is part and parcel of respect and love for God. At the same time, these forms of theism traditionally teach that those who reject God or his commandments are in some sense deserving of punishment.

Over the centuries, philosophers, theologians, and others have debated whether it is rational to believe in God. Some insist that belief in God is not supposed to be rational; it is a matter of "faith." Others argue that it is rational to believe in God. The most popular arguments for monotheism are based on the existence and orderly nature of the cosmos, on the phenomenon of religious experience or revelation, and on purported miracles. Some have argued that it is rational to believe in God because of the potential value of living the life of a believer. Still other philosophers have argued that belief in God is not rational. They argue that the cosmos can be sufficiently explained without belief in God and that religious experience is not a valid source of truth. They point to the existence of evil and suffering in the effort to show there is no God, and they argue that life is meaningful enough without a belief in God. The question of whether it is rational to believe in God remains a contested question to this day.

SEE ALSO *Atheism; Buddhism; Christianity; Hinduism; Islam, Shia and Sunni; Judaism; Lay Theories; Monotheism; Polytheism; Religion; Supreme Being*

BIBLIOGRAPHY

Armstrong, Karen. 2004. *A History of God: The 4000-Year Quest of Judaism, Christianity, and Islam.* New York: Gramercy.

Fenn, William W. 1969. *Theism: The Implication of Experience.* Ed. Dan Huntington Fenn. Peterborough, NH: Noone House.

Mascall, L. E. 1970. *He Who Is: A Study in Traditional Theism.* Hamden, CT: Archon Books.

Monson, C. H., Jr., ed. 1965. *Great Issues Concerning Theism.* Salt Lake City: University of Utah Press.

Joshua L. Golding

THEMATIC APPERCEPTION TEST
SEE *Achievement.*

THEOCRACY

The term *theocracy* signifies belief in governance by divine guidance, a form of regime in which religion or faith plays the dominant role. It denotes thus a political unit governed by a deity or by officials thought to be divinely guided. The word *theocracy* originates from the Greek *theokratia*. The components of the word are *theos*, "god," and *kratein*, "to rule," hence "rule by god" or "government by god."

The concept of theocracy was first coined by the Jewish historian Flavius Josephus (37 CE–c. 100 CE). Attempting to explain to Gentile readers the organization and political system of the Jewish commonwealth of his time, Josephus contrasted theocracy with other forms of government, such as monarchy, oligarchy, and republics: "Our legislator [Moses] had no regard to any of these forms, but he ordained our government to be what, by a strained expression, may be termed a theocracy [*theokratia*], by ascribing the authority and power to God, and by persuading all the people to have a regard to him, as the author of all good things" (Josephus 1737).

Few concepts have changed more radically over time than the concept of theocracy. According to its oldest meaning, as used by Josephus, the implication is not that ministers assumed political power. However, according to the more modern definition in the *The Shorter Oxford English Dictionary on Historical Principles*, theocracy is "a system of government by sacerdotal order, claiming divine commission" (*The Shorter Oxford English Dictionary on Historical Principles*, vol. 2, 1939, p. 2166), a state in which priests exercise political power, or, more precisely, a state ruled by ministers. In this entry, both meanings will be used.

Theocratic forms of government have existed throughout history. Theocracies were known among ancient people, as in Egypt and Tibet, where kings represented and even incarnated the deity. (In pharaonic Egypt, the king was considered a divine or semidivine figure who ruled largely through priests.) This was the case also with early American civilizations, such as the Mayas, Toltecs, Aztecs, and Natchez.

In Islam, the community established by the prophet Muhammad (c. 570–632) in Medina (622–632) was a theocracy in which Muhammad served as both temporal and spiritual leader. The communities established by Muhammad's father-in-law and successor, Abu Bakr (c. 573–634), the first caliph, were also based on theocratic government. The largest and best-known theocracies in history were the Umayyad caliphate (the first Islamic dynasty, 661–750) and the early Abbasid caliphate (the second major Muslim dynasty, 750–1258), in which state and religion were closely intertwined; the Byzantine Empire (fourth–fifteenth centuries), in which the emperor was the head of the church; and the Papal States (Stati Pontificii) during the Middle Ages, in which the pope was the ruler in a civil as well as a spiritual sense.

In Christianity during the early modern period in Europe, the republic of Florence under the rule (1494–1497) of Girolamo Savonarola (1452–1498) became a theocracy in which God was the sole sovereign and the Gospel constituted the law. After the Protestant Reformation of the sixteenth century, there were many attempts to establish theocracy. The most famous is the theocratic regime that John Calvin (1509–1564) established in Geneva when he was at the height of his power (1555–1564); Geneva's civil life was based upon total obedience to God, whose moral order is declared in the scriptures. According to Calvin, a well-ordered Christian community results from a synthesis of rule, cooperation, and order emanating from the divine laws of God; such a community is unified, organized, and structured upon the idea of advancing the glory of God in the world. The same view is evidenced in the theocratic government that Huldrych Zwingli (1484–1531) established in Zurich from 1525 to 1531. In Zurich, the city council was the lawful government of a Christian state (both church and canton) and administrated the divine commands from the Bible. For interpretation of these commands the council sought and acted on the advice of Christian ministers.

With the Puritan migration to New England during the 1630s, theocratic governments were established in what became Massachusetts and Connecticut. For the New England Puritans, theocracy was considered the best form of government in a Christian commonwealth because only this type of government acknowledged Christ as a sole ruler over the people. Spiritually saving grace was the prerequisite for admission to freemanship or citizenship in the Puritan theocracy. The Puritans' goal was not to invest ministers with political power, but rather to appoint civil magistrates who would govern according to God's word and will. Only "visible saints," or those who were able to prove the power of saving grace in their hearts, were allowed to vote, while "the ungodly," or profane people, were excluded from political power. In England too, during the Puritan Revolution (1640–1660), especially after the execution of King Charles I in 1649, many zealous Puritans strove to establish a theocratic government by introducing a "Sanhedrin of saints," or a dictatorship of the godly.

In the contemporary world, the regime that Ayatollah Ruholla Khomeini (1900–1989) established in Iran in 1979 is considered a theocracy because political power and authority is held in the hands of the imams or religious leaders. The purpose of such a fundamentalist regime is to organize society exclusively under Islamic religious law, the *shari'a*. The Taliban state in Afghanistan

(1996–2001) was similar. In the first decade of the twenty-first century, various fundamentalist Muslim groups are striving to establish theocratic forms of government in Algeria, Pakistan, Egypt, Sudan, Turkey, and other Islamic countries. There are also various fundamentalist Christian groups in the United States, Canada, and Australia who advocate aspects of theocratic government. In Israel, too, several ultra-Orthodox factions advocate restoring the theocracy of ancient times.

SEE ALSO *Government; Religion; Vatican, The*

BIBLIOGRAPHY

Belfer, Ella. 1986. *The Jewish People and the Kingdom of Heaven: A Study of Jewish Theocracy.* Ramat-Gan, Israel: Bar-Ilan University.

Clarkson, Frederick. 1997. *Eternal Hostility: The Struggle between Theocracy and Democracy.* Monroe, ME: Common Courage Press.

Josephus, Flavius. 1737. *Against Apion*, Book II. In *The Genuine Works of Flavius Josephus*, trans. William Whiston. http://wesley.nnu.edu/biblical_studies/josephus/apion-2.htm.

Nobbs, Douglas. 1938. *Theocracy and Toleration: A Study of the Disputes in Dutch Calvinism from 1600 to 1650.* Cambridge, U.K.: Cambridge University Press.

Runciman, Steven. 1977. *The Byzantine Theocracy.* New York: Cambridge University Press.

The Shorter Oxford English Dictionary on Historical Principles. 1939. 2 vols. Prepared by William H. W. Folwer, et al, rev. and ed. C. T. Onions. Oxford: Clarendon Press.

Siddiqi, Mazheruddin. 1953. *Islam and Theocracy.* Lahore, Pakistan: Institute of Islamic Culture.

Walton, Robert Cutler. 1967. *Zwingli's Theocracy.* Toronto, Canada: University of Toronto Press.

Zakai, Avihu. 1993. *Theocracy in Massachusetts: Reformation and Separation in Early Puritan New England.* Lewiston, NY: Mellen University Press.

Avihu Zakai

THEOLOGY, LIBERATION

SEE *Liberation Theology.*

THEORY

The notion of a theory is controversial in social science. A single and simple conception of theory is unlikely to apply across all fields, from mathematical economics to cultural anthropology. Still, construing *theory* broadly as any attempt to systematize and explain certain phenomena, it is clear that theories play a central role in social science. Many social-science pioneers, for example, Karl Marx, Émile Durkheim, Talcott Parsons, Sigmund Freud, Clark Hull, and Paul Samuelson, developed ambitious theories intended to explain a wide range of social phenomena. Today the tendency is toward more modest theories with narrower scope.

Philosophers of science have also adopted a more flexible and eclectic account of theorizing. For much of the twentieth-century, philosophers (and many social scientists) accepted the logical-positivist view that a theory is an axiomatized deductive system consisting of a few basic principles or laws (e.g., Newton's laws of motion constitute his theory of universal gravitation). These principles contain a theoretical vocabulary describing entities that are often unobservable (e.g., electron, utility, social role), and also bridge laws that link the theoretical vocabulary with observable things. Such theories are tested by deriving predictions from basic principles, bridge laws, and statements describing the test situation, and then determining whether those predictions come true.

By the 1960s, every aspect of the positivist view was under attack, and today few philosophers accept it. The notion of laws has come to play a smaller role in philosophical discussion and that of models a larger one. But there remains no consensus about the nature of theories in the social sciences. Some are still expressed in formal, mathematical terms, with basic principles (axioms) from which predictions are deduced. But many are less formal, with a looser connection between theory, on the one hand, and explanation and prediction, on the other. However, even relatively modest theories can be illuminating. To the extent that a theory allows one to make predictions, it provides some measure of control over the social world. Moreover, some theoretical assumptions are needed to guide exploratory research, or even mere observation, since otherwise there are potentially an infinite number of things that might be relevant.

GOALS OF SOCIAL SCIENCE

Views about the nature of theories in social science go hand in hand with views about the nature of social science itself. Naturalists (e.g., in cognitive psychology) see the social and natural sciences as continuous in their goals and methods. They aim to explain human behavior by uncovering its causal mechanisms. As objects of study, however, people are distinctive because they think about, and so guide, their own actions. Given this sort of agency, some social scientists (e.g., in cultural anthropology) hold that mechanistic theories are inappropriate for studying humans. The point of social-scientific theories is, on this view, to explain actions by interpreting them so that they are intelligible.

Interpretive scientists hold that we already have a scheme for making sense of human action: People act to get what they want (feel obliged to pursue, and so forth), given what they believe. This common-sense pattern is so fundamental that it is considered to be more than a behavioral hypothesis—it is the standard of intelligibility for action. Interpretation is a sort of translation project—people *read* the *text* of other people's actions. To understand their *language* one must empathetically immerse oneself in their concerns and situations. Like languages, conceptual schemes have conventions and norms, and fluency in both is the capacity to follow (and exploit) those conventions and norms.

Naturalists need not reject common-sense psychological principles, though historically some (e.g., behaviorists) have. Now, however, most think that it is desirable to integrate reason-based behavior into the natural-scientific picture of the world, and so they seek to find the mechanisms that underwrite common-sense psychology. It now seems clear that a person's reasons for acting are the causes of her behavior. Causal mechanisms may include preferences, values, habits, reinforcement histories, and the like.

Theories often include terms that ostensibly refer to entities involved in causal mechanisms (e.g., utilities, norms, information flows, social roles). So-called *instrumentalists* do not interpret such talk literally, but see it simply as a tool for predicting the behavior of individuals (organizations, institutions, societies, and others). They are agnostic about mechanisms—tools should pinpoint *what* will happen, but they need not say *why*. Interpreted instrumentally, however, theoretical constructs are fictions that can do no causal work. Hence, many philosophers and social scientists are *realists* about the entities posited by more successful theories.

Contrary to the views of many early-twentieth-century philosophers, causal explanation does not require appeal to, or even the existence of, precise causal laws. One can explain, for example, that the glass broke because someone dropped it, without knowing any general laws about glass or fragility. Of course some general knowledge about how things break is needed, but it need not add up to a precise exceptionless absolute (or precise probabilistic) law. Such generalizations as we do possess typically describe how a given construct or tendency would operate in isolation (e.g., rational choice theory describes how agents would act if they had clear preferences, coherent subjective probabilities, and acted to maximize their expected utility).

Behavioral mechanisms rarely operate in isolation. Outside the artificial environment of the laboratory, most social phenomena are produced by a wide variety of causal factors that differ from situation to situation and interact with each other in very complicated (frequently nonlinear) ways. Prediction in such cases is usually difficult. Even in physics, prediction is often next to impossible, because many systems of interest are nonlinear and hence chaotic. Pure, idealized cases can provide explanatory insight into the role mechanisms play in the generation of behavior despite their predictive impotence.

With the rejection of the positivist view that prediction and explanation are symmetrical (though with prediction occurring before a predicted event and explanation after the event explained), it is now clear that it is possible to have a theory that is good at one but not the other. For instance, theories that simply extrapolate correlations may be good at predicting without offering much explanatory insight into why the predictions come true. By contrast, many theories in the social sciences can offer explanations after the fact, even though they could not have predicted the phenomena beforehand. Typically they do this by pinpointing (or at least conjecturing about) the causal mechanisms that led to the thing to be explained (e.g., the bear market in U.S. stocks in the early 2000s). Even theories that are better at explaining than predicting are typically tested by their predictive power, however, and both explanatory power and predictive power are clearly desirable.

THEORY EVALUATION

Because social-scientific theories rarely underwrite precise predictions (or postdictions), they are often difficult to test. In many cases theories yield only rough qualitative predictions, and these are typically compatible with a number of competing theories. Studies in the real world often allow us to discover correlations among variables (like years of education and income), and a theory gains some support when it makes reasonably precise predictions about the strengths of such correlations. But scientists are often interested in isolating causes, and, as the truism goes, correlation is not causation. Causes are traditionally discovered by carefully designed experiments whose outcomes are evaluated using null-hypothesis significance testing. Such testing, however, has come under increasing fire from methodologists such as Lisa Harlow, Stanley Mulaik, and James Steiger.

Social-scientific theories are useful when they help isolate the mechanisms that subserve behavior. Without some idea about when such mechanisms will be triggered and how they will interact, however, predictive ability is limited. Recent work, such as that of Judea Pearl, attempts to distill causal claims from real-world correlation data (plus a few assumptions about causation). Work on path analysis and other approaches to causal modeling will probably play an increasing role in testing theories in the future.

ADMISSIBLE THEORETICAL CONSTRUCTS

Debates in the social sciences often center around identifying appropriate theoretical constructs. One classical division distinguishes the *Homo sociologicus* and *Homo economicus* pictures of human beings. A third image—*Homo psychologicus*—might be added. The first picture holds, roughly, that people are shaped by their cultures and (mostly) act in accordance with social norms. Central constructs here include norms, values, and social roles. By contrast, *Homo economicus* is a rational calculator who (normally) acts so as to secure desired outcomes. Central constructs here include preferences and subjective utilities. Thus a sociologist might explain crime in terms of the norms of a criminal's peer group, while an economist might argue that, in the agent's milieu, crime is the most sensible behavior. Those favoring a *Homo psychologicus* account are more likely to employ information-processing constructs.

No single approach has been notably successful in explaining behavior on its own. Many social scientists agree that each account supplies part of the picture: Norms can influence preferences and beliefs; economic outcomes can influence the evolution of norms and social roles. In practice, however, cooperation among social sciences has proven elusive. Integrating the insights of sociology, economics, psychology, and other social sciences is difficult because each appeals to different properties and processes. Rather than attempt any integration, different theories are often offered as competitors. As a result, disciplines often tend to be identified more with their explanatory approaches than with specific areas of interest. Cross-disciplinary theorizing is an important frontier for social science.

Another historically important debate over appropriate constructs concerns the level at which theoretical concepts and generalizations should be framed. Social scientists disagree about whether their investigations should focus on individuals or groups, but clearly they often do care about the dynamics of social groups. Scientists want to know, for example, how price levels change with world events, not just how individual consumers react. When they look for patterns at this level of aggregation they often find them. Supply shortfalls in crucial commodities result in price increases. Researchers can often detect such regularities without considering the idiosyncrasies of individuals.

French philosopher Émile Durkheim went so far as to argue that there are autonomous social facts and that social explanations should cite social properties rather than appeal to the psychology of individuals. This view has led to much fruitless debate over reductionism and the existence of social facts. Recent philosophy may help to clarify these issues. Higher level patterns are best understood as equilibria resulting from a number of actions. In a market system, for example, general price increases result from the predictable decisions of numerous agents. Accounts of supervenience, such as those by American philosopher Jaegwon Kim, make clear that the truth of generalizations at one level of analysis (e.g., biology) may depend on that of generalizations at a lower level (e.g., chemistry) without being translatable into the latter. These accounts permit reconciliation of the claim that social phenomena would not exist without the actions of individual agents with the claim that many important generalizations can only be framed in vocabulary that does not involve specific individuals.

SEE ALSO *Scientific Method*

BIBLIOGRAPHY

Davidson, Donald. 1963. Actions, Reasons, and Causes. *Journal of Philosophy* 60 (23): 685–700.

Durkheim, Émile. 1982. *Rules of Sociological Method.* Trans. W. D. Wells. New York: Free Press. (Orig. pub. 1895.)

Gigerenzer, Gerd. 2000. *Adaptive Thinking: Rationality in the Real World.* New York: Oxford University Press.

Harlow, Lisa. L., Stanley A. Mulaik, and James H. Steiger, eds. 1997. *What If There Were No Significance Tests?* Mahwah, NJ: Erlbaum.

Hargreaves Heap, Shaun, ed. 1992. *The Theory of Choice A Critical Guide.* Cambridge, MA: Blackwell.

Kim, Jaegwon. 1993. *Supervenience and Mind: Selected Philosophical Essays.* New York: Cambridge University Press.

Martin, Michael, and Lee C. McIntyre, eds. 1994. *Readings in the Philosophy of Social Science.* Cambridge, MA: MIT Press.

Pearl, Judea. 2000. *Causality: Models, Reasoning, and Inference.* New York: Cambridge University Press.

Smith, Peter. 1998. *Explaining Chaos.* Cambridge, U.K.: Cambridge University Press.

Suppe, Frederick, ed. 1977. *The Structure of Scientific Theories.* 2nd ed. Urbana: University of Illinois Press.

Stephen Ellis
Chris Swoyer

THEORY OF MIND

Theory of mind (ToM) refers to the more or less automatic tendency to impute mental states to oneself and others (Premack and Woodruff 1978). Among alternative terms such as *folk psychology, naive psychology, mind reading,* and *mentalizing* (Astington and Baird 2005), ToM has emerged as the standard terminology among psychologists, primatologists, and philosophers. ToM is at the heart of human social cognition and underlies virtually every aspect of humanity.

FOLK PSYCHOLOGY AND APE PSYCHOLOGY

Consider, for example, how biological and physical motions are perceived. The motion of a falling apple is governed by Newton's laws, and human infants as young as three months are sensitive to violations of such principles (Spelke 2000). In contrast, most human behaviors are interpreted in terms of desires, beliefs, and emotions. As a classic demonstration of how far we are ready to stretch our folk psychology, Fritz Heider and Marianne Simmel (1944) showed undergraduate students animation movies in which geometric figures moved in coordinated ways that strongly hinted intentional behaviors such as avoidance or helping. When asked to describe the scenes, participants did not hesitate to apply mentalistic attributes to circles and triangles.

Contemporary interest in ToM, however, was sparked by the mind-reading ability of Sarah, a fourteen-year-old chimpanzee who appeared to recognize intentions from behaviors. In a groundbreaking paper titled "Does the Chimpanzee Have a Theory of Mind?" (1978), David Premack and Guy Woodruff showed Sarah video vignettes of a trainer attempting in vain to achieve a goal (e.g., to exit a cage through a locked door) and then a pair of photographs depicting potential solutions (e.g., an intact key along with a broken one). Spontaneously, Sarah "recognized the videotape as problem, understood the actor's purpose, and chose alternatives compatible with that purpose" (Premack and Woodruff 1978, p. 515). The authors attributed her success to the existence of a system that represents mental states, such as desire and intent, and links them to behaviors. They further maintained that "a system of inferences of this kind may properly be viewed as a theory because such states are not directly observable, and the system can be used to make predictions about the behavior of others" (p. 515).

Some thirty years later, the field remains divided over whether chimpanzees (or any nonhuman primates) possess a theory of mind or simply a theory of behaviors. Michael Tomasello and colleagues argue that the great apes understand others as "animate, goal-directed, and intentional agents" (2005, p. 675) even though they fall short in understanding beliefs and other mental states compared to humans (Call and Tomasello 1999). Others, however, caution that we have to first rule out the possi-

bility that their responses are based on behavioral regularities (Heyes 1998; Povinelli and Vonk 2003, 2004). For example, chimpanzees spontaneously follow the gaze of others (Okamoto et al. 2002) and are attuned to what others can or cannot see (Hare et al. 2000; Povinelli and Eddy 1996). Nevertheless, it is unclear whether chimpanzees can link seeing to knowing. When competing for food, subordinate chimpanzees are reported to keep track of what dominant chimpanzees know and do not know about food locations (Hare et al. 2001). This is in stark contrast with an earlier finding that chimpanzees would beg for food indiscriminately from both trainers who could see and those who had a bucket over their head (Povinelli and Eddy 1996).

The current debate on ToM in nonhuman primates is *not* about whether they are capable of sophisticated social behaviors—yes, their abilities to keep track of and manipulate others sometimes rival those of humans. The issue is what can be concluded when their behaviors are compatible with *both* a ToM and a theory of behavioral regularities. Until a consensus is reached on this and other critical issues, the question Premack and Woodruff famously raised in their seminal work will remain unanswered.

FALSE BELIEFS AND THE DEVELOPMENT OF TOM IN HUMAN CHILDREN

In comparison, a consensus did emerge among developmental psychologists. It was suggested that an understanding of "false beliefs" is a sufficient condition for a ToM, because beliefs—unlike behaviors—are private and unobservable, and thus are beyond the scope of a theory of behaviors (Dennett 1978). And thanks to language, beliefs can be identified unequivocally in human participants.

This idea was put to a test by Heinz Wimmer and Josef Perner (1983) when the researchers told young children a story in which Maxi put his chocolate in a kitchen drawer and left. In his absence, Maxi's mom moved the candy to a different drawer. Children had to predict where Maxi would look for his chocolate on his return. While most six-year-old children correctly predicted Maxi's action on the basis of his false belief that the candy was still in the original drawer, most four- and five-year-old children in this study expected Maxi to look in the new location.

Young children's difficulties are not limited to thinking in other peoples' shoes. They appear to be oblivious about false beliefs they held a few moments earlier (Gopnik and Astington 1988). The development of ToM is remarkably consistent and robust, progressing almost uniformly from appreciating that people have different desires to understanding false beliefs, and later to differentiating apparent versus true emotions (Wellman and Liu 2004). A meta-analysis of more than 170 false-belief studies concluded that the transition in false-belief understanding takes place in the preschool years for most children (Wellman et al. 2001).

Although passing the false-belief task attests to a ToM, the converse is not true (Bloom and German 2000). For example, younger children may fail due to their inability to inhibit improper responses (Leslie et al. 2004; Leslie and Polizzi 1998). In addition, children show a range of competences before they pass the false-belief test. At three months of age, infants prefer biological motion to random motion (Bertenthal et al. 1984) and shift their eye gaze after an adult makes an eye movement (Hood et al. 1998). At around twelve months, human infants begin to follow others' line of sight and predict actions according to gaze (Sodian and Thoermer 2004). The second year of life sees the onset of joint visual attention (Butterworth and Jarrett 1991), imitation (Meltzoff 1995), and pretend play (Lillard 2002). There is even evidence that sixteen-month-old infants have an implicit understanding of false beliefs (Onishi and Baillargeon 2005). From three to five, children produce mental words such as *think* or *want*, start to appreciate jokes (Leekam 1991), and attempt to deceive (Sodian et al. 1991). ToM continues to develop; adults still fall victim to egocentrism from time to time (Keysar et al. 2003). Nonetheless, the basic apparatus for reading and reasoning about mind is largely in place early in childhood.

THEORIES OF THEORY OF MIND

What explains children's initial failure and later success in the false-belief task? The *theory theory* postulates that we reason about mental events based on a system of heuristics or if-then rules (Gopnik and Wellman 1994). The child actively constructs and revises the informal ToM based on experience. For instance, a toddler may begin with a prediction that if Maxi wants something, he will act to satisfy his desire. Experiences with false beliefs of others or herself will force the child to abandon this simple heuristic and incorporate *belief* into an adultlike theory of mind (Bartsch and Wellman 1995).

The notion of a *theory* as the basis for mind reading is challenged by the *simulation theory*, which proposes that we compute others' mental states through an automatic role-play simulation ("if I were him …"; Gallese and Goldman 1998; Gordon 1986). Young children find the impersonation difficult in a false-belief task because one has to withhold one's own belief and instead reason with the erroneous belief of the person to be simulated.

If a child has to *discover* a ToM completely on his or her own, as suggested by the theory theory, the acquisition is unlikely to be consistent and universal. Two solutions

have been proposed in the literature. One is the hypothesized *theory of mind mechanism* (ToMM; Leslie et al. 2004; Baron-Cohen 1995), an innate neurological module that automatically maps behaviors of self-propelled agents to mental states and vice versa. The ToMM is thought to mature fairly early in life and kick off the subsequent development of folk psychology. Young children's difficulty with the false-belief task is attributed to immature executive functioning, which works in conjunction with ToM to make behavioral predictions.

An alternative view traces the origin of ToM to language and culture. Everyday conversations expose children to the fact that speakers may have different knowledge and beliefs. Language also provides specific lexical terms for mental states (e.g., *see, know,* and *want*) and, in some cases, different syntactic structures for different mental states (e.g., "*I want to …*" but *not* "*I want that…*"; however "*I know that …*" but *not* "*I know to…*"; see de Villiers and de Villiers 2000). These linguistic structures invite children to think and talk about mental events in a way that is conventional in the language community. In this perspective, language and culture provide both the blueprint and building blocks for developing a ToM (Astington and Baird 2005).

MINDBLINDNESS AND BRAIN IMAGING

What would the world be without a ToM? Childhood autism is a spectrum of pervasive developmental disorders characterized by deficits in social interaction, verbal communication, and repetitive behaviors. Simon Baron-Cohen and colleagues (1985) hypothesized that autistic children have a severe deficit in the ToMM. For example, Baron-Cohen (1995) showed children a face ("Charlie") surrounded by four different kinds of candy, with Charlie's eyes looking toward one of them. When asked "which candy does Charlie want," most four-year-olds pointed to where Charlie was gazing. In contrast, children with autism responded randomly to what Charlie *wanted*, even though they had no trouble answering where Charlie was *looking*. The problem is a failure to map perception to mental states. Niki L, a high-functioning autistic person, wrote:

> Many [autistic persons] lack some sort of intuition and have a hard time guessing hidden rules many [normal] kids somehow see.… I think I eventually formed a relatively good theory of mind, but it took intentional effort. And I still have to apply it manually. It gets faster and faster as I collect many patterns in my memory, but I'm afraid it won't be automatic forever. (Blackburn et al. 2000)

Brain imaging has begun to shed light on the potential neural mechanism underlying ToM. For example, Kevin Pelphrey and colleagues (2005) reported functional MRI evidence that participants with autism are insensitive to intentions conveyed by other people's eye movements. Other imaging studies contrasted brain activities while processing mental versus physical events, for example, listening to stories involving rich mentalizing (Fletcher et al. 1995; Gallagher et al. 2000; Vogeley et al. 2001) or watching Heider/Simmel-like cartoon animations (Castelli et al. 2000). Consistently, stronger activations are found in the medial prefrontal cortex (MPFC), temporal poles, and the posterior superior temporal sulcus (STS) during mentalizing. For further information, see Frith and Frith (2003) and Baron-Cohen et al. (2000).

CONCLUSION

The prepositional phrase *theory of mind* is a linguistic oddity. Contrary to the expectation of a native English speaker, for example, the "theory of mind mechanism" is not a theory about "mind mechanism" but a mechanism for theory of mind. The strong internal cohesiveness reflects a commitment to two of its core assumptions—that behaviors are understood in mental terms and that this understanding constitutes a theory.

Although both points are under vigorous debate, ToM as a field of scholarship has thrived, and continues to thrive, beyond the imagination of Premack and Woodruff (1978). Recent reports of self-recognizing elephants and dolphins (Plotnik et al. 2006; Reiss and Marino 2001) and deception in scrub jays (Dally et al. 2005), among others, question the view that ToM is unique to a handful of primate species—if not for humans only—and instead suggest similar competences have evolved independently as an adaptation to complex social lives. Meanwhile, computer scientists find ToM essential in developing autonomous, cooperative robotic agents (Scassellati 2002), and economists are tying many aspects of social exchange and decision making to ToM (Singer and Fehr 2005). This brief survey of ToM cannot do justice to a vast and vibrant field of study. But fortunately, motivated readers should not have difficulty finding in-depth and up-to-date readings that connect ToM with their specialty—after all, where there is social interaction, there is theory of mind. At least potentially.

SEE ALSO *Child Development; Developmental Psychology; Lay Theories; Needs; Neuroscience; Primates; Psychology; Stages of Development; Wants*

BIBLIOGRAPHY

Astington, Janet Wilde, and Jodie A. Baird. 2005. *Why Language Matters for Theory of Mind.* New York: Oxford University Press.

Baron-Cohen, Simon. 1995. *Mindblindness: An Essay on Autism and Theory of Mind.* Cambridge, MA: MIT Press.

Baron-Cohen, Simon, Alan Leslie, and Uta Frith. 1985. Does the Autistic Child Have A "Theory of Mind"? *Cognition* 21 (1): 46–37.

Baron-Cohen, Simon, Howard Ring, Ed Bullmore, et al. 2000. The Amygdala Theory of Autism. *Neuroscience and Biobehavioral Reviews* 24 (3): 355–364.

Bartsch, Karen, and Henry Wellman. 1995. *Children Talk about the Mind.* New York: Oxford University Press.

Bertenthal, Bennett I., Dennis R. Proffitt, and J. E. Cutting. 1984. Infant Sensitivity to Figural Coherence in Biomechanical Motions. *Journal of Experimental Child Psychology* 37: 213–230.

Blackburn, Jared, Katja Gottschewski, Elsa George, and Niki L. 2000. A Discussion about Theory of Mind: From an Autistic Perspective. *Proceedings of Autism Europe's 6th International Congress.* http://www.autistics.org/library/AE2000-ToM.html.

Bloom, Paul, and Tim German. 2000. Two Reasons to Abandon the False Belief Task as a Test of Theory of Mind. *Cognition* 77 (1): 25–31.

Butterworth, George, and Nicholas Jarrett. 1991. What Minds Have in Common Is Space: Spatial Mechanisms Serving Joint Visual-Attention in Infancy. *British Journal of Developmental Psychology* 9: 55–72.

Call, Josep, and Michael Tomasello. 1999. A Nonverbal False Belief Task: The Performance of Children and Great Apes. *Child Development* 70 (2): 381–395.

Castelli, Fulvia, Francesca Happé, Uta Frith, and Chris Frith. 2000. Movement and Mind: A Functional Imaging Study of Perception and Interpretation of Complex Intentional Movement Patterns. *NeuroImage* 12 (3): 314–325.

Dally, Joanna, Nathan Emery, and Nicola Clayton. 2005. Cache Protection Strategies by Western Scrub-Jays *(Aphelocoma californica)*: Implications for Social Cognition. *Animal Behaviour* 70 (6): 1251–1263.

Dennett, Daniel C. 1978. Beliefs about Beliefs. *Behavioral and Brain Sciences* 1: 568–570.

De Villiers, Jill G., and Peter A. de Villiers. 2000. Linguistic Determinism and the Understanding of False Beliefs. In *Children's Reasoning and the Mind,* eds. Peter Mitchell and Kevin J. Riggs, 191–228. Hove, U.K.: Psychology Press/Taylor and Francis.

Fletcher, Paul C., Francesca Happé, Uta Frith, et al. 1995. Other Minds in the Brain: A Functional Imaging Study of "Theory of Mind" in Story Comprehension. *Cognition* 44: 283–296; 57: 109–128.

Frith, Uta, and Christopher D. Frith. 2003. Development and Neurophysiology of Mentalizing. *Philosophical Transactions: Biological Sciences* 358 (1431): 459–473.

Gallagher, H. L., Francesca Happé, N. Brunswick, et al. 2000. Reading the Mind in Cartoons and Stories: An Fmri Study of

"Theory of Mind" in Verbal and Nonverbal Tasks. *Neuropsychologia* 38: 11–21.

Gallese, Vittorio, and Alvin Goldman. 1998. Mirror Neurons and the Simulation Theory of Mind-Reading. *Trends in Cognitive Sciences* 2 (12): 493–501.

Gopnik, Alison, and Janet Astington. 1988. Children's Understanding of Representational Change and Its Relation to the Understanding of False Belief and the Appearance-Reality Distinction. *Child Development* 59 (1): 26–37.

Gopnik, Alison, and Henry M. Wellman. 1994. The Theory Theory. In *Mapping the Mind: Domain Specificity in Cognition and Culture*, eds. Lawrence A. Hirschfeld and Susan A. Gelman, 257–293. New York: Cambridge University Press.

Gordon, Robert. 1986. Folk Psychology as Simulation. *Mind and Language* 1: 158–171.

Hare, Brian, Josep Call, and Michael Tomasello. 2001. Do Chimpanzees Know What Conspecifics Know? *Animal Behaviour* 61: 139–151.

Hare, Brian, Josep Call, and Michael Tomasello. 2006. Chimpanzees Deceive a Human Competitor by Hiding. *Cognition* 101: 495–514.

Hare, Brian, Josep Call, Bryan Agnetta, and Michael Tomasello. 2000. Chimpanzees Know What Conspecifics Do and Do Not See. *Animal Behaviour* 59: 771–785.

Heider, Fritz, and Marianne Simmel. 1944. An Experimental Study of Apparent Behavior. *The American Journal of Psychology* 57 (2): 243–259.

Heyes, Cecelia M. 1998. Theory of Mind in Nonhuman Primates. *Behavioral and Brain Sciences* 21 (1): 115–148.

Hood, Bruce M., Douglas J. Willen, and Jon Driver. 1998. Adult's Eyes Trigger Shifts of Visual Attention in Human Infants. *Psychological Science* 9: 131–134.

Keysar, Boaz, Shuhong Lin, and Dale J. Barr. 2003. Limits on Theory of Mind Use in Adults. *Cognition* 89 (1): 25–41.

Leekam, Susan R. 1991. Jokes and Lies: Children's Understanding of Intentional Falsehood. In *Natural Theories of Mind: Evolution, Development, and Simulation of Everyday Mindreading*, ed. Andrew Whiten, 159–174. Oxford: Blackwell.

Leslie, Alan M., and Pamela Polizzi. 1998. Inhibitory Processing in the False Belief Task: Two Conjectures. *Developmental Science* 1: 247–254.

Leslie, Alan M., Ori Friedman, and Tim German. 2004. Core Mechanisms in "Theory of Mind." *Trends in Cognitive Sciences* 8: 528–533.

Lillard, Angeline S. 2002. Pretend Play and Cognitive Development. In *Handbook of Cognitive Development*, ed. Usha Goswami, 188–205. London: Blackwell.

Meltzoff, Andrew N. 1995. Understanding the Intentions of Others: Re-Enactment of Intended Acts by 18-Month-Old Children. *Developmental Psychology* 31: 838–850.

Okamoto, Sanae, Masaki Tomonaga, Kiyoshi Ishii, et al. 2002. An Infant Chimpanzee *(Pan troglodytes)* Follows Human Gaze. *Animal Cognition* 5 (2): 107–114.

Onishi, Kristine, and Renée Baillargeon. 2005. Do 15-Month-Old Infants Understand False Beliefs? *Science* 308 (5719): 255–258.

Pelphrey, Kevin, James Morris, and Gregory McCarthy. 2005. Neural Basis of Eye Gaze Processing Deficits in Autism. *Brain* 128 (5): 1038–1048.

Plotnik, Joshua, Frans B. M. de Waal, and Diana Reiss. 2006. Self-recognition in an Asian Elephant. *Proceedings of the National Academy of Sciences* 103 (45): 17053–17057.

Povinelli, Daniel J., and Timothy J. Eddy. 1996. Chimpanzees: Joint Visual Attention. *Psychological Science* 7 (3): 129–135.

Povinelli, Daniel J., and Jennifer Vonk. 2003. Chimpanzee Minds: Suspiciously Human? *Trends Cognitive Science* 7 (4): 157–160.

Povinelli, Daniel J., and Jennifer Vonk. 2004. We Don't Need a Microscope to Explore the Chimpanzee's Mind. *Mind and Language* 19 (1): 1–28.

Premack, David, and Guy Woodruff. 1978. Does the Chimpanzee Have a Theory of Mind? *Behavioral and Brain Sciences* 1: 515–526.

Reiss, Diana, and Lori Marino. 2001. Mirror Self-Recognition in the Bottlenose Dolphin: A Case of Cognitive Convergence. *Proceedings of the National Academy of Sciences* 98 (10): 5937–5942.

Scassellati, Brian. 2002. Theory of Mind for a Humanoid Robot. *Autonomous Robots* 12 (1): 13–24.

Singer, Tania, and Ernst Fehr. 2005. The Neuroeconomics of Mind Reading and Empathy. *American Economic Review* 95: 340–345.

Sodian, Beate, and Claudia Thoermer. 2004. Infants' Understanding of Looking, Pointing, and Reaching as Cues to Goal-Directed Action. *Journal of Cognition and Development* 5 (3): 289–316.

Sodian, Beate, Catherine Taylor, Paul Harris, et al. 1991. Early Deception and the Child's Theory of Mind: False Trails and Genuine Markers. *Child Development* 62 (3): 468–483.

Spelke, Elizabeth. 2000. Core Knowledge. *American Psychologists* 55 (11): 1233–1243.

Tomasello, Michael, Malinda Carpenter, Josep Call, et al. 2005. Understanding and Sharing Intentions: The Origins of Cultural Cognition. *The Behavioral and Brain Sciences* 28 (5): 675–691.

Vogeley, K., P. Bussfeld, A. Newen, et al. 2001. Mind Reading: Neural Mechanisms of Theory of Mind and Self-Perspective. *NeuroImage* 14: 170–181.

Wellman, Henry M., and David Liu. 2004. Scaling of Theory-of-Mind Tasks. *Child Development* 75 (2): 523–541.

Wellman, Henry M., David Cross, and Julanne Watson. 2001. Meta-Analysis of Theory-of-Mind Development: The Truth about False Belief. *Child Development* 72 (3): 655–684.

Wimmer, Heinz, and Josef Perner. 1983. Beliefs about Beliefs: Representation and Constraining Function of Wrong Beliefs in Young Children's Understanding of Deception. *Cognition* 13 (1): 103–128.

Gary Feng

THEORY OF SECOND BEST

Consider a stylized economy in which all markets are perfectly competitive, there are no distortions, no externalities, and no public goods. All resources are privately owned and all agents maximize their respective welfare, consumers maximizing utility and firms maximizing their profit. All individuals possess perfect information and there are no impediments to trade so that all markets always clear (i.e., the quantity of goods supplied always equals the quantity of goods demanded). The resulting equilibrium in this idealized world is characterized by a set of optimality conditions, known as *Pareto* optimality conditions. This equilibrium is said to be a first-best optimum in which there is no welfare-improving role for government policy.

In a seminal paper published in 1956, Richard Lipsey and Kelvin Lancaster considered the consequences of introducing into this general equilibrium system a constraint (or distortion) that prevents one or more of the optimality conditions characterizing the first-best optimum from being attained. For example, suppose a firm has monopoly power, causing it to set a price above marginal cost, thus violating one of the conditions for the first-best equilibrium to prevail. Lipsey and Lancaster then showed that while the other optimality conditions characterizing the first-best outcome may still be attainable, in general it is no longer optimal to impose them. In other words, if one of the Pareto optimality conditions cannot be fulfilled, a second-best optimum is achieved only by deviating from all other optimality conditions.

This proposition has profound implications. First, the simple intuitive efficiency conditions characterizing the first-best optimum are replaced by complex nonintuitive optimality conditions characterizing the second-best equilibrium. Consequently in general nothing can be inferred about either the direction or the magnitude of the deviations of the second-best optimum from the first-best outcome. That depends upon the entire underlying economic structure and the extent to which the distortions relate to the rest of the economy. Second, the optimality conditions may introduce nonconvexities, which call into question whether the equilibrium is indeed an optimum. Third, the existence of such constraints restores a potential welfare-improving role for economic policy.

Although the concept of "second best" is identified primarily with Lipsey and Lancaster, it in fact appeared in the economics literature well before that time. References to it in the context of free trade versus protection can be found as early as the beginning of the twentieth century in the Italian economist Vilfredo Pareto's original work on general equilibrium theory, while the concept is also discussed by Paul Samuelson in his 1947 book *Foundations*

of Economic Analysis and in more detail by James Meade in his 1955 publication *Trade and Welfare*. The main contribution of Lipsey and Lancaster is to provide a more formal analysis of the concept and to highlight the consequences for policy makers.

IMPEDIMENTS TO FIRST-BEST OPTIMUM

Several types of distortions may prevent the first-best Pareto optimal outcome from being attained. Some, such as returns to scale (the relationship between proportionate changes in inputs and the resulting change in output), are technological in nature; while others, such as monopolistic market structures and barriers to entry, may be created by the private sector. These distortions may be neutralized, at least in part, by some form of government intervention. In some cases this may take the form of economic incentives, designed to discourage the behavior causing the distortion, while in other cases it may simply be an outright legal restriction. It is also possible for the government itself to be the source of the distortion. The need to provide public goods, financed by a distortionary tax, such as an income tax, is a familiar example.

While, as Lipsey and Lancaster highlighted, externalities and distortions generally lead to divergences from the Pareto optimal outcome, simple examples also exist where no divergence is created. For example, in their 2005 study Wen-Fang Liu and Stephen Turnovsky considered a neoclassical growth model with an inelastic labor supply in which utility depends upon the agent's own consumption, together with economy-wide average consumption, a potential distortionary effect. They show that while the consumption externality influences the economy's time path for capital accumulation, for a widely employed class of utility functions it causes no deviation from the Pareto optimal time path.

The presence of the constraints that, all other things being equal, would lead to the violation of the Pareto optimality conditions need not in fact preclude the attainment of the first-best optimum. In some instances the government may be able to neutralize fully the effects of the various distortions and externalities embodied in the constraints and thus mimic the first-best equilibrium. A well-known example of this was illustrated in a 1986 study by Paul Romer. In the study he introduced an endogenous growth model, in which private agents ignore the production externality due to aggregate capital and therefore overconsume and underaccumulate capital, relative to what is socially optimal. By appropriately subsidizing the return to capital, the government can induce the agents to adjust their consumption-savings behavior and thus attain the first-best optimal growth rate.

In most cases the policy maker is likely to have insufficient policy instruments to reach the first-best outcome, in which case the resulting equilibrium will be truly second-best. In such a situation a natural question to consider concerns the policy options available to improve social welfare relative to the second-best equilibrium. In the Romer model, for example, it is likely that to attain the first-best growth rate the required subsidy to capital income is too large to be politically feasible. The policy maker may therefore decide to target a more modest growth objective that can be achieved by different combinations of tax rates and subsidies. The policy maker is faced with several second-best choices and thus with ranking the set of alternatives.

As noted, the optimality conditions characterizing the second-best equilibrium are complex and therefore, as a practical matter, may be difficult, if not impossible, to implement. This issue was addressed by Yew-Kwang Ng in *Welfare Economics: Introduction and Development of Basic Concepts* (1979) when he proposed a "third-best" equilibrium. He suggested that in cases where policy makers have insufficient information to implement the second-best policies, they should seek to correct only the known distortions and leave the optimality conditions in the undistorted markets unchanged at their first-best levels. This is sometimes also referred to as "piecemeal" policy making.

SECOND-BEST VERSUS FIRST-BEST

The issue of second-best versus first-best policy making is pervasive in economics. Early contributions were concentrated in the area of international economics and the debate between free trade versus protection. Subsequently it has played a central role in public economics, where governments face the issue of financing public goods, with the externalities they entail, using various fiscal instruments with their own distortionary effects. It has also been important in the area of applied microeconomics and industrial organization in dealing with issues related to market structure, barriers to entry, and deviations from competitive behavior. Finally, the existence of production externalities is a cornerstone of much of modern economic growth theory, where they have been important in giving the theory of the second best a dynamic dimension.

SEE ALSO *Economic Growth; Economics, Public; Equilibrium in Economics; General Equilibrium; Liberalization, Trade; Market Clearing; Meade, James; Monopoly; Pareto Optimum; Pareto, Vilfredo; Public Goods; Samuelson, Paul A.; Social Welfare Functions; Welfare Economics*

BIBLIOGRAPHY

Lipsey, Richard G., and Kelvin Lancaster. 1956. The General Theory of Second Best. *Review of Economic Studies* 24: 11–32.

Liu, Wen-Fang, and Stephen J. Turnovsky. 2005. Consumption Externalities, Production Externalities, and Long-Run Macroeconomic Efficiency. *Journal of Public Economics* 89 (5–6): 1097–1129.

Meade, J. E. 1955. *Trade and Welfare*. London: Oxford University Press.

Ng, Yew-Kwang. 1979. *Welfare Economics: Introduction and Development of Basic Concepts*. London: Macmillan.

Romer, Paul. 1986. Increasing Returns and Long-Run Growth. *Journal of Political Economy* 94 (5): 1002–1037.

Samuelson, Paul Anthony. 1947. *Foundations of Economic Analysis*. Cambridge, MA: Harvard University Press.

Stephen J. Turnovsky

THIRD WORLD

The term *third world* was coined by the French economist and demographer Alfred Sauvy to apply to the developing countries that belonged to neither the American nor the Soviet bloc during the cold war. Countries of the "first world" included the United States, its European allies, Canada, Australia, and New Zealand. Countries in the "second world" referred to the Soviet Union and its East European allies. The third world comprised the rest of the countries.

DEFINITIONS

From its very inception, the term *third world* has proven problematic. During the cold war, states such as the Philippines and Cuba, closely aligned to one or the other superpowers, nevertheless were considered third world. Even after the conception of the term broadened to include economic backwardness, poverty, and lack of power, confusion as to its meaning persisted. Included in the third world during the cold war years were states that are among the richest in the world (Saudi Arabia, Kuwait), states whose militaries were larger than those of the North Atlantic Treaty Organization (NATO) powers (Vietnam and Iran), and countries that were major powers in their own right (India). Nevertheless, the term stuck, referring loosely to the countries of Africa, Latin America, and Asia, with Israel, Japan, and China usually omitted.

The third world has always been associated with other groupings of states that share "third world" characteristics. One of the most prominent of these is the nonaligned movement, begun in 1955 by the leaders of

Egypt, India, and Yugoslavia to advance the interests of countries that sought to avoid entanglement in East-West issues. Another prominent organization was the Group of 77 established in June 1964 to promote the economic demands of poorer countries. The Group of 77, now numbering some 130 countries, is a prominent player in international institutions, particularly the United Nations, where it often clashes with the group of developed states known as the Organization for Economic Cooperation and Development (OECD). While the nations that make up these and other groups overlap with the third world, their focused agendas gave substance to what was otherwise an ambiguous term.

Once the cold war was over, whatever meaning *third world* had was further eroded. The collapse of the Soviet Union brought about the end of the second world, making the term *third world* especially difficult to justify. Making matters worse, many saw the term *third world* as pejorative, which in part explains efforts to use other terms, such as *developing countries*, the *South*, and *LDC* (for least or less developed countries).

Despite all these problems, the use of *third world* persists. In large measure this is because of the belief that the term is usefully descriptive of a class of countries that share similar characteristics. While not all third world countries manifest these characteristics to the same degree (or at all), enough do to consider retaining the category of third world.

CHARACTERISTICS

The first characteristic of third world countries is that they are relatively young. Unlike countries outside the third world that have evolved over centuries, most third world states were artificially created by others. The great majority of third world states are ex-colonies. Outside powers created states where none had existed. Although the degree to which the newly formed boundaries coincided with the boundaries of indigenous societies varies in the third world (e.g., high in Southeast Asia, low in Africa), in all cases a formal division replaced what had been a flexible demarcation. Because of the arbitrariness of their borders, many third world states began as and remain more artificial constructs than coherent units.

The artificiality of the third world states and their colonial heritage has created a situation in which groups owe allegiance to and act for interests other than the national interest. Policies by colonial powers of "divide and rule" and the destruction of existing political entities made integration and a sense of nationalism all but impossible. Instead of identifying with their states, individuals identify with ethnic, religious, or regional groupings. This narrow seeking of interests perpetuates itself by preventing the formation of a national consciousness.

Rather than transcending the differences among these different groups, the state is often simply the representative of the group that holds power in the capital.

Legitimacy is likely to be weaker for third world leaders than for leaders elsewhere. Many regimes in the third world are narrowly based, came to power through force, and use suppression to remain in power. In part this legitimacy stems from a lack of national identity. When people cannot agree on what constitutes the state, they are unlikely to agree on what constitutes legitimate uses of power within the state. Developing states often lack effective institutions for mediating political disputes, intensifying the internal conflicts that frequently arise. Most third world states are not liberal democracies. Despite the rise of nationalism, meaningful political participation and the acceptance of basic rights, such as freedom of speech and religion, toleration of minority rights, and an independent judiciary, are not found in the majority of third world countries.

The power of the third world states, as in other states, derives from the ability to distribute goods. The state in the third world is distinctive, however, in that it controls a much greater degree of wealth and power than any other group in the society. Gaining control of the state is the only means for the ambitious to meet their needs. Hence a major vulnerability of the state is that it controls a much greater degree of wealth and power than any other group in the society. At the same time those in power will mightily resist attempts at replacement because they do not want to relinquish their only opportunity for wealth and influence and because they fear for their lives.

Third world states are also characterized by economic underdevelopment. It is generally thought that third world countries' citizens are poor, ill educated, and lack access to quality medical care. The World Bank and the United Nations, which categorize nations as to income and other indicators, confirm this view. The World Bank divides countries into four categories: high income, upper-middle income, lower-middle income, and low income. Third world states make up all the low income states and none of the high income ones, with the exception of oil rich Arab countries. Moreover third world countries tend to rank low on measures of human development, such as literacy, access to education, life expectancy, and infant mortality.

One can categorize third world states by means of their self-identification. If a state considers itself to be a third world country, it is likely to have a set of attitudes and goals that are defined by its "third worldness." For example, third world states overwhelmingly supported the huge price increases in Organization of Petroleum Exporting Countries (OPEC) oil in 1974 despite the horrendous economic effects they caused. Third world solidarity has also been displayed in votes at the United

Nations, where countries seen as third world tend to vote similarly. It is possible to speak of a third world therefore because member states do and because they act in at least some ways in terms of their self-identification.

These generalizations are not set forth to suggest that all third world countries share these characteristics equally. Different states manifest different characteristics. Nor do these generalizations apply only to the third world. As demonstrated by the collapse of the second world in 1989, states outside the third world also suffer from problems such as weak legitimacy. What some say justifies considering the third world as a category is that whatever combination of factors may exist in a particular third world state, their cumulative impact makes virtually all third world leaders more vulnerable to overthrow—particularly by internal threats such as coups and rebellions—than other leaders.

Finally, the third world is not a static category. Countries formerly considered to be in the third world have left that status behind, while other states that had been second world countries find themselves increasingly being considered third world. Countries such as Taiwan can become more politically stable, or previously stable countries can plunge into chaos, as occurred with Yugoslavia. Some states, such as South Korea and Singapore, have achieved impressive levels of economic development, while others, such as many of the former Russian republics have descended into "third world" levels of poverty and despair.

There is little question that *third world* is a messy, ambiguous, and vague term. For those who demand rigor in their definitions, the category of third world has long lost its utility. And yet the persistence of the term indicates that it satisfies a need for many in describing the condition of states and peoples that is not met by any other categorization. As long as poverty and instability exist, so too will the relevance of the category "third world."

SEE ALSO *Anticolonial Movements; Cold War; Colonialism; Developing Countries; Globalization, Social and Economic Aspects of; Nation-State; Neutral States; North and South, The (Global); Poverty; South, The (USA); State, The; Union of Soviet Socialist Republics; United Nations; World Bank, The*

BIBLIOGRAPHY

Ayoob, Mohammed. 1995. *The Third World Security Predicament: State Making, Regional Conflict, and the International System.* Boulder, CO: Lynne Rienner.

Clapham, Christopher. 1985. *Third World Politics: An Introduction.* Madison: University of Wisconsin Press.

David, Steven R. 1991. *Choosing Sides: Alignment and Realignment in the Third World.* Baltimore, MD: Johns Hopkins University Press.

United Nations Development Programme. 2005. *Human Development Report 2005.* New York: United Nations.

Worsley, Peter. 1979. How Many Worlds? *Third World Quarterly* 1 (2): 100–108.

Steven R. David

THOMPSON, EDWARD P.
1924–1993

Edward Palmer ("E. P.") Thompson was an historian and social activist. His first significant publication, *William Morris: From Romantic to Revolutionary* (1955), was produced under the auspices of the Communist Party Historian's Group, of which he was an early and active member. Although this is still an enormously important work, Thompson is best remembered for his writings and activities following his resignation/expulsion from the Communist Party (CP) in 1956, which resulted from his criticism of the party's support for the Soviet invasion of Hungary. Following his departure from the party, Thompson—along with John Saville, with whom he had been publishing *The Reasoner* (renamed *The New Reasoner* in 1956), Raymond Williams, Stuart Hall, and others—founded *New Left Review* in 1960 as one of a number of endeavors to maintain and foster a non-Labour, non-CP left in Britain.

Although generally overshadowed as a theorist by Williams and Hall, Thompson's polemics on culture, history, and power in this period deserve reexamination for the manner in which they presaged developments in anthropology and literary studies some thirty years later, and his own later understanding of class.

CULTURE

Like Williams and Hall, Thompson found in the concept of culture (both in its anthropological and humanistic senses) an alternative to the economic determinism that dominated Marxist thought. Williams endeavored to expand the traditional capital *C* Culture to include the contributions of working people, which were often occluded in such discussions, effecting a mutual interpenetration of this humanistic culture with its small *c* anthropological cousin. Thompson railed against Williams's notion of culture as a "whole way of life" as being invocative of a "cozy consensus" and not going far enough. Thompson instead argued that culture was more fruitfully viewed as a "whole way of conflict"—not a more or less static, atemporal, and apolitical entity, but itself formed by and generative of social struggle.

Secondly, though both Hall and Williams would retain some form of the basis/superstructure model, Thompson sought to jettison it altogether. Thompson viewed the economic "basis" as the product of social struggle, whereby economic activity had been gradually divorced from all moral and social constraints. To this end, he deployed a generous reading of Marx's concept of production, arguing that, in effect, the economy was indistinguishable from the human beings who collectively produce a society with economic laws, and "discover," and are governed by those laws. In this stroke, one glimpses Thompson's distaste not only for political economy, but also for its left opposite number, "Structural Marxism," both of which he saw as abdicating morality, agency, and responsibility by theologizing what was itself a human production.

CLASS

Thompson brought these understandings fully to bear in his *Making of the English Working Class* (1963) (*MEWC*). Though often confused with the "advocacy" histories that came in its wake (which is *not* to say Thompson was not an advocate of his subjects), the *MEWC* should not be viewed as a treatment of how class "ought" to look, but a history of *how* the working class in England came to look as it did on the eve of Chartism. The book ranged across seemingly unconnected domains, from Methodism to the de-skilling of trades to demonstrate both the experience of the working class and its "handling" of these experiences. The emphasis of the book was squarely placed on the concept of *making*, and an argument that class is a relationship and a process, not a "thing" that could be abstracted from its historical context and studied in isolation. Class, he argued, came about over time as a result of struggle, as the realization of mutual and antagonistic interests in human society that come to be articulated in class ways. Because class is an historical process, neither the experience nor the articulation is ever "finished."

Thompson's understanding of class endeavored to bring matters down to earth, to demonstrate the role ordinary people have in making their own history—both in terms of his eighteenth-century subjects and as a sort of *ana-amnesis* for the 1960s, with its early rumblings of what would come to be known as *postmodernism*. For Thompson, history had no preordained "direction"; it was quite literally what people (based "on experiences inherited or shared") made it—that the black hats could (and often did) win out gave a sense of urgency to his subjects and, by extension, to the present. Thompson's *MEWC* was not a mining of the past for justifications in the present, however; it offered little safe ground for the reader (themselves historical subjects)—because struggle is always (at least) two-sided, and ongoing, each victory remains in jeopardy.

Thompson's sprawling, impressionistic opus had an enormous and almost immediate impact in historical studies. From a methodological standpoint, the inclusion of literary sources as a form of historical evidence was novel, as were his attention to anonymous letters and ("fumigate[d]") readings of spy reports. He viewed each in its turn as participating in what he called the "handling" of experience and in so doing managed to reposition politics in terms of the everyday.

Following the publication of *MEWC*, Thompson's historical output was scant—in addition to a study of William Blake, he produced only two further volumes of historical writing in his lifetime—*Whigs and Hunters* (1975) and *Customs in Common* (1991)—the latter consisting largely of essays that had appeared in various forms over the previous two decades. On this count, the two major essays that followed *MEWC*—"The Moral Economy of the English Crowd in the Eighteenth Century" (1971) and "Time, Work-Discipline, and Industrial Capitalism" (1967) (both collected in *Customs*)—rivaled the importance and influence of *MEWC* and deserve special mention.

Both essays drew on concepts and addressed concerns introduced in *MEWC*. In "Moral Economy," Thompson demonstrated that far from being spasmodic eruptions of hunger or "collective psychosis" (LeBon), English grain riots exhibited logic and discipline and were an attempt to enforce moral constraints upon the market. Thompson found a customary sense of fairness, a component of plebeian, and to a great extent also patrician, sensibilities being negotiated in the riots. The riots were not opposition to capitalism *per se*, as the rioters often sold seized grain at what they considered a fair price, giving the money to merchants (occasionally with magistrates looking on), but opposition to a market divorced of all moral and social concerns.

In "Time, Work Discipline, and Industrial Capitalism," Thompson examined the rationalization of labor and time over the course of the eighteenth century. Drawing on a typically impressive array of local sources, which he linked up to anthropological studies of noncapitalist societies, Thompson demonstrated that time and labor, which had been rooted in the human body and natural processes, were gradually estranged from those processes to conform to notions of abstract labor power and clock time, both of which mirrored the money form. Thompson's essay, unlike the more celebrated work of Michel Foucault on similar themes, had the merit of moving beyond the truisms of power and the tendency of human activity to increase its scope (power + resistance = power', power' + resistance = power", ...∞) by gearing analysis toward concrete forms of domination and their attenuation (also, incidentally through human activity). Put simply, while it may be the case that all roads lead to power, people have to live in a world in which the concrete forms and variable severity of "power" matter very much to them.

This sensibility informed his 1975 *Whigs and Hunters: The Origin of the Black Act*. The book was a microscopic study of the 1723 "Waltham Black Act," notorious for exploding the number of capital offenses against property in England by criminalizing traditional forms of plebeian subsistence. Though on one hand granting that the new laws represented a transparent power grab on the part of an emergent capitalist class, Thompson steadfastly refused to see the new laws as merely that. Instead, he argued that, though susceptible to ruling class interest, these laws codified a "ground" that also constrained ruling class interests and could be (and later were) used as a check against the arbitrary power of those interests.

While Thompson was perhaps one of the greatest historians of the twentieth century, his historical work was interrupted by periods of intense political activity, for which he is remembered as both a charismatic speaker and a devastating polemicist. Beginning with his exit from the CP, Thompson polemicized—first in *The New Reasoner* and *New Left Review*, and later in a myriad of mainstream newspapers and magazines—on everything from imperialism to the welfare state, but his central concern remained nuclear disarmament. Thompson, whose involvement with the Campaign for Nuclear Disarmament (CND) was early and continued, viewed the atomic bomb, and the polarization it created, as inimical to democratic institutions. He did not view the bomb as a particularly deadly "add on" to "economic man" (capitalist or "communist"), but as economic man's realization. Thompson envisioned a Pan-European, nuclear-free "third way" (not to be confused with the Blairite vision of the same name) that divested itself both of Soviet and American influence, both of which, he argued, utilized the threat of nuclear war to suppress democratic self-determination the world over. With the arrival of cruise missiles in Britain under Margaret Thatcher, he stopped his historical writing almost entirely, and devoted his energies to Europeans for Nuclear Disarmament (END). He was (to the chagrin of Thatcher, no doubt) the most recognized person in Britain after the Queen in the early 1980s, and both the Soviet Union and United States exerted a great deal of effort in insinuating that he was an "operative" for the other. Nonetheless, END's success was enormous, rallying huge numbers of both "free" and "Communist" Europeans to its cause. Seldom remarked upon in the United States, the movement exerted enormous pressure, particularly in Eastern Bloc countries, and had what his-

torians are beginning to recognize as a significant role in Soviet disengagement from those countries.

CRITICISM AND THE "CRISIS OF CLASS"

Thompson's privileging of the class "concept" as the defining historical experience began to come under fire in the early 1980s and reached something of a fever pitch following his death in 1993. Joan Scott presented "The Women in the *Making of the English Working Class*" at the American Historical Association's session honoring the twentieth anniversary of the publication of *MEWC*. She argued that class as it had been "theorized" by Thompson was a masculine concept, and Thompson had made it more so with his tendency to masculinize "it" by describing his book as a kind of "biography" of the working class from its "youth to early manhood." She further castigated Thompson's book for its treatment of the prophetess Joanna Southcott (who, among other things, claimed to be pregnant with the son of God, and whose followers Thompson had described as "deluded"). If Scott's criticism strikes the reader today as a quaint search for masculine pronouns in the guise of a critique, at the time it was (and it remains) something of a declaration of independence for feminist historians who had had an uneasy relationship with class. Scott's essay raised the possibility for many that "the class concept" was in fact hostile to feminist ambitions.

Further influential criticisms came from Dipesh Chakrabarty and Linda Colley, the first offering a postcolonial critique of Thompson, and the latter attempting to displace the notion of class with that of *nation*. Chakrabarty questioned the suitability for India of the class concept as "theorized" by Thompson, insisting on the primacy of religious identity there (particularly as opposed to the liberal traditions and institutions of "the Freeborn Englishman"). Colley, for her part, argued, by sidestepping class more or less altogether, that over Thompson's period, people came to identify themselves as "Britons" above all else.

In Chakrabarty's case, one questions the depth of engagement with Thompson's work, particularly given the primacy Thompson accords to such things as Methodism, and his insistence that the identity of "Freeborn Englishman" was not stable either in its application or content—just who this applied to and what it meant was a matter of centuries long contest. In Colley's criticism, the notions of *patriot, Briton,* and so forth tend to be stripped of their contextual specificity: The very Thompsonian questions of who is speaking, in what context, and how they mean what they are saying were generally ignored or overshadowed by the meta-identity of being "British." Though Thompson allowed in his review of Colley's *Britons* that nationalism was undertheorized and underexplored in his work, he bristled at the book's tendency to melt all concrete utterances into one nationalist soup.

Though neither Chakrabarty's nor Colley's critiques can be viewed as ultimately satisfactory from an intellectual standpoint, both have enjoyed a great deal of institutional success. Colley's *Britons*, in particular, has opened the closet door for a historical establishment in Britain that was always hostile to studies of class, if consistently unable to outflank Thompson in debate. Thus, where these historians might have been forced to address the question of class previously, they now proceed as though all were on board with the British ship of state and write "Imperial" history as though the thirty years of *MEWC*'s primacy had never occurred.

LEGACY

Thompson's legacy is difficult to determine. His self-appointed heirs have often proven sloppy in research, theoretically uninquisitive, and off-putting in argument. Others who have more closely engaged themselves with the possibilities in Thompson's work have tended to retreat into the cutting-edge hinterlands of historical study, particularly the *Journal of British Studies*, where the sort of interdisciplinary and theoretical engagement Thompson advocated is better received. Even though interdisciplinary study has flourished in recent years, the tendency has been toward a sort of compartmentalization, and for these very institutional reasons, one finds it difficult to imagine again the sort of all-out assault on received historical paradigms that *MEWC* represented.

From a political standpoint, one is again scarcely able to conceive of Thompson's moment. Thompson once wrote of a "peculiar and vengeful kind of bitterness that a certain kind of man feels for an enchanted mistress who has disappointed him" (O'Brien and Vanech 1969), and that hostility to or disenchantment with the possibility of social transformation seems the patrimony of the '68 generation. Between an academic left as convinced of an omnivorous "power" as it is of human impotence or unwitting complicity in the face of it, and a political left that no longer recognizes, much less is able to converse with working people, Thompson appears something of a relic, ironically the very "damned fool in utopia" he was labeled at his expulsion from the CP. It remains to be seen how long human beings can both go on living and being so "smart."

SEE ALSO *Anthropology; Capitalism; Class; Communism; Culture; History, Social; Humanism; Imperialism; Industrialization; Nation-State; Patriotism; Postcolonialism; Tradition; Working Class*

BIBLIOGRAPHY

PRIMARY WORKS

Abelove, Henry, E. P. Thompson, and MARHO. 1983. *Visions of History*. New York: Pantheon Books.

Thompson, E. P. 1957. Socialist Humanism: An Epistle to the Philistines. *New Reasoner* 1 (1): 105–143.

Thompson, E. P. 1958. Agency and Choice. *New Reasoner* 1 (5): 89–106.

Thompson, E. P. 1961. The Long Revolution I. *New Left Review* 1 (9): 24–33.

Thompson, E. P. 1961. The Long Revolution II. *New Left Review* 1 (10): 34–39.

Thompson, E. P. 1963. *The Making of the English Working Class*. 1st Vintage ed. New York: Vintage Books, 1966.

Thompson, E. P. 1978. *The Poverty of Theory and Other Essays*. New York: Monthly Review Press.

Thompson, E. P. 1985. *The Heavy Dancers*. New York: Pantheon Books.

Thompson, E. P. 1991. *Customs in Common*. New York: New Press.

Thompson, E. P. 1993. *Witness against the Beast: William Blake and the Moral Law*. New York: New Press.

Thompson, E. P. 1994. *Making History: Writings on History and Culture*. New York: New Press.

Thompson, E. P. 1997. *The Romantics: England in a Revolutionary Age*. New York: New Press.

SECONDARY WORKS

Bess, Michael. 1993. *Realism, Utopia, and the Mushroom Cloud: Four Activist Intellectuals and Their Strategies for Peace, 1945–1989: Louise Weiss, France, Leo Szilard, USA, E. P. Thompson, England, Danilo Dolci, Italy*. Chicago: University of Chicago Press.

Dworkin, Dennis L. 1997. *Cultural Marxism in Postwar Britain: History , the New Left, and the Origins of Cultural Studies*. Post-Contemporary Interventions Series. Durham, NC: Duke University Press.

Epstein, James. 1994. *Radical Expression: Political Language, Ritual, and Symbol in England, 1790–1850*. New York: Oxford University Press.

Epstein, James. 2003. *In Practice: Studies in the Language and Culture of Popular Politics in Modern Britain*. Stanford, CA: Stanford University Press.

Kaye, Harvey J. 1984. *The British Marxist Historians: An Introductory Analysis*. Cambridge, U.K.: Polity Press.

Kaye, Harvey J., and Keith McClelland. 1990. *E. P. Thompson: Critical Perspectives*. Philadelphia: Temple University Press.

Linebaugh, Peter. 1993. The London Hanged. *New York Review of Books* 40 (9).

O'Brien, Connor Cruise, and W. D. Vanech. 1969. *Power and Consciousness*. New York: New York University Press.

Rogers, Nicholas. 1998. *Crowds, Culture, and Politics in Georgian Britain*. Oxford: Clarendon Press; New York: Oxford University Press.

Thomas, Keith. 1992. How Britain Made It, reviews of *Britons: Forging the Nation, 1707–1837*, by Linda Colley, and *The*

London Hanged: Crime and Civil Society in the Eighteenth
Century, by Peter Linebaugh. *New York Review of Books* 39
(19).

Thomas, Keith. 1993. Response to "The London Hanged," by
Peter Linebaugh. *New York Review of Books* 40 (9).
http://www.nybooks.com/articles/2575.

Williams, Raymond. 1961. *The Long Revolution.* London:
Chatto and Windus.

Williams, Raymond. 1977. *Marxism and Literature.* Marxist
Introductions Series. Oxford: Oxford University Press.

Williams, Raymond. 1983. *Culture and Society, 1780–1950.* 2nd
ed. New York: Columbia University Press. (Orig. pub. 1958.)

Christopher J. Lamping

THOREAU, HENRY DAVID
1817–1862

Writer, naturalist, theorist of civil disobedience, and anti-slavery activist, Henry David Thoreau was born in Concord, Massachusetts, and lived there most of his life. A graduate of Harvard College, his most formative intellectual experience was his friendship with Ralph Waldo Emerson (1803–1882). The central figure of New England transcendentalism, Emerson famously called on individuals to dispense with traditional religious and intellectual authorities and seek truth and divinity for themselves. Thoreau spent his life answering Emerson's call to establish "an original relation to the universe" (Emerson 1983, p. 7).

Thoreau's most concerted effort to connect directly with the universe was his two-year sojourn in the woods at Walden Pond. Thoreau lived in a cabin of his own making, sustained himself by his own labor, looked inward, and observed nature. He recounted his experience magisterially in *Walden* (1854): "I went to the woods because I wished to live deliberately, to front only the essential facts of life, and see if I could not learn what it had to teach, and not, when I came to die, discover that I had not lived" (Thoreau 2004b, p. 90). *Walden* urges mental awakening and original perception; it also urges simple living so that one may free oneself from the relentless acquisition of material goods and the unquenchable thirst for riches.

In 1846, Thoreau had a brush with the law that spawned his other great contribution to American letters. Walking through town, he ran into the tax collector, who demanded that he pay his poll tax. Thoreau refused because he did not want his money going to support the Mexican War, which Thoreau saw as an indefensible attempt to extend the reach of American slavery. The tax collector threw Thoreau in jail; the next day an acquaintance paid the tax for Thoreau, much to Thoreau's irritation. Thoreau's night in jail became the occasion for "Resistance to Civil Government"—his 1849 essay defending his refusal to pay the tax and arguing that morally unconscionable laws are not binding. Eventually re-titled "Civil Disobedience," Thoreau's essay is the foundational text of the modern doctrine of civil disobedience: Citizens may justifiably defy laws which break with higher moral laws or with the moral foundations of the polity. In the twentieth century, Indian leader Mohandas Gandhi and American civil rights leader Martin Luther King Jr. drew inspiration from Thoreau in formulating their respective theories of nonviolent resistance. Unlike Gandhi and King, however, Thoreau was not a committed pacifist.

Thoreau gave three more noteworthy antislavery addresses before his death. In "Slavery in Massachusetts" (1854), Thoreau excoriated the recently passed Fugitive Slave Law, which required free states such as Massachusetts to assist slave-owners in the recovery of their property. In "A Plea for Captain John Brown" (1859) and "The Last Days of John Brown" (1860), Thoreau defended Brown's failed raid on the federal arsenal at Harpers Ferry, Virginia, which was part of Brown's broader attempt to incite a slave insurrection throughout the South. Despite his hatred of slavery, the carnage of the Civil War greatly disturbed Thoreau. Falling ill just before its outbreak in 1861, he said he "could never recover while the war lasted" (Harding 1992, p. 451). Thoreau never did, dying of tuberculosis at the age of forty-four.

SEE ALSO *Citizenship; Civil Disobedience; Civil Rights; Gandhi, Mohandas K.; Human Rights; Inequality, Racial; King, Martin Luther, Jr.; Pacifism; Passive Resistance; U.S. Civil War*

BIBLIOGRAPHY

Emerson, Ralph Waldo. 1983. *Essays & Lectures,* ed. Joel Porte. New York: Library of America.

Harding, Walter. 1992. *The Days of Henry Thoreau: A Biography.* Princeton, NJ: Princeton University Press.

Rosenblum, Nancy L. 1996. Introduction. In *Thoreau: Political Writings,* ed. Nancy L. Rosenblum, vii–xxxi. Cambridge, U.K.: Cambridge University Press.

Thoreau, Henry David. 2004a. *The Higher Law: Thoreau on Civil Disobedience and Reform,* ed. Wendell Glick. Princeton, NJ: Princeton University Press.

Thoreau, Henry David. [1854] 2004b. *Walden,* ed. J. Lyndon Shanley. Princeton, NJ: Princeton University Press.

Jack Turner

THORNDIKE, EDWARD
1874–1949

Although he spent his mature career in educational psychology at Columbia University's Teachers College in New York City, American psychologist Edward Lee Thorndike's most important work was done in animal learning, begun at Harvard under William James (1842–1910). Thorndike, along with Russian physiologist Ivan Pavlov (1849–1936), provided the methodological tools of behaviorism, in which psychologists used animal models to formulate theories of learning and behavior that would include humans.

When Thorndike and Pavlov began their research, comparative psychology used the so-called anecdotal method—collecting stories about animal behavior in natural and seminatural settings—in order to understand conscious animal thinking. Thorndike challenged the anecdotal method for lack of control, overestimation of animal intelligence, and tendencies to anthropomorphize the animal mind. He substituted experiments for anecdotes, establishing one of the two major paradigms for studying learning: instrumental, or operant, conditioning. Contemporaneously, Pavlov established Pavlovian, classical or respondent, conditioning. With regard to animal thought, Thorndike set out to catch the animal mind at work but concluded that animals do not reason their way to problem solutions. Rather, they engage in mindless trial-and-error learning.

In the experiments that defined instrumental conditioning, Thorndike placed young cats inside wooden cages called *puzzle boxes* from which they could escape by working a manipulandum inside the box, such as a foot treadle. Thorndike observed that cats tried out a variety of instinctive responses before accidentally hitting on the correct response. Nor did they show insight. Instead of stepping on the treadle immediately on the next trial, cats repeated erroneous responses, although the correct response emerged sooner as trials progressed until it became dominant. Thorndike described the process of learning as a gradual "stamping out" of connections between the box stimuli (S) and the incorrect instinctive responses (R), and the gradual "stamping in" of connections between S and the correct R. Hence, Thorndike called his theory of learning *connectionism*, a behavioral version of associationism.

Thorndike proposed three laws governing learning. The *law of exercise* held that using a connection strengthened it and disuse weakened it, while the *law of readiness* stated that when a connection was available, its use would be satisfying to the organism; these laws were later abandoned. Most important was the *law of effect*. Initially, the law of effect held that when a response to a stimulus led to pleasure, the S-R connection was strengthened, and

when a response led to painful punishment, the connection was weakened. Thorndike later revised the law of effect, having found that punishment did not weaken S-R connections, but inhibited their expression, a view held today.

Because Thorndike never proposed a comprehensive system of psychology, his ideas were subjected to detailed rather than systematic criticism. Most significant were critiques of the law of effect and the methodology of the puzzle boxes. Eager to purge references to mental states from psychology, behaviorists objected to Thorndike's reference to "pleasure"—a subjective conscious feeling—as the cause of learning. They substituted less mentalistic causes such as contiguity of stimulus and response (Edwin R. Guthrie [1886–1959]) or biological drive reduction (Clark Hull [1884–1952]), or they defined reinforcers functionally as events that strengthen the responses that produced them (B. F. Skinner [1904–1990]). Later, as information-processing views of learning gained strength, psychologists questioned Thorndike's law of effect in a new way (anticipated by Edward C. Tolman [1886–1959] in the 1930s). Thorndike assumed that rewards and punishments work via pleasure and pain, but they also provide information (a concept not available to Thorndike) that a response was correct or incorrect. Experiments that separate the two (e.g., making a painful stimulus indicate that a response was correct) have shown that learning depends on the information value of reinforcers more than their subjective quality.

The Gestalt psychologist Wolfgang Köhler (1887–1967) offered an important criticism of Thorndike's puzzle-box method. One of the driving issues in psychology of learning is whether learning occurs gradually or can occur suddenly via insight. Thorndike found no signs of insight in his puzzle-box studies, while Köhler found evidence of insight in his studies of problem solving by chimpanzees. Köhler argued that Thorndike's method was faulty because it made insight impossible: Trapped in the puzzle box, the cat could not see the connection between the manipulandum and the door opening, and so was forced to resort to trial and error. In Köhler's experiments, on the other hand, all the elements needed to solve a problem were available to the subject, who was able to assemble them insightfully into a solution. The force of Köhler's critique extends beyond issues of learning. Psychologists perform experiments in order to discover laws explaining behavior in real life, but experiments are necessarily artificial, and may lead psychologists to propose universal laws of behavior that are in fact laws induced by their experiments.

Nevertheless, Thorndike's influence was enormous. He initiated the S-R concept of learning elaborated by Clark Hull and his followers from the 1930s to the 1960s, which overshadowed the cognitive tradition of the Gestalt psychologists and Edward Tolman, which held that learning consisted of developing internal representations of the world, the main view in cognitive science today. The law of effect provided the basis for Skinner's principles of reinforcement, though Skinner did not view operant learning as making connections. There is today a new "connectionist" (neural network) movement, but it is not linkable to Thorndike.

SEE ALSO *Hull, Clark; Reinforcement Theories; Skinner, B. F.; Tolman, Edward*

BIBLIOGRAPHY

Leahey, Thomas H. 2004. *A History of Psychology: Main Currents in Psychological Thought.* 6th ed. Upper Saddle River, NJ: Prentice-Hall.

Thorndike, Edward L. [1911] 1965. *Animal Intelligence: Experimental Studies.* New York: Hafner. http://psychclassics.yorku.ca/Thorndike/Animal/.

Thomas Leahey

THRESHOLD EFFECTS

According to Eric Naevdal in his 2001 article "Optimal Regulation of Eutrophying Lakes, Fjordes, and Rivers in the Presence of Threshold Effects," the use of *threshold effects* is widespread in natural and social sciences alike. A *threshold* represents a gateway from one description of the world into another, which may be quite different. More precisely a threshold effect describes a process by which the magnitude of the response variable changes significantly as the triggering stimulus exceeds some critical value. One can think of threshold effects as devices to explain nonlinear phenomena.

HOW DO THRESHOLD EFFECTS WORK?

A way of understanding how threshold effects work is by means of an example. In economic growth, one of the main theories developed to explain the process of per-capita income growth in an economy is the one that allows for human capital to affect the production of output overtime. Human capital refers to the stock of knowledge that is accumulated through education and technological progress. These resources make workers more productive and able to adapt to new technologies. Most of the theoretical models that deal with the relationship between human capital and growth assume that this relationship is linear: Increasing the level of human capital should yield a higher rate of economic growth *irrespec-*

tive of the level of human capital, something, according to Pantelis Kalaitzidakis, Theofanis Mamuneas, Andreas Savvides, and Thanasis Stengos in their 2001 study, not borne by empirical evidence.

Costas Azariadis and Alan Drazen observe in their 1990 article "Threshold Externalities in Economic Development" that long-run growth rates exhibit persistent differences between more and less developed economies. Historically this derives from the "Big-Push" ideas of P. Rosenstein-Roden (1943) and Ragnar Nurkse (1953) who have noted that an economy can remain stuck in an underdevelopment state unless there is a substantial investment effort. Some low-income economies appear to be caught in a low-growth environment and lag behind countries similar in terms of endowments. The standard growth model cannot account for such persistent differences. While one can seek explanations for this stylized fact in non-economic factors, there is an economic explanation based on the existence of technological externalities with a threshold property that allows for economies with very similar structures to exhibit different growth experiences. Specifically, once human capital attains a certain threshold level aggregate production possibilities may expand especially rapidly. Economies that have not attained this threshold level may languish in a self-perpetuating state of persistent underdevelopment.

Nonlinearities due to the presence of threshold externalities in the production of human capital can lead to different growth experiences, including possible low-growth (or low-development) "traps," where low investment in human capital (education) will discourage further human capital accumulation (acquisition of additional skills) and, hence, result in a low-growth trap. Consequently, a group of countries with unequal initial educational endowments may never catch up to each other; the growth rate of ones with higher endowments will diverge from those with lower initial endowments of human capital. This suggests a role of government intervention in the educational sector to introduce policies (such as educational subsidies) that support skill acquisition and higher educational attainment.

NONLINEARITIES AND THRESHOLD EFFECTS

As explained above, threshold effects are the main cause for the presence of nonlinearities in the process that underlies economic growth. From a modeling point of view, threshold effects only produce a specific type of nonlinearity that is quite restrictive. The process that is induced by thresholds can be described by piece-wise linear segments that are individually defined by thresholds. Thresholds act as the "knots" that connect the different segments together. In that case a threshold effect is an "all or nothing" effect as values below and above the threshold result in different regimes. Alternatively, such regime change could occur gradually and not as abruptly by means of a smooth transition. The amount of smoothing done to the knots that connect the linear segments will result in different types of nonlinear effects. Assuming that smoothing is arbitrary there is a large class of such smooth transition nonlinear effects that includes threshold effects as a special case. Yet despite their limitations, threshold effects have proven to be powerful devices to introduce nonlinearity in economic modeling, especially growth theory.

BIBLIOGRAPHY

Azariadis, Costas, and Alan Drazen. 1990. Threshold Externalities in Economic Development. *Quarterly Journal of Economics* 105: 501-526.

Kalaitzidakis, Pantelis, Theofanis Mamuneas, Andreas Savvides, and Thanasis Stengos. 2001. Measures of Human Capital and Nonlinearities in Economic Growth. *Journal of Economic Growth* 6 (3): 229-254.

Naevdal, Eric. 2001. Optimal Regulation of Eutrophying Lakes, Fjordes, and Rivers in the Presence of Threshold Effects. *American Journal of Agricultural Economics* 83 (4): 972-984.

Nurkse, Ragnar. 1953. *Problems of Capital Formation in Underdeveloped Countries.* Oxford: Basil Blackwell.

Rosenstein-Rodan, P. 1943. The Problem of Industrialization of Eastern and South-Eastern Europe. *Economic Journal* 53: 202-211.

Thanasis Stengos

THURMOND, STROM
1902–2003

Strom Thurmond was born James Strom Thurmond on December 5, 1902, in Edgefield, South Carolina. He was one of six children born to John William Thurmond and Eleanor Gertrude Strom. Thurmond's father was a lawyer, farmer, community leader, and former South Carolina state senator. Strom followed in his father's footsteps by acquiring a self-taught law degree (under the tutelage of his father) and entering politics after his 1923 graduation from Clemson College (now Clemson University). In 1928 Thurmond was elected the superintendent of education for Edgefield County. In 1932 he was elected a state senator of Edgefield County. In 1938 he was sworn in as an elected state judge, but he voluntarily gave up his judgeship in 1942 to enlist in the army during World War II (1939–1945). Thurmond became governor of South Carolina in 1946 when he beat the incumbent governor, Ransome J. Williams, (and nine other candidates) in the South Carolina gubernatorial race.

Thurmond was an avid Democratic Party politician, but the 1948 presidential election became a benchmark year for what became his and southern Democratic politicians' revolt from the national party. Democratic president Harry S. Truman's 1948 reelection campaign advocated pro–civil rights legislation (abolition of the poll tax, support of an antilynching law, the creation of a permanent Federal Employment Practices Commission, and a ban on discrimination in commerce). Southern states reacted negatively to this platform by revolting from the national party to form their own, prosegregation and antiblack civil rights, wing of the party—the Dixiecrats, or States' Rights Party. Thurmond was nominated the Dixiecrat presidential candidate, officially representing the party's position that states had the right to retain segregation. Thurmond lost the election, but his staunchly southern prosegregation and antiblack civil rights positions launched him into the helm of southern political leadership.

Thurmond was elected a U.S. senator of South Carolina in 1954, and during his tenure he opposed the passage of several civil rights bills—the Civil Rights Acts of 1957 (in obstructing the bill's passage he set the record for the longest Senate filibuster—twenty-four hours and eighteen minutes), the Civil Rights Act of 1964, and the Voting Rights Act of 1965, all of which were important in advancing blacks' civil rights. His continued dissatisfaction with the Democratic Party's stance on civil rights issues led him to sever his ties with the party in 1964 and become a Republican.

Despite Thurmond's initial support for Lyndon B. Johnson (a southern Democrat from Texas) as the vice presidential candidate in 1964, Thurmond later openly opposed the national party's liberal plank on civil rights. The summer before the 1964 presidential election, Thurmond decided not to attend the Democratic national convention because of his ideological differences on civil rights, which separated him from the national party's politics. In a 1964 speech to a South Carolina audience, Thurmond denounced the Democratic Party platform and announced his realignment with the Republican Party and his support of Barry Goldwater's (a Republican senator from Arizona) 1964 presidential candidacy. Thurmond found more ideological connections with the conservative Goldwater, who, although he was not a segregationist per se, had outlined in 1961 a "southern strategy" to invite southerners to support the Republican Party as the anticivil rights political party. Thurmond's partisan realignment influenced the eventual realignment of most white southern Democrats to the Republican Party. His realignment with the Republican Party also laid the foundation for what would become a new and lifelong commitment to this political party.

During much of Thurmond's political career, his politics were marred with antiblack interests. He was an avid supporter of "freedom of choice" school desegregation plans (despite their being declared unconstitutional by the 1968 Supreme Court case *Green v. New Kent County*), which were a part of the "massive resistance" that southern governments implemented to avoid desegregation. Often, freedom of choice desegregation plans retained former segregation practices—whites who opposed desegregation chose to attend white schools (in order to avoid contact with blacks) and blacks who more than likely supported desegregation continued to attend all-black schools (in order to avoid intimidation by whites in integrated schools).

The issue of freedom of choice plans was at the center of the 1970 South Carolina gubernatorial race, and the candidate who supported the plan (South Carolina congressmember Albert Watson) lost to the candidate who opposed it (South Carolina lieutenant governor John West). This political victory attested to the significance of the candidate's more moderate views on race and his appeal among a majority of black voters. After witnessing this change in how elections could be won in South Carolina politics, Thurmond became more open to considering blacks' political interests and to broadening his constituent service to South Carolina's black electorate. He even hired a black staff member, Thomas Moss, who informed him about black political issues.

During the 1970s Thurmond continued to build his relationship with the black electorate, but despite this changed political interest in addressing black issues, Thurmond (as chairman of the Senate Judiciary Committee) initially opposed support of the 1982 Voting Rights Act, which would have extended the provisions of the Voting Rights Act of 1965 that protected blacks' voting rights. He eventually supported the act.

Over time, Thurmond climbed the political ladder, achieving high political posts such as chairman of the Senate Judiciary Committee and serving as president pro tempore (1981–1987; 1995). He was the longest-lived and longest-serving U.S. senator, having reached the age of 100 during his service. At his 100th birthday celebration, Trent Lott (R-MS) made controversial remarks about Thurmond's 1948 presidential candidacy that eventually led to Lott resigning from his position as senate majority leader. In January 2003 Thurmond retired from his senate position. He died in the same year on June 26, 2003.

Posthumously, rumors about his having fathered an African American daughter resurfaced and were confirmed when Essie Mae Washington-Williams announced that she was, in fact, Thurmond's daughter. Thurmond's fathering of an African American daughter (with the Thurmond family African American housekeeper, Carrie Butler) conflicts with a major principle of segregation—the prohibition of "race mixing," or miscegenation. According to segregationists, blacks and whites are supposed to be divided in every way of life, especially sexual relations, and antimiscegenation laws in the south banned interracial marriage and interracial sexual relations. Thus Thurmond had covertly defied the racial and sexual social mores that he publicly supported. Thurmond was married successively to Jean Crouch and to Nancy Janice Moore (with whom he had four children); both of them were (white) former Miss South Carolinas.

SEE ALSO *Civil Rights Movement, U.S.; Dixiecrats; Filibuster; Segregation; Sex, Interracial; Voting Rights Act*

BIBLIOGRAPHY

Bass, Jack, and Marilyn W. Thompson. 2003. *Ol' Strom: An Unauthorized Biography.* Columbia: University of South Carolina Press.

Bass, Jack, and Marilyn W. Thompson. 2006. *Strom: The Complicated Personal and Political Life of Strom Thurmond.* New York: Perseus.

Cohodas, Nadine. 1993. *Strom Thurmond and the Politics of Southern Change.* New York: Simon & Schuster.

Frederickson, Kari. 2001. *The Dixiecrat Revolt and the End of the Solid South, 1932–1968.* Chapel Hill: University of North Carolina Press.

Lachicotte, Alberta. 1966. *Rebel Senator: Strom Thurmond of South Carolina.* New York: Devin-Adair.

Sherrill, Robert. 1968. *Gothic Politics in the Deep South: Stars of the New Confederacy.* New York: Grossman.

Strom Thurmond Biography. Strom Thurmond Institute of Government and Public Affairs. http://www.strom.clemson.edu/strom/bio.html.

Washington-Williams, Essie Mae, and William Stadium. 2005. *Dear Senator: A Memoir by the Daughter of Strom Thurmond.* New York: HarperCollins.

Shayla C. Nunnally

TIEBOUT EFFECTS

SEE *Hedonic Prices.*

TIME

From the perspective of the natural sciences, time in and of itself causes nothing. Being but the interval between the motions of material objects, it is a gauge of change with no natural divisions. Such is not the case for most social times, where time has a causative role in shaping action and its perception. Humans mark its passage with ceremony, hope, and anxiety. The approach of a bureaucratic deadline or belief in an impending apocalypse can generate a flurry of culminating behaviors. Time is used as a reward, such as being given "time off" or promoted "ahead of time," or as punishment, when one "does time" or is placed in "time out" for moral violations. Time, in addition to space, constructs the very boundaries of social reality by ordering social life and shaping individuals' awareness of its passing.

Born without any temporal instinct or sense, human existence is largely orchestrated by external pacemakers, or *Zeitgebers*. Upon entry into the world, infants' first lessons are largely temporal as they come to internalize the rhythms of their families' language and activity schedules. With maturation, their lives become controlled by the metronomes of school, work, leisure, and community.

The most all-encompassing of these external times come from one's culture, whose tempos underlie its music, poetry, language, sports, and religion. Cultural systems can be likened to massive musical scores whose rhythms, argues anthropologist Edward T. Hall, "may yet prove to be the most binding of all the forces that hold human beings together" (1983, p. 156). Thus state-of-the-art technologies have historically been applied to time's measurement: Just as modern peoples measure time by the vibration of atoms, so prehistoric peoples constructed huge monoliths to coordinate social time with cosmological calendars.

The broadest of cultural time conceptions involve orientations toward the future and past. The "Golden Years," for example, can be collectively understood to exist either in the future (hence, time is seen as progressive and evolutionary) or in some idyllic past (as Paradise lost). The future can be in the past if the flow of time is culturally understood to be recurrent and reversible. A near universal myth holds that the world goes through cycles of destruction and regeneration (Eliade 1949), evident in beliefs about the cyclical nature of both natural and social phenomena. Where time's flow is understood to be linear and irreversible, the future can be either progressive (i.e., the outlook engendered by the Enlightenment and industrialization) or degenerative (i.e., theologians' belief in humanity's growing cultural depravity since the Fall or cosmologists' predictions of a universe increasingly filled with black holes). These two broad orientations underlie distinction between traditional and modern cultures.

Cultural times are interwoven with social needs, the predominant personality types of social members, social complexity, and technology. The smaller and more homogeneous the group, the less the need for temporal precision. Hopi-speaking Pueblo Indians have no tenses for past, present, or future events, and they think of time not as a series of unique distinct instants but rather as cumulative events. Where identities are collectivist and individuals focus on the welfare of their groups as opposed to themselves, often they think in terms of long-term goals. An Iroquois chief describes how his people's decision-making "relates to the welfare and well-being of the seventh generation to come" (Rifkin 1987, p. 65). Such cultures feature people-oriented polychronic time, which stresses human engagements and the completion of transactions rather than rigid schedules. The activities of individualistic selves, such as those in the United States, tend to be governed by monochronic time, doing things one at a time in observance of task-oriented schedules and procedures. Oriented toward immediate rewards, these people are obsessed with punctuality and deadlines (Hall 1983)—and are demeaned when higher status others make them wait (Schwartz 1975).

As the primary form of work historically shifted from the land to the machine, the rhythms of social life were decreasingly dictated by natural times (e.g., cycles of day and night and the seasons) and increasingly by artificial times, such as the sixty-minute hour or the seven-day week, which have no bases in nature. With social differentiation and specialization evolved separate institutional realms, each with its own time schedules, rules, orientation toward the future and past, and patterns of change (e.g., cycles of growth and decay and oscillations between political liberalism and conservatism, bear and bull markets, and religious revivalism and secularism).

Given the growing importance of time, social institutions invariably sought its control through their creations of duration, succession, temporal location, and uniform rates of occurrence (Zerubavel 1981). Religions created prayer times and holy days (to distinguish themselves in time as well as space, Muslims claimed Fridays, Jews Saturdays, and Christians Sundays). One of the early acts of the First Republic of France was to alter time to create a more rational secular society. In 1793 the French Revolutionary calendar was adopted, with ten-day weeks, ten-hour days, and 100-minute hours. In Britain and the United States, national railroad schedules required uniform time because each town could no longer have its own noon when the sun was directly overhead. In 1883, Standard Railroad Time went into effect, creating five time zones to replace fifty regional times. A year later it was made the national legal time. Finally, with the increased rationalities of bureaucratic organizations, time became increasingly regularized and scheduled owing to greater needs for coordination and deadline-dictated precision.

Institutional differentiation was accompanied by the proliferation of social roles, which have become increasingly age graded over the past six decades (Chudacoff 1989). Single-room schools, for instance, became age-segregated classrooms. Each of these roles, in turn, came with its own "social clock" and associated age norms. To be thirteen and still in the third grade is to be "behind schedule" and a source of shame; to be a thirteen-year-old college junior is to be "ahead of time" and a source of esteem. Sequences of these age-graded roles provide biographical pathways and timetables. In the case of the family, there exist normative "best times" for the length of courtships and when to first marry and begin parenting. In addition, there are normative patterns for how individuals' various roles are to be synchronized, such as not getting married before completing junior high school.

Finally, substantial social science research has been devoted to individuals' subjective experiences of time. Temporal orientations are, for instance, shaped by positions within the class structure, with the future-oriented middle-class being more likely than the present-oriented lower class to stress delayed gratification and thriftiness in their children's socialization. The passage of time seems to accelerate with increasing age, density of experiences, and approaching conclusions. Multiple and conflicting role demands produce the stresses of temporal scarcity. Excessive rates of social change, according to Toffler (1970), can produce "future shock." Not surprisingly, mystical significance is attributed to senses of timelessness, such as athletes being "in the zone" and in religious depictions of deathless eternities.

SEE ALSO *Christianity; Clock Time; Cultural Relativism; Industrialization; Iroquois; Machinery; Native Americans; Work; Work Day; Work Week*

BIBLIOGRAPHY

Chudacoff, Howard P. 1989. *How Old Are You? Age Consciousness in American Culture.* Princeton, NJ: Princeton University Press.

Eliade, Mircea. [1949] 1959. *The Myth of the Eternal Return: Cosmos and History.* Trans. Willard R. Trask. New York: Harper Torchbooks.

Hall, Edward T. 1983. *The Dance of Life: The Other Dimension of Time.* Garden City, NY: Anchor Books.

Rifkin, Jeremy. 1987. *Time Wars: The Primary Conflict in Human History.* New York: Henry Holt & Co.

Schwartz, Barry. 1975. *Queuing and Waiting: Studies in the Social Organization of Access and Delay.* Chicago: University of Chicago Press.

Toffler, Alvin. 1970. *Future Shock.* New York: Random House.

Zerubavel, Eviatar. 1981. *Hidden Rhythms: Schedules and Calendars in Social Life.* Chicago: University of Chicago Press.

Michael C. Kearl

TIME ALLOCATION

The international comparative time-use surveys organized by Alexander Szalai (1966, 1972) are usually seen as the first modern time-use measurements. These surveys were followed by an increasing number of time-use surveys in many countries. Initially, these data were used descriptively for the valuation of household work and for information about leisure activities, commuting, and travel behavior.

Table 1 gives the average shares of a day allocated to various activities for both males and females aged twenty to seventy-four over two years for three European countries and the United States. Depending on the country and year, market work occupies on average about 15 percent of all available time, as does household work. Tertiary time, about 45 percent, is mostly sleep and personal activities, while the remaining 25 percent is devoted to leisure.

Economic analysis of the rationale for time allocation was inspired by the pathbreaking work of a group of economists at the University of Chicago. They were led by Gary Becker (1965), who saw the household as a unit that produced utility giving commodities from market goods and time input from household members. For surveys of the first decades of time-use analysis, see F. Thomas Juster and Frank Stafford (1991) and N. Anders Klevmarken (1999).

Becker's revised theory of choice assumes that a household derives utility from commodities, say Z_i, $i = 1, \ldots, m$, such as meals, a clean house, sleep, and going to a movie, which are produced by the household according to the household production functions,

$$\begin{cases} T_i = t_i Z_i \\ x_i = b_i Z_i \end{cases} \qquad \text{(1a, b)}$$

The functions specify how much input of market time, T_i, and goods, x_i, is needed to produce Z_i. (The proportionality factors t_i and b_i are not necessarily constant.) The household is assumed to maximize utility subject to its budget and time constraints. These two constraints are not independent because time for consumption can be converted into money income by allocating more time to market work. The two constraints can be combined into one,

$$\sum_{i=1}^{m} p_i x_i + \omega \sum_{i=1}^{m} T_i = V + T\omega. \qquad (2)$$

Total expenditures on market goods and household production time valued at the wage rate ω add up to the sum of nonlabor income V and total time T valued at the wage rate. The latter sum has been called *full income*. Substituting (1a,b) into the constraint (2), it becomes,

$$\sum_{i=1}^{m} (p_i b_i + t_i \omega) Z_i = V + T\omega. \qquad (3)$$

	Germany		Italy		The Netherlands		United States	
	1991/92	**2001/02**	**1988/89**	**2002/03**	**1990**	**2000**	**1985**	**2003**
Individuals in survey	6,928	7,239	25,490	37,882	1,531	1,586	3,567	17,668
Days surveyed	2	2 or 3	1	1	7	7	1	1
All work	**0.336**	**0.306**	**0.336**	**0.309**	**0.274**	**0.275**	**0.310**	**0.329**
Market work	0.183	0.137	0.172	0.144	0.121	0.131	0.171	0.178
Household Production	0.153	0.168	0.164	0.165	0.153	0.143	0.139	0.151
Family care	0.015	0.021	0.022	0.020	0.026	0.024	0.021	0.031
Shopping	0.029	0.040	0.027	0.030	0.028	0.031	0.035	0.036
Tertiary time	**0.444**	**0.462**	**0.470**	**0.412**	**0.441**	**0.449**	**0.450**	**0.436**
Sleep	0.348	0.350	0.358	0.346	0.347	0.357	0.334	0.349
Leisure	**0.219**	**0.232**	**0.193**	**0.279**	**0.285**	**0.276**	**0.240**	**0.234**
Radio/TV	0.079	0.082	0.071	0.070	0.075	0.075	0.098	0.102

SOURCE: Adapted from Table 1.1. In Burda et al. (2006, p. 17); the source table contains means in minutes and corresponding standard errors.

Table 1. Average shares of a day (twenty-four hours) allocated to activities by country and year. All individuals aged twenty to seventy-four.

The expression in parenthesis is the full price of the ith commodity, and it is the sum of the prices of the goods and the time used per unit of the commodity i. The price of time input is the earnings forgone by using time to produce a unit commodity rather than to work in the market. If all t_i are zero, the model reduces to a conventional model of consumer choice. Becker's model thus generalizes the conventional model by including the cost of time input to produce the utility-yielding commodities.

If the wage rate, the time cost, and the cost of market goods are fixed, it follows from the maximization of the utility function under the constraint (3) that marginal utility is proportional to the full price at maximum. We can now derive a number of predictions from this model: An increase in the wage rate will increase earnings forgone, and the full price of time-intensive commodities will increase more than that of good-intensive commodities. It follows from basic choice theory that the consumer will substitute away from time-intensive commodities and toward good-intensive commodities if the increase in the price of time is income compensated. At the same time, consumption time is freed for market work, which will increase. The effect of an uncompensated increase in the wage rate will depend on the relative size of the substitution and income effects.

If productivity of consumption time increases—that is, if t_i decreases—the relative price of time-intensive commodities will decrease, and consumers will substitute toward these commodities. For instance, when time-saving techniques are introduced into household work, we do more washing, cooking, and so on than we otherwise would have done. Whether or not we use less time in these activities will, as usual, depend on the relative size of the substitution and income effects, but if these commodities also become more good intensive, more market work is

needed to generate the income required to buy the goods that go into these commodities.

Becker's model is a good conceptual model for theorizing about time allocation, but it has weaknesses as a model for empirical work: One and only one good contributes to each commodity; the wage rate and the time and good productivities are not necessarily fixed and independent of the consumer's choice; and the definition of a commodity is far from obvious. The model has been generalized to cope with these problems, but a more difficult problem is that the amount produced of each commodity is difficult if not impossible to observe. Without observations on the output from household production, it is in general not possible to identify preference parameters separately from the household production functions. All we can do is estimate mongrel time-use functions that depend both on preferences and household production technology.

In Becker's model, the household is treated as a single decision-making unit, and there is no place for the separate decisions of the household members. Although Becker obtains some results from his model concerning the division of labor within a household—for instance, those who are more efficient at market activities use relatively less time at consumption activities—this issue is better analyzed within a bargaining model (see, for instance, the survey by Behrman [1997]).

Time allocation is not only an issue of how many hours of the twenty-four-hour day or of the 8,760 hours of a year are spent on various activities; it is also an issue of *when* in a day or in a year various activities are done. One could also extend the domain of time allocation research by asking how much time is spent with whom? These issues have only recently attracted the interest of social scientists, but it is clear that when we do things and with whom is a matter of choice. These choices are some-times constrained by laws, such as those regulating the opening hours of shops; by nature—for instance, we typically sleep during the night; or by social and religious conventions, such as those associated with Christmas and Easter. For recent contributions in this domain, see Daniel Hamermesh and Gerard Pfann (2005).

SEE ALSO *Becker, Gary; Labor Force Participation; Leisure; Utility Function*

BIBLIOGRAPHY

Becker, Gary S. 1965. A Theory of the Allocation of Time. *Economic Journal* 75 (299): 493–517.

Behrman, Jere R. 1997. Intrahousehold Distribution and the Family. In *Handbook of Population and Family Economics*, ed. Mark R. Rosenzweig and Oded Stark, 126–187. Amsterdam, NY: Elsevier.

Burda, Michael C., Daniel S. Hamermesh, and Philippe Weil. 2006. The Distribution of Total Work in the EU and the US. Unpublished manuscript. http://www.eco.utexas.edu/faculty/Hamermesh/BHW4.0.pdf.

Hamermesh, Daniel S., and Gerard A. Pfann, eds. 2005. *The Economics of Time Use*. Amsterdam, NY: Elsevier.

Juster, F. Thomas, and Frank P. Stafford. 1991. The Allocation of Time: Empirical Findings, Behavioral Models, and Problems of Measurement. *Journal of Economic Literature* 29 (2): 471–522.

Klevmarken, N. Anders. 1999. Microeconomic Analysis of Time Use Data: Did We Reach the Promised Land? In *Time Use: Research, Data, and Policy*, ed. Joachim Merz and Manfred Ehling, 423–456. Baden-Baden, Germany: NOMOS Verlagsgesellschaft.

Szalai, Alexander. 1966. Trends in Comparative Time Budget Research. *American Behavioral Scientist* 9 (9): 3–8.

Szalai, Alexander, ed. 1972. *The Use of Time: Daily Activities of Urban and Suburban Populations in Twelve Countries*. The Hague, Netherlands: Mouton.

N. Anders Klevmarken

TIME AND MOTION STUDY

Time and motion study, or motion and time study, is a basic set of tools used by industrial engineers to increase operational efficiency through work simplification and the setting of standards, usually in combination with a wage-incentive system designed to increase worker motivation. Originally developed to drive productivity improvement in manufacturing plants, motion and time study is also now used in service industries.

Motion and time study is associated with the so-called scientific management movement of the late nineteenth and early twentieth centuries in the United States, primarily with the work of industrial engineers Frederick Winslow Taylor (1856–1915), Frank B. Gilbreth (1868–1924), and Lillian Gilbreth (1878–1972). Some time studies had been conducted before Taylor, particularly by French engineer Jean Rodolphe Perronet (1708–1794) and English economist Charles Babbage (1791–1871), both analyzing pin manufacturing. However, modern motion and time study was developed as part of the scientific management movement championed by Taylor and eventually became known as *Taylorism*.

The foundation of Taylorism is a system of task management in which responsibilities are clearly divided between managers and workers. Managers and engineers engage in planning and task optimization, primarily through motion and time study, while workers are responsible for carrying out discrete tasks as directed. The Gilbreths sought to find the best method to perform an operation and reduce fatigue by studying body motions, attempting to eliminate unnecessary ones and simplify necessary ones to discover the optimal sequence of motions. The Gilbreths developed the technique of *micromotion study*, in which motions are filmed and then watched in slow motion. Taylor incorporated early research from the Gilbreths in his *The Principles of Scientific Management* (1911), and subsequent industrial engineers further developed the Taylorist system.

Taylorism played a key role in the continuous productivity improvement generated by the Fordist model of work organization. The Fordist model, which is based on the supply-driven, mass production of standardized goods using semiskilled workers, achieved efficiency improvements via scale economies and detailed division of labor, both accomplished through the Taylorist separation of conception from execution, in which managers plan tasks that workers execute.

Taylor argued that such a division of labor between management and workers was a form of "harmonious cooperation" that ultimately removed antagonisms from the workplace and benefited both managers and workers. However, this process of separating conception from execution is often understood as a form of de-skilling, and Taylorism has been rejected by unions, who have denounced it as a form of speedup that harms workers and hence quality and productivity.

Debates about the effect of motion and time study on workers continue today in discussions of post-Fordism, particularly *lean production*, which employs motion and time study to set standards and achieve continuous improvement in work processes, but in a context of demand-driven production without large buffers of in-process inventory. Some workers and commentators argue that motion and time study under lean production is simply a form of work intensification that is detrimental to workers, while others argue that under lean production workers are able to contribute to problem solving and standard setting and thus prefer motion and time study under lean production to that under Fordism.

Underlying each system is a theory of worker motivation—that workers need to be coerced (in the Fordist model) or that workers want to do their best and are interested in more intellectual activity (in the post-Fordist model). In reality, there is more likely a distribution of different motivations across workers, and worker well-being is likely to depend more on the interaction between individual orientations toward work and how a given set of methods such as motion and time study are applied in a particular work context.

SEE ALSO *General Motors; Taylorism*

BIBLIOGRAPHY

Adler, Paul. 1995. "Democratic Taylorism": The Toyota Production System at NUMMI. In *Lean Work: Empowerment and Exploitation in the Global Auto Industry*, ed. Steve Babson, 207–219. Detroit, MI: Wayne State University Press.

George, Claude S., Jr. 1972. *The History of Management Thought*. 2nd ed. Englewood Cliffs, NJ: Prentice Hall.

Niebel, Benjamin W. 1993. *Motion and Time Study*. 9th ed. Homewood, IL: Irwin.

Taylor, Frederick Winslow. [1911] 1998. *The Principles of Scientific Management*. Mineola, NY: Dover.

Matt Vidal

TIME ON THE CROSS

Robert William Fogel and Stanley L. Engerman's two-volume revisionist study, *Time on the Cross: The Economics of American Negro Slavery*, is the most widely known and controversial work ever written on the subject of slavery. Indeed, it is arguably the most widely known and controversial work ever written in the entire field of economic history. The celebrity and controversy surrounding the publication of *Time on the Cross* in 1974 were related not only to its conclusions, but also to its methodology and rhetorical style, and the study has continued to spark debate since it was first published.

By the early twenty-first century, the field of economic history had lost much of the vitality it had in the 1970s. It may therefore be difficult for some to imagine a time when a technical work such as *Time on the Cross* could command space in mass-circulation newspapers and

magazines such as the *New York Times*, the *Wall Street Journal*, *Time*, and *Newsweek*, and when economic historians made the rounds on the TV talk-show circuit. But *Time on the Cross* represented a kind of harmonic convergence of method, subject, authors, readers, and cultural milieu.

During the 1960s the venerable field of economic history was reinvented, mainly by small cadres of economists who explicitly and self-consciously brought economic theory, mathematics, and formal methods to a field that had previously been dominated by scholars trained in history departments and in traditional historical approaches. As a result, practitioners of the "new economic history," such as Fogel and Engerman, spent much of the 1960s and 1970s revising and reinterpreting standard accounts of U.S. economic history. Although both Fogel and Engerman wrote on other topics, from the late 1960s on, they, along with many of their graduate students, worked assiduously on the economic history of the "peculiar institution" of slavery. In so doing, they turned the field of slavery studies upside down.

In 1974, the year *Time on the Cross* was published, the general consensus on slavery among historians of the American South was that slavery was a singularly exploitative, inefficient, and unprofitable system of labor organization. Slaves themselves were viewed as reluctant, recalcitrant, and inefficient workers, and the consensus was that their material lives were pinched, their emotional lives were stunted, and their family lives were disjointed and transient, if not incidental. For their part, slaveholders were viewed as "traditional," or "paternalistic," and nonentrepreneurial (or even anticapitalistic) in mindset and behavior. They were believed to be more concerned with aristocratic trappings and conspicuous consumption than with production, prices, and the bottom line. Moreover, despite scholarly outliers such as Frank and Harriet Owsley, who called attention to the importance of yeoman farmers and small slaveholders in the region, most students of slavery in the American South focused their attention on large planters, and this narrow focus served to render normative what was actually a very small and exceptional group. Furthermore, slavery and the slave system were said to have had deleterious long-run developmental consequences for the South as a region, rendering it poor and backward, particularly in comparison to the northern part of the United States.

Fogel and Engerman challenged all of these positions and more in *Time on the Cross*. Basing their "iconoclastic" findings on "the application of quantitative methods" (principally neoclassical economic theory, statistics, and applied mathematics) to historical materials, they concluded, among other things, that slavery was an efficient, profitable, and vibrant system of labor organization; that

African American slaves labored hard and purposively, sharing much the same work ethic that motivated free Americans; that Southern agriculture was highly productive—even more productive than agriculture in the North; that Southern slaveholders, including planters, were capitalistic, entrepreneurial, and bullish on the future; and that slaves, though exploited to a degree, enjoyed relatively good material living standards and, generally speaking, were able to sustain stable families and family ties. More broadly, they claimed that the slave economy of the South was not only healthy and growing rapidly in the antebellum period, but that it was also, in comparative terms, one of the most modern and advanced economies in the entire world at that time.

After a short honeymoon period of prizes, fawning reviews, and unstinting praise, *Time on the Cross* came under heavy critical fire from both traditional historians and some fellow "new economic historians." Fogel and Engerman's critics attacked from several different directions. Some criticized the authors' approach and methods; others attacked both the assumptions and the evidentiary base upon which the authors' findings were based; still others challenged the authors' purportedly condescending and vainglorious rhetoric; and some questioned the implications of the authors' findings, even if valid.

No wallflowers, Fogel and Engerman mounted a robust defense of their findings. In this effort, they were joined by their students and research associates, as well as by many other economic historians who found their approach, methods, and conclusions worth defending. The response to the publication of *Time on the Cross* was unprecedented in the normally quiet little field of economic history. Essays, both pro and con, proliferated in technical journals, and entire books were devoted to attacking Fogel and Engerman's findings. Conferences and symposia on *Time on the Cross* were held throughout the decade of the 1970s, and for a time the study, or at least the nontechnical first volume of the two-volume work, became a staple on reading lists and course syllabi at American universities.

By the 1980s, *Time on the Cross* had taken many direct hits from critics and fallen out of favor among many students of American slavery. Although economic historians challenged parts of Fogel and Engerman's argument on technical grounds—such as finding fault with some of their estimates, measurements, and assumptions—the most damaging blows were struck by traditional historians, who were particularly critical of Fogel and Engerman's conclusions regarding the mindset and behavior of enslaved African Americans, and of what they viewed, rightfully or wrongfully, as the authors' relatively benign depiction of the system of slavery itself.

Fogel issued an impressive rejoinder in 1989 with the publication of *Without Consent or Contract: The Rise and Fall of American Slavery*, which was followed in 1992 by two supplementary volumes of corroborative "technical papers" coedited by Fogel and Engerman. In the 1989 volume, Fogel, writing in a more subdued scholarly tone, defended much of the argument advanced in *Time on the Cross*, albeit with some qualifications, particularly in the section on the workings of the domestic slave trade.

Despite the study's many strengths, *Without Consent or Contract* did not make nearly the splash made by *Time on the Cross* fifteen years earlier. By the 1990s, the "new economic history" was no longer new, and many of Fogel and Engerman's "iconoclastic" 1974 findings on the economics of slavery seemed less jarring. Indeed, some had been more or less absorbed into the master narrative of American economic history.

If greater acceptance among the initiated helps to explain the rather subdued reception to *Without Consent or Contract*, the decline of economic history as a field of study was also a factor. By the early 1990s, few nonspecialists were paying attention to any work being done in this increasingly esoteric and marginalized area of study. Given this fact, it is not surprising that Fogel's receipt (along with Douglass C. North) of the Nobel Prize in Economic Sciences in 1993 for "applying economic theory and quantitative methods to historical puzzles" did not rekindle the high-profile debate over *Time on the Cross*. Even so, outside of the spotlight, major figures in economic history, such as Gavin Wright, have continued to spar with Fogel and Engerman over issues raised in their combustible 1974 study.

SEE ALSO *Cliometrics; Economics, Neoclassical; Engerman, Stanley; Fogel, Robert; Slave Lives, Archaeology of; Slave Resistance; Slavery*

BIBLIOGRAPHY

David, Paul, et al. 1976. *Reckoning with Slavery: A Critical Study in the Quantitative History of American Negro Slavery.* New York: Oxford University Press.

Fogel, Robert William. 1989. *Without Consent or Contract: The Rise and Fall of American Slavery.* New York: Norton.

Fogel, Robert William. 2003. *The Slavery Debates, 1952–1990.* Baton Rouge: Louisiana State University Press.

Fogel, Robert William, and Stanley L. Engerman. 1974. *Time on the Cross: The Economics of American Negro Slavery.* 2 vols. Boston: Little, Brown.

Fogel, Robert William, and Stanley L. Engerman, eds. 1992. *Without Consent or Contract: The Rise and Fall of American Slavery, Technical Papers.* 2 vols. New York: Norton.

Gutman, Herbert G. 1975. *Slavery and the Numbers Game: A Critique of* Time on the Cross. Urbana: University of Illinois Press.

Owsley, Frank L. 1949. *Plain Folk of the Old South.* Baton Rouge: Louisiana State University Press.

Smith, Mark M. 1998. *Debating Slavery: Economy and Society in the Antebellum American South.* Cambridge, U.K.: Cambridge University Press.

Wright, Gavin. 2006. *Slavery and American Economic Development.* Baton Rouge: Louisiana State University Press.

Peter A. Coclanis

TIME ORIENTATION

For centuries scientists and philosophers have been interested in the question of how the meaning of time is constructed and how people's thoughts, feelings, and behaviors are shaped by time-related considerations. In the *Critique of Pure Reason*, for instance, Immanuel Kant (1781) provides an outline of the psychological significance of time. Thus time perception is an innate ability that shapes the way people perceive the world. The emphasis on innateness, however, does not imply lack of variability across individuals. Indeed most scientists and philosophers in the early twenty-first century concur that time is a social phenomenon that is likely to be perceived and experienced differently across individuals, situations, and cultures.

Another source of inspiration for contemporary theorizing on time is the work of Kurt Lewin (1951). According to Lewin, to understand the behavior of an individual at a given time, it is necessary to consider all the forces acting on the person at that time, including past experiences in similar situations as well as his or her expectations about the future. In line with this reasoning, most models of self-regulation maintain that influences on goal pursuit can be partitioned into three time frames, namely *past experiences*, *present considerations*, and *expectations about the future*. For instance, according to Albert Bandura's (1997) self-efficacy theory, considerations about the past, present, and future are all consequential in determining people's beliefs about whether or not they can perform a behavior. Thus when people engage in a goal-driven activity, relevant past experiences as well as expectations about the future can be brought to the current stream of consciousness and affect the way they pursue their goals.

Considerations about time come into picture when people make decisions as well. Many decisions in everyday life involve a trade-off between the immediate and the delayed consequences of actions. An employee receiving a bonus, for instance, may be torn between saving this bonus for retirement (delayed gratification) and spending it right away for vacation (immediate gratification).

Confronting such a dilemma, some people focus on the immediate consequences of their actions (present-time orientation) and choose to spend the bonus for vacation; others are more concerned about the delayed outcomes of their actions (future-time orientation) and choose to add this bonus to the retirement fund. If people prefer one type of orientation over another repeatedly, these preferences may translate into habits or traitlike individual differences, which can in turn serve as cognitive biases toward being past, present, or future oriented.

Indeed various constructs have been proposed to address such differences in time orientations. For instance, the construct of *consideration of future consequences* (CFC) refers to "the extent to which people consider the potential distant outcomes of their current behaviors and the extent to which they are influenced by these potential outcomes" (Strathman et al. 1994, p. 743). Thus individuals low in CFC pay greater attention to the immediate consequences of their behaviors than to the delayed consequences of their behaviors. Individuals high in CFC, in contrast, pay greater attention to the delayed outcomes of their behaviors. The implications of CFC have been explored in a variety of contexts. For instance, future orientation has been consistently related to academic achievement, conscientiousness, less risk taking (e.g., safe sex), greater general concern with health and the environment (e.g., exercise frequently, consume less alcohol and tobacco, recycle), and more responsible consumption practices (e.g., less impulse buying). In line with this, present-time orientation has been shown to predict self-regulatory failures in a wide range of contexts. Presumably resisting temptations in a given context requires the ability to transcend that context, which is something future-oriented people seem more capable of doing than present-oriented people (for a review, see Strathman and Joireman 2005).

The fact that future orientation has been related to many positive consequences suggests that it may be the preferred time orientation. Indeed interventions have been designed to enhance future-time orientation and decrease present-time orientation. According to Philip G. Zimbardo and John N. Boyd (1999), however, encouraging people to focus on the future at the expense of the present time may not be a fruitful strategy because "life is lived in the present." Focusing too much on the future may lead people to miss out on the meaning of life. Thus a *balanced time orientation*, where people flexibly switch temporal frames depending on self-regulatory resources, situational pressures, and personal appraisals, may prove to be more adaptive than a time orientation that is exclusively biased in one direction. The implication is that somebody can be high on both present-time and future-time orientations. Thus unidimensional scales may fall short of capturing the complexity of time orientation.

SEE ALSO *Bandura, Albert; Discounted Present Value; Expectations; Farsightedness; Interest Rates; Lewin, Kurt; Risk; Scales; Self-Control; Self-Efficacy; Time Preference; Zimbardo, Philip*

BIBLIOGRAPHY

Bandura, Albert. 1997. *Self-Efficacy: The Exercise of Control.* New York: W. H. Freeman.

Kant, Immanuel. 1965. *Critique of Pure Reason.* Trans. Norman Kemp Smith. New York: St. Martin's. (Orig. pub. 1781.)

Lewin, Kurt. 1951. *Field Theory in Social Science: Selected Theoretical Papers*, ed. Dorwin Cartwright. New York: Harper.

Strathman, Alan, Faith Gleicher, David Boninger, and C. Scott Edwards. 1994. The Consideration of Future Consequences: Weighing Immediate and Distant Outcomes of Behavior. *Journal of Personality and Social Psychology* 66: 742–752.

Strathman, Alan, and Jeff Joireman, eds. 2005. *Understanding Behavior in the Context of Time: Theory, Research, and Application.* Mahwah, NJ: Erlbaum.

Zimbardo, Philip G., and John N. Boyd. 1999. Putting Time in Perspective: A Valid, Reliable Individual-Differences Metric. *Journal of Personality and Social Psychology* 77: 1271–1288.

Zeynep Cemalcilar
G. Tarcan Kumkale

TIME PREFERENCE

A person with a time preference favors having a good sooner rather than later. As a result, the person also prefers having a good immediately to having a somewhat greater good later. Having a time preference amounts to discounting the value of future goods. It may be a source of improvident behavior later regretted: Because of a time preference, someone may spend next month's rent money on a party and yet later, when the rent is due, would rather pay the rent than have had the party.

A leading member of the Austrian School of economics, Eugen von Böhm-Bawerk ([1884, 1889, 1921] 1959) appeals to time preference to justify payment of interest. Because people would rather have goods now than have identical goods later, he concludes that people who borrow capital should pay for its use. Refining this view, Irving Fisher (1930) attributes a community's interest rate, an indication of the community's preference for a dollar of present income over a dollar of future income, to time preference together with the value of investment opportunity.

Böhm-Bawerk also uses time preference to explain profits from business ventures. An employer pays for labor and other factors of production. Payments occur before products are sold. The payments plus profits equal the products' price. The profits are the employer's compensation for postponing consumption of the amount of payments until the products are sold. The prevailing rate of profit depends on the prevailing degree of time preference and is equal to the prevailing rate of interest. Although short-term profits may not equal the rate of interest, long-term profits do. Economists elaborating this view argue that time preference is just a partial explanation of profits. Other relevant factors are the uncertainty of a product's sale price and the influence of the supply of money on sale price.

Studies in psychology measure time preference. Harrell Chesson and W. Kip Viscusi (2000) infer the temporal discount rate of subjects from their choices. Subjects stated their choices between an amount of money in a fixed number of years and a gamble that pays either that amount of money in a smaller number of years or in a larger number of years. Chesson and Viscusi discovered that the subjects' choices do not maximize time-discounted expected consumption. More surprisingly, they discovered that some groups have discount rates different from the rates commonly attributed to them. For example, smokers have a lower discount rate than nonsmokers do, and therefore they do not disregard future consequences more than others do. Chesson and Viscusi conjectured that smokers simply have tastes and perceptions of risk different from those of nonsmokers. Also, contrary to the common view that youth is impatient, Chesson and Viscusi found that older subjects have higher discount rates than younger subjects have. Shorter life expectancies may explain older subjects' greater impatience to receive benefits.

Philip Trostel and Grant Taylor (2001) similarly argue that time preference increases as a person ages. Because of declining abilities, an aging person increasingly prefers consumption now to consumption later. Trostel and Taylor find that this effect is independent of a decline in the probability of survival.

Viscusi and Joel Huber (2006) examined revealed rates of time preference for public goods, such as water quality. They measured a person's impatience to receive a public good and divided that impatience into a component due to time preference and a component due to the person's perceived probability of not living long enough to benefit from the public good. According to their data, people display hyperbolic discounting rather than the exponential discounting most theorists assume. According to exponential discounting, if a good arrives in T years and the interest rate is r, then the discount rate for the good is δ^T with $\delta = 1/(1 + r)$. According to quasi-hyperbolic discounting, the form of hyperbolic discounting that Viscusi and Huber investigated, the discount rate is $\lambda\delta^T$

with a parameter λ such that $0 < \lambda < 1$. Their data show a high rate of time preference for immediate improvements and substantially lower rates of time preference for later improvements. This sharp decline in the rate of time preference is inconsistent with exponential discounting, but is consistent with hyperbolic discounting. The rate of time preference also varies among groups of subjects. Subjects who are old especially disliked delays in provision of public goods.

Economists characterize time preference as discounting future goods. Does time preference apply to goods that are dated, for example, dated commodity bundles? Because the value of a commodity bundle with a future date is already discounted for time, discounting the dated bundle for time results in an unwarranted double discount. For generality, philosophers characterize time preference as discounting future desires. A person with a time preference gives less weight now to satisfaction of a future desire than the person will give to satisfaction of the future desire when the desire occurs. The person's discount applies to reasons for acts rather than to consequences of acts.

Philosophers and economists debate the rationality of time preference. Discounting future goods because of uncertainty is plainly reasonable, so the debate considers primarily the rationality of pure time preference, that is, discounting future goods just because they are future. Robert Strotz (1956) finds that clear-thinking people display pure time preference, and so concludes that pure time preference is rational.

Paul Weirich (1981) takes doing what one knows one will regret as a sign of time preference. Acting that way discounts future desires that generate regret. Foreknowledge of regret eliminates discounting because of uncertainty. Treating only future desires that are rational eliminates another reason for discounting. Suppose that in some cases it is rational to do what one knows one will rationally regret; then it is rational to have a pure time preference. One rationally prefers satisfaction of present desires to satisfaction of future desires just because the present desires are present. Basic goals change over time. Suppose that basic goals now and in the future are similarly rational although they differ. Then one may rationally not care now about satisfying a future rational desire. Suppose that one makes decisions using rational, all-things-considered desires that take account of all relevant reasons, including promotion of future desires' satisfaction. A decision to perform an act is then rational, even if it leads to foreseen regret because of foreseen changes in basic goals. Doing what one knows one will regret, a manifestation of pure time preference, may be rational.

Derek Parfit reviews time preference's treatment by Plato, Jeremy Bentham, and David Hume (1984, pp. 158–163). He characterizes time preference as caring less about the further future, and calls it a "bias toward the near." If two future goods that are identical in features an agent cares about are separated by a period of time, a bias toward the near may lead an agent, relative to the first good, to discount the second good. Suppose that the discount increases as the first good comes nearer, and is highest when the first good arrives. Then the agent will have trouble keeping resolutions. The agent may for receipt of a sum of money agree to forego the first good and wait for the second good when both goods are far off. When the first good is imminent, the agent may pay a larger sum to have the first good rather than wait for the second. The agent's temporal discounting causes a preference reversal.

Whether an agent is subject to such preference reversals depends on the agent's type of discounting. If an agent has an exponential discount rate, and discounts the future at the same n percent per unit of time, then relative to the first good, the second good always receives the same discount no matter how near the two goods are. Given an exponential discount rate, no preference reversals arise.

Many philosophers hold that a bias toward the near, which is independent of uncertainty concerning the future, arises from lack of imagination. Because of shortsightedness, an imminent pleasure is more vivid than a remote pleasure. The difference in vividness is a poor reason for a preference, however. A person with a bias for the near, for example, postpones pains at the cost of making them worse. It is irrational to care more about the nearer future just because it is nearer. Although Parfit acknowledges that because of a foreseen change in desires one may do what one knows one will regret (p. 189), he concludes that one should care about one's self-interest in a temporally neutral way. This neutrality is incompatible with a pure time preference.

SEE ALSO *Farsightedness; Interest Rates*

BIBLIOGRAPHY

Böhm-Bawerk, Eugen von. [1884, 1889, 1921] 1959. *Capital and Interest.* Trans. George Hunke and Hans Sennholz. South Holland, IL: Libertarian Press.

Chesson, Harrell, and W. Kip Viscusi. 2000. The Heterogeneity of Time-Risk Tradeoffs. *Journal of Behavioral Decision Making* 13: 251–258.

Fisher, Irving. 1930. *The Theory of Interest.* New York: Macmillan.

Parfit, Derek. 1984. *Reasons and Persons.* Oxford: Clarendon Press.

Strotz, Robert. 1956. Myopia and Inconsistency in Dynamic Utility Maximization. *Review of Economic Studies* 23: 165–180.

Trostel, Philip, and Grant Taylor. 2001. A Theory of Time Preference. *Economic Inquiry* 39: 379–395.

Viscusi, W. Kip, and Joel Huber. 2006. *Hyperbolic Discounting of Public Goods.* Harvard Law and Economics Discussion Paper No. 543. http://ssrn.com/abstract=921425.

Weirich, Paul. 1981. A Bias of Rationality. *Australasian Journal of Philosophy* 59: 31–37.

Paul Weirich

TIME SERIES REGRESSION

Consider two random variables, *y* and *x*. A *regression* of *y* on *x* is a model of the mean (or average) of *y*, conditional on values of *x*. It is thus a common statistical tool for analyzing how *x* might influence *y*. If a sample of values of *y* and *x* is observed in sequence over a period of time, this model is called a *time series regression.*

Time series regressions are distinct from cross-sectional regressions, in which observed values vary across similar units at a point in, or averaged across, time. For example, a researcher interested in the effect of income on consumer expenditures might rely on a cross-sectional regression model of expenditures of individual households during the year 2006 on household income during that same year. On the other hand, other researchers interested in overall consumer behavior might utilize a time series regression of aggregate consumer expenditures and income as they vary from year to year.

The distinguishing aspect of time series regression models is the common presence of *serial dependence*—a correspondence of values at different points in time—which does not typically arise in cross-sectional data. In time series regressions, there is a sense in which the order of the observations matters. Indeed, one of the important functions of time series regressions is to estimate and characterize this dependence on time and to determine how different variables fluctuate together over time. Serial dependence presents practical and conceptual problems that typically do not occur in cross-sectional applications.

Regression models of the mean of a random variable trace back to Francis Galton's 1877 work on the hereditary effects of parent sweet pea seeds on their offspring. The first person to apply regression analysis to economic data is most likely Udny Yule (1895), who investigated the effect of types of government relief on pauperism in England in the late nineteenth century using cross-section data. Time series regressions and correlation analysis in economics begin to appear at about the same time in later work by Yule (1899) and in important studies by Reginald Hooker (1901) and John Norton (1902). This research grappled with many unique issues arising in time series

regressions, such as trends and time lag effects (Klein 1997, chapter 9).

In a time series regression of *y* on *x*, the random variable *y* is called the dependent variable, because the model shows how its mean depends on the vector of *k* regressors, or independent or explanatory variables, *x*. Formally, we may write the regression model as

$$y_t = \beta' x_t + \varepsilon_t, \quad t = 1 \dots T, \quad (1)$$

where β is a $k \times 1$ vector of constant parameters or coefficients (independent of time), ε is a random error with mean zero and variance σ^2, and the sample period is assumed to run from period *t* to period *T*. The subscript *t* on the random variables denotes a particular point in time or period of time, so it is understood that these random variables vary over time. Since there are *k* explanatory variables, the model is in general a multiple regression model. We interpret any particular β coefficient as measuring the marginal effect of a change in the corresponding explanatory variable at time *t* on the expected value of *y* at time *t*, holding all other explanatory variables constant.

The model in effect decomposes the random variable y_t into its mean conditional on x_t and a random error. The conditional mean is given by $E(y_t|x_t) = \beta' x_t + E(\varepsilon_t|x_t) = \beta' x_t$, in light of the zero mean assumption of ε, and is assumed to be linear in the explanatory variables. If *y* and *x* are jointly normally distributed, this linearity assumption will hold exactly. Linearity implies that the marginal effects of the explanatory variables are independent of the values of these variables.

Given a sample of time series data on *y* and *x*, the regression in (1) can be estimated. Estimation assigns specific values to the unknown parameters to identify the specific probability distribution that most likely generated this sample. Once the regression has been estimated, it can be used for making inference about theory, for forecasting, or for understanding the effects of policy actions.

The key assumption of the regression model is that the expected value of the error term is independent of the explanatory variables

$$E(\varepsilon_t | x_1, x_2, \dots, x_t) = E(\varepsilon_t) = 0, \quad (2)$$

which is assumed to hold for all *t* in the sample. This assumption is called the *strict exogeneity* of the vector *x*. It implies that the systematic relationship between *y* and *x* is fully captured by the model for conditional mean, so that deviations of *y* from this mean are purely random. It follows that under strict exogeneity the error term is *orthogonal* to each of the regressors (the expected value of their product is zero) and that the covariances between the error and each of the regressors is zero. It also implies that least squares estimates of β are unbiased in small samples—no matter the size of the sample, the expected value of this estimator of β is equal to its true value.

A common case in which strict exogeneity does not hold is the autoregressive model, in which the conditional mean of y depends on its past values (for example, $x_t = y_{t-1}$). It should be clear that $E(\varepsilon_{t-1}|x_t) = E(\varepsilon_{t-1}|y_{t-1})$ does not equal zero in this case, as required by strict exogeneity. For such lagged dependent variable models, least squares estimators are biased in small samples. However, they will be unbiased in large samples, even when strict exogeneity does not hold if the regressors are *predetermined*: $E(x_{it}\varepsilon_t) = 0$ for all $i = 1, \dots, k$.

Both strict exogeneity and predeterminedness often break down in applications in the social sciences because of *simultaneity bias*. Such bias in estimating a time series regression occurs when the explanatory variable is influenced by the dependent variable or when common factors jointly affect both dependent and independent variables. *Instrumental variables* methods are a common approach to dealing with this problem; an instrument for x is a variable related to the dependent variable y only through its association with the explanatory variable x. In general, the appropriate use of theory to guide the selection of instruments and other identifying restrictions is essential to solving the simultaneity problem.

Another important assumption of the basic time series regression model is that the error term is *serially uncorrelated*: $E\varepsilon_t\varepsilon_s = 0$ for all $t \neq s$. This condition means that past observations of the error term do not help forecast future values. If this condition holds (along with strict exogeneity), the least squares estimator of β is efficient in the sense that, of all the linear, unbiased estimators of β, the least squares estimator has the lowest sampling variance. If the error term is serially correlated, least squares estimators of β will remain unbiased as long as x is strictly exogenous, but will be inefficient. Generalized least squares methods allow efficient estimation of β in the presence of serial correlation.

The autoregressive model with lagged dependent variables noted above is an example of a more general family of time series regression models that can capture the complex dynamic interactions that typically characterize time series data in the social sciences. A dynamic regression, sometimes called a *distributed lag model*, is given by

$$
\begin{aligned}
y_t = a_0 + a_1 y_{t-1} + \dots + a_p y_{t-p} \\
+ b_0 x_t + b_1 x_{t-1} + \dots + b_q x_{t-q} + \varepsilon_t
\end{aligned}
\tag{3}
$$

Note that this model specifically accounts for serial correlation in the dependent variable through the a coefficients, while allowing direct dynamic interactions with x through the b coefficients. For example, the coefficient b_3

measures the marginal effect (holding all other variables at all other times fixed) of a small change in the value of x three periods ago on the current value of the dependent variable.

Many time series variables wander over time without an apparent tendency to revert to mean. A dynamic process exhibiting this type of behavior is called a *stochastic trend* process, an example of which is the *random walk*. The best predictor of the current value of a random walk process is last period's value; the change in a random walk is unpredictable. Time series regressions that involve random walks, or more generally stochastic trends, may lead to invalid results and inappropriate inference.

Suppose that y and x each follow a random walk. As shown by Granger and Newbold (1974), a simple time series regression of y_t on x_t will reveal a strong correspondence between the two variables, even if they are, in fact, unrelated. That is, the estimated relationship between the two independent random walks will be spurious. The common solution to this spurious regression problem in the presence of stochastic trends is to either (1) estimate the time series regression after transforming the data into first-differences (i.e., instead of regressing y_t on x_t, regress $(y_t - y_{t-1})$ on $(x_t - x_{t-1})$; or (2) regress y_t on x_t, but include lagged y and lagged x as explanatory variables.

SEE ALSO *Autoregressive Models; Regression*

BIBLIOGRAPHY

Galton, Francis. 1877. Typical Laws of Heredity. *Proceedings of the Royal Institution* 8: 282–301.

Granger, Clive W. J., and Paul Newbold. 1974. Spurious Regressions in Econometrics. *Journal of Econometrics* 2: 111–120.

Hamilton, James D. 1994. *Time Series Analysis*. Princeton, NJ: Princeton University Press.

Harvey, Andrew. 1990. *The Econometric Analysis of Time Series*. Cambridge, MA: MIT Press.

Hooker, Reginald. 1901. Correlation of the Marriage Rate with Trade. *Journal of the Royal Statistical Society* 64: 485–492.

Klein, Judy L. 1997. *Statistical Visions in Time: A History of Time Series Analysis, 1662–1938*. Cambridge, U.K.: Cambridge University Press.

Norton, John. 1902. *Statistical Studies in the New York Money Market*. New York: Macmillan.

Yule, Udny. 1895. On the Correlation of Total Pauperism with Proportion of Out-Relief. *Economic Journal* 5: 603–623.

Yule, Udny. 1899. An Investigation into the Causes of Changes in Pauperism in England, Chiefly during the Last Two Intercensal Decades (Part I). *Journal of the Royal Statistical Society* 62: 249–295.

William D. Lastrapes

TIME TRENDS

A *time trend*, or *time index*, is the ordered set of natural numbers, for example, $t = (1,2,3,4 \ldots)$, that measures the time span between observations. The slope of a time-trend line represents the growth of a variable. For example, a time-trend line may be used to illustrate growth in production or industry earnings. To predict or explain economic variables, regression equations often use time trends. There are three main reasons for introducing time trends in regression equations that use time-series data. One reason is that a time trend captures the trajectory of the variable over time, providing forecasts of an economic variable. A second reason is that a time trend captures the effect of relevant variables in the regression equation that change over time and are not directly measurable. For example, in the estimation of production functions, Thomas Cooley and Edward Prescott (1973) use a trend variable as a proxy for technological change. A third advantage is that the time trend may capture specification error in regression equations that stem from functional form choice or variable aggregation.

Both linear and nonlinear time trends may be used in regression equations. The assumption in the linear-trend model is that changes will continue into the future at the same or similar rate. This assumption is particularly restrictive when only more recent observations contribute to explaining the future. A more flexible form is a linear trend under a spline-functional form (nonlinear time trend). The spline function jointly determines the trajectory and the memory of the series by allowing the slope of the time trend to vary across time. For example, the rate of change in the price of gasoline may vary across time. In this case, a time trend in a spline function allows the forecasting model to switch the slope parameters with the current economic regime. Both linear and nonlinear time-trend functions may be used in forecasting economic series such as prices, inventories, productivity, and consumption.

In addition to its uses in forecasting, a time trend serves as a proxy for nonmeasurable variables when explaining economic relationships, and it is commonly used in consumption models as well as in models that explain production, employment, and other factors of production. For example, food consumption is often specified as a function of personal disposable income, the price of food, the price of other goods, and a time trend. The time trend captures changes in consumer preferences.

A time trend also captures omitted information from specification error that stems from functional form choice or variable aggregation in the regression equation. The effectiveness of a time trend as a proxy for the omitted information from specification error depends on its correlation to included and excluded information in the regression equation, as well as the choice of functional form for the time trend in the equation. In a simulation study, Camilo Sarmiento and Richard Just (2005) provide evidence that a time trend is able to capture variation of the aggregation error (a special form of specification error) in aggregate consumption functions more effectively than methods based on conceptually accurate, time-specific approximations.

Clive Granger (2001) indicates the potential and unexplored uses of varying coefficients to approximate functional form in applications that use time series data. A time trend as an interaction variable in the model can be used to introduce time-varying coefficients and, thus, approximate unobserved functional structure in economic models, while reducing dimensionality issues in the specification of the functional form from the *m*-dimensional space (number of explanatory variables in the model) to the simpler one-dimensional space. The functional form for the time trend as an interactive variable in the regression equation could be linear or nonlinear. Significant empirical work and simulation analysis is needed in this area.

The popularity of a time trend in many economic models stems from its simplicity and intuitive interpretation. Statistical tests may be used to evaluate the effectiveness of time trends in forecasting and regression equations. Effectiveness depends largely on the application. The choice of time trend as a tool in model building involves not only whether to include a time trend and its functional form (spline function), but also whether to include it as an interactive variable.

BIBLIOGRAPHY

Cooley, Thomas F., and Edward C. Prescott. 1973. Systematic (Non-random) Varying Parameter Regression: A Theory and Some Applications. *Annals of Economic and Social Measurement* 16: 463–474.

Granger, Clive W. J. 2001. Macroeconomics: Past and Future. *Journal of Econometrics* 100: 17–19.

Sarmiento, Camilo, and Richard E. Just. 2005. Empirical Modelling of the Aggregation Error in the Representative Consumer Model. *Applied Economics* 37: 1163–1175.

Camilo Sarmiento

TIME USE SURVEYS

SEE *Time Allocation.*

TIME-AND-A-HALF

Since 1938 the U.S. Fair Labor Standards Act (FLSA) has required that most wage earners be paid one-and-a-half times their regular hourly pay rate for weekly hours worked above forty. This rate is comparatively high. Whereas South Korea and most Canadian provinces also require a 50 percent overtime premium, France, Germany, and Italy require a smaller 25 percent, collective bargaining sets overtime premiums in the United Kingdom, and New Zealand has no overtime regulation. Countries' overtime regulations also differ in other aspects, such as the standard weekly hours beyond which the overtime premium applies, the types of jobs exempt from overtime regulations, and whether the regulation stipulates maximum weekly hours. An increasing number of countries allow employers to average work hours over the year rather than the week, greatly decreasing overtime payments.

The 1938 FLSA described its rationale as "the maintenance of the minimum standard of living necessary for health, efficiency and general well-being." It gained union support because it made union labor more competitive. However, an additional major motivation behind overtime regulations, both during the Great Depression of the 1930s and the high unemployment of Europe in the 1980s and 1990s, is to increase employment.

Whether overtime regulation indeed has a salutary impact on employment is ambiguous even in the short run. An overtime premium will immediately increase the marginal cost of additional hours per week, thus decreasing the weekly hours of those previously working more than forty hours, decreasing national work hours, and creating many jobs of exactly standard hours (e.g., forty). Whether this also increases employment depends on the substitutability between labor and capital and between different types of labor, scale effects, and on other labor regulations and institutions.

Once contracts can be renegotiated, however, economic theory suggests that an overtime premium can easily be undone by an implicit contract reducing the straight-time wage rate until workers get the same weekly pay and work the same hours as before the regulation. Consequently employment would not change. This does not apply to minimum or near-minimum wage jobs, because straight-time pay rates cannot fall sufficiently to offset the premium.

The best empirical work studies the impact of new or tightened overtime regulations. Average hours decline for those earning at or near the minimum wage or when straight-time wages are not allowed to fall for other regulatory or institutional reasons. Similarly the FLSA permanently decreased overtime hours (over forty) and increased the number of people working exactly forty hours, perhaps because of minimum wage jobs. Extensions of U.S. overtime regulations to new groups of more highly paid workers have not significantly affected weekly hours, corroborating theoretical predictions.

Studies of decreases in standard time in Europe generally find that standard time and average weekly hours move together. These studies, however, do not isolate exogenous changes and therefore should not be used to impute causality. The employment effects of lower standard hours or otherwise tighter overtime legislation in European, U.S., and Japanese labor markets have typically been found to be zero or negative, although these studies are subject to the same criticisms regarding causality.

BIBLIOGRAPHY

Hart, Robert A. 2004. *The Economics of Overtime Working.* Cambridge, U.K.: Cambridge University Press.

Trejo, Stephen J. 2003. Does the Statutory Overtime Premium Discourage Long Workweeks? *Industrial and Labor Relations Review* 56 (3): 530–551.

Shulamit Kahn

TINBERGEN, JAN
1903–1994

When the Nobel Foundation initiated an award in economic sciences in memory of Alfred Nobel, it was no surprise that the first award in 1969 went jointly to Jan Tinbergen and Ragnar Frisch (1895–1937), two leading figures in the formation of the Econometric Society and the establishment of a new branch of economics early in the twentieth century.

Jan Tinbergen, like other economic scholars, began academic studies in science, but switched to economics and carried the mathematical background that became the hallmark of the new branch of economics. He made numerous original contributions to economic analysis, theory, and practice, but his greatest single contribution was in constructing the first working econometric models of a system as a whole, first for Holland, and later, for the United States. In the latter study, he was searching for a system that would enable economists to find the most satisfactory model of the business cycle. In that respect he tried to find a statistical representation of the ideas expressed by John Maynard Keynes (1883–1946) and his followers at Cambridge University during the years of the Great Depression in the 1930s. Although he did not uncover *the* secret of the cycle, he did succeed in laying the groundwork for empirical macroeconometric model building, in spite of Keynes's dislike of Tinbergen's approach, which Keynes did not fully understand. Tinbergen's U.S. model prominently displayed the role of income distribution, the wealth effect, and some model specifications that would lead eventually to a well-established relation between wages and unemployment. The wealth effect, which is now investigated on a broad scale, came about through Tinbergen's idea that price movements on the stock exchange played an important role in explaining the U.S. downturn after 1929.

It is important to note that Tinbergen made his pioneering contribution to macroeconometric model building in a dynamic framework at a time when usable national data were sparse and computational facilities were primitive. His work is being carried on and extended now with unusually better national accounts, frequency of data reporting, improved economic concepts, and enormous computer power with speed, all to make the tasks of econometric model building for the succeeding generation much easier for those who learned basics from Jan Tinbergen.

Tinbergen made early studies of income distribution and elasticity of substitution in international trade. He was dedicated to strong pacifist views. After World War II (1939–1945) he headed the Central Planning Bureau of the Netherlands and devoted his life to many worthy social causes; at the very end of his life he was soliciting help from colleagues and friends worldwide to support efforts against exploitation of children. He had a very systematic mind and conceived principles of economic planning, based on the clever separation, and distinctive properties of economic policy *instruments* and *targets*. Many politicians fail to make the appropriate distinction. In his exposition of policy formation in economics and in his work as director of the Central Planning Bureau, he made such distinctions clear.

Throughout his career, he trained many Dutch students in economics and also attracted many from abroad, especially after World War II. He is remembered as a person who led an exemplary life with simple tastes, great generosity, and a deep social conscience. In addition to his activities aimed at protecting children worldwide, Jan Tinbergen was a founding supporter of Economists Against the Arms Race (ECAAR) during the cold war. In line with his charitable instincts, during the immediate post–World War II period he generally carried cigarettes for a supplement to service fees such as taxi fares, even though he was a nonsmoker.

BIBLIOGRAPHY

De Wolff, Pieter. 1983. Jan Tinbergen als Modellen Bouwer. *Economisch-Statistische Berichten* 68: 308–311.

Keynes, John Maynard. 1939. Professor Tinbergen's Method. *The Economic Journal* 49: 558–568.

Tinbergen, Jan. 1939. *Statistical Testing of Business Cycle Theories. II. Business Cycles in the United States of America, 1919–1932.* Geneva, Switzerland: League of Nations.

Tinbergen, Jan. On a Method of Statistical Business Cycle Research: A Reply. *The Economic Journal* 50: 141–154.

Tinbergen, Jan. 1946. Some Measurements of Elasticities of Substitution. *Review of Economic Statistics* 28 (August): 109–116.

Tinbergen, Jan. 1950. Note on the Measurement of Elasticity of Substitution in International Trade. *Review of Economics and Statistics* 32 (February): 20–21.

Tingbergen, Jan. 1951. *Business Cycles in the United Kingdom, 1870–1914.* Amsterdam: North-Holland.

Tinbergen, Jan. 1952. *On the Theory of Economic Policy.* Amsterdam: North-Holland.

Tinbergen, Jan. 1956. *Economic Policy: Principles and Design.* Amsterdam: North-Holland.

Tinbergen, Jan. 1956. On the Theory of Income Distribution. *Weltwirtschaftliches Archiv* 77: 10–31.

Tinbergen, Jan. 1959. An Economic Policy for 1936. In *Jan Tinbergen Selected Papers*, eds. L. H. Klassen, Leen M. Koyck, and H. Johannes Witteveen, 37–84. Amsterdam: North-Holland.

Lawrence R. Klein

TITO (JOSIP BROZ)
1892–1980

Josip Broz "Tito" was born in Kumrovec, Croatia, on May 7, 1892. His first contact with political and social issues came in October of 1920 when he joined a union of metallurgy workers. In 1929, because of his active participation as political agitator, he was imprisoned for five years. After his release in 1934, he became a member of the Political Bureau of the Central Committee of the Communist Party, then located in Vienna, Austria, and in 1937 he became the Secretary General of the Central Committee of Yugoslavia.

After the German invasion of Yugoslavia in 1941, Tito became the national leader in the fight against the foreign occupation. It is during this period that his role as the leader of the Yugoslav people became clear, and he was soon able to attract a much wider base of support. His charismatic personality, his successful military guerrilla tactics, and his idea of a united Yugoslavia had a wide appeal. In addition to the Communists, he was joined by various resistance groups, such as the Chetniks of Draža Mihajlović, the Serbian resistance leader. After the liberation of the country in November 1943, Tito negotiated what would become the Socialist Federal Republic of Yugoslavia and became marshall of the new Yugoslav government.

TITO'S LEGACY

Tito ruled Yugoslavia as prime minister and chief of defense from 1945 until 1980. His ruling style appealed to both communists and noncommunists, and he unified Yugoslavia in a more liberal form of communism, commonly referred to as "Titoism." However, this independence from mainstream communism created a schism between Tito and Joseph Stalin, the Soviet Communist Party leader, in 1948.

Although Tito succeeded in unifying the Yugoslav people, he faced many challenges in keeping this unification peaceful. Many viewed Yugoslavia as a single unified nation, but it was actually a federation of different republics and two autonomous regions. Tito was trying to hold this federation together by fighting nationalistic tendencies in both the Serbs and Croats. He also had to heal the wounds accumulated during the area's war-torn past. One way Tito preserved the nation was through a more liberal economic policy that enabled the Yugoslavs to travel and often work in Western European countries. This policy contributed to the stability of the period. Tito's open policy toward both the West and the East contributed to good relations with various nations that were otherwise politically opposed to each other. As a result, citizens of some communist European countries, such as Czechoslovakia or Hungary, could vacation in Yugoslavia, where they were joined by Western European tourists from Germany and Italy. Furthermore, in 1961 the first conference of the states of the Non-Aligned Movement was held in Belgrade. In 1971, Tito established a twenty-two member collective presidency, which was composed of the presidents of the six republics and the two autonomous provincial assemblies, in addition to fourteen members chosen from the republican and provincial assemblies for five-year terms. Tito was elected chairman of the new presidency.

While his policy of openness provided positive economic incentives to Yugoslavs, Croats and Slovenes benefited more than those in the other regions because of their proximity to Western Europe. Being the most economically advanced in Yugoslavia, the Croats and Slovenes resented having to transfer their profits to the poorer regions of Yugoslavia, which was a way for Tito to minimize discrepancies and redistribute wealth. This inequality between republics fueled increased nationalistic feelings from states such as Serbia and Macedonia, which did not benefit as much from the same trade. Croat and Serb nationalists who promoted independence were exiled, and many were assassinated in their new countries of exile, where they were planning insurgencies to break up Yugoslavia. Many were also sent into forced labor camps in different parts of Yugoslavia.

Tito's legacy came under threat in the 1970s. The economic downturn in the 1970s came as a consequence of rising foreign debt, inflation, and economic inefficiencies. Furthermore, Croatian nationalist secessionists were pressuring for independence, and Tito had to crack down on them by tightening the dictatorship. However, upon his death in 1980, the nationalist sentiments came to the surface and exploded in what became the Yugoslav civil war, which led to the breakup of the federation in the early 1990s.

YUGOSLAVIA AFTER COMMUNISM

As a consequence of ethnic tensions, the breakup of Yugoslavia in the 1990s was seen by some as inevitable after fifty years of Tito's suppression of the Croat and Serb nationalist movements. First, Slovenia and Croatia, the two most economically advanced republics of the federation, were no longer willing to be tightly controlled by the central government and share their economic wealth through redistribution to poorer republics. The disappearance of Tito's tight control also created an opportunity for Croats to declare independence, while the Serbian nationalists wanted to preserve a claim over Yugoslav territories, including Croatia. The war eventually spilled into the republic of Bosnia and Herzegovina, which to this day remains divided into cantons.

SEE ALSO *Communism; Non-alignment; World War II*

BIBLIOGRAPHY

Auty, Phyllis. 1970. *Tito: A Biography.* New York: McGraw-Hill.

West, Richard. 1994. *Tito and the Rise and Fall of Yugoslavia.* New York: Carroll and Graff.

Dagmar Radin

TOBACCO INDUSTRY

The tobacco industry's main tobacco products are smoking tobacco (including cigarettes, cigars, and pipe tobacco), chewing tobacco, and snuff. The use of cigarettes as a means of consuming tobacco is relatively recent, beginning around the start of the twentieth century. Six states in the United States produce most of the U.S. tobacco: Georgia, Kentucky, North Carolina, South Carolina, Tennessee, and Virginia. Internationally, the United States is in somewhat of a unique position in that it is simultaneously a big tobacco-producing and a big tobacco-consuming country. On one hand, some countries, such as Malawi and Zimbabwe, produce tobacco at low costs but consume relatively little. On the other hand, the European Union (EU) and Japan are heavy tobacco consumers but relatively little tobacco is grown there. About 100 countries produce tobacco, but Brazil, China, India, Malawi, Turkey, the United States, and Zimbabwe together produce over 80 percent of the world's tobacco. China is the biggest producer of tobacco, while the United States is the biggest tobacco exporter in the world. In 2002, unfinished tobacco and tobacco product exports contributed $1.7 billion to the U.S. trade balance (Capehart 2001).

Tobacco use across the globe remains significant. According to the World Health Organization (WHO), globally, approximately half the men and about a tenth of women smoke. Smoking in developing nations has been increasing faster than that in the developed world. Since the 1960s, governments across the world have tried to control cigarette consumption (smoking) using various measures. Most governments now have some sort of anti-smoking policies in place. Initially these policies were driven by concerns regarding the health of smokers, while more recently the health of nonsmokers (dangers of second-hand smoke) has also become a concern.

SMOKING-CONTROL MEASURES

Generally policy makers have used both price and non-price measures to combat smoking. Whereas there is now a relatively good understanding of the effectiveness of tobacco control policies in developed nations, under-standing of the effectiveness of such policies in developing nations is not so good. In addition, smoking behaviors of different population subgroups are slowly being under-stood. Price measures are primarily based on reducing smoking using higher cigarette prices driven by higher taxes. The responsiveness of cigarette demand to cigarette tax increases is at the heart of how effective tax-based smoking control policies can be. The effectiveness of price measures, however, may be limited by the habit-forming nature of cigarettes and their low price responsiveness of demand. Conversely, demand unresponsiveness provides greater opportunities for tax revenue generation by governments. Relatively speaking the few studies of developing countries have largely found a higher demand responsiveness implying that dollar-for-dollar, there may be greater smoking reduction opportunities in developing nations than in developed countries (Jha and Chaloupka 2000; U.S. Department of Health and Human Services 2000). Nonprice smoking control measures include numerous initiatives such as cigarette advertising bans (Saffer and Chaloupka 2000), health warnings on cigarette packages, and territorial restrictions (such as workplace and public-place smoking bans and restrictions on sales of tobacco products to minors).

In 1964 the U.S. Surgeon General issued a report warning about the negative health effects of smoking. While the United States was at the forefront of legislating smoking-related health warnings beginning in 1965, other countries have since enacted more restrictive requirements. There has been a ban on the broadcast advertising of cigarettes in the United States since 1971. In 1998, forty-six states in the United States and the key cigarette/smokeless tobacco products producers signed a master settlement agreement (MSA) to reimburse states for costs imposed due to negative health effects of smoking. The main provisions of the MSA include cash payments to the states, advertising restrictions, support for antismoking measures, and disbanding of tobacco-industry trade organizations. Payments were also to be made to tobacco growers to compensate them for the decrease in the tobacco demand (Capehart 2001; Viscusi 2002). In 2003 the WHO drafted a framework convention on tobacco control that included numerous restrictions on the sale and marketing of tobacco products.

EFFECTIVENESS OF SMOKING-CONTROL POLICIES

The extent of the effectiveness of these policy measures remains to be seen. Further, in spite of the stringent restrictions imposed by the various measures, technological advances, especially the spread of the Internet, make it virtually impossible to effectively regulate the marketing and sale of tobacco products. Effectiveness may be improved by comprehensive tobacco control policies in which lawmakers pay attention to consumption substitutability among tobacco products as more effective control policies are enacted on one product. At the macro level policy makers face the dilemma of replacing export revenues generated by tobacco products with other revenues. So how can curbs on domestic sales of tobacco be reconciled with encouragement of tobacco exports? The long-term future of the tobacco industry seems somewhat uncertain given all the attention and resources being devoted to smoking control. However, the habit-forming nature of their products, huge industry cash reserves, and the ability to launch newer tobacco products seem to promise a very long tobacco-control road.

BIBLIOGRAPHY

Capehart, Thomas C. 2001. U.S. Tobacco Industry Responding to New Competitors, New Challenges. *Amber Waves: The Economics of Food, Farming, and Natural Resources, and Rural America.* U.S. Department of Agriculture, Economic Research Service. www.ers.usda.gov/AmberWaves/September03/Features/USTobaccoIndustry.htm.

Chaloupka, Frank J., and Kenneth E. Warner. 2000. The Economics of Smoking. In *Handbook of Health Economics.*

Vol. 1, eds. Anthony J. Culyer and Joseph P. Newhouse, 1539–1627. Amsterdam: Elsevier.

Gallet, Craig A., and J. A. List. 2003. Cigarette Demand: A Meta-Analysis of Elasticities. *Health Economics* 12 (10): 821–835.

Jha, Prabhat, and Frank J. Chaloupka. 2000. *Tobacco Control in Developing Countries.* Oxford: Oxford University Press.

Saffer, Henry, and Frank J. Chaloupka. 2000. Tobacco Advertising: Economic Theory and International Evidence. *Journal of Health Economics.* 19 (6): 1117–1137.

U.S. Department of Health and Human Services, U.S. Public Health Service. 2000. *Reducing Tobacco Use: A Report of the Surgeon General.* Washington, DC: U.S. Government Printing Office.

Viscusi, W. Kip. 2002. *Smoke-Filled Rooms: A Postmortem on the Tobacco Deal.* Chicago: University of Chicago Press.

Rajeev K. Goel

TOBIN, JAMES
1918–2002

James Tobin, winner of the 1981 Nobel Memorial Prize in Economics, was among the leaders of postwar economics, with several significant contributions that now bear his name. Tobin was born in 1918 in Champaign, Illinois. Educated in economics at Harvard, he earned an AB in 1939, an AM in 1940, and, after a wartime role as a naval officer, a PhD in 1947. After three more years at Harvard, he departed for Yale's economics department, where he spent the rest of his career save academic leaves and eighteen months in Washington as a member of Kennedy's council of economic advisers. He remained an active member of the profession until his death in 2002.

Much of Tobin's fame is due to his contributions to monetary economics and finance. As of the early 1950s, theorists had identified two main motivations for economic agents to hold cash: a *transactions demand* from consumers, and an *investment demand* based on portfolio considerations. While these two forces had been identified, there were no careful models to justify these demands by utility-maximizing agents. Thus, monetary theory lacked an answer to its most basic question: Why should anyone hold cash at all? In two pathbreaking papers, Tobin built models for each source of demand.

In a 1956 paper Tobin showed how to quantify the transactions demand. Starting with two simple forces—the transactions cost of making cash withdrawals and the opportunity cost of forgone interest—the model shows how the transactions demand is affected by interest rates. All other things being equal, an increase in interest rates induces consumers to make smaller, more frequent with-drawals, which lowers their average cash balances and the aggregate demand for cash. In combination with related work by William Baumol, this approach became known as the *Baumol-Tobin model* and still serves as a benchmark model of transactions demand.

Two years later, Tobin published another foundational paper on monetary theory, this time focusing on the investment demand for cash. In Keynes's General Theory, the investment demand for cash was driven by investors' subjective and nonrandom expectations of future interest rates, with investors holding cash rather than bonds if they expected interest rates to rise by some critical amount. This theory was criticized by several prominent economists for inconsistency with other parts of Keynes's theory. Tobin (1958a) fixed this problem by introducing uncertainty into the portfolio problem, and then solving for the optimal portfolio of cash and bonds for an investor that cares only about the mean and variance of his portfolio returns. This "mean-variance" approach echoed the work of Harry Markowitz (1952) on portfolio optimization, with Tobin notably providing an important linkage between the financial decisions of individual investors and macroeconomic implications for money demand. Markowitz and Tobin shared their Nobel Prize in large part for this work, which provided the key building blocks for the foundational model of modern financial theory, the Capital-Asset-Pricing Model of William Sharpe (1964) and John Lintner (1965).

Tobin continued to build on the portfolio approach of the 1958 paper by adding more assets and increasingly complex economic environments for the portfolio-choice decision. This model-building continued for the remainder of his career. In two papers published in 1968 and 1969 (the first with William Brainard), investment in capital played a direct role in the portfolio decision. As a notational device, these papers used the letter *q* to represent the price of capital as normalized by its replacement cost. This appellation stuck, and *Tobin's q* is now so ubiquitous that many economists cannot name the original papers from whence it came. In it simplest interpretation, a *q* greater than 1 indicates that the market price of capital is greater than its replacement cost, and thus rational investors would choose to build new capital rather than buy existing assets. When *q* is less than 1, investors would prefer the opposite. The large amount of information packed into this simple ratio has enabled an enormous and still-growing literature in macroeconomics and finance, all with Tobin's *q* as the key valuation measure.

Early in his career, Tobin focused his research on the consumption component of macroeconomic demand. As in his work on monetary economics, Tobin attempted to build more rigorous microfoundations for Keynesian models, and in this attempt he ran into a stubborn econometric problem: For large expenditures on consumer durables such as cars, most consumers have spending of zero in most years. In these cases, ordinary-least-squares (OLS) regression will give biased results. Tobin posited that such estimations require a combination of probit analysis with OLS, and in a paper for *Econometrica* (1958b) he derived an analytical solution for such a combination. Through wordplay based on various literary antecedents, this procedure, which remains a popular tool in econometric analysis, became known as the *Tobit* regression.

In addition to making numerous contributions to economics research, Tobin also maintained an active presence in policy debates. Following his service in Washington in the early 1960s, he generated a stream of policy proposals throughout the rest of his life. The most famous of these proposals, the so-called *Tobin tax*, achieved a life of its own in the twenty-first century over the objections of its originator. Tobin taxes—small taxes on financial transactions—were proposed by Tobin as a possible mechanism for reducing speculation and volatility in foreign-exchange markets. While this proposal never garnered much empirical support and was never an important plank in Tobin's policy platform, his academic reputation made his name a valuable asset for antiglobalization activists, who saw Tobin taxes as a way to reduce international trade. In the last years of his life, Tobin actively distanced himself from this interpretation of his proposal and affirmed his lifelong support for free trade.

SEE ALSO *Economics, Nobel Prize in; Financial Markets; Interest Rates; Investment; Keynes, John Maynard; Macroeconomics; Markowitz, Harry M.; Risk; Speculation; Tobin's Q; Transaction Taxes*

BIBLIOGRAPHY

PRIMARY WORKS

Brainard, William C., and James Tobin. 1968. Pitfalls in Financial Model Building. *American Economic Review* 58 (2): 99–122.

Tobin, James. 1956. The Interest-Elasticity of the Transactions Demand for Cash. *Review of Economics and Statistics* 38 (3): 241–247.

Tobin, James. 1958a. Liquidity Preference as Behavior towards Risk. *Review of Economic Studies* 25 (2): 65–86.

Tobin, James. 1958b. Estimation of Relationships for Limited Dependent Variables. *Econometrica* 26 (1): 24–36.

Tobin, James. 1969. A General Equilibrium Approach to Monetary Theory. *Journal of Money, Credit, and Banking* 1 (1): 15–29.

SECONDARY WORKS

Lintner, John. 1965. The Valuation of Risky Assets and the Selection of Risky Investments in Stock Portfolios and Capital Budgets. *Review of Economics and Statistics* 47 (1): 13–37.

Markowitz, Harry. 1952. Portfolio Selection. *Journal of Finance* 7 (1): 77–91.

Sharpe, William F. 1964. Capital Asset Prices: A Theory of Market Equilibrium under Conditions of Risk. *Journal of Finance* 19 (3): 425–442.

Andrew Metrick

TOBIN TAX

SEE *Tobin, James; Transaction Taxes.*

TOBIN'S Q

Tobin's Q is the ratio of the stock market valuation of firms to their "replacement" costs. Economists going at least as far back as Thorstein Veblen have noted the possibility of a discrepancy between the stock market value of firms and their replacement costs. Veblen conceived of a historiography of "capital," whereby *capital* took on different meanings in accordance with various historical periods. In reference to the competitive phase of nineteenth-century capitalism, Veblen understood that crisis resulted from a "readjustment of [capital] values" ([1892] 1998, p. 112). New technologies made existing capital installations obsolete so that the "nominal accepted valuation of the capital, on which its returns are computed, exceeds its actual value as indicated by its present earning capacity" ([1892] 1998, p. 112). Here, Veblen compares a measure of capital based on "putative" earning capacity to actual expenditures on plant and equipment. That is, he formulates a measure of Q, without actually naming the ratio. According to Veblen, misalignments of valuations produce a psychological "malady of affections" in the investing class, a psychological fact that produces industrial depression ([1904] 1978, p. 237). In the transition to the great monopolies established during the Great Merger Wave of 1897 to 1903, Veblen contended that high stock valuations relative to replacement costs (i.e., high Qs) were reflective of monopoly power and a "sabotaging of production."

In stark contrast to Veblen's contention that high Qs reflect a monopolistic restriction on output and investment, modern Q theory, as elaborated by William C. Brainard and James Tobin (1977), holds that high Qs are primary forces driving new investment ahead. Tobin and Brainard's modern version of Q theory derives from John Maynard Keynes's remarks in his *General Theory of Employment, Interest, and Money* ([1936] 1953). In this famous work, Keynes noted that stock market booms would encourage investment because new plant and equipment could be "floated off on the Stock exchange at an immediate profit" (p. 151). In the aggregate, a Q greater than one indicates that the stock value of firms exceeds their replacement costs and so there is an incentive for greater investment. Conversely, stock market slumps should drag Q below one, dampening the rate of building because entrepreneurs could buy similar enterprises on the stock market for less than it would cost to build them.

IMPLICATIONS OF Q THEORY

As an investment theory, Q theory has two clear, potentially testable implications. First, stock market booms should encourage investment. Second, mergers and acquisitions should rise when the stock market slumps and should fall off during stock booms. The first implication—that investment should go up during stock booms—is a virtual truism in that stock booms generally occur during booms in the general economy. It is generally difficult, however, to measure the separate effects of causative variables when many causative variables move together. For example, high profits generally expand both stock valuations and investment, so it is difficult to isolate any separate effect of high stock valuations on investment. In early tests, Tobin found "a good relationship" of investment and Qs (1978, p. 425). Yet in more recent studies, models that have used Q as a variable to explain investment have fared no better and have often done worse than pared down models using variables other than Q (Chirinko 1993; McCarthy 2001). So it is uncertain whether Q theory operates on new investment as predicted.

The other implication—that mergers and acquisitions should move countercyclically to stock booms and busts—is clearly refuted by the evidence. In the stock boom years of the 1920s, the 1960s, the 1980s, and the 1990s, mergers and acquisitions expanded rapidly. And during stock market slumps, mergers and acquisitions declined, often spectacularly as in the Great Depression of the 1930s. Various explanations have been offered to explain these results. Some theorists have postulated that stock booms allow firms additional financing through stock issues or debt collateralized by stock, which together with merger promoters have encouraged more acquisitions (Du Boff and Herman 1989). Other theorists suggest that stock booms encourage a wider divergency in stock valuations of companies (Gort 1969; Shleifer and Vishny 2003), although such an explanation seems at variance with the fact that stock valuations decline much more severely over shorter periods of time than they expand during booms.

MARGINAL Q AND MONOPOLY POWER

In order to fully comprehend how Q operates on investment and mergers, theorists still need to derive credible estimates of what is termed *marginal Q*—the additional stock valuation consequent on additional capital installations. In regard to the building of new firms, the logic of Q theory makes sense if there is "free entry" into industries—that is, new firms can be built and sold on the stock market. But when existing firms have monopoly power, the predictions of Q theory make sense only if marginal Q and Q move together. In contemplating new investment, existing firms would ask if additional capital spending would enhance the share price of the firm by more than the cost of the investment. Estimates of marginal Q have been made, but these estimates have either relied on assumptions of perfect competition in product markets (Hayashi 1982) or assumptions that conceive of capital as separate from technological change (Abel and Blanchard 1986). These assumptions are clearly unrealistic in an economy dominated by oligopolies, which install plant and equipment that often embody certain specific kinds of technology.

Monopoly power permits a divergence of marginal Q and Q. If marginal Q could be estimated accurately, then Q theory might well be able to better predict investment as well as mergers and acquisitions. If existing firms bumped up against new investment limits during stock booms (if marginal Q fell off), then this might explain why mergers and acquisitions expand during these same stock booms (Medlen 2003). Brainard and Tobin (1977) argued that marginal Q and Q moved together, but in the absence of any credible estimates of marginal Q, the question is still open.

Q theory has also been used to gauge monopoly power (Lindenberg and Ross 1981). Industries that have persistent monopoly power would presumably enjoy abnormally high profits over time. Given that industries with persistent monopoly power are protected against new entrants, such industries should exhibit high Qs. Conversely, in competitive markets, the Q ratio should approximate one; if "free entry" exists, then any abnormally high profitability would soon be eroded as new entrants came into the market.

In addition to theoretical problems, Q theory also contains unresolved measurement problems—particularly regarding the "replacement costs" of assets. With ongoing technological change, many assets would not be replaced at all. So the measurement of replacement costs might well be of questionable value. Some theorists also question whether the concept of replacement costs make sense in an information age in which capital often takes the form of knowledge, inclusive of the knowledge of in-house specialized workers (Bond and Cummins 2000). In addition, the very concept of marginal Q has been questioned on the basis that theorists have not yet fully understood the time path of new investment, a necessary precondition for any possible measurement of marginal Q (Caballero and Leahy 1996).

SEE ALSO *Investment; Profitability; Rate of Profit; Stock Exchange*

BIBLIOGRAPHY

Abel, Andrew B., and Oliver J. Blanchard. 1986. The Present Value of Profits and Cyclical Movements in Investment. *Econometrica* 54 (2): 249–273.

Bond, Stephen R., and Jason G. Cummins. 2000. The Stock Market and Investment in the New Economy: Some Tangible Facts and Intangible Fictions. *Brookings Papers on Economic Activity* 2000, no. 1: 61–124.

Brainard, William C., and James Tobin. 1977. Asset Markets and the Cost of Capital. In *Economic Progress, Private Values, and Public Policy: Essays in Honor of William Fellner*, eds. Bela Balassa and Richard Nelson, 235–262. Amsterdam: North-Holland.

Caballero, Richard J., and John V. Leahy. 1996. Fixed Costs: The Demise of Marginal q. NBER Working Paper Series, no. 5508. National Bureau of Economic Research, Cambridge, MA.

Chirinko, Robert S. 1993. Business Fixed Investment Spending: Modeling Strategies, Empirical Results, and Policy Implications. *Journal of Economic Literature* 31 (4): 1875–1911.

Du Boff, Richard B., and Edward S. Herman. 1989. The Promotional-Financial Dynamic of Merger Movements: A Historical Perspective. *Journal of Economic Issues* 23 (1): 107–133.

Gort, Michael. 1969. An Economic Disturbance Theory of Mergers. *Quarterly Journal of Economics* 83 (4): 624–642.

Hayashi, Fumio. 1982. Tobin's Marginal *q* and Average *q*: A Neoclassical Interpretation. *Econometrica* 50 (1): 213–224.

Keynes, John Maynard. [1936] 1953. *The General Theory of Employment, Interest, and Money*. San Diego, CA: Harcourt, Brace, Jovanovich.

Lindenberg, Eric B., and Stephen A. Ross. 1981. Tobin's q Ratio and Industrial Organization. *Journal of Business* 54 (1): 1–32.

McCarthy, Jonathan. 2001. Equipment Expenditures since 1995: The Boom and the Bust. *Current Issues in Economics and Finance* 7 (9). Federal Reserve Bank of New York, New York.

Medlen, Craig. 2003. Veblen's Q-Tobin's Q. *Journal of Economic Issues* 37 (4): 967–986.

Shleifer, Andrei, and Robert W. Vishny. 2003. Stock Market Driven Acquisitions. *Journal of Financial Economics* 70 (3): 295–311.

Tobin, James. 1978. Monetary Policy and the Economy: The Transmission Mechanism. *Southern Economic Journal* 44 (3): 421–431.

Veblen, Thorstein. [1892] 1998. The Overproduction Fallacy. In *Essays in Our Changing Order*. New Brunswick, NJ: Transaction Publishers. Originally published in *Quarterly Journal of Economics* 6, no. 4 (1892): 484–492.

Veblen, Thorstein. [1904] 1978. *The Theory of Business Enterprise*. New Brunswick, NJ: Transaction Books.

Craig Medlen

TOBIT

Following James Tobin's 1958 article "Estimation of Relationships for Limited Dependent Variables," the tobit is a statistical model that is used to estimate the relationship between a limited dependent variable (y) and a vector of explanatory variables (x), usually by the method of maximum likelihood. The tobit model is warranted when the variable y is censored (i.e., when it is observed for some values above or below a certain threshold, but not in the remainder of the data). The term "tobit" was derived from Tobin's name and by adding the suffix "it," as for the 1964 probit model by Arthur Goldberger.

For example, a tobit model can be used to estimate the relationship between the number of hours worked (y) and education, age, gender, race, number of children, and so on (x). In this case, some individuals do not work at all ($y = 0$) while some work ($y > 0$), but education, age, gender, race, and the like are observed for all individuals, so that the data is censored. The advantage of using the tobit instead of the usual linear regression model is that it yields unbiased coefficient estimates for each of the variables in x. Note that the censoring need not occur at zero, nor does it need to occur below a specific value of y; the tobit also accommodates censoring above a specific value of y, and in a two-limit tobit, the dependent variable is censored both below and above a certain range of y.

CRITIQUES OF THE TOBIT MODEL

The most important critique of the tobit model is that it does not allow for the set of variables used in explaining whether y is positive or zero (say, x_1) to differ from the set of variables used in explaining the value of y conditional on y being strictly positive (say, x_2). James Heckman introduced a model in his 1979 article "Sample Selection Bias as a Specification Error," which allows such a specification as well as control for selection bias in applications. Heckman's model (or "heckit"), however, requires the use of an instrumental variable that can be excluded on theoretical grounds from the estimated equation for the values of y that are strictly positive in order to explain selection into the noncensored sample. Additionally, the tobit model is inconsistent when the error term is not normally distributed (this critique also applies to the heckit model), or when the variance of the error term is not constant, (i.e., it has unequal variances).

In a thorough survey of the literature on the tobit, Takeshi Amemiya (1984) discussed the properties of the model and provided many examples and applications of the tobit. He also outlined various estimation techniques as well as possible departures from the usual statistical assumptions and discussed generalizations of—and extensions to—the basic tobit model. G. S. Maddala suggested in his 2001 book *Introduction to Econometrics* exercising caution when considering the use of the tobit model (i.e., researchers who wish to use the tobit model should make sure that the dependent variable is, indeed, censored).

SEE ALSO *Censoring, Sample; Heteroskedasticity; Logistic Regression; Probabilistic Regression; Regression; Regression Analysis; Tobin, James*

BIBLIOGRAPHY

Amemiya, Takeshi. 1984. Tobit Models: A Survey. *Journal of Econometrics* 24 (1–2): 3-61.

Goldberger, Arthur. 1964. *Econometric Theory*. New York: J. Wiley.

Heckman, James. 1979. Sample Selection Bias as a Specification Error. *Econometrica* 47 (1): 153–161.

Maddala, G. S. 2001. *Introduction to Econometrics*. 3rd ed. New York: John Wiley.

Tobin, James. 1958. Estimation of Relationships for Limited Dependent Variables. *Econometrica* 26 (1): 24–36.

Marc F. Bellemare

TOCQUEVILLE, ALEXIS DE
1805–1859

The French statesman and political philosopher Alexis de Tocqueville was born July 29, 1805, in Paris and died April 16, 1859, in Cannes. Much of his life was devoted to scholarship and public service. He is most famous for writing *Democracy in America* (1835–1840), a sweeping and perceptive study of American democratic life. His other important work is *The Old Regime and the French Revolution* (1856). As a young man, Tocqueville studied law and began his public service by working at the courts in Versailles. Later in his life, he became active in French politics, holding several elected offices.

Tocqueville's family was part of the French *petite noblesse* and had suffered greatly during the French Revolution (1789–1799). Consequently, it is not surprising that he held some aristocratic sympathies, along with concerns about the hazards of democratic excess. Still, Tocqueville was intrigued by democratic society and its potential for advancing personal liberty. He was also convinced that the spread of democracy was irresistible. For this reason, he wanted to better understand its benefits and dangers. This interest led him to visit the United States between May 1831 and February 1832. His cross-country tour took him to seventeen of the then existing twenty-four states. He spent a great deal of time in the metropolitan areas of the Northeast. He also traveled through such regions as the Great Lakes, the Ohio Valley, the Gulf Coast, and the South Atlantic. After returning to France, Tocqueville spent several years reflecting on his experiences and doing additional research. During this period, he wrote *Democracy in America*, which was published as two volumes in 1835 and 1840.

Democracy in America is considered a classic study because of its shrewd insights into the psychological, sociological, political, and institutional nature of American democracy. The book covers an exceptionally wide range of topics dealing with the democratic condition. Underlying this extensive analysis, however, is a desire to safeguard human freedom by better understanding democratic dispositions, passions, and tendencies.

According to Tocqueville, the most fundamental characteristic of the democratic age is equality. Its effect on democratic society is ubiquitous in both the public and private spheres. "The influence of [equality] extends far beyond political mores and laws … it creates opinions, gives birth to feelings, suggests customs, and modifies whatever it does not create" ([1835–1840] 2000, p. 9). Moreover, it inspires a strong and ardent attachment among democratic citizens. The benefit of equality is that it expands the reach of liberty and opportunity. Consequently, it gives all citizens a chance to take more control of their own lives.

Although equality had a fundamental influence on American society, inequalities did exist. Slavery, in particular, was a well-established practice in the southern states. Tocqueville, however, viewed slavery as a practice in "retreat" and destined to be abolished. He claimed, "Whatever efforts the Americans of the South make to maintain slavery, they will not forever succeed…. Slavery amid the democratic liberty and enlightenment of our age is not an institution that can last" ([1835–1840] 2000, p. 363). Still, Tocqueville was pessimistic about the future of race relations in the United States. Regardless of how slavery ended, he foresaw "great misfortunes." He believed that conflict between the races could only be avoided by isolation or complete intermingling. Once slavery ended, isolation would be impossible, but white racism would prevent significant intermingling. As a result, the races would be left in a condition of precarious coexistence, producing a dangerous struggle for power.

Tocqueville also felt that equality could become dangerous if taken to an extreme. When people become too enamored with equality, they will do anything to maintain it, including sacrificing their liberty. The idea of equality can also be dangerous because it lends a daunting form of moral authority to the opinions of the majority. Because everyone is considered equal, the larger number of individuals in the majority is equated with superior judgment and greater utility. The opinions of the majority carry such great weight that they can lead to political tyranny, social conformity, and intellectual monotony.

Tocqueville argued that two other democratic dispositions, individualism and materialism, can also be threats to liberty. These inclinations are dangerous because they cause citizens to lose interest in public affairs. Individualism compels people to isolate themselves from the greater society and withdraw into small groups of family and friends. Materialism leads people to focus obsessively on their own private prosperity and to disregard public duties. The neglect of civic responsibilities can result in the development of a paternalistic despotism. Personal rights and freedoms are hindered and enervated as citizens become entangled in a network of "petty, complicated rules" ([1835–1840] 2000, p. 692).

Tocqueville claimed that it is possible to overcome these and other threats to liberty with the proper institutions, mores, and values. The presence of numerous and robust civil associations, for example, serves to protect individuals from an overbearing government. An independent press informs the public and facilitates associational activity. Religions that are able to inspire benevolence and instill a strong sense of spirituality can help counter the influences of individualism and materialism. The concept of self-interest properly understood links the performance of civic duties with private advantage. Prudent political leaders protect liberty through statecraft and soulcraft. Educated citizens are aware of the seductive dangers of extreme equality. Tocqueville concludes by noting that the future of democracy is not predestined; the people will determine if equality will lead to servitude or freedom.

The Old Regime and the French Revolution is Tocqueville's attempt to understand the origins of the French Revolution. It examines the nature of French society prior to 1789. His primary claim is that the revolution was prompted by the political centralization of the state. Moreover, the revolution itself was a failure because it also centralized political power. Although *The Old Regime* has not attracted the attention of *Democracy in America*, it is still considered an important account of the social conditions that led to the French Revolution.

Tocqueville's ideas about the democratic condition continue to exert a considerable influence on contemporary academic and political discourse. Of particular importance are his discussions of unchecked individualism and the importance of associational membership, which are frequently referenced in scholarly research on civil society and social capital. His pithy observations about democracy and democratic life are often quoted by politicians and popular commentators. The continuing relevance of Tocqueville's work should not be surprising. He provides a seminal and perhaps the best account of the dangers of democracy and its threats to liberty.

BIBLIOGRAPHY

Jardin, André. 1988. *Tocqueville: A Biography*. Trans. Lydia Davis with Robert Hemenway. New York: Farrar Straus Giroux.

Tocqueville, Alexis de. [1835–1840] 2000. *Democracy in America*. Trans. George Lawrence; ed. J. P. Mayer. New York: HarperCollins Perennial.

Tocqueville, Alexis de. [1856] 1955. *The Old Regime and the French Revolution*. Trans. Stuart Gilbert. Garden City, NY: Doubleday.

Johnny Goldfinger

TOILETS

This article is concerned with indoor conveniences: both domestic home toilets and those in the workplace and public buildings. Technological and cultural factors are discussed to understand why everyone, in the West at least, thinks it is quite normal to have a flushing toilet inside the house.

The Romans installed toilets inside their villas over 2000 years ago. But indoor plumbing was not a feature of European cities until the time of Queen Elizabeth I, for whom Sir John Harrington installed the first valve-flushing toilet in the 1590s. The majority of the population used chamber pots or relieved themselves outdoors. The wealthy had no need of domestic toilets; they had chambermaids. The few toilets that existed comprised a "privy" at the bottom of the garden, or on the outside of the castle wall hanging over the river. Privacy was not a major consideration, and men, especially, could relieve themselves anywhere inside or outside the house.

It was not until the Industrial Revolution that toilet provision became an issue. It was no longer acceptable to throw human waste on the midden outside the house. The ruling classes saw it in their own interests to enact public health reforms and to build sewers and drains because cholera is no respecter of class distinctions.

The introduction of water-based sewerage systems required the installation of flushing toilets. New paradigms of hygiene and social morality arose. The toilet had to be "tamed" and "domesticated" and brought inside the house from the yard. Toilet entrepreneurs such as Thomas Crapper in Britain, and John Randall Mann in North America, capitalized upon this new toilet market, for "every home should have one." Design was based upon the "sit" rather than "squat" style of toilet provision and exported globally. Most people in the world still squat and have no access to modern toilets or toilet paper. To have a flush-toilet in your house is a sign of great wealth, with the increasing scarcity and privatization of water supply in developing countries.

Social prudery made it taboo directly to talk about bodily functions in polite company. Americans say they are going to "the bathroom," (in a bathtubless room?), the British ask for "the little room." In Far East countries bodily functions are not seen to be as culturally and religiously dirty as in the West: So euphemisms are less necessary. Nevertheless, Japanese high-tech toilets that play music to cover embarrassing noises are popular with women users.

In the nineteenth century it was considered so shocking for a woman to need the toilet when out that little "away from home" provision was made for women. Women still have approximately half the number of toilet facilities as men, a last vestige of sex discrimination. Standardized toilet manufacturers make little allowance for different user group needs, in terms of ergonomic design. Factory and office workers also suffer from lack of workplace provision, and there is no constitutional right for employees to urinate during company time.

While householders invest in high-quality designer bathrooms, in contrast the poor quality and lack of public toilets has been the cause of great concern to user groups such as the American Restroom Association (ARA). The ARA argues the business case that "bathrooms mean business" as better public restrooms will result in more tourists, shoppers, and visitors coming to town, staying longer, and spending more.

Public toilets, because they are public, are contested spaces, offering anonymity and seclusion to drug users and deviant groups. News reports of people being born, dying, being raped, trapped, attacked, or arrested in toilets are frequent. They are one of the few places where complete strangers mix and share intimate facilities. They repel those worried about picking up a sexually transmitted disease; women warn their daughters not to sit on the seat for hygienic purposes. They attract men who are "cruising" (cottaging, or looking for a date): the subject of many sociological and criminological studies. Toilet closure is often seen as the way to reduce crime. But closure greatly inconveniences bona fide users, as evidenced by a new generation of research on the practical needs of women and other social groups that are disenabled by the design of the built environment.

One can judge a nation by its toilets. When visiting a foreign country, the first necessity that people are likely to look for is the toilet, and the image and smell remain with them. The nature of toilet provision is an indicator of whose needs are valued in society and what a society thinks about women, babies, children, workers, and its elderly and disabled citizens.

SEE ALSO *Development; Development Economics; Disease; Plumbing; Public Health; Sanitation*

BIBLIOGRAPHY

Armstrong, David. 1993. Public Health Spaces and the Fabrication of Identity. *Sociology* 27 (3): 393–410.

Gandy, Matthew. 2004. Water, Modernity and Emancipatory Urbanism. In *The Emancipatory City: Paradoxes and Possibilities*, ed. L. Lees, 178–191. London: Sage.

Greed, Clara. 2003. *Inclusive Urban Design: Public Toilets.* Oxford: Elsevier.

Kira, Alexander. 1976. *The Bathroom.* London: Cornell University Press.

Linder, Marc, and Nygaard, Ingrid. 1998. *Void Where Prohibited: Rest Breaks and the Right to Urinate on Company Time.* Ithaca, NY: Cornell University Press.

Wright, Lawrence. 2000. *Clean and Decent: The Fascinating History of the Bathroom and WC.* London: Penguin.

Clara H. Greed

TOLERANCE, DRUG

Tolerance is a decrease in the effects of a drug dose following repeated administrations. Tolerance is central to the definition of chemical dependence to some drugs (e.g., alcohol, heroin, painkillers), with theorists assigning to tolerance, or the mechanisms that produce tolerance, an important role in the genesis and maintenance of addictive drug use. Drug tolerance can be a symptom of physical dependence and a contributing factor to the severity of the physical and psychological dependence on a drug. For example, as drug users develop tolerance, they have to progressively increase their level of consumption to achieve the "high" they used to feel with lower doses during their initial stages of experimentation with the drug. Tolerance can be described as a homeostatic mechanism, or an organism's adaptive response to foreign substances. Unfortunately, tolerance may decrease the effectiveness of medication regimes, as in the treatment of chronic pain, epilepsy, or depression.

Drug tolerance has been studied as either pharmacological (physiological) or learned (psychological) phenomena. Pharmacological tolerance models distinguish between dispositional (or pharmacokinetic) and functional (or pharmacodynamic) tolerance. *Dispositional tolerance* refers to an organism's increased ability to metabolize and distribute the drug in the body. Thus, with increased dispositional tolerance, more of the drug must be taken to reach a specific concentration at the receptor sites. On the other hand, *functional tolerance* defines changes in neural functioning that result in dose-response decrements at the receptor site (i.e., the receptor responds less to a given concentration of a drug). Functional tolerance that develops to the effects of the first or second drug administration is called *tachyphylaxis* or *acute* tolerance. Functional tolerance that persists after prolonged exposure is called *acquired* or *chronic* tolerance.

Psychological or learning models distinguish between operant (or instrumental) and associative (or classically conditioned) drug tolerance. *Operant tolerance* defines the acquisition of specific skills or responses that compensate for the disruptive effects of a drug on task performance. For example, with other influencing variables being equal (e.g., genetic sensitivity to alcohol), operant tolerance theory predicts that a person who habitually drinks and drives should make fewer mistakes while driving under the influence of a relatively high dose of alcohol than a person with the same level of alcohol-use history who rarely drinks and drives.

Associative or *classically conditioned* models of drug tolerance posit that environmental stimuli reliably paired with drug delivery become conditioned stimuli that elicit conditioned responses that reduce drug effects. Perhaps the most influential of the associative tolerance models is Shepard Siegel's *compensatory response* model. In the 1970s and 1980s, Siegel conducted a number of highly influential studies to test a theory that predicted that conditioned stimuli can produce conditioned responses that are opposite to, and thus cancel or compensate for, the effects of drugs. The compensatory response model of tolerance has been used to explain why some heroin addicts may die from a heroin overdose despite having developed very high tolerance to the effects of the drug. Although overdoses are often a result of mixing heroin with other drugs, many overdose deaths appear to result from a sudden loss of tolerance. Noting that many heroin overdose deaths occurred after the drug was consumed in a new setting or a new set of circumstances, Siegel reasoned that tolerance to heroin must be partially conditioned to the environment where, and manner in which, the drug is usually taken. Therefore, taking the drug in a new environment would eliminate the presence of conditioned tolerance and lead to overdosing.

An important characteristic or difference between pharmacological and learned drug tolerance is their differential resistance to extinction following detoxification or discontinuation of a given drug administration regime. Associative drug tolerance can be maintained or "remembered" for long periods of time, whereas nonassociative tolerance disappears rapidly in the absence of a drug administration regime. This characteristic of associative drug tolerance has been linked to the construct of drug craving. Like tolerance effects, cravings can be elicited by environmental stimuli (e.g., the sight of a lit cigarette for the smoker), a phenomenon that can occur even after years of abstinence (as often reported by smokers). That is, craving and tolerance can be conceptualized as memories associated with drug effects. Future research examining the physiological mechanisms underlying the development of learned tolerance will be invaluable for the development of drug addiction treatments, as well as the creation of medications partially resistant to pharmacological and learned tolerance effects.

SEE ALSO *Addiction; Medicine; Pharmaceutical Industry; Smoking*

BIBLIOGRAPHY

Cepeda-Benito, Antonio, and Paul Short. 1997. Morphine's Interoceptive Stimuli as Cues for the Development of Associative Morphine Tolerance in the Rat. *Psychobiology* 25: 236–240.

Ramsay, Douglas S., and Stephen C. Woods. 1997. Biological Consequences of Drug Administration: Implications for Acute and Chronic Tolerance. *Psychological Review* 104: 170–193.

Siegel, Shepard. 1975. Evidence from Rats that Morphine Tolerance is a Learned Response. *Journal of Comparative and Physiological Psychology* 89 (5): 498–506.

Siegel, Shepard. 2005. Drug Tolerance, Drug Addiction, and Drug Anticipation. *Current Directions in Psychological Science* 14 (6): 296–300.

Tiffany, Stephen T., David J. Drobes, and Antonio Cepeda-Benito. 1992. Contribution of Associative and Nonassociative Processes to the Development of Morphine Tolerance. *Psychopharmacology* 109 (1–2): 185–190.

Antonio Cepeda-Benito

TOLERANCE, POLITICAL

In the social sciences, scholars have devoted a significant amount of attention to the conceptualization, measurement, and analysis of one of the primary domains of tolerance, political tolerance. Although disagreements about the nature of political tolerance remain, most political theorists contend that it is one of the central tenets of democratic theory because democracies are predicated on the assumption that people with widely differing viewpoints should be able to express their opinions and participate in political processes.

The first major empirical work on political tolerance was published in 1955 by sociologist Samuel Stouffer (1900–1960). In *Communism, Conformity, and Civil Liberties*, Stouffer reported the results of two national surveys in which he found that most U.S. adults were unwilling to extend civil liberties to unpopular left-wing groups; community leaders, however, demonstrated greater tolerance than the general public. This presented a conundrum to many political theorists who had thought that widespread tolerance was necessary for sustaining a democratic society. Later studies provided a partial explanation: U.S. adults were very supportive of civil liberties *in the abstract*, but they were much less likely to apply them to specific groups and situations.

In a groundbreaking study published in 1982, John Sullivan, James Pierson, and George Marcus offered a significant reconceptualization of political tolerance. Sullivan and colleagues defined political tolerance as "a willingness to permit the expression of ideas or interests one opposes" (Sullivan et al. 1982, p. 2). Thus, tolerance presupposes disagreement with a particular group's views. Tolerance is demonstrated when one finds a group's views objectionable, yet *still* supports the rights of the group. Sullivan and his colleagues developed the *least-liked group* approach to measuring political tolerance, in which they first asked respondents to identify their least-liked group, and then asked whether they would be willing to extend certain civil liberties to the group (recall that Stouffer had focused on unpopular left-wing groups). Their research found that while the objects of intolerance had changed since Stouffer's original study, the majority of U.S. citizens were still intolerant.

Extensive studies of political tolerance both in the United States and in countries such as Australia, Germany, Israel, New Zealand, and South Africa indicate that although the target (least-liked) groups may differ, the variables that influence tolerance tend to be the same. Individuals who support the abstract norms of democracy (e.g., free speech, majority vote) are more likely to be tolerant. Those who perceive a high level of threat from the target group, however, are less likely to be tolerant.

Tolerant stances tend to be associated with education (high), social status (elite), age (younger), religiosity (more secular), and, to a lesser extent, gender (males). Individuals who demonstrate low levels of dogmatism and authoritarianism and high levels of interpersonal trust also tend to be more tolerant.

Scholars have also identified contextual factors that promote or inhibit tolerance. Stable, longer-enduring democracies tend to provide an environment that supports tolerance; however, conflict, and particularly conflict that threatens one's group identity, tends to decrease individual levels of tolerance.

SEE ALSO *Civil Society; Conformity; Democracy; Education, USA; Groups; Ideology; Intergroup Relations; Political Correctness; Politics*

BIBLIOGRAPHY

Stouffer, Samuel. 1955. *Communism, Conformity, and Civil Liberties: A Cross-section of the Nation Speaks Its Mind.* Garden City, NY: Doubleday.

Sullivan, John L., James Pierson, and George E. Marcus. 1982. *Political Tolerance and American Democracy.* Chicago: University of Chicago.

Patricia G. Avery

TOLERANCE, REPRESSIVE

SEE *Repressive Tolerance.*

TOLMAN, EDWARD
1886–1959

The American psychologist Edward Chace Tolman was born in Newton, Massachusetts, on April 14, 1886 and died in Berkeley, California, on November 19, 1959. He received a BS in electrochemistry from the Massachusetts Institute of Technology in 1911, and a PhD in experimental psychology from Harvard in 1915. He spent the bulk of his academic career at the University of California, Berkeley, retiring in 1954. In 1937 he was elected to the National Academy of Sciences.

Tolman entered psychology in the first years of John B. Watson's behaviorist revolution, and he even dedicated his best-known book, *Purposive Behavior in Animals and Men* (1932), to the white rat, but he was never a radical behaviorist. Whereas Watson (and, later, B. F. Skinner) rejected mental states as explanatory constructs, Tolman emphasized molar behavior over molecular "muscletwitches," as well as the importance of goals and expectations intervening between stimulus and response. (Another neobehaviorist, Clark Hull, similarly stressed the importance of internal drive states.) Heavily influenced by Gestalt theory, and especially by Kurt Lewin's notion of the "life-space," Tolman viewed the behaving organism as acquiring a "sign-gestalt-expectation" that a particular behavior will achieve a particular goal in a particular "behavior space," and a general "means-end readiness," represented by a "belief-value matrix" to engage in similar behavior in the future, under similar circumstances. He construed the rat facing a maze, even on the first learning trial, as entertaining and testing a sort of hypothesis as to what it should do; as engaged in "vicarious trial and error" behavior as it considered the choice of turning right or left; and as actively "searching for the stimulus" that would indicate one choice over another.

The flavor of Tolman's experimental work, and its implications, are best illustrated by his most famous experiment, on "latent learning" (Tolman and Honzik 1930). Over twenty trials, rats who were rewarded with food took progressively less time to traverse a maze, compared to a control group that received no reward. A third group received no reward for the first ten trials, and behaved no differently than the controls. But when reward was introduced in trial eleven, they showed a precipitous drop in running time, behaving just like the rats who had been rewarded all along. Apparently, these rats had formed a "cognitive map" of the maze as a whole, but did not act on what they had learned until they had an incentive to do so. This experiment shattered the traditional view that reinforcement was crucial to learning: Reinforcement may control performance, but learning happens even in its absence. By redefining learning as the acquisition of knowledge, which organisms—rats as well as humans—could use for their own purposes, Tolman's "purposive behaviorism" set the stage for the cognitive revolution in psychology that began in the 1950s.

Tolman was a civil libertarian as well as a psychologist, and served for a time on the national board of the American Civil Liberties Union. Perhaps reflecting his Quaker background, in 1918 he was dismissed from his first faculty post, at Northwestern University, for publishing an article in a pacifist student publication; and in 1942 he published *Drives Towards War*, proposing a set of social controls that could produce a warless society. Nevertheless, he volunteered for military service in World War I, and was offered a commission in the army; and he worked for the Office of Strategic Services, forerunner to the Central Intelligence Agency, during World War II. From 1949 to 1950 Tolman led faculty opposition to a loyalty oath required by the Regents of the University of California. He (among others) was briefly dismissed from his post, taking shelter at Harvard. In *Tolman v. Underhill* (1955) the California Supreme Court invalidated the oath, and Tolman and the others were reinstated. In 1963, in recognition of his contributions to both the discipline of psychology and the cause of academic freedom, the building housing Berkeley's Department of Psychology

and the School of Education—an award-winning example of mid-twentieth-century modernism designed by Gardner Dailey—was renamed in Tolman's honor.

SEE ALSO *Behaviorism; Civil Liberties; Gestalt Psychology; Hull, Clark; Peace; Psychology; Skinner, B. F.; War*

BIBLIOGRAPHY

PRIMARY WORKS

Tolman, Edward C. 1932. *Purposive Behavior in Animals and Men.* New York: Century.

Tolman, Edward C. 1938. The Determinants of Behavior at a Choice Point. *Psychological Review* 45: 1–41.

Tolman, Edward C. 1942. *Drives Towards War.* New York: Appleton-Century-Crofts.

Tolman, Edward C. 1948. Cognitive Maps in Rats and Men. *Psychological Review* 55: 189–208.

Tolman, Edward C. 1952. Edward Chace Tolman. In *A History of Psychology in Autobiography*, vol. 4, eds. Edwin G. Boring, Herbert Werner, Heinz S. Langfeld, and Robert M. Yerkes, 323–339. Worcester, MA: Clark University Press.

Tolman, Edward C. 1955. Principles of Performance. *Psychological Review* 62: 315–326.

Tolman, Edward C., and Charles H. Honzik. 1930. "Insight" in Rats. University of California Publications in *Psychology* 4 (14): 215–232.

SECONDARY WORKS

Bower, Gordon H., and Ernest R. Hilgard. 1981. *Theories of Learning.* 5th ed. Englewood Cliffs, NJ: Prentice Hall.

Ritchie, Benbow F. 1964. Edward Chace Tolman. *Biographical Memoirs of the National Academy of Sciences* 37. New York: Columbia University Press.

John F. Kihlstrom

TOLTECS

SEE *Pre-Columbian Peoples.*

TOMMING

SEE *Uncle Tom.*

TOOLS

Stanley Kubrick's science-fiction film *2001: A Space Odyssey* (1968) opens with a scene of early hominids hammering with bones, depicting primitive tool use. While we might consider human tool use as beginning with stones shaped by man for specific tasks, it is likely that found objects such as sticks, stones, and bones were used much earlier than this. With the advent of tools being intentionally formed for specific tasks, tools not only assisted, but also represented, particular ways of doing things. In other words, the design of a tool reflects an understanding of how to use that tool and what effect using it can make on the world.

Broadly speaking, a tool is some object that extends the abilities of its user. Thus, a tool might be an object held by an animal's claws or mouth that extends the animal's ability to reach, hit, and so on. This extension is also a change in the animal's movement and activity. It is interesting to note that tool use occurs in so few species; that is, it is the exception rather than the norm in animal behavior. The problem with defining *tool use* is that often there is little need to assume that the animal has a purpose in mind—it is perfectly feasible to assume that the animal is exhibiting a stereotyped pattern of behavior that is common across the species, or in other words, the animal has little choice *but* to act in this manner. As Benjamin Beck points out in *Animal Tool Use: The Use and Manufacture of Tools by Animals* (1980), it can be difficult to separate tool use from the myriad other activities that animals perform.

An obvious route around this dilemma is to consider the manner in which objects might be used to solve problems. One cannot write about tool use without mentioning the work of Wolfgang Köhler and his studies of captive chimpanzees. His studies are interesting for introducing *Einsicht* ("insight") into the psychological literature. In his work, the chimpanzees were confronted with problems, for example, a piece of fruit was placed just out of reach and the chimpanzee was given two sticks. Köhler's thesis was that, after a period of confusion, the chimpanzee had a sudden realization (or "insight") that joining the two sticks would allow him to reach the fruit. However, subsequent research suggested that a chimpanzee, given two sticks, will spontaneously attempt to join them, as part of exploring and playing with them. Thus, it is not clear whether the "insight" led the chimpanzee to decide to join the two sticks, or whether joining two sticks provided him with a longer stick that he recognized could reach the fruit. On the one hand, if "insight" was at work, then one could assume that the chimpanzee spent some time mulling over the problem until realizing a solution—that is, viewing the solution to the problem as requiring cognitive activity. On the other hand, the physical activity of joining two sticks (because it was possible) could lead to the creation of a new object, which could have new properties that the chimpanzee could recognize. This seems to raise questions of perceiving the affordance of objects (in the manner suggested by J. J. Gibson) rather than requiring representation of a model.

There has been growing evidence from the neuropsychological community that images of objects that support grasping evoke different neural responses from other images (in both humans and apes). This suggests that the brain responds to objects that afford particular responses, such as grasping. Research from patients with apraxia (disorders of movement) suggests that objects are coded in terms of their appearance and also in terms of the sequence of actions performed with an object—lesions in specific cortical regions can impair one or another of these codings. An implication of this is that an object can be recognized as supporting a particular activity (e.g., a shoe or a stone can serve as a hammer), and that practicing the use of the object can create coordinative structures for expert performance (e.g., comparing an experienced carpenter with a novice sawing a piece of wood). This suggests that the use of tools is a complex combination of psychomotor skill with cognitive abilities to recognize objects as potential tools and to determine sequences of use of these objects.

Research on the forming of stone tools by early hominids often divides between theorists who suggest that the tools were being made to a template or model and those (more recently) who suggest that the tools could be fashioned by reacting to the appearance of the object as it was being shaped. This would be an extreme version of stone-tool creation in which the process of hammering the stone to produce a "tool" was repeated until something approaching a useful tool was produced. However, many surviving stone tools not only exhibit similar shapes, but also tend to exploit the properties of the stones being worked. This suggests that even if the toolmaker did not have a "template" of the final product, the activity was responsive to the gradually changing nature of the stone being worked. This suggests that the toolmaker was sufficiently dextrous to work the stone, and capable of recognizing the affordance of the stone as it was being worked. Consequently, rather than setting out to make a specific tool, the toolmaker might have selected a stone that would potentially yield a tool (thus, needing to recognize in an object not only the potential to be used as a tool, but also the potential to be worked into a tool) before beginning the process of working the stone. As this process unfolded, imperfections in the stone might result in unanticipated fractures that would cause the toolmaker to either abandon the stone or to modify the shape being worked. What is clear from analysis of early stone tools is that different tools were used for different purposes (often, collections of several different tools have been found on a site, implying the existence of a "tool kit" to support different activities).

If we accept that a tool, in any form, represents an extension of the user's abilities, cognitive tools can also be used to replace or at least redefine these abilities. What is interesting is that the substitution is not simply a matter of one set of activities replacing another, for example, a calculator replacing the ability to perform mental arithmetic by the ability to enter numbers on a keypad. Rather, the tool itself represents the problem that one is trying to solve, together with the manner in which to solve it. Thus, the calculator buttons invite entering numbers, even when the sum can be more quickly performed mentally. The conclusion is that a tool is not only a physical object but also the embodiment of the solution to a problem, and it also suggests the best way to approach activity.

SEE ALSO *Machinery; Production; Work*

BIBLIOGRAPHY

Baber, Christopher. 2005. *Cognition and Tool Use: Forms of Engagement in Animal and Human Tool Use.* London: Taylor and Francis.

Beck, Benjamin B. 1980. *Animal Tool Use: The Use and Manufacture of Tools by Animals.* New York: Garland.

Gibson, James J. 1966. *The Senses Considered as Perceptual Systems.* Boston: Houghton Mifflin.

Köhler, Wolfgang. 1925. *The Mentality of Apes.* London: Kegan Paul.

Oakley, Kenneth. 1972. *Man the Tool Maker.* London: Trustees of the British Museum.

Schick, Kathy, and Nicholas Toth. 1993. *Making Silent Stones Speak.* London: Weidenfeld and Nicholson.

Christopher Baber

TOPOGRAPHY

Translated literally from its Greek roots of *topos* (place) and *graphein* (to write), *topography* means "the writing of place." In modern usage, however, the term has taken on more complex significance. As J. Hillis Miller notes (1995, p. 3), the term has come to refer to both the practice of accurate, scientific representation of particular places on the earth's surface and the actual configuration of those places. In social science, topographies (both representational and actual) are of interest to researchers investigating relationships between societies and local environments. Such studies are common within the disciplines of geography, anthropology, archaeology, and sociology, and are sometimes found within economics and political science. As the diversity of disciplines with topographical interests reveals, the term *topography* addresses a fundamental aspect of human experience (place) and thus serves as a foundational category around which social inquiry can be organized.

The dominant modern usage of the term has been in reference to the material configuration of places on the earth's surface, typically with an emphasis on physical geography rather than the built environment. As Robert Christopherson makes clear (2002, p. 338), topographical studies based upon this emphasis are marked by the observation and recording of landscape features such as hill and mountain relief (dramatic or modest), slope angles (shallow or steep), drainage patterns (wetlands and rivers), and terrain characteristics (rugged or smooth, vegetated or barren) for specific locales. The goal of such studies is to define regional topographies (in the material sense) and provide the environmental knowledge (through representation) needed to facilitate land use decisions appropriate to specific social and economic goals. For instance, as Scott Kirsch (2002) outlines in an essay on John Wesley Powell's (1834–1902) survey of the Colorado Plateau and surrounding area in the 1870s, in the late nineteenth century the U.S. government was keen to gain knowledge of the arid region of the American West so that land and resource use decisions could be made for an expanding nation. In particular, Powell was charged with ascertaining the irrigation potential of the region for agrarian settlement. Due to the undulating and arid topography, he argued, the grid system of land allotment typical of the Midwestern United States was not suited to the area. Instead, he recommended that all lots should abut water sources, even if that resulted in the alienation of land in irregular shapes. By observing and recording the characteristics of the physical geography of the region and combining the information for presentation in cartographic form, Powell's work provided distant decision makers with knowledge of local environmental conditions, thereby enabling the setting of social policies regarding land allocation and resource rights. Of course, this relationship between topographical information and land and resource use marks a variety of enterprises and activities. From hikers' use of maps to navigate mountain ranges to military officers' use of electronic geographical information to locate specific place-based threats and targets, understanding the material arrangement of the physical environment of certain locales is central to decision making and interaction with places.

While modern topographical studies have tended to focus on the material configuration of places on the earth's surface in order to facilitate land and resource use, this has not been an exclusive orientation. The term *topography* has been seized upon by a variety of researchers in the social sciences and humanities who are interested in place-based human experience. The humanistic geographer Yi-Fu Tuan (1974) has written about the centrality of place to human experience, the appreciation of which he terms *topophilia*. Eugene V. Walter, in an attempt to formulate a more general understanding of humans' physiological attachment to place, has proposed the study of *topisitics* as a "framework to grasp the whole experience of space and place" (1988, p. 18). Asserting that "topostic inquiry seeks theories that represent and explain forces that make or break the integrity of located experience" (p. 18), Walter seeks to emphasize that places are more than the sum of their material components and that people's interactions with places form a central front in inquiries into both environments and the human mind. And, in his work on the relationship between literature, philosophy, and place, Miller (1995, p. 4) deploys the term *topography* to question how particular ways of knowing places have been inserted into modern Western epistemologies through language. Noting that in modern usage *topography* shifts between signifying representations of places and signifying actual characteristics of places, he highlights the connections between the production of knowledge about places and the experience of them. In different ways, then, these authors and others have moved understandings of topographies beyond concern for merely the material configuration of places and instead highlighted the multiplicity of ways in which humans become attached to and interact with places.

In an essay that brings together the human and physical aspects of place through a historical materialist approach, Cindi Katz argues for a conceptualization of *topography* as the sociomaterial terrain produced by an ever-globalizing capitalism. She insists that topographical studies "encompass the processes that produce landscapes as much as they do the landscapes themselves, making clear the social nature of nature and the material grounds of social life" (2001, p. 720). Further, Katz argues, the production of topographies "simultaneously turns on, reveals, and specifies the intricate relations among discrete places." As such, topographical studies "can provide literal and figurative grounds for developing a critique of the social and political-economic relations sedimented into space and for examining the range of social practices through which place is produced" (pp. 720–721). Ultimately, Katz points out that this framework enables the development of a series of *countertopographies*. She envisions these as "linking different places analytically in order to both develop the contours of common struggles and imagine a different kind of practical response to problems confronting them" (p. 722). In combination, Katz's conceptualization of topographies and countertopographies provides a resource for critical analyses of place that takes seriously the impacts of political and economic history in shaping local terrain.

As is evident from this survey, *topography* is a malleable and widely used term. With its focus on place and human understanding of it, the term and the studies organized around it are central to a comprehensive pursuit of social science. Whether material, social, or both, *topographies* (both representation and actual) mediate the lives people lead and help to define the places in which they are lived.

SEE ALSO *Anthropology; Archaeology; Architecture; Geography; Human Ecology; Irrigation; Natural Resources, Nonrenewable; Water Resources*

BIBLIOGRAPHY

Christopherson, Robert W. 2002. *Geosystems: An Introduction to Physical Geography.* 4th ed. Upper Saddle River, NJ: Prentice-Hall.

Katz, Cindi. 2001. Vagabond Capitalism and the Necessity of Social Reproduction. *Antipode* 33 (4): 709–728.

Kirsch, Scott. 2002. John Wesley Powell and the Mapping of the Colorado Plateau, 1869–1879: Survey Science, Geographical Solutions, and the Economy of Environmental Values. *Annals of the Association of American Geographers* 92 (3): 548–572.

Miller, J. Hillis. 1995. *Topographies.* Stanford, CA: Stanford University Press.

Tuan, Yi-Fu. 1974. *Topophilia: A Study of Environmental Perception, Attitudes, and Values.* Englewood Cliffs, NJ: Prentice-Hall.

Walter, Eugene Victor. 1988. *Placeways: A Theory of the Human Environment.* Chapel Hill: University of North Carolina Press.

David A. Rossiter

TOPOLOGY

In the social sciences, it is important to know if close-by models of human behavior and interaction entail close-by predictions. More precisely, the question is whether a sequence of models, which mirror reality in an increasingly accurate manner, yield predictions that converge to those that can be observed in the real world. *Topology* is a mathematical structure designed to express robustness, approximation, convergence, and continuity, and is thus useful in determining the relevance of a given social-science model.

For example, economies differ according to the endowments of individuals, the available production technologies, and the preferences of individuals over bundles of commodities. General Equilibrium Theory predicts the market prices that can emerge as a result of various combinations of these factors. The robustness of these predictions can then be tested through a consideration of a *topological space* of economies in which one can examine whether market prices change continuously with changes in the economies' characteristics.

Similarly, in Game Theory, Nash equilibrium is a prediction of the strategies that players will choose noncooperatively as a function of their preferences over the outcomes entailed by strategy profiles. When considering a topological space of games, one can check how Nash equilibria vary with the game specification. Alternatively, Social Choice Theory, based on normative considerations, prescribes a strategy profile that the players *should* choose collectively (rather than noncooperatively) in the social situation at hand. In a topological space of such social choice problems, one can check if close-by behavior is prescribed in close-by situations.

Formally, given a space X of model characteristics (or some other objects of interest), a topology is a system T of *open sets*, which are subsets of X with the following properties: (1) The union of any collection of open sets is open; (2) the intersection of a finite number of open sets is open; and (3) both the entire space and the empty set are open. The complement of an open set is called *close*. A space X equipped with a topology of open subsets T is called a *topological space*.

A pertinent example is the case in which the space is *metric*, i.e., when there exists a metric that defines the distance between any two objects in the space (such that the distance of an object to itself is zero; the distance from x to y is the same as the distance from y to x; and the distance from x to z is no larger than the distance from x to y plus the distance from y to z). In such a case, the unions of "open balls" constitute a topology (an open ball of radius r around a point x in the space is the set of points in the space whose distance to x is smaller than r). Moreover, a set v is open if and only if every point $x \in V$ has an open ball around it contained in V.

Hence, if for some property P of the model, the set V of characteristics at which P obtains is open, then the property P is *robust*: When a characteristic $x \in V$ is measured with a small enough error, the measurement will still have the property P.

The idea of robustness, as captured by open sets, carries over also to families of economic models whose topological structure is so rich it cannot always be compatible with a metric. Financial models of dynamic investment in continuous time, and stochastic uncertainty—over objective circumstances, as well as over others' uncertainties—are two important examples.

A sequence x_n of points in the space *converges* to the point x if for every open set V containing x there exists a stage N beyond which all points x_n, $n \geq N$ in the sequence belong to V.

This definition of convergence applies not only to sequences, but also to nets. In a *net* x_n, the indices n are not necessarily the natural numbers. Rather, they may form a *directed system*—a set where not every pair of distinct indices n, n' is characterized by one of the indices being larger than the other, but where there always exists another index n'' that is larger than them both.

Convergence of sequences and nets depends on the richness of the topology. In the *trivial topology*, containing only the empty set and the entire space X, every net converges to every point. At the other extreme, with the *discrete topology*, in which every subset is open (and, in particular, every subset containing a single point is open), a net x_n converges to x only if for some index N and onward $x_n = x$ for all $n \geq N$. Hence, the choice of topology expresses the extent to which the modeler views different points (or objects or model characteristics) in the space as distinct or similar. The more fine-detailed the distinctions are, the richer will be the topology, and fewer nets will be converging to any given point x.

When X and Y are topological spaces, we say that the function $f: X \to Y$ is *continuous at the point* $x \in X$ if for every net x_n converging to x, the net $f(x_n)$ converges to the point $f(x) \in Y$. We say that f is *continuous* if it is continuous at every point $x \in X$.

If X is a space of model characteristics and Y is a space of potential predictions, one would like the prediction function $f: X \to Y$ of the model to be continuous—otherwise a slight misspecification of the characteristics might yield wildly distinct predictions.

One can show that f is continuous if and only if for every open set $W \subseteq Y$, the set $f^{-1}(W) = \{x \in X: f(x) \in W\}$ is open in X. Thus, the richer is the topology of X and the poorer is the topology of Y, the more functions f from X to Y are continuous.

SEE ALSO *Manifolds*

BIBLIOGRAPHY

Aliprantis, Charalambos D., and Kim C. Border. 2006. *Infinite Dimensional Analysis: A Hitchhiker's Guide.* 3rd ed. Berlin and New York: Springer.

Royden, Halsey. 1988. *Real Analysis.* 3rd ed. Englewood Cliffs, NJ: Prentice-Hall.

Aviad Heifetz

TORTURE

As media accounts and images of torture, trauma, disaster, and rape permeate our daily lives, it is difficult to ignore the impact such destruction wields on the social fabric in which we live. Individuals directly affected by this devastation, such as refugees, asylum seekers, IDPs (internally displaced people), and illegal immigrants, struggle to piece their lives back together after enduring unimaginable cruelty and violence. The cruel and violent acts witnessed and experienced by these individuals come in many forms, one of the most common being torture. Though the word *torture* is commonly used without restraint in everyday language, its use should be clearly differentiated from words for inhumane and degrading actions that may fail to match the true definition of "torture."

DEFINITIONS OF TORTURE

The two most frequently cited definitions of torture are the World Medical Association's (WMA) 1975 Declaration of Tokyo and the definition given by the 1984 United Nations Convention Against Torture.

The 1975 WMA Declaration defines torture as: "The deliberate, systematic, or wanton infliction of physical or mental suffering by one or more persons acting alone or on the orders of any authority, to force another person to yield information, to make a confession, or for any other reason." The 1984 United Nations Convention Against Torture expands upon this definition, distinguishing the legal and political components typically associated with torture:

> Any act by which severe pain or suffering, whether physical or mental, is intentionally inflicted on a person for such purposes as obtaining from him or a third person information or a confession, punishing him for an act he or a third person has committed or is suspected of having committed, or intimidating or coercing him or a third person, or for any reason based on discrimination of any kind, when such pain or suffering is inflicted by or at the instigation of or with the consent or acquiescence of a public official or other person acting in an official capacity.

Currently accepted definitions of torture have two essential elements: (1) Individuals are placed in captivity and subjected to extreme mental and physical suffering; and (2) the captors have a political goal or agenda. In this way, torture as a legal definition can be distinguished from criminal acts of violence.

TYPES AND PURPOSE OF TORTURE

The most common types of torture are summarized in Table 1. Torturers use these techniques to achieve several main goals. The most obvious intention of torture is breaking down an individual both physically and mentally (frequently for military or political purposes). Secondly, torturers seek to spread collective fear throughout a particular community or culture in which the victim lives. Finally, the torturer seeks to deeply humiliate the victim's society and community. The goal of torture is essentially to render the victim nonhuman.

Table 1. Most Common Forms of Torture.

Beating, kicking, striking with objects
Beating to the head
Threats, humiliation
Being chained or tied to others
Exposure to heat, sun, strong light
Exposure to rain, body immersion, cold
Being placed in a sack, box, or very small space
Drowning, submersion of head in water
Suffocation
Overexertion, hard labor
Exposure to unhygienic conditions conducive to infections and other diseases
Blindfolding
Isolation, solitary confinement
Mock execution
Being made to witness others being tortured
Starvation
Sleep deprivation
Suspension from a rod by hands and/or feet
Rape, mutilation of genitalia
Sexual humiliation
Burning
Beating to the soles of feet with rods
Blows to the ears
Forced standing
Having urine or feces thrown at one or being made to throw urine or feces at other prisoners
(Nontherapeutic) administration of medicine
Insertion of needles under toenails and fingernails
Being forced to write confessions numerous times
Being shocked repeatedly by electrical instrument

Table 1. Most Common Forms of Torture.

One important act of torture, for example, that has only recently been recognized as such is rape, a frequently used torture practice during periods of conflict and genocide. A group with a particular agenda often executes systematic or wanton rape and sexual violence knowing that the long-term effects of this experience will be devastating to both the individual and his or her community. However, rape was only recognized globally as an act of torture after the international appraisal of violence that occurred in Bosnia-Herzegovina and Rwanda.

PSYCHOLOGICAL AND PHYSICAL EFFECTS OF TORTURE

Knowledge of the types of torture described in Table 1 enables medical doctors, mental health professionals, and other health-care workers to assess the medical and psychological impact of torture and determine appropriate treatment. Until very recently, the psychological effects of torture have remained largely invisible. This is because of the combined effects of the difficulty of assessing mental symptoms in culturally diverse populations, the unsuccessful search by human-rights organizations for a unique "torture syndrome," and the popular belief in some medical circles that extreme violence leads to the psychiatric diagnosis of post-traumatic stress disorder (PTSD). PTSD may be an appropriate diagnosis. However, this emphasis on PTSD has obscured the reality that the most common mental illness diagnosed in torture survivors is depression—often a serious and socially debilitating condition associated with serious medical consequences. While physical complaints in torture survivors are very common, usually these bodily complaints are the way people from various cultures express their pain and suffering.

Head injuries caused by beatings to the head with fists, clubs, or gun butts represent one of the most common physical effects of torture, leading to neuropsychological deficits that are rarely identified. Studies have shown that victims of all types of torture often experience persistent and pervasive sensory and memory deficits, cognitive impairment, chronic pain, and certain forms of motor impairment (as serious as paraplegia) as a result of their torture experience. Other more specific physical symptoms commonly reported include headaches, impaired hearing, gastrointestinal distress, and joint pain. Scars on the skin and bone dislocations and fractures are also typically observed.

Since sexual violence is a common form of torture, its effects, including increased risk for cervical cancer, human immunodeficiency virus (HIV) infection and AIDS, and a range of sexual dysfunction including impotence, must be identified and treated by medical professionals.

TREATMENT FOR VICTIMS OF TORTURE

Physicians and health-care providers throughout the world are frequently confronted with the need to identify and treat the physical and psychological impact of extreme violence and torture. It is estimated, for example, that 60 percent of individuals who seek asylum in the United States have been tortured, as have many refugees and migrant workers. A history of torture is common in various groups that have resettled in the United States and other countries during recent decades—Cambodians, Vietnamese "boat people," and former Vietnamese prisoners of war (POW) who arrived in the 1980s; Central Americans who immigrated in the 1980s and 1990s; and recent arrivals from sub-Saharan Africa, the Middle East, and eastern Europe. Many newcomers enter the United States not only to find economic opportunities but also to escape violence and political instability at home.

Despite routine exposure to the suffering of victims of human brutality, many health-care professionals tend to be apprehensive about confronting this reality in their clinical work. Globally, clinicians often avoid addressing torture-related symptoms of illness, believing they will not have the tools or the time to help torture survivors once they have elicited their history. As a result of this resistance, survivors and clinicians may conspire to create a relationship founded on the avoidance of all discussion of trauma.

The most effective care for torture survivors must begin with awareness. Persons who have been tortured generally do not want to be treated simply as torture survivors. Rather, they prefer a holistic approach that addresses their current reality in a culturally sensitive way. Many characteristics of the patient's background provide clues that torture may have occurred. As health-care practitioners become more empowered to ask questions such as, "Have you experienced extreme violence or torture?," it becomes easier to identify and treat the pathological symptoms of such trauma.

Torture survivors often do not recognize any relationship between the torture and current medical problems they may be experiencing. When asked about specific events, patients are usually grateful that the clinician is aware of what they have suffered, is interested in their history, and is encouraging them to talk about their story. Though clinicians often fear a patient's reaction to questions about torture, patients rarely become emotionally overwhelmed or lose control when such questions are asked. Some torture survivors, especially victims of sexual violence, may have been hiding their history out of feelings of shame or fear of stigmatization, and thus be grateful to talk to someone who cares. Others may come from cultures in which physicians are not expected to be interested in patient's personal history.

RECOVERY FOR SURVIVORS OF TORTURE

Many torture survivors recover from torture with the help of spiritual and religious practices, work, and altruistic activities that benefit themselves, their families, and their communities. These self-healing efforts need to be strongly supported by society and its health-care and mental health–care institutions. Human beings are incredibly resistant to even the most horrifying acts of human cruelty. While the majority of torture survivors recover without professional help, some do not. It has been shown that these individuals can greatly profit from proper medical and mental health care that will facilitate their return to a normal life.

A broad range of individual treatments exist that include primary health care, physical rehabilitation of torture-related disabilities, and psychological interventions aimed at eliminating traumatic memories, nightmares and chronic depression. Healing of torture survivors is also maximized when governments and the international community acknowledge the injustice they have suffered (e.g., the Truth and Reconciliation Commission in South Africa).

SEE ALSO *Guantánamo Bay; Interrogation; Justice; Post-Traumatic Stress; Refugees; Reparations; Resiliency; Restitution Principle; Sexual Harassment; Terrorism; Trauma; Traumatic Bonding; Violence; Vulnerability; War*

BIBLIOGRAPHY

Convention Against Torture and Other Cruel, Inhuman or Degrading Treatment or Punishment. 2002. Geneva, Switzerland: Office of the United Nations High Commissioner for Human Rights. http://www.unhchr.ch/html/menu2/6/cat/treaties/opcat.htm

Goldfield, Anne E., Richard F. Mollica, Barbara H. Pesavento, et al. 1988. The Physical and Psychological Sequelae of Torture: Symptomatology and Diagnosis. *Journal of the American Medical Association* 259: 2725–2729.

Krug, Etienne G., James A. Mercy, Linda L. Dahlberg, and Anthony B Zwi, eds. 2002. World Report on Violence and Health. Geneva, Switzerland: World Health Organization. http://www.who.int/violence_injury_prevention/violence/world_report/en/introduction.pdf

Mollica, Richard F. 2000. Invisible Wounds: Waging a New Kind of War. *Scientific American* 282: 54–57.

Mollica, Richard F. 2004. Surviving Torture. *New England Journal of Medicine* 351: 5–7.

Mollica, Richard F. 2006. *Healing Invisible Wounds: Paths to Hope and Recovery in a Violent World*. Orlando, FL: Harcourt.

Quiroga, Jose, and James M. Jaranson. 2005. Politically-Motivated Torture and Its Survivors: A Desk Study Review of the Literature. *Torture* 15 (2–3): 1–111.

Richard F. Mollica
Daniel Hovelson

TOTAL FACTOR PRODUCTIVITY

SEE *Growth Accounting.*

TOTALITARIANISM

Totalitarianism is a term employed by social scientists to describe a type of political regime that arose in the twentieth century. What is said to distinguish this type of regime from traditional forms of nondemocratic authority such as tyranny or dictatorship is the ability of the totalitarian state to establish and maintain a highly integrated social system that controls nearly every aspect of public and private life.

Social scientists have developed a theoretical model to delimit five essential features underlying this unique political system. First, the totalitarian state is organized around an all-encompassing ideology that subordinates all aspects of society to the logic of a teleological process that promises to culminate in the attainment of a perfect and final stage of humanity. In order to achieve the revolutionary goal, the totalitarian project systematically eliminates constraints on state power. In this manner, a totalitarian state aims to establish a permanent state of emergency (wherein the rule of law is suspended) as a legal norm, thus, in effect, codifying arbitrary power.

Second, totalitarianism destroys all social, legal, and political traditions that precede it. It transforms a pluralistic party system into the rule of a single mass party headed usually by a single dictator. The party aims to transform the ensemble of social relations into an integrated social totality by a process of perpetual revolution.

Third, if this "perpetual revolution" is to be carried out successfully, it must institutionalize a highly coordinated use of terror that shifts the epicenter of power from the army to the police. Totalitarian use of terror suppresses not only political opposition and all groups and ideas not subordinate to the substantive goals of the state, but also all social space traditionally beyond state control that exists among citizens. Such use of terror produces an environment within which individuals live with an extremely high level of uncertainty and unpredictability.

Fourth, such a regime monopolizes not only the armed forces, but all forms of mass communication as well. Seizing control over the means of communication allows the state to socialize and mobilize different segments of the population through the dissemination of mass propaganda. This mobilization entails the participation of individuals in state-sponsored social and political organizations that stage events and campaigns that often target an "enemy of the state," usually entire categories of citizens that must be eliminated. Finally, the totalitarian state seeks central control and direction of the economy.

The two outstanding historical examples of totalitarian states are Nazi Germany, particularly during the years of World War II (1939–1945), and Stalinist Russia (1927–1953). Although most commentators agree on the totalitarian nature of these two states, there is no general consensus on what other states can be declared totalitarian, but such a list could arguably include fascist Italy under Benito Mussolini (1922–1943); Communist China, particularly during the Cultural Revolution

(1966–1976); Khmer Rouge Cambodia (1975–1979); Augusto Pinochet's Chile (1973–1989); the Argentine military regime of the 1970s; and North Korea since 1953.

CAUSES OF TOTALITARIANISM

There are a number of possible causes of the rise of totalitarian states. An historically specific explanation has it that the political and economic chaos in Europe that followed World War I (1914–1918) created a climate of fear and resentment that some popular governments and movements exploited in order to seize or consolidate state power. Fascist totalitarian regimes (Mussolini's Italy and Nazi Germany) aimed at diverting attention from class conflict by ruthlessly repressing political strife and labor unrest and promoting a form of nationalism in the name of interclass solidarity. Communist systems, on the other hand, sought to end class struggle and inaugurate a classless utopia by repressing those opinions and actions deemed antithetical to a workers' state.

Another argument holds that industrialization eroded traditional social values and familial, social, and professional bonds, thereby creating a gap that was then filled by the development of a modern mass society; the latter came to be distinguished by a uniform style of life reinforced by propaganda, advertising, and mass entertainment. In such a society, individuals severed from tradition become alienated and highly susceptible to totalitarian manipulation.

An explanation popular with libertarian theorists argues that the roots of totalitarianism can be found in the gradual growth of socialism in all industrial societies. Such theorists argue that because socialism requires states to direct and control the economy, it lays the groundwork for the eventual subordination, regulation, and domination of all aspects of public and private life.

Another explanation sees a connection between the rise of totalitarianism and the influence exerted by certain traditions in political philosophy that promote a theoretical justification for the creation and preservation of an ideal state. Jean-Jacques Rousseau's concept of a "general will" and G. W. F. Hegel's exposition of "absolute spirit" in the state are often included in a larger historical narrative that isolates the origins of totalitarianism in the Enlightenment philosophers' equation of reason with the transformative powers of technology. An alternative explanation views the rise of totalitarianism as part and parcel of European imperialism and racism.

Totalitarianism differs from its equally nondemocratic and modern counterpart, authoritarianism. Whereas the former is concerned with revolutionizing the entirety of social relations, the latter is principally concerned only with exercising and maintaining direct political control. Authoritarian states do not reach into the private sphere, at least to the same extent as their totalitarian counterparts. Authoritarian states thus allow elements of civil society such as religious organizations, schools, private nonpolitical associations, and the press to retain a relative degree of autonomy. Seeking above all to ensure their own political survival, authoritarian states have neither the will nor the resources to control all aspects of social, economic, and individual life. It should be noted, however, that the theoretical distinction between these two kinds of states tends to falter when applied to actual countries. However, the inadequacy of the distinction in this context does often serve to illuminate the extent to which its use is primarily determined by the political perspective of the analyst. For example, during the cold war, conservative commentators were likely to see left-wing dictatorships as "totalitarian" and their right-wing counterparts as "authoritarian." Analyses of the right-wing military regimes of South America's Southern Cone have since questioned this easy demarcation.

HISTORY OF THE CONCEPT

Although the term *totalitarian* was first coined by the Italian fascist philosopher Giovanni Gentile in 1925, it did not come into widespread use in the social sciences until the 1940s. During this period Hannah Arendt, Carl Friedrich, and Zbigniew Brezinski were primarily responsible for expanding the use of the term so that it could serve as a means of understanding the excessive repression associated with Nazi Germany and Stalinist Russia. During the cold war the concept played a pivotal role in the formation of U.S. containment policy directed toward the Soviet Union and other communist and/or socialist states. It then fell into disuse during the 1960s, particularly among Western Sovietologists, either because it was seen as lacking conceptual rigor or, more likely, because it was viewed as more an ideological than an analytical form of typology. Nevertheless, the term was revived a decade later by neoconservative theorist Jeane Kirkpatrick, who sought to influence U.S. foreign policy makers by arguing that although totalitarian states were incapable of transforming themselves into democracies, their authoritarian counterparts could be refashioned into liberal democracies—or at least into nonthreatening realpolitik allies in the U.S. attempt to contain global communism. The appositeness of this argument abruptly expired in the wake of the unanticipated implosions of the Soviet Union and its Eastern bloc allies in the late twentieth century.

In the opening years of the twenty-first century, however, the term was redefined yet again, this time by leftist theorists who pointed to the encroachment of capitalist markets into an increasing number of sectors of liberal democratic states. This growing depoliticization of public space is viewed as indicative of a new kind of totalitarianism.

Some critics charge that the concept of totalitarianism does not account for the different forms of social totality that may exist, not all of which are tyrannical; that is, that the concept tends to conflate all forms of social totality (the expansion of the public sphere into the private) with *statist* totality (one where the state controls all aspects of life). However, other forms of social totality, such as communitarianism (in which individuals tend to see in the public realm the fulfillment of their private interests) and involuntary totality (one where pluralistic compromise requires public power to seep into the private realm, such as with the modern welfare state), enjoy widespread support. The conceptual weakness of the concept of totalitarianism lies in its reliance on the abstract liberal democratic bifurcation of society into public and private spheres, an analytical division that seems to grow less rather than more distinct when submitted to historical and theoretical scrutiny.

The concept of totalitarianism has also been faulted for overstating the monolithic nature of the regimes it explains. According to such critics, totalitarian states are more likely to resemble a "fragmented authoritarianism," where power is dispersed pluralistically among competing elites situated at various levels of government, instead of being derived from any single and totalizing source or idea. Viewed in this manner, totalitarianism no longer functions as an accurate or adequate tool to explain nondemocratic regimes. Some critics have also noted that the term readily lends itself to certain ideological and propagandistic programs; according to one argument, the concept of totalitarianism functions in liberal democratic societies as a way of preempting any theory or practice aimed at an egalitarian transformation of social and political relations. Known as the "blackmail of totalitarianism," this tactic holds that any achievements associated with a sociopolitical movement with aspirations for expanding equality would inevitably usher in a new reign of terror. Critics note that this "blackmail" attempts to limit the very possibility of egalitarian politics by isolating it as antidemocratic.

Other scholarship also has called into question the traditional juxtaposition of totalitarianism to constitutional democracy. The latter limits the power and authority of the state in order to promote pluralism, whereas the former obliterates the distinction between the state and civil society in order to consolidate its power. However, upon closer inspection, certain similarities between totalitarianism and modern mass democracy are discernible. In both, the state possesses a monopoly of military and police force. Both control certain forms of mass communication and suppress dissent, particularly in times of crisis. Some

theorists have noticed that by the early twenty-first century, democracies, not unlike their totalitarian counterparts, have invoked with increasing frequency the state of emergency as a means of preserving the legal norm. Also, as noted originally by Alexis de Tocqueville, modern democracies often engender a high level of conformity to repressive and irrational standards of social behavior—a feature also found in totalitarian states. What this suggests is that, in its own way, the modern mass democracy may be just as adept as totalitarianism at placing effective limits on individual freedom. In this sense, democracy and totalitarianism share certain features that have become hallmarks of a technically advanced mass society.

TOTALITARIANISM IN POPULAR CULTURE

By means of literature and cinema, totalitarianism has made its way into the popular imagination. An entire literary genre known as dystopian literature is dedicated to nightmarish representations of totalitarian systems. These depictions are crafted largely through the satirizing of certain trends in contemporary society. The major texts of this genre include Yevgeny Zamyatin's *We* (1922), Aldous Huxley's *Brave New World* (1931), and George Orwell's *1984* (1949). These three works vary in their views as to what elements in contemporary society are most totalitarian. Zamyatin criticizes the desire for technological efficiency and routine rooted in industrial societies by depicting the world as a single state dedicated to the static mathematical and technological routinization of all life. Huxley's novel targets the fetish of youth, the dangers of consumerism, and the manipulations of the human psyche built into commercial societies, especially the United States. Orwell's *1984* most directly targets Stalinist totalitarianism, but also includes satirical references to British capitalism. Orwell's novel is the most controversial of the three works, largely because of its mobilization during the cold war as a political attack on all utopian visions. Cinematic representations of totalitarianism include Bernardo Bertolucci's *Il Conformista* (*The Conformist*, 1970), Ridley Scott's *Blade Runner* (1982), and Terry Gilliam's *Brazil* (1985). Whereas Bertolucci and Gilliam, in quite different ways, tackle totalitarianism from the perspective of the individual's longing for escape, Scott depicts the loss of humanity in a world dominated politically by large, manipulative corporate interests. Cinematic representations of totalitarianism share the diversity and nightmarish elements of their literary cousins.

SEE ALSO *Authoritarianism; Mussolini, Benito; Repressive Tolerance; Tito (Josip Broz); Tyranny of the Majority; Union of Soviet Socialist Republics*

BIBLIOGRAPHY

Agamben, Giorgio. 2005. *State of Exception*. Trans. Kevin Attell. Chicago: University of Chicago Press.

Arendt, Hannah. 1951. *Origins of Totalitarianism*. New York: Harcourt, Brace, Jovanovich.

Friedrich, Carl, and Zbigniew Brezinski. 1956. *Totalitarian Dictatorship and Autocracy*. Cambridge, MA: Harvard University Press.

Friedrich, Carl, Michael Curtis, and Benjamin Barber. 1969. *Totalitarianism in Perspective: Three Views*. New York: Praeger.

Graziano, Frank. 1992. *Divine Violence: Spectacle, Psychosexuality, and Radical Christianity in the Argentine "Dirty War."* Boulder, CO: Westview Press.

Jacoby, Russell. 2005. *Picture Imperfect: Utopian Thought for an Anti-Utopian Age*. New York: Columbia University Press.

Kirkpatrick, Jeane. 1982. *Dictatorships and Double Standards: Rationalism and Reason in Politics*. New York: Simon & Schuster.

Zizek, Slavoj. 2002. *Did Somebody Say Totalitarianism? Five Interventions on the (Mis)Use of a Notion*. London: Verso.

Kevin Cameron

TOTEMISM

Totemism has been the subject of much discussion within the social sciences, in particular within the discipline of social anthropology, concerning both what totemism means and whether it is a valid, cross-culturally descriptive term for the range of phenomena it is often used to describe. Various definitions of totemism exist, but it is usually agreed that the word *totem* is derived from the language of the Ojibwa, an Algonquin Native American ethnic group from north of the Great Lakes region in North America. Claude Lévi-Strauss, who has produced one of the most important works on the subject, *Totemism* (1962), describes how the Ojibwa expression *ototeman* means, approximately, "He (she) is a relative of mine" ([1962] 1991, p. 18). This is significant, for a useful and broad definition of *totemism* is that it refers to the use of plants or animals by social groups as guardians or emblems that are ritually celebrated. In such a system, different social groups are identified with different species.

There have been two phases in how totemism has been considered by anthropologists. Initially, it was presented by such scholars as Émile Durkheim (1858–1917) and James Frazer (1854–1941) within an evolutionary framework—that is, totemism was seen as a unified and universal phenomenon that was a required state of the religious belief through which all societies must proceed. The second, less simplistic view allows for variety in both the classificatory systems and the symbolism evident in

totemism in different cultural contexts. The latter is best represented by the work of Lévi-Strauss. A third phase of thinking about totemism is sometimes apparent, in that totemism is at times now subsumed, usually erroneously, within the category of shamanism. As a result, the religious beliefs and practices of hunter-gatherer communities, for instance, might be referred to exclusively as those of *shamanism*, while *totemism* is suppressed or avoided. This third view might reflect the fads to which scholarship, like many other endeavors, is subject, for *shamanism* is academically fashionable at present, whereas *totemism* is not.

The archaeologist Steven Mithen has suggested that cognitive developments indicate that totemism and anthropomorphic thought developed as early as circa 100,000 years ago as a result of the integration of the domains of social and natural history intelligence (1996). This view is interesting, if difficult to prove, and the denotations of the earliest possible material indicators of totemism have been subject to debate. For example, recent interpreters of Upper Paleolithic rock art, which appeared around 40,000 years ago in Europe, see it as primarily shamanic rather than totemic. This interpretation is based upon the distribution of the images present in rock art. The species represented in a shamanic system will be widely depicted as guardians available to people in many different groups. In contrast, the species represented in totemic rock art are much more preferentially depicted within the group territory for which they serve as a totemic emblem. The later rock art of parts of Australia is usually described as totemic. The rock art of Wardaman country in the Northern Territory, for example, is linked with the "dreaming" (i.e., creation) and with totemism through the representation of painted dreaming beings such as emus, devil dogs, flying foxes, and nail-tail wallabies.

Bruno David has described the central role of totemism in various Australian aboriginal societies, as manifest in rock art but also in totemic centers and sacred objects, and their associated rituals, the whole creating "a socially meaningful, ordered world" (David 2002, p. 51). In the Australian examples, totemism is manifest across whole landscapes; in other societies, it may be prominently attested in different ways. The totem poles produced by various Native North American ethnic groups of the Pacific Northwest Coast, such as the Haida people of the Queen Charlotte Islands, provide an example of the variety that exists, affirming Lévi-Strauss's thesis, as well as the absence of a universal totemic "template." Totemism certainly continues today, in Australia and also among the Tallensi of northern Ghana, but as is usual, it forms one element of a set of religious beliefs and practices that cannot be defined as solely totemic. In fact, totemism has probably never been the sole element of any group religious practice and belief where totemism is found, but rather coexists alongside, for instance, animistic beliefs, ancestral and earth cults, or shamanism. Among New Age groups where paganism, neoshamanism, and druidism are found, totemic beliefs, as understood by the definition given above, apparently do not exist. In the United Kingdom, for instance, where druidism, paganism, and neoshamanism all prevail, totemism rarely enters the relevant vocabulary, perhaps indicating its absence or a need to refine the definition of what totemism is.

SEE ALSO *Dreaming; Lay Theories; Levi-Strauss, Claude; Magic; Myth and Mythology; Religion; Rituals; Shamans; Supreme Being; Symbols; Visual Arts*

BIBLIOGRAPHY

David, Bruno. 2002. *Landscapes, Rock-Art, and the Dreaming: An Archaeology of Preunderstanding.* London: Leicester University Press.

Layton, Robert. 2000. Shamanism, Totemism, and Rock Art: *Les Chamanes de la Préhistoire* in the Context of Rock Art Research. *Cambridge Archaeological Journal* 10 (1): 169–186.

Lévi-Strauss, Claude. [1962] 1991. *Totemism.* Trans. Rodney Needham. London: Merlin.

Mithen, Steven. 1996. *The Prehistory of the Mind: A Search for the Origins of Art, Religion, and Science.* London: Thames and Hudson.

Wagner, Roy. 1986. Totemism. In *The Encyclopedia of Religion,* ed. Mircea Eliade, vol. 14, 573–176. New York: Macmillan.

Timothy Insoll

TOURÉ, SÉKOU

SEE *Socialism, African.*

TOURISM

Tourism is a complex phenomenon that can be conceptualized on several levels. It can be considered demographically, as the flow of temporary leisure migration across international boundaries (international tourism) or within the boundaries of a given country (domestic tourism). It can be thought of institutionally, as the system of enterprises (airlines, travel companies, touring agencies, hotels, resorts, guest houses, souvenir shops, restaurants, theme parks, and so on) and organizations (travel associations, local and national tourist authorities, and international tourist organizations) that process and serve that flow. Finally, it can be conceptualized socially, as the complex of attitudes, motivations, norms, and role models that regulate and shape that flow into a distinct institutional domain.

Traveling for leisure was common in many historical and premodern societies. Tourism as a socially recognized, separate institutional domain, however, emerged in western Europe only in the course of the nineteenth century.

HISTORY

There have been two major precursors of modern tourism: (1) *pilgrimages* to sacred places, which created basic services for travelers, such as hostelries, and formed routes that prefigured the itineraries of modern sightseeing tourism; (2) *spas*, or thermal springs, at which members of the European higher classes assembled to "take the waters," which prefigured popular modern vacationing tourism on seaside beaches.

The Grand Tour of the British nobility and upper classes between the late sixteenth and the early nineteenth centuries was a form of secular pilgrimage to the centers of European antiquity and culture. In its course, an expanding core of major attractions and amenities developed, which constituted the basis of the emergent modern tourist system.

The development of modern tourism was made possible by major technological innovations in transportation, such as the steamship and the train, and later the car and the airplane, which facilitated the establishment of regular transportation services for large numbers of people. The demand for tourist services, however, was provoked by the economic and social changes that followed the Industrial Revolution: Industrial pollution and urbanization separated people from as yet unspoiled nature; the strains of modern life created demands for rest and recreation; secularization and imperial conquests led to a broadened outlook on the world and a growing interest in remote lands and people. The prosperous middle classes increasingly disposed of discretionary income, which enabled them to bear the costs of traveling, while the introduction of social benefits, such as paid vacations, enabled ever broader social strata to travel. The introduction by Cook, in 1841, of the package tour, was followed by other innovations in the organization of travel, such as the formation of travel companies and touring agencies, airlines, and hotel chains, which made traveling fast and easy, even for people with limited cultural capital.

The principal expansion of tourism took place in the second part of the twentieth century, and especially from the 1970s onward, with the emergence of mass tourism to popular destinations. Most citizens of affluent Western countries at the end of the century took at least one annual vacation abroad, and many took two or even more. Tourism from the non-Western countries, especially Japan, and, more recently, India and China, expanded at an accelerating rate; experts predict that by 2010, one hundred million Chinese will be traveling abroad.

THE TOURIST INDUSTRY

Contemporary tourism is a massive phenomenon. According to the World Tourism Organization (UNTWO), there were 808 million international tourists in 2005, up from about 25 million in 1950. The scope of domestic tourism cannot be ascertained, but it is estimated to be three or four times larger than that of international tourism, totaling about 2.5 to 3.0 billion people per year.

Tourism is one of the leading components of world trade, accounting for about 6 percent of world exports of goods and services. In 2004 the total expenditures of international tourists amounted to $623 billion, up from about $2 billion in 1951. The great majority of international border crossings remain concentrated in Europe, a phenomenon ensuing partly from the relatively large number and small size of European countries. Six European countries are among the ten leading global destinations. France tops the list, with about 70 million visitors a year.

As of 2006 global tourism is growing at about 4 percent annually, but the rate of its expansion to non-Western destinations is significantly higher than it is in the old European core. This growth manifests a marked *heliotropic* tendency, a flow of tourists from the cold North to vacationing destinations in the warm South, particularly those around the Mediterranean, Caribbean, South Pacific, and Southeast Asian coasts.

Mass tourism is an important source of significant economic benefits, particularly to less-developed countries, but these are mostly unequally distributed. It has also generated undesirable and sometimes destructive environmental, social, and cultural consequences in popular destinations, which threaten the sustainability of local tourist industries. Small countries, particularly island states, in which tourism became the dominant industry while other sectors of the economy remained underdeveloped, are often utterly dependent on tourism, and thus often exposed to financial risks created by far-away political and economic crises.

In reaction to the problematic consequences of the hegemonic tourist industry, various kinds of "alternative tourisms" have emerged, such as "green" tourism, ecotourism, low-impact tourism, and "countercultural" tourism, the latter espoused in the ideology—but not necessarily in the practice—of contemporary backpackers. Most of these alternative tourisms, however, have been eventually absorbed by the tourist industry, which has adapted its services to the particular needs and preferences of alternative tourists.

More recently, rather than seeking alternatives to the industry, environmentalists and other concerned individuals have sought to collaborate with the industry to ascertain the sustainability of tourism development projects. They thus hope to prevent the environmental and social ravages that unconcerned and often speculative developments wrought in sensitive sites in the past.

SOCIOLOGICAL APPROACHES TO TOURISM

Sociologists have been slow in realizing the growing significance of tourism. Early commentators tended to disparage rather than analyze the phenomenon. Once its study was initiated, the principal issue of concern became the relationship between tourism and modernity (and, later on, postmodernity). Dean MacCannell (1973) proposed a distinctly sociological perspective on tourism, by conceiving of the tourist as a modern individual who, alienated from his own society, travels in quest of authentic experiences in other places and other times—in pristine nature, unspoiled, simple communities, or the traces of great civilizations of the past. In MacCannell's view, however, this quest is thwarted by the locals at the destinations, who stage "authentic" tourist settings for the visitors' consumption.

Though influential as a paradigm for the sociological study of modern tourism, MacCannell's approach was also much contested. Critics argued that he essentialized "the tourist," disregarding the empirical variety of touristic phenomena; while a quest for authenticity might be a modern cultural ideal, not all tourists are believed to pursue it to the same extent. Typologies of tourists and touristic experiences were proposed (Cohen 2004). Authenticity was shown to be a socially constructed concept, rather than a given fact. Ning Wang (2000) distinguished between three kinds of authenticity: objective, constructed, and existential—the latter being a state of exaltation, of "really living," virtually independent of the nature of the tourist's surroundings. Wang's concept may help explain the attractiveness of otherwise overtly contrived attractions, such as theme parks.

The emerging discourse of postmodern tourism, or the "post-tourist" (Urry 1990), moved away from MacCannell's paradigm. In a world allegedly devoid of originals, and dominated by simulacra (Baudrillard 1988), the quest for authenticity becomes senseless. The growing interpenetration of cultures in the twin processes of globalization and "glocalization" blurs the distinction between *home* and *away*, and between ordinary leisure and tourism. Sophisticated and reflective post-tourists are said to travel in quest of enjoyment of experiences that, while familiar, are of a higher quality, more abundant, more varied (and cheaper) than those available at home. They are particularly attracted to the "world cities," such as London, Paris, or New York, which are the pacesetters in contemporary music, art, fashions, and cuisine, but they may also derive fun from visits to such contrived attractions as technologically highly sophisticated theme parks, of which the Disneylands are the prototype. Some researchers argue that the alleged fragmentation of the postmodern worldview, and of individual identities, is reflected in the post-tourists' tendency to mix diverse experiences on the same trip (Uriely 2005), thus thwarting the possibility of constructing typologies of post-tourists.

In the contemporary world, tourism often merges with other institutional domains, such as education (study tours), religion (pilgrimage-tourism), sports (*extreme tourism*), and recently even medicine. *Medical tourism*, combining vacations with medical services, emerged in the last years of the twentieth century as a rapidly expanding phenomenon, with growing numbers of people from developed countries seeking a variety of treatments and checkups in developing ones. They are pushed by the escalating costs of private medicine, and the lengthening of waiting lists for socialized medical services, in their countries of origin, and attracted by the high quality and relatively low costs of treatments offered by top hospitals in several developing countries, such as Brazil, India, Malaysia, Singapore, Thailand, and Turkey. Popular vacationing destinations, such as the islands of southern Thailand, offer package tours, combining vacations with medical checkups, cosmetic treatments, and even surgery. The phenomenon has led to an internal brain drain of qualified physicians from local to foreigner-oriented medical establishments, but it has also encouraged some who emigrated to the developed West to return to their home countries.

THE FUTURE OF TOURISM

The alleged homogenization of the world under the impact of globalization is considered by some authorities as a disincentive for tourism; however, tourist numbers are in fact growing annually, and are projected to continue to grow even more strongly in the future, with much of the expected growth coming from newly prosperous non-Western countries. The tourist system has continually expanded into new regions, though large parts of sub-Saharan Africa, Central Asia, the South American interior, and Antarctica remain as yet relatively little penetrated by it. While it will probably yet expand into most of those regions, space is expected to become the new frontier of tourism in the twenty-first century. As yet affordable only to the extraordinarily rich, and facing apparently insurmountable technological, medical, and economic constraints, space tourism might remain restricted to only a few passengers into the foreseeable future; however, the current popularity of simulated space travel and of brief, commercial flights to the edge of space, offered to the general public, attest to a demand for the "real thing." If such

a demand persists, and is no mere fad inspired by novelty, it might provide the incentive for the necessary scientific breakthroughs in the more remote future. Whether and when space travel will become affordable to broad social strata, however, remains an open question.

SEE ALSO *Cultural Tourism; Disney, Walt; Gaze, The; Leisure; Tourism Industry*

BIBLIOGRAPHY

Baudrillard, Jean. 1988. *Selected Writings.* Ed. Mark Poster. Stanford CA: Stanford University Press.

Cohen, Erik. 2004. *Contemporary Tourism: Diversity and Change.* Amsterdam: Elsevier.

MacCannell, Dean. 1973. Staged Authenticity: Arrangements of Social Space in Tourist Settings. *American Journal of Sociology* 79 (3): 589–603.

Uriely, Natan. 2005. The Tourist Experience: Conceptual Developments. *Annals of Tourism Research* 32 (1): 199–216.

Urry, John. 1990. *The Tourist Gaze: Leisure and Travel in Contemporary Societies.* London: Sage.

Wang, Ning. 2000. *Tourism and Modernity: A Sociological Analysis.* Kidlington, U.K.: Pergamon.

Erik Cohen

TOURISM INDUSTRY

Leisure tourism has long been a pursuit of the wealthy, but it is only since the 1980s that the majority of the population has become involved, either as tourists or as workers catering for their needs—a phenomenon that has raised tourism to the position of one of the world's largest industries. Domestic tourism is estimated to be ten times greater in volume than international tourism, and yet relatively little is known about it; closer attention has been paid to international tourism. With developments in world trade, better means of transport and communications, intensive marketing, rises in disposable income, improvements in political ties, technological advances, and increased leisure time, international tourism has grown rapidly, as is reflected in the global trend of inbound tourist arrivals and receipts. The number of international arrivals rose from 25 million in 1950 to 763 million in 2004, and receipts rose from $2 billion to $623 billion during the same period (World Tourism Organisation 2006).

Globalization has also contributed to the rapid expansion of tourism, via such changes as deregulation of air transport. The growth of charter flights, low-cost airlines, and package-tour holidays provided a major boost to this expansion. International and domestic tourism combined generate up to 10 percent of the world's gross domestic product (GDP) and a considerably higher share in many small nations and developing countries.

The tourism product comprises a combination of goods and services supplied by the tourism industry, as well as nonpriced features that motivate tourism, such as natural sites (such as beaches, mountains, and forests), historic sites, and cultural features. The welcome provided to tourists by industry employees and by the local population is also of fundamental importance. The tourism industry includes hospitality (e.g., accommodation, restaurants), transportation (e.g., airlines, car rental), travel facilitation and information (e.g., tour operators, travel agents, tourist information centers), and attractions and entertainment (e.g., heritage sites and theme, national, and wildlife parks). Thus the scope of tourism supply is wide-ranging and influenced by market conditions that affect the environment in which tourism businesses operate.

The market structures within which tourism businesses operate vary from highly competitive (akin to perfect competition) to monopoly. Key features indicating competitive status are the number and size of firms, degree of concentration, entry and exit conditions, pricing strategies, profit levels, product differentiation, cost structures and capacity, and interaction between firms (Sinclair and Stabler 1997). The classification of the supply components is not straightforward; for example, the transport and accommodation sectors are themselves divided into subcategories with different market structures.

The accommodation sector is dominated by large chains (e.g., Cendant Corporation, Bass Hotels, Marriott, Accor, Choice, Hilton), giving the impression of an oligopolistic structure, and each firm's strategy takes account of the past and predicted future strategies of the others. This sector also encompasses a large number of other establishments with diverse attributes, including hotels, motels, holiday centers, timeshares, and camping facilities, and the diversity of the products that they provide, and a degree of price control, indicate monopolistic competition. In contrast, a highly competitive market structure characterizes the sales of souvenirs and knickknacks by numerous small businesses, including street-based sellers, who have very limited control over the prices they can charge tourists.

Tour operators negotiate deals with hotels, airlines, and other service operators to assemble holiday packages primarily for the mass market, facilitating a link between suppliers and customers. The packages are retailed through travel agents or directly to the customer. In the United Kingdom, the inbound and outbound tour-operator organizations, UK Inbound and ABTA (Association of British Travel Agents), respectively, defend their inter-

ests. ABTA had 6,310 travel-agent office members and 1,052 tour-operator office members in 2005, generating a combined turnover of £26 billion. Eighty-five percent of all package holidays sold in the United Kingdom were sold through ABTA members. The four dominant tour operators in the United Kingdom are Thomson, First Choice, My Travel, and Thomas Cook. Large tour operators are primarily linked to the mass market, whereas specialized tour operators that cater for ecotourists, older tourists, and gay and lesbian travelers are growing rapidly. Although the large tour operator market structure is highly concentrated, suggesting an oligopolistic structure, there is relatively easy entry into and exit from the sector, so it has many of the characteristics of a competitive, contestable market. The fact that many tour operators tend to experience low profit margins also indicates a competitive structure. High sales volumes have enabled the large firms to achieve substantial economies of scale and scope, but they are experiencing intense competition from Internet travel sites.

Travel agents are, in effect, retailers providing travel services to customers for commission. Some are linked to tour operators, and others function independently. This intermediary sector has experienced substantial growth. In the United States there has been an almost fivefold increase in agency outlets since the early 1970s. In the early 1990s more than two-thirds were single-office agents, and just one-fifth were branches of multiple firms. This is in contrast with Europe, where single outlets account for no more than one-third of the total, with the major multiples owning just over one-quarter (Sinclair and Stabler 1997). Like the tour operators, travel agents are facing a major challenge from the rapidly growing Web-based companies that sell a wide range of holiday packages over the Internet.

Transport is a crucial factor in the growth of tourism. With the wide range of transport modes (air, rail, car, bus, coach, ferry), the market structure is diverse. Air travel is of key importance in terms of passengers carried and revenue generated. Since the 1960s air travel has grown tremendously, and with technological change the potential for growth has increased further. With deregulation, privatization, low-cost airlines, and globalization, competition in the air industry is fierce, although oligopolistic conditions and domestic monopoly still exist in some long-haul destinations, and airline alliances such as the Star Alliance and One World have facilitated collaboration. The structures of the bus, coach, ferry, and rail sectors are similar to the air sector's in that they have problems of high capital costs, fixed capacity, peaked demand, and the need for feeder routes to sustain profitable ones.

The source markets for international tourism are concentrated in the industrialized countries of Europe, the

Americas, and Asia and the Pacific. The main tourist-generating countries are in the world's industrial core: The United States and Germany are the major markets, followed by the United Kingdom, Japan, France, and Italy. With rising levels of disposable income many emerging economies, such as those of Central and Eastern European countries, have shown fast growth in recent decades, and China is becoming a major source market.

Europe remains the most visited of all regions of the world; since the new millennium it has received almost 60 percent of all international tourists and more than half of total tourism receipts. France is the most popular destination visited by tourists worldwide, followed by Spain, the United States, Italy, China, and the United Kingdom. In terms of international tourism receipts, the United States has been the major recipient, accounting for around 12 percent of the total, followed by Spain (8 percent) and France (7 percent).

Outbreaks of disease or political unrest or terrorist attacks have recently hit the tourism industry with some severe and unexpected downturns in demand. Examples include the Gulf War in the early 1990s, the terrorist attacks at Luxor in Egypt in 1997, the Kosovo conflict in 1999, foot-and-mouth disease in the United Kingdom in 2001, the September 11 terrorist attacks in the United States in 2001, and the tsunami in the South Pacific in 2004. All of these events had negative impacts on the number of international tourist arrivals. In 2003 world tourist arrivals were 691 million, compared with 703 million in 2002. Tourist arrivals from the United States fell from a high of 128 million in 2000 to 113 million in 2003. Despite the volatility in demand over the short term, the World Tourism Organization forecasts that international arrivals will reach more than 1.56 billion by the year 2020, with Europe being the top destination, followed by East Asia and the Pacific, the Americas, Africa and the Middle East, and South Asia.

The recent high growth in tourist arrivals and expenditures affects host destinations in various ways, contributing to higher exports of services, bringing in foreign currency, increasing the level of income, and generating tax revenue. Tourism also generates large numbers of jobs, although remuneration in many parts of the tourist industry is low compared with other industries. There is significant gender structuring in employment. For example, in the United Kingdom in 1995, 76 percent of jobs in the transport sector were filled by men, whereas 62 percent of those in accommodation and catering were undertaken by women (Purcell 1997). Furthermore, in the hospitality sector staff often live on premises and are expected to work long and "unsocial" hours. Many receive low pay, and there is a large proportion of young, female, and part-time and casual staff, as well as high staff turnover in many establishments.

Although the tourism industry has great potential for benefiting recipient countries, major criticisms have been leveled at its impact on the environment as well as on social norms and cultures. Construction of resort hotels and theme parks, for instance, has led to significant changes in the environment and some reduction in the biodiversity of native flora and fauna. Damage to coastal areas has been a cause for concern, with construction of marinas and other water-based activities. Other environmental issues relate to noise and air pollution (for example, from aircraft, vehicles, nightclubs) and to water contamination by discharges from hotels, boats, and cruise ships. These pose serious challenges for destination managers.

Industry problems, ranging from increasing competition between destinations to environmental concerns, have encouraged destinations to introduce structural changes and to think about sustainable tourism. Many destinations have stressed the importance of ecotourism. Tourism is a sensitive industry with respect to changes in economic, social, and political conditions, and tourism activities are hampered by disease, political unrest, and climatic changes. A further challenge for the tourism industry is to consider how to integrate tourism into society such that the economic benefits are equitably shared without significantly damaging the environment.

SEE ALSO *Colonialism; Development Economics; Gaze, Colonial; Gaze, Panoptic; Imperialism; Industry; Tourism; Travel and Travel Writing*

BIBLIOGRAPHY

Purcell, Kate. 1997. Women's Employment in U.K. Tourism: Gender Roles and Labour Markets. In *Gender, Work, and Tourism*, ed. M. Thea Sinclair, 35–59. London and New York: Routledge.

Sinclair, M. Thea, and M. Stabler. 1997. *The Economics of Tourism*. London and New York: Routledge.

World Tourism Organization. http://www.world-tourism.org.

Ramesh Durbarry
M. Thea Sinclair

TOUSSAINT-LOUVERTURE
1743–1803

Toussaint-Louverture was one of the most important leaders of the Haitian Revolution. He is generally considered to be the father of Haitian independence although he did not survive to see Haiti become free, and during his lifetime he claimed to be loyal to France.

Much of Toussaint's early life is shrouded in mystery. He was probably born in 1743, a slave on the Bréda plantation at Haut-du-Cap near today's Cap Haitien. There he was known as Toussaint Bréda. He served the plantation as a caretaker of livestock and a coachman, and was obviously a valuable slave who was treated with some consideration by his masters. He was allowed to marry Suzanne Simone before 1776, and they had three children. The estate manager, Antoine Bayon de Libertat, granted him his freedom, probably around 1774. By the 1780s he owned land and slaves and was a small-scale planter. He also served in the colonial militia. Haitian tradition holds that he went to Savannah, Georgia with the French army to fight in the American Revolution.

Toussaint, who knew how to read and write, became secretary to Georges Biassou (d. 1801), one of the early leaders of the slave rebels in Saint-Domingue's north province shortly after the great uprising of August 1791. He brought military professionalism and ideological and political coherence to the slave rebels' cause. After Biassou's death, Toussaint became supreme commander and led his forces to victories over a wide variety of enemies. It was at this time that he took the surname Louverture. He first fought against the French revolutionary government alongside Spanish and French Royalist troops. When in 1794 the government in Paris abolished slavery, Toussaint switched sides, taking a good-sized Spanish force by surprise and wiping it out. Then, he fought British invaders and dissident Haitian rebels before taking control of the entire island by 1801.

As governor-general of the island, he set up a system of required labor service for the former slaves that tried to respect both the human rights of the agricultural laborers and the property rights of the land owners, and to ensure the supply of tropical produce for the French market. But his system was highly unpopular among the former slaves, who did not want to go back to working on sugar plantations after they had fought a terrible war for their freedom. They refused to work, and the Haitian army had difficulty forcing them. Production of sugar remained very low.

This setback led Napoléon Bonaparte (1769–1821), now the supreme leader in France, to decide that Toussaint's liberty was not worth the price. Napoléon's wife and brother-in-law both owned property in Haiti and wanted the old system restored, and Napoléon saw the abolition of slavery as one of the excesses of the radical revolutionaries that he was determined to reverse. When he sent an army in 1802 to overthrow Toussaint and restore the old system, Toussaint and a few of his sol-

diers fought the invaders, but most of his army obeyed Napoléon's orders. The few resisters put up a tough fight but were finally defeated. Toussaint was arrested and taken to France, where he died in prison. Even as he was breathing his last, his former generals were becoming aware of Napoléon's plans and plotting a new uprising. Jean-Jacques Dessalines, Toussaint's lieutenant, led them in a terrible life-or-death struggle and won Haitian liberty on January 1, 1804.

Toussaint-Louverture became a symbol of freedom for blacks throughout the African diaspora. He inspired an 1802 sonnet by William Wordsworth, "To Toussaint Louverture," which is considered one of the founding documents of English romanticism in literature as well as an inspiration to English abolitionists. He also inspired the African American artist Jacob Lawrence to make a famous series of portraits illustrating moments in Toussaint's life. Lawrence's art played a role in the great African American cultural renaissance of the 1930s and also inspired a re-evaluation of Toussaint in modern scholarship. With *The Black Jacobins* (1938) C. L. R. James attempted to make the Haitian Revolution fit the Marxist category of bourgeois revolution, but Toussaint somehow took over the book and became the idealized tragic hero. Subsequent scholarship refined James's view, both by illuminating the repressive nature of Toussaint's regime and by showing that Toussaint was a pre-revolutionary free colored plantation owner (and so more like the bourgeois James had signally failed to paint him as). However, modern scholars and Haitian national tradition still see him as a tragic, perhaps flawed, but essentially heroic figure who deserves to be considered alongside Martin Luther King Jr., Frederick Douglass, and Marcus Garvey as one of the great heroes of black liberation. Toussaint remains the tragic hero of the Haitian Revolution who wanted to make a just, multiracial society in the French empire and ended up inadvertently creating a black American republic, Haiti, which has been a dictatorship for most of its national existence.

SEE ALSO *Haitian Revolution; James, C. L. R.*

BIBLIOGRAPHY

Bell, Madison Smartt. 2007. *Toussaint Louverture: A Biography.* New York: Pantheon.

Dubois, Laurent. 2005. *Avengers of the New World: The Story of the Haitian Revolution.* Cambridge, MA: Belknap.

James, C. L. R. [1938] 1989. *The Black Jacobins: Toussaint L'Ouverture and the San Domingo Revolution.* 2nd ed. New York: Vintage.

Stewart R. King

TOWNS

Towns have usually accommodated great social diversity, making them places of magnificent human achievements as well as sometimes-violent struggles over resources and power. The words *town* and *city* are largely interchangeable, with the former used more in Britain than in the United States, where it is typically reserved for smaller settlements. The names are applied to places with substantial clusters of residents and buildings as well as complex social and economic structures. In some times and places, towns have been independent and self-governing; in others, they have been granted limited self-government.

The earliest towns emerged in the Middle East and are known only from archaeological evidence. Jericho is sometimes identified as the first town, around 7000 BCE, but many scholars believe that the first true towns were those that arose after the development of agriculture, beginning with Sumerian cities such as Ur, around 3000 BCE. At later dates, towns also developed in productive agricultural regions of Egypt, India, China, and Mesoamerica. Early towns were typically ceremonial centers, home to priests, soldiers, and administrators as well as skilled artisans who made luxury goods for members of the ruling class. Often the demand for luxuries stimulated long-distance trade, and some towns became centers of commerce, in which merchants were among the most wealthy and powerful residents. Coastal towns devoted to trade and commerce first flourished around the eastern Mediterranean in the Phoenician and Greek civilizations, which were later conquered by the Roman Empire. After Rome lost control of the Mediterranean around the fifth century CE, and Muslim invaders subsequently conquered much of the region, many Mediterranean towns became important Islamic administrative and commercial centers, whereas Christian Europe became a much more exclusively rural civilization. Although Italian commercial towns such as Venice and Amalfi revived by the tenth century, towns remained marginal to the rural and feudal society of medieval Europe. Partial exceptions were northern Italy and the Low Countries, where commercial towns ruled much of the countryside. These towns and regions dominated the European cultural revival known as the Renaissance, which began in the fourteenth century.

URBANIZATION AND INDUSTRIALIZATION

For several centuries more, Europe, like the rest of the world, remained a place where a tiny percentage of the population lived in towns, and economies as well as political power were rural-based, with the great majority of the population working in subsistence agriculture, producing a small surplus that supported priestly, warrior, and ruling elites. These elites were sometimes based in towns, and here and there cities grew to great size, for example ancient Rome, medieval Baghdad, Tenochtitlan in Mexico, and several Chinese capitals.

A fundamental change in the role of towns came with urbanization—that is, when larger percentages of a region's or nation's population came to live in them. This shift coincided with the growth of large-scale industry, beginning in eighteenth-century England and spreading across much of Europe, and beyond, in the nineteenth century. Many towns grew rapidly as rural migrants arrived in search of work in the new factories or in other trades stimulated by urban growth and industrial wealth. Around 1800 London became the first European city with a million inhabitants; a century later, at least eight more had crossed that threshold, and London's six million made it far larger than any city in history. Outside of Europe, North America experienced the most dramatic nineteenth-century urban growth. The twentieth century, especially its second half, saw rapid urbanization in other regions, notably East Asia. Whereas the world's population was still 70 percent rural in 1950, sometime around 2007, town dwellers became a majority. By then, twenty cities, most of them in Asia, had at least ten million inhabitants.

In many poor countries, urban growth has been concentrated in a single city, typically the capital, with floods of migrants drawn by rural overpopulation, political turmoil, and the collapse of agricultural or subsistence economies. In one respect this recent phase differs fundamentally from nineteenth-century Europe: This is often urbanization without industrialization. That had been the exception in nineteenth-century Europe, characteristic of only a few of Europe's poorest cities, such as Naples and Dublin. By the late twentieth century, however, as political and economic turmoil continued to push rural people toward large cities in their home countries or foreign ones, they arrived in places where there were few industrial jobs, and they joined a vast informal sector of intermittent, insecure, and often illegal work. Following a long tradition, these migrants see towns as places of opportunity, but most of them have little chance for security or prosperity.

SOCIAL AND SPATIAL STRUCTURES

From their earliest origins, towns have been associated with complex social structures and a diversity of occupations and roles. Far more than the countryside, towns have usually encompassed extremes of wealth and poverty, with rulers and wealthy merchants living near their slaves, servants, and laborers. As a result, towns have typically been centers of economic dynamism, cultural innovation, and social and political tensions. These urban phenomena have interested social scientists since the eighteenth century, when Adam Smith's theory of the division of labor explained the great economic potential inherent in the occupational specialization found in towns. Many liberal theorists following Smith have also contended that towns fostered individual opportunity and individual identities, thus promoting economic growth as well as new doctrines of citizenship and human rights that challenged traditional barriers of caste and status. However, Karl Marx and other socialists (including Vladimir Lenin), observing the concentration of poverty and misery among urban factory workers and casual laborers, predicted that revolutionary change would begin in towns, where oppressed classes would forge bonds of solidarity.

The combination of urban growth and the breakdown of traditional hierarchies has encouraged the urban upper classes to live apart from their poorer neighbors. The modern town has thus been characterized by horizontal segregation, following two basic patterns that have developed in different times and places. In one, the prestigious town center, the traditional site of palaces and shrines, is reserved for the wealthy, and the poor live on the urban edge in suburbs or shantytowns. This arrangement became typical of many European cities (Paris is the best known) as well as former colonial cities in Asia and Latin America. Alternatively, in some places the city center became a stronghold of business and employment, not a prestigious residential district, and the wealthy moved out to suburbs. This pattern emerged in eighteenth-century England and became even more typical of the United States, where premodern urban traditions are scant. By the end of the twentieth century, suburbanization had become increasingly apparent elsewhere, as communications and transportation technology made it easy for elites to live far from their workplaces. The urban core may remain as an office center, but surrounding areas have become poor, even largely abandoned in the case of the most devastated U.S. cities. Many cities in the United States saw rapid change in the decades after World War II (1939–1945), as white working-class residents moved to the suburbs in large numbers, and industrial jobs either followed or left the area entirely. Left behind in the inner cities were concentrations of poverty, unemployment, and minority groups (mainly African Americans), with high crime rates and poor schools continuing to push upwardly mobile residents outward while making life more difficult for those left behind. By the end of the century, similar problems were becoming apparent in major cities of other wealthy countries, such as Britain and France, sometimes in poor suburbs rather than inner cities. At the same time, a countervailing trend has been the "gentrification" that has created or expanded enclaves of wealthy inner-city residents, sometimes dislodging but not necessarily reducing the concentrations of poverty.

SEE ALSO *Segregation, Residential; Sociology, Urban; Suburbs*

BIBLIOGRAPHY

Bairoch, Paul. 1988. *Cities and Economic Development: From the Dawn of History to the Present.* Trans. Christopher Braider. Chicago: University of Chicago Press.

Davis, Mike. 2006. *Planet of Slums.* London: Verso.

Hohenberg, Paul M., and Lynn Hollen Lees. 1995. *The Making of Urban Europe, 1000–1994.* Rev. ed. Cambridge, MA: Harvard University Press.

LeGates, Richard T., and Frederic Stout, eds. 2007. *The City Reader.* 4th ed. New York: Routledge.

Brian Ladd

TOWNSHIPS

A township is the land formally allocated to hosting the site of a town; the word *township* legally refers to both residential and industrial sites. Possibly the most famous townships are in South Africa and were a creation of the apartheid system and its predecessor regimes of white rule.

Apartheid was formally instituted as state policy in 1948, but dating from the white settlers' permanent landing at what is now Cape Town in 1652, racial segregation was formal practice. The townships were racially discriminatory in that "black" African, "colored" (mixed-race), and "Indian" people were ordered by the Land Act of 1913 and the Group Areas Act of 1950 to live separately. Even within black townships, ethnic groups were often segregated into separate areas for Zulus, Xhosas, Sothos, and others. These laws existed until the early 1990s, and since then there has been only gradual desegregation of formerly white, colored, and Indian areas.

In the area surrounding Johannesburg, South Africa's largest metropolis (founded with the discovery of gold in 1886), the best-known townships are Soweto (an acronym for "South Western Townships") and Alexandra. Others include Bosmont (largely colored), Daveyton, Diepsloot, Duduza, El Dorado Park (colored), Etwatwa, Evaton, Ivory Park, Kagiso, Katlehong, KwaThema, Lenasia (Indian), Orange Farm, Tembisa, Thokoza, Tsakane, Vosloorus, and Wattville. These stretch more than 30 miles (50 kilometers) east–west and north–south, and they fuse into other townships near Pretoria and the Vaal River. The area constitutes a vast peri-urban expanse with more than 10 million residents in Gauteng Province. Of the townships, which together host more than half the population, only Alexandra is relatively well located, and hour-long commutes from the distant townships to work are common.

Townships originated from South Africa's unique economic requirement for inexpensive migratory labor, and they were managed using brutal policing systems as well as British municipal administrative traditions. Debates have raged between social scientists and policy advocates since the 1980s about whether to view townships through the lens of collective consumption (as do Jeffrey J. McCarthy and Daniel P. Smit, following Manuel Castells), the urban accumulation of capital (Patrick Bond, following David Harvey), administrative and spatial power (Jennifer Robinson, following Michel Foucault), or urban efficiency (the Urban Foundation, following the World Bank). Townships also give rise to debates about South African race and class (Harold Wolpe), activist political agency (Mzwanele Mayekiso), social history from below (Charles van Onselen), and gender relations (Belinda Bozzoli).

Although Cape Town and Port Elizabeth had townships dating to the early nineteenth century, the first modern, formal townships were in Kimberley, where migrant workers came to work in the mines following the discovery of diamonds in 1867. In these early townships were the infamous hostel systems that typically housed sixteen workers per sleeping room for eleven months of the year, with a one-month break to visit families in the Bantustan homelands. Indigenous black people were lured or often forcibly compelled to move from rural areas through a variety of means common to colonialism: the dispossession of good farmland, the expropriation of livestock, "hut taxes" forcibly paid through labor, periodic wars, and other forms of manipulation. Indian workers brought to the seaport city of Durban in the nineteenth century as indentured labor for the sugar estates gradually migrated to cities.

At the turn of the twentieth century, the South African War—also known as the Boer War—was responsible for uprooting large rural populations, including white Afrikaners (people of Dutch and French origin). After gold was discovered in Johannesburg in 1886, a "poor white problem" emerged in the area during the first three decades of the twentieth century. Housing shortages, sanitation crises, and public health epidemics such as an influenza outbreak fed into racial and moral panics about the proximity of black workers, who lived in the same urban neighborhoods as whites for a time. Water-borne sanitation was first introduced in Johannesburg around 1908, but the disposal of excrement for the entire city occurred close to the black locations.

There followed in 1922 a major labor revolt, the Rand Strike, by white gold miners concerned about the erosion of racial privileges as more black workers came to Johannesburg. (By 1946 blacks had become the majority urban residents.) As white workers and farmers gained increasing influence over government policy, more laws were passed to delineate the white cities from township sites for "temporary sojourners" (i.e., black migrant workers) who lived in urban areas so long as they had a job and a passbook to comply with the Pass Laws.

Real-estate property ownership by blacks was forbidden except in two townships near central Johannesburg that preceded the 1913 Land Act, Alexandra and Sophiatown. The latter, renamed Triomph, was destroyed in the 1950s, and residents were forcibly moved to Soweto. The Public Health Act of 1919 gave local administrative powers in some townships to the Department of Health. The Natives (Urban Areas) Act of 1923 provided for formal township (also known as "location") planning, and the Slums Act of 1934 provided for urban forced removals.

Townships sprouted across Johannesburg and the other main urban centers—Cape Town, Durban, Pretoria, Port Elizabeth, East London, the Vaal, Bloemfontein, and Pietersburg—as firms sought an unending stream of black workers during the high-growth era of the 1930s through the 1960s. Housing, transportation, and rudimentary health facilities were built by mining companies and other large employers.

In this process, several kinds of divisions endemic to South Africa and southern Africa were exacerbated, including class, race, gender, and rural-urban. In particular, women suffered in rural areas across the region by helping to inexpensively reproduce cheap labor through the Bantustan system and migrant labor. Women in these areas provided the kinds of child care, home schooling, home-based medical aid, and care for the elderly that ordinarily would have been provided by tax-based or benefit-based public and private educational, medical, and pension systems in a normal capitalist labor market. Because the women tended to remain in the rural areas caring for their families and communities, the townships had a much higher proportion of male dwellers, and firms were able to keep wages and employee benefits at inordinately low levels.

There were many important anti-apartheid protests in townships, including the famous 1955 Bus Boycott that required long walks by black workers into white towns. Many protests targeted living conditions. The typical township house was a "matchbox" of 430 square feet (40 square meters) with rudimentary plumbing but, until the 1980s, without electricity.

One reason for the adverse socioeconomic conditions was the inadequate tax base—often just beer-hall revenues—for the administratively distinct black townships. In contrast, black workers labored in white cities where employers paid taxes to white authorities, which offered first world amenities to white residents. In protest, community activists raised the demand, "One city, one tax base!" during the 1980s and insisted on integrated metropolitan authorities, in contrast to those who intended to maintain geographical segregation using U.S.-style suburban planning techniques.

Although the June 16, 1976, Soweto uprising against Afrikaans language education in the schools was the iconic moment of township protest, the nationwide mass uprisings from 1984 to 1986 and from 1989 to 1993 finally gave rise to South Africa's democracy, born in 1994. The apartheid-era black councilors chosen by white provincial authorities, especially between 1983 and 1994, were universally considered puppet collaborators, and many were forced to resign by anti-apartheid activists. At the same time, late-apartheid policymakers turned to the World Bank and the pro-business Urban Foundation for central advice on privatization of urban-housing stock and services. Public-housing construction ground to a halt by the early 1980s in black townships.

Even after apartheid was overthrown, however, restrictive macroeconomic conditions and neoliberal microeconomic policies meant that living conditions remained uncomfortable in most black townships. Statistics South Africa released a report in October 2002 confirming that in real terms, the average black household income declined 19 percent from 1995 to 2000 while white household income increased 15 percent. The official measure of unemployment rose from 16 percent in 1995 to 31.5 percent in 2002. Add to that figure frustrated job seekers, and the percentage of unemployed people rose to 43 percent. Moreover, at least 10 million people had their water disconnected for nonpayment, and a similar number experienced disconnection for not paying electricity bills.

The first post-apartheid housing minister, Joe Slovo (1926–1995), adopted World Bank advice that included smaller housing subsidies than were necessary and more reliance upon banks for credit. The policy was to give developers $2,000 per unit, leaving scant funds for good building materials, sound construction, and full services. Ironically, due to such neoliberal policies, the new township housing provided by the government in the early 2000s was half as large and constructed with flimsier materials than during apartheid, was located even farther from jobs and community amenities, and had lower-grade state services, including rare rubbish collection, inhumane sanitation, dirt roads, and inadequate storm-water drainage.

By the early 2000s, there were more protests per person in South Africa than in any other country: more than 5,800 counted in one year by police, mostly in the townships. A new set of urban social movements arose in Durban, Johannesburg, and Cape Town that were reminiscent of the civic associations of the 1980s and 1990s.

SEE ALSO *Apartheid; Boer War; Coloreds (South Africa); Diamond Industry; Discrimination, Racial; Gold Industry; Migration; Mining Industry; Protest; Segregation, Residential; Separatism; Social Movements; White Supremacy; World Bank, The*

BIBLIOGRAPHY

Bond, Patrick. 2000. *Cities of Gold, Townships of Coal: Essays on South Africa's New Urban Crisis*. Trenton, NJ: Africa World Press.

Bozzoli, Belinda. 1983. Marxism, Feminism and South African Studies. *Journal of Southern African Studies* 9 (2): 139–171.

Castells, Manuel. 1983. *The City and the Grassroots: A Cross-Cultural Theory of Urban Social Movements*. Berkeley: University of California Press.

Foucault, Michel. 1979. *Discipline and Punish: The Birth of the Prison*. Trans. Alan Sheridan. New York: Vintage.

Harvey, David. 1985. *The Urbanization of Capital: Studies in the History and Theory of Capitalist Urbanization*. Baltimore, MD: Johns Hopkins University Press.

Mayekiso, Mzwanele. 1996. *Township Politics: Civic Struggles for a New South Africa*. New York: Monthly Review Press.

McCarthy, Jeffrey J., and Daniel P. Smit. 1984. *South African City: Theory in Analysis and Planning*. Cape Town, South Africa: Juta.

Robinson, Jennifer. 1995. *The Power of Apartheid*. Oxford and Boston: Butterworth-Heinemann.

Urban Foundation. 1990. Regional Development Reconsidered. *Policies for a New Urban Future Series*, no. 3. Johannesburg, South Africa: Urban Foundation and the Private Sector Council.

Van Onselen, Charles. 1976. *Chibaro: African Mine Labour in Southern Rhodesia, 1900–1933*. London: Pluto.

Wolpe, Harold, ed. 1980. *The Articulation of Modes of Production: Essays from Economy and Society*. London: Routledge and Kegan Paul.

World Bank. 1991. *Urban Policy and Economic Development: An Agenda for the 1990s*. Washington, DC: World Bank.

Patrick Bond

TOXIC WASTE

The safe disposal of toxic waste has become a global challenge. Each year, world nations produce 440 million tons of toxic waste. This is a highly conservative estimate, given the clandestine nature of the enterprise and fluid definitions of what constitutes hazardous or toxic waste (the terms are used interchangeably). The U.S. Environmental Protection Agency defines hazardous waste as "a waste with properties that make it dangerous or potentially harmful to human health or the environment" (U.S. Environmental Protection Agency 2006). Hazardous waste can be liquids, solids, contained gases, sludge, byproducts of manufacturing processes, or simply discarded commercial products, like cleaning fluids or pesticides.

An international trade has arisen to transfer toxic waste from developed to developing nations. The United Kingdom exported spent mercury to South Africa throughout the 1990s, which claimed at least three lives at a mercury recycling plant, where mercury is removed from waste sludge for reuse. Similarly, the U.S. chemical firm Holtrachem Manufacturing attempted to export 260,000 pounds of spent mercury waste from its U.S. plant in Maine to India in September 2000. The U.S. government defined the spent mercury as a metal with trade value and exempted it from regulations on waste exports. Pressured by environmental advocacy groups, the Indian government refused the shipment and returned it to the United States.

LAWRENCE SUMMERS'S MEMO

Some leaders of global financial institutions have offered economic rationale for trade in toxic waste between developed and developing countries. On December 12, 1991, Lawrence Summers, who served as chief economist at the World Bank, wrote an internal memo that stated the World Bank should "be encouraging more migration of the dirty industries to the LDCs," referring to less developed countries (Vallette 1999). His argument was threefold: First, "a given amount of health impairing pollution should be done in the country with the lowest cost, which will be the country with the lowest wages." Second, as "under-populated countries in Africa are vastly under-polluted, their air quality is probably vastly inefficiently low compared to Los Angeles or Mexico City." Third, "the concern over an agent that causes a one in a million change in the odds of prostrate [sic] cancer is obviously going to be much higher in a country where people survive to get prostrate cancer than in a country where under 5 mortality is 200 per thousand" (Vallette 1999). After the memo became public in February 1992, Brazil's secretary of the environment, José Lutzenberger, wrote to Summers: "Your reasoning is perfectly logical but totally insane" (Vallette 1999). Lutzenberger was forced from office shortly afterward.

As indicated in Summers's memo, according to the Trade and Environment Database,

> poor African nations have served as the dumping ground for toxic hazardous waste materials, i.e. raw sewage, sludge, incinerated ashes, contaminated oils, chemical substances, acids, poisonous solvents ejected by chemical, pharmaceutical and fertilizer producing plants in the industrialized world.... Uncontrolled dumping of toxic wastes in Africa has been traced back to the early 1970s, when reports of clandestine deals between African

countries and companies in the United States, France, Germany, the United Kingdom, Switzerland, Italy, and the former U.S.S.R. began surfacing (Trade and Environment Database 1996).

The worst victims of this waste shipment have been the African nations of Benin, Nigeria, and Somalia, which became a tempting target for cost-conscious waste traders. On average, the cost of processing toxic waste is as high as $3,000 per ton in industrialized countries, whereas it drops to $5 per ton in developing countries, according to the Trade and Environment Database. In 1987 the United Nations Environment Programme (UNEP) adopted the Cairo Guidelines and Principles for the Environmentally Sound Management of Hazardous Waste, which require toxic-waste exporters to ensure that disposal sites in waste-importing countries meet the safety requirements of national and international regulations.

BASEL CONVENTION AND BASEL BAN AMENDMENT

Two years after the UNEP adopted the Cairo Guidelines, the leaders of 118 governments met in the Swiss town of Basel in 1989 and signed the first-ever global treaty regarding toxic waste, the Basel Convention on the Control of Transboundary Movements of Hazardous Wastes and Their Disposal. As of November 2006, more than 165 countries had ratified it to become international law. The Basel Convention was resented by waste-exporting industries and world governments, however, and they tried to cripple its enforcement. To prevent such efforts, the Basel Convention was amended to ban the trade in toxic waste with immediate effect. In all, 83 countries signed on to the 1995 amendment to the Basel Convention, which is now known as the Basel Ban Amendment. This amendment criminalizes all toxic-waste exports from member nations of the Organization of Economic Cooperation and Development (OECD) to non-OECD countries, even for recycling. According to the Basel Action Network, more than 90 percent of toxic-waste exports from OECD to non-OECD countries were meant for recycling.

Interestingly, the United States, which is the single largest producer of toxic waste, has ratified neither the Basel Convention nor the Basel Ban Amendment. The country's refusal rests on the argument that U.S. laws effectively regulate toxic-waste exports. It is true that the United States has one of the toughest legal regimes to protect the environment, including the Atomic Energy Act of 1954, the Resource Conservation and Recovery Act of 1976, and the Comprehensive Environmental Response, Compensation, and Liability Act, or Superfund Act, of 1986. These legal regimes, however, ensure safe disposal of toxic waste only within the United States, and their impact is diluted in regulating waste exports outside the country.

Even the Basel Convention and the Basel Ban Amendment are marred by several loopholes that allow the toxic-waste trade to continue. Some nations try to circumvent the ban on toxic-waste exports by resorting to bilateral agreements, which they argue fall outside the purview of the Basel Ban Amendment. Japan, which is the world's second-largest economy after the United States, signed bilateral economic partnership agreements (EPAs) in the early 2000s with Singapore, Malaysia, and the Philippines to evade the ban on toxic-waste exports. These EPAs list hazardous wastes as tariff barriers, which Japan believes need be eliminated. Japan is also using free trade agreements to promote free trade in hazardous wastes. Similarly, some governments and industries attempt to nullify the banned designations of toxic wastes under the Basel Convention under one pretext or another, or define them down to continue toxic-waste exporting. The ultimate enforcers, however, are individual governments that allow waste imports. They can defeat international legislation on toxic-waste trade by being lax in the enforcement of the Basel Ban Amendment for short-term economic gains. A vigorous civic engagement by national and international public interest groups is, therefore, crucial to hold the governments of waste-importing countries to their commitments to halt trade in toxic waste. More important, clean production, minimum waste generation, and waste management within the national limits of waste-producing countries can bring an end to the global trade in toxic waste.

SEE ALSO *Disease; Environmental Kuznets Curves; Love Canal; Public Health; Resources; World Bank, The*

BIBLIOGRAPHY

Basel Action Network. 1998. Why the U.S. Must Ratify the *Entire* Basel Convention (or Not at All). Briefing Paper No. 2. Seattle, WA: Basel Action Network. http://ban.org/Library/briefing2.html.

Basel Action Network. 1999. The Basel Ban: A Triumph for Global Environmental Justice. Briefing Paper No. 1. Seattle, WA: Basel Action Network. http://ban.org/Library/briefing1.html.

Clapp, Jennifer. 2002. Seeping through the Regulatory Cracks: The International Transfer of Toxic Waste. *SAIS Review* 22 (1): 141–155.

Japanese Citizen Groups Joint Statement. 2007. Japanese Citizen Groups Urge the Japanese Government to Remove Wastes from EPAs with Developing Countries and to Seek National Self-Sufficiency in Waste Management. February 11. http://www.ban.org/Library/070211_letter.html.

Knight, Danielle. 2000. Outcry over U.S. Toxic Chemical Shipment to India. Inter Press Service, December 11. http://www.ban.org/ban_news/outcry.html.

Knight, Danielle. 2001. Controversy around Mercury Shipment from U.S. to India. Inter Press Service, January 25. http://ban.org/ban_news/controversy.html.

Kockott, Fred. 1994. Wasted Lives: Mercury Waste Recycling at Thor Chemicals. Waste Trade Study No. 4. Amsterdam, Netherlands: Greenpeace International and Earthlife Africa.

Trade and Environment Database. 1996. Africa Waste Trade. Case No. 315. http://www.american.edu/TED/oauwaste.htm.

U.S. Environmental Protection Agency. 2006. Hazardous Waste. http://www.epa.gov/epaoswer/osw/hazwaste.htm.

Vallette, Jim. 1999. Larry Summers' War against the Earth. New York: Global Policy Forum. http://www.globalpolicy.org/socecon/envronmt/summers.htm.

Tarique Niazi

TRACKING IN SCHOOLS

Educational tracking refers to the placement of students into different kinds of educational programs according to a defined criterion of similarity or dissimilarity, such as interest, ability, or achievement. There are various types of tracking in schools, including vocational tracks, college preparatory tracks, honors tracks, and the ability tracks of remedial and gifted and talented. Vocational tracks channel students into classes that develop the skills needed to enter the labor market directly after graduation from secondary school. College preparatory tracks channel students into classes that will prepare them to attend institutions of higher education. College preparatory tracks in American high schools also frequently offer advanced classes that provide opportunities for college credit before graduation. Honors tracks channel students into more rigorous classes for college preparation but also enhance these students' chances of attending the college of their choice by giving them opportunity to achieve honors distinction and a higher class ranking upon graduation. The ability tracks of remedial and gifted and talented channel students into programs of study designed to accommodate unusually low or high aptitudes, respectively.

Critics of tracking argue that the tracking process restricts the educational exposure of students in the lower tracks. The earlier tracking occurs, the greater the educational restrictions. The placement of students into vocational, college preparatory, or honors tracks usually occurs upon entrance to secondary school. Because these tracks significantly affect chances for higher education, the tracks restrict the range of future occupational choices as early as age twelve or thirteen. For students who are tracked according to ability, the impact on educational exposure and future life opportunities is even greater. Ability tracking into remedial or gifted and talented classes often occurs in the primary school grades. In many ability tracking systems, those in the different tracks are exposed to differential amounts of knowledge. Students in remedial tracks are assumed to be slow learners, so they are exposed to less information within a school year than other students; students in gifted and talented tracks are assumed to be fast learners and so are exposed to more information. The longer students are ability tracked, therefore, the progressively greater are the gaps of knowledge between the tracked students and their peers and the fewer are the chances for remedial students to catch up with their peers. Conversely, the gifted and talented students progressively exceed their peers in knowledge, which increases their scores on standardized achievement tests, thereby enhancing their relative chances in future college placements and college career performance.

A more insidious effect of educational tracking that compounds the problem of differential knowledge is differential development of cognitive abilities by track. College preparatory, honors, and gifted and talented tracks provide greater opportunities to develop the higher-order skills of abstract, critical, and creative thinking. The ability to think and solve problems by abstract principles increases scores on college aptitude tests and contributes to successful performance in college classes. Abstract, critical, and creative thinking also contribute to success in professional careers and to effective decision-making in many areas of life, including consumer and voting choices. Students in remedial tracks, especially, have less opportunity to develop these higher-order thinking skills in a formal educational setting. This not only decreases their chances of college and occupational achievement, it reduces their logical capabilities to make successful life choices.

A profound effect of educational tracking is the labeling of students by track, which produces differential performance expectations and subsequent differences in self-images and behaviors. Children in remedial tracks, especially, are labeled negatively by their school administrators, teachers, peers, and, most significant, themselves. They consequently receive less encouragement to achieve, and their self-esteem is lowered. The latter contributes to a self-fulfilling prophecy in which the students expect to fail, so they do not make the effort necessary to succeed.

Another criticism of ability tracking is that it tends to be involuntary. In many societies, such as Japan, the assignment to a vocational or college preparatory track is based on standardized achievement test scores. Honors eligibility is determined by past academic achievement or scores in standardized achievement tests. Ability tracks are determined by students' performance on tests designed to measure their academic aptitudes.

Educational track placement is strongly correlated with socioeconomic status and race and ethnicity. Students of higher socioeconomic status are substantially more likely to be placed in college preparatory, honors, and gifted and talented tracks; children of lower socioeconomic status, in vocational and remedial tracks. Black children and, with the exception of Asian minorities, ethnic minorities are more likely to be placed in vocational and remedial tracks. The reasons for these differences are varied. Evidence indicates that school counselors are less likely to encourage lower-class and minority children to choose the college preparatory track. Evidence also suggests that class and minority group differences in cultural and social capital contribute to track placement. Parents of lower income children may be less aware of the importance of and opportunities for their children to pursue a college education. In addition, middle class or upper class students are more likely to be eligible for honors programs because they have parents who are able to help with schoolwork or secure tutors for their children. Perhaps the most pernicious effect of socioeconomic and cultural minority differences, however, is that the purported "ability tests" that determine ability track placement do not actually measure native aptitude but rather cultural exposure or, in the terms of the French sociologist Pierre Bourdieu (1930–2002), cultural capital. Students with less exposure to the majority group culture of the middle or higher classes are likely to score lower on the tests.

The consequences of these educational tracking differences by social class and racial and ethnic minority group status is that lower class and racial and ethnic minority students receive a more restricted education that reduces their level of knowledge, the development of their cognitive potential, and their opportunities to attain a high quality college education. Educational tracking thereby relegates a relatively high proportion of the lower classes and racial and ethnic minorities to lower level occupations. It also creates de facto racial or ethnic segregation within the schools, which in turn breeds false stereotypes and prejudice. Tracking in schools consequently serves to reproduce the socioeconomic and racial and ethnic inequalities that already exist in modern societies.

SEE ALSO *Achievement; Achievement Gap, Racial; Cognition; Curriculum; Education, Unequal; Education, USA; Equal Opportunity; Gifted and Talented; Inequality, Gender; Inequality, Racial; Inequality, Wealth; Pedagogy; Stratification*

BIBLIOGRAPHY

Alexander, Karl L., and Doris R. Entwistle. 1996. Educational Tracking during the Early Years: First Grade Placements and Middle School Constraints. In *Generating Social*

Stratification: Toward a New Research Agenda, ed. Alan C. Kerckhoff, 75–106. Boulder, CO: Westview.

Choe, Lena Domyung. 1999. Separate and Still Unequal: Legal Challenges to School Tracking and Ability Grouping in America's Public Schools. In *Race Is—Race Isn't: Critical Race Theory and Qualitative Studies in Education*, ed. Laurence Parker, Donna Deyhle, and Sofia Villenas, 231–250. Boulder, CO: Westview.

Mickelson, Roslyn Arlin. 2005. How Tracking Undermines Race Equity in Desegregated Schools. In *Bringing Equity Back: Research for a New Era in American Educational Policy*, eds. Janice Petrovich and Amy Stuart Wells, 49–76. New York: Teachers College Press.

Rosenbaum, James E. 1976. *Making Inequality: The Hidden Curriculum of High School Tracking*. New York: Wiley.

David Dietrich

TRADE

Trade is the exchange of goods between locations. For example, bananas from Honduras exchange for automobiles from the United States. International trade between locations in different nations receives far more attention than does domestic trade because nations discriminate against foreigners with international policies that are contested. For example, in 2005, the U.S. Congress ratified a Central American Free Trade Agreement in a hotly contested vote.

Trade also means the exchange of services of factors of production such as labor and capital. For example, Bangalore call centers provide telemarketing labor to U.S. marketers, while U.S. computer engineers maintain hardware and software in Bangalore. Trade in services is quantitatively important, but the distinction between trade in services and trade in goods is often not important. For many purposes, the distinction between international and intranational trade is similarly irrelevant. This essay uses the term *trade* to mean international trade in goods, but much of its content also applies to intranational trade in goods and services. The distinction is crucial when international trade policy—discrimination against foreigners—is important. (Domestic trade is affected by domestic policy, but seldom controversially.)

The key questions are: What explains the pattern of trade? Is liberal trade policy a good thing? The householder's answer to the first question is that nations import goods that are unavailable domestically or are cheaper than potential domestic substitutes and export goods that are unavailable or more expensive abroad. There are gains from this exchange, to answer the second question—voluntary transactions must be beneficial or they would not

be made, once familiarity acquaints participants with exchange.

Economic analysis embeds the householder's insight in an equilibrium system. Crucially, householders take prices as given in their decisions. When all households together react to a new market opportunity, they will necessarily have an impact on prices. International trade theory provides an answer to what makes a nation's goods cheaper or more expensive in a world where the act of trade changes prices. It also provides an analysis of the gains from trade in complex, many-household production economies. Since all prices normally will change, some households will gain (for example, owners of property or specific skills in the expanding export sector of the economy) while others will lose (for example, owners of property or specific skills in the contracting import sector). Trade theory shows that the gains to the gainers must ordinarily be larger than the losses to the losers.

The answers convince the vast majority of economists about the desirability of trade, provided some compensation for losers from trade is made. But the explanation of how international trade affects the overall well-being of society is also subtle and sometimes misunderstood by a portion of the general population that tends to oppose liberal trade. Opposition to trade liberalization may also arise from well-informed opponents, including lobbies representing workers and firms that might be harmed by liberalization, as well as persons sympathetic to those workers and firms who are skeptical that fair compensation will be provided.

THE PATTERN OF TRADE

Imports are goods and services purchased by domestic households and firms from firms located in foreign countries. Exports are goods and services sold to foreign households and firms by domestic firms. Imports must be paid for by exports, so the market for a nation's imports is linked to the market for its exports. The price of imports cannot be isolated from the price of exports. Moreover, exports increase the demand for factors such as labor used to produce them, while imports reduce demand for factors used to produce import substitutes. Thus factor markets at home and abroad are linked through the mechanism of trade. (If exports pay for imports every year, trade is balanced. This simplification does no real harm to the analysis. Unbalanced trade has international borrowing or lending as a counterpart, and in this setting exports must pay for imports over time, in present discounted value terms.)

The balanced trade requirement implies that the relative price of exports, the terms of trade, is equal to the volume of imports divided by the volume of exports. Thus trade determines relative prices and, conversely, relative prices determine trade. The cause of trade must be sought in relative price differences between countries. Indeed, with frictionless trade (that is, international trade without tariffs, quotas, or other barriers to trade), these must be the price differences that would prevail in the absence of trade (autarky).

Compare the relative price (of, for example, wine in terms of cheese) at home to the same relative price abroad in a prior equilibrium with no trade (autarky) or restricted trade. The country with the lower relative price of wine is said to have a comparative advantage in wine, while the other country has, symmetrically, a comparative advantage in cheese. Trade theory predicts that countries will export the good in which they have the comparative advantage. Krugman and Obstfeld (2005) cite a recent study showing that Japan's opening to trade in the 1850s reveals data consistent with the prediction.

Comparative-advantage differences between nations are explained in trade theory by differences between countries in either technology or factor supplies. Both are realistic—Canada exports grain because its large endowment of agricultural land makes land relatively cheap, but its better technology also provides an edge relative to land-abundant Ukraine. Notice that the mechanism run by relative price differences implies that economy-wide forces (exchange-rate manipulations, environmental or labor standards) that tend to cause uniform (over goods) national differences in costs will tend to cancel out and have no effect on trade patterns.

Absolute, or "competitive," advantage should be distinguished carefully from comparative advantage, as the former is the source of much fallacious reasoning. For example, suppose there are two countries considering whether they should trade with each other. Prior to the opening of trade, a naïve observer would compare the domestic prices or production costs in the two countries good by good and predict that the country with the lower cost, having an absolute or "competitive" advantage, will export the good. But economic theory establishes that this method fails whenever one country could undersell the other for all goods, since the importer could not pay for the imports by exporting. Instead, prices of goods and factors must change so that in the trade equilibrium each country is competitive in its export industry, in which it has a comparative advantage. In equilibrium, prices must clear markets for all goods and factors in the world economy, and exports must pay for imports.

Differences between countries can arise endogenously from their economic interaction, in contrast to the differences which are given prior to trade in the preceding account of comparative advantage. Differences which arise as a result of trade lead to theories of trade that do not necessarily imply comparative advantage—difference

in relative prices in the absence of trade. One theory is based on economies of scale, whereby the wider markets brought by trade will confer a cost advantage on one of the countries. Another theory is based on monopolistic competition, whereby the wider markets brought by trade increase product variety as buyers seek the special characteristics of foreign brands.

GAINS FROM TRADE

There are gains from trade in all these models. Each nation can act through trade policy to take more, leading to destructive trade wars with mutual losses. International institutions such as the World Trade Organization (WTO) act to restrain the destructive tendencies of unilateral action.

Within national economies, some members of a nation must lose from trade. For example, factors of production used intensively in export sectors of the economy tend to gain disproportionately when trade expands, while factors used intensively in import competing sectors tend to lose disproportionately. This gives insight into the widespread political resistance to trade that occasionally erupts into protectionism. National institutions act to redistribute some of the gains (U.S. Trade Adjustment Assistance) or provide temporary relief from losses due to trade (antidumping, escape-clause protection). In equilibrium the gains must outweigh the losses; there are gains from trade on average. On the way to equilibrium, it is theoretically possible that losses may temporarily exceed gains, justifying temporary relief measures. Extensive investigation of U.S. cases suggests that losses from trade are small and of short duration and are swamped by the gains from trade.

Most professional economists support liberal trade because there must be gains on average. The average is a "typical" household. Suppose that in autarky equilibrium, the home (domestic) typical householder is willing to swap 2 units of cheese for 1 unit of wine. That is, he would be indifferent to moving his consumption and production a small distance to offer the market 2 cheese for 1 wine or 1 wine for 2 cheese. Suppose that a typical foreign country household in the autarky equilibrium is willing to swap 2 wine for 1 cheese. Now allow frictionless trade, and suppose that the new equilibrium price is equal to 1. Each home household offers cheese to foreign households. Formerly it cost 2 cheese for 1 wine, but now the 2 cheese will procure 2 wine, a gain from trade. Similarly, each foreign household can obtain 2 cheese for 2 wine, where formerly this would procure only 1 wine. Both households gain from trade.

What if losers are not compensated? A person must decide for or against liberal trade by weighing individual gains and losses. Ethical considerations give more weight to the poor. The case for liberal trade is strengthened because the illiberal trade policies of rich countries hurt the poor disproportionately, as documented by Edward Gresser (2002). Poor countries have comparative advantage based on cheap low-skilled labor, hence discrimination against their exports harms the poor citizens of poor countries. At home in rich countries, protection makes food and clothing more expensive, a regressive tax on poor consumers. Among the poor, losers from protection surely outweigh gainers.

Much opposition to liberal trade is based on confusion and ignorance. The confusion of absolute advantage with a valid theory of trade sows fear that a nation must protect itself from overwhelming competition. Ignorance of the harm done to the world's poor by protection persuades many who favor income redistribution in rich countries to support protection of rich country import-competing workers, who tend to be relatively poor.

SEE ALSO *Barriers to Trade; Liberalization, Trade; North American Free Trade Agreement; Quotas, Trade; Tariffs; Trade, Anglo-Portuguese; Trade, Bilateral*

BIBLIOGRAPHY

Gresser, Edward. 2002. Toughest on the Poor: America's Flawed Tariff System. *Foreign Affairs* (November/December): 9–14.

Krugman, Paul, and Maurice Obstfeld. 2005. *International Economics.* 7th ed. Boston: Addison Wesley Longman.

James E. Anderson

TRADE, ANGLO-PORTUGUESE

Anglo-Portuguese trade figures prominently in seventeenth- and eighteenth-century economic literature because it was a central linkage in the Portugal–England–Americas triangular trade, which raised monetary issues ranging from workings of exchange rates and the balance of payments to the effects of money changes on domestic output. These issues overlap with the perennially relevant and wide-ranging questions of how slavery, trade, and European expansion contributed to economic growth and the Industrial Revolution.

England supported the Brazanga (or Bragança) house after the Duke of Bragança staged a palace coup and took the throne as João IV. Commercial-diplomatic relations evolved within the context of successive Anglo-Dutch and Anglo-French conflicts. England's trade with Portugal was largely an indirect trade with Brazil, which increased considerably in the late seventeenth century as exports of Brazilian sugar were augmented by gold from Minas Gerais and Portuguese fortified wine. In return, England exported light woolens, and at times grain, to Portugal and onwards.

Exempt from Portuguese prohibitions on the export of gold, English naval ships and packet boats carried Portugal's trade deficit back to London in gold. Richard Cantillon's "Essay on the Nature of Commerce in General" (in French, 1720s) illustrated the workings of the foreign-exchange market with the London rate of exchange against Portugal and argued that laws against the export of specie raised prices to Portuguese consumers. David Hume's *Political Discourses* (1752) reiterated aspects of Cantillon's position, but also emphasized that imported New World gold had increased output and employment in England.

Adam Smith steered clear of this in *The Wealth of Nations* (1776). Smith substituted national savings for the balance of trade as a causal factor behind economic growth and harshly criticized the 1703 Methuen Treaty with Portugal. The treaty lowered tariffs on English textiles, ending a brief period in which Portugal had protected manufacturing; in exchange, England guaranteed Portuguese wine a lower tariff than French—a policy Smith portrayed as likely to reduce savings and growth by increasing the cost of wine consumption.

Napoleon's 1808 invasion led the Portuguese royal house to flee to Brazil and ushered in direct British trade and investment. Nevertheless, David Ricardo famously chose to illustrate the gains from international trade in his *Principles of Political Economy* (1817) with an exchange of English cloth for Portuguese wine. In his example Ricardo supposed Portugal to be more efficient than England at producing both textiles and wine, but he demonstrated that trade could leave both nations better off—both could have cheaper commodities in greater abundance. Part of this gain would be devoted to savings and capital formation. This aspect of trade ran parallel to Ricardo's wider argument that British growth was suffering from diminishing returns to capital and labor in agriculture and would revive only if cheap grain were imported. Friedrich List highlighted the asymmetric aspects of this trade pattern in his *National System of Political Economy* (in German, 1841). In his view, Portugal had allowed itself to become trapped in the production of agricultural goods, whereas England enjoyed continuing technological progress and manufacturing supremacy.

SEE ALSO *Trade; Trade, Bilateral*

BIBLIOGRAPHY

Cantillon, Richard. [1720s] 2001. *Essays on the Nature of Commerce in General.* Trans. Henry Higgs. New Brunswick, NJ: Transaction Publishers.

Darity, William A., Jr. 1987. The Hume Process, Laws of Returns, and the Anglo-Portuguese Trade. *Southern Economic Journal* 54 (1): 119–133.

Fisher, H. E. S. 1963. Anglo-Portuguese Trade, 1700–1770. *Economic History Review* 2nd series 16 (2): 219–233.

Hume, David. [1752] 1987. *Essays, Moral, Political, and Literary*, ed. Eugene F. Miller. Indianapolis, IN: Liberty Classics.

Ricardo, David. [1817] 1981. *The Works and Correspondence of David Ricardo*, eds. Piero Sraffa and M. H. Dobb. Cambridge, U.K.: Cambridge University Press.

Smith, Adam. [1776] 1976. *An Inquiry into the Nature and Causes of the Wealth of Nations*, eds. R. H. Campbell and A. S. Skinner. Oxford: Clarendon Press.

John Berdell

TRADE, BILATERAL

Trade is the exchange of goods or services within market conditions. A synonymous term is *commerce*, which involves individuals, companies, or even governments and countries when they seek to buy or sell goods and services mainly for profit. Bilateral trade is a form of trade that takes place between two traders or two countries, or two trading blocks, or a trading block and a country.

Initially, people used a bilateral barter system of trade, that is, exchanging goods and services for other goods and services. Money was introduced as a means of exchange as trade developed over time. The development of trade was facilitated and promoted by money, which first took the form of coins and later banknotes, then checks, or bills of exchange, and finally "plastic money" (credit cards). There are many reasons why bilateral trade further expands. As time passes, labor is specialized and divided into discrete activities as people decide to concentrate on the production of a specific good or even a part of a good, and then sell it to purchase other goods. As well, countries differ in comparative advantage for the production and supply of goods or services. On the basis of the theory of comparative advantage proposed by David Ricardo (1817), international free trade is lucrative for all countries. Comparative advantage (relative cost advantage) as a basis for bilateral trade contrasts with Adam Smith's absolute advantage (absolute cost advantage), or the proximity effects associated with the gravity model. (The gravity model may predict bilateral trade flows based on distance, economic size, diplomatic relationships, income level, and trade policies between two countries, although the model could be subsumed under relative transportation costs.)

Bilateral trade has evolved through human history. As the most valuable of commodities, metals were a great incentive to trade. The extensive deposits of copper on Cyprus brought the island much wealth from about 3000 BCE. The first extensive trade routes were initially the long rivers (e.g., the Nile, the Tigris), which became the foundation of early civilizations. From the third millennium BCE there is evidence that long-range trade routes existed. The eastern Mediterranean was the first region to develop extensive maritime trade. The presence of Greeks in Mesopotamia and the eastern Mediterranean encouraged a new trade route. Goods were put on board ships after arriving in caravans from Mesopotamia. An ancient trade route existed between China and the Mediterranean Sea linking China with the Roman Empire—the Silk Road, which was not a trade route that existed solely for the purpose of trading in silk; many other commodities were also traded, from gold and ivory to exotic animals and plants. During the Dark Ages (500–1000 CE) trade almost collapsed. The Portuguese expeditions of the fifteenth century brought European ships for the first time into regular contact with sub-Saharan Africa. The Netherlands promoted the free movement of goods, and became the center of free trade in the sixteenth to eighteenth centuries, together with Spain and England. In 1776, the famous economist Adam Smith contributed to trade theory by arguing against mercantilism (that government should protect the economy from international trade through the use of tariffs to achieve a positive trade balance) by pointing out that economic specialization is as advantageous to nations as it is for firms. In 1799, the Dutch East India Company, the world's largest company at that time, became bankrupt, mainly due to increased competition in free international trade. By the nineteenth century the adoption of free trade was based on absolute advantage until David Ricardo in 1817 demonstrated that all countries can benefit from international trade based on the theory of comparative advantage. In the twentieth century, the Great Depression brought a considerable decrease in trade. The Bretton Woods Agreement, which was signed in 1944 by forty-four countries, aimed at the removal of national trade barriers. In 1947 twenty-three countries made an agreement, the General Agreement on Tariffs and Trade (GATT), to advance free trade. The World Trade Organization (WTO) was formed through the GATT Marrakech Agreement in 1994.

Bilateral trade is a part of each country's gross domestic product (GDP). A country's *balance of trade* is the amount of goods and services that the country exports minus the amount of goods and services that the country imports. The term *bilateral trade agreement* denotes an agreement on trade issues between two countries or two trading blocks (e.g., the European Union and Mercosur) or a trading block and a country (e.g., the EU and China). The main aim of a bilateral trade agreement is the elimination of barriers in trade and the facilitation of the movement of goods and services across the national or regional borders to encourage expansion and diversification of trade. Other decisive goals of bilateral trade agreements can be the promotion of fair competition conditions; the substantial increase of investment opportunities; the provision of protective measures concerning intellectual property rights; and the creation of procedures that will secure the implementation and application of the bilateral agreement. All the abovementioned goals are achieved by the bilateral jointed administration of the agreement and the removal of disagreements, together with the establishment of a framework that will further trilateral, regional, and multilateral cooperation in order to promote the advantages of the bilateral trade agreement.

Throughout history bilateral trade has been standard practice. However, the importance it carries economically, socially, and politically has increased substantially recently. This is due to industrialization, advanced transportation, globalization, multinational corporations, and outsourcing (Bitzenis 2004). High tariffs, governmental quotas, and restrictions are usually used to regulate bilateral international trade. Although tariffs are usually imposed on imports, it is not unusual for a country with a protectionist policy to impose export tariffs or provide subsidies. Such restrictions are known as *trade barriers*; free trade exists in a situation where a government does not impose any trade barriers. Countries are sometimes punished economically by other nations through the implementation of trade sanctions against it. The term *embargo*—that is, externally imposed isolation that is severe—refers to the total absence of trade between the two countries. An example is the United States's trade embargo on Cuba, which has lasted for more than forty years.

A preferential trade agreement (PTA) may exist between two trading partners in a bilateral trade agreement, creating a preferential trading area. In this case, the two trading partners (the two countries or the two trading blocks, or one trading block and a country) reduce tariffs between each other, but do not necessarily abolish them completely; this is the weakest form of economic integration. States that are not party to the PTA do not usually benefit from such reductions. PTAs may have adverse effects on multilateral trade liberalization. Since the creation of the GATT and its successor, the WTO, 362 regional trade agreements have been reported to the WTO; of these, 211 were in force in mid-2006 (Lamy 2006). Agreements with services provisions are more and more common. Trade provisions in sectors not controlled multilaterally are a part of an increasing number of bilateral agreements. According to a World Bank study, *Global Economic Prospects 2006: Economic Implications of Remittances and Migration* (2005), the percentage of trade that takes place under preference treatment varies from 15 to 40 percent (Lamy 2006). The situation of trade under preference treatment undermines substan-

tially the principle of the "most-favored nation," which is one of the cornerstones of the WTO.

SEE ALSO *Absolute and Comparative Advantage; Barriers to Trade; Free Trade; Liberalization, Trade; North American Free Trade Agreement; Quotas, Trade; Tariffs; Trade*

BIBLIOGRAPHY

Bitzenis, Aristidis. 2004. Is Globalisation Consistent With the Accumulation of FDI Inflows in the Balkan Countries? Regionalisation for the Case of FDI Inflows in Bulgaria. *European Business Review* 16 (4): 406–425.

Lamy, Pascal. 2006. Lamy Warns Bilateral Agreements Are Not the "Easy Way Out" From the Suspended Talks. Annual Memorial Silver Lecture, Columbia University, New York, October 31.
http://www.wto.org/english/news_e/sppl_e/sppl46_e.htm.

Ricardo, David. 1817. *Principles of Political Economy and Taxation*. 3rd ed., 1821. London: John Murray.

Aristidis Bitzenis
John Marangos

TRADE, SLAVE

SEE *Slave Trade.*

TRADE CREATION

SEE *Customs Union.*

TRADE DEFICIT

A trade deficit—that, is, a deficit on flows of goods and services in a country's international balance of payments—occurs when a country imports more than it exports. Because the concept of the trade deficit depends intimately on its two component flows of exports and imports, what motivates these cross-border, that is, international, transactions? If a country buys more than it sells, how does it pay for the excess purchases? Does the concept of the trade deficit give a complete picture of a country's international relationships and flows?

People and firms trade because they want different things, have different skills and technologies, and earn different amounts of money. People and firms value goods and services differently, depending on their income, tastes, and needs. Countries are the aggregation of individual actions by firms and individuals. So, countries differ from one another in terms of resources (such as land, minerals, and educated workers) and the techniques firms use to produce goods and services (such as how much information technology is used in the factory or office), and in terms of tastes and preferences for products (due to, for example, the presence of immigrants or to level of income). These differences are reflected across countries as differences in costs of production, and in prices for goods and services. Because costs and prices differ across countries, it makes sense for a country to trade some of what it holds less dear and produces most cheaply to people who want it more and for whom production is costly or even impossible. Although this is most obvious in the case of goods, the concept holds as well for services, and it is applicable to rich and poor, large and small countries alike.

When individuals and firms buy and sell from each other, international trade takes place. When a country, which is the aggregated activity of firms and individuals, sells goods and services across its international borders, these are termed *exports*. When a country buys goods and services from abroad, these are termed *imports*. A trade deficit occurs when the cost of imports exceeds the value of exports. A trade deficit can be measured either on a bilateral basis—when country A imports more from country B than it exports to country B—or on a global basis—when country A's total exports to all countries is less than country A's total imports from all countries.

What factors can lead to a trade deficit, where one country buys more from abroad than it sells? A country growing relatively more rapidly than other countries in the world tends to import more than it exports, particularly if the country tends to consume and invest a lot at home, if the price of imports is low compared to the domestic price of similar products, if the country's residents and firms have a particular taste for imported products, and if there are few barriers to inhibit the purchase of imports. A rapid pace of domestic consumption and investment tends to draw in goods and services from other countries in order to satisfy domestic demand. A relatively low price of imports compared to domestic goods and services (which may be a consequence of the international exchange value of a country's currency) makes it cheaper for residents and firms to buy the imported product than a similar one from the home producer. Some countries have large immigrant populations or intricate supply chains of production, which can boost imports, all else being equal (although these also can support more exports). Finally, as trade barriers fall, so do the cost of imported products.

Which of these factors is most important to increasing imports relative to exports depends on the particular country. For the United States, which has run a trade deficit for more than twenty-five years, the most impor- tant factor is its relatively faster growth of domestic consumption and investment. For some periods over this time span, the exchange value of the currency has further aug- mented imports and restrained exports.

If a country systematically buys more than it sells, it has to pay for the excess by selling financial assets of the country, or by borrowing. These financial inflows are one counterpart to the trade flows in the international balance of payments. But international financial flows also take place because investors want to diversify their wealth port- folios, increasing their rate of return and changing the IR risk profile. Just as countries differ in resources, technolo- gies, and tastes (thus generating trade flows), countries differ in offerings of and preferences for risk and return on financial assets. So, not only are countries linked through international trade flows, they also are linked through international flows of financial assets.

Whereas a trade deficit implies that there must be some international financial inflow as a balancing entry in the international accounts, there are also large interna- tional flows of financial assets that are independent of the trade flows. For the United States, international capital flows both into and out of the country amount to trillions of dollars each year—far more than the cross-border trade flows. Moreover, even as the country as a whole borrows to finance the trade deficit, the inflow of financial capital generally exceeds the trade deficit, as foreign investors purchase U.S. assets and U.S. investors buy foreign assets.

A trade deficit that persists implies that borrowing also rises, as does foreign ownership of domestic financial assets. How long such a country can, or should, import more than it exports might be a policy concern. If the imports and net borrowing are invested in such a way as to increase the capacity of the economy to produce and therefore repay its international financial obligations, then there are few worries. However, if imports and financial inflows do not so augment the economy's capacity to pro- duce, then there is less support for more imports and financial inflows. In such a situation, the country's ability to attract financial inflows is at risk, and economic forces such as a depreciation in the exchange value of the cur- rency or a rise in interest rates in the domestic market work to change the growth in imports and exports and bring the trade deficit back into trade balance.

SEE ALSO *Mundell-Fleming Model; Trade Surplus*

BIBLIOGRAPHY

Caves, Richard E., Jeffrey A. Frankel, and Ronald W. Jones. 1990. *World Trade and Payments: An Introduction.* Glenview, IL: Scott, Foresman and Little Brown Higher Education.

Feenstra, Robert C. 1998. Integration of Trade and Disintegration of Production in the Global Economy. *Journal of Economic Perspectives* 12 (4): 31–50.

Helpman, Elhanan, and Paul R. Krugman. 1985. *Market Structure and Foreign Trade.* Cambridge, MA: MIT Press.

Levich, Richard M. 1998. *International Financial Markets: Prices and Policies.* Boston: Irwin/McGraw-Hill.

Mann, Catherine L. 1999. *Is the U.S. Trade Deficit Sustainable?* Washington, DC: Institute for International Economics.

Catherine L. Mann

TRADE DIVERSION

SEE *Customs Union.*

TRADE SURPLUS

A trade surplus occurs when a country's trade balance is in surplus, or positive. The trade balance, which is also referred to as net exports, is the difference between the value of a country's exports of goods (EX) and services to other countries and the value of imports of goods and services from other countries (IM):

$$TB = EX - IM$$

Thus, the trade balance is in surplus when exports exceed imports.

The trade balance is part of a country's gross domestic product (GDP), which measures the market value of all final goods and services produced in a country. GDP is equal to the sum of the domestic residents' absorption, A (which is given by the sum of private consumption, private investment, and government consumption), and net exports, TB. This implies that the trade balance can also be described as the difference between a country's GDP and its domestic absorption:

$$TB = \text{GDP} - A$$

A country therefore runs a trade surplus when its gross domestic product exceeds its domestic absorption.

From an economic point of view, a trade surplus arises when the demand for a country's export goods is higher than the country's demand for import goods from the rest of the world. In the traditional, partial equilibrium view of trade flows, export demand depends positively on the economy's price competitiveness, approximated by the real exchange rate, which is given by the ratio of the price of foreign goods to domestic goods (in foreign currency), and positively on aggregate demand conditions, which are approximated by foreign income. The idea is that when export goods are relatively cheap (i.e., price competitiveness is high), the demand for them will be higher. And when the income of foreign consumers increases they will also consume more goods,

which will also increase the demand for the domestic economy's export goods. By the same token, a country's import demand is assumed to depend negatively on its price competitiveness and positively on domestic income. A country's trade balance would therefore improve when a country experiences an improvement in its price competitiveness via a depreciation of its exchange rate or lower inflation than the rest of the world, or when domestic income expands at a slower pace relative to the rest of the world. Whether such developments will give rise to a trade surplus depends, of course, on how pronounced these developments are, on the strength of their effect on export and import demand, and on initial conditions.

Changes in domestic and foreign income and the exchange rate that influences the trade balance are in turn the result of macroeconomic fluctuations, such as a monetary policy or government expenditure shocks, which affect domestic and foreign economies. The textbook workhorse model for the analysis of the effects of such shocks is the Mundell-Fleming (*MF*) model (Mundell 1968; Fleming 1962). The model assumes that prices are fixed in the short run, so that short-run production is demand determined. As a result, shocks to aggregate demand affect aggregate income and the real exchange rate and thereby the trade balance via their effect on export and import demand as well as relative prices. The net effect of macroeconomic shocks on the trade balance in the *MF* model is not always clear-cut and also depends on the exchange rate regime in place. For a textbook exposition of the Mundell-Fleming model see Paul R. Krugman and Maurice Obstfeld (2006).

The more recent class of models of the so-called "New Open Economy Macroeconomics" (NOEM) also builds on the assumption of short-run price stickiness in the analyses of the effects of macroeconomic shocks on the dynamics of exchange rates, trade balances, and other macroeconomic variables. The NOEM models are based on a microfounded intertemporal optimising model framework (see Obstfeld and Rogoff 1995 and 1996 and for an overview of the NOEM framework Lane, 2001). In this setup, trade balance surpluses (deficits) arise because of consumption smoothing. The trade balance is essentially the buffer that allows a country to insulate consumption from short-run income fluctuations. While the assumption of short-run price rigidity is similar to the fix price assumption in the Mundell-Fleming model, the implications of the NOEM framework can differ substantially. The effect of macroeconomic shocks on the trade balance depends in these models on many factors, like the assumptions made regarding the pricing scheme of export firms, the degree of home bias in consumption, whether shocks have been expected or not, or whether they are expected to be transitory or permanent.

Movements of the trade balance are closely linked to financial flows between countries. This becomes clear when looking at the balance of payments identity. The balance of payments records all of a country's transactions with countries abroad and is equal to the current account balance (CA) plus the capital account balance (KA) less the change in a country's net foreign reserves (ΔFR) and is by definition equal to zero:

$$BP = CA + KA - \Delta FR = 0$$

The capital account balance records all of a country's capital transactions with countries abroad (sales and purchases of assets), and the change in foreign reserves is the change in a country's central bank holding of gold and foreign exchange. The current account balance records all of a country's current transactions with countries abroad including trade in goods and services and a country's net factor income from abroad; that is net factor income earned on the return on capital invested abroad and net international income receipts, NFI:

$$CA = TB + NFI.$$

The previous two equations show that, as part of the current account, the trade balance is an important determinant of a country's net foreign asset position, because the current account balance is equal to the change in its net foreign asset position, which is given by the change in foreign reserves less the capital account balance.

When a country exports more to the rest of the world than it imports (i.e., the country is a net exporter and runs a trade surplus), it produces more than it consumes and sells this production surplus to the rest of the world. In order to finance the transaction, the country is lending to the rest of the world and, as a consequence, improves its net foreign asset position by accumulating foreign assets or repaying outstanding debts that were received from the rest of the world in earlier periods.

The trade balance is an important determinant of a country's international solvency. The previous equation illustrates that the sum of a country's trade surplus and its net international income receipts equal the country's current account balance. This implies that if a country runs perpetual current account deficits, its net foreign asset position is negative and the country is a net debtor to the rest of the world. Thus, the country must generate trade balance surpluses in the future in order to service its foreign debt obligations. Therefore, the international solvency and creditworthiness of a country depends on its ability to meet its foreign debt obligation by generating trade balance surpluses in the future.

SEE ALSO *Balance of Payments; Balance of Trade; Exchange Rates; Macroeconomics; Mercantilism; Mundell-Fleming Model; Trade Deficit*

BIBLIOGRAPHY

Fleming, J. M. 1962. Domestic Financial Policies under Fixed and Floating Exchange Rates. IMF Working Paper No. 9.

Krugman, Paul R., and Maurice Obstfeld. 2006. *International Economics: Theory and Policy*. 7th ed. Boston: Addison Wesley.

Lane, Philip R. 2001. The New Open Macroeconomics: A Survey. *Journal of International Economics* 54 (2): 235–266.

Mundell, Robert A. 1968. *International Economics*. New York: Macmillan.

Obstfeld, Maurice, and Kenneth Rogoff. 1995. Exchange Rate Dynamics Redux. *Journal of Political Economy* 103 (3): 624–660.

Obstfeld, Maurice, and Kenneth Rogoff. 1996. *Foundations of International Macroeconomics*. Cambridge, MA: MIT Press.

Obstfeld, Maurice, and Kenneth Rogoff. 2000. New Directions for Stochastic Open Economy Models. *Journal of International Economics* 50: 117–153.

Mathias Hoffmann
Boris Hofmann

TRADE UNIONS

SEE *Unions.*

TRADE-OFFS

Given finite resources and limited productive capacity, economies are inevitably constrained with respect to their production and consumption options, particularly in the short run, and consequently must choose among alternatives. These constraints apply both to private individuals in the allocation of their budgets and to the government in its decisions over the provision and financing of public goods. By choosing to have more of one good, an economic agent must be willing to accept less of something else, thus defining a trade-off between the two alternatives. An important challenge facing economic decision makers is to allocate resources efficiently subject to the constraints imposed by the trade-offs they face.

At the aggregate economy-wide level, the constraints imposed by fully utilized finite resources can be represented by a production possibility curve. In his pioneering 1958 textbook *Economics*, Paul Samuleson described this in terms of the choice between "guns" and "butter." An economy can have more butter only if it is willing to have fewer guns. The number of guns one forgoes in order to obtain an extra unit of butter is referred to as the "opportunity cost" of an extra unit of butter. Not only is this trade-off negative, but it is generally assumed to be concave with respect to the origin. This implies that each extra marginal unit of butter requires the economy to forgo increasing quantities of guns and is known as the law of increasing costs. This is a consequence of the economy's factors of production being imperfect substitutes in the production of the two commodities. As resources are increasingly transferred from gun production to butter production, they are increasingly more suited for gun production and less efficient for producing butter.

THE PHILLIPS CURVE

The concept of trade-offs is generic, and some of the most important trade-offs relate to policy making. Among the most celebrated is the so-called Phillips curve, named after the New Zealand economist A. W. Phillips. In 1958 Phillips used British data to find a pronounced negative relationship between the rate of unemployment and the rate of (wage) inflation. This was interpreted as confronting policy makers with a trade-off between inflation and economic activity. Introducing an expansionary fiscal policy to reduce unemployment, according to Phillips, will also raise inflation, forcing the policy makers to choose some combination of these two responses.

In the 1960s and 1970s, as economists scrutinized the unemployment-inflation relationship in more detail, the nature of the trade-off was questioned. First, with rising inflation during that period the Phillips curve appeared to be unstable, shifting out over time. Several authors, most notably Milton Friedman in his 1968 article "The Role of Monetary Policy" and Edmund Phelps in his 1967 article "Money-Wage Dynamics and Labor-Market Equilibrium," argued that the Phillips curve should be augmented to include anticipated inflation. As a result the trade-off between current inflation and unemployment would still shift out over time as past inflation was increasingly incorporated in anticipated inflation. However, in the absence of "money illusion" (the tendency of people to evaluate their wages in nominal terms rather than in real terms), they argued that the trade-off was only temporary. In the long run expectations will be fully realized, and anticipated inflation will fully reflect actual inflation. Unemployment will converge to the "natural rate" of unemployment, a rate determined by the structural characteristics of the economy and independent of conventional monetary and fiscal policy instruments, so there is no long-run unemployment-inflation trade-off. The "rational expectations" revolution led to an even more drastic conclusion. If economic agents are smart and understand the structure of the economy, they will internalize government policy into their inflationary expectations and thus negate the trade-off even in the short run.

OTHER TYPES OF TRADE-OFFS

In contrast to the static (but possibility shifting) trade-offs associated with the Phillips curve, other trade-offs are fundamentally intertemporal or occur over time. The most basic of these is the relationship between investment and consumption. To increase current investment an economy needs to increase its current savings, and with fixed output this involves giving up current consumption. Over time, as the increase in investment augments the capital stock, the economy's productive capacity is increased, thus increasing future consumption; the trade-off is therefore between *current* consumption and *future* consumption. In deciding on the intertemporal allocation of resources, an economic agent needs to weigh the short-run consumption losses against the long-run consumption gains.

By its nature investment is also risky and therefore is associated with another important trade-off, that between risk and return, a crucial element in financial decision making. Assuming agents are risk averse, the riskier an investment the higher its return will need to be to compensate the investor for the additional risk. This trade-off between risk and return is the basis for the pricing of risky assets and is central to the theory of corporate finance.

Trade-offs exist in other dimensions as well. Almost all economic decisions have differential effects on different segments of the economy. Some groups inevitably benefit more than others, who may often be adversely affected. This is particularly true of trade policy. A tariff designed to stimulate an import-competing industry, through its effect on the real exchange rate, will affect other sectors of the economy adversely, again giving rise to a trade-off in benefits, this time across industries. Moreover in the presence of externalities, the social opportunity cost may differ from the private opportunity cost, in which case the social and private trade-offs will diverge.

Finally, some trade-offs are more controversial. Some economists argue that devoting resources to improve environmental standards will harm the productive capacity of the economy, implying a trade-off between economic performance and environmental quality. Others argue precisely the opposite; devoting resources to the environment will stimulate employment, increase the efficiency of the economy's productive inputs, and enhance economic performance, thus denying the presence of any trade-off in this case.

SEE ALSO *Choice; Phillips Curve; Production Frontier; Samuelson, Paul A.; Scarcity*

BIBLIOGRAPHY

Friedman, Milton. 1968. The Role of Monetary Policy. *American Economic Review* 58 (1): 1–17.

Phelps, Edmund S. 1967. Money-Wage Dynamics and Labor-Market Equilibrium. *Journal of Political Economy* 76: 678–711.

Phillips, A. W. 1958. The Relation between Unemployment and Money Wage Inflation in the United Kingdom, 1861–1957. *Economica* 25: 265–277.

Samuelson, Paul A. 1958. *Economics: An Introductory Analysis.* 4th ed. New York: McGraw-Hill.

Stephen J. Turnovsky

TRADITION

A key term in the study of culture, *tradition* refers most often to the collective customs and knowledge of a group or society. Tradition is a source of basic learning, occurring even before formal education begins and continuing throughout life. Its usual connotation is a social process of "handing down" knowledge from generation to generation, especially by oral and customary means. It therefore is associated with precedent and culturally is linked often to a group's "heritage," although unlike referring to history, which suggests a time and place in the past, tradition carries a sense of social and cultural patterns—ways of doing things—that continuously occurred "before." The term has other meanings as well, referring to the substantive results of this process, such as a story or ritual, a custom given social importance through repeated practice, knowledge whose official source cannot be verified but is held widely, or a concept (i.e., a mode of thought or behavior) characteristic of people generally. Social sciences scholarship may therefore refer to *a tradition in a culture* as a specific song passed down in a group through time or *the tradition of a culture* more broadly as a way of thinking and acting.

Culture in the past was a reference to place, often to a language group bounded in space, whereas traditions were more variably social—possibly referring to family, age, and gender—and migratory. In academic circles, tradition is more broadly defined than is culture, as in the use of such terms as *Western tradition* and *Eastern tradition*; here *tradition* is used as a synonym for *pattern*. Culture, by contrast, is applied to all types of associations as well as bounded groups. The view persists that traditions define a culture, rather than the reverse, and the "science of tradition" in European American intellectual history—whose purpose is to objectify and organize tradition—has been associated with folklore and ethnological studies. As a result, many genres and groups labeled "folk" are often considered "traditional" or "tradition-oriented."

The reverence commonly afforded to tradition indicates that people follow it, willingly or not, and—significantly for social sciences—may define themselves or their group through its presence. Whether following tradition means unconsciously adhering to a severe form of cultural authority or choosing from a tradition that one finds appropriate can be a cause for dispute among social scientists. Implied in this difference is a questioning of whether tradition forces stability and conformity or fosters change and progress. Inherent in the concept is a duality that is constantly negotiated in society: tradition's reference on the one hand to precedent (as the source of knowledge and action) and on the other hand to the present (as living practice, often adapted and adjusted for particular needs and conditions).

MODERNITY AND CREATIVITY

For social scientists viewing tradition as providing the cultural authority of precedent, there is often an implication that tradition is a contrast to modernity, the latter characterized by individualism (with free will and choice), mobility, and progress. A tradition-oriented, or folk, society in anthropological and sociological scholarship (e.g., on groups such as the Amish, Japanese, Hutterites, and Bedouins) usually has the characteristics of valuing social interdependence, filial and ancestral piety, communitarian stability, and harmony or "group orientation." Many folklorists, however, theorize that the role of tradition is essential to everyday life in modern complex societies, often enacted through cued and framed speech, narrative, and custom to express social identities within a mass culture or to provide a sense of control for individuals (e.g., dressing and athletic rituals).

Another duality with tradition has been with creativity, particularly in studies of artistic traditions. It is often assumed that "traditional" or "folk" art means repetition or imitation of precedent by a community, whereas "fine" or "creative" art represents individuality and novelty. The former is viewed as primitive or ordinary, whereas the latter is elite and refined. A modern philosophy of the arts incorporating tradition since the twentieth century considers tradition and creativity as intertwined in the artistic process, viewable in everyday practice as well as expressive culture.

CONTESTED AND NATIONAL TRADITIONS

Rather than use tradition to describe national or hemispheric patterns, many social scientists apply it to minority cultures and small groups. Arguably, national traditions have been categorized as histories, whereas marginal groups have often been described in terms of tradition. In public or political discourse in the United States, tradition may be invoked in proposals for maintaining national or majority "traditional values" or preserving the sanctity provided by tradition for institutions of the nuclear family and religion in daily life. Debates arose through the late twentieth century and into the twenty-first century over virtues that constituted the basis of U.S. culture. Associations such as the Traditional Values Coalition, Toward Tradition, and Citizens for Traditional Values took on the label of tradition to represent conservative religious groups in lobbying for prayer and religious programming in the schools, prohibitions on gay marriage, public support for parochial institutions, and school voucher programs. Although sounding secular and broad-based, *traditional* in the organizational titles came to stand for an orthodox morality upholding the centrality of religion in public life. It invoked the merit of traditional to describe national "values" proven worthy by time and by popular usage. The implication by advocates of traditional values is that rapid social change has undermined "mainstream" or national values, while opponents argue for establishment of new or multiple traditions that are culturally relative and legitimate even if they are different from the mainstream. Sometimes the culturally relative keyword of *multiculturalism*, implying that traditions are created anew in contemporary life, may be set against the concept of *culturalism*, connoting the stability of values passed from generation to generation. Both views, sometimes stated as sides in a U.S. "culture war," invoke tradition for social legitimacy.

In other countries facing rapid social change and diversity, tradition has been a publicly contested term for viewing different priorities of building national unity and multicultural community. Modifiers to tradition such as *national, ethnic, religious, folk, cultural, family,* and *local* have implied a need to place a feeling of social connectedness, a collective memory, in an identified niche within mass society. In the Netherlands, a society with a tradition of tolerance toward minorities, a rapid rise of ethnic and religious minorities (e.g., Muslims from Turkey and Morocco) starting in the late twentieth century caused social scientists to notice political and cultural responses to define and celebrate Dutch traditions (e.g., *Koninginnedag* [Queen's birthday], *Sinterklaas* or St. Nicholas Day) nationally as a way to mollify fears of losing "Dutchness." While creating a sense of cultural norming, applications of tradition have also been interpreted in social science as a process of "othering"—characterizing groups and individuals who do not conform. Subcultural difference can also be normed, as can be seen in the common Dutch social scientific attention to regional traditions of speech, architecture, and customs to show a type of cultural diversity, even within a small country.

The way that social scientists approach tradition can vary across national lines. It has often been argued that Japan and the United States, for example, provide contrasting views of tradition. In Japanese scholarship, tradi-tion is associated with the reverence given to ancient customs and myths, the system of intimate group life established in hierarchical village social structures, and the everyday expressions of social relations based on rank and filial piety (e.g., different performances of respect to elders and superiors in bowing and speech). Tradition is considered the basis of a unified society, and the concept of modernization is integrated with tradition (technological progress and mobility while maintaining a group orientation). In the United States, tradition is tied to the recent past and is viewed as more varied, befitting a multicultural country. It is a more malleable, privatized concept, with less force of authority, and indeed is often seen as "threatened" or "nostalgic" in a postmodern society. Tradition in the United States is more often associated with religion than public life, although American social scientists frequently discuss organized efforts to "construct" tradition (e.g., folk revivals, ethnic and social movements, "roots" organizations, nationalistic movements).

ADAPTED AND INVENTED TRADITIONS

A binary has emerged in cross-cultural studies of tradition between the naturalistic associations of genuine/authentic and the artificial connotations of invented/organized. The concept of "invented tradition," defined by the social historian Eric Hobsbawm as "a set of practices, normally governed by overtly or tacitly accepted rules and of a ritual or symbolic nature, which seek to inculcate certain values and norms of behaviour by repetition, which automatically implies continuity with the past" (Hobsbawm 1983, p. 1), suggests a linkage of organizers'/inventors' motivations for creating practices that invoke tradition and instill senses of the past and of belonging, especially within national contexts concerned with the modern displacement of heritage and community. These invented traditions usually are of recent origin but appear or claim to be old. They also try to construct cultural meanings in the public marketplace, which can be contested, such as the ritual of national founding principles in the American Thanksgiving marked by a twentieth-century reenactment of "Pilgrims' Progress" celebrating the seventeenth-century settlement of the New World and protested by a simultaneously held "National Day of Mourning" sponsored by Native American groups starting in 1970.

Set against the background of change, tradition's role in the way people live and view the world commands renewed attention as new forms of communication arise. As industrialization and urbanization supposedly ushered in a "break with tradition" in the twentieth century, in the twenty-first century trends of computerization and globalization raise questions anew about the processes of tradition for individuals and the various groups with which they identify, many of which have emerged only recently with invented traditions to promote bonding and expression. Social science inquiry has thus taken up tradition as a concept of social existence relating to modernization, diversity, and identity.

BIBLIOGRAPHY

Bronner, Simon J. 1998. *Following Tradition: Folklore in the Discourse of American Culture.* Logan: Utah State University Press.

Bronner, Simon J. 2002. *Folk Nation: Folklore in the Creation of American Tradition.* Lanham, MD: Rowman and Littlefield.

Bronner, Simon J., ed. 1992. *Creativity and Tradition in Folklore: New Directions.* Logan: Utah State University Press.

Finnegan, Ruth. 1991. Tradition, but What Tradition and for Whom? *Oral Tradition* 6 (1): 104–124.

Gailey, Alan. 1989. The Nature of Tradition. *Folklore* 100 (2): 143–161.

Glassie, Henry. 2003. Tradition. In *Eight Words for the Study of Expressive Culture*, ed. Burt Feintuch, 176–197. Urbana: University of Illinois Press.

Hobsbawm, Eric. 1983. Introduction: Inventing Traditions. In *The Invention of Tradition*, eds. Eric Hobsbawm and Terence Ranger, 1–14. Cambridge, U.K.: Cambridge University Press.

Shils, Edward. 1981. *Tradition.* Chicago: University of Chicago Press.

Simon J. Bronner

TRAGEDY OF THE COMMONS

In 1968 the ecologist Garrett Hardin (1915–2003) published the article "The Tragedy of the Commons," in which he argued that the problem raised by population growth had only a moral solution. His use of the word *tragedy* was meant to emphasize the inevitableness of destiny and the remorseless working of things. He used the celebrated example of a pasture open to all to illustrate what he considered to be a problem facing the human race in general.

Suppose that a pasture is used freely by herdsmen owning their cattle privately. Acting rationally and selfishly, each herdsman chooses the size of his herd so as to maximize his private gain. Adding one animal yields a positive component reflecting the proceeds from selling the animal. It also involves a cost: if pasture space is scarce, the additional animal results in overgrazing. However, that cost is shared by all herdsmen and is only minimally felt by the particular decision maker. The tragedy unfolds when all decision makers disregard the costs imposed on others, which leads all the herdsmen to own too many animals. Heavy overgrazing results, and the cattle are underfed and fetch low prices. In this scenario, herdsmen will add to their herd until they derive no benefit from the additional animal. This is called *rent dissipation*. With free access, the magic of Adam Smith's (1723–1790) invisible hand does not work.

In "The Economic Theory of a Common Property Resource: The Fishery" (1954), H. Scott Gordon provided a technical analysis of the problem well before Hardin gave it celebrity. Gordon described a situation in which a private fisherman does not benefit from restraining his activity: the fish he leaves in the water is likely to be caught by some other fisherman. As a result, valuable fish stocks are often overfished, and fishermen are often poor. The collapse of the North Atlantic cod fishery at the end of the twentieth century, as well as the collapse of the Chilean anchovy fishery two decades earlier, are just two dramatic examples.

The particular conditions inducing waste and rent dissipation that are typical of the tragedy of the commons arise either progressively when populations increase their pressure on a common-access resource, or more suddenly when a resource is discovered or when some technological breakthrough makes its exploitation easier. This is why some such tragedies appear as historical events. For example, whales were not endangered before the introduction of harpoon guns reduced the cost of catching them at the same time that they had become valuable for uses other than food for Inuit. In the early twentieth century, oil was discovered and exploited in common pools in the United States. This led to overextraction as one operator rushed to exploit a pool before others could deplete it. In "The Simple Economics of Easter Island" (1998), Jim Brander and M. Scott Taylor interpret the rise and collapse of that island's civilization as an instance of tragedy of the commons. Climate change is another example: emitters of greenhouse gases treat the atmosphere as an open-access resource, not taking into account the costs borne by present and future humans (not to mention other species).

While pervasive, is the tragedy of the commons inevitable, as implied by Hardin? Gordon's analysis identifies common property as the culprit. Were the fishery controlled by a single owner who decided how much fish should be caught, that single owner would bear the consequences of overfishing privately and would properly weigh such costs against the benefits of higher current catches. The outcome would be Pareto efficient under perfect competition.

There are many examples of private property rights solving the tragedy of the commons. The enclosures episode which witnessed the construction of fences around previously open-access areas in eighteenth- and nineteenth-century England is a celebrated though disputed example. Coase's theorem indicates that any system of property rights, by defining a framework for bargaining, will solve externality problems provided costs of transactions are negligible. In *Governing the Commons* (1990), Elinor Ostrom analyzes many instances where societies have devised institutions other than private property and markets to secure or induce efficient resource use.

A simple look at the organization of economic and social life shows many potential tragedies being avoided thanks to property rights or other social rules: We accept that we must pay for food that we buy in a supermarket; most of the time, cars do not get robbed while parked on the street; we do not freely cut trees in forests for firewood.

Yet solutions or improvements are not easy to come by. The creation or enforcement of property rights, whether private or otherwise, may be institutionally or technologically difficult. Ideally, property rights must be designed in such a way that they cause decision makers to act in the interest of society as a whole in the use of the resource. In many situations, this is not possible either because the required information is not available at a reasonable cost, or because it will not be revealed to the regulator by decision makers, or because there is no authority with the power to impose the required behavior. In such cases, Coase's theorem does not apply because transaction costs are not negligible. Yet, stakeholders may be aware of the collective costs associated with the tragedy of the commons. They can try to improve the situation by signing contracts or treaties, sometimes involving cooperation. They will do so with due consideration for their position in the status quo as determined by their power.

SEE ALSO *Coase Theorem; Externality; Overfishing; Property, Private; Rent*

BIBLIOGRAPHY

Brander, Jim A., and M. Scott Taylor. 1998. The Simple Economics of Easter Island: A Ricardo-Malthus Model of Renewable Resource Use. *American Economic Review* 88 (1): 119–138.

Gordon, H. Scott. 1954. The Economic Theory of a Common-Property Resource: The Fishery. *Journal of Political Economy* 62: 124–142.

Hardin, Garrett. 1968. The Tragedy of the Commons. *Science* 162: 1243–1248.

Ostrom, Elinor. 1990. *Governing the Commons: The Evolution of Institutions for Collective Action.* Cambridge, U.K.: Cambridge University Press.

Pierre Lasserre

TRAIL OF TEARS

Andrew Jackson's 1828 election as U.S. president presaged congressional approval of the Indian Removal Act, which initiated processes that led in the mid- and late 1830s to the notorious Trail of Tears. Although Jackson justified his actions in compelling relocation of southeastern Indian tribes to plains west of the Mississippi River as "a just, humane, liberal policy," implementation led to widespread suffering, cruel deprivation, and painful deaths for many. All told, perhaps 60,000 Choctaws, Chickasaws, Cherokees, Creeks, and Seminoles found themselves uprooted from traditional homes; the ordeal experienced by Cherokees stands out as emblematic of the policy's inhumanity.

Understanding of the Trail of Tears and its impact requires recognition of circumstances then prevalent in the United States and of the targets of Jackson's policy other than Native Americans. For example, beginning with the 1803 Louisiana Purchase certain national leaders including Thomas Jefferson and, later, John C. Calhoun had argued for relocation as the only "permanent solution" to "the Indian problem." Controversy greeted such calls, but national policy by the time of the Jackson presidency offered Native Americans a strictly limited number of options: acculturation, relocation, or extermination.

Meanwhile, egalitarian and antislavery tides of the American Revolutionary period had subsided in the wake of profound changes in American life. First, a rising tide of immigration had begun to swell the nation's northern cities. This created competition for livelihoods between the new arrivals, particularly the Irish, and free blacks at a time when Jackson and his allies courted the white immigrant vote. Extension of the "Cotton Kingdom" in the South coincidentally created huge demands for new lands and slave labor, as well as for enhanced governmental protections for chattel slavery. Further accelerating the processes at play were European intellectuals who formulated supposedly scientific theories regarding race, racial superiority, and racial inferiority. As a result, the nation found itself accepting new racist concepts that countenanced harsh and arbitrary treatment of Indians and black Americans.

Finally, Jackson's personal experiences contributed to the implementation of racist policy. He repeatedly had invaded Spanish Florida to suppress challenges to southern expansion posed by the defiance of Upper (or Red Stick) Creek warriors and of maroon fighters later called Black Seminoles. His troops had destroyed the Apalachicola River Negro Fort in 1816; battled maroons at the Suwannee River in 1818; and, through the agency of Lower Creek raiders, obliterated the Tampa Bay area sanctuary known as Angola in 1821. Having failed to subdue his nemeses, Jackson aimed early implementation of the removal policy at Florida. By 1835 his actions led to the outbreak of the Second Seminole War, the longest Indian war and, arguably, the largest slave uprising in U.S. history. As noted by General Thomas Jesup, "[This is] a negro and not an Indian War." Eventually, the Black Seminoles accepted western relocation but mostly after negotiated surrender rather than by military defeat. Thus, the Trail of Tears saw African Americans, as well as Native Americans, paying dearly for political and social changes that had placed the nation on the road to Civil War.

SEE ALSO *American Indian Movement; Native Americans; Tribalism; Tribes*

BIBLIOGRAPHY

Brown, Canter, Jr. 2005. Tales of Angola: Free Blacks, Red Stick Creeks, and International Intrigue in Spanish Southwest Florida, 1812–1821. In *Go Sound the Trumpet! Selections in Florida's African American History*, eds. David H. Jackson Jr. and Canter Brown Jr., 5–21. Tampa, FL: University of Tampa Press.

Ehle, John. 1988. *Trail of Tears: The Rise and Fall of the Cherokee Nation*. New York: Doubleday.

Landers, Jane. 1999. *Black Society in Spanish Florida*. Urbana: University of Illinois Press.

Porter, Kenneth W. 1996. *The Black Seminoles: History of a Freedom-Seeking People*. Gainesville: University Press of Florida.

Rivers, Larry Eugene. 2000. *Slavery in Florida, Territorial Days to Emancipation*. Gainesville: University Press of Florida.

Larry Eugene Rivers

TRAIT INFERENCE

Does this person deserve my help? Why is she being so hostile? Should I trust that politician? Is he someone I would like to get involved with romantically? The answers to questions such as these that people ask themselves about others depend to a great extent on their beliefs about others' personal characteristics. In other words, trait inferences—judgments made about people's stable underlying characteristics, also referred to as stable dispositions—play an important role in interpersonal behavior. Social and personality psychologists have extensively investigated the trait inference process.

Research in the 1960s and 1970s started from the assumption that people make trait inferences both carefully and logically. Attribution theory predicted that in order to infer that a certain man is rude, one would have to gather information indicating that he is rude to people in general, is ruder than others, and has consistently behaved rudely over an extended period. Trait inferences are sometimes based on systematic thinking of this kind,

but researchers recognized early on that trait inferences are messier and more biased than that. For example, people are often motivated to infer that individuals have certain traits and not others; one would probably more readily infer that a stranger is untrustworthy than that a good friend is. In addition, people are very quick to infer that others' behaviors are reflections of stable dispositions even when other obvious explanations exist for those behaviors (the correspondence bias). To illustrate, a nervous-looking woman might be perceived as being a generally anxious person even if she is in a situation that would clearly make anyone nervous.

People infer traits from others' behavior so readily that they often do so unintentionally and without even being aware of it. In other words, people infer traits effortlessly, spontaneously, and automatically when interacting with others. As a result, one is often unable to bring to mind any evidence to support one's beliefs about others' traits. Unfavorable traits (such as selfishness and unfriendliness) are inferred more quickly than favorable ones (such as generosity and friendliness). The reason for this seems to be that although favorable behaviors could reflect favorable traits, they could also have many other causes (such as a desire to make a good impression on other people). Unfavorable behaviors, it is assumed, are more likely to reflect people's true underlying natures.

Research conducted since the 1980s, however, indicates that the heavy emphasis on traits as causes of behavior is more characteristic of people in individualistic cultures (found primarily in North America and western Europe) than of people in collectivistic cultures (found in East Asia and South America, among other places). People in collectivistic cultures are more sensitive to the social and situational pressures that affect people's behavior.

Despite all of the biases that creep into the trait inference process, people's impressions of others' traits can still be very accurate. When researchers ask a number of a person's acquaintances to make judgments about that person's traits, they typically find high levels of agreement.

SEE ALSO *Attribution; Person-Situation Debate; Trait Theory*

BIBLIOGRAPHY

Gilbert, Daniel T. 1998. Ordinary Personology. In *The Handbook of Social Psychology*, 4th ed., eds. Daniel T. Gilbert, Susan T. Fiske, and Gardner Lindzey, vol. 2, 89–150. Boston: McGraw-Hill.

Jones, Edward E. 1990. *Interpersonal Perception*. New York: W. H. Freeman.

Leonard S. Newman
Aliza Silver

TRAIT THEORY

Personality traits describe individual differences in human beings' typical ways of perceiving, thinking, feeling, and behaving that are generally consistent over time and across situations. Three major research areas are central to trait psychology. First, trait psychologists have attempted to identify sets of basic traits that adequately describe between-person variation in human personality. Second, social scientists across disciplines use personality traits to predict behavior and life outcomes. Third, trait psychologists attempt to understand the nature of behavioral consistency and the coherence of the person in relation to situational influences.

DESCRIBING INDIVIDUAL DIFFERENCES: TRAIT STRUCTURE AND HERITABILITY

There are two prominent approaches to identifying the basic personality traits and their organizational structure (McCrae and John 1992). The *lexical approach* emphasizes the evaluation of personality trait adjectives in the natural language lexicon and assumes that those personality descriptors encoded in everyday language reflect important individual differences, particularly if they are found across languages. The *questionnaire approach* attempts to assess important traits derived from psychologically based and biologically based personality theories. Self- and peer-ratings on sets of lexically derived or theoretically derived traits have typically been subjected to factor analysis to develop hierarchical organizations of traits reflecting a small number of broad superordinate dimensions overarching a large number of narrow-band traits. At the superordinate level, contemporary trait structural models vary in the number of dimensions necessary to organize lower-order traits, ranging from two to sixteen. Each of these models can be assessed via self- and peer-report using reliable and well-validated questionnaires and rating forms.

In the most influential and widely used structural model, thirty traits are hierarchically organized into five broad bipolar dimensions, reflecting a convergence of the *Big Five* lexical traits (Goldberg 1990) and the questionnaire-based *five-factor model* (FFM; Costa and McCrae 1992). The Big Five/FFM dimensions are neuroticism, extraversion, openness, agreeableness, and conscientiousness. Adherents of the Big Five/FFM model assert that these dimensions can be found across languages and personality measures, providing a comprehensive and parsimonious account of individual differences in personality.

Contemporary research on the heritability of traits has focused on the Big Five/FFM dimensions. Behavioral genetic studies have found substantial heritability ranging from 41 percent to 61 percent for the broad dimensions, with little evidence of shared environmental effects (Jang, Livesley, and Vernon 1996). Heritability of the narrow-band traits of the FFM is more modest, ranging from 30 percent to 50 percent. It is widely believed that traits are influenced by multiple genes; molecular genetic studies, however, have not replicated results linking specific genes to personality traits. In addition to the genetic correlates of traits, promising new efforts by neuropsychologists using functional brain imaging and electroencephalogram (EEG) recordings have begun to reveal the neural basis for traits.

PREDICTING BEHAVIOR AND LIFE OUTCOMES

Personality trait theory has been used in almost every branch of social science and practice. Researchers in clinical psychology have effectively used trait theory to predict both symptom-based psychopathology and personality disorders. Trait theories have also been used in treatment planning, as well as for understanding psychotherapy processes and outcomes.

Beyond clinical psychology, trait theory has been applied to industrial/organization psychology where it has been used to predict employee satisfaction and job performance. Personality traits have also been of interest to forensic psychologists in predicting psychopathic and deviant behavior. Other areas in which traits have been successfully employed include: predicting mate selection as well as marital satisfaction, social psychology, counseling, studies of human development across the lifespan, cross-cultural studies, learning and educational outcomes, and health-related behaviors and outcomes.

THE PERSONALITY TRIAD: BEHAVIORAL CONSISTENCY, INDIVIDUAL COHERENCE, AND SITUATIONAL INFLUENCE

Trait theory implies that personality and behavior exhibit levels of temporal stability and cross-situational consistency. There is strong empirical support demonstrating that the rank order of individuals on various trait dimensions is stable (Roberts and DelVecchio 2000), as well as support that individuals' behavior is relatively consistent across situations (Funder and Colvin 1991). It is also quite evident, however, that situational influences also impact stability and variability of behavior. For many years, the "person–situation debate" generated significant advances in the study of behavioral consistency and variability (Kenrick and Funder 1988), leading to contemporary interactionist models.

Since the early 1990s, evidence has accumulated supporting conceptions of within-person behavioral variability as classes of stable individual differences at the level of both psychological states and behaviors. While evidence of variability was first interpreted as support of situational influences, contemporary views propose a comfortable coexistence of large within-person variability and large between-person stability in the study of personality (Fleeson 2001; Fleeson and Leicht 2006; Funder 2006). This has recast the person–situation debate into an effort to integrate personality variability and stability.

These contemporary integrative models involve contextualization of within-person behavioral variability and between-person consistency within the situation and include the cognitive-affective personality system (Mischel and Shoda 1995), knowledge-and-appraisal personality architecture (Cervone 2004), the density distribution of states approach (Fleeson and Leicht 2006), and the latent state-trait theory (Steyer, Schmitt, and Eid 1999). At varying levels of specificity, these models all employ intrapersonal perceptual and meaning-making processes (e.g., explicit cognitive and affective subsystems are often proposed). As suggested by David C. Funder (2006), the future success of such approaches also requires identification of the psychologically salient aspects of situations.

SEE ALSO *Nature vs. Nurture; Personality; Person-Situation Debate; Temperament*

BIBLIOGRAPHY

Cervone, Daniel. 2004. The Architecture of Personality. *Psychological Review* 111 (1): 183–204.

Costa, Paul T., Jr., and Robert R. McCrae. 1992. Normal Personality Assessment in Clinical Practice: The NEO Personality Inventory. *Psychological Assessment* 4 (1): 5–13.

Fleeson, William. 2001. Toward a Structure- and Process-Integrated View of Personality: Traits as Density Distributions of States. *Journal of Personality and Social Psychology* 80 (6): 1011–1027.

Fleeson, William, and Christine Leicht. 2006. On Delineating and Integrating the Study of Variability and Stability in Personality Psychology: Interpersonal Trust as Illustration. *Journal of Research in Personality* 40 (1): 5–20.

Funder, David C. 2006. Towards a Resolution of the Personality Triad: Persons, Situations, and Behaviors. *Journal of Research in Personality* 40 (1): 21–34.

Funder, David C., and Randall C. Colvin. 1991. Explorations in Behavioral Consistency: Properties of Persons, Situations, and Behaviors. *Journal of Personality and Social Psychology* 60 (5): 773–794.

Goldberg, Lewis R. 1990. An Alternative "Description of Personality": The Big-Five Factor Structure. *Journal of Personality and Social Psychology* 59 (6): 1216–1229.

Jang, Kerry L., John W. Livesley, and Philip A. Vernon. 1996. Heritability of the Big Five Personality Dimensions and Their Facets: A Twin Study. *Journal of Personality* 64 (3): 577–591.

Kenrick, Douglas T., and David C. Funder. 1988. Profiting from Controversy: Lessons from the Person-Situation Debate. *American Psychologist* 43 (1): 23–34.

McCrae, Robert R., and Oliver P. John. 1992. An Introduction to the Five-Factor Model and Its Applications. In The Five-Factor Model: Issues and Applications. Spec. issue, *Journal of Personality* 60 (2): 175–215.

Mischel, Walter, and Yuichi Shoda. 1995. A Cognitive-Affective System Theory of Personality: Reconceptualizing Situations, Dispositions, Dynamics, and Invariance in Personality Structure. *Psychological Review* 102 (2): 246–268.

Roberts, Brent W., and Wendy F. DelVecchio. 2000. The Rank-Order Consistency of Personality Traits from Childhood to Old Age: A Quantitative Review of Longitudinal Studies. *Psychological Bulletin* 126 (1): 3–25.

Steyer, Rolf, Manfred Schmitt, and Michael Eid. 1999. Latent State-Trait Theory and Research in Personality and Individual Differences. In Personality and Situations. Special issue, *European Journal of Personality* 13 (5): 389–408.

Aaron L. Pincus
Mark R. Lukowitsky

TRAIT-SITUATION CONTROVERSY

SEE *Person-Situation Debate.*

TRANSACTION COST

Economists use the term *transaction cost* to refer to costs arising from actions that hinder the ability of two (or more) individuals to achieve mutually desirable objectives or resolve disputes. Originally conceived as the costs of conducting market transactions, recognition that exchange and cooperation also take place within firms (between employers and employees), within legislatures (among politicians trading votes over preferred legislation), and even within families has led to the broadening of the term to include costs incurred in interactions within any institutional or organizational setting.

Transaction costs have been described broadly as "the costs of running the economic system" (Arrow 1970) and have been compared to the frictions that occur in mechanical systems (Williamson 1985, p. 19). Examples include costs arising out of such activities as discovering or communicating opportunities for trade (information, search, and marketing costs), of reaching and describing agreements (bargaining and contracting costs), and of making sure that agreements are honored (monitoring and enforcement costs). The concept also includes costs of litigation (to enforce property rights or contracts or to determine liability for an accident, for example), lobbying (to influence legislation), and the management or administration of firms and government agencies. Although transaction costs are distinguishable from production costs, unnecessary or excessive production costs incurred to improve one's bargaining position, or to protect oneself from losses that would result if a trading partner reneged on a deal, are also appropriately regarded as transaction costs.

The logic for focusing on transaction costs derives from an observation by 1991 Nobel laureate Ronald Coase (subsequently dubbed "the Coase theorem") that, were it not for transaction costs, all possible gains from trade and cooperation would be achieved through voluntary agreements regardless of the particular institutions, legal rules, or organizational forms in place. It follows that if institutions and organizational forms do matter, it must be because transaction costs are significant. And because transaction costs reduce the gains from trade and cooperation available to transactors, institutions and organizational forms that generate lower transaction costs will generally be preferred to alternatives with higher transaction costs.

Early use of transaction costs to explain observed institutional and organizational arrangements were often criticized on the grounds that because transaction costs can be difficult to measure—and cannot be observed at all for institutions and organization forms that are not adopted—claims that observed arrangements minimized transactions costs were easy to make and impossible to refute. If companies are observed producing their own inputs, it must be because the transaction costs of procuring those inputs on the market are too high; if legislators enact strict liability standards for product liability, it must be because a negligence rule would generate excessive transaction costs.

Beginning in the 1970s, economists, led by Oliver Williamson (1985), began to address this criticism by relating the size of transaction costs under different forms of organization to observable characteristics of transactions such as the complexity of the transaction and the degree to which transactions require investments that are "relationship specific," that is, are designed or located for use in a particular relationship and consequently have a lower value if used for some other purpose. Since then, transaction cost reasoning has been applied to a wide array of organizational forms and institutions. Although its most extensive development has occurred in the analysis of the boundaries of firms and the design of contracts, the theory of transaction costs has also been used to explain the evolution of political institutions and legal rules and the implications of those structures for the economic performance of nations (North, 1991).

SEE ALSO *Coase, Ronald; Coase Theorem; Economics, Institutional; Neoinstitutionalism; Organization Theory; Organizations; Transaction*

BIBLIOGRAPHY

Arrow, Kenneth J. 1970. The Organization of Economic Activity: Issues Pertinent to the Choice of Market versus Non-market Allocation. In *Public Expenditure and Policy Analysis*, eds. R. H. Haverman and J. Margolis, 51–73. Chicago, IL: Markham.

Coase, Ronald H. 1937. The Nature of the Firm. *Economica* 4 (16): 386–405.

Coase, Ronald H. 1960. The Problem of Social Cost. *Journal of Law and Economics* 3: 1–44.

North, Douglass C. 1991. Institutions. *The Journal of Economic Perspectives* 5 (1): 97–112.

Williamson, Oliver E. 1985. *The Economic Institutions of Capitalism: Firms, Markets, Relational Contracting*. New York: The Free Press.

Scott E. Masten

TRANSACTION TAXES

Although transaction taxes can be taxes imposed on any transaction, the term generally refers to the taxes imposed on trading of currencies, stocks, and other financial instruments by economists.

One of the most influential transaction tax is the Tobin tax. After the United States's suspension of convertibility from U.S. dollars to gold and the collapse of the Bretton Woods system in the early 1970s, James Tobin, an economist who later won the Nobel Memorial Prize in Economics in 1981, proposed a charge on all exchange transactions between currencies in all countries. The proposed charge is called the "Tobin tax." The purpose of the Tobin tax is to discourage short-term speculation in global foreign-exchange markets and thus reduce the exchange-rate volatility, or, in Tobin's words, "to throw some sand in the wheels of our excessively efficient international money markets" (Tobin 1978, pp. 154–155). Because the Tobin tax is to be levied on all currency-exchange transactions worldwide, it has been suggested that an international organization such as the United Nations, the International Monetary Fund, or the World Bank would manage the Tobin tax, which would be used to stabilize the international economy and promote peace and reduce poverty. Opponents of the Tobin tax argue that such taxes would reduce the liquidity in the exchange markets and actually lead to more volatile exchange rates.

Another type of transaction taxes, securities transaction taxes (STT), has been proposed and implemented in many equity markets. STT are taxes imposed on the trading of stocks, bonds, futures contracts, and option contracts. Unlike the Tobin tax, the implementation of STT does not require international cooperation. Proponents of STT argue that in addition to generating revenues, these taxes may reduce excess volatility. However, opponents argue that the taxes may reduce market liquidity, decrease market efficiency, and drive trading to other countries. G. William Schwert and Paul Seguin (1993) provided an overview of the costs and benefits of STT. John Campbell and Kenneth Froot (1994) reviewed some international experiences associated with securities transaction taxes and found that the behavioral responses from investors are large in the sense that investors move a significant portion of the trading to markets with lower STT. In the United States, the then House Speaker Jim Wright proposed a "stock transaction tax" in 1987. The 1994 Clinton budget proposal contained a fee of 14 cents for each contract bought and sold on an organized futures exchange. But such taxes have never been passed by Congress. Empirical evidence on the subject has been mixed. Some researchers found that a higher transaction tax leads to a more volatile stock market, contrary to what the proponents claim. The transaction tax can be viewed as part of the transaction costs, which may include broker fees and stamp duty, among other costs associated with trading of stocks, bonds, futures, and options.

SEE ALSO *Financial Markets; Speculation; Taxes; Tobin, James*

BIBLIOGRAPHY

Buiter, Willem H. 2003. James Tobin: An Appreciation of His Contribution to Economics. *Economic Journal* 113: 585–631.

Campbell, John Y., and Kenneth A. Froot. 1994. International Experiences with Securities Transaction Taxes. In *The Internationalization of Equity Markets*, ed. Jeffrey A. Frankel, 277–308. Chicago: University of Chicago Press.

Schwert, G. William, and Paul J. Seguin. 1993. Securities Transaction Taxes: An Overview of Costs, Benefits, and Unsolved Questions. *Financial Analysts Journal* 49: 27–35.

Tobin, James. 1978. A Proposal for International Monetary Reform. *Eastern Economic Journal* 4: 153–159.

Dong Li

TRANSACTIONS MOTIVE

SEE *Money, Demand for.*

TRANS-ATLANTIC SLAVE TRADE DATABASE

SEE *Slave Trade.*

TRANSCENDENTALISM

SEE *Buddhism.*

TRANSCULTURATION

SEE *Ortiz, Fernando.*

TRANSFER PRICING

Tax avoidance by multinational companies poses a serious problem for governments. Governments began to grow aware of eroding tax bases as multinational business expanded in the late 1960s. Since tax systems differ from country to country, multinational companies can reduce their tax burden by shifting profits to countries with relatively low tax rates.

Transfer pricing is one method of tax avoidance. A transfer price is a price used for transactions among affiliates. Multinational companies can move income among affiliates located in different countries by manipulating the transfer price used in intrafirm transactions. For example, suppose a parent company in the United States sells goods to a subsidiary in Germany. Suppose also that the corporate tax rate in the United States is higher than the corporate tax rate in Germany. Assuming that a multinational company maximizes joint after-tax profits earned in the two countries, the company reduces its tax payments by using a lower transfer price. A lower transfer price allocates less profit to the United States parent company and more profit to the German subsidiary. The transfer pricing benefits the company via increased after-tax profit. However, the U.S. government suffers a decrease in tax revenue.

Tax avoidance, as outlined above, has also been brought to the public's attention as an equity issue. Domestic companies are subject to higher effective corporate tax rates when compared to multinational companies. Domestic companies are not able to manipulate their profits, as multinational companies do, for tax-saving purposes.

Corporate tax laws address illegitimate income allocation among a company's related affiliates. For example, in the United States, Section 482 of the Internal Revenue Code regulates income allocation among affiliates. Many countries employ similar regulations on this type of transaction among affiliates. These regulations require companies to use the so-called arm's length price for the purpose of filing a tax return. The arm's length price is defined as the transfer price that would have been used if the intrafirm transaction took place between nonassociated parties in the market. However, determining the arm's length price is not straightforward, especially when transactions involve intangibles and services.

In 1991 the Advanced Pricing Agreement (APA) was introduced by the U.S. Internal Revenue Service to resolve disputes associated with determining the arm's length price. The purpose of the APA is to allow taxpayers and tax authorities to reach a consensus regarding the arm's length price before taxpayers file a tax return. The APA has been extended to the Bilateral Advanced Pricing Agreement (BAPA), which aims to coordinate the confirmation of the arm's length price between two countries. The necessity of coordination results from efforts to eliminate international double taxation, which occurs when tax authorities in each jurisdiction apply a different arm's length price.

Transfer pricing can also occur when transactions between affiliates take place in the same country, though the term usually refers to tax evasion across national borders. The United States has a long history of regulating transfer prices, since transfer price manipulation allows companies to allocate income among affiliates located in different states. Regulation pertaining to interstate transaction dates back to 1928.

The U.S. government has been leading transfer pricing discussions in the Organisation for Economic Cooperation and Development (OECD), an international organization that coordinates tax policies across countries. The OECD has made several proposals for transfer pricing solutions, one being the Model Tax Convention on Income and on Capital. Providing an outline when two countries enter into a tax treaty, the Model is a suggestion and is not legally binding. The first draft was published in 1963, and the committee on fiscal affairs accepted it in 1977. Since then, the contents of the Model have been periodically updated.

Tax legislation for multinational businesses prompted numerous studies as it became one of the critical policy issues presented by economic globalization. The earlier literature of the 1970s and 1980s tried to provide a theoretical framework for the decision making of multinational companies under different tax rates across countries. The literature demonstrated that multinational companies could increase global income by shifting their profits to lower-taxed jurisdictions by transfer price manipulation. While it is clear that the mechanism of transfer pricing can serve as an arbitrage device to reduce the tax burden of companies, these studies treated tax policies as exogenous.

The literature of the 1990s studied policy planning as it applied to a less-informed government that was attempting to regulate tax evasion. Transfer pricing information is private and generally beyond government control. The literature proposed an analysis of mechanism design using a principal-agent model. The question posed was how to implement tax policies that induce appropriate transfer prices from multinational companies.

The policy concern became one of efficiency loss rather than information constraints after the introduction of the APA and BAPA. The literature in the early 2000s argues that the BAPA system causes efficiency losses since multinational companies, while integrated under common control, cannot internalize the costs of intrafirm transactions. The BAPA separates the profits earned by two different affiliates within the same company for the purposes of imposing taxes in each country. Corporate profits (and tax revenue) will, consequently, be lower.

SEE ALSO *Markup Pricing; Taxes; Transaction Taxes*

BIBLIOGRAPHY

Organisation for Economic Co-operation and Development. 2001. *Transfer Pricing Guidelines for Multinational Enterprises and Tax Administrations.* Paris: Author.

Tomohara, Akinori. 2004. Inefficiencies of Bilateral Advanced Pricing Agreements (BAPA) in Taxing Multinational Companies. *National Tax Journal* 57 (4): 863–873.

Akinori Tomohara

TRANSFLECTIVE DISPLAYS
SEE *Symbols.*

TRANSFORMATION, STRUCTURAL
SEE *Structural Transformation.*

TRANSFORMATION PROBLEM

The so-called transformation problem has to do with an apparent contradiction between Marx's labor theory of value and the tendency of profit rates to equalize across industries. The labor theory of value, which assumes that labor is the source of both value and surplus value (or profit), seems to imply that "labor-intensive" industries would have a higher rate of profit than "capital-intensive" industries. Marx claimed to have resolved this apparent contradiction in Part 2 of Volume 3 of *Capital* with his theory of prices of production, which may be very briefly summarized as follows:

1. The general rate of profit is determined by the ratio of the total surplus value to the total capital invested in the economy as a whole ($R = S / [C + V]$) (in Volume 1 of *Capital*, the total surplus value is determined by the labor theory of value).

2. The average profit in each industry is determined by the product of the general rate of profit and the capital invested in each industry ($\Pi_i = R [C_i + V_i]$).

3. The price of production for each industry is determined by the sum of the constant capital and variable capital in each industry and the average profit in each industry ($PP_i = C_i + V_i + \Pi_i$).

In this way, Marx claimed, each industry receives the same rate of profit in a way that is consistent with the labor theory of value.

A long-standing criticism of Marx's theory of prices of production is that he "failed to transform the inputs" of constant capital and variable capital from values to prices of production. According to this interpretation, constant capital and variable capital are derived from given physical quantities of means of production and means of subsistence (they are first determined as the values of these groups of commodities in Volume 1, and then determined as their prices of production in Volume 3). The criticism is that Marx failed to make this transformation of constant capital and variable capital in Volume 3, but instead left these inputs in value terms. Marx's theory is therefore logically incomplete and inconsistent: Output prices are prices of production, but input prices are values. It is further argued that Marx's mistake can be corrected, using a method first suggested by Ladislaus von Bortkeiwicz in 1905 and popularized by Paul Sweezy in 1942, but this correction has damaging consequences for Marx's theory. This is because Marx's two aggregate equalities (total price of production = total value, and total profit = total surplus value) cannot both be true simultaneously, and because the rate of profit changes (so that the "value rate of profit" ≠ "price rate of profit"). These results mean that individual prices and profits are not merely the redistribution of aggregate amounts of value and surplus value, as Marx claimed. This alleged logical inconsistency has been the main reason for the rejection of Marx's theory over the last century by mainstream economists and others. The Sraffian interpretation of Marx's theory (Steedman 1977) has reinforced these criticisms.

Most Marxists have largely accepted these criticisms of Marx's theory of prices of production (that he failed to transform the inputs, and that the two aggregate equalities cannot both be true at the same time), although they draw different conclusions. Marxists have generally argued that

these are minor problems, requiring only minor modifications, and that they are not sufficient reason to reject Marx's theory, especially when compared to mainstream theories of profit, which have much more serious logical problems and much less explanatory power.

Since the 1980s, there have been several new reinterpretations of the transformation problem that have provided stronger defenses of Marx's theory. The best known and most influential of these new works on the transformation problem has been called the "new interpretation." It was presented originally, and independently, by Duncan Foley in 1982 and Gerard Duménil in 1983 and 1984. The main innovation of the new interpretation is that it argues that variable capital is not derived from a given quantity of means of subsistence, but is instead taken as given, as the actual quantity of money capital advanced to purchase labor power in the real capitalist economy, and that this is equal to the price of production of the means of subsistence, not the value of the means of subsistence. Furthermore, this same quantity of variable capital is taken both in the theory of value and in the theory of prices of production. In other words, variable capital does not change in the transformation of values into prices of production. It follows from this interpretation of variable capital that total profit is always equal to total surplus value. The new interpretation also redefines the aggregate price equality in terms of the "net price" of commodities, rather than the "gross price," and it assumes that this net-price equality is always true. Therefore, according to the new interpretation, both of Marx's two aggregate equalities, redefined in this way, are always true simultaneously. However, the new interpretation continues to accept the standard interpretation of constant capital, so that constant capital changes in the transformation of values into prices of production, and Marx's gross aggregate price equality is not satisfied (and the rate of profit also changes).

The "macro-monetary" interpretation presented by Fred Moseley in 2000 extends the new interpretation to constant capital as well as variable capital. Moseley argues that both variable capital and constant capital are taken as given, as the actual quantities of money capital advanced to purchase means of production and labor power in the real capitalist economy, and that these are equal to the price of production of the means of subsistence and the means of production, respectively. The crucial point is that these same quantities of constant capital and variable capital are taken as given in both the theory of value and the theory of prices of production. It follows from this interpretation of the initial givens in Marx's theory that both of Marx's two aggregate equalities are always true simultaneously, and also that the rate of profit does not change.

Similar interpretations have been presented by Richard Wolff, Antonio Callari, and Bruce Roberts (1984), and by Andrew Kliman and Ted McGlone (1988), although these interpretations are also different in some respects. It remains to be seen whether these recent reinterpretations will be accepted by the majority of Marxist economists and by the critics of Marx. But a new phase in the long debate has been opened up, which could lead to different conclusions concerning the logical consistency of Marx's theory.

SEE ALSO *Forces of Production; Labor Theory of Value; Value*

BIBLIOGRAPHY

Bortkiewicz, Ladislaus von. [1905] 1952. Value and Price in the Marxian System. *International Economic Papers* 2: 5–60.

Duménil, Gerard. 1983-1984. Beyond the Transformation Riddle: A Labor Theory of Value. *Science and Society* 47 (4): 427–450.

Foley, Duncan. 1982. The Value of Money, the Value of Labor Power, and the Marxian Transformation Problem. *Review of Radical Political Economics* 14 (2): 37–49.

Kliman, Andrew, and Ted McGlone. 1988. The Transformation Non-Problem and the Non-Transformation Problem. *Capital and Class* 35.

Moseley, Fred. 2000. The "New Solution" to the Transformation Problem: A Sympathetic Critique. *Review of Radical Political Economics* 32 (2): 282–316.

Steedman, Ian. 1977. *Marx after Sraffa*. London: New Left Books.

Sweezy, Paul. 1942. *Theory of Capitalist Development*. Chapter 7. New York: Modern Reader Paperbacks.

Wolff, Richard, Antonio Callari, and Bruce Roberts. 1984. A Marxian Alternative to the Traditional "Transformation Problem." *Review of Radical Political Economics* 16 (2–3): 115–135.

Fred Moseley

TRANSGENDER

Transgender is an umbrella term that describes different ways in which people transgress the gender boundaries that are constituted within a society. Groups encompassed by this term include people who have an atypical gender expression, sex, sexual identity, or gender identity. An understanding of *transgender* requires an awareness of the difference between the terms *sex* and *gender*—terms that often are conflated.

Sex is a biological construct. It refers to a person's physical anatomy, usually determined by their genetics and exposure to hormones. While sex often is considered dichotomous, so that individuals are classified as *male* if they have a penis and as *female* if they have a vagina, *intersexed* persons are an exception to this dichotomy because they have features of both sexes (Fausto-Sterling 2000). The debate about the treatment of intersexed infants whose sex organs do not appear traditionally male or female has been heated. On one side, people feel that genital surgery should be performed early so that the infant has the genitalia of one sex and can be raised without confusion about their *sexual identity*—that is, without confusion about how they understand and label their own sex. On the other side, organizations of intersexed people, such as the Intersex Society of North America, have protested this practice on the grounds that the sex assigned to the child in surgery may not correspond with their sexual identity as they mature. Instead, they argue that intersexed children should be raised with their genitalia unaltered until they are old enough to determine if they would like genital surgery and, if so, to select which sex is a better fit for them.

Unlike sex, *gender* is a social construct. Within social groups, sets of traits are linked together come to form genders, such as *masculinity* and *femininity*, through repeated performance and symbolism. The set of traits may depend upon the culture and time, such that enacting femininity in one country may appear different from doing so within another country or within another era. While many cultures recognize two genders attributed to male or female physical sexes, other cultures have formed genders that are based upon a combination of the sexes and personalities of individuals. For instance, some Native American tribes recognized "two-spirit" people as having distinct genders with valued social roles—so "masculine women" might become warriors and "feminine men" healers (Feinberg 1996).

In most cultures, however, gender is thought to be dictated by one's physical sex, without any recognition of the cultural assignment of gender traits to one sex or another. When people fall outside the norms of gender transgression—that is, enacting traits that are attributed to the other sex—they may fall into one of the categories of transgender identity. People who adopt *gender expressions* (i.e., appearances that reflect gendered traits) that are not consistent with their sex by wearing clothing that is associated with the other sex may identify as *cross-dressers* or as *transvestites*. Because women are permitted a broader range of apparel in the West, male cross-dressers are more common and noticeable than female cross-dressers. Cross-dressing does not indicate a person's sexual orientation; in fact, most male cross-dressers identify as heterosexual (Docter and Prince 1997).

Transsexual people have a sexual identity that does not match their physical sex. While some desire sex-reassignment surgery so that their anatomy can match their sense of self, not all transsexuals want to change their bodies. Surgery is costly, and can have mixed results. Hormone therapy may be used as well, as a complement to surgery or independently, and is less costly. To receive services, many clinics require that transsexual people first meet the Harry Benjamin Standards of Care (Meyer et al. 2001), which detail a list of steps that people complete to show that they are ready for surgery—such as living for a year as the other sex. *Transmen* or *FTM* (female-to-male) and *transwomen* or *MTF* (male-to-female) are common labels to describe the sex of those who transition from one sex to the other.

Sexual orientation refers to one's emotional, physical, and sexual attraction to another person. Individuals who are attracted to the other sex are *heterosexual,* to the same sex are *homosexual,* and to both sexes are *bisexual.* While having a sexual orientation other than heterosexual does not necessitate a transgender sexual identity or gender expression, there are forms of gender or gender expression within some nonheterosexual communities that fall under a transgender rubric. For instance, being *in drag* is slang that connotes appearing and acting, for entertainment purposes, in a way that is typical for the other sex—with *drag queens* being men emulating women and *drag kings* being women emulating men (Volcano and Halberstam 1999). Within lesbian communities, terms like *butch* and *femme* describe the gender identities of women who display different sets of gendered traits. Although they often are misunderstood as mimicking heterosexual genders, these genders are composed of traits that do not fall neatly into masculine or feminine genders but have unique meanings within those communities (Levitt and Hiestand 2004).

People who are transgender tend to experience more discrimination and harassment than those who are not, even when compared to gay or lesbian people who are not transgender (Herek 1995; Levitt and Horne 2002). There is debate within the psychological community on how to understand transgender. A diagnosis for *gender identity disorder* remains listed in the 2000 edition of the *Diagnostic and Statistical Manual of Mental Disorders* of the American Psychiatric Association. Many mental health professionals believe that this diagnosis should be abolished because it is based upon a false understanding of gender and that treatment should focus on creating supportive environments for transgender youth rather than pathologizing them (Hiestand and Levitt 2005). At the same time, others believe that the diagnosis is necessary so people can obtain insurance coverage for treatments (Brown and Rounsley 1996), and still others persist in conceptualizing transgender as a mental disorder inherent to the individual.

Groups of transgender people have organized to fight for supportive legislation and medical and mental health treatments that meet their needs and respect diversity within gender experiences. Such organizations as the International Foundation for Gender Education and the National Center for Transgender Equality also work to educate the public about transgender issues and concerns.

SEE ALSO *Discrimination; Gender; Gender, Alternatives to Binary; Harassment; Sexual Orientation, Determinants of; Sexual Orientation, Social and Economic Consequences; Sexuality*

BIBLIOGRAPHY

American Psychiatric Association. 2000. *Diagnostic and Statistical Manual of Mental Disorders* (*DSM*-IV-TR). 4th ed., text rev. Washington, DC: Author.

Brown, Mildred L., and Chloe Ann Rounsley. 1996. *True Selves: Understanding Transsexualism—For Families, Friends, Coworkers, and Helping Professionals.* San Francisco: Jossey-Bass.

Docter, Richard F., and Virginia Prince. 1997. Transvestism: A Survey of 1032 Cross-dressers. *Archives of Sexual Behavior* 26 (6): 589–605.

Fausto-Sterling, Anne. 2000. *Sexing the Body: Gender Politics and the Construction of Sexuality.* New York: Basic Books.

Feinberg, Leslie. 1996. *Transgender Warriors: Making History from Joan of Arc to Dennis Rodman.* Boston: Beacon Press.

Herek, Gregory M. 1995. Psychological Heterosexism in the United States. In *Lesbian, Gay, and Bisexual Identities Over the Lifespan: Psychological Perspectives,* eds. Anthony R. D'Augelli and Charlotte J. Patterson, 321–346. New York: Oxford University Press.

Hiestand, Katherine, and Heidi M. Levitt. 2005. Butch Identity Development: The Formation of an Authentic Gender. *Feminism and Psychology* 15 (1): 61–85.

International Foundation for Gender Education. http://www.ifge.org.

Intersex Society of North America. http://www.isna.org.

Levitt, Heidi M., and Katherine Hiestand. 2004. A Quest for Authenticity: Contemporary Butch Gender. *Sex Roles: A Journal of Research* 50 (9–10): 605–621.

Levitt, Heidi M., and Sharon G. Horne. 2002. Explorations of Lesbian-Queer Genders. *Journal of Lesbian Studies* 6 (2): 25–39.

Meyer, Walter, III (Chairperson), Walter O. Bockting, Peggy Cohen-Kettenis, et al. February 2001. The Standards of Care for Gender Identity Disorders–Sixth Version. *The International Journal of Transgenderism* 5 (1). http://www.symposion.com/ijt/soc_2001/index.htm.

National Center for Transgender Equality. http://www.nctequality.org.

Volcano, Del LaGrace, and Judith "Jack" Halberstam. 1999. *The Drag King Book.* New York: Serpent's Tail.

Brandy L. Smith
Heidi M. Levitt

TRANSGRESSION

SEE *Sin.*

TRANSNATIONALISM

Although the idea of transnationalism is widely employed in the social sciences to describe long-distance networks, there is little agreement about its precise definition. The concept of transnationalism describes a situation in which nations and communications are connected, regardless of the geographical distances that separate them, typically by new communication technologies that facilitate flows and networks of people, goods, and services. Transnationalism is therefore also associated with such notions as "network society" (Castells 2000) and with international mobility (Urry 2000). Transnationalism can also be used simply as a substitute for the notion of globalization (Held et al. 1999). It is therefore important to distinguish between internationalism and transnationalism. The former refers to cooperation between nation states and encompasses the international relations between governments that are regulated by treaties and agreements. Transnationalism refers to global cooperation between people and can evolve into a global social movement that advocates harmony, multiculturalism, and cosmopolitanism.

Transnationalism is said to be manifest in certain characteristic social phenomena. These include preeminently the global development of ethnic diasporas as a consequence of the international flow of legal and illegal migrants. The growth of such networks of dispersed communities is also associated with the development of transnational crime and with terrorist networks. These cross-border activities involve not just the trade in capitalist goods and services but include drugs, weapons, contraband, and people. The trade in women as prostitutes is part of a larger pattern of global slavery. It is also claimed, primarily in cultural studies, that transnationalism has given rise to new forms of consciousness because migrants have multiple identities and hybrid cultures. The analysis of these global cultural flows is closely associated with the anthropological investigations of Arjun Appadurai (1996, 2001). These fragmented and multiple identities become part of a transnational imaginary that creates fictive communities of membership and belonging. Because these cultural identities and images are drawn from multiple sources, it is claimed by writers such as Homi Bhabha (1994) that many modern cultures are going through a process of hybridization.

Alongside cultural transnationalism, there is the emergence of economic transnationalism, which is manifest in the transnational corporation that produces and sells in global markets beyond the controls of the nation state. There is also, as a result, an international capitalist class that is highly mobile and a transnational working class whose remittances to countries like Pakistan and the Philippines represent a significant contribution to the national economy. These movements of labor now also include large numbers of women, resulting in both the feminization of migrant labor—for example the Filipino maids of Singapore and the Gulf states—and the growth of the transnational marriage (Yeoh et al. 2000). These migratory roots also become the sites of international business communities that can exploit these ethnic ties, however weak and dispersed, to create economic opportunities for global accumulation, as Aihwa Ong (1999) has demonstrated with respect to the diasporic Chinese business community.

Unsurprisingly, transnationalism is thought to have significant political consequences resulting, for example, in the global city as a site of power that can challenge the nation state, or giving rise to a global democracy and a global public sphere (Held 1995) or to new forms of citizenship or "mutations of citizenship" (Ong 2006) and "transnational citizenship" (Bauböck 1994). Transnational migration in creating guest workers and permanent residents has required a reassessment of the relevance of national citizenship to the rights of migrant workers and their families. The legal and political status of migrants as quasi citizens is often ambiguous, because national citizenship is based on both rights and duties. It is often unclear whether migrants, refugees, or asylum seekers should be expected to fulfill the duties of citizens, such as paying taxes or undertaking military service.

Transnationalism is also associated with the idea of cosmopolitanism, and it has been assumed that the porous boundaries of the modern state, along with international cooperation through such institutions as the United Nations, might fulfill Immanuel Kant's (1724–1804) dream of "perpetual peace" and international harmony (Kant [1795] 1991). However, with growing fear of terrorism after the attack on the World Trade Center in New York in 2001 and the increasing emphasis on domestic and international securitization, many governments are attempting to control the transnational flow of illegal people, goods, and services. One state response is to build walls to contain such flows—for example, between Mexico and the United States. In October 2006 U.S. president George W. Bush signed the Secure Fence Act, which anticipates the creation of a 700-mile barrier to deter illegal migrants. However, walls are also being constructed between Brazil and Paraguay, between Saudi Arabia and Iraq, and between Israel and its Palestinian neighbors. The city council of Padua in Italy has created a steel barrier to divide the respectable side of the city from the high-crime neighborhoods, which are said to be rife with illegal drugs associated with an influx of Nigerian and Tunisian migrants. Sociologists have argued therefore that modern states, perceiving transnationalism as a threat to their sovereignty and security, have created an "immobility regime" and that increased surveillance and regulation of populations is resulting in an "enclave society" rather than transnational integration (Turner 2007).

SEE ALSO *Citizenship; Corporations; Cosmopolitanism; Cultural Studies; Globalization, Social and Economic Aspects of; Immigrants to North America; Immigration; Kant, Immanuel; Nationalism and Nationality; Networks*

BIBLIOGRAPHY

Appadurai, Arjun. 1996. *Modernity at Large: Cultural Dimensions of Globalization.* Minneapolis: University of Minnesota Press.

Appadurai, Arjun, ed. 2001. *Globalization.* Durham, NC: Duke University Press.

Bales, Kevin. 2005. *Understanding Global Slavery: A Reader.* Berkeley: University of California Press.

Bauböck, Rainer. 1994. *Transnational Citizenship: Membership and Rights in International Migration.* Aldershot, U.K.: Elgar.

Bhabha, Homi. 1994. *The Location of Culture.* New York: Routledge.

Castells, Manuel. 2000. *The Rise of the Network Society.* 2nd ed. Oxford: Blackwell.

Held, David. 1995. *Democracy and the Global Order: From the Modern State to Cosmopolitan Governance.* Cambridge, U.K.: Polity.

Held, David, Anthony McGrew, David Goldblatt, and Jonathan Perraton. 1999. *Global Transformations: Politics, Economics, and Culture.* Cambridge, U.K.: Polity.

Kant, Immanuel. [1795] 1991. Perpetual Peace. In *Kant: Political Writings*, ed. Hans Reiss; trans. H. B. Nisbet, 93–130. 2nd ed. Cambridge, U.K.: Cambridge University Press.

Ong, Aihwa. 1999. *Flexible Citizenship: The Cultural Logics of Transnationality.* Durham, NC: Duke University Press.

Ong, Aihwa. 2006. Mutations in Citizenship. *Theory Culture & Society* 23 (2–3): 499–531.

Sassen, Saskia. 1996. *Losing Control? Sovereignty in an Age of Globalization.* New York: Columbia University Press.

Turner, Bryan S. 2007. The Enclave Society: Towards a Sociology of Immobility. *European Journal of Social Theory* 10 (2): 287–303.

Urry, John. 2000. Mobile Sociology. *British Journal of Sociology* 51 (1): 185–203.

Yeoh, Brenda, Shirlena Huang, and Katie Willis. 2000. Global Cities, Transnational Flows, and Gender Dimensions: The View from Singapore. *Asian Studies Review* 28: 7–23.

Bryan S. Turner

TRANSPARENCY

The use of the concept of transparency has become widespread across multiple fields and subfields in the social sciences. In most instances, it is used to describe the ability of one actor to access information from another actor. More simply, transparency can be understood as the opposite of secrecy. "Government transparency" refers to the ability of societal actors to access government-held information. Democratic theory has long emphasized that an accountable, truly democratic polity must make its decisions public to its citizens. Such arguments can be traced as far back as the writings of Jeremy Bentham (1748–1832), who used the concept of "publicity" rather than "transparency," and James Madison (1751–1836), who argued that "a popular government, without popular information, or the means of acquiring it, is but a prologue to a farce or a tragedy" (Madison 1973, p. 473).

Some authors differentiate between the "openness" of a political system and the transparency of the government. Openness is a reflection of the free flow of information *among* societal actors (e.g., through a free press). Transparency, on the other hand, reflects the flow of information *from* governments *to* society.

The need for government transparency has become part of the broader social science debates on the "principal-agent problem." Government officials are seen as "agents" who need to act on behalf of citizens (their "principals"). Their actions need to be known and approved by the public. The main opposition to government transparency comes from government bureaucrats, because greater public access to information about bureaucrats' work increases the likelihood for their mistakes to become visible. Also, lack of transparency sometimes allows government officials to reap "rents" by disclosing information only to individuals friendly to them or their organizations.

Transparency is closely related to the concept of accountability. Accountable governments need first to inform the public of their actions and intentions and, second, to offer mechanisms through which they can be punished for not being representative. Transparency is thus considered a necessary, albeit not sufficient, condition for accountability.

Transparent political systems are considered to be more effective economically and more stable politically; governments that are not transparent are generally more corrupt. Whether corruption is present or not, a secretive political system leads people to assume that government officials have something to hide, so lack of transparency reduces citizens' faith in the performance of democratic governments and slows down democratic consolidation. Lack of government transparency in many new democracies is one of the factors that can lead to incomplete consolidation or even reversals to authoritarianism.

Transparency is best assured through the adoption of "freedom of information" (FOI) laws. The few existing gauges of government transparency are in fact based on the existence and completeness of such laws. In 1766 Sweden was the first country to adopt freedom of information legislation, as part of its press freedom act. Finland (in the 1950s) and the United States (in the 1960s and 1970s) were the next countries to adopt such laws. In 1990 only fourteen countries had legislation pertaining to citizens' access to information. From 1991 to 2000, during what Thomas Blanton in "The World's Right to Know" (2002) called the "decade of transparency," that number more than doubled. While many of the countries adopting freedom of information laws in the 1990s were new democracies, some consolidated democracies such as the United Kingdom, Italy, and Japan also adopted FOI legislation.

The literature suggests two possible reasons for the increased transparency in the post–cold war era: the emergence of a general "norm of transparency" and technological advances such as the development of personal computers, word processing, photocopying, and, especially, the Internet. Such technologies have led to an increased ability to generate, store, and, more importantly, disseminate information to a large number of citizens. The costs of offering information to the public—one of the long-standing problems associated with government transparency—have been reduced substantially due to such new technologies. But even with the improvements brought by new information technology, many government agencies still struggle with the implementation of freedom of information legislation. In the United States, for example, more than half a million requests for information are made every year under the Freedom of Information Act (FOIA). The FOIA offices that deal with such requests in individual agencies do not have the necessary funds and staff to deal with them, and therefore become backlogged.

Transparency is limited not only because it is costly and time-consuming for government officials, but also because there are limits to the kinds of information that can be made available. Virtually all the countries that allow public access to government information have some restrictions on that access, such as exempting from scrutiny information that endangers national security or individual privacy. Yet a truly transparent government is one that

1. makes clear that access to information is the norm and exemptions are to be resorted to only in exceptional cases;

2. has legislation with precise definitions of the exemptions to the right of access;

3. provides for an independent review of denials of access to information; and

4. requires minimal or no fees for the requested information.

While the literature on transparency still focuses overwhelmingly on the relationship between governments and citizens, the concept is now also used increasingly to describe the ease with which information flows between other types of actors. For example, during international negotiations a state can be characterized as transparent if it offers information about its preferences and intentions to another state; a corporation is transparent when it allows investors access to financial data; an international organization is transparent if states or the public can access information about its workings. This implies that, when discussing transparency, one needs to specify the actor that is offering information *and* the one who is receiving such information.

The relationship between information and power has long been acknowledged. In the contemporary information age it is only natural that there is a growing interest in who controls information and how they control it. The increased focus on transparency is a reflection of such interests in multiple disciplines in the social sciences.

SEE ALSO *Accountability; Bureaucracy*

BIBLIOGRAPHY

Blanton, Thomas. 2002. The World's Right to Know. *Foreign Policy* 131: 50–54.

Finel, Bernard, and Kristin Lord, eds. 2000. *Power and Conflict in the Age of Transparency.* New York: St. Martin's Press.

Florini, Ann. 1998. The End of Secrecy. *Foreign Policy* 111: 50–63.

Florini, Ann. 2003. *The Coming Democracy: New Rules for Running a New World.* Washington, DC: Island Press.

Madison, James. 1973. *The Mind of the Founder: Sources of the Political Thought of James Madison*, ed. Marvin Meyers. Indianapolis, IN: Macmillan.

Alexandru Grigorescu

TRANSPORTATION INDUSTRY

Transportation services move people or freight from one location to another. These services are a near necessity for successful operations of businesses and governments. Efficient transportation systems contribute to businesses fulfilling purchase orders in a timely fashion. They also increase residency options for employees because workers are not restricted to living in close proximity to their jobs. Government services also benefit from the use of efficient transportation networks by enhancing governments' ability to respond to national emergencies.

Different modes of transportation are available to satisfy business, government, and commuter demands. Shipping volume and geography dictate the most efficient type of transportation service. For example, trucking, rail, and inland water barges generally transport freight within a country or region. Cost advantages from hauling relatively small shipments of 80,000 pounds or less are associated with trucking carriers primarily because such operations face small fixed costs. Often the major source of fixed costs for many trucking carriers is the leasing of trucks. The investment in more trucks and employment of more drivers to meet high volume demand at best is associated with unit costs remaining the same. In contrast, the unit costs of providing shipping service by rail and inland barges declines as volume increases due in large part to the high fixed costs of providing transport. For instance, fixed costs such as the cost of locomotives and barges are substantial and allow for additional freight volume beyond the typical 80,000-pound limit in trucking. Labor costs associated with operating such transport equipment increase less than proportionately with increasing volume given the large hauling capacity of trains and barges.

The shortcoming of trucking, barge, and rail is their inability to provide overseas service. As an alternative, international shippers rely on the services of ocean liners and air carriers. The introduction of containerized shipping by the American entrepreneur Malcom McLean in 1956 contributed to ocean liners' capacity advantage over aircraft when shipping large quantities of bulk products. In contrast, aircrafts typically transport small packages and parcels. Air transport service also offers the advantage of faster delivery compared to ocean liner service.

Excluding trucking, the major modes of freight transport also provide passenger service. This service constitutes a large share of air transport business. The ability to provide relatively fast transport across long distances makes this mode of travel a superior choice over rail and water passenger service. Light rail service is more cost effective than air transport for service within localities with high population density. Along with bus transport, rail provides an alternative to the use of private automobiles for local commutation. The benefits associated with rail and bus public transit in high-density areas are the easing of traffic congestion and the reduction of pollution emissions. Commuter demand for privacy and scheduling flexibility, however, makes the private use of automobiles a viable option for local commutes.

The economic significance of transportation services is further highlighted by its large share of national output. For instance, transportation's share of total trade of commercial import services varies from a low of 16.7 percent in North America to a high of 28.6 percent in Asia, according to World Trade Organization statistics published in 2004. Transportation services' share of total trade of commercial exports varies from a low of 22.3 percent in Western Europe to a high of 38.5 percent in Africa. The interest of governments in the development of transportation services is universally strong given that these services are a major source of economic growth. Hence, the remainder of this entry explores the twentieth-century history of governments' influence on the provision of efficient transportation services.

GOVERNMENT POLICY TOWARD TRANSPORTATION SERVICES

For the majority of the twentieth century, many countries provided state-owned transportation services. Ownership gave governments the power to offer universal service at affordable rates. Other countries such as the United States imposed economic regulation on private transportation operations. Local U.S. governments' role in the provision of public transit did resemble that of other countries. Typically U.S. municipalities owned and operated local rail and bus services.

U.S. regulation of transportation services from the 1920s to the mid-1970s restricted carrier competition and set rates along routes. The rationale for limiting competition in rail, air, and water transport was that their high fixed costs made them susceptible to destructive competition. Competition in this type of market leads to periods of carrier foreclosure as firms are unable to cover costs when facing competitive price pressures. Setting the terms for service rates gave rate-makers the opportunity to promote affordable service for a large group of potential customers. Regulation did contribute to reaching policymakers' goals of avoiding ruinous price competition and providing extensive network service at affordable prices. For example, minimum freight hauling rates were imposed on railroad carriers to help them avoid financial disaster. Entry restrictions, though, required these carriers to service nonlucrative routes to rural agricultural areas. Rate regulation for trucking and airline carriers were set as mark-ups over cost. Market pressure to keep costs low in trucking did not arise since entry restrictions significantly limited entry of potential rivals along routes. Indeed, potential entrants were often limited to offering service to newly formed routes, and even then incumbent carriers were given the initial opportunity to provide such service. This approach toward entry regulation gave established carriers the opportunity to reject servicing potentially nonlucrative routes. A different regulatory approach was taken for airline carriers as they were required to service low demand locations at the rate charged for high demand locations. Compared to rate regulation in the transportation sectors previously mentioned, ocean liners experienced less government control over rates. Ocean liners were given antitrust immunity in negotiating port-to-port rates for lines involving U.S. foreign commerce.

State-owned operations achieved the goal of providing universal and affordable service by using government revenue to subsidize transit operations. Subsidization of commuter transit was not limited to publicly provided services as commuters using their own motor vehicles drive on roads constructed and maintained with significant financial support from government revenue.

TRANSPORTATION LABOR HISTORY IN A REGULATED BUSINESS ENVIRONMENT

While incumbent transportation carriers, consumers in rural areas, and commuters were the intended beneficiaries of regulation and state ownership, transportation workers also enjoyed significant benefits from these policies. Transportation labor markets became highly unionized following regulatory reform in the early part of the twentieth century. The restriction of competitive entry into transportation services contributed to a large share of these industries' work forces belonging to a union.

Three years following enactment of the 1935 Motor Carrier Act, the number of trucking employees belonging to the International Brotherhood of Teamsters rose to 370,000 compared to 75,000 in 1933, according to a 1986 report by Charles Perry. Union membership reached 920,000 by 1948. The Teamsters' membership was concentrated in the highly profitable intercity carriage sector, where 80 percent of workers in that sector belonged to the Teamsters by 1940. Representation of such a large group of workers contributed to the Teamsters ability to negotiate lucrative contracts for its members. Rate regulation that allowed trucking carriers to pass on costs to shippers further contributed to the Teamsters ability to negotiate high wages. Indeed, researchers reveal that union truck drivers received wages 30 to 50 percent above wages paid to nonunion drivers working in less lucrative sectors of the trucking industry.

Union growth in rail, airlines, and ocean shipping differed from trucking. Rather than a single dominant union representing the work force, workers belonged to several unions. Labor law guidelines of the 1926 Railroad Labor Act influenced union development in rail and airlines. This act prohibited rail and airline unions representing different occupational groups of workers employed by the same carrier. Most rail workers belonged to the United Transportation Union, the Brotherhood of Maintenance of Way Employees, and the Transportation Communications Union. Negotiating with several unions presented rail carriers with the opportunity to target the weakest union and use that settlement as a pattern for successful negotiations with other rail carriers. Rail unions addressed this problem in 1973 by collectively negotiating with a group of major carriers. Shifting to group negotiations contributed to union rail workers receiving lucrative contracts.

In contrast to rail, labor relations in the airlines were characterized by the proliferation of more than 100 bargaining units across industry carriers under the administration of the Railroad Labor Act. Such a large number of units made it difficult for airline unions to cooperate among each other. Even though the industrial relations environment for airline workers lessened the negotiation strength of the industry unions, workers were able to attain relatively high wages because the major occupations such as pilots and mechanics are vital to carrier operations and command lucrative compensation.

Philosophical differences among union leaders led to the 1937 development of two major U.S. ocean shipping unions. The International Longshore and Warehouse Union (ILWU) under the leadership of Harry Bridges split from the International Longshoreman's Association (ILA) and negotiated contracts primarily for workers on the West Coast. Both unions were able to negotiate high wages even though their members faced significant risk of job loss due to technological innovation. The ILA and ILWU's monopolistic control over the supply of workers on the coasts contributed to their ability to secure high wages for their members.

INEFFICIENCIES ASSOCIATED WITH TRANSPORTATION REGULATION

Using regulation and state ownership as government approaches to promote universal and affordable transportation services unintentionally helped create a business environment that fostered inefficient operations and poor financial performance. Faced with rate regulation that removed price competition, transportation carriers often engaged in costly nonprice competition. For example, airline carriers provided passengers the convenience of nonstop service with frequent daily departure times as a strategy for distinguishing their service from that of rivals. This type of nonprice competition reduced carriers' ability to fly with a significant number of seats filled per flight.

Rate regulation of ocean liners influenced carrier profitability by prohibiting them from directly negotiating low rates with inland transport carriers. Poor financial performance was much more severe in rail and air transport as carriers in these industries were required to charge relatively high rates on high demand routes to subsidize servicing less profitable locations.

TRANSPORTATION SERVICES FOLLOWING DEREGULATION AND PRIVATIZATION

The potential for enhancing efficiency by promoting competition led to the deregulation and privatization of transportation sectors in the last quarter of the twentieth century. Deregulation gave carriers greater freedom to set rates and to enter markets previously restricted to incumbent carriers. This more competitive environment created a greater incentive for carriers to adopt cost-saving strategies across all transportation sectors. For instance, the introduction of the "hub-and-spoke" distribution system in the airlines industry resulted in a marked increase in the percentage of seats filled per flight. This type of system transports travelers from originating cities into a major airport, which is the airline's hub. From the hub travelers from different originating cities are grouped together to take connecting flights to a common destination.

Postderegulation efficiency gains in the railroad industry were achieved in part by consolidating operations through mergers and by abandoning low-use routes. Efficiency gains in rail were further enhanced by carriers' adoption of labor saving technologies such as electronic-based communications and information systems. New communications technologies in tandem with logistics software contributed to enhanced productivity in the trucking industry by allowing carriers to coordinate efficient delivery and pick-up schedules. Deregulation in the ocean liner sector facilitated efficiency gains by allowing these carriers to negotiate "door-to-door" rates. Such negotiations set rates for the international delivery of cargo to the final destination terminal inclusive of any inland transportation. These rates differ from the pre-deregulation requirement of "port-to port" negotiations that limit rate determination for transport freight from one port directly to another. Setting rates for the final destination allows liners to take advantage of economies of scale by choosing ports with the capacity to service large container ships and also provide intramodal service to the final destination point.

Privatization of public transit operations encourages cost savings by granting operating rights to low-bid service providers. Private providers are thought to have an advantage when competing for the provision of public services because managers in this sector are subject to more demanding incentives than those faced by their public sector counterparts. Evidence of public transit efficiency gains indicate cost savings in the range of 9 to 23 percent in the U.S., according to a 1988 report by Roger Teal. Similar cost savings from privatization are also reported for other countries.

SOCIAL IMPACT OF STEPPED-UP COMPETITION IN TRANSPORTATION

The labor market for transportation workers has been substantially influenced by the more competitive postderegulation and pro-privatization business environment. The pressure to lower costs led to declining work force sizes in U.S. rail and ocean shipping. The shift to greater efficiency and lower costs in ocean shipping also facilitated job loss in other countries. In 2006 James Peoples and colleagues reported that the introduction of new technology in the United Kingdom contributed to a 49 percent job reduction from 1989 to 1992. Ocean shipping jobs declined up to 66 percent at six major French ports following work rule reforms in 1992. Waterfront reforms introduced by the Australian government in 1989 contributed to a 42 percent reduction in stevedore jobs by 1991.

The approach toward labor cost savings did not result in a shrinking work force in U.S. trucking and airlines. Rather, the work force in these industry sectors grew over 70 percent in twenty years following deregulation, according to a 1998 report by Peoples. Declining labor costs in trucking and airlines were the result of eroding union wage premiums.

Transportation labor market changes influence other aspects of social welfare. For instance, the growing number of truck drivers on the road poses greater risk of environmental degradation from the emission of pollutants and greater risk of traffic accidents. Demand for quick service that places scheduling pressure on transportation operators further contributes to dangerous roads. Concerns over the social impact of increasing transportation demand promoted the enactment of several safety and environmental regulations following deregulation. In conjunction with safety-enhancing technologies, regulation limiting hours of operating service and regulations setting minimum standards for attaining driving permits helped the trucking industry avoid increasing injury rates following economic deregulation. Stiffer fuel efficiency standards and requirements for cleaner burning fuel have been enacted to help protect the environment from the debilitating health effects of emission pollutants.

In sum, the role of transportation services as an engine of economic growth will gain in importance during the twenty-first-century trend toward economic globalization. Those economies that are able to provide easy access to affordable services will enjoy a competitive advantage over other economies. In the future, such success will rely heavily on the ability to make efficient use of non-renewable energy sources in addition to the ability to develop new energy alternatives.

SEE ALSO *Aviation Industry; Industry; Railway Industry; Shipping Industry*

BIBLIOGRAPHY

Bitzan, John, and Theodore Keeler. 2003. Productivity Growth and Some of its Determinants in the Deregulated U.S. Railroad Industry. *Southern Economic Journal* 70 (2): 232–253.

Card, David. 1998. Deregulation and Labor Earnings in the Airline Industry. In *Regulatory Reform and Labor Markets*, ed. James Peoples. Boston: Kluwer Academic Publishers.

Grimm, Curtis, and Robert Windle. 1998. Regulation and Deregulation in Surface Freight, Airlines, and Telecommunications. In *Regulatory Reform and Labor Markets*, ed. James Peoples. Boston: Kluwer Academic Publishers.

Hendrick, Wallace, Peter Feuille, and Carol Szersen. 1980. Regulation, Deregulation, and Collective Bargaining in Airlines. *Industrial and Labor Relations Review* (34): 67–81.

Hirsch, Barry. 1988. Trucking Regulation, Unionization, and Labor Earnings: 1973–85. *Journal of Human Resources* (23): 286–319.

Jenks, Christopher. 1998. *International Transit Studies Program Report on the Spring 1997 Mission Public-Private Partnerships and Innovative Transit Technologies in Scandinavia.* Washington, DC: Transportation Research Board.

Kay, John, and David J. Thompson. 1986. Privatization: A Policy in Search of a Rationale. *Economic Journal* 96 (1): 18–32.

MacDonald, James, and Linda Cavalluzzo. 1996. Railroad Deregulation: Pricing Behavior, Shipper Responses, and the Effects on Labor. *Industrial and Labor Relations Review* (50): 80–91.

Monaco, Kristen, and Dale Belman. 2004. An Econometric Analysis of the Impact of Technology on the Work Lives of Truck Drivers. In *Transportation Labor Issues and Regulatory Reform*, eds. James Peoples and Wayne Talley. Amsterdam: Elsevier Science.

Moore, Thomas Gale. 1986. Rail and Trucking Deregulation. In *Regulatory Reform: What Actually Happened?*, eds. Leonard Weiss and Michael Klass. Boston: Little, Brown.

Morrison, Steven, and Clifford Winston. 1986. *The Economic Effects of Airline Deregulation.* Washington, DC: The Brookings Institution.

Peoples, James. 1998. Deregulation and the Labor Market. *The Journal of Economic Perspectives* 12 (3): 111–130.

Peoples, James, Wayne Talley, and Pithoon Thanabordeekij. 2006. Shipping Deregulation's Wage Effect on Low and High Wage Dockworkers. In *Port Economics*, eds. Kevin Cullinane and Wayne Talley. Amsterdam: Elsevier Science.

Perelman, Michael. 1994. Fixed Capital, Railroad Economics and the Critique of the Market. *Journal of Economics Perspectives* 8 (3): 189–195.

Perry, Charles. 1986. *Deregulation and the Decline of the Unionized Trucking Industry.* Philadelphia: Wharton School's Industrial Research Unit.

Rose, Nancy. 1987. Labor Rent-Sharing and Regulation: Evidence from the Trucking Industry. *Journal of Political Economy* 95 (6): 1146–1178.

Savage, Ian. 2004. Trends in Transportation Employee Injuries Since Economic Deregulation. In *Transportation Labor Issues and Regulatory Reform*, eds. James Peoples and Wayne Talley. Amsterdam: Elsevier Science.

Talley, Wayne. 2000. Ocean Container Shipping: Impacts of a Technological Improvement. *Journal of Economic Issues* 34 (4): 933–948.

Talley, Wayne. 2002. Dockworker Earnings, Containerization and Shipping Deregulation. *Journal of Transport Economics and Policy* 36 (3): 447–467.

Talley, Wayne, and Anna Schwartz-Miller. 1998. Railroad Deregulation and Union Labor Earnings. In *Regulatory Reform and Labor Markets*, ed. James Peoples. Boston: Kluwer Academic Publishers.

Teal, Roger. 1988. Public Transit Service Contracting: A Status Report. *Transportation Quarterly* 42 (2): 207–222.

Winston, Clifford. 1998. U.S. Industry Adjustment to Economic Deregulation. *The Journal of Economic Perspectives* 12 (3): 89–110.

World Trade Organization. 2004. *International Trade Statistics.* http://www.wto.org/english/res_e/statis_e/its2004_e/its04_by sector_e.htm#CommercialSevices.

James Peoples

TRANSSEXUALS

SEE *Transgender.*

TRAUMA

Until the middle of the nineteenth century, the word *trauma* was used primarily to designate physiological injury emanating from an external event. Beginning in the 1860s, however, the term acquired additional significance when survivors and witnesses of industrial accidents began to show symptoms of trauma in the absence of any observable physical injury. These symptoms typically included mutism, amnesia, tics, paralysis, recurrent nightmares, and, in some extreme cases, psychic dissociation. Observing a pattern that linked exposure to an overwhelming event with forms of mental disorder, doctors coined the term *traumatic neurosis.*

One of the most remarked-upon features of this neurosis was the incapacity of the victim to recall the event that precipitated it, coupled with a simultaneous sensation of its recurrence in the present. For this reason, trauma quickly became understood not merely as a psychic injury but also as a wound in the memory. It therefore demanded particular techniques of memory recovery, which ranged over the century from hypnosis to narcotic therapies.

FREUD AND HIS FOLLOWERS

The crisis of memory was variously understood as a function of repression and/or nonsymbolic apprehension of an event. In Austrian Sigmund Freud's (1856–1939) later writings, trauma was conceived as the result of extreme psychic excitement, in which the mind's consciousness—which he analogized as a protective shield—was traversed by overwhelming stimuli, which were then registered in a different part of the mind, namely its unconsciousness. Precisely because the traumatic event had never become an object of consciousness, Freud theorized, it was unavailable for narration, objective reflection, and the analytic distance of the kind that would secure the subject against its frightening effects. For this reason, treatment focused on the method of abreaction, an induced revival of the event in which a subject, working with the therapist, would be able to render it conscious. The abreaction was also intended to produce a discharge, which then relieved the patient of a crippling, nervous energy.

Whether the efficacy of the treatment lay in the revival and cognitive apprehension and contextualization of the event or in the simple emotional relief obtained from the process was a matter of some controversy. Some argued that any event, even a false or confabulated one, could serve the purpose of treatment if its recall relieved patients of their symptoms. In the 1980s and 1990s, debates about the dubious validity of the "recovered memories" used in cases of alleged satanic or mass sexual abuse in the United States can be traced to this history of confabulation, coupled with the centrality of hypnosis in the treatment of trauma. Freud and his followers nonetheless insisted that the purpose of treatment was an intellectual reconciliation with the truth of experience, and hence the cathartic function of abreaction was played down in favor of a synthetic narrative or "talking cure."

Freud and his followers developed their theories and treatments largely in response to two kinds of phenomena, namely female hysteria (initially believed by Freud to be caused by sexual seduction of the girl) and "war neuroses." In both cases, charges of dissimulation (fakery) were often leveled against sufferers, and it was for this reason that Freud argued so fervently against the therapeutic deployment of fiction.

During wartime, the possibility of dissimulated illness acquired additional salience because soldiers who manifested acute forms of traumatic neurosis were relieved of their military duties. It was, in fact, the prolif-eration of cases of war neuroses (or "shell shock") that led to the burgeoning study of trauma in the early twentieth century. The centrality of war in the development of trauma theory has continued unabated since then.

POST–WORLD WAR II DEVELOPMENTS

Since World War II (1939–1945), two major developments have affected trauma theory: the experience of mass or collective trauma, especially that associated with the Nazi death camps, and the recognition of delayed developments of traumatic symptoms, or post-traumatic stress disorder (PTSD). In the first instance, individual experience has become paradigmatic of a general historical condition, and a person's incapacity to represent traumatic events has been translated into a suspicion of historical narratives that claim to represent the truth of collective violence. In the second, a historically verifiable event has been used to liberate individuals for recognition, treatment, and material compensation.

In some cases, events of mass suffering—such as the Holocaust, the atomic bombing of Hiroshima and Nagasaki, the Middle Passage of slavery, or the rape camps of Bosnia—are deemed uniquely unrepresentable. This is an argument of scale, but an ethico-political injunction emanates from it, prohibiting or restricting efforts to represent such horrors on the grounds that their actuality would be betrayed or diminished in the process. In some versions of this argument, the question of scale is either linked to or substituted with one of structure, according to which all representation is deemed inadequate or incommensurate with actual historical events (Caruth 1996). For proponents of this position, the purpose of historical narration is the communication of traumatic effects to others—secondary witnesses and historical heirs—a process that is said to facilitate identification between those who have survived and those who have not. This argument has been widely criticized, however, because it fails to differentiate between those who suffered or witnessed events firsthand and those whose encounters with trauma were mediated by narratives of others who suffered them in actuality.

The question of PTSD has attracted similarly widespread debate. Observing that the syndrome was recognized only through advocacy on behalf of U.S. military veterans (PTSD was added to the *Diagnostic and Statistical Manual of Mental Disorders* of the American Psychiatric Association in 1980), some have suggested that presentation of symptoms and prevalence rates are influenced by the possibility of compensation for injuries. Moreover, as the authority of PTSD and American psychiatry has assumed international dimensions, new questions have arisen about the cross-cultural validity of the concept of trauma. In Vietnam, for example, there is considerable resistance to the idea of veterans suffering from PTSD. In Japan the diagnosis was rarely made prior to the Kobe earthquake of 1995, despite the country's long experience of acute postwar ailments.

Two factors explain the differential diagnosis of PTSD on a global scale, one cultural, the other politico-economic. First, there are many culturally distinct vocabularies and methodologies for identifying and treating shock and its psychosomatic aftermath. In some Buddhist societies of Southeast Asia, a sudden fright or accident is said to cause a dissociation of the person's spiritual being and requires rituals that call back or rebind dislodged spiritual essences. In parts of Africa and in aboriginal America, shock may be adduced as a causal factor in some illnesses and is often said to precipitate birth crises. It may be treated with combinations of naturopathic and ritual methods.

Second, the widespread recognition of shock as a source of injury and the prevalence of ideas of dissociation that accompany vernacular knowledge about shock resonate strongly with Western medical concepts of trauma, though Western medicine increasingly attributes the disturbing symptoms of PTSD to chemical transformations of the brain, especially in the hippocampus, amygdala, and cerebral cortex. The diagnosis of PTSD, however conceived, has nonetheless been promoted by international humanitarian organizations as a mechanism for obtaining financial resources and mental health services for populations—displaced by war and natural disaster—that would otherwise lack them. Invoking PTSD as a basis for claiming human rights is not without risks, however. The inherent focus on traumatic events in its diagnosis (which requires that the symptoms of hyperarousal and/or withdrawal be linked to an originating event) often displaces concern for the structural sources of long-term social and psychic suffering, including that caused by homelessness, poverty, unemployment, or long-term political oppression. Moreover, the proliferating tendency to invoke trauma as a synonym for unpleasant experiences in popular media and public discourse threatens to dissipate the term's medical as well as its ethico-political force. Beyond the risks that it is subject to both trivialization and economic utilitarianism, however, most theorists agree that trauma is a phenomenon whose increasing occurrence is inextricably tied to the industrialization of war and the massifications of modernity.

BIBLIOGRAPHY

Antze, Paul, and Michael Lambek, eds. 1996. *Tense Past: Cultural Essays in Trauma and Memory.* New York: Routledge.

Bracken, Patrick J., and Celia Petty, eds. 1998. *Rethinking the Trauma of War.* London: Free Association.

Breslau, Joshua. 2004. Introd. to Cultures of Trauma: Anthropological Views of Posttraumatic Stress Disorder in International Health. Spec. issue, *Culture, Medicine, and Psychiatry* 28 (2): 113–126.

Caruth, Cathy, ed. 1995. *Trauma: Explorations in Memory.* Baltimore, MD: Johns Hopkins University Press.

Caruth, Cathy. 1996. *Unclaimed Experience: Trauma, Narrative, and History.* Baltimore, MD: Johns Hopkins University Press.

Ferenczi, Sándor. 1988. *The Clinical Diary of Sándor Ferenczi,* ed. Judith Dupont. Trans. Michael Balint and Nicola Zarday Jackson. Cambridge, MA: Harvard University Press.

Freud, Sigmund. 1955a. *Beyond the Pleasure Principle.* In Vol. 18 of *The Standard Edition of the Complete Psychological Works of Sigmund Freud.* Trans. and ed. James Strachey. London: Hogarth Press. (Orig. pub. 1920.)

Freud, Sigmund. 1955b. Introd. to *Psycho-Analysis and the War Neuroses.* In Vol. 17 of *The Standard Edition of the Complete Psychological Works of Sigmund Freud.* Trans. and ed. James Strachey. London: Hogarth Press. (Orig. pub. 1919.)

Kardiner, Abram. 1941. *The Traumatic Neuroses of War.* Washington, DC: National Research Council.

Laplanche, Jean. 1976. *Life and Death in Psychoanalysis.* Trans. Jeffrey Mehlman. Baltimore, MD: Johns Hopkins University Press.

Leys, Ruth. 2000. *Trauma: A Genealogy.* Chicago: University of Chicago Press.

Young, Allan. 1995. *The Harmony of Illusions: Inventing Post-Traumatic Stress Disorder.* Princeton, NJ: Princeton University Press.

Rosalind C. Morris

TRAUMATIC BONDING

In contrast to normative bonds and attachments, which are characteristically affectionate and protective, traumatic bonding refers to a counterintuitive variation in which one member of the bonded pair intermittently victimizes or traumatizes the other person. The term *traumatic bonding* was first employed to describe a powerful and destructive bond that is sometimes observed between battered women and their abusers, or between maltreated children and their caregivers (Dutton and Painter 1981). It has since been applied more generally to describe strong emotional ties that may form between victims and their oppressors across a range of relationships and types of abuse (e.g., the Stockholm Syndrome; see Strentz 1980).

The necessary conditions for traumatic bonding are that one person must dominate the other and that the level of abuse chronically spikes and then subsides. The relationship is characterized by periods of permissive, compassionate, and even affectionate behavior from the dominant person, punctuated by intermittent episodes of intense abuse. To maintain the upper hand, the victimizer manipulates the behavior of the victim and limits the victim's options so as to perpetuate the power imbalance. Any threat to the balance of dominance and submission may be met with an escalating cycle of punishment ranging from seething intimidation to intensely violent outbursts. The victimizer also isolates the victim from other sources of support, which reduces the likelihood of detection and intervention, impairs the victim's ability to receive countervailing self-referent feedback, and strengthens the sense of unilateral dependency.

The traumatic effects of these abusive relationships may include the impairment of the victim's capacity for accurate self-appraisal, leading to a sense of personal inadequacy and a subordinate sense of dependence upon the dominating person. Victims also may encounter a variety of unpleasant social and legal consequences of their emotional and behavioral affiliation with someone who perpetrated aggressive acts, even if they themselves were the recipients of the aggression.

Theoretical explanations for this phenomenon are divergent and controversial. Psychodynamic theorists have employed concepts such as masochism, repetition compulsion, and identification with the aggressor (van der Kolk 1989; Young and Gerson 1991) to explain how such seemingly self-destructive relationships can be formed. A central developmental tenet of this perspective is that a proclivity toward abusive relationships and traumatic bonds is rooted in the victim's traumatic childhood attachments. Attachment theory has also been applied to explain traumatic bonding as an unresolved form of insecure attachment (Saunders and Edelson 1999) in which the capacity for self-regulation has been impaired by the alternately abusive and protective actions of an attachment figure. Each of these perspectives has persuasive elements, but the explanatory mechanisms are difficult to operationalize and have therefore gone untested.

Learning theory offers an explanation based on the consistent finding that intermittent reinforcement schedules can strengthen and maintain behavior even during periods when the reinforcer is absent. In the cycle of relational behavior attributed to traumatic bonding, the victimizer applies intense punishment, then negatively reinforces compliant behavior from the victim by ceasing the punishment, and soon after shifts to lavishing the victim with various forms of noncontingent positive reinforcement. This pattern of punishment and reinforcement may constitute a particularly powerful form of double-bind or vicious cycle, especially given the victim's legitimate fear of being injured or killed in retaliation for any act of defiance.

Little empirical research has been published examining the individual and situational characteristics that predict the development and maintenance of traumatic

bonding. Some support has been found both for the construct of traumatic bonding and for the importance of the intermittency element for predicting postrelationship distress among victims (Dutton and Painter 1993). But the most perplexing and counterintuitive aspect of traumatic bonding—the victim's feelings of affection and longing toward the victimizer following termination of the abusive relationship—has not been studied with the kind of rigor that would provide definitive findings, and the sociopolitical and philosophical aspects of this phenomenon make it particularly difficult to address from a scientific perspective.

SEE ALSO *Illness, Mental; Mental Health; Stress; Trauma*

BIBLIOGRAPHY

Dutton, Donald G., and Susan L. Painter. 1981. Traumatic Bonding: The Development of Emotional Attachments in Battered Women and Other Relationships of Intermittent Abuse. *Victimology: An International Journal* 6 (1–4): 139–155.

Dutton, Donald G., and Susan Painter. 1993. The Battered Woman Syndrome: Effects of Severity and Intermittency of Abuse. *American Journal of Orthopsychiatry* 63 (4): 614–622.

Saunders, Eleanor A., and Jill A. Edelson. 1999. Attachment Style, Traumatic Bonding, and Developing Relational Capacities in a Long-Term Trauma Group for Women. *International Journal of Group Psychotherapy* 49 (4): 465–485.

Strentz, Thomas. 1980. The Stockholm Syndrome: Law Enforcement Policy and Ego Defenses of the Hostage. *Annals of the New York Academy of Sciences* 347 (1): 137–150.

Van der Kolk, Bessel A. 1989. The Compulsion to Repeat the Trauma: Re-Enactment, Revictimization, and Masochism. *Psychiatric Clinics of North America* 12 (2): 389–411.

Young, G. H., and S. Gerson. 1991. New Psychoanalytic Perspectives on Masochism and Spouse Abuse. *Psychotherapy: Theory, Research, Practice, Training* 28 (1): 30–38.

Gilbert Reyes

TRAUMATIC STRESS DISORDER

SEE *Post-Traumatic Stress; Traumatic Bonding; Trauma.*

TRAVEL AND TRAVEL WRITING

Modern notions of travel have their roots in a diverse history of developments; groups of people have moved across landscapes for the purposes of migration, pilgrimage, trade, exploration, and colonization. For example, humans have migrated for resettlement for a million years, and for agricultural reasons for tens of thousands of years. Similarly, pilgrimages have been the cornerstone of most major religions: Just as the ancient Greeks sought the oracle at Delphi, Buddhists travel to the city of Buddha's birth, Muslims make the hajj to Mecca, and Christians visit Jerusalem. In another parallel flow of travel, trade routes flourished between Europe and China from the rise of Greek civilization to the fall of the Roman Empire.

MODES OF TRAVEL THROUGH HISTORY

The Mediterranean, which served as a vast network of people and places enriching communities for centuries, spurred commerce and exploration as twin historical processes—climaxing in the Age of Exploration between the fifteenth and seventeenth centuries. New technologies of cartography, navigation, warfare, and shipbuilding allowed travelers and traders to extend their reach beyond the Mediterranean—notably, Christopher Columbus's (1451–1506) arrival in the New World in 1492 and Vasco da Gama's (c. 1469–1524) trip around the Cape of Good Hope in 1498. Just as religion compelled pilgrimages, it has also inspired exploration and colonialism, either through evangelism or through groups fleeing religious persecution.

One of the first organized forms of travel that was neither explicitly religious nor commercial was the "grand tour." Beginning in the mid-1600s, it became fashionable for young British elites to take an expedition, as both a rite of passage and a duty. The grand tour was an extended journey through Europe, wherein a young man would travel in order to become more cultured and educated. Because of its courtly manners, high fashion, rich history, and sophisticated language, Paris was a common stop, but Italy, Switzerland, and Germany were also preferred destinations.

Industrialization, however, brought this trend to an end and ushered in a new era. Travel in the modern age can be traced to Thomas Cook (1808–1892), who would transport up to five hundred people at a time on train trips across England beginning in 1841. While tours from the ancient age through the grand tour tended to be a privilege of the rich, Cook's standardized tours aimed at mass appeal. Shadowing the ancient tradition, but also forecasting the powerhouse industry to come, Cook packaged trips to Egypt that followed the exact route the Romans traveled in 19 CE. Mass production of travelogues and improved transportation sparked the collective imagination and made travel more accessible to the masses.

The rise of cities brought about a newfound curiosity in urban life that also echoed more ancient times. Just like the Romans, nineteenth-century New Yorkers regularly toured their own city for entertainment, desiring brief, controlled exposure to "the other half," with its commoner struggles, immigrant communities, and what was seen as deviant sexual practices (which inspired slumming parties, wherein people would pay to rub elbows with Lower East Side homosexuals). Similarly, international visitors like Charles Dickens (1812–1870), Alexis de Tocqueville (1805–1859), and Frances Milton Trollope (1779–1863) were coming as early as the end of the American Revolution (1775–1783) to write travelogues of the national social experiment—with its racial and cultural mix, class inequalities, and vast geography.

Originally the purview of the elite, diplomats, and rugged explorers, travel since the 1960s has become widely available to working and middle-class people. By 2000, tourism and travel had become the world's largest industry, which, according to the World Travel and Tourism Council, produces up to 10 percent of the world's economic output and employment.

TRAVEL WRITING

Along with travel comes the parallel cultural production of travel writing. While Petrarch's (1304–1374) description of his ascent of Mount Ventoux in 1336 is often traced as a progenitor of travel writing, the practice blossomed with the consolidation of British hegemony in the 1800s, when expansion and empire matched eager public fascination as stories of Native Americans and the Opium Wars with China were produced for the masses. The impact of travel writing as a newfound form of nonfiction valorizing British economic and political values can be found in the works of writers such as Dickens, William Thackeray (1811–1863), Joseph Conrad (1857–1924), and Rudyard Kipling (1865–1936).

Perhaps no writing of that era was more dramatic, popular, and controversial as that of explorer, writer, poet, and diplomat Sir Richard F. Burton (1821–1890). Stirring public fascination with his adventures, Burton (who made the first English translations of *Arabian Nights* and the *Kama Sutra*) traveled disguised as an Afghani physician throughout the Middle East. "Passing" well enough to have entered Mecca, the heart of the Muslim world, in 1853, he gave the Western readers their first glimpse into that unknown land. Travel writing has always been particularly keyed toward the cultural translation of "unknowns," and Burton often displayed his dual roles of explorer and poet as he communicated the connections and differences between disparate cultures to his Victorian readers: "the pigeons of Mecca resemble those of Venice" (Burton [1855] 1964, p. 174).

The notion of cultural translation infuses problems of representation, and cultural theorists, ethnographers, and postcolonial thinkers have questioned the colonizing and misguided gaze of the Western observer (Clifford and Marcus 1986). The dialectic of cross-cultural exchange has been criticized as being imbued with power relations that predominately favor the more dominant cultures. Burton, for example, had to serve the imperialist economic and political needs of the Royal Geographical Society and the British East India Company, as well as his own desires for exploration and translation. Missionaries of the British Empire were similarly wrought with tensions as they wrote of their travels: On the one hand, they attempted to fulfill their religious and moral duties as benevolent evangelicals, and on the other hand they had to maintain the interests of the crown.

Such pressures are found throughout travel writing, as authors aspire for objectivity yet struggle with their own subjective experiences and moral concerns—whether they toured Bali or New York's Bowery. This perspective is perhaps best evidenced in the scholarly realm by Claude Lévi-Strauss's ambiguous narratives of *Tristes Tropiques* (1955), a text often used by those wishing to criticize the colonizing power of ethnography and travel. Just as the grand tour served as a form of education and entertainment, those dual functions also play important roles for both the traveler and travel writing, in and out of the scholarly realm.

The contemporary moment is marred for many in the field, as they dread increasing "homogenization," "commodification," and "banalization" of culture—what some have called Disneyfication. While making travel and travel writing more accessible, industrialization and mass production have also caused some cultures to be carefully packaged in order to attract visitors, as tourism and culture scholars like Dean MacCannell (1976) have noted. Mass travel and travel writing, it is feared, summarizes culture and cities into "sets" of a few places and experiences that prejudice the visitor into particular expectations before arrival. This, however, is an ahistorical perspective, as even ancient Romans would feel contented to have seen the world so long as they had gazed upon each of the Seven Wonders—the original "best-of" list devised by an unknown scholar in the third century BCE. There was also Homer's *Iliad*, another form of writing that established a path around which a travel infrastructure could sprout: hotels and restaurants to fill basic needs, and droves of guides ready for hire to present the alleged armor of Trojan War heroes, the beach where Greek ships landed, or where Achilles and Ajax were buried. These antiquarians kept close to the beaten path, seeking out the perceived cornerstones of their own cultures (Casson 1974).

It is, perhaps, because of this juggernaut tourism and travel industry that travel writing has returned to the journeys of earlier epochs. Several popular press books trace the paths of Captain James Cook (1728–1779), antiquarian

tourists, the Indian god Rama, and a Buddhist monk's seventh-century journey down the Silk Road. These travel writings match up contemporary journeys with those of their ancient forebears. Such a trend is evident in the social sciences as well: Indian anthropologist Amitav Ghosh (1993), for example, blends a contemporary narrative as he attends school in Alexandria, Egypt, with the story of a twelfth-century Jewish merchant and his Indian slave.

SEE ALSO *Colonialism; Columbus, Christopher; Cook, James; Cultural Tourism; Empire; Gaze, Colonial; Imperialism; Leisure; Levi-Strauss, Claude; Missionaries; Narratives; Other, The; Tourism; Vacations; White Supremacy*

BIBLIOGRAPHY

Burton, Richard F. [1855] 1964. *Personal Narrative of a Pilgrimage to al-Madinah and Meccah.* Vol. 1. New York: Dover.

Casson, Lionel. 1974. *Travel in the Ancient World.* London: Allen & Unwin.

Clifford, James, and George Marcus, eds. 1986. *Writing Culture: The Poetics and Politics of Ethnography.* Berkeley: University of California Press.

Ghosh, Amitav. 1993. *In an Antique Land.* New York: Knopf.

Lévi-Strauss, Claude. [1955] 1961. *Tristes Tropiques.* Trans. John Russell. New York: Criterion.

MacCannell, Dean. 1976. *The Tourist: A New Theory of the Leisure Class.* Berkeley: University of California Press.

Jonathan R. Wynn

TREASURY VIEW, THE

In April 1929 the British chancellor of the exchequer, Winston Churchill (1874–1965), defended "the orthodox Treasury doctrine which has steadfastly held that, whatever might be the political and social advantages, very little additional employment, and no permanent additional employment can, in fact, and as a general rule, be created by state borrowing and state expenditure" (House of Commons 1929, p. 54). Churchill's comment, made during the 1929 general election campaign, was designed to blunt opposition proposals for large-scale public works to reduce unemployment. Churchill's view was reinforced the next month by a white paper restating the practical and doctrinal objections to public works. The issues were aired again in an examination by the economist John Maynard Keynes (1883–1946) of the senior Treasury official Sir Richard Hopkins (1880–1955) before the Committee on Finance and Industry (established by Labour prime minister Ramsay MacDonald [1866–1937] in 1929 to examine the impact of the financial system on the economy).

Britain did not launch an expansionist policy against unemployment (comparable to that implemented in Sweden after 1936), and some have identified the "Treasury view" as the main obstacle. Histories of economic thought published during the "Keynesian era" (such as Michael Stewart's *Keynes and After* [1969]) blamed the grip of outmoded ideas on senior Treasury officials. The opening of Britain's public records brought a new agenda to the debate. A number of historians found in interwar Treasury papers little doctrinal argument but many practical administrative difficulties, most of which related to the Treasury's management of public finance. However, the (delayed) release of further Treasury papers to the Public Record Office in mid-1986 allowed Peter Clarke (1990) to create a more complex analysis. He demonstrated that in the early 1920s senior Treasury officials believed that British prosperity depended upon firm commitment to the liberal international order: the gold standard, free trade, and the balanced budget. This was the "knave-proof" fiscal constitution that senior British officials had deployed against the grandiose, expansionist ideas of cabinet ministers from 1918 to 1919. It held that the ultimate causes of unemployment lay in lagging exports and could be remedied by industrial modernization, lower unit labor costs, and higher foreign lending (within limits). Thus, diverting money into home investment would exacerbate the problem.

Personnel changes, growing recognition that the gold standard adjustments had not worked, and the impact of the return from Harvard University of the economist R. G. Hawtrey (1879–1975, a senior Treasury official but with limited day-to-day influence over policy) brought a new, more flexible approach from 1930. Hawtrey demonstrated the stickiness of the gold standard adjustment processes, underlined the possible effectiveness of reflationary finance, and encouraged Hopkins and others to think more creatively and flexibly about economic relationships. This paved the way for a still more productive interchange between Treasury officials and leading economists in the 1930s, as noted by Susan Howson and Donald Winch (1977).

Unfortunately, econometric work has suggested that "Keynesian" policies offered only a palliative to Britain's interwar unemployment problem. T. Thomas's macro-model (1981) of the interwar economy and Sean Glyn and Peter Howells's calculation (1980) of the interwar multiplier both pointed to the extreme improbability that unemployment could be reduced to "normal" levels by monetary and fiscal policy. Thus, one is left with the conclusion that the Treasury view may have acted as a barrier to independent, expansionist policies at a critical

moment, but it was only one of a number of impediments, and the bold assumptions of Keynes and the Keynesians, both at the time and during the 1950s and 1960s, that there was an easy solution to unemployment were misplaced.

SEE ALSO *Keynes, John Maynard; Policy, Fiscal; Policy, Monetary; Unemployment*

BIBLIOGRAPHY

Clarke, Peter. 1990. The Treasury's Analytical Model of the British Economy Between the Wars. In *The State and Economic Knowledge: The American and British Experiences*, eds. Mary O. Furner and Barry Supple, 171–207. Cambridge, U.K.: Cambridge University Press.

Glynn, Sean, and Peter Howells. 1980. Unemployment in the 1980s: The "Keynesian Solution" Reconsidered. *Australian Economic History Review* 20: 28–45.

Hatton, T. J. 1985. Unemployment in the 1930s and the "Keynesian Solution": Some Notes of Dissent. *Australian Economic History Review* 25: 129–148, 149–157.

House of Commons. 1929. *Memoranda on Certain Proposals Relating to Unemployment*, Cmd 3331. London: HMSO (His Majesty's Stationery Office).

Howson, Susan, and Donald Winch. 1977. *The Economic Advisory Council, 1930–1939: A Study in Economic Advice during Depression and Recovery*. Cambridge, U.K.: Cambridge University Press.

Stewart, Michael. 1969. *Keynes and After*. Harmondsworth, U.K.: Penguin. 3rd ed., 1986.

Thomas, T. 1981. Aggregate Demand in the United Kingdom, 1918–45. In *The Economic History of Britain since 1700*. Vol. 2: *1860 to 1970s*, eds. Roderick Floud and Donald McCloskey, 332–346. Cambridge, U.K.: Cambridge University Press.

Alan Booth

TREATY FEDERALISM

Treaty federalism, also referred to as treaty constitutionalism, is a concept that explicitly identifies negotiated agreements between aboriginal people and other sovereign actors as constitutional documents. In this interpretation, treaties are considered founding political documents between two sovereign parties that at once establish a delegation of power or areas of shared responsibility as well as a retention of autonomy for each signatory. Treaties therefore establish a constitutional order that gives force to the central concept of federalism: a constitutionally guaranteed system of both shared and self-rule.

Using treaties or negotiated agreements as the primary mechanism for establishing and defining a political relationship between sovereign parties has important historical precedents in both nonaboriginal and aboriginal contexts. In British North America, intra-aboriginal political relationships were thus established among the Mi'kmaq, the Iroquois, and the Blackfoot. The use of treaties to establish political relationships and to define land rights between the British Crown and aboriginal people found strong expression in King George III's Royal Proclamation, 1763. A period of historical treaty making continued in what are now former British colonies, with these periods concluding in the United States in 1871, Canada in 1923, and New Zealand in 1840. This historical practice was not universal, however, as British colonial powers did not recognize aboriginal rights in Australia and no treaty-making practice was there established. A contemporary round of negotiated agreement making was reestablished in Canada in 1973 and in New Zealand in 1989. Australia's Native Title Act, first enacted in 1993, establishes a statutory framework for negotiated agreement making, and there is ongoing political discussion regarding the meaning and effect of a treaty between Australian governments and aboriginal peoples.

The concept of treaty federalism pushes the standard interpretation of the founding constitutional order of many countries. It argues that treaties between aboriginal people and the states of the New World are the source of these states' constitutional legitimacy and territorial sovereignty. Following from this view, states are considered fundamentally illegitimate if treaties are not respected or inadequately implemented. It also follows that states that have not negotiated with the descendent communities of its prior occupants exercise state sovereignty on illegitimate grounds.

The arguments raised by the treaty constitutionalist position point to a very different conception of the appropriate constitutional and legislative relationship with aboriginal people. As historical treaties were largely limited documents and did not include provisions over many aspects of aboriginal life, territory, and governance, it is argued that those areas outside the treaties remain within the exclusive jurisdiction of aboriginal people. As they did not cede or delegate responsibility over many issues to colonial powers, a treaty constitutionalist position holds that the jurisdiction to address these areas remains with aboriginal people according to aboriginal laws. It also necessarily holds that state action in areas not mentioned within the treaties would be ultra vires, or outside its jurisdiction.

In states that are constitutionally federal—ones that are divided into two levels of government, each guaranteed a degree of autonomy—the treaty constitutionalist position argues that the assignment of constitutional responsibility for aboriginal affairs to either the federal or subnational level of government cannot be interpreted as an assignment of constitutional power or sovereignty *over* aboriginal people. For instance, it would deny that section 91(24) of Canada's Constitution Act, 1867, granted the Canadian federal government the power to legislate for "Indians, and Lands reserved for Indians" without their consent. Treaty constitutionalists argue instead that the scope of section 91(24) is constitutionally limited to those issues explicitly delegated under the treaties and that in no way would those issues include a complete delegation of aboriginal sovereignty. In this reading, section 91(24) merely identifies the federal government, not the provinces, as having the responsibility of implementing existing treaty obligations and negotiating future agreements with aboriginal people, as befitting a nation-to-nation political relationship.

A treaty constitutionalist position necessarily implies that the judicial review of existing and future treaties between aboriginal people and other governments should be governed by conventions of constitutional interpretation, a higher standard of interpretation than that regarding normal contract law.

SEE ALSO *Anticolonial Movements; Constitutions; Diplomacy; Federalism; Indigenous Rights; Land Claims; Native Americans; Natives; Settlement, Negotiated; Sovereignty*

BIBLIOGRAPHY

Henderson, James Youngblood. 1995. Empowering Treaty Federalism. *Saskatchewan Law Review* 58: 241–329.

Ladner, Kiera. 2003. Treaty Federalism: An Indigenous Vision of Canadian Federalisms. In *New Trends in Canadian Federalism*, 2nd ed., eds. François Rocher and Miriam Smith, 167–196. Peterborough, Ontario, Canada: Broadview Press.

Tully, James. 1995. *Strange Multiplicity: Constitutionalism in an Age of Diversity.* Cambridge, U.K.: Cambridge University Press.

Christa Scholtz

TREATY OF TIENTSIEN
SEE *Opium Wars.*

TREATY OF VERSAILLES
SEE *Interwar Years.*

TRENDS

A trend is a relatively smooth and unidirectional pattern in data that arises from the accumulation of information over time. Many of the time series in economics and in other social sciences exhibit a smooth (upward or downward) tendency. In developed economies, the macro-socioeconomic time series, such as gross national product, consumption, income, and population, are characterized by an upward trend. Though in the short run the economy goes through expansions and recessions, in the long run there is growth. This is due to technological progress and/or population growth. The trend arises from the accumulation of socioeconomic activity from one period to the next. For instance, the time series of the U.S. population has an upward trend over time because the number of births exceeds the number of deaths and/or because the number of immigrants exceeds the number of emigrants.

From an econometric point of view there is a distinction between deterministic and stochastic trends, depending on whether the accumulation of information is due to a deterministic or to a random component. Suppose that an economic variable Y_t, for instance national product, can be represented by a model such as $Y_t = a + bt + \varepsilon_t$ for $t = 1,2,3,\ldots$. In this case, the trend is a line $a + bt$ with a as intercept and b as slope, which is also the growth rate. Because $t = 1,2,3,\ldots$ is purely deterministic, the trend is deterministic. An example of an exponential deterministic trend is the time series of the U.S. population. Conversely, a stochastic trend is generated by the accumulation of random components. An example of a model with a stochastic trend is $Y_t = \varepsilon_t + \varepsilon_{t-1} + \varepsilon_{t-2} + \ldots \varepsilon_1$ where $\{\varepsilon_t\}$ is a collection of normal random variables. An example of a stochastic trend is the time series of speculative prices such as stock prices or exchanges rates. The time series generated by deterministic trend models tend to be smoother than those generated by a stochastic trend.

Deterministic trends may have different shapes. Among these, the most common are linear, quadratic, exponential/logarithmic, and logistic. Only when the trend is linear is the growth rate constant. In any other specification, the growth rate will depend on the time period under study. Models with a deterministic trend are also known as trend-stationary models because all the unconditional moments, with the exception of the mean, are time-invariant. Their estimation and testing is straightforward because standard statistical results apply. In the linear trend model specified above, the parameters a and b can be estimated by Ordinary Least Squares (OLS), assuming that the error term is well-behaved. Hypothesis testing relies on tests that have standard asymptotic distributions, such as the t-ratio and F-tests.

Stochastic trends are more complicated than deterministic trends because they are non-stationary. Their statistical analysis requires the use of non-standard asymptotic distributions, which need to be obtained by simulation techniques. The model introduced above, $Y_t = \varepsilon_t + \varepsilon_{t-1} + \varepsilon_{t-2} + \ldots \varepsilon_1$, has the following equivalent representation $Y_t = Y_{t-1} + \varepsilon_t$, which is an autoregressive process of order one with an autoregressive parameter equal to one. This model is also known as a unit root process or random walk without drift. If the model includes a constant such as $Y_t = c + Y_{t-1} + \varepsilon_t$, one says that the process is a random walk with drift. The drift produces a smoother upward (or downward) tendency. Unit root processes are non-stationary because the unconditional moments (mean, variance, and covariances) are increasing functions of time. The autocorrelation function of a unit root is very characteristic with autocorrelation coefficients of any order asymptotically equal to one.

From an empirical perspective it is important to differentiate a deterministic trend model from a stochastic trend model. There are two main reasons for this: the need to conduct the correct statistical inference, and the construction and interpretation of the correct forecast. Consequently, the first step in empirical research is testing for unit root, which is a test of non-stationarity versus stationarity. In a model such as $Y_t = c + \varphi Y_{t-1} + \varepsilon_t$, the null hypothesis is set as $H_0: \varphi = 1$ (non-stationarity) versus an alternative $H_1: \varphi < 1$ (stationarity). Under the null, the standard t-ratio is not normally distributed but has a non-standard distribution, which is known as the Dickey-Fuller (DF) distribution. The DF critical values are tabulated by numerical simulation. A rejection of the null in favor of the alternative hypothesis means that the process does not have a stochastic trend. On the contrary, failure to reject the null hypothesis means that there is not enough evidence against the unit root process and a stochastic trend in the data should be entertained.

From a forecasting perspective, a deterministic trend model produces a forecast along the time trend specification. The uncertainty associated with the forecast is bounded regardless of how far into the future one wishes to predict. However, a forecast from a stochastic trend model has unbounded uncertainty as the variance of the forecast is an increasing function of time.

A pervasive problem in empirical research in the social sciences during the 1970s and 1980s is the case of spurious regression. Regression is spurious when two (or more) variables, Y_t and X_t, are found to be correlated but in fact they are not. This finding arises because Y_t and X_t are non-stationary (unit root processes) and a regression of Y_t on X_t does not take into account the stochastic trend. The diagnosis of spurious regression is relatively simple. If the R-squared of the regression is extremely high, around 0.90 and above, the t-statistics are exceptionally large, and the Durbin-Watson statistic is low, it is highly likely that the regression of Y_t on X_t is spurious and, consequently, there is no correlation between them. The correct approach to analyze the correlation between Y_t and X_t is first to remove the stochastic trend and then to run the regression. By first-differencing the data, the stochastic trend is removed. For instance, if Y_t and X_t have a unit root, for example $Y_t = Y_{t-1} + \varepsilon_t$ and $X_t = X_{t-1} + \nu_t$, the first difference of Y_t is $\Delta Y_t = \varepsilon_t$ and the first difference of X_t is $\Delta X_t = \nu_t$. The proper regression is to regress ΔY_t on ΔX_t. However, if Y_t and X_t have a deterministic trend, the data should not be first-differenced but the regression of Y_t on X_t should contain a deterministic trend specification. There is only one instance in which a regression of Y_t on X_t, being both unit root processes, is meaningful. This is the case of cointegration, in which Y_t and X_t share the same stochastic trend. In this instance there is a long-run equilibrium between both processes.

SEE ALSO *Autoregressive Models; Least Squares, Ordinary; Random Walk; Regression Analysis; Time Series Regression; Unit Root and Cointegration Regression*

BIBLIOGRAPHY

Dickey, David A., and Wayne A. Fuller. 1979. Distribution of the Estimators for Autoregressive Time Series with a Unit Root. *Journal of the American Statistical Association* 74: 427–431.

Hamilton, James D. 1994. *Time Series Analysis.* Princeton, NJ: Princeton University Press.

Gloria González-Rivera

TRIARCHIC THEORY OF INTELLIGENCE

SEE *Multiple Intelligences Theory; Intelligence.*

TRIBALISM

The concept of *tribalism*, like that of the *tribe*, is difficult to define precisely, as it is closely interwoven with the context in which it is used. Tribalism may be defined as the maintenance by a tribal society of its organization, ways, and autonomy in the face of change. But tribalism may be defined differently when a tribe's claim of identity has less to do with its primitivism or indigeneity than with its ethnic discreteness and cultural distinctiveness for gaining material or political advantages. In fact, tribalism does not exist in any objective sense—hence the problem in defining the concept.

Early ethnographic writings offer examples of "we-feeling" among the members of a particular tribe that set it apart from neighboring tribes. Ethnographers called this tribalism and linked it to the notion of ethnocentrism, but particularly associated with tribal people. For example, when the Zulu people of South Africa name themselves as *isizwe*, meaning a nation or a people different from other tribes, or the Birhor of India distinguish themselves as *hor* or people from *diku*, an explicit reference to tribalism is made. Therefore, tribalism is the manifestation of a collective group identity based on common natural impulses such as fear, desire, necessity, or ethnic distinctiveness.

Vine Deloria Jr. proposes in his 2003 book that, from the Native American perspective, tribalism has four dimensions: spatial, social, spiritual, and experiential. The spatial dimension connects the tribes with their land, which is for them a precious possession. The social dimension refers to the social cohesion that binds the members of the tribe together. The spiritual dimension refers to the idea of the people as a religious conception. The experiential dimension is the sharing of history, culture, rituals, and traditions. For Deloria tribalism has to be practiced; it is more than a philosophy, it is a way of life.

Since the late twentieth century, tribalism in the Middle East, Africa, and South and Southeast Asia has generated some dangerous and divisive tendencies. Tribalism is positive when the complete allegiance of a collectivity is geared toward the collective good—nation building, preserving the group identity as a single cohesive unit that fosters ethnic solidarity, seeking new dimensions of development. Contrarily, tribalism is negative when it generates ethnic hatred and war. The intertribal warfare and ethnic divide in Africa is tribalism's worst manifestation. Another example of negative tribalism is the disintegration of Yugoslavia in the early 1990s into smaller competing states. Whereas positive tribalism needs to be fostered for the sake of collective tribal identity, negative tribalism that threatens to give rise to terrorism and political turbulence must be thwarted. The genocide of nearly one half million Tutsis by the Hutu extremists in 1994 in Rwanda and the ethnic cleansing in the former Yugoslavia in the 1990s are painful commentaries on negative tribalism.

Given both its positive and negative manifestations, tribalism is closely related to ethnic solidarity and ethnocentrism. But it is one step ahead of racism, as the conflicts of the early twenty-first century in Somalia, India, Pakistan, Afghanistan, Sri Lanka, Turkey, and Indonesia are between ethnic groups or tribes rather than between the races.

In his 2006 article, Howard Campbell discusses two major approaches to tribalism that suggest revisions to anthropological notions of tribes and indigeneity from a Native American perspective. According to one approach, "ethnic identity is never essential and ... identity change is quite common" in tribal cultures; the second approach asserts that native tribes persist "by production of symbolic representations" rather than through the "performance of aboriginal traditions in everyday life" (Campbell 2006, p. 296). In view of the rising trend of neotribalism in India, with similarities to the Native American experience, "protective discrimination" has consolidated hitherto dispersed tribal groups into organized pressure groups to fight for their legitimate constitutional rights. In 2005 the Indian state of Sikkim recognized the Lepcha community as the "Most Primitive Tribe"—a distinction that signals the tribe's relatively high standard of living and confers status and privileges. Sometimes it becomes necessary for a tribe to reinvent itself, as in the case of the Ngati Kuri of New Zealand, whose name did not appear in the list of the country's recognized tribes. Tribalism, therefore, is a fluid concept with both positive and negative connotations that must be understood with reference to specific contexts.

SEE ALSO *Anthropology; Ethnicity; Ethnocentrism; Ethnography; Natives; Primitivism; Racism; Representation; Solidarity; Symbols; Tribe*

BIBLIOGRAPHY

Adhikary, Asim. 1991. The Tribal Worldview: Changing Perspective. In *Tribal Thought and Culture*, ed. Baidyanath Saraswati, pp. 105–120. New Delhi: Concept Publishing House.

Campbell, Howard. 2006. Tribal Synthesis: Piros, Mansos and Tiwas through History. *Journal of the Royal Anthropological Institute* 12 (2): 293–311.

Deloria, Vine, Jr. [1972] 2003. *God Is Red: A Native View of Religion*. Golden, CO: Fulcrum.

Lewis, I. M. 1968. Tribal Society. In *International Encyclopedia of Social Sciences*, vol.16, ed. David L. Sills, pp. 146–151. New York: The Macmillan Company.

Mafeje, Archie. 1971. The Ideology of "Tribalism." *Journal of Modern African Studies* 9 (2): 253–261.

Kamal Misra

TRIBE

Despite its popular as well as academic usage, *tribe* is a contentious concept. In popular imagination, *tribe* is associated with "primitivism" and "backwardness," clearly referring to non-Western or indigenous groups inhabiting the countries of Asia, Africa, and Latin America or to American Indian reservations. In 1951 the Royal Anthropological Institute defined the tribe as a "politically or socially coherent and autonomous group occupying or claiming a particular territory" (1951, p. 66). Scholars since then have contested the notions of coherence, autonomy, and territorial segregation as only ideal constructs, devoid of much empirical support. Although it is unlikely that this definition would apply perfectly to any single tribe, theoretically *tribe* is construed as a group or community sharing a common territory, speaking a common language or dialect, sharing a culture and religious tradition, united under a single political organization, and having a common economic pursuit. Therefore, as André Béteille (1981) observes, the existence of a tribe fitting any theoretical definition is at best an anthropological imagination.

Morton Fried suggests that what anthropologists study today is "tribe as a secondary sociopolitical phenomenon, brought about by the intercession of more complex ordered societies, states in particular.... The 'pristine tribe,' on the other hand, is a creation of myth and legend, pertaining either to the golden age of the noble savage or romantic barbarism" (1975, p. 114). As Archie Mafeje notes, in Africa "the indigenous population has no word for 'tribe'... Traditionally, people were identified by territory—'Whose [which Chief's] land do you come from'" (1971, p. 254). This is true also for India, where there is no lexical equivalent of the English word "tribe"; it began to be used by the British administrator-anthropologists only for administrative convenience.

In the United States and India, tribes today refer to the indigenous or autochthonous people, legally recognized groups that enjoy some degree of autonomy and state protection. In India, for example, the Constitution makes special provisions for the protection and welfare of its "Scheduled Tribes," a legal-administrative category within the nation.

HISTORY AND DEVELOPMENT OF THE CONCEPT

When European colonial expansion was at its peak during the sixteenth and seventeenth centuries, the writings of missionaries, traders, and adventurers resulted in the genre of ethnography of the peoples they encountered, whom they called tribes. The tribes were deceptively painted to be in the primal stage of human cultural evolution, the culmination of which was, in the minds of the Europeans, advanced European civilization. The legacy of this Eurocentric notion was inherited by the anthropologists of the eighteenth and nineteenth centuries. In the latter half of the nineteenth century, within the domain of anthropology, unilineal or classical evolutionists like Lewis H. Morgan (1818–1881) hypothesized tribe as a transient stage in the process of cultural evolution from early hunters and foragers to agrarian societies. With the collapse of classical evolutionism at the beginning of the twentieth century and the consolidation of the field of anthropology in Great Britain, scholars like E. E. Evans-Pritchard used a structural definition of tribe, particularly in the context of segmentary societies like the Nuer of Sudan, which he discussed in his 1940 book. Later, Marshall Sahlins, in his 1968 study, characterized tribes with segmentary lineages that were different from centralized chiefdoms.

Taking cue from Wilson and Wilson, Lewis introduced the concept of "scale" in characterizing a tribe. He contended, "Ideally, tribal societies are small in scale, are restricted in the spatial and temporal range of their social, legal, and political relations, and possess a morality, religion, and world view of corresponding dimensions" (1968, p. 147). In the 1970s the Marxist anthropologist Maurice Godelier, while attempting a critique of the concept, cautioned that "tribe" was used as a tool by the powers who dominated the Third World and warned that "we cannot silently bury it with a mere death sentence, or stigmatize those who continue to use it with the epithet 'infamous' empiricism." Godelier argued that new concepts would not resolve the problem; thus the "concept of the 'tribe' will continue to be used in more or less refined forms and will deliver the same goods and the same kind of bad service" (1977, pp. 95–96). Despite Godelier's exhortation, in subsequent decades post-structuralist, postmodern, and feminist theorists such as Lila Abu-Lughod and Michael Gilsenan deconstructed the colonial legacy of the concept and pleaded for a more reflexive and dialogic ethnography. All these controversies notwithstanding, there is nothing wrong in using the term *tribe*, so long as it conveys the real sociopolitical formation and cultural distinctiveness of a group rather than myths, stereotypes, and prejudices. However, anthropologists have come to prefer the term *ethnic groups* over *tribes*.

For many, as Susana Devalle (1992) notes, tribe is understood as a "colonial category" to promote specific colonial interests and is largely associated with the Western colonial power structures and discourses. Yet Fried (1975) persuasively argues that in the past in many expansionist states, such as China, the relatively weaker peoples conquered by the stronger groups were given pejorative terms on a par with "tribe."

BASIC CHARACTERISTICS

In the absence of a clear-cut definition, it is useful to examine the ways in which tribes are characterized. A tribe is ideally designated as having a common territory, a common name and culture, speaking a common language, practicing endogamy, with an autonomous political organization and close-knit kinship ties, the members of which are believers of a common religion. The classical anthropological depiction of tribes, as put forward by Mafeje, as "self-contained,

autonomous communities practicing subsistence economy with no or limited external trade" (1971, p. 257) is highly polemical, as ethnographies hardly support this utopian construction. Far from being autonomous or self-contained, tribal communities have more often fostered multitribal units that functioned as bigger kingdoms or confederacies. The Luapula Kingdom of Kazembe in Central Africa, the Zulu empire in South Africa, the Ashanti Confederacy in West Africa, and the Gond kingdoms of India are good examples of, in Mafeje's term, "super-tribes." Realistically, tribal communities as "little traditions" in the civilizational model of Robert Redfield (1956) have interacted politically, economically, and ritually with larger sociopolitical formations in their neighborhoods. The process of Sanskritization suggested by M. N. Srinivas (1966), Nirmal K. Bose's model of Hindu methods of tribal absorption (1967), and Surajit Sinha's case studies on state formation in tribal India (1987) are classical examples of the fact that neither in the past nor at present have tribes remained secluded or insulated either politically or culturally, despite having their own chiefs or heads, territorial affiliations, and customary laws.

Tribes also economically interact with other neighboring tribes and nontribes, and yet have their own means of subsistence. Many of them still practice hunting and foraging (the !Kung of Botswana and Namibia), pastoralism (the Masai of Kenya and the Nuer of Sudan), swidden agriculture (the Pgakenyaw and Lua of Thailand, Uma' Jalan of East Kalimantan), settled cultivation (the Kikuyu of Kenya and the Munda and Santal of India), or traditional crafts (the Uraali Kurumas of South India), or more realistically, a combination of them. Although tribal societies may not be stratified, primordial forms of social differentiation do exist in them, as noted by Kamal Misra (1991); and despite practicing many different faiths, animism still forms the bedrock of their religion.

SCHEDULED TRIBES IN INDIA

Approximately 8.2 percent of the total Indian population has been designated as "Scheduled Tribes" (STs), according to the Indian census of 2001. The official Web site of the Ministry of Tribal Affairs, Government of India, states that "the Scheduled Tribes are the tribes or tribal communities or part of or groups within these tribes and tribal communities which have been declared as such by the President through a public notification." The Indian government regards retention of "primitive" traits, geographical isolation, possessing distinct culture, shyness of contact with the community at large, and economic backwardness as the essential characteristics of Scheduled Tribes. However, most of these communities are in close proximity and constant interaction with the neighboring Hindu peasants. Some of the tribal groups are now almost extinct—the Great Andamanese number only twenty persons—whereas others, like the Gonds, number more than five million. They are still at different stages of economy, from hunting and foraging to industrial labor and white-collar jobs. According to the census, the tribal literacy rate is 47.1 percent. The Government of India has designated seventy-five communities among the STs as Primitive Tribal Groups (PTGs), for whose development specific microprojects have been designed and implemented. Despite constitutional protection, Scheduled Tribes in India are still impoverished and marginalized.

TRIBES, INTERNATIONAL CONVENTIONS, AND HUMAN RIGHTS

Many tribes have come to symbolize the most victimized segments of societies. It is a strange paradox that although they inhabit the most resource-rich regions of the world, many of them are in a state of impoverishment. They are the most severely affected victims of induced development, such as the establishment of mega-hydroelectric projects, conservation through parks, sanctuaries and bio-reserves, mining and allied activities, urbanization and industrialization, ecotourism projects, and so on. As John Bodley notes in his 1988 study, these activities cause involuntary displacement, alienation from natural resources, cultural disorganization, and disengagement with the intense community life, eventually pushing them into abject poverty and squalor. Their problems are compounded by the penetrating regime of globalization and a competitive market economy. The Jarawa of the Andaman Islands, the Yanamami group of tribes of South America, and others are now vulnerable to new diseases like measles and mumps because of their exposure to the people outside their habitat.

Concern for the plight of the tribes and indigenous peoples is growing in many quarters, and efforts are being made to protect them and preserve their cultural heritage. The International Decade of the World's Indigenous People (1995–2004), declared by the United Nations; the International Labor Organization conventions 107 (1957) and 169 (1989); and the Convention on Biological Diversity (1992) have made special provisions for protecting the civil and political rights of the tribes and indigenous people. Tribal empowerment and participatory development have become buzzwords in the field of tribal development, and efforts are being made to reverse the trend of marginalization of tribes all over the world.

SEE ALSO *Animism; Colonialism; Darwinism, Social; Ethnicity; Ethnography; Evans-Pritchard, E. E.; Human Rights; Indigenous Rights; Marxism; Native Americans; Natives; Postmodernism; Poststructuralism; Sahlins, Marshall; Stratification; Third World; Tribalism*

BIBLIOGRAPHY

Béteille, André. 1981. The Definition of Tribe. In *Tribe, Caste and Religion in India*, ed. Romesh Thapar, 7–14. Delhi: Macmillan Co. of India.

Bodley, John H., ed. 1988. *Tribal Peoples and Development Issues: A Global Overview*. Mountain View, CA: Mayfield Publishing.

Bose, Nirmal Kumar. 1967. *Culture and Society in India*. Bombay, London, and New York: Asia Publishing Co.

Devalle, Susana B. C. 1992. *Discourses of Ethnicity: Culture and Protest in Jharkhand*. New Delhi and Newbury Park, CA: Sage.

Evans-Pritchard, E. E. 1940. *The Nuer: A Description of the Modes of Livelihood and Political Institutions of a Nilotic People*. Oxford: Clarendon Press.

Fried, Morton H. 1967. *The Evolution of Political Society: An Essay in Political Anthropology*. New York: Random House.

Fried, Morton H. 1975. *The Notion of Tribe*. Menlo Park, CA: Cummings Publishing.

Godelier, Maurice. 1977. *Perspectives in Marxist Anthropology*. Trans. Robert Brain. Cambridge, U.K., and New York: Cambridge University Press.

Lewis, I. M. 1968. Tribal Society. *International Encyclopedia of the Social Sciences*, vol. 16, ed. David L. Sills, 146–151. New York: The Macmillan Company.

Mafeje, Archie. 1971. The Ideology of "Tribalism." *Journal of Modern African Studies* 9 (2): 253–261.

Misra, Kamal K. 1991. Dynamics of Inequality in an Unstratified Society: A Case Study of the Juang. *Man in India* 71 (2–3): 363–372.

Redfield, Robert. 1956. *Peasant Society and Culture: An Anthropological Approach to Civilization*. Chicago: University of Chicago Press.

Royal Anthropological Institute of Great Britain and Ireland. 1951. *Notes and Queries on Anthropology*. 6th ed. London: Routledge and K. Paul.

Sahlins, Marshall D. 1968. *Tribesmen*. Englewood Cliffs, NJ: Prentice-Hall.

Sinha, Surajit, ed. 1987. *Tribal Polities and State Systems in Pre-Colonial Eastern and North Eastern India*. Calcutta: K. P. Bagchi.

Srinivas, M. N. 1966. *Social Change in Modern India*. Berkeley: University of California Press.

Suzuki, Peter T. 2005. Tribe: Chimeric or Polymorphic? In *Tribal Situation in India*, vol. 6 of *Contemporary Society: Tribal Studies*, eds. Georg Pfeffer and Deepak Kumar Behera. New Delhi: Concept.

Kamal Misra

TRIGUEÑO

The term *trigueño* is derived from *trigo* (wheat) and literally means "wheat-colored." The term seems to have gained currency in twentieth-century Puerto Rico and elsewhere in Spanish-speaking Latin America (Argentina, Bolivia, Cuba, the Dominican Republic, Ecuador, Mexico, Peru, and Venezuela) to describe people with a tan or brown skin tone (*piel morena*). However, its meaning and social uses contain the same ambiguities inherent in all so-called race-related concepts as *race* is not an objective fact of nature but what might be called a social fact, subject to power dynamics and the social hierarchies of racism. Thus, in the Hispanic Caribbean, *trigueño* is also deployed as a euphemism for *Negro* (black). This is to avoid the pejorative connotations derived from the association of *Negro* with slave status. This use of *trigueño* is similar to the more old-fashioned term *de color* (colored), which is also used euphemistically to refer to black people. However, *trigueño* can also be used in Puerto Rico and in Cuba to describe a light-skinned person with a slightly tanned complexion.

The term therefore covers a wide variety of skin-color types: black, lighter than black, or darker than white. Which meaning is ascribed will depend on factors such as who says it, in what context, in what country, and how the person's skin color is perceived in combination with other phenotypic markers. In Puerto Rico, for example, two individuals might have the same dark-brown skin, but if one has kinky hair and the other has straight hair, the person with straight hair will probably be called *Indio* (Indian) and the person with coiled hair *trigueño*.

The application of *trigueño* also can be influenced by the relationship between the person describing and the one who is being described and by their perception of blackness. For example, if two people do not know each other well, one person might describe a black person as a *trigueño(a)* for reasons of social etiquette. This "polite" euphemistic use presumes and does not challenge the negative connotations associated with *Negro*. People who proudly assert a black identity, therefore, might dislike other people using *trigueño* to describe them or others because it assumes their blackness should be hidden or whitened by this euphemistic expression.

In a different context, a person might use *trigueño* to describe someone considered neither black nor white. In such cases, applying *trigueño* is not necessarily informed by the belief that *Negro* is offensive. Rather, it shows an attempt to make an accurate description in a social context where *trigueño* is associated with a mixed-race individual and is set apart from other racial types that are understood as less hybrid, such as *blanco* or *Negro*.

Depending on who uses it, how, and to whom they apply it, therefore, the use of *trigueño* can be interpreted as a polite gesture, as the sign of a condescending attitude toward black people, or as a phenotypic marker of racial mixture that lies somewhere between the white and black poles of a racial continuum.

SEE ALSO *Blackness; Colorism; Moreno/a; Mulattos; Negro; Pardo; Phenotype; Preference, Color; Race; Racism; Stratification; Whiteness*

BIBLIOGRAPHY

Stephens, Thomas M. 1999. *Dictionary of Latin American Racial and Ethnic Terminology*. 2nd ed. Gainsville: University Press of Florida.

Vargas-Ramos, Carlos. 2005. Black, Trigueño, White …? Shifting Racial Identification among Puerto Ricans. *Du Bois Review: Social Science Research on Race* 2 (2): 267–285.

Isar P. Godreau

TRILATERAL COMMISSION

Constituted of over three hundred leading politicians, businesspeople, and intellectuals from Western Europe, Japan, and North America, the Trilateral Commission was founded in 1973 by David Rockefeller, then chairman of Chase Manhattan Bank. Rockefeller had called for the establishment of the organization in a 1972 speech before the Bilderberg Group, a secretive post–World War II (1939–1945) discussion forum regularly attended by heads of state and other "influentials" from Europe and the United States.

In the wake of the collapse of the Bretton Woods system in the early 1970s, many members of the Bilderberg Group were concerned that the unilateralist foreign and economic policies of U.S. President Richard Nixon (1913–1994) were jeopardizing the cold war liberal order. Launched in 1946, the system was constituted by a set of multilaterally agreed-upon rules for regulating commercial and financial relations among the world's most powerful states. Given the rise of Japan and West Germany as economic powers and the decreased capacity of the U.S. state to direct world affairs, they feared a return to the "beggar-thy-neighbor" interstate rivalry that had characterized the interwar years. As such, they believed that the responsibility to lead would now have to be shared among the advanced nations.

The Trilateral Commission was established to bring together leading intellectuals and policymakers from the United States, Europe, and Japan in order to forge among them such consensus as necessary for the successful "collective management" of the world economy. The chairmen of the Commission detailed the group's philosophy of international cooperation in the foreword to a collection of the Commission's early Triangle Papers (task force reports). There they suggested that Trilateral cooperation should be based not on "coercion and arm-twisting, but on the mutuality of interest and indeed on the longer-term interest of mankind" (Berthoin, Smith, and Watanabe 1977, p. viii).

The first public statement of the Trilateral Commission was issued in Tokyo in October 1973. It spoke of both the "new problems" confronting nation-states under conditions of complex interdependency and the "special responsibility" of the Trilateral countries for "developing effective cooperation, both in their own interests, and in those of the rest of the world." Moreover, it set out the agreed-upon rules and procedures to govern the official interactions between Trilateral countries. It stipulated that they should work with each other "on the basis of equality" and avoid any such unilateral interaction as would be "incompatible with their interdependence." In closing, it elaborated the "creative role" of the Commission in generating consensus among its constituent states through a "sustained process of consultation and mutual education" (Trilateral Commission 1973, pp. 1–2).

The highlight of the Trilateral Commission's year is its annual plenary meeting. These sessions are supposed to build collegiality among the members, allowing them to develop trust in each other and familiarity with each other's customs. Among the agenda items generally discussed at plenaries are the reports of special "task forces," directions in future research, and possible new members. The preparation of task force reports is an essential part of Commission activity. Task forces focus on a variety of topics, from such immediate concerns as currency market fluctuations and arms control, to more long-term issues like the impact of technological transformation on world affairs.

Founded as a nonpermanent organization, the Trilateral Commission must regularly meet to review its purposes and determine if it wishes to continue operation. Such reviews happen every three years (every "triennium," in the official jargon). The business of each region is steered by a chairperson, with daily activities managed by a director. An Executive Committee provides overall direction and initiates the Commission's policy studies. There is also a Program Advisory Board that advises the director and regional chairpersons on policy studies.

Criticisms of the Trilateral Commission have been issued from both the left and the right. Left-wing critics see the organization as a booster club for transnational elite interests. Stephen Gill (1990), for example, argues that the Commission is an "ideological apparatus" developed by a transnational capitalist class in response to the general crisis of American hegemony presented by the end of the Bretton Woods system.

Critics on the extreme right, like Lyndon LaRouche, argue that the Trilateral Commission is part of a global network of "Anglo-American Liberal Establishment" organizations that constitute the "shadow government" of the United States. In 1980 LaRouche accused George W. Bush of being an agent of the Trilateral Commission in order to help Ronald Reagan (1911–2004) win the Republican presidential nomination (see Berlet and Lyons 2000).

Large portions of the American delegations to the Trilateral Commission are often drawn from the political elite. Many of the original U.S. delegation went on to serve in the Jimmy Carter administration (1977–1981), including President Carter himself, Vice President Walter Mondale, security advisor Zbigniew Brzezinski, and Secretary of State Cyrus Vance (1917–2002). In 2007, Vice President Dick Cheney was also a member. Representatives of the U.S. delegation are often also members of the Council on Foreign Relations, an influential Washington, D.C., think tank.

SEE ALSO *Diplomacy; Multilateralism; Unilateralism*

BIBLIOGRAPHY

Berlet, Chip, and Matthew N. Lyons. 2000. *Right-Wing Populism in America: Too Close for Comfort.* New York: Guilford.

Berthoin, Georges, Gordon S. Smith, and Takeshi Watanabe. 1977. Foreword. In *Trilateral Commission Task Force Reports: A Compilation of Reports from the First Two Years of the Trilateral Commission,* 1–7. New York: New York University Press.

Gill, Stephen. 1990. *American Hegemony and the Trilateral Commission.* Cambridge, U.K.: Cambridge University Press.

Trilateral Commission. 1973. Statement of Purposes. *Trialogue: A Bulletin of North American-European-Japanese Affairs* 2: 1–2.

Nicholas J. Kiersey

TRILATERALISM

Unlike related terms such as *multilateralism, internationalism,* or *unilateralism,* the term *trilateralism* carries with it little connotation of an underlying methodological or ideological approach to managing international disputes or negotiations, though this was not always the case. At its most basic level, trilateralism is simply a way to describe more specifically international interaction among three entities (usually nation-states) so as to differentiate between bilateral or multilateral formats when discussing trade, security, or other international policy issues. There are several examples of such arrangements, including the trilateral negotiation in the early 1990s over the North American Free Trade Agreement (NAFTA) by the United

States, Canada, and Mexico, and a formal series of meetings by South Korea, Japan, and the United States over four years ending in 2003 regarding foreign policy coordination vis-à-vis North Korea (known as the Trilateral Coordination and Oversight Group, or TCOG).

The use of the term *trilateral* to describe a specific subset of multilateral events essentially began in the 1970s, due primarily to the establishment of the Trilateral Commission by citizens of North America (United States and Canada), Western Europe, and Japan. At this time, *trilateralism* did have an ideological connotation, as it became closely associated with the commission's core emphasis on reaching beyond the established trans-Atlantic relationships to draw Japan into a three-region coalition of so-called industrial democracies whose political and corporate elite would work together to promote liberalism, open markets, and economic interdependence. To critics, these trilateralists were trying to dominate the global economy and to exploit weaker nations, whereas proponents viewed this as a well-intentioned effort to develop a broader coalition of leaders focused on mitigating international conflict and isolationism by promoting common interests and values.

As economic interdependence accelerated and blossomed into globalization throughout the 1980s and 1990s, however, many new potential coalition partners emerged, such as South Korea, Mexico, Singapore, and Taiwan, thereby introducing greater complexity and diluting the broader triangular image. The collapse of the Soviet Union in 1991 accelerated this trend. Trilateralism lost its ideological flavor, but it endured as a convenient way to describe a variety of new three-way interactions. An early post-Soviet example is the so-called Weimar Triangle, launched in Weimar, Germany, in 1991 by the foreign ministers of Germany, France, and Poland as a loose alliance to promote Poland's emergence from Communist rule.

Trilateralism coexists with other dialogue formats because it offers some advantages in certain situations. For international trade negotiations, such as NAFTA, three-way agreements can be easier for governments to navigate compared to broader multilateral initiatives that must reconcile the nations' conflicting interests and proposals; yet they can offer greater benefits or efficiency than a collective set of three bilateral agreements. In addition to formal negotiating forums, trilateralism can describe less structured gatherings of national representatives dedicated to issues of common concern. The Weimar Triangle is one example, but there are many other groups of countries that promote trilateral dialogue about such issues as trade, investment, immigration, transportation, environment, and security, including the Trilateral Wadden Sea Cooperation group involving the Netherlands, Germany,

and Denmark (starting in 1978), as well as tripartite cooperation by Japan, South Korea, and China, starting around 1999, which promotes a broad agenda of regional economic, social, and political initiatives. Small multilateral gatherings of more than three entities (but usually not more than five or six) can be considered *minilateral* meetings and offer some of the same advantages as trilateral forums.

Occasionally these trilateral meetings become institutionalized and self-sustaining; other trilateral experiments are more beholden to particular founding individuals or diplomatic moods and consequently their relevance fluctuates over time (or they disappear altogether). The TCOG, for example, was an active forum for policy coordination vis-à-vis North Korea for almost four years, but it essentially dissolved when the policy approaches of three countries diverged too widely following leadership changes.

Another use of trilateralism is as an attempt by three states or other entities to present a united front on a given issue of collective concern or to otherwise form a de facto caucus within a larger multilateral organization. Macedonia, Croatia, and Albania, for example, began formal collaboration in 2003 to promote their collective entry into the North Atlantic Treaty Organization (NATO) and the European Union (EU). Finally, trilateral meetings are also sometimes arranged as a means of formal dispute resolution, whereby one participant acts as a mediator or facilitator between two conflicting parties. A well-known example is the negotiation of the Camp David Accords in 1978 by U.S. President Jimmy Carter, Egyptian President Anwar Sadat, and Israeli Prime Minister Menachem Begin.

SEE ALSO *Alliances; Bilateralism; Coalition; Internationalism; Multilateralism; Trilateral Commission; Unilateralism*

BIBLIOGRAPHY

Owada, Hisashi. 1980–1981. Trilateralism: A Japanese Perspective. *International Security* 5 (3): 14–24.

Ullman, Richard H. 1976. Trilateralism: "Partnership" for What? *Foreign Affairs* 55 (1): 1–19.

James L. Schoff

TRIUMPHALISM

Triumphalism consists of the warrantless assertions that the decline or defeat of an adversary is caused by an antagonist and that the antagonist's success is a sign of superior virtue. In the post–World War II period, for instance, the political and economic collapse of the Soviet empire is often attributed to a competitive loss to Western European and North American capitalist powers. The fall of the Soviet Union is alleged proof of the superiority of those economic and political institutions over their Soviet counterparts.

Triumphalism is a combination of two mistaken assertions. The first assertion, that the defeat of one is due to the effort of another, is what classical rhetoricians since Aristotle have called a fallible sign. Not only is the assertion open to refutation, but its certainty can never be reliably established beyond doubt. The second assertion, that the adversary's defeat establishes the virtue of the victor, is a value judgment. As such, no credible facts can be derived from the perspectives of the victor or the loser that are not tainted by their interests. Thus facts cannot validate values, only facts.

The German sociologist and economist Max Weber is perhaps most responsible in the social sciences for stressing the ultimate dependence of the constitution and relevance of facts on values. His student, the Hungarian sociologist Karl Mannheim, showed how class interests were particularly important in forming worldviews whereby both values and facts attained cultural significance. In modern philosophy the American Thomas Kuhn's argument that knowledge is normative and writer Hilary Putnam's (b. 1926) insistence on the inseparability of judgments about facts and values have contributed additional support to a more general view that there can be no such thing as a *value-free* estimation of the world and its virtues. This position would view triumphalism as logically untenable.

If one starts with individual values, some difficulties can be avoided. Take the phenomenon of increased economic inequality in post-Soviet Russia. A believer in competitive capitalism valuing individual freedom in economic pursuits, for instance, would find growing economic inequality in post-Soviet Russia perhaps a necessary condition for the success of an enterprising minority. A socialist from the Soviet era, in contrast, would find the growth in economic inequality in post-Soviet society iniquitous. Thus in this case the *fact* of increased economic inequality in post-Soviet Russia takes on a differential significance, based upon one's basic values.

There are, however, more difficult scenarios. Suppose two persons or groups claim to agree on basic values but do not count as significant the same facts. In the United States people for and against therapeutic abortions value the sanctity of human life. The antiabortionists count fetal deaths as the indispensable marker for valuing human life. The pro-abortionists count the health of the pregnant woman as the vital measure of human well-being. Neither

accepts the facts of the other as valid counters in valuing the sanctity of human life.

These two instances do not exhaust the logical possibilities of the problems entailed in assessing facts via values and vice versa. They do suggest, however, how triumphalism as a theoretical practice is undercut by its reliance on unwarranted assertions on both sides of a given fact-value equation.

SEE ALSO *Abortion; Capitalism; Civilizations, Clash of; Cold War; Idealism; Kuhn, Thomas; Mannheim, Karl; Popper, Karl; Socialism; Weber, Max*

BIBLIOGRAPHY

Blim, Michael. 1997. Can NOT-Capitalism Lie at the End of History, or Is Capitalism's History Drawing to an End? *Critique of Anthropology* 17 (4): 351–363.

Fukuyama, Francis. 1992. *The End of History and the Last Man.* New York: Free Press.

Higgott, Richard, and Nicola Phillips. 2000. Challenging Triumphalism and Convergence: The Limits of Global Liberalization in Asia and Latin America. *Review of International Studies* 26: 359–379.

Kuhn, Thomas. 1970. *The Structure of Scientific Revolutions.* 2nd ed. Chicago: University of Chicago Press.

Mannheim, Karl. 1936. *Ideology and Utopia.* Trans. Edward Shils and Louis Wirth. New York: Harcourt, Brace.

Peet, Richard, and Michael Watts. 1993. Introduction: Development Theory and Environment in an Age of Market Triumphalism. *Economic Geography* 69 (3): 227–253.

Putnam, Hilary. 1981. *Reason, Truth, and History.* Cambridge, U.K.: Cambridge University Press.

Schrecker, Ellen, ed. 2004. *Cold War Triumphalism: The Misuse of History after the Fall of Communism.* New York: New Press.

Singer, J. David. 2000. Triumphalism and Reality in U.S. Cold War Policies. *Peace Review* 12 (4): 613–617.

Weber, Max. 1949. "Objectivity" in Social Science and Social Policy. In *Max Weber on the Methodology of the Social Sciences.* Trans. Edward Shils and Henry Finch, 49–112. Glencoe, IL: Free Press.

World Bank. 2001. *Transition—The First Ten Years: Analysis and Lessons for Eastern Europe and the Former Soviet Union.* Washington, DC: Author.

Michael Blim

TROTSKY, LEON
1879–1940

Leon Trotsky (Lev Davidovich Trotskii [Bronshtein]) was a leading Russian revolutionary. Born into a Jewish farming family in present-day Ukraine, Trotsky became a Marxist publicist and organizer in the 1890s. During

Russia's 1905 Revolution, he became chairman of the St. Petersburg Soviet of Workers' Deputies just before its suppression by the tsarist government. Forced to flee Russia, he spent the next several years as a journalist in Europe.

After 1917's February Revolution overthrew the tsarist regime, Trotsky returned to Russia. Despite fifteen years of disputes with Vladimir Lenin, Trotsky now found their views congruent, and joined Lenin's Bolsheviks to help lead the October coup d'état that overthrew Russia's provisional government. Trotsky served briefly as Soviet foreign minister before shifting in spring 1918 to building the Soviet military to fight the Russian civil war. After the Red Army's 1920 victory, Trotsky struggled against other Bolsheviks to take the ailing Lenin's place as head of the Soviet Union. For some historically conscious Bolsheviks, Trotsky's talent, military authority, and arrogance raised the specter of a new Bonaparte; a coalition of enemies, led by Joseph Stalin, first removed him from power then exiled him in 1929.

Trotsky produced a remarkable amount of work, including history, military theory, and even literary criticism, but his key contribution is his concept of *permanent revolution* (perhaps more aptly termed *uninterrupted revolution*). According to classical Marxism, proletarian revolution can take place only after a successful bourgeois revolution and the consequent long-term development of capitalism create material abundance, socioeconomic polarization, and a self-conscious working class. After the 1905 Revolution, however, Trotsky suggested that in Russia, the bourgeoisie alone was too weak to overthrow the autocracy and establish bourgeois capitalism. This created an opportunity for the proletariat to hijack the bourgeois revolution, by collaborating with the bourgeoisie to overthrow the tsarist regime, then immediately destroying the bourgeoisie and establishing a proletarian government—precisely what Lenin and Trotsky later did in 1917. Though Trotsky's theory had a specifically Russian context, he noted its applicability to other backward societies.

Russian backwardness was, however, a double-edged sword. While it allowed direct transition from bourgeois to proletarian revolution, it produced a socialist regime in an underdeveloped country. Without accompanying revolutions in industrially advanced countries, the new Soviet state was vulnerable. This led Trotsky after 1917 to promote revolution abroad to protect Soviet Russia, a stance Stalin distorted. Painting Trotsky as pessimistic about Soviet prospects, Stalin used nascent Soviet nationalism against him. Soviet backwardness also led Trotsky to push industrialization, if necessary at the peasantry's expense. Though Stalin attacked this policy during the struggle for power, he adopted it upon consolidating victory.

Trotsky's theoretical work continued in exile. Trotsky did not attribute his defeat to Stalin, who he dismissed as a nonentity, but instead to Russian backwardness. Material want and a scarcity of class-conscious workers, Trotsky argued, created the conditions for the ascendance of the Soviet bureaucracy, which employed Stalin as a tool to solidify its own position. In analyzing the bureaucracy, Trotsky anticipated later criticisms that suggested that Marxist revolutions merely substituted a new exploitative ruling class for the old one. Trotsky, however, did not see the Soviet bureaucracy as a class, for that would mean that Russia's proletarian revolution had failed. Though deformed and twisted by the bureaucracy, the Soviet Union remained for Trotsky a genuine workers' state, the fruit of a true proletarian revolution.

Trotsky's opposition to Stalin led to his assassination in 1940 by a Stalinist agent in Mexico City. He was a nonperson for the rest of the Soviet Union's existence, his achievements expunged from the historical record. Elsewhere, however, his charisma, anti-Stalinism, rhetorical flair, and reputation as the *ne plus ultra* of the revolutionary left ensured that Trotskyism remained an important force on the far left.

SEE ALSO *Bolshevism; Bureaucracy; Communism; Industrialization; Lenin, Vladimir Ilitch; Marxism; Revolution; Socialism; Stalin, Joseph; Stalinism; Union of Soviet Socialist Republics*

BIBLIOGRAPHY

Day, Richard B. 1973. *Leon Trotsky and the Politics of Economic Isolation*. Cambridge, U.K.: Cambridge University Press.

Deutscher, Isaac. 1954. *The Prophet Armed: Trotsky, 1879–1921*. New York: Oxford University Press.

Deutscher, Isaac. 1959. *The Prophet Unarmed: Trotsky, 1921–1929*. New York: Oxford University Press.

Deutscher, Isaac. 1963. *The Prophet Outcast: Trotsky, 1929–1940*. New York: Oxford University Press.

Knei-Paz, Baruch. 1978. *The Social and Political Thought of Leon Trotsky*. Oxford: Clarendon Press.

David R. Stone

TROTSKYISTS

SEE *Neoconservatism; Trotsky, Leon.*

TROUBLES, THE

SEE *Irish Republican Army.*

TROUILLOT, MICHEL-ROLPH
1949–

Few scholars actually practice the discursively much-touted interdisciplinarity of early-twenty-first-century social science. Michel-Rolph Trouillot, an anthropologist whose intellectual homes are history and philosophy, is one. Haitian by birth and in sensibility, he came to the United States by chance but chose to become a Caribbeanist. His work on Dominica and Haiti, though steeped in the details of time, place, event, and person that some carelessly dub *local color*, embraces the Americas and the world through a radical yet discerning critique of the West and capitalism. Some fifty publications, in three languages and spanning the usual text types, display Trouillot's unusual capacities for sophisticated, politically engaged theorizing and careful empirical observation. Trouillot's conference presentations, undergraduate courses, graduate seminars, editing of scholarly book series or journals, and informal conversations have also been important pathways for his critique's cumulative movements.

FAMILY HISTORY AND EDUCATION

Since Haiti's independence in 1804, many Haitian families have had black and mulatto wings with rural or urban staves in the peasantry, the middle and working classes, and the elite. By the mid-twentieth century, the black middle class Trouillots of Port-au-Prince included intellectually inquisitive and politically active professionals. Trouillot's father, attorney Ernest Trouillot (1922–1987), deftly practiced the historian's craft as an avocation. His paternal uncle, Hénock Trouillot (1923–1988), arguably Haiti's most prolific, subtle, and influential *Noiriste* historian, was a professor and for many years director of the Archives Nationales d'Haïti. Michel-Rolph, born on November 26, 1949, the second of four children, grew up in a household full of ideas and lively argument about things of this world—literature, science, art, economics, music, politics—and about how the past shapes those things in the present.

At age five, Trouillot enrolled in Port-au-Prince's Petit Séminaire Collège Saint-Martial and, under the tutelage of its progressive Pères du Saint-Esprit, completed the Baccalaureate II (Philosophy) in 1968. In the same year, he began courses at L'École Normale Supérieure. However, the Duvalier dictatorship's escalating repression of student activists compelled Trouillot to join hundreds of young compatriots who sought refuge in New York City, which was then host to the Haitian Diaspora's largest population. Trouillot received a bachelor's degree (BA) in Caribbean history and culture at Brooklyn College, City

University of New York (CUNY) in 1978, driving cabs to pay for his education and support his wife and children. He devoted spare time (not *free*, he would emphasize) to reading, Haitian Diaspora politics, and writing poetry and journalism. In 1977 he completed his first book, *Ti difé boulé sou istoua Ayiti*, an incisive Marxist analysis of the Haitian Revolution and politico-ideological developments immediately after Haitian independence, presented in the playful style of Haitian Creole dialogues. At the same time, he initiated research for two papers on coffee production in Saint-Domingue/Haiti that would alter Caribbeanists' thinking about the sociology, economics, and politics of slavery and freedom around the turn of the nineteenth century.

In 1978, anthropologists Sidney W. Mintz and Richard Price recruited Trouillot for the Johns Hopkins University Program in Atlantic History and Culture, and he completed a PhD in anthropology in 1985. By that time, Trouillot was already an assistant professor at Duke University (1983–1988), working closely with colleagues in other departments to establish the University's Caribbean Studies program and planning revisions of his dissertation, which became his second book, *Peasants and Capital* (1988), a detailed ethnographic and historical study of how Dominica's peasantry copes with the global banana industry. Trouillot subsequently returned to Johns Hopkins, first as associate professor, then as Krieger/Eisenhower Professor of Anthropology and founding director of the Institute for Global Studies in Culture, History, and Power. Since 1998, he has been professor of anthropology at The University of Chicago.

WORK AND INFLUENCE

Haitian relatives and intellectuals aside, Karl Marx is Trouillot's main source of inspiration in the study of world history. However, his work also reflects lessons learned from an international, multidisciplinary cohort of predecessors including Mintz, Eric R. Wolf, Price, David W. Cohen, Immanuel Wallerstein, Fernand Braudel, C. L. R. James, Antonio Gramsci, Jean-François Lyotard, Michel de Certeau, and Hayden White. This list omits Trouillot's contemporaries, diversely self-identified interlocutors in the social sciences and philosophy whose influences he generously acknowledges in books and articles. He also constructively appraises their scholarship in reviews or review essays, and subjects it to illuminating commentary in symposia and workshops.

Synthesizing diverse lineages of ideas, Trouillot routinely unsettles taken-for-granted dichotomies concerning concepts and data in research on political economy, society, and culture by historicizing and contextualizing them. Nevertheless, three binary oppositions establish a purchase for understanding the scope and depth of his work:

stasis/movement or flow, agency/contingency, and articulation/separation or plural integration. Trouillot relentlessly zigzags across the boundaries of these concepts to gauge relations of dominance and determination between the canalizing effects of material conditions and the creative potential of structures and processes of signification.

Polemics against empiricism, parochialism (e.g., exceptionalism, individualism, and subjectivism) and idealist or realist cultural approaches to symbolism (including identity politics) animate Trouillot's work. He is especially critical of the common, though naïve, assumption that the purposes of study, objects of observation (or units of description and analysis), and sites of inquiry are homologous. Carefully crafted operational definitions of concepts and categories for a research project, one imagines, might overcome naïveté. Yet Trouillot rejects operational definitions, insisting that they fetter serious investigation of the play of concepts and categories, and the search for relevant evidence.

These two moves puzzle methodologically oriented scholars who view theory as an indispensable guide to empirical research, but do not consider theory construction its sole or primary goal. The point holds even for core subject matters of Trouillot's best-known works. One example is the concept of the State, particularly in countries once called third world or peripheral but now forming the Global South. Another is the productivity of varied forms of power in history that precipitates privileged narrators along with mentions and silences in narratives about selected information from the past. Likewise, Trouillot had probed the savage slot by placing the presuppositions, propositions, and consequences of anthropology's mission to study "primitive" peoples, cultures, and societies in a world-historical context. Therefore, he responds with a knowing smile to the malaise among anthropologists concerning epistemology, ethnographic authority, and incursions into their traditional turf, fieldwork. As disciplinary boundaries crumble and global flows accelerate, Trouillot laconically proclaims that academic disciplines are what their practitioners do.

The dust jacket of *Silencing the Past* (1995) dubs Trouillot "one of the most prominent Haitian scholars in the United States." Although true, the statement conceals as much as it reveals. All scholars will find in Trouillot's work buoys on troubled waters—the intellectual demimonde's fitful struggle to make interdisciplinarity yield knowledge and understanding of the late-modern world's historicity. Since 2003, Trouillot has been recuperating from aneurysms; this has unfortunately interrupted his ambitious research projects, conscientious training of doctoral candidates, and wise contributions as a board member or editor to scholarly organizations and publications.

Scholars who have learned from his work await its next movements.

SEE ALSO *Anthropology; Behaviorism; Caribbean, The; Causality; Coffee Industry; Collective Memory; Critical Theory; Durkheim, Émile; Empiricism; Freud, Sigmund; Gramsci, Antonio; Haitian Revolution; Hull, Clark; James, C. L. R.; Marx, Karl; Marxism; Memory; Methodology; Mulattos; Naturalism; Norms; Parsons, Talcott; Philosophy; Philosophy of Science; Popper, Karl; Positive Social Science; Positivism; Power; Prediction; Probability; Psychology; Samuelson, Paul A.; Science; Social Science; State, The; Wallerstein, Immanuel; Wolf, Eric*

BIBLIOGRAPHY

Trouillot, Michel-Rolph. 1977. *Ti difé boulé sou istoua Ayiti.* Brooklyn, NY: Kolèksion Lakansièl.

Trouillot, Michel-Rolph. 1981. Peripheral Vibrations: The Case of Saint-Domingue's Coffee Revolution. In *Dynamics of World Development*, ed. Richard Rubinson, 27–41. Beverly Hills, CA: Sage.

Trouillot, Michel-Rolph. 1982. Motion in the System: Coffee, Color, and Slavery in Eighteenth-Century Saint-Domingue. *Review* 5 (3): 331–388.

Trouillot, Michel-Rolph. 1986. *Les Racines Historiques de l'État Duvaliérien.* Port-au-Prince: Éditions Deschamps.

Trouillot, Michel-Rolph. 1988. *Peasants and Capital: Dominica in the World Economy.* Baltimore, MD: Johns Hopkins University Press.

Trouillot, Michel-Rolph. 1990. *Haiti, State against Nation: The Origins and Legacy of Duvalierism.* New York: Monthly Review Press.

Trouillot, Michel-Rolph. [1991] 2003. Anthropology and the Savage Slot: The Poetics and Politics of Otherness. In *Global Transformations: Anthropology and the Modern World*, 7–28. New York: Palgrave Macmillan.

Trouillot, Michel-Rolph. 1992. The Caribbean Region: An Open Frontier in Anthropological Theory. *Annual Review of Anthropology* 21:19–42.

Trouillot, Michel-Rolph. 1995. *Silencing the Past: Power and the Production of History.* Boston: Beacon Press.

Trouillot, Michel-Rolph. 1997. A Social Contract for Whom? Haitian History and Haiti's Future. In *Haiti Renewed: Political and Economic Prospects*, ed. Robert I. Rotberg, 47–59. Washington, DC: Brookings Institution Press; Cambridge, MA: World Peace Foundation.

Trouillot, Michel-Rolph. 2003. *Global Transformations: Anthropology and the Modern World.* New York: Palgrave Macmillan.

Drexel G. Woodson

TRUDEAU, PIERRE ELLIOT

SEE *Quebecois Movement.*

TRUMAN, HARRY S.
1884–1972

Harry S. Truman was the thirty-third president of the United States of America. He was born on May 8, 1884, in Lamar, Missouri, and died on December 26, 1972, in Kansas City, Missouri. His middle initial, *S*, does not begin a middle name because of a family disagreement over whether his middle name should be "Solomon" or "Shipp(e)." Truman's family moved to Independence, Missouri, in 1890. After graduating from high school in 1901, Truman worked at several clerical jobs and in 1905 joined the Missouri National Guard. He worked at his family's farm from 1906 until 1916.

During World War I, Truman served as an artillery captain in France. Truman was respected by his troops for his bravery in combat and leadership ability. After he returned to Missouri, Truman married Elizabeth "Bess" Wallace. Truman and an army friend, Edward Jacobson, opened a haberdashery in Kansas City. It was a popular place for veterans to socialize, but the business suffered during the 1921–1922 recession and went bankrupt.

James Pendergast, a veteran of Truman's artillery unit, persuaded his uncle, machine boss Tom Pendergast, to ask Truman to run for a seat on the county "court," actually a public works commission. With the support of the Pendergast machine, Truman was elected as a Democrat to the Jackson County court in 1922, 1926, and 1930. Despite his affiliation with the Pendergast machine, Truman earned a reputation for honesty and efficiency, especially in the construction of new roads and a new courthouse. He accepted Tom Pendergast's offer to run for the U.S. Senate and was elected in 1934.

Upon his arrival in the Senate in 1935, Truman was initially dismissed by his colleagues as the "Senator from Pendergast" because of his association with the notorious political machine. Truman was frustrated and disappointed by President Franklin D. Roosevelt's apparent indifference and occasional hostility toward him. While generally supporting New Deal legislation, Truman also backed Roosevelt's failed, controversial "court-packing" bill, higher defense spending, military aid to Great Britain, and military conscription before the United States entered World War II. At Truman's suggestion, the Senate created a special committee to investigate waste, fraud, and mismanagement in defense contracts and appointed Truman as its chairman. The Truman Committee saved

$11 billion in defense spending and made Truman a respected national political figure.

By 1944 a growing number of Democratic politicians and campaign contributors wanted Roosevelt to replace Vice President Henry A. Wallace with Truman as his running mate in the 1944 presidential election. Truman reluctantly accepted Roosevelt's offer to be his running mate. During and after the 1944 election, Truman was concerned that the ailing Roosevelt rarely consulted him and did not confer with him about major war policies and postwar plans. Truman's brief vice presidency ended with Roosevelt's death on April 12, 1945.

TRUMAN'S PRESIDENCY

Truman's first few months as president were a whirlwind of major world events and presidential decisions. Germany surrendered on May 7, 1945. From July 17 until August 2, Truman conferred with Winston Churchill and Joseph Stalin in Potsdam to determine the postwar occupation of Germany and the trial arrangements for Nazi war criminals. One week later, Truman ordered the dropping of atomic bombs on Japan. Japan formally surrendered on September 2. On September 8, Truman ordered American troops to be stationed in South Korea.

During his first year as president, Truman also confronted labor disputes, inflation, and public demands for a more rapid demobilization of troops and reconversion to a civilian economy. Truman became known for his blunt rhetoric and unequivocal decision-making style, epitomized by the catchphrases "The Buck Stops Here" and "Give 'em Hell." Nonetheless, Truman's declining public approval ratings and the public perception of his inferiority to Roosevelt helped the Republicans to win control of Congress in 1946.

With regard to foreign and defense policies, Truman had a fairly productive and effective relationship with the Republican-controlled 80th Congress. Truman and Congress enacted the Marshall Plan for the economic reconstruction of Western Europe and a similar plan for Japan, sent military and economic aid for the Greek and Turkish governments fighting communist aggression, reorganized the Department of Defense, and established the foundation of the North Atlantic Treaty Organization (NATO) for the collective security of Western Europe.

In the area of domestic policy, however, Truman often had disagreements with Republicans and conservative Southern Democrats in Congress. In 1947 the Taft-Hartley Act, which reduced the legal powers and privileges of labor unions, became law over Truman's veto. Southern Democrats and some Republicans rejected Truman's civil rights legislation for African Americans.

Most Republicans in Congress disagreed with Truman on tax, housing, price control, and agricultural issues.

Truman's campaign in the 1948 presidential election repeatedly denounced the "do-nothing Republican 80th Congress" on domestic issues and implicitly linked it to Governor Thomas E. Dewey of New York, the moderately liberal Republican presidential nominee. Friendly crowds encouraged Truman to "give 'em hell." Meanwhile, the Democratic Party splintered further. The most anti-civil rights Southern Democrats supported Governor J. Strom Thurmond of South Carolina as the presidential nominee of the States Rights Democrats, or "Dixiecrat" party. Anti-cold war liberals and leftists supported the Progressive Party's presidential nominee, Henry A. Wallace.

With a comfortable lead in public opinion polls, Dewey avoided sounding antagonistic toward Truman and addressing specific issues that might reveal his differences with more conservative Republicans in Congress. Major newspapers and magazines predicted Dewey's victory and speculated on his future policies and cabinet appointments. The *Chicago Tribune*'s top headline on Election Day famously announced, "Dewey Defeats Truman." Nonetheless, Truman won an upset victory. The Democrats also won control of Congress.

In his 1949 message to Congress, Truman proposed what he called "a Fair Deal for all Americans." His major policy proposals included civil rights, national health insurance, and repeal of the Taft-Hartley Act. Except for the Housing Act of 1949, Congress rejected all of the major Fair Deal legislation.

Republicans charged that the Truman and Roosevelt administrations had failed or refused to uncover and prevent communist influence on American foreign and defense policies; in response, Truman created loyalty review boards to find communists in the federal government, especially the state department. The Truman administration's reputation was also tarnished by congressional and media investigations of corruption on the part of some officials. These issues were overshadowed, however, by the communist takeover of mainland China in 1949, the Soviet detonation of an atomic bomb, and the outbreak of the Korean War in 1950.

Truman secured a decision from the United Nations (UN) authorizing the United States and other UN members to support South Korea. He appointed General Douglas MacArthur commander of the American and other UN forces in Korea. After MacArthur publicly defied Truman's strategy of limiting the war to Korea and avoiding a war with China, Truman removed MacArthur from command. Truman's removal of MacArthur and the ensuing stalemate in the Korean War proved to be unpopular. Truman spent the remainder of his presidency defending his policies in Korea and supporting the Democratic presidential campaign of Illinois governor Adlai Stevenson in 1952.

After Republican presidential nominee Dwight D. Eisenhower easily defeated Stevenson, Truman spent the early years of his retirement supervising his presidential library in Independence, Missouri, and writing his memoirs. On December 26, 1972, Truman died of complications from pneumonia in a Kansas City hospital. During his retirement and after his death, Truman's historical reputation steadily improved, especially for his integrity and major foreign policy decisions.

SEE ALSO *Dixiecrats; Eisenhower, Dwight D.; Korean War; Roosevelt, Franklin D.; Thurmond, Strom; World War II*

BIBLIOGRAPHY

McCoy, Donald R. 1984. *The Presidency of Harry S. Truman.* Lawrence: University Press of Kansas.

McCullough, David. 1992. *Truman.* New York: Simon and Schuster.

Savage, Sean J. 1997. *Truman and the Democratic Party.* Lexington: University Press of Kentucky.

Sean J. Savage

TRUST

Trust, the general sense of well-being in relation to one's self and toward others, is an essential attribute of human character as well as of interpersonal interaction. The attainment of a sense of trust has long been thought by ego psychologists to be the first human developmental task and is based largely on the infant's growing expectation that the mothering figure will become a constant source of nurturing and satisfaction in the individual's life. Good nurturing thus disposes the individual to anticipate positive encounters with the environment and with other persons.

There is common agreement that trust is an essential factor in successful social environments and interactions. Persons need to feel secure in their expectations for good outcomes as they go about their daily lives. For instance, they need to assume that an elevator is functioning normally, that they will be understood linguistically if they cry for help, and that a medical professional will try to do them good rather than harm. So important is what could be called "background trust" that experimentally breaching it, as sociologist Harold Garfinkel has shown, by speaking nonsense when a person asks for directions or help, causes subjects to become extremely angry and anxious. If one has a flat tire, and the experimenter replies to a call for help by asking what a tire is, rage on the subject's part is sure to follow. Hence there is strong reason to think that trust is an interaction imperative, up to and including dealing with one's enemies, as the history of the cold war suggests.

The greater the degree of trust in social transactions, it is believed, the more optimal are the satisfactions for participants. Relations between members of households and kin networks, for instance, are typically characterized as high in trust, and it is notable how solutions to the most difficult problems of human dependency, such as infancy, old age, and disability, are undertaken at great sacrifice within their confines. Trustworthy expectations also flow through social networks such that they are an important source of economic opportunities such as job finding and job getting.

Trust and exchange, used here in the broadest sense, are intimately related. Exchange creates trust, and trust facilitates exchange. Among members of small-scale societies, gift giving creates the necessity of reciprocity and generates in the giver the expectation of being a receiver and thus a beneficiary of a gift in a future transaction. Bonds of mutual expectation are formed and can often support the exchange of purely economic goods, as the classic investigation of anthropologist Bronislaw Malinowski (1884–1942) among the Trobriand Islanders of the Pacific a century ago showed.

The depth of trust among participants also affects exchanges in markets. At minimum, most economists recognize trust as a helpful externality: that is, trust is a noneconomic element that improves economic efficiency by increasing the speed of transaction and limiting the need for costly conditions to ensure mutual compliance. Its absence increases economic risk and may foster opportunism among buyers and sellers that limits the scope of market transactions. Lack of trust between producers and suppliers has been argued as a primary motivation for the growth of large, vertically integrated industrial firms. If firms cannot trust their suppliers to deliver quality goods in a timely and cost-effective fashion, they reason it is better to produce the goods internally or purchase the supplying firm outright.

On the other hand, trust, it has been argued, can be misplaced. Exclusive trust in kin or in personal and social networks often signifies lack of trust in other persons, networks, and institutions outside their purview. This diffidence toward others can create economic and political troubles. Politically, Robert D. Putnam has argued, for instance, that trust is an indispensable good for building a successful civil society and, by implication, a functioning democracy. In a world economy dominated by large corporations, the temporary advantages afforded by a high degree of internal trust found among families and kin

groups that stimulate high levels of personal dedication, income pooling, and personal sacrifice can become overwhelmed by such problems as small firm size, stunted organizational growth, and lack of access to capital markets for expansion. If mistrust in the face of outsiders in markets leads to out-and-out hostility, deviant economic combinations, such as the mafia and what Max Weber (1864–1920) called "pariah capitalism," can arise. A market where neither the expectation nor the reality of fair treatment, both reliant on background trust, is met tends to founder and shrink. Moreover, exploitation of others outside the bounds of exclusive trust becomes highly likely.

Exclusive bonds of trust need not be overtly hostile to be exploitative. Cartels and trusts, historic fetters on economic efficiency, are precisely the products of relations of trust developed among nominally competing firms. Through the reciprocal exchange of information, favors, and market opportunities, they effectively charge a tax on their transactions with other buyers and sellers outside their circle.

As world society and the world economy become more integrated, *globalized* in a word, the need for, as well as evidence of, a more generalized interpersonal trust have been noted. Mass travel and migration, unprecedented collective reliance on large bureaucratic organizations for all kinds of commodities and services, and the rise of communication and information technologies necessitate increased contact with impersonal, anonymous persons, providers, and interlocutors. The sense of well-being and the expectation of gratification embodied in the concept of trust take on even greater importance. There are many instances in which this sense of globalized background trust can be observed, from the casual use of the credit card to the ease with which one can trade, borrow, and travel in ever grander geographical and social spaces. Inside large organizations, the same expectations of good interactions are created through rewards and training, though employee trust can be lost easily through the abuses of hierarchy and corporate economic power.

SEE ALSO *Reciprocity*

BIBLIOGRAPHY

Arrow, Kenneth. 1974. *The Limits of Organization.* New York: Norton.

Erikson, Erik. 1963. *Childhood and Society.* 2nd ed. New York: Norton.

Fukuyama, Francis. 1995. *Trust: The Social Virtues and the Creation of Prosperity.* New York: Free Press.

Garfinkel, Harold. [1967] 1984. *Studies in Ethnomethodology.* Cambridge, U.K.: Polity Press.

Giddens, Anthony. 1990. *The Consequences of Modernity.* Stanford, CA: Stanford University Press.

Granovetter, Mark. 1995. *Getting a Job: A Study of Contacts and Careers.* 2nd ed. Chicago: University of Chicago Press.

Malinowski, Bronislaw. [1922] 1984. *Argonauts of the Western Pacific.* Prospect Heights, IL: Waveland.

Putnam, Robert D., Robert Leonardi, and Raffaella Y. Nanetti. 1993. *Making Democracy Work.* Princeton, NJ: Princeton University Press.

Weber, Max. [1905] 2001. *The Protestant Ethic and the Spirit of Capitalism.* Trans. Talcott Parsons. New York: Routledge.

Michael Blim

TRUTH, SOJOURNER
c. 1797–1883

Sojourner Truth was born a slave in Ulster County, New York. Her masters at birth were the Hardenburgh family, descendents of Dutch "patroon" planters, and she was named Isabella Baumfree at birth. During her lifetime she was sold several times, married Thomas Dumont, another slave, and had at least four children with him. In 1827 New York freed all remaining slaves, but Isabella had already left her owners. After the abolition of slavery, she successfully sued her former owners to obtain the freedom of one of her children, whom they had transferred to Alabama.

The 1830s were a time of great religious ferment, called the Second Great Awakening. Isabella was caught up in the movement, and she traveled around the northeast and settled in several religious communes. It was about this time that she began calling herself Sojourner Truth and became an itinerant preacher.

In the 1840s she became active in the abolitionist movement, and she worked with many abolitionist leaders such as Frederick Douglass (1817–1895) and William Lloyd Garrison (1805–1879). She was in great demand as a speaker, and her memoir *The Narrative of Sojourner Truth, a Northern Slave,* was dictated to and edited by abolitionist author Harriet Beecher Stowe (1811–1896).

Sojourner Truth also became involved in women's rights issues. Like many abolitionists, she saw a connection between the issues of women's liberation and freedom for blacks. Her most famous speech, "Ain't I A Woman?," was delivered at a women's rights conference in 1851. The speech was transcribed by another woman abolitionist, Frances Gage, who published it almost thirty years later. Gage's text is the only record of Sojourner Truth's oratorical style, and it is written in nonstandard English. It is unclear if that is really the way Sojourner Truth spoke. Contemporaries, both black and white, always described her as a riveting speaker, and nobody ever suggested that her English was poor or difficult to understand. Nonetheless, the speech as transcribed shows some of the power of Sojourner Truth's oratory: the biblical or theological arguments mixed with homely, rural simile, the chatty tone, the repetition of "and ain't I a woman?" and other rhetorical elements that have made this speech a classic of early feminism.

When the Civil War (1861–1865) broke out, Sojourner Truth worked for better conditions for blacks in the Union military and against segregation in northern cities. After the war she called for the establishment of a "Negro state" in the west. She also supported the Freedman's Bureau and tried to help black war refugees and the newly freed people in the South find jobs and housing. She continued to work for women's rights, civil rights for blacks, and temperance (laws restricting alcohol consumption) until her death in 1883.

Sojourner Truth is important because she helped set the terms of reference for the debate over slavery, civil rights for blacks after the Civil War, and women's rights in the United States in the mid-nineteenth century. She is probably as important a figure as any of the other well-known abolitionists—Douglass, Garrison, Beecher Stowe—especially because as a black woman she has inherent credibility on both black and women's issues. She is also important as an example of a little-appreciated phenomenon, the link between Protestant evangelical Christianity, abolitionism, and women's liberation. It is important to realize that in the middle of the 1800s, evangelical Christians were more likely to be radicals than conservatives. Finally, she deserves attention because of her lively speaking style. There is a reason that she stood out as a speaker and sold many books in that era, so well provided with great speakers and writers.

SEE ALSO *Civil Rights; Feminism; Fundamentalism; Fundamentalism, Christian; Slavery; Social Movements; Suffrage Movement, Women's; U.S. Civil War*

BIBLIOGRAPHY

Painter, Nell Irvin. 1996. *Sojourner Truth: A Life, a Symbol.* New York: W. W. Norton.

Truth, Sojourner. 1998. *Narrative of Sojourner Truth.* New York: Penguin Classics.

Stewart R. King

TRUTH AND RECONCILIATION COMMISSIONS

Many countries with histories of widespread human rights abuses in the past have turned to truth and reconciliation commissions as an institutional solution to the problem of transitional justice and attempted democratization. Although these commissions take many forms—and are assigned a variety of mandates—each is charged with investigating the truth of past events with the hope that knowing about the truth will contribute to "reconciliation." Roughly two dozen such commissions have been created (including one in Greensboro, North Carolina, charged with discovering the truth of what happened during a political riot in 1979). Many more such tribunals are being considered in countries trying to confront their troubled pasts (e.g., Iraq).

Nearly all truth commissions have the aim of creating a collective memory about the past. This ranges from official versions of "who did what to whom" to macrohistorical treatises (e.g., what role did religious organizations play in the maintenance of apartheid in South Africa?). The objective of truth commissions is to get widespread acceptance of a historical narrative, typically under the assumption that battling continually over whether historical injustices actually took place (e.g., Holocaust deniers) is not productive.

Some truth commissions are empowered to grant amnesty to gross human rights violators. The theory is that, with amnesty, perpetrators will come forward and admit their crimes, allowing a collective memory to be constructed. Amnesty schemes are controversial because by definition they create a retributive justice deficit. Amnesty provisions vary widely, from individual to blanket amnesties, and are often accompanied by selective prosecutions of those not qualifying for amnesty (e.g., those who committed their crimes without political motives). Many social scientists believe that amnesties play a valuable role in democratization processes by allowing the forces of the ancien régime to retire from politics and to refrain from acting as "spoilers" of the transition. Others, however, point to the failure to achieve retribution as a crucial flaw in amnesty programs and argue that, without the punishment of wrongdoers, little deterrent to future human rights abuses exists.

Reconciliation is a more complicated concept, in part because some would limit reconciliation to the relationship between victims and perpetrators, whereas others treat the concept as referring to entire societies. The South African Truth and Reconciliation Commission, for instance, was charged with transforming South African society—which, of course, was overwhelmingly comprised of bystanders, not victims and perpetrators of gross human rights violations. Generally, reconciliation requires that people of disparate political views tolerate one another and agree to limit political competition to peaceful and democratic means.

The form that truth commissions take—their structure, functions, and powers—is typically hotly contested by competing political factions, which makes such tribunals hard to establish in the first place. A key issue in such disputes concerns the evenhandedness of the commission's activities, and in particular whether all sides in political struggles should be held accountable to the same human rights standards. Some distinguish between "victor's justice" and "transitional justice," with the latter being characterized by a willingness to cast blame for human rights atrocities broadly across all combatants. With truth commissions crucially situated to shape political transitions on a broad scale, it is no wonder that getting agreement from those formerly at war with each other is difficult, and in many instances impossible.

By almost universal agreement, the most successful truth commission in the world is that of South Africa. Led by the cleric and anti-apartheid activist Desmond Tutu, and fully backed by Nelson Mandela, the first president of the country to be elected after the end of apartheid (but not backed by the governing political party, the African National Congress), South Africa's TRC adopted societal transformation as one of its most important objectives. Although widely known (and often criticized) for granting amnesties to some of the apartheid regime's worst assassins and criminals, the TRC held hearings throughout the country involving enormous numbers of citizens, produced a massive documentary history of apartheid and human rights abuses, fought the battle to provide compensation to victims, and generally contributed to tolerance and reconciliation in the country. Consequently, the South African TRC is widely copied by those seeking to move beyond the past toward a more democratic future. Reconciliation and democracy are not synonymous, but without some degree of reconciliation, it is difficult for countries to put the violent conflicts in the past and agree that political competition will be limited to peaceful and democratic means.

SEE ALSO *African National Congress; Apartheid; Collective Memory; Genocide; Human Rights; Justice; Justice, Social; Reparations; Slavery; Terror; Violence*

BIBLIOGRAPHY

Barkan, Elazar, and Alexander Karn, eds. 2006. *Taking Wrongs Seriously: Apologies and Reconciliation.* Stanford, CA: Stanford University Press.

Boraine, Alex. 2000. *A Country Unmasked: Inside South Africa's Truth and Reconciliation Commission.* Cape Town and New York: Oxford University Press.

Gibson, James L. 2004. *Overcoming Apartheid: Can Truth Reconcile a Divided Nation?* New York: Russell Sage Foundation.

Hayner, Priscilla B. 2002. *Unspeakable Truths: Facing the Challenge of Truth Commissions.* New York: Routledge.

James L. Gibson

TRYPTOPHAN

SEE *Serotonin.*

TSE-TUNG, MAO

SEE *Mao Zedong.*

T-STATISTIC

SEE *Student's T-Statistic.*

TSUNAMI

SEE *Disaster Management; Natural Disasters.*

TUBMAN, HARRIET
1822–1913

Born Araminta "Minty" Ross on the plantation of Anthony Thompson, in Dorchester County, Maryland, in 1822, Harriet Tubman was one of nine enslaved children of Harriet "Rit" Green and Benjamin Ross, both slaves. During the mid-1820s, Thompson's stepson, Edward Brodess, took Rit and the children ten miles away to his own farm in Bucktown after he inherited them from his deceased mother. Over the next twenty-five years, Tubman endured painful separations from her family while being hired out to cruel masters who beat and starved her. Brodess sold several of her sisters, permanently tearing apart her family.

While working as a field hand as a young teen, Tubman was severely wounded by a blow to her head from an iron weight thrown by an angry overseer at another fleeing slave. This left her suffering from headaches and epileptic seizures that affected her for the rest of her life. About 1844 she married a local free black named John Tubman, shedding her childhood name in favor of Harriet.

Upon Brodess's death in 1849, Tubman determined to take her own liberty rather than risk being sold to set-tle Brodess's debts. She tapped into an Underground Railroad network operating on the Eastern Shore of Maryland: Using the North Star and assistance from white and black helpers, she found her way to freedom in Philadelphia. Once safely there, Tubman worked as a domestic to support herself and save enough money to help family and friends escape from the Eastern Shore of Maryland.

Through a variety of familial, social, and abolitionist networks, Tubman was able to exploit secret and reliable communication and support systems and craft her own Underground Railroad networks to freedom. These networks included many free and enslaved African Americans and antislavery whites who lived and worked near crucial access points to food, transportation, and shelter in Maryland, Delaware, Pennsylvania, and New York. Unable to read or write, Tubman also used a variety of disguises and ruses to affect her multiple escape missions. In spite of debilitating seizures, Tubman returned about thirteen times during the 1850s, bringing away roughly seventy friends and family members, while giving instructions to scores more who found their way to freedom independently. Miraculously, Tubman was never betrayed and never "lost a passenger."

The Fugitive Slave Act of 1850 left many runaway slaves vulnerable to recapture. Tubman brought numerous freedom seekers to safety in St. Catharines, Ontario, Canada, where they became part of a growing community of refugees from slavery. Her dangerous missions won her the biblical name "Moses" and the admiration of abolitionists throughout the North, including Frederick Douglass, William Lloyd Garrison, Lucretia Mott, Gerrit Smith, and Susan B. Anthony, among others, who supported her and sought her counsel. Tubman collaborated with the legendary John Brown as he planned for an attack on Harpers Ferry, West Virginia, in 1859.

During the Civil War (1861–1865), Tubman traveled to Port Royal, South Carolina, to support Union activities. She nursed wounded black soldiers and conducted important spying missions behind Confederate lines. She became the first woman to command an armed military expedition when she guided Colonel James Montgomery and his black troops on a successful raid in June 1863.

After the war, Tubman moved to Auburn, New York, where William Henry Seward, President Abraham Lincoln's secretary of state, had sold her a home and where she had settled her aged parents and other family members. There, she intensified her fight for women's rights and civil rights for African Americans. After John Tubman died in Maryland, Harriet Tubman married Nelson Davis, a veteran, in 1869. She struggled financially the rest of her life. Denied her own military pension, she eventually received a widow's pension and, later, a Civil War nurse's pension.

Rising above social, economic, and physical adversity, Tubman continued her humanitarian work with the opening of the Harriet Tubman Home for the Aged in 1908 in Auburn. She continued to appear at local and national suffrage conventions until the early 1900s. She died at the age of ninety-one on March 10, 1913, in Auburn.

Since her death, Tubman has been memorialized and commemorated in many ways, including the naming of schools, roads, nonprofit social-service organizations, and state days of recognition. In 1944 the U.S. Maritime Commission launched the Liberty ship SS *Harriet Tubman*, and in 1978 and again in 1995 the U.S. Post Office issued postage stamps in her honor. Tubman has earned international acclaim as a symbol of the struggle for freedom, equality, and justice from oppression and discrimination, and has become one of America's most enduring historical figures.

SEE ALSO *Slavery*

BIBLIOGRAPHY

Humez, Jean M. 2003. *Harriet Tubman: The Life and the Life Stories*. Madison: University of Wisconsin Press.

Larson, Kate Clifford. 2004. *Bound for the Promised Land: Harriet Tubman, Portrait of an American Hero*. New York: Ballantine.

Kate Clifford Larson

TULIP MANIA

SEE *Great Tulip Mania, The.*

TULSA RIOT

On the evening of May 31, 1921, a mob of people appeared at the Tulsa County Courthouse in Tulsa, Oklahoma. They were drawn by rumors afoot in the community that Dick Rowland, a nineteen-year-old black man, would be lynched. Those rumors, in turn, were started by a story on the front page of the *Tulsa Tribune* that Rowland had been arrested for attempting to assault an orphaned white girl in an elevator in a building in downtown Tulsa the day before. Rumors of lynching drew black men, veterans of World War I (1914–1918), to the courthouse as well. They hoped to prevent what they feared would be a lynching of Rowland. In the late evening hours, around 10 p.m., the black men who had shown up to prevent the lynching clashed with police and the mob. And the riot began. By the time it ended around noon the next day, thirty-five blocks of the prosperous black section of Tulsa had been burned, leaving thousands homeless and thousands of black people in custody.

Tulsa was the last of the terrible World War I–era riots that began in East Saint Louis, Illinois, in 1917 and continued in Chicago and many other cities in 1919. The Tulsa riot was also likely the worst in terms of loss of life. Like the other riots of the era, Tulsa had its origins in the rising prosperity of the black community, as well as its rising aspirations, which caused the black community to come into conflict with the white community. People in Greenwood, as the black section of Tulsa was known, were doing well; there was a weekly newspaper, churches, rooming houses, schools, stores, even two movie theaters. And many of the Greenwood residents were men who had fought in World War I. They had traveled the world and seen that life might be organized differently from how it was in Tulsa. They returned, as one newspaper said in the riot's aftermath, "from the war in France with exaggerated notions of social equality and thinking [they could] whip the world" (*Tulsa Tribune* 1921). Thus, people in Greenwood participated in the national renaissance of black culture and pride. They read the vehicles of the renaissance, like W. E. B. Du Bois's *The Crisis* and the sensational *Chicago Defender*. When they heard that Rowland was in danger, they acted to protect his life. And in doing so they put in motion events that led to the destruction of their own community.

After the riot began, the Tulsa police department acted to put down what was called at the time a "negro uprising." The police chief deputized hundreds of men and told them to get a gun and "get a nigger." The police department worked in conjunction with local units of the National Guard to disarm Greenwood residents and take them to what newspapers called "concentration camps" around the city. Those who refused to give up their weapons peacefully were shot. The arrests and fighting continued throughout the night, but around dawn of June 1, the deputies, working in conjunction with a mob and the police and National Guard, swept through Greenwood. First, residents were arrested and disarmed; then looters followed and, once they had taken everything of value, homes and businesses were burned.

In the aftermath of the riot, virtually every African American resident of Tulsa was left homeless. Thousands left the city, never to return. Others vowed to rebuild, even in the face of opposition from the city. The mayor wanted to relocate the black section of Tulsa farther away from the city and to convert the burned area into an industrial and railroad center. "I'll keep what I have until I get what I lost" was the rallying cry of many in

Greenwood. And, despite receiving little assistance from the city, Greenwood was rebuilt. Meanwhile, an all-white grand jury blamed the riot on African Americans. About the same time as the riot, the Ku Klux Klan was gaining membership throughout the state. Riot victims could not hope for justice through the courts at the time.

The Tulsa riot has received renewed attention due to the Oklahoma legislature's Tulsa Riot Commission, which in 2001 recommended that the surviving victims receive reparations from the state. In 2003 a team of lawyers led by Harvard Law School Professor Charles Ogletree filed a federal lawsuit on behalf of riot victims, which was dismissed in 2004. The few remaining Tulsa riot victims and their lawyers continue to seek compensation from the state legislature and elsewhere.

SEE ALSO *Racism; Reparations; Riots; Wilmington Riot of 1898*

BIBLIOGRAPHY

Brophy, Alfred L. 2002. *Reconstructing the Dreamland: The Tulsa Riot of 1921—Race, Reparations, Reconciliation.* Oxford: Oxford University Press.

Brophy, Alfred L. 2006. The Functions and Limitations of a Historical Truth Commission: The Case of the Tulsa Race Riot Commission. In *Taking Wrongs Seriously: Apologies and Reconciliation*, eds. Elazar Barkan and Alexander Karn, 234–258. Stanford, CA: Stanford University Press.

Ellsworth, Scott. 1982. *Death in a Promised Land: The Tulsa Race Riot of 1921.* Baton Rouge: Louisiana State University Press.

Ellsworth, Scott, and John Hope Franklin, eds. 2001. *Tulsa Race Riot: A Report by the Oklahoma Commission to Study the Tulsa Race Riot of 1921.* http://www.okhistory.org/trrc/freport.htm.

Tulsa Tribune. 1921. Negro Tells How Others Mobilized, at 1. June 1.

Alfred L. Brophy

TURGOT, JACQUES
1727–1781

Born in 1727 in Paris, economist Anne-Robert-Jacques Turgot, Baron de l'Aulne, received a thorough education, especially in philosophy, and then studied theology at the Sorbonne. In 1750 he was elected to the office of prior. In the same year, he published his *Philosophical Review of the Successive Advances of the Human Mind*, which contained a four-stage theory of human development. After the death of his father in 1751, Turgot began an administrative career. In the late 1750s he contributed several entries to the *Encyclopédie* edited by Denis Diderot (1713–1784).

His friendship with the Marquis de Gournay (1712–1759), a French economist, merchant, and government official, had a lasting impact on Turgot's interests and acquainted him with contemporary English political economy. In the late 1750s Turgot met with the head of the physiocratic school, François Quesnay (1694–1774), whose work he admired. He also became friendly with another leading member of that school, Pierre-Samuel du Pont de Nemours (1793–1817), and with Voltaire (1694–1778) and the mathematician and philosopher J. A. N. Caritat de Condorcet (1743–1794).

In 1761 Turgot was appointed intendant of Limoges, a post he held until 1774. He was in charge of the collection of direct taxes, justice, economic and social policy, infrastructure, and so forth. In this period, he composed what may be called his magnum opus, *Reflections on the Production and Distribution of Wealth*, which was not published until 1769 and 1770 in serial form in the *Ephémerides*. In addition, he wrote essays on several economic themes, including taxation, public administration, mines and quarries, the grain trade, and the rate of interest. During his visits to Paris he met, among others, David Hume (1711–1776) and Adam Smith (1723–1790).

With Louis XVI's (1754–1793) succession to the throne in 1774, Turgot was appointed minister of finance. He carried out a number of reforms, including the restoration of domestic free trade of grain, an act that caused the grain riots of early 1775, and the abolition of other constraints on trade (Faccarello 1994). A retrenchment of the influence of the guilds and a replacement of the corvée with a more general land tax followed in January 1776. These measures met with fierce opposition, causing Turgot's dismissal in May 1776. In 1778 he was elected president of the Académie des Inscriptions et Belles Lettres. He died in Paris in 1781.

Turgot was arguably one of the most important economists of the eighteenth century. In important respects, he developed the physiocratic doctrine and anticipated some of the ideas subsequently elaborated by the English classical economists from Adam Smith to David Ricardo (1772–1823). In the *Reflections*, he expounded central economic concepts, including the idea that in conditions of free competition the rate of return on capital tends to uniformity across all employments. In his view, self-interest constrained by competitive conditions can be expected to yield desirable economic outcomes. He therefore advocated laissez-faire and is considered a "patron saint" of the French liberal economics tradition of the middle of the nineteenth century (Groenewegen 1977). His writings had an impact on a number of economists, including the Austrian Eugen von Böhm-Bawerk (1851–1914). Joseph A. Schumpeter's (1883–1950) contention that Turgot anticipated in important respects the so-called marginal revolution is, however, difficult to sustain.

SEE ALSO *Austrian Economics; Laissez Faire; Liberalism; Physiocracy; Quesnay, Francois; Ricardo, David; Smith, Adam*

BIBLIOGRAPHY

Faccarello, Gilbert. 1994. *Nil repente!* Galiani and Necker on Economic Reforms. *European Journal of the History of Economic Thought* 1 (3): 519–550.

Groenewegen, Peter, ed. and trans. 1977. *The Economics of A. R. J. Turgot.* The Hague, Netherlands: Martinus Nijhoff.

Meek, Ronald, ed. and trans. 1973. *Turgot on Progress, Sociology, and Economics.* Cambridge, U.K.: Cambridge University Press.

Schelle, Gustave. 1913–1923. *Oeuvres de Turgot et documents le concernant.* Paris: Félix Alcan.

Turgot, Anne Robert Jacques. 1844. *Oeuvres de Turgot.* New ed. Eds. Eugène Daire and Hyppolite Dussard. Paris: Guillaumin.

Heinz D. Kurz

TURNER, NAT
c. 1800–1831

Abolitionist and rebel Nat Turner was born circa October 2, 1800, on the Virginia plantation of Benjamin Turner, the child of an enslaved woman named Nancy (the name of Nat's father is unknown). Little is known about either parent. Family tradition holds that Nancy landed in Norfolk five years before in 1795, the slave of a refugee fleeing the revolt in Saint Domingue. Evidence indicates that after being purchased by Turner, Nancy was used as a domestic servant. Later in life, Nat Turner insisted that his father ran away when he was still a boy.

Early on, blacks and whites alike came to regard Nat as unusually gifted. Upon being given a book, the boy quickly learned how to read, "a source of wonder to all in the neighborhood" (Greenberg 1996, p. 45). As a devout Methodist, Benjamin Turner was not only aware of Nat's literacy, he even encouraged him to read the Bible, as did his paternal grandmother, Old Bridget, who Nat later said was "very religious, and to whom I was much attached" (p. 44). Even assuming that some of what Nat later told to attorney Thomas R. Gray was exaggerated bravado—or that the white lawyer's editorial hand helped shape the pamphlet published as *The Confessions of Nat Turner* (Baltimore, 1831)—there is little reason to doubt Nat's assertion that he spent every possible childhood moment "either in prayer" (p. 45) or in reading books purchased

for white children on nearby Southampton County farms and estates.

Aware of his unique abilities, young Nat "wrapped [himself] in mystery" (Greenberg 1996, p. 45). When not doing light work in the fields, Nat kept to himself and "studiously avoided mixing in society" (Greenberg 1996, pp. 44–45). Unlike other enslaved boys, he neither played practical pranks on others nor touched liquor. Told by both his mother and grandmother that he was "intended for some great purpose," the unusually serious child devoted his limited leisure moments to "fasting and prayer" (Greenberg 1996, pp. 44–45). As was later said of abolitionist Frederick Douglass, whites spoke of Nat as being too clever to be raised in bondage, and Benjamin Turner once remarked that the boy "would never be of service to anyone as a slave" (Greenberg 1996, p. 44).

In 1809, Benjamin Turner's oldest son Samuel purchased 360 acres two miles away. Nancy, Nat, Old Bridget, and five other slaves were loaned to Samuel to help him establish his cotton plantation, a move that became permanent the following year when Benjamin died during a typhoid epidemic. It may have been at this point that Nat adopted the surname of Turner as a way of linking himself to his ancestral homeplace rather than as an act of homage to the deceased Benjamin Turner. Although the evidence for a spouse is circumstantial, the Richmond *Constitutional Whig* later reported that Turner married a young slave woman; this may have been Cherry, who in 1822 was sold to Giles Reese when Samuel died and his estate was liquidated. Turner was sold to Thomas Moore for $400, an indication he was regarded as a prime field hand. Despite being short of stature and a little knock-kneed, Turner's shoulders were broad and well muscled from more than a decade of hard labor.

Embittered by the forced separation from his wife, Turner turned to fasting and prayer. He avoided large spiritual gatherings on Sundays, but at night in the quarters he willingly described what he had discovered during his solitary readings of the Bible. Sometime in 1825, while working in the fields, Turner had his first vision. "I saw white spirits and black spirits engaged in battle," he later recalled, "and the sun was darkened—the thunder rolled in the Heavens, and blood flowed in streams" (Greenberg 1996, p. 46). Certain that he was ordained to bring about Judgment Day, Turner began to conduct religious services at Barnes's Church near the North Carolina border. Most whites scoffed, but at least one man, Etheldred T. Brantley, an alcoholic overseer on a nearby plantation, asked Turner to baptize him before an interracial crowd at Pearson's Mill Pond.

On May 12, 1828, Turner experienced his most epochal vision to date. "I heard a loud noise in the heavens," he remembered, "and the Spirit instantly appeared to me" (Greenberg 1996, p. 46). The voice instructed Turner to take up the "yoke" of Christ, "for the time was fast approaching when the first should be last and the last should be first" (Greenberg 1996, p. 47). Warned not to act until given a further sign by God, Turner was instructed to continue teaching but not to breathe a word of his plans to his family or friends.

Several months later, Thomas Moore died, and Turner became the property of Thomas's nine-year-old son Putnam. When the boy's mother remarried to Joseph Travis, a local wheelwright, Turner and the other sixteen slaves on the Moore plantation found themselves under the supervision of yet another new master. When an eclipse of the sun took place in February 1831, Turner concluded that the time was near to act. He recruited four trusted lieutenants, Hark Travis, Nelson Williams, Henry Porter, and Sam Francis. Turner had known Travis for years, as he was also a slave on the Moore plantation and now under the supervision of Joseph Travis. The five initially established July 4 as the date of the uprising, but Turner fell ill, due perhaps to fasting, and the target day passed. Since evidence exists that Turner was merely part of a much larger, two-state revolt, it is also possible that he was waiting for bondmen across the border to rise first.

Turner's precise goals remain unclear. He may have planned to establish a maroon colony within the Dismal Swamp, or the black evangelical may have preferred to leave the next step in his plan to God's will. But once the town of Jerusalem was within the grasp of his army, he could either fortify the hamlet and wait for word of the rising to spread across the countryside or retreat into the swamp and establish a guerrilla base in the interior. According to the *Norfolk Herald*, Turner later confessed that he planned to conquer "the county of Southampton [just] as the white people did in the revolution" (Greenberg 1996, p. 48).

The rebels began around 2:00 A.M. on Monday, August 22. Turner struck the first blow, but failed to kill Joseph Travis with his hatchet. Hark finished the work, while others killed the four other whites in the house, including the Travis baby in its cradle. By noon the slave army had grown to roughly seventy armed and mounted men. They had sacked fifteen houses and killed sixty whites; Turner killed only Margaret Whitehead. As they neared Jerusalem, a column of eighteen volunteers attacked the insurgents. Turner's men waded into the group, but the tide turned when reinforcements arrived. During the fighting, six of Turner's men were wounded, and several others, too drunk to continue, abandoned the army and made their way back to the quarters. By Tuesday, only twenty rebels remained. In hopes of bolstering their numbers, Turner rode for the plantation of Dr. Simon Blunt, who owned sixty bondpeople. Under-

standing that the revolt had failed, Blunt's slaves cast their lots with the winning side. When they attacked the rebels with clubs and pitchforks, Turner's army collapsed. Among those badly wounded was Hark Travis, who survived only to be hanged on September 9.

The conventional wisdom that Turner was mentally unstable began immediately following his death on November 11, 1831. Southampton authorities refused to dignify his theology with the term "religion" and instead insisted that his desire to be free was "instigated by the wildest superstition and fanaticism." At the height of the Jim Crow era, area whites still spoke of seeing Turner's skull, which was retained as a curiosity. Most described it as abnormal. The publication of William Styron's Pulitzer Prize–winning fiction, *The Confessions of Nat Turner* (1994), only contributed to the modern characterization of the slave general as a dangerously irrational rebel. But rural Americans in the antebellum years would have had an equally difficult time understanding the rationalist tone of Styron's world. During the Jacksonian era, many Americans, white and black, devoutly believed that the end of time was near, and that Christ would soon return to rule his earthly kingdom. To that extent, Turner was well within the popular millenarian religious tradition of the period and was hardly abnormal for his time.

SEE ALSO *Gabriel (Prosser); Mysticism; Religion; Slave Resistance; Slavery; Vesey, Denmark*

BIBLIOGRAPHY

Genovese, Eugene D. 1979. *From Rebellion to Revolution: Afro-American Slave Revolts in the Making of the Modern World.* Baton Rouge: Louisiana State University Press.

Greenberg, Kenneth, ed. 1996. *The Confessions of Nat Turner and Related Documents.* Boston: Bedford Books.

Greenberg, Kenneth, ed. 2003. *Nat Turner: A Slave Rebellion in History and Memory.* New York: Oxford University Press.

Oates, Stephen B. 1975. *The Fires of Jubilee: Nat Turner's Fierce Rebellion.* New York: Harper and Row.

Douglas R. Egerton

TURNER, VICTOR
1920–1983

One of the most influential and respected anthropologists of the mid- to late twentieth century, Victor Turner made his name as an ethnographer of south-central Africa, and in doing so, became known as a theorist on social structure and process, with particular emphasis on ritual, symbol, and performance. In more than a dozen books and numerous articles he authored, co-authored, or edited, he concentrated on topics including social drama, social fields, symbolic action, symbolic multivocality (or compression), transition, liminality, *communitas*, and structure and anti-structure (a term he coined).

Born May 28, 1920, in Glasgow, Scotland, to a stage acting mother and an electronic engineer father, Victor Witter Turner attended Bournemouth Grammar School in England and did undergraduate study in modern and classic literature at University College, London (1938–1941). His studies were interrupted by war, in which, as a conscientious objector, he served as a noncombatant soldier in London. During the war, in 1943, he married Edith Lucy Brocklesby Davis Turner, with whom he would build a lifelong working partnership and parent six children between 1944 and 1963—five to reach adulthood. Drawn to anthropology from about the time of the war's end in 1945, Victor Turner studied in London under Daryll Forde and other leaders in the discipline, proceeding for his doctorate as part of the University of Manchester department coalescing around the South African-born Max Gluckman. This study took him to Africa as a Research Fellow of the Rhodes-Livingstone Institute and back to Manchester, where, upon receiving his doctorate in 1955, he stayed to write and lecture in anthropology for several years.

During this period he dropped and added some important affiliations. Having been active in the Communist Party of Great Britain in youth, he withdrew, disaffected, by his mid-thirties, or by about 1956, when the Soviet military crushed dissidence in Hungary, upsetting pacifists abroad. Between then and 1958, he and Edith joined the Roman Catholic Church in Stockport, near Manchester. In Catholicism they found ritual, and evidently faith, to fill a void left after leaving those to which they had become exposed in Africa. (Some other leading British anthropologists, notably Edward Evans-Pritchard and Godfrey Lienhardt, were similarly drawn to Catholicism after studying African cultures and their religious dimensions.) In their new faith and practice, the Turners also found solace after the death of their afflicted fourth child, Lucy, in her infancy in 1959. Identifying with Catholicism, however, cost Victor Turner the favor of some of his Manchester colleagues.

After a year's research fellowship at Stanford University (from 1961) and a return to Manchester, the Turners moved to the United States, where Victor wrote more than half of his books and Edith several more. There Victor served consecutively as professor of anthropology at Cornell (from 1964), professor of anthropology and social thought at the University of Chicago (from 1968), and professor of anthropology and religion at the University of Virginia (from 1977 until his death in 1983).

Intellectual influences on Turner were diverse. Most centrally they included his parents (especially his mother, on drama and performance); his wife Edith; Max Gluckman (on social structure and process, and on the ritual expression and resolution of conflict); and Arnold van Gennep (whose work on rites of passage became a keystone for his own on that topic and related ones). He also gained inspiration from anthropologist Clifford Geertz, sociologist Kurt Lewin, psychoanalysts Sigmund Freud and Carl Jung, philosopher Wilhelm Dilthey, and drama scholar Richard Schechner. Not least, Turner gained intellectual guidance from informants and guides in Africa, including individuals he identified as Samutamba, Sakazao, Kajima, Windson Kashinakaji, Muchona, and Ikelenge—some of whose lives and interactions he wove into his writing.

RESEARCH IN AFRICA

Turner's career was built upon his studies in Northern Rhodesia (later Zambia), which he carried out as a Research Officer of the Rhodes-Livingstone Institute toward the end of the period of British colonial rule. With Edith he conducted ethnographic research by interview, participant-observation, and other means among the Ndembu (part of the larger Lunda population—all classed as Bantu-speaking). This they did from December 1950 to February 1952 and from May 1953 to June 1954, mainly in Mukanza village, Mwinilunga District. About the Ndembu people he wrote, over many years and with much help from Edith, a chain of overlapping, theoretically innovative ethnographies that together comprised one of the most detailed and integrated records then available on any small society living in Africa south of the Sahara.

The roughly 17,000 Ndembu people practiced shifting agriculture, hunting, and gathering in forests and clearings, and some lived in mining and trading towns. Their plateau homeland lies within the so-called matrilineal belt that crosses the southern middle of Africa. Among rural Ndembu, Turner construed matriliny (tracing descent through the female line) and virilocality (wives' moving to their husbands' homes upon marriage) as together causing social stresses and strains. He found, for instance, fathers' loyalties torn between their sisters' offspring (their own known biological kin) and their wives' offspring (less surely so). As the Ndembu and others in the Lunda region had been involved in a series of regional conquests and colonizings, including by the British, he supposed Ndembu patterns of kinship and leadership might be in a period of transition.

But it was their immediate lifeways, and especially their rituals, that captured his attention. To Turner they represented social drama, but not just that. Periods of crisis, he saw, brought social and micropolitical tensions into the open, forcing rifts or reconciliations. Typically, he found, the process had four phases: breach, crisis, redressive action, and reintegration. His doctoral thesis, published in 1957 as *Schism and Continuity in an African Society*, built on Gluckman's work on ritual-political process; but to it he added elements of willful decision making and contingency, including what he came to call purposive "symbolic action."

Social ills tie into other ills, too, Ndembu people showed the Turners. Divination, healing, and exposure rituals (rituals of affliction) conducted on an ad hoc basis, contrasted with the more predictable, elaborate, and formulaic life-crisis rituals (a kind of rite of passage)—for instance, among Ndembu, the *nkang'a*, a girls' puberty ritual and celebration of matriliny. Affliction rituals address bodily malfunctions, psychological troubles, and social schisms, or indeed all these at once. Turner argued in *The Drums of Affliction* (1968) that in a society surrounded by dangers and disease—and one that is also disrupted by seemingly arbitrary, indirect colonial rule—rituals provide security, reconciliation, emotional catharsis, and also some sense of transcendence over uncertainty. Rituals have reason, he argued. They serve current needs, not just dead traditions. No ethnographer had analyzed social structure and process with closer attention to emotion.

RITUAL PROCESS AND SYMBOLIC ACTION

Following van Gennep's broadly comparative work in a more geographically limited but topically holistic way, Turner perceived in rites of passage three stages or subtypes: separation, margin (or limen—a threshold "like a tunnel" of transition), and reaggregation. In his most influential book, *The Ritual Process* (1969)—a collection of essays—he elaborated van Gennep's concept of liminality: a condition of limbo, of suspension betwixt and between, sometimes following symbolic death and preceding symbolic rebirth, and sometimes occurring in seclusion or on a journey. He contrasted social structure (a more ordinary condition of hierarchies and dividedness) with what he named anti-structure (a more amorphous condition of flux, equality, and potential growth) that he discerned in liminal conditions. Often in the latter he perceived what he called *communitas*: the temporary condition and feeling of unity, submission, and liberation existing in times and places where usual social barriers were brought down and internal differences of rank and status were erased.

As Turner saw things, symbols work in ways more complex than mere signs. In *The Forest of Symbols* (1967) and other works, he described ritual and religious symbols as "multivocal" or polysemous—that is, as being given

many meanings and interpretations. Sometimes they are phased with a single ritual—but they can refer to more than one thing simultaneously, evoking what may not be clearly known or consciously perceived. The color triad of white, red, and black, given prominence in sacred or religious rituals around the world, also, in Turner's view, carried local, culturally specific meanings, interpretable only in terms of each other and of other local values. For instance, to Ndembu people, the *mudyi* tree with its white latex, figuring in girls' puberty rites (*nkang'a*), stood for breast, milk, matriliny, feminine distinctiveness and solidarity, continuity of tribal custom, and unified opposition, among other things. But some of its meanings were activated only in relation to other objects, colors, words, or acts. Symbols crystallize polarities and unify disparate significata (by metaphorically linking different domains of experience). Individuals manipulate symbols and their meanings in rituals. Understanding of how this happens can require insiders' (both expert and lay) perspectives for "exegetic meaning," an outsider's perspective for "operational" meaning (for instance, in terms of social structure), and a broad outlook for "positional" meaning—for instance as part of a system of objects, actions, and understandings.

Turner's later works led him beyond contemporary Ndembu into world history and into broad public culture. Turner was struck by commonalities between the liminal phases of ritual in small-scale societies and religious pilgrimages, as periods of submission on the way to greater status or power. But he also noted instances of more enduring liminality in monasteries, convents, and communes. In *Dramas, Fields, and Metaphors* (1974), as in *The Ritual Process* before, he likened crisis episodes in the nascent periods of many world religious movements to the transient conditions giving rise to the rock counterculture and antiwar protests in larger movements during the 1960s and early 1970s. In such diverse movements he noted criticism of broader society and its hierarchies and inequities, as well as a potential for willful social change. But whereas in smaller, tribal societies' initiation rites a liminal phase or condition was obligatory, in larger-scale ones, participation in dramas such as concerts and theater plays—other sites of potential criticism from which change might originate—was more optional, and hence not strictly liminal yet still limin*oid*. Although he generalized rather more and made bolder leaps of association in his later works than in his earlier ones, it was the books on Ndembu and Africa that remained the focal points of his renown.

SCOPE OF INFLUENCE

Victor Turner defies easy classification. Never was he just an empiricist or a theorist, but always something of both.

As an anthropologist he drew upon a closely focused and fieldwork-intensive British functionalist approach that remained important from about the early 1920s until the 1960s, as well as upon a broadly comparative French structuralist approach influential in the 1960s and 1970s. But he devoted more attention to diachronic process, individual choice, and emotion than either functionalists or structuralists typically did. His work tied French, English, and American schools of thought to African realities, integrating more than compromising. All this moved him from the liminal status of fieldworker to the prominent posts he held in major centers of the anthropological profession. Even when involved in party politics in youth, and in church religion in adulthood, Turner sometimes tested authority and contravened orthodoxy, as if both needing hierarchic structure and wanting a way of release from it. In any case Turner remained a political idealist throughout his career, and something of a spiritualist. He hoped for a more unified and just society, arguing for recognition of the sense and dignity of tropical African lifeways, including their symbolic and religious elements, and tracking the hopeful elements of popular political and religious movements. Turner's colleagues (who usually called him Vic) and his students generally deemed him nurturing, peaceable, and conciliatory. In these ways he represented to them something like what one of his favorite symbols, the milk of the *mudyi* tree, represented to Ndembu.

Even social and cultural anthropology's great breadth of topics could scarcely contain the range of his eclectic interests, from ancient history to experimental drama to brain science (these last two traceable to his parents' seemingly disparate interests). His musings, late in life, that the complementary functions of the brain's hemispheres might relate somehow to the symbolic polarization he had long observed in ritual and aesthetic life remained hypothetical, untested, and unsung. Arguably his neuropsychological interest was ahead of his time, but he was hardly alone in his quest to conjoin, or at least reconcile, the arts and the sciences.

Turner's legacy can be taken as a whole or in parts, and construed as the product of a lifetime, a marriage, or a transcontinental collaboration. While strong waves of critical political-economic scholarship on race, class, gender, and international linkages nearly submerged his early work on micropolitics from the early 1970s on, other aspects of his work proved more buoyant in the shifting currents. He re-explained them while widening his comparisons in his later works, and in those his widow Edith continued editing and publishing after his death in 1983. In his work on ritual process, liminality, communitas, and symbols with multiple meanings, his influence extends far beyond African and Euro-American studies, and beyond anthropology into psychology, sociology, comparative religion, public health, and other fields.

SEE ALSO *African Studies; Anthropology; Anthropology, British; Communism; Community Power Studies; Ethnography; Neuroscience; Observation, Participant; Religion; Rituals; Symbols*

BIBLIOGRAPHY

PRIMARY WORKS

Turner, Victor. 1957. *Schism and Continuity in an African Society: A Study of Ndembu Village Life*. Manchester, U.K.: Manchester University Press, for the Institute for African Studies, University of Zambia. 1972.

Turner, Victor. 1967. *The Forest of Symbols: Aspects of Ndembu Ritual*. Ithaca, NY and London: Cornell University Press.

Turner, Victor. 1968. *The Drums of Affliction: A Study of Ritual Processes among the Ndembu of Zambia*. Ithaca, NY and London: Cornell University Press, 1981.

Turner, Victor. 1969. *The Ritual Process: Structure and Anti-Structure*. Chicago: Aldine.

Turner, Victor. 1974. *Dramas, Fields, and Metaphors: Symbolic Action in Human Society*. Ithaca, NY and London: Cornell University Press.

Turner, Victor. 1986. *On the Edge of the Bush: Anthropology as Experience*, ed. Edith L. B. Turner. Tucson: University of Arizona Press.

Turner, Victor, and Edith L. B. Turner. 1978. *Image and Pilgrimage in Christian Culture*. New York: Columbia University Press, 1995.

Turner, Victor, and Edith L. B. Turner. 1992. *Blazing the Trail: Way Marks in the Exploration of Symbols*. Tucson: University of Arizona Press.

SECONDARY WORKS

Deflem, Mathieu. 1991. Ritual, Anti-Structure, and Religion: A Discussion of Victor Turner's Processual Symbolic Analysis. *Journal for the Scientific Study of Religion* 30 (1): 1–25.

Engelke, Matthew. 2004. The Endless Conversation: Fieldwork, Writing, and the Marriage of Victor and Edith Turner. In *Significant Others: Interpersonal and Professional Commitments in Anthropology*, ed. Richard Handler, 6–50. Madison: University of Wisconsin Press.

Gluckman, Max. 1955. *Custom and Conflict in Africa*. Oxford: Blackwell.

Pritchett, James A. 2001. *The Lunda-Ndembu: Style, Change, and Social Transformation in South Central Africa*. Madison: University of Wisconsin Press.

Turner, Edith. 2006. *Heart of Lightness: The Life Story of an Anthropologist*. New York: Berghahn.

Van Gennep, Arnold. 1908. *The Rites of Passage*. Trans. Monika B. Vizedom and Gabrielle L. Caffe. Chicago: University of Chicago Press, 1961.

Werbner, Richard. 1984. The Manchester School in South-Central Africa. *Annual Review of Anthropology* 13: 157–185.

Parker Shipton

TUSKEGEE SYPHILIS STUDY

From 1932 to 1972, the U.S. Public Health Service (USPHS) sponsored an observational study of syphilis in black men in Macon County, Alabama. This trial has come to be known as the Tuskegee syphilis study. Six hundred black men, 399 with syphilis and 201 without, were observed for forty years to chart the effects of untreated syphilis. Perhaps the most famous example of unethical modern medical research in the United States, three features of the Tuskegee syphilis study are instructive: its racism, its perseverance, and its lack of scientific value.

RACISM

The racism of the Tuskegee syphilis study is evident in its design, its justification, and its implications. The misguided popularity of social Darwinism at the turn of the twentieth century is perhaps the most generous explanation available for the views expressed by Joseph Earle Moore (1892–1957), one of the nation's leading venereologists, and Taliaferro Clark (1867–1948), chief of the USPHS Venereal Disease Division. Previously, Moore had argued for the treatment of syphilis to (1) diminish its effects on the patient and (2) limit its possible spread. In reviewing the design for the Tuskegee syphilis study, he suggested, surprisingly, that it would be a laudable study. Perhaps to mollify any concerns about the racist nature of the design, Moore suggested that syphilis in the black male would be an almost entirely different disease than syphilis in the white male. It is unclear why he made this claim, but even if it were true, it would not diminish the effects on the patient or eliminate the spread of the disease, primarily, of course, to other blacks. In the buildup to the syphilis study, Clark offered a more overtly racist justification for the experiment. He argued that the low intelligence of blacks meant that they would not seek treatment for syphilis. Observing, and not treating, was justified because these men would not choose to be treated anyway.

Offering dubious or overtly racist justifications, the Tuskegee syphilis study condemned these black men and their sexual partners to continual exposure to syphilis and its painful effects. The study also condemned Macon County, a primarily black county, to a robust population of syphilitic men and thereby guaranteed the continued presence and spread of the disease.

PERSEVERANCE

The Tuskegee syphilis study faced a number of obstacles and setbacks that could have easily ended the study. For starters, it was difficult to entice subjects to be tested and, once tested, to return for other exams. Ironically, the researchers successfully enticed subjects to enter the trial by offering them treatment. This, of course, is a surprising turn because (1) treatment was the very thing that the investigators had predicted the black population would not seek, and (2) it was a lie—there was no plan to treat these men for syphilis.

The covert nature of the experiment precluded telling the men that getting treated elsewhere would be detrimental to the study. Accordingly, there was also a constant risk that these men would get treatment through other sources. To eliminate this possibility, the USPHS secured the agreements of local doctors, the Alabama Health Department, and the U.S. Army. Each group agreed to exclude subjects of the study from the antisyphilitic treatments they offered (or, in the case of the Army, required of) others. In the 1950s, penicillin became the standard treatment for syphilis. Though it cannot undo previous complications, penicillin does prevent the disease from producing further complications. By and large, though, subjects failed to procure adequate doses of penicillin during the course of the study.

This study was also under the purview of the Center for Disease Control and could have been cancelled at any given review point. In 1965 the study was reviewed, and the reviewers concluded that it should continue and that the "race issue," if it were brought up at a later date, could be deflected.

SCIENTIFIC VALUE

The scientific value of the Tuskegee syphilis study was limited by its aim, its execution, and its origin. At the time the study was planned, there already existed some modestly effective treatments for syphilis. This, at the very least, raises serious questions about the value of an observational study. Without any clear benefits for the subjects or the possibility of promising scientific knowledge, the aim of the trial is unclear. That no improvement on existing diagnostic or treatment options was being pursued is further confirmed by the researchers' response to the introduction of a highly effective treatment for syphilis (penicillin)—they did all they could to keep the subjects from taking it.

During the execution of the trial, control subjects, who started the study without evidence of syphilitic infection, were transferred to the study group if, at a later date, they were positively diagnosed with syphilis. As any student of science can attest, transferring subjects from the control group to the study group is sure to muddy the results.

The origins of the Tuskegee syphilis study are as significant as any other limit on its ultimate scientific value. The planning of the study depended upon a particularly racist version of social Darwinism. Without critiquing this view, one can still note that the trial continued even after this view was no longer accepted in the scientific community. Designed around a problematic and ultimately untenable perspective, the results of the study lack any scientific or medical value.

A LESSON FOR RESEARCH ETHICS

In courses on medical ethics and research ethics around the country (and perhaps even further), the Tuskegee syphilis study, alongside the Nazi experiments during World War II (1939–1945) and the Willowbrook studies of hepatitis in mentally disabled children from 1956 to 1971, is used as an example of medical research gone wrong. The difference is that the Nazi experiments and the Willowbrook studies both produced useful knowledge (the Nazi experiments produced a wide array of knowledge about the physiological workings and limits of the human body, and the Willowbrook studies correctly identified the distinction and the possibility of inoculation for hepatitis A and B), while the syphilis study produced nothing of value. The Tuskegee syphilis study reminds us that medical research can use ethically impermissible methods to achieve many things, but medical research can also fail to accomplish anything more than an expression of the worst of our social views.

SEE ALSO *Disease; Ethics in Experimentation; Ethno-epidemiological Methodology; Experiments, Human; Informed Consent; Racism*

BIBLIOGRAPHY

Brandt, Allan M. 1978. Racism and Research: The Case of the Tuskegee Syphilis Study. *Hastings Center Report* 8 (6): 21–29.

Jones, James H. 1993. *Bad Blood: The Tuskegee Syphilis Experiment*. Expanded ed. New York: Free Press.

Lombardo, Paul A., and Gregory M. Dorr. 2006. Eugenics, Medical Education, and the Public Health Service: Another Perspective on the Tuskegee Syphilis Experiment. *Bulletin of Medical History* 80: 291–316.

Abraham P. Schwab

TUTU, DESMOND

SEE *Apartheid; Mandela, Winnie; Truth and Reconciliation Commissions.*

TVERSKY, AMOS

SEE *Rationality.*

TWIN STUDIES

In the social sciences, the twin study has become an important source of information about the contribution of "nature" to human traits and dispositions. Twin studies are particularly used in clinical and psychological research aimed at attempting to find the genetic component of certain disorders, such as schizophrenia, as well as of intelligence and various personality traits. The British scientist Francis Galton (1822–1911) was the first to suggest that the study of twins might unlock the mysteries of nature. In the 1870s Galton, who sought a methodology that could conclusively show the primacy of hereditary factors in human nature, suggested that the life histories of twins could be used to weigh the relative powers of both nature and nurture. However, Galton cannot be credited with the invention of what is now known as the *classical twin study* because he merely collected life histories from twin pairs in England through the use of self-report surveys.

The first two classical twin studies, published in 1924, were conducted in Germany and the United States. In the context of understanding the pathologies of races, families, and twins, the German dermatologist Hermann W. Siemens (1891–1969) suggested comparing the correlations (r) of identical or monozygotic (MZ) twins on a given trait to correlations of fraternal or dizygotic (DZ) twins on the same trait. The American psychologist Curtis Merriman (1875–1975), who at this time still needed to convince his readership that two distinct types of twins actually existed, reported correlations of identical and fraternal twins on a number of attributes, with the former showing higher correlations than the latter. Several statistical calculations for estimating the *heritability coefficient* have been reported, the most basic being $2\,(r_{Mx} - r_{Dz})$. This formula provides an estimate of the total variance of a given trait that may be attributed to genetic variance.

Twin studies are used to estimate the heritability of a trait, although the concept of heritability is often misunderstood. It was first described in 1936 by Jay Lush (1896–1982), a professor of animal breeding. Lush distinguished between two types of heritability: *broad* (H^2) and *narrow* (h^2). Narrow heritability is of most interest to the social sciences. The heritability coefficient obtained through the classical twin study is an estimate of h^2. Narrow heritability can be understood as the proportion of the variance in a given population on a given trait that can be attributed to genetic variance.

This definition encompasses the following important points. (1) Heritability refers to variance within a population; it does not describe the relative importance of genetic factors at an individual level. (2) Heritability is an estimate of genetic variance in a specific population, at a specific point in time, under specific environmental conditions; these estimates are variable over time, location, and population. (3) Estimates of heritability describe the genetic variance within a given population; they are not valid for comparisons between different populations. (4) Environmental conditions may improve the strength of the heritability estimates. (5) Heritability does not necessarily measure the genetic contribution to a trait. Suppose, for example, a researcher is interested in using the classical twin-study method to find a heritability estimate for the condition of having two eyes. The researcher would find that, in most cases, all of their MZ and DZ participants have two eyes, thereby expressing no variance, and resulting in a heritability estimate of zero.

Calculating h^2 from classical twin studies rests on an important premise: the *equal environment assumption* (EEA). Since MZ twins share 100 percent of their genetic material, and DZ twins share on average only 50 percent, one might assume that any observed differences between the two types of twins are due to genetic variance. However, in order to calculate h^2 from classical twin studies, researchers must first assume that MZ twins and DZ twins share the same environment, thus allowing researchers to isolate the magnitude of genetic influences on a trait without environmental confounds. Critics of twin studies have long pointed out that MZ twins generally experience environmental conditions and treatment that are more similar than that experienced by DZ twins, particularly if the DZ twins are of different genders.

In response to such criticism, twin-study proponents reformulated the EEA into the *equal trait-relevant environment assumption* (trait-relevant EEA), which assumes that MZ and DZ twins have equal exposure to only those environmental influences of known relevance to the trait under study. But critics of the trait-relevant EEA argue that MZ twins spend more time together, are more likely to engage in similar activities, are similarly treated by others, and are more likely to have similar friends than DZ twins. Therefore, since MZ twins experience a more similar environment than DZ twins overall, they are also more likely to have greater exposure to environmental influences that affect a given trait than DZ twins.

In addition to the classical twin study, other methodologies are available for comparing the differences between twins. The *co-twin control method* is the only twin-study design that attempts to manipulate environmental influences. In this type of study, the genetic component is held constant, and the researcher manipulates the environment. Only MZ twins can be used in such a study. One twin becomes the control participant, while the other is given an environmental intervention. Scores on the trait of interest are measured before and after environmental manipulation. The correlation between the twin pairs before the intervention is measured against the correlation in their scores afterward. The resulting coeffi-

cient is a measure of the effects of the environment on the trait under study. This method, however, has largely been discontinued due to its history of misuse, most notably in the twin studies conducted by Nazi doctor Josef Mengele (1911–1979) at the Auschwitz concentration camp during World War II (1939–1945).

Adoption studies are often referred to as *twins-reared-apart studies*, since one or both of the twins is separated from the biological parents and placed with a relative or an adoptive or foster family. Typically, MZ twins who are reared apart (MZA) are compared to MZ twins reared together (MZT). In adoption studies, correlations of MZAs on a given trait are compared to MZTs. Occasionally, DZ twins reared apart are used as well. In most cases, researchers are interested in establishing trait similarity across a number of different measures. The underlying assumption of adoption studies is that twins have been placed randomly into homes, with minimal or no contact with each other. Although this assumption is almost never accurate, the results from twins-reared-apart studies have been very influential in the social sciences.

The most significant twin-study findings resulted from two large-scale systematic adoption studies: the Minnesota Study of Twins Reared Apart (beginning in 1983) and the Swedish Adoption/Twin Study of Aging (beginning in 1984). These studies reported medium to high correlations between MZAs and MZTs on a number of variables, including IQ, physical traits, and a long list of personality traits. In addition, the Swedish Adoption/Twin Study found moderate to high correlations for processes specifically related to aging, such as memory decline. The conclusion reached in these studies is that genetics are responsible for trait similarity, and that environmental factors have little influence. Critics of these results have pointed to researcher bias, vague or missing data, the denial of access to collected raw data, and the dubious separation of the twins involved in the studies.

Genetics research has at times generated heated ethical and political debates. For example, some authors have commented that studying the genetic components of traits will lead to a resurgence in the eugenics movement and, in particular, the misuse of heritability research on intelligence by some proponents of genetic engineering. Despite these concerns, twin studies and the field of behavioral genetics have had an undeniable impact in the sciences and culture. The progress of this field of research has helped to shift the public discourse on genetic research in favorable directions. With advances in microgenetic research and the continuing development of genomic sciences—particularly as they relate to health promotion and disease prevention—twin studies are likely to become a less-prominent technique for estimating genetic effects than they have been in the past. In any case, because of the methodological shortcomings of twin studies, the estimates that such studies provide for the heritability of attributes and processes should be analyzed carefully and critically.

SEE ALSO *Determinism, Biological; Determinism, Environmental; Eugenics; Genomics; Heredity; IQ Controversy; Nature vs. Nurture; Sibling Relationships; Social Science; Trait Inference; Trait Theory*

BIBLIOGRAPHY

Bouchard, Thomas J., Jr., David T. Lykken, Matthew McGue, et al. 1990. Sources of Human Psychological Differences: The Minnesota Study of Twins Reared Apart. *Science* 250 (4978): 223–228.

Joseph, Jay. 2004. *The Gene Illusion: Genetic Research in Psychiatry and Psychology Under the Microscope.* New York: Algora.

Merriman, Curtis. 1924. The Intellectual Resemblance of Twins. *Psychological Monographs* 33 (4): 1–58.

Plomin, Robert, and Gerald E. McClearn, eds. 1993. *Nature, Nurture, and Psychology.* Washington, DC: American Psychological Association.

Siemens, Hermann Werner. 1924. *Die Zwillingspathologie: Ihre Bedeutung, ihre Methodik, ihre bisherigen Ergebnisse.* Berlin: Springer.

Laura C. Ball
Thomas Teo

TWINS

SEE *Multiple Births.*

TWO-SECTOR MODELS

Broadly speaking, the two-sector model is an analytical framework that embodies stylized dynamic economies with two production processes. Each sector is devoted to the production of a unique good, and there are usually two factors of production that can freely move across sectors. This analytical framework abandons the rather limiting restriction of the one-sector model, in which the same aggregate good is devoted to both consumption and capital. The two-sector framework allows for the study of dynamic effects of economic policies on each sector and the possible interactions between the two sectors. These effects can also be studied in models with several sectors of production, though in these latter models the analysis may not be tractable. Two-sector models are found in many areas of economics. In international economics, the two-sector framework arises naturally in economies with tradable and non-tradable goods. In analyses of economic growth, the distinction is usually between consumption and capital. More recent research has focused on other pairings: physical and human capital, physical production and R&D, home and market goods, and cash and credit goods.

John R. Hicks (1937) introduced a two-sector model for examinations of consumption and investment, as a way to compare the predictions of newly developed Keynesian theories with what he then viewed as the "typical classical theory." In this model, there are two production processes that are represented by two production functions. Each production function contains only one factor, labor, which can be shifted at no cost from one sector to the other. There is a given relative price at which the consumption good can be exchanged for investment. This relative price is determined by the functional forms of the two production functions. The value of output or aggregate production is then the sum of the values of consumption and investment. Similarly, Santi K. Chakrabarti (1979) argues that Keynes's theories should be studied in a two-sector framework and reformulated in terms of wage units.

Hicks's model is concerned with short periods of time, because the quantity of physical capital available in the economy is taken as fixed. James E. Meade (1961) and Hirofumi Uzawa (1963) provide early analyses of the dynamics of two-sector models examining consumption and capital. Another two-sector model is considered by James Tobin (1965). In Tobin's model, one sector produces the physical good, which can be consumed or invested. The other sector is a monetary asset issued by the government to finance public spending. The creation of money affects the capital-labor ratio in the economy. This ratio varies with the rate of inflation. In this second group of models the economy is assumed to save a fixed proportion of income. A further step is taken by Duncan K. Foley and Miguel Sidrauski (1971), who postulate a nonconstant saving rate—according to them, the propensity to save may depend on the interest rate and total income. Still, this saving function is *ad hoc* in that it is not derived as the solution of a behavioral maximization process. The formulation of the optimal amount of savings was posed by Frank P. Ramsey (1928) as a one-sector planning problem. This approach was later extended to two-sector models. Thus, at each moment in time a representative individual may decide on the level of consumption and investment, and the optimal amounts of production in the two sectors.

There are three main types of production functions that have been used to describe the production processes in two-sector models. The first models used von Neumann linear production function in which output is proportional to the amount of labor and capital used. A second generation of models used Harrod-Domar production functions, where the two factors of production are perfect complements, and therefore the amounts of capital and labor needed to produce a unit of output must be in a fixed proportion. The third type of production function is the neoclassical production function, which drops the assumption of a fixed capital-labor ratio to produce a unit of output and assumes that the same amount of output can be produced with different combinations of the production factors. The neoclassical production function also exhibits constant returns to scale, which implies that if we double the amounts of production factors then output produced is also doubled. This production function has been extensively used in growth theory and many other areas of economics, and it is a centerpiece of current research. However, it has been criticized because of the difficulty of measuring the capital stock. This is known as the *Cambridge capital controversy*. If the assumption of one single good is abandoned, then aggregate capital cannot be measured independently of the interest rate. There is therefore a circularity in the determination of aggregate capital and the interest rate; moreover, the demand for capital may not be downward sloping.

The early 1990s witnessed a new surge of growth models intended to analyze why some countries are richer than others or why they may grow faster. This new generation of so-called endogenous growth models considers one sector devoted to physical capital and consumption and a second sector devoted to education or human capital accumulation. The available non-leisure time can be spent either to produce physical good or on education. The time spent on education increases the productivity of labor in the future. Therefore, the tradeoff for non-leisure time is between producing physical good today or increasing future labor productivity. The main feature of this model is that it endogenizes technological progress, and hence the growth rate of the economy. Another way to endogenize the growth rate of the economy is to include an R&D sector instead of an educational sector. There are also hybrid models of endogenous and exogenous growth. Endogenous growth may make sense when we consider the world as a whole. However, a small country may take the growth of productivity in the world economy as exogenous, and search for an optimal allocation of production across sectors to increase its total value of output.

Recent research has also analyzed models with heterogeneous agents, external effects from physical and human capital, market frictions, and government interventions. The predictions of these models are generally explored by both mathematical analysis and scientific computing. The progressive development of numerical methods has allowed researchers to investigate quantitative properties of optimal allocations and effects of economic policies. Several recent studies have been concerned with effects of fiscal variables (i.e., public expenditure, taxes on capital, labor and consumption, and subsidies to education) on economic aggregates such as output growth, consumption, capital accumulation, and worked hours. The two-sector model also appears in several recent papers on monetary theory, exchange rates, and asset pricing.

SEE ALSO *Cambridge Capital Controversy; Economic Model; Economics, Keynesian; Optimal Growth; Production Function*

BIBLIOGRAPHY

Chakrabarti, Santi K. 1979. *The Two-Sector General Theory Model*. Delhi: Macmillan.

Foley, Duncan K., and Miguel Sidrauski. 1971. *Monetary and Fiscal Policy in a Growing Economy*. New York: Macmillan.

Hicks, John R. 1937. Mr. Keynes and the "Classics": A Suggested Interpretation. *Econometrica* 5 (2): 147–159.

Meade, James E. 1961. *A Neo-Classical Theory of Economic Growth*. New York: Oxford University Press.

Ramsey, Frank P. 1928. A Mathematical Theory of Saving. *Economic Journal* 38 (152): 543–559.

Tobin, James. 1965. Money and Economic Growth. *Econometrica* 33 (4): 671–684.

Uzawa, Hirofumi. 1963. On a Two-Sector Model of Economic Growth II. *Review of Economic Studies* 30 (2): 105–118.

Fernando García-Belenguer
Manuel S. Santos

TWO-STATE SOLUTION

The two-state solution refers to the idea that the most practical solution to the Palestinian-Israeli conflict is one that divides the land historically called *Palestine* between a Jewish and a Palestinian Arab state. Part or all of the West Bank, the Gaza Strip, and East Jerusalem, which were captured by Israel in the 1967 Six-Day War, would become the Palestinian state. Israel, which has existed since 1948, could see its borders adjusted to fit a new reality. Such an arrangement could effectively end the state of war that has existed between Israel and its Arab neighbors since Israel's establishment and bring a degree of stability to a region that has suffered four major Arab-Israeli wars, two Palestinian uprisings, cross-border raids and instability, as well as the continuing cycle of violence fed by suicide bombings and targeted assassinations.

HISTORY

The first two-state solution proposal was made in 1937 by the Peel Commission, sent by the British, who then ruled the area, to investigate the motives for Arab unrest. Jewish immigration from Europe, driven by anti-Semitic violence and seemingly backed by the British, provoked Arab fears of Jewish dominance in historical Palestine, which was overwhelmingly populated by Arabs. The Peel Commission Report claimed that Arab-Jewish coexistence in a single state was impossible because of the unyielding mutual hostility and the conflicting demands for statehood made by the two communities. The report proposed the creation of a Jewish and an Arab state, but the plan was never implemented due to continued Arab rioting.

In 1947 the United Nations voted to partition Palestine into Jewish and Arab states and to internationalize Jerusalem. The Jewish state would comprise 56 percent of Palestine, although Jews only comprised 31 percent of the population, at most, and owned only 20 percent of the land designated for the Jewish state, a fact that caused the Arabs to angrily reject the plan. Zionists, however, argued that many Jews had recently escaped extermination in Europe and had no place to go, and the long history of violent anti-Semitism had demonstrated the need for a Jewish state. The Zionists, therefore, accepted the UN partition plan, if somewhat reluctantly, since they had hoped for more territory.

The 1947 UN partition plan was not fully implemented since no peacekeeping troops enforced the decision. Instead, from 1947 to 1949, war determined the outcome on the ground. In what is called in Israel the War of Independence and by Palestinians the Nakba (Disaster), Zionist forces managed to fight back Palestinian irregulars and military contingents sent by six Arab states to capture more territory than that allotted by the 1947 UN plan. The territory allotted to the Palestinians was taken over by Jordan and Egypt, so no Palestinian state was created. Over half of the Palestinian people fled their homes, creating a massive refugee crisis.

A long stalemate endured until 1967, when Israel captured the remaining parts of historical Palestine from Jordan and Egypt, as well as the Golan Heights from Syria and Sinai from Egypt in the Six-Day War. This war marked a turning point in the history of the two-state solution. Henceforth, the conflict was primarily over the recovery of lands taken in 1967, rather than attempting to reverse the effects of the 1947–1949 war. This turning point became much more apparent in the political arena during the 1980s. The Palestinian leadership gathered in Algiers, Algeria, in November 1988 to both formally recognize Israel and symbolically proclaim a Palestinian state in the West Bank and Gaza, the first time that the two-state solution was officially accepted by the Palestinians. Since this time, efforts to solve the conflict on the basis of the two-state solution have been undermined by violent extremists on both sides, as well as diplomatic quibbling over the details of an agreement.

The Oslo Accords of 1993 represented another attempt to solve the conflict based on the principle of "land for peace," the concept that underlies the two-state solution; however, Oslo was an interim agreement and did not explicitly make provisions for a Palestinian state. Nevertheless, it was widely expected that the final status arrangements that were to be concluded by 1998 would result in the establishment of a Palestinian state. Negotiations broke down before the final status agreement could be concluded. In July 2000 Israeli prime minister Ehud Barak and Palestinian president Yasser Arafat (1929–2004) attempted to reach a peace agreement at a summit held at the U.S. presidential retreat in Camp David, Maryland, with the mediation of U.S. president Bill Clinton. Although many far-reaching proposals were considered, the negotiations were ultimately unsuccessful.

LATER DEVELOPMENTS

International efforts to solve the conflict have revolved around the "Road Map," a plan sponsored by the United States, the United Nations, the European Union, and Russia. According to the plan, if the Palestinians cease violence against Israelis and reform their political system, a Palestinian state will be created with provisional borders, to be adjusted during later negotiations. For their part, the Israelis must stop settlement activity in Palestinian lands. As of 2006, the Road Map had not resulted in a peace agreement. Nevertheless, Prime Minister Ariel Sharon's unilateral "disengagement" from Gaza, in which Israel withdrew its forces from the Gaza Strip and evacuated Israeli settlements there, reinvigorated interest in peace efforts such as the Road Map.

The 1990s saw the rise of a challenge to the two-state solution in the binational (one-state) principle. There is more than one version of the one-state solution, but common to all is the vision of both Palestinians and Israelis sharing the entire land of Palestine as equal citizens, rather than dividing it between them into two states. The binational solution has risen in popularity, particularly among Palestinians and some leftist Israelis due to the increasing difficulties of implementing the two-state solution. Because the growing number of Israeli settlements on Palestinian land, including Arab East Jerusalem, as well as the "separation barrier" that Israel began constructing in 2002, may drastically reduce the territory available for a Palestinian state, proponents argue that the two-state solution is no longer viable and a shared state is preferable. Such a solution would eliminate the Jewish character of the state, since its Jewish majority would soon disappear under Palestinian demographic pressure, a problematic proposition from an Israeli standpoint. The binational solution does not have the significant international or domestic support that the two-state solution currently enjoys, but it increases in popularity with each failure of the two-state solution.

SEE ALSO *Arab-Israeli War of 1967; Palestinians*

BIBLIOGRAPHY

Bard, Mitchell G., ed. 2001. *Myths and Facts: A Guide to the Arab-Israeli Conflict.* 2nd ed. Chevy Chase, MD: American-Israeli Cooperative Enterprise.

Smith, Charles D. 2004. *Palestine and the Arab-Israeli Conflict.* 5th ed. Boston and New York: Bedford/St. Martin's.

Thomas, Baylis. 1999. *How Israel Was Won: A Concise History of the Arab-Israeli Conflict.* Lanham, MD: Lexington Books.

Sherry R. Lowrance

TYRANNY OF THE MAJORITY

Although the specter of an unwise and unrestrained majority has haunted the democratic imagination since the trial of Socrates (c. 470–399 BCE) in ancient Greece, the concept of majority tyranny dates to the modern age of democratic revolutions. The emergence of large groups of individuals from the "lower" classes of society as political actors in the English civil wars of the seventeenth century prompted philosopher John Locke (1632–1704) to articulate the first conception of majority rule in his *Two Treatises of Government* (1690). A century later, the revolutionary experiences in America in 1776 and France in 1789 cast the prospect of rule by "the people" in a new, more threatening, light. The phrase "tyranny of the majority," first coined by French historian and political theorist Alexis de Tocqueville (1805–1859) in his seminal two-volume study *Democracy in America* (1835–1840) and memorialized by John Stuart Mill (1806–1873) in his classic 1859 treatise *On Liberty*, represented to this generation the fear and deep distrust of rule by an uneducated democratic mob.

Democracies were thought vulnerable to two distinct forms of majority tyranny. The first is political or legal tyranny that operates through the formal procedures of majoritarian rule. Where all aspects of government, from public opinion and juries to the legislature, the executive, and even some judges, are a function of the majority, its power is absolute. As Tocqueville put it in the first volume of *Democracy in America* (1835), "politically speaking, the people have a right to do anything" ([1835–1840] 1990, p. 259). This political tyranny was the primary concern of American founder James Madison (1751–1836) in *The Federalist Papers* (1788), especially No. 10, in which he famously sought to quell anxieties that a majority "fac-

tion" would impose its biddings on an enlightened minority by calling attention to the natural obstacle of the diversity of opinions in a large republic.

The second type is the moral or social tyranny the majority exercises through custom and the power of public opinion. "As long as the majority is still silent," Tocqueville observed, "discussion is carried on; but as soon as its decision is irrevocably pronounced, everyone is silent." More insidious than the overt tyranny long practiced by monarchs and despots, which was physically brutal but powerless to inhibit the exercise of thought, under this new form of "democratic despotism," as Tocqueville would come to call it, "the body is left free, and the soul is enslaved" ([1835–1840] 1990, pp. 263–264).

In *On Liberty* (1859), his famous defense of individual freedom, Mill deepened Tocqueville's diagnosis of this second type of tyranny by warning against the "despotism of custom" and "collective mediocrity" endemic to egalitarian societies, while defending expressions of individuality not in harmony with the "tyranny of prevailing opinion and feeling" ([1859] 1982, pp. 136, 131, 63). Yet Mill had reviewed each volume of *Democracy in America* as they appeared in English translation two decades earlier, and he emendated Tocqueville's account in important ways. While very sympathetic on the whole, in his review of volume two Mill suggested that Tocqueville had overgeneralized by associating all the causes of this new form of majority tyranny with the rise of democracy. Drawing on insights from his own 1836 essay "Civilization," composed after reviewing Tocqueville's first volume the year before, Mill argued that the "growing insignificance of individuals in comparison with the mass" was less the result of a transition from aristocracy to democracy than of the progressive growth of wealth and industry he termed "Civilization." The ills identified by Tocqueville emanated not from an omnipotent democratic majority per se but from an emergent commercial class. "The most serious danger to the future prospects of mankind," Mill concluded, "is in the unbalanced influence of the commercial spirit" ([1840] 1962, p. 155).

As far as Tocqueville could see, there were no barriers against the absolute sovereignty of the majority. None, at least, that naturally would attend it; "precautions" needed to be actively pursued. Still, despite the omnipresence of majority power, Tocqueville believed the "secondary affairs of society" in the "townships, municipal bodies, and counties" were outside its reach. More specifically, the class of lawyers, rendered "very hostile to the revolutionary spirit and the unreflecting passions of the multitude" by the rigors of their legal training, are offered as a bulwark to the tyranny of majority opinion, along with the educating influence of jury service, which cultivated in citizens a capacity for judgment and a notion of right

([1835–1840] 1990, vol. 1, pp. 271–273). In his *Considerations on Representative Government* (1861), Mill advocated reforms like educational qualifications, proportional representation, plural voting, and an open ballot to preempt majority political tyranny.

Against tyranny of the second type, which was entirely "an affair of the mind," remedies were more complicated. Here the problem was less one of political procedure than a question of the formation of individual character. Dropping the language both of majority and tyranny, Tocqueville despaired in volume two of *Democracy in America* of not having an appropriate term to describe the new "species of oppression." In chapter 6 of book 4, he wrote powerfully of "an immense and tutelary power" that "compresses, enervates, extinguishes, and stupefies" rather than tyrannizes, reducing each nation to "nothing better than a flock of timid and industrious animals, of which the government is the shepherd." The "rare and brief exercise" of free choice offered by periodic elections would not be enough to prevent citizens "from gradually losing the faculties of thinking, feeling, and acting for themselves, and thus gradually falling below the level of humanity" ([1835–1840] 1990, pp. 318–321). Sharing this diagnosis, Mill sought, most memorably in *On Liberty*, to remedy the deficiency of "personal impulses and preferences" by fostering an environment of diverse, conflicting opinions where more robust individual characters could grow. In addition, he insisted upon support for a "contrary spirit" to check the dominant commercialism, which he found in the agricultural, leisured, and learned classes of society.

Because they perceived that in the United States the majority did not, as European aristocrats had feared, use their political sovereignty to make laws against the rich, Tocqueville and Mill saw the second kind of tyranny as the far greater threat. Other than the wealthy, they believed, all other political minorities were fluctuating; therefore, "he who is in the majority today is in the minority tomorrow," ([1835] 1962, p. 205) as Mill put it, though he did point out that the antipathies of race and religion were an exception. The racially divided society of twentieth-century America has given the first type of tyranny of majority a renewed relevance. Legal scholar Lani Guinier (1994) has written eloquently about the problem of permanent and fixed minorities. Though fair in principle, the procedures of winner-take-all majority rule ensure in practice that ethnic or racial minorities will be perpetually powerless. Guinier has outlined a more cooperative style of decision making based on the "principle of taking turns," which alleviates political tyranny by compelling majorities to confer with minority groups in the hope of generating a more inclusionary politics that is not a zero-sum game.

SEE ALSO *Civil Liberties; Freedom; Liberty; Mill, John Stuart; Pluralism; Society; Tocqueville, Alexis de*

BIBLIOGRAPHY

Guinier, Lani. 1994. *The Tyranny of the Majority: Fundamental Fairness in Representative Democracy*. New York: Free Press.

Locke, John. [1690] 1964. *Two Treatises of Government*, ed. Peter Laslett. Cambridge, U.K.: Cambridge University Press.

Madison, James, Alexander Hamilton, and John Jay. [1788] 1982. *The Federalist Papers*, ed. Garry Wills. New York: Bantam.

Mill, John Stuart. [1835] 1962. Tocqueville on Democracy in America, Vol. I. In *Essays on Politics and Culture*, ed. Gertrude Himmelfarb. Garden City, NY: Anchor.

Mill, John Stuart. [1836] 1962. Civilization. In *Essays on Politics and Culture*, ed. Gertrude Himmelfarb. Garden City, NY: Anchor.

Mill, John Stuart. [1840] 1962. Tocqueville on Democracy in America, Vol. II. In *Essays on Politics and Culture*, ed. Gertrude Himmelfarb. Garden City, NY: Anchor.

Mill, John Stuart. [1859] 1982. *On Liberty*, ed. Gertrude Himmelfarb. New York: Penguin.

Tocqueville, Alexis de. [1835–1840] 1990. *Democracy in America*. 2 vols., ed. Phillips Bradley. New York: Vintage.

Christopher Voparil

U

UBERMENSCH

SEE *Nietzsche, Friedrich.*

U-CURVES,
ENVIRONMENTAL

SEE *Environmental Kuznets Curves.*

UJAMAA,
VILLAGIZATION

SEE *Socialism, African.*

UNCERTAINTY

In neoclassical theory, markets are portrayed as stable economic systems, with changes in variables having their desired effects: There is a strong tendency for the economic system to converge toward a position of equilibrium. Economic agents are assumed to have all reliable information for decision making, and the future is known with certainty. Any "uncertainty" regarding future events or outcomes is reduced to a probabilistic distribution.

In heterodox economics, and in post-Keynesian theory in particular, however, markets and economic systems are chaotic and unpredictable (Moore 2006). The economic system is set in what is called "historical time"; that is, the past is known and cannot be changed, but the

future is unknown and cannot be predicted. This also suggests that we do not simply move from one position of equilibrium to another: The passage of time implies that during the interval when we are shifting, other variables may also be changing, such that a final position of equilibrium is difficult to predict and may never even exist. In other words, the economy is path-dependent: It is continuously moving such that there is no final position of rest.

The source of this instability is the uncertain future and how it affects motives and the decision making of all agents. Indeed, fundamental uncertainty is a central argument of post-Keynesian theory. It is defined as a situation in which agents do not know the future: It is the pure absence of knowledge. This was a central feature in Keynes's theory of effective demand (see also Knight 1921; Shackle 1967). As Keynes tells us in this memorable passage (1973, p. 113):

> We have, as a rule, only the vaguest idea of any but the most direct consequences of our acts.... By "uncertain" knowledge, let me explain, I do not mean merely to distinguish what is known for certain from what is only probable. The game of roulette is not subject, in this sense, to uncertainty.... The sense in which I am using the term is that in which the prospect of a European war is uncertain, or the price of copper and the rate of interest twenty years hence.... About these matters there is no scientific basis on which to form any calculable probability whatever. We simply do not know.

As Keynes makes clear, uncertainty is not the same as risk. In such a situation, outcomes are usually known, or at least the probability of possible outcomes known with certainty. But let us be clear: Uncertainty is not a situation in which agents cannot compute possible outcomes or probabilities or do not have sufficient information. Gathering more information does not make the future less uncertain.

Uncertainty affects decision making in many ways. For instance, if firms do not know the future or cannot predict future levels of effective demand or growth rates, how can they take a rational decision regarding investment? If central banks cannot know with certainty future levels of inflation or output, how can they correctly take decisions about interest rates? Similarly, how can banks lend to potential borrowers if they do not know whether they will be able to repay their loans, given the uncertain levels of effective demand in the future? The presence of uncertainty also leads to the emergence of power and hierarchical relationships: Faced with uncertainty, agents will try to capture the biggest share of wealth by exerting power over other individuals and social groups (Monvoisin and Rochon 2006).

Despite the pervasive nature of uncertainty, it does not lead to nihilism. Post-Keynesians have developed theories and policies that incorporate uncertainty (see Rochon 2006). Indeed, even when faced with uncertainty, agents, of course, still make decisions. Agents rely on "rules of thumb": They will rely on past decisions, assume the near future is relatively similar to the present, follow the decisions taken by others, or simply postpone taking a decision.

SEE ALSO *Economics; Economics, Post Keynesian; Expectations; Risk; Subjectivity: Analysis*

BIBLIOGRAPHY

Davidson, Paul. 1978. *Money and the Real World,* 2nd ed. New York: Wiley.

Keynes, John Maynard. 1973. *The General Theory and After: Part II Defence and Development.* Vol. 14 of *The Collected Writings of John Maynard Keynes,* ed. Donald Moggridge. London: MacMillan and St. Martins Press.

Knight, Frank. 1921. *Risk, Uncertainty and Profit.* London: The London School of Economics and Political Science.

Monvoisin, Virginie, and Louis-Philippe Rochon. 2006. Economic Power and the Real World. *International Journal of Political Economy* 35 (4): 5–28.

Moore, Basil. 2006. *Shaking the Invisible Hand: Complexity, Endogenous Money and Exogenous Interest Rates.* London: Palgrave Macmillan.

Rochon, Louis-Philippe. 2006. Endogenous Money, Central Banks and the Banking System: Basil Moore and the Supply of Money. In *Complexity, Endogenous Money and Macroeconomic Theory: Essays in Honour of Basil J. Moore,* ed. Mark Setterfield, 220–243. Cheltenham, U.K.: Edward Elgar.

Shackle, G. L. S. 1967. *The Years of High Theory: Invention and Tradition in Economic Thought, 1926–1939.* Cambridge, U.K.: Cambridge University Press.

Louis-Philippe Rochon

UNCLE TOM

Uncle Tom is associated with negative, self-denigrating attributes. An Uncle Tom is a black person who is submissive, docile, self-effacing, a race traitor, and psychologically dependent on, nonthreatening to, and always anxious to please, and gain the validation of, whites. Though Uncle Tom is associated with negative qualities, its history is much more complex. Its origin is traced to two major works. The first is the 1849 autobiography of a black slave, Josiah Henson, whose experiences and personality supposedly inspired the second, Harriet Beecher Stowe's 1852 novel *Uncle Tom's Cabin.* Henson was a slave on a plantation in Montgomery, Maryland, owned by Amos Riley. His autobiography catalogued the cruelties of slavery. He escaped to Canada in 1830, settling in Dresden, Ontario, Canada, where he started the Dawn Settlement, which provided opportunities for fugitives to learn skills. He also assisted in establishing the British American Institute, an industrial school for the education of fugitives.

Written in angry response to the Fugitive Slave Act of 1850, which authorized the capture and re-enslavement of fugitives, Stowe's novel was a scathing indictment of slavery. The central character, Tom, is spiritually and morally superior to his white owners. Tom's life revealed, in horrific details, the atrocities of slavery. He was repeatedly whipped for refusing his owner's order to whip fellow slaves. He was sold several times, his last owner beating him to death for refusing to divulge the whereabouts of two fugitive slaves. Even as he lay dying, Tom prayed for, and forgave, his owner.

Stowe came from a white New England abolitionist family and lived in Cincinnati, Ohio, in the 1830s, across the bridge from slaveholding Kentucky. She taught at a school for former slave children and witnessed the atrocities of slavery. Returning to New England in 1850, she decided to write a book detailing her thoughts about slavery. Her depiction of Tom and of other black characters in the book as people who confronted degradation with submission became the source of the concept of Uncle Tom. Tom's humility, Christian character, and forgiving nature led to the modern association of his name with attributes of compromise and self-denigration.

The paradox of Uncle Tom, however, is that neither of the two characters with which the concept is associated embodied such negative qualities. Stowe's Tom resisted, albeit in a passive way. He disobeyed orders he deemed inhumane and refused to betray fellow slaves even at the risk of punishment and death. He once risked his life to save a drowning little white girl. Henson's life reflected similar heroism and nobility. Riley was so incompetent that Henson was left in charge of the operations of the farms. Threatened with seizure by creditors, Riley entrusted Henson with transferring his slaves to Kentucky for safekeeping. For Henson, personal freedom was not an end. He worked hard to help others not only become free but also acquire the skills to make freedom meaningful. These qualities of courage and nobility conflict with the use of Uncle Tom as an epithet for blacks who betrayed their own race or who are deemed submissive and deferential to whites. During the civil rights movement, Malcolm X frequently referred to Martin Luther King Jr. and other civil rights leaders as Uncle Toms. Black officials who oppose affirmative action or race-based policies are tagged Uncle Toms. In 2002 the *American Directory of Certified Uncle Toms* was published. It ranked over fifty black leaders according to a five-star Uncle Tom rating. Uncle Tom thus became a means of cultural policing to determine who is authentically black.

There are two modern versions of Uncle Tom. The first is the docile, loyal, contented person who accommodates lowly status. The second is the ambitious black person who seems willing to be subordinate to whites in order to achieve a more favorable status. Both characters overtly identify with whites either because of fear or opportunism. It is important, however, to distinguish between Uncle Tom the character and Uncle Tom the concept. Neither the historical (Henson), nor literary (Tom) Uncle Tom was a betrayer or compromiser. Their lives demonstrated courage, rebellion, and nobility. They both resisted. Henson escaped and created the institutions that helped other fugitives adjust to life in freedom. Tom disobeyed orders he deemed inhumane and sacrificed his life rather than betray fellow slaves. Critics have nevertheless mistaken their peaceful strategies and nobility for meekness and compromise. Hence, while the concept Uncle Tom might be negative, depicting a coward and compromiser, the characters from whom it originated did not fit into such negative constructions. Furthermore, the "Tom" epithet is not necessarily a negation of the person's blackness. It disparages behavioral and idiosyncratic dispositions that contradict perceived collective interests of blacks.

BIBLIOGRAPHY

Kauremszky, Ilona. 2005. Uncle Tom Was a Real Person; His Cabin Is in Canada. *Christian Science Monitor*, January 26: 11. http://www.csmonitor.com/2005/0126/p11s02-trgn.html.

Laurence, Richard. 2002. *American Directory of Certified Uncle Toms.* New York: CBIA Publishing.

Stowe, Harriet Beecher. 1994. *Uncle Tom's Cabin: Authoritative Text, Backgrounds and Contexts, Criticism,* ed. Elizabeth Ammons. New York: Norton.

Stuteville, George. 2005. "Uncle Tom" Today: From Slavery to Obscurity? *National Geographic*, February 17. http://news.nationalgeographic.com/news/2005/02/0217_05 0218_ngm_uncletom.html.

Tunde Adeleke

UNCONSCIOUS, THE

SEE *Psychoanalytic Theory; Psychotherapy.*

UNCONSCIOUSNESS

SEE *Psychoanalytic Theory; Psychotherapy.*

UNDERACHIEVERS

In general underachievement is defined as a discrepancy between potential (what a student ought to be able to do) and actual performance (what a student is demonstrating). However, there is little consensus about how best to define underachievement, particularly among gifted students. In some instances an underachieving gifted student is defined broadly, in others cases it is defined as limited to specific criteria. One definition of the underachieving gifted student, for example, is when a gap exists between a student's achievement test scores or academic grades and intelligence test scores. Such a broad delineation would result in a comparatively large number of students identified as gifted. In contrast, a more specific definition of the underachieving gifted student is one who has a Stanford-Binet (IQ test) score of 132 or above and a percentile ranking of 75 or below on the California Test of Basic Skill. This definition limits the underachieving gifted student to only a handful of students.

Professionals whose responsibility it is to identify underachieving gifted students (UGS) for intervention must keep in mind that whatever definition is decided upon will determine the instruments and types of selection procedures used. The definitions, instruments, and selection procedures will ultimately determine who receives special education programs and who does not.

IDENTIFICATION PROCESS

Typical methods of identifying UGSs rely on standardized measures (for example, IQ tests, achievement tests), teacher perceptions (for example, checklists, grades, assessment of motivation, assessment of daily work, comparisons with other students), and self-perceptions (for example, personal information and insight, comparisons with peers). The most common method of identifying UGSs in the early twenty-first century involve examining the difference between achievement test scores and intelligence test scores. According to the psychologist Anne Anastasi (1976), the statistical nature of achievement and intelligence tests "assures" a percentage of underachievers. Anastasi claims that categorizing students by comparing achievement scores with intelligence scores is a misuse of the test results, since no two tests correlate perfectly (Dowdall and Colangelo 1982). The psychometrician Robert L. Thorndike (1963) further discounted the use of intelligence tests for identifying gifted students, warning that IQ scores should not be used to assume a particular level of performance (Dowdall and Colangelo 1982).

Another method of identifying UGSs is teacher observations. A teacher's judgments and grades have the advantage of being based upon direct experience with the student. The disadvantage of these measures is that they are often biased. The discrepancy between potential and classroom achievement as measured by teacher assessments often reflects nonachievement factors, such as neatness, good behavior, motivation, and teacher attitudes, rather than pure academic ability. Research has consistently found that teachers tend to rate students who are most similar to themselves in social, racial, and economic background as more desirable and successful compared to students who are dissimilar to the teachers. Another problem with the identification process is an indiscriminate use of the tests to identify the "prototypical gifted student." This practice is based on the assumption that gifted students are a homogeneous group, all of whom can profit equally from a common curriculum.

Some scholars point out that a more beneficial approach may be to use the information gleaned from achievement and intelligence tests to diagnostically determine the strengths and needs of the individual student, regardless of how the student is classified. With individualized information, curricular modules and activities could be developed that address the particular strengths and weaknesses of each student.

GIFTED UNDERACHIEVERS' TRAITS

Overall the literature consistently reports positive qualities of interpersonal effectiveness, independence, and self-assurance for academically gifted students and the reverse for UGSs. UGSs appear to have more in common with underachieving average students than with gifted students. Both UGSs and underachieving average students tend to be male and exhibit more social immaturity, more antisocial behavior, and lower self-esteem than gifted students. In addition UGSs and underachieving average students are also more likely to come from unstable, lower income, single-parented homes. The only consistent difference between UGSs and underachieving average students is the high scores of UGSs on standardized IQ and achievement tests.

UNDERACHIEVEMENT CAUSES

A variety of factors contribute to the underachievement of high ability students, including emotional and social problems, lack of an appropriate curriculum, and learning and self-regulation difficulties. The attitudes of teachers and counselors toward a child may also be responsible for the gap occurring between student potential and performance.

Other researchers contend that the underachieving gifted problems are deeply rooted in family interaction patterns or attitudes toward education. Educational psychologists have suggested that underachievement for gifted students is a choice, a form of social self-defense because of strong cultural or peer identification. This phenomenon of "deliberate underachievement" has been found to be particularly evident among gifted adolescent females, as a response to perceived sex-role expectations, and among African American gifted students involved in the process of adolescent impression management, as an attempt to control the perceptions other people form of them.

Other scholars contend that for UGSs it is not an issue involving attitudes so much as one of skills (more precisely, the lack of such) or creativity. Given the wide variety of factors contributing to underachievement in high ability students, it is understandable the students thus affected may demonstrate unique learning needs.

INTERVENTION APPROACHES

Published research on intervention with UGSs can be grouped into two conventional areas. The first group focuses on intensive counseling to address problems of low self-image and feelings of inferiority, while the second group focuses on manipulating the classroom environment.

An overview of the counseling intervention with UGSs indicates that such procedures have not been shown to be consistent or effective. A 1979 study that did report limited success concluded that intensive counseling can be effective only when: (a) counselors are specifically selected and trained, (b) a small number of students are treated, (c) objectives are clearly delineated, and (d) methodology is carefully developed.

Research on the second type of intervention—focusing on altering or modifying the classroom environment—also reported limited success. Critics of these interventions point out that generally such interventions have not begun until high school, although the most crucial time to intervene is during the elementary years. Critics also state that while classroom sizes and ability grouping have been manipulated, teaching strategies, expectations, and curriculum content have not been altered.

Programs that have taken an individualized holistic approach have reported promising results. One such intervention, Joseph Renzulli's Enrichment Triad Model, is an active process in which students choose to learn. In order to facilitate students becoming creative producers, this model capitalizes on the student's potential by using an interest-based curriculum, bringing together the student's ability, interest, learning styles, and a supportive student-teacher relationship.

Given that professionals cannot agree on a definition or the antecedents of underachievement, the adoption of one common intervention is unrealistic. Effective interventions are those that are designed to address the uniqueness of the UGS student in a holistic fashion.

SEE ALSO *Anxiety; Depression, Psychological; Neuroticism; Overachievers; Self-Presentation; Stereotype Threat*

BIBLIOGRAPHY

Baum, Susan M., Joseph S. Renzulli, and Thomas Hébert. 1995. The Prism Metaphor: A New Paradigm for Reversing Underachievement. National Research Center on the Gifted and Talented. Report CRS-95310. ERIC no. ED402711.

Dowdall, Cynthia, and Nicholas Colangelo. 1982. Understanding Gifted Students: Review and Implications. *Gifted Child Quarterly* 26 (4): 179–184.

Ford, Donna Y., and Antoinette Thomas. 1997. Underachievement among Gifted Minority Students: Problems and Promises. Council for Exceptional Children. http://www.ericdigests.org/1998-1/gifted.htm.

Frasier, Mary M., Scott L. Hunsaker, Jongyeun Lee, et al. *Educators' Perceptions of Barriers to the Identification of Gifted Children from Economically Disadvantaged and Limited English Proficient Backgrounds*. National Research Center on the Gifted and Talented. Report RM95216. ERIC no. ED402711.

Carolyn B. Murray

UNDERCLASS

The term *underclass* was used by Charles Murray in 1984 to describe a permanent or persistent poverty population whose lower-income status passes from one generation to the next because of intrinsically dysfunctional behaviors. This social class is described by Ken Auletta (1982) as a group, largely concentrated in urban areas, that is cut off from society, marginalized, and lacks the skills or the behaviors needed in order to find jobs in the modern economy. William Julius Wilson (1985) defines the underclass as those who lack training or skills, are out of the labor force or long-term unemployed, and who engage in deviant behavior. Wilson also incorporates in his definition family instability and welfare dependency. Erol Ricketts and Isabel Sawhill (1988) produce an empirically operational definition of an underclass area where a census tract has rates of high school dropouts, male labor-force nonattachment, welfare recipiency, and female-family headship one standard deviation above the mean for the country as a whole. A person who lives in such a census tract and who engages in socially deviant behavior is considered by Ricketts and Sawhill to be in the underclass.

These definitions of the underclass share many of the features of earlier conceptualizations of populations at the lowest rungs of the social and economic ladder. Karl Marx described the *lumpenproletariat* as "the lowest sediment of the relative surplus population," an unproductive and regressive portion of the population unable or unwilling to work (Darity et al. 1994, p. 16). The underclass, in this sense, is "the continuously deprived fraction of the working class … comprised of the persons most frequently relegated to the 'disposable reserve army,' often found without work even during times of accelerated capitalist accumulation" (Darity 1982, p. 135).

Ken Auletta, referring to a 1980 report by the Manpower Development Research Corporation, writes that:

> These people have been excluded from the regular labor market and find, at most, sporadic employment. Though relatively few in number, they have become a considerable burden to themselves and the public—as long-term recipients of welfare, and as the source of much violent crime and drug addition…. There is nothing new about such a social class. There have always been pirates, beggars, vagrants, paupers, illiterates, street criminals and helplessly, sometimes hopelessly, damaged individuals. (Auletta 1982, p. 25)

A key element of the underclass definition is the superfluous nature of the population and its status as permanently unemployed, underemployed, or unemployable (Myrdal 1963, 1970). The underclass, in this sense, is the stagnant portion of the relative surplus population (Darity 1982, p. 135). Darity writes, furthermore, that in the managerial society the underclass is more comprehensively viewed as superfluous by the dominant social class than is the case under capitalism. The surplus population serves a function under capitalism; it serves no function in managerial society (Darity, 1990, pp. 248–249).

CAUSES

Two broad sets of causal factors have been offered to explain the existence, size, and growth of the underclass. One set of factors involves behavioral and attitudinal deficits. These include decisions to bear children out of wedlock; participation in illegitimate activities—often destructive, violent activities; and inability or unwillingness to work or obtain the necessary skills in order to become productive members of the labor force. Another set of causal factors offered to explain the underclass are termed *structural factors*. These include residential segregation that produces concentrations of poverty and pathology, deindustrialization, and the shift of jobs from the inner city to the suburbs (Wilson 1987; Darity et al. 1994). Both the structural and behavioral explanations predict pathological behaviors.

For Murray (1984), the responsibility for criminal involvement, children born out of wedlock, joblessness, and dependency on welfare rests upon the shoulders of members of the underclass themselves. The underclass reproduces its behavior from one generation to the next, just as it perpetually reproduces itself, through excessive unwanted births to teenage mothers and unemployed or unemployable fathers.

For Wilson (1987), the underlying causes are more broadly found in the larger context of structural transformations in the economy. Joblessness in the inner city arises in part from the flight of low-skilled and semiskilled jobs from their historic location in central cities. Social isolation and concentration of poverty are but consequences of these structural transformations. Other structural factors suggested in the literature include sentencing reforms during the 1980s and the rising use of imprisonment as a vehicle for reducing labor surpluses (Darity et al. 1994; Myers and Sabol 1987).

SIZE OF THE UNDERCLASS

One view is that the size of the underclass in the United States is relatively small. The underclass population, in this view, ranged from less than one million in 1970 to somewhere between 2.5 and 3.5 million in 1990. By 2000, using the Ricketts-Sawhill empirically driven definition of underclass, Paul Jargowsky and Sawhill estimate that only about 2.2 million persons lived in underclass areas. They write:

> The underclass areas are disproportionately minority, and concentrated primarily in large urban areas, especially in the mid-Atlantic and

Midwest areas of the country.... The underclass grew dramatically in the 1970s, edged up further in the 1980s and declined sharply in the 1990s (although not to its 1970 level.) The immediate reasons for the decline were reductions in the number of census tracts with high levels of dropping out of high school and high levels of public assistance receipt. (Jargowsky and Sawhill 2006)

The sharp drop in the relatively small numbers of underclass persons is attributed to welfare reforms during the 1990s that resulted in significant declines in welfare rolls and to inner-city education reforms that helped to fuel graduation rates.

Charles Murray (1999) disputes these conclusions. He feels that the underclass grew during the 1990s. Murray tracks data on persons under correctional supervision, labor-force dropouts, and illegitimacy ratios. There were 1.8 million persons under correctional supervision in 1980 in the United States. By 1997 this number had risen to 5.7 million. In 1985, 5.2 percent of black adults were under correctional supervision. By the end of 1996, there were 9 percent of black adults under correctional supervision. Murray points to statistics showing an increase in the share of black males who are labor-force dropouts and the share of all black births that are illegitimate to underscore his claim that the underclass continued to grow throughout the 1990s. For example, he reports that in 1982, 58 percent of black children were born out of wedlock. In 1997, 69 percent of black children were born out of wedlock. Murray's earlier concept of underclass as arising from poverty and the perverse incentives associated with welfare is later replaced with the concept of intergenerationally and genetically determined transmittal of poverty status. (Herrnstein and Murray, 1994). Murray's change in conceptualization of underclass helps him reconcile how the black underclass could grow even during a period of welfare retrenchment.

RACE AND THE UNDERCLASS

Inextricably intertwined with the definition of the underclass is race. Using 1980 U.S. census data, Ricketts and Sawhill (1988) calculate that 59 percent of persons in underclass areas were black. Ricketts and Mincy (1990) compute that this share dropped from 77 percent in 1970. Murray's definition of underclass points to the disproportionate share of blacks who meet the criteria selected for inclusion.

Even though pains are often taken to clarify that not all underclass areas are black or even poor, it is generally understood that underclass areas are disproportionately poor and black. Indeed, the term *black underclass* is often used synonymously with the term *underclass*. This is so because blacks are disproportionately found among each of the key definitional components of the underclass: concentrations of poverty and labor-force withdrawal; high rates of criminality; and high rates of female-family headship.

Race is highly correlated with place. Low social capital and deviant behavior can be thought of as a manifestation of place or a concentration of pathology in particular neighborhoods. Location in particular neighborhoods, though, could be traced to redlining, mortgage discrimination, and other housing barriers that can be seen as manifestations of race (Wilson 1987; Stoll 2005; Massey and Denton 1993; Jargowsky 1997).

HOW THE UNDERCLASS HAS SHAPED PUBLIC POLICY

Much of the debate about the causes and consequences of the growth of the underclass surrounds the impacts of culture, or shared values, attitudes, and beliefs on the perpetuation of poverty and dependency on welfare. This debate is reminiscent of the culture-of-poverty debates, wherein the behaviors and attitudes of the poor themselves cause their poverty. This notion that the intergenerational transmission of poverty rests in the culture of poverty populations has direct implications for what to do about poverty.

Writing on behalf of the Committee for Research on the Underclass of the Social Science Research Council, Michael Katz summarizes how the term *underclass* evolved into a metaphor for discussions about inner-city crises and the attendant policy responses. The destructive violence, the threats to law-abiding citizens, and the substantial social costs associated with teenage pregnancies and dependency on welfare invoke the image of a group, mostly blacks, permanently stuck in concentrations of poverty in inner-city areas. The eruption of riots, the dependency on drugs, the distance from conventional morals, and the apparent inability of this population to lift itself out of poverty evoke concerns about policy responses and the social transformations that accompany these changes. According to Katz, "the underclass is a metaphor of social transformation. It asserts the emergence of a new social grouping within America's inner cities" (1993, p. 22). The term *underclass* itself evokes images of the undeserving poor, those whose behaviors contribute to their own distress. And, thus, the underclass designation signals a significant turn toward policies designed to eliminate the incentives to reproduce undesirable behaviors.

Policy prescriptions that presume that underlying behaviors respond to incentives and disincentives—the core of the microeconomic-behavioral model of the underclass—suggest that welfare restrictions and increased deterrence through law enforcement and imprisonment will reduce the size of the underclass population. Policy prescriptions that presume that the underlying problems rest in structural transformation require greater reliance on the matching of jobs and residences, reductions in housing segregation, and the breakup of concentrations of low-income and public housing in affected areas. But, both the aforementioned behavioral and structural explanations assume that the underclass is not functionally necessary. An alternative view is that the underclass is permanent in part because of its centrality in maintaining the managerial society (Darity et al. 1994).

SEE ALSO *Benign Neglect; Class; Crime and Criminology; Culture of Poverty; Determinism; Determinism, Genetic; Deterrence; Ghetto; Lumpenproletariat; Marx, Karl; Microeconomics; Pathology, Social; Prison Industry; Prisons; Public Policy; Race; Surplus; Surplus Population; Unemployable; Unemployment; Welfare; Wilson, William Julius*

BIBLIOGRAPHY

Auletta, Ken. 1982. *The Underclass*. New York: Random House. Rev. and updated ed., 1999, Woodstock, NY: Overlook.

Darity, William A., Jr. 1982. Economists, the Minimum Wage, and the Underclass: 133-156. In *Race, Poverty, and the Urban Underclass*, ed. Clement Cottingham. Lexington, MA: Lexington Books.

Darity, William A., Jr. 1990. Racial Inequality in the Managerial Age: An Alternative Vision to the NRC Report. *The American Economic Review* 80(5): 247–251.

Darity, William A., Jr., and Samuel Myers, with Emmett Carson and William Sabol. 1994. *The Black Underclass: Critical Essays on Race and Unwantedness*. New York: Garland.

Herrnstein, R. J., and Charles Murray. 1994. *The Bell Curve*. New York: The Free Press.

Jargowsky, Paul A. 1997. *Poverty and Place: Ghettos, Barrios, and the American City*. New York: Russell Sage Foundation.

Jargowsky, Paul A., and Isabel Sawhill. 2006. The Decline of the Underclass. CCF Brief no. 36. Washington, DC: Brookings Institution. http://www.brookings.edu/es/research/projects/wrb/publications/pb/pb36.htm.

Katz, Michael B., ed. 1993. *The "Underclass" Debate: Views from History*. Princeton, NJ: Princeton University Press.

Massey, Douglas S., and Nancy A. Denton. 1993. *American Apartheid: Segregation and the Making of the Underclass*. Cambridge, MA: Harvard University Press.

Murray, Charles. 1984. *Losing Ground: American Social Policy, 1950–1980*. New York: Basic Books.

Murray, Charles. 1999. *The Underclass Revisited*. Washington, DC: AEI Press.

Myrdal, Gunnar. 1963. *Challenge to Affluence*. New York: Pantheon.

Myrdal, Gunnar. 1970. *The Challenge of World Poverty: A World Anti-Poverty Program in Outline*. New York: Vintage.

Myers, Samuel, and William Sabol. 1987. Business Cycles and Racial Disparities in Punishment. *Contemporary Economic Policy* 5: 46–58.

Ricketts, Erol, and Ronald Mincy. 1990. Growth of the Underclass: 1970–1980. *Journal of Human Resources* 25: 137–145.

Ricketts, Erol, and Isabel Sawhill. 1988. Defining and Measuring the Underclass. *Journal of Policy Analysis and Management* 7: 316–325.

Stoll, Michael. 2005. Geographic Skills Mismatch, Job Search, and Race. *Urban Studies* 42 (4): 695–717.

Wilson, William Julius. 1985. Cycles of Deprivation and the Underclass Debate. *Social Science Review* 59: 541–559.

Wilson, William Julius. 1987. *The Truly Disadvantaged.* Chicago: University of Chicago Press.

Samuel L. Myers Jr.

UNDERCONSUMPTION

Underconsumption is a macroeconomic phenomenon of deficient aggregate demand resulting from the failure of consumption expenditure to keep pace with rising output. It might equally be described as oversaving. Most (but not all) theorists of underconsumption explain it by reference to a parallel failure of real wages to keep pace with rising labor productivity, so that the wage share in national income tends to decline. Because non-wage-earners save much of their income—unlike wage-earners, who spend all (or nearly all) of their incomes on consumer goods— the ratio of consumption expenditure to total income also declines.

This "low-wage" version of underconsumption theory can be traced back to J. C. L. Simonde de Sismondi and Robert Owen in the 1820s; the slightly earlier theories of Robert Malthus and the Earl of Lauderdale are rather different. It is generally agreed that low-wage underconsumption formed part of Karl Marx's complex and poorly articulated theory of capitalist crisis. The doctrine certainly reappeared in the writings of his followers, from Karl Kautsky and Rosa Luxemburg before 1914 through to the theory of "monopoly capital" developed by Paul Baran and Paul Sweezy in the 1960s. A slightly different version of underconsumption theory was energetically propagated in the 1920s by the American writers William T. Foster and Waddill Catchings.

In the Marxist tradition underconsumption is seen as a fundamental contradiction of capitalism and a root cause of the Great Depression. It can be overcome only when capitalism itself is transcended through socialist revolution. Many Marxists, however, remain skeptical about underconsumption and emphasize other causes of economic crises, especially capital-intensive technological change that reduces the rate of profit but also (in certain circumstances) militant labor pressure on the profit share.

There is a reformist variant of underconsumption theory, associated with J. A. Hobson, in which it is argued that underconsumption can be avoided through comprehensive measures of social reform. Beginning in the 1890s, New Liberals and social democrats advocated redistribution of income through the tax system, labor market regulation to raise real wages, and the development of a comprehensive welfare state. Hobson and his coauthor Alfred Mummery (1889) had already argued that underconsumption was the principal cause of trade depression, which seriously damaged the interests of the workers, and supported a range of measures to increase real wages (including emigration, trade unionism, and a statutory eight-hour day). Subsequently Hobson argued that the consequences of failure to reform the system might be severe. He believed that capitalist imperialism was very largely a response to underconsumption: Colonial territories offered market opportunities that were unavailable at home because of the restricted purchasing power of the mass of the population. Hobson's ideas had a profound influence on Lenin and other Marxian theorists of imperialism.

Underconsumption has always been rejected by orthodox macroeconomists on the grounds that the economy has powerful adjustment mechanisms that remove any tendency toward chronic demand deficiency. Say's Law was originally formulated, by Jean-Baptiste Say himself and by James Mill, largely in response to early advocates of underconsumption, and the law formed the analytical core of pre-Keynesian macroeconomics. Any tendency toward underconsumption, or oversaving, would in this view be eliminated through the inevitable reduction in the rate of interest that would occur; this would induce people to save less and thus to consume more. In equilibrium, output and employment are constrained by supply considerations and not by aggregate demand.

John Maynard Keynes denied that such a self-correcting mechanism could be relied upon because saving depends on income rather than on the interest rate and total output is normally constrained by demand. Not surprisingly, therefore, Keynes had considerable sympathy with underconsumptionist ideas, though he emphasized deficient investment rather than excessive saving and was therefore inclined to believe that increased investment expenditure could (at least in principle) generate enough effective demand to maintain full employment. The Keynesian growth theorists Roy Harrod and Evsey Domar denied this possibility because the capital stock cannot profitably be continually increased relative to consumption expenditure. This criticism is implied by the accelerator principle, which links investment to the growth of consumption; thus, the accelerator is closely linked to underconsumptionist ideas.

Another important heterodox economist with links to underconsumption theory was Michał Kalecki, who famously identified "the tragedy of investment." Investment adds both to aggregate demand and to productive capacity, but in a capitalist economy, where there is no planning or coordination of investment decisions, it is only by accident that investment spending will be in exactly the correct proportion to consumption expenditure. Kalecki's version of underconsumption has affinities with both the Marxist and the Keynesian schools.

The revival of pre-Keynesian macroeconomics since 1970, however, has restored belief in Say's Law and pushed underconsumptionist ideas back into the theoretical undergrowth. Today mainstream macroeconomists regard underconsumption as a faintly ludicrous radical heresy.

SEE ALSO *Consumption; Overproduction; Stagnation*

BIBLIOGRAPHY

Baran, Paul A., and Paul M. Sweezy. 1966. *Monopoly Capital: An Essay on the American Economic and Social Order.* New York: Monthly Review Press.

Bleaney, Michael F. 1976. *Under-Consumption Theories: A History and Critical Analysis.* New York: International Publishers.

Mummery, A. F., and J. A. Hobson. 1889. *The Physiology of Industry: Being an Exposure of Certain Fallacies in Existing Theories in Economics.* London: J. Murray.

Schneider, Michael P. 1996. *J. A. Hobson.* Basingstoke, U.K.: Macmillan.

J. E. King

UNDERDEVELOPMENT

The theory of "underdevelopment" became popular during the 1970s within development studies, an important subfield within the social sciences. It addresses the question of why economic growth has been elusive in postcolonial countries. Is it primarily because of *internal* factors, such as local culture, religion, lack of skills, lack of institutions, corruption, and patrimonial relations? Or is it primarily the result of *external* factors, particularly the power relations within a world capitalist system dominated by a core of industrialized countries exploiting a periphery of poor countries in a form of "neocolonialism"?

Before the 1970s it was common within the modernization school of thought, which arose out of Western Keynesian and neoclassical economic thinking, to regard colonial and postcolonial countries as being "*un*developed." In this perspective, internal factors were emphasized, and these countries were encouraged to follow particular stages of economic growth in order to catch up and "develop" in a manner similar to that of the Western industrialized countries. The more postcolonial countries integrated within the world capitalist system, it was argued, the more they would reap the benefits through increased aid, trade, and investment.

In contrast, a school of thought emerged which argued that the colonized world was actively *under*developed by its contact with imperial powers. According to the underdevelopment perspective, which has close links to the dependency and world-systems perspectives, the economies of colonized countries were distorted to meet the needs of emerging capitalism in Western Europe. This was particularly so during the phase of industrialization, when capitalist firms in competition with each other needed cheap labor, raw materials, and new markets for their products. The colonial and postcolonial regions became satellites (or peripheries) of the industrialized countries that formed the metropoles (or centers) of a world system of capitalist expansion, through relations of economic dependency.

The theory of underdevelopment arose within Marxism but as a departure from the classical Marxist view that capitalism, while it exploits and destroys, also develops. As Karl Marx (1818–1883) said in *Capital* (Vol. 1): "The country that is more developed industrially only shows, to the less developed, the image of its own future" (1954, p. 19). The Russian-born American economist Paul A. Baran (1910–1964) wrote in 1957 that, on the contrary, postcolonial societies were blocked from development by the peculiar manner in which they came into contact with industrialized countries. For Baran, the origins of underdevelopment can be traced back to the plunder and enforced trade of the seventeenth and eighteenth centuries. This was a time, he argued, when Western European colonization of the rest of the world began on behalf of merchant capitalists, to be later followed by producer capitalists. Imperialism, as famously stated by V. I. Lenin (1870–1924), is the "highest stage of capitalism," as it grows out of the inevitable tendency toward the creation of monopolies. Competition among capitalist firms eventually results in the more successful firms destroying or swallowing the less successful.

Baran argued, however, that monopoly capitalism faced a crisis of overproduction due to the lack of effective demand in the capitalists' home countries. The economic surplus generated had to be productively absorbed by the capitalism system if a crisis was to be avoided. Parts of this surplus were absorbed through military expansion, state expenditure (for example, building a welfare state to prevent the working class at home from revolting), and technological innovation. However, this was not sufficient to absorb the massive surplus and create the conditions for the continued accumulation of capital, which is the motor force of capitalism (i.e., accumulation for the sake of accumulation). Capitalism had to conquer new markets and create new investment opportunities, argued Baran, and this could only be achieved through expansion into new territories in the form of colonialism (political and economic dominance) and neocolonialism (economic dominance over politically "independent" countries).

According to Baran, the class interests that came to dominate within these countries, foreign and local, benefited from this state of dependency in various ways. These beneficiaries included domestic landowners, merchants and monopoly capitalists, and the foreign capitalists—none of whom had any real interest in the development of a domestic market that would generate a developmental dynamic within the satellites. Foreign capital in particular was mainly interested in primary resource extraction, where profits are repatriated to the metropoles. This resulted in the development of modern enclaves to serve a very small domestic market composed of expatriates and domestic elites, who aspire to mimic the consumption patterns of the metropolis. The rest of the periphery was composed of an expanding "reserve army of cheap labor" living in poverty in the countryside and in urban slums.

The theory of cumulative causation developed by the Swedish economist and sociologist Gunnar Myrdal (1898–1987) also arose during the 1950s and covered similar ground but from a non-Marxist perspective. Myrdal (1957) laid emphasis on the cumulative development path of industrial countries that had made breakthroughs in science, technology, and industrial production. These countries had large domestic markets with a high demand for goods and services, thus attracting capital into their economies. Poor countries, on the other hand, fell into a downward spiral of stagnation and impoverishment due to, among other things, low savings, small domestic markets, and the low skills and poor health of the work force. Low tax revenue meant that the governments of poor countries could not invest in social and economic infrastructure, except in small export enclaves that benefit foreign capital. These conditions lead to rising intranational as well as international inequality, thus perpetuating the underdevelopment of the periphery.

While Baran favored Soviet style state planning to overcome underdevelopment, Myrdal saw the solution in state-led industrialization and market regulation, where infant industries are protected from foreign competition.

These ideas were popularized and refined by a number of neo-Marxist thinkers, such as Andre Gunder Frank (1967), Samir Amin (1970), and Walter Rodney (1971), who argued that the development of Europe rested on the underdevelopment of Africa. This perspective found a ready audience among revolutionary nationalist leaders in the postcolonial world who were not necessarily Marxists. To mitigate the negative impact of neocolonialism and dependency, many countries used the postcolonial state as an active agent of development, with policies ranging from import substitution to a relative delinking from the world capitalist system in the pursuit of self-reliant development.

These strategies during the 1960s and 1970s did achieve some success in growing a domestic market, achieving respectable growth rates, and improving health and education services in many African, Latin American, and Asian countries. However, these achievements were also accompanied by an overreliance on increasingly authoritarian, corrupt, and unaccountable states, and massive borrowing that resulted in an unsustainable debt crisis beginning in the 1980s. This, and the declining fortunes of Soviet state socialism, helped pave the way for the ideology of "free market" neoliberalism to penetrate the periphery.

This period saw the resurgence of modernization theory, albeit couched in the language of "globalization." During the 1990s, development studies seemed to be in crisis, as globalization theory, whether from the Right or the Left, posited that a "global village" of open economies was being created. National boundaries, it was argued, were being eroded; the state was being replaced by "the market" (i.e., private firms) as a key agent of development, and there was no longer an industrialized core in the "first world" and an impoverished periphery in a "third world." Instead, global inequality was becoming "deterritorialized" as investment and jobs flowed increasingly to the periphery, leading to increased economic growth and employment, while the industrialized countries experienced greater unemployment and inequality. The only exception is much of sub-Saharan Africa, which remained marginalized from the process of global integration.

The 1997 East Asian economic crisis and subsequent crises elsewhere in the world exposed the vulnerability of the newly industrializing economies, forcing a retreat from neoliberal policies, and the reemergence of the state as a critical actor in development. Writers such as Samir Amin insist that the core-periphery model remains valid. Only two countries, namely South Korea and Taiwan, have risen out of their periphery status, largely because of the privileges they received as U.S. allies during the cold war. For the rest, including fast-developing China and India, rapid industrial growth has followed the pattern of enclave development. These countries are still reservoirs of cheap labor and seas of extreme poverty. On the other hand, the industrialized "triad" of the United States and Canada, the European Union, and Japan continues to dominate the world economy at the core, with the United States performing the hegemonic role with the help of the World Trade Organization, the International Monetary Fund, and the World Bank. These institutions impose rules on underdeveloped countries that undermine efforts at domestic development, in the interests of transnational corporations that remain firmly based in industrialized countries.

There is now increased recognition that both internal and external factors are responsible for the inability of poor countries to rise out of their conditions of underdevelopment. Poor countries are challenged to democratize internally, develop local capacities, and spread the benefits of economic growth to all citizens. At the same time, they need to act in concert with other countries and civil society organizations to reap the benefits of globalization. Some emphasize regulating capitalism at a global level through transformed global institutions that are reoriented toward the needs of poor countries. Others urge a focus on strategic delinking, especially from the financial markets dominated by the financial institutions of the triad, in pursuit of a "polycentric negotiated globalization" that is governed by democracy, disarmament, and a new system of international law that respects national and regional autonomies.

SEE ALSO *Caribbean, The; Colonialism; Dependency; Development Economics; Globalization, Social and Economic Aspects of; Imperialism; Neocolonialism; North-South Models; Poverty; South, The (USA)*

BIBLIOGRAPHY

Amin, Samir. [1970] 1974. *Accumulation on a World Scale: A Critique of the Theory of Underdevelopment.* Trans. Brian Pearce. New York: Monthly Review Press.

Baran, Paul. 1957. *The Political Economy of Growth.* New York: Monthly Review Press.

Frank, Andre Gunder. 1967. *Capitalism and Underdevelopment in Latin America: Historical Studies of Chile and Brazil.* New York: Monthly Review Press.

Marx, Karl. 1954. *Capital.* Vol. 1. London: Lawrence & Wishart. (Orig. pub. 1887).

Myrdal, Gunnar. 1957. *Economic Theory and Under-developed Regions.* London: Duckworth.

Rodney, Walter. 1972. *How Europe Underdeveloped Africa.* London: Bogle-L'Ouverture. Rev. ed., 1981. Washington, DC: Howard University Press.

Devan Pillay

UNDEREATING

Undereating is a relative term. It refers to a negative energy imbalance that results when energy intake is less than energy that is expended. This negative energy imbalance can occur as a consequence of social conditions (e.g., poverty), medical conditions (e.g., cystic fibrosis), or psychological conditions (e.g., depression). It can also occur during any developmental period, such as in *failure-to-thrive* infants and in the elderly, who can suffer fat loss as part of normal aging processes. In these instances, undereating is considered to be involuntary because it is attributable to impecuniousness, nutrient malabsorption, or loss of appetite. Undereating, however, can also be intentional, as in self-starvation. Most notably, intentional undereating is pathognomonic in the eating disorder *anorexia nervosa*.

Anorexia nervosa is characterized by refusal to maintain at least 85 percent of normal body weight for one's age, height, and gender; fear of weight gain; disturbance in body perception; and self-worth based on body weight and shape. These core symptoms cause the individual to relentlessly pursue caloric restriction through behaviors such as dieting, fasting, excessive exercise, and vomiting. Anorexia can also include purging after binge-eating. It is often comorbid with other psychopathology such as depression and substance abuse. Other adverse medical consequences of undereating include emaciation, anemia, tooth decay, hair loss, bone loss, heart and kidney failure, and even death.

As of 2007, the lifetime prevalence rate of anorexia nervosa is estimated to be approximately 1 percent. It is most prevalent in adolescents and young adults who are white, female, and of mid-to-upper socioeconomic status. It is, however, increasingly being diagnosed at younger ages, in males, across U.S. ethnic minorities, and at all levels of socioeconomic status. The research, though limited, suggests that self-starvation is more prevalent in Western countries but that it is on the rise in non-Western countries.

The apparent general increase in prevalence of anorexia across groups and cultures likely reflects the strong influence of regnant sociocultural values. With globalization, the Western media exert a powerful and pervasive influence, conveying explicit and implicit messages that uphold the thin body as the ideal to which many females feel they should aspire. Although sociocultural explanations of anorexia are compelling, studies show that a predisposition to anorexia may be genetically based. Psychological factors such as early trauma (e.g., abuse), a major negative life event (e.g., parental divorce), or a critical transition (e.g., college) may then precipitate disease onset in individuals who are susceptible. It has been suggested that, although maladaptive, the ability to tightly control one's caloric intake may serve to restore an individual's sense of power over his or her life.

Anorexia is viewed as both a medical and psychological condition and is notoriously intractable to treatment, with relapse common. A multidisciplinary approach is recommended. When patients are very underweight, hospital or day-program treatment is required, consisting of psychological counseling, nutritional education, and a supervised diet of from 2,000 to 4,000 calories per day. Cognitive-behavioral therapy and family-systems therapy appear to be the most widely used psychotherapeutic approaches. Research is needed, however, to identify the approach that is most effective. Psychopharmacotherapy to treat anorexia has so far met with little success, but research is ongoing in this regard.

SEE ALSO *Body Image; Disease; Food; Malnutrition; Obesity; Overeating; Self-Esteem*

BIBLIOGRAPHY

American Psychiatric Association. 2000. *Diagnostic and Statistical Manual of Mental Disorders* (DSM-IV-TR). 4th ed., text rev. Washington, DC: Author.

Hudson, James I., Eva Hiripi, Harrison G. Pope Jr., and Ronald C. Kessler. 2007. The Prevalence and Correlates of Eating Disorders in the National Comorbidity Survey Replication. *Biological Psychiatry* 61: 348–358.

Makino, Maria, Koji Tsuboi, and Lorraine Dennerstein. 2004. Prevalence of Eating Disorders: A Comparison of Western and Non-Western Countries. *Medscape General Medicine* 6 (3): 49.

Joan K. Orrell-Valente

UNDEREMPLOYMENT

The labor force concept of *underemployment* can be defined as a comprehensive way to identify and measure the underutilization of labor resources. In this sense, it goes beyond plain unemployment—being jobless while looking for work—to further include different forms of inadequate employment, such as being discouraged or subemployed, or employed involuntarily in part-time and low-income jobs with marginal or unstable labor market attachments.

The globalization of the world economy and the corresponding industrial restructuring of developed countries—away from manufacturing and towards services—have had a considerable impact on the composition and characteristics of the labor market. While labor force participation has increased, it has also resulted in an important rise in employment hardship with the emer-

gence, among a considerable portion of the labor force, of unstable, poorly paid, and often involuntarily part-time jobs. This new situation has led labor-market researchers to point out the need for a new term (beyond *unemployment*) to better capture all meaningful forms of employment hardship.

Interestingly, the origin of this researchers' concern can be traced back to the 1930s in the work of British economist Joan Robinson (1903–1983). At that time, she wisely argued that in a society where no regular system of unemployment benefits exists and where poor households are unlikely to be supported by social institutions (i.e., a social welfare system), individuals who are out of work and who cannot find a job fitting their skills will naturally employ their time as usefully as they possibly can.

> Thus, except under peculiar conditions, a decline in effective labor demand which reduces the amount of employment offered in the general run of industries will not lead to unemployment in the sense of complete idleness, but this surplus of labor will rather get employment into a number of occupations still open to them … [where] their productivity is less than in the occupations that they have left. (Robinson 1936, p. 226)

Robinson referred to this phenomenon as *disguised unemployment*. Other researchers later drew attention to the existence of such disguised unemployment in certain economic sectors (e.g., agriculture), particularly in the economies of developing countries (Moore 1953; Lewis 1954) where the presence of an unlimited supply of labor makes its marginal productivity negligible, zero, or even negative.

Sponsored by the International Labor Organization, labor statisticians have gathered on numerous occasions to discuss and develop concrete measures of underemployment. In this ongoing discussion, American sociologist Philip Hauser (1909–1994) made an important contribution by developing what became widely known as the *labor utilization framework* (LUF) to capture a more accurate picture of employment, acknowledging both the official forms of unemployment, as well as different categories of economically inadequate employment based on hours (involuntarily part-time work) and wages (poverty-level pay) (Hauser 1974). The LUF has evolved through time and now has both a substantial literature and a more elaborated set of subcategories (Clogg 1979; Sullivan 1978) to better capture the employment situation and to adapt more efficiently to datasets other than the U.S. *Current Population Survey* (CPS, compiled monthly by the U.S. Census Bureau for the Bureau of Labor Statistics), where all the original empirical work came from.

Nevertheless, the operational definitions of states of underemployment typically used by researchers can be summarized as follows, from the most to the least severe:

Subunemployed is a proxy for "discouraged workers" and includes individuals who are not currently working and who did not look for work during the previous four weeks because they felt no jobs were available.

Unemployed follows the official definition and includes those not working but who (1) have looked for work during the previous four weeks, or (2) are currently on layoff.

Underemployed by low hours (or involuntary part-time employment) parallels the official definition of those who are working "part-time for economic reasons" and includes those who are working less than thirty-five hours per week because they cannot find full-time employment.

Underemployed by low income (or *working poor*) includes those whose labor market earnings during the previous year, adjusted for weeks and hours worked, were less than 125 percent of the official poverty threshold for an individual living alone.

Underemployed by occupational mismatch (or overeducated) includes those whose educational level (measured as years of schooling) is greater than one standard deviation above the mean education for workers with the same occupation.

All other workers are defined as *adequately employed*, while those who are not working and do not want to be working are defined as *not in the labor force*.

Of course, no standardized measure of any important concept will be perfect, and underemployment is not without flaws. Some of these deficiencies are related to problems with the operationalization itself (e.g., using poverty thresholds that ignore cost-of-living differences), while others have to do with other related forms of employment hardship, such as job security, which are not included in the definition. Notwithstanding, these criticisms are minor since underemployment provides a useful way to analyze trends over time, as well as inequality between groups in the prevalence of employment hardship.

In all years, these trends are unequivocally countercyclical, a phenomenon reflected in the fact that underemployment rose and then fell over the 1990s owing to the recession early in the decade and subsequent economic expansion. Inequality between groups in the risk of underemployment is often striking and should be an issue of great policy concern. Women, minorities, the young, and those with low educational attainment are all espe-cially vulnerable to underemployment. Moreover, these vulnerabilities are often particularly acute among residents of rural areas and central cities. As a result, economists continue research (both theoretical and empirical) on the topic to further contribute to the understanding of these trends in employment hardship over time and between groups.

SEE ALSO *Unemployable; Unemployment*

BIBLIOGRAPHY

Clogg, Clifford C. 1979. *Measuring Underemployment: Demographic Indicators for the United States.* New York: Academic Press.

Hauser, Philip M. 1974. The Measurement of Labor Utilization. *The Malayan Economic Review* 19: 1–17.

Lewis, W. Arthur. 1954. Economic Development with Unlimited Supplies of Labor. *Manchester School of Economic and Social Studies* 22: 139–191.

Moore, Wilbert E. 1953. The Exportability of the "Labor Force" Concept. *American Sociological Review* 18 (1): 68–72.

Robinson, Joan. 1936. Disguised Unemployment. *Economic Journal* 46 (182): 225–237.

Sullivan, Teresa A. 1978. *Marginal Workers, Marginal Jobs: The Underutilization of American Workers.* Austin: University of Texas Press.

Esperanza Vera-Toscano

UNDEREMPLOYMENT RATE

Underemployment generally refers to one of several situations that result in employment in an economically inadequate position. In this context the underemployment rate refers to the fraction of those employed who are "underemployed." Some scholars utilize an alternative version of this definition by considering some nonemployed individuals as underemployed. Regardless of the definition of underemployment, the concept evolved from inadequacies in the unemployment rate in capturing work-related hardships (Jensen and Slack 2003, p. 25).

Ignoring for now the definition of underemployment that includes nonemployed individuals, the underemployed work while incurring some form of employment-related hardship. This includes individuals working in occupations with an insufficient number of hours, individuals working in positions with insufficient pay, individuals working in occupations below their levels of educational attainment, and individuals working in positions involving some combination of the above scenarios. Because they have employment they are not considered to be unemployed according to the standard definition of unemployment.

First, underemployment refers to a situation where employees work fewer hours than they desire. Such an event may occur because of real-world labor-market rigidities such as a fixed-hour workweek. For example, workers desiring a thirty-hour workweek at a job that requires forty hours for full-time employees or twenty hours for part-time employees will be considered underemployed if they accept the part-time position. A similar case occurs when workers accept part-time employment without choice, often referred to as "involuntary part-time." This is the most widely cited reference to the underemployment rate, perhaps because it is easier to measure than the other types of underemployment. John Ham (1982) estimates that in the United States in 1970 over a quarter of the labor force was either unemployed or underemployed according to the hours worked measurement of underemployment.

Alternatively, workers may accept positions that offer the desired workweek but with low pay. In this case workers will be considered underemployed when their expected wages—based on personal (i.e., educational attainment, experience) and job-specific characteristics—are higher than their actual wages. This type of underemployment may occur within the context of either full-time or part-time employment. In a sense, workers accept such employment rather than become unemployed. Measuring the underemployment rate by this definition is difficult due to the need for an empirical estimation of one's expected wage.

Some scholars consider all working-poor individuals to be underemployed, thereby eliminating the need for wage estimates. Such scholars would likely categorize a full-time employee earning the minimum wage as underemployed. Other researchers note that this need not be the case if the earnings of low-wage individuals are consistent with their level of human capital. Among those who consider all working poor as underemployed, a debate exists as to what the threshold level of income should be. Frequently a percentage of the official poverty threshold (either 100% or 125%) or a fraction of the median wage (from one-third to two-thirds) is utilized. Critics contend that such levels are arbitrarily determined.

Moreover, some workers are in occupations with an adequate workweek and pay but are not using all of their human capital, most notably by not fully using their educational qualifications. For example, individuals with a bachelor's degree working in positions requiring only a high-school diploma are considered underemployed when compared to degree holders with higher-level jobs. As noted by Stephen Rubb (2005), the same individuals are considered "overeducated" when compared to others in their own occupational category. Measuring the underemployment rate by this definition is difficult due to the need for an estimation of the required level of education (and other human capital characteristics) for various occupations. Implicit in such a calculation of an "occupational mismatch" is the idea that all jobs within an occupational category are homogenous and that educational quality is uniform. Many scholars find such assumptions objectionable. Due to such complexities, researchers tend to focus on underemployment from other categories. A similar concept is "disguised unemployment" introduced by Joan Robinson (1937, p. 84) "where workers' productivity is less than in the occupation they have left," presumably because the worker's new occupation does not make full use of their human capital.

It should be noted that many scholars (e.g., Jensen and Slack 2003) use underemployment to capture *all* forms of employment hardship, including those associated with nonemployment. As such, their definition of underemployment includes both discouraged and unemployed workers in addition to those employed in inadequate situations. For such scholars, the underemployment rate is the fraction of the labor force that is "underemployed" with a slight adjustment to include "discouraged workers" as part of the labor force. Discouraged workers are individuals who are neither employed nor looking for work, and typically they are not counted as part of the labor force. Using such a definition, Jensen and Slack find that in the United States in 2000 the overall underemployment rate was 13.5 percent, and that it was notably higher during the global recession in the early 1990s. In their model the most common type of underemployment is the working poor. This is followed by unemployment, insufficient hours, and discouraged workers as the second, third, and least common types of underemployment. They do not estimate the level of occupational mismatches in their calculation of the underemployment rate. Researchers who include nonemployed workers in their estimates of the underemployment rate tend to also automatically include working-poor individuals in their calculation. In general, their work tends to focus on issues involving the equitable distribution of income. Other researchers disagree with the inclusion of discouraged and unemployed workers in the estimates of the underemployment rate, contending that underemployment implicitly infers employment.

SEE ALSO *Natural Rate of Unemployment; Unemployment*

BIBLIOGRAPHY

Ham, John C. 1982. Estimation of a Labour Supply Model with Censoring Due to Unemployment and Underemployment. *Review of Economic Studies* 49 (3): 335–354.

Jensen, Leif, and Tim Slack. 2003. Underemployment in America: Measurement and Evidence. *American Journal of Community Psychology* 32 (1/2): 21–31.

Robinson, Joan. 1937. Disguised Unemployment. In *Essays in the Theory of Employment*. London: Macmillan.

Rubb, Stephen. 2005. Overeducation, Undereducation, and the Theory of Career Mobility: A Comment and a Note on Underemployment. *Applied Economic Letters* 12: 115–118.

Stephen Rubb

UNDERGROUND ECONOMY

SEE *Informal Economy.*

UNDERREPRESENTATION

Underrepresentation occurs when members of discernible groups are not consistently present in representative bodies and among measures of well-being in numbers roughly proportionate to their numbers within the population. These underrepresented groups are discernable based on a shared history and an ongoing legacy of disenfranchisement, usually marked by gender, race, ethnicity, class, sexuality, and religion. Underrepresentation in basic social and economic measures, such as adequate housing, income, education, and physical health, generally coincides with a history of disregard, deprivation, and even violence. Access to these basic social goods is necessary to pursue a dignified life and is a prerequisite for the enjoyment of the political liberties of democratic citizenship. When access to these goods coincides with markers of social and political marginalization or exclusion, the exercise of political rights and obligations and the opportunity to achieve a good life, however defined, is severely compromised.

The dimensions of underrepresentation in any society coincide with the access to and exercise of power. Historically, those with power use their influence to define full membership in the polity to include themselves and similar subjects while excluding those they designate as different. This "difference" is not without judgment but is defined as inferior to the privileged groups and as corrosive to the community. In some instances, groups want to assert their social difference but seek to change how a community values it. This is often the case with ethnicity, where an ethnic group wishes to maintain its cultural way of life but demands fair recognition and accommodation of its existence from the state and other members of the polity. However, in other instances members of disadvan-

taged social groups regard their "group" status as illegitimate altogether and strive to dismantle its very meaning and any associated punishments. The goal in this regard is elimination of their status as a "group." Some consider gender to be an appropriate example of this perspective.

Fair political representation in democratic societies is essential because it is a key democratic activity geared toward generating legitimacy, setting agendas, and establishing the practices and policies under which people live. When identifiable groups of citizens are not present in representative bodies in adequate numbers over time, their interests and concerns tend to be absent, and thus a state of underrepresentation exists. A situation in which women and racial, ethnic, religious, and sexual minorities are overrepresented on the lowest ends of most measures of social and political well-being, while remaining underrepresented on the higher measures, raises the specter of *structural inequality*. Structural inequality occurs when measures of a good life and indicators of deprivation are visibly and measurably stratified along these lines.

One of the most potent ways to address structural inequality is through political participation and representative government. Yet women and minorities are politically underrepresented across the globe—both in terms of their presence in representative bodies and the interests those bodies address. Some scholars argue that to create more inclusive representative bodies, democratic societies should adopt a semiproportional electoral system that utilizes cumulative voting (Guinier 1994). Others advocate proportional representation through the single transferable vote (as in Ireland and Malta), party-list quotas for women and minorities (Phillips 1995), reserved seats in legislatures for marginalized groups (as in India and Tanzania), and public funding for minorities to organize and select their own slates of candidates (Christiano 1996).

Is it fair to consider an individual's race, class, gender, or sexuality when deciding on the allocation of scarce goods or opportunities? Is it fair not to? If it is fair, then how should social difference be considered, and what weight should it be accorded? Who decides? If societies maintain that the distribution of goods should be solely based on merit, then how should they determine what is "meritorious" achievement; how should they address what is sure to be an increase in the existing inequality between, for example, whites and nonwhites, men and women, and the economically privileged and the struggling; and who should make these determinations?

If social difference cannot be ignored without serious deleterious consequences but according it too much weight, or too little, is associated with even more negative outcomes than not considering it at all, then the stakes are very high for arriving at any conclusion. At the same time, answering these complex questions regarding difference and disagreement is a matter of democratic judgment. That judgment cannot be truly democratic or just, however, unless all relevant members of the polity are fully included at all stages of deliberation and decision making.

Experiments with policies aimed at achieving a greater presence of members of historically marginalized groups in representative bodies show promise in India on local councils and in Scandinavian countries on national legislatures. In the United States, experiments at local and state levels, as well as within the national party structures, have produced policies, expanded agendas, and altered the very terms of the debate, which likely would have otherwise remained unchanged. How to go about increasing the presence of marginalized groups, however, is a highly complex endeavor fraught with potential, but very real, dangers.

Hannah Pitkin writes, "We show a government to be representative not by demonstrating its control over its subjects but just the reverse, by demonstrating that its subjects have control over what it does" (1967, p. 232). But this statement begs the questions of *who* or *what* is to be represented, and under *what conditions* representation can be understood as democratic, or even just? All political representation is about the representation of some group; to some degree, whatever proxy is used for the interests (be it geography, party, identity, or some other indicator), one runs the risk of subverting intragroup disagreement and even cementing differences. It is not enough to argue that a particular approach to representation holds the capacity to freeze differences because, to varying degrees, they all do. Any system in which a part stands for the (often heterogeneous) whole is assured to get it wrong on occasion. The challenge is for the part to represent the whole as faithfully and justly as can be made possible through fair and inclusive procedures and processes.

SEE ALSO *Electoral Systems; Gerrymandering; Representation; Tyranny of the Majority*

BIBLIOGRAPHY

APSA Task Force on Inequality and American Democracy. 2004. *American Democracy in an Age of Rising Inequality. Perspectives on Politics* 2 (4): 651–666.

Christiano, Thomas. 1996. *The Rule of the Many: Fundamental Issues in Democratic Theory.* Boulder, CO: Westview.

Guinier, Lani. 1994. *The Tyranny of the Majority: Fundamental Fairness in Representative Democracy.* New York: Free Press.

Phillips, Anne. 1995. *The Politics of Presence: Issues in Democracy and Group Representation.* New York: Oxford University Press.

Pitkin, Hanna Fenichel. 1967. *The Concept of Representation.* Berkeley: University of California Press.

Angela D. Ledford

UNEMPLOYABLE

A person is said to be unemployable if he or she is unsuitable for any job. More precisely, someone is unemployable if there exists an absolute mismatch between his or her personal characteristics or attributes (including, for example, education, skills, experience, or physical fitness) and those currently demanded by employers. Unemployable persons are either chronically unemployed or else do not participate in the labor force at all.

Three important features of the contemporary view of unemployability can be associated with the definition given above. First, as is obvious from the definition, being unemployable is identified with the inability to secure any employment. Second, it is commonplace to focus on acquired characteristics (that are amenable to change) rather than innate characteristics (that are taken as given) when accounting for an individual's status as unemployable. Third, following from the previous point, unemployability is viewed as a state that can and should be remedied by means of appropriate policy interventions. Unemployability has not always been viewed in this way, however. Historically, it has been associated with the ability to gain *some* employment, but for material reward that is insufficient to support an "adequate" standard of living. Moreover, there has, in the past, been a greater emphasis on innate rather than acquired characteristics when explaining the state of unemployable persons. This, in turn, encouraged a view of the unemployable as morally repugnant persons who needed to be dissociated from the "mainstream" labor force. These sentiments are evident to some degree even in the writings of radical or reform-minded critics of capitalism, such as Karl Marx, William Beveridge, and Beatrice and Sydney Webb.

Because unemployable persons are defined as lacking the attributes desired by employers—and in particular, the sort of human capital firms require—the inevitable tendency is to focus on individual choice and behavior as the ultimate cause of unemployability. However, it is possible that events beyond an individual's control induce personal characteristics that make the individual unemployable. For example, the family environment and/or schooling that contribute to early childhood development may be responsible for making some individuals unemployable. Alternatively, chronic unemployment may cause skills to atrophy or even come to be regarded by employers as, in and of itself, a negative credential. This can result in an unemployed person eventually becoming unemployable. In this case, rather than unemployability resulting in chronic unemployment, it is chronic unemployment that causes a person to become unemployable—a process anticipated by Beveridge that is now associated with modern views of hysteresis in the labor market. Finally, the mismatch between individual attributes and employers' requirements characteristic of unemployability may not arise because of any literal deficiency of individual attributes at all. Consider, for example, the effects of the geography of deindustrialization coupled with the relative geographical immobility of labor. It is possible for the skill set in which a geographically concentrated group of workers has invested to be rendered redundant by the decline or relocation of a regionally concentrated industry. This leaves workers with the wrong skills rather than no skills—too few for some remaining jobs, but too many for others—and thus suffering the absolute mismatch between individual attributes and employers' requirements that renders them unsuitable for any job (at least within a regional context).

Whatever its causes, unemployability can be associated with a variety of social problems. Most obviously, since most individuals depend on the labor market for most of their income, unemployable persons may suffer severe material hardship. Since work also lends meaning and definition to the lives of most people, isolation from work caused by unemployability can lead to dissociative, antisocial behaviors such as violence and crime. It is not surprising, then, that numerous policy measures have been proposed to address the problem of unemployability. Some of these—such as welfare (or workfare) programs and earnings subsidies—are essentially permanent income maintenance schemes designed to *offset* the condition of unemployability. Other policies, however, seek to *remedy* the condition itself. For example, the strong association between unemployability and human capital deficiencies means that training schemes are a prominent feature of policy proposals to reduce the number of unemployable persons. If, however, former workers are made unemployable by geographically concentrated structural change as described earlier, broader regional development policies that focus not only on changing individual attributes (through retraining, for example) but also on the level and variety of economic activity in a region may have a role to play in redressing the problem of unemployability.

SEE ALSO *Underemployment; Unemployment*

BIBLIOGRAPHY

Gray, D. 1996. Are Displaced Manufacturing Workers Unemployable? An Analysis of Sectorally Based Adjustment Costs in France. *Canadian Journal of Economics* 29 (Special Issue: Part 1): S84–S88.

Komine, A. 2004. The Making of Beveridge's *Unemployment* (1909): Three Concepts Blended. *European Journal of the History of Economic Thought* 11 (2): 255–280.

LeBlanc, G. 2004. Optimal Income Maintenance and the "Unemployable." *Journal of Public Economic Theory* 6 (3): 509–535.

Scitovsky, T. 1996. My Own Criticism of *The Joyless Economy*. *Critical Review* 10 (4): 595–605.

Mark Setterfield

UNEMPLOYED, HARD CORE

SEE *Hard-core Unemployed.*

UNEMPLOYMENT

A person is unemployed when he or she is willing and able to work given the prevailing terms and conditions of employment but does not currently have a job. Depending on its causes, unemployment can pose severe problems for both individuals and societies alike. For example, since most households derive most of their income from participation in the paid labor market, unemployment can be a source of considerable material hardship and distress. Furthermore, unemployment can challenge the sense of identity and self-worth that individuals derive from their jobs. Finally, unemployment represents, in the aggregate, a waste of productive resources: society as a whole would be better off if the unemployed were engaged in productive activity.

MEASUREMENT OF AND VARIATIONS IN UNEMPLOYMENT

Because of its importance, economists have long had an interest in the accurate measurement of unemployment. But unemployment statistics are subject to several measurement problems. For example, official statistics usually measure unemployment by requiring that a person's willingness to work be demonstrated by evidence that they are actively searching for a job. Some economists, however, identify *discouraged workers*—those who are willing and able to work, but have ceased to search for work because they do not believe that jobs are available—as being unemployed. Despite this, discouraged workers are not included in official measures of unemployment because they are not actively looking for work. They are instead categorized (along with full-time students, retirees, and others) as not participating in the labor force.

Another measurement problem is associated with *disguised unemployment*. This was originally identified as a condition afflicting developing countries, wherein individuals might engage in very low-productivity work in the agricultural sector for want of a job that would more fully utilize their productive potential. But some economists now identify involuntary part-time or temporary work—that is, part-time or temporary work performed by those who would prefer a full-time, year-round job—as a form of disguised unemployment. Once again, disguised unemployment is not reflected in official measures of unemployment. This is because all those who have jobs are automatically categorized as employed, regardless of whether or not the jobs they perform fully utilize their productive potentials or satisfy their preferences with respect to the number of hours of paid work they perform.

Whatever their potential flaws, official unemployment statistics reveal a number of important stylized facts about unemployment. First, it has long been established that unemployment varies over the course of the business cycle, rising when the economy enters a recession and falling during a boom. Second, a more recently established stylized fact is that unemployment varies over time between lengthy "episodes" of higher or lower unemployment. For example, average annual unemployment rates in the major industrialized economies were much lower during the 1950–1973 period than they were during the preceding interwar period (1918–1939) or than they have been since 1973. Third, unemployment rates differ across countries at any particular point in time and during the episodes of high or low unemployment referred to above. Prior to 1973, for instance, it was commonly observed that unemployment in the United States was higher than that in Europe. Since the 1980s, however, the United States has tended to experience unemployment below the average rates witnessed in Europe. Finally, unemployment rates differ by age, sex, and race. Unemployment is typically highest among the young (ages sixteen to twenty-five) and members of racial or ethnic minorities. Older workers and women also frequently experience more unemployment than prime-age males, although since the 1970s, unemployment rates for women have become comparable to those for men in some of the major industrialized economies.

EXPLANATIONS FOR UNEMPLOYMENT

What factors cause unemployment and so explain the stylized facts described above? According to some economists, the labor market operates like any commodity market, with variations in the level of wages serving to "clear" the market—that is, equate the supply of and demand for labor. But even when the labor market clears in this fashion, unemployment will exist. This *frictional unemployment* is often associated with the normal workings of the labor market. It arises because even if the number of jobs available is exactly sufficient for the number of job seekers at currently prevailing wages, the process of matching employers with employees takes time. It is therefore pos-

sible for some workers to be without jobs at any point in time. The amount of frictional unemployment is affected by a variety of factors, including the choices of workers themselves. For example, a currently unemployed person might decline to accept an offer of employment in anticipation of a superior subsequent offer. Unemployment that is the product of individual choice in this fashion is termed *voluntary*.

Other economists, however, claim that labor market clearing is a special case, sometimes called *full employment* (although not all economists who use the term *full employment* would agree that it is best conceptualized in terms of labor market clearing). These economists claim that observed unemployment is largely involuntary. According to the conventional definition, *involuntary unemployment* occurs when the labor market does not clear but is instead characterized by a surfeit of job seekers relative to the number of jobs available at currently prevailing wages. In this situation of "too many workers chasing too few jobs," the unemployed are without work not by virtue of individual choice but as a result of a constraint that exists on their ability to sell labor. Some economists locate the source of this constraint on the supply side of the economy. For example, there may be impediments to the workings of the price mechanism that prevent wages from varying in the manner required to equate the demand for and supply of labor. Or alternatively, the stock of capital accumulated by firms may be insufficient to warrant the employment of all those willing to work, given the number of workers that need to be combined with a single unit of capital to produce a unit of output.

Other economists, however, locate the source of involuntary unemployment on the demand side of the economy. They argue that the demand for labor (and hence the quantity of employment offered by firms) is derived from the quantity of goods that firms can profitably produce and sell, so that the aggregate demand for goods is the ultimate determinant of employment and unemployment. According to this view, even when wages are free to vary and output can be produced by different combinations of capital and labor inputs (so that the existing stock of capital does not determine the level of employment that can be achieved), it is possible for an insufficient aggregate demand for goods to give rise to an insufficient derived demand for labor relative to the number of persons who wish to work at currently prevailing wages. This is the theory of employment and unemployment originally developed by John Maynard Keynes (1883–1946). Its most important feature is that it identifies as the source of involuntary unemployment a deficient demand for goods, rather than any problems with the functioning of the aggregate labor market that might prevent the latter from clearing.

The distinction between supply-side and demand-side theories of involuntary unemployment leads to a further distinction between classical and Keynesian unemployment. Classical unemployment—which includes frictional unemployment and supply-side involuntary unemployment—is determined on the supply side of the economy and is unresponsive to variations in aggregate demand. Classical unemployment is often associated with the concept of a natural rate of unemployment or a nonaccelerating inflation rate of unemployment (NAIRU). Keynesian unemployment, meanwhile, is determined on the demand side of the economy and does respond to variations in aggregate demand.

It is possible in principle for voluntary and involuntary or classical and Keynesian unemployment to exist within the same economy. However, economists disagree as to what extent observed unemployment is voluntary, involuntary, classical, or Keynesian, and hence on the extent to which these categories, and the theories of unemployment associated with them, are useful for explaining the stylized facts outlined earlier.

POLICY IMPLICATIONS

The policy implications of unemployment depend greatly on the theorized causes of unemployment. For example, if unemployment is a product of individual choice (i.e., a voluntary condition), it would not appear that any form of policy intervention is merited. Even if unemployment is entirely frictional, however, it may be prudent to use public policy to reduce unemployment—including voluntary unemployment—by improving the process whereby employers and employees are matched. In this case, supply-side, microeconomic policies designed to affect the choices or attributes of job seekers are appropriate. Unemployment insurance programs might be altered to influence the propensity of those searching for work to accept job offers, or training programs might be established in an effort to imbue the unemployed with the sorts of skills required by currently vacant jobs. If unemployment is involuntary and Keynesian, however, an altogether different approach to policy intervention is required. In this case, macroeconomic policies (such as a reduction in interest rates or an increase in government spending) are needed to raise aggregate demand in order to remedy the deficient demand for goods and hence the deficient derived demand for labor that is the ultimate cause of unemployment. As with the theories of unemployment from which these policy interventions derive, the appropriate policy response to unemployment is—and will likely remain—a subject of controversy among economists.

SEE ALSO *Keynes, John Maynard; Lucas, Robert E.; Marx, Karl; Natural Rate of Unemployment; Underemployment; Voluntary Unemployment*

BIBLIOGRAPHY

Cornwall, John, and Wendy Cornwall. 2001. *Capitalist Development in the Twentieth Century: An Evolutionary-Keynesian Analysis.* Cambridge, U.K.: Cambridge University Press.

Davidson, Carl. 1990. *Recent Developments in the Theory of Involuntary Unemployment.* Kalamazoo, MI: Upjohn Institute for Employment Research.

Friedman, Milton. 1968. The Role of Monetary Policy. *American Economic Review* 58 (1): 1–17.

Keynes, John Maynard. 1936. *The General Theory of Employment, Interest, and Money.* London: Macmillan.

Lawlor, Michael S., William A. Darity, Jr., and Bobbie L. Horn. 1987. Was Keynes a Chapter Two Keynesian? *Journal of Post Keynesian Economics* 9 (4): 516–528.

Lucas, Robert E., Jr. 1978. Unemployment Policy. *American Economic Review* 68 (2): 353–357.

Mark Setterfield

UNEMPLOYMENT, DISCOURAGED

SEE *Discouraged Workers.*

UNEMPLOYMENT, INVOLUNTARY

SEE *Involuntary Unemployment.*

UNEMPLOYMENT, NATURAL RATE OF

SEE *Natural Rate of Unemployment.*

UNEMPLOYMENT RATE

There are two dimensions of the unemployment rate that sit uneasily with each other. First, national statisticians produce the "official" unemployment rate that policy makers, lobby groups, and media commentators use to summarize the state of the labor market. Second, economists attempt to explain the unemployment rate using microeconomic and macroeconomic models, which do not correspond directly with the statisticians' framework. The various explanations of unemployment remain highly contested.

DEFINING AND CALCULATING THE UNEMPLOYMENT RATE

Prior to the Great Depression, limited efforts were made to collect labor market data. For example, the gainful worker framework in the United States used the ten-year census to enumerate employment activities with little attention being paid to unemployment. A worker was defined as "a person who works for money" (Smuts 1960, p. 71).

The mass unemployment in the 1930s created a demand for a broader enumeration system, and the modern concept of the labor force framework emerged after World War II (1939–1945) in response. This framework is made operational through the International Labour Organization (ILO) and the conference of International Labour Statisticians. These conferences develop procedures (definitions) for generating national labor force data (see http://laborsta.ilo.org/ for sources and methods). National statistical agencies implement these definitions in periodic sample surveys (usually monthly) and publish labor force estimates. The application of these definitions varies from country to country.

Figure 1 sketches the labor force framework. The labor force concept has two components: (a) criteria defining activity—specifically, willingness and search; and (b) a time period for assessing activity. The working-age population (persons above fifteen years, although some countries exclude those above sixty-five years) dichotomizes into

active (the labor force) and nonactive (not in the labor force). The labor force divides between employment and unemployment. A person is considered employed if he or she works at least an hour during the survey week. A person not working and actively searching for and willing to work is classified as being unemployed.

The official unemployment rate is the number of unemployed persons as a percentage of the labor force. While a rising rate usually indicates the economy is wasting resources and sacrificing income by not utilizing willing labor, it may also reflect a strengthening economy if the labor force is growing faster than employment.

International comparisons are difficult because countries vary the ILO definitions. However, the Organization for Economic Cooperation and Development (OECD) publishes standardized unemployment rates that reflect common definitions, and the U.S. Bureau of Labor Statistics publishes labor force statistics that convert foreign aggregates into estimates consistent with U.S. definitions.

HOW USEFUL IS THE OFFICIAL UNEMPLOYMENT RATE?

The official unemployment rate's ability to portray accurately the condition of the labor market is challenged because it is a narrow measure of labor underutilization. Critics call for broader measures to be published. There are many issues relating to the labor force concept itself, including whether unpaid workers should be included in the labor force and whether defense personnel and persons who are institutionalized should be included in the working-age population. Decisions made by national statistical agencies with respect to these cohorts influence the size of the labor force estimate and in turn the unemployment rate estimate.

In this section we concentrate on the issues arising from marginal workers and underemployment. Total labor underutilization (wastage) of willing labor resources arises for a number of reasons that can be divided between two broad functional categories: (a) unemployment or its near equivalent, which includes the official unemployed under ILO criteria and those classified as being not in the labor force on search criteria (discouraged workers), availability criteria (other marginal workers), and more broadly still, those who take disability and other pensions as an alternative to unemployment (forced pension recipients). These workers share the characteristic that they are jobless and desire work if vacancies were available. They are, however, separated by the statistician on other grounds; (b) suboptimal employment relations, where workers are classified as being employed but suffer "time-related underemployment," such that there are insufficient hours of work. Suboptimal employment also arises from an "inadequacy of the employment situation" when

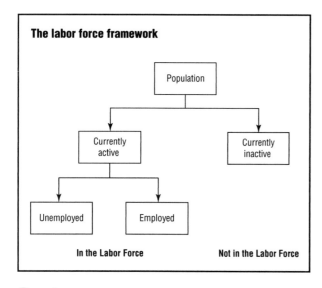

Figure 1

skills are wasted, income opportunities denied, and/or workers are forced to work longer than they desire.

The official unemployment rate captures only a portion of this wastage. Broadening the concept of labor wastage involves recognizing other cohorts within the working-age population that share some similarities with the official unemployed.

First, focus on the rise of underemployment in many countries is increasing. While both sources of underemployment ("time-related" and "inadequacy of the employment situation") are possible to measure, in practice, estimates of time-related (or visible) underemployment are more easily obtained. Involuntary part-time workers face constraints similar to those confronting the unemployed. As estimated underemployment has risen around the globe, the official unemployment rate measured as the percentage of persons in the labor force not employed underestimates the extent of labor wastage. Governments that extol the virtues of employment growth generated under their watch rarely express it in terms of full-time equivalents and thus rarely admit that, in part, people are shifting from unemployment to underemployment.

Second, workers who are not working but have abandoned active search because they perceive there are insufficient job opportunities are classified as not in the labor force. These "hidden unemployed" or discouraged workers are similar to the official unemployed because they would accept a job offer immediately. They are also unlike others who are not in the labor force such as retirees.

A broad rule of thumb is that the true labor underutilization rate (including underemployment and hidden unemployment) is estimated by doubling the official unemployment rate.

We can consider two other working-age population cohorts that are less attached to the labor force but who nonetheless, by their size, provide some guide to the potential labor resources available to any country. First, persons who desire work but are unable to start immediately and are not actively searching are called marginal workers and are excluded from the labor force. But with some institutional changes (such as improved child or aged care) this cohort would accept immediate offers of employment. Second, in many countries the number of disability pension recipients has increased. These persons are excluded from the labor force on activity grounds. The increasing trend is arguably the result of health professionals and/or governments easing their interpretations of what constitute a disability when job prospects are low. Given that many of these persons are at the bottom of the labor queue (especially older males), pushing them out of the labor force reduces the unemployment rate and is thus politically beneficial in times of recession. In recent years, in strong employment-growth countries (for example,

Australia) new measures have been introduced to induce this cohort back into the labor force in recognition that their disabilities may not preclude some capacity to work.

The justification for considering the broader underutilization concepts relates to the concept of labor efficiency. An economy that cannot provide enough hours of work to match the preferences of the available labor supply and/or institutional structures to maximize the participation of its potential labor resources is less efficient than one that can achieve these goals.

THE COSTS OF UNEMPLOYMENT

Is high unemployment a problem? Involuntary unemployment imposes heavy costs on the economy in the form of forgone output of goods and services and associated income. Economists typically ignore the social costs of unemployment. Unemployment also exacerbates social ills such as crime, family breakdown, and physical and mental health problems. Human capital (skills) atrophies when unemployment persists.

Strong spatial impacts reinforce the loss of income that accompanies unemployment. As a region's unemployment rate rises, more mobile workers (the youth and educated) leave such that skills are lost, making it hard to attract new business investment.

Many economists (mostly those who advocate a voluntarist conception) claim that unemployment is not a significant policy problem because it reflects the normal functioning of the labor market whereby job seekers use spells of unemployment to search for information about the career prospects that are available to them before settling into a career path. They specifically note that high youth unemployment is merely information-seeking behavior.

Focusing on short unemployment spells may be misleading given that many workers drop out of the labor force when they cannot find a job. Further, the transition by youth from a sequence of casual jobs to a higher paying career-oriented job is largely confined to those who combined schooling with casual employment while they acquire the skills necessary to satisfy entry into the chosen career path. While the casual work may have provided them with generic skills such as punctuality and grooming, the issue remains that those locked into the casual labor market and not combining work with schooling do not make such career transitions. Instead they sequence through a range of dead-end, low-paying jobs interspersed with spells of unemployment. For them unemployment provides no information.

WHAT CAUSES UNEMPLOYMENT?

Economists have used various taxonomies to help explain unemployment but remain in deep disagreement about its causes. A major debate during the Great Depression centered on the extent to which unemployed individuals were acting voluntarily (classical position) or whether macroeconomic spending deficiencies imposed systemic constraints (lack of jobs) on individuals who become involuntarily unemployed (Keynesian position). Marx had earlier provided analysis supporting the demand-deficient explanation. In his 1936 *General Theory*, Keynes turned this idea into a full-blooded rejection of classical employment theory, and Keynesian theory subsequently dominated macroeconomics until the mid-1970s. It provides the most accessible unemployment taxonomy for the layperson by distinguishing between frictional, structural, and cyclical unemployment.

Jobs are continuously being created and destroyed as industries grow and wane, and these processes generate huge flows of workers moving between jobs. So even when demand for goods and services is strong, there will be a coincidence of unfilled vacancies and unemployed persons. This unemployment is called frictional because it arises from frictions that accompany job turnover. Workers take time to find and move to new jobs, and firms take time to locate required labor. While it clearly represents an irreducible minimum level, there is some confusion between this level of unemployment, which is likely to be low, and the concept of natural rate of unemployment, which is explained below. Both have been referred to as the irreducible level of unemployment.

Keynesian theory considers firms' supply output and hires workers in response to the demand for goods and services. Demand-deficient or cyclical unemployment arises when the demand for labor overall (indicated by unfilled vacancies) drops below the number of workers who desire employment. The lack of jobs is experienced across all regions and industries. Cyclical unemployment reflects a systemic failure, with individuals powerless to improve their job prospects. Most economists agree that cyclical fluctuations in unemployment are caused by changes in the demand for labor rather than shifts in workers' attitudes to work. As a result, most would agree that mass unemployment is involuntary. The policy solution to demand-deficient unemployment is to use expansionary fiscal and/or monetary policy.

The concept of structural unemployment sits uneasily within this framework. It reflects a mismatch between the requirements of available jobs and the characteristics of job seekers and arises even if there is no overall demand deficiency. This mismatch could be in terms of skills and/or locations and is of concern because the retraining and relocation of labor take time and resources. Structural mismatch may arise as changes in industry composition, reflecting changing consumer spending patterns, cause regional dislocation as growing industries seek new labor skills and declining industries shed skills. Adjustment is slow because the social settlement (where people live) is less mobile than the economic settlement (where jobs are created).

Technological change also creates skill obsolescence and a demand for new skills. A particular variant of this idea is found in the emergence in the 1970s of the deindustrialization literature, which focused on manufacturing decline (and to some extent the decline of mining) and the simultaneous rise of services. The amorphous concept of globalization is interwoven into these discussions to explain job loss in particular regions and industries as a result of employment being "exported" to lower cost regions and countries. If there is structural unemployment, expansionary policies will come up against bottlenecks and invoke inflationary impulses. Instead, training and mobility incentives are required to ease the mismatch. In this sense, structural unemployment is a microeconomic problem.

However, the boundaries between cyclical and structural causes are blurred. For example, theories of hysteresis conclude that the current state of the economy reflects where it has been. Accordingly, cyclical fluctuations create structural imbalances, which can be reversed through macroeconomic expansion. For example, recession generates skill obsolescence as old capital is scrapped and/or long-term unemployment causes skills to atrophy. This structural problem is reversed as the economy resumes growth because firms lower their hiring standards and provide training opportunities as a way around perceived skill shortages.

Clearly, the idea that individuals can experience involuntary outcomes underpins this taxonomy and overlaps with the voluntary/involuntary taxonomy that was central to the "Keynes versus Classics" debates in the 1930s and persists today. The Great Depression spawned macroeconomics as a new and distinct field of study, and center stage was the concept of involuntary unemployment, which challenged the neoclassical orthodoxy. The neoclassical competitive model postulated that the equilibrium unemployment rate is determined by the intersection of labor supply and demand, both functions of the real wage. As labor supply reflects workers' preferences between labor and leisure (real wage is the opportunity cost of leisure) and labor demand reflects the marginal productivity of labor (profit-maximizing firms equilibrate the real wage with the marginal product), flexible real wages guarantee full employment. At the full employment real wage, any firm can find a suitable worker and any worker can find a suitable job. Any observed unemployment is deemed voluntary (worker preference for leisure). When the real wage is above the full employment level, the resulting unemployment is caused by real wage rigidities such as excessive legislated minimum wages and trade unions wage setting power.

This type of unemployment is termed classical and is solved by real wage cuts to restore the equilibrium level where labor demand equals labor supply. During the Great Depression, the government tried neoclassical remedies without success. In the 1930s, Kalecki and Keynes, building on the earlier work of Marx, challenged this dominant view. They saw mass unemployment as a systemic failure in demand for goods and services—that is, cyclical. Deficient effective demand causes firms to lay off workers. Neoclassical remedies would exacerbate this Keynesian unemployment because real wage cuts reduce worker incomes, further eroding effective demand. As firms adjusted to the lower activity by producing and employing less, an exogenous force in the form of expansionary fiscal and/or monetary policy was needed to push the economy toward higher activity levels.

Keynesian unemployment is involuntary because an individual unemployed worker cannot improve his or her job prospects in the face of employment rations imposed by deficient effective demand. This concept challenges the centerpiece of neoclassical theory known as Say's law, which holds that aggregate demand always absorbs production, given price flexibility. Keynes showed that even with flexible prices, unemployment would persist until the deficient demand was eliminated. This observation underpinned the so-called Keynesian revolution that dominated the next thirty years of policy making. The period of full employment up until the mid-1970s gave policy makers confidence that the business cycle had been tamed.

Neoclassical economists argue that the concept of involuntary unemployment is implausible because it implies irrational behavior by individuals. Why would workers not simply accept lower real wages? Keynesians respond by arguing that workers prefer higher money wages at each real wage level because they have large nominal commitments (such as mortgages). Resisting a money wage cut was rational even if real wages were falling (via general price-level rises) because nominal commitments could be maintained. Keynesians also argue that workers are unable to engineer a real wage cut by accepting a lower money wage because the lower costs would lead to competitive price-cutting with no guarantee of a lower real wage. But this was moot because even if real wages fell, firms would still not hire if the cheaper labor produced goods and services that could not be sold (given deficient demand).

The major policy challenge for Keynesians in a period of full employment was inflation as economies approached full capacity. A vast literature has emerged since the late 1950s examining the relationship between the unemployment rate and inflation—the so-called Phillips curve (Phillips 1958). Policy makers came to believe that they faced a stable trade-off between the twin evils of unemployment and inflation and sought to choose the combination that maximized social welfare.

The challenge to the Keynesian macroeconomic consensus was ignited by the "monetarist" contributions of Friedman (1968) and Phelps (1967). They disputed the existence of a stable Phillips curve that could be exploited using aggregate demand policy. For example, the misperceptions hypothesis (Friedman 1968) considers that workers possess less short-run information than employers about the relationship between relative and absolute price levels. Accordingly, workers can be induced to supply more labor than is optimal given their preferences for as long as they are confused about their real wage level. They thus believe that a nominal wage rise is a real wage rise and supply more labor accordingly. Once they learn the truth, they withdraw this supply and equilibrium is restored. So any policy-induced reductions in the unemployment rate bought by tricking workers into supplying more labor than was optimal would evaporate. The long-term implication was that there is a "natural" unemployment rate that reflects the underlying microeconomic structure of labor supply and labor demand, and any attempts by fiscal and monetary authorities to drive unemployment below this equilibrium generate ever increasing rates of inflation.

The essence of all supply-side explanations is that workers quit when times are bad despite all evidence to the contrary. The pro-cyclicality of quitting challenges the very core of the neoclassical labor market model.

However, the rising inflation associated with the Vietnam War and the oil price hikes in the early 1970s provided a fortuitous empirical backdrop to the growing backlash against Keynesian demand management policies. While there was scant empirical support to associate rising inflation with the mechanisms that underpinned the natural rate hypothesis, the revival of Say's law was broadly accepted by economists and policy makers.

Keynesians such as Clower (1965) and Leijonhufvud (1968) provided resistance to the natural rate hypothesis by showing that no market signals accompanied mass unemployment such that firms would hire more workers, even though these workers had notional demands for their products. The problem was that without income these demands were not effective. The market coordination implicit in Say's law failed in these situations, leaving the economy stuck in an under-full-employment equilibrium.

By the 1970s, the "new labor economics" reinstated neoclassical notions of voluntarism in explaining unemployment, a view that still dominates labor market policy today. Accordingly, unemployment arises from workers' need to search for new jobs and jobless spells are voluntary, maximizing strategies in pursuit of career improvement. Workers balance the costs of search (time and forgone earnings) with the gains in future earnings that emerge from successful search. Importantly, welfare benefits are seen as subsidizing search and encouraging long-term unemployment.

The reality is that while most job search activity is done on the job, many unemployed workers experience frequent spells of unemployment interspersed with low-skill, low-paid employment. Segmented labor market theory uses this observation to argue that structural rigidities, principally due to hiring policies of employers, discriminate against disadvantaged groups and confine them to marginal jobs and status (Doeringer and Piore 1971).

MODERN DEBATES ABOUT CAUSES OF AND REMEDIES FOR UNEMPLOYMENT

The breadth of the acceptance of the new labor economics by economists and policy makers was expressed in the influential 1994 OECD Jobs Study, which provided a policy blueprint for economic policy reform aimed at reducing unemployment following the deep recession in 1991. Its theoretical foundations can be found, for example, in Layard, Nickell, and Jackman (1991), LNJ for short. While, economists such as LNJ mimicked the traditional neoclassical concern about trade union power and legislated minimum wages, they also focused on welfare payments as a cause of persistent unemployment. They argued that the provision of unemployment assistance subsidized inactivity by reducing the intensity and effectiveness of job search. As a result of this subsidy, the wage necessary to induce the worker to abandon unemployment and accept work (the so-called reservation wage) is higher. Further, various government charges on employment (such as superannuation and termination payments) drive a wedge between what the worker receives and what the firm pays, which discourages firms from increasing employment. It was also argued that the long-term unemployed had deficient skills and required retraining to improve their employability.

The Jobs Study concluded that long-term unemployment was the outcome of government intervention, other institutions (such as trade unions), and/or negative attitudes to work of the unemployed that created rigidities in labor supply. The Jobs Study advocated extensive supply-side reform with a particular focus on the labor market to eliminate rigidities that were inhibiting the capacity of economies to adjust, innovate, and be creative. Governments variously adopted the reform agenda. It was typically accompanied by a narrowing of the focus of monetary policy to inflation control, which used unem-

ployment as an instrument to achieve price stability rather than as a policy target. Further, governments adopted fiscal conservatism (for example, the Stability and Growth Pact in Europe) to passively support their inflation-first monetary policy emphasis. Policy makers believed that disinflation policy would allow the economy, after an adjustment phase, to settle at the natural rate optimum, and as a consequence they did not worry about any alleged "short-run" negative impacts of disinflation on unemployment. They considered that the micro focus of the Jobs Study would ensure there were no impediments to reaching this supposed natural rate.

However, high unemployment persisted in many countries during the 1990s, which prompted critics of the OECD position to say that governments had been encouraged to abandon full employment in favor of full employability. The critics said that unemployment existed long before unions had grown and welfare transfers operated. They also said that it was implausible to interpret the mass unemployment of the Great Depression as a sudden labor supply withdrawal.

In recent years, partly in response to the reality that active labor market policies have not solved unemployment and have instead created problems of poverty and urban inequality, some notable shifts in perspectives are evident among supporters of the OECD approach. Various econometric studies sought to establish the empirical veracity of the OECD Job Study relationships between unemployment, real wages, welfare payments, and the like. They also sought to evaluate the effectiveness of active labor market program spending. Many construct their analyses in ways that are most favorable to the null that the OECD view is valid. The overwhelming conclusion to be drawn from this literature is that there is no consensus view (see Freeman 2005; Baker, Glyn, Howell, and Schmitt 2005).

In the face of the mounting criticism and empirical argument, the OECD has now significantly shifted its position. In the 2004 *OECD Employment Outlook*, it admitted that the evidence underpinning the neoclassical relationship between real wages and unemployment was fragile. In the 2006 *OECD Employment Outlook*, which followed a comprehensive econometric study of employment outcomes across twenty OECD countries between 1983 and 2003, the OECD (2006) found that:

- There is no significant correlation between unemployment and employment protection legislation;

- The level of the minimum wage has no significant direct impact on unemployment; and

- Highly centralized wage bargaining significantly reduces unemployment.

These conclusions undermine the basic causality in the Jobs Study. They also confound those who have relied on the OECD's previous work, including the Jobs Study, to push through harsh labor market reforms, retrenched welfare entitlements, and policies aimed at reducing the role of trade unions.

Internationally, sentiment is growing that paid employment measures must be a part of the employment policy mix if unemployment is to be reduced. The lack of consideration given to job creation strategies in the unemployment debate stands as a major oversight. Recognition is growing that programs to promote employability cannot, alone, restore full employment and that the national business cycle is the key determinant of regional employment outcomes (Mitchell 2001; Peck 2001).

SEE ALSO *Business Cycles, Real; Natural Rate of Unemployment; Underemployment; Unemployable; Unemployment*

BIBLIOGRAPHY

Baker, D., A. Glyn, D. Howell, and J. Schmitt. 2005. Labor Market Institutions and Unemployment: A Critical Assessment of the Cross-Country Evidence. In *Fighting Unemployment: The Limits of Free Market Orthodoxy*, Chapter 3, ed. D. Howell. Oxford: Oxford University Press.

Clower, R. J. 1965. The Keynesian Counterrevolution: A Theoretical Appraisal. In *The Theory of Interest Rates*, eds. F. H. Hahn and F. P. R. Brechling. 103–125. London: Macmillan.

Doeringer, P. B., and M. J. Piore. 1971. *Internal Labor Markets and Manpower Analysis*. Lexington, MA: Heath.

Freeman, R. 2005. Labour Market Institutions Without Blinders: The Debate over Flexibility and Labour Market Performance. *International Economic Journal* 19 (2): 129–145.

Friedman, M. 1968. The Role of Monetary Policy. *American Economic Review* 58: 1–17.

Hauser, P. M. 1949. The Labor Force and Gainful Workers-Concept, Measurement, and Comparability. *American Journal of Sociology* 54 (4): 338–355.

Layard, R., S. Nickell, and R. Jackman. 1991. *Unemployment, Macroeconomic Performance and the Labour Market*. Oxford: Oxford University Press.

Leijonhufvud, A. 1968. *On Keynesian Economics and the Economics of Keynes: A Study in Monetary Theory*. New York: Oxford University Press.

Mitchell, W. F. 2001. The Unemployed Cannot Find Jobs That Are Not There! In *Unemployment: The Tip of the Iceberg*, eds. W. F. Mitchell and E. Carlson, 85–116. Sydney, Australia: CAER/UNSW Press.

Organisation for Economic Cooperation and Development. 1994. *The Jobs Study*. Paris: OECD.

Organisation for Economic Cooperation and Development. 2006. *Employment Outlook: Boosting Jobs and Incomes*. Paris: OECD.

Peck, J. 2001. *Workfare State*. New York: Guilford.

Phelps, E. S. 1967. Phillips Curves, Expectations of Inflation and Optimal Unemployment over Time. *Economica* 34: 254–281.

Phillips, A. W. 1958. The Relation Between Unemployment and the Rate of Change of Money Wage Rates in the United Kingdom, 1861–1957. *Economica* 25: 283–299

Smuts, R. W. 1960. The Female Labor Force: A Case Study in the Interpretation of Historical Statistics. *American Statistical Association Journal* 55(289): 71–79.

William Mitchell

UNEMPLOYMENT, VOLUNTARY
SEE *Voluntary Unemployment.*

UNEQUAL DEVELOPMENT
SEE *Unequal Exchange.*

UNEQUAL EXCHANGE

The liberal theory of free trade based mainly on the theory of comparative advantage is regarded as a win-win situation without any limitations. During the 1950s, however, development theorists presented a challenge to this well-established neoclassical theory. The theory of *unequal exchange* is a reaction to the naïve theory of comparative advantage. It provides a Marxist notion of the exploitation that is embedded in the comparative advantage theory.

The development of the theory of unequal exchange has followed several directions. First, some writers, including Andre Gunder Frank in *Capitalism and Underdevelopment in Latin America* (1967), argued that comparative advantage is not a natural endowment; rather, it is created by historical power relations through the exploitation of nations.

Second, some researchers examined the distributional inequalities of trade. Thus, the Prebisch-Singer thesis reveals that the terms of trade work against developing countries. This well-known issue of dependency theory was systematically developed in the 1950s (Ghosh 2001).

Third, on the basis of assumptions of the restricted mobility of labor and the perfect mobility of capital, Arghiri Emmanuel (1969) formally developed the theory of unequal exchange. He argued that under a situation of perfect competition, trade between developed and developing countries involves a transfer of surplus from the latter countries. In a situation of equal productivity in developed countries (DCs) and less developed countries (LDCs), but lower wages in the LDCs, high-priced products of the DCs are exchanged for low-priced products of the LDCs. Hence, the exchange is unequal. Emmanuel noted that since wages are institutionally determined, they are exogenous to the model. However, in DCs, trade unions have a critical role in raising wages. But this is not the case in LDCs. In the process of unequal exchange, there is a transfer of value from a country with low capital intensity (often a developing country) to a country with high capital intensity in production (as in a typical developed country).

Emmanuel, an Italian Marxist, has used the Marxian theory of transformation of value into prices to show that LDCs are compelled to sell their goods at prices below their value and to purchase goods from DCs at prices above their value. In the process, the advanced countries appropriate more labor time than they generate in production. In other words, DCs can get commodities from LDCs at lower prices than would have been available in their own countries. In this process of exchange, LDCs stand as losers, and DCs as gainers.

Emmanuel's analysis has been subjected to severe criticism by many scholars, including Paul Samuelson, who tried to demonstrate that the argument developed by Emmanuel is preposterous. According to Samuelson, Emmanuel concentrated simply on the circulation sphere and failed to recognize the productivity differentials between core and peripheral countries. Emmanuel is also criticized on the grounds that he treated wages as an exogenous variable.

Samir Amin (1970) presented a new version of unequal exchange by considering wages as an endogenous variable, and he showed that unequal exchange allowed capitalist countries to protect profits. To him, the dominance of foreign capital in LDCs means distorted export activity and the hypertrophy of the tertiary sector. Peripheral countries thus incur heavy debts to core countries, become necessarily dependent on them, and become linked with the world capitalist system.

In the new world order, trade is organized largely by powerful multinational companies without any regard for small peasants and poor workers. The social cost of trade in terms of damage to the environment and human rights is much greater in LDCs. Even in a situation of trade based on comparative advantage, the gains from trade are not equally distributed. Because of the many structural differences between the LDCs and the DCs, factor price equalization is not possible. Domestic wages are falling in

LDCs due to the *race to the bottom* and the informalization of labor markets (Ghosh and Guven 2006). The advantage of productivity gains through higher wages has never trickled down to LDCs through the channel of trade. Unequal competition and dissimilar bargaining powers between these two groups of countries make the theory of unequal exchange still relevant.

SEE ALSO *Amin, Samir; Marx, Karl; Prebisch, Raúl; Prebisch-Singer Hypothesis; Samuelson, Paul A.; Singer, Hans; Terms of Trade; Trade*

BIBLIOGRAPHY

Amin, Samir. 1974. *Accumulation on a World Scale: A Critique of the Theory of Underdevelopment.* Trans. by Brian Pearce. New York: Monthly Review Press.

Emmanuel, Arghiri. 1972. *Unequal Exchange: A Study of the Imperialism of Trade.* Trans. by Brian Pearce. New York: Monthly Review Press.

Frank, Andre Gunder. 1967. *Capitalism and Underdevelopment in Latin America: Historical Studies of Chile and Brazil.* New York: Monthly Review Press.

Ghosh, B. N. 2001. *Dependency Theory Revisited.* Aldershot, U.K.: Ashgate.

Ghosh, B. N., and H. Guven, eds. 2006. *Globalisation and the Third World.* London: Palgrave-Macmillan.

B. N. Ghosh

UNICAMERALISM

SEE *Bicameralism.*

UNIDENTIFIED FLYING OBJECTS

Any discussion of unidentified flying objects (UFOs) invokes multiple, often contradictory, meanings. In popular culture the UFO is an emblem of atomic-age anxiety and desire. Nonetheless, there were unidentified airship sightings in late nineteenth century America and scholars have documented striking parallels between UFO encounters and traditional fairy lore. Some UFO believers describe UFOs as prophetic missives from spiritual realms while other equally passionate believers locate UFOs in scientific and political quests.

An aura of marginality is an essential feature of UFO believers. Simultaneously, however, fascination with UFOs is mainstream. A 2002 Roper poll sponsored by the Science Fiction Channel suggested that a majority of

Americans believe in the existence of UFOs. Groups based on interest in UFOs (such as the research oriented Mutual UFO Network; support groups for alien abductees; and Internet communities) encompass multiple aesthetic and epistemological affinities spanning generational, class, racial, and geographic boundaries. Interpretations of UFOs are made to fit into larger patterns of belief ranging from anti-government conspiracies to Christian eschatology (i.e., the end of the world). UFOs are said to be involved in unknown phenomena such as mysterious patterns appearing in grain fields—crop circles—and cattle mutilation. Perhaps the only fixed feature of the UFO is its openness as a symbol; always remaining "unidentified" has made the UFO an icon for uncanny elements of life in a rationalized age.

A major theme in UFO discourse is the paucity of official scientific research into extraterrestrial visitation. (UFOlogy is the study of UFOs.) Reports of UFO encounters have been studied through official venues, though these results tend to further the division between UFOlogy practiced by amateurs and authoritative forms of power and knowledge. In 1947 the Army Air Force began one of three investigative studies into reported UFO sightings. The final investigation, Project Blue Book, ended in 1969 with the conclusion that natural phenomena accounted for most UFO sightings. As with many UFO-related conclusions, however, this one remained open. One of its own participants, astrophysicist J. Alen Hynek, was dismayed by the investigation's lack of scientific rigor and open-mindedness, especially regarding ambiguous reports that could not be explained as natural phenomena ([1972] 1998). Hynek assumed the rationality of most UFO witnesses and renounced his initial skepticism to become a major figure of UFOlogy.

In social science UFO belief has been studied for insights into religion, memory, psychology, and culture. Scholars of "new religions" make no claim as to the reality or falsity of UFOs but track religions or "cults" that arise out of the belief. In recent studies in psychology and memory at Harvard, researchers found abduction memories were linked to common brain states between sleeping and waking (Clancy 2005). Scholars in anthropology and cultural studies have also studied UFOs in the context of larger social and cultural meanings (Dean 1998, Battaglia 2005). Beginning with psychologist Carl Jung (1875–1961) to the beginning of modern UFO belief in the mid-twentieth century, scholars of psychology, religion, and culture emphasized the mythic elements of UFO belief. UFO history itself is organized through large stories of events that come to function like origin myths. Such narratives include the "first sighting," the "first crash" and the "first abduction."

THE "FIRSTS": ORIGIN NARRATIVES

UFOs are often said to enter American life through Kenneth Arnold, a respectable businessman and pilot who was flying solo in Washington State on a clear afternoon, on June 24, 1947. After Arnold saw nine unidentifiable objects flying over the Cascade Mountains he told a reporter the objects moved in the sky like saucers, thus coining a lasting term. Although other strange flying objects had been reported in the year before Arnold's sighting, his sighting became the originary narrative of UFO culture and was the impetus for the military's first UFO investigations. In the U.S. government, there was worry about both extraterrestrials and a possible secret weapon in development. From this beginning, UFOs were entangled with technological military development.

Weeks after Arnold's sighting a crashed flying saucer was reported from Roswell, New Mexico, the only military base with an atomic bomb unit. A rancher named Mac Brazel had discovered mysterious wreckage scattered over the countryside, including pieces covered in what appeared to be hieroglyphics. Sometime in the next few days, amid the excitement of flying saucer talk around America, Brazel reported his find to the local sheriff, who in turn reported it to the Army Air Field's (AAF) intelligence officer, Jesse Marcel. The AAF issued a press release that led the Roswell *Daily Record* to report on July 8 that a flying saucer had been captured by the Air Force near Roswell. But within a day, Brigadier General Roger Ramey called the press, changing the UFO explanation to that of a crashed high-altitude weather balloon.

STORIES OF CONSPIRACY

The incident receded. Its uncanny and conspiratorial elements emerged in the late 1970s when Stanton Friedman, a UFO researcher with a background in nuclear physics, happened to meet Marcel and began to investigate the case. Friedman claimed that the government had been hiding evidence of this crashed UFO for decades. In subsequent research by Friedman and other researchers, one part of the story grew especially salient: Alien bodies had been recovered and hidden by the government for research. Reports grew of the military threatening witnesses. Friedman used testimony from a recently-emerged witness to propose that two extraterrestrial crafts had crashed in the area, and the government had secreted the crafts along with the alien bodies. In another twist, a former Pentagon official and army colonel named Philip Corso claimed not only that he had seen alien bodies from the Roswell crash but that the United States had developed modern technology, such as the integrated circuit and the laser, by studying the extraterrestrial craft. There was speculation that the UFOs had made their way to

Area 51, a top-secret high technology military base bordering the Nevada nuclear test site.

In 1994 Representative Steven Schiff of New Mexico requested the release of government files on Roswell under the Freedom of Information Act. To Schiff, the files were unsatisfactory, containing scant and redacted pages. Finally, however, Schiff's appeals to the Congressional General Accounting Office led to revelations about a secret cold war program in 1947 called Project Mogul. Scientists from New York University had launched balloons in New Mexico carrying devices meant to track nuclear tests by the Soviet Union. One of these had disappeared near Roswell during the appropriate time period. The balloons had some of the physical qualities described by witnesses fifty years earlier, such as tape containing symbols that could have been mistaken for alien hieroglyphics. This explanation has created controversy among UFO researchers, some of whom are convinced and some of whom still believe in the extraterrestrial hypothesis.

The original story of the first abduction contained themes that set a pattern for subsequent cases. In September 1961 a couple from New Hampshire named Betty and Barney Hill experienced "missing time" while driving in the White Mountains. Strange dreams and Barney's anxiety prompted them to seek out hypnotherapy, which revealed memories of having been abducted. According to the Hills, the couple had seen a UFO approaching and their car engine had failed. Like most alleged abductees, the Hills described a medical violation of their bodies, especially their sexual organs.

ABDUCTION PATTERNS

Since the case of the Hills, many abduction narratives have followed a similar pattern of clinical experimentation and violation based on human reproduction. Some people recall seeing "hybrids," offspring between humans and extraterrestrials.

Budd Hopkins (1981) and David Jacobs (1992) have been at the forefront of this narrative's circulation for twenty years, often relying on hypnosis to elicit traumatic abduction memories. Symptoms of abduction that might lead one to seek hypnotic regression include missing time, unexplained marks on the body, unexplained mechanical failures, strange dreams, and "screen memories" of things representing extraterrestrials. In one famous case, logger Travis Walton says he was abducted from Arizona by extraterrestrials for several days. In most instances documented by Hopkins and Jacobs, however, the missing time is hours, not days, and there are rarely witnesses.

While many people who claim to be abductees portray abductions as terrifying, it is often more complex. A belief in benevolent spiritual extraterrestrials, prevalent in the mid-twentieth century, became an ambivalent, complex discourse of personal transformation. The process of post-traumatic spiritual enlightenment undergone by "alien abductees" is best known from the work of two men: Whitley Strieber, who in the 1980s turned from writing best-selling science fiction and fantasy novels to writing a nonfiction account of his own encounters with extraterrestrials; and John Mack, a Harvard psychiatrist who, late in a distinguished academic and clinical career, began working with people who said they had memories of alien abduction and experienced great spiritual growth.

SEE ALSO *Cults; Ethnology and Folklore; Lay Theories; Myth and Mythology; Popular Culture; Science Fiction*

BIBLIOGRAPHY

Battaglia, Debbora, ed. 2005. *E.T. Culture: Anthropology in Outerspaces.* Durham, NC: Duke University Press.

Bullard, Thomas E. 1989. UFO Abduction Reports: The Supernatural Kidnap Narrative Returns in Technological Guise. *Journal of American Folklore* 102, no. 404 (April/June): 147-170.

Clancy, Susan A. 2005. *Abducted: How People Come to Believe They Were Kidnapped by Aliens.* Cambridge, MA: Harvard University Press.

Corso, Philip J. (with William J. Birnes). 1997. *The Day After Roswell.* New York: Pocket Books.

Dean, Jodi. 1998. *Aliens in America: Conspiracy Cultures from Outerspace to Cyberspace.* Ithaca, NY: Cornell University Press.

Friedman, Stanton, and Don Berliner. 1992. *Crash at Corona: The US Military Retrieval and Cover-Up of a UFO.* New York: Paragon House.

Fuller, John G. 1993 [1966]. *The Interrupted Journey: Two Lost Hours "Aboard a Flying Saucer."* Alexandria, VA: Time-Life Books.

Harding, Susan. 2005. Living Prophecy at Heaven's Gate. In *Histories of the Future*, 297–320. Durham, NC: Duke University Press.

Hopkins, Budd. 1981. *Missing Time: A Documented Study of UFO Abductions.* New York: R. Marek Publishers.

Hynek, Allen J. [1972] 1998. *The UFO Experience: A Scientific Inquiry.* New York: Marlowe and Company.

Jacobs, David. 1992. *Secret Life: Firsthand Documented Accounts of UFO Abductions.* New York: Simon and Schuster.

Jung, Carl Gustav. [1953] 1979. *Flying Saucers: A Modern Myth of Things Seen in the Skies.* Princeton, NJ: Princeton University Press.

Korff, Kal K. 1997. What Really Happened at Roswell. *Skeptical Inquirer*, (July/August). http://www.csicop.org/si/9707/roswell.html.

Lepselter, Susan. 2005. *The Flight of the Ordinary: Narrative, Poetics, Power and UFOs in the American Uncanny.* Doctoral Dissertation: University of Texas at Austin.

Lewis, James R., ed. 1995. *The Gods Have Landed: New Religions from Other Worlds.* Albany: State University of New York Press.

Mack, John. 1999. *Passport to the Cosmos: Human Transformation and Alien Encounters.* New York: Crown Publishers.

Patton, Phil. 1998. *Dreamland: Travels Inside the Secret World of Roswell and Area 51.* New York: Villard Books.

Peebles, Curtis. 1994. *Watch the skies!: A Chronicle of the Flying Saucer Myth.* Washington, DC: Smithsonian Institution Press.

Rojcewicz, Peter. 1987. The "Men in Black:" Experience and Tradition - Analogues with the Traditional Devil Hypothesis. *Journal of American Folklore* 100: 148–160.

Saler, Benson, Charles A. Ziegler, and Charles B. Moore. 1997. *UFO Crash at Roswell: the Genesis of a Modern Myth.* Washington, DC: Smithsonian Institution Press.

Sci Fi.com. Roper Poll: UFOs & Extraterrestrial Life. September 2002. Sci Fi Channel. http://www.scifi.com/ufo/roper.

Strieber, Whitley. 1988. *Communion.* New York: Avon Books.

Vallee, Jacques. [1969] 1997. *Passport to Magonia: On UFOs, Folklore, and Parallel Worlds.* New York: McGraw Hill.

Susan Lepselter

UNIFORM BERTRAND'S PARADOX

SEE *Distribution, Uniform.*

UNILATERALISM

The term *unilateralism* describes an approach toward conducting foreign policy in which a country does not subordinate its aims or actions to the wishes of other countries or the constraints of international agreements. While few would advocate discarding all multilateral commitments, there is disagreement over the degree to which a country (and especially, a hegemon like the United States) ought to pursue its foreign policy in a unilateral fashion.

Although the debate over unilateralism became heated during the administration of President George W. Bush, the concept has a long history in U.S. foreign policy. In his 1796 farewell address, President George Washington (1732–1799) urged the United States to "steer clear of permanent alliances with any portion of the foreign world, so far … as we are now at liberty to do it." Advocates of unilateralism emphasize that such a policy does not imply isolationism. Nor does it imply that the ends sought by a country are narrowly defined or that they neglect the interests of other countries. Indeed, Charles Krauthammer celebrates a "new unilateralism" that, he argues, "is clear in its determination to self-consciously and confidently deploy American power in pursuit of … global ends" (2002/2003, p. 14), such as promoting democracy and maintaining peace and stability. In this view, the hegemon has unique responsibilities in managing the international system that other states may not share or even support.

Countries with less power naturally seek to restrain the hegemon. Robert Kagan, for instance, argues that "Europe's military weakness has produced a perfectly understandable aversion to the exercise of military power" (2002, p. 10). Ideology, economic interests, domestic politics, or honest disagreement about the wisdom of a particular policy may also lead smaller powers to oppose the hegemon's unilateralism. As a result, there may simply be little the hegemon can do to assuage smaller countries. Furthermore, American unilateralists argue that the United States should not, as President Bush remarked in his 2004 State of the Union address, "seek a permission slip to defend the security of our country."

A unilateral approach does not shun allies, but it counsels against adjusting one's policies to accommodate the views of other states. As U.S. Secretary of Defense Donald Rumsfeld said in 2002: "The mission must determine the coalition, and the coalition must not determine the mission. If it does, the mission will be dumbed down to the lowest common denominator, and we can't afford that." According to Rumsfeld, exercising strong leadership will eventually bring countries on board. As Krauthammer argues, "no one wants to be left at the dock when the hegemon is sailing" (2002/2003, p. 17).

By contrast, critics argue that acting unilaterally reduces a country's ability to achieve its interests and increases the associated costs of its foreign policy. Part of the reason why unilateralism is such an inefficient way to achieve national goals lies in its lack of legitimacy. As a result, other states will be less likely to support or cooperate with such policies, reducing the probability of success. Power is less costly to exercise when it takes the form of authority, combining power with consent from others. Moreover, other countries find a hegemon's unilateralism threatening and are thus more likely to balance against it. By contrast, multilateralism signals that a state is taking the interests of other countries into account in formulating its own foreign policy; this poses less of a threat to other countries and reduces the chances that they will align against the hegemon. Although there is much debate over whether such counterbalancing occurs, survey evidence makes clear that the United States is perceived by much of the world as acting unilaterally and that this has generated widespread resentment since the late 1990s.

Advocates of unilateralism answer critics by pointing out that while there may be costs to unilateralism, there are also costs to multilateralism. John Bolton, the U.S. ambassador to the United Nations during George W. Bush's second term, argued that "the costs [of multilateralism] to the United States—reduced constitutional autonomy, impaired popular sovereignty, reduction of our international power, and limitations on our domestic and foreign policy options and solutions—are too great, and the current understanding of these costs far too limited to be acceptable" (Bolton 2000, p. 221). Similarly, in an overview of the case against unilateralism from the standpoint of international relations theory, Stephen G. Brooks and William C. Wohlforth (2005) argue that most scholars oppose unilateralism on substance grounds and have provided only weak theoretical reasons to criticize the approach on more general procedural grounds.

In economic relations, the term *unilateralism* is used more specifically to refer to trade policies, frequently carried out by the United States during the 1980s and 1990s, that involve imposing sanctions on countries whose markets are deemed to be closed to foreign products. Proponents of this approach argue that only this pressure can pry open previously closed markets; thus, unilateralism could increase the total amount of international trade and improve world welfare. In particular, they argue that countries such as Japan that are characterized by structural or informal trade barriers often do not respond to multilateral rules and thus require more forceful measures— such as results-oriented managed trade—to break into their markets.

Critics of so-called aggressive unilateralism, such as Jagdish Bhagwati (1990) and Douglas A. Irwin (1994), respond by questioning whether in fact these countries are really acting "unfairly." To the extent that powerful countries, responding to domestic pressure, threaten sanctions against allegedly closed markets, the targeted state might respond by satisfying the complaining state, thereby diverting trade from countries with less political clout. The result would thus not be more trade, but rather discrimination in favor of the powerful. Within the target country, the power of bureaucrats would be expanded rather than reduced—an effect that would slow down the country's integration into the world trading system. Most seriously, when powerful countries determine for themselves whether other states are acting unfairly, the rule of law in the international trading system is undermined. As Bhagwati writes, "the world trading regime should not be built on the assumption that any one player, no matter how dominant, can impose its own rules, unilaterally claiming social legitimacy for them" (1990, p. 36). In fact, the spread of this policy was an important factor in building support for the creation of a stronger World Trade Organization (WTO). Since the creation of the WTO, such resorts to unilateralism have declined. Nonetheless, as the controversy over antidumping duties suggests, the issue has by no means disappeared.

SEE ALSO *Bilateralism; Internationalism; Multilateralism; Trilateralism; United Nations*

BIBLIOGRAPHY

Bhagwati, Jagdish. 1990. Aggressive Unilateralism: An Overview. In *Aggressive Unilateralism: America's 301 Trade Policy and the World Trading System*, eds. Jagdish Bhagwati and Hugh T. Patrick, 1–45. Ann Arbor: University of Michigan.

Bolton, John. 2000. Should We Take Global Governance Seriously? *Chicago Journal of International Law* 1 (2): 205–222.

Brooks, Stephen G., and William C. Wohlforth. 2005. International Relations Theory and the Case against Unilateralism. *Perspectives on Politics* 3 (3): 509–524.

Bush, George W. State of the Union Address. 2004. http://www.whitehouse.gov/stateoftheunion/2004/index.html.

Irwin, Douglas A. 1994. *Managed Trade: The Case against Import Targets*. Washington, DC: AEI Press.

Kagan, Robert. 2002. Power and Weakness. *Policy Review* 113: 3–28.

Krauthammer, Charles. 2002/2003. The Unipolar Moment Revisited. *National Interest* 70 (winter): 5–17.

Rumsfeld, Donald. 2002. Twenty-First Century Transformation. Remarks delivered at National Defense University, Fort McNair, Washington, DC, January 31. http://www.defenselink.mil/speeches/2002/s20020131-secdef.html.

Washington, George. 1796. Farewell Address. U.S. Department of State International Information Programs: Basic Readings in U.S. Democracy. http://usinfo.state.gov/usa/infousa/facts/democrac/49.htm.

Jonathan Crystal

UNION OF SOVIET SOCIALIST REPUBLICS

The Soviet Union was the world's first Communist state, the West's principal adversary during the cold war, and a dominant force in international affairs until its collapse in 1991. Moreover, the Soviet Union was the world's largest country stretching from the Baltic and Black Seas to the Pacific Ocean. It also had over one-hundred distinct nationalities living within its borders, making it extremely diverse. Thus, it is not surprising that almost every social science subfield devoted much time and effort to studying various aspects of the Soviet Union. This makes the amount of social science research produced on it almost impossible to quantify.

The history of the Soviet Union begins with the Russian Revolution of 1917. In February of that year the wartime decay of Russia's economy and morale triggered a spontaneous popular uprising in Petrograd. This culminated in the imperial government of Czar Nicholas II (1868–1918) being overthrown. After the formation of a provisional government, workers councils, known as soviets, began to sprout up throughout the country to protect the rights of the working class. This allowed the Bolsheviks (Communists) to arouse widespread interest in a socialist revolution. Eventually, in November 1917, the Bolsheviks, led by Vladimir Lenin (1870–1924), seized power from the provisional government and established the world's first Communist government.

Immediately after the Bolsheviks came to power a civil war erupted between the Communist Red Army and the loosely allied anti-Communist White Army. Despite struggling for survival throughout the bitterly fought civil war, there was no doubt that the Communists would emerge victorious by the end of 1920. Finally, after securing power, the Bolsheviks officially established the Soviet Union in December 1922. Lenin, as head of the party, became the de facto ruler of the country.

Under Lenin, the new government centralized its control over the political, economic, social, and cultural lives of the Soviet people by prohibiting other political organizations and inaugurating one-party rule. However, Lenin realized that a radical approach to communism did not suit existing conditions and jeopardized the survival of his regime. In turn, under the program that came to be known as the New Economic Policy, the state sanctioned partial decentralization of the economy; market forces and the monetary system regained their importance, but heavy industry remained under state control.

As the Communist Party continued to consolidate its authority throughout the country, it became a monolithic presence. However, in May 1922 after Lenin became temporarily incapacitated by a stroke, the unity of the Communist Party fractured. This facilitated Joseph Stalin's (1879–1953) rise to power, and he became general secretary in April 1922. Lenin's death in January 1924 cemented Stalin's dominance over the Politburo, the executive committee of the Communist Party.

THE STALIN ERA

Transformation and terror best characterize the first decade of Stalin's rule. Beginning in the late 1920s, Stalin began carrying out a program of intensive socialist construction by rapidly industrializing the economy and nationalizing all industry and services. At the same time, Stalin began purging from the Communist Party all leaders and their followers deemed disloyal. The most prominent leader was Leon Trotsky (1879–1940), a Bolshevik revolutionary and a founding member of the Politburo.

Soviet foreign policy also underwent a series of changes. Lenin realized that the Soviet government required normal relations with the Western world for it to survive. Stalin, by contrast, aimed to exasperate social tensions in Europe to produce conditions favorable to Communist revolution. Nevertheless, the dynamics of Soviet foreign relations changed drastically after Stalin recognized the danger Nazi Germany posed. In turn, to constrain Germany, the Soviet Union built coalitions that were hostile to fascism. Furthermore, it gave assistance to antifascists in the Spanish Civil War (1936–1939).

After France and Britain acquiesced to Adolph Hitler's (1889–1945) demands for Czechoslovak territory at Munich, Germany, in 1938, Soviet foreign policy shifted again; Stalin decided to come to an understanding with Germany. This culminated in the Nazi-Soviet Nonaggression Pact of August 23, 1939, which called for absolute neutrality in the event one of the parties became involved in war. However, after World War II (1939–1945) broke out, Hitler began preparing for war against the Soviet Union. Germany finally declared war on the Soviet Union in June 1941. Although the Great Patriotic War, as World War II was referred to in the Soviet Union, began inauspiciously for the Soviet Union, the war with Germany ended triumphantly for the Soviets.

The Soviet Union rebuilt its economy during the immediate postwar period and continued to maintain strict centralized control over state and society. It also emerged from the war as a world superpower along with the United States. In turn the Soviet Union began taking an active role in the United Nations as well as in other major international and regional organizations. However, as it turned many Eastern European countries into satellite states and set up the Warsaw Pact and Comecon (economic and military organizations of Central and Eastern European Communist states), the Soviet Union's relations with the West became extremely tense. This led to the protracted geopolitical, ideological, and economic struggle between capitalism and communism known as the cold war.

FROM STALIN'S DEATH TO GORBACHEV'S REFORM

Stalin died on March 5, 1953. Since Stalin did not name an heir, a factional power struggle broke out within the party. After the succession struggle abated, Nikita Khrushchev (1894–1971) emerged as first secretary. By the beginning of 1956, Khrushchev was the most important figure within the Soviet leadership. Khrushchev even denounced Stalin and launched a campaign to ease the repressive controls over party and society. But, Khrushchev did face significant opposition in the Presidium, or Politburo, which threatened much needed economic reform and the de-Stalinization campaign. The

Presidium even voted Khrushchev out of office in June 1957, but the Central Committee (the highest body of the Communist Party of the Soviet Union to which the Politburo reported to) overturned the decision and expelled Khrushchev's opponents. After becoming prime minister in March 1958, Khrushchev's position in the state and party was solidified.

Khrushchev attempted to carry out domestic reform in a range of fields, but economic difficulties and political disarray remained. At the same time, events such as the suppression of democratic uprisings in Hungary and Poland in 1956 hurt the Soviet Union's international stature. Furthermore, Khrushchev's efforts to improve relations with the West suffered many setbacks, especially after the Cuban Missile Crisis (a cold war conflict between the United States and the Soviet Union regarding a Soviet buildup of nuclear missiles in Cuba). These events highlighted the fact that Khrushchev never exercised the high level of authority that Stalin did.

In October 1964 the Presidium voted Khrushchev out of office again. Khrushchev's removal from office was followed by another period of rule by collective leadership. During this time, the Soviet leadership experimented with economic reform and several individuals contended for power. This situation lasted until Leonid Brezhnev (1906–1982), who attained the post of first secretary in 1964, became the most important figure within the Soviet leadership in 1971. During Brezhnev's sixteen years as first secretary, economic and political reform was nonexistent. The Soviet Union also stepped up its repression against political dissidents and even tolerated popular expressions of anti-Semitism.

Soviet relations with the West first improved in the years after Khrushchev, which led to *détente*, or a relaxing of strained relations, in the early 1970s. Although the international community viewed this as a positive development, the use of force in Eastern Europe to suppress reform movements, attempts to broaden its influence in the Middle East, and its expanding influence in the developing world in accordance with the strategy of non-alignment caused improved relations to be short-lived. Finally, détente appeared dead when Brezhnev sent armed forces into Afghanistan in December 1979 to shore up the Communist government there. This along with economic stagnation proved to be formidable challenges for the Soviet leadership after Brezhnev's death in 1982.

After the rapid succession of Yuri Andropov (1914–1984) and Konstantin Chernenko (1911–1985), the reform minded Mikhail Gorbachev (b. 1931) became general secretary in March 1985. To fix the crumbling Soviet political and economic structures, Gorbachev implemented the *perestroika* program to improve living standards and worker productivity and *glasnost*, which

freed public access to information after decades of government regulations. This reinvigorated détente allowed Gorbachev to develop a strong relationship with President Ronald Reagan (1911–2004) of the United States. However, the impact the policies had on the Soviet Union's political and economic structures was not so positive.

THE SOVIET UNION'S DEMISE

Although there is debate over what exactly caused the Soviet Union's demise, it is clear that the policies of *perestroika* and *glasnost* led to unintended consequences that greatly contributed to this. This is because the relaxation of censorship on the media brought to light many of the severe social and economic problems the Soviet government claimed did not exist; events such as the ongoing war in Afghanistan and the Chernobyl nuclear power plant disaster in 1986 exasperated this. These negative aspects of Soviet life, in turn, undermined the faith of the people in the Soviet system and eroded the Soviet Union's identity and integrity. Moreover, improved relations with the West infuriated Soviet hardliners.

This led to upheaval throughout the Soviet Union and in its Eastern European satellite states. In the late 1980s nationalism was rising throughout the Soviet republics, which reawakened ethnic tensions throughout the Union thereby discrediting the idea of a unified Soviet people. The Soviet Union, in turn, lost all control over economic conditions. At the same time, Moscow disowned the Brezhnev Doctrine in favor of nonintervention in the internal affairs of its Warsaw Pact allies. This was significant given that the Brezhnev Doctrine had modeled Soviet foreign policy since 1968; the Brezhnev doctrine stated that if any hostile force tried to turn the development of any socialist country towards capitalism, it would become the problem and concern of all socialist countries. Eventually, many Soviet satellite states began asserting sovereignty over their territories with some even declaring independence. By 1991 revolution had swept through Eastern Europe bringing down several Communist governments.

In February 1990 the unintended consequences of Gorbachev's reforms forced the Central Committee of the Soviet Union to give up its monopoly of power. Even though the Communists were not going down without a fight, a unionwide referendum saw approximately 78 percent of voters approve the retention of the Soviet Union in an altered form. Presidential elections followed in June; Boris Yeltsin defeated the Gorbachev-backed Nikolai Ryzhkov.

Gorbachev attempted to restructure the Soviet system into a less centralized state. But in August 1991, the vice president, prime minister, defense minister, KGB (the Soviet security agency) chief, and other senior officials acted to prevent the signing of the union treaty. The coup organizers put Gorbachev under house arrest at his vacation home in the Crimea and attempted to restore the Union to its former state. However, public sympathy for their actions was largely against them and the coup ultimately failed. After the coup the Soviet republics accelerated their process toward independence. Finally, on December 8, 1991, Soviet leaders decided to dissolve the Union and established the Commonwealth of Independent States, which is an alliance that is open to all former Soviet republics. The Soviet Union ceased to exist by the end of December.

BEYOND THE SOVIET IMPERIUM

The dissolution of the Soviet Union led to numerous political, economic, and social changes within the region. Democratization and economic liberalization began throughout the post-Soviet sphere. However, the transition from communism in the former Soviet Union only sometimes led to democracy; some states abandoned communism for democracy, while others turned to authoritarian rule. Many of the post-Soviet republics also saw their economies collapse during the transition to capitalism. Corruption, weak property rights protection, and political instability were just a few of the reasons for this. Russia, in particular, struggled in its transition to a market economy. This precipitated a return to more interventionist economic policies by the government. Further, numerous ethnic and religious conflicts erupted. There are a number of de facto, but internationally unrecognized, states as a result of this.

Several global changes that have occurred since the Soviet Union's demise are also worthy of note. There are no longer two clear-cut superpowers dominating international political life. Nuclear disarmament and reconfigured security arrangements are the salient themes in this "new world order." Economic interdependence and political integration are also being seen everywhere. However, the most important global change since the Soviet Union's demise is the ever-increasing threat of terrorism, especially Islamic fundamentalism. The events of September 11, 2001, indicate that this has officially replaced nuclear war as the greatest threat to peace.

There is no doubt that the Soviet Union was one of the most powerful countries in the world during its period of existence, especially from 1945 to 1991. At its peak it consisted of fifteen republics making it one of the most strongly centralized federal unions in the history of the world. Furthermore, the Soviet Union became a primary model for future Communist states; some states, such as Cuba, exemplify the Soviet tradition. All of this suggests that it is likely that few topics will generate as much social science research as the Soviet Union did.

SEE ALSO *Berlin Wall; Bolshevism; Castro, Fidel; Cold War; Communism; Confederations; Cuban Missile Crisis; Cuban Revolution; Decentralization; Deterrence, Mutual; Economies, Transitional; Glasnost; Gorbachev, Mikhail; Hitler, Adolf; Industrialization; Khrushchev, Nikita; Lenin, Nikolai; Lenin, Vladimir Ilitch; Leninism; Nationalism and Nationality; Nationalization; Nation-State; Nonalignment; Reagan, Ronald; Russian Revolution; Socialism; Stalin, Joseph; Third World; Trotsky, Leon; United Nations; Weaponry, Nuclear; World War II; Yeltsin, Boris*

BIBLIOGRAPHY

Aron, Leon. 2006. The "Mystery" of the Soviet Collapse. *Journal of Democracy* 17 (2): 21–35.

Hosking, Geoffrey. 1992. *The First Socialist Society: A History of the Soviet Union from Within.* 2nd ed. Cambridge, MA: Harvard University Press.

Hough, Jerry F. 1977. *The Soviet Union and Social Science Theory.* Cambridge, MA: Harvard University Press.

Laibman, David. 2005. The Soviet Demise: Revisionist Betrayal, Structural Defect, or Authoritarian Distortion? *Science and Society* 69 (4): 594–606.

Nogee, Joseph L., and Robert H. Donaldson. 1992. *Soviet Foreign Policy since World War II.* 4th ed. New York: Macmillan Publishing.

Sakwa, Richard. 1999. *The Rise and Fall of the Soviet Union: 1917–1991.* New York: Routledge.

Service, Robert. 2005. *A History of Modern Russia: From Nicolas II to Vladimir Putin.* Cambridge, MA: Harvard University Press.

Zickel, Raymond E., ed. 1991. *Soviet Union: A Country Study.* 2nd ed. Washington, DC: The Division.

David Mastro

UNION SHOP

SEE *Labor Law.*

UNIONS

Unions are organizations of wage earners designed to better working conditions and give laborers a collective voice in the contract bargaining procedure.

Unions emerged from the early trade associations built by workers confronting the effects of the industrial revolution. In 1790, New York City was a center of commerce, but not yet an industrial city. It was also a city divided by class, property, and power. On the one hand, a wealthy class of traders and financiers had developed during the pre-revolutionary period and controlled the city's international commerce. They were merchant capitalists who made their money through import and export, buying commodities cheaply in Europe, Asia, Africa, and the Americas, and selling them dearly in the United States; or they bought native-made products and exported them for profit to the rest of the world. Through this process they accumulated wealth, or capital, that they then reinvested in their businesses.

On the other hand, there were artisans, skilled craftsmen (including printers, blacksmiths, brick-layers, and carpenters) who produced many of the commodities necessary for early urban life. These artisans inhabited a world of tradition inherited from the guild systems of Europe. Rather than hiring employees, the master craftsmen took on apprentices who worked for a given period of years (usually six or seven), receiving room and board as recompense rather than a wage or salary. After the apprenticeship ended, workers became journeymen. After several years of wage labor, the journeymen, in turn, expected to become master craftsmen. Finally, there were unskilled laborers who worked for a wage. During this early republican period, craft workers created trade associations. Carpenters organized together, print-makers, and brick-layers. These early trade associations included masters, journeymen, and apprentices; and all three groups of skilled workers felt a unity of purpose, a community of art, and a common social bond. But these associations were not yet trade unions.

EMERGENCE OF TRADE UNIONS

Modern trade unions emerged only after the industrial revolution began to take shape. Because of New York's pivotal place as a trading center in the world economy, the merchant class began to accumulate capital. With their coffers enriched by the import-export trade, some of these merchants began to set up their own workshops to manufacture the goods usually made by skilled craftsmen. These workshops proved to be efficient and highly profitable. Thus, some of the wealthier artisans followed suit, transforming their own tradition-bound workshops into early modern versions of the manufacturing plant. While in the older craft workshops, the apprentice and the journeyman were bound to the master by traditional ties and communal associations, in these new proto-industrial workshops, the relationship between the master and the journeyman or apprentice was increasingly governed by a wage. The master hired the men he needed, paid them by the hour, and dismissed them if they were unnecessary. As masters became increasingly wealthy, the social and economic space between masters and journeymen likewise increased.

Soon the journeymen were organizing their own associations; and by the 1820s, journeymen associations began to strike against their masters for higher wages, better working conditions, and rudimentary social benefits. From these early journeymen associations, the modern trade union movement was born.

At the same time, as a direct result of these new economic forces, poverty increased, male laborers found their livelihoods increasingly precarious, and women began to enter the formal workforce. Excluded from the all-male craft associations, New York women worked in occupations generally associated with the household labor that they had done for centuries. They became street corner vendors, provisioners selling prepared foods, prostitutes, midwives, nurses, and seamstresses. As the workshop system advanced, and as technological change and new machines transformed textile labor, women textile laborers increasingly worked in early factories. In New York, in Baltimore, in Philadelphia, and in Massachusetts, women in various trades began organizing their own trade unions. And in 1825, New York seamstresses organized the first all-women's strike in the United States.

At first, these women trade unionists enjoyed considerable support from male wageworkers and male dominated trade unions. But that soon changed. Between 1834 and 1836, one of the first attempts to affiliate all trade unions within the borders of the United States took place with the conventions of the National Trades' Union (NTU). The NTU addressed the issue of women wage earners. While many of the conventions' delegates were labor radicals who advocated the abolition of the wage system and a rudimentary notion of economic democracy, these male trade unionists also objected to the "degradation" of women in factory work. Constructing a discourse based upon what one labor historian has called "a species of radical paternalism," the NTU delegates sought to "protect" women from the ravages of capitalism. But that "protection" amounted to nothing less than an exclusion of women from union activity, except in a supporting or auxiliary role, as the wives, mothers, and daughters of good union men. The brief moment of inter-gender trade union cooperation ended and would not reappear in full force for another hundred years.

THE KNIGHTS OF LABOR

Despite early attempts at a national organization, such as the NTU, it was not until 1869 that laborers were able to come together in a truly effective national trade union, the Knights of Labor. During this period, employers and the state attempted to repress union organization through legal and extralegal means, including blacklisting, court injunctions, labor spies, and firings. Thus the Knights were originally a quasi-secret organization. But by the

1880s, with almost one million members, the Knights shed much of their secrecy and became one of the most influential labor organizations of the late nineteenth century. The Knights actively recruited women, African American, and Hispanic workers. They fought for and helped effect the abolition of child labor, the eight-hour workday, equal pay for equal work, women's rights, and the Labor Day holiday. They advocated combining all craft associations into one big union that would protect the rights of all working people.

The power of the Knights of Labor ended in 1886, during the Haymarket Affair. After the Knights helped organize a general strike in Chicago, police fired into a large protest rally held by workers, killing four people. The next day, a group of anarchists held a rally in Haymarket Square protesting police actions. Someone—it is still unclear whether it was a police spy or an anarchist protester—threw a bomb into a group of police officers, killing eight. In turn, the police fired into the crowd of protesters, killing another eight and wounding more than one hundred others. In the following days, radicals, anarchists, and unionists were rounded up by state and local authorities; some were indicted and tried for conspiracy. The age of the Knights of Labor came to an end with one of the first "Red Scares" in American history. This was a pattern that would be repeated over and again for the next sixty years.

THE AFL AND THE IWW

As the twentieth century approached, the Knights of Labor left an ambiguous legacy for the American labor movement. On the one hand, their repression by the government led to the moderate craft unionism of the American Federation of Labor (AFL). On the other hand, the forms of radical solidarity promoted by the Knights found a new life in the syndicalism of the Industrial Workers of the World (IWW), known as Wobblies.

Samuel Gompers founded the American Federation of Labor in 1886 as a craft union federation that organized skilled workers. In other words, the AFL attempted to protect the privileges of a small segment of the American working class, often at the expense of less privileged, unskilled wage-workers. When the First World War began, the AFL issued a no-strike pledge, promising to keep industry working for the war effort. In return, the Woodrow Wilson administration began to actively support union organizing efforts. Between 1915 and 1920, union membership in the United States doubled. But the AFL's increasing reliance upon governmental support further encouraged the moderate, responsible unionism that already distinguished this organization from the more radical efforts of the Knight of Labor.

In contrast, the Industrial Workers of the World (IWW), founded in 1905 by a group of radical activists and Socialist Party leaders, had a vision of unionization far different from the moderate program advanced by Gompers's AFL. While the AFL sought to organize and protect the privileges of skilled craft workers, the Wobblies promoted the organization of all industrial workers, skilled and unskilled, into one big union. Further, the Wobblies were influenced by the European syndicalist tradition. A close cousin of anarchism, syndicalism was a set of political ideologies that sought to transform capitalism through direct action at the point of production. With slow-downs, work-to-rules actions, sabotage and strikes, syndicalists argued that workers themselves could challenge the control of industry by capitalists. And for the syndicalists in the IWW, unions that utilized these tactics were a means toward the broader end of social transformation. While the AFL sought to win higher wages and benefits for its members, the IWW attempted to overthrow capitalism itself. Although the IWW participated in or led important strikes in Lawrence, Massachusetts; Patterson, New Jersey; and throughout the lumber camps of the Northwest, it never had the influence or power of the American Federation of Labor. Because of its radical politics and unconventional tactics, the IWW was a target for constant surveillance and repression and was eventually destroyed by the forces arrayed against it.

But in the political environment of the early twentieth century, even the moderate AFL was a target of state-sanctioned repression. Because of government support, the AFL came out of the First World War stronger than ever before. And after the war ended, workers who had sacrificed much for the national effort sought some recompense for their troubles. During the summer of 1919 a strike wave washed across the United States, paralyzing industry on a national scale. Beginning just two years after the Bolshevik Revolution in Russia, what became known as the American Red Summer provoked profound fears among American capitalists and within the U.S. government. This Red Summer led directly into a new red scare. After his house was bombed, he claimed, by anarchists, U.S. Attorney General Alexander Palmer ordered the round-up and arrest of thousands of immigrant unionists. What followed was a series of legal and extralegal forms of political repression and in the years directly following 1919, there was a 30 percent drop in overall union membership.

THE CIO

The union movement went into retreat. But that changed after the stock market crash of 1929 and the beginning of the Great Depression. Because of its moderate, craft orientation, the AFL proved incapable of taking advantage of the economic downturn to expand its base of support. A series of general strikes (in San Francisco, Toledo, and Minneapolis), a national textile strike, militant street actions, rent strikes, and general protests led the Roosevelt administration to enact the National Labor Relations Act (or Wagner Act) in 1935. This law gave legal support to labor's right to organize and bargain collectively. Buoyed by new legislative openings, John L. Lewis, Philip Murray, Sidney Hillman, and other labor leaders already dissatisfied with the limits of the AFL's craft unionism founded the Congress of Industrial Unions (CIO). Like the Knights of Labor and the IWW before it, the CIO set out to organize workers along industrial lines and had early success unionizing the steel and rubber industries. The early phase of this movement culminated in a 1936–1937 wave of sit-down strikes, beginning at the General Motors plant in Flint, Michigan. At the GM plant and elsewhere across the country, unionists sat down at their machines and occupied factory floors.

Following the sit-down wave, the CIO became increasingly close to the Roosevelt administration. When the United States entered the Second World War, the CIO offered a no-strike pledge in return for continued support from the government apparatus. While this no-strike pledge could not stop the many wartime wildcat work actions, it did have the effect of alienating the more militant and energetic local workers and leaders from the national CIO. If the government apparatus were to continue to support union efforts, the militancy of the early CIO had to be surrendered to the quest for industrial order. In place of class conflict, the CIO had to pursue a path of business-government-labor cooperation. This path, however, necessarily led to the decline of internal democracy, as unions increasingly became mechanisms for disciplining the shop floor. As one contemporary observer, C. Wright Mills, put it in his *The New Men of Power*, unions increasingly became "shock-absorbers" for both management and workers (p. 224).

After the war, workers and returning soldiers had confidence in their union strength and a sense of entitlement derived from having sacrificed so much for the national cause. This led to another postwar strike wave. In a now familiar pattern, this postwar strike wave was followed by a new red scare, political repression, and, most importantly for labor, the passage of the 1947 Taft-Hartley law. Taft-Hartley bureaucratized union grievance procedures, outlawed secondary boycotts, and required all union leaders to sign an oath that they were not Communists. This last provision forced the federation to expel many militant and radical organizers and to disaffiliate radical unions. Taft-Hartley made the militant actions that characterized the early days of the CIO extremely difficult.

THE IMPACT OF GLOBALIZATION

Despite this latest wave of government-sponsored repression, almost 35 percent of the American industrial workforce was unionized by mid-century. Because the new, moderate unionism of the CIO no longer differed in character from the AFL, the two unions affiliated in 1955. The AFL-CIO had considerable power between 1955 and 1973, making possible the formation of an American blue-collar middle class. Union workers bought houses, automobiles, and sent their children to college. And union prosperity benefited many American workers left out of direct unionization campaigns through pattern bargaining and by setting an ideal American standard of living that pressured non-union firms to provide better pay and benefits to their employees. But often, this American standard of living came at the expense of non-American workers. Now integrated into the government apparatus, the AFL-CIO supported American anticommunism around the world, working with the CIA to undermine radical unions in the Third World and helping to prop up right-wing dictators.

Beginning in the 1970s, new laws and new trade agreements that made capital increasingly mobile ushered in the age of globalization. In order to remain competitive with international firms, American companies increasingly sought out cheaper labor sources, moved production operations to the Third World, and, when they remained within the United States, demanded concessions and givebacks from their union workers. American unions were decimated, declining to the point that in 2007 approximately 8 percent of American workers were in a union. Although the AFL-CIO attempted to deal with this setback through a new emphasis upon organizing communities of previously unorganized workers in the service sector (janitors, hotel staff, and restaurant workers), its lack of success resulted in another split in the movement. Led by the Service Employees International Union (SEIU), a group of dissatisfied labor organizations formed a new federation, the Change To Win (CTW) coalition. Like the AFL-CIO, CTW promised a new emphasis upon organizing and militant action; and, most significantly, it has set out to organize Wal-Mart workers. To date, CTW has shown little progress in that direction, but its efforts continue.

At the same time, as American corporations increasingly outsourced production, they produced industrial zones in formerly underdeveloped nations. For instance, throughout the twentieth century RCA sought sources of cheaper labor. When its plant in Camden, New Jersey, organized, RCA opened a new production center in the non-union town of Bloomington, Indiana. When the Bloomington plant unionized, RCA opened a new manufacturing facility in the open-shop town of Memphis,

Tennessee. When the Memphis plant organized, RCA outsourced production to Ciudad Juarez, in Mexico. Soon afterward, the Juarez plant began organizing. In each case, as production relocated, unionization movements followed. In the early twenty-first century, many Third World countries became hotbeds of union activity. And in 2002, a former union leader, Luiz Ignatio "Lula" DeSilva, was elected president of one of the largest democracies in the Americas, Brazil. In these industrializing nations, union movements have successfully adopted tactics similar to those used by unions in the United States and Europe. But one important constraint on union activity remains. In these new industrial regions, unions have prospered under democratically elected governments. But authoritarian regimes continue to repress union activity through imprisonment, the murder and torture of union activists, and various other state-sanctioned methods. Consequently, the future of the international union movement may well hinge on the ability of activists and organizers to penetrate rapidly industrializing authoritarian countries such as China; and whether such a possibility exists under current political conditions is an open question.

SEE ALSO *Blue Collar and White Collar; Capitalism; Class Conflict; Great Depression; Industrialization; Labor; Labor Demand; Labor Supply; Labor Union; Middle Class; Organizations; Social Movements; Socialism; Syndicalism; Wages; Work; Work Week; Working Class; Working Day, Length of*

BIBLIOGRAPHY

Barrett, James R. 1999. *William Z. Foster and the Tragedy of American Radicalism.* Urbana: University of Illinois Press.

Chan, Anita. 2001. *China's Workers Under Assault: The Exploitation of Labor in a Globalizing Economy.* Armonk, NY: M.E. Sharpe.

Cowie, Jefferson. 1999. *Capital Moves: RCA's Seventy-Year Quest for Cheap Labor.* Ithaca, NY: Cornell University Press.

Foner, Philip S. 1965. *The Industrial Workers of the World, 1905–1917.* Vol. 4 of *History of the Labor Movement in the United States.* New York: International Publishers.

Klein, Jennifer. 2003. *For All These Rights: Business, Labor, and the Shaping of America's Public-Private Welfare State.* Princeton, NJ: Princeton University Press.

Lichtenstein, Nelson. 2002. *State of the Union: A Century of American Labor.* Princeton, NJ: Princeton University Press.

Mills, C. Wright. 2001. *The New Men of Power.* Introduction by Nelson Lichtenstein. Urbana: University of Illinois Press. (Orig. pub. 1948).

Montgomery, David. 1979. *Workers Control in America: Studies in the History of Work, Technology, and Labor Struggles.* Cambridge, U.K. and New York: Cambridge University Press.

Murray, R. Emmett. 1998. *The Lexicon of Labor.* New York: New Press.

Roediger, David. 1991. *The Wages of Whiteness: Race and the Making of the American Working Class.* New York: Verso.

Shorrock, Tim. 2003. Labor's Cold War. *Nation* 276 (19): 15–22.

Silver, Beverly J. 2003. *Forces of Labor: Workers' Movements and Globalization since 1870.* Cambridge, U.K. and New York: Cambridge University Press.

Stansell, Christine. 1987. *City of Women: Sex and Class in New York 1789–1860.* Urbana: University of Illinois Press.

Wilentz, Sean. 1984. *Chants Democratic: New York City & the Rise of the American Working Class 1788–1850.* New York: Oxford University Press.

Graham Cassano

UNIT ROOT AND COINTEGRATION REGRESSION

The study of the evolution through time of a variable or group of variables has existed since the dawn of empirical analysis in the mid-seventeenth century. The formulation of explicit statistical models for a time series process $\{y_t\}$ is typically in the form of an *autoregressive moving average model*

$$
\begin{aligned}
y_t - a_1 y_{t-1} - \dots - a_p y_{t-p} \\
= b + \epsilon_t + \theta_1 \epsilon_{t-1} + \dots + \theta_q \epsilon_{t-q}
\end{aligned}
\tag{1}
$$

where the *innovation* or *shock* ε_t is assumed independently, identically distributed with mean zero and variance σ^2.

When the roots of $1 - \sum_{j=1}^{p} a_j z^j = 0$ lie outside the unit circle, the process $\{y_t\}$ is *stationary* in the sense that y_t has a fixed mean and variance for all t, and the covariance between any pair of values depends only on their distance apart in time, not on their absolute location. When the roots lie inside the unit circle, the process $\{y_t\}$ is *explosive* in the sense that it quickly becomes unbounded as t increases. If there are d unit roots for the solution $1 - \sum_{j=1}^{p} a_j z^j = 0$, and others are outside the unit circle, the process is called *integrated of order d, I(d)*, because the process can be interpreted as a d-fold partial sum of stationary process $y_{d,t} = \sum_{s=1}^{t} y_{d-1,s}$, for $d = 1, \dots,$ where $y_{d-1,t} = (1-L)^d y_t$, L denotes the backward shift operator, $L^s y_t = y_{t-s}$ (Box and Jenkins 1970). When there is only one unit root ($d = 1$), it is called an *I(1) process* or a *unit root process*; thus when all the roots are outside the unit circle, it is also called an *I(0) process*.

Unit root process is intermediate between stationary and explosive process. Nelson and Plosser (1982) have found that many economic and financial time series are $I(1)$ or $I(2)$. There are many reasons that a time series of a variable is integrated. For instance, real business-cycle models predict that many real economic variables would contain a unit root. There is also the efficient market hypothesis in which the best predictor of tomorrow's price y_{t+1} is today's price y_t (Fama 1970).

When $y_{t+1} = y_t + \varepsilon_t$, it is commonly referred to as a *random walk process*. Hall's consumption function theory (1978) implies that, under a simple version of the permanent income hypothesis, future changes in consumption are unpredictable, so consumption follows a random walk. The predictions of these theories often extend to multivariate relations. For example, if income has a unit root, then consumption as a function of income will also have a unit root. The residuals that can be viewed as a linear combination of consumption and income will not have a unit root. When some linear combination of $I(d)$ variables has a lower order of integration, these variables are *cointegrated*, in Engle and Granger's terminology (1987).

UNIT ROOT PROCESS

If a variable, say y_t, has a unit root, the shock to the variable never dies out. A unit root process can be written as the sum of past shocks plus an $I(0)$ current shock. Because the sum of past shock is a dominant term in y_t, this permanent component constitutes a *stochastic trend*. Information on the degree of persistence in a time series and, in particular, on its order of integration, can help to guide the construction or testing of economic theories.

Box and Jenkins (1970) proposed an informal data-analytic basis for the choice of *d*. Formal testing of a unit root is usually conducted by fitting a *p*-th order autoregressive form

$$y_t = \sum_{j=1}^{p} a_j y_{t-j} + \varepsilon_t, \qquad (2)$$

or its *error-correction* representation,

$$\Delta y_t = \rho y_{t-p} + \sum_{j=1}^{p-1} a_j^* \Delta y_{t-j} + \varepsilon_t \qquad (3)$$

where $\delta = (1 - L)$, and $a_j^* = \sum_{i=1}^{j} a_i - 1$. The null that $\sum a_j = 1$ is equivalent to the null $\rho = 0$.

Time series regressions that include integrated variables have statistical properties that are very different from the time series regressions with stationary variables. The least squares estimator of ρ when the regressor is $I(1)$ converges to its true value 0 at the speed T, not at speed $T^{1/2}$, and has a limiting distribution that is a functional of Brownian motion (Chan and Wei 1988). Dickey and Fuller (1979) derive the *t*-statistics for the null hypothesis $\rho = 0$ by considering the limiting behavior of quadratic forms. The distribution of Dickey-Fuller *t*-statistic is tabulated by Dickey (1976).

Applying Dickey-Fuller procedure to the first difference of y_t provides a test of $I(2)$ against $I(1)$. When the process $\{y_t\}$ may possess two or more unit roots, Dickey and Pantula (1987) recommend a "downward," sequential *t*-test procedure starting with the greatest suspected number of unit roots, *d* (i.e., transform (2) into equivalent formulation (3) in terms of $\delta^d y_t$), because the "upward" testing procedure starting with a test for a single unit root is an inconsistent test. Pantula (1989) proves that the distribution of the relevant *t*-statistic under each null has the standard Dickey-Fuller (1979) distribution.

From the perspective of empirical work, (2) may be overly restrictive. The process $\{y_t\}$ may also be a function of trend and serially correlated $I(0)$ errors. Moreover, $\{y_t\}$ may be subject to trend breaks or structural breaks with unknown breakdays, or trend may be misspecified (Perron 1989). The bulk of the large literature on tests for unit roots has been to propose tests that (1) are asymptotically similar under the general $I(1)$ null, in the sense that the null distribution depends neither on the parameters of the trend process nor the parameters describing the short-run dynamics of ε_t (Phillips and Perron 1988); (2) have good power in large samples; and (3) exhibit small size distortions. Although the asymptotic size and power vary greatly across the proposed test statistics, the Monte Carlo findings for finite sample yield similar conclusions: The proposed tests have relatively low power against $I(0)$ alternatives, and there are substantial size distortions for the tests. For instance, with 100 stationary observations, the one-sided 5 percent significance level Dickey-Fuller *t*-test has a power of only 0.19. On the other hand, processes that are $I(1)$ but which have moderate negative autocorrelation in first difference are incorrectly rejected with high probability. (For detail, see Stock 1994).

COINTEGRATION REGRESSION

Multivariate time series methods are widely used by empirical economists. One important implication of economic theory is that certain ratios are stable. For instance, in response to growth in productivity and population, neoclassical growth models (King, Plosser, and Rebelo 1988) predict that output (y), consumption (c), and investment (i) will grow in a balanced way. That is, even though y_t, c_t, and i_t increase permanently in response to increases in productivity and population, there are not permanent shifts in $c_t - y_t$ or $i_t - y_t$. In other words, these variables are *cointegrated*.

For ease of exposition, here we shall only focus on the classical analysis of $I(1)$ and $I(0)$ systems. Let $\{w_t\}$ be a sequence of $m \times 1$ vector of $I(1)$ time series observations. Vector autoregressive model (VAR) of the form

$$W_t = \Pi_1 W_{t-1} + \ldots + \Pi_p W_{t-p} + v_t \qquad (4)$$

provides a flexible and tractable framework for analyzing w_t (as in Hsiao 1979 and Sims 1980). Transforming (4) into an *error-correction* form provides a framework for analyzing both long-run and short-run economic relations

$$\Delta W_t = \sum_{j=1}^{p-1} \Pi_j^* \Delta W_{t-1} + \Pi_p^* W_{t-p} + v_t \qquad (5)$$

where $\Pi_j^* = \sum_{i=1}^{j} \Pi_j - I_m$, $j = 1, \ldots, p$, and I_m denotes the m-rowed identity matrix. If there are m unit roots, $\Pi_p^* \equiv 0$, each series in the system is governed by a different stochastic trend. When there are fewer than m unit roots in (4), say n, then rank $(\Pi_p^*) = r$, $r = m - n$, $1 \leq n \leq m$. When rank $(\Pi_p^*) = r$, one can write $\Pi_p^* = \alpha\beta'$ where α and β are $m \times r$ full column rank matrices. Since w_t is $I(1)$, δw_t is $I(0)$, $\beta' w_{t-p}$ must be $I(0)$ to ensure compatibility between the left-hand and right-hand side of (5). Therefore, the matrix β' is called the *cointegrating matrix* that describes "equilibrium" or "long-run" relations within a fully dynamic framework. The matrix α transmits the deviations from the long-run relations, $e_t = \beta' w_t$, into respective elements of w_t. The matrix Π_j^*, $j = 1, \ldots, p-1$, describes the short-run adjustment pattern that provides information on how soon the "long-run equilibrium" is restored after any of the variables in the system are perturbed by a shock. In economics, the existence of long-run relations and the strength of attraction to such a state depends on the actions of a market or on government intervention. The concept of *cointegration* has been applied in a variety of economic models including the relationship between capital and output, real wages and labor productivity, and so on (King, Plosser, Stock, and Watson).

Several issues arise from the cointegration analysis. First, because $\beta' w_t$ is $I(0)$, w_t must be driven by some common trends. In other words, cointegration signifies comovements among trending variables. However, only the rank of cointegration can be uniquely determined. The cointegrating matrix β' is not uniquely defined. Any linear combination of cointegrating vector is a cointegrat-

ing vector or $\Pi_p^* = \alpha C^{-1} C \beta'$ for any $r \times r$ nonsingular constant matrix C. (Therefore, the maximum number of linearly independent cointegrating vectors in a system of m $I(1)$ variable, is $(m - 1)$). Normalization rule for the unique determination of the cointegrating matrix has to be used.

Second, although the least squares estimator with integrated regressor is consistent, it has very different statistical properties from the least squares estimator with stationary regressors (Chan and Wei 1988; Phillips and Durlauf 1986). Some of the estimated coefficients of (4) converge to the true values at speed $T^{1/2}$ and are asymptotically normally distributed; some converge to the true values at speed T and have non-normal asymptotic distributions (Sims, Stock, and Watson 1990). This raises the issue of statistical inference because in some instances the usual test statistics can be approximated by chi-square distributions while in other circumstances, they cannot.

Third, to overcome the miscentering and skewness of the usual test statistics because of the issues of unit root distribution, one can either condition on the innovations driving the common stochastic trends of the system (Phillips 1991) or use the *reduced rank* regression technique (Johansen 1988; 1991). In a system of m $I(1)$ variables, the possible common trends vary between 1 and m. However, the knowledge of the rank of cointegration or nonstationarity (location of unit roots) is not generally known *a priori*. Johansen (1991) proposes likelihood-based tests for the rank of cointegration by considering the likelihood function of (5), whereas Stock and Watson (1988) propose a rank test for $\frac{1}{T^2}\sum_{t=1}^{T} w_t w_t'$ based on the fact that if there are r linearly independent cointegrating relations, then w_t are driven by $m - r$ common trends, hence the sum of cross-products of w_t divided by T^2 can only have rank $m - r$. Unfortunately, neither method provides reliable inference in finite sample. Many Monte Carlo studies show that there are serious size and power distortions (Ho and Soresen 1996; Gonzalo and Pitarakis 1999).

The literature on unit root and cointegration analysis has greatly enhanced our understanding of dynamic econometric modeling of economic time series and provides a useful repertoire of tools for empirical analysis. However, unit root tests and cointegration analysis also raise serious finite sample issues. Tests with better finite sample size and power remain to be developed. More attention to economic theory and integrating economic analysis with time series analysis could also be fruitful.

SEE ALSO *White Noise*

BIBLIOGRAPHY

Banerjee, Anindya, Juan J. Dolado, John W. Galbraith, and David F. Hendry. 1993. *Cointegration, Error-Correction, and the Econometric Analysis of Non-Stationary Data.* Oxford: Oxford University Press.

Bierens, Herman J. 2001. Unit Roots. In *A Companion to Theoretical Econometrics*, ed. Badi H. Baltagi, 610–633. Oxford: Blackwell.

Box, George E. P., and Gwilym M. Jenkins. 1970. *Time Series Analysis, Forecasting, and Control.* San Francisco: Holden Day.

Chan, Ngai H., and Ching Z. Wei. 1988. Limiting Distributions of Least Squares Estimates of Unstable Autoregressive Processes. *Annals of Statistics* 16: 367–401.

Dickey, David A. 1976. Estimation and Testing of Nonstationary Time Series. PhD diss., Iowa State University.

Dickey, David A., and Wayne A. Fuller. 1979. Distribution of the Estimators for Autoregressive Time Series with a Unit Root. *Journal of the American Statistical Association* 74: 427–431.

Dickey, David A., and Sastry G. Pantula. 1987. Determining the Order of Differencing in Autoregressive Processes. *Journal of Business and Economic Statistics* 5: 455–462.

Diebold, Francis X., and Marc Nerlove. 1989. Unit Roots in Economic Time Series: A Selective Survey. In *Advances in Econometrics: Cointegration, Spurious Regressions, and Unit Roots*, vol. 8, eds. Thomas B. Fomby and George F. Rhodes, 3–69. Greenwich, CT: JAI Press.

Engle, Robert F., and Clive W. J. Granger. 1987. Cointegration and Error Correction: Representation, Estimation, and Testing. *Econometrica* 55: 251–276.

Fama, Eugene F. 1970. Efficient Capital Markets: A Review of Theory and Empirical Work. *Journal of Finance* 25: 383–417.

Gonzalo, Jesus, and J. Y. Pitarakis. 1999. Dimensionality Effect in Cointegrated Systems. In *Granger Festschrift*, eds. Robert Engle and H. White, 212–229. Oxford: Oxford University Press.

Hall, Robert E. 1978. Stochastic Implication of the Life Cycle-Permanent Income Hypothesis: Theory and Evidence. *Journal of Political Economy* 86: 971–987.

Ho, Mun, and Bent Sørensen. 1996. Finding Cointegration Rank in High Dimensional Systems Using the Johansen Test: An Illustration Using Data Based on Monte Carlo Simulations. *Review of Economics and Statistics* 78: 726–732.

Hsiao, Cheng. 1979. Autoregressive Modelling of Canadian Money and Income Data. *Journal of the American Statistical Association* 74: 553–560.

Johansen, Søren. 1988. Statistical Analysis of Cointegration Vectors. *Journal of Economic Dynamics and Control* 12: 231–254.

Johansen, Søren. 1991. Estimation and Hypothesis Testing of Cointegration Vectors in Gaussian Vector Autoregressive Models. *Econometrica* 59: 1551–1580.

King, Robert G., Charles I. Plosser, and Sergio T. Rebelo. 1988. Production Growth and Business Cycles II: New Directions. *Journal of Monetary Economics* 21: 309–342.

Nelson, Charles R., and Charles I. Plosser. 1982. Trends and Random Walks in Macroeconomic Time Series: Some Evidence and Implications. *Journal of Monetary Economics* 10: 139–162.

Pantula, Sastry G. 1989. Testing for Unit Roots in Time Series Data. *Econometric Theory* 5: 256–271.

Perron, Pierre. 1989. The Great Crash, the Oil Price Shock, and the Unit Root Hypothesis. *Econometrica* 57: 1361–1401.

Phillips, Peter C. B. 1991. Optimal Inference in Cointegrating Systems. *Econometrica* 59: 283–306.

Phillips, Peter C. B., and Pierre Perron. 1988. Testing for a Unit Root in a Time Series Regression. *Biometrika* 75: 335–346.

Sims, Christopher A., James H. Stock, and Mark W. Watson. 1990. Inference in Linear Time Series Models with Some Unit Roots. *Econometrica* 58: 113–144.

Stock, James H. 1994. Unit Roots, Structural Breaks, and Trends. In *Handbook of Econometrics*, vol. 4, eds. Robert F. Engle and Daniel L. McFadden, 2739–2841. Amsterdam: North-Holland.

Stock, James H., and Mark W. Watson. 1988. Testing for Common Trends. *Journal of the American Statistical Association* 83: 1097–1107.

Watson, Mark W. 1994. Vector Autoregressions and Cointegration. In *Handbook of Econometrics*, vol. 4, eds. Robert F. Engle and Daniel L. McFadden, 2844–2915. Amsterdam: North-Holland.

Cheng Hsiao

UNITED ARAB REPUBLIC

The United Arab Republic (UAR) was founded in 1958 as a political union between Syria and Egypt. The union reflected a sense of Arab nationalism and solidarity (Pan-Arabism). It was largely driven by a desire to overcome dividing borders viewed by many as an artificial creation of European colonial powers. However, the union eventually collapsed in 1961 due to widespread sentiments in Syria that it had become a vehicle for furthering Egyptian hegemony.

PAN-ARABISM

A major driving force behind the formation of the UAR was Pan-Arabism. Sentiments of collective Arab nationalism had already emerged in the Middle East in the early twentieth century. These attitudes were largely motivated by a desire to shake off the corrupt, inefficient, and alien rule of the Ottoman Empire. Shared experience coupled with a common language and culture engendered collective sentiments that spread throughout the Arab-speaking Middle East.

After conquering the Middle East during World War I (1914–1918), the colonial powers divided the Arabs by drawing previously nonexistent political frontiers. Among other things, segmentation enabled the victorious Europeans to reward friendly Arab leaders with a state that they could govern. Thus, local leaders, whose support for the Europeans during the war was initially driven by encompassing Arabism and the desire to rid themselves of the foreign Ottoman rule, now had an incentive to continue cooperating with the Europeans and encourage loyalties to the smaller, newly created states. In almost every Arab country, schemes for regional Arab unity were countervailed with efforts to instill a sense of patriotic solidarity and identification with the new state through the creation of a national flag, an anthem, and other local symbols. Nonetheless, modern technology, mobility, and newspapers and other printed materials enhanced the sense of collective Arabism that transcended the new political boundaries. Furthermore, the new regimes found that by appealing to sentiments of Arabism, they could increase local support and further their legitimacy.

Attempts to balance the tension-laden tendencies of Pan-Arabism and local regime interests continued to shape Arab politics and society well into the decades that followed. The foundation of the UAR and its demise were a product of such dynamics.

PRINCIPLE ACTORS OF THE UNION

The principle actors behind the union were the Ba'thists and Nasserites in Syria and President Gamal Abdel Nasser (1918–1970) of Egypt. When Syria became a democracy in 1954, mass public support for a new, all-encompassing Arab state got reflected in the platforms of rival political parties. Both the Communists and the Muslim Brotherhood supported transcending frontiers, although the Communists preferred closer ties with the Soviet Union. The growing merchant class in Syria saw economic opportunities in the abolition of borders and, thus, also viewed a union favorably. These domestic dynamics led the powerful Syrian Ba'th Party, headed by Michel 'Aflaq (1910–1989) and Akram Hourani (1912–1996), to propose the idea of a united republic with Egypt. In particular, the Ba'thists, espousing an ideological platform that combined Arab nationalism, socialism, and secularism, found itself in domestic struggles for power against the strengthening Communists. The party hoped that the union would lead to the collapse of its competitors.

In Egypt, meanwhile, the "Officers' Coup" in 1952 saw Colonel Nasser seize power from King Farouk (1920–1965) and emerge as the new Egyptian president. Nasser's firm stance against the British presence in the Suez and the nationalization of foreign property had made him an admired leader throughout the Arab world. After surviving the Anglo-French and Israeli invasion of 1956, Nasser was depicted as a great, modern-day Arab hero capable of defending the interests of the Arab world against the imperialist powers. His popularity made him an agreed-upon candidate for leading the union, although Nasser himself was initially reluctant to merge the two countries. He feared problems associated with merging the two very different economic systems and with unifying the civil and military institutions. The Ba'thists in Syria, on the other hand, were optimistic. They believed Nasser would entrust them with the governance of Syria. Ultimately, they managed to convince him of the feasibility of the union.

THE RISE AND DEMISE OF THE UNION

In February 1958 President Nasser of Egypt and President Shukri al-Kuwatli (1891–1967) of Syria signed the unification treaty. Following a referendum held simultaneously in both countries, the two countries were integrated and the UAR was born with a new federal constitution, with Cairo as its capital, and with Nasser as its president. Separate Egyptian and Syrian citizenship was abolished. The UAR adopted the Egyptian flag with an addition of two stars to represent the two members of the union. The birth of the union was greeted with such enthusiasm throughout the Middle East that it was followed by a series of attempts by pan-Arabists elsewhere to overthrow regimes perceived as pro-Western. Indeed, following a coup d'état in 1958, Iraq declared its intent to join the UAR. That same year, the United Arab States, a loose federation of the UAR and Yemen, was also established.

Although the union was initially received with immense enthusiasm in both of the UAR's member countries, disillusionment soon took over popular attitudes in Syria. The disparity of power between Egypt and Syria made the former the undisputable hegemonic force, despite the formal federal structure of the new republic. The authority bestowed on the president made Nasser extraordinarily powerful and allowed him to impose unpopular economic and social policies in Syria. Even though the Ba'thist Hourani was named one of four vice presidents, he was practically powerless and resigned in protest as early as December 1959. Egypt's political superiority left very little room for Syrian input in administering the affairs of the union. Leading figures from the Syrian regime, particularly the military, were transferred to Cairo. This way, Nasser could ensure they were isolated from their power bases. Officials and military personnel from Egypt were reassigned to Syria, where they in practice took control of the Syrian bureaucracy and security forces.

In addition, the Ba'th Party dissolved itself in compliance with the ban on all political parties other than Nasser's Arab Socialist Union, a condition that Nasser presented before consenting to the merger and which the Ba'thists accepted under the misguided assumption that Syria would preserve a degree of autonomy in the new institutional framework. The Communists and the Muslim Brotherhood, meanwhile, were brutally repressed as the Egyptians increasingly asserted their authority. Similarly, the Syrian press was seized by the new regime. Furthermore, attempts to impose Egypt's socialist policies in Syria left the Syrian merchant class not only without access to Egyptian markets but also facing stiff limitations on its ability to maneuver within the Syrian part of the UAR. Likewise, land reforms made large landowners unhappy. In short, Syrians of all political and social streams were left disenchanted and feeling as though they were ruled by outsiders.

A 1961 coup d'état in Syria led to its withdrawal from the union and a renewed assertion of its independence. A short time later, the United Arab States was abolished following Yemenite criticism of Nasser's heavily socialist policies. Witnessing the Syrian experience, the Iraqi regime too decided to stay out of the union, despite its initial vow of commitment to join. Egypt retained the name of UAR until 1971.

Following yet another coup d'état in 1963 in Syria, unity talks were again undertaken, but without results. The failure of the UAR left many leaders in Syria and the rest of the Arab world determined never to allow their country to be pushed into such a subordinate position. Thus, despite continuing widespread sentiments of Arabism, the demise of the UAR brought about an end to any real chance of integrating Arab countries into a single state. And by the end of the 1980s, notions of pan-Arab unity had all but disappeared.

SEE ALSO *Cold War; Communism; Coup d'Etat; Gulf States; Nation-State; Stability, Political; Union of Soviet Socialist Republics*

BIBLIOGRAPHY

Batatu, Hanna. 1999. *Syria's Peasantry, the Descendants of Its Lesser Rural Notables, and Their Politics.* Princeton, NJ: Princeton University Press.

Jankowski, James P. 2002. *Nasser's Egypt, Arab Nationalism, and the United Arab Republic.* Boulder, CO: Lynne Reinner.

Peretz, Don. 1994. *The Middle East Today.* 6th ed. Westport, CT: Praeger.

Oded Haklai

UNITED NATIONS

The United Nations (UN) is a global organization of states that aims to find cooperative solutions for international security, economic, and social problems. The first formal use of the term *United Nations* appeared in the Declaration by the United Nations (January 1, 1942), in which twenty-six Allied countries pledged to defeat the Axis Powers and subscribed to the principles of the Atlantic Charter (August 14, 1941) during World War II (1939–1945). These principles included "the establishment of a wider and permanent system of general security."

From August to October 1944, delegates from the United States, the Soviet Union, the United Kingdom, and the Republic of China met at the Dumbarton Oaks estate in Washington, D.C., to negotiate the formation of a new organization to replace the League of Nations. Most of the outstanding issues were settled at the Yalta Conference (February 4–11, 1945) among the leaders of the "Big Three" nations: U.S. president Franklin D. Roosevelt (1882–1945), British prime minister Winston Churchill (1874–1965), and Soviet general secretary Joseph Stalin (1879–1953). Shortly thereafter, delegates of fifty nations met in San Francisco to finalize the negotiations, culminating in the signing of the UN Charter on June 26, 1945. On August 8, 1945, the United States became the first country to ratify the Charter. The United Nations Organization came into being on October 24 (celebrated since 1948 as United Nations Day) when the majority of original signers, including the great powers (the four Dumbarton Oaks conveners and France), had ratified the Charter.

STRUCTURE

Although the UN Charter opens with the famous phrase "We the peoples of the United Nations," the United Nations is primarily an organization of sovereign states. Membership is open to all "peace-loving states" (Article 4), but disputes over the admission of new members fell victim after World War II to the cold war conflict. In 1955 the United States and the Soviet Union reached a compromise that allowed for the admission of sixteen new members. Still, controversy persisted over the membership status of the partitioned states of Germany, Korea,

Vietnam, and China. Both German states were admitted in 1973 and both Korean states in 1991. Vietnam entered as a single state in 1977. Nationalist China (Taiwan) represented China until November 1971, when the United States ended its objection to the membership of the People's Republic of China. In 2006 the United Nations had 191 member states.

The UN Charter also established the six "principal organs" of the United Nations: the General Assembly, the Security Council, the Economic and Social Council, the Trusteeship Council, the International Court of Justice, and the Secretariat. The General Assembly is the United Nations' plenary body. Aside from occasional special sessions, it meets in annual sessions that usually start in September and last for three months. The General Assembly oversees subsidiary bodies, calls international conferences, approves the budget, and adopts nonbinding resolutions on a wide variety of issues. General Assembly decisions are taken by majority vote based on a one-state–one-vote principle. Since 1987, after lobbying by the United States, critical votes on the budget are taken by unanimity rule (instead of the historical two-thirds majority) in an effort to curtail large annual budget increases. Budget assessments are made on a capacity-to-pay basis. As of 2005, the United States was responsible for 24 percent of the UN budget, followed by Japan (19 percent) and Germany (8 percent). Countries do not always meet their budget obligations in a timely manner: In September 2005 member states owed the United Nations $3 billion in outstanding peacekeeping and regular budget payments ($1.2 billion from the United States alone).

The Security Council has primary responsibility for the maintenance of international peace and security. Under chapter VII of the UN Charter, the Security Council can adopt coercive measures, including economic sanctions and the use of force, which are binding on individual member states. The Security Council has five permanent members (China, France, the Russian Federation, the United Kingdom, and the United States) and ten nonpermanent members that are elected for two-year, nonrenewable terms by the General Assembly. (Until 1965, the Security Council only had six nonpermanent members.) Security Council resolutions require an affirmative vote of nine members, including the five permanent members. By 2005 the permanent members had exercised their veto right 244 times, but on only twenty occasions since 1990. The veto threat is, however, still a powerful tool to block unwanted resolutions.

The Economic and Social Council coordinates and supervises the work of numerous commissions and expert bodies on economic and social matters, including human rights. Members are elected for three-year terms by the General Assembly. The Economic and Social Council's membership has gradually expanded from eighteen to fifty-four. The Economic and Social Council has limited powers other than its ability to submit recommendations to the General Assembly (by majority vote). Formally, the Economic and Social Council coordinates the activities of various specialized agencies, including the World Bank Group and the International Monetary Fund (IMF). Developing countries have long, and unsuccessfully, pushed for a greater role for the Economic and Social Council vis-à-vis these organizations. Other specialized UN agencies, each with its own budget, membership, and charter, include the International Labor Organization (ILO), the Food and Agriculture Organization (FAO), the United Nations Educational, Scientific, and Cultural Organization (UNESCO), and the World Health Organization (WHO).

The Trusteeship Council was set up to monitor UN trust territories that were not designated as strategic by their administrating powers (strategic trust areas were the Security Council's responsibility). The Trusteeship Council ceased its operations on November 1, 1994, when the last remaining trust territory (Palau) became independent.

The International Court of Justice, located in The Hague, Netherlands, issues advisory opinions on legal questions brought to it by other UN organs and settles legal disputes submitted to it by member states. Its fifteen judges are elected for nine-year terms by the General Assembly and Security Council. By 2005 the International Court of Justice had delivered twenty-five advisory opinions and eighty-seven judgments on contentious cases, primarily on border and maritime disputes. The binding nature of International Court of Justice opinions depends on whether state parties have previously agreed to its compulsory jurisdiction.

The Secretariat is the United Nations' bureaucracy. In 2005 it employed around nine thousand international civil servants who answer to the United Nations alone for their activities. While most civil servants are stationed at the UN headquarters in New York, the United Nations also maintains staffed offices elsewhere. The Secretariat is headed by the secretary-general, a prestigious post that has been occupied by Trygve Lie (Norway, 1946–1952), Dag Hammarskjöld (Sweden, 1953–1961), U Thant (Burma [Myanmar], 1961–1971), Kurt Waldheim (Austria, 1972–1981), Javier Pérez de Cuéllar (Peru, 1982–1991), Boutros Boutros-Ghali (Egypt, 1992–1996), Kofi Annan (Ghana, 1997–2006), and Ban Ki-moon (South Korea) who was sworn in on December 14, 2006, and began serving on January 1, 2007. Critics have charged that the demands of being the world's primary diplomat sometimes undermine the secretary-general's ability to also be an effective manager of a large bureaucracy.

PEACE AND SECURITY

When states sign the UN Charter, they agree not to use or threaten force "against the territorial integrity or political independence of any state, or in any manner inconsistent with the Purposes of the United Nations" (Article 2). There are two circumstances under which force is consistent with the United Nations' purposes: when it is exercised in self-defense (Article 51) and when the Security Council approves a collective action under chapter VII. The first important authorization of a collective action occurred in 1950 (July 7), when the Security Council authorized the United States to install a central command under the UN flag to restore peace and security following the armed attack by the Democratic People's Republic of Korea (North Korea) against the Republic of Korea (South Korea).

UN action in Korea was possible only because the Soviet Union had temporarily vacated its Security Council seat in protest against nationalist China's representation. After the Soviet delegate returned, the General Assembly adopted the "Uniting for Peace" resolution, which allowed the General Assembly to circumvent a deadlocked Security Council through special emergency sessions. This procedure has been invoked ten times, most notably in 1956 to order the French and British to end their military intervention in the Suez Canal and to create the UN Emergency Force (UNEF I) to provide a buffer between Egyptian and Israeli forces.

UNEF I was the first large-scale example of *peacekeeping*, an activity not mentioned in the Charter. During the cold war, peacekeeping missions were generally limited to providing a buffer between warring parties at the invitation of those parties, prime examples being the long-standing UN forces in Cyprus and Lebanon. An exception was the more ambitious 20,000-person force employed in the Congo between 1960 and 1964. This operation failed to achieve its main objectives, led to a protracted conflict about peacekeeping financing, and cost respected Secretary-General Hammarskjöld his life when his plane crashed in the Congo on September 18, 1961.

UN activity in international security was reinvigorated with the end of the cold war. In 1988 and 1989, for the first time in a decade, the Security Council authorized new peacekeeping missions that were sent to cold war hotspots such as Afghanistan, Angola, Namibia, and Nicaragua. A transformation in UN collective security occurred with the adoption of Security Council Resolution 678 on November 29, 1990, which authorized the use of "all necessary means" if Iraq would not vacate Kuwait by January 15, 1991. The resolution conferred legitimacy on the use of force against Iraq by a U.S.-led coalition. Since then, the Security Council has granted similar authorizations to (groups of) states in eleven cases, including East Timor (with Australia as the leading state) and Haiti (with the United States as leader).

A second significant shift occurred in 1992, when the Security Council authorized the deployment of large peacekeeping forces to end civil wars in Cambodia and Yugoslavia. This was merely the prelude to increased UN involvement in domestic conflicts across the globe. Between 1991 and 2005, the Security Council authorized forty-eight peacekeeping and other multinational uses of force, almost all concerning civil conflicts rather than interstate wars. These efforts were not without risk: more than two thousand UN peacekeepers have lost their lives, most since 1991. The United Nations has also become actively involved in postwar reconstruction and has even run transitional administrations, most notably in East Timor and Kosovo. Moreover, it has created international tribunals to try war crimes in Rwanda, Sierra Leone, and the former Yugoslavia.

Despite its active record since the cold war's end, the United Nations' contribution to the preservation of peace and security has come under serious scrutiny. First, the United Nations has been unable to prevent genocides in Rwanda (1994) and the Sudan (2005). Second, the Security Council has been deadlocked on important cases and has not been able to prevent states or coalitions of states from going it alone in the absence of UN authorization, as illustrated by the intervention of the North Atlantic Treaty Organization (NATO) in Kosovo in 1999 and the U.S.-led invasion of Iraq in 2003. Third, weak and understaffed UN missions have occasionally done more harm than good, as illustrated by the United Nations' failure to maintain the promised safe haven of Srebrenica (1995). Fourth, UN-imposed sanctions on Iraq caused much suffering among the Iraqi population while failing to resolve the conflict. Moreover, the UN "Oil for Food" office allowed massive fraud to occur in the administration of the sanctions.

Some critics justifiably lament UN bureaucratic and peacekeeping practices, as acknowledged by the United Nations' remarkable Brahimi Report (2000). Yet, the United Nations ultimately remains an organization of states. The United Nations can be a useful vehicle for cooperation on those issues where states are committed, but it has few means beyond persuasion to compel states to make committed efforts. In all, most analysts believe that the United Nations has had a modest but significant positive impact, especially on the resolution of civil wars.

OTHER ISSUES

The United Nations has played an active role on a large range of other issues. The United Nations was an important arena for the transformation of former colonies into sovereign states. To many new states, UN membership served as the affirmation of their sovereignty. Moreover, General Assembly Resolution 1514 (December 14, 1960) became the most influential political declaration of the existence of a right to self-determination and the illegitimacy of colonial rule.

The 1948 Universal Declaration of Human Rights provides the foundation for the treatment of human rights in the United Nations. The United Nations administers other global human-rights instruments, such as the Convention Against Torture and Other Cruel, Inhuman, or Degrading Treatment or Punishment (1987), and organizes global conferences, such as the Beijing Women's Conference (1995), that set the normative debate on human rights. It has, however, few enforcement mechanisms other than public shaming through the Human Rights Commission, which critics charge is political and selective.

The United Nations has also provided a forum for arms control negotiations and administers important disarmament treaties. An independent agency, the International Atomic Energy Agency (IAEA), monitors observance of nuclear treaties and can refer violators to the Security Council, which can then decide on coercive measures.

The United Nations also plays an important role in economic development and humanitarian relief, primarily through special programs and funds, such as the UN Children's Fund (UNICEF), the UN Development program (UNDP), and the Office of the UN High Commissioner for Refugees (UNHCR). UNHCR provides a crucial coordinating role in providing relief to the world's refugees (around twenty million in 2005). UNDP is most active in the development and monitoring of the UN Millennium Development goals: an ambitious set of development targets to be achieved by 2015.

The most difficult issue for the United Nations continues to be the Middle East. The United Nations was instrumental in creating the state of Israel and in resolving the 1956 Suez crisis. Yet, its ability to play a constructive role has been compromised by increased politicization. Israel and its defenders charge that the United Nations regularly adopts inflammatory resolutions that unfairly target Israel. For example, between 1975 and 1991, the General Assembly annually adopted a resolution that equated Zionism with racism, a charge that resurfaced at the World Conference Against Racism, Racial Discrimination, Xenophobia, and Related Intolerance, held in Durban, South Africa, in 2001. Defenders of Palestine contend that Israel has repeatedly ignored General Assembly and Security Council resolutions, as well as International Court of Justice rulings.

Reform is also perennially on the United Nations' agenda. Reform attempts generally involve the creation of a blue-ribbon committee, including the High-Level Panel on Threats, Challenges, and Change, established in 2003. The recommendations of these committees rarely lead to fundamental changes. Instead, the United Nations regularly reinvents itself in response to major events and the ensuing new demands on the organization.

SEE ALSO *League of Nations; Multilateralism; Peace; Peace Process; World War II*

BIBLIOGRAPHY

Atlantic Charter. 1941. U.S. Department of State International Information Programs: Basic Readings in U.S. Democracy. http://usinfo.state.gov/usa/infousa/facts/democrac/53.htm.

Charter of the United Nations. 1945. http://www.un.org/aboutun/charter/.

Claude, Inis L. 1971. *Swords Into Plowshares: The Problems and Progress of International Organization.* 4th ed. New York: Random House.

Doyle, Michael, and Nicholas Sambanis. 2000. International Peacebuilding: A Theoretical and Quantitative Analysis. *American Political Science Review* 94 (4): 779–801.

Malone, David, ed. 2004. *The UN Security Council: From the Cold War to the 21st Century.* Boulder, CO: Lynne Rienner.

Report of the Panel on United Nations Peace Operations (Brahimi Report). 2000. http://www.un.org/peace/reports/peace_operations/.

Roberts, Adam, and Benedict Kingsbury, eds. 1993. *United Nations, Divided World: The UN's Roles in International Relations.* 2nd ed. Oxford and New York: Oxford University Press.

Schlesinger, Stephen. 2003. *Act of Creation: The Founding of the United Nations.* Boulder, CO: Westview.

Ziring, Lawrence, Robert E. Riggs, and Jack A. Plano. 2004. *The United Nations: International Organization and World Politics.* 4th ed. Belmont, CA: Wadsworth.

Erik Voeten

UNITED NATIONS MILLENIUM DEVELOPMENT GOALS

SEE *Gender and Development; Health in Developing Countries.*

UNIVARIATE AUTOREGRESSIVE PROCESSES

SEE *Time Series Regression.*

UNIVERSAL DECLARATION OF HUMAN RIGHTS

SEE *Civil Rights; Human Rights; Suffrage, Women's.*

UNIVERSALISM

Universalism is the proposition that there exist single objective standards, independent of culture, by which moral and epistemological questions are each correctly judged. Broad universalism includes any concept or doctrine that applies to the totality of the relevant set, such as human beings. Some religions have doctrines that are believed to apply to all humanity.

Moral universalism posits a unique ethic that applies to all human beings and is comprehensive for all human action, including action that affects nonhumans. Because the universal ethic is independent of culture, it cannot derive from the beliefs of any culture or any generalization from practices and actions. A universal moral standard can be derived only from premises that apply to all human beings, such as human nature. Moral universalism is implied in the concept of human rights and such documents as the United Nations 1948 Universal Declaration of Human Rights.

The concept of a universal ethic or "natural moral law" in European philosophy was developed by the ancient Greek Platonists and Stoics. German philosopher Immanuel Kant based his moral philosophy on the concept that rules can be universalized. Utilitarian moral philosophy, based on what is best for society, is also intended to apply universally. Universalism is also present in the philosophy of natural rights and associated with natural moral law as a standard for judging legislation.

Philosopher John Locke described natural moral law in his work on political philosophy, *Two Treatises of Government* ([1690] 1947). In the *Second Treatise*, Locke states as his premise for the "law of nature," or natural law, that human beings are all equal and independent.

Human beings are biologically independent, for feeling and thinking and choosing take place individually. Equality means that the capacity for reason and choice is common to the human species and that there is no biological basis for one set of humans to be regarded as superior to others. Nihilists, relativists, and supremacists deny the equality premise, while those with a holistic philosophy dispute the independence premise.

Locke's "law of nature" prescribes that it is morally evil to harm others in their lives, health, liberty, or possessions. The existence of such a universal ethic can be claimed by setting criteria for the ethic and then arguing that if a derived ethic fits the criteria, then it exists, just as we can set criteria for the existence of airplanes, and then if a machine fits the criteria, we must conclude that airplanes exist. The criteria could be the following four propositions:

1. The ethic is universal to all humanity.
2. The ethic is comprehensive, applying to all human action.
3. The ethic is logically consistent.
4. The ethic is not arbitrary, not merely based on the whims or beliefs of one or more persons.

Another strand of natural moral law is based on the ethical philosophy of Aristotle, which has been revised by libertarian scholars such as Murray Rothbard and by Objectivist philosophers starting with Ayn Rand. They posit some natural end inherent in human nature such that actions that are inconsistent with this end are immoral. Other philosophers, such as Jürgen Habermas, base universalist concepts on communicative action or a dialectical process, through which a consensus can be achieved by dialogue.

Epistemological universalism posits the existence of objective knowledge that human beings are able to learn. Objectivists and realists in epistemology claim that human beings have the cognitive ability to observe and explain the universe as it actually is rather than merely forming subjective interpretive beliefs. In contrast, hermeneutics, relativists, and particularists such as Michel Foucault claim that human minds have bounded cognition, not just making errors but necessarily interpreting observations using prior beliefs, making absolute objectivity impossible. Some philosophers seek a middle ground between relativism and objectivism, such as the belief that human beings can achieve knowledge but that it is not certain or comprehensive. Universalists can argue that the proposition that there are no universals is itself either universal or not; if so, the proposition is self-contradictory, and if not, then it has no general impact.

Universalists have explained the human capacity to obtain objective knowledge from evolution, which selected for beings whose survival depends on beliefs consistent with their environmental reality. Knowledge can come from a priori insights such as the concept of cause and effect, and from the capacity to reason, using logic and evidence from observation. Most scientists evidently believe in epistemological universalism, in being able to discover theories that explain reality.

Economics, for example, presumes premises that apply universally to all humanity. Economic axioms include diminishing marginal utility, economizing to maximize benefits or minimize costs, and the physical constraint of scarce resources. If economics as a social science is founded on these premises, then it must be possible to know these premises and their implications, and such knowledge must consist of shared beliefs that can be learned. Moral universalism is connected to epistemological universalism in that if human beings can know science, there is no reason to exclude moral philosophy from what can be objectively known.

Subjectivism and objectivism are not necessarily opposites in moral philosophy. In economics, we can posit that the values placed on goods are purely subjective, based on individual interests. Yet these values result in bids and offers in a market, which create objective prices and, together with other premises such as scarcity, form the basis of an objective theory of prices. Likewise in ethics, we can accept that each person has subjective values about human action and situations but that these values form the basis of an objective ethic if we also have premises such as that all human beings have an equal moral worth or that their values have an equal moral standing.

SEE ALSO *Aristotle; Cosmopolitanism; Epistemology; Ethics; Habermas, Jürgen; Hermeneutics; Libertarianism; Locke, John; Morality; Natural Rights; Objectivism; Philosophy; Realism; Religion; Utilitarianism*

BIBLIOGRAPHY

Foldvary, Fred. 1980. *The Soul of Liberty: The Universal Ethic of Freedom and Human Rights.* San Francisco: The Gutenberg Press.

Locke, John. [1690] 1947. *Two Treatises of Government.* Ed. Thomas I. Cook. New York: Hafner Press.

Nozick, Robert. 2001. *Invariances: The Structure of the Objective World.* Cambridge, MA: Harvard University Press.

Peikoff, Leonard. 1991. *Objectivism: The Philosophy of Ayn Rand.* New York: Dutton.

Popper, Karl R. 1972. *Objective Knowledge: An Evolutionary Approach.* Oxford: Oxford University Press.

Rorty, Richard. 1991. *Objectivity, Relativism, and Truth.* Cambridge, UK: Cambridge University Press.

Fred Foldvary

UNIVERSITY OF OXFORD

In company with the other twelfth-century universities of Paris and Bologna, Oxford can claim to be among the oldest of the European universities. Its foundation date, often a matter of fantastic speculation, remains unclear. All that can be said is that Oxford recognizably became a university between 1192 and 1200. Located in a river valley fed by tributaries of the Thames River, the town and the university were named for the river crossing (oxen-ford). Since no new university was established in England (although four or five in Scotland) until the formation of the University of London in the 1820s, Oxford and Cambridge (collectively termed Oxbridge or less frequently Camford) long held a duopoly on the education and training of leading politicians, Roman Catholic and afterward Church of England clergy and bishops, civil service administrators at home and abroad, and representatives of the arts and sciences. Even the Scots, with their own fine university traditions, attended the ancient universities in order to take advantage of their connections and networks.

Oxford in the twenty-first century remains one of a handful of world universities correctly described as *collegiate.* It is a federation of some seven permanent private halls and thirty-nine self-governing and endowed colleges scattered about the city of Oxford. A good number of these are twentieth-century foundations, updating ancient traditions to take advantage of new subjects and new kinds of students. The first colleges appeared in the thirteenth century, but most were founded later. Historically associated with teaching and student residence, the first college to actually admit undergraduates was New College in the fourteenth century. Women's colleges date from the 1860s. Infamously, however, women did not receive degrees until 1920 (or 1948 at Cambridge). Only Saint Hilda's College, founded in 1893, is restricted to women.

Responsibility for teaching and scholarship is divided between colleges and the university, between tutors (called *dons* from the Latin *dominum* or master) and professors, but from the sixteenth century (the early modern period) until recently the colleges were dominant. That was mainly, if not entirely, a consequence of the Protestant Reformation, expanded royal government, and international trade and rivalry. Loyal and well-educated administrators were required for service in church and state. The small size of the colleges and their systems of personal instruction and discipline in a residential setting were well suited for the education of potential leaders. The new elites were heavily drawn from established families. The collegiate university primarily bestowed its blessings on those already favored; in particular, the scions of landed society influenced the tone of the university by their often careless but also glamorous habits well into the nineteenth century.

In recent decades, considerable scholarly attention has been directed to the social composition of Oxford through the ages, a reflection of current concerns about access to higher education. However, owing to the absence of university matriculation records, estimates of the social composition of Oxford are harder to provide for the period before 1565. Entries afterward are listed by hierarchical status rankings, rather than by social or occupational groupings, as is present practice, and historians disagree on how to interpret them. The earlier records kept by colleges are often incomplete or confusing.

In the broadest terms, it can be said that until very recently wealth and privilege were always accorded a warm reception at Oxford. The numbers of recruits from the poorer sections of English society, meaning the children of farm laborers in the earliest centuries or industrial workers in the later ones, were generally in short supply. To give an example from Lincoln College from 1680 to 1799, of 972 admits, over half came from landed or gentlemanly families and another 266 from clergy, to include the higher ranks. Only 155 were listed as *plebeian*, a catchall category difficult to refine. A more complete analysis of the entire university for the 1901–1975 period, comprising 3,512 entries, more clearly indicates the changes. Professional families accounted for 1,564 admits; 1,059 were from commerce, finance, and industry, and 217 from white-collar families. Only 182 can be called skilled workers, and only several dozen fit the description of unskilled or manual workers.

As a generalization, it can be ventured that Oxford's social transformation from a university serving mainly the sons of landed and clerical families began to shift from about 1850, when professional and business families started to become dominant. This was the pattern that could be expected of most elite institutions. Gradually but firmly Oxford ceased to be a university of the traditionally privileged and became instead the destination of new generations of outstanding undergraduates from middle-income families, befitting the economic transformations that had occurred as a result of industrialism and the expansion of the urban professions.

As a center of learning and scholarship, Oxford's reputation declined in the Age of the Enlightenment. Enrollments fell, teaching was neglected, and one famous undergraduate, the future historian Edward Gibbon (1737–1794), characterized the dons of his day as addicted to "port and prejudice." More recently, historians have uncovered evidence for greater intellectual vitality than previously supposed. Yet it is the case that a serious and almost total educational transformation of the university and its colleges did not occur until the next century. The first step around 1800 was a demanding and subsequently famous honors examination in the subject of *literae humaniores* (called "Greats"). Composed of classical languages, philosophy, and history, it became the prototype of later competitive examinations. For a long while, "Greats" was regarded as the leading subject, attracting the best and most success-minded students. To begin with, improvements in teaching and examining were internal reforms, but criticisms persisted that the university and its colleges tolerated weak students, gave scholarships to the unworthy, failed to impose needed discipline, were slow in furthering the advance of modern and scientific subjects, and misused plentiful endowments. Oligopoly control of the colleges and central administration was attacked. By the middle of the nineteenth century, public opinion demanded radical reforms. For some twenty years thereafter, royal and other commissions recommended, and Parliament introduced, changes affecting all aspects of governance, financing, and the curriculum. Research was added to teaching as an academic mission, and professorial chairs were created in new subjects. If Cambridge led the way in the mathematical sciences, Oxford excelled in classical languages, ethical philosophy, and medieval history. At present, Oxford is well represented in all fields of intellectual inquiry.

Repeal of two inherited restrictions in the Victorian period furthered the process of renewal and scholarly excellence. Celibacy was abolished as a condition of holding college teaching appointments, a major step in the formation of professional academic careers; and non-Anglican undergraduates were admitted without being required to take an oath of allegiance to the Thirty-Nine Articles of the Church of England. Since half the kingdom adhered to other denominations, the pool of worthy candidates widened. However, a certain element of snobbery persisted well into the Edwardian period, not only toward the few working-class undergraduates in attendance but also toward students of Jewish origin or from India and Africa.

In the nineteenth and twentieth centuries, Oxford was also renowned as the training ground of *proconsuls*, the distinguished imperial administrators in the heyday of the British Empire. Under Benjamin Jowett (1817–1893), its legendary master, Victorian Balliol College acquired a reputation as the nursery of prime ministers, but the great William Gladstone (1809–1898), who became prime minister in 1868, had studied at Christ Church, the most aristocratic of the colleges, although he was not descended from landed gentlemen.

Protesting a growing secularism and religious tolerance, John Henry Newman (1801–1890), a fellow of Oriel College, left Oxford in 1842 and converted to Roman Catholicism. His subsequent reflections and lectures, published under the heading of *The Idea of a University* (1853), became among the most influential and lasting books ever written on the purpose of a liberal education. But Newman was right. Oxford had indeed changed. Once described as the "home of lost causes," a reference to the university's sometime attachments to deposed monarchs and High Church principles, or, romantically, as a place of "dreaming spires," an allusion to its distance from social realities, Oxford was once again at the center of the transformed educational and intellectual life of a modern Britain. Oxford dons helped establish new universities, such as Bristol, and fully participated in outreach or extension movements. Rhodes Scholarships, a bequest by the imperialist Cecil Rhodes (1853–1902) at the turn of the twentieth century, brought overseas students to the university, as did the introduction of advanced research degrees. Oxford's influence spread throughout the English-speaking world, indeed, everywhere.

The list of distinguished men and women who studied or taught at Oxford is endless. In the fourteenth century, William of Ockham (c. 1285–1349) added to the luster of the university's fame in logic. In the same century, John Wycliffe (c. 1330–1384), master of Balliol, challenged the papacy by advocating a Bible in the vernacular. The seminal philosopher John Locke (1632–1704) was at Oxford in the late seventeenth century. In the following century, Edmund Halley (1656–1742) gave his name to a comet, and starting in 1729 John Wesley (1703–1791) and Charles Wesley (1707–1788) initiated practices that resulted in the birth of Methodism. Romantic poets like Percy B. Shelley (1792–1822, expelled for atheism) and Matthew Arnold (1822–1888) were at Oxford in the nineteenth century. Two celebrated twentieth-century graduates were Lord Curzon (1859–1925), viceroy of India and chancellor of the university, and Vera Brittain (1893–1970), who studied at Somerville College (founded in 1879) and became a leader of the women's emancipation movement. Closer to the present, A. H. Halsey put sociology on the Oxford map. The political philosopher Isaiah Berlin (1909–1997) was one of the most respected and admired Oxford personalities of the twentieth century.

The British Isles (to include Ulster) currently possess well over a hundred institutions denominated *universities* and numerous polytechnics, specialized schools, and further education colleges. Yet despite competition, Oxford's superior reputation remains. Its long history, endowments, magnificent libraries and collections of art, exquisite gardens, splendid architecture, and distinguished graduates at home and abroad provide advantages that guarantee its continued presence among the top five or ten research universities in the world as measured by peer approval.

In the twenty-first century Oxford recruits more broadly than ever before. The collegiate system is intact but less dominant. High technology, laboratory science, medicine, and postgraduate research are more closely associated with the professors than with the tutors, and with the university more than with the colleges. New market-based initiatives for financing have enhanced the importance of the central administration. However, as the bulk of Oxford's income is derived from the government, institutional independence and academic freedom are serious issues for the twenty-first century. Universities everywhere are being called upon to address multiple social problems, generate wealth, and improve national efficiency in a global environment. However challenging these conditions, it is abundantly clear that contemporary Oxford has little interest in becoming a home for lost causes.

SEE ALSO *Cambridge University; University, The*

BIBLIOGRAPHY

Adams, Pauline. 1996. *Somerville for Women: An Oxford College, 1879–1993.* Oxford: Oxford University Press.

Aston, T. H., ed. 1984–2000. *The History of the University of Oxford.* 8 vols. Oxford: Clarendon.

Cobban, Alan B. 1988. *The Medieval English Universities: Oxford and Cambridge to c. 1500.* Berkeley: University of California Press.

Halsey, A. H. 1992. *Decline of Donnish Dominion*: *The British Academic Professions in the Twentieth Century.* Oxford: Clarendon.

Newman, John Henry, ed. [1853] 1976. *The Idea of a University: Defined and Illustrated,* ed. I. T. Ker. Oxford: Clarendon.

Pantin, W. A. 1972. *Oxford Life in Oxford Archives.* Oxford: Clarendon.

Shattock, Michael. 1994. *The UGC and the Management of British Universities.* Buckingham, U.K.: Open University Press and the Society for Research into Higher Education.

Symonds, Richard. 1986. *Oxford and Empire: The Last Lost Cause?* New York: St. Martin's Press.

Sheldon Rothblatt

UNIVERSITY OF TEXAS INEQUALITY PROJECT

A new body of empirical literature on economic inequality emerged in the early- and mid-1990s that sought to establish cross-country and timewise analysis of the relationship between economic growth, income levels, and income distribution. At a fundamental level, this literature was concerned with exploring questions posed by Simon Kuznets in the mid-1950s about the relationship between income and inequality levels. His hypothesis was that if one were to plot inequality levels against income levels over the long run, this relationship could be described by an inverted U curve. As countries grew from an agricultural to an industrial economy, inequality would go up initially, with few people working in the high-productivity and high-income industrial sector. As more and more people transitioned from agriculture to industry, the increase in inequality would decelerate, stop, and eventually reverse when the majority of the population worked in the industrial sector.

The new empirical studies of the early 1990s related to the Kuznets hypothesis but also to newer conjectures that predicted either positive or negative relationships between inequality and growth. Some theories, such as those of Alberto Alesina and Dani Rodrik, were based on political economy arguments, while others, such as the work of Abhijit Banerjee and Andrew Newman, were based on the effect of inequality in impeding access to credit.

This work generated a large demand for data on inequality that were internationally comparable and that spanned as long a time series as possible. While such data had long been available for income and growth, there was a paucity of global data on income distribution. Klaus Deininger and Lyn Squire, then at the World Bank, were pioneers in setting up and making available a compilation of inequality measures that were broadly comparable across countries and over time. Their dataset, based on household surveys, reported Gini coefficients—a summary measure of income inequality that ranges from 0, for perfect equality, to 100, when all income goes to a single individual, which is the most unequal of all possible distributions of income. Other similar, more comprehensive efforts followed, including that by the United Nations University's World Institute for Development Economics Research (WIDER) center.

As Andrea Bradonlini and Anthony Atkinson noted in the late 1990s, these comprehensive datasets had promise but also pitfalls. Some of the main shortcomings involved the lack of long and dense time series of inequality for many countries, especially developing countries. Cross-country comparability was also an issue. These factors made empirical work using these datasets difficult. Under the leadership of James K. Galbraith, the University of Texas Inequality Project (UTIP) was created initially as an effort to offer other sources of measures of inequality that addressed some of the shortcomings of these datasets.

UTIP's initial proposal was to derive measures of within-country inequality using internationally comparable pay data, collected for industrial statistics released by the United Nations Industrial Development Organization (UNIDO). An issue with this dataset was that pay data were reported only at the industry level, and thus the within-industry distribution was unknown. Thus the use of the Theil index—the most widely used measure of a family of inequality measures that are perfectly decompos-

able into a within-group and between-group distribution—emerged as the most natural choice. For between-industry pay, the Theil index generated long and dense measures of inequality that were broadly comparable across countries.

In addition to releasing this global dataset, the work of UTIP involved exploring the methodological issues associated with the chosen measure of inequality. Using this dataset as well as data from national sources, Galbraith led innovative work on the interactions between inequality and several economic and political issues, ranging from conflict to financial crises. In fact, the use of the Theil index was expanded beyond global measures of interindustry inequality pay into other fields where issues of aggregation made the Theil index the natural measure to use. For example, when income or pay data are available at several levels of geographic aggregation (as in the United States, for example, at the national, state, and county levels), the Theil index enables the construction of decomposable aggregate measures into the contributions of the lower levels of aggregation. Insights into the dynamics of the contributions to aggregate inequality from lower levels of aggregation can then be established. Galbraith and colleagues at UTIP did pioneering work in using the Theil index to "aggregate upward." For example, while inequality in the United States is often compared with that of other countries, it has rarely been compared with inequality in, say, Europe or European Union countries. By aggregating national measures of inequality upward, it is possible to construct a European-wide measure of inequality that may be more analytically appropriate to use in comparisons with the United States than that of individual countries.

More recently the UTIP-UNIDO measures of manufacturing-pay inequality were used, with other information, to estimate measures of household income inequality. This was accomplished by taking advantage of the systematic relationship between the UTIP-UNIDO estimates and those of Deininger and Squire. The residuals from this exercise provided a map to problematic estimates in the Deininger and Squire data, and the estimated coefficients enabled the construction of a new panel dataset of estimated household income inequality.

SEE ALSO *Deininger and Squire World Bank Inequality Database; Income Distribution; Inequality, Income; Kuznets Hypothesis; Theil Index*

BIBLIOGRAPHY

Alesina, Alberto, and Dani Rodrik. 1994. Distributive Politics and Economic Growth. *Quarterly Journal of Economics* 109 (2): 465–490.

Atkinson, Anthony, and Andrea Brandolini. 2001. Promise and Pitfalls in the Use of "Secondary" Data-Sets: Income

Inequality in OECD Countries as a Case Study. *Journal of Economic Literature* 39: 771–799.

Banerjee, Abhijit, and Andrew F. Newman. 1993. Occupational Choice and the Process of Development. *Journal of Political Economy* 101: 274–298.

Deininger, Klaus, and Lyn Squire. 1996. New Ways of Looking at Old Issues: Inequality and Growth. World Bank. Unpublished paper.

Galbraith, James K., and Pedro Conceição. 1998. Constructing Long and Dense Time-Series of Inequality Using the Theil Index. UTIP Working Paper No. 1. http://utip.gov.utexas.edu/papers/utip_01.pdf.

Galbraith, James K., and Hyunsub Kum. 2005. Estimating the Inequality of Household Incomes: A Statistical Approach to the Creation of a Dense and Consistent Global Data Set. *Review of Income and Wealth* 51 (1): 115–143.

Kuznets, Simon. 1955. Economic Growth and Income Inequality. *American Economic Review* 45 (1): 1–28.

United Nations University. 2005. WIDER World Income Inequality Database V 2.0b. http://www.wider.unu.edu/wiid/wiid.htm.

Pedro Conceição

UNIVERSITY, THE

The modern social sciences, as well as all other forms of knowledge, are primarily studied and taught in universities. Not all the social sciences disciplines can trace their origins directly back to the twelfth century when universities first appeared. Many evolved indirectly from subjects taught at the original universities, such as law, logic, philosophy, and medicine. But the university's main role in the development of the social sciences is primarily the result of manifold changes occurring in the second half of the nineteenth century. Demographic and urban growth, industrialization, democracy, and religious pluralism provided new arenas for academic inquiry and problem-solving and produced the array of disciplines commonly united under the heading of the social sciences. Economics, sociology, anthropology, demography, psychology, city planning, and scientific history came of age as autonomous university-based disciplines.

ORIGINS, CURRICULUM, AND SPREAD OF UNIVERSITIES

As a special type of educational institution, universities emerged almost unnoticed in three locations: Bologna, Paris, and Oxford. The circumstances were propitious. Trade had improved, cities were expanding, and municipal, imperial, and ecclesiastical authorities were in need of trained talent. Cities provided the necessary population, the facilities, the markets, and the career opportunities.

Student fees, gifts, and ecclesiastical resources supported teaching, and universities were expected to help define and encourage religious belief. Until approximately the nineteenth century, most graduates of universities entered clerical careers, and most academics were ordained priests and ministers. Secularism and pluralism called into question many religious assumptions. At the same time universities embraced new forms of critical and scientific thinking, and as a consequence theology became just another subject rather than a primary focus, even within faith-based colleges.

In the beginning, the intellectual, philosophical, and scientific starting point of all teaching and learning was the corpus of encyclopedic writings mainly but not solely derived from Aristotle, preserved by Arabic scholars and transmitted to Italy in what historians have called the Renaissance of the Twelfth Century. This was the first of two revivals of ancient Greek and Latin learning in the Western world, the second commencing with the Italian Renaissance of the late fourteenth and fifteenth centuries. The medieval curriculum itself derived from the seven Roman liberal arts of logic, rhetoric, grammar, dialectic, astronomy, music, geometry, and arithmetic, but these were regarded as preparation for the professions of medicine, law (civil and canonical), and divinity rather than subjects in their own right. All were grouped into administrative structures called "faculties." Although at first glance the seven liberal arts appear to be limited to mathematical and language studies, the process of teaching and expounding them furthered their development as multifaceted disciplines.

By the early modern period hundreds of universities had been founded in Europe by both secular and religious authorities, spreading from the Atlantic to Russia. During the ages of exploration Spain and Portugal established universities in their New World colonial territories, primarily to train imperial administrators and priests. Further north, the British settlements, beginning with Massachusetts, established university colleges to provide the colonies with an educated class. The first university in Japan came at the end of the nineteenth century, and in China in the twentieth. By the nineteenth century the utility of universities and college alternatives was so clearly accepted that governing elites associated their existence with the health of a modern bureaucratic state and economy.

NEW KNOWLEDGE AND STRUCTURES

There is a popular tendency to regard universities as conservative institutions and resistant to change. Academic costumes, rituals, and ceremonies provide an impression of unbroken tradition through the ages, as do the forms of teaching. But the conservatism of universities is merely apparent. Sometimes deliberately, but often accidentally, the pursuit of learning by its very nature yields new conceptions, methods of inquiry, and startling intellectual movements. Two of the most closely studied are the scientific revolution of the sixteenth and seventeenth centuries and the transformation of the liberal arts during the Italian Renaissance.

In both cases examples can be found of innovations that grew out of the scholarly methods taught at universities. But there was also internal resistance. The heliocentric universe described by the Polish astronomer Copernicus (1473–1543) and publicized by the Italian physicist Galileo (1564–1642) undermined theological assumptions about the purpose, scale, and physical laws governing the cosmos. As a consequence, subsequent generations of scientists gravitated to newly establish royal societies where they could work unimpeded. In the same way, humanistic scholars using new critical methods of historical analysis founded academies where the liberal arts could be taught from a different perspective. Ruling elites were in favor. They desired education more closely focused on statecraft and better suited to the growing individualist cultures of the Renaissance. Yet intellectual cooperation between universities and the outside world never altogether ceased.

Disciplines alter over time, but so does the organization of teaching. Within a century or two of the founding of universities, colleges joined faculties as centers of instruction, improved discipline, and residence for students and instructors. Colleges were either freestanding or connected to existing universities, and among the most academically enterprising and successful were the Jesuit foundations of the Counter-Reformation. By the nineteenth century, however, colleges had largely disappeared from Europe, except for Oxford and Cambridge, where they remain, or in America with its distinct family of liberal arts colleges. Other examples of new administrative and teaching structures that arose, especially in the later centuries, are disciplinary departments, scientific laboratories, botanical gardens, observatories, art museums, marine biological stations, and ethnographical institutes. Libraries continued to buttress all pedagogical efforts.

Eventually the radical curricular changes associated with the early modern period were fully embraced by universities. As a consequence, the thrust of universities changed from places that mainly preserved and disseminated inherited learning, however modified in practice, to places devoted to discovering new knowledge. Research as the primary missions of universities is usually said to have started in Germany with the foundation of the University of Berlin in 1809; there were, however, earlier manifestations. Yet universal adoption of the research ethic was a phenomenon of the second half of the century, burgeoning in the century that followed.

ACADEMIC FREEDOM

The universities of the Middle Ages were genuinely international. The curriculum was similar, and the language of instruction was Latin. Students migrated to the leading centers from all corners of Europe. But the spread and popularity of vernacular languages, combined with political and religious divisions in the early modern period, altered the patterns of student mobility. Universities became more conspicuously national. Regarded as extensions of state power, the political loyalty of academics was under continual scrutiny.

Academic commitment to religious orthodoxy was also closely watched during the early modern period. The wars between Protestants and Roman Catholics created church and state alliances unknown in the centuries of a universal Christendom. But no matter how threatening the new conditions to academic freedom and institutional autonomy were, they did not compare to the calamities inflicted on universities, teaching, and freedom of inquiry by totalitarian regimes and nondemocratic governments of the twentieth century and afterward. The historical lessons clearly show that knowledge growth requires both external and internal freedom. Although universities originally developed as self-governing institutions with the right to own and dispose of property, they are only as free and independent as their societies and governments allow. And they are only as tolerant and open-minded in teaching and learning as are the devotion to those ideals of professors and students.

BIBLIOGRAPHY

Anderson, Robert D. 2004. *European Universities from the Enlightenment to 1914.* New York: Oxford University Press.

Bender, Thomas, ed. 1988. *The University and the City, from Medieval Origins to the Present.* New York: Oxford University Press.

Clark, Burton R., and Guy R. Neave, eds. 1992. *The Encyclopedia of Higher Education.* 4 vols. New York: Pergamon Press.

De Ridder-Symoens, Hilde, ed. 1992. *Universities in the Middle Ages.* Vol. 1 of *A History of the University in Europe.* Cambridge, U.K.: Cambridge University Press.

De Ridder-Symoens, Hilde, ed. 1996. *Universities in Early Modern Europe.* Vol. 2 of *A History of the University in Europe.* Cambridge, U.K.: Cambridge University Press.

Heilbron, John L. 2006. *Coming to Terms with the Scientific Revolution.* Uppsala, Sweden: Uppsala University, Office for the History of Science.

Hofstadter, Richard, and Walter P. Metzger. 1955. *The Development of Academic Freedom in the United States.* New York: Columbia University Press.

Marsden, George M. 1994. *The Soul of the American University: From Protestant Establishment to Established Nonbelief.* New York: Oxford University Press.

Rashdall, Hastings. 1987. *The Universities of Europe in the Middle Ages*, eds. F. M. Powicke and A. B. Emden. New York: Oxford University Press.

Sheldon Rothblatt

UNLIMITED SUPPLIES OF LABOR

SEE *Labor, Surplus: Conventional Economics; Lewis, W. Arthur.*

UNRESTRICTED STOCKS

SEE *Stocks, Restricted and Unrestricted.*

UNTOUCHABLES

SEE *Dalits.*

UPWARD MOBILITY

Upward mobility is the experience of moving up into a more privileged economic position in society. Social scientists study the rates of upward mobility across different groups and societies because upward mobility is associated with notions of meritocracy and equality of opportunity. In a meritocratic or "open" society, all that is required for upward mobility is an education and hard work. Success in this type of society is determined by individual achievement rather than family background. In closed societies, on the other hand, there is little or no upward mobility. For example, children from working-class parents are likely to end up in working-class occupations themselves, and one's educational attainment is determined in large part by the educational achievements of one's parents.

There are two general types of upward mobility: *intragenerational* and *intergenerational* mobility. Upward mobility across generations, or intergenerational mobility, is commonly studied and often used as an indicator of a society's openness or fluidity. People also often experience upward mobility over the course of their own careers, which is known as intragenerational mobility. For example, someone may start out working in a low-paying job

and then move up into a higher-paying job within the same company after a few years. In addition, a person may go back to school in midcareer to earn a college or graduate degree in order to move into a higher-status occupation, such as a professional or manager.

MEASURING UPWARD MOBILITY

Social scientists measure upward mobility in surveys in a variety of ways. In order to measure upward mobility, the researcher must decide on a measure of economic well-being or status. Several common measures of economic status include: individual earnings, family income, wealth, educational attainment, occupational status or prestige, and social class. Economists often measure the degree of mobility as the strength of the association between the income or earnings of fathers and their sons. A *strong* association between fathers' and sons' income indicates a *low* rate of upward mobility. On the other hand, a *weak* association indicates a *high* rate of upward mobility because children are not limited in their future economic success by the success of their parents. While these studies of intergenerational income mobility are informative, they are also limited in a few respects. First, focusing on income or earnings ignores other aspects of economic success, such as educational attainment and occupational prestige or status. Second, these studies also tend to ignore racial differences in upward mobility, which scholars such as Dalton Conley and Tom Hertz have pointed out.

Sociologists tend to measure upward mobility in terms of occupational or class "origins" and "destinations." While the definition of class is contested in the literature, several definitions involve the nature of the employment relationship and the degree of skill, autonomy, and ownership someone has. This definition is similar to the one developed by Robert Erikson and John Goldthorpe in their book, *The Constant Flux* (1992). Sociologists within the status attainment tradition examine the importance of class origins in determining class destinations. Class origin, often measured by the father's occupation, is taken as an indicator of the degree of *ascription* or inherited success, whereas educational attainment is taken as an indicator of *achievement* or earned success. The relative importance of earned versus inherited economic status reveals the amount of potential there is for upward mobility. An increase in the importance of individual achievement regardless of class origin should translate into an increased rate of upward mobility. However, there is also the potential for downward mobility in an open society, which may be the result of economic downturns and organizational restructuring or individual decisions regarding education and different career paths.

UPWARD MOBILITY ACROSS COUNTRIES

Rates of upward mobility vary across countries. Under the rule of Mao Zedong (1893–1976) in China from 1949 to 1976, there was very little social mobility of any kind. As Yanjie Bian notes in his article in the *Annual Review of Sociology*, "it was rare to change an individual's social position in Mao's status hierarchy because of the rigid institutional walls" (2002, p. 104). In such a closed society, one is born into a particular economic status and destined to remain in that status group. However, with the economic reforms in China since 1978, social mobility is now possible and educational attainment is beginning to play an important role in determining occupational status.

The changing pattern of upward mobility in China highlights the importance of political and economic systems in explaining differences in mobility across countries. In general, advanced capitalist countries have greater potential for upward (and downward) mobility than socialist countries. Several formerly socialist countries in central and eastern Europe have begun to experience increasing mobility and inequality since the revolutions between 1989 and 1991. However, the transition from socialism to capitalism does not necessarily mean that the potential for upward mobility will increase. As Theodore Gerber and Michael Hout discuss in their 2004 article in the *American Sociological Review*, there is evidence that social mobility actually declined during Russia's market transition in the 1990s. Gerber and Hout found that the association between class origins and destinations strengthened during the transition to a capitalist economy in part because the deregulation of the state labor market allowed elites to pass on benefits to their children with greater ease (2004, p. 696).

There are other scholars, such as Erikson and Goldthorpe, who contend that advanced industrial countries with similar occupational structures will have similar rates of social mobility. According to this view, all modern societies will display some association between class origin and class destination. This does not suggest that upward mobility does not exist. However, it is limited by certain laws, customs, and norms that serve to reproduce systems of stratification across generations. Despite these similarities across countries, many scholars agree that countries such as Sweden exhibit a higher degree of social mobility than the average country, and others, such as the United States, exhibit lower degrees of mobility (Solon 2002). However, the reasons behind these differences are still not clear, and the issue is complicated even further by measurement differences across countries. A substantial amount of research remains to be done on the topic of country differences in upward mobility.

RACE AND UPWARD MOBILITY

Rates of upward mobility also vary substantially across different social groups within countries. Different racial and ethnic groups in the United States have dramatically different experiences with upward mobility. In his study of race and economic mobility, Tom Hertz finds that the association between parents' and children's income "is driven to a large extent by black families' especially low rate of upward mobility from the bottom of the income distribution" (2005, p. 165). The "rags to riches" transition popularized by the Horatio Alger novels is twice as likely for whites as it is for African Americans in the United States. Being born into a family in the bottom income bracket has very different implications for whites and African Americans. For African Americans, it means that one is likely to end up living in a low-income household as an adult as well. However, whites have a fair chance of moving up into at least the middle of the income distribution later in life. Therefore, the United States is a fluid and open society for whites with a lot of potential for upward mobility. However, for African Americans, it is often a rigid and closed society with little potential for mobility.

Explanations for racial differences in social mobility in the United States range from racial discrimination in the educational system and the labor market to differences in individual aspirations and abilities. In his book, *Being Black, Living in the Red* (1999), Dalton Conley examines racial differences in several indicators, such as income, education, and family structure. Conley's major conclusion is that racial differences in income and wealth are primarily due to the dramatically different class backgrounds of whites and African Americans. In particular, differences in wealth between white and African American families are responsible for subsequent racial differences in the labor market. As Conley notes, it is easier to pass on wealth across generations than income or education (1999, p. 14). Solutions to the problem do not center on increasing access to educational institutions. According to Conley, what is needed is a race-based asset policy that promotes property ownership for African Americans (p. 138).

Research on upward mobility has benefited from recent studies that incorporate racial differences. However, there are several limitations to these studies. The most important limitation is the absence of any discussion of the mobility patterns of Asians, Latinos, and other racial and ethnic groups. Latinos are now the largest racial or ethnic minority group in the United States, and an investigation of the potential barriers they face to upward mobility is needed.

UPWARD MOBILITY OVER TIME

Upward mobility also changes over time. However, there is a debate in the literature about how much change has occurred and why. According to the liberal theory of industrialism, rates of social mobility should converge over time across countries as they reach similar levels of industrialization. Richard Breen and Jan Jonsson observe in their 2005 article in the *Annual Review of Sociology* that there is evidence of at least modest increases in mobility in several different countries since the 1970s. Additionally, the relationship between class origins and destinations may be weakening over time in several countries, which suggests greater potential for upward mobility in the future based solely on individual achievements. However, other scholars, such as Erikson and Goldthorpe, see temporal changes in social mobility as short-term fluctuations rather than long-term trends (1992, p. 36).

The trajectory for upward mobility in the future is complicated by several different factors. First, the strength of the association between class origins and destinations will play an important role. Despite the popularity of the "rags to riches" stories from Horatio Alger novels in the late 1800s and the image of most modern societies as meritocracies, family background continues to have a strong influence on one's economic success today. Growing up in a wealthy family with educated parents puts children in an advantaged position because of the resources and values that are passed down, which children from economically disadvantaged backgrounds often do not receive. Therefore, as long as class inequality persists, so too will the limits on upward mobility.

However, there is also reason to believe that rates of upward mobility may increase in the future in several countries. Education is increasingly important in the postindustrial world, and the worldwide expansion of educational opportunity may help to provide opportunities for people to move up into higher-status occupations regardless of their social origins. Even in Communist countries such as China, educational attainment is increasingly responsible for what type of job someone works in and the income they receive. Although equalizing access to education would increase the potential for upward mobility, it would not lead to completely open or fluid societies. Equality of opportunity does not guarantee an equal or "just" society. It merely guarantees "an equal chance to leave the less fortunate behind in the personal quest for influence and social position" (Rawls 1999, p. 91). Inequalities of condition, such as wealth inequality, are likely to persist and limit the potential for upward mobility. Only policies aimed explicitly at limiting the degree of inequality in property and assets, such as redistributive taxes on wealth, are likely to make a significant difference.

SEE ALSO *Achievement; Achievement Gap, Racial; Alger, Horatio; Blau, Peter M.; Class; Discrimination; Duncan, Otis Dudley; Equal Opportunity; Equality; Hierarchy; Inequality, Income; Inequality, Wealth; Intergenerational Transmission; Meritocracy; Rawls, John; Stratification*

BIBLIOGRAPHY

Bian, Yanjie. 2002. Chinese Social Stratification and Social Mobility. *Annual Review of Sociology* 28: 91–116.

Blau, Peter M., and Otis Dudley Duncan. 1967. *The American Occupational Structure*. New York: Wiley.

Breen, Richard, and Jan O. Jonsson. 2005. Inequality of Opportunity in Comparative Perspective: Recent Research on Educational Attainment and Social Mobility. *Annual Review of Sociology* 31: 223–243.

Conley, Dalton. 1999. *Being Black, Living in the Red: Race, Wealth, and Social Policy in America*. Berkeley: University of California Press.

Erikson, Robert, and John H. Goldthorpe. 1992. *The Constant Flux: A Study of Class Mobility in Industrial Societies*. Oxford: Clarendon.

Gerber, Theodore P., and Michael Hout. 2004. Tightening Up: Declining Class Mobility during Russia's Market Transition. *American Sociological Review* 69 (5): 677–703.

Hertz, Tom. 2005. Rags, Riches, and Race: The Intergenerational Economic Mobility of Black and White Families in the United States. In *Unequal Chances: Family Background and Economic Success*, eds. Samuel Bowles, Herbert Gintis, and Melissa Osborne Groves, 165–191. New York: Russell Sage Foundation.

Rawls, John. 1999. *A Theory of Justice*. Rev. ed. Cambridge, MA: Harvard University Press.

Solon, Gary. 2002. Cross-country Differences in Intergenerational Earnings Mobility. *Journal of Economic Perspectives* 16 (3): 59–66.

Andrew Fullerton

URBAN ECOLOGY

SEE *Human Ecology.*

URBAN FOUNDATION

SEE *Townships.*

URBAN LEGENDS
SEE *Rumors.*

URBAN POVERTY
SEE *Poverty, Urban.*

URBAN RENEWAL

Urban renewal is a cooperative effort by public officials and private interests to improve a city's structural, economic, and social quality. Major American cities were economically and socially devastated by the stock market crash of 1929 and the ensuing Great Depression of the 1930s. Most cities had narrow tax bases that relied excessively on property tax revenues, which sharply declined because of widespread business failures and mortgage foreclosures. High rates of unemployment, poverty, and homelessness overwhelmed scarce local resources and contributed to a decline in essential local services, such as public schools and police protection.

The urban-centered New Deal programs of President Franklin D. Roosevelt (served 1933–1945) addressed the immediate economic crisis of American cities instead of their long-term improvement. In particular, New Deal programs such as the Works Progress Administration (WPA) and Public Works Administration (PWA) used public-works jobs to reduce unemployment, stimulate local economies, and subsidize state and local relief for the unemployable poor. The Social Security Act of 1935 included unemployment insurance and Aid to Dependent Children (ADC). Nonetheless, these New Deal programs did cause some major long-term changes in the structure and design of major cities, such as the construction of the Triborough Bridge in New York City and a new city hall for Houston, Texas.

The Housing Act of 1934 created the Federal Housing Authority (FHA), and the U.S. Housing Authority was established in 1937. These federal agencies eventually became the major bureaucratic components of the U.S. Department of Housing and Urban Development (HUD), created in 1965. Influenced by the perspectives of local banking, real estate, and construction interests, the FHA encouraged and solidified the practice of redlining, in which poor African Americans and Latinos were segregated in federally subsidized public housing projects and experienced discrimination in the sale and rental of private housing in white neighborhoods.

During World War II (1938–1945), major cities experienced severe housing shortages and strains on local public services and infrastructure. There was a sharp increase in the number of poor and working-class residents, especially African Americans from the South and whites from rural areas, who moved there to work in defense industries. There also existed a scarcity of materials and labor for civilian construction needs.

The Housing Act of 1949 was the first act of Congress that included federal funds and guidance for urban renewal in addition to providing federal funds and regulations for building more affordable private and public housing and clearing slums. This law also had the effect of continuing and expanding the practice of redlining as more whites, assisted by federally subsidized home mortgages for veterans, moved from cities to suburbs and a larger percentage of urban populations consisted of low-income African Americans and Latinos.

During the 1950s, other federal policies, especially the interstate highway program, accelerated the economic and social decline of major cities, especially in the Northeast and Midwest, as more middle-class homeowners lived in suburbs and commuted to cities for work or moved to growing metropolitan areas of the South and West. Under President Dwight D. Eisenhower (served 1953–1961), the federal government financed a limited number of competitive block grants to help cities revitalize their downtown business districts and clear slums. Led by Mayor Richard Lee, the ambitious urban renewal project of New Haven, Connecticut, was a prominent beneficiary of this federal aid. Toward the end of his presidency, however, Eisenhower vetoed Democratic legislation intended to economically revitalize chronically depressed cities and rural areas on a more expensive, comprehensive basis.

By the 1960s, major urban renewal projects had been completed in Pittsburgh, Boston, and New Haven. Under the leadership of parks commissioner Robert Moses, New York City continued to construct new highways, expressways, bridges, tunnels, office buildings, and public housing and to force the migration and dispersal of residents and small businesses from working-class and poor neighborhoods. Jane Jacobs's 1961 book, *The Death and Life of Great American Cities*, galvanized greater public opposition to urban renewal policies, especially in New York City. Jacobs argued that comprehensive, aggressive urban renewal policies, like those of Moses, often destroyed the social cohesion and quality of life of urban neighborhoods. Critics of urban renewal referred to it as "Negro removal" for adversely affecting urban black neighborhoods in particular. Poor and elderly blacks were forced to move to public housing projects while middle-class black professionals and business owners often moved to suburbs.

Partially influenced by Jacobs, some of the Great Society programs of President Lyndon B. Johnson (served 1963–1969) tried to ameliorate the social problems caused or worsened by urban renewal. Programs such as Model Cities, Head Start, Community Action, Legal Services, and Job Corps were intended to help urban residents, especially low-income African Americans and Latinos, to improve their social, economic, and educational conditions and redress their grievances against local officials and businesses. The Fair Housing Act of 1968 addressed the increasing residential segregation of poor African Americans and Latinos in major cities by prohibiting racial discrimination in the sale and rental of both public and private housing. Nonetheless, major race-related urban riots occurred during the 1960s.

The Republican administrations of presidents Richard M. Nixon (served 1969–1974) and Gerald R. Ford (served 1974–1977) eliminated or reduced funding for the most urban-oriented Great Society programs. However, they increased total federal aid to cities by introducing General Revenue Sharing (GRS) and Community Development Block Grants (CDBG). GRS and CDBG increased federal aid to cities while reducing federal control, and CDBG gave local business interests greater discretion in using CDBG funds for urban renewal. By the 1980s, the percentage of local government budgets consisting of federal aid peaked at 30 percent.

Determined to reduce federal spending and intervention in urban affairs, President Ronald W. Reagan (served 1981–1989) eliminated GRS by 1987 and reduced the number of block grants. Instead, the Republican administrations of Reagan and President George H. W. Bush (served 1989–1993) emphasized the use of tax credits and other market-based incentives to encourage the ownership of public housing units by their residents and to subsidize the construction of affordable private housing through HUD grants. By 1990 the percentage of local government budgets derived from federal aid declined to 17 percent.

With a Republican-controlled Congress during most of his administration, Democratic president William J. Clinton (served 1993–2001) did not introduce a major new role for the federal government in urban renewal. Instead, Clinton's policies sought to improve the quality of life for the urban working poor, especially racial and ethnic minorities, through earned income tax credits, the Welfare Reform Act of 1996, greater access to Head Start and public health services for poor, urban children, and more federal aid for law enforcement and public safety. By 2000 federal aid as a percentage of local government budgets had modestly increased to 20 percent. With steady economic growth during most of the 1990s and early twenty-first century, "gentrification" became the primary objective of urban renewal as local officials and business interests sought to attract young, affluent professionals as new residents and more tourists, conventions, and cultural activities to downtown areas.

SEE ALSO *Cities; Community Power Studies; Dahl, Robert Alan; Gentrification; Ghetto; Jacobs, Jane; Johnson, Lyndon B.; Moses, Robert; Neighborhoods; Planning; Segregation; Segregation, Residential; Urban Riots; Urban Studies; Urbanization*

BIBLIOGRAPHY

Banfield, Edward C. 1970. *The Unheavenly City.* Boston: Little, Brown.

Caro, Robert A. 1975. *The Power Broker: Robert Moses and the Fall of New York.* New York: Random House.

Harrigan, John J., and Ronald K. Vogel. 2006. *Political Change in the Metropolis,* 8th ed. New York: Longman.

Jacobs, Jane. 1961. *The Death and Life of Great American Cities.* New York: Random House.

Judd, Dennis R., and Todd Swanson. 2002. *City Politics: Private Power and Public Policy,* 3rd ed. New York: Longman.

Mollenkopf, John H. 1983. *The Contested City.* Princeton, NJ: Princeton University Press.

Sean J. Savage

URBAN RIOTS

A riot happens whenever a crowd engages in collective violence such as beatings, murder, looting, or arson. Riots are far more likely to occur in urban than in rural areas because the density of population increases the supply of potential participants, as well as targets of attack. The state's role in a riot ordinarily is to squash it using police or military force, but in some instances the police or government officials may provoke a riot for political ends. Generally, countries have laws against rioting, as well as rules of engagement that govern the use of deadly force to quell a disturbance. A riot may spread through media reports or if rioters contact their compatriots in other cities, urging them to start a disturbance. The odds of rioting may be increased or decreased by nature: A hot summer night may cause tempers to flare, whereas a thunderstorm may disperse a crowd otherwise bent on mayhem.

Riots have underlying and proximate causes. The underlying causes are grievances, real or perceived, that rioters hold against social or political institutions, usually (but not always) where the riot occurs; or against other groups of people on racial, ethnic, or religious grounds. The proximate cause can almost always be identified after the fact—an incident of police brutality or a racial, ethnic, or religious slur. Riots may have economic, social, or political consequences. A riot of a majority against a minority may cause the latter to move away from particular neighborhoods in a city or to different cities. A riot may change expectations of future economic growth in a city, causing capital to be allocated elsewhere.

Urban riots have been widespread throughout modern history and across countries. Riots over food shortages were common in seventeenth- and eighteenth-century Europe. Riots fueled by religious conflict have occurred quite regularly in the Middle East, India, and the Far East. As discussed below, racial rioting erupted at unprecedented levels in the United States in the 1960s. In the 1980s urban riots broke out in England. In the early twenty-first century, rioting by disaffected minority youth was particularly violent in suburban areas of French cities.

Governments react to the aftermath of riots in diverse ways. A dictator may react by repressing the dissenting minority harshly, although this may entail a subsequent risk of revolution. In democracies rioting may also influence the course of national politics by enhancing the political clout of politicians on the left or right. In the United States, for example, Spiro Agnew, a conservative Republican from the state of Maryland, came to prominence on a "law and order" platform in the aftermath of riots in Baltimore in the 1960s. Democratic governments may also react by creating special commissions to study the causes of the rioting such as the famous *Kerner Commission Report* (Kerner et. al. 1968), which studied the causes of the 1960s riots in the United States. Ameliorative policies may be adopted in the hope of stemming future violence. Richard Nixon's so-called "Black Capitalism" agenda (Weems and Randolph 2001) and expansion of affirmative action in the early 1970s can be seen in this light.

1960s RIOTS: THE UNITED STATES

The United States possesses a long, terrible history of racial rioting. Until World War II, the vast majority of urban riots involved white-on-black violence. Perhaps the most infamous example during the nineteenth century was the 1863 riot in New York City, during which immigrants angry over the Civil War draft in the North attacked and killed scores of African Americans. As African Americans left the rural South and moved to Northern cities they increasingly competed with whites for housing and jobs. Racial tension sometimes escalated into white-on-black riots such as those in St. Louis and Chicago in 1919. In 1943 riots broke out in Newark and Detroit that in character bear a resemblance to those that occurred in the 1960s, including clashes between African Americans and police, as well as looting and arson of businesses in African American neighborhoods. Even when viewed against the backdrop of the 1940s riots, those occurring in the 1960s were without historical precedent. From the early 1960s through the early 1970s, hundreds of riots originating in African American neighborhoods

broke out in American cities. Since the 1960s the United States has not been completely immune to racial riots, as examples in Miami (1980), Los Angeles (1992), Cincinnati (2001), and Benton Harbor, Michigan (2003), attest.

The standard academic definition of a 1960s race-related riot, as originally put forth by Spilerman (1970, 1971), was a "spontaneous" occurrence with a minimum of thirty participants, some black, that resulted in violent outcomes, such as arson, looting, or death. With this definition in mind, social scientists have collected information on the location, timing, and severity of the 1960s riots. Currently, the most comprehensive data set is that collected by Carter (1986), which covers the period 1964 to 1971 and includes the dates and locations of more than 700 civil disturbances, as well as numbers of deaths, injuries, arrests, and occurrences of arson. The peak years of riot activity were 1967 to 1969, especially 1968 in the aftermath of the assassination of Martin Luther King Jr. Most riots were not severe, in the sense of widespread loss of life or property destruction, but a small number were extraordinarily violent. By far the deadliest riots were those in Detroit in July 1967 (43 deaths), Los Angeles in August 1965 (34 deaths), and Newark in July 1967 (24 deaths).

Social scientists have long tried to identify city-level factors associated with the incidence and severity of the 1960s riots. In general, after accounting for each city's black population size in 1960 and for region, little or no variation in incidence and severity can be accounted for by pre-riot city-level measures of African Americans' absolute or relative (black-to-white) economic status. The point is not that the 1960s riots had no underlying causes but rather, if the black population in a given city was of a sufficient size, a riot could happen at almost any time in the mid-to-late 1960s if there was an appropriate spark. Most sparks were local—for example, in the Watts, Los Angeles, riot in 1965, the arrest of an intoxicated black motorist led to a wider altercation with neighborhood residents and eventually a huge riot. By contrast, the King assassination was a national spark that had the potential to incite rioting across the country.

The King riots figure importantly in two recent studies of the economic impact of the 1960s riots in urban areas (Collins and Margo 2004a, 2004b; King 2003). In the several weeks following that assassination, more than 100 riots erupted. However, riots did not occur everywhere, and a key factor in determining the likelihood and severity of a post-King riot was the level of rainfall. A high level of rainfall in April 1968 significantly reduced rioting and is a source of exogenous variation across cities. Using predicted severity based on rainfall, Collins and Margo show that the various economic outcomes for African

Americans—for example, median household income, employment rates, and the value of owner-occupied housing—declined sharply between 1960 and 1970 in cities that experienced severe riots. Moreover, these declines persisted and in some cases worsened in the 1970s. Collins and Smith (2007) extend the cross-city analysis to a case study of Cleveland, showing that black neighborhoods that bore the brunt of the rioting experienced economically significant and persistent declines in property values and population that were not continuations of trends in place prior to the violence.

THE FRENCH RIOTS OF 2005

In the United States the poor tend to live in the central cities of metropolitan areas, but in France (as in other western European countries) the poor are concentrated in suburban rings around a wealthy core. Since the 1970s French suburbs have been increasingly populated by immigrants from North Africa (the Maghreb), sub-Saharan West Africa, and the French West Indies. Most immigrants live in public housing built in the 1950s and 1960s. Their list of grievances is long—high unemployment, racism, police brutality, and inadequate educational opportunities.

In the fall of 2005, serious rioting broke out in the town of Clichy-sous-Bois in suburban Paris. The spark that caused the riot was the accidental electrocution of two minority youths who were fleeing the police. News of the electrocution spread quickly, and rioting commenced. The principal form of violence was arson, primarily directed against automobiles, but also some schools, day care centers, and businesses. As news of the violence was broadcast on French television (indeed, throughout the world) and by the Parisian rioters using the Internet and other electronic media, rioting spread to the suburban peripheries of other French cities. Nationwide, the rioting lasted for two weeks before finally petering out. On the first anniversary of the riots there were sporadic outbreaks of violence, but no full-scale reoccurrence of rioting.

BIBLIOGRAPHY

Carter, Gregg Lee. 1986. The 1960s Black Riots Revisited: City Level Explanations of Their Severity. *Sociological Inquiry* 56: 210–228.

Collins, William J., and Robert A. Margo. 2004a. *The Economic Aftermath of the 1960s Riots in American Cities: Evidence from Property Values.* National Bureau of Economic Research Working Paper No. 10493, Cambridge, MA.

Collins, William J., and Robert A. Margo. 2004b. The Labor Market Effects of the 1960s Riots. In *Brookings-Wharton Papers on Urban Affairs 2004*, eds. W. G. Gale and J. R. Pack, 1–46. Washington, DC: Brookings Institution.

Collins, William J., and Fred H. Smith. 2006. A Neighborhood Level View of Riots, Property Values, and Population Loss: Cleveland, 1950–1980. *Explorations in Economic History* http://www.sciencedirect.com/science/article/B6WFJ-4M3RP9M-3/2/574f2d33a6df4d93e500e0dd63fc1317.

Kerner, Otto, et al. 1968. *Report of the National Advisory Commission on Civil Disorders.* New York: New York Times Company.

King, Mary C. 2003. "Race Riots" and Black Economic Progress. *Review of Black Political Economy* 30 (4): 51–56.

Spilerman, Seymour. 1970. The Causes of Racial Disturbances: A Comparison of Alternative Explanations. *American Sociological Review* 35 (4): 627–649.

Spilerman, Seymour. 1971. The Causes of Racial Disturbances: Test of an Explanation. *American Sociological Review* 36 (3): 427–442.

Weems, Robert E., Jr., and Lewis A. Randolph. 2001. The Ideological Origins of Richard M. Nixon's "Black Capitalism" Initiative. *Review of Black Political Economy* 29: 49–61.

Robert A. Margo

URBAN SPRAWL

Urban sprawl may be defined as the low-density, haphazard housing development that spreads out around modern towns and cities. The terms *sprawl* and *suburbia* are often used interchangeably and pejoratively to describe inferior forms of development, compared, presumably, with the ideal model of the compact urban form of the historical European city. Urban sprawl is typified as "bad," physically because it is so spread out with a lack of local facilities; socially because of boredom among residents and a lack of community identity; economically because of residents' dependency on the motorcar and thus upon politically sensitive international oil supplies; and environmentally because of the impact on agriculture and native habitats and the increased generation of pollution and urban waste.

Until the nineteenth century, towns and cities were generally limited in extent because local facilities and employment had to be within walking distance of home, while longer journeys utilizing horse transport were time-consuming and often dangerous. The coming of the railways enabled people to "escape" the city and live further from their workplace. But residential density and expansion were still constrained by accessibility to the nearest train station. The development of the motorcar, and the growth of public transport omnibus routes, meant that transport was no longer limited to fixed-track systems. Potentially, people could live anywhere. Factors that hastened suburban sprawl included cheap vehicle fuel and mass production of motorcars, mass commercial housebuilding, cheap mortgages, weak urban-planning control, a cultural desire to have "a home of one's own," and the trend for aspiring households to abandon the inner city and move "up and out."

While suburban development was rapid, extensive, and encouraged in North America, Western European governments were anxious to control expansion because their countries are so much smaller and there is simply not the space to expand or to give the motorcar and road-building projects unfettered freedom. For example, the land area of the British Isles fits into Texas alone six times, and France fits four times. By the 1930s, regulations were being introduced to control urban sprawl, to protect farmland, and to prevent the tentacles of "ribbon development" house-building alongside intercity highways, invading the countryside. Retaining enough agricultural land to be self-sufficient in food was recognized as vital following World War II (1939–1945) shipping blockades of the British Isles. In the postwar period, strict spatial-planning legislation was introduced to prevent the town from engulfing the countryside. For example, "green belts" were designated around major cities to act as cordons to prevent further outward development.

Recognition of "urban sprawl" as a problem is relative, depending on the size of a country's population and its land area. Some countries have maintained a laissez-faire approach toward urban sprawl. In New Zealand, a country of comparable size to Britain but with only four million inhabitants (in contrast to Britain's fifty-nine million), large tracts of low-density, single-story "bungalow" development surround the major cities, and new "subdivided" residential developments have mushroomed with little apparent planning control within scenic rural areas. Although there may be lots of space to expand, environmental considerations now have to be taken into account under resource-management planning legislation. Likewise, in Australia there are increasing demands to protect koala bear habitats from encroachment by house builders. Houses built on the edges of cities alongside wilderness areas are in danger of being destroyed by forest fires, which can take hold rapidly during the dry season, as has been witnessed in recent years on the outskirts of Sydney, Australia; San Diego, California; and also in southern France and Portugal.

The low-density, spread-out nature of suburban sprawl, creates many practical problems too. Residents are completely dependent upon the motorcar to get from one land-use and amenity to another. Distances are often too great to contemplate walking to school or work. Retail provision is likely to be in an out-of-town shopping mall (Kunstler 1994), rather than along a "Main Street" (as fondly re-created by the Disney Company in the town of Celebration, Florida). Some North American housing developments are designed with no footpaths or sidewalks alongside the roads, making it impossible for residents to

walk around their area. Land-use zoning regulations, introduced to protect the quality of an area, often result in miles and miles of nothing but housing with no other uses allowed. Socially, such areas are just "dormitory suburbs," which people leave each day to commute downtown to work. Many sociological studies, including feminist research (Hayden 2002), have shown that housewives, mothers, children, young teenagers, and the elderly may feel trapped in the suburbs, with little chance of accessing the outside world. There is little room for social diversity and minority considerations (Reeves 2005). Environmentally, urban sprawl is not sustainable either. Major infrastructural investment is required to provide roads, water, sewerage, drainage, garbage disposal, power, and other utilities and services to dispersed housing developments. Water shortages and power outages, exacerbated by climate change as a result of global warming, have become a common feature of some such residential areas (Lees 2004).

Urbanization and suburbanization are major global trends (Greed 2002). The rate of growth is far greater in the developing world, where a less affluent but pervasive form of urban sprawl is taking place: namely, the shanty town, as found, for example, in Latin America, where both Mexico City and São Paolo, Brazil, have populations of over twenty million. Unregulated development may cover a larger land area than the existing city, as people move in from the countryside to seek jobs in the town. Unlike affluent Western urbanization, third-world sprawl is generally high-density, socially deprived, lacking infrastructure, and relatively carless. But, unlike Western suburbanites, barrio dwellers may have a strong sense of community and local neighborhood identity, albeit brought about by shared adversity.

What are the alternatives to urban sprawl? There is a need to create cities that are more environmentally, economically, and socially sustainable. European planners have suggested the ideal of "the city of everyday life," which would be based on higher densities, multiple functional local centers, walking distances, and public transport (Greed 2002). Likewise, the postmodern "new urbanism" in North America promotes a greater sense of community and a more human scale of design (Ellin 1999). Meanwhile planners stress the importance of urban renewal, infill, and higher densities. But the Anglo-American urban cultural tradition still favors low-rise, low-density housing solutions, in contrast to the European tradition of high-density apartment living and Asian high-rise solutions. The majority of the populations of the United States, the United Kingdom, Canada, Australia, and New Zealand live in the suburbs. The reality is that ordinary people with families want to live in the suburbs, and are willing to put up with long congested commutes to work to do so. But suburban sprawl is not a sustainable option. The challenge for the future is to create more compact cities, which are nevertheless pleasant and acceptable places to live, work, and relax.

BIBLIOGRAPHY

Ellin, Nan. 1999. *Postmodern Urbanism*. Rev. ed. New York: Princeton Architectural Press.

Greed, Clara. 2002. *Introducing Planning*. London and New Brunswick, NJ: Athlone.

Hayden, Dolores. 2002. *Redesigning the American Dream: The Future of Housing, Work, and Family Life* Rev. ed. New York: Norton.

Kunstler, James Howard. 1994. *The Geography of Nowhere: The Rise and Decline of America's Man-Made Landscape*. New York: Simon and Schuster.

Lees, Loretta, ed. 2004. *The Emancipatory City? Paradoxes and Possibilities*. London and Thousand Oaks, CA: Sage.

Reeves, Dory. 2005. *Planning for Diversity: Policy and Planning in a World of Difference*. London and New York: Routledge.

Clara Greed

URBAN STUDIES

Urban studies is the umbrella for several disciplines engaged in studies of the city, including sociology, geography, economics, political science, anthropology, urban planning, architecture, and urban design. Practitioners of these linked disciplines study urbanization and issues surrounding metropolitan dynamics, the process that links cities with the wider economy, their governance, and their spatial structure and change expressed in physical, economic, social, and cultural dimensions. These disciplines use distinctive epistemologies in understanding the city, but the issues they address typically cut across disciplines.

APPROACHES, CONCERNS, AND DISCIPLINES

The major traditions or approaches in urban studies are locational analysis, spatial network analysis in the management of cities, and sociocultural, institutional, political economy, and postmodern methods (Paddison 2001). Locational analysis, identified primarily with the work of urban economists and urban geographers, is concerned with intraurban spatial patterns of urban land use and the accessibility of central business districts. William Alonso (1964) developed the seminal bid-rent theory for urban land markets. Network studies examine the spatial distribution of systems of cities and their specialization and development. Walter Christaller's ([1933] 1966) central place theory and subsequent works by August Lösch

([1944] 1954) and Walter Isard (1956) are the key early works in this urban studies thread. More recent studies of spatial networks focus on the formulation of linkages in the world economy, urban economic restructuring, and globalization (Friedmann and Wolff 1982; Sassen 1991).

Sociocultural and institutional approaches have been developed by urban sociologists, urban anthropologists, and political scientists. Key elements of these approaches are understanding the meaning of urban social life, grasping human ecology, analyzing social areas, using techniques of factorial ecology, and conducting empirical studies on "ways of life." Early social scientists contributing to these trends included Ferdinand Tönnies ([1883] 1995), who defined community and society ideal-types; Max Weber (1905), who identified ideal city-types as loci of civilization and historical change; and Lewis Mumford (1938), who pioneered the study of urban culture.

The Chicago School, the first school of urban analysis, was established in the 1920s in the Sociology Department of the University of Chicago. It was uniquely concerned with urban life and developed the human ecology approach to describe the structure and processes of urban ethnic neighborhood change. Robert Park (1916, 1952) derived principles of competition, succession, and invasion by which groups use or dominate city spaces. Members of the Chicago School studied Chicago as an urban laboratory. Along with Ernest W. Burgess and Roderick D. McKenzie, Park (1925) explored social patterning and the concentric patterning of urban growth. Louis Wirth (1938) formulated principles of size, density, and heterogeneity and defined *urbanism* as a way of life. Eshref Shevky and Wendell Bell (1955) contributed to the development of social analysis by linking urban industrialism to sociospatial differentiation. Duncan Timms (1971) applied factorial ecology techniques to identify sociospatial patterning.

Ethnographic studies include research on the distinctive "ways of life" of different urban marginal groups (including hobos, gangs, and immigrants), the techniques of self-reporting life histories (Thomas and Znaniecki 1918–1920), and the utilization of official data, including census reports and housing/welfare records, to create maps of the location and range of such urban problems as crime, poverty, and juvenile delinquency. W. E. B. Du Bois (1899) pioneered the use of direct surveys, while E. Franklin Frazier (1932) charted new ground in understanding the dynamics of urban social classes. Later ethnographic studies on gangs and immigrant groups in Boston and Chicago are well-known examples of the application of the participant-observer methodology developed by the Chicago School (Anderson 1978, 1990; Whyte 1943). These techniques have now become standard in various urban studies fields, the former in economics and geography and the latter in sociology and anthropology. Jane Addams's (1910) fieldwork on immigrants and on the living conditions of African Americans in segregated cities added considerable voice to the movement for direct policies for urban reform.

The institutional approach explores community life, community power, and urban power. Research on the development of communities includes the detailed empirical studies of community life and community power by Robert Lynd and Helen Lynd (1929, 1937). Focused community studies by Michael Young and Peter Willmott (1957) and the early community/urban power studies of the 1960s, Floyd Hunter's (1952) study of local elites, and Robert Dahl's (1961) formulation of dispersed/pluralist sources of power established the core of metropolitan governance studies. John Rex and Robert Moore (1967) researched the role of institutions and agency in influencing social outcomes. R. E. Pahl (1970) formulated urban managerialism/gatekeeping as control mechanisms for access to key resources. Clarence Stone's (1989) regime analysis argued that the operation of metropolitan politics in the Atlanta area was based on political networks among the fragmented metropolitan governments and that managing these networks had become the essence of governance. Addressing class stratification in urban areas with this approach is indirect; if cities succeed in the global marketplace through well-developed urban management, the theory argues, prosperity will trickle down to the urban poor.

The political economy tradition links urban challenges to underlying inequalities in power and property in the process of urban development. Marxist analysis of urban issues and development (Engels [1844] 1973; Harvey 1973; Gordon 1978), the analysis of urban government as a local state (Cockburn 1977), evaluations of urban ideology and collective consumption conflicts (Castells 1977), and applications of dependency theory to urban problems are examples of this vital trend in urban studies. This approach generally argues that the rigid stratification in cities is a reflection of the broader class structures in society and that revolutionizing national and international class relations is a requirement for significant urban transformation.

Researchers from urban planning, urban design, and architecture focus their concerns on the management and structure of cities. Modernist visions of the city were applied in the New York Regional Plan (1922) and Greater London Plan (1944). William Whyte (1955) studied public use of urban parks and plazas to identify the types of architecture and spatial design that promote a certain pattern of behavior. "New Urbanism" considered American small towns as imagined urban models, where busy and lively sidewalks help cities thrive as safe and healthy places. According to Jane Jacobs's (1961) "vibrant city" concept, lively street life supports a creative and diverse economic base, but rigid planning smothers urban social life and entrepreneurialism. Where planners have called for detailed planning processes, usually engaging the affected communities, economists have argued for a greater role for market forces in determining the location and density of activities. Both generally accept existing patterns of class stratification.

Postmodern approaches confront the assumptions of positivism and the theory of modernist planning and study different aspects of city life. Postmodernists have analyzed cities as centers of consumption (Mort 1996), centers of recreation (Hannigan 1998), and centers of image (Gottdiener 1995). Jane M. Jacobs (1996) developed the concept of "representational cities," where messages encoded in the environment can be read as texts. Postmodernists, however, offer few concrete suggestions on ameliorating the conditions of the poor; increasing diversity and participation in social life, they believe, would be an important component of enhancing the quality of life for all city dwellers.

DIFFERENTIATION, DISPLACEMENT, EXCLUSION, AND GLOBALIZATION

Urban scholars today are tackling the issue of globalization's impact on urban spaces and populations from many perspectives, building on the field's past insights into such urban processes as the differentiation of urban populations due to social and economic inequalities, the displacement of the less affluent, and the exclusion of the poor from public amenities. Many urban scholars now feel that the ever-growing world-wide mobility of capital and labor—globalization—is causing populations to sort themselves into rigidly segregated global class hierarchies.

Cities have been in the process of constant economic restructuring since the beginning of industrialization. John Kain's (1968) "mismatch hypothesis" and William J. Wilson's works (1987, 1996) on "the underclass" provided frameworks within which to understand suburbanization (in both economic and sociologic dimensions) as a process that increases differentiation and exclusion. The emergence of employment centers or "edge cities" (Garreau 1991) in the suburbs showed that the loss of low-skill jobs in the central cities is not easily reversible. Globalization, driven by international flows of capital and information, has created a new system of city networks (Castells 1989; Sassen 1991).

Thomas Sugrue (1996) documented how economic restructuring in Detroit has been extremely painful and dislocating for African Americans who lost their middle-class jobs in the automotive industry. Lack of economic opportunities increased the size of the underclass in Detroit. Saskia Sassen (1991), H. V. Savitch and Ronald Vogel (1996), and John Mollenkoph and Manuel Castells (1991) showed that New York City has become a "dual city," where skilled workers work in the specialized industries and immigrant workers take lower-paying service jobs and live in distinctly separate urban environments. Globalization coupled with urban renewal programs resulted in gentrification or displacement of some poor inner-city urban residents by higher income groups. Mike Davis (1990) argued that globalization has also opened urban land markets to global capital. Los Angeles, for example, restructured its industrial base and maintained its prosperity through participation in the Pacific Rim postindustrial order (Scott and Soja 1996), but the associated flood of capital from Asian countries increased land prices and made housing unaffordable for virtually all middle-class residents in Los Angeles. Globalization and privatization of public space in Los Angeles have excluded the lower and middle classes from most of the urban space.

Urban studies today continues to grapple with such challenges. Economists urge a reliance on market forces for improvements, while planners call for detailed "smart growth" plans. Political scientists focus on enhancing and democratizing governance as the pathway to progress, while institutionalists urge the federal government, not just the locality, to address the underlying social ills confronting the poor in cities. Similarly and more radically, political economists argue that urban challenges cannot be successfully addressed as long as the national class structure maintains an unequal, exploitative regime. Taken as a whole, then, urban studies is a terrain of contention among schools of thought, with many alternative policy recommendations to address the challenges of the city.

SEE ALSO *Sociology, Urban; Stratification; Urbanization*

BIBLIOGRAPHY

Addams, Jane. 1910. *Twenty Years at Hull House.* New York: MacMillan.

Alonso, William. 1964. *Location and Land Use: Toward a General Theory of Land Rent.* Cambridge, MA: Harvard University Press.

Anderson, Elijah. 1978. *A Place on the Corner.* Chicago: University of Chicago Press. 2nd ed., 2003.

Anderson, Elijah. 1990. *Streetwise: Race, Class, and Change in an Urban Community.* Chicago: University of Chicago Press.

Castells, Manuel. 1977. *The Urban Question: A Marxist Approach.* London: Edward Arnold.

Castells, Manuel. 1989. *The Informational City: Information Technology, Economic Restructuring, and the Urban-Regional Process.* Cambridge, MA: Blackwell.

Christaller, Walter. [1933] 1966. *Central Places in Southern Germany.* Trans. Carlisle W. Baskin. Englewood Cliffs, NJ: Prentice Hall.

Cockburn, Cynthia. 1977. *The Local State: Management of Cities and People.* London: Pluto.

Dahl, Robert A. 1961. *Who Governs? Democracy and Power in an American City.* New Haven, CT: Yale University Press.

Davis, Mike. 1990. *City of Quartz: Excavating the Future in Los Angeles.* London and New York: Verso.

Du Bois, W. E. B. 1899. *The Philadelphia Negro: A Social Study.* New York: Lippincott.

Engels, Friedrich. [1844] 1973. *The Condition of the Working Class in England in 1844.* Moscow: Progress Publishers.

Frazier, Edward Franklin. 1932. *The Negro Family in Chicago.* Chicago: University of Chicago Press.

Friedmann, John, and Goetz Wolff. 1982. World City Formation: An Agenda for Research and Action. *International Journal of Urban and Regional Research* 6: 309–344.

Garreau, Joel. 1991. *Edge City: Life on the New Frontier.* New York: Doubleday.

Gordon, David. 1978. Capitalist Development and the History of American Cities. In *Marxism and the Metropolis: New Perspectives in Urban Political Economy,* 2nd ed., eds. William Tabb and Larry Sawers, 21–53. New York: Oxford University Press.

Gottdiener, Mark. 1995. *Postmodern Semiotics: Material Culture and the Forms of Postmodern Life.* Cambridge, MA: Blackwell.

Hannigan, John. 1998. *Fantasy City: Pleasure and Profit in the Postmodern Metropolis.* London and New York: Routledge.

Harvey, David. 1973. *Social Justice and the City.* London: Edward Arnold.

Hunter, Floyd. 1952. *Community Power Structure.* Chapel Hill: University of North Carolina Press.

Isard, Walter. 1956. *Location and Space Economy: A General Theory Relating to Industrial Location, Market Areas, Land Use, Trade, and Urban Structure.* Cambridge, MA: MIT Press; New York: Wiley.

Jacobs, Jane. 1961. *The Death and Life of Great American Cities.* New York: Random House.

Jacobs, Jane M. 1996. *Edge of Empire: Postcolonialism and the City.* London: Routledge.

Kain, John. 1968. Housing Segregation, Negro Employment, and Metropolitan Decentralization. *Quarterly Journal of Economics* 82 (2): 175–197.

Lösch, August. [1944, 2nd ed.] 1954. *The Economics of Location.* Trans. William H. Woglom and Wolfgang F. Stolper. New Haven, CT: Yale University Press.

Lynd, Robert, and Helen Lynd. 1929. *Middletown: A Study in Contemporary American Culture.* New York: Harcourt Brace.

Lynd, Robert, and Helen Lynd. 1937. *Middletown in Transition: A Study in Cultural Conflicts.* New York: Harcourt Brace.

Mollenkoph, John, and Manuel Castells, eds. 1991. *Dual City: Restructuring New York.* New York: Russell Sage Foundation.

Mort, Frank. 1996. *Cultures of Consumption: Masculinities and Social Space in Late Twentieth-Century Britain*. London: Routledge.

Mumford, Lewis. 1938. *The Culture of Cities*. New York: Harcourt Brace.

Paddison, Ronan. 2001. Studying Cities. In *Handbook of Urban Studies*, ed. Ronan Paddison, 1–9. London: Sage.

Pahl, R. E. 1970. *Whose City? And Other Essays on Sociology and Planning*. Harlow, U.K.: Longman.

Park, Robert E. 1916. The City: Suggestions for Investigation of Human Behavior in the Urban Environment. *American Journal of Sociology* 20: 577–612.

Park, Robert E. 1952. *Human Communities*. Glencoe, IL: Free Press.

Park, Robert E., Ernest W. Burgess, and Roderick D. McKenzie. 1925. *The City*. Chicago: University of Chicago Press.

Rex, John, and Robert Moore. 1967. *Race, Community, and Conflict: A Study of Sparkbrook*. London: Oxford University Press.

Sassen, Saskia. 1991. *The Global City: New York, London, Tokyo*. Princeton, NJ: Princeton University Press.

Savitch, H. V., and Ronald Vogel, eds. 1996. *Regional Politics: American in a Post-City Age*. Thousands Oaks, CA: Sage.

Scott, Alan, and Edward Soja. 1996. Introduction to Los Angeles: City and Region, in *The City: Los Angeles and Urban Theory at the End of the Twentieth Century*, eds. Alan Scott and Edward Soja. Berkeley: University of California Press.

Shevky, Eshref, and Wendell Bell. 1955. *Social Area Analysis: Theory, Illustrative Application, and Computational Procedures*. Stanford, CA: Stanford University Press.

Stone, Clarence. 1989. *Regime Politics: Governing Atlanta, 1946–1988*. Lawrence: University of Kansas Press.

Sugrue, Thomas J. 1996. *The Origins of the Urban Crisis: Race and Inequality in Postwar Detroit*. Princeton, NJ: Princeton University Press.

Thomas, William I., and Florian Znaniecki. 1918–1920. *The Polish Peasant in Europe and America: Monograph of an Immigrant Group*. Chicago: University of Chicago Press.

Timms, Duncan. 1971. *The Urban Mosaic: Towards a Theory of Residential Differentiation*. Cambridge, U.K.: Cambridge University Press.

Tönnies, Ferdinand. [1883] 1995. *Community and Society*. New York: Harper.

Weber, Max. 1905. *The City*. London: Heinemann.

Whyte, William F. 1943. *Street Corner Society: The Social Structure of an Italian Slum*. Chicago: University of Chicago Press. 2nd ed., 1955.

Wilson, William J. 1987. *The Truly Disadvantaged: The Inner City, the Underclass, and Public Policy*. Chicago: University of Chicago Press.

Wilson, William J. 1996. *When Work Disappears: The World of the New Urban Poor*. New York: Knopf.

Wirth, Louis. 1938. Urbanism as a Way of Life: The City and Contemporary Civilization. *American Journal of Sociology* 44: 1–24.

Young, Michael, and Peter Willmott. 1957. *Family and Kinship in East London*. London: Routledge and Kegan Paul.

Rodney D. Green
Haydar Kurban

URBANITY

Over the course of the nineteenth century in Europe and North America, urbanity came to be conceived as a personality trait. According to Richard Sennett (1974), public experience outside the private sphere of the home became an obligation for the self-development of men. Conversing in cafés or walking the busy streets, just like traveling, was a means to acquire sophistication and to become comfortable with diversity. Urbanity, cosmopolitanism, and sophistication were almost synonymous. For women, on the other hand, exploring the public sphere was considered immoral. Moving about the city alone and freely was associated with loose sexual behavior. It was in the sphere of the bourgeois home in the city that women acquired the manners and accent of urbanity. Present-day standards of politeness, such as the notion that each person has the right to be left alone when in public or norms on proper English and proper dress, were derived from the social control of the urban bourgeois home.

Indeed, urbanity is often conceived as the cultural capital of higher social classes. As a personality trait, it is used for exclusion in jobs and for residential segregation. For instance, the speaking accent of youth living in the French *banlieue* (suburbs) acts as a serious barrier to employment in a discriminatory environment. In addition to their relegation in housing projects outside cities, these youths are not seen as endowed with enough urbanity and sophistication to work and they are often tagged with a lack of civility.

For Pierre Bourdieu (1979), cultural capital provides people with a structure of predispositions transmitted by their family; urban, white, middle-class youth would thus be better equipped to succeed than their poor, suburban counterparts. There are three forms of cultural capital, each of them closely associated with the notion of urbanity. Firstly, embodied capital refers to investments in self-improvement; it is thus focused on urbanity as a personality trait that can be developed. Secondly, objectified cultural capital is represented by material objects such as a nice car or a house in a trendy neighborhood; it is thus closely related to the politics of space (who has the right to be in the city?). Thirdly, institutionalized cultural capital provides certain people with access to decision-making powers affecting everyday life in the city.

White, middle-class, urban dwellers endowed with these three forms of cultural capital have a discriminatory and exclusionary impact on other city dwellers. They can shape the city to their own image. Derelict landscapes in central cities are regenerated, pushing away poorer residents for processes of gentrification. The revamping of Times Square in New York City, for instance, is an example of what Neil Smith (1996) calls *revanchist* urbanity, whereby the white middle-class appropriates spaces in the city for their own pleasure and the fulfillment of their own urbanity. In the name of economic growth and safety, former New York mayor Rudy Giuliani went on with this model of what Sharon Zukin has called "pacification by cappuccino" (1995, p. 28), eliminating greasy mom-and-pop joints and other venues that were not attractive to the white middle class.

As a personality trait enhanced by spatial practices and institutional power, urbanity is used as a means of exclusion. However, more and more voices are rising to claim other forms of urbanity that would not be linked to class and ethnicized cultural capital. This became particularly visible in the wake of the worldwide urban revolts of the late 1960s. Henri Lefebvre (1968) wrote then about the rights to the city—that is, the right to be in the city and to have decent living conditions, but also the right to define the codes and norms of social life in a manner closer to everyday practices than to technocratic power.

In fact, according to Lefebvre (1970), after the agricultural, mercantilist, and industrial ages, we are now going through an urban revolution. This does not only mean that more than half of the world population lives in cities that cover more and more land, but also and mostly that the way we conceive of the world has become urban. For Lefebvre, personalities, economic behavior, spiritual beliefs, modes of social interaction, all aspects of human life have become urban. Urbanity, in this second definition, is not confined to a personality trait of the white middle class but is a general characteristic of the world since the 1970s. Even for peasants in a country of the "global south," Lefebvre would argue, urbanity is part of their life, their values, and their mental schemes.

In this sense, urbanity can be defined by a set of distinctive social characteristics, regardless of geographical location. Diversity of people, beliefs, and histories is the most important of these characteristics. Whether it is celebrated, commercialized, tolerated, or oppressed, diversity is a trait of urbanity that is very different from rurality (which is often associated with homogeneity). Other related characteristics of urbanity are speed, flows of people, information, and goods, and mobility, as well as concentration and density. Combined, these traits are sometimes seen as having pervasive effects, such as deviant behavior or alienation. Yet, the tenuous social bonds and anonymity often associated with urbanity in contrast to rurality are caused not so much by life in cities as by what Lefebvre calls *technocratic control*. Obsession with rational planning, rather than privileging the spontaneity and diversity of everyday life, has individualization and alienation effects.

SEE ALSO *Culture, Low and High*

BIBLIOGRAPHY

Bourdieu, Pierre. [1979] 1984. *Distinction: A Social Critique of the Judgement of Taste*. Trans. Richard Nice. Cambridge, MA: Harvard University Press.

Lefebvre, Henri. [1968] 1996. *Writings on Cities*, trans. and eds. Eleonore Kofman and Elizabeth Lebas. Oxford: Blackwell.

Lefebvre, Henri. [1970] 2003. *The Urban Revolution*. Trans. Robert Bononno. Minneapolis: University of Minnesota Press.

Sennett, Richard. 1974. *The Fall of Public Man*. New York: Norton.

Smith, Neil. 1996. *New Urban Frontier: Gentrification and the Revanchist City*. New York: Routledge.

Zukin, Sharon. 1995. *The Cultures of Cities*. Cambridge, U.K.: Blackwell.

Julie-Anne Boudreau

URBANIZATION

Urbanization—the transformation of social life from rural to urban settings—is the seminal process in defining the course of civilization. Urban life evolved approximately ten thousand years ago as a result of sophisticated agricultural innovations that led to a food supply of sufficient magnitude to support both the cultivators and a new class of urban residents. These agricultural innovations, mainly irrigation-based public works, required a more complex social order than that of an agrarian village. Urbanization at its base is thus distinguished from the settled agrarian life that preceded it in two important respects: it embodies a multifaceted social hierarchy and relies on sophisticated technologies to support the activities of daily living (Childe 1936). These uniquely urban characteristics consistently define both urbanization and civilization from the past to the present.

Just as civilization emerged from urbanization in the past, so too does the future course of civilization hinge on our ability to incorporate the reality of contemporary urbanization into our responses to twenty-first-century challenges that include climate change, the elimination of severe poverty, ecological balance, the conquest of communicable diseases, and other pressing social and environmental problems. This is the case because since 2007 more than half of the world's population resides in urban settings—a historic first.

Urban life can be defined, following Louis Wirth (1938), as life in permanent dense settlements with socially diverse populations. According to Lewis Mumford (1937), the city plays a critical role in the creation and maintenance of culture and civilization. Finally, following Henri Pirenne (1925), the crucial role of trade and production should be stressed. Thus urbanization involves an ongoing threefold process: (1) urbanization geographically and spatially spreads the number and density of permanent settlements; (2) settlements become comprised of populations that are socially and ethnically differentiated; and (3) these urban populations thrive through the production and exchange of a diverse array of manufactured and cultural products.

THE CONTEMPORARY SPREAD OF URBANIZATION

Although city life extends back at least ten millennia, the shape and size of modern urban settlements have roots that extend back only about 250 years to the Industrial Revolution, which marked a significant transformation in the role of cities as loci of critical productive activity and not just as cultural and political centers for a surrounding agrarian countryside. The present characterization of the world as predominantly urban is the cumulative result of this urbanization-industrialization trend. Industrial urbanization emerged first in the countries of the West, then in the countries of Latin America and the Caribbean, and is now strongly evident in Asia and Africa (Garau et al. 2005).

According to United Nations projections, by 2030 the increase of 2.06 billion in net global population will occur in urban areas. Over 94 percent of that urban total (1.96 billion) will be in the world's less-developed regions (UN Population Division 2004). This means that virtually all of the additional needs of the world's future population will have to be addressed in the urban areas of the poorest countries.

UN-Habitat, the United Nations agency responsible for promoting sustainable urban development, estimates that roughly one-third of the current urban population of about three billion live in places that can be characterized as slums. The UN classification schema for slums is a five-fold measure: lack of access to safe drinking water, lack of access to sanitation, inadequate shelter, overcrowding, and lack of security of tenure. If a place of residence meets any one of these measures, it is classified as a slum. By the year 2030, if nothing is done, the proportion of the urban population living in slums will rise to 43 percent (1.7 billion in an urban population of 3.93 billion). All of these people will be living in the urban slums of countries in the developing world, mainly in sub-Saharan Africa and Southeast Asia (UN-HABITAT and Global Urban Observatory 2003).

DENSITY, DIVERSITY, AND URBANIZATION

Urbanization is most powerfully observed through physical density (comparatively large numbers of people living in comparatively small areas). The ratio of population size to land area is the standard metric for evaluating density. It is a precise measurement that is not easily interpreted because neither the numerator (population size) nor the denominator (land area) is static. Political boundaries are only marginally helpful in defining the effective size of an urban settlement because at any moment changes in communications and transport technology alter the size of the relevant space over which urban residents live and work. Until the end of the eighteenth century, cities were spatially compact places with a radius of about one to two miles—the distance an individual could comfortably walk in carrying out daily activities. With the arrival of industrialization, effective urban size spread rapidly through the nineteenth and twentieth centuries. Contemporary urban or, more properly, *metropolitan* settlements easily encompass radii of 50 miles or more. This is a result of the continual improvement in rapid overland and even air travel modes and digital and wireless communications technology. The exact spatial configuration of any metropolitan settlement is a compromise between activities that must remain within walking distance and those for which residents are willing to travel (Schaeffer and Sclar 1980).

These spatially widening metropolises are not uniform in terms of their residential population densities. Hence density measurements alone tell us little about the quality of urban life. This quality can vary widely within the comparatively small confines of any metropolitan area. It is especially important to understand that high density per se is not an indicator of compromised living conditions. Metropolitan New York, which includes both the central city and the surrounding suburbs, has an average population density of over 5,300 people per square mile (ppm^2), but the wealthiest part of the region, Manhattan Island, has a density that exceeds 66,000 ppm^2. By way of comparison Nairobi, Kenya, has a citywide density of over 1,400 ppm^2, but its centrally located slum, Kibera, considered the largest in Africa, has an estimated population density of at least 100,000 ppm^2. While Kibera's density significantly exceeds Manhattan's, the major determinant of the differences in quality of life relate to the quality of shelter and the ancillary urban services, such as water, sanitation, public safety, and most importantly transportation. Very poor urban residents must exchange life in high-density, poorly serviced places for the ability to walk to the places in the urban center where they earn a livelihood.

The major urban challenge of the twenty-first century concerns the ability of governments to effectively provide adequate shelter and to plan and deliver services for metropolitan-wide areas in developing countries. The difficulty in meeting the challenge is rooted in part in the fact that the historical political boundaries of the central city and suburban (i.e., satellite city) subunits of government typically derive from an earlier century, before contemporary transport and communications technology redefined effective spatial relationships. The urban economies of modern metropolises now run beyond the legal jurisdictions of the subunits of government responsible for infrastructure and public services. The insistence of international financial agencies and donors on governmental decentralization in developing countries has only served to exacerbate this problem because it has left these governmental subunits with the responsibility but without either the technical ability or revenue sources. The result is that necessary regional planning and infrastructure investment to address the challenges of urbanization are often stymied.

Urban population growth is largely migration driven. On one side there is the push of rural poverty and on the other the pull of urban opportunity. This migration-driven growth is further exacerbated by natural rates of urban population increase (birth rates that exceed death rates). Social life in urban settlements is thus more complex than its village counterpart. The transactions of daily living in villages are governed by a social economy where goods and services are exchanged on the basis of social roles and rules of reciprocity rooted in longstanding customs and religious observances. The transactions of urbanization that confront the new arrivals are, in whole or in part, defined by the impersonal exchange relationships typical of a market economy. This transition is never a simple one-for-one exchange.

Because urban populations are continually in flux and often simultaneously expanding, they are often characterized by a multiplicity of informal and formal social relationships and institutions in a similar state of flux. The variations among an informal social economy and a formal market economy in any city at any moment in time are highly reflective of the larger external forces, such as globalization and migration, that are continually redefining the roles of different cities in a world of complex trading and production relationships. In the slum of Kibera, many of the activities of daily life, including the provision of vital public services such as water, sanitation, and public safety, are governed by an informal local, but powerful, social economy (Lowenthal 1975). In contrast, life in the working-class neighborhoods of cities in developed countries is typically an amalgam of informal social institutions imbedded in formal mechanisms of municipal public-service delivery. For the wealthiest residents of these same cities, virtually all the services they consume are provided via the formal institutions of government or market exchanges.

URBANISM AND THE GLOBAL ENVIRONMENT

Many of the patterns of contemporary urban development are extensions of those set in place in the nineteenth and twentieth centuries. These patterns were based on three assumptions: (1) energy was relatively inexpensive; (2) safe drinking water was abundant; and (3) the environment could absorb all the waste products of urbanization. None of these assumptions is any longer valid. Consequently, urbanization in the twenty-first century will have to be reconceived in both social and environmental terms. The world cannot afford the political instability and social costs of massive pockets of urban slum dwellers, nor can it accommodate urban growth through a further spatial spread that relies on urban transport powered by carbon-based energy sources and the discharge of waste products into both the local and global atmosphere. A healthy and vibrant environment is now a scarce but vital good.

Environmental problems are principally generated by the disorderly sprawl of urban settlements into the surrounding countryside. In the developed world, metropolitan areas organized around private automobile travel among low-density suburbs and tied to a central business district generate high volumes of automobile travel in the absence of tight land-use regulation and good public transport. This development pattern has led to increased mobile source pollution within the metropolitan areas and significant greenhouse gas emissions that endanger the whole planet. Sprawl requires an ever-increasing spread of impermeable (i.e., paved) ground surfaces. This in turn leads to the runoff of polluted waters into the groundwater supplies. The paved surfaces absorb heat from the sun and create urban heat islands that require more energy consumption and the emission of pollution and greenhouse gases to cool homes and offices. In addition, there are inadequate landfills to collect all the refuse of these high-consumption urban centers.

In the developing world, the problems are similar but more acute in their direct manifestation. The high rates of population growth lead to a pattern in which urban settlement runs ahead of infrastructure improvement. This leads to the establishment of informal settlements (i.e., slums) characterized by an absolute lack of safe drinking water and sanitation. The lack of adequate public transport and public health protection systems leads to a congestion of private cars and informal transports in the center of cities, which exacerbates the air quality problems and greenhouse gas emissions. The social costs of the lack of these services fall disproportionately on the poorest residents of these burgeoning metropolitan areas. These costs take the form of excessive mortality and morbidity rates, low rates of labor productivity, and the reinforcement of an ongoing trap of urban poverty.

Climate change generated by greenhouse gas emissions adds yet another layer of special urgency to these pressing social problems. It is the very concentrated nature of cities—their population densities and their centrality in social functioning—that makes them and their residents so vulnerable to the hazards and stresses that climate change is inducing. Rising sea levels and warming water make serious climatic assaults on cities more frequent. Devastating storms and floods that hit once in a century now occur in far shorter cycles. The impacts are not equitably distributed. The poorest urban residents tend to live in the riskiest portions of the urban environments—flood plains, unstable slopes, river basins, and coastal areas.

Although the challenges of urbanization are formidable, the technical knowledge for their solutions exists. The question for the twenty-first century involves the ability of the international community, nations, and local governments to create institutions of urban planning and democratic governance that can effectively apply these solutions at a sufficiently broad scale that they can make a measurable difference.

SEE ALSO *Cities*

BIBLIOGRAPHY

Childe, V. Gordon. 1936. *Man Makes Himself.* London: Watts.

Garau, Pietro, Elliott Sclar, and Gabriella Carolini (lead authors). 2005. *A Home in the City.* UN Millennium Project: Task Force on Improving the Lives of Slum Dwellers. London and Sterling, VA: Earthscan.

Lowenthal, Martin. 1975. The Social Economy of the Urban Working Class. In *The Social Economy of Cities*, eds. Gary Gappert and Harold M. Rose, 447–469. Beverly Hills, CA: Sage.

Mumford, Lewis. 1937. What Is a City? *Architectural Record* 82: 58–62.

Pirenne, Henri. [1925] 1948. *Medieval Cities: Their Origins and the Revival of Trade.* Trans. Frank D. Halsey. Princeton, NJ: Princeton University Press.

Schaeffer, K. H., and Elliott Sclar. 1980. *Access for All: Transportation and Urban Growth.* New York: Columbia University Press.

UN-HABITAT and Global Urban Observatory. 2003. *Guide to Monitoring Target 11: Improving the Lives of 100 Million Slum Dwellers.* Nairobi, Kenya: Author.

United Nations Department of Economic and Social Affairs: Population Division. 2004. World Urbanization Prospects: The 2003 Revision. New York: Author.

Wirth, Louis. 1938. Urbanism as a Way of Life. *American Journal of Sociology* 44: 1–24.

Elliott D. Sclar

URUGUAY ROUND

The Uruguay Round, which took place between September 20, 1986, and December 15, 1993, was the eighth round of multilateral trade negotiations conducted under the General Agreement on Tariffs and Trade (GATT). The "Final Act Embodying the Results of the Uruguay Round" was signed by 124 governments and the European Communities on March 15, 1994, at a ministerial conference in Marrakesh, Morocco. The act expanded the multilateral trade regime by establishing rules for the further liberalization of trade in goods, introducing new rules for services and intellectual property rights and establishing the World Trade Organization (WTO).

Prior to the Uruguay Round, seven rounds of multilateral trade negotiations that progressively lowered tariffs on goods were held between 1947 and 1979 under the auspices of the GATT, a provisional treaty. By the early 1980s, changing trade practices, increases in trade in services, the need for stronger intellectual property rights, and a growing membership of developed and developing countries made the weaknesses of the GATT apparent. A ministerial conference held in Geneva, Switzerland, from November 24 to 29, 1982, failed to launch a new round of trade negotiations as planned but initiated the process of agenda setting.

The Uruguay Round was launched at a ministerial conference held in Punta del Este, Uruguay, from September 15 to 20, 1986. The ambitious agenda included tariffs, nontariff barriers, agriculture, textiles, services, intellectual property rights, investment, and dispute settlement (see Table 1).

The Uruguay Round negotiations encountered significant delays, due in part to the political and economic sensitivity of the issues for developed and developing member governments. A ministerial conference held in Montreal, Canada, from December 5 to 9, 1988, was suspended after a deadlock developed between the United States and the European Communities over the liberalization of agriculture. Nonetheless, this meeting resulted in concessions on tropical products, revisions to dispute-settlement provisions, and the establishment of a trade policy review mechanism. The collapse of a ministerial conference held in Brussels, Belgium, from December 3 to 7, 1990, over the issue of agriculture jeopardized the Uruguay Round negotiations.

Following nearly a year of further technical preparation within the various working groups, GATT director-general Arthur Dunkel (1932–2005), a Swiss diplomat, tabled a draft of the "Final Act" on December 20, 1991. The draft was used as a basis for continuing the negotiations. The United States and the European Communities resolved their differences over agriculture with the Blair

Fifteen negotiating sectors of the Uruguay Round.

tariffs	services	dispute-settlement provisions
nontariff measures	intellectual property rights	GATT system
agriculture	investment measures	GATT articles
tropical products	natural resource protection	antidumping measures
textiles and clothing	subsidies	Tokyo Round codes

Figure 1

House Accord of December 20, 1992. A meeting of the Quad (the trade ministers from the United States, the European Communities, Canada, and Japan) resulted in an agreement on a critical market-access package on July 7, 1993. Progress continued under the leadership of the next GATT director-general, Irish diplomat Peter Sutherland. In early December 1993, the United States and the European Communities compromised on antidumping measures and "agreed to disagree" for the time being on their remaining differences on audiovisual, financial, and shipping services, as well as subsidies. On December 15, 1993, although minor issues remained to be finalized, the member governments of the GATT agreed to conclude the Uruguay Round negotiations.

Following the ratification of the Uruguay Round agreements, a permanent WTO was established on January 1, 1995. The organization incorporated stronger dispute-settlement procedures and regular trade policy reviews of its members. The WTO governs the implementation of revised GATT multilateral rules on goods, including agricultural goods, and new rules covering services and intellectual property rights; manages the work program as outlined in some of the Uruguay Round agreements; and serves as a forum for multilateral trade negotiations.

SEE ALSO *General Agreement on Tariffs and Trade; Multilateralism; World Trade Organization*

BIBLIOGRAPHY

Schott, Jeffrey. 1994. *The Uruguay Round: An Assessment.* Washington, DC: Institute for International Economics.

World Trade Organization. 1998 (rev. 2001). *Trading into the Future.* 2nd ed. Geneva, Switzerland: WTO Information and Media Relations Division. http://www.wto.org/english/res_e/doload_e/tif.pdf.

Heidi Ullrich

U.S. CIVIL WAR

The Civil War (1861–1865) broke out in the early hours of April 12, 1861, when Confederate cannons opened fire on Fort Sumter in South Carolina's Charleston Harbor. The battle over the fort, which had become a symbol for both North and South, was both an end and a beginning. The assault marked the conclusion of years of spiraling hostility and suspicions between the North and South and of a series of escalating political, legal, and even physical altercations over the question of slavery. Slavery had been a point of contention since the inception of the United States, with the founders arguing over it in the debates over both the Declaration of Independence and the Constitution. In the interest of building the nation, however, they agreed to compromises that left the question of what to do about slavery to another generation. From that point until the 1840s, the matter stood, simmering, on the back burner.

REASONS FOR THE CIVIL WAR

The Mexican War gave the subject new urgency. Defeated, Mexico in 1848 ceded half a million square miles of territory to the United States (including the present-day states of California, Nevada, and Utah; most of New Mexico and Arizona; and parts of Colorado, Oklahoma, and Wyoming). Now the nation would have to decide whether—or what parts of—this new territory would be free or slave. Aside from the abolitionists, who were considered a radical fringe group, few people in the North disputed slavery in the states where it already existed because the Constitution protected the peculiar institution there. Congress, however, had the power to dictate whether the territories would be free or slave.

Thus the 1850s became a time of increasing hostility and suspicion between North and South as the nation wrestled with the issue of slavery in the territories. A new party, the Republicans, formed on the platform of opposing the expansion of slavery into the territories. By the time Abraham Lincoln won the presidency in 1860, the sectional divisions had grown so great that many Southerners refused to believe the president-elect when he said that he was interested in eliminating slavery only in the territories. Seven Southern states seceded in the months after Lincoln's election and declared themselves the Confederate States of America. Four more would leave the Union and complete the Confederacy after the attack on Fort Sumter.

Over the years, historians have blamed a number of forces for secession—including the industrializing North versus the rural South, cultural differences between the sections, and myopic and self-serving political leadership—but since the 1960s most historians have come to agree that while those factors may have contributed to secession, the fundamental cause was slavery.

BLOODY BATTLES

After the attack on Fort Sumter, people on both sides of the Mason-Dixon line enthusiastically greeted the news of war. The common belief on both sides was that this would be a 90-day war. The first notable battle came July 21, 1861, at Manassas, Virginia, about 20 miles west of Washington, D.C. The battle was a Confederate rout that sent picnicking observers from the capital and green Union troops alike flying back to Washington. This loss would haunt most of the upper command of the Army of the Potomac for the rest of the war, imbuing them with a defeatist attitude that only Ulysses S. Grant was able to shake in 1864.

General Grant first came to the fore in early 1862 with major wins at Forts Henry and Donelson in Tennessee. His victory at Shiloh, Tennessee, in April was the first harbinger of how costly the war was going to be, however. After nearly losing the field on April 6, Grant battled back the next day. Casualties (killed, wounded, missing, and captured) on both sides approached 24,000. The toll was the highest in the history of the hemisphere, but by the end of the war Shiloh would rank as only the seventh bloodiest battle.

Robert E. Lee was appointed commander of the Virginia forces in June 1862 after General Joseph E. Johnston was seriously wounded at the Battle of Seven Pines. Lee quickly took control of what he now called the Army of Northern Virginia and unleashed it on the Army of the Potomac in the Seven Days' Battles. Two months later he again scored a searing victory against the Northerners at a second encounter at Manassas (also known as Second Bull Run). From there, Lee began to move into Maryland. He saw this as an opportunity to pull the occupying enemy out of Virginia and to allow his hungry troops to live off the Northern countryside. He clashed again with the Yankees on September 17 at Antietam, a ferocious battle that remains the single bloodiest day in American history, with about 23,000 casualties.

Antietam was a draw, but Lincoln claimed it as a victory—one that gave him an opportunity to issue the preliminary Emancipation Proclamation that had been sitting in his desk drawer since July. For the first year of the war, Lincoln believed the South held a significant number of Unionists who would rise up against the government of Confederate president Jefferson Davis. As the war proceeded, however, Lincoln learned he was wrong. Unwilling to abolish slavery early in the war, Lincoln came to see emancipation as a way to strike at the heart of the Confederacy: Freedom for the slaves would deprive the South of its labor force and give the North an addi-

tional pool from which to draw soldiers and laborers for its own armies. Moreover, emancipation promised to keep the European powers, France and England, from formally recognizing the Confederacy and therefore kept them out of the war. It is impossible to know how European intervention might have affected the war's outcome, but the assistance the French provided the Patriots during the American Revolution suggests that neutrality in this war was an important development in favor of the North. The Emancipation Proclamation, issued as a war measure, went into effect January 1, 1863. Slavery would be permanently abolished in 1865 with the ratification of the Thirteenth Amendment.

The winter of 1862–1863 was a dismal one for the Union. Lee crushed the Yankees at Fredericksburg in December. A month later the Army of the Potomac tried to move around Lee but got stuck in the mud and had to turn back. Grant's efforts to gain Vicksburg, Mississippi, "the Gibraltar of the West," were fruitless. The one bright spot for the Union was the Battle of Stones River, at Murfreesboro, Tennessee, over the New Year's holiday.

Lee had more in store for the bluecoats. In early May 1863, he staged his most audacious victory, at Chancellorsville, Virginia, defeating a Union army nearly twice the size of his own. This success came with tremendous cost for the rebels, however. After a night reconnaissance, General Thomas "Stonewall" Jackson—more beloved in the South even than Lee at that time—was shot by his own jittery troops as he approached his lines. He died eight days later.

TIDE TURNS AGAINST CONFEDERATES

Lee took advantage of his win at Chancellorsville to move into the North again, this time into Pennsylvania. This again would be a chance to move the Union army out of Virginia and allow his own men to forage off the North's bounty. It is not known where Lee intended to go, but when an advance column on July 1 bumped into Union cavalry on the west side of Gettysburg, Lee decided to fight. His decision on the third day of the battle to send thousands of men across about 1,300 yards of open ground against an entrenched enemy was suicidal. In fifty minutes, Lee suffered about 50 percent casualties, including three brigadier generals (James L. Kemper, Lewis A. Armistead, and Richard B. Garnett). Major General Isaac R. Trimble was badly wounded and had his leg amputated. The three days of battle would be the most costly of the war, claiming 51,000 casualties, and Lee, who favored offensive warfare, would spend the rest of the war on defense.

More bad news came for the Confederacy. On July 4, the day after Gettysburg ended, Grant finally succeeded in taking Vicksburg. Now the Mississippi River was entirely open to the Federals, and the Confederacy was cut in half.

Grant had emerged as the North's long-sought hero general, and when Lincoln promoted him to command all the armies in March 1864, many in the war-weary North thought that victory was certain and would come soon. They were wrong. Grant went on the attack, engaging Lee in a series of bloody battles in the spring of 1864, losing 64,000 men in six weeks. The fighting came to a halt at Petersburg, Virginia, where the two sides settled in for a siege that would last nine months.

Public sentiment turned on Grant and soured on Lincoln, too, as General William T. Sherman stalled outside of Atlanta and General Nathaniel Banks was turned back from an effort to move into Texas. Many people in the North were "wild for peace," as one Republican politico said. Lincoln would not accept peace without the dual conditions of reunion and emancipation. Davis had just one requirement: independence. The two leaders were at loggerheads.

In the South, food shortages had plagued the Confederacy since 1862, and people at home began to starve the following year. Desertion became a problem for the Southern armies as men drifted home to help their families. By the summer of 1864, when Lincoln's political fortunes tanked, many Southerners pinned their hopes for victory less on their armies' winning than on Lincoln losing in the fall elections.

BEGINNING OF THE END

Like many others in the North—Republicans and Democrats—Lincoln was certain his bid for re-election would fail. Buoyant Democrats met at the end of August, pronounced the war a failure, and called for an immediate cessation of hostilities. But two days after the convention ended, Sherman took Atlanta, and Northerners were suddenly convinced the war was nearly won. Riding the tide of good feeling, Lincoln won by a landslide.

Just after the election, Sherman set out on his march across Georgia. His goal was to destroy the Southern civilians' continuing will to wage war. Moving to Savannah in a 60-mile-wide swath, he succeeded. Meanwhile, the rebel army that had been in Atlanta moved toward Nashville, hoping to draw Sherman north. The effort failed disastrously when the Federals decimated the army on November 30 at Franklin, Tennessee. From this point on, Lee's was the only viable army remaining in the Confederacy.

From Savannah, Sherman turned north in January 1865 and began a devastating march through South Carolina. Union soldiers unleashed their wrath on the people they held responsible for starting the war. Sherman continued to move north, ultimately intending to hook up with Grant and squeeze Lee in a pincer movement. Grant, meanwhile, was busy cutting all of Lee's supply lines. On April 2, Lee decided to move to the west. Deprived of its military protection, Richmond, the capital, quickly fell.

With Grant in pursuit, Lee's starving, ragged, and depleted army headed southwest. The chase lasted a week, until Grant cut Lee off at Appomattox Court House. There the two men signed a surrender that for all practical purposes ended the war that had claimed 620,000 lives (although fighting would go on for several weeks thereafter in other theaters). Clearly, Union victory was not inevitable. Lincoln's tenacious commitment to victory, even if it cost him the presidency, was a key factor in the North's success. Another critical factor was the willingness of generals such as Sherman, Phil Sheridan, and especially Grant to press the war ruthlessly on Confederate armies and civilians, even—in Grant's case—at the cost of their own men's lives. While one cannot discount the industrial, financial, and manpower advantages the North had over the South, ultimately the men in blue defeated the men in gray.

The last casualty of the war was Lincoln, who was shot in a theater on April 14—Good Friday—by John Wilkes Booth, an actor and Confederate sympathizer. Lincoln died the next morning. Standing at his bedside, his secretary of war said, "Now he belongs to the ages."

SEE ALSO *Confederate States of America; Grant, Ulysses S.; Lee, Robert E.; Lincoln, Abraham; Slavery*

BIBLIOGRAPHY

Glatthaar, Joseph T. 1985. *The March to the Sea and Beyond: Sherman's Troops in the Savannah and Carolinas Campaigns.* New York: New York University Press.

Grimsley, Mark. 1995. *The Hard Hand of War: Union Military Policy toward Southern Civilians, 1861–1865.* New York: Cambridge University Press.

McPherson, James M. 2001. *Ordeal by Fire: The Civil War and Reconstruction.* 3rd ed. Boston: McGraw Hill.

McPherson, James M. 2002. *Crossroads of Freedom: Antietam.* New York: Oxford University Press.

Weber, Jennifer L. 2006. *Copperheads: The Rise and Fall of Lincoln's Opponents in the North.* New York: Oxford University Press.

Jennifer L. Weber

USER COST

User cost refers to the expenses borne by the owner or renter of a capital asset resulting from the use of the asset for a given period of time. The user cost of capital also is sometimes referred to as the "implicit rental price" or the "price of capital services." A capital asset in theory can be any asset that is long-lived, which typically means it has a service life of more than one year. Durable goods such as machinery, factories, automobiles, computers, and even houses are examples of "tangible" capital assets. There are also "intangible" capital assets such as a business's technological knowledge base built up by past research and development (R&D) activity or the value of its brand(s) built up by past marketing efforts.

Along with labor input, the service flows from capital assets are used by businesses to generate revenue. For many applications in economic research, such as measuring "multifactor" productivity or evaluating the potential effect on investment of changes in tax policy, one needs to measure the prices of capital and labor services. For labor, measuring this price is easy: It is simply the wage. For capital, though, measuring the price of a unit of service, that is, the user cost, can be much more complicated. If the firm leases a car for a year, for example, then, as with "renting" labor, the user cost is simply the rental price. This rent compensates the car's owner for "wear and tear" (depreciation) inflicted on the car over the year, taxes on the rental income, the decline in its market (e.g., "blue book") value over the year, and the foregone interest the owner could have earned if she had instead sold the car and invested those funds. Most capital assets used by a firm, however, are owned by the firm. Nonetheless, one can think of the firm as renting these assets to itself at an "implicit" rental price, equal to what the firm would get if it rented these assets out to other firms. In fact, government statistical agencies and others attempting to measure the user costs of specific capital assets often measure them by the prices observed in rental markets.

Most types of capital, however, do not have active rental markets. In these cases, the user cost is often measured by appealing to the neoclassical model and the seminal work of Robert Hall and Dale Jorgenson (1967). Hall and Jorgenson derived the formula for the user cost based on the neoclassical model's proposition that the price of a capital asset should be equal to the present value of the rental income stream generated by the asset net of taxes and depreciation. From this equation, one can solve for the rental income per period, that is, the user cost, as a function of the price of the capital asset, the expected change in its price over the period, the interest rate, the depreciation rate, and taxes. Because these values are either known or can be estimated reasonably well, the user cost can be calculated using this formula.

It should be noted that this neoclassical concept of user cost is distinct from Keynes's concept of user cost, which, roughly speaking, is the total cost to a firm of using capital in production (whereas the neoclassical user cost can be thought of as the price of a unit of services from that

capital). The Keynesian user cost captures the value of capital that is "used up" or "consumed" in the production process. In Keynes's production framework, the sum of labor ("factor") cost and user cost equals the total ("prime") cost of production (see chapter 6, Keynes 1936).

SEE ALSO *Keynes, John Maynard*

BIBLIOGRAPHY

Hall, Robert E., and Dale W. Jorgenson. 1967. Tax Policy and Investment Behavior. *American Economic Review* 57 (2): 391–414.

Keynes, John Maynard. 1936. *General Theory of Employment, Interest, and Money.* London: Macmillan.

Daniel J. Wilson

USE VALUE

SEE *Exchange Value.*

UTILITARIANISM

Utilitarianism is an intellectual movement in the social sciences and in philosophy. It is founded on the principle that individual actions, as well as laws, economic decisions, and social policies should promote the "greatest happiness." Jeremy Bentham (1748–1832), an English legal theorist and political reformer, first outlined the utilitarian theory in his *Introduction to the Principles of Morals and Legislation* (1789). Human beings are governed, according to Bentham, by "two sovereign masters, pain and pleasure." Actions are to be judged by their utility—that is, by a "felicific calculus," or reckoning of the benefits and harms they produce. Bentham held that such a calculus must take into account the number of persons whose interests are affected, as well as the intensity, duration, and degree of certainty of the expected pleasure or pain. In addition, one should take into account the nearness or remoteness in time, as well as the likelihood that an initial pleasure will be followed by pain, or a pain by pleasure. Whether an action or the adoption of a social policy is judged to be "good" or "bad" depends on the result of this calculation.

Bentham built on the work of thinkers such as John Locke (1632–1704), Claude-Adrien Helvétius (1715–1771), and Adam Smith (1723–1790), and himself became the center of a group of intellectuals and social reformers that included James Mill (1773–1836), William Godwin (1756–1836), and the economists David Ricardo (1722–1823) and Thomas Malthus (1776–1834). On the grounds of social benefit, "radical" utilitarian reformers called for changes to the laws governing parliamentary elections, the prison system, treatment of the poor, and other matters. Early utilitarians aimed at abolishing unnecessary suffering and promoting individual happiness through the rational study of the long-term consequences of policies and actions. For example, they believed it necessary to control the procreative impulses that can lead to rampant population growth. Because of their unsentimental approach to questions of moral and social life, utilitarians gained a popular reputation as lacking spontaneity, emotion, and artistic sensitivity. Charles Dickens's *Hard Times* (1854) includes a memorable portrayal of utilitarianism in the character of Thomas Gradgrind, whose insistence on educating his children only in "facts" rather than "fancy" (imagination) leads to unhappiness for all concerned.

John Stuart Mill (1806–1873) was the son of Bentham's associate James Mill. J. S. Mill's early education was based on Benthamite principles, and in his *Autobiography* (1873) he criticized his upbringing for its overemphasis on developing the analytic powers at the expense of educating the emotions. Despite these reservations about his own education, Mill adopted utilitarian principles and became the movement's most articulate spokesperson, developing the theory in works such as the *Principles of Political Economy* (1848). In *On Liberty* (1859) Mill defended the importance of individual freedom of thought and action, arguing that the individual is the best judge of his or her own good and that society benefits from the experimentation that occurs in an atmosphere of liberty. In *Utilitarianism* (1863) he went beyond Bentham's famous statement in *The Rationale of Reward* (1825) that "Prejudice apart, the game of push-pin is of equal value with the arts and sciences of music and poetry. If the game of push-pin furnish more pleasure, it is more valuable than either" (p. 253). In contrast to Bentham, Mill argued that there are qualitative differences among pleasures that affect their value. In *The Subjection of Women* (1869) Mill evidenced the radical bent of utilitarianism, challenging deeply held prejudices against women's capacity for intellectual development and self-governance. He argued that it is impossible to know whether women are innately less capable than men without giving women the same educational opportunities that men have.

Among the well-known later defenders of utilitarian philosophy were the English philosophers Henry Sidgwick (1838–1900) and George Edward Moore (1873–1958). In the late twentieth century utilitarian ethics was further developed by philosophers including J. J. C. Smart (b. 1920) and Peter Singer (b. 1946). Singer's contributions include highlighting the utilitarian concern for the interests of nonhuman animals. He used the term *speciesism* to refer to the view (which he opposes) that nonhuman animals deserve less consideration than human beings solely on the basis of species membership.

VARIETIES OF UTILITARIANISM

Utilitarianism is still the most prominent form of *consequentialism*, the view that actions should be morally judged on the basis of their good or bad results, rather than on their intrinsic rightness or wrongness. Within utilitarianism, different schools of thought have arisen in response to debates over the implications of the basic theory. *Act utilitarians* argue that each individual action should be judged by its beneficial or harmful results, so, for example, it may be morally permissible or even morally necessary to tell a lie in order to save an innocent life. *Rule utilitarians*, in contrast, evaluate not individual actions but social rules or types of actions. For a rule utilitarian, because telling lies generally results in more harm than benefit, lying is generally prohibited. In addition to the act versus rule debate, utilitarians have disagreed over whether utilitarianism is based on an empirical description of human motivation or a vision of how individuals ought to be motivated, and also over the question of how far the interests of individuals and those of social groups can and should be harmonized. The various versions of utilitarianism agree, however, on the need for impartial and equal consideration of the interests of all those affected by any decision.

OBJECTIONS TO UTILITARIANISM

Utilitarianism has met with numerous objections. First, some object that utilitarianism is unconcerned with how benefits and harms are to be distributed, as long as the maximum amount of total satisfaction is achieved and as long as no individual's interests are weighed more heavily than anyone else's. Utilitarianism seems more concerned with how the aggregate of individuals fares, even if a minority must suffer undeservedly in order to provide satisfaction to the majority. A related criticism was made by economist Amartya Sen in *On Economic Inequality* (1973). Sen argued that, despite the fact that utilitarianism is often believed to lead to economic egalitarianism, or an equal distribution of income, under certain circumstances it leads to just the opposite. If person A, for example, derives greater utility than person B from the same amount of income (perhaps because person B suffers from a chronic illness or a disability and person A does not), utilitarianism seems to lead to the paradoxical conclusion that person A should be given more resources than person B, in order to increase the amount of utility of the group as a whole. It is because utilitarianism concerns itself with the good of the aggregate, also known as sum-ranking, that it leads to paradoxical results in this and similar cases.

The utilitarian commitment to equal consideration of individuals' interests thus appears to be in tension with its practice of judging the goodness of a particular situation by measuring the aggregate of individual utilities.

A second objection is that utilitarians make ethical decisions based on the satisfaction of human preferences. Preferences are notoriously subjective and malleable, and they differ according to the circumstances to which individuals are accustomed. For example, someone who is used to great wealth may experience a sense of deprivation under circumstances that would seem acceptable or even luxurious to someone accustomed to severe poverty. Moreover, because preferences are of many different types, it may not be possible or appropriate to treat them as commensurable (measurable by a single standard). For example, it may not be possible to weigh the happiness gained from friendship against the happiness gained from having good health. Third, some object that utilitarianism demands excessive sacrifices from its adherents. For example, it appears that in order to bring about the greatest happiness for all people, those who are relatively well-off would be obliged to sacrifice their own material well-being, and that of their dependents, to the point at which they attain a level of satisfaction equal to that of the least well-off person who could be assisted by such a sacrifice. A fourth objection is that utilitarianism allows or even requires the performance of certain actions that are ordinarily considered unethical, such as breaking a promise, making a false accusation, or even killing an innocent person, if that action could bring about a benefit sufficiently great to outweigh its harmful effects.

Despite these and other criticisms, utilitarianism continues to exert an influence on ethics and social policy. Whenever a cost-benefit analysis is performed in order to assess the worth of a particular course of action, utilitarian thinking is at work. The appeal of utilitarianism lies in its affirmation of individual equality and its view that the goal of both personal ethics and public policy is to bring about a preponderance of benefit over harm to all who are affected by human actions.

SEE ALSO *Democracy; Social Contract*

BIBLIOGRAPHY

Bentham, Jeremy. [1789] 1996. *Introduction to the Principles of Morals and Legislation*, eds. J. H. Burns and H. L. A. Hart. Oxford: Oxford University Press.

Bentham, Jeremy. [1825] 1962. The Rationale of Reward. In *The Works of Jeremy Bentham*. Vol. 2, ed. John Bowring. New York: Russell & Russell.

Halévy, Elie. 1966. *The Growth of Philosophic Radicalism*. Trans. Mary Morris. Boston: Beacon Press.

Mill, John Stuart. [1863] 2002. *Utilitarianism*. 2nd ed. Ed. George Sher. Indianapolis, IN: Hackett.

Mill, John Stuart. [1873] 1957. *Autobiography*. Indianapolis, IN: Bobbs-Merrill.

Sen, Amartya. 1997. *On Economic Inequality*. Expanded ed. Eds. James E. Foster and Amartya Sen. Oxford: Clarendon Press.

Stephen, Leslie. [1900] 1997. *The English Utilitarians*. London: Thoemmes Continuum.

Paulette Kidder

UTILITY FUNCTION

"Economics is the science which studies human behavior as a relationship between given ends and scarce means which have alternative uses." This definition of economics, stated by Lionel Robbins in his landmark work *An Essay on the Nature and Significance of Economic Science* (1932), established the fundamental nature of economics. Given a population with seemingly unlimited wants and needs, the questions of how goods and services are consumed, produced, and distributed are the primary ones to be answered. As a consequence, the amount of satisfaction or happiness derived from consuming resources is of particular interest. Are goods and services being distributed and consumed so as to provide the greatest amount of happiness to individuals and society as a whole? To address this problem, economists require some way of measuring the happiness that is attained from consumption. *Utility* can be defined as the amount of usefulness or satisfaction or happiness gained by consuming goods and services. Utility is dependent on the bundles of goods consumed by an individual, with greater quantities of goods representing greater levels of happiness or utility. Thus, we can define a utility function as a positive relationship between the consumption of goods and services and the amount of utility received from that consumption. If a utility function can be clearly defined, then it is possible to address the question of maximizing an individual's utility, based on the size of their consumption bundle. Comparisons can also be made between different bundles, and we can make conclusions regarding individual's preferences, based on their ranking of various bundles. A well-defined utility function is also relevant when considering the welfare of an entire society. It enables social planners to determine how to distribute goods to individuals so as to maximize the total utility of a society.

The concept of utility and the doctrine of utilitarianism are rooted in Jeremy Bentham's *Principles of Morals and Legislation* (1789). In that work's introduction, Bentham declares that humans are placed "under the governance of two sovereign masters, pain and pleasure" and that the "principle of utility recognizes this subjection, and assumes it for the foundation of that system, the object of which is to rear the fabric of felicity by the hands of reason and of law" (p. 1). Bentham's "felicific calculus" was an attempt to construct a measure of utility, based on the following dimensions of pleasure and pain: intensity, duration, certainty or uncertainty, and propinquity or remoteness. The difficulties associated with such measurements were enormous, however. There was no clear way to compare feelings that were qualitatively unlike each other, nor any way to measure the intensity of feelings, much less make any comparison between the feelings of different individuals. Nonetheless, by the 1870s utility theory had come to be widely accepted, due to the independent contributions of William Jevons, Carl Menger, and Léon Walras, the leaders of the so-called Marginalist Revolution. Their works initiated a movement away from the classical theory of value set forth by Adam Smith and David Ricardo, among others, which held that the value of a product was based on its production costs. Following Jevons, Menger, and Walras, the emphasis came to be placed on the perceived value of a good and the utility a consumer would receive from the consumption of the good. The existence of utility was accepted by all three; however, the problem of the measurability of utility and the issue of defining the exact form of the utility function remained. None of the three explicitly addressed the problem of measurability; they either merely assumed the existence of such measurements, or stated that utility was measurable but not at the present time.

There were, however, attempts to develop the utility function, which is based on the quantities of the goods consumed. For the goods $x_1, x_2, x_3, \ldots$ an individual's utility was written as a function of those goods that represented ordinal utility: $\varphi (x_1, x_2, x_3, \ldots)$. This generalized form was proposed by Vilfredo Pareto, who called it an *index function*, and then also later on by Francis Edgeworth. Greater levels of consumption were believed to provide greater levels of utility. Consumers were assumed to have rationally ordered preferences and to choose a consumption bundle so as to maximize utility. Utility was also assumed to diminish with each additional unit consumed of each good. Additional units consumed of a good will increase an individual's total utility, but at a diminishing rate. In the works of several economists, including William Lloyd, N. W. Senior, and Richard Jennings, clear statements of diminishing marginal utility were given. By using the concept of diminishing marginal utility, Adam Smith's water/diamonds paradox—water is necessary for life and diamonds are not, but the price of diamonds is many times higher—could now be resolved. The relative abundance of water versus the relative scarcity of diamonds is the key here, along with the marginal utility of the last unit consumed of each good. Water is abundant enough that the marginal utility obtained from the last gallon consumed is rather low, compared to the marginal utility of the last diamond consumed.

The concept of diminishing marginal utility led in turn to the concept of the downward sloping demand curve. Walras successfully established the link between utility and demand, by using equations expressing maximum satisfaction for an individual. For some given number of m commodities, he derived the demand function as a relationship between the quantity and price of a commodity and the prices of all the other commodities, *ceteris paribus*—that is, with all other variables (such as money income and tastes) held constant. In 1892 Pareto rigorously showed that diminishing marginal utility directly implied negatively sloped demand curves. Alfred Marshall's *Principles of Economics*, first published in 1890, also formally constructed a demand curve based on utility and marginal utility. Marshall stated that "[t]here is then one law and only one law which is common to all demand schedules[,] … that the greater the amount to be sold, the smaller will be the price at which it will find purchasers" (pp. 159–160)—a conclusion he drew from the concept of diminishing marginal utility. Eugen Slutsky and John Hicks, both working with the assumptions that the utility function was additive and that consumers faced the diminishing marginal utility of consumption, also derived the downward sloping demand curve. The total change in demand for a good could be decomposed into two elements: the substitution effect and the income effect. For instance, if the price of a good increases the substitution effect dictates that a consumer will substitute consumption for a cheaper good in place of the now more expensive good. The income effect dictates that due to the price increase, a consumer effectively has less real income to spend, and will therefore consume less of both goods. For a normal good, this means that a price increase will mean a decrease in quantity demanded, and thus the demand curve will be downward sloping.

Another important extension of the utility function is the *indifference curve*, devised initially by Edgeworth. Consider a case involving two goods, and the levels of utility gained from consuming various combinations of the goods. A three-dimensional graph of this function, with two coordinates representing quantities of the two goods, and the third coordinate representing utility level, will give a *utility surface*, which rises with increasing quantities of the two goods consumed. For varying levels of utility, an indifference curve can be represented by "slices" of the utility surface that are parallel to the plane of the two commodities. An indifference curve is a two-dimensional graph of all the possible combinations of two goods that will give a consumer a given amount of utility. The downward slope of an indifference curve indicates the rate of tradeoff between the two goods, known as the *marginal rate of substitution*. Because a consumer is assumed to experience diminishing marginal utility for each additional unit consumed, decreasing consumption of one good must be offset by increasingly greater consumption of the other good, if the same level of utility is to be maintained. This fact gives rise to the shape of the indifference curve, which is convex to the origin. A graph of indifference curves for varying levels of utility is known as an *indifference map*. Consumers prefer to be on higher indifference curves, because these represent greater levels of consumption bundles and therefore greater levels of utility. Paul Samuelson's revealed preference theory was another area of work that described consumer behavior. Instead of assuming the existence of a utility function and establishing its properties, Samuelson stated that consumers revealed their preferences by what goods they purchased. From observing consumer behavior, preference relationships between bundles of goods could be established, and downward sloping indifference curves could be constructed, based on diminishing marginal utility associated with increasing consumption.

The advent of modern utility theory came with the publication of John von Neumann and Oskar Morgenstern's *Theory of Games and Economic Behavior* in 1947. In this work, it was established that individual agents make decisions so as to maximize the expected amount of utility they received from their choice of a consumption bundle. Because these choices are assigned probabilistic outcomes, utility theory could be considered to have a game theoretic framework that includes risk and an individual's attitudes toward risk-taking. Decisions regarding utility-maximization are influenced by the probabilities of outcomes. If a consumer's utility is assumed to be based on consumption as a whole and not just on one good, measures of risk aversion can be written in the form developed by economists Kenneth Arrow and John Pratt. Measurements of risk aversion are of particular importance in analyzing the behavior of consumers who make investment decisions under conditions of uncertainty.

In addition to examining economic activity as it is, without value judgment, the discipline of economics also attempts to establish normative guidelines, based on how things ought to be. Welfare economics considers the normative aspects of economic outcomes and analyzes whether these outcomes can be improved through benevolent social planning. Thus, the question of maximizing social utility becomes relevant. Edgeworth and Marshall, among others, assumed that utility was *cardinal*—that is, measurable in absolute terms—and that it was possible to make interpersonal comparisons of individual utility functions. This led to their conclusion that a social welfare function could be constructed based on a summing of all individual utility functions. Pareto, Hicks, and Nicholas Kaldor took a different approach, using an *ordinal utility*, which considers only the rankings of different bundles of goods. Social welfare was analyzed on the basis of *Pareto efficiency*, the principle that a society's condition was optimal if no further improvements in the allocation of goods could be made without making someone worse off. *Kaldor-Hicks efficiency* was an extension of Pareto efficiency. In this model, an outcome could be improved if the individuals who would be made better off by a reallocation of goods compensated those who would be made worse off.

SEE ALSO *Bentham, Jeremy; Expected Utility Theory; Marginalism; Objective Function; Pareto, Vilfredo; Preferences; Preferences, Interdependent; Principal-Agent Models; Representative Agent; Ricardo, David; Risk; Smith, Adam; Social Welfare Functions; Utilitarianism; Utility, Objective; Utility, Subjective; Utility, Von Neumann-Morgenstern; Von Neumann, John; Walras, Léon*

BIBLIOGRAPHY

Bentham, Jeremy. [1789] 1876. *An Introduction to the Principles of Morals and Legislation.* Oxford: Clarendon Press.

Edgeworth, Francis Ysidro. 1961. *Mathematical Psychics: An Essay on the Application of Mathematics to the Moral Sciences.* New York: A. M. Kelley.

Jevons, William Stanley. [1871] 1911. *The Theory of Political Economy.* London: Macmillan.

Marshall, Alfred. [1890] 1997. *Principles of Economics.* Amherst, NY: Prometheus Books.

Page, Alfred N., ed. 1968. *Utility Theory: A Book of Readings.* New York: John Wiley & Sons.

Robbins, Lionel. 1932, 1935, 1984. *An Essay on the Nature and Significance of Economic Science.* London: Macmillan.

Samuelson, Paul. 1938. A Note on the Pure Theory of Consumers' Behaviour. *Economica* 5 (17): 61–71.

Schumpeter, Joseph. 1954. *History of Economic Analysis*, ed. Elizabeth Boody Schumpeter. New York: Oxford University Press.

Smith, Adam. [1776] 1937. *An Inquiry into the Nature and Causes of the Wealth of Nations*, ed. Edwin Cannan. New York: Modern Library.

Stigler, George J. 1950. The Development of Utility Theory. *Journal of Political Economy* 58 (4–5): 307–327, 373–396.

Von Neumann, John, and Oskar Morgenstern. [1944] 2004. *Theory of Games and Economic Behavior.* Princeton, NJ: Princeton University Press.

Walras, Léon. 1954. *Elements of Pure Economics; or, The Theory of Social Wealth.* Trans. William Jaffe. London: Allen & Unwin.

Chonghyun Christie Byun

UTILITY, OBJECTIVE

Utility is value. *Objective utility* is nonrelative value. It may attach to a good for a person without being relative to the person's attitudes. For example, a baby's health has high objective utility although the baby is too young to value health.

Utilitarian moral theorists such as Jeremy Bentham ([1789] 1996) and John Stuart Mill ([1861] 2006) formulated accounts of objective utility. According to Bentham it is pleasure, and according to Mill it is happiness. Some contemporary utilitarians such as Fred Feldman (1986) accommodate pluralism about values. They recognize nonhedonistic basic values such as justice.

Objective utility contrasts with *subjective utility.* Subjective utility is a person's rational strength of desire at any time. It varies from person to person because of differences in goals and information. John von Neumann and Oskar Morgenstern (1944) define subjective utility in terms of coherent preferences concerning gambles. Such preferences ground quantitative comparisons of a person's attitudes toward the gambles' possible outcomes.

The relation between objective utility and subjective utility is twofold. First, subjective utility is a component of objective utility. It is good that a person satisfy sensible desires. Second, a person should desire the good and have an aversion to the bad. If an event is good, then a person has a reason to desire its occurrence. Objective utility influences subjective utility.

Information and rationality make subjective utility respond to objective utility. Consider the role of information. A person's desires depend on her information. Giving a person full information moves her subjective utility assignment closer to an objective utility assignment. Next, consider the role of rationality. Rationality regulates basic preferences and information's generation of derived preferences. It imposes structural constraints such as consistency of preferences, procedural constraints such as the requirement to taste flavors before forming preferences among them, and substantive constraints such as the requirement to prefer happiness to unhappiness, other things being equal. An informed, rational, cognitively ideal agent whose basic goals are intrinsic goods has a subjective utility assignment that matches an objective utility assignment.

Fields such as welfare economics use objective utility to evaluate public policies. As W. Kip Viscusi (1998) explains, government regulatory agencies seek cost-effective means of reducing risks of injury and death. A good regulation increases objective utility by promoting the public's interests rather than by catering to the public's wishes. For example, consumers want labeling of genetically modified food. Nonetheless, the U.S. Food and Drug Administration does not require labeling because its benefits do not compensate for its costs. Objective utility guides regulation.

Applications of objective utility often use a function that assigns numbers to objects evaluated. The higher the number is, the more value the object has. In some cases numbers assigned represent only a ranking, but in other cases they represent quantitative comparisons. The value of saving two lives may not only be greater than but may also be twice as great as the value of saving one life.

Measures of objective utility vary. One measure uses contribution to realization of basic goods. Life is a basic good. Water is necessary for life. So water has high objective utility using this measure. Market-value is another measure of objective utility. That people want an object is a sign that it has value. Market-value may not indicate contribution to basic goods, however. Water has low market-value because it is plentiful. The labor invested in a product is a common measure of objective utility. According to this measure, a handwoven rug has more objective utility than a gold spoon if more labor went into its fabrication. These methods of measuring objective utility have limited ranges of application and yield only approximate results. To formulate an account of objective utility, Amartya Sen (1985) uses capabilities to function and Daniel Kahneman (2000) uses momentary pleasurable experiences.

According to some theorists, objective utility attaches to physical objects such as land. A parcel of land's objective value depends on factors such as fertility. According to other theorists, objective utility attaches to realization of a proposition's truth, that is, an event or a state of affairs. The objective utility of a person's owning a parcel of land may replace the objective utility of the parcel of land. Because the value of a peasant's owning a parcel of land differs from the value of a land baron's owning the same parcel, attributing objective utilities to states of affairs involving the land's ownership makes objective utility sensitive to the variety of factors affecting value.

Value theory distinguishes intrinsic and extrinsic value, as Michael Zimmerman (2001) explains. An object with intrinsic value is good for its own sake. An object with extrinsic value is good because it leads to objects with intrinsic value. Intrinsic value is basic, and extrinsic value derives from intrinsic value. Traditional examples of intrinsic values are pleasure, justice, liberty, knowledge, beauty, and achievement. Traditional examples of extrinsic values are money, time, and power. A proposition's realization has intrinsic value in virtue of features that the proposition's realization entails rather than features its realization causes. Objective utility depends on both intrinsic and extrinsic value.

Being good for a person is not the same as being good according to a person. Health is good for a person even if he is indifferent to his health. Promoting a person's interest, well-being, or welfare is good for the person. Some accounts of objective value claim that it rests exclusively on value for sentient beings. Hedonism supports this view because all pleasure resides in a sentient being. Pluralism accommodates objective value that is independent of value for sentient beings. For example, social equality may have objective value without being good for any person.

A common criticism of objective utility is that non-relative value does not exist, or is unknowable. Persistent disagreements about values are grounds for this criticism. Another criticism is that some values are nonquantitative and incomparable so that a quantitative representation of all values is impossible. For example, one person's delight in music may not be comparable to another person's recovery from a cold. Then objective utility's interpersonal comparisons of value lack a foundation. Objective utility, despite criticisms, maintains a role in moral theory and the social sciences.

SEE ALSO *Bentham, Jeremy; Expected Utility Theory; Mill, John Stuart; Needs, Basic; Rationality; Regulation; Sen, Amartya Kumar; Utilitarianism; Utility, Subjective; Utility, Von Neumann-Morgenstern; Value; Welfare Economics*

BIBLIOGRAPHY

Bentham, Jeremy. [1789] 1996. *An Introduction to the Principles of Morals and Legislation*, eds. James H. Burns and Herbert L. A. Hart. Oxford: Clarendon.

Feldman, Fred. 1986. *Doing the Best We Can: An Essay in Informal Deontic Logic*. Dordrecht, Netherlands: Reidel.

Kahneman, Daniel. 2000. Experienced Utility and Objective Happiness: A Moment-Based Approach. In *Choices, Values, and Frames*, eds. Daniel Kahneman and Amos Tversky, 673–692. Cambridge, U.K.: Cambridge University Press.

Mill, John Stuart. [1861] 2006. *Utilitarianism*. In *The Blackwell Guide to Mill's Utilitarianism*, ed. Henry R. West, 61–113. Oxford: Blackwell.

Sen, Amartya. 1985. *Commodities and Capabilities*. Amsterdam: Elsevier.

Viscusi, W. Kip. 1998. *Rational Risk Policy: The 1996 Arne Ryde Memorial Lectures*. Oxford: Oxford University Press.

von Neumann, John, and Oskar Morgenstern. 1944. *Theory of Games and Economic Behavior*. Princeton, NJ: Princeton University Press.

Zimmerman, Michael. 2001. *The Nature of Intrinsic Value*. Lanham, MD: Rowman & Littlefield.

Paul Weirich

UTILITY, SUBJECTIVE

In economic theory, subjective utility is the satisfaction a consumer perceives to have received from consuming a product. Subjective utility is usually referred to simply as "utility." The early economists Jeremy Bentham and John Stuart Mill maintained that the goal of society is to maximize the total utility of its members. In the early twenty-first century economists refer to this as *welfare maximization.* Utility theory begins with assumptions as to individuals' preferences. When a consumer is willing to trade off one product or product attribute for another (for example, less engine power in exchange for improved gas mileage), it is said that the person has *compensatory* preferences. When a consumer is unwilling to trade off one product or product attribute for another regardless of the quantity of the second product offered (for example, a family of six needs a car with six seats no matter what the other attributes of the car are), it is said that the person has *non-compensatory* preferences. Economists typically assume compensatory preferences because they are intuitively justifiable, are easier to represent mathematically, and reflect the vast majority of true preferences. Preferences are typically represented by utility functions, which map consumption to utility.

Utility can be regarded as *ordinal* or *cardinal.* Cardinal utility is a numeric measure of utility, where units of utility are called *utils.* Ordinal utility is an ordering of objects according to utility. For example, an ordinal utility function might show a consumer deriving more utility from apples versus oranges, while a cardinal utility function might show a consumer deriving 100 units of utility from apples versus 80 units from oranges. Thus while ordinal utility is more realistic than cardinal utility in that it is difficult to measure utility numerically, cardinal utility can describe differing strengths of preference that ordinal utility cannot. Economists who use cardinal utility to describe consumer preferences note that, while consumers do not actually measure utility numerically, consumers behave (in the aggregate) as if such a measure were possible.

While utility cannot be directly measured, it is possible to obtain indirect measures by determining how much money a person must be given to compensate that person for the loss of a unit of product. For example, in an experiment a subject who has not eaten breakfast and who knows he or she will not eat dinner is given three slices of pizza for lunch. The person is then offered successively greater amounts of money in exchange for giving up one slice of pizza. The minimum amount of money the subject is willing to accept in exchange for the pizza is the dollar equivalent of the utility the subject expects to obtain from the slice of pizza.

Central to consumer theory is the idea of *declining marginal utility. Marginal utility* is the additional utility a consumer obtains from consuming one more unit of a product. Marginal utility is assumed to decline as more units of a product are consumed. For example, to a hungry person the first slice of pizza eaten yields significant marginal utility. The second slice yields less marginal utility, because the person has already consumed one slice of pizza and so is less hungry than he or she was prior to consuming the first slice. After consuming the second slice of pizza, the person's total utility is the marginal utility he or she received from the first slice plus the marginal utility he or she received from the second slice. The third slice of pizza yields less marginal utility than the second because the person is even less hungry than he or she was prior to the second slice. Eventually the person will have had enough slices of pizza that he or she does not want any more, even if the pizza is free. At this point the person's marginal utility has declined to zero (or may even be negative), consuming an additional slice of pizza will not increase the person's utility.

The phenomenon of declining marginal utility can be said to occur because consumers obtain utility from two sources: the good consumed and the *variety* the good represents. The level of variety measures how different the good is from other goods the consumer has consumed recently. For example, someone who is eating potato chips may stop eating not because he or she is full but because he or she is "tired" of potato chips and now seeks something different (like a soft drink). Without having had a drink, as the person eats more and more potato chips, the marginal utility of an additional potato chip falls because an additional potato chip is more and more like what the person has already consumed. Meanwhile the marginal utility of a soft drink rises because an additional soft drink is less and less like what the person has already consumed. Utility from variety explains why consumers tend to like to consume together things that are markedly different: beer and pizza, hot apple pie and cold ice cream, hot peppers in a sweet sauce.

If consumers can consume at no charge, they will seek out the goods that yield the greatest marginal utility. When consumers must pay for what they consume, they seek out the goods that yield the greatest *marginal utility per dollar*. This is the phenomenon that results in beer drinkers suddenly becoming scotch drinkers when the drinks are on the house. The consumer obtains greater marginal utility from a scotch than from a beer. But the difference in marginal utilities between the two drinks does not compensate for the difference in price between the two drinks. The consumer is said to attain the *optimal consumption combination* when the marginal utility per dollar for each of the goods the consumer is consuming is the same. For example, suppose a consumer obtains a marginal utility of 10 from 1 more cup of coffee and a marginal utility of 6 from 1 more bagel. If the bagel costs $2 and the cup of coffee costs $1, the consumer will purchase the bagel because the marginal utility per dollar for the bagel (6 / 1 = 6) is greater than that for the coffee

(10 / 2 = 5). But having consumed the bagel, the consumer's marginal utility for another bagel falls to (for example) 4. Now the marginal utility per dollar for the bagel (4 / 1 = 4) is less than that for the coffee (10 / 2 = 5). So the consumer buys a cup of coffee. Whenever the marginal utility per dollar for one good exceeds that of another good, the consumer consumes more of that good. In the extreme the consumer spreads his or her consumption dollars among many goods such that the marginal utility per dollar is the same for all the goods.

In the presence of uncertainty, consumers are said to maximize *expected utility*. Expected utility is the level of utility the consumer expects to obtain following resolution of the uncertainty. For example, suppose a person is offered a choice between $50 cash and a lottery ticket that carries a 50 percent chance to win $100 and a 50 percent chance to win nothing. The *expected value* of the lottery ticket is $50 ($50 = 0.5 × $100 + 0.5 × $0). The expected value of the lottery ticket is the same as the value of the cash. However, some consumers will choose the lottery ticket, while others will choose the cash. The consumers who choose the lottery ticket can be said to expect more utility from the lottery ticket than from the $50 cash. These consumers are called *risk preferential* or *risk lovers* because, apart from the utility they would receive from the money, they receive additional utility from the existence of uncertainty. More formally, the utility the risk preferential consumer expects to get from the lottery ticket exceeds the utility the consumer would get from what he or she expects to win. A risk preferential person will tend to seek out risks even when there is a negative expected return associated with the risk. Similarly a *risk averse* consumer is one who, apart from the utility he or she would receive from the money, receives disutility from the existence of uncertainty. A risk averse person will tend to avoid risks even when there is a positive expected return associated with the risk. A *risk neutral* consumer is one who receives neither utility nor disutility from risk. A risk neutral person will neither seek out nor avoid risk for its own sake but will consider only the expected return associated with the risk. If the expected return is positive, the risk neutral person will undertake the risk. If the expected return is negative, the risk neutral person will avoid the risk.

Evidence suggests that people's attitudes toward risk change depending on the size of the uncertainty relative to their wealth and whether the uncertainty involves gains or losses. On average, the less a person's wealth, the more risk preferential the person tends to be. Also people tend to be more risk preferential with respect to potential gains but risk averse with respect to potential losses. Hence, the same person may both play the lottery (an activity that increases risk but involves potential gain) and purchase insurance (an activity that decreases risk but involves a reduction in potential loss).

SEE ALSO *Expected Utility Theory; Marginalism; Ordinality; Risk; Risk Neutrality; Risk Takers; Uncertainty; Utility Function; Utility, Objective; Utility, Von Neumann-Morgenstern*

BIBLIOGRAPHY

Samuelson, Paul A. 1938. The Empirical Implications of Utility Analysis. *Econometrica* 6 (4): 344–356.

Varian, Hal R. 1992. *Microeconomic Analysis.* New York: Norton.

Von Neumann, John, and Oskar Morgenstern. 1944. *Theory of Games and Economic Behavior.* Princeton, NJ: Princeton University Press.

Walsh, Adrian, and Tony Lynch. 2003. The Development of Price Formation Theory and Subjectivism about Ultimate Values. *Journal of Applied Philosophy* 20 (3): 263–278.

Antony Davies

UTILITY, VON NEUMANN-MORGENSTERN

Von Neumann–Morgenstern utility considers decision making under risk. It concerns choice when the probabilities of the possible outcomes of that choice are objectively known. This decision framework differs from decision making under certainty and decision making when probability is subjective. John von Neumann and Oskar Morgenstern (1947) follow a behavioral framework analogous to the revealed preference framework developed by Paul A. Samuelson (1938 and 1947). Quasi-operational experiments are envisioned where people's behavior is held to satisfy key behavioral axioms.

The formal treatment of expected utility began with Daniel Bernoulli (1738) in his formulation of the St. Petersburg Paradox. In this paradox, a game is considered that has an infinite expected value. The paradox is that people will not pay a large sum to play this game. The game is one in which a fair coin (equal probability of a heads or tails) is tossed. If a head occurs the coin is tossed again and again until a tail occurs. Once a tail occurs the game is over. The payoff from playing the game depends on the number of consecutive heads that occurs. The payoff for H heads is defined as $\sum_{i=1}^{H} 2^i$. That is, if one head occurs, \$2 is paid; if two heads occur, \$2 + \$4 = \$6 is paid; and so forth. The probability of at least one head is $\frac{1}{2}$, the

probability of at least two consecutive heads is $\frac{1}{4}$, and so forth. Consequently, the expected value of the game is

$$\sum_{i=1}^{\infty} 2^i \cdot (1/2)^i = \sum_{i=1}^{\infty} 1 = \infty.$$

Despite the infinite expected payoff, few would pay large sums to play this game. Bernoulli provided an answer to this paradox in terms of diminishing marginal utility. He argued that it is the utility of the gains and not the monetary gains from the game that are relevant to the person's decision whether or not to play the game. With diminishing marginal utility, the gains from the game could be finite and small.

Von Neumann–Morgenstern utility can be illustrated by considering lotteries with two possible prizes, A and B, and a cost for playing the lottery, Y, with $A \prec Y \prec B$. Let P be the probability of the most favorable prize, B, and $(1 - P)$ be the probability of the less favorable prize, A. Six key assumptions (Luce and Raiffa 1957) will assure that a utility function can be defined from the revealed preferences of players. These assumptions assure that a probability can be found for every lottery where the decision maker is indifferent between the price of the lottery ticket and the lottery. In other words,

$$U(Y) = (1 - P)U(A) + PU(B), \text{ or}$$
$$U(Y) = U(A) + (U(B) - U(A))P.$$

Suppose we rank every possible outcome of any lottery from W, the worst possible, to B, the best possible and assign an ordinal number to $U(W)$ and $U(B)$ representing this ranking. Then $U(Y)$ for any Y can be found as a linear transformation of these two extreme outcomes. Hence, Von Neumann–Morgenstern utility is cardinal but only because it represents a linear transformation of the probabilities in the lotteries. It is not cardinal utility in any other context.

SEE ALSO *Expected Utility Theory; Gambling; Revealed Preference; Utility, Objective; Utility, Subjective; Von Neumann, John*

BIBLIOGRAPHY

Bernoulli, Daniel. 1738. *Specimen Theoriae Novae de Mensura Sortis.* Trans. Louise Sommer in *Exposition of a New Theory on the Measurement of Risk. Econometrica* 22, no. 1 (January 1954): 23–36.

Luce, R. Duncan, and Howard Raiffa. 1957 *Games and Decisions.* New York: Wiley.

Samuelson, Paul A. 1938. A Note on the Pure Theory of Consumer's Behavior. *Economica* 5: 61–71.

Samuelson, Paul A. 1947. *Foundations of Economic Analysis.* Cambridge, MA: Harvard University Press.

Von Neumann, John, and Oskar Morgenstern. 1944. *The Theory of Games and Economic Behavior*, 2nd ed. Princeton, NJ: Princeton University Press, 1947.

Michael P. Shields

UTOPIANISM

Utopianism refers simultaneously to social issues and to questions of the imagination. In fact, utopianism can be seen in action anytime the imagination is put to the use of remaking social life. The term describes a tendency to think of the world as a place to be made more perfect. The utopian impulse in history can be understood as posing the question of how else humans might organize themselves. It is generally agreed that the first utopian society in Western thought is to be found in Plato's *Republic* (c. 400 BCE), a realm where philosopher-kings govern. The term *utopia* was coined by Sir Thomas More (1478–1535) in *Utopia*, first published in 1516. The writing of More's *Utopia* corresponds to the period of discovery by Europeans of what was called the New World, with all that it ushered in to Europe's political economies and social imagination.

Ambiguous from the outset, the term *utopia* could be read as a joining of the Greek prefix *ou* with the word *topos* (place), which would translate as "no place." The first syllable could equally be understood as the Greek prefix *eu*, rendering utopia the "good place." Later writers, notably William Morris (1834–1896) in England, who titled his utopian fiction *News from Nowhere* (1891), recognized that the improved society they envisioned is, in principle, impossible to find or perhaps even to construct. However, this problem has never stopped utopian thinkers from casting their visions in print and in fact. Utopian societies or communities, though usually short-lived, have been founded in countries across the globe, especially in times of revolutionary change. And utopian manifestos and programs have been written and promulgated in such times as well.

Whether cast as prelapsarian or millenarian, the tense of the utopian narrative is inevitably the future and the mood is subjunctive, as utopians speculate about what may come to be. Even Edward Bellamy's (1850–1898) *Looking Backward* (1888), the most popular late nineteenth-century utopian novel, describes the imaginary future through a fictionalized past. Throughout the nineteenth century, utopian movements arose that looked forward to how lives might be improved by the Industrial Revolution. Other such movements looked backward with nostalgia for ways of life that had been lost due to the same irrevocable changes. Labor was no longer primarily

agricultural but industrial, and cities were rapidly growing, making the lost pastoral a focus of cultural longing. By the mid-twentieth century, such impulses toward the "good place" had been brought up short by world events, leading to a period of *dystopian* thinking. Two key texts representing this perspective are *Brave New World* (1932) by Aldous Huxley (1894–1963) and *1984* (1949) by George Orwell (1903–1950).

A strategic moment in the history of utopianism is the shift from early nineteenth-century thinkers such as Charles Fourier (1772–1837) in France and Robert Owen (1771–1858) in England, who proposed a form of utopian socialism, to the writings of Karl Marx (1818–1883) and Friedrich Engels (1820–1895), who differentiated their ideas as scientific socialism. This conceptual divide leads some to see utopianism as a way of thinking that is impossibly idealistic. Of course, utopianism was, in some sense, never intended to be of this world; hence the weakness of many utopian communities, whether those of the Levelers or Diggers of mid-seventeenth-century England or the Branch Davidians of the late twentieth-century United States. Just as visions of possible futures arose out of political thought, numerous vibrant utopian experiments often emerged from religious splinter groups, whose promise of a better life both in the here and now and in the hereafter drew multiple generations of adherents. Examples of such groups are as different as the eighteenth-century Shakers (with their doctrine of celibacy) and the Church of Latter-Day Saints or Mormons (whose beliefs included plural marriage). Millenarian beliefs are common in utopian thinking, linking utopianism both to revolutionary and reactionary forms.

Between the hopeful utopianism of the nineteenth century and its opposite, the dreadful dystopianism of the mid-twentieth century, it is crucial to note a new form of utopian thinking and writing that arose during the first wave of feminist political struggle for suffrage at the turn of the nineteenth century. *Herland* (1915), a utopian fiction by the American reformer Charlotte Perkins Gilman (1860–1935), is a key text of this period of numerous writings by women that imagine a better place. However, it was the reissue of Gilman's novel in 1979 that connected the first wave of feminist activism and imagination to the second wave of the later twentieth century. A noteworthy publication phenomenon of the 1970s and into the 1980s was the outpouring from mainstream and alternative presses of feminist utopian fictions. One of the best known is Marge Piercy's *Woman on the Edge of Time* (1976).

The most important utopian thinker of the twentieth century is the German philosopher Ernst Bloch (1885–1977), whose magnum opus, *The Principle of Hope* (1954–1959), is a three-volume study of how hope heralds the new and the "not-yet" as it emerges in political and imaginary realms. Given the speculative nature of utopianism, it is not surprising that such thinking continues to evolve in the realm of political criticism and in genre writing, especially science fiction. An effort to keep up with utopianism and utopian criticism is maintained by the Society for Utopian Studies, which has been in existence since 1975. The society publishes a journal and a newsletter, sponsors an annual conference, and recognizes that utopianism emanates from disciplines as diverse as engineering, architecture, literature, and economics.

SEE ALSO *Marxism*

BIBLIOGRAPHY

Bloch, Ernst. 1986. *The Principle of Hope.* 3 vols. Trans. Neville Plaice, Stephen Plaice, and Paul Knight. Cambridge, MA: MIT Press.

Gilman, Charlotte Perkins. [1915] 1979. *Herland.* New York: Pantheon.

Manuel, Frank E., and Fritzi P. Manuel. 1979. *Utopian Thought in the Western World.* Cambridge, MA: Belknap.

More, Thomas. 1516. *Utopia.* http://gutenberg.net/etext/2130.

The Society for Utopian Studies. http://www.utoronto.ca/utopia.

Frances Bartkowski

UZAWA, HIROFUMI
1928–

Hirofumi Uzawa was a native of Yonago, northwest Tottori Prefecture, on Honshu. His father was a schoolteacher. At the age of four, Uzawa and his brother moved with their parents to Tokyo, where they grew up. In 1948 he enrolled in the Department of Mathematics at the University of Tokyo, where he was chosen as a Special Research Fellow in the department. He received the BS degree in mathematics at the age of twenty-three in 1951, having majored in algebraic number theory. After receiving the BS Uzawa entered graduate school and taught mathematics at the University of Tokyo for five years.

To fully appreciate Uzawa's formative years, one must keep in mind that when he was born the ruling power in Japan was the militaristic Meiji dynasty. This dynasty engineered the Japanese defeat of Russia in 1904, Japanese control of South Korea and Taiwan through League of Nations mandates after World War I (1914–1918), and Japan's attack on Pearl Harbor in 1941. After Japan's defeat, the U.S. military occupied the country from 1945 until 1952, and Japan was ruled by a military governor during that period. Japan's September 1945 surrender

resulted in its loss of control of South Korea and Taiwan, both of which then were occupied by U.S. troops. During its occupation of Japan, the United States engaged in a war in Korea, across the Sea of Japan from Uzawa's birthplace. These events are implied in Uzawa's autobiographical sketch, especially in his discussion of poverty, starvation, and underdevelopment in Japan.

While studying undergraduate mathematics and seeking to become a professional mathematician, Uzawa was led by the postwar poverty of Japan to study economics. He and several others began a systematic reading of Marxian economics. He contemplated joining the Japanese Communist Party but was advised by a friend who was already a member that he could not pass the entrance examination given to prospective members. He therefore decided to quit mathematics and study economics so that he could learn enough to pass the examination. But he did continue studying mathematics until he earned a degree.

After Uzawa graduated in 1951, he secured a job with the Institute of Statistical Mathematics at the Ministry of Education, and subsequently as a statistician with a life insurance company. During 1955 and 1956, he published four articles in the institute's quarterly publication. The first two were purely statistical theory. The third was on Leontieff input-output models. The last was "A Note on Preferences and Axioms of Choice." Three years later, he published "Preference and Rational Choice in the Theory of Consumption."

During the early 1950s, Uzawa remained actively affiliated with the University of Tokyo. He joined a small group of economists in the Faculty of Economics and read Keynes's *General Theory of Employment, Interest and Money* and Kenneth J. Arrow's *Social Choice and Individual Values.* He worked for six months in 1954 as an assistant to Everett E. Hagen (1906–1993) of MIT, who was in Japan with a mission of the World Bank. Hagen was in charge of macroeconomic analysis, and on this project, Uzawa first learned about Keynesian economic policy administration. In the summer of 1954, he also attended the annual joint University of Tokyo–Stanford University seminar conducted by Dutch economist Hendrik Houtakker (b. 1924) of Stanford on demand analysis. In this seminar, Uzawa was reintroduced to the work of Arrow of Stanford, and this time read everything he could by Arrow, including especially his work with Leonid Hurwicz on the feasibility and stability of the "allocative mechanism" of a socialist economy.

In economics, Uzawa studied under Hyoe Ouch (1888–1980), who led the fight to resuscitate the Ohara Institute for Social Research after World War II (1939–1945). This institute studied labor economics, Marxian economics, and social issues and published the

Journal of the Ohara Institute for Social Research, the *Labor Yearbook*, pamphlets, and a publications series. Keynesian economics in Japan began with Keynes's *The Economic Consequences of the Peace*, and *A Treatise on Money*.

In 1955, through Houthakker, Uzawa reviewed the unpublished manuscript of Kenneth J. Arrow and Leonid Hurwicz's article on local stability. Expanding on this article on his own, Uzawa wrote "Gradient Method for Concave Programming II: Global Stability in the Strictly Convex Case." His manuscript led to the receipt in 1955 of an invitation from Arrow to work with him at Stanford. Having become interested in pursuing a career in economics rather than mathematics, in 1956 he applied for and received a Fulbright Fellowship to finance the Arrow enterprise. He was a research assistant at Stanford from 1956 to 1964. Here, he was exposed to a rigorous mathematical treatment of neoclassical economics, Keynesian theory, and general equilibrium theory rather than Marxist economics. Uzawa published at least three papers in the Technical Reports series of the Stanford economics department between 1956 and 1958. Two of these papers contributed to the Houthakker research program in consumer economics, specifically his interest in preference functions.

In 1958 Uzawa, Arrow, and Hurwicz published *Studies in Linear and Non-Linear Programming* with the support of the U.S. Office of Naval Research. In this book, Uzawa presented a general mathematical theory. This book was concerned with deriving existence proofs for solutions to programs in linear topological spaces. These proofs involved the theory of convex polyhedral cones (CPC) in point-set topology, which are treated algebraically by means of analytical geometry. Using set theory and linear algebra, Uzawa presented the theory of topology on which the editors based the application to programming in the remainder of the book. Uzawa defined CPC conventionally as "the intersection of a finite number of half-spaces," that is, affine spaces bounded by hyperplanes. In the linear programming problem, the intersection of half-spaces creates a pyramid. The linear constraints of the problem constitute the edges of the polyhedron. The intersections of these edges constitute the vertices of the polyhedron. The solution algorithm evaluates each vertex in turn to find the one constituting the maximum or minimum. In the case of the pyramid, or three-dimensional polyhedron, four or five vertices must be evaluated, depending upon whether the base is a triangle or a square.

The gradient [slope] method is defined as the solution set to a system of differential or difference equations. The gradient is the ratio of the change in the slope of the plane triangle constituting one side of the pyramid. Further, the gradient method is applied to several particular problems, including economic development and growth. It is found that it is slower than the simplex method because it calculates all surface vectors to a linear programming problem, while the simplex method calculates only the optimum vectors, that is, only vertices. A simplex is the simplest form that can be constructed between points in a given space.

Uzawa remained away from Japan for thirteen years, serving on the faculties of the University of California at Berkeley (1960–1961), Stanford (1961–1964), Cambridge (1964–1965), and the University of Chicago (1965–1969). He was thoroughly immersed in the project to mathematize neoclassical economic theory. He left Stanford to attain intellectual independence. By 1960, he was married to his wife, Hiroko, and had children.

In 1968 Uzawa returned to the University of Tokyo as professor of economics until retiring to emeritus status in 1993. In 1973 and 1976, his interest shifted to the short-run fluctuations of a capitalist economy, or business cycles, and he published papers on Keynesian theory. In 1976, he served as president of the Econometric Society. Beginning around 1970, and continuing to the present, he has been senior advisor to the Research Institute of Capital Formation of the Development Bank of Japan. He also taught at Niigata University, Chuo University, United Nations University, and Doshisha University. From about 2003 to 2005, he was director of Doshisha University's Research Center of Social Overhead Capital.

Uzawa's general equilibrium analysis concluded that Walrasian *tâtonnement* mechanism is globally stable. This again was part of the project to study the nature of equilibrium mathematically but also of the project to renew general equilibrium analysis. Uzawa is most renowned, though, for the development of two-sector neoclassical endogenous growth models, and for a theory of economic growth. His method was taken from Marx's two-department model of simple reproduction in volume 1 of *Das Kapital*. The language and categories employed, however, were those of neoclassical economics. In these growth articles, he was disaggregating the one-sector models of Robert M. Solow (b. 1924) and T. W. Swan (1918–1989). The two sectors were a consumption sector and an investment sector, each using labor and capital to produce an output. The investment sector produced a capital good, and the consumption sector produced a consumption good. The production functions for each sector exhibited diminishing returns to scale. Technological change was not included in the Solow-Swan model, and so was exogenous. Uzawa included terms for technology in his model, thus endogenizing technological change. His articles stimulated an explosion of research into growth models in the 1960s, but this interest subsided thereafter. The practical motivation driving his interest in growth was the underdeveloped state of the Japanese economy as he perceived it.

SEE ALSO *Economic Growth; Economics; Economics, Keynesian; Industrialization; Lucas, Robert E., Jr.; Mathematical Economics; McFadden, Daniel L.; Solow, Robert M.; Underdevelopment; World War II*

BIBLIOGRAPHY

Solow, Robert M. 1961. Note on Uzawa's Two-Sector Model of Economic Growth. *Review of Economic Studies* 29: 48–50.

Uzawa, Hirofumi. 1958. Gradient Method for Concave Programming II: Global Stability in the Strictly Convex Case. In *Studies in Linear and Non-Linear Programming,* ed. Kenneth J. Arrow, Leonid Hurwicz, and Hirofumi Uzawa, 127–132. Stanford, CA: Stanford University Press.

Uzawa, Hirofumi. 1961. On a Two-Sector Model of Economic Growth, I. *Review of Economic Studies* 29: 40–47.

Uzawa, Hirofumi. 1963. On a Two-Sector Model of Economic Growth, II. *Review of Economic Studies* 30: 105–118.

Uzawa, Hirofumi. 1964. Duality Principles in the Theory of Cost and Production. *International Economic Papers* 5: 216–220.

Uzawa, Hirofumi. 1964. Optimal Growth in a Two-Sector Model of Capital Accumulation. *Review of Economic Studies* 31: 1–24.

Uzawa, Hirofumi. 1969. Optimum Fiscal Policy in an Aggregative Model of Economic Growth. In *The Theory and Design of Economic Development*, eds. Irma Adelman and Erik Thorbecke, 113–139. Baltimore, MD: Johns Hopkins Press.

Uzawa, Hirofumi, and Kenneth J. Arrow. 1988. *Preference, Production, and Capital: Selected Papers of Hirofumi Uzawa.* Cambridge, U.K.: Cambridge University Press.

Julian Ellison

V

VACATIONS

The term *vacation* describes a moment of rest and recreation during sacred and secular holidays or a period of leisure time away from routine domestic responsibilities, school, or work, as allowed by present-day laws and labor regulations. The modern idea of vacationing is often linked to making a pleasure journey away from home, ranging from a simple daytrip nearby to a voyage around the world. In many countries, the notion is used interchangeably with the concept of holidays. As suggested in the volume edited by Graham Dann *The Tourist As a Metaphor of the Social World* (2002), understanding contemporary vacationing practices provides insight in the value systems of the modern world.

The notion of having a vacation is not universal. Even in industrialized societies, it did not exist until the 1850s, when the concept arose in response to time-regulated forms of labor. The clear bounding of work time was the product of victories by workers pressing for shorter workdays and scattered vacation days. The English entrepreneur Thomas Cook was the first to commercialize inexpensive package tours, designed for the short vacation time of the working class. From the 1930s, and accelerating in the postwar period, paid vacations in most European countries had been politically secured and came to be understood as a right of citizenship and part of a new social contract. In the United States modern vacations developed as a privilege accorded to workers as part of their employment package. During the 1970s and 1980s disposable incomes and annual days of vacation rose in developed countries, while the cost of travel remained more or less constant in real terms. This consequently led to a phenomenal rise in international tourism.

Legislation granting yearly vacation periods with pay and collective agreements providing for such holidays is increasingly common worldwide. Moreover, as standards of living improve, there is a marked tendency for the minimum annual vacation to be increased. The actual length of time is dependent on the length of service and provisions of the collective agreement. It can range from only a couple of days to more than six weeks. The rise in the number of international tourists from Asia—mainly the newly industrialized countries—illustrates the exportability of the vacation model to those countries where certain minimum requirements are met in terms of the availability and distribution of disposable income.

What people do during their vacation has changed over time, just as it has varied from country to country. Although vacationing has been democratized, vacations are still separate functions of differentials in income, social class, race, occupation, gender, and education. As Pierre Bourdieu described in great detail in his *Distinction: A Social Critique of the Judgment of Taste* (1984), there are substantial disparities in leisure consumption between people from different socioeconomic backgrounds. While working-class people often choose cheaply packaged mass tourism activities, the higher-class elites try to distinguish themselves by opting for expensive, individually tailored tours. Even if there is a clear global convergence in certain kinds of vacation consumerism, great local differences remain.

Vacationing is often thought of as a temporary reversal of everyday activities. It is a no-work, no-care, no-thrift situation. However, in itself it is believed to be devoid of deeper meaning: It is a vacation; that is, vacant time. In a way, time is suspended (or put in parentheses) and many people believe to live a kind of absolute break of their habitual time. Conspicuous vacation is meant to be non-productive consumption of time, an indication of distance from environmental and productive needs, and thus a sign of wealth. The growing frequency of vacation travel in the developed world has ensured that vacation time is increasingly recognized as one of the experiences that people value in terms of quality of life.

The annual vacation trip in industrialized countries is a repetitive, predictable, timed break that allows people recreation and marks the progress of cyclical time. Therefore, vacations can also be characterized as a kind of ritual process that reflect a society's deeply held values about health, freedom, nature, and self-improvement. In this view, vacations can be interpreted as the modern equivalent for secular societies of the annual and lifelong sequences of festivals and pilgrimages in more traditional, religious societies. Fundamental is the contrast between the ordinary/compulsory work state spent at home and the non-ordinary/voluntary (sacred) state away from home.

According to Orvar Löfgren in *On Holiday: A History of Vacationing* (1999), vacationing frequently involves temporal tensions and relations between past, present, and future. Traveling across space is frequently experienced as a movement across time to relive mythical periods of history, or former ways of life, or past stages from our life. Thus, it is not surprising that getting back to nature, to a more simple life, or to childhood—in other words freezing time—are common utopias of vacationers. Löfgren sees the world of vacationing as a place where tourists are able "to use the important cultural skills of daydreaming and mindtraveling ... [in] an arena in which fantasy [is] an important social practice" (p. 7). The perceptions of vacationers are thus closely related to fictional worlds and, for the same reasons, to the world of dreams. The colloquial expression "dream vacation" did not appear without precedent.

Members of industrialized societies define their lives not only through their work but also increasingly through their consumption of vacations. The latter serve as a form of escape from the stresses, pressures, and demands of everyday life. People believe that the promise of personal freedom, one of the most expansive modern myths, can be fulfilled much more on vacation than in everyday life. Vacations become the ideal moment of self-realization in which people construct their own world according to their individual preferences. However, throughout the relatively short history of leisure travel, people have quickly learned how to be vacationers and to move, often according to social dictate, through different types of artificially created vacation worlds like theme parks and beach resorts. In many countries, a system of social sanctions is in place that variously codifies vacationing as "normal" or even expected behavior.

SEE ALSO *Leisure; Travel and Travel Writing*

BIBLIOGRAPHY

Bourdieu, Pierre. 1984. *Distinction: A Social Critique of the Judgment of Taste.* Trans. R. Nice. Cambridge, MA: Harvard University Press.

Dann, Graham M. S., ed. 2002. *The Tourist As a Metaphor of the Social World.* New York: CABI Publishing.

Löfgren, Orvar. 1999. *On Holiday: A History of Vacationing.* Berkeley: University of California Press.

Noel B. Salazar

VAGABONDS

The English term *vagabond* derives from Latin and Anglo-Latin sources. The word literally meant to wander from bondage, but more idiomatically to escape from bondage. The etymology of *bondage* is also significant. Historically, forms of bondage in the West included slavery; serfdom, a system of partially unfree labor in rural societies; apprenticeship, which regulated entrance into and the practice of trades in towns; and systems of domestic service. To depart from any of these work situations without an employer's permission was to risk charges of "vagabondage." The Latin noun *vagabundus* appears in late medieval English manorial records, and according to the *Oxford English Dictionary* the English terms *vagabond* and *vagrant* date from the early 1400s. Since the fifteenth century, the same source shows, these words have been employed to describe anyone who was without fixed abode, unemployed, itinerant, or in an unlicensed trade. Of course, the terms *vagabond* and *vagrant* have also been used as terms of abuse, as have the synonyms *beggar, bum, hobo, loafer,* and *tramp.*

There are varying interpretations of vagabondage. One can be called the realist position, because it postulates that vagabondage reflected real economic and social causes, that the numbers of vagabonds were great and growing, that they were an underworld organized in gangs that engaged in professional crime, and that they posed genuine threats to the social and political order. A second interpretation emphasizes the power of the normative, especially notions about moralism and patriarchalism vis-à-vis dependents, including workers, which led to a growth of state intervention to enforce those norms. This position stressed the distinctions between the worthy and the unworthy poor and contained an impetus to reform the latter group. This normative interpretation, in turn, readily accommodates theories of law and criminality that maintain that some offenses, including vagrancy, are products of governmental initiatives leading to "status criminality" and "social control." The third view of vagabondage, which is the one favored here, is that the phenomenon was a combination of the real and the normative.

At the core of the concept of vagabondage were two key elements—voluntary unemployment and itinerancy—both of which, historically, were connected with labor and residence obligations of medieval serfdom. It cannot be a coincidence that European governments first began acting against vagabonds in the 1350s after the Black Death severely cut the population and made it possible for laborers to reject the obligations of serfdom. When population levels recovered after 1500, western European governments continued to enforce policies against vagabondage, which they found were useful weapons in the control of a workforce now largely liberated from serfdom. To police the labor force, vagrancy laws, Bridewells (houses of correction), and later workhouses were instituted from the sixteenth through the eighteenth century. These institutions lasted into the nineteenth century and were exported overseas to European colonies.

The policies against vagabonds also reflected a normative shift that desanctified the poor. Before this change the prevalent notion of the poor, inspired by the powerful example of St. Francis, idealized them as representing holiness, and Christians were encouraged to live like them. But in the thirteenth century some canon lawyers began to question whether the voluntary poor should be given relief. After 1350, moreover, Renaissance humanists argued for the positive benefits of wealth, which they argued allowed one to be a benefactor to one's community. They also attacked the notion that poverty was a holy condition, pointing to the sins, disorders, and diseases that it fostered. They derided the hypocrisy of friars living in luxury and pilgrims wallowing in dissipation and called for the moral reform of the undeserving poor through institutionalization, including punishment and work-regimes.

Homelessness is obviously a less value-laden term than *vagabond* and is appropriate in a society in which the poor without permanent residences are no longer quite so demonized as they once were, but we should remember that *homeless* is a neologism that, like *vagabond*, requires analysis. In this respect, the term *vagabond* is more historically relevant during the approximately six hundred years of world history when it was applied to a great variety of people leading itinerant lives. The significance of the word lies in its rhetorical power and its suggestion of subversion of the social order. Ultimately, its power is its explicitness

about the fact that governments criminalized and punished itinerants, who faced a two-fold challenge—homelessness to be sure, but also official demonizing and harassment.

What of the vagabonds themselves? They were not the simple equivalent of the homeless poor of the twenty-first century. Rather they resembled the "underclass" in society, in part because the authorities believed they had a distinctive culture that was opposed to respectable society. There were elements of a counterculture among vagabonds, including their use of slang, or cant, and some of them took part in organized crime. But for the most part their key characteristics arose from the structure of the economy and the labor system, particularly high unemployment and underemployment. Not all vagabonds were unemployed and begging, however; many practiced trades that were banned or subject to licensing, including unlicensed actors, itinerant healers, musicians, peddlers, practitioners of white magic, and sailors and soldiers. Overall, the key element in the lives of vagabonds was insecurity, which Olwen Hufton neatly summed up as living in an "economy of makeshifts." Like gangs in modern cities, they were overwhelmingly young males, which frightened governments wary of violence and disorder. While foreign-born Romanies or "gypsies" were sometimes singled out in anti-vagrancy laws, the overwhelming majority of vagabonds were native-born.

SEE ALSO *Hobos*

BIBLIOGRAPHY

Beier, A. L. 1985. *Masterless Men: The Vagrancy Problem in England, 1560–1640*. London: Methuen.

Hufton, Olwen H. 1974. *The Poor of Eighteenth-Century France, 1750–1789*. Oxford: Oxford University Press.

Jütte, Robert. 1994. *Poverty and Deviance in Early Modern Europe*. Cambridge, U.K.: Cambridge University Press.

Mollat, Michel. 1986. *The Poor in the Middle Ages: An Essay in Social History*. Trans. Arthur Goldhammer. New Haven and London: Yale University Press. Originally published as *Les pauvres au Moyen Age* (Paris: Hachette, 1978).

Oxford English Dictionary. 1989. 2nd ed. Oxford: Oxford University Press.

A. L. Beier

VAISYAS

An upper class in the Hindu tradition, the Vaisyas are the lowest level of the "twice-born" (*dvijas*). They are commoners, but not a servant group. They undergo the sacred thread ceremony (*Yajnopavita*), as do the Brahmins and

Kshatriyas. But while male Vaisyas "take the thread," it is made of a fiber different from that of the two castes above them (Brahmins and Kshatriyas). As part of the cosmic order of dharma, they have been assigned the role of merchants and craftspeople.

Vaisyas are described in the *Laws of Manu* (a Hindu sacred book) as being given at creation the duties to tend cattle, bestow gifts, offer sacrifices, trade, lend money, cultivate land, and study the Vedas. It is sacrilegious for a Vaisya to refuse to keep cattle. In trading it is the duty of Vaisyas to know the value of pearls, coral, metals, and other commodities.

The *Laws of Manu* charge Vaisyas with acquiring skills in good management of those they employ. They need to know languages, proper wages, and how to operate a business so that goods are properly stored and traded. These tasks are also to be done with exertion so that the wealth of the Vaisyas can increase, but in a righteous manner. It is also a Vaisya duty to give food to all creatures. Additionally, the *Laws of Manu* includes rules for accepting the testimony of Vaisyas and for their purification or their punishment in cases of adultery, murder, or other crimes.

Within the Vaisya caste there are subcastes of bakers, sheepherders, cowherders, agriculturalists, musicians, metal workers, and as well as traders and businessmen. All are people with a skill, trade, or profession.

In the myth of Purusha the Vaisyas were made from the god's stomach. The Vaisyas resemble the Platonic people of bronze who are the people of the "belly." They are the farmers, herders, merchants, and businesspeople who produce and distribute food and other needed goods to society.

The Bhagavad Gita assigned the Vaisyas the duties of farming, protecting the cows of India, and conducting business. Their way of life demands labor, study, sacrifice, and the giving of alms. On special days, giving to the Brahmin is a common practice. According to the Bhagavad Gita, Vaisyas are such an essential element in society that it cannot survive without them.

Vaisyas were expected to be specialists in the trading of jewelry, precious metals, spices, or other goods. They were often vegetarians and very devout practitioners of their religion. Many are devotes of Laksmi, wife of Vishnu and the goddess of wealth.

An important Vaisya subcaste are the Mahuri Vaisyas. They are believed to have emigrated from around the city of Mathura as well as from Vrindavan and Gokul to the Bengal area during the time of the Mughal Empire (1526–1827). They also comprise a religious community worshipping Mata Mathurashani Devi, an incarnation of the goddess Shakti.

Some of the Mahuri claim that they originated from the creative work of Krishna who made them as *gopas* and *gopis* (cowherders), but then gave them the task of earning their living from trading. Their surnames are derived from the names of the forest villages where they were originally placed. These surnames include Athaghara, Badgaway, Barahapuriya, Bhadani, Charanpahari, Ekghara, Gowardhan, Kandhaway, Kapasimey, Krishan-kunda, Kutariyaar, Lohani, Pawanchaudaha, Seth, Tarway, and Vaishakhiyar. Each clan has legendary stories that tell of their origins in remote areas where in some cases there are still temples dedicated to cows. Besides folklore, however, there is little that can be substantiated about them that is more than four hundred years old.

Around 1750, many Vaisyas migrated to the Chota Nagpur Plateau where they still maintain villages. Others are now located in western Bengal and Orissa. Many are also traders in New Delhi, Chennai, and Mumbai (Bombay). Small numbers are located around the world.

Modern Vaisyas practice business and agriculture but with ethical practices in keeping with the modern global society. They practice environmentally sound agriculture that entails protecting the environment rather than exploiting it. This is an application of their role as cow protectors.

SEE ALSO *Brahmins; Business; Caste; Caste, Anthropology of; Dalits; Hierarchy; Hinduism; Kshatriyas; Sudras*

BIBLIOGRAPHY

Das, Abinas Chandra. 1903. *The Vaisya Caste.* Calcutta: A. K. Roy.

Gupta, K. C. 1988. *Vaishyas in India.* Hyderabad: All India Vaish Samai.

Mullick, Promatha Nath. 1985. *History of the Vaisyas of Bengal.* New Delhi: Usha. (Orig. pub. 1902.)

Smith, Brian K. 1994. *Classifying the Universe: The Ancient Indian Varna System and the Origins of Caste.* New York: Oxford University Press.

Andrew J. Waskey

VAJPAYEE, ATAL BIHARI
1924–

Former Indian prime minister Atal Bihari Vajpayee is renowned for his political, literary, and professional achievements both in India and internationally. His major noteworthy accomplishments, prior to more than four decades of political participation and dynamic leadership, include his education at Victoria College (now Laxmibai) in Gwalior and DAV College in Uttar Pradesh, editing of several Indian periodicals, and composition of a variety of literary works. Vajpayee holds a Master of Arts degree in political science. He served as editor of the monthly *Rashtra-Dharma*, the weekly *Panchajanya*, and the daily *Swadesh* and *Veer Arjun* periodicals. His own major publications, including *Lok Sabha Mein Atalji, Mrityu Ya Hatya, Amar Balidan, Kaidi Kavirai Ki Kundalian, New Dimensions of India's Foreign Policy, Jana Sangh Aur Musalman, Three Decades in Parliament, Amar Aag Hai, Meri Ekyavan Kavitayen,* and *Four Decades in Parliament,* range from books to collections of poems and compilations of speeches.

Vajpayee was born on December 25, 1924, in Gwalior, in what is now Madhya Pradesh, India. In the early 1940s he first became interested in the Indian independence movement. His first party affiliation was as a member of the Quit India Movement, which was lobbying for the end of British control of India. A devout Hindu, in 1951 he was a founding member of the Bharatiya Jana Sangh (BJS) Parliamentary Party, and because of his dynamic pro-Hindu, right-wing political leadership, he led the party for over two decades, from 1957 to 1977. He was briefly imprisoned during the Indian Emergency of 1975 to 1977 because of opposing Prime Minister Indira Gandhi's state of emergency. After the BJS was merged into the Janata Party, Vajpayee was elected minister of external affairs. In 1980 he was elected president of the Bharatiya Janata Party (BJP), another Hindu fundamentalist party, a post he held until 1986. He then rose to become the leader of the National Democratic Alliance (NDA), which from 1998 through 2004 was the ruling coalition of India, and from this position he was named prime minister. In addition to championing the cause of Hindu nationalism, Vajpayee has also actively worked on behalf of women and children's welfare, and the elevation of lower caste and tribal people. His advocacy in these areas might seem paradoxical and contradictory if only seen within his attachment to the BJP, but one should consider that, more than anything else, Vajpayee was a popular intellectual leader seeking to expand his political power. So his advocacy for social justice can be viewed in part within his larger effort to advance both his political power and the BJP's influence. His advocacy in these areas might seem paradoxical and contradictory if only seen within his attachment to BJP, but one should consider that, more than anything else, Vajpayee was a popular intellectual leader seeking to expand his political power. Undermining 50 percent of the Indian population would have jeopardized both his power and BJP's rising influence. This paradox can also be seen in the case of Indira Gandhi, who was a well known left winger female leader, but with much less practical sympathy for women's welfare and social justice.

In addition to serving twice as prime minister of India, Vajpayee is the only person to have been elected nine times to the Lok Sabha, or Indian House of the People. He was first elected to the second Lok Sabha in 1957, and most recently to the thirteenth Lok Sabha in 1999. Twice he was elected to the Rajya Sabha, or House of the States. He was the only leader besides Pandit Jawaharlal Nehru to be elected prime minister by three consecutive terms in office (in 1996, 1998, and 1999). During his tenure as prime minister, he successfully managed the political fragmentation that has typically plagued the Indian government. Under his leadership, in spite of an economic recession, India logged impressive growth in various economic indicators, including foreign exchange reserves, agricultural production, and gross domestic product.

Vajpayee has participated in numerous parliamentary committees, social and cultural associations, and Indian delegations to the European Parliament, the UN General Assembly, Human Rights Commissions, and other international conferences.

In December 2005, Atal Bihari Vajpayee expressed a decision to entrust the future of Indian politics to other capable leaders, formally announcing his retirement from electoral politics.

SEE ALSO *Affirmative Action; Caste; Fundamentalism; Hinduism; Janata Party; Nehru, Jawaharlal; Right Wing*

BIBLIOGRAPHY

Raghavan, G. N. S., ed. 1997. *New Era in the Indian Polity, A Study of Atal Bihari Vajpayee and the BJP.* New Delhi, India: Gyan Publishing House.

Sharma, Chandrika Prasad. 1998. *Poet Politician: Atal Bihari Vajpayee: A Biography.* New Delhi, India: Kitab Ghar Prakashan.

Vajpayee, Atal Bihari. 2000. *Prime Minister Atal Bihari Vajpayee, Selected Speeches.* 2 vols. New Dehli, India: Publications Division, Ministry of Information and Broadcasting, Government of India.

Vajpayee, Atal Bihari. 2005. *Atal Bihari Vajpayee: Poet and Ex Prime Minister.* New Delhi, India: Pentagon Press.

Jalil Roshandel

VALIDATION

Before social scientists can study the feelings, thoughts, behaviors, and performance of individuals, and before practitioners (such as therapists, case managers, or school staff) can respond to clients' problems in those areas, they must be able to measure the phenomena in question. Measurement tools include measures, instruments, scales, indices, questionnaires, and surveys. Complex social constructs such as "depression," "worker satisfaction," or "reading achievement" cannot be assessed with one question. A depression scale, for example, requires multiple questions (or items) to fully capture depression's affective, cognitive, and physical dimensions. An individual's responses to multiple items on a scale are typically combined (e.g., averaged or summed) to give one composite score. Measurement validation is the process of demonstrating the quality of a measure, the scores obtained with the measure, or the interpretation of those scores. Validation is necessary because scores from measures may be inaccurate. Respondents may misunderstand items, deliberately provide inaccurate responses, or simply lack the knowledge or ability to provide accurate responses. Specific items or the scale as a whole may not accurately reflect the target construct.

A common textbook definition of validity focuses on how accurately and completely a measure captures its target construct. From this perspective, measures can be sufficiently validated based on evidence of content validity, criterion validity, and/or construct validity (see Table 1). Validity is considered a characteristic of measures and is a demonstrable goal. For example, a scale developer might claim that a new worker-satisfaction scale is valid after presenting results of analyses of content and criterion validity.

This approach to validation as it is commonly applied has a number of shortcomings. First, it focuses narrowly on item content and score performance. Second, as elaborated by Kenneth A. Bollen (1989), it ignores potential problems with traditional correlational analyses, including the possibly erroneous assumption that scores from the existing measures used for comparison are valid. Third, it relies on indirect methods of assessing whether respondents interpreted items and response options as intended.

A broader view of validation defines it as an ongoing process of building a case that (1) scores obtained with a measure accurately reflect the target construct and (2) scores obtained with the measure can be interpreted and used as intended. This view implies that validation is an unending, multifaceted process and that it applies to the interpretations of scores obtained with a measure, not the measure itself. It also suggests that evaluating how scores are interpreted and used is essential to the validation process. This last point implies a legitimate role for values and ethics in the evaluation of measures. Proponents of elements of this broader view include measurement scholars from numerous social science disciplines—for example, Robert Adcock and David Collier (2001), Kenneth A. Bollen (1989), Lee J. Cronbach (1988), Samuel Messick (1988), and Howard Wainer and Henry I. Braun (1988), as well as a trio of social science professional organizations: the American Educational Research Association, the American Psychological Association, and the National Council on Measurement in Education (American Educational Research Association et al. 1999). From this broad view of validation and validity, the approach to validation presented in Table 1 is inadequate.

Table 2 presents components of a broad view of measurement validation. The components of Table 1 are present (in rows 1 and 2), but other evidence is considered necessary to validate the interpretation and use of scores. Additional statistical procedures that are often used in scale development but less often presented as evidence of validity are also included (in rows 1 and 3). Corresponding categories of validation evidence described in the *Standards for Educational and Psychological Testing* (1999) are listed

---

Narrow view of validation

	Definition	Source of evidence	Example
Content validity	Items on a measure capture all major dimensions of a construct	Examination of existing literature and measures, and expert feedback	A depression scale contains items related to the cognitive, affective, and physical aspects of depression
Criterion validity	Scores obtained with a measure are related to scores from existing measures of the same construct	Analysis of scores obtained from the measure and scores from one or more existing measures of the same construct	SAT scores are correlated with high school grades (concurrent) and college grades (predictive)
Construct validity	Scores obtained with a measure are related to scores from existing measures of other constructs, as expected based on theory and prior research	Analysis of scores obtained from the measure and scores from one or more existing measures of other constructs	Scores on a measure of worker satisfaction are correlated with scores on a measure of worker productivity

Other assumptions commonly associated with this view: Measures are validated; validity can be "proven"; there are different types of validity.

Table 1

Broad view of validation*

	Evidence	Source of evidence
1. Content validation "Evidence based on test content" "Evidence based on internal structure"	Items on a measure capture all major dimensions of a construct Established dimensions of the construct are supported by statistical relations among items	Examination of existing literature and measures, and expert feedback Factor analysis of scores
2. Score performance validation "Evidence based on relations to other variables"	Scores obtained with a measure are related to scores from existing measures of the same construct and scores from other constructs as expected by theory and prior research	Analysis of scores obtained from the measure and scores from one or more existing measures of the same construct and other constructs
3. Respondent-related validation "Evidence based on response processes" "Evidence based on internal structure"	The content and format of the measure are appropriate for intended respondents' abilities and experiences The statistical qualities of the measure apply to all intended respondent groups	Analysis of direct feedback from and observation of test subjects who are similar to intended respondents Multiple-group factor analysis of scores
4. Practice-related validation Partly "evidence based on consequences of testing"	Scores fill a knowledge gap of users, are relevant to the outcomes of interest in the setting, and are related to the intervention strategies available in the setting Use of scores benefit respondents	Analysis of qualitative or quantitative data from intended users of the measure, and of outcome data on respondents

Other assumptions commonly associated with this view: Score interpretations are validated; validation is a process that is never finished; evidence of validity can be presented, but validity cannot be "proven"; instead of types of validity there are types of validation or validation evidence.

*The table is not meant to be an exhaustive list of types of validation evidence.

Table 2

---

under the terms in the first column. It is unlikely that any validation process will include all elements in the table, but the more sources and methods used, the stronger the case for validation will be.

RESPONDENT-RELATED VALIDATION

A direct method of assessing whether a scale measures what it is intended to measure is to interview pilot test subjects about their interpretation of items. Gordon B. Willis (2005) and Stanley Presser et al. (2004) provide detail on cognitive interviewing techniques. Data collected can be analyzed (usually qualitatively) to identify problem words or concepts and evidence that items or response options were misunderstood. Establishing that respondents interpret original or revised items as intended can contribute significantly to the validation case for a measure's score interpretations.

Demonstrating that respondents understand, interpret, and respond to items as intended is evidence of what Kevin Corcoran (1995, p. 1946) has referred to as the "suitability and acceptability" of a measure for its intended population. More specifically, it may constitute evidence of developmental validity (the content and format of a scale are appropriate for the cognitive, attentional, and other abilities of individuals). Natasha K. Bowen, Gary L.

Bowen, and Michael E. Woolley (2004) and Michael E. Woolley, Natasha K. Bowen, and Gary L. Bowen (2004) discuss the concept of developmental validity and a sequence of scale-development steps that promote it. The process may also generate evidence of cultural validity (the content and format of a scale are appropriate in relation to the experiences of individuals that may vary based on language, nationality, race/ethnicity, economic status, education level, religion and other characteristics). Although these examples are presented as types of validity, they are easily reframed as evidence of validation that supports confidence in the interpretation of scores obtained from respondents with different characteristics.

Certain statistical analyses of scores obtained with a measure, such as multiple group factor analysis, can also support respondent-related validation. The analyses may provide statistical evidence that scores obtained from members of different groups (e.g., males, females; members of different cultural groups) can be interpreted the same way.

PRACTICE-RELATED VALIDATION

Some measurement scholars, such as Cronbach (1988) and Messick (1988), stress that the uses and consequences of scores must be considered in the validation process. Messick states: "The key validity issues are the interpretability, relevance, and utility of scores, the import or value implications of scores as a basis for action, and the functional worth of scores in terms of social consequences of their use" (p. 33). Practice-related validation requires researchers to examine the context in which a measure is to be used—the setting, the users, and the intended uses of the measure. As demonstrated by Natasha K. Bowen and Joelle D. Powers (2005), practice-related validation of a school-based assessment might include evidence that the construct measured is related to achievement, evidence that school staff who will use the scores currently lack (and want) the information provided by the measure, and evidence that resources exist at the school for addressing the threats to achievement revealed in the obtained scores.

As pointed out by Cronbach (1988), evaluation of the context and consequences of score interpretations necessarily involves a consideration of values. The consequences of decisions based on scores may determine "who gets what in society" (p. 5). Standardized school test scores, college entrance exams scores, and mental health screening scores, for example, may be used to determine, respectively, who gets what instructional resources, who goes to college, and who receives mental health services. Given how the use of scores from social science measures affects the distribution of resources and the opportunities of individuals to succeed, a broad, thorough, ongoing approach to the validation process is an ethical necessity for social scientists.

SEE ALSO *Mechanism Design; Psychometrics; Reliability, Statistical*

BIBLIOGRAPHY

Adcock, Robert, and David Collier. 2001. Measurement Validity: A Shared Standard for Qualitative and Quantitative Research. *American Political Science Review* 95 (3): 529–546.

American Educational Research Association, American Psychological Association, and the National Council on Measurement in Education. 1999. *Standards for Educational and Psychological Testing.* Washington, DC.: American Educational Research Association.

Bollen, Kenneth A. 1989. *Structural Equations with Latent Variables.* New York: John Wiley & Sons.

Bowen, Natasha K., Gary L. Bowen, and Michael E. Woolley. 2004. Constructing and Validating Assessment Tools for School-Based Practitioners: The Elementary School Success Profile. In *Evidence-Based Practice Manual: Research and Outcome Measures in Health and Human Services*, eds. Albert R. Roberts and Kenneth R. Yeager, 509–517. New York: Oxford University Press.

Bowen, Natasha K., and Joelle D. Powers. 2005. Knowledge Gaps among School Staff and the Role of High Quality Ecological Assessments in Schools. *Research on Social Work Practice* 15 (6): 491–500.

Corcoran, Kevin. 1995. Psychometrics. In *The Encyclopedia of Social Work*, 19th ed., ed. Richard L. Edwards, 942–1947. Washington, DC: NASW.

Cronbach, Lee J. 1988. Five Perspectives on the Validity Argument. In *Test Validity*, eds. Howard Wainer and Henry I. Braun, 3–17. Hillsdale, NJ: Lawrence Erlbaum.

Messick, Samuel. 1988. The Once and Future Issues of Validity: Assessing the Meaning and Consequences of Measurement. In *Test Validity*, eds. Howard Wainer and Henry I. Braun, 33–45. Hillsdale, NJ: Lawrence Erlbaum.

Presser, Stanley, Jennifer M. Rothgeb, Mick P. Couper, et al., eds. 2004. *Methods for Testing and Evaluating Survey Questionnaires.* Hoboken, NJ: John Wiley & Sons.

Wainer, Howard, and Henry I. Braun. 1988. Introduction. In *Test Validity*, eds. Howard Wainer and Henry I. Braun, xvii–xx. Hillsdale, NJ: Lawrence Erlbaum.

Willis, Gordon B. 2005. *Cognitive Interviewing: A Tool for Improving Questionnaire Design.* Thousand Oaks, CA: Sage.

Woolley, Michael E., Gary L. Bowen, and Natasha K. Bowen. 2004. Cognitive Pretesting and the Developmental Validity of Child Self-Report Instruments: Theory and Applications. *Research on Social Work Practice* 14 (3): 191–200.

Natasha K. Bowen

VALIDITY, STATISTICAL

A study is valid when it actually measures what it claims to measure and when there are no logical errors in the drawing of conclusions from the data. There are many labels for different types of validity, but all concern threats that undermine the meaningfulness of research. Some early writers simply equated validity with establishing that a construct's scale correlated with a dependent variable in the intended manner, and, indeed, a scale might be considered valid as a measure of anything with which it correlated (Guilford 1946). Types of validity were codified in 1954 by the American Psychological Association (APA), which identified four categories: *content* validity, *construct* validity, *concurrent* validity, and *predictive* validity. Each type corresponded to a different research purpose: Content validity had to do with subject-matter content testing; construct validity with measuring abstract concepts like IQ; concurrent validity with devising new scales or tests to replace existing ones; and predictive validity with devising indicators of future performance. A 1966 update to the APA typology combined the last two types under the label *criterion-related* validity. Later, Lorrie Shepard (1993) was among those who argued that both criterion and content validity were subtypes of construct validity, leaving only one type of validity.

The unified view of validity supported the notion that only rarely could a researcher establish validity with reference to a single earlier type. Moreover, Lee Cronbach's (1971, p. 447) earlier argument that validity could not be established for a test or a scale, but only for interpretations that researchers might make from a test or a scale, also became widely accepted in the current era. Some researchers, such as Samuel Messick (1989), accept construct validity as the only type of validity, but argue for multiple standards for assessing it, including relevant content based on sound theory or rationale, internally consistent items, external correlation with related measures, generalizability across populations and time, and explicitness in social consequences (e.g., racial bias). In a nutshell, since about the mid-twentieth century, the concept of validation has evolved from the establishing of correlation with a dependent variable to the idea that researchers must validate each interpretation of each scale, test, or instrument, and do so in multiple ways that taken together form the whole of what validity testing is about.

The outline below largely accepts the unified view of validity, centering on construct validity, but adds to it separate coverage in three areas: (1) content validity, focusing on the labeling of constructs; (2) internal validity, focusing on research design bias; and (3) statistical validity, focusing on meeting the assumptions of empirical procedures. While all three might be (and by some are) considered subtypes of construct validity, they do not fall neatly in its two major subdomains—convergent and discriminant validity—and so have been treated here separately.

CONSTRUCT VALIDITY

Under construct validity (or *factorial* validity), a good construct has a theoretical basis that is translated through clear operational definitions involving measurable indicators. A poor construct may be characterized by lack of theoretical agreement on content, or by flawed operationalization such that its indicators may be construed as measuring one thing by one researcher and another thing by a second researcher. To the extent that a proposed construct is at odds with the existing literature on related hypothesized relationships using other measures, its construct validity is suspect. The more a construct is used, in more settings with more outcomes consistent with theory, the more its construct validity.

Convergent Validity Researchers should establish both of the two main types of construct validity: convergent and discriminant. Convergent validity is assessed by the correlation among items that make up the scale or the instrument measuring a construct (*internal-consistency* validity); by the correlation of the given scale with measures of the same construct using scales and instruments proposed by other researchers and, preferably, already accepted in the field (*criterion* validity); and by the correlation of relation-

ships involving the given scale across samples (e.g., racial tolerance using subject data versus spousal data) or across methods (e.g., survey data versus archival data).

Internal-consistency validity seeks to establish at least moderate correlation among the indicators for a concept. Cronbach's alpha is commonly used, with .60 considered acceptable for exploratory purposes, .70 adequate for confirmatory purposes, and .80 good for confirmatory purposes. Other tests used to demonstrate convergent validity include demonstrating a simple factor structure, employing the one-parameter logistic models developed by Georg Rasch (1960), or using the average variance extracted (AVE) method developed by Claus Fornell and David Larcker (1981).

Criterion validity (or *concurrent* validity) has to do with the correlation between measurement items and accepted measures. Ideally, the criteria are direct, objective measures of what is being assessed (e.g., how well does survey-reported voting correlate with actual voting in voting records?), but correlation with well-accepted related scales is an alternative criterion.

External validity has to do with possible bias in the process of generalizing conclusions from a sample to a population, to other subject populations, to other settings, or to other time periods. The questions raised include: "Are findings using the construct scale consistent across samples?" and "To what population does the researcher wish to generalize conclusions, and is there something unique about the study sample's subjects—the place where they lived and worked, the setting in which they were involved, the times of the study—that would prevent valid generalization?" When a sample is nonrandom in unknown ways, the likelihood of external validity is low, as in the case of convenience samples. External validity may be increased by cross-validation, where the researcher develops the instrument on a calibration sample and then tests it on an independent validation sample.

Discriminant Validity Discriminant validity, the second major type of construct validity, refers to the principle that the indicators for different constructs should not be so highly correlated as to lead one to conclude that they measure the same thing. This could happen if there is definitional overlap between constructs.

Discriminant validity analysis may include correlational methods, factor methods (Straub 1989), the AVE method, and structural equation modeling (SEM) approaches. In confirmatory factor analysis within SEM, if goodness-of-fit measures for the measurement model are adequate, the researcher concludes that the constructs in the model differ. A more rigorous and widely accepted SEM-based alternative is to run the model unconstrained and also constraining the correlation between constructs to 1.0. If the two models do not differ significantly on a chi-square difference test, the researcher will fail to conclude that the constructs differ (Bagozzi et al. 1991).

CONTENT VALIDITY

Content validity (or *face* validity) exists when items measure the full domain indicated by their label and description. A *naming fallacy* exists when indicators display construct validity, yet the label attached to the concept is inappropriate (e.g., satisfaction with outcomes is measured but is labeled as effectiveness of outcomes). A *domain fallacy* exists when indicators are restricted in value (e.g., "monetary incentives" may be the label of an indicator in a small group simulation, but the indicator would be more accurately labeled "small monetary incentives" due to restricted range; the label "large monetary incentives" may have a very different effect).

INTERNAL VALIDITY

Internal validity concerns defending against sources of bias arising in research design. When there is lack of internal validity, variables other than the independent(s) being studied may be responsible for part or all of the observed effect on the dependent variable(s). If there is no causal phenomenon under study, internal validity is not at issue.

Common issues related to internal validity are:

Hawthorne effect (experimenter expectation): The expectations or actions of the investigator may contaminate the outcomes.

Mortality bias: Attrition of subjects later in the research process may render the final sample no longer representative.

Selection bias: The subjects may not reflect a random sample, and when multiple groups are studied, there can be differential selection of the groups associated with differential biases with regard to history, maturation, testing, mortality, regression, and instrumentation (i.e., selection may combine differentially with other threats to validity).

Evaluation apprehension: Study sponsorship, phrasing of the questions, and other steps taken by the researcher may not suffice to mitigate the natural apprehension of subjects, encouraging a bias toward responses the researcher is thought to want to hear.

Special problems involving control groups include:

Control awareness: If the control group is aware it is not receiving the experimental treatment, it may exhibit compensatory rivalry, resentful demoralization, or other traits that may contaminate study results.

Compensatory equalization of treatments: Researchers may compensate for the control group's lack of benefit from treatment by providing some other benefit, such as alternative experiences, thereby introducing unmeasured variables.

Unintended treatments: Researcher attention, the status of the testing locale, and other testing experiences may constitute unmeasured variables.

Likewise, special problems exist for before-after and time series studies:

Instrumentation change: Measurement of variables may shift in before-after studies, as when the observers, through experience, become more adept at measurement.

History: Intervening events that are not part of the study may occur between measurement intervals, affecting results.

Maturation: Invalid inferences may be made when the maturation of subjects between intervals has an effect.

Regression toward the mean: If subjects are chosen because they are above or below the mean, there is a statistical tendency that they will be closer to the mean on remeasurement, regardless of the intervention.

Test experience: The before-study impacts the after-study in its own right, or multiple measurement of a concept leads to familiarity with the items and hence a history or fatigue effect.

STATISTICAL VALIDITY

Statistical validity concerns basing conclusions on a proper use of statistics, and in particular whether the assumptions of statistical procedures are met (e.g., normality, homoscedasticity, independence, and other traits may be required). Statistical invalidity also occurs when the researcher has not properly specified the model, has not taken interaction and nonlinear effects into account, or has misinterpreted the causal direction of relationships.

When significance tests are employed, they may be invalid if data are not randomly sampled, if an inappropriate alpha level has been selected (e.g., .05 is common in social science but is too liberal for medical research), if the test has an inadequate power level, or if a post hoc "shotgun" approach is used in which large numbers of relationships are examined without taking into account that multiple a posteriori tests require a higher operational alpha significance level to achieve the same nominal level.

BIBLIOGRAPHY

American Psychological Association. 1954. Technical Recommendations for Psychological Tests and Diagnostic Techniques. *Psychological Bulletin* 51 (2, suppl.): 201–238.

American Psychological Association. 1966. *Standards for Educational and Psychological Tests and Manuals.* Washington, DC: Author.

Bagozzi, Richard P., Youjae Yi, and Lynn W. Phillips. 1991. Assessing Construct Validity in Organizational Research. *Administrative Science Quarterly* 36 (3): 421–458.

Campbell, Donald T., and Julian C. Stanley. 1963. *Experimental and Quasi-experimental Designs for Research.* Chicago: Rand-McNally.

Carmines, Edward G., and Richard A. Zeller. 1979. *Reliability and Validity Assessment.* Newbury Park, CA: Sage.

Cook, Thomas D., and Donald T. Campbell. 1979. *Quasi-experimentation: Design and Analysis Issues for Field Settings.* Boston: Houghton Mifflin.

Cronbach, Lee J. 1971. Test Validation. In *Educational Measurement*, ed. Robert L. Thorndike. 2nd ed. pp. 443-507 Washington, DC: American Council on Education.

Fornell, Claus, and David F. Larcker. 1981. Evaluating Structural Equation Models with Unobservable Variables and Measurement Error. *Journal of Marketing Research* 18 (1): 39–50.

Guilford, Joy P. 1946. New Standards for Test Evaluation. *Educational and Psychological Measurement* 6 (5): 427–439.

Messick, Samuel. 1989. Validity. In *Educational Measurement*, ed. Robert L. Linn, 13–103. 3rd ed. New York: American Council on Education and Macmillan.

Rasch, Georg. [1960] 1980. *Probabilistic Models for Some Intelligence and Achievement Tests.* Expanded ed. Chicago: University of Chicago Press.

Shadish, William R., Thomas D. Cook, and Donald T. Campbell. 2002. *Experimental and Quasi-experimental Designs for Generalized Causal Inference.* Boston: Houghton Mifflin.

Shepard, Lorrie A. 1993. Evaluating Test Validity. In *Review of Research in Education*, ed. Linda Darling-Hammond, vol. 19, 405–450. Washington, DC: American Educational Research Association.

Straub, Detmar W. 1989. Validating Instruments in MIS Research. *MIS Quarterly* 13 (2): 147–166.

G. David Garson

VALIDITY IN PSYCHOLOGY

SEE *Validity, Statistical.*

VALIUM

SEE *Psychotropic Drugs.*

VALUE

In the work of Karl Marx the term *value* is defined as the labor embodied in the production of commodities, where commodities are goods produced for sale on the market. The concept of value applies only to commodity-producing economies, and the value of any particular commodity is the amount of labor required for its production according to the prevailing technological standards, assuming that the total output level is appropriate to market demand for the good. The embodied labor that defines the values of commodities includes that required to produce the intermediate goods needed in the production of these commodities as well as the direct labor inputs involved. Thus machines are regarded as passing on the labor embodied in them during their own production to what they themselves help produce. Different forms of direct labor are reduced to a common standard by applying a similar principle in calculating the amount of labor required to produce the various skills of different types of labor. More highly skilled labor therefore contributes more value to the production of commodities than does less skilled labor.

It follows that the value of any commodity can be divided into two parts: the dead labor inherent in the intermediate goods employed in production, and the living labor arising from the use of workers of various levels of skill. Marx also subdivides the value contributed by direct labor into a magnitude equal to the value of the commodities contained in the wages received by workers, and a residual magnitude called surplus value which, he believed, constituted the basis of nonwage incomes in capitalism: profits, interest, and rents.

Marx's concept of value is distinct from any notion of use-value, or utility. He knew that commodities are useful in production or consumption, but he believed that their usefulness has nothing to do with their value, which is determined solely by their conditions of production. Value as Marx defined it is also distinct from exchange value, or price. However, Marx used his value categories to provide a theory of prices in competitive capitalism. He made no claim that values directly determine prices, in the sense of being equal to, or even proportionate to, the prices of the commodities in question. The determination is more complex, and the prices Marx was concerned to explain are only long-period equilibrium prices. These are the prices that prevail in a situation where supplies are fully adjusted to demands in all lines of production, and the rate of payment of all inputs of the same type is equal in all lines of production. He conceived of long-period equilibria as centers of gravitation to which market prices tend, and in doing so Marx placed himself in a long tradition of economic thought that took labor costs to be the key to a proper understanding of such prices, including Adam Smith in the late eighteenth century and David Ricardo in the early nineteenth. This history is examined in great detail and with considerable lucidity by Ronald Meek in his *Studies in the Labor Theory of Value* (1976). However, Marx also argued that the concept of value and derivative concepts, like surplus value, provided the basis for the correct understanding of much more than equilibrium prices.

In the three volumes of *Capital*, written in the 1860s, he also made the following three claims. First, surplus value represents exploited (unpaid) labor and all forms of property income in capitalism derived from this. Second, capitalism is therefore an economic system based upon the extraction of unpaid labor from producers by nonproducing classes and, thus, is analogous to systems of production based on slavery and serfdom. Third, as a result, the conflict between workers and property-owners has a structural foundation comparable to the class conflicts of earlier modes of production that had helped to destroy them. Marx argued for these three propositions at considerable length and with great sophistication. But the basic message is straightforward: While capitalism appears to be very different from other types of economy in being grounded in free contract rather than coerced labor, the reality is less dissimilar. Capitalism, too, has an exploitative character and generates conflicts that will contribute to its transcendence.

Like Smith and Ricardo before him, Marx was well aware that values could not account for prices in any simple way. Outside of special circumstances, all three theorists recognized that equilibrium prices would not be equal to values. Smith believed that when property incomes (profits, interest, and rents) existed, values could not provide any explanation of prices whatsoever; they were relevant for understanding prices only in so-called "early and rude" societies where property had not been privatized. However, Smith continued to believe (in some unspecified sense) that labor was the only "true" cost of production, and he sometimes measured prices by the labor they could command in exchange. He was followed here by Thomas Malthus. David Ricardo proved more insightful, refuting Smith's claim that the very existence of property incomes undermined the capacity of values to explain equilibrium prices. But outside of special circumstances he, too, recognized that values would not be equal to, or proportional to, prices. Some commodity prices would exceed their values and some would fall short of their values, since in equilibrium an equal rate of profit on capital is paid in all lines of activity and the equilibrium

price has to be sufficient to allow payment of this rate of profit whatever the capital-intensity of production. It followed from this that the surplus value generated in any line of production would not typically correspond to the property incomes derived from that line of production. Marx sought to resolve this problem by showing that, for capitalism as a whole, prices are transformed values and property incomes are transformed surplus values. Values and surplus values are reallocated between lines of production according to the requirements of long-period equilibrium. So, he maintained, for the capitalist system as a whole, values and surplus values really do determine prices and property incomes. This was the basis for his social and historical claims concerning the exploitative and conflictual nature of capitalism.

CRITICISMS

Marx's arguments for the illuminating power of value theory have not proved to be robust, although the central analytical difficulties came to light only in the 1960s, and most earlier criticisms have turned out to be rather weak in comparison. Marx himself was unable to specify rigorously the exact relationship between value magnitudes and price and income magnitudes. His critics, beginning with Ladislaus von Bortkiewicz in 1907, were much more successful. On the basis of reasonable assumptions about technology (as judged by the standards then prevailing in economics), Bortkiewicz and others proved that Marx's claims with regard to the transformed nature of prices and incomes can be justified. In their *The Political Economy of Marx* (1988) authors Michael C. Howard and John E. King have outlined the technicalities of the proofs; and they have explained the proofs' historical development in their two-volume *A History of Marxian Economics* (1989 and 1992). Despite this, Marx's claims are true only under restrictive assumptions. Most particularly, when technologies involve joint production, in which more than one type of output results from a production process, or when there are alternative techniques for producing any particular commodity, there may be no sensible way in which commodity values can be computed. Furthermore Ian Steedman, in his work *Marx After Sraffa* (1977), showed that even when commodity values can be determined, they may not be able to provide a coherent theory of exploitation in terms of surplus value, so that property incomes and class conflicts cannot be explained in the way Marx believed.

It might reasonably be expected that the flaws in a theory as grand as Marx's value theory would only succumb to something equally grand, not to the mundane fact commodities can be produced jointly in a single process, or that there are alternative processes in which they can be produced. But Marx was not alone in this.

Many of the propositions in Smith's economics, and even more in that of Ricardo, are also undermined. Similarly, Austrian capital theory and aggregate versions of neoclassical economics do not survive unscathed, as is proved with great economy and elegance in *Production of Commodities by Means of Commodities* (1960) by Piero Sraffa. Scholars of all schools made the huge mistake of believing that the complexities inherent in joint production and alternative production processes would not undermine results deduced from analyzing simpler and less realistic technologies. An element of irony is also present. Von Bortkiewicz and others who attempted to show rigorously that prices were transformed values, and property incomes were transformed surplus values, were not supporters of the political project of Marxism, while those who elucidated the destructive consequences of joint production technologies and alternative techniques of production were much more sympathetic to socialist politics.

However, the weakness of Marx's value theory does not fatally undermine Marxism as an intellectual force. Some scholars have continued to defend modified impressive versions of Marx's account of equilibrium prices, exploitation, and conflict, but without utilizing the concepts of value or surplus value. Three versions are Heinz Kurz and Neri Salvadori's *Theory of Production: A Long Period Analysis* (1995); John Roemer's *A General Theory of Exploitation and Class* (1982); and Gerry Cohen's *Karl Marx's Theory of History: A Defense* (2000). The ideas presented in these books and other works in the same vein are discussed in the second volume of *A History of Marxian Economics* by Howard and King. Also Marx's account of capitalist development and crises can be formulated in terms that are entirely independent of his theory of value and is thus unaffected by the difficulties that this theory has encountered.

SEE ALSO *Exchange Value; Labor Theory of Value; Surplus Value; Transformation Problem*

BIBLIOGRAPHY

Cohen, Gerry A. 2000. *Karl Marx's Theory of History: A Defense.* 2nd ed. New York: Oxford University Press.

Howard, Michael C., and John E. King. 1988. *The Political Economy of Marx.* 2nd ed. New York: New York University Press.

Howard, Michael C., and John E. King. 1989 and 1992. *A History of Marxian Economics.* 2 vols. Princeton, NJ: Princeton University Press.

Kurz, Heinz D., and Neri Salvadori. 1995. *Theory of Production: A Long Period Analysis.* Cambridge, U.K.: Cambridge University Press.

Meek, Ronald L. 1976. *Studies in the Labor Theory of Value.* 2nd ed. New York: Monthly Review Press. (Orig. pub. 1956).

Roemer, John E. 1982. *A General Theory of Exploitation and Class.* Cambridge, MA: Harvard University Press.

Michael Howard
John E. King

VALUE ELICITATION

SEE *Value, Subjective.*

VALUE, OBJECTIVE

Within the social sciences, the concept of *value* was initially associated with the discourses of classical political economy, modern economics, and the Marxist critique of capitalism, and was later extended to refer to ideas of what is morally or ethically "right" or "important" in social life and in individual behavior. Thus, *value* can refer to both "economic values" and "cultural values"—that is, to the valuation of goods and services being bought and sold in the market, as well as to the ideals, principles, and goals that people define for themselves as they pursue the "good life" and the "good society." An *objective value* is a value that has a universal, transhistorical, or transcultural foundation. As such, it is a concept in opposition to the notion that values are always subjective and relative, and reflect the predilections, choices, and preferences of individual social or economic actors.

OBJECTIVE VALUE IN ECONOMIC THEORY

The idea that a good or service produced for sale in the market possesses a value that is distinct from its price is fundamental to all theories of economic value. All such theories proceed from the assumption that a commodity's value is in some sense the "center of gravity" around which its price generally oscillates. For the physiocrats, this center of gravity was the productivity of agricultural labor; for the Smith-Ricardo classical school, the labor expended in the commodity's production; for Marx, the abstract labor required for the commodity's reproduction as measured by socially necessary labor time; for John Stuart Mill, the commodity's costs of production; and for the marginalists, its marginal utility to a prospective buyer.

Prior to the marginalist revolution in modern economic thought, the concept of value was treated invariably as an "objective" one. The value of a commodity was conceived as the sum of the value of the objective inputs to its production (living labor, raw materials, energy, and fixed capital depreciation). Sometimes these inputs were subsumed under one or another version of the "labor theory of value" and sometimes under a "cost of production" theory. But it was generally taken for granted that an intimate connection existed between the "objective value" represented by, or embodied in, a commodity and its market price.

The most important theorist of objective economic value was Karl Marx, who recognized the revolutionary implications of the idea that value exists as a definite (objective) quantitative magnitude that sets parametric limits on prices, profits, and wages. Transforming the classical labor theory of value, Marx argued that living labor was the sole source of new value and that the contradictions inherent in the "law of value" were at the heart of the "laws of motion" of the capitalist mode of production. As living labor is displaced from commodity production as a result of technological innovation and capitalist competition, the capitalist system deprives itself of the "social substance" (labor value) that is its lifeblood, and the rate of profit falls, setting the stage for capitalist crisis and ultimately social revolution. Hence, Marx's understanding of the "objectivity" of economic value as rooted in historically specific relations of production is integral to his account of the decline of capitalism and its supersession by a new socialist society that will be liberated from the tyranny of the law of value.

If Marx's theory represented the logical outcome of the classical school's commitment to a theory of objective economic value, it is unsurprising that economists committed to the perpetuation, reform, or fine-tuning of modern capitalism were eager to abandon it. The marginalist school of Carl Menger, William Stanley Jevons, and Léon Walras transformed the concept of economic value into an essentially subjective one, insisting that a good's value is determined solely by its marginal utility and that value is merely a psychological relation between a commodity and a potential purchaser.

OBJECTIVE VALUE AS A CULTURAL PHENOMENON

Friedrich Nietzsche was the first modern thinker to project the concept of value outside the sphere of economics (and mathematics) to the sphere of culture, arguing that individuals were motivated less by the "virtues" celebrated by classical philosophy than by "values" that reflected their own interests, proclivities, and tastes. His subjective concept of value was to deeply influence the social theory of Max Weber, for whom the subjective value orientation of individual social actors was a fundamental starting point of sociological analysis.

The concept of objective cultural or moral values developed in reaction to the relativism and subjectivism of Nietzschian philosophy and Weberian social theory. Both liberal-democratic and Marxist-socialist versions of the concept have been elaborated, but they are united by the idea that some core human values transcend location, time, and culture and that these values therefore possess an "objective" character.

SEE ALSO *Economics, Classical; Labor Theory of Value; Marginalism; Marx, Karl; Mill, John Stuart; Ricardo, David; Smith, Adam; Value; Value, Subjective*

BIBLIOGRAPHY

Clarke, Simon. 1982. *Marx, Marginalism, and Modern Sociology: From Adam Smith to Max Weber*. London and Basingstoke, U.K.: Macmillan.

Himmelfarb, Gertrude. 1995. *The De-Moralization of Society: From Victorian Virtues to Modern Values*. London: Institute of Economic Affairs.

McLellan, David, and Sean Sayers, eds. 1990. *Socialism and Morality*. London: Macmillan.

Smith, Murray E. G. 1994. *Invisible Leviathan: The Marxist Critique of Market Despotism beyond Postmodernism*. Toronto: University of Toronto Press.

Murray Smith

VALUE, SUBJECTIVE

The concept of subjective value is that each individual has their own preferences for objects or actions. This concept is applied by economists to understand behavior and operates "behind the scenes" of observed behavior. That is, preferences are part of a theoretical structure to explain behavior that is latent and are assumed to model the observed behavior. Thus it is common for economists to make statements such as "the individual is assumed to behave as if he or she has subjective preferences and values for this outcome" and then test the implications of that assumption. It is not the case that one can directly observe subjective preferences or subjective value. Instead, auxiliary assumptions are needed to infer subjective preferences or value.

The justification for subjective value is primarily a priori. It is easy to just imagine that people have different preferences for the same goods or actions; for example, one person likes red wine with most food, and another likes beer with most food.

What leads to the assumption of subjective value is that people seem to make different consumption decisions, even when the circumstances are otherwise the same. Imagine people deciding between two types of cars but having the same incomes and facing the same car prices. If we observe people choosing different cars or one person not buying a car at all, how do we explain this outcome? We could claim that there are some unobserved differences in people's constraints—for example, one person might live close to good public transport. Should one always ascribe differences in behavior to differences in subjective value or, instead, assume constraints that are specific to the decision maker but not observable to others? The answer to this question is one of the practical considerations that comes up repeatedly in theoretical and empirical work in economics (e.g., Stigler and Becker 1977; Becker 1993).

The concept of subjective value has direct implications for the manner in which we determine what valuations people have. This is the area of subjective value elicitation. It also has implications for how we design policy. The concept of consumer sovereignty flows naturally from thinking about subjective value: We value what is a good wine by seeing what people are willing to pay for it. But there are two concerns with the notion of consumer sovereignty that flows from thinking of values as subjects. First, what if those values are "constructed" by others, such as marketing, or the addiction that comes from some drugs? Second, it is possible, and indeed likely in some settings, that subjective value is not based on a complete processing of all of the relevant information about the consequences of actions. Hence society may want to adopt valuations that differ from those that individuals would adopt.

WHY ELICIT SUBJECTIVE VALUES?

Economists are interested in eliciting subjective values at the level of the individual because market values do not provide the information needed to measure consumer surplus, value new products, or value goods that have no market. Why do we need to elicit values? The prices observed on a market reflect, on a good competitive day, the equilibrium of marginal valuations and costs. They do not quantitatively reflect the infra-marginal or extra-marginal values, other than in a severely censored sense. We know that infra-marginal values are weakly higher and extra-marginal values are weakly lower, but beyond that one must rely on functional forms for utility or demand to extrapolate. For policy purposes this is generally insufficient to undertake cost-benefit calculations.

When producers are contemplating a new product or innovation, they have to make some judgment about the value that will be placed on it. New drugs, and the research and development underlying them, provide an important example. Unless one can heroically tie the new product to existing products in terms of shared characteristics and somehow elicit values on those characteristics, there is no way to know what price the market will bear. Value elicitation experiments can help fill that void, com-

plementing traditional marketing techniques (see Hoffman et al. 1993).

Many goods and services effectively have no market, either because they exhibit characteristics of public goods or because it is impossible to credibly deliver them on an individual basis. These nonmarket goods have traditionally been valued using surveys, where people are asked to state a valuation "contingent on a market existing for the good." The problem is that these surveys are hypothetical, in terms of the deliverability of the good and the economic consequences of the response, and this understandably generates controversy about their reliability (Harrison 2006).

It does not follow that subjective values are those that society should use for decisions that have public consequences. For example, when public goods are being provided, the subjective value that is elicited may entail "free riding," which occurs when one person rationally understates his or her private valuation for the good in the expectation that others, in aggregate, will be willing to pay it. In this case subjective values will understate true values, and society would end up with too little investment in public goods if it relied on consumer sovereignty. We are interested in understanding when the subjective values we elicit are biased in relation to true subjective values. In such settings we may adjust the elicited subjective values in some way.

A related example might be the subjective values that an addict would place on some drug. Even if we elicit the value reliably, it is not obvious that we should use that value when deciding on policy on the drug. In this case society may take a longer-term perspective on the subjective value of the drug, even its subjective value to the addict (e.g., Becker and Murphy 1988). Or it might consider the effects of the addict's consumption of the drug on others, such as the addict's family or society as a whole. Consumer sovereignty should not be abandoned lightly, because it constrains politicians and bureaucrats from asserting value in the absence of any "market test."

PROCEDURES FOR MEASURING SUBJECTIVE VALUES

Direct methods for value elicitation include auctions, auction-like procedures, and "multiple price lists." Sealed-bid auctions require the individual to state a valuation for the product in a private manner and then award the product following certain rules. For single-object auctions, the second-price (or Vickrey) auction awards the product to the highest bidder but sets the price equal to the highest rejected bid. It is easy to show, to students of economics at least, that the bidder has a dominant strategy to bid his or her true value: Any bid higher or lower can only end up hurting the bidder in expectation. But these incentives are not obvious to inexperienced subjects.

A real-time counterpart of the second-price auction is the English (ascending bid) auction, in which an auctioneer starts the price out low and then bidders increase the price to become the winner of the product. Bidders seem to realize the dominant strategy property of the English auction more quickly than in comparable second-price sealed-bid auctions, no doubt due to the real-time feedback on the opportunity costs of deviations from that strategy (see Rutström 1998; Harstad 2000). Familiarity with the institution is also surely a factor in the superior performance of the English auction: First encounters with the second-price auction rules lead many noneconomists to assume that there must be some "trick."

Related schemes collapse the logic of the second-price auction into an auction-like procedure due to Gordon Becker, Morris DeGroot, and Jacob Marschak (1964). The basic idea is to endow the subject with the product and to ask for a "selling price." The subject is told that a "buying price" will be picked at random and that if the buying price that is picked exceeds the stated selling price, the product will be sold at that price and the subject will receive that buying price. If the buying price is equal to or lower than the selling price, the subject keeps the lottery and plays it out. Again it is relatively transparent to economists that this auction procedure provides a formal incentive for the subject to truthfully reveal the certainty equivalent of the lottery. One must ensure that the buy-out range exceeds the highest price that the subject would reasonably state, but this is not normally a major problem. One must also ensure that the subject realizes that the choice of a buying price does not depend on the stated selling price; a surprising number of respondents appear not to understand this independence, even if they are told that a physical randomizing device is being used.

Multiple price lists present individuals with an ordered menu of prices at which they may choose to buy the product or not. In this manner the list resembles a menu, akin to the price comparison Web sites available online for many products. For any given price, the choice is a simple "take it or leave it" posted offer, familiar from retail markets. The set of responses for the entire list is incentivized by picking one at random for implementation, so the subject can readily see that misrepresentation can only hurt for the usual revealed preference reasons. Refinements to the intervals of prices can be implemented to improve the accuracy of the values elicited (see Andersen et al. 2006). These methods have been used widely to elicit risk preferences and discount rates as well as values for products (see Holt and Laury 2002; Harrison et al. 2002; Andersen et al. 2007).

Indirect methods work by presenting individuals with simple choices and using a latent structural model to infer valuations. The canonical example comes from the theory of revealed preference and confronts the decision maker with a series of purchase opportunities from a budget line and asks them to pick one. By varying the budget lines one can "trap" latent indifference curves and place nonparametric or parametric bounds on valuations. The same methods extend naturally to variations in the nonprice characteristics of products and merge with the marketing literature on "conjoint choice" (e.g., Louviere et al. 2000; Lusk and Schroeder 2004). Access to scanner data from the massive volume of retail transactions made every day promises rich characterizations of underlying utility functions, particularly when merged with experimental methods that introduce exogenous variation in characteristics in order to statistically condition and "enrich" the data (Hensher et al. 1999). One of the attractions of indirect methods is that one can employ choice tasks that are familiar to the subject, such as binary "take it or leave it" choices or rank orderings. The lack of precision in that type of qualitative data requires some latent structure before one can infer values, but behavioral responses are much easier to explain and motivate for respondents.

One major advantage of undertaking structural estimation of a latent choice model is that valuations can be elicited in a more fundamental manner, explicitly recognizing the decision process underlying a stated valuation. A structural model can control for risk attitudes when choices are being made in a stochastic setting, which is almost always the case in practical settings. Thus one can hope to tease apart the underlying deterministic valuation from the assessment of risk. Likewise nonstandard models of choice posit a myriad of alternative factors that might confound inference about valuation: Respondents might distort preferences from their true values, they might exhibit loss aversion in certain frames, and they might bring their own homegrown reference points or aspiration levels to the valuation task. Only with a structural model can one hope to identify these potential confounds to the valuation process. Quite apart from wanting to identify the primitives of the underlying valuation free of confounds, normative applications will often require that some of these distortions be corrected for. That is only possible if one has a complete structural model of the valuation process.

A structural model also provides an antidote to claims that valuations are so contextual as to be an unreliable will-o'-the-wisp. If someone is concerned about framing, endowment effects, loss aversion, preference distortions, social preferences, and any number of related behavioral notions, it is impossible to generate a scientific dialogue without being able to write out a structural model and jointly estimate it.

SEE ALSO *Addiction; Auctions; Consumer; Demand; Economics, Neoclassical; Free Rider; Marginalization;*

Markets; Maximization; Opportunity Cost; Preferences; Prices; Public Goods; Structural Equation Models; Utility Function; Value, Objective; Variables, Latent

BIBLIOGRAPHY

Andersen, Steffen, Glenn W. Harrison, Morten Igel Lau, and E. Elisabet Rutström. 2006. Elicitation Using Multiple Price Lists. *Experimental Economics* 9 (4): 383–405.

Andersen, Steffen, Glenn W. Harrison, Morten Igel Lau, and E. Elisabet Rutström. 2007. Valuation Using Multiple Price List Formats. *Applied Economics* 39: 675–682.

Becker, Gary S. 1993. Nobel Lecture: The Economic Way of Looking at Behavior. *Journal of Political Economy* 101 (June): 385–409.

Becker, Gordon M., Morris H. DeGroot, and Jacob Marschak. 1964. Measuring Utility by a Single-Response Sequential Method. *Behavioral Science* 9 (July): 226–232.

Becker, Gary S., and Kevin M. Murphy. 1988. A Theory of Rational Addiction. *Journal of Political Economy* 96 (August): 675–700.

Harrison, Glenn W. 2006. Experimental Evidence on Alternative Environmental Valuation Methods. *Environmental and Resource Economics* 34: 125–162.

Harrison, Glenn W., Ronald M. Harstad, and E. Elisabet Rutström. 2004. Experimental Methods and Elicitation of Values. *Experimental Economics* 7 (2): 123–140.

Harrison, Glenn W., Morten Igel Lau, Melonie B. Williams. 2002. Estimating Individual Discount Rates for Denmark: A Field Experiment. *American Economic Review* 92 (5): 1606–1617.

Harstad, Ronald M. 2000. Dominant Strategy Adoption and Bidders' Experience with Pricing Rules. *Experimental Economics* 3 (3): 261–280.

Hensher, David, Jordan Louviere, and Joffre D. Swait. 1999. Combining Sources of Preference Data. *Journal of Econometrics* 89: 197–221.

Hoffman, Elizabeth, Dale J. Menkhaus, Dipinkar Chakravarti, et al. 1993. Using Laboratory Experimental Auctions in Marketing Research: A Case Study of New Packaging for Fresh Beef. *Marketing Science* 12 (3): 318–338.

Holt, Charles A., and Susan K. Laury. 2002. Risk Aversion and Incentive Effects. *American Economic Review* 92 (5): 1644–1655.

Louviere, Jordan J., David A. Hensher, and Joffre D. Swait. 2000. *Stated Choice Methods: Analysis and Application.* New York: Cambridge University Press.

Lusk, Jayson L., and Ted C. Schroeder. 2004. Are Choice Experiments Incentive Compatible? A Test with Quality Differentiated Beef Steaks. *American Journal of Agricultural Economics* 86 (2): 467–482.

Rutström, E. Elisabet. 1998. Home-Grown Values and the Design of Incentive Compatible Auctions. *International Journal of Game Theory* 27 (3): 427–441.

Stigler, George J., and Gary S. Becker. 1977. De Gustibus Non Est Disputandum. *American Economic Review* 67 (March): 76–90.

Train, Kenneth E. 2003. *Discrete Choice Methods with Simulation.* New York: Cambridge University Press.

Glenn W. Harrison

VALUES

The word *value* appears in two forms. The first is as a noun meaning core ideals and norms, as in, for example, "independence is a core value in contemporary U.S. society." The second form of value is a verb meaning the process by which things acquire importance or economic price, which is sometimes understood as valuation, as in, for example, "the ball was valued at $1.29 for quick resale" or "group members value her participation." Most social theory has focused on values as nouns that represent key ideas for a given culture, perform certain functions for society, or figure in ideological systems of power. However, an additional consideration of valuation can bring into focus issues of value change and the relationships between cultural and economic values.

Émile Durkheim (1858–1917) articulated a model of society in which social norms and values arose from the increasing specialization of social roles and labor in the emerging industrial societies of the time. Values and norms of behavior provide the social integration that allows individuals to function in society (Durkheim [1893] 1997), providing cohesiveness, trust, and stability. Durkheim's model of integration provided the background for Talcott Parsons's mid-twentieth century theory of society, which emphasized the functionality of values and rules, particularly in maintaining the equilibrium and stability of society (see especially Parsons 1951). Culture and a system of values form one of four dimensions of society, the others being social structure, relation to environment, and achievement of goals. For Parsons, the value system must be integrated into people's personalities and will then guide appropriate behavior. For example, competitiveness and autonomy, or individualism, are key values that are important for people to adopt to be successful in a capitalist economy, and much effort in schooling and media is spent on inculcating those ideals.

This view of values is easily critiqued for its prioritization of system stability over the possibility of social change, and for reducing the scope of agency for individuals who are seemingly programmed by social institutions to adhere to norms and uphold values. While Durkheim's work on values clearly contributed to the functionalism of Parsons, Durkheim took a view of crime and criminality

(*On the Normality of Crime*, 1895) that prefigures more critical approaches to values and norms, particularly what has been known as labeling theory (Becker [1963] 1997), and also critical approaches to deviance, such as those of Michel Foucault (1977). Labeling theory argues that acts are not inherently deviant but are labeled deviant by others, particularly powerful groups that articulate normative systems to protect social stability and their interests. For example, civic unrest may be treated by the state as sign of the deviance of protestors. But unrest may nonetheless hold value as a release for social tension and further may indicate that systematic injustice on the part of the state requires response and remediation and that alternative or neglected values should be given consideration.

Values are thus a part of systems of social power, providing the ideological frame that shapes public discourse about how the social world is operating and how it should operate. For example, when individualism as a value is prevalent, explanations for social troubles are often laid upon the shoulders of individuals: Joblessness is taken as a sign of individual lack of effort rather than diminished regional economy; mental illness as weakness or individual pathology rather than as outcome of stress and conflicting social expectations. Values are associated with and defined by those with the greatest social power. For example, in Western contexts rationality and authority are associated with masculinity, while emotionality and dependence are stereotypically associated with femininity. This means that, for example, female professors may have more difficulty in establishing authority in a classroom: If they engage in conduct considered normal for a male professor, they are seen as breaking gender norms and dismissed as cold or shrill, whereas if their behavior adheres to stereotypically feminine norms of conduct, they are not taken seriously as experts. Other social stereotypes and the values attributed to ascribed characteristics such as race, gender, or attractiveness lead to forms of discrimination both subtle and obvious.

The differential effects of values are thus an issue for formal politics and public policy as well as informal arrangements of social power. While technocracy (rule by experts) has its appeal as a seemingly neutral form of governance, it cannot itself define social priorities and thus still relies upon values to direct the efforts of the state. For example, while scientists may be able to describe the phenomenon known as global warming with mathematical tools with no obvious bias or values, it is still a matter of values to identify the potential social and environmental changes as harmful to human objectives.

Values also intersect with public policy in that negative values used to portray social groups may lead to discrimination and impede more useful ways of addressing problems. For example, groups that value social solidarity and tradition over competitiveness (whether Native American, Amish, or urban African American) come to be seen as having a "culture of poverty" and are blamed for their "backwardness" and lack of economic achievement. Recent research suggests that while values and attitudes are relevant factors, socioeconomic or class background is far more important in shaping potential success in education and work. Specifically, African American families do not possess some pathological set of values that prevents their economic achievement: Income and educational disparities can be attributed to both mechanisms of social reproduction that make it difficult for poor people of any race to achieve intergenerational social mobility and to ongoing processes of racial discrimination that result in lower wages for persons with similar qualifications (Mason 2007).

Because the media continues to circulate social stereotypes and uncritically reflects normative ideologies of value, it has a large role in supporting existing structures of power at the expense of productive social and value change. Whether relying on racial stereotypes or on common narratives of "the self-made man," television programming reinforces value systems. Media may use representations of deviance to titillate and sell, but this is done with the sense that the actions or characters represented are not normal, and sometimes to make specific points about morality. Most police dramas, whether fictional or "reality"-based, play on this process. Of course, advertisements sell products based on their value, both in the sense of monetary cost and utility, and as representations of larger ideas: Car commercials sell freedom and individualism, household cleaners sell cleanliness and domestic harmony. People in the United States will apparently buy anything that is marketed as "convenient" even if it really is not, or even if it undermines other values such as environmental sustainability or community (Tierney 1993).

As markets continue to globalize, both products and values will travel to new areas. To do this, products need to be legible to consumers. John Evans (1998) argues that processes that simplify and standardize everything, from units of land and property laws, to sizes of clothing and other units of measure, can either be products of state regulation or of capitalist needs for stability and regularity. Values, too, will travel as people learn to want to participate in global economies as producers and consumers. George Ritzer (2004) argues that the need to remove anything controversial and to reduce the identity of consumer products to their "lowest common denominator" to ensure the widest possible sales will strip away all but the most trivial of meanings from commodities and cultural products.

Legibility is a property of things to be read and measured. Its establishment involves a set of processes by which units and systems of notation are formulated and provide metrics for the evaluation of things. These processes also connect issues of law and custom as the economic values of things interact with moral or cultural values. What is the value of a human life and how is it to be measured? Or of a sacred site, or an animal species? Legibility is a form of valuation, which may be tied to economic scales of value established by assessing costs and profits, but also to processes whereby variations in human lifestyles are labeled worthwhile, normal, or deviant. Alternative lifestyles are illegible and perceived as deviant by the mainstream, as unable to be understood or valued, and are not protected by law (Butler 1993). Legibility and economic valuation are ways of establishing and reading value and measure and are closely intertwined, suggesting that production and consumption and social or cultural reproduction and economic reproduction are more closely intertwined than traditional theories of political economy have suggested (Joseph 1998).

BIBLIOGRAPHY

Becker, Howard Saul. [1963] 1997. *Outsiders: Studies in the Sociology of Deviance.* New York: Simon & Schuster.

Butler, Judith. 1993. *Bodies That Matter: On the Discursive Limits of "Sex."* New York: Routledge.

Durkheim, Émile. [1893] 1997. *The Division of Labor in Society.* Trans. W. D. Halls. New York: Free Press.

Foucault, Michel. 1977. *Discipline and Punish: The Birth of the Prison.* Trans. Alan Sheridan. New York: Pantheon.

Joseph, Miranda. 1998. The Performance of Production and Consumption. *Social Text* 16 (1): 25–61.

Mason, Patrick L. 2007. Intergenerational Mobility and Interracial Inequality: The Return to Family Values. *Industrial Relations* 46 (1): 51–80.

Parsons, Talcott. 1951. *The Social System.* New York: Free Press.

Ritzer, George. 2004. *The Globalization of Nothing.* Thousand Oaks, CA: Pine Forge Press.

Scott, James C. 1998. *Seeing Like a State: How Certain Schemes to Improve the Human Condition Have Failed.* New Haven, CT: Yale University Press.

Tierney, Thomas F. 1993. *The Value of Convenience: A Genealogy of Technical Culture.* Albany: State University of New York Press.

Jennifer L. Croissant

VALUES, FAMILY

SEE *Family Values.*

VANILLA INDUSTRY

Natural vanilla flavoring is a product of the fruity pods of the vanilla vine, a tropical plant of the genus *vanilla* of the orchid family (*orchidaceae*). There are many varieties, *v. planifolia, v. pompona,* and *v. tahiiensis* being the most common. Initially native to the forested highlands of Mexico, vanilla was found in other tropical areas of the globe after its transport to European colonies in Africa and Asia in the sixteenth century by explorers, botanists, priests, and colonial administrators.

The global world market for natural vanilla is approximately 1,000 metric tons, of which the United States is the largest consumer. However, the market for vanilla from vanilla beans is dwarfed by the use of synthetic vanilla, which is well over 95 percent of the total tonnage used in the global flavorings industry and approximately one hundredth of the cost of vanilla from beans. Synthetic vanillin is extracted from cloves and coal tars as well as lignin from paper processing. Although it is a safe flavoring product, vanillin as the signature component of vanilla lacks the subtlety and complexity of natural vanilla, which has additional flavor components and is much prized by home cooks, gourmet chefs, and food processors for which the designation of "real" is important to brand identity.

Vanilla orchids in their native Mexico are pollinated by hummingbirds and a species of small bee. In its other production contexts, this has led to vanilla being one of the most labor-intensive crops in the world, as the orchid flowers must be hand-pollinated to produce beans. Because the flowers last for only one day, farmers must daily tend to their vanilla vines, which are generally looped upon trees that provide shade and protection. Upward of 70,000 small farmers in Madagascar make at least part of their living managing vanilla vines, which can grow to be nearly thirty-five meters in length. There is a three- to five-year time period from transplanting vanilla cuttings or seedlings until the first fruiting, and the healthy maturity of vanilla vines requires effective climbing or trellising supports that provide some shade, adequate rainwater (approximately one meter per year), stable and rich soils, and temperatures remaining above fifty degrees Fahrenheit even at the coldest part of the year. The beans take several months to develop after pollination. They are harvested while green and after harvesting are processed to mature and stabilize the flavors. This ripening process generally takes several months, and the beans are carefully tended by hand.

Until the mid-1980s Madagascar and the islands of Reunion and Cormoros off the eastern coast of Africa held a virtual monopoly on natural vanilla production. Mexico's vanilla market collapsed at the end of the nineteenth century, with political turmoil disrupting production, and only began to reorganize in the late twentieth century. The Madagascar cartel controlled an extremely inflated price on the open world market, which provided significant revenues for the government and for exporters. Price controls included export restrictions and the occasional destruction of tons of crops to keep the market price high (as high as US$500 per kilogram). Natural vanilla is a high value–low volume crop, which makes it attractive for biotechnology innovations. Attempts to reproduce natural vanilla through tissue cloning of ripened bean cells seemed to be making progress until new producers, particularly Indonesia and China but also smaller producers such as Uganda, Thailand, Tahiti, and Kenya, broke the monopoly of the Madagascar-based cartel and drove the world market price of vanilla to low levels (as low as US$20 per kilogram). Madagascar remains the largest exporter of vanilla. The world price continues to fluctuate as weather and the emergence of other producing nations interacts with changing demand, but it generally brings about US$50 per kilogram.

The control that the flavor industry maintains in grading and certifying vanilla as real versus synthetic, in labeling laws, and in consumer preferences for natural products are all part of the vanilla industry's complexity. When natural vanilla prices have been consistently high, there are many more attempts at using biotechnology to produce substitutes, old-fashioned attempts to cut or dilute real vanilla with synthetic vanilla, and ventures for new natural production. Like other botanical products from developing nations, vanilla plants have been a focus of bioprospecting, from taking cuttings out of the country to mapping the genome of valued plants.

Consumer interest in products for which the global commodity chain is used to demonstrate authenticity is part of the new market for vanilla. Knowledge of the origins of a given crop with a particular farmer, through a documented set of links between processors and distributors, adds both cachet and value to vanilla products. Because the small farmers who labor to grow vanilla bear nearly all of the risks of failed crops, decreasing demand, or bad weather yet receive the smallest part of the profits collected by exporters and distributors, there is also a growing interest in fair-trade vanilla. The vanilla orchid is such an environmentally sensitive plant that it fits well into models of ecologically sustainable development. With attention to issues of fair trade and the distribution of risks and profits from vanilla sales, vanilla is sometimes seen as a model for an integrated social and environmentally sustainable production. However, the emergence of multiple small producers in tropical nations that hope to provide revenues for small farmers threatens to again lower the market value of natural vanilla.

SEE ALSO *Agricultural Industry; Food; Industry; Monopoly; Trade*

BIBLIOGRAPHY

Ecott, Tim. 2005. *Vanilla: Travels in Search of the Ice Cream Orchid.* New York: Grove.

Gereffi, Gary, and Miguel Korzeniewicz, eds. 1993. *Commodity Chains and Global Capitalism.* Westport, CT: Greenwood.

Rain, Patricia. 2004. *Vanilla: The Cultural History of the World's Favorite Flavor and Fragrance.* New York: Tarcher/Penguin.

Jennifer L. Croissant

VANITY

SEE *Narcissism.*

VARIABILITY

Variation is one of the most important concepts in quantitative social science research. Associated terms include *statistical variation*, *statistical variability*, and *dispersion*. A dataset containing identical measurements has no variation, whereas a set containing widely dispersed measurements has high variation. There are several different summary statistics that describe, using a single value, the magnitude of the variation (variability) in a set of measurements. In other words, the summary statistics provide a synopsis of the degree to which a set of measurements lacks uniformity.

Among the most popular measures of variation are the *range*, the *mean absolute deviation*, the *variance*, and the *standard deviation*. Scholars use one or more of these measures to parsimoniously summarize the uniformity of a dataset rather than presenting the set in its entirety because presenting the entire set typically would require too much space and would be inconvenient to examine, particularly when the dataset is large. The disadvantage to using one or more of these summary statistics rather than presenting the entire set is the loss of information. The information loss occurs because summary statistics can be equal across datasets that contain different sequences of numbers. Each summary method attempts to provide important information about the degree to which the set lacks uniformity while minimizing the amount of information lost by not presenting the entire set of measurements. In general, the methods used to describe variability that present more information are more difficult to interpret for those without statistical training.

The measure of variability that most people consider the easiest to interpret is the *range*, which textbooks often define as the highest number in the set minus the lowest number. More commonly, scholars describe the range as the spread of numbers between the lowest and highest values. The set of numbers {1, 2, 8, 12, 15}, for example, has a range of 14, although many scholars would report the range as 1 through 15. Although the range is easy to understand, it is determined only by the two extreme values in each dataset, one or both of which may simply be errors in data entry. For this reason, the range contains less information than alternative variability measures.

Other methods that summarize the degree of variation in a set of measurements provide more information than the range but are more difficult to interpret. These alternatives describe in slightly different ways how far away each number in the set is from the mean of the measurements. The *mean absolute deviation* (or average absolute deviation) is one such summary statistic. After the range, it is the easiest to calculate and understand. The first step in calculating the mean absolute deviation is to subtract each number in the set from the set's mean. As the name implies, the absolute value of each deviation from the mean is subsequently summed, and the sum is then divided by the number of measurements to produce an average. In the example set {1, 2, 8, 12, 15}, the mean absolute deviation is 4.88.

The *variance* is a slightly more complex summary of variability. The preliminary step to calculating the variance is the same as calculating the mean absolute deviation—determine the distance of each measurement in the set from the set's mean. Subsequently, each deviation is then squared, and the sum of the squared deviation scores is then averaged. The variance of the example number set {1, 2, 8, 12, 15} is 29.8. When compared to the mean absolute deviation, the variance places more weight on values further from the mean, while not being as decidedly affected only by the two extreme values that are used to calculate the range. Scholars typically modify the variance formula when attempting to estimate the variance of a population of values based upon the variability of a sample of values drawn from the population. Instead of dividing the sum of deviation scores by the number of values in the sample, the sum of the scores is divided by the number of values minus one. This alteration provides a better estimate of the population's variance, because the variation observed in a sample of measurements is often less than the variation in the population from which the sample is drawn. For a large set of measurements, however, this added complexity makes little difference. Using this modified formula, the variance of the example number set is 37.3.

The most commonly used measure of variability in scholarly writing is the *standard deviation*, which is simply the square root of the variance. The standard deviation is typically denoted by the Greek letter sigma (σ) or the abbreviation *SD*. The standard deviation of the example set {1, 2, 8, 12, 15} is 6.1 when the modified formula noted above is used.

Scholars often attempt to explain the variability of one set of measurements (the dependent variable) by considering additional measurements (the independent variables) through the use of more complex statistical methods. For example, we can explain a proportion of the variation in human height by understanding that humans differ in biological sex. This can be visualized by considering that if we calculated the standard deviation of men and women separately, the variability of either group would be less than the overall variability in heights when we do not take gender into account. In other words, because we know that men tend to be taller than women, we can partially explain why the heights of individuals differ. If we wanted to understand more about the variability in human height, we would want to consider factors in addition to biological sex that are associated with height, such as age, parental height, ethnicity, and nutrition. When these explanatory (or independent) variables are found, we say that consideration of the independent variable(s) reduces the *unexplained* variation in the dependent variable.

Scholars rarely are able to explain all of the variation in any set of measurements, particularly in the social sciences. In fact, in the social sciences it is uncommon to explain more than half of the variation in any variable of interest.

SEE ALSO *Mean, The; Measurement; Mode, The; Regression Analysis; Social Science; Standard Deviation; Variance; Variation*

BIBLIOGRAPHY

Agresti, Alan, and Barbara Finlay. 1997. *Statistical Methods for the Social Sciences*. 3rd ed. Upper Saddle River, NJ: Prentice Hall.

Babbie, Earl R. 2006. *The Practice of Social Research*. 11th ed. Belmont, CA: Wadsworth.

Blalock, Hubert M., Jr. 1979. *Social Statistics*. Rev. 2nd ed. New York: McGraw-Hill.

Neuman, W. Lawrence. 2006. *Social Research Methods: Qualitative and Quantitative Approaches*. 6th ed. Boston: Allyn and Bacon.

Jeffrey Ackerman

VARIABLES, LATENT

Latent variables are commonly used in the social sciences. Whether it is psychological measures such as depression, or sociological concepts such as socioeconomic status, many variables cannot be directly measured. Factor analysis, latent class analysis, structural-equation models, error-in-variable models, and item-response theory illustrate models that incorporate latent variables.

The basic statistical concept of latent variables analysis is simple. These variables refer to an abstract level of analysis that cannot be directly observed and measured. In order to estimate the numerical values of the parameters from empirical data, we must use observable indicators to link the unobservable conceptual variables. An example of a formative model, the measurement model for socioeconomic status (SES), may make clearer this distinction between conceptually abstract and observable levels of analysis. A researcher may observe the variables income, educational level, and neighborhood as indicators (manifest variables) of SES (latent variable). Latent variable models provide a means to parse out measurement errors by combining across observed variables (using correlations among variables), and they allow for the estimation of complex causal models. Those measurement errors may include faulty respondent memory or systematic errors made in the survey process.

Latent variable analysis is parallel to factor analysis. In modern test-theory models, the relation between the latent variable and the observed score (item responses) is mathematically explicit. The form for the relation is a generalized regression function of the observed scores on the latent variable. This regression function may differ in form—a linear pattern for the factor models and a logistic one for the probabilistic models (Mellenbergh 1994). Researchers should decide whether to treat the underlying latent variable(s) as continuous or discrete. Further discussion can be found in Tom Heinen's demonstrations (1996).

In psychological studies, researchers may adopt a reflective model rather than a formative model because it is the standard conceptualization of measurement in psychology. This model specifies a pattern of covariation between the indicators, which can be fully explained by a regression on the latent variable. That is, the indicators are independent after conditioning on the latent variable (this is the assumption of local independence). An example of a reflective model in the latent variable of depression may use item responses on items like, "I am sad all the time," "I often feel helpless," and "I often feel my life is empty." In the reflective model of depression, it implies that a depressed person will be more inclined to answer the question affirmatively than a mentally healthy person. In ordinary language interpretation, depression comes first and "leads to" the item responses. In the mathematical term, it implies a regression of the indicators on the latent variable, while in the SES model (a formative model), the relationship between indicators and the latent variable is reversed. In other words, variation in the SES indicators now precedes variation in the latent variable; SES changes as a result of an increase in income and/or education and not the other way around.

In sum, latent variable theory signifies both realism and constructivism. Latent variables of the formative model are more a summary of the observed variables, while a reflective model implies entity realism about the latent variable. A causal implication between observable indicators and the latent variable thus is not a strong assumption. It is suggested that researchers be cautious when interpreting the relation in empirical studies (Borsboom et al. 2003).

SEE ALSO *Depression, Psychological; Factor Analysis; Realism; Regression Analysis; Social Science; Sociology; Structural Equation Models; Variables, Random*

BIBLIOGRAPHY

Borsboom, Denny, Gideon J. Mellenbergh, and Jaap van Heerden. 2003. The Theoretical Status of Latent Variables. *Psychological Review* 110 (2): 203–219.

Heinen, Tom. 1996. *Latent Class and Discrete Latent Trait Models: Similarities and Differences.* Thousand Oaks, CA: Sage.

Mellenbergh, Gideon J. 1994. Generalized Linear Item Response Theory. *Psychological Bulletin* 115: 300–307.

Cheng-Hsien Lin

VARIABLES, PREDETERMINED

This entry explains when a variable is a predetermined variable and how identification and inference require a variable to be predetermined. In social science, researchers often try to explain a phenomenon or an event using one or more explanatory variables. For example, how much an individual earns can be explained (to some degree) by his or her education level, and how much an individual consumes can be explained by his or her income and wealth. In many cases, a social scientist will formulate a model in which one variable is a function of another variable. For example, the following is a model that relates consumption to income and wealth:

$$\text{Consumption} = c_0 + c_1 \cdot \text{income} + c_2 \cdot \text{wealth}$$

where c_0, c_1, and c_2 are numbers. For example, $c_0 = \$10,000$, $c_1 = 0.7$, and $c_2 = 0.05$. This model implies that a one-dollar increase of income causes consumption to increase by $\$c_1$ (that is, consumption increases by seventy cents if income increases by one dollar). In order to estimate this model, we need to extend the model with an error term. This error term captures variables other than income or wealth. Let

Consumption $= c_0 + c_1 \cdot$ income $+ c_2 \cdot$ wealth $+ \varepsilon$

where the error term ε is assumed to be uncorrelated with income and wealth. If ε is assumed to be uncorrelated with income and wealth, then income and wealth are exogenous variables. No correlation means that we cannot use the regressors to predict the error term, that is, $E(\varepsilon|$income, wealth$) = 0$. If all the explanatory variables are exogenous variables, then the coefficients can be given a causal interpretation. Suppose that a social science researcher does not have access to data on wealth and, therefore, estimates the model

Consumption $= d_0 + d_1 \cdot$ income $+ u$.

Note that the new error term u consists of the old error term ε plus $c_2 \cdot$ wealth. Wealth and income are correlated so that income is correlated with u. Therefore, we cannot give a causal interpretation to d_1. In particular, an estimate of d_1 is likely to overstate the effect of income on consumption. Suppose that we have data on consumption and income for N individuals, $\{$Consumption$_i$, income$_i\}$ where $i = 1, \ldots, N$. Consider the least squares estimator for d_1. This estimator minimizes $\Sigma_i($Consumption$_i - d_0 - d_1 \cdot$ income$_i)^2$ with respect to d_0 and d_1. The least squares estimator for d_1 has the following form,

$$\hat{d}_1 = \frac{\Sigma_i (\text{income}_i - \overline{\text{income}}) \cdot \text{Consumption}_i}{\Sigma_i (\text{income}_i - \overline{\text{income}})^2}$$

$$= d_1 + \frac{\Sigma_i (\text{income}_i - \overline{\text{income}}) \cdot u_i}{\Sigma_i (\text{income}_i - \overline{\text{income}})^2}$$

where $\overline{\text{income}}$ denotes the mean of income, $\overline{\text{income}} = \frac{1}{N} \Sigma_i$ income$_i$. If income and the error term u are uncorrelated, then (1) the expectation of the last term, $\dfrac{\sum_i (\text{income}_i - \overline{\text{income}}) \cdot u_i}{\sum_i (\text{income}_i - \overline{\text{income}})^2}$, is zero so that $E(\hat{d}_1) = d_1$, and (2) this last term is very small for large N (the technical term is that $\dfrac{\sum_i (\text{income}_i - \overline{\text{income}}) \cdot u_i}{\sum_i (\text{income}_i - \overline{\text{income}})^2}$ converges in probability to zero so that $\hat{d}_1$ is a consistent estimator for d_1). However, in this example, the error term u_i depends on wealth. Wealth and income are correlated so that the assumption exogeneity (i.e., that all regressors are uncorrelated with the error term) is violated. As a result, the estimate for d_1 cannot be given a causal interpretation. In particular, the expectation of the estimator, $E\hat{d}_1$, will be larger than 0.7 because of the positive correlation between income and wealth.

The exogeneity assumption is very strong and can be relaxed somewhat. Consider the following model that describes the squared daily return of a stockmarket (e.g., the daily return of the Standard & Poor's 500 index),

Squared Return$_t = f_0 + f_1 \cdot$ Squared Return$_{t-1}$.

As before, this model can be extended to include an error term,

Squared Return$_t = f_0 + f_1 \cdot$ Squared Return$_{t-1} + v_t$.

Suppose there are T data points so that $t = 1, 2, \ldots, T$. Rather than assuming that the correlation between the squared return and the error term is zero, that is, that $E(v_t|$Squared Return$_1, \ldots,$ Squared Return$_T) = 0$ for all t, we now make the weaker assumption that, given the past values of the squared return, the expectation of the error term is zero, that is, $E(v_t|$Squared Return$_1, \ldots,$ Squared Return$_{t-1}) = 0$ for all t. Note that the past values of the squared return for error term v_t consist of the squared return of the first period, Squared Return$_1$, through period t $- 1$, Squared Return$_{t-1}$. Regressors that have the property that the error term has zero expectation given past values of the regressor are called *predetermined regressors* or *predetermined variables*. Consider the least squares regressor again to see how predeterminedness helps the estimator,

$$\hat{f}_1 = \frac{\Sigma_t (\text{Squared Return}_{t-1} - \overline{\text{Squared Return}}) \cdot \text{Consumption}_t}{\Sigma_t (\text{Squared Return}_{t-1} - \overline{\text{Squared Return}})^2}$$

$$= f_1 + \frac{\Sigma_t \text{Squared Return}_{t-1} \cdot v_t - \overline{\text{Squared Return}} \, \Sigma_t v_t}{\Sigma_t (\text{Squared Return}_{t-1} - \overline{\text{Squared Return}})^2}$$

$$= f_1 + \frac{T}{\Sigma_t (\text{Squared Return}_{t-1} - \overline{\text{Squared Return}})^2} \frac{\Sigma_t \text{Squared Return}_{t-1} \cdot v_t}{T}$$

$$- \frac{T}{\Sigma_t (\text{Squared Return}_{t-1} - \overline{\text{Squared Return}})^2} \frac{\overline{\text{Squared Return}} \, \Sigma_t v_t}{T}.$$

The term $\dfrac{\sum_t \text{Squared Return}_{t-1} \cdot v_t}{T}$ is zero in expectation since $E(v_t|$Squared Return$_1, \ldots,$ Squared Return$_{t-1}) = 0$. Moreover, for large T, this term, as well as $\dfrac{\overline{\text{Squared Return}} \sum_t v^t}{T}$, will be small so that the estimate $\hat{f}_1$ is close to the true value f_1. This model of squared returns is an ARCH (auto regressive conditional heteroscedasticity) model and can be used to study volatility. In particular, a large decline of the stockmarket in period $t - 1$ means that the stockmarket will be more volatile in period t. Tim Bollerslev, Robert Engle, and Daniel Nelson (1994) discuss other ARCH models.

An endogenous regressor has the property that $E(v_t|$Squared Return$_1, \ldots,$ Squared Return$_{t-1}) \neq 0$. Thus, an endogenous regressor cannot be a predetermined regressor. Endogeneity (i.e., having an endogenous regressor) occurs if there is a third unobserved variable that affects both the regressor and the error term. For example, how much an individual earns can be partly explained by his or her education. Data on earnings and education levels are not hard to collect, but reliable data on intelligence are difficult to obtain. For this reason, earnings are usually regressed on the education so that intelligence is part of the error term. However, intelligence will also affect education levels so that the regressor education and the error term are correlated. In other words, there is an unobserved variable that affects both the regressor and the error term so that $E(v_t|\text{Squared Return}_1, \dots, \text{Squared Return}_{t-1}) \neq 0$. Therefore, least squares cannot be used to estimate the effect of education on income. Econometricians have developed another technique, namely, two-stage least squares.

In nonlinear models, a slightly different definition of exogeneity and predeterminedness is sometimes used. In particular, the regressors are exogenous if the regressors and the error term are statistically independently distributed. That is, if the density of the error term conditional on the regressors, $p(\text{error term}|\text{regressors})$ is the same as the unconditional density of the error term, $p(\text{error term})$. Similarly, the regressors are predetermined if the density of the error term of period t conditional on the past regressors, $p(\text{error term}_t|\text{regressors}_1, \dots, \text{regressor}_{t-1})$, is the same as the unconditional density of the error term, $p(\text{error term}_t)$ for all t. Robert De Jong and Tiemen Woutersen (2006) use these definitions when they estimate a model to predict monetary policy.

SEE ALSO *Autoregressive Models; Causality; Econometric Decomposition; Identification Problem; Probability; Regression; Regression Analysis; Statistics*

BIBLIOGRAPHY

Bollerslev, Tim, Robert F. Engle, and Daniel B. Nelson. 1994. ARCH Models. In *Handbook of Econometrics*, Vol. 4, eds. Robert. F. Engle and Daniel McFadden, 2961–3031. Amsterdam: North Holland.

De Jong, Robert, and Tiemen Woutersen. 2006. Dynamic Time Series Binary Choice. Working Paper. Baltimore: MD: Johns Hopkins University.

Greene, William H. 2002. *Econometric Analysis*. 5th ed. Upper Saddle River, NJ: Prentice Hall.

Stock, James H., and Mark W. Watson. 2006. *Introduction to Econometrics*. 2nd ed. Boston: Addison-Wesley.

Tiemen Woutersen

VARIABLES, RANDOM

A *random variable* is a real-valued function that maps a sample space into the real line. The sample space, denoted by $\Omega = \{\omega\}$, is the set of possible outcomes of some chance phenomenon (e.g., acts of individuals, an experiment). To illustrate, consider the familiar example of tossing a coin. There are only two possible outcomes; hence $\Omega = \{H, T\}$. Here, the symbols H and T are used to denote the outcomes "head" and "tails." A random variable Y can be defined by setting $Y = 1$ if H occurs, or $Y = 0$ if T occurs. The use of the word *if* here is important; if a coin is actually tossed, "heads" is observed, and $Y = 1$ is recorded, then this value is a realization of the random variable Y. The number 1 is not random but is simply a number. The variable Y is considered random unless it is observed. If the coin is "fair," then the probability that $Y = 1$ (on a toss that has not been observed yet) equals the probability that $Y = 0$; both probabilities equal 0.5. Alternatively, one could also define a random variable X, equal to -1 if heads occurs, and equal to 1 if tails occurs; in fact, any pair of distinct values could be used to define a random variable describing the outcome of a coin toss.

The concept of random variables was introduced by Pafnuty Chebyshev (1821–1894), who in the mid-nineteenth century defined a random variable as "a real variable which can assume different values with different probabilities" (Spanos 1999, p. 35). The concept is closely tied to the theory of probability, which has been studied since the seventeenth century. However, the modern understanding of random variables and their relation to probability arrived more recently, dating to the work by Andrey Kolmogorov (1933).

Random variables may be either discrete or continuous. In the discrete case, the elements of Ω are countable, although perhaps infinite in number. In the continuous case, elements of Ω are not countable, implying that there are infinitely many elements. The elements ω_j of Ω are called *elementary* events; collections of the elementary events are called simply *events*.

To formalize the definition of random variables, first consider the case where Ω contains a finite number of elements. An event A is a subset of Ω, that is, $A \subseteq \Omega$. The complement of A (with respect to Ω) is defined by $\bar{A} = \Omega - A$. Then Ω is the certain event, while $\emptyset = \bar{\Omega}$ is the impossible, or null event. Let $\mathfrak{F}$ be the set of all events (including Ω and $\emptyset$) defined on the sample space $\Omega = \{\omega_1, \dots, \omega_m\}$; $\mathfrak{F}$ is a *field* in the sense that it is closed under the formation of unions and complements (i.e., if $A, B \in \mathfrak{F}$ then $A \cup B \in \mathfrak{F}$; if $A \in \mathfrak{F}$ then $\bar{A} \in \mathfrak{F}$). Then the probability of the event $A \in \mathfrak{F}$, denoted $P(A)$, is a set function onto the closed interval $[0,1]$ satisfying

i. $0 \leq P(A) \leq 1$ for all $A \in \mathfrak{F}$;

ii. $P(\Omega) = 1$; and

iii. $P(A \cup B) = P(A) + P(B)$ if $A \cap B = \emptyset$.

The triple $(\Omega, \mathfrak{F}, P)$ is called a *probability space.*

If Ω contains infinitely many elements (either countable or non-countable), $\mathfrak{F}$ is required to be a σ-field, meaning that $\mathfrak{F}$ is closed under the formation of complements and unions of *countably* many events. In addition, the set function P must be *countably additive* so that condition (iii) above becomes

iii. If $A_1, A_2, \ldots$ are disjoint members of the σ-field

$$\mathfrak{F}, \text{ then } P(\bigcup_{j=1}^{\infty} A_j \sum_{j=1}^{\infty}) = P(A_j).$$

With the preceding concepts, a formal definition is possible. Suppose $(\Omega, \mathfrak{F}, P)$ is a probability space in which Ω is not necessarily countable. Then a random variable Y defined on this space is a function mapping Ω into the real line such that the set $\{\omega \mid Y(\omega) \leq y\} \in \mathfrak{F}$ for every real y. Hence for each $\omega \in \Omega$, $Y(\omega)$ is a real number.

Many examples of random variables appear in the social sciences. Linear regressions involve an attempt to explain the meaning of a continuous random variable; the error term in such equations is a random variable with 0 mean, reflecting statistical noise. Schmidt and Witte (1989) considered the (random, continuous) time that elapses between a criminal's release from prison and his subsequent conviction for another crime. Nakosteen and Zimmer (1980) examined not only workers' incomes (continuous) but also their decisions to move to a location or to stay at their current location (discrete). Others have considered counts of durable goods purchased by households; decisions of graduating high-school students to continue their education in college, enlist in the military, or enter the labor force; and other issues.

SEE ALSO *Probability; Statistical Noise*

BIBLIOGRAPHY

Kolmogorov, Andrey N. 1933. Grundbegriffe der Wahrscheinlichkeitrechnung. *Ergebnisse der Mathematik* 2 (3). Translated as *Foundations of the Theory of Probability* by N. Morrison. New York: Chelsea, 1956.

Nakosteen, Robert, and Michael Zimmer. 1980. Migration and Income: The Question of Self-selection. *Southern Economic Journal* 46: 840–851.

Schmidt, Peter, and Ann Dryden Witte. 1989. Predicting Criminal Recidivism Using Split Population Survival Time Models. *Journal of Econometrics* 40: 141–159.

Spanos, Aris. 1999. *Probability Theory and Statistical Inference: Econometric Modeling with Observational Data*. Cambridge and New York: Cambridge University Press.

Paul W. Wilson

VARIANCE

The variance is a measure of variability among scores. In describing any set of data, one uses three characteristics: the form of the distribution, the mean or central tendency, and the variability. All three are required because they are generally independent of one another. In other words, the mean indicates nothing about the variability.

Variability is a characteristic of all measures. In the social sciences the people or groups that are studied may be exposed to the same treatment or conditions but will show different responses to that treatment or those conditions. In other words, all the scores of the people would be different. The goal of the scientist is to explain why the scores are different. One can think of a score as having two parts: the mean and a deviation from the mean (Hays 1973). If everyone were exactly the same, the variability among scores (deviations from the mean) would be zero.

In manipulating conditions or treatments it is possible to explain different scores between groups by looking at the variability between the groups and also within each group. If the groups are different enough, it is said that they are statistically significantly different. Statistical significance is determined by looking at the probability (odds) that a difference could have occurred by chance. One analyzes the data by looking at the variability of the data and breaking down that variability into its component parts.

There are several methods for measuring variability among scores. The range is the difference between the highest and lowest scores and is limited because it is based on only two scores. It is not very useful because it is influenced easily by extremes among the scores. The mean deviation score sometimes is used as a measure of variability but also is limited in terms of its usefulness in additional mathematical calculations. The standard deviation is used commonly; it is simply the square root of the variance.

The variance is the most useful of these methods. It is defined as the sum of the squared deviations from the mean divided by the number of squared deviations. The equation for the variance is $var = \dfrac{\Sigma(X - M)^2}{N}$, where var is the variance, X is a raw score, M is the mean of the scores, X–M represents the deviation of a score from the mean, and N is the number of scores. Many different symbols have been used to represent the elements of this equation, but in all cases the variance is the average of the squared deviations from the mean.

A simple numerical example can illustrate the variance. There is a small set of five scores: 8, 7, 6, 5, and 4. The sum of those scores is 30, and the mean is 6. The numerator in the variance equation is called the sum of the deviation scores squared (often abbreviated SS for sum of squares). One takes each score and subtracts the mean (i.e., $8 - 6 = 2$; $7 - 6 = 1$; $6 - 6 = 0$; $5 - 6 = -1$; and $4 - 6 = -2$). Next, the deviation scores are squared to eliminate the minus signs ($2^2 = 4$; $1^2 = 1$; $0^2 = 0$; $-1^2 = 1$; and $-2^2 = 4$). Then one simply adds the deviation scores squared (4; 1; 0; 1; and 4) to get the SS, which is equal to 10. Finally, the variance is calculated by dividing the SS by the number of scores (N), which in this example is $10/5 = 2$. The variance for this small set of five scores is 2.

This example illustrates an important point: The variance is not a clear indicator of variability. Consider the scores in the example above as inches. The variance is 2 squared inches. How would one make sense out of a variability of squared inches? In the social sciences how would one interpret a variability of squared IQ, conformity, opportunity costs, and so on? The variance has no simple or particularly useful explanation in everyday language or in the technical jargon of the social sciences.

However, the variance is an essential mathematical step in describing parametric variability. The variance has the advantage of being additive, something that is not true for its square root, the standard deviation (Games and Klare 1967). This means that in working with more than one group and looking for a measure of pooled or average variability among the groups, one can add variances. This is done in many inferential parametric statistical tests.

The variance is an essential element of much social science data analysis but is not easily interpretable. The standard deviation, which is the square root of the variance, is used commonly to provide a more readily understandable indicator of variability.

SEE ALSO *Regression; Regression Analysis; Standard Deviation; Statistics; Test Statistics; Variation*

BIBLIOGRAPHY

Games, Paul A., and George R. Klare. 1967. *Elementary Statistics: Data Analysis for the Behavioral Sciences.* New York: McGraw-Hill.

Hays, William Lee. 1973. *Statistics for the Social Sciences.* 2nd ed. New York: Holt, Rinehart and Winston.

Samuel K. Rock Jr.

VARIANCE-COVARIANCE MATRIX

The variance-covariance matrix is a convenient expression of statistics in data describing patterns of variability and covariation. The variance-covariance matrix is widely used both as a summary statistic of data and as the basis for key concepts in many multivariate statistical models.

VERBAL DEFINITION

The variance-covariance matrix, often referred to as Cov(), is an average cross-products matrix of the columns of a data matrix in deviation score form. A deviation score matrix is a rectangular arrangement of data from a study in which the column average taken across rows is zero. The variance-covariance matrix expresses patterns of variability as well as covariation across the columns of the data matrix. In most contexts the (vertical) columns of the data matrix consist of variables under consideration in a study and the (horizontal) rows represent individual records. Variance-covariance matrices may, however, be calculated from any pairwise combination of individuals, measurement occasions, or variables. Even this by no means exhausts the possible covariance matrices that may be considered for a statistical model (see Cattell [1988] for an extensive list of the possibilities involving several dimensions).

MATHEMATICAL DEFINITION

If k variables are assumed in a study and letting X denote a raw score version of the data matrix and μ_k a vector of means for the variables under consideration, the covariance matrix is defined as $E(X'X) - \mu_k'\mu_k$, where $E()$ denotes the expectation operator. If the columns of X are centered to a mean of 0, the variance-covariance matrix is more conveniently expressed as $E(x'x)$. Within linear algebra, covariance matrices belong to the class of matrices known as nonnegative-definite symmetric matrices.

CALCULATION

The sample covariance matrix can be calculated as $1/n * 1_k * (X'X - \bar{\mu}_k'\bar{\mu}_k)$ if raw score matrix X is used, $\bar{\mu}_k$ denotes a vector of sample means, and where ' denotes the transpose operator. If data are expressed in column-centered form, $x = (X - \bar{X})$, Cov(x) is calculated as $1/n * 1_k * x'x$, where 1_k denotes a k-column vector of 1s and n denotes the number of observations. The sample variance-covariance matrix, although efficient, is a biased estimate of population variability. As a result, the estimated population covariance matrix divides by the reciprocal of $n - 1$ of n. If the x matrix is further transformed to have a variance of 1 (usually termed Z_x), the resulting sample Cov() matrix is known as a *correlation matrix*. If the X matrix is retained in raw score form and an additional unit column is added to the data, $1/n * 1_k * X'X$ is referred to as an *average sum of squares* and *cross-products* matrix, a data summary convenient for models in which overall elevation as well as patterns of covariation are of interest, as often occurs in longitudinal studies of growth.

PROPERTIES

The Cov() matrix has as many rows and columns as the columns of *X* and is symmetric (meaning that the value associated with the *j* th row and *k* th column in Cov() is equal to the value in the *k* th row and *j* th column). Diagonal elements of Cov() represent the variances of the column variables; off-diagonal elements represent covariances or, if based on Z_x, correlation coefficients.

ADDITIONAL MATHEMATICAL PROPERTIES

Covariance of a sum: Assuming three matrices *x*1, *x*2, and *y*,

$$\text{Cov}(x1 + x2, y) = \text{Cov}(x1,y) + \text{Cov}(x2,y).$$

Covariances involving matrix products: Assuming two conformable matrices *A* and *B*,

$$\text{Cov}(AX,BX) = A\,\text{Cov}(X,X)B'$$ where ' denotes the transpose operator.

USES

As mentioned before, covariance matrices, by themselves, are compact summaries of the variability and covariation present in data. More generally, the covariance matrix and vector of means constitute sufficient statistics for models that assume a multivariate normal distribution. As such, the covariance matrix may be used in lieu of the raw data in calculating a number of multivariate statistical models, such as confirmatory and exploratory factor analysis (assuming the diagonal of the matrix is appropriately adjusted by the estimated communality), path analysis, or other general linear models, including the special cases of multiple regression, analysis of variance, and repeated measures analysis of variance or MANOVA. In many statistical models, finding an optimal basis for representing the covariance matrix in a compact fashion is of primary interest. Such reduced or optimal bases are referred to as *principal components analysis* (PCA), or in image processing as the *Karhunen-Loève transform*, which has time series applications within psychology (Molenaar and Boomsma 1987). Covariance matrices alone are not sufficient statistics for other more sophisticated models, such as those involving weighted least squares, sampling weights, or other categorical or distributional adjustments to reflect the dichotomous, polytomous, or other distributional characteristics of the variables under consideration.

SEE ALSO *Classical Statistical Analysis; Covariance; Econometric Decomposition; Inverse Matrix; Least Squares, Ordinary; Matrix Algebra; Ordinary Least Squares Regression; Path Analysis; Regression; Regression Analysis; Statistics*

BIBLIOGRAPHY

Cattell, Raymond B. 1988. The Meaning and Strategic Use of Factor Analysis. In *Handbook of Multivariate Experimental Psychology*, eds. John R. Nesselroade and Raymond B. Cattell, 174–243. 2nd ed. New York: Plenum.

Molenaar, Peter C. M., and Dorrett I. Boomsma. 1987. The Genetic Analysis of Repeated Measures. II: The Karhunen-Loève Expansion. *Behavior Genetics* 17 (3): 229–242.

Phillip K. Wood

VARIATION

Variation refers to the degree of dispersion, diversity, or inequality in a distribution: the extent to which observations of an attribute are similar to or different from one another. Applications of variation in the social sciences include income inequality, the degree to which incomes are concentrated among a few households or spread broadly across a population, and religious diversity, which describes whether a single religion dominates the cultural landscape or multiple religions exist side by side.

COMPONENTS AND MEASURES OF VARIATION

Popular quantitative measures of variation include the following:

Range : The difference between extreme values.

Variance : The sum of the squared distances from each observation to the mean divided by the number of observations (for a population) or divided by one less than the number of observations (for a sample).

Standard deviation : The square root of the variance. The standard deviation is the average distance between a set of observations and the mean.

Coefficient of variation : The standard deviation divided by the mean. Graphically the coefficient of variation describes the peakedness of a unimodal frequency distribution. Because the coefficient of variation scales to the mean, this measure often is used in comparative analysis.

Gini coefficient : Bounded by zero and one, where lower values correspond to greater equality, the Gini coefficient is defined as twice the area between the Lorenz curve and an equality diagonal. (To construct a Lorenz curve, one ranks the observations from lowest to highest on the variable of interest and then plots the cumulative proportion of the population against the cumulative proportion of the variable of interest.)

Theil's T statistic: Particularly appropriate for hierarchical, nested, or aggregate data, Theil's T statistic is the product of the population share of each observation, the quotient of the observation and the population average, and the natural logarithm of the quotient of the observation and the population average, summed over all observations. Unlike the Gini coefficient and the coefficient of variation, Theil's T statistic is sensitive to the number of underlying observations.

In addition to these widely used metrics, researchers sometimes create original measures to isolate a particular type of variation. For example, in *American Apartheid* (1993), Douglas Massey and Nancy Denton develop five dimensions of variation to identify racial "hypersegregation" in U.S. metropolitan areas.

Whereas measures of central tendency, such as the mean, median, and mode, describe the center of gravity of a distribution, measures of variation express how concentrated the observations are around the average. Both types of measures are necessary to describe most social science data sets. For instance, with regard to the test scores in a school, the median expresses the score of a typical student. Schools desire high median scores. However, a high level of variation in test scores indicates that some students excel, while others lag behind their peers. This could suggest differences among students in family resources, native intelligence, or other characteristics over which a school has little control, but high variation also can result from inconsistent teacher quality or administrative choices to overallocate resources to high-achieving students and/or underallocate resources to low-achieving students.

The ease of computing variation can hide the difficulties in its interpretation. Although variation reflects differences among individuals, it is a property of a group, not an individual. Correlation between variation and another group-level variable does not imply a corresponding relationship across individuals; improperly asserting that it does is an instance of the ecological fallacy. Similarly variation is relative. A measure of variation can only be described as high or low in comparison to the variation of another group, the same group in a different time period, or a predefined standard value.

USE OF VARIATION IN SOCIAL SCIENCES

Whether variation in a particular attribute is preferred is an issue of context and perspective. A high degree of variation may be preferable, as in the case of racial diversity within communities, in which variation may imply integration rather than segregation. A low degree of variation may be preferable; for instance, a good medical intervention consistently will improve the health of those who receive treatment and have few side effects. Alternatively, preference for high or low variation may depend on one's theoretical or ethical perspective. For instance, one view of income inequality is that higher levels of variation reflect a more efficient economic system that rewards hard work (or talent) and punishes laziness (or ineptitude). An alternative view is that income inequality suggests nondemocratic use of monopoly power or outright oppression of the poor.

One way to reduce subjective judgment is to view variation as a predictor variable rather than an outcome variable. An example of such an application is research that relates economic inequality to population health. In a 1975 article Samuel Preston popularized this issue by pointing out an inherent nonlinearity in the relationship of health to income. For individuals with low incomes, an increase in economic resources will be accompanied by significant health gains, but as an individual's income rises to the top of the distribution, subsequent increases in income will yield diminishing returns in terms of health. Thus at least among nations with high average incomes, lower variation of incomes should be associated with better health. Although subsequent scholarship seemed to confirm this correlation, there is debate over causation. Some scholars assert that inequality leads to stress and stress leads to poor health. Other researchers point to mediating factors, such as race and access to care, to explain the correlation between inequality and health.

Individuals with low incomes are more likely to have poor health, and individuals with high incomes are more likely to have good health, on average. Thus the suggestion that an increase in inequality that results from the poor getting poorer would decrease population health seems reasonable. However, advocates of the inequality hypothesis also must explain why an inequality increase that occurs when the rich get richer also would reduce health. Until they address this seeming paradox, the burden of proof lies with those who claim that income variation is an operative factor for health. This exemplifies the central challenge in using variation in social science analysis; to be a useful tool, variation must be both measurable and meaningful.

SEE ALSO *Gini Coefficient; Standard Deviation*

BIBLIOGRAPHY

Kachigan, Sam Kash. 1991. *Multivariate Statistical Analysis: A Conceptual Introduction*. 2nd ed. New York: Radius.

Massey, Douglas S., and Nancy A. Denton. 1993. *American Apartheid: Segregation and the Making of the Underclass.* Cambridge, MA: Harvard University Press.

Mullahy, John, Stephanie Robert, and Barbara Wolfe. 2004. Health, Income, and Inequality. In *Social Inequality*, ed. Kathryn Neckerman, 523–544. New York: Russell Sage Foundation.

Preston, Samuel H. 1975. The Changing Relation between Mortality and Level of Economic Development. *Population Studies* 29: 231–248.

J. Travis Hale

VASECTOMY

SEE *Sterilization, Human.*

VATICAN, THE

The term *Vatican*, like the word *Washington*, has multiple meanings. Geographically, it is one of the Seven Hills of Rome, located west of the Tiber River. Politically, it is an independent state within the city of Rome. Ecclesiologically, it is the bureaucracy that serves the pope in governing the Catholic Church.

With the collapse of the Roman Empire in the West, the people of Italy turned to the Church for leadership when Constantinople was unable to defend them against the barbarian invasions. Even before the Papal States formally existed, popes were raising armies, maintaining public order, and providing government services. By 590, Gregory the Great was the de facto ruler of Italy. With Lombards attacking from the north and a weak and unsympathetic imperial government in the south, Pope Zacharias backed Pepin as king of the Franks. In exchange, Pepin defended Rome and presented the pope with the Papal States in 773. His son, Charlemagne, was crowned in Rome by Pope Leo III in 800, establishing the Church as a major source of political legitimacy in Europe.

For the next 1,100 years, through diplomacy and war, the popes fought to preserve or expand the Papal States, which they saw as the only way to maintain the political and financial independence of the Church in a precapitalistic agrarian society. The power and wealth of the Papal States, however, corrupted the papacy as much as it protected it. The loss of the Papal States in 1870 proved to be an unanticipated blessing for the Church because it freed the papacy to pursue its spiritual goals without having to worry about governing 16,000 square miles of Italy. The normalization of relations between the Vatican and Italy in 1929 left the pope with 108.7 acres.

Under international law, the Vatican is a sovereign state headed by the pope, who has supreme legislative, executive, and judicial authority. It has its own army (Swiss Guard), flag, passports, stamps, post office, Internet domain extension (.va, as in vatican.va.), and the right to mint a limited number of coins. Criminals are normally turned over to Italy for prosecution and punishment. Citizenship is given on a temporary basis to about 500 people working for the Vatican, about half of whom are members of the Vatican diplomatic service. Another 100 are members of the Swiss Guard. The governance of Vatican City is delegated to the Pontifical Commission for the Vatican State (five cardinals), which is headed by a cardinal president appointed by the pope. Under the president, a lay delegate acts as a city manager and runs the day-to-day affairs of Vatican City, which employs about 1,300 people for administration, maintenance, police, stores, and its world-class museums. The Vatican City budget is normally in the black even though it has no taxes because of income from the museums, post office, supermarket, gasoline station, and other stores.

Located in the Vatican is the Instituto per le Opere di Religione, commonly known as the IOR or Vatican Bank, founded in 1887 after the fall of the Papal States as a way of keeping Vatican finances independent of Italian control. Its depositors are now limited to the Vatican agencies, Vatican employees, dioceses, religious orders, and other Church entities. Although in the past some depositors used it to launder money, since 1993 the bank has cooperated with police investigations. Like any bank, it invests its deposits; the profits are used at the discretion of the pope. Its involvement in one investment scandal caused it to pay $244 million to Banco Ambrosiano creditors. This scandal led to the reform of the bank, which is now governed by a committee of cardinals whose principal function is to select a supervisory council of financial experts from around the world to supervise the bank and hire its lay director-general. No financial report is made public.

The Vatican Curia is the bureaucracy that helps the pope in his ministry as head of the Catholic Church (he has a separate bureaucracy for the diocese of Rome). The oldest bureaucracy in the world, it is shaped more by history than organizational theory and still has many of the trappings of a medieval court. It has about 2,500 employees. The professional staff (mostly priests) is recruited from all over the world, but the support staff is mostly Italian. It is financed by donations and income from investments. The official language is Latin, but the working language is Italian. Most offices have people who can communicate in the other major European languages.

The top official under the pope is the secretary of state, who is more like a prime minister than a U.S. secretary of state. The secretary of state has two offices: the

First Section for General Affairs, headed by the *sostituto* (substitute), and the Second Section for Relations with States, headed by the secretary for relations with states. Although there are numerous exceptions, the principal work of the First Section is internal Church affairs, while the Second Section deals with international issues. Both sections are relatively small; for example, the Second Section has only about forty people.

The First Section is divided into language desks, with the *sostituto* acting as the pope's chief of staff. Practically all paper going to and from the pope goes through this office, making the *sostituto* one of the most powerful men in the Vatican, although he is not a cardinal.

The Second Section, divided into country desks, is the Vatican's foreign ministry, with the secretary acting as the foreign minister. Practically every nation in the world sends an ambassador to the Holy See (the major exception is China). The Vatican stresses (and legal scholars agree) that diplomatic relations are with the Holy See and that the pope would have the right to them under international law even if the State of Vatican City (*Stato della Città del Vaticano*) ceased to exist. Vatican foreign policy has supported international cooperation through the United Nations, the peaceful resolution of international disputes, human rights, disarmament, and aid to refugees and poor countries, while opposing international financing of abortion. But its principal concern is the promotion of religious freedom and the good of the Church. Historically it has attempted to protect the rights of local churches through international treaties (concordats) with countries.

Other dicasteries (offices) of the curia are organized as congregations or councils. They are committees of prelates (some working in Rome, others heading dioceses around the world), which meet under the leadership of a prefect (for congregations) or president (for councils). The prefects and presidents also head the staffs of their congregations and councils, which do the day-to-day work of the curia. The older congregations tend to deal with internal Church affairs: doctrine, liturgy, Eastern (non-Latin) Catholic churches, canonization of saints, appointment of bishops, evangelization, clergy, members of religious orders, and Catholic education. The newer councils are a mixed bag of offices dealing with issues that have concerned the Church since Vatican II: laity, ecumenism, family, justice and peace, health-care workers, canon law, communications, culture, and interreligious dialogue. Most staffs are quite small. They relate to Catholic dioceses around the world either directly or through the Vatican diplomatic representatives (nuncios) in each country.

The Congregation for the Doctrine of the Faith (formerly the Inquisition) is the most powerful office. It must review and approve the doctrinal content of documents from other offices before publication. It also attempts to control the teaching and writing done by Catholic theologians around the world. The congregations for bishops and evangelization of peoples propose names to the pope for episcopal appointments around the world, in a process that screens for orthodoxy and loyalty to the pope.

From at least the time of Constantine, the papacy has been an instrument of political legitimacy in Europe. This has given the Church political power, which it often used for good—to mediate disputes, insist on the observance of law, and protect the powerless—but sometimes used for evil—to suppress heresy and enrich itself. This power and wealth, however, made it a target of political intervention, whether imperial, feudal, or totalitarian. Beginning with Leo XIII in the nineteenth century, the Church began developing a social teaching that was more appropriate for a pluralistic democratic world. The contemporary political role of the papacy was epitomized in John Paul II (1920–2005), who through his support of Solidarity and the Polish freedom movement began the landslide that wiped out communism in Eastern Europe and ultimately the Soviet Union. He was also an outspoken defender of religious freedom, human rights, refugees, migrants, the environment, and the unborn. He spoke of the responsibility of the rich to help the poor and advocated forgiveness of Third World debt. He opposed both Persian Gulf wars. He was critical of unbridled capitalism and a culture of individualism, greed, and consumerism. Although lacking the political skills of John Paul, Benedict XVI (b. 1927) has not strayed far from his foreign policy positions.

Papal opposition to birth control and abortion have been controversial. While most Catholic moral theologians oppose abortion, a number consider making it illegal a debatable issue. John Paul did not shrink from giving Communion to pro-choice Italian politicians, although this became an issue for a few U.S. bishops in 2004. Most theologians, priests, laypeople, and even some bishops do not accept the pope's teaching on birth control, with the result that many Catholic countries such as Italy and Spain now have falling birthrates. Also controversial both inside and outside the Church has been the questioning of condoms as a means of fighting AIDS. This dissent on Church teaching led the Vatican to investigate, reprimand, and silence many priest theologians. It also led to the appointment of bishops known for their loyalty and support for Church teaching. But with the exception of abortion, birth control, and condoms, the Vatican's position of international issues has been far to the left of most American politicians.

SEE ALSO *Politics; Religion; Roman Catholic Church*

BIBLIOGRAPHY

Beal, John P., James A. Coriden, and Thomas J. Green, eds. 2000. *New Commentary on the Code of Canon Law.* New York: Paulist Press.

Graham, Robert. 1959. *Vatican Diplomacy: A Study of Church and State on the International Plane.* Princeton, NJ: Princeton University Press.

John Paul II. June 28, 1988. *Pastor Bonus.* Vatican City: Apostolic Constitution. http://www.vatican.va/holy_father/john_paul_ii/apost_constit utions/documents/hf_jp-ii_apc_19880628_pastor-bonus-index_en.html.

Reese, Thomas J. 1996. *Inside the Vatican: The Politics and Organization of the Catholic Church.* Cambridge, MA: Harvard University Press.

Thomas J. Reese S.J.

VEBLEN, THORSTEIN
1857–1929

Thorstein Bunde Veblen, an economist and sociologist (social critic and social and cultural theorist), was born to a Norwegian immigrant couple and grew up in rural Minnesota. He attended Yale University for graduate work in philosophy, where he met the sociologist William Graham Sumner (1840–1910). Upon graduation Veblen was not able to find academic employment. He eventually went to Cornell University to study economics, then taught at the University of Chicago (1891), later moving to Stanford University (1906), the University of Missouri (1911), and the New School for Social Research (1919). Veblen's troubles with university administrations stemmed from his disregard for the norms of dress for "proper professors," his uncommon living conditions (he lived in a shack of his own construction at one point), his classroom presentations (he often spoke softly in monotone or displayed unorthodox behavior), and his unconcealed extra-marital affairs. At one point in his career he taught a class entirely in the Icelandic language to make the point that modern education was useless. Veblen saw himself as outside both Norwegian and American cultures and specifically asked those who knew him not to write his biography after his death.

Veblen posited certain human instinctual drives (mediated by cultural norms) that allow for technological and social advance, social organization, and social evolution: the instinct of workmanship, which is the most productive instinct for well-being, being an underlying creative impulse to manipulate the world with productive labor; the instinct of parenting, which leads to a concern for the well-being of others and an identification with

community; and the instinct of idle curiosity, which leads to the development of knowledge. His use of the word *instinct* does not correspond to standard understandings from biology. Rather, he used *instincts* as socially refracted modifications of desire (Veblen 1914).

SOCIETY

Influenced by Darwin's theory of evolution, Veblen was interested in the historical and evolutionary development of society and argued that humans interpret the world using categories based in biographic and historically shaped "habits of the mind," which in turn are the basis for cultural norms passed on through socialization. Activities formed around these norms Veblen called "institutions," with changes in productive activity leading to changes in society (Veblen 1914).

Veblen formulated a scale of three evolutionary stages of society based on changes in material forms of production: "savagery" (a peaceable, isolated, and stable society); "barbarianism" (a warlike and conquest-oriented society, hierarchical and dominated by religion, with distinct predatory and industrious classes and a surplus of wealth); and "civilization" (a modern, economically developed society that is rational and instrumental, with machine technology, mass production, and a high division of labor). For Veblen, the business class in modern society is "predatory" in that its livelihood is based on the acquisition of personal wealth and competitive capitalist profit making (Veblen 1914). In other words, Veblen labeled modernity as a form of latter-day barbarism.

Veblen is most famous for his book *The Theory of the Leisure Class* (1899), which some view as a satire of American elite society but others interpret as a "coded" social criticism that was a product of his marginal social status (Riesman 1995). In either case, it establishes Veblen's commitment to the idea that culture shapes economics, and as opposite from Marxist-derived, where Marx thought economics shaped society, it is an alternate analysis of society based on an understanding of production and consumption, material life, and economic stratification. In it Veblen shows the social and cultural causes and effects of economic changes (or economic evolution) and includes class, gender, and ethnicity in his economic analysis. He uses a materialistic approach in that he analyzes the changes in habit of productive activity.

Veblen's social analysis draws a distinction between two classes of people. The first, the privileged, elite class of businesspeople and captains of industry, survive through the parasitic exploitation of the productive class and engage in pecuniary activities that detract from the further evolution of society. This is his critique of capitalism, which includes an attack on industrialists he labeled as "robber barons." Veblen viewed this class as militant and predatory because its members do not engage in productive work; instead, they live off of the innovations of other people. The second class, made up of industrious workers, engineers, and inventors, produces both the wealth and useful goods for society. This class is focused on the well-being of society as a whole and includes women. Veblen tended to associate predatory culture with patriarchy and peaceful, productive culture with women—in this sense, David Riesman regards Veblen as an early feminist. In a capitalistic society within an economic price system, individuals are rewarded not for creative entrepreneurship but for ideals of competition, which for Veblen leads to "sabotage" rather than the advancement of the ideals of production (Veblen 1921). Hence Veblen critiques modernity as latter-day barbarism because of the wastefulness of capitalistic production (Veblen 1904).

For Veblen, competition exists within society due to individuals' fear of loss of self-esteem. Patterns of consumption and conduct are seen as having symbolic significance and the latent function of enhancing status—Robert K. Merton (1910–2003) drew upon Veblen when writing about manifest and latent functions (Merton 1957). Veblen provides a theory about how individuals symbolize their own social status in the struggle for competitive advantage. Heightened self-evaluation comes with conspicuous consumption, conspicuous leisure, conspicuous waste, and conspicuous display of symbols that indicate high status, all of which are used to communicate social position and improve social standing. Conspicuous leisure indicates elite status and must be expensive because it is a symbolic message that one is above laboring. Conspicuous consumption and waste, demonstrated by the socially visible consumption and display of expensive items, fashion, exotic pets, and so on, also sends the message that one does not participate in productive labor; thus the more wasteful a person is, the more prestige he or she has. Lower-status groups emulate higher-status practices in an attempt to increase their own status, and Veblen calls these habits of competitive display and consumerism wasteful.

Veblen argued that women are exploited by men through *vicarious* conspicuous consumption, waste, and leisure; that is, the conspicuous activity is performed by the female to benefit the status of the male. Ideals of feminine beauty (e.g., frailty, weakness, and paleness, indicating inability to labor), certain restrictive fashions that prevent laboring, and the removal of women from socially visible, productive labor enhance the status of the male and the good name of the household and its master.

ECONOMICS

In *The Theory of Business Enterprise* (1904) Veblen gives an account of the business enterprises of the 1900s, with a theoretical analysis of the large-scale corporation and the institutions of U.S. capitalism. This analysis highlights the associations of business and industry, the making of money and the making of goods, ownership and technology, pecuniary and industrial employment, and the roles of those who perform social functions versus those whose behavior leads to waste. Veblen highlights the individual businessperson, the powers he or she holds and what he or she can accomplish with those powers, and his or her effect on the economic and social community as a whole. Veblen looks at the world community as it enters into the industrial age, which is dominated by what he calls the "machine process," and shows the importance of machines and their relation to business enterprise. This discussion is important for modernization theory. Interestingly, *The Theory of Business Enterprise* links stock market valuation to aggregate investment in the economy, prefiguring James Tobin's Q model.

In *Absentee Ownership* (1923) Veblen attempted to explain U.S. business after World War I (1914–1918) and before the Great Depression, providing a theoretical analysis of absentee ownership and credit and the economic circumstances associated with economic growth and change through the late nineteenth century. He discussed the rise and fall of the captains of industry and the notion of sabotage associated with entrepreneurs.

Finally, in his essays on education Veblen argues that universities, colleges, and even elementary schools increasingly fall under the spell of predatory habits drawn from the business world. Even in the era in which he lived, he found trends such as the increase of administrative expense over funds devoted to teaching, competition and rating among teachers based upon business models of productivity, the rivalry among universities as if they were corporations based upon the profit motive, and so on. He regarded all these trends as the opposite of what education should represent, namely, "idle curiosity"—interest in knowledge for its own sake, not for profit.

WAR, PEACE, AND NATIONALISM

In *The Nature of Peace* (1917) Veblen looked at the material conditions necessary to induce modern warfare as well as the varied meanings of patriotism within modern society. He saw militarism, nationalism, and patriotism as "predatory" in that they do not benefit the well-being of society as a whole, and he was concerned about military conflict and the patriotic exploitation of the industrious class.

In both *Imperial Germany and the Industrial Revolution* (1915) and *The Nature of Peace* (1917) Veblen developed the ideal-type of the "dynastic state" to describe Germany's and Japan's hierarchical organization and identification combined with the subservience of their underlying populations. This situation, he argued, results in militant aggressive nationalism and finally war; indeed, he criticized nationalism itself because it involves honor and prestige and is therefore barbaric. Veblen used a historical comparison of Germany and Great Britain before, during, and after the Industrial Revolution to show the difference in their developments due to history and context that focused on material causes as well as social-psychological states, and he claimed that when a culture industrializes more rapidly, the country will use this industrialization to produce weapons because of the honor and prestige in being warlike. Militarism is barbaric because it enforces the values of obedience and is obsessed with honor and prestige. Hence if a nation becomes militaristic, this is a sign that it is crossing the border to barbarianism, where war is a natural outcome.

VEBLEN AS CULTURAL THEORIST

Veblen has been interpreted as a cultural theorist, most recently by Stjepan G. Mestrovic (2003) in his analysis of narcissism as central to understanding the unifying strand in Veblen's approach to culture. Others have used Veblen's ideas in cultural theory as well. For example, Riesman integrated Veblen's thought with his own concept of marginal differentiation by the other-directed type and the striving for status by the inner-directed type (Riesman 1953). Riesman and Jean Baudrillard are influenced by Veblen's idea that all forms of waste must be "conspicuous," which is to say reflected in the opinions of the mass media and the peer group. These insights led to Riesman's concept of "fake sincerity," performed to gain approval from others, and eventually to Baudrillard's notion of simulacra. The doctrine of separate spheres widely used in feminist theory, the notion of public versus private, was challenged by Veblen's connection of social spheres through consumerism and status, reflecting a cultural whole with causally linked underlying economic and social class realities (e.g., domination, production, and consumption). Thus Veblen provided an opportunity to understand culture in terms of economics and vice versa. Perceived status and hierarchical social distinctions make status comparisons and symbolic representations central to Veblen's theorizing.

Veblen had a particular influence in the social sciences with his symbolic representation of social class and social position, use of modernization theory, and analyses of economics (production, consumption, technology, business and industry, and economic growth and change). Veblen's influence is wide-ranging. C. Wright Mills used Veblen's work to develop his own ideas about leisure and social status in *White Collar* (1956) and updated Veblen's theory of the dominant sociopolitical elite (the predatory business class) in *The Power Elite* (1956). Chris Rojek incorporated Veblen's work into leisure studies with his analysis of leisure as taking on the characteristics of work (Rojek 1994), and

Theodor Adorno used Veblen when discussing the aesthetics of ostentatious display. The French postmodern Baudrillard developed his own consumption theory concerning the significance of objects and images of consumption in designating prestige, where consumption and leisure should not be understood only as pleasure but also as a ranking and classification system of status itself.

SEE ALSO *Business; Business Cycles, Real; Capitalism; Class, Leisure; Conspicuous Consumption; Economics; Modernity; Stratification; Tobin's Q*

BIBLIOGRAPHY

PRIMARY WORKS

Veblen, Thorstein. 1904. *The Theory of Business Enterprise.* New York: Scribner.

Veblen, Thorstein. 1914. *Instinct of Workmanship and the State of Industrial Arts.* New York: Macmillan.

Veblen, Thorstein. 1915. *Imperial Germany and the Industrial Revolution.* New York: Macmillan.

Veblen, Thorstein. 1917. *An Inquiry into the Nature of Peace and the Terms of Its Perpetuation.* New York: Macmillan.

Veblen, Thorstein. 1921. *The Engineers and the Price System.* New York: B. W. Huebsch.

Veblen, Thorstein. 1923. *Absentee Ownership and Business Enterprise in Recent Times.* New York: B. W. Huebsch.

Veblen, Thorstein. [1899] 1994. *Theory of the Leisure Class.* New York: Penguin.

SECONDARY WORKS

Baudrillard, Jean. 1981. *For a Critique of the Political Economy of the Sign.* St. Louis, MO: Telos.

Coser, Lewis A. [1971] 1977. *Masters of Sociological Thought: Ideas in Historical and Social Context.* New York: Harcourt, Brace, Jovanovich.

Heilbroner, Robert L. 1955. *The Worldly Philosophers.* New York: Simon and Schuster.

Merton, Robert K. 1957. *Social Theory and Social Structure.* Glencoe, IL: Free Press.

Mestrovic, Stjepan G. 2003. *Thorstein Veblen on Culture and Society.* London: Sage.

Mills, C. Wright. 1956. *The Power Elite.* New York: Oxford University Press.

Mills, C. Wright. 1956. *White Collar: The American Middle Class.* New York: Oxford University Press.

Mills, C. Wright. 1959. *The Sociological Imagination.* New York: Oxford University Press.

Riesman, David. [1953] 1995. *Thorstein Veblen.* Introduction by Stjepan G. Mestrovic. New Brunswick, NJ: Transaction Publishers.

Rojek, Chris. 1994. *Decentering Leisure: Rethinking Leisure Theory.* London: Sage.

Ryan Ashley Caldwell

VECTOR AUTOREGRESSION

Vector autoregression (VAR) models were introduced by the macroeconometrician Christopher Sims (1980) to model the joint dynamics and causal relations among a set of macroeconomic variables. VAR models are useful for forecasting. Consider a univariate autoregressive model—for example, an AR(1) $Y_t = \alpha + \beta Y_{t-1} + \varepsilon_t$—which describes the dynamics of just one random variable Y_t (i.e., national income) as a linear function of its own past. Based on this model, the forecast of national income will depend just on its past history. However, economic variables such as national income, employment, prices, money supply, interest rates, and so on interact with each other. For instance, movements in interest rates affect the level of employment, which in turn affects the level of national income. In this multivariate setting, the forecast of national income will be a function of a larger *information set* that combines not only the history of national income but also the histories of many other variables, such as interest rates and employment. A VAR is the generalization of the univariate autoregressive model to a vector of economic variables.

DEFINITION

An *n*-variable vector autoregression of order p, VAR(p), is a system of *n* linear equations, with each equation describing the dynamics of one variable as a linear function of the previous p lags of every variable in the system, including its own p lags. A simple case is a VAR(2) ($p = 2$) for a vector of two variables ($n = 2$), say $\{Y_t, X_t\}$:

$$
\begin{aligned}
Y_t = {} & \alpha + \beta_{11}Y_{t-1} + \beta_{12}Y_{t-2} \\
& + \gamma_{11}X_{t-1} + \gamma_{12}X_{t-2} + \varepsilon_{1t} \\
X_t = {} & \alpha_2 + \beta_{21}Y_{t-1} + \beta_{22}Y_{t-2} \\
& + \gamma_{21}X_{t-1} + \gamma_{22}X_{t-2} + \varepsilon_{2t}
\end{aligned}
\tag{1}
$$

The *innovations* are assumed to be zero-mean random variables, $E(\varepsilon_{1t}) = E(\varepsilon_{2t}) = 0$, with constant variance, $\mathrm{var}(\varepsilon_{1t}) = \sigma_1^2$ $\mathrm{var}(\varepsilon_{2t}) = \sigma_2^2$, possibly correlated, $\mathrm{cov}(\varepsilon_{1t}, \varepsilon_{2t}) = \sigma_{12} \neq 0$, and with normal *probability density functions*.

The components of the definition are:

1. The *n*-dimension of the vector: number of variables to model, which is equal to the number of equations in the system.

2. The *p*-lag structure: identical number of lags for each of the *n* variables in the right-hand side of each equation.

3. The *linear* autoregressive specification.

4. The assumptions on the statistical properties of the innovations.

The joint dynamics are captured in two ways: (1) each variable is explained by the past history of every variable—Y_t is a function of its own past and the past of the other variables in the system $\{Y_{t-1}, Y_{t-2}, \dots Y_{t-p}, X_{t-2}, \dots X_{t-p}, \dots\}$; and (2) the innovations may be contemporaneously correlated, that is, $\sigma_{12} \neq 0$.

ADVANTAGES

Easy implementation. Since every equation in the VAR has the same number of variables on the right-hand side, the coefficients $\{\alpha_1, \alpha_2, \dots, \beta_{11}, \beta_{21}, \dots, \gamma_{11}, \gamma_{21}, \dots\}$ of the overall system are easily estimated by applying *ordinary least squares* (OLS) to each equation individually. The OLS estimator has the standard asymptotic properties. In large samples, the OLS estimator is *consistent* and *asymptotically normal* distributed.

Classical inference. Since the OLS estimator has standard asymptotic properties, it is possible to test any linear restriction, either in one equation or across equations, with the standard t and F statistics. Suppose that one is interested in whether the second lag is relevant in the first equation. One writes the null hypothesis as H_0: $\beta_{12} = \gamma_{12} = 0$. This is a restriction involving only the first equation. It is also possible to test for restrictions involving more than one equation. Suppose that one is interested in whether the coefficients corresponding to Y_{t-2} are identical across equations, that is, H_0: $\beta_{12} = \beta_{22}$. In both cases, an F-statistic will be appropriate.

The lag length p is also chosen by statistical testing or by minimizing some *information criteria*. Suppose that one starts by assuming $p = 2$. One writes the null hypothesis as H_0: $p = 2$ against an alternative hypothesis $p > 2$, say H_1: $p = 3$. The VAR model is estimated under the null and under the alternative, and testing is carried out by constructing either the F-statistic (based on the comparison of the sum of squared residuals for the restricted and unrestricted specifications) or an *asymptotic likelihood test* (based on the comparison of the value of the likelihood function for the restricted and unrestricted specifications).

Testing for Granger causality. It is of interest to know whether one or more variables have predictive content to forecast the variable(s) of interest. For instance, in system (1) one could ask whether X is helpful in predicting Y. The corresponding null hypothesis is that all the coefficients on the lags of X are zero, that is, H_0: $\gamma_{11} = \gamma_{12} = 0$. If these coefficients are statistically zero, one says that X does not Granger-cause Y or, equivalently, X does not have any predictive content to forecast Y. The null hypothesis can be tested with a standard F-statistic.

Impulse-response function and variance decomposition. An important use of VAR is to quantify the effects over time of economic policy. Suppose that the monetary authority shocks interest rates. The questions become: When, for how long, and how much does the shock to interest rates impact employment and output? Impulse-response functions are designed to answer these questions. An impulse-response function describes the response over time of each variable in the VAR to a one-time shock in any given variable while keeping all others constant. For the system described in (1), one has four impulse-response functions: the impact and future effects on Y and on X of a unit shock to ε_1, and the impact and future effects on Y and on X of a unit shock to ε_2.

Closely associated with the impulse-response function is the *variance decomposition.* This decomposition refers to the contribution of each innovation to the variance of the forecast error associated with the forecast of each variable in the VAR. Standard time series software provides both impulse-response functions and variance decomposition.

SHORTCOMINGS

Ad hoc specification. VAR models are criticized because they do not shed any light on the underlying structure of the economy. Though this criticism is not important when the purpose of VAR is forecasting, it is relevant when the objective is to find causal relations among the macroeconomic variables. A *structural* VAR is a system of *simultaneous equations* that aim to analyze causal relations. For each variable in the system, there is an equation that accounts for simultaneous as well as dynamic interactions among the full set of variables. A structural VAR(2) for $\{Y_t, X_t\}$ corresponding to the system described in (1) looks like:

$$
\begin{aligned}
Y_t = {} & a_1 + b_1 X_t + \phi_{11} Y_{t-1} + \phi_{12} Y_{t-2} \\
& + \varphi_{11} X_{t-1} + \varphi_{12} X_{t-2} + \nu_{1t} \\
X_t = {} & a_2 + b_2 Y_t + \phi_{21} Y_{t-1} + \phi_{22} Y_{t-2} \\
& + \varphi_{21} X_{t-1} + \varphi_{22} X_{t-2} + \nu_{2t}
\end{aligned}
\tag{2}
$$

where ν_1 and ν_2 are known as the structural innovations. With matrix algebra, it is possible to solve for $\{Y_t, X_t\}$ in the structural VAR. The solution is known as the *reduced form*, which is the VAR in (1) subject to some parameter restrictions. The question becomes: Is it possible to recover the structural parameters from the estimated parameters of the reduced form? This is known as the *identification* problem. The structural VAR in (2) has fourteen parameters (twelve coefficients and the variances of the two innovations, assuming that the covariance is

zero), while the VAR in (1) has thirteen parameters (ten coefficients, two variances, and one covariance of the innovations). To uniquely identify the structural parameters, the investigator needs one restriction on the structural VAR. Which restriction should be used?

Identifying restrictions. This is a point of debate in structural VAR modeling. The ideal view is that economic theory should dictate which restrictions to impose. However, Sims argued that economic theory was not informative about the appropriate identifying restrictions, and therefore the estimation of the reduced form was the most that one could accomplish. Some researchers impose restrictions on the coefficients of the contemporaneous variables (Sims 1980). Others impose restrictions on the covariance of the structural innovations (Hausman, Newey, and Taylor 1987), or on the long-run multipliers (Blanchard and Quah 1989).

The most popular identifying restriction is the *recursive parameterization* or *lower triangularization* of the matrix of contemporaneous coefficients. In the structural VAR(2) described in (2), this restriction is $b_1 = 0$, which implies that exogenous shocks to X will not contemporaneously affect Y. If X is money and Y is output, the restriction $b_1 = 0$ means that a shock to the money supply will not affect output instantaneously, though it will affect output with some delay depending upon the dynamics specified in the VAR model. The lower triangularization is the most popular restriction in the time series computer packages.

Ordering of the variables. When the innovations $\{\varepsilon_{1t}, \varepsilon_{2t}\}$ are contemporaneously correlated, the impulse-response functions will depend on the ordering of the variables. A common solution is to transform the innovations (for instance, using the *Cholesky decomposition*) such that the transformed innovations are uncorrelated. The implication is that now one can trace the response of the system to an innovation shock in isolation without disturbing the rest of the innovations. The transformation also has implications for the specification of the system because now the first equation will have only one current innovation, the second equation will have two current innovations, the third equation will have three, and so on. Therefore, the ordering of the variables matters. There are no rules on how to choose the ordering of the variables. Economic theory may shed some light, but eventually the choice of the ordering will depend on the questions that the forecaster aims to answer.

SEE ALSO *Cholesky Decomposition; Lags, Distributed; Linear Systems; Properties of Estimators (Asymptotic and Exact); Regression; Specification Tests; Student's T-Statistic; Test Statistics*

BIBLIOGRAPHY

Blanchard, Olivier, and Danny Quah. 1989. The Dynamic Effects of Aggregate Demand and Aggregate Supply Disturbances. *American Economic Review* 79: 655–673.

Granger, Clive W. J. 1969. Investigating Causal Relations by Econometric Models and Cross-Spectral Methods. *Econometrica* 37 (3): 424–438.

Hamilton, James D. 1994. *Time Series Analysis.* Princeton, NJ: Academic Press.

Hausman, Jerry A., Whitney K. Newey, and William E. Taylor. 1987. Efficient Estimation and Identification of Simultaneous Equation Models with Covariance Restrictions. *Econometrica* 55 (4): 849–874.

Sims, Christopher. 1980. Macroeconomics and Reality. *Econometrica* 48 (1): 1–48.

Gloria González-Rivera

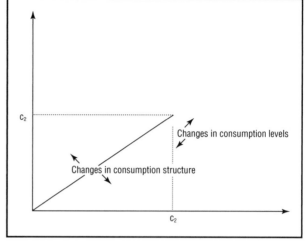

Figure 1

VECTOR ERROR CORRECTION MODEL

SEE *Unit Root and Cointegration Regression.*

VECTORS

It is well known that any point in the plane can be represented by a pair of numbers, its *coordinates.* If one draws a horizontal axis, labeled the x axis, and a vertical axis, labeled the y axis, then one can represent any point uniquely by giving its x coordinate and its y coordinate *in order.* Point (a, b) is the point that lies directly on a vertical passing by the point marked a on the x axis and on level with the point marked b on the y axis. Naturally, a or b can be negative. Note that the *order* of the coordinates is important. Points represented by (a, b) and (b, a) are *not* the same (unless $a = b$).

There is a complete correspondence between geometrical objects, namely, points of the plane, and purely algebraic objects, namely, ordered pair of numbers. Such algebraic objects that correspond exactly to points are called *vectors.* Thus a vector is a pair of any numbers (x, y). More precisely, one should call such pairs *two-dimensional vectors* because the concept can be easily generalized to *n-dimensional vectors*, geometrical representation being of course limited to three-dimensional space; nonetheless, the illustrations herein are limited to two-dimensional space.

Economic applications of vectors are quite important and numerous. The presentation herein deals with consumption first, production and activity analysis second, and then finally, temporal processes.

Consumption structures can be easily presented using vectors. The consumption of consumer C_i consists of n different quantities or bundles of different commodities (meat, bread, beer, tea …), represented by $C_i = (c_{i1}, c_{i2}, … (c_{in})$. When for simplicity of presentation one deals with two commodities, then $n = 2$ and $C_i = (c_{i1}, c_{i2})$, which can be represented with quantities consumed on relevant axes, as in Figure 1. The length of the vector represents the level of consumption, and its slope represents the structure of composition. Level changes of the "consumption basket" will be represented by an increase or a decrease of the vector length; changes in structure, depending on consumer preferences, revenue, and market prices, will modify the vector slope.

Vector analysis can also be useful to present problems of accumulation with heterogeneous capital goods, a technique dating as far back as Karl Marx's analysis of "reproduction schemes" found in the second volume (1885) of *Das Kapital.* John von Neumann (1946) and Wassily W. Leontief (1941) have contributed important modern examples of this technique.

For an example of a production analysis, one might begin by defining an "activity," "process," or "production method" representing production of one commodity, say "corn," using labor, iron, and corn (for seed needs). For one unit of labor time (one hour, one day, or labor time available in the economy), one can obtain a given amount of corn, called b_{11}, using a_{11} amount of corn and a_{21} of iron. Consequently, activity can be represented by vector $\vec{OM_1}$ (see Figure 2). The first coordinate of M_1 is $b_{11} - a_{11}$, representing "net" production of corn, that is, "gross" production of corn (b_{11}) less intermediate consumption of corn (a_{11})—the seeds; the second coordinate, a_{21}, represents the intermediate consumption of iron; vector $\vec{OM_1}$,

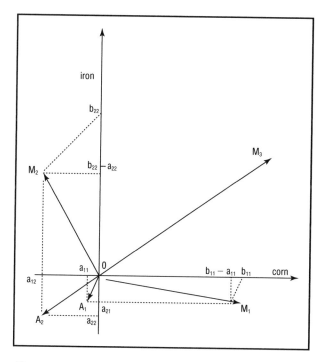

Figure 2

representing the "net product" of activity (1), can be easily constructed by vectoral summation of, first, gross production of corn represented by vector $O\bar{b}_{11}$ and second, D, vector $O\bar{A}_1$, itself sum of inputs of corn and iron.

In a similar way, let iron be produced by another activity producing b_{22} units (tons …) of iron using a_{22} units of iron, a_{12} units of the other commodity (corn here in this very simplified model), and one unit of labor. Vector $O\bar{M}_2$ represents the "net product" of this activity.

One may note that $O\bar{M}_1$ and $O\bar{M}_2$ have just one positive component, both activities being "specialized" in the production of one and only one commodity. Such a case is called "simple production"; but one may have a different case in which one activity produces two commodities simultaneously (say, wool and milk); in such a case, named "joint production," both coordinates of M_3 may be positive, as indicated in Figure 2 (this vector is shown only for mathematical illustration as it is quite difficult to imagine a method producing jointly iron and corn).

When both activities are specialized, one comes to matrix representations such as:

$$A = \begin{bmatrix} a_{11} & a_{12} \\ a_{21} & a_{22} \end{bmatrix} \quad B = \begin{bmatrix} b_{11} & 0 \\ 0 & b_{22} \end{bmatrix}$$

which are square matrixes largely used in *input-output* systems, or Leontief models—*2 × 2* in the simplified model used here, but *n × n* in a more general treatment. The $i^{ème}$ column vector represents conditions of production of the $i^{ème}$ commodity (production of b_{11} units of commodity i necessitates intermediate consumption of a_{11} units of itself and a_{21} units of second commodity, and so on); the $i^{ème}$ line vector represents utilization of the $i^{ème}$ commodity by the entire system, as intermediate consumption (a_{11} representing intermediate consumption of first commodity by the first production process, a_{12} intermediate consumption of the same commodity by the second production process, and so on).

Von Neumann models are more complicated and more general. First, there is the possibility of joint production. Second, the matrix may be rectangular because there is the possibility of production systems with un-equality between the numbers of processes (line vectors) and commodities (column vectors).

It should be noted that when economic systems can be characterized by a "square matrix," one can define and characterize eigenvectors that have a special structure associated with matrix characteristics. Such vectors play a special role in economic analysis because they can be useful to characterize, on the one hand, special accumulation regimes—with maximum uniform growth rates—and, on the other hand, special price systems—with minimum uniform interest rates.

Vectors can also be useful in presenting and generalizing about temporal interdependencies. Simple "autoregressive" models involve the dependence of variable x on the anterior value of the same variable, for instance, $x_t = f(x_t - 1)$, with any kind of relevant function.

Vector autoregressive (VAR) models are a generalization of such simple autoregressive models. Consider two stationary variables x_{1t} and x_{2t}; each variable depends on its own past values but also on the present and past values of the other one. VAR models are very important in contemporary econometrics. They have been introduced by Christopher A. Sims (1980) as an alternative to macroeconometric models with a Keynesian flavor.

SEE ALSO *Eigen-Values and Eigen-Vectors, Perron-Frobenius Theorem: Economic Applications; Input-Output Matrix; Linear Systems; Matrix Algebra*

BIBLIOGRAPHY

Leontief, Wassily W. 1941. *The Structure of American Economy, 1919–1929: An Empirical Application of Equilibrium Analysis.* Cambridge, MA: Harvard University Press.

Neumann, John von. 1946. A Model of General Equilibrium. *Review of Economic Studies* 13 (1): 1–9. (Orig. pub. 1937.)

Sims, Christopher A. 1980. Macroeconomics and Reality. *Econometrica* 48 (1): 1–48.

Gilbert Abraham-Frois

VEDA

SEE *Brahmins.*

VEIL, IN AFRICAN AMERICAN CULTURE

The veil in African American culture is a mystical dimension of a spiritual belief system that traveled with slaves on the Middle Passage. An infant "born with a veil" of fetal membrane enveloping the head was interpreted as supernaturally gifted with a second sight, an ability to see into the future. Likewise, the seventh child of a seventh child would also be gifted with spiritual powers. The veil, also called a caul, like roots, charms, and conjurers, is a vivid aspect of African American spiritual, literary, and folklore tradition.

Moving beyond the mystical, African American sociologist W. E. B. Du Bois explored the notion of the veil from a societal perspective, using the metaphor of being "born with a veil" to describe black life in America, particularly the plight of the black American experience and the challenges facing African American culture. In his 1903 masterpiece *The Souls of Black Folk*, Du Bois articulates with poetic beauty and poignant accuracy the pain and confusion felt by an entire race of people as it sought self-understanding.

A sense of duality surrounds Du Bois's veil metaphor: First is the physical delineation of blackness and whiteness, that semipermeable border that separates black and white cultures and forces blacks to learn to function in both worlds. Second is white people's inability to view blacks as worthy Americans. Du Bois often felt despised by whites and was regularly asked, indirectly, "How does it feel to be a problem?" (1903, p. 1). This obstruction of vision is twofold, for the veil also refers to black people's inability to see themselves beyond the prescipted image projected onto them by whites. Realizing his racial identity, Du Bois states, "Then it dawned upon me with a certain suddenness that I was different from the others; … shut out from their world by a vast veil. I had thereafter no desire to tear down that veil, to creep through" (p. 2).

Faced with this problematic veil that separated the two worlds of black and white, blacks were forced to create a "twoness" or "double-consciousness."

> The Negro is a sort of seventh son, born with a veil, and gifted with second-sight in this American world—a world which yields him no true self-consciousness, but … this double-consciousness, this sense of always looking at one's self through the eyes of others… One ever feels his twoness,—an American, a Negro; two souls, two thoughts,

two unreconciled strivings; two warring ideals in one dark body. (p. 3)

But also drawing upon the positive spiritual qualities of the veil, Du Bois notes that a black person seeks "to merge his double self into a better and truer self" (p. 3).

A century later, Du Bois's metaphor veil lives on in *Behind the Veil: Documenting African American Life in the Jim Crow South*, a comprehensive research project associated with the Center for Documentary Studies at Duke University. Historians conducted nearly 1,300 oral interviews with everyday men and women from the Jim Crow era, resulting in a book and audio documentary titled *Remembering Jim Crow: African Americans Tell about Life in the Segregated South* (2001). Much like the dualism of *The Souls of Black Folk*, *Behind the Veil* has its own dualism: to convey the oppression experienced by African Americans during Jim Crow but also their incredible hope and monumental efforts.

SEE ALSO *African Americans; Du Bois, W. E. B.; Ethnography; Inequality, Racial; Jim Crow; Mysticism*

BIBLIOGRAPHY

Chafe, William H., Raymond Gavins, and Robert Korstad, eds. 2001. *Remembering Jim Crow: African Americans Tell about Life in the Segregated South.* New York: New Press.

Du Bois, W. E. B. 1903. *The Souls of Black Folk.* New York: Bantam, 1989.

Judy L. Isaksen

VEIL, IN MIDDLE EASTERN AND NORTH AFRICAN CULTURES

The veil—or *hijab*—is attire that is said to be women's religious duty as well as a cultural requirement of personal modesty. Across the Muslim countries of the Middle East and North Africa, the veil takes varied forms: the headscarf, loose jacket, and long skirt ensemble seen in Egypt; the black cloak (*chador*) in Iran; the brightly-patterned silk scarf and long coat worn by Islamic women in Turkey; and the full *niqab* that covers the face and hands, which is worn by women affiliated with Islamist movements as well as many women in the Gulf countries. Not all Muslim women veil, and governments have taken different positions on veiling. For example, veiling in government agencies and universities is forbidden in Turkey and Tunisia but is compulsory in Iran and Saudi Arabia. Still, polemics surrounding *hijab* abound in every country, and scholars have written about the increasing observance of the veil in the Middle Eastern and North African countries. Immigrant communities in Europe and North America also have seen veiling, leading to national debates and policy formulations. Commentaries and popular images depict the veil variously as symbolizing women's oppression or as a Muslim woman's cultural right.

During the era of early modernization and postcolonial nation-building, when national progress and the emancipation of women were considered synonymous, the veil was associated with national backwardness and with female illiteracy and subjugation. This viewpoint entailed discouragement of the veil and encouragement of schooling for girls. At certain times in Middle Eastern modern history the veil has been convenient to militants and political activists. In the Algerian war for independence against the French in the 1950s and the Iranian revolt against the shah in 1978, women used the veil to hide political leaflets and arms. But a paradox of the 1980s was that more and more educated women, including university students and working women, donned the veil. In Egypt, *hijab* included both modest dress and the more extreme *niqab* (Badran 1994).

Observers have raised a number of questions about veiling. Is veiling merely a matter of convenience and individual choice, or does social pressure play a part? If veiling is a "voluntary" identity marker of "The Muslim Woman," what larger message does it send about women's bodies and hair? What is the relationship between veiling/reveiling, the growth of Islamist movements, and the policies of Islamist states? In the case of compulsory veiling, veiling is clearly tied to state policy and its patriarchal gender regime. But what of the expansion of veiling in Algeria, Egypt, Turkey, and among the Palestinians, where veiling is not mandated by the state?

One response has been to emphasize Muslim women's "agency" in the decision to veil (El-Guindi 1981; Hoodfar 1991). In this view, veiling permits public roles for women from conservative families that would otherwise not allow "their women" access to higher education or employment. *Hijab* is a form of "protection" that allows the educated, professional woman to participate in public life and be both modern and Islamic. There is also some evidence that voluntary veiling is not always an expression of affiliation with or support for an Islamist political movement; it could represent rejection of parental and patriarchal authority among rebellious young women. Some young women from nontraditional families who adhere to *hijab* aspire to personal autonomy and a more serious mien, especially at coeducational colleges.

Others have argued that the response of some women who are compelled to work for low wages has been an intensification of traditional modesty markers, such as veiling. Reluctantly working outside the home, and thus "exposed," middle-class and low-income women must use every symbolic means at their disposal to signify that they continue to be "respectable" and worthy of protection. Arlene MacLeod (1991) called this "accommodating protest."

The expansion of Islamist movements and the ideology of political Islam have led to increased veiling in at least three ways. First, Islamism places a high premium on sex segregation, a preference for the confinement of women to the private sphere of the family, male guardianship over women, and the veiling of women in public or before men who are not closely related—norms that Islamists in power have legislated. The wives, daughters, sisters, and other women supporters of Islamist movements all have been veiling. Second, the ideological exhortation that to be an authentic Muslim woman is to veil has created a political environment and cultural climate that have compelled many non-Islamist women to veil. The insistent message that veiling is a moral and religious requirement constitutes an effective ideological pressure. Third, in some instances Islamists have used intimidation and physical force against unveiled women—this has occurred in Algeria and among the Palestinians (Moghadam 2003).

Veiling reflects and encourages notions of women's vulnerability, of their "difference," and of the presumed dangers of the female body. Fatima Mernissi has pointed out that women's bodies and their sexuality are regarded as potential sources of *fitna* (moral or social decay) and as such, veiling is meant to protect men, not women. In the same way that many feminists have decried the underdressing of women in Western contexts (Hollywood, the fashion industry, MTV, and so on) because of the way that this reduces a woman to her sexuality, so feminists regard the veil as reinforcing the idea of women's bodies as sexual, dangerous, and a source of temptation (Mernissi 1987; Sabbah 1983).

Other scholars have noted that women's bodies are the site of contestation over religious, national, and cultural identity (Kandiyoti 1991; Moghadam 1994). Islamists in Algeria, Iran, Jordan, Palestine, and elsewhere have exhorted women to veil, to have more children, and to steer clear of "alien" ideologies. Women who do otherwise are branded as cultural traitors, morally repugnant, and religiously damned. The concept of *gharbzadegi*—widely used in postrevolutionary Iran and variously translated as "Westoxication" or "Westitis"—illustrates this point. Through those members who are "struck by the West," notably women, imperialism can penetrate the society and wreak havoc on the culture. The claim was made that by depriving women of chastity, modesty, and honor through notions of autonomy, sex appeal, and so on, colonialists and imperialists had been able to weaken

Muslim cultures. This is said to have happened in Algeria under French colonialism and in Iran during the rule of the pro-American shah. It follows that the main antidote to the virus of *gharbzadegi* is the veil. Furthermore, veiling must be compulsory in order to protect the cultural identity and integrity of the group and of its female members (Najmabadi 1991; Tohidi 1994). A similar exhortation was made by the Ikhwan Muslemin (Muslim Brothers) of Jordan: "How can God's victory prevail when women adorn themselves openly and mix with men, and when defiance of God's law continues day and night? The enemy relies on you, my sister, to strike at this nation from within, as if the stabs we receive from the outside were not enough" (Taraki 1995, p. 660).

Faegheh Shirazi (2001) notes that veiling is heavy with meaning; it has been a symbol of cultural identity, religious assertion, gender oppression, and sexual mystery. The "fetishism of the veil" is found among Westerners and Islamists alike. She argues that while the veil has "semantic versatility" it often serves political agendas. In Iranian politics, and especially during the war with Iraq in the 1980s, the connection between *hijab* and jihad was maintained through the strategic use of postage stamps, posters, banners, billboards, and other print material depicting veiled women as strong supporters of the war. She also describes the preoccupation with *bad-hijabi* (malveiling) on the part of the Islamic authorities in Iran.

In its most innocuous form, veiling is a sign of piety and a form of protection against the male gaze. Increasingly, it is the line of demarcation between the Islamist/Islamic community and non-Muslim communities, a shield against the slings and arrows of imperialists, and protection against the dangers of female sexuality. Veiling can symbolize the imposition of identity and "morality." In the Islamic Republic of Iran, even non-Muslim citizens—Christian, Jewish, and Zoroastrian women—have been forced to veil in public. Whether compulsory or "encouraged," veiling has been a mechanism of social control: the regulation of women.

BIBLIOGRAPHY

Badran, Margot. 1994. Gender Activism: Feminists and Islamists in Egypt. In *Identity Politics and Women: Cultural Reassertions and Feminisms in International Perspective*, ed. Valentine M. Moghadam, 202–227. Boulder, CO: Westview.

El-Guindi, Fadwa. 1981. Veiling *Intifah* with Muslim Ethic: Egypt's Contemporary Islamic Movement. *Social Problems* 8: 465–485.

Hoodfar, Homa. 1991. Return to the Veil: Personal Strategy and Public Participation in Egypt. In *Working Women: International Perspectives on Labour and Gender Ideology*, eds. Nanneke Redclift and M. Thea Sinclair, 104–124. London and New York: Routledge.

Kandiyoti, Deniz, ed. 1991. *Women, Islam, and the State*. Philadelphia: Temple University Press; London: Macmillan.

MacLeod, Arlene Elowe. 1991. *Accommodating Protest: Working Women, the New Veiling, and Change in Cairo*. New York: Columbia University Press.

Mernissi, Fatima. 1987. *Beyond the Veil: Male-Female Dynamics in Modern Muslim Society*. 2nd ed. Bloomington: University of Indiana Press.

Moghadam, Valentine M., ed. 1994. *Identity Politics and Women: Cultural Reassertions and Feminisms in International Perspective*. Boulder, CO: Westview.

Moghadam, Valentine M. 2003. *Modernizing Women: Gender and Social Change in the Middle East*. 2nd ed. Boulder, CO: Lynne Rienner.

Najmabadi, Afsaneh. 1991. Hazards of Modernity and Morality: Women, State, and Ideology in Contemporary Iran. In *Women, Islam, and the State*, ed. Deniz Kandiyoti, 48–76. London: Macmillan.

Sabbah, Fatna A. 1983. *Woman in the Muslim Unconscious*. Trans. Mary Jo Lakeland. New York: Pergamon.

Shirazi, Faegheh. 2001. *The Veil Unveiled: The Hijab in Modern Culture*. Gainesville: University Press of Florida.

Taraki, Lisa. 1995. Islam is the Solution: Jordanian Islamists and the Dilemma of the "Modern Woman." *British Journal of Sociology* 46 (4): 643–661.

Tohidi, Nayereh. 1994. Modernity, Islamization, and Women in Iran. In *Gender and National Identity: Women and Politics in Muslim Societies*, ed. Valentine M. Moghadam, 110–147. London: Zed.

Valentine M. Moghadam

VEIL OF IGNORANCE

SEE *Rawls, John.*

VELOCITY OF CIRCULATION

SEE *Quantity Theory of Money.*

VELOCITY OF MONEY

SEE *Money, Demand for.*

VENTURE CAPITAL

Venture capital (VC) is capital used by private equity funds to support the creation and growth of businesses; it is characterized by a tradeoff between high risk and high rates of return. Most VC has been invested in technology-oriented companies and projects. Because it is independent and professionally managed, VC is a crucial equity type of external financing for privately held companies that seek to grow rapidly. As a result, VC investments play a critical role in economic development.

Newly created firms that are expected to grow quickly into big companies often do not have sufficient funds to finance their projects and thus need outside financing. These firms are subject to potential capital constraints; that is, they have difficulty receiving bank loans and other types of standard financing because of a limited track record and uncertain future prospects. VC is a professionally managed pool of money raised for the specific purpose of making equity investments in such companies. In addition to providing new capital during critical stages of development, professional management adds value to expansion through screening, monitoring, and aiding in decision-making. A typical VC firm receives many proposals per year, but only approves a very small percentage.

The first formal private equity fund was formed in 1946 in Boston to provide financing to several companies that had developed new technologies during World War II (1939–1945). The first VC limited partnership was formed in 1958. Even though several other VC companies were established later on, the total average annual VC investment did not exceed a few hundred million dollars until the end of the 1970s. During the 1980s, VC firms provided capital to the most successful high-technology companies, such as Cisco Systems and Microsoft. Since then, the private equity industry has been experiencing tremendous growth in the United States, both in terms of the amount of capital invested and in terms of returns. VC market growth also spread abroad, first to the U.K. and then to continental Europe and beyond. Differences in the nature of financial markets from country to country are the main reasons for the varying maturity of VC markets. For instance, there is a clear institutional separation between investment banks and the VC industry in the United States, but in countries with relatively young financial markets, the functions of VC firms are often performed by major investment banks as well as private equity partners. Whereas VC firms provide funds to firms at early stages of their development in the United States, in Europe and in developing countries VC companies prefer firms that have already developed and started marketing their products.

The supply of VC is determined by investors' willingness to provide funds to venture firms. This willingness depends on the expected rate of return on investments. High-tech companies with the potential to grow rapidly are also highly risky investments. VC firms that become major equity owners in such new firms are only willing to finance high-reward investment proposals because they also have responsibilities to several other funding sources, such as individual investors, investment bankers, subsidiaries of banks, and other corporations. In order to make money on their investments, a VC fund needs to turn the illiquid stakes in private companies into realized return, for example by taking a company public. The most profitable exit opportunity for VC firms is an initial public offering (IPO). In an IPO, the VC fund assists the company in issuing shares to the public for the first time. The exit is an important aspect of the VC business because investors in a VC need a way to evaluate the performance of VC funds in order to decide whether to provide further capital. On the stock exchange, the success of existing strategy is demonstrated by lower underpricing (the difference between offer price and first-day trading price) and by high long-term performance (measured against certain benchmark investments). Empirical research shows that VC backing reduces the degree of IPO underpricing, and that the long-term stock returns (up to five years) of companies backed by VC funds are substantially better than those of companies without VC.

SEE ALSO *Cooperatives; Firm; Investment; Risk Takers; Risk-Return Tradeoff; Stock Exchanges*

BIBLIOGRAPHY

Barry, Christopher B., Chris J. Muscarella, John W. Peavy, and Michael R. Vetsuypens. 1990. The Role of Venture Capital in the Creation of Public Companies: Evidence from the Going-Public Process. *Journal of Financial Economics* 27 (2): 447–472.

Bygrave, William D., and Jeffry A. Timmons. 1992. *Venture Capital at the Crossroads.* Boston: Harvard Business School Press.

Halit Gonenc

VER

SEE *Import Penetration.*

VERBA, SIDNEY
1932–

Sidney Verba is Carl H. Pforzheimer University Professor of Government at Harvard University and was director of the University Library from 1984 to 2007. Professor Verba has held many important positions in the discipline of political science, including chairman of the American Political Science Association and coordinator of national research committees. Verba is also a fellow of a number of academies and learned societies and has received numerous prizes, including the 2002 Johan Skytte Prize in Political Science at Uppsala University in Sweden.

Verba is one of the leading scholars in the field of political behavior. Since the mid-twentieth century, this branch has become so internalized in the way political scientists conduct their research that they no longer think of it as a special subdiscipline. Verba's textbook, *Designing Social Inquiry* (1994), authored with Gary King and Robert Keohane, beautifully summarizes how research problems in political science should be formulated, how variables are identified, how data is collected, and how hypotheses are tested and conclusions drawn.

Verba's contribution to political science is basically of a substantive nature. In one of his most famous books, the prize-winning *Participation in America* (1972), written with Norman H. Nie, Verba stresses that participation constitutes the very core of democracy—the more participation, the more democracy. Participation widens citizens' horizons and teaches them responsibility for others. Participation has consequences—for power and influence and for what issues are pursued and decided upon. However, participation is not equally distributed between social groups. Socioeconomic status is the best explanation for the variation in participation—the SES (socioeconomic status) model. There is a conflict between participation and representation. When new channels are opened up for political participation, those citizens who have time and money increase their influence further. The well-to-do are thus overrepresented in political parties and organizations, and they are especially among the most active in the Republican Party. But there are also countervailing powers. Verba underscores the political consciousness of black citizens, which he saw in the 1970s as an important political potential.

The level of political inequality also varies between countries. It is especially striking in the United States, whereas the correlation between social status and participation is much less marked in such countries as Great Britain, Italy, Mexico, and Germany. These nations were included in Verba's *The Civic Culture* (1963), a book that took a pathbreaking classificatory approach to the comparative study of political systems, published by Verba in cooperation with political scientist Gabriel Almond (1911–2002). In Europe, the political mobilization of the underprivileged by the labor movement has leveled out but not obliterated differences in participation; the SES model is still valid.

Verba's ongoing interest in political equality is reflected in the titles of many of his books: *Participation and Political Equality* (1978), *Equality in America* (1985), and *Voice and Equality* (1995). In *The Private Roots of Public Action* (2001), written with Nancy Burns and Kay Lehman Schlozman, Verba draws attention to another important source for the variation in political participation—the lack of equality between the sexes.

SEE ALSO *Almond, Gabriel A.; Behaviorism; Culture; Democracy; Democracy, Representative and Participatory; Inequality, Gender; Inequality, Political; Participation, Political; Political Science, Behavioral*

BIBLIOGRAPHY

Verba, Sidney, and Gabriel Almond. 1963. *The Civic Culture: Political Attitudes and Democracy in Five Countries.* Princeton, NJ: Princeton University Press.

Verba, Sidney, and Norman H. Nie. 1972. *Participation in America: Political Democracy and Social Equality.* New York: Harper and Row.

Verba, Sidney, and Gary R. Orren. 1985. *Equality in America: The View from the Top.* Cambridge, MA: Harvard University Press.

Verba, Sidney, Nancy Burns, and Kay Lehman Schlozman. 2001. *The Private Roots of Public Action: Gender, Equality, and Political Participation.* Cambridge, MA: Harvard University Press.

Verba, Sidney, Gary King, and Robert O. Keohane. 1994. *Designing Social Inquiry: Scientific Inference in Qualitative Research.* Princeton, NJ: Princeton University Press.

Verba, Sidney, Kay Lehman Schlozman, and Henry E. Brady. 1995. *Voice and Equality: Civic Voluntarism in American Politics.* Cambridge, MA: Harvard University Press.

Verba, Sidney, Norman H. Nie, and Jae-on Kim. 1978. *Participation and Political Equality: A Seven-Nation Comparison.* Cambridge, U.K.: Cambridge University Press.

Leif Lewin

VERDOORN'S LAW

Productivity growth is the key to economic development. The continuous increase in labor productivity, defined either as the output per worker or the output per hour worked, is what allows human societies to experience a rise in their per capita income even in face of a growing population. Productivity growth is usually associated with technological innovations, but since the beginning of the Industrial Revolution in the eighteenth century, it became clear to social scientists that economic growth itself may foster productivity growth through the division of labor, as pointed out by Adam Smith in 1776. However, despite the direct evidence that productivity rises with the level of output in manufacturing, the concept of increasing returns was ignored through most of the nineteenth century in the mainstream economic literature because the hypotheses of decreasing marginal returns to capital and labor and constant returns to the scale of production became preponderant in neoclassical economic theory.

The importance of increasing returns for economic growth was revitalized only in the early twentieth century by Allyn A. Young (1928), who emphasized not only the reduction in the average cost of production brought by output growth in manufacturing but also the product diversification that characterizes an increase in the division of labor. Verdoorn's law, an attempt to quantify this relationship, is named after the Dutch economist P. J. Verdoorn, who published a paper in 1949 in which he measured the impact of economic growth on labor-productivity growth in manufacturing for a group of countries in the late nineteenth century and early twentieth century.

In general terms, Verdoorn's law implies the existence of a stable and positive causal relationship from the growth rate of output to the growth rate of productivity in manufacturing in the long run. More formally, let p and q represent the growth rates of labor productivity and output in manufacturing, measured in logarithmic terms. Verdoorn's law was originally estimated as $p = a + bq$, where b is a positive parameter that measures the elasticity of labor productivity to output. The estimate of b, known as the "Verdoorn coefficient," in most empirical studies takes a value around 0.5. The intuitive meaning of this result is that an additional one percentage point increase in the growth rate of output leads to a half percentage point increase in productivity in manufacturing. Since $p = q - n$, where n is the growth rate of employment in manufacturing, Verdoorn's law can also be estimated as $n = -a + (1 - b)q$.

The theoretical foundation of Verdoorn's law is the existence of economies of scale in manufacturing, that is, the fact that the average cost of production falls with an increase in the amount of goods produced. The sources of economies of scale within a firm or industry are usually divided into two categories: static or dynamic. Static economies of scale come from the fact that most processes of production incur a fixed cost, that is, a cost that has to be paid no matter whether anything is produced. As a result, the higher the level of production, the lower the average fixed cost per unit produced and consequently the higher the economy of scale. It should be noted that static economies of scale are reversible because, if production is reduced, the average fixed cost rises. Dynamic economies of scale come from the productivity gains associated with innovations brought about by the increase in production. The intuition here is that the dynamic economies arise from learning by doing and as such are irreversible. Even if the level of production falls, the new knowledge acquired from experience does not vanish.

Verdoorn's (1949) study of productivity growth was published in Italian and went unnoticed by the majority of the economic profession until Nicholas Kaldor (1966) drew attention to it. As summarized by Anthony P. Thirlwall (1983), Kaldor proposed that three growth laws characterized economic development: (1) the higher the growth rate of output in manufacturing, the higher the growth rate of gross domestic product (GDP); (2) the higher the growth rate of output in manufacturing, the higher the growth rate of labor productivity in manufacturing, as proposed by Verdoorn; and (3) the higher the growth rate of output in manufacturing, the higher the growth rate of labor productivity outside manufacturing.

In its broadest sense, Verdoorn's law implies the possibility of endogenous or induced technical change, which forms the basis of theories of economic growth based on increasing returns. In neoclassical theories economic growth is usually explained from the supply side, and Verdoorn's law tends to appear as a learning function that links the growth rate of labor or multifactor productivity to the growth rate of the stock of human and physical capital. In nonmainstream theories of Keynesian inspiration, economic growth is usually determined from the demand side, and therefore Verdoorn's law tends to appear as the explanation of how demand problems can result in uneven development, that is, in permanent growth divergences across countries or regions.

The logic of demand-driven growth divergences is clear and intuitive. If productivity growth is a positive function of economic growth, then an initial increase in aggregate demand can set off a cumulative process along the lines proposed by Gunnar Myrdal (1957), in which productivity gains increase profits and wages, which in its turn leads to another round of demand expansion and so on. The main economic implication of Verdoorn's law is therefore that growth may be self-reinforcing, especially if we bring international trade into the analysis. The basic idea here is that fast-growing economies may be able to maintain their international competitiveness because of the fast productivity growth induced by income growth itself. By analogy, slow-growing economies may not be able to break out from their situation because of the slow productivity growth induced by their very own poor growth performance.

Since its revitalization by Kaldor, Verdoorn's law has been the object of many studies, and the empirical debate tends to revolve around four main issues. First, if productivity growth is exogenous across regions, Verdoorn's law may be spurious because it may be productivity that drives output instead of the other way around. The solution for this possible reverse causation is to investigate whether Verdoorn's law holds across regions that share the same technology. Second, it may also be the case that productivity growth depends on the level of capital per worker, so that Verdoorn's law finds an influence of output growth on productivity growth because the former functions as a proxy of capital growth. The solution for this problem is to include the capital per worker as a separate explaining variable when estimating Verdoorn's law. Third, Verdoorn's law may actually be a misspecified labor demand function, that is, a demand function that ignores the impact of the real wage in the determination of employment. The obvious solution for this problem is to include the real wage as a separate explaining variable when estimating Verdoorn's law. Finally, because firms do not adjust employment as fast as output in the face of demand fluctuations, productivity tends to increase during upswings and fall during downswings because of labor hoarding. If that is the case, Verdoorn's law may actually be just a short-run phenomenon resulting from business fluctuations, known as Okun's law in economics. The natural solution to this problem is to control for changes in the business cycle when estimating Verdoorn's law.

As usually happens in economics, after decades of empirical studies there is evidence both in favor of and against Verdoorn's law. From the many studies on North America and Europe surveyed by John McCombie, Maurizio Pugno, and Bruno Soro (2002), the balance seems to confirm Verdoorn's law. When we consider developing economies, Vaishali Mamgain (1999) finds evidence in favor of Verdoorn's law only in one of six newly industrializing countries of East Asia, whereas Thirlwall and Heather Wells (2003) find evidence in support of Verdoorn's law for a sample of forty-five African countries. In Latin America, E. Luis Lemos Marinho, Cláudio André Gondim Nogueira, and Antonio Lisboa Teles da Rosa (2002) find mixed evidence for Brazil. It will probably take some time until the increasing number of applied studies on developing economies tend one way or another.

SEE ALSO *Cumulative Causation; Development Economics; Economic Growth; Industrialization; Industry; Myrdal, Gunnar; Productivity; Returns, Increasing*

BIBLIOGRAPHY

Kaldor, Nicholas. 1966. *Causes of the Slow Rate of Economic Growth of the United Kingdom.* London: Cambridge University Press.

Mamgain, Vaishali. 1999. Are the Kaldor-Verdoorn Laws Applicable in Newly Industrializing Economies? *Review of Development Economics* 3 (3): 295–309.

Marinho, E. Luis Lemos, Cláudio André Gondim Nogueira, and Antonio Lisboa Teles da Rosa. 2002. Evidências empíricas da lei de Kaldor-Verdoorn para a indústria de transformação do Brasil (1985–1997). *Revista Brasileira de Economia* 56 (3): 457–482.

McCombie, John, Maurizio Pugno, and Bruno Soro, eds. 2002. *Productivity Growth and Economic Performance: Essays on Verdoorn's Law.* New York: Palgrave Macmillan.

Myrdal, Gunnar. 1957. *Economic Theory and Under-Developed Regions.* London: Duckworth.

Thirlwall, Anthony P. 1983. A Plain Man's Guide to Kaldor's Growth Laws. *Journal of Post-Keynesian Economics* 5 (3): 345–358.

Verdoorn, P. J. 1949. Fattori che regolano lo sviluppo della produttività del lavoro. *L'Industria* 1: 3–10.

Wells, Heather, and Anthony P. Thirlwall. 2003. Testing Kaldor's Growth Laws across the Countries of Africa. *African Development Review* 15 (2–3): 89–105.

Young, Allyn A. 1928. Increasing Returns and Economic Progress. *Economic Journal* 38: 527–542.

Nelson H. Barbosa-Filho

VERIFICATION

SEE *Validation.*

VESEY, DENMARK
c. 1767–1822

The man later known as Denmark Vesey was born around 1767, probably on the Caribbean island of Saint Thomas. Joseph Vesey, a Carolina-based slaver, purchased the boy in 1781 as part of a cargo of 390 bondpeople. During the passage to the French colony of Saint-Domingue (Haiti), Vesey noticed the child's "beauty, alertness, and intelligence" and employed him as a cabin boy. But when the ship reached Cap François, the captain "had no use for the boy" and turned him over to his colonial agents. Either traumatized by his new life in Saint-Domingue or feigning illness, the child began to display "epileptic fits." Returned to the docks, a physician "certified that the lad" was unwell, which cancelled the sale. When Joseph Vesey returned to Cap François on April 23, 1782, with a new cargo of Gold Coast slaves, he was forced to take the child back. The fits promptly ceased, and Vesey decided to keep him as a servant.

Charleston authorities later described the child as a person of "superior power of mind & the more dangerous for it." The captain saw only the value of a tall, muscular boy already conversant in two languages. Vesey gave the boy a new name, Telemaque, after the son of Homer's Odysseus; over time, Carolina bondmen either punned or corrupted the name into Denmak, and then finally Denmark.

In the spring of 1783, following the British evacuation of South Carolina, Joseph Vesey settled into Charleston as a ship chandler. At some point during this period, Denmark married an enslaved woman named Beck. Beck had several masters over the course of her life, but she remained married to Denmark long enough to give birth to at least three of his children. Two of his sons were named Polydore and Robert; a third, Sandy, would be the only child to be implicated in his 1822 plot. Toward the end of his life, Denmark Vesey married again. His last wife, Susan, was born a slave around 1795. She was the only woman to carry his surname. Some historians have speculated that Vesey practiced polygamy, although no evidence exists to support the theory.

On September 30, 1799, Denmark happened upon a handbill announcing the "East-Bay Lottery," and bought a ticket. In November, Charleston newspapers declared his ticket the winner. The prize was $1,500, a princely sum that slaves who hired their time would take ten years to acquire. Joseph Vesey agreed to sell Denmark his freedom for $600; the contract was signed on December 31, 1799. After seventeen years as a Charleston slave, the thirty-three-year-old Denmark was free.

Chained to the South by family ties, Denmark remained in the city and apprenticed himself to a carpenter, an easy trade to learn and a lucrative business as Charleston expanded up the peninsula. At the same time, he adopted Vesey as a surname, probably as a linguistic tie to an established businessman whose name could help to secure clients. Vesey threw his enormous energies into his business, and according to one former slave, Denmark labored "every day at de trade of carpenter" and "soon became much [re]spected" and "esteem[ed] by de white folks." But because of competition from white carpenters, free mulattoes (whose fathers provided business contacts), and enslaved craftsmen (who lived with their masters and paid no rent), Vesey barely maintained a modest income. Despite published claims made in 1822 that he died a rich man worth nearly $8,000, there is no evidence that Vesey ever owned a single piece of property.

Around 1818 Vesey joined the city's new African Methodist Episcopal congregation, the center of Charleston's enslaved community. Sandy Vesey also joined, as did four of Vesey's closest friends: Peter Poyas, a literate ship carpenter; Monday Gell, an African-born Ibo who labored as a harness maker; Rolla Bennett, the manservant of Governor Thomas Bennett; and "Gullah" Jack Pritchard, an East African priest and woodworker purchased in Zinguebar in 1806. The temporary closure of the church by city authorities in June 1818 and the arrest of 140 congregants, one of them presumably Vesey,

reinforced the determination of black Carolinians to maintain a place of independent worship and established the motivation for Vesey's conspiracy. In 1820 several "Negroes was taken up" for holding a late-night service at the church, and city authorities warned that they would not tolerate class leaders conducting instructional "schools for slaves," as "the education of such persons was forbidden by law." The "African Church was the people," Gell replied. He and Pritchard had considered insurrection in 1818, "and now they had begun again to try it."

At the age of fifty-one, Vesey briefly thought about emigrating to the English colony of Sierra Leone. But as Beck's children remained slaves, Vesey resolved instead to orchestrate a rebellion, followed by a mass exodus from Charleston to Haiti. President Jean-Pierre Boyer had recently encouraged black Americans to bring their skills and capital to his beleaguered republic. Vesey did not intend to tarry in Charleston long enough for white military power to present an effective counterassault. "As soon as they could get the money from the Banks, and the goods from the stores," Rolla insisted, "they should hoist sail" for Saint-Domingue and live as free men.

Vesey planned the escape for nearly four years. His chief lieutenants included Poyas, Gell, Rolla Bennett, and "Gullah" Jack Pritchard. Although there are no reliable figures for the number of recruits, Charleston alone was home to 12,652 slaves. Pritchard, probably with some exaggeration, boasted that he had 6,600 recruits on the plantations across the Cooper and Ashley rivers. The plan called for Vesey's followers to rise at midnight on Sunday, July 14—Bastille Day—slay their masters, and sail for Haiti and freedom. As one southern editor later conceded: "The plot seems to have been well devised, and its operation was extensive."

The plot unraveled in June 1822 when two slaves revealed the plan to their owners. Mayor James Hamilton called up the city militia and convened a special court to try the captured insurgents. Vesey was captured at Beck's home on June 21 and hanged on July 2, together with Rolla, Poyas, and three other rebels. In all, thirty-five slaves were executed. Forty-two others, including Sandy Vesey, were sold outside the United States; some, if not all, became slaves in Spanish Cuba. Robert Vesey lived to rebuild the African Church in the fall of 1865.

SEE ALSO *Slavery*

BIBLIOGRAPHY

Egerton, Douglas R. 1999. *He Shall Go Out Free: The Lives of Denmark Vesey.* Madison, WI: Madison House.

Freehling, William W. 1994. *The Reintegration of American History: Slavery and the Civil War.* New York: Oxford University Press.

Lofton, John. 1964. *Insurrection in South Carolina: The Turbulent World of Denmark Vesey.* Yellow Springs, OH: Antioch.

Paquette, Robert L. 2002. Jacobins of the Lowcountry: The Vesey Plot on Trial. *William and Mary Quarterly* 59: 185–192.

Douglas R. Egerton

VETO

The veto is the power to block or reject a proposed decision. In Latin, the word *veto* literally means "I forbid." The veto is generally an executive prerogative, as in the power of a chief executive to reject a bill or resolution that is proposed by the legislature. This power may also extend to an official authority or body, such as an international organization (e.g., the United Nations). While executive veto power is often discussed in conjunction with the authority granted to governors or presidents in the United States, it is a hallmark of a variety of separation-of-powers systems in other countries. The veto provides an important check on the power of the legislature in the lawmaking process.

In the United States, veto power is given to the chief executive by the U.S. Constitution. Even though this executive power has existed since America's founding, its use was often construed narrowly. Prior to the administration of President Andrew Jackson (1829–1837), the veto was not used by presidents to object to legislation that was viewed as questionable on policy grounds. Rather, legitimate use of the executive veto involved objecting to legislation that was either poorly drafted or clearly unconstitutional. Following Jackson's presidency, however, this practice changed, and modern U.S. presidents routinely veto legislation to which they object for political reasons. In contemporary American politics, the incidence of presidential vetoes is almost always greater under divided government, where the executive is controlled by one political party and (at least one chamber of) the legislature by the other.

Although vetoes occur relatively rarely in the legislative process, scholars are drawn to study them because vetoes carry clear policy implications. Indeed, the use of the veto by an executive is an ideal example of negative agenda control. The veto creates an opportunity to block legislative action, but it does not give the executive the power to alter proposed legislation after the fact. Nonetheless, Charles Cameron (2000) asserts that chief executives regularly engage in bargaining with legislators in an attempt to shape legislative outcomes at various stages of the process. In many respects, a credible veto

threat may be sufficient to force compliance on the part of reluctant legislators who would prefer not to prolong a legislative battle over a controversial bill or resolution. To avoid "losing" to the president, one or both chambers of the legislature may be willing to make concessions if the price of passage necessitates it.

Although veto power is usually associated with the executive office, legislatures may hold veto power as well. In a bicameral legislature where both chambers must pass legislation in identical form before it is sent to the executive for approval, for instance, either chamber can block legislation, which is the equivalent of a veto. Moreover, a veto does not always require action on the part of an executive to effectively block legislation. If the U.S. Congress sends a bill to the president and adjourns prior to the ten days given to the president to sign or veto the measure, the bill essentially dies through what is known as a *pocket veto.* Conversely, the measure will automatically become law without the president's signature if Congress remains in session past the ten-day limit. Thus, inaction on the part of the executive still can have tangible legislative consequences, contingent on the behavior of the legislature.

Veto power is by no means absolute. Consistent with the notion of both shared and separated powers, the legislature is typically given the opportunity to override an executive veto if members can garner the necessary votes. The override authority granted to legislatures provides an opportunity for offsetting an executive veto in an attempt to alter policy outcomes. In many cases, a legislative override requires a supermajority. In the U.S. Congress, for instance, two-thirds of both chambers must successfully vote to override an executive veto. While most override attempts fail as a result of the supermajority requirement, David Rohde and Dennis Simon (1985) maintain that the uncertainty associated with a potentially successful override provides an important check on unilateral power on the part of the executive.

SEE ALSO *Constitution, U.S.; Monarchy, Constitutional; Power; Presidency, The; Separation of Powers; United Nations*

BIBLIOGRAPHY

Cameron, Charles M. 2000. *Veto Bargaining: Presidents and the Politics of Negative Power.* New York: Cambridge University Press.

Ingberman, Daniel E., and Dennis A. Yao. 1991. Presidential Commitment and the Veto. *American Journal of Political Science* 35: 357–389.

Rohde, David W., and Dennis M. Simon. 1985. Presidential Vetoes and Congressional Response: A Study of Institutional Conflict. *American Journal of Political Science* 29: 397–427.

Spitzer, Robert J. 1988. *The Presidential Veto: Touchstone of the American Presidency.* Albany: State University of New York Press.

Jamie L. Carson

VIDEO GAMES

The very mention of video games conjures a myriad of different thoughts, emotions, and concerns. Originally, video games were released for the Atari gaming system in 1973, and for the Apple 2c (1984) and Apple 2gs (1986). Coin-operated gaming machines surfaced in shopping malls and in various stores during the late 1970s and early 1980s. Nintendo debuted video games as early as 1976. Although games have appeared on computer systems in the past and continue to flourish today, the two major gaming systems that paved the way for today's famous systems were the original Sega and the Nintendo gaming system. Nintendo is the oldest of the game systems companies and is currently the leader in handheld console sales. Sega offered the GameGear handheld during the 1990s. Nintendo's first offering had been Game Boy, and as of 2007 the graphically intense DS was for sale at retail outlets. The original Nintendo saw games in production from 1983 to 1994, Super Nintendo remained in production from 1990 to 2000, Nintendo 64 from 1996 to 2002, and GameCube from 2001 to 2007.

The games released may seem primitive relative to those on the market in 2007, but for the players they represented something prodigious. Games such as Pac-Man, Galaga, Pong, Budokan, Ultima, Might and Magic, Zillion, Rocky, The Adventures of Zelda, Donkey Kong, and the cult favorite, Super Mario Brothers, have entertained and delighted millions around the world. Donkey Kong was released exclusively for the Nintendo system in 1981, and the prototype for future Super Mario Brothers games appeared on the market in 1983. The Legend of Zelda became another instant classic after its arrival in early 1986.

The cult favorite game Mike Tyson's Punch-Out arrived to much fanfare in 1987. Even family restaurants welcomed the coin-machine version of the game into their establishments. The very mention of Mike Tyson in association with a video game proved to be a brilliant advertising mechanism. Meanwhile, Nintendo's Super Mario Brothers games, a smash hit when they arrived in 1985, have been criticized because they contain violent images. The objective is to slay the evil serpentine "end-guys" at the end of each level and jump on the mushroom men. To achieve this goal a player searches for special character upgrades such as the chance to wield fireballs, to be able to

fly, and the like. Meanwhile, Nintendo's competitor Sega flooded the market with games as early as 1981. Developed originally as a prototype for U.S. servicemen stationed overseas, it too achieved popularity. Although many of the games offered for the Sega system did not receive as much acclaim as those invented by Nintendo, many gamers have heralded its superior game play and controllers. Sega's smash video game hits included Rocky (1987), Zillion (1987), Phantasy Star II (1989), and the ultimate game of strategy and surprise, Herzog Zwei (1990).

Nintendo's second smash hit system, Super Nintendo, was even more successful. Super Nintendo offered Super Mario Land, an adaptation and graphically superior version of its prototype. Recently, Nintendo has capitalized on the success of these games by introducing Super Mario Brothers for their handheld system, the Nintendo DS. Additionally, Nintendo's third hit system, the Nintendo 64, offered a variety of Mario Brothers games in 3-D.

The inundation of the market with video consoles has not come without scrutiny from various sectors of society. One area of concern is that young males favor video game play more than females do. Critics and watchdog groups believe this leads to aggression and violent impulses in men. As early as the late 1980s studies showed that male characters vastly outnumbered female protagonists or heroines. Conversely, scholars have recently argued that those who grew up playing video games may actually fare better in the workplace, having gained valuable knowledge and insight into cognitive behavior and how to socialize with coworkers. As technology has advanced, so have the messages propounded in the games themselves. With the ability to command ostensibly real-life armies and to dictate bombing campaigns and infantry showdowns, skilled game players may act as mock generals. Although this may lead to an artificially enhanced sense of self-power, it can also serve as a lesson about the viciousness of warfare, the consequences of failure, and the large number of casualties experienced during a heated battle. Sports games such as NBA Live, Madden NFL, Smackdown! vs. RAW, and NHL are interactive and promote athletes as supermen and role models, and game players often aspire to become professional entertainers as a result.

As early as 2000, video games had finally become mainstreamed in society. Teenage boys are not the only group interested in acquiring and playing the big three: Microsoft's Xbox 360, Sony's PlayStation 3, or Nintendo's newest console, the Wii. The competition is on for these companies to produce high-definition-ready systems and games to correspond with this capability. Regardless, the popularity of these systems has been a cause for concern for social and civil rights groups. The most infamous game in the market has continued to be the series Grand Theft Auto, a lucrative series developed by Rockstar Games. A player may purchase prostitutes, destroy private property, wreck other people's automobiles, and essentially wreak havoc on the streets of a major city. This has captured the attention of city councils, Congress, and any number of outraged advocacy groups. As portrayed in the game, mimicking and glorifying gang behavior is disruptive and dangerous. Two staff writers for the *Washington Post,* Eric M. Weiss and Jose Antonio Vargas, have pointed out that these games are often sold or rented to children (2005). Although the revenue for game sales may be extraordinary, the social consequences are regarded by some as dire. Psychologist Craig Anderson has published findings asserting that adolescents playing violent video games experience accelerated heart rates and adrenaline rushes that may translate into violent behavior in real life.

Many of the most educational games are offered as PC games and are frequently priced lower than those created exclusively for one of the big three systems. Games such as Battle Chess or Chessmaster offer tutorials in how to improve one's chess skills. Colonization and Civilization are examples of intellectually stimulating games that have been offered in the past. Players of these games learn about world history, world leaders, inventions, architecture, the development of civilizations, and how to defeat an opponent by exercising the mind.

Clearly, video games raise awareness of the level of violence and crude sexuality that exist in contemporary society. However, it must not be ignored that these games serve several important purposes. Video games display images that brighten the imaginations of children, many are educational, and the old cliché about hand and eye coordination being sharpened through repeated game play is scientifically valid. When examining and engaging in discourse about societal problems, video games deserve to be discussed in a balanced manner and with the full spectrum of perspectives in order to recognize their positive impact on society as a whole.

SEE ALSO *Adolescent Psychology; Cultural Studies; Entertainment Industry; Leisure; Microelectronics Industry; Popular Culture; Sexuality; Sports; Sports Industry; Violence*

BIBLIOGRAPHY

Beck, John, and Mitchell Wade. 2006. *The Kids Are Alright: How the Gamer Generation Is Changing the Workplace.* Boston: Harvard Business School Press.

Provenzo, Eugene. 1991. *Video Kids: Making Sense of Nintendo.* Cambridge, MA: Harvard University Press.

Sohn, Emily. 2004. The Violent Side of Video Games. *Science News For Kids.* January 14.

http://www.sciencenewsforkids.org/articles/20040114/Feature1.asp.

Weiss, Eric M., and Jose Antonio Vargas. 2005. Video Games' Chaos Echoed in Streets, D.C. Leaders Say. *Washington Post.* February 4, 2005: A-1.

Jonathan Jacobs

VIE

SEE *Import Penetration.*

VIET MINH

SEE *Ho Chi Minh.*

VIETNAM WAR

The Vietnam War has been permanently singed into the American consciousness, and its impact will be felt for years to come in foreign policy debates. The conflict produced four million killed or wounded Vietnamese—one-tenth of the combined population of North and South Vietnam at the onset of the war—and ranks as the United States' longest and costliest overseas conflict, with the loss of 57,939 American lives and $150 billion in U.S. military spending. Moreover, Vietnam was a critical issue in the foreign policy of six successive U.S. presidential administrations.

BACKGROUND

A thorough understanding of the Vietnam War must begin with the end of World War II (1939–1945) and the onset of the cold war. To be sure, Communist Vietnam and the United States had interacted before 1946, notably when Ho Chi Minh requested Vietnamese self-determination at the 1918 Versailles Peace Conference ending World War I (1914–1918) and when he made his 1945 independence speech, which quoted the U.S. Declaration of Independence as a band played the "Star Spangled Banner." But it was the specter of a strengthened Soviet Union threatening Asia that spurred U.S. involvement in Indochina, the French colonial holdings that comprised present-day Vietnam, Cambodia, and Laos. In 1945 France had petitioned for the return of Indochina, which it had surrendered to the Japanese earlier in World War II. A year earlier, U.S. president Franklin Roosevelt, a fervent anticolonialist, had written to the British ambassador that he believed "Indochina should not go back to the French, but that it should be administered by international trusteeship."

But by the summer of 1950, four years into the French Indochina War, Roosevelt was long dead, Harry Truman had assumed office, and the geopolitical landscape looked remarkably different: the Soviet Union had detonated an atomic bomb, Chinese communists had completed their conquest of the mainland, Senator Joseph McCarthy had initiated his now infamous campaign against "softness" toward communism, and the United States was involved in a full-scale war against a Soviet satellite in Korea. In such a political climate the United States regarded Ho Chi Minh and his organization the *Viet Minh* (the abbreviation for the Vietnam Independence League, formed in 1941) as part of a wider communist threat. The image of France in U.S. policy circles also had evolved with the changing times; the country was no longer a nation of greedy imperialists, but a stalwart opponent of the spread of the "red menace" in Asia. Thus, in much the same spirit as the Berlin airlift (1948–1949) and the postwar provision of monetary assistance to Greece and Turkey, the United States offered financial support to France in its quest for repossession of Vietnam. The allotment in 1950 started at $10 million, but it rapidly grew to $1.06 billion by 1954. In fact, a full 80 percent of the French war effort was paid for by the United States.

Despite the substantial U.S. support, the French were unable to prevail, and they eventually withdrew entirely after the battle of Dien Bien Phu in spring 1954. The resounding defeat (13,200 of the 16,000 French soldiers were either killed or captured) drove both sides to the bargaining table (along with, among others, the United States, China, and Soviet Union) at the 1954 Geneva Conference, where an agreement was reached to temporarily partition the country at the seventeenth parallel. A demilitarized zone (DMZ) now divided two governments: the communist North (the Democratic Republic of Vietnam) led by the Viet Minh, and the anticommunist South (the Republic of Vietnam) under the emperor Bao Dai.

The seeds of war were sown in the very language of the Geneva Accords, which called for an election to take place in July 1956 to choose the government of a reunified Vietnam. There was considerable consternation that a Communist government could prevail in a democratic election: Ho Chi Minh had become a popular revolutionary figure throughout Vietnam and, more importantly, no southern leaders had emerged with the charisma to best him in an election. Certainly, few Vietnamese would be willing to support an emperor who owed his very position to French colonialism. A Communist win would pose a setback to Eisenhower's global strategy of "rolling back" the Communist threat, and U.S. officials warned that the loss of Vietnam would cause a chain reaction, much like the falling of dominoes, as other Southeast Asian nations succumbed to Communist pressures. Recent scholarship has refuted this "domino theory" by arguing that the United States' military advantage over the Soviet Union at that time demonstrates that important U.S. policymakers such as Secretary of State John Foster Dulles were less afraid of fending off Communist insurgencies and more interested in projecting U.S. power in the region.

Eventually the United States chose to throw its support behind Ngo Dinh Diem, the prime minister of South Vietnam, who was nominated in 1954 by Emperor Bao Dai in the midst of the Geneva Conference. Although he possessed staunch anticommunist credentials, Diem was handicapped by his Catholicism (a religion shared by only 15% of the country's population), his residence in the United States during the war against the French (which prevented him from capitalizing on the nationalist fervor), and his lack of many political allies other than his own powerful family. He needed help to build a political base and popular support before he could possibly succeed in an election. The United States was willing to offer that assistance, in part because of Diem's cultivation of important political figures such as intelligence officer Colonel Edward G. Lansdale, and it began channeling aid through Diem, informing all potential rivals that future assistance hinged on Diem's position at the helm. The gamble to support Diem until he could consolidate power and institute democratic reforms was the means by which the United States found itself inextricably linked to the southern regime.

THE POLICE ACTION

The issue of which side first violated the Geneva Accords will forever remain the fault line dividing historians of the war. Did South Vietnam violate the accords by postponing the elections, claiming (with U.S. support) that free and fair elections could never take place under a Communist government? Or did North Vietnam violate the terms of the accords through its military assistance to Communist guerrillas in the South, the National Liberation Front (NLF)? Although some have claimed that the NLF (also called the *Vietcong*) was always composed of northern agents and controlled by Hanoi, and not an indigenous popular movement of the South, there was no clear political relationship between the northern government and the growing insurgency in the South until northern leaders decided in May 1959 that they needed to take control of the movement.

Whatever the answer, the South found itself embroiled in a deadly conflict with the NLF, which had entrenched itself in the Mekong Delta as early as 1957 and in the central highlands by 1958. Afraid that Diem's power might be threatened by the conflict, the United States almost immediately lent him military assistance. The first deaths recorded on the U.S. Vietnam War Memorial are from 1957, but for the most part the U.S. military's role remained minor until May 1959, when U.S. military advisors were placed with South Vietnamese regiments as part of a police action. Although the United States described this move as aiding an anti-Communist ally, North Vietnam interpreted the assistance as a continuation of the Western colonialism begun by the French.

The U.S. commitment to Vietnam expanded under the Kennedy administration at the end of 1961 after a series of incidents (most notably the Bay of Pigs) allowed the Republican opposition to portray him as soft on Communism. Consequently, Kennedy chose to take a hard line against the advance of Communism in Southeast Asia, expanding the number of military advisers from 900 to 3,200 by the end of 1961 and then to 11,300 by the end of 1962. Despite these large increases in advisers and despite optimistic Defense Department reports to the contrary, little progress was being made in quelling the insurgency. Prominent U.S. officials began to blame this failure on Diem, claiming that rampant corruption by his friends and family, lack of progress on land reform, and, above all else, an anti-Buddhist policy, were causing him to lose favor with Vietnamese citizens. Diem's relationship with Buddhists was highlighted by a May 1963 incident in Hue when a deputy provincial chief gave orders to fire on 20,000 Buddhists at a religious celebration. Nine people were killed, and the Buddhist monk Quang Duc was prompted to burn himself a month later, calling for Diem to "show charity and compassion to all religions." Photographs of his self-immolation appeared in U.S. newspapers and were thought to undermine support for the war effort. Small-scale opposition to the war, mainly on U.S. college campuses, erupted not long after the incident.

Putting pressure on Diem, the United States called for South Vietnamese military leaders to act against Diem's excesses. How much the United States knew of the southern military's true plans is a matter of intense debate, but on November 2, 1963, Diem was overthrown in a coup and executed, and General Duong Van Minh (or Big Minh) came to power. (Minh lasted less than two months before another military coup installed Nguyen Khanh.) The overthrow of Diem was followed by an announcement on November 15 that the United States would begin withdrawing 1,000 troops. The withdrawal never happened because a week later Kennedy was assassinated and Vice President Lyndon Johnson assumed the presidency. More optimistic about the potential for U.S. victory, Johnson increased the number of U.S. advisers to 21,000.

THE ONSET OF WAR

The Gulf of Tonkin incident served as the catalyst to full U.S. military involvement in Vietnam. On August 2, 1964 the USS *Maddox* was conducting a routine reconnaissance mission in the gulf when it was fired on by North Vietnamese coastal defense forces. The *Maddox* easily repelled the attack with air support from the nearby USS *Ticonderoga*, destroying one torpedo boat in the encounter. President Johnson, who was mired in a tough election campaign, chose a firm but restrained response, rejecting reprisals against the North but warning Hanoi that "grave consequences" would result from further unprovoked military attacks. Then, on August 4, the *Maddox* and USS *Turner Joy* picked up radar signals of an apparent torpedo attack from North Vietnamese vessels, and for two hours the ships responded with a torrent of fire against radar targets and took a series of evasive actions. Johnson ordered retaliatory air strikes on North Vietnamese targets and used the event to persuade Congress to pass the August 7 Gulf of Tonkin resolution that authorized the president "to take all necessary steps, including the use of armed force."

Recent scholarship has examined whether the North Vietnamese ever actually attacked during the Tonkin incident. *Maddox* captain John J. Herrick conceded that the radar signal may have been nothing more than an "overeager sonar man" who "was hearing the ship's own propeller beat." The National Security Agency admitted to translation errors in intercepted Vietnamese transmissions that were used as grounds for the second attack. Senator William Fulbright confessed that he felt hoodwinked by the information presented in the 40-minute Senate debate. Most importantly, the scholar Gareth Porter in *Perils of Dominance* (2005) claimed that important information that cast doubt on the attack may have been concealed from Lyndon Johnson by Robert McNamara, his own secretary of defense.

Thus began the Vietnam War. The United States convinced Australia and New Zealand to contribute troops and material support, and in March 1965 began a series of bombing raids on North Vietnam known as "Rolling Thunder," with the intention of bringing the Hanoi leadership to the bargaining table. An initial 3,500 ground troops were designated for combat rather than advisory duty in Vietnam; through incremental escalation, the number of U.S. troops in Vietnam grew to 184,000 by the end of 1965 and to 429,000 by the end of 1966.

As the United States geared up for war, young Americans sensed that there would be a return to the draft lottery. The National Committee to the End the War in Vietnam staged the first burning of a draft card in the United States in October 1965. After the Tonkin incident there was also turmoil in South Vietnam, where Nguyen

Khanh tried to exploit the new situation with a series of repressive decrees that led to riots in the street and a series of plots and counterplots until Nguyen Van Thieu and Nguyen Cao Ky grabbed power in the spring of 1965.

North Vietnam attempted to match the U.S. escalation with incursions by its regular army into the central highlands, but a setback with the battle of Ia Drang Valley in November 1965 curtailed the use of their regular army in favor of guerrilla tactics. Even so, at Ia Drang 240 Americans were killed and 450 wounded, sending a shocking signal to the United States that the war would not be won easily or on the cheap.

Most U.S./South Vietnam military activity after Ia Drang focused on three areas. First, search and destroy missions, a favorite of General Westmoreland, the head of U.S. forces in the country, were part of his attrition strategy to kill and capture Vietcong forces in the South. Second, "pacification" was the securing of the South Vietnamese countryside by means of a combination of military protection and development assistance. Finally, efforts were made to cut the Vietcong's supply line that came down the Ho Chi Minh Trail, a dense network of forest paths running through Laos into South Vietnam. Although the CIA began to pick up evidence of enemy activity along the trail as early as 1959, the route was of limited value to the North until 1963, when at the behest of Colonel Bui Tin it was expanded to accommodate trucks and large movements of North Vietnamese regulars. The original intention of Rolling Thunder was to disrupt traffic on the trail, but the bombing raids did not have the desired effect because the North Vietnamese showed remarkable ingenuity in repairing damaged roads and bridges. Moreover, the United States' use of toxic chemical defoliants such as napalm and Agent Orange along the trail and in other areas to cut back the dense brush and expose Northern forces had devastating effects on Vietnamese civilians; news of this bolstered the antiwar movement in the United States, and protesters and police clashed violently at the University of Wisconsin in October 1967.

The United States attempted again to disrupt the supply network in January 1968 by setting up a fire base along the Laotian border near the town of Khe Sanh. The U.S. marines at the base soon found themselves under heavy attack from North Vietnamese regulars. Only in April did the siege finally end, after an incessant barrage of U.S. artillery and air strikes equivalent to five Hiroshima-sized atomic bombs. Khe Sanh served to distract U.S. attention from North Vietnam's preparations for its largest and best coordinated operation of the war, lasting from January 1968 to July 1969. Known as the Tet Offensive because it occurred during the *Tet Nguyen Dan* (the Vietnamese name for the Chinese New Year), the operation had North

Vietnamese troops driving to the center of South Vietnam's seven largest cities and attacking thirty provincial capitals from the deep South to the DMZ. The goal of the attacks was to ignite a popular uprising that would result in the overthrow of the South Vietnamese government and withdrawal of U.S. forces. In the first days of the offensive several cities were overrun and a nineteen-man suicide squad managed to seize the U.S. embassy in Saigon for six hours before they were routed. In most areas the U.S. and South Vietnamese forces repulsed the attacks immediately, but in Saigon the fighting lasted almost a week and in Hue bloody house-to-house combat consumed the two sides for over a month. Eventually, Hue was recovered, and Westmoreland declared that allied forces had killed more enemy troops in the last seven days of fighting than the United States had lost since the beginning of the war.

Although North Vietnam's military objectives had not been achieved in the Tet Offensive, the psychological impact on the American home front was considerable. Many U.S. citizens who had supported the war were shocked by the ferocity of the attack and concluded that the government was misleading them. Members of Johnson's own cabinet began to turn against the war and resisted calls for more troops. Soon Westmoreland was replaced in Vietnam by Creighton Adams, and that same year, 1968, Johnson announced an "October surprise"—a complete cessation of all air, naval, and artillery bombardment of North Vietnam north of the twentieth parallel as a symbolic gesture to encourage the peace talks taking place in Paris. The Paris talks broke down eventually, as did Johnson's fortitude. He chose not to run for president in the 1968 election, which was marred by intense antiwar protests at the Democratic Convention in Chicago, and eventually won by the Republican candidate Richard Nixon, in part because of his "secret plan" to remove the United States from the war with honor.

THE WIND DOWN

Nixon's secret plan rested on two pillars. First, "Vietnamization" consisted of the gradual strengthening of the South Vietnamese military until they could hold their own against the NLF and North Vietnamese Army. It was hoped that reducing the combat load of U.S. troops would lessen popular opposition to the war stateside. Second, Nixon's foreign policy of rapprochement with both China and the Soviet Union, in the midst of the Sino-Soviet split, had the effect of limiting their assistance to North Vietnam.

The diplomatic success was undermined by the negative publicity surrounding two notorious events: the 1968 My Lai massacre, which occurred when a platoon led by William Calley killed several hundred Vietnamese women and children and burned a small town to the ground; and the bombing of Cambodia in 1969, which was intended to destroy NLF sanctuaries and supplies hidden along the Cambodian border. The latter action prompted more protests on U.S. college campuses—four students were shot and killed by National Guard troops during demonstrations at Kent State University in Ohio. On the warfront, one unintended effect of the bombing campaign was to push Communist forces deeper into Cambodia, which destabilized the country and in turn may have encouraged the rise of the Khmer Rouge, who seized power in 1975.

In an effort to help assuage opposition to the war, Nixon announced on October 12, 1970 that the United States would withdraw 40,000 more troops before Christmas. But on October 30th, the worst monsoon to hit Vietnam in six years caused large floods, killed close to 300, left 200,000 Vietnamese homeless, and brought the war effort to a standstill. On January 15, 1973, citing progress in peace negotiations, President Nixon suspended offensive operations in North Vietnam, then followed with a unilateral withdrawal of U.S. troops from Vietnam. The Paris Peace Accords were signed on January 27, 1973, officially ending U.S. involvement in the Vietnam conflict. For their efforts, Secretary of State Henry Kissinger and North Vietnamese lead negotiator Le Duc Tho were awarded the Nobel Peace Prize. But the fighting in Vietnam continued unabated. In December 1974 the U.S. Congress passed the Foreign Assistance Act of 1974, thereby cutting off all military funding to the Saigon government and rendering the peace terms negotiated by Kissinger unenforceable. By 1975 the South Vietnamese army stood alone against the powerful North Vietnamese, and Saigon famously fell on April 30, 1975 when two tanks crashed through the gates of the presidential palace as South Vietnamese who had cooperated with the United States desperately tried to flee the country.

THE AFTERMATH

Vietnam became a unified nation after the war, but at a great cost in terms of human lives and infrastructure, and in 1975 it was one of the world's poorest countries. Although the population still suffers effects of Agent Orange and unexploded ordinance, economic reform (*Doi Moi*) begun in 1986 has drastically reduced poverty from over 70 percent of the population to less than 20 percent and spurred impressive long-term growth throughout the nation. Foreign investment also has played a major role in Vietnam's economic upturn, with an increasing amount coming from the United States after the normalization of relations in 1995. For South Vietnamese connected with the former regime, the end of the war was a time of fear and resentment. Many highly skilled and educated South Vietnamese fled the country at the fall of Saigon and for

years after, severely depleting the nation's human capital. The new Communist government promptly sent connected South Vietnamese to hard-labor camps for "reeducation," many for several years. Persecution and poverty prompted an additional two million people to flee Vietnam as "boat people" over the fifteen years following unification. To deal with the severe refugee crisis in the 1980s and 1990s, the United Nations established refugee camps in neighboring countries to process them. Many of these refugees resettled in the United States, forming large Vietnamese American emigrant communities with a decidedly anticommunist viewpoint.

In the United States the war had profound psychological effects, dividing the American public over the contentious issues of the humiliating withdrawal, perceived inequities in the draft, the schism in society created by the antiwar movement, knowledge of the devastation wrought on an impoverished country, and, most importantly, a profound sense of distrust in government, as many Americans believed their elected officials had not been forthcoming about the difficulties of the encounter while young citizens died in unprecedented numbers. Civil military relations were damaged because many soldiers and officers believed a winnable war had been undermined by civilian leadership and politics, and politicians felt that a runaway military had supplied it with misleading reports about the success of operations (particularly pacification). Finally, the role of the media was forever altered by reporters, photographers, and television crews who delivered coverage of the war into American living rooms. Some would hold the media up as heroic truth-tellers; others would blame it for supplying fodder to unpatriotic war protesters.

SEE ALSO *Anticolonial Movements; Bay of Pigs; Communism; Coup d'Etat; Domino Theory; Guerrilla Warfare; Imperialism; Johnson, Lyndon B.; Kennedy, John F.; Khrushchev, Nikita; Minh, Ho Chi; Peace; Union of Soviet Socialist Republics*

BIBLIOGRAPHY

Bowman, John S. 2005. *The Vietnam War Almanac.* New York: Barnes and Noble.

Economist. 2005. Vietnam: Changing Gear. November 26: 49–50.

Ely, John Hart. 1993. *War and Responsibility: Constitutional Lessons of Vietnam and Its Aftermath.* Princeton, NJ: Princeton University Press.

Herring, George C. 1996. *America's Longest War: The United States and Vietnam, 1950–1975.* New York: McGraw-Hill.

Levy, David W. 1995. *The Debate over Vietnam.* Baltimore, MD: Johns Hopkins University Press.

Marr, David G. 1945. *Vietnam 1945: The Quest for Power.* Berkeley: University of California Press.

Miguel, Edward, and Gerard Roland. 2005. The Long Run Impact of Bombing Vietnam. National Bureau of Economic Research working paper no. 11954. Washington, DC.

Porter, Gareth. 2005. *Perils of Dominance: Imbalance of Power and the Road to War in Vietnam.* Berkeley: University of California Press.

Scott, Shane. 2005. Vietnam War Intelligence " 'Deliberately Skewed,' " Secret Study Says. *New York Times*, December 2.

Van Arkadie, Brian, and Raymond Mallon. 2003. *Vietnam: A Transition Tiger?* Canberra: Asia Pacific Press at Australia National University.

Edmund J. Malesky

VILLA, FRANCISCO (PANCHO)
1878–1923

The memory of Francisco (Pancho) Villa evokes contradicting sentiments. Villa has been extolled as a trustworthy revolutionary. He has also been vilified as a cruel, dishonest bandit. Nevertheless, Villa remains a significant figure in Mexican history. His memory remains alive through Mexican ballads known as *corriodos*, poetry, and film. This article examines the life of Villa—the bandit and the revolutionary—and his contributions to Mexican political history.

Villa was born José Doroteo Arango Arámbula on June 5, 1878, in the northern state of Durango. (In *The Life and Times of Pancho Villa*, Friedrich Katz states that baptism records show he was baptized as Doroteo Arango, while Francisco Caudet Yarza claims in *Pancho Villa* that he was baptized as José Doroteo.) Villa came from a poor background. His parents, Agustín Arango and Micaele Arambula, worked as sharecroppers on one of the largest haciendas in Durango. Villa's father died when Villa was young. Consequently, Villa, the oldest of five children, had to work to support the family at the expense of a formal education.

Villa was a bandit by the 1890s. The reason he decided to live the harsh life of a bandit in the mountains of Durango is unknown. In his memoirs Villa recounts that he fled into the mountains of Durango when he was sixteen years old out of fear that he would be incarcerated for shooting and injuring Agustín López Negrete, the owner of the hacienda on which he lived and worked (Katz 1998, p. 3). Villa allegedly shot the owner to protect the honor of one of his younger sisters.

However, some biographers question whether or not Villa's attack on the hacienda owner actually took place (Braddy 1948, p. 349; Garfias, 1985, p. 15; Katz 1998,

p. 65). Celia Herrera, whose relatives had been killed by Villa, recorded that he became a bandit upon murdering a friend during an altercation (Katz 1998, p. 6). Regardless of its validity, the incident remains a part of Villa's story.

Doroteo changed his name to Francisco, or Pancho, Villa as an outlaw. The new name was probably an adoption of the name of his biological grandfather, Jesús Villa, and changed to evade the federal army and state authorities in Durango. Legendary tales impart that Villa adopted the name of a famous bandit, Francisco Villa, who died after being severely injured during an attack by local citizens in the mountains of Durango.

The description of Villa's life during this time has varied. Some individuals viewed him solely as a violent, ruthless bandit. Celia Herrera's *Francisco Villa ante la historia* describes Villa as one who led a life of crime and vengeance in which he killed friends, beat women, and tortured those who refused to cooperate when he demanded their money (Katz 1998, p. 6). Villa admitted to killing many men in his memoirs but denied being a cold-blooded murderer. Rather, the men were killed in self-defense or out of retaliation for betrayal (Katz 1998, p. 5).

On the other hand, Villa has been perceived as a benevolent champion of the poor. His memoirs reveal that he had stolen money and given it to the poor, including family members. These altruistic acts earned him the label of "Robin Hood of the Mexicans" (Brandt 1964, p. 153; Caudet 1998, p. 35; Katz 1998, p. 7).

By 1910 Villa had transformed from a bandit into a revolutionary. Abraham González, the leader of the Anti-Reelectionist Party in Chihuahua, recruited Villa and a military leader, Pascual Orozco, into the revolutionary movement against President Porfirio Díaz (Katz 1998, p. 73). González's decision to recruit an outlaw to support the revolutionary efforts of Francisco Madero remains questionable. Regardless, the revolution was successful. President Díaz was forced to resign after thirty years of dictatorial rule, and Madero became the president of Mexico. Villa earned a promotion to honorary general, and he fought against the counterrevolutionaries, led by Orozco, in 1912.

Villa was also an important figure in U.S.-Mexican relations. His relationship with the United States was initially amicable. The United States allowed arms to be smuggled to Villa in January 1914, and President Woodrow Wilson ended the U.S. arms embargo against Mexico shortly thereafter, which allowed Villa to buy ammunition legally from the United States (Katz 1998, p. 250). President Wilson even offered Villa political asylum in the United States in 1915 (Katz 1998, p. 535). These actions illustrated the United States' confidence in Villa's abilities as a leader.

The positive relationship between Villa and the United States took a turn for the worse by 1916, when Villa attacked Columbus, New Mexico. The reasons for Villa's attack remain under debate. A letter from Villa indicates that the attack was meant as revenge for an act of betrayal by President Wilson during his war against the troops of President Venustiano Carranza of Mexico (Katz 1998, p. 552). Whatever the reason, the attack caused Wilson to send American troops to Mexico to capture Villa and destroy his forces (Sandos 1981, p. 303).

Villa was murdered on July 20, 1923, while driving to a village in Chihuahua. Two weeks after Villa's assassination, Jesús Salas Barraza claimed sole responsibility for Villa's murder. He said he killed Villa on behalf of the many people in his district, El Oro, who had been victimized by Villa (Katz 1998, p. 773). Salas was sentenced to twenty years in prison on September 13 but was pardoned and released a few months later. No one else was accused or arrested for Villa's murder.

An examination of Villa's life reveals that he probably was neither the devil nor the angel that many chose to label him. Instead, he is a complex figure whose memory continues to flourish in both Mexico and the United States.

SEE ALSO *Mexican Revolution (1910–1920); Revolution; Social Movements; Zapata, Emiliano*

BIBLIOGRAPHY

Braddy, Haldeen. 1948. Pancho Villa, Folk Hero of the Mexican Border. *Western Folklore* 7 (4): 349–355.

Brandt, Nancy. 1964. Pancho Villa: The Making of a Modern Legend. *Americas* 21 (2): 146–162.

Caudet Yarza, Francisco. 1998. *Pancho Villa.* Madrid, Spain: Dastin.

Garfias M., Luis. 1981. *Verdad y leyenda de Pancho Villa.* Mexico, D.F.: Panaroma Editorial.

Herrera, Celia. 1981. *Francisco Villa ante la historia.* 3rd ed. Mexico, D.F.: Costa Amic Editores.

Katz, Friedrich. 1998. *The Life and Times of Pancho Villa.* Stanford, CA: Stanford University Press.

Sandos, James A. 1981. "Pancho Villa and American Security: Woodrow Wilson's Mexican Diplomacy Reconsidered." *Journal of Latin American Studies* 13 (2): 293–311.

Sarita D. Jackson

VINDICATION

"Vindication" describes a style of political and intellectual discourse that motivates certain social movements. Adherents of vindicationist movements believe that their group is undervalued by the broader society, and they seek to rehabilitate and elevate their collective reputation. Vindicationist rhetoric argues that the minority group possesses qualities and abilities that are equal to or superior to those of the dominant group and that the dominant group's prejudice against the minority is thus based on false premises. Vindicationism functions to motivate potential followers of the movement while simultaneously scolding the dominant group for failing to appreciate the admirable character and qualities of the people for whom the movement is advocating. Vindicationism is most commonly found in the ideologies of feminist movements and racial-ethnic nationalist movements.

An early example is Mary Wollstonecraft's *A Vindication of the Rights of Woman* (1792), a pioneering feminist treatise. Mary Wollstonecraft argued on behalf of women's natural talents and abilities and held that women should not be measured according to essentially male standards. She asserted that men needed to change in order to end women's oppression. Many of the ideological roots of twentieth-century liberal feminism trace back to Wollstonecraft.

A significant strain of vindicationism emerges in early African American political thought. Black abolitionist David Walker's famous "Appeal" (1829) argued for the humanity and inherent rights of African Americans. Walker traces African American heritage back to ancient Egypt, whose cultural achievements demonstrate racial abilities equal or superior to those of whites.

The vindicationist sentiment found in nineteenth-century African American political writing influenced the anticolonial ideologies of twentieth-century Africa. Not surprisingly, vindicationism appeared first in Sierra Leone and Liberia, the two West African countries most heavily populated by freed slaves from North America. A contemporary influence on African anticolonialist vindicationism was American author W. E. B. Du Bois's *The World and Africa: An Inquiry into the Part That Africa Has Played in World History* (1947).

Vindicationist ideology is also central to white Southern nationalism in the United States. Immediately following the Civil War, Confederate apologists began to recast the causes of the war, in what became known as the "Lost Cause" narrative. This narrative denies the role of proslavery ideology as a significant motive behind secession. Instead, it argues that "state's rights" were the primary instigating factor. This permits Confederate apologists to situate the secession not as a rebellion but instead as advocacy of core American values as expressed in the Constitution. The other major component of Lost Cause vindicationism is the argument that the South lost the Civil War because of the North's overwhelming numbers and resources, and not because of Northern soldiers' superior bravery or tactical skill. Thus, for Southern nationalists invested in the Lost Cause narrative, the Confederacy can be honored in historical memory not as a rebellion motivated by a dishonorable motive, not as a military failure, but as a noble Lost Cause whose ultimate purpose was to uphold the best of American values.

Lost Cause vindicationism found an organizational home around the turn of the twentieth century with the establishment of the United Daughters of the Confederacy (UDC). The UDC embarked on a number of educational and symbolic campaigns to cement the Lost Cause ideology in American historical memory. The early 1990s saw the foundation of the League of the South (LoS), an explicitly separatist southern nationalist movement. By 2005, the neo-Confederate nationalism of the LoS had also suffused the Sons of Confederate Veterans, a much older, larger, and wealthier organization.

Many vindicationist ideologies develop elements of supremacism. This rhetorical move begins with an essentialist argument, holding that we—the vindicated group—are essentially different from the dominant group. The argument then asserts that the differences between the dominant group and the vindicated minority demonstrate the minority's superiority to the dominant group. The essentialist strain in contemporary feminism at its extremist fringes verges into female supremacism. The lesbian separatist feminism that emerged in the 1970s is the most prominent example.

The early black abolitionist David Walker argued that blacks "never were half so avaricious, deceitful and unmerciful as the whites" (1829). In the mid-twentieth century, Elijah Muhammad (1897–1975) preached to African Americans that they are divine, while whites are a race of devils that were created by an evil black scientist. Muhammad's arguments persist today in the theology of the Nation of Islam. The group's current leader, Louis Farrakhan, has said that "White people are potential humans…they haven't evolved yet" (Raghavan 2000, p. B1).

The use of "vindication" among social scientists to refer to a particular expression of minority grievances begins with Wollstonecraft's feminism. The most common application of the "vindication" adjective has historically been to describe African American political writings of the nineteenth and early twentieth centuries. However, a recent shift has emerged in the social science community's use of the concept. Political scientists now apply the term "vindicationism" to attempts by the United States to remake the world to conform to American values. This body of research locates the origins of American vindicationism in the Spanish-American War of 1898 and traces it through subsequent foreign interventions by the United States during the twentieth century. The vindicationist approach to foreign policy reached a peak with the wars in

Afghanistan and Iraq, as advocated and prosecuted by the George W. Bush administration and its neoconservative advisors (McCartney, 2004).

SEE ALSO *Bush, George W.; Confederate States of America; Feminism; Ideology; Iraq-U.S. War; Nationalism and Nationality; Social Movements; U.S. Civil War; White Supremacy*

BIBLIOGRAPHY

Du Bois, W. E. B. 1947. *The World and Africa: An Inquiry into the Part which Africa Has Played in World History.* New York: Viking.

McCartney, Paul T. 2004. American Nationalism and U.S. Foreign Policy from September 11 to the Iraq War. *Political Science Quarterly* 119 (3). http://www.ciaonet.org/olj/psq/psq_fall04/.

Raghavan, Sudarsan. 2000. Farrakhan exhorts student leaders to fight oppression. *Philadelphia Inquirer*, March 19, p. B1.

Walker, David. 1829. *Walker's Appeal, in Four Articles; Together with a Preamble, to the Coloured Citizens of the World, but in Particular, and Very Expressly, to Those of the United States of America, Written in Boston, State of Massachusetts, September 28, 1829.* Boston: Author. http://docsouth.unc.edu/nc/walker/walker.html.

Wollstonecraft, Mary. 1792. *A Vindication of the Rights of Woman: With Strictures on Political and Moral Subjects.* Boston: Peter Edes for Thomas and Andrews.

Thomas F. Brown

VINTAGE MODELS

Capital goods that are constructed at different moments in time embody the state of technology at the moment of their construction, thus giving rise to the notion of individual vintages of capital goods. These vintages differ in intrinsic "productive quality" because of ongoing technological progress, just like different vintages of wine can differ in quality. The basic idea underlying a vintage model is that the potential of *technical change* as an idea can only be realized in practice by first incorporating that idea in a piece of machinery and subsequently using that machinery to produce output. Because technical change is therefore *embodied* in individual pieces of machinery and equipment, vintage models emphasize the fact that complementary investment has to take place in order to realize the productivity promises of new ideas. There is also technical change not linked to investment that comes in the form of new ideas about the organization of production; this is called *disembodied* technical change in a vintage context. By contrast, an *aggregate production function*, which is still the most popular way of representing technology in large-scale macroeconomic models, assumes that capital is homogeneous and that the process of technical change can be represented as a continuous shift of the per capita production function that is independent of the rate of investment. Hence, all technical change is thought of as disembodied, and technology-induced reductions in unit production costs are therefore assumed to be independent of the actual level of investment.

The main focus of a vintage model is on the *diffusion* of technical change as opposed to endogenous growth theory that focuses on the source of technical change. The embodiment of technical change results in a capital stock that is heterogeneous in terms of the factor-productivity (hence the unit operating cost) associated with individual vintages. Depending on the type of vintage model on hand, the arrival of new superior technologies may render the old ones obsolete, leading to the *economic scrapping* of inferior equipment. It is through investment and disinvestment at both ends of the vintage spectrum that the average productivity characteristics of the capital stock can be made to change, though only relatively gradually.

Since the arrival of vintage models in the late 1950s and 1960s (see, for example, Johansen 1959; Salter 1960; Solow 1960; Phelps 1962, 1963; Jorgenson 1966; Solow et al. 1966), they have been used by economists interested in the connection between technical change and economic growth, because they highlight a number of important insights regarding the complementarity between productivity growth and investment. Firstly, productivity growth is positively influenced by gross investment. In the aggregate production function approach, labor productivity growth is as much the result of the growth in capital per capita (and is therefore linked to net investment per capita rather than gross investment) as it is the result of (labor-saving) technical change itself. Secondly, vintage models stress the idea that technical change has to be bought and paid for, rather than falling freely like "manna from heaven." Consequently, anything that reduces incentives to invest in new machinery—for example, increasing uncertainty or a higher *user cost of capital*—will reduce the speed of diffusion of technical change. Thirdly, under the embodiment assumption, the average productivity characteristics of the total capital stock will change only gradually as new capital goods fill the gaps left by the *technical decay* and *economic scrapping* of old capital goods. Hence, if one wanted to change the average characteristics of capital stock in a noticeable way, one would either have to engage in nonmarginal replacement investment, or start promoting investment in new technologies sooner rather than later.

There are different types of vintage models, ranging from *putty-putty* (Solow 1960; Phelps 1962), to *putty-clay* (Johansen 1959; Salter 1960; Phelps 1963), to *clay-clay*

models (Kaldor and Mirrlees 1962; Solow et al. 1966). Even *putty-semi-putty* models exist (Fuss 1978). The somewhat far-fetched names come from the world of pottery (Phelps 1963). The term *putty* refers to clay that is still soft enough to change shape, whereas *clay* refers to the hard-baked state of that shape that cannot be changed anymore without breaking it. When applied to a technology, *putty-ness* describes a state in which there are many different techniques associated with a specific technology that one could choose to implement, whereas *clay-ness* implies that there is just one implementation of a technology available, and that it is impossible to change it without "breaking" it (and, thus, effectively discarding it). The first word (*putty* or *clay*) in the name of a vintage model refers to the size of the set of potentially available techniques before the moment that the actual hardware embodying the technique is installed (i.e., *ex ante*), and the second word (*putty* or *clay*) refers to the set of techniques still left after installation (i.e., *ex post*). A putty-clay model, therefore, covers a situation with (infinitely) many choices *ex ante*, and just one *ex post* (i.e., the one technique that has actually been implemented after making a choice from many techniques *ex ante*). Putty-putty models have infinitely many choices *ex ante* and *ex post*. A clay-clay model has just one technique to choose from, both *ex ante* and *ex post*. The putty-clay model is generally considered to be the most realistic vintage model because it recognizes that one generally has several production techniques to choose from, but also that once the machinery has been built and installed the choice for that technique can not be undone. *Ex post* "clay-ness" therefore represents the impossibility of reversing decisions made *ex ante*.

This irreversibility of investment *ex post* implies that one would have to try to forecast changes in factor prices *ex ante*, and incorporate these forecasts into the factor proportions that are to be embodied in the new vintage under consideration. For example, a rise in wages not properly foreseen would result in a labor intensity of production *ex ante* that is *too* high (with hindsight), and that would lead to an *economic lifetime* that is consequently too short (the economic lifetime of a vintage is equal to the duration of the period over which it would be most profitable to operate that vintage; see Malcomson 1975). In putty-putty models, such lifetime effects of forecasting errors do not exist, as one can continuously and costlessly adjust factor proportions (i.e., production techniques) to the current factor price situation on every vintage installed, from the newest to those installed in the distant past. Obviously, the latter situation is less relevant in practice, even though elegant in theory.

From a policy point of view, the irreversibility of investment is important, as it implies that humanity's trust in technical change to solve some of its problems—

for example, global warming—may involve high investment costs. The latter are routinely ignored in an aggregate production function setting, as technical change is assumed to take place regardless of the level of investment. Consequently, an aggregate production function approach would tend to underestimate the real cost of technical change while neglecting the positive link between the effective pace of technical change (insofar as the latter is embodied in machinery and equipment), and the rate of investment. In a putty-clay setting, on the other hand, a large volume of replacement investment would be required to change the energy consumption characteristics of the aggregate capital stock in a nonmarginal way. Thus, either one would be forced to bear very large (just-in-time) adjustment costs, or, from a risk-diversification point of view, one would have to promote investment in new energy-saving technologies sooner rather than later. Interestingly, Schumpeterian endogenous growth theory (see, for example, Aghion and Howitt 1998) points out that the expectation of new technological breakthroughs that might or might not arrive just in time may actually have the opposite effect—namely, the postponement of investment. In any case, the embodiment of technical change in combination with the irreversibility of investment underlines the potential role of policymakers in reducing adjustment costs and smoothing transition shocks that are largely ignored in aggregate production function settings.

SEE ALSO *Investment; Machinery; Production Function; Schumpeter, Joseph; Solow, Robert M.; Technological Progress, Economic Growth; User Cost*

BIBLIOGRAPHY

Aghion, Philippe, and Peter Howitt. 1998. *Endogenous Growth Theory.* Cambridge, MA: MIT Press.

Fuss, Melvyn A. 1978. Factor Substitution in Electricity Generation: A Test of the Putty-Clay Hypothesis. In *Production Economics: A Dual Approach to Theory and Applications*, eds. Melvyn A. Fuss and Daniel McFadden, 187–213. Amsterdam: North-Holland.

Johansen, Leif. 1959. Substitution versus Fixed Production Coefficients in the Theory of Economic Growth: A Synthesis. *Econometrica* 27 (2): 157–176.

Kaldor, Nicholas, and James A. Mirrlees. 1962. A New Model of Economic Growth. *Review of Economic Studies* 29 (3): 174–192.

Malcomson, James M. 1975. Replacement and the Rental Value of Capital Equipment Subject to Obsolescence. *Journal of Economic Theory* 10 (1): 24–41.

Phelps, Edmund S. 1962. The New View of Investment: A Neoclassical Analysis. *Quarterly Journal of Economics* 76 (4): 548–567.

Phelps, Edmund S. 1963. Substitution, Fixed Proportions, Growth, and Distribution. *International Economic Review* 4 (3): 265–288.

Salter, W. E. G. 1960. *Productivity and Technical Change.* Cambridge, U.K.: Cambridge University Press.

Solow, Robert M. 1960. Investment and Technical Progress. In *Mathematical Methods in the Social Sciences, 1959; Proceedings*, eds. Kenneth J. Arrow, Samuel Karlin, and Patrick Suppes, 89–104. Stanford, CA: Stanford University Press.

Solow, Robert M., James Tobin, Carl Christian von Weizsäcker, and Menahem Yaari. 1966. Neoclassical Growth with Fixed Factor Proportions. *Review of Economic Studies* 33 (2): 79–115.

Adriaan H. van Zon

VINYL RECORDINGS

Vinyl is more than simply a material used to make disc records; the term is shorthand for a culture, a lifestyle, a set of attitudes about music technology, even an object of obsession and addiction. Vinyl, specifically polyvinyl chloride (PVC), became the standard material in the manufacture of records with the introduction of 33 1/3 and 45 RPM discs in 1948, replacing the shellac 78 RPM records that had been in use since the 1890s. The vinyl record remained standard until the 1980s and early 1990s, when it was largely replaced by the compact disc (CD).

Although relegated to the margins, vinyl continues to hold a special place for a certain segment of listeners and performers in the twenty-first century. Listeners value vinyl records both for their sound and as objects to be collected. Many audiophiles claim that the "warm" analog sound of a pristine record played on a fine turntable is superior to the "cold" digital perfection of any compact disc. The appeal of records, however, is perhaps more a function of their materiality than their actual sound. With the invention of the record came the advent of record collecting, and soon after came the obsessive collector who seeks rare or unusual records with extreme devotion. In the 1920s the "disease" known as "gramomania" (derived from "gramophone," the British term for phonograph) was facetiously identified, and "vinyl addicts" continued to figure in the popular imagination throughout the century (e.g., in Nick Hornby's 1995 novel *High Fidelity* and its eponymous film adaptation in 2000). Although such "addicts" represent a small fraction of those who collect records, their example reveals that there is more to vinyl than simply music. Record collecting is about the thrill of the hunt, the accumulation of expertise, the display of wealth, the visual and tactile sensation of artifacts, and the creation and cataloging of memories.

A certain type of musician—the disc jockey (DJ)—also values vinyl, not simply as a means for reproducing existing sounds, but for creating new music. DJs are often thought to do little more than play records, but the ways in which many hip-hop and electronic dance music (EDM) DJs in particular manipulate records elevate them to the status of musicians. DJs may combine the sounds of multiple records, alternate between discs in complex counterpoint, or "scratch" them (move them back and forth underneath the stylus), all of which can create new sounds not contained on any single one of the manipulated discs. EDM DJs often combine dozens of individual songs into a seamless musical flow that may last several hours, while hip-hop DJs (also known as turntablists), may take a single passage from a record and manipulate it into an extended composition.

The standard equipment for most DJs has been two turntables and a mixer (a machine that regulates the signal being sent from the two machines to the speakers). In the 1990s, however, various companies began developing and refining CD turntables. The advantages of these players are clear. It is a much simpler matter to find, repeat, and shape particular recorded passages than with traditional turntables, and one need not worry about replacing cartridges or wearing out records. (With digital turntables, the DJ manipulates a simulated record platter, whose movements—even scratching—are converted into signals that transform the sound of the CD.) Moreover, with inexpensive CD burners, DJs can easily compile their own individualized records from other CDs or from digital files, such as MP3s.

Despite these advantages many DJs have resisted the incursion of CD turntables. This resistance is strongest among hip-hop DJs, and can be explained with a single word: vinyl. Because vinyl was present at, and largely responsible for, the birth of hip-hop (which developed around the art of the DJ), it is considered a precious substance, one that carries with it the whole history, the DNA, of hip-hop. Moreover, with traditional turntables, the DJ handles the sound directly, essentially touching the music; CD players remove the immediacy and tactility of vinyl. Nevertheless, as CD turntables continued to improve in the early 2000s, DJs increasingly began turning to digital machines. Some have argued that DJing transcends vinyl and must evolve with changing technologies.

In the early years of the new millennium, vinyl finds itself both cherished and embattled. It continues to be collected and manipulated, and coexists, sometimes uneasily, with digital technologies. Although it plays an important role in the lives of many listeners and performers, its place in the musical life of the future is uncertain.

BIBLIOGRAPHY

Eisenberg, Evan. 2005. *The Recording Angel: Music, Records and Culture from Aristotle to Zappa*. 2nd ed. New Haven, CT: Yale University Press.

Fikentscher, Kai. 2000. The Cult and Culture of the DJ. In *You Better Work!: Underground Dance Music in New York City*. Hanover, NH: University Press of New England.

Katz, Mark. 2004. The Turntable as Weapon: Understanding the DJ Battle. In *Capturing Sound: How Technology Has Changed Music*. Berkeley: University of California Press, 2004.

Milano, Brent. 2003. *Vinyl Junkies: Adventures in Record Collecting*. New York: St. Martin's Press.

Schloss, Joseph G. 2004. Materials and Inspiration: Digging in the Crates. In *Making Beats: The Art of Sample-Based Hip-Hop*. Middletown, CT: Wesleyan University Press.

Straw, Will. 1997. Sizing Up Record Collections: Gender and Connoisseurship in Rock Music Culture. In *Sexing the Groove*, ed. Sheila Whiteley, 3–16. London: Routledge.

Mark Katz

VIOLENCE

Though violence has been characterized as the use of force by and against one or more social subjects with the intention to inflict bodily harm, the study of violent processes over the past three decades has broadened the concept by underscoring its varying forms, which emerge from the struggle for power between modern states, elites and subalterns, and recently formed communities. Interstate war, discourse and the coercive apparatuses of the state, epistemic violence, ethnic conflict, collective recovery, and terrorism represent intellectual signposts in the scholarship on violence, although they emerge from different trajectories of inquiry that do not belong to a single genealogical tradition or discipline.

WAR, THE STATE, AND COERCION

Violence is identified as an effect of competitive war-making in early modern Europe, which produced a bureaucratic apparatus that could secure the material and human resources required for managing warfare. Such bureaucratic apparatuses would form the institutional skeleton of modern national states from the seventeenth century onward (Tilly 1990). The link between war, the state, and violence is reflected in Max Weber's remark that a striking feature of the modern state is, ideally, its "monopoly of the legitimate use of physical force" and, therefore, its ability to sanction the use of force (Gerth and Mills 1946, p. 78). However, this is not to say that modern states only seek to stem forms of unsanctioned violence, especially those that appear to threaten its authority. Michel Foucault's inquiries (1963, 1966, 1975) reveal that modern welfare states also strive to redefine, regulate, and channel the use of force in order to achieve social order. This insight marked a watershed in the study of violence and shifted the focus of research on the phenomenon from interstate war to the subtle manners in which coercion and the "measured" use of force are deployed by state agencies in order to shape the social identities of individuals.

Foucault's studies of institutions of criminal punishment and rehabilitation, schools and hospitals, and the spaces of economic production underscore the discourses that organize these institutions, in order to socially produce docile subjects whose utility would, ostensibly, advance societal welfare and maintain order. Competing legal, penal, medical, and academic disciplines converge to define, discursively, what forms of violence are criminal, why they are socially immoral or harmful, and how their perpetrators should be punished or rehabilitated. Far from remaining ideological platitudes that are applicable only to those labeled as "criminals" or "insane," these social meanings of deviance are authoritative because they are articulated as categories of objective knowledge, and they become a metric by which to measure—and curb—our own deviant and violent tendencies. Foucault not only demonstrates how social control is achieved from above, he also reveals the political utility of microdimensions of violence, which enable the reproduction of a predictable social order by conditioning individuals to coerce themselves through conformity to institutionally sanctioned categories of "normal behavior."

Ironically, the very institutional apparatuses and discourses that seek to discipline subjects can also be the source from which to innovate new strategies for resisting violent and coercive regimes. Studies of collective violence associated with popular revolution in western Europe, for example, reveal that tactics employed by protesters borrowed heavily from the police forces' own methods of employing violence to suppress collective protest. Similarly, these investigations also point to the manner in which episodes of collective violence directed against monarchical power were morally legitimated by perpetrators through the appropriation and redeployment of political concepts like *popular sovereignty*. Anthropologists, historians, and sociologists attentive to the discursive dimensions of collective movements enrich the meaning of the concept of violence by tracing the manner in which knowledge, as a means of exercising social power, can animate and constrain collective forms of resistance that employ the use of force.

EPISTEMIC VIOLENCE

Inquiries into the creation of social order under European colonization identify epistemic forms of violence that radically essentialized social identities and dismantled previously existing social solidarities. This body of literature marks a departure from a previous form of anthropological study that accepted the "traditional culture" of non-Western societies as an essentially differentiating feature and one that necessitated methods of exhaustive description as a form of analysis. Anthropologists and historians interrogating the cultural objects of "tradition" demonstrate that in the name of crafting effective procedures of political rule, colonial administrators set about to objectify "native traditions." Such a project involved the production of systematized bodies of objectified knowledge that documented the "cultures and traditions" of colonial subjects; rather than learning about their dynamism, the European project reduced their complexity and then enabled their ossification (Cohn, 1987, 1996; Dirks, 1987, 2001; Chatterjee, 1986, 1993). Working with Orientalist assumptions about "the traditional East," these bodies of knowledge taxonomically classified categories and practices of social identity in new and singular relationships with Western notions of religion, ethnicity, or clan. Importantly, the concept of violence in this domain of research is considered a historical process that involved supplanting the previously existing "fuzzy" character of social identity, which was shaped by numerous sources of competitive influence, with rigid conceptions of identity (Kaviraj 1992, p. 20).

Having epistemologically fixed such "traditions" as the primary source of native identity, colonial rulers applied these taxonomies to form key state undertakings spanning law and policing, education, urban planning, the fine arts, and census-taking operations. State projects aimed to stabilize the colonial state's task of maintaining social order, creating the conditions for profitable and taxable economic production, while representing—ostensibly—only a latent imposition on the social and cultural practices of colonial subjects. In fact, these brutal processes of colonial rule would engender more violent social transformations and political conflicts.

COMMUNAL AND ETHNIC CONFLICT

Institutionalizing such rigid conceptions of identity in the state's operations created the conditions for political forms of violence by sharpening—and rendering incommensurable—the perceived cultural differences between novel "traditional" communities that consequently began to form. This was especially palpable in the context of emerging native leaders who were able to cultivate new supportive constituencies, in terms of their imagined traditional commonalities, and call for the state to arbitrate when conflicts with rival communities arose. As historians of colonial Asia and Africa demonstrate, despite the state's quest to maintain social order, communal and "tribal" conflict became a bloody and conspicuously recurring phenomena in this era.

The emergence of competing traditional communities became a mobilizational resource—and source of tension—when native elites began to organize collective resistance to colonialism. Such communities were rallied behind the call for national sovereignty through movements of cultural nationalism. For native elites, political independence was a corresponding entitlement of these traditional communities who now aspired to the status of nationhood. Of course, such cultural forms of nationalism were riddled with tensions, often manifesting in violent internal conflict. Though statehood was eventually achieved for most colonies, the process was often characterized by territorial partition, bitter campaigns of violence, and the unprecedented displacement of people (as in the case of India and Pakistan). In other instances, the hollowness of constitutional arrangements based on "multiculturalism" was exposed when domestic politics spiraled into intense ethnic violence or agonistic competition over political and economic resources. Such violence emerges historically out of—and through—the commission of epistemic forms of violence.

COLLECTIVE INJURY AND TERRORISM

The study of violence associated with contemporary episodes of ethnic cleansing and genocide has revealed much about the dynamics of collective recovery. Scholars in this subfield have shown how testimonies relating to experiences with violence are often shaped by an implicit requirement that frayed ethnic or national solidarities be restored. Testimonials are burdened with the tasks of reestablishing familial-communal honor, identifying perpetrators, and securing state resources for communal rehabilitation. Strikingly, the analysis of collective memory and recovery points to the difficulty of articulating pain as an experience and how the depth of it is necessarily reduced when it is articulated as a collective and social form of suffering (Das 1997).

The theme of collective injury is also salient to discussions of more recent forms of violence associated with terrorist groups, particularly those movements that seem to be morally organized by a religious ethos. Scholars have shown that the moral justifications employed by such movements draw upon earlier forms of cultural nationalism that challenged foreign occupation and imperialism, as well as "heretical" regimes and moral "waywardness." Many current-day militant movements draw their moral authority from religious reform movements from the colonial era that placed an emphasis on the correct observance of religious rituals. The Taliban, for example, trace their genealogy to the Deoband movement in late-colonial-era India, which initiated and institutionalized the *madrassa*-based study of Islamic law and the upholding of Muslim ritual practices (dress, morality, and regular prayer) as a means to achieve a virtuous way of life.

Tellingly, the focus of such religious reform movements was transformed during the Cold War period when "insurgents" were recruited, trained, and armed by alliances of Western states and their clients to fight "communism." Militant and globally dispersed movements that turn noncombatants into targets of political violence are the products of proxy wars that were waged between the superpowers in Asia, Africa, and Latin America.

In summary, the study of culture and ideology has transformed the meanings of *violence* by shifting away from an emphasis on interstate war and physical harm to an exploration of the more insidious ways in which highly regulated forms of violence and coercion—presented as socially productive methods of reform and development—are sanctioned by the state in order to govern the actions of individuals. Examinations of the formation of discourses, as loci in which social power is exercised through claims to disciplinary knowledge and truth, reveal how epistemic forms of violence reduce the complexity of social identity and, in the colonial sphere, artificially classify non-Western societies as premodern. Ironically, the history of nationalist and political movements from the end of European colonial rule through the Cold War and afterward is marked by forms of communal and ethnic conflict that reinforce the social and political salience of tradition. Terrorism—and the predominantly Orientalist public debate surrounding it—is a contemporary example of the ways in which religion and politics can come to be mutually dependent and, moreover, of how many of the most dynamic cultural and logistical strategies that organize violence rest outside the domain of the state.

SEE ALSO *Anticolonial Movements; Colonialism; Decolonization; Foucault, Michel; Genocide; Orientalism; Terrorism*

BIBLIOGRAPHY

Brass, Paul R. 2003. *The Production of Hindu-Muslim Violence in Contemporary India.* Seattle: University of Washington Press.

Chatterjee, Partha. 1993. *The Nation and Its Fragments: Colonial and Postcolonial Histories.* Chicago: University of Chicago Press.

Chatterjee, Partha. 2004. *The Politics of the Governed: Reflections on Popular Politics in Most of the World.* New York: Columbia University Press.

Cohn, Bernard S. 1987. *An Anthropologist among the Historians and Other Essays.* Oxford: Oxford University Press.

Cohn, Bernard S. 1996. *Colonialism and Its Forms of Knowledge: The British in India*. Oxford: Oxford University Press.

Das, Veena. 1995. *Critical Events: An Anthropological Perspective on Contemporary India*. New Delhi: Oxford University Press.

Das, Veena. 1997. Language and Body: Transactions in the Construction of Pain. In *Social Suffering*, eds. A. Kleinman, Veena Das, and M. M. Lock. Berkeley: University of California Press.

Das, Veena. 1998. Official Narratives, Rumour, and the Social Production of Hate. *Social Identities* 4: 109–130.

Das, Veena, et al., eds. 2001. *Remaking a World: Violence, Social Suffering, and Recovery*. Berkeley: University of California Press.

Dirks, Nicholas B. 2001. *Castes of Mind: Colonialism and the Making of Modern India*. Chicago: Chicago University Press.

Feldman, Allen. 1991. *Formations of Violence: The Narrative of the Body and Political Terror in Northern Ireland*. Chicago: Chicago University Press.

Foucault, Michel. 1971. *The Order of Things: An Archeology of the Human Sciences*. Trans. Alan Sheridan. New York: Pantheon Books. (Originally published as *Les mots et les choses: Une archéologie des sciences humaines*. Paris: Gallimard, 1966.)

Foucault, Michel. 1973. *The Birth of the Clinic: An Archeology of Medical Perception*. Trans. A. M. Sheridan Smith. New York: Pantheon Books. (Originally published as *Naissance de la clinique: Une archéologie du regard médical*. Paris: Presses Universitaires de France, 1963.)

Foucault, Michel. 1977. *Discipline and Punish: The Birth of the Prison*. Trans. Alan Sheridan. New York: Pantheon Books. (Originally published as *Surveiller et punir*. Paris: Gallimard, 1975.)

Gerth, H. H., and Mills, C. Wright, eds. 1946. *From Max Weber: Essays in Sociology*. New York: Oxford University Press.

Kaviraj, Sudipto. 1992. The Imaginary Institution of India. In *Subaltern Studies*, vol. VII. New Delhi: Oxford University Press.

Mamdani, Mahmood. 1996. *Citizen and Subject: Contemporary Africa and the Legacy of Late Colonialism*. Princeton, NJ: Princeton University Press.

Mamdani, Mahmood. 2001. *When Victims Become Killers: Colonialism, Nativism, and the Genocide in Rwanda*. Princeton, NJ: Princeton University Press.

Mamdani, Mahmood. 2004. *Good Muslim, Bad Muslim: America, the Cold War, and the Roots of Terror*. New York: Pantheon.

Metcalf, Barbara. 2004. Piety, Persuasion, and Politics: Deoband's Model of Social Activism. In *The Empire and the Crescent: Global Implications for a New American Century*, ed. Aftab Ahmad Malik, 156–147. Bristol, U.K.: Amal Press.

Pandey, Gyanendra. 1990. *The Construction of Communalism in Colonial North India*. New Delhi: Oxford University Press.

Pandey, Gyanendra. 2001. *Remembering Partition: Violence, Nationalism, and History in India*. Cambridge, U.K. and New York: Cambridge University Press.

Scott, David. 1999. *Refashioning Futures: Criticism after Postcoloniality*. Chicago: Chicago University Press.

Sewell, William H., Jr. 1996. Historical Events as Transformations of Structures: Inventing Revolution at the Bastille. *Theory and Society* 25 (6): 841–881.

Tambiah, Stanley. 1996. *Leveling Crowds: Ethnonationalist Conflicts and Collective Violence in South Asia*. Berkeley: University of California Press.

Tilly, Charles. 1990. *Coercion, Capital, and European States, AD 990–1990*. Cambridge, U.K.: Blackwell.

Tilly, Charles, Louise Tilly, and Richard Tilly. 1975. *The Rebellious Century, 1830–1930*. Cambridge, MA: Harvard University Press.

Verdery, Katherine. 1999. *The Political Lives of Dead Bodies: Reburial and Postsocialist Change*. New York: Columbia University Press.

Warren, Kay B. 1993. *The Violence Within: Cultural and Political Opposition in Divided Nations*. Boulder, CO: Westview Press.

Arafaat A. Valiani

VIOLENCE, FRANTZ FANON ON

According to the Martinican author and political theorist Frantz Fanon (1925–1961), violence fundamentally defined the meaning and practice of colonialism, and as such violence was central to the effort to resist and overthrow colonial rule. For Fanon, violence was both the poison of colonialism and its antidote.

Fanon arrived at this view on violence largely through his work as a psychiatrist. He was born in Martinique and trained in France, later working in a hospital in Algiers, the capital of Algeria, under the auspices of the French colonial administration. Most of his psychiatric patients were native Algerians, many suffering from the mental and physical turmoil of colonial degradation, including the experience of torture at the hands of French interrogators. Some of these French torturers were also his patients, and by working with them Fanon learned how the "disease" of colonialism also infected the mind of the colonizer. Beyond the hospital walls, Fanon saw how the constant presence of French police stations and military barracks conveyed to the Algerians the clear message that they were little more than animals, to be beaten, dehumanized, and contained for the sake of colonial interests. He thus gained first-hand knowledge of the damage that colonialism inflicted on the minds and bodies of African people.

On November 1, 1954, leaders of the embryonic Algerian national movement, known as the Front de Libération Nationale (FLN), began the armed struggle for independence with violent attacks against French military and civilian targets, thereby rejecting the path of negotiation and compromise that had been followed to this point. His experiences treating the sufferings of Algerians and witnessing this explosion of violent anticolonialism led Fanon to join the nationalist movement and advocate for the Algerian revolution as a militant activist and writer. He resigned his post at the hospital in 1957, unable to tolerate working for the colonial administration any longer.

Fanon's clearest and most thorough articulation of his views on colonialist and anticolonialist violence can be found in the chapter "Concerning Violence" in *The Wretched of the Earth*, published in 1961, his last work before his death. In it, Fanon argues that anticolonialism must be revolutionary rather than reformist. Colonialism, he explains, is "not a thinking machine, nor a body endowed with reasoning faculties. It is violence in its natural state, and it will only yield when confronted with greater violence" (Fanon 1963, p. 61). Since violence fundamentally defined the colonizing society's existence, only "absolute violence" could get the colonizers' attention. Absolute violence meant that no meaningful distinction was to be made between the French civilian settlers in Algeria and the French police and military forces. According to Fanon, they were all complicit in some way and thus all subject to anticolonial violence. This view of colonialism reflected Fanon's Manichean understanding of the relationship between the colonizers and the colonized. The two were as opposed as white and black; in fact, they were white and black, and no middle ground or negotiated withdrawal was possible if the colonized were to ever be truly liberated. True liberation could only arrive when the binary categories of white and black were destroyed, expunged from the earth.

Fanon believed that anticolonial violence was required in order to achieve two intimately connected objectives: the expulsion of the colonizer and the mental "decolonization" of native Algerians. To Fanon, this latter aim was fundamental because institutional independence from the colonizer would mean little if the people remained psychologically trapped within a self-image as colonized, dehumanized objects. Fanon observed that Algerians were indeed violent under colonial rule, but this violence was directed toward other Algerians as an expression of self-hatred in which "black-on-black" violence represented a futile effort to negate the dehumanized identity imposed upon them. In the movement, led by the FLN, to redirect this violence toward the colonizer, Fanon conceived of a way to construct and affirm a positive political identity infused with a national consciousness liberated from the colonized mindset: "At the level of individuals, violence is a cleansing force. It frees the native from his inferiority complex and from his despair and inaction; it

makes him fearless and restores his self-respect" (Fanon 1963, p. 94).

Individually and collectively, anticolonial violence for Fanon was an act of rebirth—"the veritable creation of new men" (Fanon 1963, p. 36)—that simultaneously bound the people together in an expression of national solidarity in which all are implicated in the struggle. Thus, violence was to shape the Algerian national consciousness as the people became collectively responsible for, and thus asserted popular authority over, the anticolonial struggle itself and its immediate product, an independent nation built upon socialist principles and institutions. Fanon argued that this expression of solidarity should not end at the national borders; the anticolonial struggle united the African continent as a whole, as Africans looked forward to the unique and varied postcolonial contributions that they would make on the world stage.

SEE ALSO *Anticolonial Movements; Fanon, Frantz; Postcolonialism; Revolution; World War II*

BIBLIOGRAPHY

PRIMARY WORKS

Fanon, Frantz. 1963. *The Wretched of the Earth*. Trans. Constance Farrington. New York: Grove Press.

Fanon, Frantz. 1965. *A Dying Colonialism*. Trans. Haakon Chevalier. New York: Grove Press.

Fanon, Frantz. 1967a. *Black Skin, White Masks*. Trans. Charles Lam Markmann. New York: Grove Press.

Fanon, Frantz. 1967b. *Toward the African Revolution: Political Essays*. Trans. Haakon Chevalier. New York: Grove Press.

Kevin Bruyneel

VIOLENCE, ROLE IN RESOURCE ALLOCATION

Violence, or the threat of violence, is a source of political and economic power, a means of acquiring either assets, income, or influence over their use and distribution. It is, however, not the only source of power, though perhaps it is the most familiar.

Simple acts of violence, such as robbery, can achieve short-term gain, or they can achieve long-term gain by setting precedents to support future threats. Well-established threats are the basis for systems of tribute or "protection money." The difference between these two approaches is that robbery is typically furtive, making use of stealth to compensate for a lack of real superiority in force. In contrast, a tribute system is public to the extent that the violent agent is confident of superiority in force, so that general knowledge of the threat offers little protection for others and instead increases income from collections. What the two approaches share in common is that violence can take the crudest forms and be effective, since the goal is to acquire finished goods without involvement in the production process.

If the use or threat of violence is to be involved in the actual process of production, matters get more complicated. The goal shifts from collection to coercion, and both the exercise and threat of violence need to be more carefully calibrated parts of a program of supervision, as in the case of slavery and other forced labor systems.

A great many societies until recent times, including most colonial regimes, have had economic arrangements centered on threats of violence in order either to collect finished goods and money as tribute or to coerce labor services.

In modern capitalist societies, violence continues to play a role in the defense of property and enforcement of contracts, but under normal conditions it remains in the background while the law occupies the foreground. Violence seems to have played a key role in the acquisition of property during the centuries preceding the modern era, a process sometimes referred to as "original accumulation." It still can play that role during periods of war or other severe crisis, but this use of violence is rarely acknowledged as a regular part of modern economic arrangements.

Critics of violence, in every social arrangement from ancient to modern, point to the suffering and destruction it causes. Some simply insist that no countervailing benefit could ever compensate for the horrors of violence, and they push at every juncture for its elimination. Others argue that both the destruction caused by violence and the parasitism of those who live off acts of violence constitute economic waste.

Apologists of violence usually claim that its elimination is an unachievable dream and that the best hope lies in channeling it instead, at least to minimize harm but possibly to do some good. To those who decry its economic wastefulness, they reply that this waste is more than compensated for, insofar as it leads to additional productive activity. In a world where most people are viewed as wasting time—and this is a view that many colonial rulers had of their subjects—apologists can argue that unless rulers' demands for tribute or labor are excessive, little more than this wasted time is actually lost, while production in the meantime is increased.

Perspectives on violence can depend somewhat on what theories people hold on how it arises. In classical economic theory, competition for scarce resources can give rise to violence in the form of wasteful strife and warfare. In this view it is desirable and efficient to develop a state structure with a monopoly on violence—as Thomas Hobbes most vividly advocated in *Leviathan* (1651)—and to use it to build a legal system of property rights and contract enforcement that encourages resource allocation through markets instead. Böhm-Bawerk (1914) painstakingly showed that once property rights are secure and contracts enforceable, introduction of additional force in an effort to control market dynamics was futile and wasteful, and this has been the neo-classical view ever since.

In certain political realist theories, such as those of Eugen Dühring (criticized by Friedrich Engels in *Anti-Dühring*, 1894) in the last century, violence arises more from its own profitability: The resources expended in a violent campaign to extract goods or labor yield a return as good as or better than from any other use. Because property rights and contracts are not here assumed to be firmly established, this in itself would not contradict the classical view, but political realists go further to argue that violence can be efficient also on the macro level, primarily because of its function in extracting productive labor from people that otherwise would not have been performed. According to those views, the state with its monopoly on violence contributes to economic activity by institutionalizing the labor extraction function, leaving to the market a decidedly secondary role of efficiently allocating resources thus extracted. Perhaps where land and resources are abundant and hard to dominate, a property system might be inferior to a tribute or slave system in terms of productivity.

Georges Sorel (1906) explored the potential for violence to liberate the oppressed, suggesting that the huge problem of organization could at least in principle be overcome by a general strike of all workers. According to him, the general strike, constructed as a myth as well as organized as much as possible in reality, represents the socialist answer to oppressive violence from above.

According to other theories, including certain psychological views, such as those expressed by Sigmund Freud in *Civilization and Its Discontents* (1930), most violence cannot be accounted for by either of the above economic theories. Roughly put, violence instead arises from protracted and intense frustration brought about by all kinds of social experience, such as role conflict or inhibition of biological impulses, and it is best understood as an expressive rather than instrumental phenomenon. In other words, in the view of these theories, rather than a rational act for gain, violence is a kind of lurch into irrationality engaged in by someone for whom no rational option appears.

Finally, some theories are inspired by biology, claiming that violent behavior that is irrational at the individual level might appear rational at the species level. The survival prospects of the species are enhanced even though those of particular individuals appear not to be, and therefore some mechanism of natural selection might breed in a certain amount of violent tendencies that could not otherwise be accounted for.

SEE ALSO *Accumulation of Capital; Capitalism; Colonialism; Competition; Confiscation; Freud, Sigmund; Giddens, Anthony; Hobbes, Thomas; Imperialism; Primitive Accumulation; Property; Property Rights; Slavery; Urban Riots; Violence; War; Weber, Max*

BIBLIOGRAPHY

Böhm-Bawerk, Eugen von. 1914. Control or Economic Law? Trans. J. R. Mez. In *Shorter Works of Eugen von Böhm-Bawerk*. South Holland, IL: Libertarian Press, 1962.

Engels, Friedrich. 1894, 1947. *Anti-Dühring: Herr Eugen Dühring's Revolution in Science*. Trans. Emile Burns. Moscow: Progress Publishers.

Freud, Sigmund. 1930. *Civilization and Its Discontents*. Trans. James Strachey. New York and London, W. W. Norton & Co., 1961.

Giddens, Anthony. 1987. *The Nation-State and Violence*. Cambridge, UK: Polity Press.

Hobbes, Thomas. 1651. *Leviathan: or the Matter, Forme and Power of a Commonwealth Ecclesiasticall and Civil*. New York: Collier, 1962.

Sorel, Georges. 1906. *Reflections on Violence*. Trans. T. E. Hulme and J. Roth. Glencoe, IL: Free Press, 1950.

Weber, Max. 1951. *Economy and Society*, eds. Guenther Roth and Claus Wittich. Berkeley: University of California Press, 1978.

Michael J. Brun

VIOLENCE IN TERRORISM

While there are many definitions of terrorism and no single accepted one, the research literature assumes three main components: (1) use or threat of violence; (2) injury to noncombatants; and (3) a symbolic effect designed to attract attention. Violence is an integral part of terrorism and is present in every incident.

Several factors influence the decision to use violence within the terrorism framework: (1) violence must be faced by the target power, and the target power's response may violate its own values and draw criticism at home and abroad; (2) violence attracts attention to the terrorist organization's agenda, obliging the targeted regime to confront the problems raised and try to solve them; and (3) the use of violence arouses fear and horror in the civilian population. The perpetrators of the violence try to make the population pressure the regime into solving the terror problem, and sometimes even to meet the demands of the terrorist group.

Even though terror is considered the weapon of the weak, it should be stressed that the use of violence in the framework of terror is also common between sovereign states, and not only between illegal groups operating against certain other groups or states. State terrorism is terror perpetrated by states against their citizens or via specific groups that enjoy state support, whether covert or overt. Totalitarian regimes such as that of Augusto Pinochet in Chile or Saddam Hussein in Iraq used their own secret police forces to terrorize their citizens. These regimes operated against their own citizens, employing kidnappings, torture, and extrajudicial executions. Other regimes, mainly in South America, had armed militias that perpetrated acts of terror against their citizens and which were supported or tacitly approved by the state.

Despite this reality, there is disagreement regarding the inclusion of state-sanctioned acts of violence against citizens in the definition of terror. The main dispute concerns the fact that state violence instigated in its own territory is considered legitimate and justified in the struggle against hostile elements, and therefore cannot be defined as terror. The significance of this is that the definition of state-sanctioned acts as terror depends on the attitude of the international community toward the methods used by the state, the conditions under which the violence is used, whether in an armed conflict facing the state or during peacetime.

According to David Rappoport's 2003 work, there have been four separate waves in the use of terror since the 1880s. The first lasted about thirty years, from the 1880s to the 1920s. The groups active during this period espoused a revolutionary antimonarchy ideology, using force mainly in assassination attempts against representatives of the royalty; for example, the People's Will, Narodnaya Volya in Russia, or the Black Hand in Serbia. Notable among the events of this period were the assassinations of Czar Alexander II by Russian revolutionaries on March 13, 1881, and of Franz Ferdinand, heir to the Austrian throne, on June 28, 1914, the incident that sparked World War I.

The second wave continued from the 1920s to the 1960s. In this wave, terror was used mainly by ethnic groups in their struggles for independence from colonial powers—the EOKA in Cyprus and the Etzel and Lehi, Hebrew acronyms for National Military Organization and Fighters for Israel's Liberty, respectively, in British Mandate Palestine. The activities in this second wave differed from those in the first wave in that their targets were military and government installations, similar to the guerrilla warfare of the Force de Libération Nationale (FLN) in Algeria in the mid-1950s.

The third wave was concentrated in the 1960s and 1970s and was employed by ideological groups on the radical left trying to change the ruling regimes in their own countries, like the Red Brigades in Italy. For the first time, these groups were active in countries other than their own. They cooperated with like-minded foreign organizations and for the first time launched international terrorist activities, such as when the Palestine Liberation Organization (PLO) cooperated with the Japanese Red Brigade in Jordan, Lebanon, Israel, and Libya, among other countries.

The fourth wave began in the 1980s. The political ideology of the 1960s and 1970s has been largely replaced by religion as a background for acts of violent terrorism and its targets. Most perpetrators come from Islamic countries, although today's terrorism is not unique to Islam. The main tactics are kidnappings and suicide attacks in numbers that rose from 40 in the 1980s to 125 in the 1990s, and dozens of attacks per year since 2000. The most notable terrorist group is Al-Qaeda, which recruits and operates worldwide. Its network-based structure and use of the Internet for communication between cells in different countries make it completely different from the typical groups of previous decades.

In the early twenty-first century accelerated technological development and computerization throughout the world have increased terror that is less conspicuously violent, such as cyber-terrorism. This involves attacks against a country's computer systems and civilian and military communications. As such, researchers are not in agreement as to whether this is actually terrorism, since it does not involve violence.

SEE ALSO *Al-Qaeda; Guerrilla Warfare; Terrorism; Violence*

BIBLIOGRAPHY

Rappoport, David C. 2003. The Four Waves of Rebel Terror and September 11. In *The New Global Terrorism: Characteristics, Causes, Controls*, ed. Charles W. Kegley. Upper Saddle River, NJ: Prentice Hall.

White, Jonathan R. 1998. *Terrorism: An Introduction*. Belmont, CA: Wadsworth Publishing Company.

Ami Pedahzur
Alexandr Bialsky

VIRGIN OF GUADALUPE

SEE *Symbols.*

VIRGINS

Virgins are individuals of both sexes who have never had sexual intercourse, most commonly defined as vaginal penetration. Historically, virginity—particularly female—has been important in many cultures. The virginity of a bride has often been regarded as a mark of her purity, a sign of her family's honor, and as a means of guaranteeing the passage of her husband's bloodlines to her children. For Christians, male and female virginity has long been associated with spiritual purity, and most Christian religions today still place a high value on premarital virginity, even in societies where the vast majority of individuals do not remain virgins until marriage. In many contemporary societies, particularly in Africa and the Middle East, premarital female virginity still has tremendous cultural significance. In other cultures, especially North American and European societies, it is uncommon for people to remain virgins much past late adolescence. However, in such societies, there remains a double standard that encourages women to remain virgins longer than men.

In the United States, contemporary definitions of virginity are fluid. Some regard any sexual activity short of vaginal penetration as compatible with maintaining virginity, whereas others believe that participation in oral or anal sex constitutes a loss of virginity. Although heterosexuals are more likely to link virginity to vaginal penetration, most homosexuals do not consider those who have engaged in oral or anal sex to be virgins. For some, whether one gives or receives oral sex affects the potential loss of virginity. Similarly, in the case of anal sex between two men, there is sometimes debate as to whether one must penetrate or be penetrated in order to lose one's virginity.

In most cases one's status as a virgin is linked to lack of experience with certain sexual activities. In some instances, however, virginity is more closely tied to emotional or spiritual definitions. Some men and women, including many victims of rape, do not believe that nonconsensual sexual intercourse can be counted as losing one's virginity. Certain Christians who, after losing their virginity, decide to abstain from sex before marriage, consider themselves to have regained their virginity, becoming "born-again virgins" and thereby tying the notion of virginity to a personal spiritual state rather than a physical act.

In the United States today, loss of virginity is much less likely to be considered medically than emotionally or physically. In many cultures (and in earlier U.S. history), however, loss of virginity has been associated with the breaking of the hymen, a ring of tissue partially occluding the vagina. Though there is no necessary correlation between virginity and an intact hymen, some women have opted to undergo vaginal reconstruction surgery, which repairs or replaces the hymen. Although some do equate this procedure with a restoration of virginity, many others believe that restoring the hymen cannot make one a virgin.

Female virginity has long been of great importance to many cultures. Anthropologists suggest that a society's attitude toward virginity is an indication of the social roles of men and women: In traditional, patriarchal societies a woman's virginity is often considered a commodity that enhances a woman's desirability, enables a prestigious marriage, cements interfamily alliances, and ensures the legitimacy of heirs. In the Kanuri society of Africa virginal brides were considered more prestigious than older, divorced women because they were believed to be more submissive to their husbands. In China, well into the twentieth century, a bride's virginity was thought to be something owed to her husband; a man would consider it beneath his dignity and honor to wed a woman who was not a virgin.

In societies that place a high value on virginity, ritual verification of a bride's virginity were common; such tests persist in some traditional cultures. In many cultures throughout the world the virginity of a woman was verified on or before her wedding night. As late as the 1950s the bedsheets of Kurdish brides were examined after the wedding night, and a handkerchief smeared with hymenal blood was presented to the groom's mother as evidence of the bride's virginity. A bride who failed to prove her virginity was returned to her family, where she was killed. African Amhara women who were discovered to not be virgins on their wedding nights were returned to their families to be beaten. Brides among the Bulgarian Gypsies and the African Twi were required to present proof of virginity, in the form of stained bedclothes, to their husbands' families after the wedding night. Bedouin men tested their brides' virginity with togas wrapped around their forefingers. Though such rituals of virginity verification are rare in North American and European societies and disappearing in other areas of the world, some cultures, particularly in Africa and the Middle East, continue to practice them.

SEE ALSO *Gender; Human Sacrifice*

BIBLIOGRAPHY

Blank, Hanne. 2007. *Virgin: The Untouched History.* New York: Bloomsbury.

Carpenter, Laura M. 2005. *Virginity Lost: An Intimate Portrait of First Sexual Experiences.* New York: New York University Press.

Chozick, Amy. 2005. U.S. Women Seek a Second First Time with Hymen Surgery. *Wall Street Journal,* December 15.

Holtzman, Deanna, and Nancy Kulish. 1997. *Nevermore: The Hymen and the Loss of Virginity.* Northvale, NJ: Jason Aronson.

Maureen Lauder

VISUAL ARTS

Art comes from the Latin word *ars*, meaning skill, thus the term *visual arts* describes those skills that are visible to the human eye, including drawing, painting, sculpture, architecture, graphic art, decoration, and later photography and film. The visual arts are the expression of human creativity, a visualization of the way we see life and the world around us. Standing midway between what is perceived and what is believed, they stem from a need to make sense of human existence and explain it, both internally and externally.

One of the earliest forms of communication, the visual arts form a language through which humans speak about the world. This language is tempered by the society from which it springs, conditioned by its beliefs, its rituals, and its social codes. Pablo Picasso's painting *Guernica* (1937), for example, can be fully understood only when related to the environment of the Spanish civil war (1936–1939). Likewise, every work of art has to be rooted in its own context, which is what gives it shape, function, and relevance—only then is it truly alive. During World War II (1939–1945) a Nazi officer showed Picasso a reproduction and asked, "Is it you who did that?" Picasso is said to have replied, "No, it is you."

HISTORY

It is believed that the history of the visual arts begins with sculpture, the creation of a three-dimensional form. One of the earliest examples was the Lion-Human of Hohlenstein-Stadel, Germany (c. 30,000 BCE), a fantastic form carved from mammoth ivory. Half human and half beast, it marks the meeting of external reality with internal reality, and it is at this juncture that visual art occurs.

The decorative arts have always served both an ornamental and a functional purpose. Originating with the daubing of the body, it was an impulse that led to the fashioning of jewelry, pottery, glassware, textiles, and furniture. By 7000 BCE ceramic ware was already in use, and as decoration became more skilled and sophisticated different types of materials were adopted to create all kinds of objects. One of the most skilled and intricate early pieces was the Great Lyre from Mesopotamia (c. 2550–2400 BCE), which was created in the form of a bull's head. Combining gold, silver, lapis, shell, and wood, it was both functional and beautiful.

Some of the most important elements of the visual arts are drawing, the creation of an image, and painting, the application of color to a surface. At Chauvet, in southwestern France, there are caves full of early drawings and paintings of animals (dating from 25,000 to 17,000 BCE). A visual expression of the world in which early humans lived, these pictures depict the beasts that were hunted and worshipped, and whose bones provided tools and weapons. Located far away from the living area, in the darkest part of the caves, these paintings evidently had a ritual and symbolic purpose. It is clear that both images and pictures were once things of power and that art itself played an important role in the everyday struggle of living; only today has it been relegated to a purely aesthetic role.

Beginning with the cave, architecture—"the enclosure of spaces"—also dates back to prehistoric times. As skills developed and resources increased, architecture became a statement about religion, power, and spectacle. The giant pyramids of Giza (c. 2601–2515 BCE) were the forerunners of today's skyscrapers. Soaring toward the heavens, they proclaimed the divine status of the pharaohs and glorified the wealth, prestige, and stability of Egypt's rulers. At 792 feet high, the Woolworth Building in New York (1911–1913) is almost twice the height of the tallest pyramid, yet the message it sends out is much the same. Built not from brick, but from steel, glass, and concrete, like the pyramid, it dominates the skyline. Imposing a sense of order and control, it proclaimed the supremacy of the United States as the richest, most powerful, and most technologically advanced society on Earth.

Despite its importance, advanced or sophisticated technology was not an essential requirement for artistic achievement. Fewer resources did not mean lesser skill. Although they did not use iron or steel, the Moche people of ancient Peru (200 BCE–600 CE) were exceptional potters and metalworkers. The Moche potters were renowned for making vessels in the form of human heads. Many of these heads are strikingly true to nature, and they show a mastery of the human face.

This highlights the fact that the development of the visual arts is not primarily a story of technical progress but a story of changing ideas. Each culture had its own idea of the world. This was embodied in images and structures that were far more potent than words could ever be.

For a long time art reflected the domination of knowledge over vision. Based not on what artists could see at any given time, it was conditioned by what they knew was there. It was the Greeks who first began to use their eyes, as their sculptors, artists, and craftsmen began to rely more and more on what they could see, feeling free to represent nature and the human body the way they saw it. This transition from knowledge to the visual marked the beginning of innovation.

In Europe, it was during the Italian Renaissance (fourteenth through seventeenth centuries) that the visual arts really began to mirror a fragment of the real world. The adoption of scientific perspective, the knowledge of anatomy, and the rediscovery of the inheritance of Greece and Rome added to the armory of artists, helping them master the portrayal of nature and enabling them to represent the world around them. Led by Leonardo da Vinci (1452–1519), artists began to explore the visible world, experimenting and searching nature as a means of deepening their understanding.

CHINA

In China principles of theory and aesthetics were formulated as early as 500 CE by the scholar Xie He (500–c. 536). The emperor himself practiced painting, and schools were developed where art was taught as a subject. The first academy was established at the Song court in the early thirteenth century. The visual arts were thus placed on the same footing as the literary arts, and painters finally achieved a status equal to that of court officials.

The idea of art for art's sake was also well established in China, and a distinction was made between amateurs and professionals, between those who worked for money and those for whom personal expression mattered most. This philosophy was first articulated by Ni Zan (1301–1374), one of the most famous painters of the Yuan dynasty, who was the first to assert the independence of the artist: "What I call painting does not exceed the joy of careless sketching with a brush. I do not seek formal likeness but do it simply for my own amusement" (Bush and Shih 1985, p. 266).

POWER, PATRONAGE, AND PROPAGANDA

Artists had always worked for patrons and institutions who specified what they wanted and rewarded the artist accordingly. In eighteenth-century Europe the initiation of regular exhibitions where artists sold their work completely changed the traditional pattern. Instead of working for patrons, artists now relied on exhibitions to sell their work, appealing to critics, connoisseurs, and the general public. Artists could now go their own way and make their own choices.

In Mayan society (350 BCE–900 CE) artists had enjoyed high status because of their ability to record, and for most of its history the visual arts had played an essential role in supporting the status quo. Around 1840 the discovery of photography transformed the artist's position. Photography, the process of making pictures through the action of light, liberated the arts from the propagandist role that they had to play. There was now no need for painting to perform a task that a mechanical device could do far more effectively, and the camera took over as the principle means of recording, leaving artists free to criticize, comment, and give voice to their conscience and their creativity.

As a rule patrons and patronage systems did not encourage criticism of the existing social order. In societies such as Soviet Russia (1917–1991), where the state was supreme, the arts were run by government organizations, and artistic freedom was curtailed in order to promote the new social order. Patronage and the status quo also played a critical role in freer, more democratic societies. In 1932 the Mexican artist Diego Rivera (1886–1957) was commissioned to paint a fresco for the Rockefeller Center in New York, one of the most ambitious urban designs of the century. Rivera, however, included a portrait of Vladimir Lenin, leading John D. Rockefeller (1839–1937) to cancel the commission and have the unfinished mural destroyed.

MATERIALISM

The advent of the Industrial Revolution had a profound impact on the decorative arts. The workshop gave way to the factory, while craftspersons and their individual skills succumbed to the machine and mass production. During the twentieth century, movements such as the Bauhaus (1919–1933) in Germany did their best to combat the effects of this trend. Combining the schools of art and craft, Bauhaus revived the creation of unique handmade objects. In an age driven by technology, the effect of these developments has been to place a premium on cost and time. This has made the possession of a handmade object even more desirable and even more exclusive than ever before.

As the expression of a living society, the nature of art was very closely tied to its material context. Economics often defined what artists could do, what they aspired to do, and the way in which their work was received. Centralization, urbanization, political stability, and control of resources were all key factors in this equation.

In Japan the growth of peace and prosperity during the Edo period (1603–1867 CE) fostered a vibrant cultural atmosphere. Literacy was widespread and the demand for art was so extensive that it could no longer be confined to a single group of patrons. This demand found its outlet in the affordable new medium of woodblock prints, which become the most popular art form of the day. Known as *ukiyo-e* (pictures of the floating world), they were filled with everyday subjects, reflecting the lives of the people who bought them. The two most famous series, Utagawa Hiroshige's *Fifty-three stages of the Tokaido* (1833) and Katsushika Hokusai's *Thirty-six Views of Mount Fuji* (c. 1826–1833), became the most popular sets of graphic art ever printed.

CHANGE

A striking characteristic of the visual arts is the way it often accompanies momentous changes in politics, economics, and science. The upheaval of the twentieth century led to revolutionary developments in art and culture.

Photography had compelled artists to explore areas where the camera could not go, encouraging them to discard convention and experiment. Like the scientists who discovered penicillin and atomic power, and the inventors who created the telephone, the car, the airplane, and the computer, artists too committed themselves to a process of experimentation and discovery. As they did so, they questioned the nature of art itself.

Led by Paul Cézanne (1839–1906) and Vincent van Gogh (1853–1890), and then Picasso (1881–1973) and Georges Braque (1882–1963), artists deliberately abandoned the previous attitudes toward accurate representation. It was no longer important to represent what people see; humankind had gained such mastery over the appearance of reality that the only way forward lay in abstraction and nonrepresentation, the reality behind realism.

Visual art now aspired to create something more relevant, more meaningful, and more lasting than a copy of an object or a depiction of nature. In this cause new techniques and materials were adopted that resulted in the breakdown of the distinctions between art and everyday life. This search led to a new feeling for the arts of Africa, Australasia, and America, where art was charged with an almost magical power and had a living function in society.

"FOLK" PRACTICE AND "HIGH CULTURE"

In Nigeria, the Yoruba people still believe that a parent's love can reach a dead child through the medium of art. Nigeria has one of the highest rates of twin births in the world; when a Yoruba twin dies, a wooden image, *ere ibeji*, is carved and kept in the house by the parents. A symbol of hope for the future, the image is bathed and fed in the hope that the dead twin will bring the parents good luck. Described as "folk" practice, many of these art forms were the product of a community with a shared view of the world and a shared way of life. Rooted in tradition and less open to change, this art did not question but merely reflected the values of its society.

"Folk" art or practice was distinct from what was called *high culture*, a term that implies a more rarified culture with a greater level of luxury and sophistication and perhaps a different kind of patronage. Fostered by the state and the ruling elite for its own enjoyment, it also served to display power and glory. Unlike folk culture, high culture was not static or tied to tradition. Based on knowledge, experience, and understanding, it was, like art during the Italian Renaissance, in a constant state of evolution. This capacity to grow made it capable of change, and it was able to explore new issues and to question and break barriers. As the product of a community, many forms of folk art did not have a single author. High culture in contrast was often the product of individual discovery and endeavor. However this apparent difference may have been more the result of poor records and historiographic bias. What we do know is that the "high art" of Renaissance Italy was the result of individual genius, the work of such men as Leonardo da Vinci, Michelangelo (1475–1564), and Raphael (1483–1520), and as such its many forms were different and distinctive. The ceilings of the Sistine Chapel (1508–1512) in Rome, for example, would not have been painted in the same fashion by any artist other than Michelangelo.

FILM

The social impact of the visual arts is best summed up through the metaphor of film, the art of the motion picture. The youngest of the arts, the motion picture represents the logical development of everything that has come before. It was produced by recording a series of images with cameras and then showing them in rapid succession, thus giving an illusion of motion. Since the first commercial motion picture was made in 1898, the addition of sound and then color have made film arguably the most potent and popular art form of all. More so than other visual arts, it has an almost universal power of communication, possessing an ability to entertain, educate, enlighten, and inspire across countries and cultures.

Through film, culture has become truly global. Today the Coca-Cola logo is recognizable the world over in numerous languages. The visual arts are no longer indigenous—the product of one particular culture or experience. A universal language has become or is in the process of becoming a universal experience.

SEE ALSO *Aesthetics; Cultural Relativism; Culture; Culture, Low and High; Distinctions, Social and Cultural; Film Industry*

BIBLIOGRAPHY

Bush, Susan, and Hsio-yen Shih, eds. 1985. *Early Chinese Texts on Painting.* Cambridge, MA: Published for the Harvard-Yenching Institute by Harvard University Press.

Gombrich, E. H. 1984. *The Sense of Order: A Study in the Psychology of Decorative Art.* Oxford: Phaidon Press.

Gombrich, E. H. 1995. *The Story of Art.* 16th ed. London: Phaidon Press.

Honour, Hugh, and John Fleming. 2006. *The Visual Arts: A History.* 7th ed. Upper Saddle River, NJ: Prentice Hall.

Hughes, Robert. 1991. *The Shock of the New: Art and the Century of Change.* Rev. ed. London: Thames and Hudson.

Stokstad, Marilyn. 2005. *Art History.* 2nd ed. Upper Saddle River, NJ: Pearson/Prentice Hall.

SinhaRaja Tammita-Delgoda

VODOU

Based primarily on an amalgamation of spirit and ancestor cults and healing traditions brought by African slaves to the New World, and secondarily on African and European forms of folk Catholicism, Vodou (Voodoo) is the most popular religion among Haiti's eight million citizens, most of whom are peasants. It is also practiced by a sizable minority of the two million Haitian immigrants (and a small number of converts of diverse ethnic backgrounds) in the Dominican Republic, the Bahamas, and North American cities like Miami, New York, and Montreal. The first Vodou practitioners in the United States were the African and Creole slaves of French plantation owners fleeing the violence of the Haitian Revolution (1791–1804), who settled mainly in New Orleans, where the religion remains part of the city's religious fabric, sometimes practiced in concert with Hoodoo, a form of African American folk spirituality that is also based on ancient African traditions. Like any religion, Vodou is a system of symbols, beliefs, and practices that provides its adherents, whether in Haitian or American society, with a sense of meaning and purpose in life, a means of communing with the sacred, moral guidelines, a source of personal identity and group solidarity, and the courage to face life's struggles.

Vodou emerged in the sixteenth century among enslaved Africans and their descendants in the western region of the Spanish Caribbean colony of Santo Domingo, which became the French colony of Saint-Domingue in 1697 and eventually the Republic of Haiti in 1804. Although possessing deep roots in West Africa and Central Africa, the religion is more correctly identified as *African-derived* or *African-based* rather than *African,* even if the term *vodou* (whose original meaning in the West African Fon language is "spiritual entity") was reappropriated by practitioners of traditional African religions in West Africa in the twentieth century to designate their own religion. Like Santería and other major African-derived religions in the Americas, Vodou is an example of *diffused monotheism,* meaning that the sacred power of a single creator god, called Bondye (Good God) or Granmèt (Great Master), is diffused through a pantheon of divinities, which in Vodou are called *lwa,* and throughout nature. As such, the *lwa* are deeply enmeshed in nature, and each *lwa* is associated with some natural force or feature, like rivers, rainbows, the earth, and the sea.

From the beginning of the sixteenth century to the end of the eighteenth century, a total of some 800,000 enslaved Africans were brought to Santo Domingo/Saint-Domingue, the majority from the West African Fon and Central African Kongo ethnic groups. Numbering relatively few and facing opposition by slaveholders, Catholic missionaries managed little success in evangelizing slaves beyond administering the legally required sacrament of baptism. The syncretism that would thereafter characterize Vodou thus resulted, as Catholic saints merged with African spirits, and crosses, holy water, and rosaries joined spiritual forces with amulets that slaves refashioned from African traditions, which proved remarkably resilient in the face of the unspeakable oppression of slavery.

Prior to the Haitian Revolution, a multiplicity of African religious traditions thus persevered in Saint-Domingue, whose sugar plantations made it Europe's most lucrative colony. To speak of Vodou prior to the revolution is therefore somewhat anachronistic, as three of the religion's cornerstones were not laid until the second half of the eighteenth century and the first half of the nineteenth century: (1) the unity of purpose of the Haitian Revolution, as exemplified by the powerful ceremony at Bwa Kayman in August 1791, led by a prototypical Vodou priest named Boukman Dutty, which is widely credited with having sparked the revolution; (2) the integration of essential African religious traditions that were being practiced during the colonial era in clandestine maroon settlements of escaped slaves in the island's mountains and forests; and (3) the acceleration of the adoption of Catholic elements (especially hagiography) during the period of the "great schism" between Haiti and Rome from 1804 to 1860, when the Vatican refused to send Catholic priests to the young nation. After the schism, the Catholic Church, in alliance with the Haitian government, orchestrated several formal campaigns to suppress Vodou. These ultimately failed, however, and today the religion enjoys protection under the 1987 Haitian constitution, while in 2003 its baptisms and marriages gained legal recognition in Haiti.

Vodou has always been heterogeneous and decidedly uncentralized, relying on neither the teachings of a founder, nor scripture, nor formal doctrine. In some parts of Haiti, for example, the religion is primarily characterized by ancestor veneration, and elsewhere by cults of spirits of West African origins, such as Ezili, the female *lwa* of love, sensuality, and feminine power, and Ogou, the male *lwa* of iron and all powers associated with metals. The Vodou pantheon is divided into two principle rites: the *rada*, whose *lwa* are "cool" and serene; and the *petwo*, whose *lwa* are "hot" and feisty. Many *lwa* have manifestations in each rite. *Rada* and *petwo* cults are supplemented for most practitioners by the veneration of their ancestors (*zanset* or *lemò*, "the dead"). Collectively, the *lwa*, *zanset*, and *lemò*, along with angels and Catholic saints, are identified simply as the "mysteries" (*mistè*).

Principal forms of communication and contact with Vodou's *mistè* include prayer, praise, ablutions, offerings, spirit possession, drum and dance ceremonies, divination, and animal sacrifice. These rituals' overarching aim is to ensure, establish, or reestablish harmony between practitioners and the *mistè*, or to protect practitioners from sor-

cery (*wanga*). In the event of bad things happening, Vodouists consult with ritual specialists (female: *manbo*; male: *oungan*), who perform divination and orchestrate ceremonies (which most often take place either in temples (*ounfò*), family burial compounds, or public cemeteries) to provoke spirit possession and thereby enter into communication with the *mistè* in order to discover the cause of the underlying discord, disease, problem, or misfortune, and to determine and prescribe means of reestablishing harmony, healing, or achieving relevant solutions. Further drum ceremonies may be prescribed, while others are held according to a liturgical calendar derived from Catholicism.

Harmony between humans and the *mistè* and healing comprise Vodou's raison d'être. In general, such harmony requires the ritual appeasement of the *mistè*, whether through splendidly artistic communal drum and dance ceremonies, animal sacrifice, or more frequent personal devotions such as praising and feeding the *lwa*. Healing, meanwhile, often involves herbalism and ritual baths. Leaves, water, song, dance, drums, blood, healing, and communion with the sacred are thus what Vodou is truly about. It is a dignified and complex religion of survival, resistance, and African roots that is quite the opposite of the ignorant and racist stereotypes that malign Vodou in Western imagination and media.

SEE ALSO *Haitian Revolution; Peasantry; Religion; Rituals; Roman Catholic Church; Santeria; Slavery; Zombies*

BIBLIOGRAPHY

Desmangles, Leslie G. 1992. *The Faces of the Gods: Vodou and Roman Catholicism in Haiti*. Chapel Hill: University of North Carolina Press.

Hurbon, Laënnec. 1995. *Voodoo: Search for the Spirit*. Trans. Lory Frankel. New York: Abrams.

Hurston, Zora Neale. 1995. *Folklore, Memoirs, and Other Writings*. New York: Library of America.

Métraux, Alfred. [1959] 1972. *Voodoo in Haiti*. Trans. Hugo Charteris. New York: Schoken.

Terry Rey

VOICE AND LOYALTY

SEE *Exit, Voice, and Loyalty.*

VOLTAIRE
1694–1778

François Marie Arouet was born in Paris in fall 1694 and died there in spring 1778. "Voltaire," the name by which he is most widely known today, was a pen name that François invented for himself, most likely in 1718. It is believed to be an anagram of the Latinized form—"Arovet le leune"—of his name "Arouet le jeune" ("Arouet the younger," because Voltaire's father, a notary, was also named François). Voltaire is the best known of the *philosophes* of the French Enlightenment, and there is an industry of modern scholarship on his life and thought, including hundreds of monographs, as well as the multiple-volume series *Studies on Voltaire and the Eighteenth Century* and the *Complete Works of Voltaire*, both published in Oxford by the Voltaire Foundation. A champion of religious tolerance and human reason, a "philosophical historian" and popularizer of social history, Voltaire was clearly one of the Age of Enlightenment's most influential contributors to what would become known as the social sciences.

Like many eighteenth-century men of letters, Voltaire wrote in several genres, in both prose and verse. When measured against the literary output of his enlightened contemporaries, Voltaire's staggering productivity—amounting to some 15 million words—stands out. Historians typically divide his life into five periods, or phases, based on his literary projects and his place of residence.

The first period of Voltaire's life is defined by his youth, his education at the hands of the Jesuits of the College of Louis-le-Grand, and the publication of his early poems and plays, including his first important publication, the tragic play *Œdipe* (1715). It was also a period that saw the young Voltaire imprisoned in the Bastille for eleven months for writing libelous verse insulting to the king. In his youth, and throughout his long life, Voltaire was plagued by poor health, and he complained so frequently to his correspondents that modern scholars have identified hypochondria as one of his conditions.

The second stage of Voltaire's life was determined by his fleeing to England in spring 1726. His "exile" was occasioned by his having traded insults with the chevalier de Rohan. In England he mixed with Henry St. John, Viscount Bolingbroke (1678–1751), whose literary talents he admired and who introduced Voltaire to other writers, including Alexander Pope (1688–1744) and Jonathan Swift (1667–1745). Voltaire also read the works of the fathers of the English Enlightenment—Francis Bacon (1561–1626), John Locke (1632–1704), and Isaac Newton (1642–1727), whose burial at Westminster Abbey he attended. Voltaire's *Lettres philosophiques sur les Anglais* [Letters concerning the English nation] (1733) came out of this period, and he would long admire the English for what he perceived as their religious toleration, their defense of liberty, and their support of men of letters, such as Newton. It was also while in exile in England that Voltaire began to give serious attention to historical writings. While in England he published *Essay Upon the Civil Wars of France* (1727) and, more importantly, was probably working on the manuscripts that would become his *Histoire de Charles XII* [History of Charles XII] (1731) and *Le Siècle de Louis XIV* [The Century of Louis XIV] (1752), and also thinking about the history of the English constitution. Those activities continued after he returned to France in 1729.

The third period of Voltaire's life was the time of his residence at Cirey-en-Champagne, the château of the marquise du Châtelet (1706–1749), Voltaire's learned and witty mistress. Living there from 1733, Voltaire wrote poetry and plays, biblical criticism, popularizations of science such as *Eléments de la philosophie de Newton* [Elements of Newton's philosophy] (1738), and fiction, including *Zadig* (1747). These were also years in which he was working on *Essai sur les moeurs et l'esprit des nations* [Essay on the manners and spirit of nations] (1756), and frequently traveling throughout France, but also to Brussels. Voltaire's career was on the rise. In 1745 he was appointed *historiographe du roi* (historian to the king), largely owing to the support of Madame de Pompadour (1721–1764), and in 1746 he was elected to the French Academy.

With Madame du Châtelet's death in 1749, Voltaire accepted an invitation to take up residence at the court of Frederick II (1712–1786), the Great of Prussia, with whom Voltaire had corresponded from the mid-1730s. Frederick once claimed of Voltaire, "this great man alone was worth an entire Academy" (quoted in Aldridge 1975, p. 411). This fourth phase of Voltaire's life saw the publication of Voltaire's *Le Siècle de Louis XIV* [The Century of Louis XIV], (1752), an account that praised the French king for his support of literature and art, and also work on his *Dictionnaire philosophique* [Philosophical Dictionary] (1764). Voltaire also was involved in shady business deals, arousing Frederick's anger and helping to bring his stay in Prussia to an end only three years after it had begun. This was not the first of Voltaire's financial schemes, nor would it be the last. As Ben Ray Redman puts it in his introduction to *The Portable Voltaire*, Voltaire's "fingers began to itch whenever he thought there were sous to be made" (1949, p. 19).

The final stage of Voltaire's literary career was spent in Geneva, where Voltaire moved in 1755, and at Ferney, an estate he purchased in France near the French-Swiss border, in 1758. During these years he wrote *The Lisbon Earthquake* (1755) and contributed to the greatest of French Enlightenment publications, the *Encyclopédie* edited by Denis Diderot (1713–1784) and Jean le Rond d'Alembert (1717–1783). Voltaire also published his *Essai sur les moeurs* (1756), worked on his *History of the Russian Empire Under Peter the Great* (1759, 1763), and published *Candide* (1759), which is perhaps the best known of his works. It was during his years at Ferney that Voltaire penned his famous cry *"écrasez l'infâme!"* ("crush the infamy!"), the precise meaning of which historians continue to debate. It was also during this period that Voltaire became more vocal in his deism and more involved in several public events, including the Calas affair, in which he used his pen to defend the reputation of Jean Calas, a Huguenot who was tortured and executed in 1762. In 1764 Voltaire published *Dictionnaire philosophique*. His literary reputation was growing in the 1760s and 1770s, and the aging Voltaire was often visited by guests from around the world. In winter 1778, when Voltaire was eighty-four, his play *Irène* (1776) was celebrated in Paris. He died soon afterwards, the most famous man of letters of the Age of Enlightenment.

Voltaire's social and political thought is found throughout his satires, pamphlets, and voluminous correspondence, but it is his historical writings that contain some of his most important contributions to the social sciences. As an historian, Voltaire was forward looking, and he saw himself to be presenting history in a new way. Writing with a critical spirit similar to those of Pierre Bayle (1647–1706), François Fénelon (1651–1715), Bernard le Bovier de Fontenelle (1657–1757), and Henri de Boulainvilliers (1658–1722), Voltaire was less credulous than the humanist historians of the seventeenth century, and it is largely for that reason that he is considered by some to be the forerunner of modern historiography. He aimed to incorporate more sources and a greater variety of sources than did most of his contemporaries, even though some, such as Edward Gibbon (1737–1794), thought Voltaire did not go far enough in this regard. In his efforts to expand the subject matter of history in the direction of social and cultural history, Voltaire shared a common concern with other great Enlightenment historians, such as David Hume (1711–1776). In his "An Essay on Universal History" (1756), for example, Voltaire dispensed with Christian structure to tell the story of the rise and fall of civilizations, beginning with the ancient Chinese and also including America. In that grand narrative and in other historical works Voltaire showed little concern with military events and the rule of princes, but he found a primary role for economics. As J. H. Brumfitt summarizes in *Voltaire: Historian*, "more than his predecessors, and more than many of his contemporaries, who are often involved in abstract political theorizing, he succeeds in giving to economic developments a place in the narrative of history not too far removed from that which they occupy today"(1958, p. 70). Again in a notably modern way, Voltaire aimed to go beyond history as the recital of disparate and unconnected events. In the *Siècle*, for example, he attempted to integrate economics, politics, and the arts and sciences, and to present all of that in a unified whole. Part of Voltaire's appeal as an historian, then and now, was his realist's approach to change over time. As the historian Peter Gay put it in *Voltaire's Politics: The Poet as Realist*, Voltaire was "a practical hard-headed political man" (1959, p. xi). Near the core of Voltaire's historical thought, as with his philosophical writing, was an unrelenting attempt to appeal to reason at the expense of fable, myth, superstition, and religion. That tendency, more than anything else, explains why Voltaire was, as Theodore Besterman summed up in *Voltaire*, "the most famous, the best loved and the most fanatically hated man in Europe" (1969, p. 528).

SEE ALSO *Civilization; Constitutions; Enlightenment; Hume, David; Locke, John; Realism*

BIBLIOGRAPHY

PRIMARY WORKS

Voltaire. [1764] 1984. *Philosophical Dictionary*. Trans. and ed. Theodore Besterman. London: Penguin.

Voltaire. 1949. *The Portable Voltaire*, ed. Ben Ray Redman. New York: Penguin.

Voltaire. 1968–. *Complete Works of Voltaire*. Vol. 30 of a planned 85. Ed. Theodore Besterman et al. Oxford: Voltaire Foundation.

SECONDARY WORKS

Aldridge, A. Owen. 1975. *Voltaire and the Century of Light*. Princeton, NJ: Princeton University Press.

Besterman, Theodore. 1969. *Voltaire*. London and Harlow, U.K.: Longmans, Green.

Brumfitt, J. H. 1958. *Voltaire: Historian*. Oxford: Oxford University Press.

Gay, Peter. 1959. *Voltaire's Politics: The Poet as Realist*. Princeton, NJ: Princeton University Press.

Schlereth, Thomas J. 1977. *The Cosmopolitan Ideal in Enlightenment Thought: Its Form and Function in the Ideas of Franklin, Hume, and Voltaire, 1694–1790*. Notre Dame, IN: University of Notre Dame Press.

Wade, Ira O. 1969. *The Intellectual Development of Voltaire*. Princeton, NJ: Princeton University Press.

Mark G. Spencer

VOLUNTARY ASSOCIATIONS

SEE *Associations, Voluntary.*

VOLUNTARY UNEMPLOYMENT

In principle, a voluntarily unemployed person is a jobless worker refusing an available vacancy for which the wage is lower than a certain threshold known in the literature as *reservation wage.* John Maynard Keynes, in his *The General Theory of Employment, Interest, and Money* (1936), when describing the classical view of unemployment, introduces the notion of voluntary unemployment as "a refusal or inability of a unit of labor [...] to accept a reward corresponding to the value of the product attributable to its marginal productivity." According to this definition, frictional unemployment due to job searching would be voluntary, while unemployment determined by demand factors would be involuntary.

Robert E. Lucas Jr. criticizes this view, since "there is an involuntary element in all unemployment, in the sense that no one chooses bad luck over good; there is also a voluntary element in all unemployment, in the sense that however miserable one's current work options, one can always choose to accept them" ([1978] 1981). Unemployment should then always be viewed as voluntary, as alternative activities are always available in the economy. This interpretation is consistent with Ludwig von Mises that states, "Unemployment in the unhampered market is always voluntary. In the eyes of the unemployed man, unemployment is the minor of two evils between which he has to choose" (1949).

However, the question of voluntary versus involuntary unemployment should not be overemphasized. Indeed, for the majority of workers there is often a chance of being employed at a certain wage level. Nevertheless, even if a worker would refuse such a job offer, this does not seem to be enough to classify him as merely voluntarily unemployed.

Richard Layard, Stephen Nickell, and Richard Jackman (2005) make the example of the unskilled workers, for whom the number of well-paid jobs with good working conditions is far below the number of potential applicants. Therefore, the majority of the unskilled turn to jobs that pay less and are in general of worse quality. These jobs are easier to find and in some cases offer the possibility of immediate employment.

The labor market can then be divided into two sectors. One is identified as primary, where the best jobs are available, and the other is called secondary, where jobs are on average lower pay and of lower quality. In the secondary sector the labor market is said to clear, as vacancies are filled very quickly, the skills needed for the jobs are modest, and the wages are too low to appeal to a large number of applicants. In the primary sector the labor market does not clear, and job rationing results. Some of the workers excluded from the primary sector are subsequently employed in the secondary sector while others remain unemployed, according to the reservation wage of each individual.

Assuming that total labor force is equal to L and that all workers are willing to be employed in the primary sector, we can assume a negatively sloped labor-demand curve in the primary sector DD_1. The latter identifies the primary sector employment N_1 corresponding to the real wage W/P_1 resulting from union bargaining or firms' efficiency-wage policies. The number of workers available for secondary-sector jobs is then $L - N_1$. The positively sloped labor-supply curve in the secondary sector, SS_2, is determined by the reservation wages of these workers and is affected by the characteristics of the unemployment benefit system. The negatively sloped labor-demand curve in the secondary sector, DD_2, illustrates the demand of secondary-sector labor for any given level of real wage in that sector W/P_2. The market-clearing equilibrium is then reached when $SS_2 = DD_2$ and the employment level in the secondary sector N_2 is determined. The resulting unemployment level is then $U = L - N_1 - N_2$.

The nature of unemployment U is questionable. From one point of view, the workers in U are voluntarily unemployed because they are not willing to work in the secondary sector for a real wage that is below a certain threshold given by their reservation wage. However, they are also involuntarily unemployed because they are willing to work in the primary sector at the prevailing real wage but are not able to do so.

In a dynamic setting, the relative importance of the primary and the secondary sector varies according to aggregate as well as idiosyncratic shocks. Workers move within the three states (primary sector, secondary, and unemployed). Some of them will search for primary-sector jobs while unemployed, while others will become employed in the secondary sector.

It is the primary-sector real wage, which is the result of union bargaining or wage-efficiency policies, that will determine primary-sector employment, the crucial element in this representation. The entity and duration of unemployment will result from the general equilibrium of the economy.

SEE ALSO *Dual Economy; Involuntary Unemployment; Natural Rate of Unemployment; Underemployment; Unemployment*

BIBLIOGRAPHY

Keynes, John Maynard. 1936. *The General Theory of Employment, Interest, and Money.* New York: Harcourt Brace.

Layard, Richard, Stephen Nickell, and Richard Jackman. 2005. *Unemployment: Macroeconomic Performance and the Labour Market.* 2nd ed. Oxford: Oxford University Press.

Lucas, Robert E. Jr. [1978] 1981. Unemployment Policy. In *Studies in Business Cycle Theory*, ed. Robert E. Lucas Jr., 240–247. Cambridge, MA: MIT Press.

Mises, Ludwig von. 1949. *Human Action: A Treatise on Economics.* New Haven: Yale University Press.

Luca Nunziata

VOLUNTEER PROGRAMS

According to the Corporation for National and Community Service (CNCS), 65.4 million Americans reported that they volunteered in 2005 (the latest year for which data are available), almost 30 percent (28.8 percent) of the U.S. population (CNCS 2006). In 2000 the substantial volume of time volunteered by Americans was the equivalent of 9.1 million full-time employees (based on 1,700 hours per year per employee). The total assigned dollar value of volunteer time in that year was 239.2 billion dollars, which grew to an estimated 280 billion dollars in 2005 (Independent Sector 2001).

Volunteering is, of course, not limited to the United States; although variations exist across countries (Salamon and Sokolowski 2001), volunteering has emerged as "an international phenomenon" (Anheir and Salamon 1999). According to Salamon and Sokolowski's research on volunteering in twenty-four countries (2001), volunteering constitutes 2.5 percent of non-agricultural employment on average. In their study, this percentage ranged from a low of 0.2 percent in Mexico to a high of 8.0 percent in Sweden.

In the past, volunteering was mainly regarded as work or activities contributed to private charitable or religious organizations. However, volunteers have become a crucial resource for various types of organizations not only in the nonprofit sector but also in the public sector. As an example, the 1992, 1990, and 1988 Gallup surveys on volunteering in the United States show that a significant portion of volunteer efforts went to government organizations (Brudney 1999).

Having such a large amount of time directed to volunteer work does not assure that desirable results are attained for host organizations or volunteers, or for the targets of their well-intentioned efforts. Different issues may arise depending on the types of volunteering activities or on the social and organizational context, and even the nation where volunteering occurs. A 2004 survey on volunteering policies and partnerships in the European Union, for example, suggests that volunteer regulations, policies, and laws differ substantially cross-nationally (Van Hal, Meijs, and Steenbergen 2004).

Attaining beneficial outcomes from volunteer involvement for participants, clients, organizations, and the community requires a programmatic structure. Below we explain how to provide this structure for volunteer programs. To do so, we elaborate and extend a model proposed by Young-joo Lee and Jeffrey L. Brudney (2006), based on the essential challenges that all volunteer programs must meet.

CHALLENGES CONFRONTING VOLUNTEER PROGRAMS

A volunteer program is a systematic effort to involve volunteers in the work, outputs, and outcomes of an organization. Several authors have proposed models to guide volunteer programs (Boyce 1971; Dolan 1969; Kwarteng et al 1988; Lenihan and Jackson 1984; Penrod 1991; Vineyard 1984). A review of these models shows that they are quite similar, being grounded in a set of core functions that these programs typically perform, such as selection, orientation, and job design. Rather than considering the activities conducted, the challenge model focuses on the goals that must be met to achieve successful performance with volunteers. Although research on the validity of volunteer program design models is scant, a study based on a heterogeneous sample of government volunteer programs suggests that various elements of the challenge model are related empirically to the perceived effectiveness of these programs (Hager and Brudney 2004; Brudney 1999).

Lee and Brudney's *A New Challenge Model of a Volunteer Program* (2006), developed originally to guide school volunteer programs, can be extended to the design of volunteer programs in general. These researchers outline six principal challenges that confront volunteer programs:

1. recruiting citizens for volunteer service;

2. engaging the community in the volunteer program;

3. gaining acceptance from organizational members;

4. maintaining accountability, to ensure that volunteers adhere to the values and goals of the organization;

5. managing the program effectively through structural design;

6. evaluating the program's processes and results.

Figure 1 presents the challenge model of a volunteer program. The article discusses, in turn, each challenge a volunteer program must meet.

Recruiting Citizens Perhaps the greatest challenge to an effective volunteer program is attracting people willing and able to donate their time and expertise. Volunteerism expert Susan Ellis (1996b, pp. 5–6) cautions that "recruitment is not the first step" in a program; a volunteer program must have a clear purpose or goal and meaningful work for volunteers to carry out. Yet, without sufficient volunteers, a program cannot be sustained.

It is important to provide potential volunteers with incentives to participate in the program. A powerful motivation for most volunteers is the idea that their efforts will provide a benefit to the recipients of volunteer service, which in turn will bring them a sense of fulfillment. Most

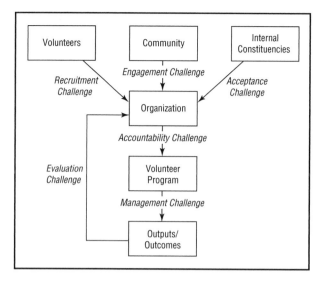

Figure 1. A New Challenge Model of a Volunteer Program (Lee and Brudney 2006)

volunteers say that they volunteer to "help other people" or "do something useful" (Brudney 2005, p. 329). Thus, an emphasis on the benefits of a volunteering program would likely prove an effective volunteer recruitment strategy. Another incentive is the benefit to volunteers themselves. Research has shown that there are positive effects of volunteering for volunteers, such as improved health, increased occupational skills, greater networking and social support, and enhanced self-confidence and self-esteem (Wilson and Musick 1999).

The most effective recruitment strategy is to *ask* people to volunteer. Research findings show that people volunteer far more frequently when they are asked to do so. For instance, the Independent Sector reported that 71.3 percent of the people who volunteered had been asked to volunteer, compared to just 28.7 percent of the non-volunteers (Independent Sector 2002, p. 68). To recruit volunteers, experts recommend targeting groups or organizations with a membership of potential volunteers. For instance, recruitment efforts can be made in workplaces, churches, and synagogues, and directed at neighborhood groups, civic associations, and other institutions in the community (Ellis 1996b).

Engaging the Community As more organizations, including nonprofit, government, and even for-profit, have implemented volunteer programs, an evolution has occurred in the traditional population of volunteers (Smith 1994). Volunteers are no longer predominantly middle-aged, middle-class white women. Instead, they embrace a much wider segment of the community,

including males, youth, seniors, people of color, and so forth (CNCS 2006).

A significant consequence of the growth in the number of volunteer programs and an increasingly diverse volunteer pool is that host organizations must compete for volunteers with other nonprofit, government, and corporate volunteer programs. In order to attract volunteers, volunteer programs must emphasize the contribution or impact of a program, its uniqueness, and its connection to the community. Competition also requires volunteer programs to network with other organizations to gain resources and support, such as funding, legitimacy, volunteer opportunities, in-kind contributions, and publicity.

Gaining Acceptance As Brudney (1994) points out, satisfying an organization's internal constituencies is a prerequisite to setting up an effective volunteer program. Prior to establishing a program, proponents must gain acceptance from, among others, paid staff, board members, clients, and affiliated organizations, such as labor unions and professional associations (if they exist). Without the commitment and support of these stakeholders, the success of a volunteer program is questionable. The likelihood of gaining acceptance increases with the benefits the program may offer, not only to the clients of the program, but also to internal constituencies, volunteers, and the larger community. These benefits can be substantial and include: more attention to clients, greater opportunity for innovation, higher levels of service, increased fund-raising capability, enhanced cost-effectiveness, more satisfying and professional work opportunities, and greater community knowledge, feedback, and involvement (Brudney 2005).

Maintaining Accountability A host organization must make sure volunteers understand the work to be done and the authorized organizational methods and procedures for carrying it out. Accountability makes it possible to recognize and reinforce superior performance by volunteers and, correspondingly, to identify and make changes where performance is inferior or lacking.

In order to ensure accountability, organizational leadership should appoint or hire a volunteer administrator (or coordinator or director) responsible for the overall management and participation of volunteers (Brudney 1996; Ellis 1996, p. 55). The position is usually part-time or constitutes a portion of the duties of a full-time position. Studies find that organizational support for this position is strongly associated with the success of a program (Urban Institute 2004).

Establishing accountability for the volunteer program also includes having a program structure that organizes and integrates the volunteer effort. The program should have job descriptions for volunteer administrators as well as for the volunteer positions to be filled (Brudney 1996). In the United States, the Volunteer Protection Act of 1997 (Public Law PL105–119) strongly encourages organizations to have job descriptions for their volunteers. In addition, written policies and procedures should be on file that specify the rules and regulations concerning volunteer involvement, including the rights and responsibilities of volunteers as well as appropriate behavior and norms on the job (for example, confidentiality, reliability, and attire).

Managing the Program As several authors have noted, managing volunteers is not the same as managing employees (Farmer and Fedor 1999; McCurley and Lynch 2006). For example, volunteers are far less dependent on the organization than paid employees and contribute far fewer hours. Given these differences, the volunteer administrator assumes a critical role in the program. Ideally, volunteer administrators should have the following qualifications (Ellis 1996b, p. 60):

1. background in volunteerism or volunteer administration;

2. ability and/or experience in management;

3. proficiency in job design and analysis;

4. skills in leadership;

5. understanding of the needs of those to be assisted through volunteer effort;

6. familiarity with community resources;

7. interest in outreach to the community.

The volunteer administrator's job typically includes recruiting, screening, orienting, training, placing, supervising, evaluating, and recognizing volunteers. This official also has to attend to risk management (Graff 2003). Liability with respect to volunteer programs applies to situations in which a volunteer is harmed while performing his or her duties, as well as when a third party is harmed by a volunteer (Lake 1997). Given the distinctive duties of volunteer administrators, the literature endorses specialized training and preparation for the volunteer administrator position (Ellis 1996b; McCurley and Lynch 2006).

Evaluating the Program Evaluation provides the ultimate justification for a volunteer program. Brudney (1996, p. 201) defines evaluation as "collecting systematic information on the processes and results of the volunteer program and applying these data toward program assessment and, hopefully, program improvement." To evaluate the effectiveness of volunteer involvement, Brudney recommends focusing on three target audiences: the clients or intended beneficiaries of the volunteer program, internal constituencies, and the volunteers themselves. A variety of

methods exist for evaluation of volunteer programs (Gaskin 2003; Goulborne and Embuldeniya 2002).

Of all the challenges, evaluation apparently receives the lowest priority in volunteer programs (Brudney 1999), perhaps as a consequence of the donated nature of volunteer effort. Organizations may be wary of questioning the involvement or effectiveness of citizen volunteers. Nevertheless, just as with any systematic activity, organizations should assess volunteer programs and learn from the results. As Figure 1 shows, the information gained from evaluation should be fed back to the organization and used to improve the volunteer program.

CONCLUSION

A volunteer program requires an investment on the part of an organization, internal constituencies, and volunteers. Some may ask whether this investment is worth the effort. Indeed it is: Volunteerism benefits all parties involved. Benefits to clients include receiving needed services and the feeling that someone is interested in and cares about them. Benefits to organizations include increasing cost-effectiveness, expanding programs, and raising service quality. Benefits to communities include enhanced civic participation and awareness.

Research has shown that, with respect to the monetary return on investment, volunteer programs routinely yield more in dollar value than organizations expend on them (Gaskin 2003). For clients, volunteers, and communities, the social and psychic benefits are likely to be far greater.

SEE ALSO *National Service Programs; Philanthropy*

BIBLIOGRAPHY

Anheier, Helmut K., and Lester M. Salamon. 1999. Volunteering in Cross-National Perspective: Initial Comparisons. *Law and Contemporary Problems* 62 (4): 43–66.

Brudney, Jeffrey L. 1994. Volunteers in the Delivery of Public Services: Magnitude, Scope, and Management. In *Handbook of Public Personnel Administration*, eds. Jack Rabin, Thomas Vocino, W. Bartley Hildreth, and Gerald J. Miller, 661–686. New York: Marcel Decker.

Brudney, Jeffrey L. 1996. Designing and Implementing Volunteer Programs. In *The State of Public Management*, eds. Donald F. Kettl and H. Brinton Milward, 193–212. Baltimore, MD: Johns Hopkins University Press.

Brudney, Jeffrey L. 1999. The Effective Use of Volunteers: Best Practices for the Public Sector. *Law and Contemporary Problems* 62 (4): 219–255.

Brudney, Jeffrey L. 2005. Designing and Managing Volunteer Programs. In *The Jossey-Bass Handbook of Nonprofit Leadership and Management*, 2nd ed., eds. Robert Herman et al., 310–344. San Francisco: Jossey-Bass.

Corporation for National and Community Service (CNCS). 2006. *Volunteering in America: State Trends and Rankings: A Summary Report.* Washington, DC: CNCS.

Dolan, Robert J. 1969. *The Leadership Development Process in Complex Organizations.* Raleigh: North Carolina State University.

Ellis, Susan J. 1996a. *From the Top Down: The Executive Role in Volunteer Program Success.* Rev. ed. Philadelphia: Energize.

Ellis, Susan J. 1996b. *The Volunteer Recruitment Book (and Membership Development).* Philadelphia: Energize.

Farmer, Steven M., and Donald B. Fedor. 1999. Volunteer Participation and Withdrawal: A Psychological Contract Perspective on the Role of Expectations and Organizational Support. *Nonprofit Management and Leadership* 9 (4): 349–367.

Gaskin, Katherine. 2003. VIVA in Europe: A Comparative Study of the Volunteer Investment and Value Audit. *Journal of Volunteer Administration* 21 (2): 45–48.

Goulborne, Michele, and Don Embuldeniya. 2002. *Assigning Economic Value to Volunteer Activity: Eight Tools for Efficient Program Management.* Toronto: Canadian Center for Philanthropy.

Graff, Linda. 2003. *Better Safe: Risk Management in Volunteer Programs and Community Service.* Ontario, Canada: Linda Graff and Associates.

Hager, Mark A. 2004. *Volunteer Management Capacity in America's Charities and Congregations: A Briefing Report.* Washington, DC: Urban Institute.

Hager, Mark A., and Jeffrey L. Brudney. 2004. *Balancing Act: The Challenges and Benefits of Volunteers.* Washington, DC: Urban Institute.

Independent Sector. 2002. *Giving and Volunteering in the United States: Findings from a National Survey.* Washington, DC: Independent Sector.

Independent Sector. 2006. Value of Volunteer Time. http://www.independentsector.org/programs/research/volunteer_time.html#value.

Kwarteng, Joseph A., Keith L. Smith, and Larry E. Miller. 1988. Ohio 4-H Agents' and Volunteer Leaders' Perceptions of the Volunteer Leadership Development Program. *Journal of the American Association of Teacher Educators in Agriculture* 29 (2): 55–62.

Lake, Jaime. 2001. Screening School Grandparents: Ensuring Continued Safety and Success of School Volunteer Programs. *Elder Law Journal* 8 (2): 423–431.

Lee, Young-joo, and Jeffrey L. Brudney. 2006. School-Based Volunteer Programs: Meeting Challenges and Achieving Benefits. *The Reporter,* Georgia Association for Supervision and Curriculum Development.

Lenihan, Genie O., and Louise Jackson. 1984. Social Need, Public Response: The Volunteer Professional Model for Human Services Agencies and Counselors. *Personnel and Guidance Journal* 62 (5): 285–289.

McCurley, Steve, and Rick Lynch. 2006. *Volunteer Management: Mobilizing All the Resources of the Community.* 2nd ed. Philadelphia: Energize.

Penrod, Kathryn M. 1991. Leadership Involving Volunteers: The L-O-O-P Model. *Journal of Extension* 29 (4): 3–9.

Salamon, Lester M., and S. Wojciech Sokolowski. 2001. Volunteering in Cross-National Perspective: Evidence from Twenty-Four Countries. Comparative Nonprofit Sector Project Working Paper no. 40. Baltimore, MD: Johns Hopkins Center for Civil Society Studies.

Smith, David H. 1994. Determinants of Voluntary Association Participation and Volunteering: A Literature Review. *Nonprofit Voluntary Sector Quarterly* 21: 243–263.

Van Hal, Tirza, Lucas Meijs, and Marijke Steenbergen. 2004. *Volunteering and Participation on the Agenda: Survey on Volunteering Policy and Partnerships in the European Union.* Utrecht, Netherlands: CIVIQ.

Vineyard, Sue. 1984. Recruiting and Retaining Volunteers … No Gimmicks, No Gags! *Journal of Volunteer Administration* 2 (3): 23–28.

Wilson, John, and Marc A. Musick. 1999. The Effects of Volunteering on the Volunteer. *Law and Contemporary Problems* 62 (4): 141–168.

Jeffrey L. Brudney
Young-joo Lee

VOLUNTEERISM

Volunteerism refers to a broad range of activities that benefit another person, group, or cause and that are carried out by individuals by their own choice and without pay. Individuals engaged in volunteerism are referred to as *volunteers.* Examples of volunteerism include serving on the board of a museum, organizing a protest meeting against environmental pollution, preparing food in a soup kitchen, caring for the elderly in a nursing home, looking after pets or mail for a neighbor, and the donation of blood at a blood center. However, also more controversial activities like distributing flyers for an extremist political party and providing shelter to illegal immigrants may qualify as examples of volunteerism.

A common distinction is made between *formal* and *informal* volunteerism. Formal volunteerism is carried out in an organization, usually a nonprofit organization. Informal volunteerism is not carried out in an organization and usually benefits specific individuals or groups with whom the volunteer has personal connections. Informal volunteerism is also called *social support* or *helping behavior.* Informal volunteerism that benefits colleagues or one's employer is called *organizational citizenship behavior.*

In sociology and political science volunteerism is considered a form of civic engagement and an expression of cohesion or social capital in society (Putnam 2000). Formal volunteerism has received more attention in these disciplines than informal volunteerism, although the two are related empirically (Wilson and Musick 1997). The focus on formal volunteerism is apparent in the frequent measurement of engagement in voluntary associations in general household surveys. These surveys contain lists of types of organizations, for each of which the respondent answers to what extent he or she is engaged in the organization (not engaged, passive member, active member, volunteer). In some household surveys respondents report the frequency of informal helping behaviors. Informal volunteerism is commonly measured in questionnaires on social support networks. Respondents indicate whether they have people ("alters") available to them with whom they discuss important matters (emotional support) or who can assist them in practical matters like small repairs (practical support).

Volunteerism is more common among married persons, whites, the middle-aged and elderly, the higher educated, more frequent church attendees, rural residents, children of volunteers, and extraverted persons (Bekkers 2005, 2007; Penner et al. 2005; Putnam 2000; Wilson 2000). Differences between whites and blacks differ from study to study (contrasting findings in Wilson and Musick 1997 and Carson 1987). Among other things, volunteerism is more common among the higher educated because they have more civic skills, more knowledge, and a stronger feeling of efficacy (Brady et al. 1995; Nie et al. 1996). Individuals with more civic skills and knowledge are more able to understand arguments, to express their views, and to convince others. These are useful qualities that lower the cost and increase the expected benefit of volunteerism. Individuals with a stronger feeling of efficacy are more likely to think their volunteerism makes a difference for the beneficiary of their volunteerism, which increases its expected benefit. Formal volunteerism in turn enhances civic skills, knowledge, and self-efficacy. Beyond paid work, voluntary associations are an important context in which people gain experience in organizing meetings, learn to understand others, and gain confidence in their abilities.

Volunteerism is also linked with a variety of other benefits. Volunteers are known to live longer and to be healthier in old age than nonvolunteers. In addition volunteerism contributes to mental health and may contribute to success in paid labor in the long run (Penner et al. 2005; Wilson and Musick 2000). At the macro level voluntary associations strengthen civil society and democracy (Putnam 2000).

Because of these benefits, schools increasingly include service learning and community service programs in their curricula. Completing a service learning program, which itself is usually not a form of volunteerism because it is obligatory, may promote civic skills and volunteerism in the future, depending on several characteristics of the program. More beneficial programs have a moderate level of freedom for pupils in selecting service activities, require a higher level of reflection from pupils, and are supervised by more enthusiastic teachers (Metz and Youniss 2005). Voluntary programs do not have more beneficial effects than required programs (Schmidt et al. 2006). Voluntary programs draw an audience that consists mostly of young people with a social background that facilitates volunteerism: parents volunteer themselves, are religious, and have higher socioeconomic status (Metz and Youniss 2005). Given that required service learning programs also have beneficial effects among youths from less-favorable backgrounds and perhaps even more so than among youths from advantaged backgrounds, required service learning programs may reduce social inequality in volunteerism and civic engagement in the long run.

SEE ALSO *Altruism; Altruism and Prosocial Behavior; Associations, Voluntary; Civil Society; Nongovernmental Organizations (NGOs); Philanthropy; Prevention Science; Putnam, Robert; Social Capital; Verba, Sidney; Volunteer Programs*

BIBLIOGRAPHY

Bekkers, René. 2005. Participation in Voluntary Associations: Relations with Resources, Personality, and Political Values. *Political Psychology* 26: 439–454.

Bekkers, René. 2007. Intergenerational Transmission of Volunteerism. *Acta Sociologica* 50 (2): 99–114.

Brady, Henry E., Sidney Verba, and Kay Lehman Schlozman. 1995. Beyond SES: A Resource Model of Political Participation. *American Political Science Review* 89: 271–294.

Carson, Emmett D. 1987. The Charitable Activities of Black Americans: A Portrait of Self-Help? *Review of Black Political Economy* 15 (3): 100–111.

Metz, Edward C., and James Youniss. 2005. Longitudinal Gains in Civic Development through School-Based Required Service. *Political Psychology* 26 (3): 413–437.

Nie, Norman H., Jane Junn, and Kenneth Stehlik-Barry. 1996. *Education and Democratic Citizenship in America.* Chicago: University of Chicago Press.

Penner, Louis A., John F. Dovidio, Jane A. Piliavin, and David A. Schroeder. 2005. Prosocial Behavior: Multilevel Perspectives. *Annual Review of Psychology* 56: 365–392.

Putnam, Robert D. 2000. *Bowling Alone: The Collapse and Revival of American Community.* New York: Simon and Schuster.

Schmidt, Jennifer A., Lee Shumow, and Hayal Kackar. 2006. Adolescents' Participation in Service Activities and Its Impact on Academic, Behavioral, and Civic Outcomes. *Journal of Youth and Adolescence* 35 (2): 127–140.

Wilson, John. 2000. Volunteering. *Annual Review of Sociology* 26: 215–240.

Wilson, John, and Marc A. Musick. 1997. Who Cares? Toward an Integrated Theory of Volunteer Work. *American Sociological Review* 62: 694–713.

Wilson, John, and Marc A. Musick. 2000. The Effects of Volunteering on the Volunteer. *Law and Contemporary Problems* 62: 141–168.

René Bekkers

VON NEUMANN, JOHN
1903–1957

John von Neumann (born December 28, 1903 in Hungary, died February 8, 1957 in Washington, D.C.) was a versatile scholar whose path-breaking ideas have enriched various disciplines. In social sciences his contributions to game theory, economic growth, and consumers' choice are of special importance.

Von Neumann's talents showed up early, and outstanding mathematicians tutored him individually. In 1923 he entered MSc chemistry studies in Zürich and at the same time studied for a doctoral degree in mathematics in Budapest. In 1926 and 1927, as an assistant to David Hilbert in Göttingen, he laid down the axiomatic foundations of quantum mechanics. His reputation grew rapidly, and he was invited to several universities. He visited Princeton University first in 1929 and became a professor of mathematics at its Institute for Advanced Study in 1933. He became a leading expert on shock and detonation waves, which became significant during World War II (1939–1945), when von Neumann became involved in important projects such as the Manhattan Project. It was mainly the complex nonlinear problems that emerged in these projects that made him realize the importance of computers, and he made key contributions to formulating the basic principles of computer science.

Von Neumann made major scientific contributions to the social sciences as well. As always, he was interested in comprehensive structures, and focused on the core problems in the field. He was the first to prove the existence of equilibrium for two-person zero-sum games in 1928, based on his famous minimax theorem. Using a similar mathematical structure he formulated a multisectoral model of balanced economic growth (first presented in 1932), which was a brilliant mathematical synthesis of some classical ideas concerning the production and price proportions of economic equilibrium. He was the first to employ a fixed-point theorem in the proof of existence of competitive equilibrium, on the one hand, and an explicit duality approach, recognizing the symmetry of the conditions that characterize the choice of optimal activities and the equilibrium price system sustaining it under the conditions of a competitive equilibrium, on the other. His model allows for different theoretical interpretations (classical, Marxist, neoclassical, etc.) indicating its general nature.

Although his model was a prototype of the highly abstract models used in modern economics, he cautioned often against the potential deterioration of such an approach into intellectual games. He saw this danger threatening not only the development of economics but also mathematics itself. He repeatedly criticized economists for not using more appropriate mathematics, and he emphasized the need for more comprehensive tools than those borrowed from classical physics.

Von Neumann set an excellent example for such a novel approach in his work with Oskar Morgenstern on game theory. In their book, *Theory of Games and Economic Behavior* (1944), they laid down the foundations of modern game theory and initiated a new discipline almost from scratch. It was in this connection that they developed the axiomatic theory of expected utility, which states that under certain conditions the preferences of a rational individual can be represented by a function of the expected utility form. The use of the von Neumann–Morgenstern expected utility function became universal in economics because it is analytically very convenient and its normative character may provide a valuable guide to rational actions. Although he darted only briefly into its domain, von Neumann's tremendous influence on the development of modern economics has been widely acknowledged.

SEE ALSO *Game Theory; Neoclassical Growth Model; Optimal Growth; Utility, Von Neumann-Morgenstern*

BIBLIOGRAPHY

Von Neumann, John. 1945. A Model of General Economic Equilibrium. *Review of Economic Studies* 13: 1–9. (Published first in German, 1937.)

Von Neumann, John, and Oskar Morgenstern. 1944. *Theory of Games and Economic Behavior*. Princeton, NJ: Princeton University Press.

Zalai, Ernő, guest ed. 2004. A Special Issue on John von Neumann. *Acta Oeconomica* 54 (1): 1–96.

Ernő Zalai

VOODOO
SEE *Vodou.*

VOTE, ALTERNATIVE

The alternative vote is an electoral method wherein voters rank candidates, and the winner is determined by a sequential count in which the weakest candidate is repeatedly eliminated until one candidate has secured a majority of the vote. Electoral-law terminology is unfortunately nonuniform, but the alternative vote can be regarded as a special case of the "single-transferable vote" or the "preferential vote," with the conditions that only one candidate is elected per district, and election requires an absolute majority. Most real-world examples of this system come from Australia, but it has also seen use elsewhere.

An example from the 1952 election in the Canadian province of British Columbia (Table 1) clarifies how it works.

Voters could rank as many of the four candidates as they liked, and the "first count" column shows how many placed each candidate in first place. None of the four had the necessary majority (5,771) immediately, so the last-place candidate, the Progressive Conservative (P.C.), was eliminated. The second-count "transfer" column shows how the 1,690 ballots on which Wright was ranked first were then redistributed: 169 of those ballots had no further rankings, and were thus discarded; 937 of them had Turnbull ranked second; and so on. Following elimination of the candidate from the Co-operative Commonwealth Federation (C.C.F), the Social Credit (S.C.) candidate, Robert Sommers, ultimately won the seat on the third count.

Advocates of the alternative vote often stress that it tends to be more proportional than simple plurality election, wherein voters pick one preferred candidate and whichever candidate wins the most votes wins the seat. In other words, the proportions of votes and seats won by the parties are usually more nearly equal under the alternative vote system. Again, British Columbia illustrates. The 1952 and 1953 elections were held using the alternative vote ("vote" in Table 2 refers to first count), whereas later elections awarded seats by plurality.

Unlike proportional-representation electoral rules, which ensure very close equality between seat and vote shares, the alternative vote merely tends not to exaggerate the support for large parties when turning votes into seats as drastically as does plurality.

One criticism of the alternative vote is that getting higher rankings can actually cause a candidate to lose a seat. The example in Table 3, devised by Steven Brams and Peter Fishburn, demonstrates this surprising trait. Candidates A, B, C, and D are competing for the seat, and the voters fall into four types, according to their preference rankings.

The outcome is a win by candidate A, as shown in Table 4 (since all voters ranked all candidates, exhausted ballots play no role).

Now suppose that the Type-IV voters move A up from last place to first place, so that their rank ordering is A, D, C, B. If all other voters remain the same, the outcome is now shown in Table 5.

Candidate (Party)	first count	second count transfer	second count result	third count transfer	third count result
Turnbull (Liberal)	3,331	+937	4,268	+535	4,803
Wright (P.C.)	1,690	−1,690	—	—	—
Johnson (C.C.F.)	2,541	+259	2,800	−2,800	—
Sommers (S.C.)	3,979	+325	4,304	+1,613	5,917
exhausted ballots	—	169		652	
TOTAL (minus ex'd)	11,541		11,372		10,720
required majority	5,771		5,687		5,361

Table 1: Rossland-Trail Electoral District

	1952 vote %	1952 seat %	1953 vote %	1953 seat %	1956 vote %	1956 seat %	1960 vote %	1960 seat %
Conservatives	17	8	6	2	3	0	7	0
Liberals	24	13	24	8	22	4	21	8
C.C.F.	31	38	31	30	28	19	33	31
Social Credit	27	40	38	58	46	75	39	62
other	1	2	1	2	1	2	0	0

Table 2

	Type I (7)	Type II (6)	Type III (5)	Type IV (3)
rank 1st	A	B	C	D
rank 2nd	B	A	B	C
rank 3rd	C	C	A	B
rank 4th	D	D	D	A

Table 3

Candidate	first count	second count transfer	second count result	third count transfer	third count result
A	7		7	+6	13
B	6		6	−6	—
C	5	+3	8		8
D	3	−3	—		—

Table 4

Candidate	first count	second count transfer	second count result	third count transfer	third count result
A	10		10		10
B	6		6	+5	11
C	5		5	−5	—
D	0	−0	—		—

Table 5

Candidate B wins. Candidate A did worse (losing, not winning) because some voters gave him a *higher* ranking. If voters recognize the possibility of outcomes like this, they have incentives to misrepresent their preferences. Surprisingly, however, all electoral systems are vulnerable to such strategic voting.

SEE ALSO *Elections; Electoral Systems; Voting; Voting Schemes*

BIBLIOGRAPHY

Farrell, David M. 1997. *Comparing Electoral Systems.* London: Prentice Hall.

Lijphart, Arend, and Bernard Grofman, eds. 1984. *Choosing an Electoral System: Issues and Alternatives.* Westport, CT: Praeger.

Brian J. Gaines

VOTING

Voting is the central act of democracy, the method by which citizens influence the policy of the state by holding the leaders who represent them accountable for their decisions. It is also the means by which elected leaders make decisions in legislatures, and it is used outside government in businesses, civic organizations, social groups, and families in every modern society. This entry focuses on voting for elected offices because that type of voting defines democracy.

WHY DO PEOPLE VOTE?

Does voting make a difference? Almost all political scientists agree that political leaders in democracies respond to voters in a way that leaders in undemocratic, or "authoritarian," countries do not. Because representatives in democracies are accountable to voters, they are much more likely to do things that benefit large sectors of society (rather than their friends and families)—for example, providing public goods such as infrastructure, public safety, and education and adhering to the rule of law rather than relying on arbitrary decisions about who should have access to government resources.

Political leaders in authoritarian countries are not entirely unaccountable to ordinary citizens. They must provide at least minimal government services or they eventually will face revolt or at the very least citizens who express their displeasure by cheating the system, refusing to do what they are told when no one is watching, and engaging in other subtle forms of resistance. When politicians must compete against one another for votes, the degree of accountability to ordinary citizens is much higher, much as merchants in a competitive marketplace offer better prices and higher quality than does a seller with a monopoly.

Though voting is clearly important for society as a whole, the question of why individuals vote is more problematic: One vote among thousands seems to matter very little. This is a classic example of a collective action problem in which many people working together can produce something that benefits them all but any individual's contribution adds little to the whole and its absence will not be missed; as a result any particular person has little incentive to contribute. For the individual, then, voting appears to be irrational because one vote would not change the outcome but voters and nonvoters alike share the results.

In some political systems politicians solve this problem by trading money or favors to the citizens who are willing to vote for them, a practice known as patronage. Although this strategy motivates people to vote, most scholars believe it compromises the nature of democracy. Another strategy is to instill civic pride and responsibility in voters so that they see voting as an important part of their role in the community. This strategy also can work for dedicated groups within a larger society, such as labor unions, which often expend a great deal of effort encouraging their members to vote. Some societies even adopt compulsory voting, forcing citizens who do not vote to pay fines. Also, whatever people perceive the benefits of voting to be, they are more likely to vote if casting a vote is easy to do.

In part because politicians, parties, and governments in different countries have adopted different strategies to encourage citizens to vote and in part because of differences in political cultures among countries, levels of voter turnout vary dramatically from one country to the next and often change over time. The United States, for example, had lower voter turnout rates throughout the twentieth century than those of most other rich democracies, and that pattern continued into the twenty-first century; however, turnout rates in most Western European countries declined after the 1970s, whereas U.S. rates remained stable over that period among eligible voters (though the presence of increasing numbers of noncitizens and disenfranchised convicts in the population created the appearance of a decline in U.S. turnouts). Especially low turnouts can call the legitimacy of elections into question because actual voters may not be representative of society as whole. Because poorer and less educated voters are less likely to turn out than are their fellow citizens, low turnouts harm parties that draw more support from those voters.

THE HISTORY OF VOTING

Voting dates at least from ancient times, with well-known examples including the Greek city-state of Athens, the republic of Rome, and the direct ancestors of modern legislatures: the assemblies, or parliaments, of medieval Europe. In all those cases the only people allowed to vote were males who held important social positions (members of the nobility or clergy) or owned a certain amount of property; the vast majority of adults, including women, could not vote.

The fight to create democratic government in Europe was therefore as much a fight over who got to vote as it was a fight over whether the king or the parliament would be supreme. Disenfranchised groups placed the right to vote at the forefront of their fights for equality both for its symbolic importance as the mark of full citizenship and because it gave them the political power to pursue other goals. During the nineteenth and early twentieth centuries pressure from the lower classes, often organized by labor unions, resulted in the lowering of property qualifications until finally universal male suffrage became the norm throughout Europe and the Americas. Beginning in the late nineteenth century, those countries witnessed a push to give women the right to vote, and by the late twentieth century nearly every country in the world had adopted universal suffrage.

As a result the right to vote ceased to be the true measure of democracy because authoritarians found ways to give people the right to vote without turning over real political power. One example was the American South, where the United States freed black slaves and gave them the right to vote after the Civil War ended in 1865. Strict requirements such as literacy tests and poll taxes (requirements usually waived for poor, uneducated whites) prevented blacks from voting until those measures were overturned by the Voting Rights Act of 1965. In the first decade of the twenty-first century laws in many U.S. states that prevented convicts and even ex-convicts from voting continued to affect blacks disproportionately.

A far more popular strategy has been to ban all political parties other than the ruling party or to make it difficult for other parties to organize and campaign. A more subtle method to reduce the power of the vote is the practice of patronage, or "machine" politics, in which politicians trade money or favors for votes; this practice was easier to implement before the secret ballot was adopted in most countries in the late nineteenth century, but politicians have devised numerous ways to reward loyalty and punish disloyalty even when votes are secret. Those politicians are accountable to voters, but there is little political competition; the politicians are political monopolists and are less responsive to voters than are politicians in a competitive system.

In a society with deep ethnic, racial, or national divisions, the members of each ethnic group typically vote only for politicians and parties of their own group. Some scholars consider ethnic solidarity in voting a reasonable

exercise in self-determination, especially when minority groups attempt to oppose an oppressive majority. However, other scholars argue that not only does this situation produce a monopolistic relationship between leaders and voters that encourages patronage, but when the majority as well as the minority votes along ethnic lines, the majority wins every election and the minority has little reason to participate in the political system, a situation that leads to conflict that may turn violent.

In some countries legislators represent districts with unequal numbers of constituents, giving voters in smaller districts more power. This normally happens for historical reasons (for example, when people move from rural districts to urban ones), but parties with strong support in the smaller districts typically oppose any changes. In addition, officeholders sometimes "gerrymander" district boundaries, drawing them so that even if districts are equal in size, they tend to favor the election of one party or of incumbents in general.

Even when everyone has an equal right to vote and elections are competitive, casting votes may be difficult. In the United States citizens must register to vote before an election, and this requires extra time and effort. By contrast, in many countries all adult citizens are automatically eligible to vote. The actual act of voting may be problematic as well, especially when elections are held on working days or transportation to the polls is difficult to obtain. Low levels of education also may pose a barrier because people who cannot read or understand complex political concepts may have little ability to choose candidates wisely and little interest in doing so. Negative campaign ads and bad weather discourage many voters, strengthening the role of the most dedicated (and typically most extreme). Some scholars have argued that voters can grow apathetic as a result of "election fatigue" resulting from multiple elections within a specific period or multiple races at each election. The United States, with its many state and local as well as national elections, provides a clear example of this problem. Because many barriers to voting disproportionately affect the poor and less educated, efforts to raise or lower those barriers often become the objects of political dispute, with parties that draw more votes from the affected groups arguing for lower barriers.

At the other end of the spectrum the ability to provide campaign contributions or mobilize voters may give rich individuals and well-organized groups a more powerful voice in elections. Though all countries have restrictions on these sorts of activities, it seems unlikely that those advantages can be eliminated completely, and some scholars argue that private funding of political causes is necessary to provide true opposition to the government in power.

ELECTORAL SYSTEMS

Except in a few small communities where citizens vote directly on every issue, voters elect representatives to a legislature and, in some countries, executive offices such as the presidency. The first traditional method of electing legislatures is single-member districts (SMDs), in which the candidate who receives the most votes is elected; in countries with presidential systems presidents usually are elected this way. SMDs tend to produce two-party systems because parties with similar ideologies are more likely to win in each district by uniting. This system encourages direct accountability of representatives to a set of constituents, and this can make individual politicians more important than parties; however, the presence of only two parties gives voters a clear choice.

The other traditional form of voting is proportional representation (PR), in which each district elects many representatives and people vote for parties rather than individual candidates, with each party receiving a share of seats in the legislature proportional to its vote (in a rare variant known as the single transferable vote system [STV] voters actually vote for individual candidates, listing them in order of preference, but the system nonetheless produces proportional representation of parties). PR produces multiparty systems, requiring parties to form coalitions to rule. Because people vote for parties in PR systems, parties are usually strong and have clear platforms. In addition, voters never fear that their votes will be wasted as a result of their living in districts where their parties are always in the minority.

Because of this, it is thought that PR systems favor minorities whose members are spread evenly across geographical districts: In an SMD system a minority that is a minority in every district will win no seats, whereas in a PR system it will win a percentage equal to its share of the population. In practice, however, a minority that would lose every seat in an SMD system would end up with a minority in a PR system and thus, despite having symbolically important seats in the legislature, would be unable to pass legislation unless it could take part in a coalition (and a coalition would work equally well to gain a majority in SMDs), though in most legislatures a sizable minority may be able to block certain legislation or at least prevent constitutional amendments.

This concern applies most clearly when an electoral minority is a permanent one, as is the case in an ethnically divided country. In a competitive democracy, whether SMD or PR, the greatest barrier to "tyranny of the majority" is that no majority is permanent and therefore the members of the current majority have incentives both to treat potential future allies in the current minority well and to institutionalize respect for the minority because they themselves will be in the minority eventually.

Some countries have adopted other systems in an attempt to combine the best features of SMDs and PR. An open-list PR system allows voters to choose specific candidates within each party. An SMD system with a primary election allows voters to choose among competing candidates with similar ideologies in the primary. This narrows the choice in the general election to a clear one between two (or at most a few) candidates; holding a runoff if no candidate wins a majority in an election works in much the same way. Multiple voting allows each voter to vote for several different candidates in one district; each voter receives a number of votes equal to the number of offices to be filled, with all candidates competing against one another. An SMD system with alternative voting lets voters rank candidates in order of preference, allowing someone to support a first-choice party without hurting the chances of a second-choice party to win out over parties the voter dislikes; like STV, this is a rare variant. A few countries have adopted a mixed system in which some representatives are chosen in SMDs and others are elected by PR.

Older democracies tend to use one system or another for historical reasons. Newer democracies and those that have undergone major constitutional reforms are more likely to use systems like those of neighboring countries or their former colonial rulers (SMDs in the Americas and PR in Europe, for example) or to use one of the new systems.

In addition to electing representatives and executive officers such as presidents, voters sometimes vote directly on important issues, especially constitutions or constitutional amendments. This practice, called a referendum, was pioneered by Switzerland and has become increasingly common throughout the world.

ELECTORAL SYSTEMS IN LEGISLATURES AND OUTSIDE GOVERNMENT

Voting is also important within legislatures: Governments and laws must be approved by a majority of representatives. Secret ballots are uncommon in legislatures because they make it difficult for constituents to hold legislators accountable. In addition, when parties are strong, legislators almost always vote as their party leaders direct. The result is that a government in a system with strong parties wins nearly every vote, especially in the typical parliamentary system, where a government must have a majority of the seats in the legislature to take power in the first place.

The electoral systems used outside government often mimic governmental systems. For example, the members of a large club usually elect a board of directors and a president and other executive officers. However, there may be important differences. For example, many organizations use open voting rather than a secret ballot, and in corporations the shareholders have as many votes as they own shares rather than one vote each.

HOW DO PEOPLE DECIDE WHOM TO VOTE FOR?

Many factors enter into citizens' decisions about how to vote, and with the exception of ethnicity in an ethnically divided country no single factor overshadows the rest. Profession and economic class, religion, gender, region, the values instilled by parents, and longtime identification with a party can all play a role, as can events during the lifetime of a voter, such as the Great Depression and the 9/11 attacks. This complexity is probably for the best because having voters pulled in many different directions by cross-pressures tends to moderate conflicts and forces politicians to compete for votes.

Researchers generally agree, however, that except in patronage systems, voters rarely vote on the basis of narrow self-interest; they are more likely to vote on the basis of the interests of a large social group or the country as a whole. Citizens also tend to vote retrospectively, rewarding or punishing incumbents for the results of previous years, especially economic results, rather than guessing how candidates may perform in the future.

SEE ALSO *Compulsory Voting; Democracy; Elections; Electoral Systems; Party Systems, Competitive; Political Parties; Suffrage, Women's; Vote, Alternative; Voting Patterns; Voting Rights Act; Voting Schemes; Women's Movement*

BIBLIOGRAPHY

Campbell, Angus, Philip E. Converse, Warren E. Miller, and Donald E. Stokes. 1960. *The American Voter.* New York: Wiley.

Lawson, Steven F. 2003. *Civil Rights Crossroads: Nation, Community, and the Black Freedom Struggle.* Lexington: University Press of Kentucky.

LeDuc, Lawrence, Richard G. Niemi, and Pippa Norris, eds. 2002. *Comparing Democracies 2: New Challenges in the Study of Elections and Voting.* Thousand Oaks, CA: Sage.

Niemi, Richard G., and Herbert F. Weisberg, eds. 2001. *Controversies in Voting Behavior.* 4th ed. Washington, DC: CQ Press.

Popkin, Samuel L. 1994. *The Reasoning Voter: Communication and Persuasion in Presidential Campaigns.* 2nd ed. Chicago: University of Chicago Press.

Rae, Douglas W. 1967. *The Political Consequences of Electoral Laws.* New Haven, CT: Yale University Press.

Weatherford, Doris. 1998. *A History of the American Suffragist Movement.* Santa Barbara, CA: ABC-CLIO.

Scott D. Orr

VOTING, COMPULSORY

SEE *Compulsory Voting.*

VOTING, MAJORITY

SEE *Majority Voting.*

VOTING, PARADOX OF

SEE *Paradox of Voting.*

VOTING PATTERNS

Political scientists often study voting patterns to determine partisan preferences among selected voter groups. Voter groups, such as those based on income levels, education levels, gender, age, regional location, religion, race, or ethnicity, have historically changed their partisan preferences at times in a process called realignment.

Political scientist V. O. Key Jr., in "A Theory of Critical Elections" (1955), defined realignment as occurring when cross-cutting issues tear apart old partisan alliances and create new ones during an election cycle. For instance, in the 1930s, American president Franklin Roosevelt's New Deal policies of union rights, government jobs programs, and social welfare caused large groups of voters who had previously voted Republican to switch to the Democrats.

Political scientist Walter Dean Burnham (1970) elaborated on the critical election theory of American politics, finding a cyclical pattern of every thirty to forty years for such a phenomenon and stating that such elections tend to create a new majority political party for decades afterward.

Because no critical election has been apparent in modern American politics, more recent political science studies of voting patterns tend to focus on the more gradual realignment processes that appear to have occurred since the 1950s or on the concept of dealignment, a belief that partisan attachments among voters are in decline. Studies of modern voting patterns outside of the United States also usually examine long-term realigning processes or a decline of long-term partisan attachments among voters.

Throughout history, democratic elections and partisan divisions around the world have often been organized along regional, ethnic, and religious lines. Class distinctions in voting patterns became important in many countries in the late nineteenth and early twentieth centuries. And by the end of the twentieth century, partisan voting differences related to race, educational level, age, and gender also became apparent in many countries.

While specific issues are important in explaining some of the partisan divisions and voting patterns, shared cultural attitudes toward government, society, and other groups often provide a stronger explanation. Examples are plenty among democracies of one group in society favoring a political party while another group in historical, social, or political opposition to the first group favors another political party.

AMERICAN HISTORICAL VOTING PATTERNS

In the United States, regional divisions became strong immediately prior to and after the Civil War of 1861–1865. Following the war, many northern parts of the United States, which had favored the abolition of slavery, supported the new Republican Party, while most white voters in the southern United States, who had opposed abolition, favored the Democrats. While the South also had a large African American population, most of that population was prevented from voting through intimidation and legal measures for much of the period between 1877 and 1965.

These regional divisions strengthened in the 1890s when a Populist agrarian and fundamentalist Christian movement took over the Democratic Party, and most Catholic immigrant populations in the northern United States joined northern Protestants in voting solidly Republican for the following forty years. However, Catholic voters in New York City remained mostly Democratic, and by the 1910s and 1920s, the majority Republican Party had split between a conservative wing and a progressive wing.

During the years of the Great Depression in the 1930s, Democratic president Franklin Roosevelt put together a "New Deal coalition" of support for the now majority Democratic Party by supporting new social welfare programs and union rights for working-class Americans, including Catholics, Jews, and African Americans in the North, as well as government reforms to appeal to progressive, educated voters and infrastructure spending to continue the support from southern white voters.

However, a party that tried to create a coalition of northern progressive voters, African Americans, and southern white conservative voters in the United States was doomed not to last, and by the 1960s, the Democratic New Deal coalition fell apart over such issues as equal rights for African Americans, the Vietnam War, environmental and consumer regulations, religious and family values, and gun control and responses to crime.

Prior to the 1960s, both the Democrats and the Republicans in the United States were catchall parties containing members and politicians from all ideological

persuasions. But the realignment that began in the 1960s made the Republicans into a clearly conservative party favoring less government regulation, more military spending, imposition of the death penalty for violent crimes, opposition to limits on gun ownership, and support for traditional cultural values such as prayer in schools and opposition to gay marriage. Much of this shift in Republican ideology came from the strengthened role of southern politicians and voters in the party. The Democrats took stances opposite to the Republicans on most of those issues. Moderates did remain in each party, however, sometimes taking positions closer to the majority from the other party.

MODERN AMERICAN VOTING PATTERNS

This change in U.S. voting patterns has led to what many in the American media labeled the division of the "red states and the blue states," named for a color-coded map used in the 2000 presidential election showing which states voted for the Republican presidential candidate and which voted for the Democratic candidate. On this map, Republican states were red, with Democratic states blue.

American voting patterns had evolved in the early twenty-first century to the regional opposite of what they had been a hundred years earlier. In the four presidential elections occurring between 1992 and 2004, the Democratic Party swept almost entirely the states of the Northeast and Pacific Coast areas as well as the states bordering on the Great Lakes in the Midwest region. The Republican Party during those elections swept almost entirely the states of the South and of the center of the country west from the Great Lakes through the Rocky Mountain region.

Strong racial and religious voting patterns also emerged in the United States over the period after the 1950s, with African Americans and Jewish Americans overwhelmingly supporting the Democrats, and the most religious white Americans strongly favoring Republicans.

While a majority of higher income U.S. voters continued to support the Republican Party in the early twenty-first century because of the party's stance on low taxes, voting patterns based on educational levels began to change after the 1950s. Over the following fifty years, while the voters with the lowest educational levels and lowest incomes tended to remain as Democratic supporters, the voters with the highest educational levels, with graduate degrees, also became more Democratic, making the party to some extent a coalition of the most educated and least educated. The Republicans were at their strongest among those who had completed some years of university but had not finished.

A gender gap also opened up in the United States during the 1980s and continued into the twenty-first century. In every presidential election from 1988 to 2004, women preferred the Democratic presidential candidate, while men preferred the Republican presidential candidate, according to polls.

The presidential election of 2004 also showed the beginning of a possible new generation gap in American voting patterns, with voters under age thirty preferring the Democratic candidate for president, and older voters preferring the Republican.

MODERN VOTING PATTERNS AROUND THE WORLD

Such voting patterns and divisions of voter groups can be found in most other countries with democratic elections. Traditional economic class divisions between working-class voter support for left-wing parties and middle- and upper-class support for right-wing parties in Europe were common for much of the twentieth century, but many of those divisions began to blur by the end of the century as some voters focused more on noneconomic issues.

Regional divisions in voting patterns have been strong in many countries. In Canada, the Conservative Party dominated in the western part of the country in the early twenty-first century, while the Liberal Party dominated the most populous province of Ontario, and parties advocating independence for Quebec tended to dominate politics in that province.

In the United Kingdom, the Conservative Party in the early twenty-first century had trouble winning any parliamentary seats in the northern part of England, and in Scotland and Wales, limiting its ability to form a new majority in the House of Commons. Voting patterns in many other European countries showed a strong regional basis in the early twenty-first century, with a former Communist party winning many votes in the former East Germany in German elections, a Northern League regional party in Italy participating in government coalitions, and Basque and Catalan regional nationalist parties winning a number of seats in the Spanish Cortes Generales.

VOTER TURNOUT

Voter turnout is a political phenomenon related to voting patterns, with voter turnout usually being defined as the percentage of the voting-age population who participate in an election, though the exact method by which turnout is measured can vary by country. In general, the United States and Switzerland have long had the lowest voter turnout among economically advanced countries, in part because of the frequency and complexity of elections in those countries. In the United States, only about half of adults were voting in presidential elections by the end of the twentieth century, with far lower numbers for other types of elections.

While turnout in other economically advanced democracies was generally much higher than in the United States during the 1900s, the trend in most countries has been toward declining turnout closer to the American tradition, with younger and less educated voters in particular among the least likely to participate in elections. Such a global decline in voter turnout may also have implications for changes in voting patterns throughout the twenty-first century.

SEE ALSO *Conservative Party (Britain); Democratic Party, U.S.; Elections; Electoral Systems; Gender Gap; Great Depression; Jim Crow; New Deal, The; Politics, Black; Politics, Southern; Reconstruction Era (U.S.); Republican Party; Slavery; Voting*

BIBLIOGRAPHY

Burnham, Walter Dean. 1970. *Critical Elections and the Mainsprings of American Politics.* New York: Norton.

Flanigan, William H., and Nancy H. Zingale. 2006. *Political Behavior of the American Electorate*, 11th ed. Washington, DC: CQ Press.

Karvonen, Lauri, and Stein Kuhnle, eds. 2001. *Party Systems and Voter Alignments Revisited.* London and New York: Routledge.

Key, V. O., Jr. 1955. A Theory of Critical Elections. *The Journal of Politics* 17 (1): 3–18.

Mehra, Ajay K., D. D. Khanna, and Gert W. Kueck, eds. 2003. *Political Parties and Party Systems.* New Delhi, India, and Thousand Oaks, CA: Sage.

Speel, Robert W. 1998. *Changing Patterns of Voting in the Northern United States: Electoral Realignment 1952–1996.* University Park: Pennsylvania State University Press.

Sundquist, James L. 1983. *Dynamics of the Party System: Alignment and Realignment of Political Parties in the United States.* Rev. ed. Washington, DC: Brookings Institution.

Robert W. Speel

VOTING RIGHTS ACT

On July 27, 2006, President George W. Bush signed the Fannie Lou Hamer, Rosa Parks, and Coretta Scott King Voting Rights Reauthorization and Amendments Act of 2006 into law. That act extended several key but nonpermanent parts of the Voting Rights Act (VRA) of 1965 and its subsequent amendments.

The renewal was preceded by debates about whether the VRA was still necessary. The VRA is and has been one of the most important laws in American history. Aimed at eradicating systematic discrimination against minorities and specifically at securing their voting rights, the VRA enabled the federal government to take affirmative steps toward ensuring racial equality and political fairness. Nonetheless, the renewal and extension of the VRA in July 2006 indicated that the battle to achieve nationwide political fairness was not over.

BACKGROUND AND GENESIS

The Voting Rights Act was signed into law by President Lyndon Johnson on August 6, 1965. The act was passed essentially to enforce the provisions of the Fifteenth Amendment, which states, "The right of citizens of the United States to vote shall not be denied or abridged by the United States or by any State on account of race, color or previous condition of servitude." Despite the passage of the Fifteenth Amendment, along with the Thirteenth and Fourteenth Amendments to the Constitution, blacks systematically had been denied access to the franchise and the free exercise of their constitutional rights for the better part of a century.

The president's determination to introduce the VRA was crystallized by the events of February and March 1965. The Reverend Martin Luther King had been arrested in Selma, Alabama. Peaceful protest marches ensued as King and other civil rights workers attempted to organize resistance to the institutionalized system of racial discrimination known as Jim Crow. The peaceful marches were met and dispersed by police violence. Clergy and other marchers were beaten and in some cases killed.

On March 7 marchers seeking to march from Selma to Montgomery were stopped on the Edmund Pettus Bridge leading out of Selma. There the marchers were beaten in another outbreak of police violence. This time, however, the violence was broadcast on national television.

On March 15, 1965, President Johnson spoke to a special joint session of Congress. In that speech he acknowledged that despite the passage of the Fifteenth Amendment black voters had been prevented systematically from exercising the franchise: "Experience has shown that the existing processes of law cannot overcome systematic and ingenious discrimination. No law that we now have on the books—and I have helped to put three of them there—can ensure the right to vote when local officials are determined to deny it" (Johnson 1965).

THE VOTING RIGHTS ACT OF 1965

The key provisions of the VRA were as follows:

- Section 2 of the act essentially restated the Fifteenth Amendment: "No voting qualification or prerequisite to voting, or standard, practice, or procedure shall be imposed or applied by any State or political subdivision to deny or abridge the right of any citizen of the United States to vote on account of race or color."

- Section 4 explicitly forbade the use of literacy tests or other devices to deny citizens access to the franchise or the polling booths.

- Section 5 imposed "preclearance requirements" on any state or political subdivision that as of November 1, 1964, had used literacy tests and in which less than 50 percent of the voting-age population was registered to vote or in which less than 50 percent of registered voters voted in the presidential election of 1964.

In any political subdivision that met those criteria Section 5 required that the government submit any change to a "voting qualification or prerequisite to voting, or standard, practice, or procedure with respect to voting different from that in force or effect on November 1, 1964" to the United States District Court for the District of Columbia or the United States Department of Justice for approval. Section 5 thus was designed to prevent surreptitious or invidious attempts by local or state governments to continue to disenfranchise minority voters despite the intent of the VRA.

CONTROVERSIES

Several controversies arose as a result of the VRA, and all of them led to Supreme Court litigation. The first dealt with the scope of the act. What actually constituted a "voting qualification or prerequisite to voting, or standard, practice, or procedure with respect to voting"? Local officials who tried to resist the VRA took advantage of that ambiguity to craft subtle but effective practices that would limit the capacity of minorities to vote. As Abigail Thernstrom noted in 1987, "By 1969 public officials in Mississippi and elsewhere had made all too plain their readiness to alter the electoral environment by instituting, for instance, county-wide voting, eliminating the single member districts from which some blacks were likely to get elected" (Thernstrom 1987, p. 4).

In 1969 in *Allen v. State Board of Elections* the Supreme Court heard challenges to such laws passed by several southern states. The states argued that because the changes had no impact on black voters' access to the polls, they were not covered by the VRA. However, in striking down those laws, the Supreme Court ruled that the franchise entailed more than mere access to the polls. The challenged laws included the following:

- A 1966 Mississippi law that allowed counties to change the manner in which their boards supervisors were elected. Instead of using districts, they could use at-large elections.

- Another Mississippi law that allowed the boards of education in eleven counties to appoint the superintendent of education (instead of electing the superintendent).

- A Mississippi law that changed the requirements for independent candidates running in general elections.

- A Virginia law that changed the requirements for casting write-in ballots.

In striking down those laws, the Court ruled:

The Voting Rights Act was aimed at the subtle, as well as the obvious, state regulations, which have the effect of denying citizens their right to vote because of their race. Moreover, compatible with the decisions of this Court, the Act gives a broad interpretation to the right to vote, recognizing that voting includes "all action necessary to make a vote effective." We are convinced that in passing the Voting Rights Act, Congress intended that state enactments such as those involved in the instant cases be subject to the 5 approval requirements. (*Allen v. State Board of Elections*, 565–566, internal citations omitted)

Thus, the Court expanded the scope and definition of the franchise to protect it from pernicious attempts to constrain its exercise.

Another major controversy arose in 1982. As it originally was written, the VRA could have been interpreted to require plaintiffs to forbid only those electoral arrangements which had been passed with the *intent* of diluting minority voting power. In 1982 Congress rewrote Section 2 to require only a demonstration that a challenged law had the *effect* of diluting minority voting strength. Legislative intent did not matter.

In *Thornburg v. Gingles* (1986) the Supreme Court sustained the new effects standard. *Gingles* thus placed a great deal of pressure on the states. It led to extensive efforts by the Justice Department to require states to draw legislative and congressional districts in a manner that would allow minority voters to constitute an electoral majority. That practice led to the creation of so-called majority-minority districts with truly bizarre shapes and gave rise to another controversy: If districts drawn to shut minority voters out of politics were unconstitutional, could districts drawn to ensure their chances of election survive constitutional scrutiny?

In *Shaw v. Reno* (1993) the Court ruled that a redistricting scheme that was "unexplainable" on grounds other than race would violate the equal protection clause

of the Fourteenth Amendment. If the record indicated that racial considerations had played a determining role in the construction of a challenged district *and* if the district's shape indicated that the legislature had forsaken "traditional districting principles" to such an extent that its outline was "highly irregular," "bizarre," and "irrational on its face" (*Shaw*, 648), the redistricting plan would run afoul of the equal protection clause of the Fourteenth Amendment.

Shaw rewrote the rules of the districting process. *Gingles* had indicated that if states did not draw districts to enhance minority representational opportunities, they were guilty of vote dilution in violation of Section 2 of the VRA. According to *Shaw*, if they went too far in drawing majority-minority districts, particularly in states that did not have large demographic concentrations of African American voters, they risked a Fourteenth Amendment challenge.

SHAW AND THE DOUBLE STANDARD OF VOTING RIGHTS

After *Shaw* voting rights law was based on a double standard. Districts drawn to harm minority voters were unconstitutional, but districts drawn to help them were also unconstitutional even though it was constitutionally permissible to draw them to help other groups, such as incumbents, urban and rural voters, Democrats and Republicans, and other ethnic groups. In subsequent rulings the Supreme Court resolved that double standard by modifying its stand against racial gerrymandering.

In *Miller v. Johnson* the Court declared congressional districts in Georgia unconstitutional because the legislative record clearly demonstrated that they had been drawn with the explicit intent of maximizing the number of majority-minority districts. In her concurrence, however, Justice O'Connor indicated that the double standard in *Shaw* was problematic:

The standard [for assessing the constitutionality of districts] would be no different if a legislature had drawn the boundaries to favor some other ethnic group; certainly the standard does not treat efforts to create majority-minority districts *less* favorably than similar efforts on behalf of other groups…. Application of the Court's standard does not throw into doubt the vast majority of the Nation's 435 congressional districts, where presumably the States have drawn the boundaries in accordance with their customary districting principles. That is so even though race may well have been considered in the redistricting process. (*Miller*, 928–929, O'Connor, J., concurring)

O'Connor thus acknowledged that factors such as race and ethnicity are part of the redistricting process.

But, she said, the *Shaw* standard at least allowed the Court to police "extreme instances of gerrymandering."

ERADICATING *SHAW*'S DOUBLE STANDARD

A majority of the Court finally acknowledged the tensions in its voting rights jurisprudence. In *Easley v. Cromartie* (2001) the Court declared majority-minority congressional districts in North Carolina constitutional despite their bizarre shapes because they were the product of a multitude of factors only one of which was race. In so doing, the Court set forth a standard of proof that made it easier for states to avert a *Shaw* challenge while simultaneously upholding the goals of the VRA.

So long as states could demonstrate that some other factor besides race played an important role in the drafting of legislative district lines, they could defend a districting scheme by explaining that race did not "predominate" (*Easley*, 258). The Court thus drew upon a statement made by Justice O'Connor in *Bush v. Vera*: "If district lines merely correlate with race because they are drawn on the basis of political affiliation, which correlates with race, there is no racial classification to justify" (*Bush v. Vera*, 968). Thus, the Court explained that "the Constitution does not place an *affirmative* obligation upon the legislature to avoid creating districts that turn out to be heavily, even majority, minority. It simply imposes an obligation not to create such districts for predominantly racial, as opposed to political or traditional, districting motivations" (*Easley*, 248).

Easley allowed courts to look at a racially remedial gerrymander and declare it nothing more than a partisan or incumbent one. By declaring that race had to be the predominant factor in a redistricting plan, the Court enabled states to defend their plans by offering a plausible partisan alternative explanation for their districting decisions. In this respect the states could cloak a racial gerrymander in partisan clothing and move on.

RETROGRESSION AND PRECLEARANCE

Although the line of cases from *Shaw* to *Cromartie* addressed the manner in which states and the Justice Department could remedy claims of vote dilution, the Supreme Court also had to address key issues concerning the preclearance provision in Section 5. Specifically, the Court had to determine the scope and definition of "retrogression." In *Georgia v. Ashcroft* (2003) the Supreme Court ruled that a reduction in the number of majority-minority districts in a covered jurisdiction did not necessarily amount to a retrogression in minority voting power. In some cases states could draw so-called minority "influence" districts. In those districts, it was argued, minority candidates could win even though the districts were not composed of a majority of minority voters.

The development of this strategy for enhancing minority voting strength was a reaction to the *Shaw* line of cases. Scholars such as Sam Hirsch (2002) had demonstrated that minority candidates could win elections in minority influence districts if their campaigns were crafted carefully. Insofar as such districts were not drawn to ensure that minority voters constituted a majority of the population, they did not run afoul of the standard set forth in *Shaw*. Speaking for the Court, Justice O'Connor stated:

> a court should not focus solely on the comparative ability of a minority group to elect a candidate of its choice. While this factor is an important one in the § 5 retrogression inquiry, it cannot be dispositive or exclusive … to maximize the electoral success of a minority group, a State may choose to create a certain number of "safe" districts, in which it is highly likely that minority voters will be able to elect the candidate of their choice. Alternatively, a State may choose to create a greater number of districts in which it is likely—although perhaps not quite as likely as under the benchmark plan—that minority voters will be able to elect candidates of their choice. (*Ashcroft*, 480)

She concluded: "Section 5 gives States the flexibility to choose one theory of effective representation over the other" (*Ashcroft*, 482).

IMPLICATIONS AND FEARS

In some aspects the decisions in *Easley v. Cromartie* and *Georgia v. Ashcroft* represent a great victory and resonate with the spirit of the VRA. They permit the practice of drawing districts to help racial and ethnic minority voters gain representation that has benefited other groups of voters throughout American history. However, they do so in a manner that prevents unabashed attempts to draw electoral districts that are guaranteed to produce a particular result. In this respect they manifest a bizarre irony: The battle to end discrimination against minority voters by gerrymandering electoral districts has been won by giving minorities the same chance as every other political group to gerrymander electoral districts in their favor.

The controversy surrounding ways to define and prevent minority vote dilution and retrogression remains a key focus of the VRA. However, although academic debates about the superiority of majority-minority districts or minority influence districts endure, they demonstrate the positive impact of the VRA. Instead of fighting to protect minority voting rights, scholars and practitioners now debate how best to protect the franchise.

Despite these advances the possibility that some parts of the VRA might have expired in 2007 generated controversy and debate. Studies by many organizations ranging from the American Civil Liberties Union to the National Commission on the Voting Rights Act demonstrated that in many ways many Americans still were unable to exercise the franchise freely.

The renewal of the language provisions manifested the scope and complexity of expanding voting rights protections further. As the election of 2000 and the passage of the Help America Vote Act demonstrated, many obstacles to the truly free exercise of the franchise have continued to exist. They range from making sure that non–English speakers are able to register and vote to ensuring that voting procedures are not confusing and that voting machines function properly.

Thus, although the VRA and the ensuing Supreme Court decisions have resulted in a fairer process of drawing voting districts and a means by which the federal government can be called on to oversee changes in local election laws, the renewal of the nonpermanent provisions of the act in 2007 demonstrates the need to continue policing the electoral process and the renewed national commitment to preserving the integrity of American democracy.

SEE ALSO *Gerrymandering; Jim Crow; King, Martin Luther, Jr.; Politics, Black; Politics, Southern; Protest; Race; Racism; Supreme Court, U.S.; Violence*

BIBLIOGRAPHY

Allen v. State Board of Elections, 393 U.S. 544. 1969. http://caselaw.lp.findlaw.com/cgi-bin/getcase.pl?court=US&vol=393&invol=544.

Bush v. Vera, 512 U.S. 952. 1996. http://caselaw.lp.findlaw.com/scripts/getcase.pl?court=US&vol=517&invol=952.

Easley v. Cromartie, 532 U.S. 234. 2001. http://law.onecle.com/ussc/532/532us234.html.

Frederickson, Caroline, and Deborah Vagins. 2006. *Promises to Keep: The Impact of the Voting Rights Act in 2006*. Washington DC: American Civil Liberties Union.

Georgia v. Ashcroft, 539 U.S. 461. 2003. http://caselaw.lp.findlaw.com/cgi-bin/getcase.pl?navby=case&court=US&vol=539&invol=461.

Hirsch, Sam. 2002. Unpacking *Page v. Bartels*: A Fresh Redistricting Paradigm Emerges in New Jersey. *Election Law Journal* 1: 7–23.

Johnson, Lyndon B. 1965. Special Message to Congress: The American Promise. March 15. National Archives and Records Administration, Lyndon Baines Johnson Library and Museum, Austin, TX. http://www.lbjlib.utexas.edu/johnson/archives.hom/speeches.hom/650315.asp.

Karlan, Pamela S. 2004. *Georgia v. Ashcroft* and the Retrogression of Retrogression. *Election Law Journal* 3: 21–36.

National Commission on the Voting Rights Act. 2006. *Protecting Minority Voters: The Voting Rights Act at Work, 1982–2005*. Washington DC: Lawyers' Committee for Civil Rights under Law.

Raskin, Jamin. 1998. The Supreme Court's Racial Double Standard in Redistricting: Bizarre Jurisprudence, Bizarre Scholarship. *Journal of Law and Politics* 14: 591–666.

Rush, Mark E. 2006. The Voting Rights Act and Its Discontents. In *The Voting Rights Act: Securing the Ballot*, ed. Richard M. Valelly, 145–160. Washington, DC: CQ Press.

Shaw v. Reno, 509 U.S. 630. 1993. http://caselaw.lp.findlaw.com/scripts/getcase.pl?court=us&vol=509&invol=630.

Thernstrom, Abigail M. 1987. *Whose Votes Count? Affirmative Action and Minority Voting Rights*. Cambridge, MA: Harvard University Press.

Thornburg v. Gingles, 478 U.S. 30. 1986. http://supreme.justia.com/us/478/30/.

Valelly, Richard M., ed. 2006. *The Voting Rights Act: Securing the Ballot*. Washington, DC: Congressional Quarterly.

Mark Rush

VOTING SCHEMES

Voting schemes are methods of combining individual preferences to arrive at the aggregate preferences of the group. The study of the effects of different voting schemes is called *social choice theory*. Perhaps the seminal work in the modern study of voting schemes is Kenneth Arrow's *Social Choice and Individual Values* (1951). In that work, Arrow lays out five attributes that ought to exist in any fair and just voting scheme, then goes on to say that no scheme can simultaneously incorporate all five attributes.

Arrow's *impossibility theorem* implies that there is no one best voting scheme. To that end, democracies have experimented with a number of different voting schemes. The question of which voting scheme to use is not merely trivia, because the type of voting scheme that is adopted almost certainly has effects on electoral outcomes. For example, consider the following election with three candidates, one hundred voters, and three types of voters:

- There are thirty-five type-one voters who prefer candidate A most, then candidate B, then candidate C.

- There are thirty-three type-two voters who prefer candidate C most, then candidate B, then candidate A.

- There are thirty-two type-three voters who prefer candidate B most, then candidate C, then candidate A.

It is easy to see that the election above is not decisive under majority voting, since no candidate garners a majority of votes. Two very popular voting schemes are *plurality rule*, whereby the candidate who receives the most votes wins, and *majority rule with runoff*, whereby the top two vote-getters in the first election compete in a second election to determine the winner. Under plurality rule, which is used in countries such as Great Britain and Canada, candidate A would win with 35 percent of the vote. Under majority rule with runoff, which is used in countries such as France and Brazil, candidates A and C would go to the runoff election, where candidate C would win with 65 percent of the vote (since all type-three voters would join with type-two voters in supporting candidate C).

One important determinant of the voting scheme is the country's type of regime. Democracies can differ on a number of variables. For example, in *unitary* systems, the country is governed in a single unit, often the parliament, which elects a prime minister to serve as an executive. Great Britain, Israel, and Chile are examples of unitary states. At the same time, other countries are *federal* systems, whereby governing authority is held in different locations. Often, states or provinces share governing authority with a national government. Examples of federations include the United States, Russia, and Brazil. Smaller countries often tend to be unitary systems, whereas larger ones are more likely to be federations, although there are exceptions. For example, Switzerland is a relatively small country, but has a federal system.

Many unitary countries use *proportional representation* (PR) electoral systems, although Great Britain and other Westminster systems are notable exceptions. In PR systems, parties receive representation in the nation's legislature that is proportionate to the percentage of votes the party received in the last election. In these systems, parties prepare lists of candidates. In *open-list* systems, such as those of Chile and Sweden, voters can choose individual candidates from the parties' lists. In contrast, voters in *closed-list* systems, such as that of Israel, select only the party, and the choice of the candidates is left up to party leaders. PR systems tend to have very disciplined parties within their legislatures, meaning that party members virtually always vote the same way on legislative proposals. This is because parties control the lists, and can therefore punish rogue representatives by keeping them off the lists.

On the other hand, many federal systems and some unitary systems use *winner-take-all* elections, whereby one candidate wins an election to represent the people living in a particular geographic area. This is how elections work in, for example, the United States and Great Britain. According to Duverger's law (1963), systems that use winner-take-all elections, sometimes called *first-past-the-post*

elections, tend to have only two parties. This is because such systems provide no incentive for coming in second place. In winner-take-all systems, a candidate who receives 45 percent of the vote wins nothing, whereas such a candidate would receive about 45 percent of the legislative seats in a PR system. For this reason, politicians are better off coalescing into two parties prior to an election in winner-take-all systems, but do not face that same incentive in PR systems. As a result, PR systems tend to have many small parties, whereas winner-take-all systems tend to have only two.

Furthermore, political activists often advocate for implementing new voting schemes because the voting scheme selected has such a strong effect on the political landscape of a democracy. For example, we saw above that voting schemes affect the number of parties in an electoral system. Other systems are advocated because they could increase the amount of representation minority groups receive. For example, *cumulative voting* is a voting scheme in which voters elect several representatives, and have the same number of votes as there are empty seats to fill. Voters may opt to use those votes to vote for different candidates, or they may cumulate their votes onto one candidate whom they most prefer. In this way, advocates argue, members of minority groups can cumulate their votes onto one candidate, thereby increasing the chances that their one candidate will win. At the same time, advocates of *approval voting* argue that their system encourages voters to accurately report their true preferences, rather than misstating them in an effort to gain some strategic advantage. In this type of system, voters deem each candidate either "approved" or "not approved," and the candidate with the most "approved" votes wins. Furthermore, advocates of *single transferable voting*, often called *instant runoff voting*, argue that their system discourages negative campaigning and provides incentives for sincere voting. In this system, voters provide a ranking of candidates from most to least favored. Counting votes entails adding up all of the most-favored votes and dropping the candidates with the lowest number of votes. Then, the votes of all those who ranked the dropped candidate first transfer to their next-most-preferred candidate, and the process continues until a winner is determined.

SEE ALSO *Elections; Electoral Systems; Vote, Alternative; Voting; Voting Patterns*

BIBLIOGRAPHY

Arrow, Kenneth. [1951] 1963. *Social Choice and Individual Values.* 2nd ed. New Haven, CT: Yale University Press.

Duverger, Maurice. 1963. *Political Parties: Their Organization and Activity in the Modern State.* 2nd English ed. Trans. Barbara North and Robert North. New York: Wiley.

Riker, William H. 1982. *Liberalism against Populism: A Confrontation between the Theory of Democracy and the Theory of Social Choice.* Prospect Heights, IL: Waveland.

Saari, Donald G. 2001. *Decisions and Elections: Explaining the Unexpected.* Cambridge, U.K.: Cambridge University Press.

Kristin Kanthak

VOUCHERS, SCHOOL

SEE *School Vouchers.*

VULNERABILITY

The concept of vulnerability is derived from the Latin *vulnus* or "wound." Its etymology signifies the human potential to be wounded, that is, to experience physical trauma. In modern usage, the notion refers to both physical and psychological harm: It indicates human exposure to psychological harm, moral damage, or spiritual threat. *Vulnerability* more generally includes our ability to suffer psychologically, morally, and spiritually rather than simply a physical capacity for pain from our exposure to the physical world. Our common human vulnerability as illustrated by our morbidity and mortality can be regarded as the basis for shared human rights, such as the right to life itself. Modern revulsion against torture in international legal codes illustrates the common theme of vulnerability running through human rights declarations.

In referring to hazards and disasters, the notion of vulnerability draws attention to the risky relationship between people and their natural environments. Various major disasters in modern times—Hurricane Katrina (2005), the tsunami disaster (2004), the earthquake in Kobe, Japan (1995), and severe droughts across Africa—have encouraged governments and international agencies to seek improved measures of risks and vulnerabilities.

More recently, vulnerability refers in computer sciences to weaknesses in a system that permit an attacker to compromise the integrity, security, and confidentiality of the system, its data, and its applications. Computer vulnerability of a construct exists when many program faults can be traced to it. One important task of computer software programs is to devise appropriate tools that can assist in the discovery and removal of such vulnerabilities as input validation errors.

Various attempts have been made to create standardized measurement systems to provide accurate information on risks and vulnerability. For example, in the realm of information technology security, the U.S. National Infrastructure Advisory Council has promoted the Common Vulnerability Scoring System, which provides universal standard ratings of vulnerabilities. The challenge is to get these measurement criteria universally accepted. In 1973 the United Nations University was created and now incorporates the Institute for Environment and Human Security (UNU-EHS), which exists to study acute environmental hazards. Its journal, *SOURCE*, has published research that attempts to provide coherent and unified criteria for understanding hazards.

Vulnerability research covers a range of complex fields, such as political ecology, security studies, and disaster and risk management. This research is important for organizations trying to reduce vulnerability. Major research questions are concerned with measuring, assessing, and preventing vulnerability. Although much of this research is concerned with assessing environmental risk, social vulnerability is an important branch of vulnerability research. In this context, vulnerability research considers how different social groups are exposed to natural hazards and major social disruptions. One example is research on the vulnerability of isolated elderly men in the inner-city areas of Chicago who were found to suffer an "excess" of fatalities (as compared to other social groups in the city) during the heat wave of July 1995.

Social risk management (SRM) is a developing academic field associated with attempts to limit poverty and analyze the causes of poverty, including the interaction between empowerment, security, opportunity, and poverty. The threat of SARS (severe acute respiratory syndrome) and avian influenza has illustrated the vulnerability of modern societies, especially in the developing world, to the globalization of acute infections, to which traditional quarantine techniques are inadequate policy responses. There is a close relationship between SRM and world development programs that attempt to predict poverty and address its causes. These developments now fall under the general heading of *prevention science*, which applies the social sciences to a broad range of modern crises on the model that has been developed by public health strategies.

Risk assessment of vulnerable groups plays an important role in public health programs. An early illustration can be taken from the research of George Brown and Tirril Harris (1978) into the social causes of depression among young women in London. They found that the "vulnerability factors" included the loss of a mother before the age of eleven, lack of employment, and three or more children at home under the age of fourteen. The most significant protection against depression was the presence of an intimate friend. An effective social network lowers the risk of clinical depression. Adolescent children are at risk, and suicides among young people have in recent years increased dramatically. In the United States, suicide is the third leading cause of death for twenty-four-year-olds and the sixth leading cause of death for children between the ages of five and fourteen. Various agencies—the American Psychological Association, Usenet newsgroups, and the National Clearinghouse on Child Abuse and Neglect Information—provide checklists to assess behavioral changes in young people that might indicate increasing risk of self harm, including suicide, such as a change in eating and sleeping habits, withdrawal from friends, violent behavior, and drug use. The Behavioral Risk Factor Surveillance System (BRFSS) is the world's largest ongoing telephone health survey system tracking health conditions and risk behavior in the United States through fifty state health departments.

With the aging of populations in developed societies, the leading causes of death have changed from infectious disease in infants to geriatric conditions—stroke, heart attack, and cancer—among the elderly. For example, the American Heart Association has identified several risk factors associated with heart disease, such as increasing age, male sex, and hereditary. There are also lifestyle factors that make people vulnerable, such as smoking, physical inactivity, obesity, and diabetes mellitus. Starting with research in the 1950s, psychologists argued that there was an "executive disease" among white-collar employees in the corporate world. American cardiologists claimed that *type-A* men were competitive and ambitious, and their corporate lifestyle made them vulnerable to heart attack as a consequence of high levels of stress. Medical debate has concentrated on assessing whether vulnerability to disease is produced by environmental factors (such as pollution) that can be modified by legislation and political intervention, or whether the primary causes are genetic, where medical intervention (such as genetic counseling for Huntington's disease) involves long-term strategies. The evidence suggests that disease is a product of both environmental and genetic causes, and requires appropriate strategies to address both social and genetic dimensions.

The growth of prevention sciences (for consistency with above changes) can be seen as a response to the common perception that the world is becoming increasingly risky. The economic and social assessment of risk arose from attempts to calculate profit and loss in the growing international trade in the sixteenth and seventeenth centuries. With modernization, there is greater interconnectivity between societies, making the rapid spread of infectious disease more problematic. With technological development, the risks of industrial pollution and hazard are much greater. With growing sophistication in military technology, the risk of intended and unintended military disaster is also much greater. In short, with modern social change, human vulnerability and institutional precariousness increase.

These social and technological changes were summarized by sociologist Ulrich Beck in his *Risk Society*, which was originally published in Germany 1986. The concept of a "risk society" greatly stimulated social science research into uncertainty, risk, and hazard. Beck developed a sociological perspective to show why disasters such as the chemical leak at Bhopal (1984), accidents at the nuclear power plants at Three Mile Island (1979) and Chernobyl (1986), and global warming were products of modernization, involving the intensive application of technology to transform the environment to satisfy human needs. Such risks were the unintended consequences of technological modernization. The modern growth of "green" political parties and their electoral successes can also be treated as an indication that the general public is aware of modern vulnerabilities, of which the prospect of global warming is probably the most significant.

SEE ALSO *Coping; Death and Dying; Depression, Psychological; Disaster Management; Disease; Global Warming; Mental Illness; Morbidity and Mortality; Obesity; Personality, Type A/Type B; Pollution; Prevention Science; Resiliency; Risk; Smoking; Stress*

BIBLIOGRAPHY

Bankoff, Greg, George Frerks, and Dorothea Hilhorst. 2004. *Mapping Vulnerability: Disasters, Development, and People.* Sterling, VA: Earthscan.

Beck, Ulrich. 1992. *Risk Society: Towards a New Modernity*, trans. Mark Ritter. London: Sage.

Brown, George W., and Tirril Harris. 1978. *Social Origins of Depression: A Study of Psychiatric Disorder in Women.* London: Tavistock.

Klinenberg, Eric. 2002. *Heat Wave: A Social Autopsy of Disaster in Chicago.* Chicago: University of Chicago Press.

Turner, Bryan S. 2006. *Vulnerability and Human Rights.* University Park: Pennsylvania State University Press.

Bryan S. Turner